THE BUSINESS OF SPORTS

Edited by
SCOTT R. ROSNER
The Wharton School
University of Pennsylvania

KENNETH L. SHROPSHIRE
The Wharton School
University of Pennsylvania

JONES AND BARTLETT PUBLISHERS
Sudbury, Massachusetts
BOSTON   TORONTO   LONDON   SINGAPORE

World Headquarters
Jones and Bartlett Publishers
40 Tall Pine Drive
Sudbury, MA 01776
978-443-5000
info@jbpub.com
www.jbpub.com

Jones and Bartlett Publishers Canada
2406 Nikanna Road
Mississauga, ON L5C 2W6
CANADA

Jones and Bartlett Publishers International
Barb House, Barb Mews
London W6 7PA
UK

Production Credits
Acquisitions Editor: Jacqueline Ann Mark
Production Editor: Julie Champagne Bolduc
Editorial Assistant: Nicole Quinn
Marketing Manager: Ed McKenna
Manufacturing Buyer: Therese Bräuer
Composition: Graphic World
Cover Design: Kristin E. Ohlin
Cover Images: (top) LiquidLibrary, (bottom) Image Gap/Alamy Images
Printing and Binding: Malloy, Inc.
Cover Printing: Malloy, Inc.

Library of Congress Cataloging-in-Publication Data
The business of sports / [edited by] Scott Rosner, Kenneth Shropshire.
    p. cm.
  ISBN 0-7637-2621-4
    1. Sports administration—United States. 2. Professional sports—United States—Management.
  I. Rosner, Scott.   II. Shropshire, Kenneth L.
GV713.B87 2004
796′.06′91—dc22   2004000685

Printed in the United States of America

08 07 06 05 04   10 9 8 7 6 5 4 3 2 1

CONTENTS

PREFACE

"Within the framework of what you've been taught, this business makes no sense."

— Wendy Lewis, Vice President, Strategic Planning, Recruitment and Diversity,
Major League Baseball, at MBA Media and Entertainment Conference,
Stern School of Business, New York University,
February 21, 2003

THE BUSINESS OF SPORTS: THE FOUNDATIONS OF A UNIQUE INDUSTRY

The Ford Motor Company and General Motors Corporation operate under a general business model of selling as many vehicles as possible with the greatest profit margin possible. In the end, Ford and General Motors are competitors who want to sell product. There is no interest, and it is in fact illegal, to cooperate in a manner that allows both companies to be more profitable. Any traditional business could be used to illustrate the contrast that is important here. Yet, as the epigraph notes, the sports business has been different from the beginning.

In almost every sports venture, the competitors must cooperate for the venture to be profitable. In the nascent stages of team sports, the hat was passed among the spectators at local playing fields. A percentage of the take was distributed among the still sweat-drenched and muddy players from the two squads, and the man (it was almost always a man) who organized the outing took a higher percentage. It was in everyone's interest to have a bigger pie to split, but even if they cooperated to make attendance as high as possible, they still competed vigorously to be the sole winner on the field. Following the competition, all went back to their jobs during the week. This competitive-cooperative model is now the standard in the National Football League (NFL), Major League Baseball (MLB), National Basketball

Association (NBA), National Hockey League (NHL), and other sports leagues and professional sports ventures around the world.

Other visionaries saw ways to exploit athletes labeled *amateurs* by putting together athletic spectacles and reaping the profits. The cash was kept away from those amateurs. The value and need for amateurism was embellished by Greek mythology and class-centered Victorian logic. These amateurism concepts would eventually evolve into the National Collegiate Athletic Association (NCAA) and the Olympic Games. The modern Olympiad was founded by Baron Pierre de Coubertin in 1896 and, shortly thereafter, the NCAA was founded by a group of college presidents convened by then U.S. President Theodore Roosevelt. The application of the amateur ideal took hold, and student-run sports were taken over by universities, and so too were the revenues. From the labor standpoint, a large segment of the sports industry has found a way, unlike the automobile and other industries, to avoid paying for labor.

But winning at any cost is not allowed at any level, at least when the cost is something other than money. Every modern sports business has sets of defined rules and regulations that may even, in many instances, be grounded in law. For example, even if it could be argued that steroids and dietary supplements can make athletes better players, most sports business enterprises have banned their use.

Profit at any cost is similarly problematic. At various times studies have shown that, at the margin, an additional white player on a squad will bring in more fans than an additional black player. Most sports businesses will go for the win rather than the racial slight; or will they?

As these ventures grew, new players became part of the industry: radio, television, commercial endorsers, licensees, and sponsors. Lawyers and agents came into the picture to pull these deals together. The business went beyond just what happened during the competition. The business model was expanding. The primary revenue source was no longer limited to just the fans who could put money in the hat or, later, the fans who bought tickets.

By the time sport began to be referred to as a business, it was also clearly entertainment too; as such, different rules of business and law applied. Not all parties were able to move away from the concept of these businesses being little more than glorified games. There is a continuing conflict about whether the business of sports should be treated differently.

The stadiums and arenas where teams played or wanted to play became big parts of the business too. Interestingly, public money has been used to build many of these facilities. Ford and GM can only dream of that type of aid from the public coffers. There are seldom public battles between cities bidding to build a bigger plant to host an automaker.

Athletes too have realized that it is all more than a game, and they have unionized in the team sports, like much of the rest of working class America. That became an ironic position as average salaries surpassed $1 million and then $2 million per year in some leagues. Without a doubt, some of the highest paid union members in the world are those involved in professional sports leagues.

There are social issues uniquely impacting the sports industry too. These see the light of day in sports more than elsewhere, because the business is subject to constant scrutiny. Beat writers cover every aspect of the game, looking for that unique story, and those stories go far beyond whatever is happening on the field, court, or ice.

As in other industries, women are still not treated with parity in sports. Initially, it was not "appropriate" for women to participate in sports. Apart from their absence in any highly visible professional sport, the disparity was especially visible in the Olympics. It was not until 1984 at the Olympics in Los Angeles that women competed in a marathon event. Health reasons, decorum, and the need to be at home were cited. The passage of Title IX in 1972 has helped create new business opportunities in women's professional sports by allowing women to participate in sports in a meaningful way. Many women's leagues have started and failed. A long dominant men's league, the National Basketball Association started and financed the Women's National Basketball Association (WNBA). The reasons for doing so were all based on business. Beyond professional sports, Title IX has also had a dramatic effect on the business of collegiate sports. It is now so long an ingrained part of the culture that at least one of the beneficiaries has never heard of it: When asked a question about Title IX at the 2002 U.S. Open tennis tournament, tennis star Jennifer Capriati replied, "I have no idea what Title IX is. Sorry." She was a lifetime beneficiary at the age of 26. Today, women's professional tennis is a sport in better shape than men's professional tennis.

Many argue that sports led the way for American business on diversity with the racial integration of Major League Baseball in 1947 and that sports are still leading the way today. Approximately one-third of the players in the big leagues are of Latin American origin. There is, however, a dearth of diversity in management. Omar Minaya was the lone Latino general manager in baseball in 2003. Professional sport has become a global business in a manner similar, yet different from, other businesses. On the one hand the concepts of larger markets and cheaper labor can certainly be pointed to. In the NBA and Major League Baseball, the expanded talent pool is a genuine reality as well.

This is an industry where the issues that make headlines are the sharing of revenues, salary caps, luxury taxes, luxury boxes, and the search for the next corporate sponsor. The business model for the automobile may have evolved since the Model T, but not with the same level of public scrutiny and angst as has occurred in sports. Probably most uniquely, this business has an extraordinary level of dependence on the selling of a product to broadcasters, as opposed to getting customers to "purchase" the product by walking in the gate.

With that said, many of the rules are the same. The bottom line of the enterprise is ultimately important. As applied to team sports, there is just a different way of getting there. This is the case even though some individual owners (whether people or entities) can afford to lose seemingly endless amounts of money, citing reasons ranging from marketing the larger enterprise, to controlling content for the enterprise, to fattening up the enterprise for sale. The value of sport as strategic content was probably best exemplified in the structuring of YankeeNets. That venture went beyond the named enterprises to also include the New Jersey Devils and even internationally to include Manchester United. Though that specific entity ultimately failed, its structure will doubtlessly be repeated by future sports organizations.

This book is designed for current and future sports business leaders as well as those interested in the inner-workings of the industry. Through original introductions, carefully selected readings with editors' notes updating relevant text, and incisive questions, this book gives the reader insight into this unique business. The business of sports is interdisciplinary in nature. As such, the major business disciplines of management, marketing, finance, information technology, accounting, ethics, and law are all encompassed in the materials that follow. The readings provide this insight from the perspective of a variety of stakeholders in the industry. We have attempted to edit the selections in the book in a manner such that the reader will not be overburdened with the jargon of any specific discipline. Where possible, cumbersome citations are deleted as well, to provide for a smoother read. Where we deemed it necessary for reference purposes, the citations were retained. The original note numbering is retained in many selections.

This book is not meant to cover all aspects of every topic involved in the sports industry. Nonetheless, it does provide the reader with a fairly comprehensive overview of many of the major sports business issues. In order to do so most effectively, the book has been divided into three broad sections: professional, Olympic, and intercollegiate sports. The major issues that impact each of these broad categories of sports are subsequently addressed within each section. In addition, there are separate sections on both sociological considerations and the future challenges facing the sports industry. These two sections include all three of the aforementioned categories of the sports business — professional, Olympic, and intercollegiate sports. Though all sports are not discussed in each section, the message that is gleaned from a selected reading is typically instructive for understanding the issues as they impact other sports. As the first comprehensive collection of readings to focus on the business of sports, it is our hope that this book will provide a framework for understanding the business of sports and the dilemmas faced by today's sports business leaders.

However, we recognize that no work is perfect. This book is no different. In researching this book, we found a dearth of existing works on the business aspects of the Olympic Games and intercollegiate athletics, even though much attention has been given to the sociological aspects of both of these topics. Similarly, a glaring lack of attention has been given to the ethical aspects of the business of sports, as well as the involvement of Latinos, women, and people with disabilities. These shortcomings are likely a product of the fact that the serious study of sports as a business is relatively new, with the first academic articles appearing in the 1950s and the advent of college sports management programs occurring little more than 30 years ago. Nonetheless, these neglected subjects warrant further study.

As we were completing the manuscript, Michael Lewis's book *Moneyball* was released. As many sports fans know by now, that book is largely about achieving success in sports by thoroughly understanding the business, while also stepping back and taking a brand-new approach. Our hope is that both current and future business leaders will take both the facts and viewpoints expressed here and apply their own creativity to take their particular focus in sports to an even higher level.

ACKNOWLEDGMENTS

T his book is the culmination of thousands of hours of thinking, researching, talking, and writing about the business of sports. We have attempted to provide a comprehensive overview of this industry in a novel manner. In interspersing our own narrative with significant existing works, we seek to "tell the story" of the business of sports so that it is accessible to a wide audience. It is our hope that sports industry practitioners, academics, students, business people, and sports fans alike will find this to be a useful resource and learning tool.

This project could not have been completed without the help of many others. Tamara English, Tiffany Fujioka, Cherly Vaughn-Curry, and Nesha Patel provided outstanding administrative and editorial assistance, and Lowell Lysinger's technological support greatly facilitated the completion of the book. It is difficult to imagine a more talented, dedicated, or nicer group of support staff anywhere. Josh Cohen, Jason Gershwin, and Matt Mezvinsky spent a significant amount of time researching and providing important feedback on the early drafts of the book as well as the ideas for many of the discussion questions. Amy Pietrasanta, Mori Taheripour, and Winnie Wu of Wharton West provided invaluable input on the text and charts and provided coherent model answers for the discussion questions. Their work on the MBA independent study project was exceptional. The members of the Wharton School's 2004 MBA sports industry class provided model answers to both the discussion questions and sample exam questions found in the instructor's manual.

We also have a list of individuals that we'd like to thank on a personal basis.

For Ken:

My list is brief on this one. As always, thanks to my family for their support, time, and otherwise in allowing me to complete this project. But this is probably the best place to acknowledge that the lion's share of the effort in this book is Scott's. I certainly hauled a great deal of the water, but Scott's name goes first on this for more than alphabetical reasons. Even with that, I'll share the blame for any perceived shortcomings.

For Scott:

I learned of the need for this book when teaching courses on the business of sports, first at Seton Hall University and now at the Wharton School. Finding no appropriate textbook, I subjected the students in these courses to a constantly evolving collection of readings, many of which are now excerpted in this book. This book never would have happened without their "suffering" and willingness to enthusiastically engage in my folly. I thank my students profusely, as I have certainly learned more from them than I have taught them.

Of course, this book also would not have happened without the authors whose works we have included. We are grateful for their diligence and contributions to the "business of sports."

I first met Ken Shropshire while I was a second-year law student in January 1996, and I have not left him alone since. Starting as his teaching and research assistant, Ken has been my mentor for over eight years and is the individual who has had the single most influence on my career. Working with him on this project has been a highlight. Ken is a great academic and an even better friend. It is an honor to work with him.

I have dedicated this book to my family. My parents, Sandy and Jay Rosner, have inspired me more than they could ever know. As it pertains to this project, their passion for education and sports has become mine, and I can only hope to display their work ethic as well. My other parents, Phyllis and Ken Konner, have offered unending encouragement and support. My brother-in-law, Jon Sherman, has been a valued friend whose strength has been nothing short of remarkable and similarly inspirational.

My wife and best friend, Kim Rosner, is a woman whose courage, intelligence, work ethic, passion, love, and sense of humor would make any man's life complete. I am lucky that I get to be the one. (And I'm not just writing that because I have to . . .)

Finally, I'd like to acknowledge Lorin Sherman, my sister and friend. A sweet and beautiful soul, a promise of the future, and an enormous part of my family was lost when she passed away, but her spirit and memory endure. To Lorin, I offer the prayer of Bruce Springsteen's "Into the Fire":

May your strength give us strength
May your faith give us faith
May your hope give us hope
May your love bring us love . . .
May your love bring us love

READING CREDITS

CHAPTER 1

Page 5: From *The Rich Who Own Sports* by Don Kowet, pp. 3–8, copyright © 1977 by Don Kowet. Used by permission of Random House, Inc.

Page 8: James P. Quirk and Rodney D. Fort. *Pay Dirt: The Business of Professional Team Sports,* pp. 96–116. Copyright © 1992 by Princeton University Press. Update for paperback edition © 1997 by Princeton University Press. Reprinted by permission of Princeton University Press.

Page 15: Eugene J. Stroz, Jr. Public Ownership of Sports Franchises: Investment, Novelty, or Fraud? 53 *Rutgers Law Review,* 517, Winter 2001. Copyright by Rutgers School of Law-Newark. Online. Used with permission. All rights reserved.

CHAPTER 2

Page 23: Moag and Company. The Sports Industry's Resistance to Bear Markets, published online. Copyright by John A. Moag, Jr. Used with permission. All rights reserved.

Page 26: Gerald W. Scully. *The Market Structure of Sports,* pp. 3–26, 31–40. The University of Chicago Press. Copyright 1995 by The University of Chicago Press. Used with permission. All rights reserved.

Page 34: Michael Danielson. *Home Team: Professional Sports and the American Metropolis,* pp. 83–96. Copyright © 1997 by Princeton University Press. Reprinted by permission of Princeton University Press.

Page 38: Stephen F. Ross and Stefan Szymanski. Open Competition in League Sports. 2002 *Wisconsin Law Review* 625; Copyright 2002 by The Board of Regents of the University of Wisconsin System; Reprinted by permission of the Wisconsin Law Review.

CHAPTER 3

Page 47: Richard G. Sheehan. *Keeping Score: The Economics of Big-Time Sports,* pp. 155–179. Copyright 1996 by Diamond Communications. Used with permission. All rights reserved.

Page 54: Daniel S. Mason. Revenue Sharing and Agency Problems in Professional Team Sport: The Case of the National Football League. *Journal of Sport Management* 11 (3): 203–222 (1997). Adapted by permission.

Page 62: Richard C. Levin, George J. Mitchell, Paul A. Volcker, and George F. Will. Report of The Independent Members of the Commissioner's Blue Ribbon Panel on Baseball Economics. Copyright 2001 by Major League Baseball Properties.

CHAPTER 4

Page 77: Richard Stein and Jerry Gorman. Keeping the Financial Scorecard. *CPA Journal.* June 1992. Copyright 1992 by *CPA Journal.* Used with permission. All rights reserved.

Page 81: Paul L.B. McKenney and Eric M. Nemeth. The Purchase and Sale of a Sports Team: Tax Issues and Rules. *Michigan Bar Journal,* June 2001. Copyright by Michigan Bar Journal. Used with permission. All rights reserved.

Page 96: Robert Reilly. The Challenges of Professional Sports Franchise Purchase Price Allocations. Copyright by Willamette Management Associates. Used with permission. All rights reserved.

Page 99: Ralph C. Anzivino. Reorganization of the Professional Sports Franchise. *Marquette Sports Law Review*, Fall 2001. Copyright by Marquette University. Used with permission. All rights reserved. 12 *Marq Sports L Rev* 9.

CHAPTER 5

Page 113: Martin J. Greenberg. *The Stadium Game,* ScheerGame. ScheerGame Sports Development, LLC. Copyright 2000 by ScheerGame Sports Development, LLC. Used with permission. All rights reserved.

Page 127: Martin J. Greenberg and April R. Anderson. The Name Is the Game in Facility Naming Rights. *The Sports Lawyer 2000.* Copyright by Sports Lawyers Association. Used with permission. All rights reserved.

Page 135: Kenneth L. Shropshire. *The Sports Franchise Game: Cities in Pursuit of Sports Franchises, Events, Stadiums, and Arenas,* pp. 7–12. Copyright 1995 by the University of Pennsylvania Press. Used with permission. All rights reserved.

CHAPTER 6

Page 143: Stanley J. Baran. Sports and Television. From *Encyclopedia of Television*, 1997. Copyright by Museum of Broadcast Communications (MBC). Used with permission. All rights reserved.

Page 147: Jere Longman. Pro Leagues' Ratings Drop; Nobody Quite Sure Why. *New York Times,* July 29, 2001, p. 1. Copyright © 2001 by The New York Times Co. Reprinted by permission.

Page 152: John Fortunato. The NBA Strategy of Broadcast Television Exposure: A Legal Application. 12 *Fordam Intellectual Property, Media & Entertainment Law Journal,* 133. Copyright © 2001 Fordham Intellectual Property, Media & Entertainment Law Journal and John Fortunato.

Page 159: David K. Stotlar, Vertical integration in sport. *Journal of Sport Management,* 14 (1): 1–7 (2000). Adapted by permission.

Page 163: John Beech, Simon Chadwick, and Alan Tapp. Toward a Schema for Football Clubs Seeking an Effective Presence on the Internet. *European Journal of Sport Management* Vol. 7, July 2000, 30–50. Special Issue. Copyright © European Journal of Sport Management.

Page 173: Mark McDonald, Toru Mihara, and Jinbae Hong. Japanese Spectator Sport Industry: Cultural Changes Creating New Opportunities. *European Sport Management Quarterly,* 2001, 1 (1): 39–60. Copyright © European Sport Management Quarterly.

CHAPTER 7

Page 179: Lisa Pike Masteralexis, Carol A. Barr, and Mary A. Hums. *Principles and Practice of Sport Management,* pp. 409–424. Copyright © 1998, Jones and Bartlett Publishers, Sudbury, MA, www.jbpub.com. Reprinted with permission.

Page 183: Brandon L. Grusd. The Antitrust Implication of Professional Sports' League-wide Licensing and Merchandising Arrangements. 1 *Virginia Journal of Sports and the Law* p. 1, Spring 1999. Copyright by University of Virginia School of Law. Used with permission. All rights reserved.

Page 188: James M. Gladden and George R. Milne. Examining the Importance of Brand Equity in Professional Sport. *Sport Marketing Quarterly* 8 (1): 21–29. Copyright 1999 by Fitness Information Technology. Reproduced with permission of Fitness Information Technology in the format Other Book via Copyright Clearance Center.

Page 194: James M. Gladden and Daniel C. Funk. Understanding Brand Loyalty in Professional Sport: Examining the Link Between Brand Associations and Brand Loyalty. *International Journal of Sports Marketing and Sponsorship*, March/April 2001, pp. 67–94. Copyright © International Journal of Sports Marketing and Sponsorship.

CHAPTER 8

Page 202: Mark Conrad. Blue Collar Law and Basketball, pp. 90–103. From *Basketball Jones, America Above the Rim*, edited by Todd Boyd and Kenneth L. Shropshire. Copyright © 2000 New York University Press. Used with permission. All rights reserved.

Page 209: Jeffrey S. Moorad. Major League Baseball's Labor Turmoil: The Failure of the Counter-Revolution. 4 *Villanova Sport & Entertainment Law Journal* 53 (1997). Copyright by Villanova Sport & Entertainment Law Journal. Used with permission. All rights reserved.

Page 218: Adam Heller. Creating a Win-Win Situation Through Collective Bargaining: The NFL Salary Cap. 7 *Sports Lawyers Journal* 375, Spring 2000. Copyright by Sports Lawyers Association. Used with permission. All rights reserved.

CHAPTER 9

CHAPTER 10

CHAPTER 11

Page 331: Arthur T. Johnson. *Minor League Baseball and Local Economic Development,* pp. 10–33. Copyright 1993 by Board of Trustees for the University of Illinois. Used with permission of the University of Illinois Press.

Page 338: Orlando Predators Entertainment, Inc. Annual Report for the Fiscal Year Ended September 30, 2002.

Page 349: Rachel Elyachar and Lauren Moag. The Growth of Women's Sports, published online. Copyright by John A. Moag, Jr. Used with permission. All rights reserved.

CHAPTER 12

Page 361: Michael Leeds and Peter von Allmen, *Economics of Sports*, pp. 69–105. Copyright © 2002 Pearson Education Inc. Reprinted by permission of Pearson Education. Inc. Publishing as Pearson Addison Wesley.

Page 367: Eric Thornton. How to Value Professional Sports Franchise Intangible Assets. Copyright by Willamette Management Associates. Used with permission. All rights reserved.

Page 376: Scott Levine. The Impact of Stadium Economics on the Value of the Professional Sports Franchise. Copyright by Willamette Management Associates. Used with permission. All rights reserved.

Page 380: Gerald W. Scully. *The Market Structure of Sports,* pp. 100–139. The University of Chicago Press. Copyright 1995 by The University of Chicago Press. Used with permission. All rights reserved.

Page 385: Neil Begley, David Hamburger, and Robert Konefal. Moody's Methodology for Rating Sports-Related Enterprises. Copyright © Moody's Investors Services, Inc. and/or its affiliates. Reprinted with permission. All rights reserved.

CHAPTER 13

Page 401: Jean-Loup Chappelet. Management of the Olympic Games: The Lessons of Sydney. *European Journal for Sport Management*, Special Issue 2001, Vol. 8, pp. 128–136. Copyright © European Journal for Sport Management.

Page 407: John A. Lucas. *The Future of the Olympic Games,* pp. 73–83. Copyright 1992 by Human Kinetics. Used with permission. All rights reserved. Adapted by permission.

Page 415: Holger Preuss. *Economics of the Olympic Games: Hosting the Games 1972–2000,* pp. 198–201. Copyright © 2000 Walla Walla Press. Reprinted with permission.

CHAPTER 14

Page 423: Rodney K. Smith. A Brief History of the National Collegiate Athletic Association's Role in Regulating Intercollegiate Athletics. *Marquette Sports Law Review.* Copyright by Marquette University. Used with permission. All rights reserved. 11 *Marq Sports L Rev* 9 (2000).

Page 430: Lisa Pike Masteralexis, Carol A. Barr, and Mary A. Hums. *Principles and Practice of Sport Management,* pp. 166–181. Copyright © 1998, Jones and Bartlett Publishers, Sudbury, MA, www.jbpub.com. Reprinted with permission.

Page 436: Ray Yasser, James R. McCurdy, C. Peter Goplerud, and Maureen A. Weston. *Sports Law: Cases and Materials,* 4th ed., pp. 92–99. Copyright 2000 by Anderson Publishing Co. All rights reserved.

Page 447: Daniel F. Mahony, Janet S. Fink, and Donna L. Pastore. Ethics in Intercollegiate Athletics: An Examination of NCAA Violations and Penalties: 1952–1997. Vol. 7 (2): 53–74 (1999) Copyright by *Professional Ethics: A Multidisciplinary Journal.* Used with permission. All rights reserved.

CHAPTER 15

Page 469: James V. Koch, The Economic Realities of Amateur Sports Organizations. 61 *Indiana Law Journal* 9 (1985). Copyright 1985 by the Trustees of Indiana University. Reprinted by permission.

Page 477: Roger C. Noll. The Business of College Sports and the High Cost of Winning. *Milken Institute Review*, pp. 24–37, Third Quarter, 1999. Copyright by The Milken Institute Review. Used with permission. All rights reserved.

Page 492: Rodney Fort and James Quirk. The College Football Industry. In Fizel, Gustafson, and Hadley. *Sports Economics: Current Research,* pp. 11–23. Copyright © 1999 and reproduced with permission of Greenwood Publishing Group, Inc., Westport, CT.

Page 500: John L. Fizel and Randall W. Bennett. Telecasts and Recruiting in NCAA Division I Football: The Impact of Altered Property Rights. *Journal of Sport Management*, 10 (4): 359–372 (1996). Adapted by permission.

Page 503: Andrew Zimbalist. *Unpaid Professionals: Commercialism and Conflict in Big Time College Sports,* pp. 90–124. Copyright © 1999 by Princeton University Press. Reprinted by permission of Princeton University Press.

Page 516. NCAA. NCAA 2002–03 Revenue Distribution Plan. Copyright by NCAA. Used with permission. All rights reserved.

Page 522: Timothy D. DeSchriver and David K. Stotlar. An Economic Analysis of Cartel Behavior Within the NCAA. *Journal of Sport Management*, 10, (4): 388–400 (1996). Adapted by permission.

CHAPTER 16

Page 533: Murray Sperber. *Beer and Circus: How Big-Time College Sports Is Crippling Undergraduate Education*, pp. 219–229, 255–261, Copyright © 2000 by Murray Sperber. Reprinted by permission of Henry Holt and Company, LLC.

Page 540: Brian Goff. Effects of University Athletics on the University: A Review and Extension of Empirical Assessment. *Journal of Sport Management*, 14 (2): 85–104 (2000). Adapted by permission.

Page 551: Robert Litan, Jonathan Orszag and Peter Orszag. The Empirical Effects of Collegiate Athletics: An Interim Report, pp. 2–7. Reprinted with permission from the authors.

CHAPTER 17

CHAPTER 18

Page 670: James L. Shulman and William G. Bowen. *The Game of Life: College Sports and Educational Values,* pp. 258–267. Copyright © 2001 by Princeton University Press. Reprinted by permission of Princeton University Press.

Page 678: Knight Foundation Commission, 2001 Report. A Call to Action: Reconnecting College Sports and Higher Education. Copyright by John S. and James L. Knight Foundation. Used with permission. All rights reserved.

CHAPTER 19

Page 703: Edward Rimer. Discrimination in Major League Baseball: Hiring Standards for Major Managers: 1975–1994. *Journal of Sport & Social Issues* 20 (2):118, copyright © 1996 by Sage Publications. Reprinted by Permission of Sage Publications, Inc.

Page 711: Kenneth L. Shropshire. Diversity, Racism and Professional Sports Franchise Ownership: Change Must Come from Within, 67 *University of Colorado Law Review* 47 (1995). Reprinted with permission of the University of Colorado Law Review.

Page 714: Lawrence M. Kahn. The Sports Business as a Labor Market Laboratory. *Journal of Economic Perspectives*, 14 (3): 75–94, Summer 2000. Copyright by American Economic Association. Used with permission. All rights reserved.

Page 718: Angel Vargas. The Globalization of Baseball: A Latin American Perspective. *Indiana Journal of Global Legal Studies* 8 (1):21. Copyright © 2000 by Indiana University Press.

CHAPTER 20

Page 727: Mary A. Hums, Carol A. Barr, and Laurie Gullion. The Ethical Issues Confronting Managers in the Sport Industry. *Journal of Business Ethics*, May 1999, 20 (1): 51–66. Copyright © 1999 by the *Journal of Business Ethics*, with kind permission from Kluwer Academic Publishers.

Page 733: John Milton Smith. The Olympics and the Search for Global Values. *Journal of Business Ethics*, January 2002, 35 (2): 131–142. Copyright © 2002 by the *Journal of Business Ethics*, with kind permission from Kluwer Academic Publishers.

CHAPTER 21

Page 741: Richard G. Sheehan. *Keeping Score: The Economics of Big-Time Sports,* pp. 328–336. Copyright 1996 by Diamond Communications. Used with permission. All rights reserved.

Page 746: Daniel F. Mahony and Dennis R. Howard. Sport Business in the Next Decade: A General Overview of Expected Trends. *Journal of Sport Management*, 2001, 15 (4): 275–296. Adapted by permission.

Page 757: James M. Gladden, Richard L. Irwin and William A. Sutton. Building Brand Equity. *Journal of Sport Management*, 2001, 15 (4): 297–317. Adapted by permission.

PART I

PROFESSIONAL SPORTS

CHAPTER 1

OWNERSHIP

INTRODUCTION

A key to the direction of the sports business are the faces of the individuals or entities that own the various sports enterprises. League founders have long preferred to work with individuals that they can look directly in the eye at a meeting and with whom they can make decisions on the spot. League commissioners and owners prefer to deal with an individual rather than an unwieldy corporate board. Leagues want to make decisions now, not when the schedules of two dozen corporate boards allow, or worse yet, those of thousands of shareholders. However, with the exception of the National Football League, all leagues have evolved from this individual ownership model to the operationally less desirable corporate format.

While it is debatable whether this evolution is good or bad for the sports industry, there can be no doubt what is motivating this change: money. While owners have always been wealthy, escalating franchise prices and operating costs have simply made ownership by individual "moms and pops" more difficult. The game has become too risky and expensive for many of them to play. Estate planning has also led to the divestiture of sports franchises by individual owners. Even when individual owners have remained, the rationale for their involvement may have changed. Though some venerable owners like George Steinbrenner remain, a new breed of individual owners such as Dan Snyder, Jerry Jones, Mark Cuban, Ted Leonsis, and Jeffrey Lurie has infused professional sports.

In addition to the financial benefits that can result from the ownership of professional sports franchises, there is a very high consumption value involved as well. Individual owners have long received significant psychological benefits, such as an ego boost, publicity, fun, access to athletes and other powerful individuals, membership in an exclusive fraternity or club, and the opportunity to be a real-life "fantasy team" owner. Yet, even the motivations of individual owners have changed, as there is an ongoing shift in focus to the synergies that ownership can provide. Bob Johnson, the owner of the Charlotte Bobcats NBA expansion franchise, explained it this way:

> It's not the sports side of me that drives ownership, it's the business side. Owning an asset like this creates the potential for opportunities beyond the business itself. There are opportunities to develop relationships with other team owners. These are entrepreneurs who like to do things outside of the box.

1

There may be other things I can do with [Dallas Mavericks owner] Mark Cuban or [Denver Nuggets owner] Stan Kroenke. It's just a good club to belong to.[1]

In recent years, the ownership entity has thus evolved from the gritty, individual model embodied by Art Rooney and George Halas to the current presence of both individuals and corporations — particularly media, entertainment, and communications companies — looking for synergies to exploit. Indeed, 20% of all teams are now owned by corporations, many of which have shares in more than one team (and usually in teams that share the same facility). The Tribune Company, Rogers Communications, Comcast, and Cablevision are among the media companies involved in the ownership of sports franchises. Ownership of professional sports franchises is attractive to corporations with interests in the media, communications, and entertainment business, because sports team programming has significant content value due to the franchise's strong audience loyalty and brand visibility.

Viewing sports franchises as entertainment assets, corporations have attempted to use them to garner additional revenues through the team's playing facility and media rights. In theory, the ownership of the team and both its playing facility and programming rights allow the corporate owner to enhance its value through the exploitation of a wide range of synergies, including cross-promotional opportunities, the creation of additional distribution outlets, and higher visibility in the marketplace, as well as risk reduction and cost savings through economies of scale. For this reason, as revenues and costs grow larger and values keep increasing, expect the number of corporate owners to increase. Nonetheless, this strategy has not been successful for every corporation that has attempted it. It is likely that corporate owners with a local or regional focus will be more successful than those with a national or global focus. Politician Tip O'Neill's statement that "all politics is local" seems to apply to corporate ownership of professional sports franchises as well. There have been some notable flameouts among internationally focused corporate owners. Both Disney and AOL Time Warner abandoned their "sports strategies," at least partially because they were unable to capitalize on their ownership of professional sports franchises. Disney's failure is likely attributable to its inability to effectively capture the media-related revenues available through its sports franchises, which resulted in the company incurring a $100 million loss during its ownership tenure of the Anaheim Angels and Mighty Ducks. To AOL Time Warner, the value of owning professional sports franchises was in its ability to charge national advertising rates for the broad cable distribution of local team broadcasts via its TBS Superstation. When this value diminished as the company grew from a local broadcasting interest to a global venture through a series of mergers and acquisitions, and investor pressure grew for the company to reduce its debt load in a difficult economy, AOL Time Warner began withdrawing from ownership of its sports franchise holdings. With the exception of a handful of teams, local sports franchises do not have much impact on a national or international level, where audience loyalty is unlikely to be strong and cross-promotional opportunities limited. Locally focused corporations avoid these problems, and can retain the additional revenues that are available through the ownership of professional sports franchises.

In addition to this mix of old-school and corporate owners are anomalies such as the Green Bay Packers, a franchise long held in a public ownership form. Recently, there has been a smattering of public offerings as well. The public offering structure has provided a cash infusion to existing sports enterprises, including several North American franchises and numerous European soccer clubs.

There has also been the adoption of the single-entity structure. Major League Soccer (MLS) was the first entity to use this model, in which an entire league is controlled by a single operating company.

Investments are made in this company, rather than in a particular franchise. This format was developed to avoid the self-destructive behavior displayed by owners in other nascent sports leagues whose desire to win led them to pay more than they could afford for athlete services. This ultimately contributed to the demise of these leagues, as so many teams went out of business that the league could no longer survive. By adopting a single-entity structure, competitive bidding among owners for players is eliminated, and a major cause of league failure is sidestepped. In addition, this structure allows sports leagues to evade the application of antitrust laws in management–labor disputes. Following the lead of MLS, every other new league has since adopted this operating structure. Despite its strengths, the model may not prove to be an effective method of running a mature league. It places a disincentive on individual investors to engage in entrepreneurial behaviors, as the benefits of such tactics are likely outweighed by their costs. The sum may be weaker than the whole of its individual parts.

The readings that follow examine these various ownership models and the business issues impacting individuals involved in each. There is emphasis on the functionality of each model. Beyond impact and functionality, the valuable lessons come in understanding who the successful owners have been and who the most successful owners of the future might be.

The chapter opens with an excerpt from *The Rich Who Own Sports.* The focus there is on the old-school owners. It describes these individuals as well as the earliest ventures of corporate franchise ownership.

The excerpt from *Hard Ball: The Abuse of Power in Pro Team Sports* touches on this ownership history but also provides an overview of modern-day owners like Paul Allen and the Tribune Company. The excerpt also focuses on how these owners fit into the modern-day sports league. This is a discussion that will be carried out in more depth in Chapter 12, "Sports Franchise Valuation." Importantly too, the excerpt discusses the "why" of ownership both in monetary and nonmonetary terms.

The final excerpt focuses on the initial public offerings. This format, which has received a good deal of attention, seems to be more of a novelty than an important long-term business model. These are faceless owners, but similar to the broader corporate model used for raising funds for business success. After a brief flurry, it seems that the use of this novel approach to ownership has fizzled in North America, though the model endures in Europe.

Among the related readings in other sections of the book, three might be of particular interest. In Chapter 6, "Media," there is a discussion of vertical integration. In Chapter 11, "Start-Up Leagues and Niche Sports," a selection focuses on the single-entity model of league operation. In Chapter 19, "Diversity," the excerpt from the article "Diversity, Racism, and Professional Sports Franchise Ownership: Change Must Come from Within" focuses on the diversity issue as it relates to ownership.

REFERENCES

1. Phil Taylor (quoting Bob Johnson), "Franchise Player," *Sports Illustrated,* May 5, 2003, 36.

Personalities and Motivations

The Rich Who Own Sports

Don Kowet

Once upon a time, in the ancient republic of Rome, people were caught up in a fad called *hippomania* — a madness for horses. The leading chariot drivers enjoyed the adulation showered today on Joe Namath and Reggie Jackson and Rick Barry and Bobby Orr. The drivers belonged to four teams — Whites, Blues, Reds and Greens. They dressed in "uniforms" — tunics dyed in their team colors. Nearly every Roman citizen rooted for one team or another; White fans, for example, wore white tunics and white scarves to broadcast their allegiance. Fans at the Circus Maximus sat in groups, shouting encouragement, waving placards and team insignias, just the way fans do today in stadiums and arenas across the country. Each team was owned by a large corporation, similar to those that own, say, the Dallas Cowboys and the Kansas City Chiefs. And all four teams were organized into a league run by the four corporations, just the way modern baseball owners run the major leagues.

As the popularity of the races soared, the drivers started making demands. Almost two thousand years before Catfish Hunter got $3.75 million for switching teams, an ex-slave named Diocles got 35 million sesterces ($1.8 million) for switching stables. "Decent men groan to see this former slave earn an income that is one hundred times that of the entire Roman Senate," moaned one contemporary sportswriter.

Eventually, as the empire replaced the republic, the league expanded. Races were increased to twenty-four a day, and eight franchises were added, then another four, for a total of sixteen. The owners of Roman franchises had discovered that by charging millions of sesterces in entry fees, they could turn selling franchises into a profitable business. To make the sport more exciting, as expansion had made it more profitable, the owners began to tolerate, and finally to encourage, violence for its own sake. Just as in modern hockey, the chariot races became marred by collisions and fistfights and deliberate fouls and injuries. The day of the gladiators wasn't far off. In A.D. 79, to attract fans to the newly built Roman Colosseum, promoters staged a bizarre spectacle: a team of Amazon women fought a team of Pygmy men, to the death. Fortunately, the stakes were lower in 1973, when — to attract fans to the newly built Houston Astrodome — an Amazon named Billie Jean King beat a pygmy named Bobby Riggs at tennis.

The Roman franchise owners, of course, didn't have TV to promote their product. Ten years ago *[1967]* the three networks were broadcasting between 540 and 550 hours of sports a year. Now *[1977]* the three commercial networks bombard us with 1,000 hours of baseball and table-top tennis and football and demolition derby and basketball and barrel jumping and ice hockey and dart throwing. TV created a new set of Dioclesses, whose cost-accounted grins gleam at us above cans of shaving cream, under a lathery shampoo. It created new leagues. In promoting the modern version of *hippomania,* TV turned our Sundays from days of rest into days of anxiety. It caused Kiwanis clubs and Boy Scout troops and Parent–Teacher Associations to reshuffle their Monday night meetings, so entranced had their members become by the hypnotic monotone of Howard Cosell. As they had in Rome, multimillionaire tycoons infiltrated American sports, joining the old guard who had started their franchises as a hobby, on a shoestring.

. . . .

It took Walter O'Malley to bring a modern method to the madness of sports ownership. O'Malley expanded baseball's horizon to the West Coast, and provided an early object lesson to modern owners when he brought the Los Angeles City Council to its knees over the issue of a stadium in Chavez Ravine. Then came two millionaires from Texas: Lamar Hunt, frustrated in his effort to start a new team, invented a whole new *league,* while he was still in his twenties; Clint Murchison, only a few years older, started a new team, then invented a new way to operate it — with computers, and an alert eye for collateral profits. At the same time, Roy Hofheinz, a man with more political clout than cash, was brokering an alliance between Texas and professional baseball; he built the first domed stadium, then saw his empire crumble, all the while indulging his bizarre taste for period furniture.

Perhaps the most striking figure among . . . owners is a man who made an unexpected fortune selling health insurance to doctors. Charlie Finley never gained much fame in insurance, but once he bought a baseball team his wildly contradictory behavior made him more famous than most players. He was by turns the advocate of new promotional stunts and fan comfort, deserter of a city, enemy of the Players Association, firer of managers, critic of the press, enemy of the Commissioner and defender of owner rights. And his baseball team happened to be just about the best in the game.

Two other owners who came to wealth late in their lives showed themselves almost as irrepressible as Finley himself. Ewing Kauffman became owner of a baseball team on a fortune made from ground-up oyster shells. And Ray Kroc, whose hamburgers are sold at every crossroads in America, once grabbed the public-address microphone at his team's first home game and denounced his players for their inept performance. (See Table 1 for the Forbes List of Wealthiest Sports Franchise Owners.)

. . . .

The whole boom in sports and the wild increase in the number of teams available to own was the work of the one-eyed monster called television. Noticing this fact, corporate businessmen in the 1960s declared sports a part of the entertainment industry. The Madison Square Garden Corporation, once merely the owner of a malodorous arena and the teams that played there, built a new complex suitable for ice shows, circuses, live musical events, movies, and political conventions. Their hockey and basketball players played alternate nights with acrobats and trained seals. CBS, the original patron of televised pro football, even got into the ownership business, paying the bills for the fast-declining

TABLE 1.

ALL-STAR OWNERS				
Name	All-star value ($mil)	Team	Team value ($mil)	Net worth ($mil)
Paul Allen	28,923	Seattle Seahawks; Portland Trail Blazers	440; 283	21,000
Philip Anschutz	9,789	Los Angeles Kings	189	9,600
Micky Arison	4,848	Miami Heat	248	4,600
William Davidson	2,550	Tampa Bay Lightning; Detroit Pistons	120; 230	2,200
Richard DeVos	1,876	Orlando Magic	176	1,700
William Ford	1,623	Detroit Lions	423	850
Mark Cuban	1,611	Dallas Mavericks	211	1,400
Thomas Hicks	1,323	Texas Rangers; Dallas Stars	356; 207	725
Malcolm Glazer	1,322	Tampa Bay Buccaneers	582	750
Stephen Bisciotti	1,144	Baltimore Ravens	544	600

Source: http://www.forbes.com/2002/03/28/0327allstarowners_print.html.

baseball Yankees for a few years before selling the team at a loss. The marriage of broadcasting and sports seems more stable on a local level. . .

. . . .

History may not spin in cycles. The twentieth-century franchise owner may not, after all, be leading pro sports down the perilous path cleared by his Roman counterpart. But there are some eerie resemblances. The Super Bowl and the World Series seem to have at least as much pomp and pageantry as a Roman circus. The increasing strife between players and owners is mirrored by Diocles' statement two millennia earlier: "I do not care that I am exploited," he said. "I exploit those that exploit me." And an unusual number of the new "emperors" of sport were at one time professional musicians: Ray Kroc and Jack Kent Cooke were dance-band pianists; Gene Autry, a Western singer. We can only be thankful that none of them was a fiddle player.

Hard Ball: The Abuse of Power in Pro Team Sports

James P. Quirk and Rodney D. Fort

. . . . There was a time in the far distant past when owners were ordinary, run-of-the-mill individuals who made their living, such as it was, from their teams. The list of early owners of baseball teams included several prominent ex-players such as Cornelius McGillicuddy (Connie Mack), who caught for the Washington and Philadelphia NL clubs and for Buffalo in the Players League, and ended up owning the old Philadelphia Athletics; Clark Griffith, a star pitcher for the Yankees, later owner of the Washington Senators; John McGraw, third baseman for the Baltimore NL team and then long-time manager and minority owner of the New York Giants; and Charles Comiskey, first baseman and manager for the St. Louis Browns team, which dominated the American Association when it was a major league in the 1880s, followed by his long stint as owner of the Chicago White Sox. In the NFL, George Halas owned and coached his Chicago Bears and played end as well during the 1920s, participating in every way in those memorable early matchups with the Green Bay Packers, where Curly Lambeau was also a player-coach-owner during the first few years of that team. But that is all a thing of the past now. The single most important thing an owner needs today is neither playing nor coaching experience, nor even any knowledge whatsoever of the game. What he needs, pure and simple, is money — lots of it — and the current crop of owners certainly has this in spades. . . .

Heading the list of present-day owners is Paul Allen, the Microsoft multibillionaire who owns the NBA Portland Trail Blazers and the NFL Seattle Seahawks. But there are lots of others on the Forbes 400 list of the richest in the country. Philip Anschutz made his money in fiber optics and now owns the NHL LA Kings and the NBA LA Lakers. . . . Ted Turner of CNN fame owns the NBA Atlanta Hawks and the NL Atlanta Braves. . . . *[The author's discussion of other sports owners and the source of their wealth is omitted.]*

The payoffs to a rich owner from owning a sports team might come mainly from the fun of being involved with the sport itself and with the players and the coaches, rather than from the profits the team generates. There is also the publicity spotlight that shines on the owner of any team — Carl Pohlad is much better known in the Twin Cities for the Twins than for his Marquette National Bank. . . . And all of the fun and publicity is that much more intense when the team you own is a winner.

This view of owners as "sportsmen" ignoring bottom-line considerations has its attractions, and there have been owners who really seem to have fit this image — Tom Yawkey of the Boston Red Sox of the 1930s and 1940s is one who comes immediately to mind. Still, it pays to be a little skeptical. Billionaires don't get there by throwing their money around recklessly — they tend to be the people who let someone else pick up the tab for lunch. As important as winning is to them, it might well be a matter of ego and personal pride that they manage to do this while pocketing a good profit at the same time.

A competing view of the owners is that, their loud protestations to the contrary, they actually are minting money from their teams' TV contracts and high-priced luxury boxes and preferred seating licenses. According to this view, owners would very much like to field winning teams if there's any money in it, but otherwise, they're quite content to load up the roster with low-priced talent and have no qualms about moving the team if fans don't flock to watch a second-division turkey.

Whatever view you have of the matter, there is no doubt that almost all of the huge amount of money that pro team sports generates, through gate receipts, TV income, stadium revenues, and sales of memorabilia, passes first through the hands of the owners. But how much stays there, and how much gets passed on in the form of player and coaching salaries, traveling expenses, administrative costs, stadium rentals, and the like? To answer this question authoritatively would require access to the books of sports teams and their owners. Unfortunately, we do not have that access. There are a few — the Boston Celtics, Cleveland Indians, and Florida Panthers — that are publicly traded businesses, so their revenues, costs, and profits are public information. *[All three teams have since been purchased by private individuals and taken off the public market.]* But most sports teams are closely held businesses, organized as limited partnerships or subchapter S corporations, with no legal requirement to open their books to the rest of us. What we have instead is a set of estimates of income of the various sports teams, prepared on an annual basis since 1990 by *Financial World* magazine. . . .

The first thing that is abundantly clear . . . is that, with just a handful of exceptions, pro team sports does not appear to be a terribly profitable business. In major league baseball, where teams were selling in the $100 to $175 million range between 1990 and 1996, an average operating income of $3.6 million per team per year over the same period wouldn't represent much of a return on investment for an average owner, even if he or she didn't have any interest costs at all — and most owners, especially the most recent ones, have substantial interest costs associated with financing the purchases of their teams. The same is true for the NFL ($5.0 million average operating income per year, teams selling for $150 to $200 million) and the NHL ($3.7 million average per year, with teams worth $50 to $100 million). Only in the NBA do owners appear to be doing much better than breaking even, with an $8.6 million average operating income (and with team prices in the early- to mid-1990s in the $75 to $125 million range). . . .

The figures seem to make mockery of the notion that owners are making out like bandits. At most only a few teams in each league are showing impressive book profits, and they are generally the ones that all of us would have predicted . . .

Another aspect of the financial picture of sports leagues . . . is the division between the haves and the have-nots. . . .

The large numbers of have-nots in baseball and hockey reflect the fact that winning is more important to the bottom line in these sports than in basketball or football. NFL and NBA teams derive most of their gate revenue from season ticket sales, whereas in baseball, walk-in ticket sales are an important share of the team's gate revenues and are much more sensitive to the team's won–lost record. In the NHL, there are the regular season and the "second season," the playoffs. Playoff ticket sales are a critical part of any NHL team's finances, so missing the playoffs almost certainly means financial problems for the team.

Add to this the fact that the value of local TV rights is sensitive to the playing success of a team and that local TV plays a larger role in baseball and hockey than in the other two sports. Thus, a larger share of revenue is sensitive to the won–lost record of baseball and hockey teams, which tends to increase the value of star players to teams, so that salary costs are adversely affected as well.

The large number of have-not teams also provides a clue as to why it was major league baseball and the NHL that experienced long debilitating work stoppages in 1994 and early 1995, with the have-not owners holding out for radical changes in the rules governing their leagues' player markets. Of course, it is also true that the baseball strike in 1994 and 1995 and its after-effects account for part of the dismal operating income figures for baseball teams. If the two strike-related years are thrown out, then average income for MLB teams over the 1990–96 period rises to $5.6 million, still not much to crow about.

. . . .

What does this suggest about the profit orientation of team owners? We would argue that the pressures that free agency has imposed on the bottom line in sports, as indicated by operating income figures, have made it all the more important for teams to act like profit maximizers, ferreting out every possible source of revenue and exploiting it to the hilt, while paring away at costs with a vengeance. It is much more expensive to be a sportsman-owner today than it was in Tom Yawkey's days, and this lesson is well known to everyone who owns a sports team. The drive for stadium subsidies and tax rebates and the hard-line stands in labor negotiations are just a few of the obvious consequences of the tightening of profit margins in sports.

Does this mean that we should be passing the hat again for Paul Allen . . . , or that we should erect statues to owners for their selfless and profitless task of bringing quality athletic entertainment to the masses? Well, maybe not. Let's try to count some of the ways in which an owner can still break even or do better than that, even with an operating income that is negative or barely on the plus side.

First, it is commonplace for an owner to take on a salaried job with his team, as president or chairman of the board. It's the owner's team so he can pay himself whatever salary he wishes. . . .

. . . . In the years when Calvin Griffith owned and operated the Minnesota Twins, it was widely reported that there were Griffith relations galore on the payroll of the team. There is nothing illegal or immoral about this, of course; in fact, to the contrary, it makes Griffith seem like what he in fact was, a very family-oriented person. However, it does mean that book figures on team revenues, costs, and profits for the Twins understated the income that the owner and his family derived from the team.

Second, more and more often, team owners today have complex financial interrelationships with their teams. For example, the Tribune Company owns the Chicago Cubs and also televises Cub games on its superstation, WGN. The value of the Cubs' TV rights can appear as revenue for the team; or a part can be shifted to WGN, which would have the effect of lowering the revenue and hence the operating income of the team. It's all up to the executives of the Tribune Company, who have free range to allocate the revenue where they wish. There are often incentives to shift income away from the team and to the TV station instead.

In the case of the Florida Marlins, when Wayne Huizenga owned the team, he also owned the stadium (Professional Players Stadium) in which the team played as well as the Miami TV station that aired Marlin game telecasts. Into which of Huizenga's several pockets did the stadium rental or the local TV revenue go? Questions like this have become much more than merely academic matters for the players in the NFL and NBA operating under salary cap rules, because those rules guarantee players a stated minimum percent of league revenues. League revenues will vary depending on whether the team gets the full market value of its TV revenues, or instead a part is transferred to the station, network, or superstation owned by the team owner. (See Table 2 for a list of the high profile and publicly traded corporations that own sports franchises.)

. . . .

Third, ownership of a sports team provides tax sheltering opportunities that are not available to most other businesses, so that what appears to be a before-tax loss by the team can, in certain circumstances, be converted into an after-tax profit for the owner. The idea behind the tax shelter was one more contribution to the sports industry by the fertile and conniving mind of Bill Veeck, baseball's greatest hustler and team owner. Back in 1950, Veeck was in the process of selling his Cleveland Indians team to a syndicate headed by his friend Hank Greenberg, the great Tiger outfielder. Veeck convinced the IRS that the purchaser of a team should be allowed to assign a portion of the purchase price of the team to the player contracts that the team owned, and then to treat this as a wasting asset, depreciating the contracts over a period of five years or less. That was an important bit of convincing, because the IRS already had in place rules allowing teams to write off as current costs signing bonuses, scouting costs, losses of minor league affiliates, and all the other costs incurred by a team in replacing its current roster of players with young players coming into the sport.

By allowing a new owner to assign a part of the purchase price of a team to player contracts and then depreciate them, the IRS in effect was allowing a team to double-count the cost of replacing players. And, since depreciation is a noncash cost, just a bookkeeping entry, this could allow the owner to convert a pretax book loss to an after-tax profit. Without getting into too much detail, an example can illustrate things.

Suppose someone buys an NFL team for $200 million. The new owner assigns 50 percent of the purchase price to player contracts (the maximum allowed under the law) that is, $100 million, and then depreciates the contracts over 5 years at $20 million per year. Suppose that revenue is $100 million per year and that costs, exclusive of player contract depreciation, are $90 million. Then, for the first five years of operation of the team, the books of the team will look like this:

Revenue	$100 million
Less costs	90 million
Less depreciation	20 million
Pretax profits	−$10 million

First, note that depreciation of $20 million is simply a bookkeeping entry, with no actual cash expended to cover this expense. Thus, even though the team will report a loss of $10 million to the IRS, the owner will have a positive cash flow of $10 million ($100 million in revenue minus $90 million in cost) from the operation of the team.

Suppose that the team is operated as a partnership, so that the operating income of the team becomes a part of the taxable income of the owner, which includes his or her income from outside sources. (The reason that teams are often organized as [limited] partnerships rests in large part on this fact.) As the comments earlier make clear, most owners have lots and lots of income from sources other than their teams. Suppose the owner is in the 33 percent tax bracket. Because operating income is negative, the owner can use the $10 million pretax loss to reduce his total taxable income from other sources by $10 million, thus saving him $3.3 million on his tax bill.

By the magic of accounting and the Veeck tax shelter, the team shows a loss of $10 million per year, but the owner has in fact earned $13.3 million in after-tax income from the team, equal to the

TABLE 2.

LIST OF HIGH PROFILE AND PUBLICLY TRADED CORPORATIONS THAT OWN SPORTS FRANCHISES		
Company	*Symbol*	*Teams*
AOL Time Warner	AOL	Atlanta Braves
Cablevision Systems	CVC	NY Knicks, NY Rangers
Comcast Corp.	CMCSK	Philadelphia 76ers Philadelphia Flyers
New York Times	NYT	Boston Red Sox
Rogers Communications	RG	Toronto Blue Jays
Tribune Co.	TRB	Chicago Cubs

Source: http://money.cnn.com/2002/10/04/commentary/column_sportsbiz/public_teams/.

$10 million cash flow from the team's operations plus the $3.3 million the owner has saved in taxes on his outside income.

The owner can continue to do this each of the first five years he owns the team, after which contract depreciation is exhausted. Moreover, because the IRS permits the team to write off the out-of-pocket costs of actually replacing players, the team should be every bit as strong on the field after five years as it was when it was purchased, despite the fact that, on the books of the team, the value of the player contracts has now been completely written off.

. . . .

Owners typically plead poverty by quoting net operating losses as the value of the team. And, for people in their wealth class, even 7 percent does not seem like an extraordinary return. Harold Seymour, the eminent baseball historian, quotes Charles Ebbets on baseball operations: "The question is purely one of business; I am not in baseball for my health." But before we agree that sports are not a high-return investment for rich people, let's remember the other values of owning a team. Profit-taking can occur under the "other salaries" heading. Most of the rest of the costs may actually be revenues, or generate even larger revenues, in other nonsports business operations of the owners. Business and government associations made during ownership tenure are valuable. And there is, after all, the fun of owning a team. Given all of these benefits, a 7 percent rate of return generating $5 million annually after taxes looks pretty good to us. Now, if only we could come up with that initial $75 million. . . .

. . . . A team can show a book loss, yet pay owner-management quite well while they run the team, generate many other values not captured in the team's income statement, and end up as a very valuable commodity at sale time. After all, any subsequent owner will be starting the player roster depreciation process all over again while buying in on the same stream of value over time. The essential lesson from this analysis . . . is that you can expect owners of a pretty good team to be happy for about three or four years. After that, player contract depreciation plays out, the value of ownership falls, and owners start making public statements about the losses they are suffering and the need for some sort of revenue boost in order to remain competitive in the league.

. . . .

Finally, offsetting the bad news about operating income is the good news about the continuing increases in the prices of sports teams themselves. The capital gains that an owner gets from selling his team can more than offset the losses, if any, that the team has shown from its ongoing operations. In fact, this has been true in practically all cases involving recent sales of sports teams. . . .

. . . .

The fact that the market prices of teams keep going up, even while operating income figures remain at very low levels, raises the question as to whether what we are observing is a "bubble," much like the bubble in California real estate in the 1980s. In a bubble, the current price of an asset is determined not by what the asset is expected to earn in the future, but by what people today think buyers in the future will be willing to pay for the asset. A bubble is fueled by the "greater fool" argument: "Sure, I know this house isn't worth $300,000, but a year from now, I'll be able to sell it to some other real estate speculator for $500,000 because he'll be expecting the price the year after he buys it to be $600,000." The price is what it is today because everyone expects a "greater fool" to come around tomorrow to take the item off your hands at an even higher price.

All that economists know for sure about bubbles is that, eventually, they burst, and it's like the old game of musical chairs — whoever gets stuck with the overvalued asset at the time the bubble bursts has nowhere to get rid of it. There is a classic story about the stock market that goes something like this:

> A broker touted a small company's stock to a client and convinced him to buy 1,000 shares at $10 per share. A week later, the broker reported that the price was up to $12, and the client opted for another 1,000 shares. The price kept going up and the client kept buying for several more weeks. When the broker reported the price at $25 per share, the client said, "I'm not greedy. I'll just take my profits now. So sell my shares." There was a pause and then the broker asked, "To whom?"

If it really is a bubble that we are observing in the market for sports teams, the problem is that there isn't any way to know beforehand just when the bubble will burst. Those unlucky people who happen to be holding title to the overvalued team franchises will simply have to eat their losses and live with them. But if it is a bubble, it's been going on for quite a long time. Historical records of franchise sales in sports indicate that over the past thirty years or so, on average, NBA teams have been increasing in price at a rate of around 26 percent per year, MLB teams at around 14 percent per year, and NFL teams at around 22 percent per year.

The fact that the rates of increase in franchise prices in the 1990s, while in the double-digit range, still are lower than those in earlier years indicates that if there is a bubble in these markets, at least it is tapering off. Actually, over the period of the mid-1990s, investors were making a better rate of return simply "buying the market" with an indexed stock fund than were sports entrepreneurs with their high-visibility team investments.

Rather than being simply a bubble phenomenon, the continuing increase in team prices in sports and the capital gains being captured by owners no doubt reflect a range of factors at work in the sports industry. There are the "fun and games" and publicity aspects of ownership of a sports team. These have been increasing over time along with the media exposure that sports receives. The "spill-over" benefits of owning a sports team, those after-tax returns identified earlier that don't show up as operating income for a team, have been increasing over time as well, and get reflected in higher team prices. And there is undoubtedly something of a speculative bubble present as well, a common belief among present and prospective owners that because almost no one in the past has sold a team for less than its purchase price, future capital gains are more or less assured.

In summary, pro sports teams are now selling in the $150 to $250 million range; thus the current owners of sports teams are, by and large, very wealthy individuals. But, with teams being as expensive as they are, ownership of a team is a significant investment, even for a wealthy owner. The returns to ownership, as measured by operating income, are below market rates of return from investments of comparable risk in all sports with the possible exception of the NBA. A prime reason for the weak operating income performance of teams is free agency and the continuing escalation of player salaries. This suggests that bottom-line considerations play a critical role in team decision making, perhaps looming larger for today's owners than for owners of the past. On the one hand, this provides incentives for owners to act as aggressively as possible in attempting to exploit whatever local monopoly power the team possesses — if we don't squeeze out every cent of money from local fans and tax-payers, how can we afford to compete with the teams that do? On the other hand, the concentration on the bottom line makes it more difficult for teams to act cooperatively as members of a sports league in addressing problems of mutual interest to all teams in the league. What team can afford to sacrifice some of its income for the "common good" in a world in which lots of red ink is waiting just around the bend for any team that loses a star player to injury or ticket sales to bad weather?

There have been exceptional owners such as Phil Wrigley, who refused to schedule night games at Wrigley Park when he owned the Cubs, to keep nighttime noise, traffic, and confusion out of the north side neighborhood of the park; and Ewing Kauffman, who heavily subsidized his Kansas City Royals when he was alive and then set up a committee of leading local citizens to operate and then sell the team after his death, to ensure that the team stayed in town. But everything about the current and historical record of pro sports suggests that if you are trying to understand what is going on in sports, your best bet is to assume that owners will be motivated by bottom-line considerations, however wealthy they are. Wayne Huizenga's decision to sell off his Florida Marlins, one by one, and then the team franchise itself after the team won the 1997 World Series but reportedly lost $30 million at the gate fits the mold nicely.

The contribution of owners to the problems of pro team sports does not arise, however, because they operate their teams to make money. After all, one of the fundamental reasons why we in America enjoy the living standards we do is that all those businessmen out there are free to operate to make as much money as they can. The argument in favor of a free enterprise, profit-oriented economy is that the way a businessman makes money is by producing the goods that consumers want, in the style and quantity that they want, at the lowest possible price. And if a businessman doesn't do this, he should be prepared to be steamrollered by other businessmen who do a better and cheaper job of producing that product.

Once again, the problem with the sports industry is the fact that leagues operate as monopolies, so that team owners in sports are not subject to the same intense market pressures to perform well as if they had to face competition from rivals. The local monopoly power of teams is limited, of course, by the availablity of substitutes. NFL football has to compete with the college game, with other pro sports such as the NBA and the NHL, and with alternative forms of entertainment. But, when combined with the monopoly power of the league it belongs to, the local monopoly power of a team is certainly significant, as evidenced, for example, by the success of teams in their campaigns for new, highly subsidized stadiums financed by cities and states. . . .

New Models

Public Ownership of Sports Franchises: Investment, Novelty, or Fraud?

Eugene J. Stroz, Jr.

A recent phenomenon . . . is the offer and sale of interests in professional sports franchises to the "public" in initial public offerings. There are examples of such offerings in each of the major American sports. The National Football League's ("NFL") Green Bay Packers sold their first share to the public in 1923. The Boston Celtics of the National Basketball Association ("NBA"), the Florida Panthers of the National Hockey League ("NHL"), and the Cleveland Indians of Major League Baseball ("MLB") have all recently offered and sold diluted interests in their franchises to the public. Have these owners discovered a way for fans to become more involved in their team's performance, both on and off the field, or have they simply advanced a more elaborate, relatively risk-free means of lining their own pockets at the further expense of the fans?

Sinking hard-earned money into sports stocks is not generally regarded as a good investment. It is widely viewed as nothing more than the purchase of a novelty item which does little more than show support for the team. It is at best a questionable practice and at worst a fraud perpetrated on the fans. One must question why our legitimate capital-raising markets are being used by these sports franchises to sell nothing more than elaborate novelty items.

In theory, our federal securities laws exist to protect the investing public from such situations. However, neither Congress nor the Securities and Exchange Commission ("SEC") . . . is in the business of regulating substance. Disclosure is the method by which Congress has chosen to protect investors, sophisticated and unsophisticated alike. Therefore, as long as an issuer fully discloses what it is selling, it can sell just about anything.

Although not technically fraudulent under the current securities regulation regime, these offerings of sports stocks have difficulty passing a simple "smell test." The best interests of the fans and the best interests of shareholders in a franchise are strikingly divergent. Marketing and selling these securities to sports fans creates a situation of inherent conflict. . .

II. OVERVIEW: WHY GO PUBLIC?

There are several advantages and disadvantages that must be considered when contemplating the sale of interests in a public offering. The primary advantage to a public offering is the ability to raise capital on favorable terms. Another important advantage is the liquidity that a public offering brings to the owner's value in the enterprise. Although the owner will be subjected to administrative regulations limiting the immediate ability to realize the value of the enterprise, over time the owner will be able to realize most, if not all, of the wealth of the business without necessarily ceding complete control.

There are also many disadvantages to consider. When a company goes public, lost is much of the flexibility that the autonomous owner of a private company enjoys. Generally, once the company is public the owner will relinquish a certain amount of control over the business, which, depending on how much the owners sells, could make the company susceptible to a hostile takeover. Additionally, the expenses of public offerings are quite large, as are the expenses that a public company incurs on a continuing basis. In short, the decision of whether to take a business public is not an impetuous one. Some of the pitfalls, such as loss of control, are understandably more troubling to the owner of a sports franchise.

The considerations do not end with the decision to sell interests in the company to the public. Once that decision has been made, another major hurdle must be cleared. The owner must find a suitable investment bank willing to underwrite the public offering. In evaluating candidates for public offerings, investment bankers consider a number of factors, including a company's size, its product lines, growth potential, financial ratios, historical performance, management, market conditions, and — most importantly for sports franchises — its public appeal. The underwriting investment bank, among other things, provides the basic strategy of the public offering, organizes the syndicate and selling group, and generally manages the mechanics of the offering process.

III. BACKGROUND: THE PUBLICLY HELD SPORTS FRANCHISES

A. The Green Bay Packers

Since 1923 the Packers have completed four separate offerings of "stock." The first sale was in 1923 and was for $5.00 per share. In contrast, their fourth and most recent stock sale was intended to raise up to $200 million at $200 per share. The Packers were only able to sell about 120,000 shares and raised about $24 million in revenue, far below the minimum of 400,000 shares they expected to sell.

In return for their $200 per share, purchasers were entitled to not much more than "becom[ing] a part of the Packers' tradition and legacy." Each purchaser also received an "official" stock certificate, presumably suitable for framing. The shares did include minimal voting rights, but these shares are more notable for what they did not include. No dividends will ever be paid, the shares cannot appreciate in value, shares are nontransferable and can only be redeemed by the Packers at a substantial loss, no shareholder is permitted to own more than 200,000 shares, and, in stark contrast to the original offering in 1923, there were no "special benefits," such as season ticket privileges associated with ownership of shares. These shares bear a striking resemblance to the PSL, a noteworthy dissimilarity being that the shares are devoid of the only "benefit" of a PSL — the right to purchase a seat. In a sense, they are nothing more than "personal certificate licenses" because they do little more than permit the purchaser to receive a certificate.

The principal, and perhaps only, benefit enjoyed by Packers shareholders is that, by virtue of the fact that over half of the outstanding shares are owned by Wisconsin residents, it is unlikely that the Green Bay Packers would ever be able to relocate or sell the team because a majority vote of shareholders would be required. However, in reality, purchasers of Packers shares are primarily interested in boasting about their ownership of the team and attending the annual meeting which is held annually at Lambeau Field.

B. The Boston Celtics

In 1986, the Boston Celtics became . . . the only NBA team to sell interests in their franchise in a public offering. Units in the Boston Celtics Limited Partnership are traded on the New York Stock Exchange under the ticker symbol "BOS." The Celtics offering had a few similarities to Packers' offering, but there were many notable differences as well.

Similar to a purchase of Packers stock, the Celtics purchaser did not receive many privileges beyond that of receiving a framable certificate. However, it is important to note the additional rights that Celtics unitholders retain. Holders of Celtics units actually can receive annual dividends distributed out of accumulated earnings. The Celtics have not paid a cash dividend since December 1998, but prior to that, cash distributions were made to unitholders on at least an annual basis. Also, holders of Celtics shares have the ability to sell their shares and have access to the capital markets to do so. Notwithstanding such rights, these securities are largely considered stocking stuffers. It must be noted that, unlike the Packers' shareholders, Celtics' unitholders have no voice in how the business is conducted. They have absolutely no say in how the business is run.

Also noteworthy is that the big winners in the Celtics offering were the existing owners of the Celtics, not the partnership itself. Interestingly, the offering was a secondary offering, not a primary offering. The Boston Celtics Limited Partnership received none of the proceeds from the offering — it was the existing owners who individually reaped all of the proceeds from the sale. *[The Celtics were taken private in 2003.]* In contrast, the Green Bay Packers can only use the proceeds of their offerings for very specific purposes as laid out in their by-laws, primarily for renovations to Lambeau Field and other related expenses.

C. The Florida Panthers

Florida Panther Holdings, Inc. represents more of a traditional investment as it has diversified its operations into more than just ownership of the hockey team. It also attempted to minimize the novelty value of its stock by providing for a minimum purchase of 100 shares in the initial public offering. This may not prevent souvenir seekers from looking to the open market, but most trades on the open market are in minimum blocks of 100 shares. Florida Panther Holdings, Inc. Class A Common Stock currently trades on the New York Stock Exchange under the ticker symbol "RST."

Similar to the Packers, the Panthers will not be paying dividends, and, like the Celtics, the Panthers have restricted shareholder voting rights. Each of the 32,599,965 shares of Class A Common Stock outstanding at the time of the initial public offering is entitled to one vote at any shareholder meeting. This sounds remarkable until one realizes that each of the 255,000 outstanding shares of Class B Common Stock (all of which are held by H. Wayne Huizenga, the principal owner) is entitled to 10,000 votes at any shareholder meeting, amounting to an aggregate of 2.55 billion votes. This voting structure was apparently a byproduct of certain NHL voting control requirements.

Although a more diversified company may appeal to the conventional investor, one must query whether this is what the fan-as-investor truly desires when acquiring sports stocks. Boca Resorts, Inc. (formerly known as Florida Panthers Holdings, Inc.) has expanded its operations into hotels, resorts, golf courses, and other leisure- and recreation-related business areas. *[Boca Resorts has since sold its ownership of the Panthers to a group of individual investors. The team is no longer publicly traded.]* The more diversified these enterprises get, the more diluted and indirect the investment in the sports franchise becomes to the fan-as-investor. Cablevision Systems Corp. owns the New York Rangers and the New York Knicks, but does one acquire part ownership in the Knicks or Rangers when purchasing shares of Cablevision stock? A tenuous argument might be undertaken until confronted with the fact that the Knicks and the Rangers combine to account for less than four percent of Cablevision's assets. In other words, buy Cablevision stock with the goal of investing in a sports franchise and "at most, you're buying a couple of Knicks road jerseys."

D. The Cleveland Indians

In 1998, Cleveland Indians Baseball Company, Inc. offered and sold 4,600,000 shares of Class A Common Stock in a public offering. While they were publicly traded, they were traded on the Nasdaq National Market under the ticker symbol "CLEV." The Cleveland Indians appear to have gleaned much from their publicly traded brethren — incorporating the most one-sided features from each of the aforementioned offerings.

They emulated the Packers by stating their intention not to pay any dividends on the Class A Common Stock, instead choosing to retain all earnings for reinvestment purposes. They mimicked the Panthers by adopting their voting structure. Similar to the Celtics offering, the net proceeds wound up lining the pockets of the owners, most significantly the Indians' principal owner, Richard (Dick) E. Jacobs, not in the coffers of the company. Although the net proceeds of the offering were technically received by the company, as they were in the Celtics offering, they were used solely to purchase existing limited partnership interests from Mr. Jacobs.

For the better part of two years, Cleveland Indians Baseball Company, Inc. languished as a public company with "little enthusiasm for its stock from the serious investment community." In May 1999, Dick Jacobs decided to sell the Indians and subsequently hired two investment banking firms to find a buyer. At this point, the stock rallied and began to trade at or above the initial public offering price for the first time. Ultimately, Dick Jacobs found a buyer in Larry Dolan and agreed to sell the company for $320 million. The acquisition was structured as a cash-out merger, which meant that all of the shareholders — Class A and Class B holders alike — were required to tender their shares back to the company for cash consideration in an amount equal to $22.61 per share. The merger closed in February 2000, at which point Cleveland Indians Baseball Company, Inc. ceased to exist.

What is it that the purchasers of these securities were actually buying anyway? The Celtics offering was sold directly to the public, making the shareholders, in a collective sense, limited partners. Alternatively, the Cleveland Indians created an entity — Cleveland Indians Baseball Company, Inc. — which offered and sold shares of Class A Common Stock to the public. With the proceeds of the offering, Cleveland Indians Baseball Company, Inc. purchased limited partnership interests in Cleveland Indians Baseball Co. Limited Partnership from entities controlled by Dick Jacobs for an aggregate of $55.8 million.

Purchasers of the Class A Common Stock were not actually buying the Cleveland Indians, they were buying shares of an entity which was formed to own limited partnership interests in the limited partnership which actually owned the Cleveland Indians. In essence, Cleveland Indians Baseball Company, Inc. was nothing more than an undiversified mutual fund. Although the purchasers had a pecuniary interest in the Cleveland Indians, it could best be described as indirect and attenuated. As such, the Cleveland Indians were not a publicly owned entity, rather they were owned by a public entity. The sole factor distinguishing the Indians' ownership situation with that of the Knicks and the Rangers is that the sports franchise made up a higher percentage of the total assets of the company, but even that was subject to change since the Indians' prospectus left the door open for an expansion of its business. Dick Jacobs and the Cleveland Indians have escalated the phenomenon of "public ownership" of sports franchises, started innocently enough by the Packers in 1923, to a disturbingly complex and elaborate level.

 . . . . *[The author's discussion of federal securities laws and related discussion is omitted.]*

At first glance, there appears to be a natural synergy — owners desiring to sell and fans-as-investors eager to buy — and in theory, giving fans an interest in their favorite franchises is a terrific idea. In reality, however, it creates more problems than it solves. The seemingly perfect synergy turns out to be nothing more than the proverbial square peg in the round hole.

The fundamental problem with public ownership of sports franchises lies not in its viability — as it has proven to be a feasible option for the owners — but rather with its implementation, its impurity, and its startling lack of synergy. The implementation quandary stems from the plundering mentality of the owners, and the impurity results from the increasingly restrictive provisions that our fan-as-investor has been subjected to, such as the complete lack of voting rights and the absence of dividends — all of which lead to a transaction amazingly devoid of synergy. However, the issue remains unresolved as to whether a purchase of interests in a sports franchise is analogous to an investment, akin to buying a sports novelty item, or a fraud perpetrated on our fan-as-investor.

 . . . . *[The author's discussion of novelty versus investment and fraud is omitted.]*

VI. CONCLUSION

If this subject matter were to be analogized in terms of criminal law, it might be characterized as a "victimless" crime, involving fans who are more than willing to part with hard-earned dollars for the novelty and prestige of part ownership in a sports franchise and unscrupulous owners who are more than willing to accept their money. However, in our hypothetical analogy, although "victimless," they would still be "crimes." Is it germane that the fans enter willingly into these transactions? There are several areas of the law that afford protection to the willing yet unwitting participant in a one-sided transaction.

The Green Bay Packers offerings are quite perplexing in this regard. In some aspects, they are troublesome primarily because there is absolutely no investment value. However, for that same reason they might be the least distressing. The Packers did not even attempt to market their shares as investment securities. They made it clear to their purchasers that a purchase of the shares was tanta-mount to a donation to a fund which will be used exclusively for stadium repairs to Lambeau Field. However, the Packers' offerings are less troublesome since the purchases actually have a bottom-line effect in the shareholders' favor. They make the likelihood of a franchise relocation of the Green Bay Packers nearly impossible. The only bottom-line effect of the Indians and Celtics offerings was encountered by the selling owners — who pocketed millions while ceding next to nothing.

At least one commentator has suggested that, although these offerings might be misleading and bad investments for the fans, it is more appropriate to target the fans of a sports franchise for financing

— as opposed to holding an entire city hostage for stadium financing, subsidies, and abatement packages. It is suggested here that these offerings will not be conducted in lieu of municipal assistance, but will be conducted in addition to whatever municipal assistance the team can garner. This is exactly what Dick Jacobs did in Cleveland. He conducted the public offering and pocketed his $55 million dollars after getting a $180 million "sweetheart deal" to build Jacobs Field four years earlier.

Fans will likely get more enjoyment out of framing their stock certificate, bragging of their ownership to friends, and attending the annual meetings (with or without the ability to vote) than they will from a return on the investment. The dilemma is inherent: the fans do not require or expect a return on their investment, and even if an investment in a sports franchise actually turns a profit — as in the case of the Cleveland Indians when they were sold — the shares have to be tendered, something the typical fan-as-investor is not interested in doing. They just want to feel that they are a part of their favorite sports franchise. The owners, however, have not relinquished any control over the team and have left the fans with nothing more than an indirect, pecuniary interest in the team, one that will not likely appreciate in value to any large degree.

Are these offerings legitimate investments? Are they elaborate schemes? Are they innocuous novelties? It is hard to say because they have attributes of all three. A telling sign may be the reaction shareholders had when informed by Dick Jacobs at the Indians' annual shareholders meeting that a sale of the Cleveland Indians would bring a healthy return on their investment. The "investors" were singularly concerned with whether or not they would have to tender their shares. When Dick Jacobs informed them that it was likely, their only reaction was a sigh of disappointment.

The headline in the *Cleveland Plain Dealer* the day after the Indians' public offering described the situation — not only of the Indians, but also of public ownership of sports franchises in general — with such succinct clarity that no further comment or explanation is necessary. The headline simply read: "Indians Stock Is a Hit with Fans, Jacobs Gets Millions, but Share Price Slips."

DISCUSSION QUESTIONS

1. What is the likely view of public ownership by league commissioners?
2. Why do small investors buy shares of sports franchise stocks?
3. What are the unique characteristics of the Green Bay Packers public ownership structure?
4. Do you think public ownership of sports franchises will continue to grow?
5. How does sports franchise ownership differ from corporate ownership?
6. Is sports franchise ownership profitable?
7. Are sports franchise owners still "sportsmen?"
8. Which sports are the most profitable? Why?
9. What is the single factor that has proved to be most important in the "boom" of professional sports?
10. Discuss the difference in importance in winning hockey and baseball versus football and basketball. What are the major reasons for this difference?
11. Is the bottom-line motivation of most owners bad for sports?
12. Given the economic concept of market efficiency, is Stroz correct in arguing that the sale of stock by professional sports franchises is at best a questionable practice and at worst a fraud on the public?

LEAGUES: STRUCTURE AND BACKGROUND

INTRODUCTION

Professional sports leagues are unique business structures in a free market economy. As was mentioned in the introduction to this book, leagues combine elements of cooperation and competition and allow independent team owners to seek monetary gains that might otherwise be unavailable if pursued unilaterally through the playing of disparate contests. Indeed, it is doubtful whether professional team sports could survive in the absence of leagues. Leagues offer an enticing, profit-maximizing structure to teams both on and off the playing field. Though professional sports teams are clearly competitors on the field, leagues benefit owners by providing organized regular and championship seasons of play and offering a unitary set of playing rules, both of which are designed to maximize fan interest and, consequently, team profits. Off the field, competition among teams is generally limited to the pursuit of scarce playing and managerial talent. Professional sports leagues are cooperative endeavors away from the playing field, with teams jointly engaging in numerous practices that maximize the profits of the collective entity.

There exists only one league in each of the major professional sports. This has important public policy implications. The league structure allows teams to establish constitutions that govern the locations of their franchises, conditions of entry into the league and relocation within the league, the labor market for players, and rules of the game, as well as permitting teams to pool their broadcast rights for negotiation and sale. This cartel behavior has been widely criticized. However, it is possible that this off-the-field cooperation among teams allows the on-field competition between teams to endure. It is also important to note in a free market economy that professional sports leagues have adopted many characteristics of an alternative economic system — socialism — particularly with respect to planning and the redistribution of income. Indeed, it seems that the higher the degree of socialism, the stronger the league. The collective strength of the league is more important than that of the individual teams within the league. Revenue sharing in leagues is discussed in Chapter 3.

In the first reading, the sports advisory firm Moag and Company examines the sports industry's resistance to downturns in the United States economy. While a soft economy is often cited by members of sports organizations as a cause of declines in both fan attendance and franchise values, this report provides evidence that the sports industry is more resistant to bear markets than other sectors of the economy.

In the second selection, Gerald Scully reviews the economics of professional sports leagues, focusing on the restrictions that these leagues place on their products. Particular attention is given to league-wide television contracts and player salaries.

In the third excerpt, Michael Danielson provides a comprehensive analysis of the role of leagues in the business of professional sports. After giving an overview of league structures, the author then discusses the importance of both on-field competition and territorial exclusivity for the individual teams within the league. Danielson subsequently addresses the issue of geographic exclusivity in professional sports leagues in great detail.

In the next selection, an alternative to the league structure embraced by North American professional sports is presented by Stephen Ross and Stefan Szymanski. The system of promotion and relegation utilized in the majority of the global professional sports leagues has numerous advantages over the closed ventures that are found domestically. The specific case of English professional football (soccer) is presented as an example.

POSITIONING OF SPORTS IN THE U.S. ECONOMY

THE SPORTS INDUSTRY'S RESISTANCE TO BEAR MARKETS

Moag and Company

In response to the recent decline in the U.S. economy, Moag and Company has examined the impact of declining economies on the sports industry in the United States. Our analysis focuses on the U.S. economy from 1970 through November 2001, when the S&P 500 grew at a compound annual growth rate ("CAGR") of 8.4%. During this 30-year period, however, five bear markets have occurred. . . . Based on our analysis, we conclude that the sports industry has performed better during the broader effects of a declining economy, and is therefore an attractive investment during both robust and declining economies.

Businesses in most industries experience dramatic declines in value during bear markets and periods of market instability.

During these same periods of uncertainty, however, businesses in the sports industry experience either no decline or less of a decline than the broader market. One, therefore, may classify sports businesses as "bear resistant." In some cases, during poor broad market conditions, the values of franchises and other sports-focused companies actually prosper as fans turn to sports-related pursuits as an entertaining distraction from the nervousness of economic doubt.

. . . .

PART I: PROFESSIONAL SPORTS FRANCHISE VALUES

Professional sports franchises currently are valued at their highest levels ever. This analysis presents franchise values as both specific comparative data versus bear market performance and as a general reflection of the value of sports content in the marketplace. We examine franchise values according to attendance, ticket prices, and franchise sale values during the last 30 years.

A. Attendance

Fan attendance at professional sports events is a primary revenue driver for sports franchises. Attendance-related revenue depends upon the volume of tickets sold, the price of tickets, and the number of "bodies in seats."

Ticket Sale Volume for Paid Attendance.   Since 1970, overall attendance at regular season sports events in the NBA, NFL, NHL, and MLB has grown 163%, from 49 million fans in 1970 to 128 million fans in 2000. Moreover, each of the four major professional sports leagues has experienced significant growth in attendance, with the NHL and NBA producing 214% and 362% growth respectively.

A portion of the rise in attendance is related to the entrance of expansion teams. But expansion teams notwithstanding, the fact remains that a larger body of consumers is attending professional sports events, and attendance figures continue to grow.

Regular season attendance figures during the five identified bear market periods indicate that even during periods of poor economic performance, fans continue to attend professional sports events. . . . In fact, during the five bear markets since 1970, fan attendance at sports events actually has grown more often than it has decreased. . . .

In four of the six instances for which attendance decreased during a bear market, the decline is more likely to have been a direct result of a labor dispute during the bear market than a decrease in the number of fans attending events due to tightening economic conditions. . . .

. . . .

Ticket Prices.   The average ticket price for a professional sports event has grown at an 8.7% CAGR since 1995, or 62%. Average ticket prices in both the NFL and the NBA have surpassed the $50 mark, and the NHL is quickly approaching that range. Major League Baseball remains the lowest-priced average ticket among the four major professional leagues. . . .

Attendance Trends and Ticket Prices.   Even during bear markets, sports franchises benefit from two significant trends: (1) an expanding fan base, and (2) increasing ticket prices. Either of these trends would by itself provide sports franchises with increased revenue on an annual basis, but the real significance of these trends and their effect on professional sports franchise values is their simultaneous occurrence during bear markets. More fans attend sports events during declining economies despite rising ticket prices. This market dynamic reflects an insatiable consumer demand for sports entertainment that resists pressures to reduce personal consumption during bear markets.

B. Franchise Sale Values

Values paid in franchise transactions have increased consistently under various market conditions over the last 30 years. The increases in values paid for professional sports franchises continue even during depressed economies.

Since 1970, investments in sports franchises have provided a greater return on investment than the market return during the same transaction period. On a broad scale, investments in franchises grew at an average rate of 18.8% per year since 1970, outpacing the average 8.4% growth of the S&P 500 during the same period.

While the general return on investment in sports franchises is favorable versus the broader market, the returns during bear markets are remarkable. . . .

Bear Market Franchise Returns vs. S&P 500. Fifteen of the 17 franchise transactions that have occurred during bear markets have exhibited a greater percentage return for their investors than the market percentage return during the same period. . . .

Franchise Returns: Bull vs. Bear Market Sales. Further evidence that sports franchise values endure despite declining economies is derived from a comparison of investment returns from sales of franchises in bear markets versus returns from franchise sales in the year preceding and the year following a bear market. Franchises that have been sold during the most recent five bear markets have provided excellent returns to the franchise owners. The most recent sales, however, have provided the greatest returns, indicating the dramatic increase in franchise values that have occurred recently. When comparing franchise percentage returns to market percentage returns, four of the five highest franchise returns over market returns have occurred in the last two years. Remarkably . . . the average CAGR of a franchise sale during a bear market is comparable to, and in three of the five bear markets, better than the CAGR of the franchise sales which occurred in the year prior to and the year after the bear market.

. . . . *[The author's discussion of publicly traded companies is omitted.]*

CONCLUSION

Our research concludes that businesses in the sports industry maintain an attractive resistance to the broader market declines that occur during bear markets. Barring labor issues and or work stoppages, attendance across the four leagues has grown consistently every year. Simultaneously, ticket prices across the four leagues have increased year after year. Finally, the investment returns that franchises have provided during bear markets have generally outperformed the returns of the market during the same time period.

. . . . The sports industry prospers during poor economic conditions. . . .

The sports industry has developed into a dynamic and valuable segment of the U.S. economy. Based on our analysis, it appears that most sports-focused businesses thrive regardless of the present economic conditions. In both robust and declining economies, people turn to sports out of loyalty, passion, and a need for an entertaining distraction from the regularities of life. Accordingly, the sports industry represents an attractive investment opportunity.

Overview of the Professional Model

The Market Structure of Sports

Gerald W. Scully

A financial golden age in professional sports has existed for the last fifteen years or so. Club revenues and player salaries have skyrocketed. . . . Rapid revenue growth has fostered aggressive bidding for free agents: average player salary has risen twentyfold in baseball and tenfold in basketball. As a class, professional athletes in team sports are among the most highly paid in society.

. . . . The prospects for robust revenue and salary growth . . . have dimmed. Attendance may rise somewhat, but with so many sellouts, its growth rate will decline. Luxury boxes will be added, and ticket prices increased, but revenue growth from these and other fan-related expenditures is marginal. The fact is that ticket prices are set so as to maximize gate receipts. Except for championship clubs, ticket prices tend to rise at about the inflation rate. The prospects for rapid growth in broadcast revenue are not promising. Network audience shares have declined drastically . . . depressing advertising revenues. The networks are less than enthusiastic about bidding aggressively for sports-broadcasting rights. The conventional wisdom is that the value of the national broadcast rights might fall. It is certain that the value of these rights will not grow by much. Some leagues have sought joint production with network television, where leagues and television share risk and profits from televised games. Pay-for-view of play-off and championship games may eventually come for the leagues. While this is technologically feasible . . . , early trials . . . have not been promising. Each league is waiting for the other to make the plunge. Through the grace of Congress (the Sports Broadcasting Act of 1961), leagues are allowed to collude in the sale of broadcast rights, but that antitrust exemption can be revoked. Wide media coverage of sports and viewer resistance may make it politically difficult for the leagues to exploit the opportunity of pay-for-view. Thus the era of 20–25 percent annual growth in revenue is over for a time. . . .

Club costs have been rising more rapidly than revenue in recent years. With the rapid rise in player salaries, the player share of revenues has been climbing. There is no hard evidence that the player share has reached an upper bound, despite owner complaints . . . that there is not much more room for growth of average player salaries beyond revenue growth. The implication of the rhetoric is that the bidding for free agents will be less aggressive in baseball and basketball. There is some evidence for this view. . . . Now that football has veteran free agency, player salaries have risen steeply, and it is likely that they will converge toward those in baseball and basketball.

. . . Sports leagues are unique in the range of anticompetitive practices tolerated in both the product and players' market. While the degree of anticompetitiveness in these markets has been attenuated over the years, the practices have not been eliminated. Owners have always claimed that restrictions on competition were necessary for the protection of their investments and for competitive balance on the playing field. . . .

. . . .

RESTRICTIONS IN LEAGUE PRODUCT MARKETS IN THE MODERN PERIOD

All professional sports leagues restrict entry, assign exclusive franchise territory, and collude on a revenue-sharing formula. In general, public policy tolerates this collusion. Baseball is formerly exempt from the antitrust statutes since a unanimous court in *Federal Baseball v. National League et al.* [259 U.S. 200 (1922)] ruled that baseball was not engaged in interstate commerce and was therefore exempt from the antitrust statutes. The legal standing of collusion in baseball has been reaffirmed in several decisions since then. The other team sports do not enjoy formal exemption except in two important matters. When a collective bargaining agreement exists or remains in force despite a labor dispute, player–league disputes are exempt from antitrust under the labor exemption. Second, in 1961 Congress passed the Sports Broadcasting Act (amended in 1966), which extends the antitrust exemption to the negotiation of the sale of league broadcasting rights. Thus the league packaging of broadcast rights for sale to the broadcast networks is perfectly legal.

Team sports are naturally collusive at some minimal level. A game or a contest is a joint output. To produce it, the teams must agree on a set of rules governing the contest and on the division of revenues. All sports began with barnstorming clubs. Some clubs emphasized entertainment, and frequently contests with the locals were mismatches. The Harlem Globetrotters are the only remaining club with a barnstorming tradition. The limited commercial appeal of a single contest or a series of contests between the same two teams led to the rise of groups of teams formed as leagues. A league is the natural unit of economic organization. While still having entertainment value, league play is different. A club's financial bottom line depends on its performance against clubs of similar quality over a season. Sports fans appear most interested in organized championships with a high caliber of play among the contestants.

Leagues establish constitutional agreements governing the geographical markets of their franchises, conditions of entry and franchise relocation, the market for players, and playing regulations. These agreements, or league operating rules, tend to be privately joint-wealth maximizing* and collusive. While barriers to entry . . . exist in other industries (e.g., gate space in the airline industry, shelf space in supermarkets), permission of the current firms in the industry is not a condition of

---

* A rule or agreement is joint-wealth maximizing if in its presence the value of the new firms (teams) party to the rule rises. For example, the value of a franchise is greater under a reserve clause in the players' market because players earn less than their incremental contribution to team revenue. . . .

entry for new firms. In order for new teams to enter a league or for existing franchises to relocate, permission of the existing members must be secured. The Oakland Raiders moved to Los Angeles in 1982, and the Clippers moved from San Diego to Los Angeles in 1984 without league permission. The Raiders won the antitrust suit with the NFL, the Clippers paid $6 million to the NBA for invading the Lakers' territory. Since these unilateral moves, the ability of leagues to legally enforce territorial restrictions is ambiguous, but leagues still exercise considerable monopoly power in the geographical markets in which contests are held.

Leagues provide contests with a degree of uncertainty of outcome. A set of rules governing the contest must be formulated and followed by the teams to insure the ordered outcome of the games. These consist of uniform rules of play, scoring, scheduling of games, use of equipment, and so on. Without such rules, disputes about the outcomes of games would be widespread and championships would be suspect. Teams must therefore collude to some degree, if only to establish uniform playing rules and establish a credible champion. If all teams within a league were of equal playing strength, the schedule of contests would not be relevant to the establishment of a champion. When wide variation exists in team quality within a sport, league organization and scheduling ensure that each competitor engages a similar number of teams in a similar number of contests.

League rules that define membership, conditions of entry, division of territorial rights, and division of revenues from contests are not necessary for the provision of games but exist in the interest of rent-seeking. Owners have argued that these collusive agreements are justified to protect franchise values. While such rules are wealth-maximizing for the existing club owners, they are unique in American business. Under common law such cartel agreements are not enforceable, nor is competition recognized as a tort. Thus a dry cleaner on a particular city block has no standing in a court of law for recovery of lost value of his assets when a competitor locates next door. Second, even though the price of an existing franchise might be as high as $250 million, the purchase consists largely of player contracts and the right to be the exclusive provider of games in a geographical market, not meaningful physical assets.

A more compelling economic argument for these restrictions on the number of clubs and for exclusive territory is that in their absence the quality of team contests would be lower. Quality of play in team sports has two dimensions: absolute and relative. The absolute quality of play is its level, and that depends on the quality of athletic talent fielded. While minor league baseball, college baseball, football, and basketball, and the various amateur leagues may be exciting in their own right, the absolute quality of play is lower. If the supply of high-quality playing talent were perfectly elastic, the number of major leagues or teams within a league would have no effect on the absolute quality of play. But prime athletic talent is scarce. The huge differential in player pay versus the player's next best occupational wage is evidence of the low elasticity of supply of prime athletic talent. Because the addition of teams to a league dilutes the quality of play by spreading a more or less fixed supply of star players over a greater number of teams, restrictions on the number of teams increase the absolute quality of play. Similarly, the rise of a competing league reduces the absolute quality of play. From the perspective of the fans, some restrictions on the number of leagues in a sport and teams within a league may be socially desirable.

In the course of time, leagues have expanded. . . . Further domestic expansion of the various leagues, while contemplated (e.g., in football and hockey), will be difficult for several reasons. The remaining potential sites tend to be in small population centers or in larger metropolitan areas that already have clubs. The expansion fees are very high, mainly to cover the present value of reduced national broadcast revenues. The prospect for robust growth in revenues is dim, and with free agency in baseball, basketball, and now football, an investor can no longer get into a sport cheaply.

These leagues have not expanded because of a desire to supply contests in a market previously not served, but to preempt entry by a new league. If, say, eight teams is the minimum size for a league, sufficient population growth in eight other locations that would financially support a league brings the threat of the formation of a rival. New leagues are not signatory to existing league cartel agreements. Players precluded from moving to teams within leagues can gain financially by jumping to the new league. Of course with veteran free agency in three of the sports, the incentive for jumping to a new league is reduced, but not eliminated. Competition for player talent leads to large increases in average player salaries that threaten the financial stability of the leagues. By expanding judiciously, existing leagues can preclude the entry of a competing league. However, demand is never fully satisfied. It pays leagues to keep several sites open. This induces cities without franchises to compete with cities that have them for an existing franchise. . . . Such teams threaten to move or do relocate to acquire new stadium facilities or other benefits on more favorable terms. . . .

The second dimension of playing quality is relative. Relative playing quality is measured by the dispersion in team standings. A distribution of team standings in which team A always beat team B, team B always beat team C, and so on would yield a very large variance in team standing. Such games would not be contests, but exhibitions, and there would be little fan interest in the games of such a league. On the other hand, if each team had an equal chance of beating another, then team records would be .500, with a small variance due to random factors. Knowing that it was simply luck or the erroneous decisions of referees and umpires that caused a team to be the champion or the bottom finisher would also reduce fan interest in the contests of such a league. This suggests that there is an optimal degree of uncertainty or variance in team standings that maximizes fan interest, revenue, and profits to the clubs. Fans want their home team to win under uncertainty. Some degree of uncertainty of outcome is a necessary feature of competitive team sports, and this uncertainty is largely determined by the relative playing strengths of the teams within a league. Greater equality of playing strengths and hence more uncertainty about the outcome of games, up to some level, is wealth-maximizing. League attendance and probably Nielsen ratings are higher when team standings are closer within a league over a season.

The relative playing strength of a team depends on the financial strength of the team and the owner. Teams earn revenue from ticket sales, concession income, and the sale of broadcast rights. The main cost for a team is for the player roster. Teams face the same supply function for player services (incremental cost), but different demand functions for games. The restrictive practices of the sports cartels in the product market and the rule on revenue division among the teams in a league have implications for the dispersion of team standings.

Prior to the rise of television, teams earned revenues from ticket sales. Attendance is determined mainly by franchise market size (measured crudely by SMSA population size) and the club win–loss record. Because teams are located in cities of markedly different sizes, the ability to field a competitive team is affected by franchise market size and the cartel rule on the division of the gate receipts. Consider the extreme cases. In basketball and hockey the home team gets all of the gate receipts, the visitor gets nothing. . . . Obviously, given the unequal size of cities, the more unequal the division of the gate receipts, the more unequal the division of revenues among the clubs within a league.

The long-run, steady-state win percent of a club is that record that maximizes profit.* Technically, this is a condition where incremental revenue from wins equals the incremental cost of producing that win record. Because population size differs among clubs, assuming that the fans' demand for wins is geographically variant, average and incremental revenue differ by a scalar among the clubs. Teams in cities with large populations have maximum profits with records above .500: teams in cities with small populations have maximum profits with records below .500. It is no accident that large-city teams historically have dominated as championship teams. . . .

THE CARTELIZATION OF BROADCAST RIGHTS

In the early years broadcast rights were negotiated locally. Most clubs simply sold their rights to a station that packaged the games. Some clubs purchased air time and put the games on themselves. In a few instances clubs sold their rights to sponsors who put the games on the air. In all instances restrictions were placed on the use of the rights. By reciprocal agreement among the clubs, broadcasts to the home market were blacked out when the team was playing at home; only away games were broadcast. In 1946 the major leagues adopted a rule preventing the broadcast of other clubs' games into the home territory when games of the club were at home. Clearly, this practice was anticompetitive. Under pressure from the Justice Department, the leagues modified the rule in 1950. While a number of anticompetitive practices arose in the 1950s, the fact that several networks or stations competed among themselves and with a large number of providers of broadcast rights had implications for the distribution of rents between clubs and television. . . .

The first league-wide packaging of rights was between the National Basketball Association and NBC TV in 1954. Baseball followed suit with "Game of the Week." In 1960 the American Football League pooled its rights and sold them to ABC. The NFL and CBS had a similar agreement in 1961. By pooling broadcast rights, the leagues eliminated interclub competition in their sale and increased their share of the rents relative to the networks' share. The ban on the broadcast of home games remained. Leagues shopped the networks for the best deal, and because broadcast rights are very valuable each network increased its offer in each successive round of negotiation. While one network emerged a winner by locking up the broadcasts of a particular sport for a few years, the other networks were unsatisfied and a potential source of trouble if a rival league emerged. . . .

. . . . What the courts undid, however, Congress permitted. On September 30, 1961, Congress passed the Sports Broadcasting Act, which permitted leagues to act as cartels in the negotiation and sale of their broadcast rights, and to be free of any antitrust sanction. The league sale of rights to a specific network for a specific period of time continued, but the NFL later moved to an arrangement in which all of the networks got some of the games, some of the time. The great advantage of this arrangement was that all of the networks had an interest only in NFL games. There was no unsatisfied demand that a potential rival league could exploit to improve its chances of surviving.

---

* There is no denying that owners may have different motives other than the profitability of the club. At a time when ownership of a club was the sole source of income for the owner, the altruistic motive to "win at any price" was not sustainable, because it meant a loss of wealth. In more modern times ownership of clubs may be a strategy to improve net income in other lines of business. August Busch bought the St. Louis Cardinals to increase beer sales. Some teams (e.g., Chicago, Atlanta) are owned by broadcast interests and are an all important part of programming. The bottom line on the balance sheet of the clubs owned for these purposes may be of secondary importance to larger corporate interests.

From the point of view of the fans, who are interested in the chances of their local team having a winning season, the various arrangements in the sale of broadcast rights have had both positive and negative consequences. When broadcast rights were sold on a club-by-club basis, the fans got to see their local team's away games, but not much else. Because the value of local broadcast rights is a function of broadcast market size, big-city clubs obtain much more revenue than small-city clubs. Television increased the dispersion in club revenues, and to the extent that financial inequality promotes inequality on the playing field, it increased further the gap between wins and losses among clubs. Local rights remain an important source of variation in club revenues in baseball and basketball.

. . . .

There are two important, interconnected antitrust issues in professional team sports. First, entry restriction and exclusive territory preclude a larger number of clubs except by voluntary expansion, so that expansion will at best be limited. Second, the collusive arrangement between the existing leagues and television largely precludes the formation of rival leagues. Because of the Sports Broadcasting Act, the cartel arrangement in the sale of broadcast rights acts as a powerful barrier to the entry of a potential rival league. Sports programming is extremely valued by the television networks. The demographic profile of viewers is attractive to a certain class of advertisers, whose willingness to pay some of the highest advertising fees in the industry has propelled the growth of network television revenues to the leagues. By allocating games to all three networks, the NFL has co-opted the networks as a partner in the enterprise. Further, the contract stipulates that other professional football games cannot be broadcast by the networks within forty-eight hours of an NFL game. This relegates any competing league's games to mid-week, which is hardly attractive to the networks.

Television appears to increase the demand for attendance at games, and thus indirectly increases gate receipts. Certainly the effect of television is to build team recognition and loyalty among fans. . . .

Access to television may be a necessary condition for the survival of a new league. The NFL has an exclusive multiyear contract with the networks. Only at the time of that contract's expiration is there a possible point of entry, but that implies that the networks would find the games of a new league to be suitable substitutes for NFL games. New leagues are inferior to established leagues in the quality of play (consider the quality of the games of the World League, an NFL creation manned with players who could not make an NFL club), and it takes many seasons of play for them to achieve parity. It is entirely possible that the viewing audience would be smaller for the games of a competing league, giving the networks little incentive to substitute the games of a new league for NFL games.

. . . .

If entry was unrestricted in sports, what would the sports markets look like? Would this be in the interest of fans, club owners, and players? Under a completely free market, it is possible that clubs in the existing leagues might relocate to larger metropolitan markets (e.g., more clubs in New York, Los Angeles, Chicago) and that new leagues would be formed. Many cities without clubs might have them. In the interest of self-preservation, such clubs would probably sort themselves out into regional leagues that contained clubs of more or less comparable quality, as in collegiate sports. Let me continue to speculate on a structure that might be attractive to sports fans. Pennant winners in such regional leagues could engage in a series of play-offs with each other, as divisional winners currently do in the existing leagues. A World Series or Championship Series would follow from these playoffs. Thus, in principle, a world-champion club could be established in sports organized in a free market. With complete freedom of competition, including the market for players' services, no club would dominate for long in a sport.

As the fan base was spread over a larger number of teams, however, revenues would fall, and the value of the existing franchises would plummet. Salaries would fall as club revenue fell. . . . On average, players' pay would be more comparable to the average pay in the economy; their opportunity cost. Premier players would earn a premium, as high achievers do elsewhere in the economy, but a star would earn only a few times, not fifty times, what a rookie earned. Players in professional clubs therefore have as much at stake in maintaining the anticompetitive restrictions of the existing leagues as do the owners.

Would a free market in professional sports benefit fans? That is hard to say. If absolute quality of play means more to them than having a hometown club, fans would suffer. Clearly the absolute quality of play would decline. Say that one hundred of the regular roster players in baseball are the stars. These players would be spread over many more teams. On the other hand, if having a local club means more than restricted access to high-quality clubs, fans would benefit.

The fact that so many rival leagues in professional team sports have failed can be interpreted as evidence that absolute quality of play matters to fans (and that relative quality of play matters also, since competitive balance frequently was absent). . . . We do not know what trade-off fans would make between absolute quality of play and an expansion in the number of clubs. Certainly the existing size of the big leagues is not a reflection of that trade-off. League expansion is governed by the constraint of not adversely affecting current franchise values. Only a free market (free entry and exit by clubs) in professional team sports would tell us the fans' preferred trade-off between absolute quality of play and the number of professional clubs.

THE PLAYERS' MARKET

Historically, teams were invested with exclusive bargaining rights with the players. All of the leagues established collusive agreements that governed the selection, contractual arrangements (exclusive contracts with the signing club, which then owned the rights to the players' services), and distribution of players among the clubs. Collectively these powers granted a great degree of monopsony power to the clubs in the various sports. Monopsonistic exploitation (pay less than a player's incremental contribution to club revenue) of baseball players was in effect from 1879 to 1976, in basketball until the mid-1970s, and in football until recently. The only other important example of monopsony was in the market for actors and actresses in motion pictures.

Substantial reforms in the market for players have improved player initiated movement among teams, but by no means is there an open and competitive market for player services. Rather, an elaborate set of rules determines which teams can negotiate with which players for their services. These agreements also are collusive and anticompetitive.

Athletes enter professional sports through a drafting procedure. The various types of drafts are intended to distribute the rights to the acquisition of amateur players to the professional clubs. The common feature of the drafts is that they grant to the team exclusive bargaining rights for the services of the prospective player. Once drafted, the athlete negotiates with that team. While these rules have been weakened somewhat over the years, they still impede aggressive bidding for amateur players. Once a player has come to terms with the drafting team, he must sign a standard players' contract.

The contract restricts the sale of his services to the team holding the contract (until death in baseball during the era of the reserve clause, and for a fixed length of time today). . . .

There are considerable differences in the average pay and in the distribution of pay between players in the various sports. The differences are correlated with the degree of restrictiveness of player-initiated mobility, the nature of the production function in the sport, and the arrangement for dividing the revenues among the teams. When the players' market was very restricted, players made somewhat more than the average American worker, and salaries were more or less equal across team sports. . . .

. . . The economic justification for a fairly wide salary differential in professional sports is as an incentive to induce all players to perform at their maximum level. Rather than monitor player performance, although this is easier in sports than in other occupations, players signal their own quality. In essence they are offered a two-part contract. One part is payment for expected performance. The other part is a prize: the probability of becoming a superstar and earning the salary and perquisites of stardom. The probability is endogenously determined by the player's performance. Thus the high pay of superstars arises less from owner altruism than from the fact that it shifts the cost of ensuring player performance at maximum levels to the players themselves. . . .

The relatively high starting salary of rookie players . . . is also economically rational. Certainly the average salary of a player's next best alternative occupation is a fraction of the rookie salary. But the probability of making a professional team is small. Hence rookie salaries times the probability of making a team (expected salary) must exceed average nonsport salaries to insure an adequate pool of athletic talent.

Owners have always claimed that restrictions on player movement were necessary to maintain competitive balance and to protect franchise values. Economists have always been skeptical of the motives and of the evidence. Economists and owners always agreed that there would be a tendency for star players to wind up on big-city teams, but restrictions on player-initiated movement have no bearing on the distribution of playing talent within a league. If players are free to move between teams, holding preferences for location constant, they will tend to play for the team that pays the most. Obviously there are exceptions. . . . The team that will pay the most is the one that expects the largest increment in revenue from that player's service. Because an increment in the win record brings more fans into the stadium or arena in New York than in Kansas City, the very best players tend to go to the big-city teams. . . . Absent a league ban on player sales for cash, the small-city franchise will have an incentive to sell the player's contract to the big-city team and capture some portion of the differential rents. Thus players are allocated by highest incremental revenue, with or without restrictions on player-initiated movement. This is not to say that all of the star players wind up on big-city clubs. The marginal revenue product of stars declines with the number of star players on the roster (i.e., a .700 record does not generate that much more attendance than a .600 record). . . . While these restrictions have little implication for the allocation of player talent within a league, they dramatically affect the division of rents between owners and players. Under free agency, the players receive most of the rents arising from their scarce talent; under league restrictions on player-initiated transfers, the owners get most of the rents.

. . . .

THE SUCCESSFUL STRUCTURE

HOME TEAM

Michael Danielson

The business of professional team sports requires organization of teams into leagues. Leagues bring together a set of places that provide the primary market for the collective product; they provide the framework in which teams meet to produce games; they structure games into seasons, playoffs, and championships. Customers prefer organized games among teams competing for pennants, division titles, or a place in postseason play. As Commissioner Pete Rozelle constantly reminded NFL owners, "if you didn't belong to a league, and just had teams arranging scrimmages against one another, you couldn't expect many people to watch."[1]

The necessity for teams to be organized as leagues structures relations between professional sports and places. Leagues exercise controls over the location and relocation of teams, territorial rights, suitability of places for teams, the number of places that can have franchises, and who can own teams. They determine how revenues will be shared among members, negotiate national broadcasting arrangements, and bargain collectively with players. These league activities raise complicated issues of public policy, whose outcomes shape the way places connect with teams and leagues.

STRUCTURING THE GAME

In performing their functions, leagues have developed a common organizational structure, composed of individual teams operating collectively under direction of a commissioner. . . .

Leagues are associations of teams rather than independent entities; they exist to promote the common interests of their member teams, which are separately owned and operated firms. League rules are determined by member teams, and are only effective as long as individual teams abide by them. Teams collectively make league decisions on relocation, expansion, revenue sharing, and network broadcasting contracts. Extraordinary majorities usually are required on important questions like moving or adding teams. These special voting requirements increase the power of individual owners or small groups of teams with common interests, such as large-market teams desirous of protecting their territories from competition and their revenues from sharing arrangements.

34

Team interests often conflict with the collective welfare of a league. Revenue sharing reduces income for some clubs in the interest of lessening economic differences among all teams in a league. Few teams can resist the attractions of unshared revenues from luxury boxes, better stadium and concessions deals, and broadcasting income outside league control, even though these revenues tend to increase disparities within a league. Conflict has been intensified by the rapidly increasing economic stakes of professional team sports. Newer owners who pay hefty prices for their teams and carry substantial debts are particularly interested in maximizing team revenues, which intensifies conflicts within leagues over revenue sharing, broadcasting deals, labor contracts, and expansion fees.

Differences among league members are amplified by the people who own major league franchises. Most are rich and powerful individuals who have been successful in other businesses and are used to having their way. Strong egos and personal animosities among owners exacerbate conflicts within leagues over relocation, expansion, and sharing revenues. Baseball owners, in the words of one, "never learned how" to be "both competitors and partners off the field."[2] Owners in the NFL have been more willing to subordinate individual for collective interests; they were the first to adopt an amateur playing draft, and developed the most extensive revenue-sharing arrangements in professional team sports. Still, sustaining collective concerns has been a constant struggle within the NFL. . . .

Leadership has been an important factor in the interplay of league and team interests. Formidable political and public relations skills enabled Pete Rozelle to expand league authority despite an increasingly diverse and contentious set of NFL owners. Another strong leader, David Stern, revitalized the NBA, turning a league plagued by drugs, weak franchises, and declining television appeal into a vibrant organization that pioneered the development of salary caps and league marketing, while expanding successfully and securing lucrative network television contracts. Under Stern, the NBA has emphasized league interests and league services to teams in marketing, promotions, and local broadcasting. National broadcasting revenues also have boosted the power of league officials. The dependence of NFL owners on the commissioner's ability to make good television deals greatly enhanced Rozelle's authority over all aspects of the game.

. . . . League officials are concerned about a set of places; they worry about market coverage and being in major markets. Increasingly, the focus of leagues is national and international, while teams are preoccupied with their metropolitan and regional market. David Stern promotes the NBA as an entity rather than a set of teams. . . . In Stern's approach, individual teams become units of the business like Disneyland or Disney World, and places where they play are the sites of particular business units in the same sense that Anaheim and Orlando are for the Disney empire. Of course, there are critical differences between the NBA and Disney; each of the NBA's twenty-nine teams is individually owned and operated, most play in public arenas, and the owners collectively hire and fire the league commissioner as well as pass judgment on league decisions affecting ownership of teams, relocation of franchises, expansion of leagues, suitability of arenas, national broadcasting deals, and sharing of revenues.

COMPETITIVE LEAGUES

Professional teams have a collective interest in producing games that involve enough uncertainty to sustain the interest of their customers. Competitive leagues are good business; close pennant races and more teams in contention for postseason play increase attendance and broadcast audiences. A league's ability to produce competitive games, teams, and seasons determines how many places will have successful teams at least some of the time. . . .

A league's collective interest in competitiveness coexists uneasily with the desire of individual teams to be successful. Team success means doing better than other clubs by winning more games and championships. Winning teams attract more customers, command more local broadcast revenues, earn additional revenues from postseason play, and make more money for their owners. Both winning teams and competitive leagues are good for business, but teams that win most of the time reduce league competitiveness. This situation leads to arguments that teams have a rational interest in winning, but not so often as to dominate a league and undermine the viability of weaker teams. . . . Winning, however, can be a profitable business strategy even if a team dominates its league. Great teams and dynasties usually are good business for the triumphant team, if not the league. . . .

For most teams, the incentives to win also are more powerful than the rewards of increased competitiveness. Although closely contested games, pennant races, and championships are collectively desirable, individual teams understandably are wary of the risks inherent in highly competitive enterprises. . . . Noneconomic considerations reinforce the attractions of winning teams over competitive leagues. Most people who own teams are highly competitive; they are used to success, and success in professional sports is measured by won–lost records and championships rather than profits and losses. . . . Fans reinforce the drive for victory; fans care more about rooting for winners than whether the home team plays in a competitive league. And winning itself increases pressures to win again, heightening expectations of players for bigger contracts, of fans for another victorious season, and of owners for the thrill of another championship.

Among the four sports, the NFL has been most committed to increasing competitiveness. League control of television and sharing of most revenues were acceptable to NFL owners because these policies promised a more attractive product by increasing the ability of teams to compete regardless of market size. The NFL also uses scheduling to increase competitiveness, matching teams for games outside their division with opponents with similar records during the previous season. . . . However . . . only one team can win the World Series, Super Bowl, Stanley Cup, or NBA championship. Leagues, however, can create more winners by increasing opportunities to participate in postseason play. Leagues can be subdivided into conferences and divisions whose winners make the playoffs, and "wild card" teams can be added to increase the number that advance to postseason play.

. . . . *[The author's discussion of owners is omitted. See Chapter 1 for a discussion of this topic.]*

TERRITORIAL RIGHTS

Teams in a league have substantial shared interests in the location of franchises. As a result, league control of franchise locations has been a cardinal feature of professional team sports from the start. The National League limited franchises to cities with populations of 75,000, with each team granted exclusive territorial rights in its market area. The National League and American Association agreed in 1883 to preserve exclusive territories for teams in each league. Contemporary territorial rights generally include the city where a team plays and the surrounding area within fifty or seventy-five miles of the team's home turf. Each NFL team has "the exclusive right within its home territory to exhibit professional football games played by teams of the League," with two teams in the same territory, as in the New York area, having equal rights.[20] Territorial rights include broadcasts within a team's area, except for games covered by league contracts with national networks.

Territorial exclusivity enables teams to avoid competition for local fans, viewers, media, and broadcasting and advertising dollars. Exclusive territories focus fan loyalty and support for the home team. . . . Territorial controls are the basic instruments by which teams and leagues regulate their relations with places. Exclusive franchises are based on the notion that places belong to a league and its teams; territories are staked out and controlled by private league rules. Territorial controls are vigorously defended as indispensable to professional team sports. . . . Without these protections, professional sports are seen as facing economic ruin and places could lose their teams. . . .

Territorial rights have been relatively static during the rapid expansion of metropolitan areas and urban regions. Fifty or seventy-five miles, which once extended the control of most teams well beyond the urbanized portion of their home territory, now encompass a diminishing portion of the far-flung regions that supply teams with customers and viewers. . . .

Territorial rights have the most substantial impact on the location of professional teams in large metropolitan areas; with or without exclusive territories, smaller areas can sustain only one team in a sport.

. . . .

Because territorial exclusivity primarily protects franchises in the largest markets from competition, these rights reinforce the advantages of teams in the major urban centers. Limiting the number of teams in large metropolitan areas exacerbates market differences by forcing most owners to operate in smaller areas with less revenue potential. League controls also severely constrain the ability of small-market teams to move to larger markets that could sustain another franchise or support a more successful team. . . . The other side of this coin, of course, is that more places have teams because the number of franchises in the largest metropolitan areas is limited by leagues.

Territorial restrictions also reduce competition among teams to be in a particular place, thus increasing the leverage of teams on places. Most places have to deal with a single team in each sport. In the absence of competition from other teams for stadiums and arenas, holders of exclusive franchises are able to drive harder bargains with public agencies for leases, tax concessions, and other subsidies. Franchise controls, however, do not guarantee that a team will be able to capitalize on its market monopoly.

REFERENCES

1. Ross Atkins, "With Super Bowl Settled, Comes Another Showdown," *Christian Science Monitor,* Jan. 26, 1981.
2. John Fetzer of the Detroit Tigers, quoted in Thomas Boswell, "Baseball: Riches or Ruin?" *Washington Post,* Dec. 21, 1980.
20. National Football League, Constitution & Bylaws, Sec. 4.2 (1970).

An Alternative Model

Open Competition in League Sports

Stephen F. Ross and Stefan Szymanski

In North America, sports leagues are closed ventures. Membership in the league is a gift from the existing members, who typically grant the right of entry only in exchange for a substantial fee. . . . This is fundamentally different than the structure of team sports in the rest of the world. Elsewhere, sports leagues are usually open: membership in the league is contingent on success. Professional sports leagues in soccer, rugby, basketball, and cricket are organized in ascending tiers (generally called divisions), and every year the teams with the worst record are relegated to a lower division and replaced by the most successful teams from that lower division.

This structural difference has significant consequences for the conduct and performance of sports leagues. . . .

. . . The practice of "promotion and relegation" tends to raise consumer welfare by increasing effective competition among the teams in a league. Teams that are relegated to a lower division after an unsuccessful year will play a lower standard of competition and generate less interest among fans, and therefore will reduce the revenue-generating potential for their owners. Because teams seek to avoid relegation as well as to win championships, they have a greater incentive to invest in players than teams participating in closed competitions. For lesser teams in lower divisions, the allure of promotion to the top division enhances the incentive to invest in players and provides fans with new and innovative professional league competition, distinct from and qualitatively superior to the current minor leagues. Moreover, promotion provides a market-based means of permitting new entry, which will check the power of incumbent clubs to exercise market power. These effects involve a direct gain for consumers (sports fans), since the additional efforts of their team enhance the quality of play, while at the same time the excitement of promotion and relegation struggles add an extra dimension to league competition.

The competitive check provided by new entry is particularly significant in the sports industry, because the particular interdependence that sports teams have with other economically separate firms within the same league has led courts to be much more permissive in their antitrust scrutiny of trade restraints among members of sports leagues than in the case of most businesses. Rules involving limitations on competition for players and sharing revenue between rival clubs, as well as restrictions on entry into the league joint venture, on the sale of broadcast rights, and on the internal business structure of member clubs, are all tolerated unless demonstrably unreasonable in the sports context. Yet such rules would probably be unacceptable under the antitrust laws if employed in other industries. This legal generosity stems from the recognition that teams need to cooperate to some degree in order to produce their output and that a more balanced competition requiring cooperation is more interesting to consumers. Restraints that promote balance are therefore deemed justifiable, and reasonable forms of those listed above have all been accepted as legitimate.

. . . .

I. THE ECONOMICS OF PROMOTION AND RELEGATION

In general, a larger league is more attractive than a smaller one. A world championship title is more prestigious than a national title, which is more prestigious than winning a regional competition. The more inclusive the competition, the more gratifying the victory. However, there are limits to the optimal size of a league. If the clubs all play each other at least once during a season, there are limits imposed by the physical ability of the players to perform in a sequence of matches, and by the total supply of talent. A larger league leads to a skewed distribution of talent, creating more unbalanced contests. If expansion leads to more unbalanced contests, it can be argued that very large leagues will sacrifice quality for quantity. Finally, even if player talent were evenly spread across all clubs, the talent level for each team would be diluted. Although in many cases the value-added for the fans of the additional clubs outweighs the marginal decline in attractiveness for the fans of the existing teams, at some point this ceases to be the case. These are reasons why members of a league would want to control access in order to maintain an optimally sized league, and why society's laws should find such control to be desirable.

However, there are reasons to suppose that league members will tend to restrict access to a point below the socially optimal level. The major North American sports leagues are organized as joint ventures, where entry and other major business decisions are made jointly by clubs seeking to maximize their own profits, as opposed to a "single entity," where entry and other decisions would be made by an executive or board seeking to maximize overall league profits. Thus, while a single entity league would ordinarily be expected to expand franchises until the point where marginal revenue equals zero, the objective of teams in the league will be to choose the number of franchises so as to maximize average revenue per club. This is analogous to prior observations by labor economists that a labor-managed firm will not expand employment as far as a profit-maximizing firm.

Even though expansion franchises can be assessed a fee to compensate the existing teams for the loss of expected income (reduced probability of winning a championship, reduced percentage of revenue from league-wide ventures), there are several reasons why leagues will still tend to engage in under-expansion. Transaction costs in estimating and agreeing upon expected losses from future entry may lead the league to set the fee too high to attract efficient entry. Most significantly, league members have an incentive to expand sub-optimally in order to provide clubs with a credible threat to move to economically viable open markets unless local taxpayers provide generous tax subsidies. Any expansion can be expected to remove the most viable markets as threatened relocation sites, thus reducing the ability to acquire subsidies. . . .

. . . .

In contrast to the closed league structure featured in North America, an open league system with promotion and relegation will significantly dissipate rents, as well as inefficient rent-seeking activity such as the creation of sub-optimal entry restrictions, without causing the problems that might be associated with over-expansion. The prospects of demotion for teams in the major leagues and promotion for teams in the junior league both induce an increase in investment, raising the quality of competition. Not only will individual clubs have a greater incentive to improve the quality of their product by obtaining better players, but the total talent level is likely to increase as well. Even if all the best baseball, basketball, football, and hockey players in the entire world already play in the North American major leagues, the existing talent pool is likely to improve through increased expenditure on training and coaching. This is driven by the fact that failure would potentially involve a significantly heavier price than simply "waiting until next year." An additional advantage of promotion and relegation would be a consistent average talent level in the major leagues, in contrast to alternatives that rely on significant expansion.

The system of promotion and relegation will also significantly increase the quantity as well as the quality of competition. The system will introduce an entirely new level of competition available for mid-sized cities, suburban areas, and growing metropolitan areas, that is qualitatively distinct from and superior to that provided by minor league farm teams, where young players compete solely to develop skills to be used at the discretion of the parent club.

Another advantage of promotion and relegation is a significant increase in the attractiveness of the second half of each season for fans of teams not in contention for the championship, by creating a new aspect of competition: avoiding relegation. The problem of end-of-season ennui has become even more acute in recent years, as teams that have lost hope rush to trade players whose contracts are expiring to pennant contenders in return for young prospects, thus rendering the remainder of their season even less interesting for fans.

One of the most significant economic implications of the system of promotion and relegation is its effect on the opportunity for incumbent clubs to obtain rents because of franchise scarcity. It is arguably efficient to extract the quasi-rents associated with maintaining a team of high quality through some form of public subsidy (like the fixed fee of a two-part tariff), to the extent that teams cannot extract, through conventional means of ticket pricing, broadcasting rights sales, and merchandising, the consumer surplus associated with reading about the local team in the newspaper or talking about it with friends. However, it is socially wasteful to extract pure economic rents by threatening to relocate unless a heavily subsidized facility is provided. This wasteful extraction is possible only because of franchise scarcity, and the amount of the rent extracted matches the willingness to pay of the unserved location (and if this is larger than the willingness to pay of taxpayers/voters in the current location, the team moves). The existence of an unserved location enables all of the teams to extract economic rents from their existing location, whether or not any of them actually move.

Once a system of promotion and relegation is instituted, all credible locations will be served, even if only by teams competing in a lower tier. The threat of relocation would then have limited value. The only credible relocation scenario in the open system would arise when a team in a small drawing location currently in the top tier offers to relocate to a large drawing area. However, the amount of rent would be much smaller, because: (a) second-tier competition has a value; (b) a second-tier team can be promoted in the future (and will be likely to do so if it is from a large drawing area that will generate revenue sufficient to support investment in a major league payroll); and (c) a team currently in the top tier might end up getting relegated at some point in the future. All of this suggests that relocation is quite unlikely with a system of promotion and relegation.

Compare the economic choices facing civic officials wishing to obtain a major league franchise under the two systems. In a closed system, the government will likely have to construct a new stadium at public expense and provide it to an existing or expansion franchise on heavily subsidized terms. Even then, a local owner will have to be found who is willing to invest a significant amount of capital in paying an expansion fee or purchasing an existing franchise. In an open system, several local owners anxious to eventually enter the major leagues may well compete for the local land development rights to build a new stadium (or, if civic officials choose to build a public stadium, to pay market-based rent). The winning owner's investment will not be used to pay a huge fee to other owners, but rather to acquire the front-office and on-field talent necessary to succeed in the junior league and secure promotion to the major league.

. . . .

The foregoing analysis also suggests that promotion and relegation is a more efficient and consumer-responsive means of allocating franchises than allowing the owners of a fixed league to accept or reject requests for individual franchises to relocate. Teams would be optimally located in markets where consumer demand for major league sports is most intense. With closed leagues, relocating to reflect a change in demand requires: (a) an owner's ability to identify the change; (b) the owner's willingness to incur transaction costs to make the change; and (c) the other owners' willingness to agree to the change. With open leagues, local entrepreneurs who may have better information about their market's ability to support a major league team, and who may have ancillary reasons for wanting to bring a major league club to their town, can do so at a lower cost. Modern architectural techniques permit the construction of modest-sized stadia viable for junior league competition that can, without prohibitive expense, be expanded to accommodate major league capacities.

. . . .

II. PROMOTION AND RELEGATION IN ENGLISH SOCCER

. . . .

English soccer provides a case study to evaluate the impact of promotion and relegation on league structure and performance. . . .

Mobility between the divisions is more than a theoretical possibility. In any one year, there are ninety-two league clubs, and over the seasons 1976–77 to 1997–98 there have been ninety-nine teams participating in four professional divisions (there have been a small number of demotions to the lower semi-professional divisions). Of these ninety-nine teams, only five were never relegated or promoted over the period. Furthermore, over the same period, more teams have moved between three divisions (forty-three) than have played only in two (thirty-two), while twelve teams managed to visit all four divisions over the space of twenty-two years. Moreover, many promoted teams become championship contenders even in their first year after promotion. . . . In all, 50% of all promoted teams succeeded in surviving at least one season in the top division over the decade, with 27% of these teams finishing in the top half of the table.

Expenditure on players represented the largest single cost item for all teams. In the Premier (top-tier) League, salaries accounted for 52% of total income, while wages in the second-tier league (confusingly called the Football League First Division) averaged 68% of income. In the Second and

Third Divisions, teams traded at a loss, spending respectively 84% and 97% of their income on salaries. Only three Premier League teams reported an average operating surplus in excess of $10 million per year over the five seasons between 1993 and 1998. Of the ninety-two teams comprising the top four tiers of English soccer, only eight reported an operating surplus at all. Of all the English clubs, only Manchester United can be considered to have reported significant and consistent profits.

These figures, representing modest profitability, were reported not against a background of relative decline, but one of considerable growth. Between 1990 and 1998, aggregate attendance at league matches rose by 27% to 24.7 million. In 2001, capacity utilization averaged nearly 93% in the Premier League and almost 69% in the First Division. Ticket prices rose at an annual rate of around 15% in the 1990s, well in excess of the rate of inflation, and by the late 1990s the average ticket price for a Premier League match (when tickets were available) was around $40. Television broadcasting income rose from less than $10 million per year (for the entire league) in 1983 to a more plausible figure of around $250 million per year in 2001. Furthermore, low profit figures are explained in part not only by high levels of player spending, but also by significant increases in stadium expenditure made by the clubs themselves, which has in part made possible the increasing levels of match attendance.

. . . . In mid-1999, only three teams had a market capitalization in excess of $100 million (Manchester United, Newcastle, and Chelsea). Of the remaining Premier League teams, those that seldom fall into the bottom of the division had capitalizations just under the $100 million mark (Tottenham, Leeds, and Aston Villa). Three teams that have recently moved between divisions or repeatedly faced the threat of relegation (Sunderland, Leicester, and Southampton) had market capitalizations of $50 million, $20 million, and $17 million, respectively, which is little different from comparable teams in the (lower tier) First Division.

The relatively low market value of teams at the bottom of the Premier League does not simply reflect the fact that England is a smaller market than North America. Since 1998, Manchester United has been valued at over $1 billion, making it the most valuable sports team franchise in the world. The income of clubs at the bottom of the Premier League is between five and ten times smaller than that of Manchester United, but in 1998 still amounted to around $30 million per year, whereas the average baseball club's income approached $80 million in the same year. Yet the least valuable baseball franchise would sell for well in excess of two and a half times the market value of an English club threatened with relegation. Conversely, there can be little doubt that if Leicester City or Southampton were promised perpetual membership in the Premier League, their market values would rise sharply.

. . . .

In sum, despite the strong monopoly position of English soccer, a brief overview of the economic performance of English soccer teams supports the economic theory that promotion and relegation will dissipate monopoly rents and increase relative spending on players. An industry where profits are plowed back into improving the quality of the product for sports fans would appear to be better for overall economic welfare than one where profits are pocketed by owners. . . .

DISCUSSION QUESTIONS

1. Advise a potential team owner of both the benefits and concerns of league membership that he or she will face as an owner of a professional sports team.

2. If you were the commissioner of a new professional sports league, what considerations would you have to keep in mind to ensure both a competitive and a profitable league?

3. As an MLB, NBA, or NHL owner, would you rather sweep the championship series or have it come down to a close Game 7? Why?

4. In which sport is there the greatest likelihood that a rival league will emerge to challenge the established league? Explain.

5. What are some examples used by Moag and Company that promote the argument that the sports industry is resistant to bear markets?

6. What evidence could be used to prove that sports are not as resistant to bear markets as Moag and Company would lead the reader to believe?

7. What are some examples of how leagues use their monopolistic power?

8. Why do leagues expand into new territories?

9. Explain how consumers are both benefited and harmed by restrictions on the number of sports leagues and league teams.

10. Scully makes the argument, "Television appears to increase the demand for attendance at games, and thus indirectly increases gate receipts." What are some arguments that would support this theory?

11. What incentives exist for individual franchises to win?

12. Why aren't there more barnstorming teams like the Harlem Globetrotters?

13. How does a team operating within a league structure resemble that of another entertainment company, like Disney? What are the advantages of a team operating within a league structure resembling another entertainment company, like Disney? What are the disadvantages?

14. Are dynasties good or bad for sports leagues?

15. Explain the dichotomy that exists between winning and not completely dominating a league.

16. What are the effects of winning versus not dominating a league on franchises? Owners? Players? Leagues? Commissioner?

17. What are the advantages and disadvantages of the system of promotion and relegation?

18. Is a transition to this type of structure feasible in the established North American leagues? Is it feasible in a newly created league? Why or why not?

19. How would the adoption of the system of promotion and relegation in Major League Baseball affect the minor leagues? How would it affect NCAA Division I basketball and football?

CHAPTER 3

LEAGUES: REVENUE SHARING AND SELF-ANALYSIS

INTRODUCTION

With an understanding of the background and structure of leagues, the reader can give attention to the intraleague revenue-sharing policies in place in each league. While the leagues vary as to the degree of revenue sharing that they engage in, it is safe to say that there is a fair amount of dispute within each league as to the appropriate level of revenue sharing. The NFL has the most aggressive revenue-sharing system, a product of historical necessity and the foresight and leadership of longtime commissioner Pete Rozelle. The NHL has the least amount of revenue sharing and the largest number of struggling franchises of any of the leagues. Over the years, various proposals to increase the level of revenue sharing in the NHL have been met derisively by the owners, with the typical response beginning with an owner standing up and saying, "Comrades!" This is in reference to the highly socialistic nature of revenue sharing. Revenue sharing in the NBA and Major League Baseball falls between these two extremes.

In the first selection, Richard Sheehan examines the revenue-sharing practices that have been adopted by professional sports leagues, as well as the economic principles upon which these profit-maximizing endeavors are based. The author proposes a two-part tax on a franchise's costs and its win–loss record to enhance the effectiveness of these revenue-sharing models.

After Sheehan's passage, the broad revenue-sharing model adopted by the National Football League is considered by Daniel Mason. The development of the NFL's revenue-sharing system is instructive for current sports business leaders, as the league's revenue-sharing plan is considered a significant part of why the NFL is currently considered to be the most successful of the professional sports leagues. Despite this success, the system is not without its problems, including the threats posed by opportunistic owner behavior.

Finally, the issues facing Major League Baseball are addressed by examining various aspects of the Report of the Independent Members of the Commissioner's Blue Ribbon Panel on Baseball Economics. Though the lack of player representation on this panel has caused its report to be criticized for its partisan nature, its content is significant. Indeed, other leagues might be encouraged to follow the lead of Major League Baseball and engage in a greater degree of self-analysis in order to remain responsive to the changing environments in which sports leagues operate. An in-depth review of baseball provides an understanding of the complexity of the problems that professional sports leagues can face when operating with a suboptimal economic system and offers possible solutions to these difficulties.

KEEPING SCORE: THE ECONOMICS
OF BIG-TIME SPORTS

Richard G. Sheehan

First, all four leagues on average have been and remain very profitable. The average return to major league professional franchises has been greater than the average return to stocks. Second, profits are not evenly distributed. In each league, some franchises earn substantial profits while other franchises barely break even or lose money. . . . Third, owners have different motives for buying and owning a professional sports franchise. Some are in it primarily for the money while others are in it primarily for wins or ego or civic pride. And fourth, not all major league franchises are competently managed. Some franchises . . . have not been well run, assuming that the objective is to make money or to win games.

The conclusions that each league makes a substantial profit but that the profit is unevenly distributed suggests that some revenue sharing may be appropriate. When a league has an average profit rate over 15 percent but some teams are losing money, there might be a problem in the distribution of league profits, and some mechanism to share league revenues might be appropriate. In fact, each league already has some revenue sharing. For example, all leagues equally divide national television revenues, regardless of a team's number of TV appearances, record, or drawing power. Another example is a league's centralization of the licensing process. . .

This chapter considers three questions on revenue sharing. First, how much revenue has been shared in each league. Second, why should any revenue be shared? That is, is there an economic justification underlying revenue sharing and how can the problems associated with revenue sharing be overcome? And third, is there a specific proposal for revenue sharing that begins to address two of the most important problems facing professional sports: (1) How can revenues be split between rich franchises and poor without destroying the incentives for the rich to keep generating prolific revenues? (2) And how can anyone reconcile the split among owners where some focus primarily on the bottom line and others focus primarily on winning? . . .

CURRENT REVENUE-SHARING ARRANGEMENTS

What revenues currently are shared? For all leagues, the ground rules are strikingly alike. National media money is shared while local media money generally is not; licensing money accrues to the league and is shared while any local advertising money is not; sharing of gate receipts varies by league while luxury box income generally is not shared. NFL gate receipts are split 60-40, with the home team receiving a greater amount justified on the basis of the costs of putting on the game. At the other extreme, the NHL home team retains the entire gate. In the NBA the home team keeps 94 percent of the gate while the league receives the other 6 percent.

. . . .

. . . . In terms of total revenue generated per franchise, the NFL leads all leagues. . . Major League Baseball (MLB) is second in revenues. . . . Gate receipts are the largest component of MLB receipts . . . followed by other revenues (primarily stadium revenues) . . . and local media . . . The NBA's two largest income sources are gate revenues . . . and national media. . . . The NHL relies most heavily on gate revenues . . . and other revenues (again, primarily stadium revenues) . . . .

Comparing the leagues, the advantage of the NFL clearly lies in its television contracts. Without them, the NFL would have lower revenue than the NHL. Based on national media revenues, MLB is no longer the national pastime and is not even number two. The NBA now has that honor. . . . Where baseball is still the most popular is in terms of attendance and gate receipts, where it easily outdistances all other leagues. Perhaps the surprises here are that the NHL has the second highest gate receipts, surpassing the NBA, and that the NFL with so few games still has close to the same gate receipts as other leagues.

. . . . In the NFL, the two largest revenue categories, TV money and gate receipts, are split relatively equally. Thus, the NFL has the greatest degree of revenue sharing. . . . In contrast, the NHL has the smallest national media revenues, the smallest licensing revenues, and no split of gate revenues. Thus NHL revenue sharing was the lowest. . . MLB and the NBA fall between these two extremes. . . . In the NBA, the percentage sharing of the gate is relatively small, but national media money is shared and is relatively more important for NBA franchises than for MLB franchises.

Another perspective on the distribution of revenues is given by the range of revenues in a league. How do the revenues of the richest and poorest franchises compare? . . . The results indicate a wide range for all four leagues, smallest in the NFL and widest in the NHL. . . Given the importance of TV money to the NFL, this result should not be a surprise. Regardless of how a franchise is run, TV money gives all NFL teams a solid revenue base.

. . . .

What may be most noteworthy about the maximum and minimum revenue numbers is the observation that New York City teams lead in all leagues except the NFL, the league with the most revenue sharing. New York City teams have natural revenue advantages over . . . Buffalo and Salt Lake City. However . . . this revenue advantage has not led to more victories and has led to only marginally greater financial success. New York City teams have both higher revenues and higher costs. . . . Market size may play a minor role, but it is a long way from the whole explanation of profits, wins, or anything else. Whether a team wins and whether it is well run both contribute more to financial success.

THE ECONOMIC LOGIC UNDERLYING REVENUE SHARING

Should there be revenue sharing? Is there any economic justification underlying revenue sharing? For an economist the answer is simple. In MLB, for example, the Yankees and the Brewers take the field to play a game. They create a win, a loss, and entertainment. It is a classic example of a joint product. The fans and the media pay for the entertainment while one of the teams ends up with a win and the other gets a loss. The product obviously is shared, and since the Yankees and Brewers must cooperate to produce it — in terms of agreeing on ground rules — the financial rewards are appropriately shared. But how are the Yankees and Brewers to split the revenues?

Three issues underlie this apparently simple question. First, you have a set of accounting issues: do you split gross revenues or net and how do you define the revenues to be shared? . . .

Second, there are equity concerns. What is a "fair" split of the revenues between the Yankees and the Brewers? . . . Efficiency arguments made below weigh heavily against an equal split of local revenues. Before considering efficiency, however, there is an equity argument against equally splitting local revenues. In any league we should expect the first franchises to be located in the most profitable cities. New York, Chicago, and Los Angeles have franchises in all leagues (temporarily except the NFL) and sometimes multiple franchises. Detroit, Boston, Philadelphia, and San Francisco also have franchises in all leagues. When you buy an expansion franchise, you should know that it is unlikely to generate the revenue stream of many "old guard" franchises. Thus, it would be disingenuous in MLB for expansion franchises in Colorado or Florida to argue that they deserve a share of Yankees' or Dodgers' revenues when the new owners should have known at the outset that they would be among the marginal franchises in the league. . . .

Third and most importantly, how can you undertake revenue sharing while not destroying economic incentives? How can you undertake revenue sharing and give owners or potential owners a greater incentive to pursue profits, victories, and the long-run economic health of the league? From an economic perspective, the interesting question about revenue sharing is its efficiency implications. The simplest way of viewing revenue sharing is to think of it as a tax. The general rule in economics is that any tax will distort economic incentives. In this case, we can put the distorting effects of taxes to an advantage. Many things could be taxed, for example, total costs, total revenues, player payrolls (the owners' favorite), or even wins and losses. What is taxed will effect how owners will react to the tax and will impact how owners, players, and fans will fare.

. . . .

. . . . There are fixed costs associated with running a franchise. For example, a MLB franchise has a minimum payroll of $2.5 million *[now $7.5 million]* given the roster size and the minimum salary. Taxing this amount or any fixed cost has no impact on a franchise's operations and is incompatible with revenue sharing. A tax on anything other than incremental costs or revenues is simply bad economics as far as changing incentives is concerned.

A second example of how not to tax has been proposed by some small-market MLB owners. This tax would split all local media money equally among all franchises. . . . More problematic is the question of incentives. What would happen the next time the New York Yankees' media contract is up for renegotiations? How much incentive do the Yankees have to bargain aggressively for a higher fee . . . ? The moral: equally splitting local revenues would likely have devastating long-run impacts on those revenues. Thus this tax also is bad economics.

ECONOMICALLY JUSTIFIED TAXES TO IMPLEMENT REVENUE SHARING

So how can we set a tax that would be good economics? Let me state the requirements for a good tax system, given the problems facing all leagues. (1) Profits are healthy but are unevenly distributed. Implication: some revenue sharing is necessary, and a tax must fall more heavily on profitable franchises. (2) Owners have different goals; some focus more on wins and others on profits. Implication: two types of taxes are necessary, one on those seeking victory and another on those seeking profits. (3) Taxing revenue will make owners reluctant to take steps to "grow" revenues coming into the league. Implication: avoid taxing revenues; where possible, tax costs instead. (4) Taxes should allow markets to operate without introducing additional distortions. Implication: when players' salaries are determined in a competitive market, there is no need to separately tax this component of costs.

With these suggestions, let us consider a two-part tax, on a franchise's total costs and on its win–loss record. First, consider the "cost" tax and three fundamental questions. Why tax costs rather than revenues? What costs should be taxed? And how high a tax rate is appropriate?

Revenue sharing could be undertaken either by taxing a franchise's revenues or its costs. To date, revenue sharing in all leagues has been done by taxing revenues. . . . Taxing a franchise's revenues ultimately depresses the league's revenues and both owners and players suffer in the long run. In contrast, taxing costs strengthens owners' existing desires to control costs and to increase profitability. Owners will be better off even if players are not.

What costs should be taxed? Any tax would appear appropriately levied with respect to all costs and not just player salaries, assuming owners are serious about getting a handle on costs and are not simply out to break a union. . . . While the focus is on all costs, the tax itself should be levied only on incremental costs. For example, if the average costs in a league were $50 million, it would make sense to tax a franchise only on its costs in excess of $50 million, or on its incremental or marginal costs. The goal of the tax is to provide an incentive to keep expenditures below some level.

Now the focus on incremental costs requires some additional explanation, and that explanation is related to how high the tax rate should be and what is the need for revenue sharing in the first place. The tax rate cannot be too high or it will have ugly incentive effects. With a high enough tax rate we could have all franchises fielding a whole new team of rookies each year. But we do not need a tax rate all that high to obtain the desired effect of restricting costs. The main point underlying revenue sharing is that a game creates both a win and a loss and the winner receives more revenues than the loser. Thus, the winner imposes an economic cost on the loser. What is that cost? The answer varies by sport and even by team within [a] sport. . . .

There is some question on what costs should be taxed. The argument made earlier emphasized placing the tax on all costs rather than just on players' salaries. There remains a question of whether this tax should be placed only on costs above some threshold, a so-called "luxury tax" or whether it should be placed on all costs. . . . For simplicity assume all clubs spend the same amount and are equally competitive. Then one owner attempted to buy a championship by increasing spending. His additional expenditures make his team more competitive and presumably cost other owners money. Those incremental expenditures should be subject to a tax. There is no reason why only expenditures, say, 30 percent above the average impose costs on other franchises.

 . . . . Two numbers are important. First, how much does it cost to win one more game? . . . Second, how much revenue does a franchise lose when the team loses one more game? . . . The appropriate tax rate is simply the ratio of the revenue sacrificed with one additional loss divided by the cost of winning one more game, or how much one owner's incremental expenditures cost another in lost revenues.

. . . .

Perhaps the most important feature of this type of tax is that it begins to address one of the major problems underlying much economic strife in sports: the problem of differing owner desires. Some owners primarily want profits and some victories. How does this tax address that? Owners that want victories and championships will still choose to spend more. . . . As they spend more and perhaps win more they also impose costs on other owners that place a higher value on profits. Presumably the money from the tax on costs will be used to reimburse those owners who choose not to increase spending and who end up losing more frequently. Owners that want championships can still attempt to buy them if they wish, but only to the extent that they compensate other owners for the costs of losing.

Now this "cost" tax by itself is not the entire solution. Of course, all owners want both wins and profits, but the relative importance placed on each may differ dramatically. The tax above is on those that want to win and are spending freely to do it. They have to pay a penalty for the costs they are imposing on those that want profits. Those who want to win can still spend as freely as they want, but they must internalize the costs they impose on other owners. But owners who primarily want profits also impose costs on other owners. Why? They have little incentive to field a competitive team unless profits are at stake. . . .

League revenues will be higher in the long run when the games and the races are tight, although any one team might be able to reduce short-term expenditures and lose games but gain profits. What can be done to reduce this incentive? One suggestion: tax less-successful franchises. Give owners who focus only on profits a greater incentive to win. In some cases, franchises have effectively stopped trying to field a competitive team. . . . Taxing their losses would likely stimulate more interest in winning and may increase league profitability.

The first tax takes the Steinbrenners and Turners and taxes them for their free-spending ways. The second takes the Bill Bidwells (owner of the Arizona Cardinals) and Tom Werners (former owner of the Padres) and says field a competitive team or pay a price. The former says of the win-at-all-cost owners pay attention to those concerned with profits. The second says of the only-profits-count owners that you must also be concerned with the on-the-field competition. Thus both sets of owners must move closer to a common middle ground that explicitly gives weight to both controlling costs and fielding a competitive team. Both types of owners may continue with their original focus, but the economic incentives push them toward a compromise. Furthermore, a compromise between the owners is a prerequisite for an agreement with the players.

. . . .

. . . . What is to be done with this revenue? Given that all leagues face a problem not of insufficient profits but of an unequal distribution of profits, it would seem reasonable to take the revenue raised and return it to franchises with revenue below the league average. What mechanism you employ should not seriously weaken poorer franchises' incentives to generate their own revenues. Consider a mechanism that returns taxes proportionately to all franchises with revenues less than the league average. . . . These franchises have experienced real financial difficulties. This system of taxes and revenue sharing would help them all. It would not guarantee them profits, however.

. . . .

The nature of these taxes is to subsidize teams that are well run and yet still have difficulty making ends meet. . . . This tax system, with low tax rates and a carefully selected base, cannot bail out a club . . . that is awash in red ink. It can do two things, however. It can and does reward those clubs that are "doing things right" or fielding a competitive team at a relatively low cost. It also provides an even greater incentive for owners to be financially prudent and exercise appropriate oversight over fielding competitive teams. In a word, this set of taxes cannot give all owners the same set of incentives. However, it does bridge the current chasm between those in the league primarily as a business and those in it primarily as a hobby.

. . . .

REVENUE SHARING IN THE NFL

Virtually all NFL franchises have been quite profitable. One can make the argument that the NFL's success is rooted in their revenue sharing, even as different owners appear to have very different objectives. With the NFL's current revenue sharing arrangements, there is little reason or justification for additional revenue sharing. There is, however, a strong case against allowing owners like Jerry Jones to cut their own deals with whomever they choose. Ultimately, Jones' deals with Nike and Pepsi, for example, reduce the value of the league's deals with Reebok and Coke. When the league's deals through its marketing arm, NFL Properties, come up for renewal they will be negotiated downward and total league revenue may fall.

. . . .

Jerry Jones quite likely can make more money marketing the Cowboys on his own than he will receive from the Cowboys' share of NFL Properties income. Jones may well have the panache to run NFL Properties substantially better than it currently is being run. Jones, however, is totally off base when he says that the average franchise is better off doing its own marketing than going through NFL Properties. With 30 franchises each doing its own marketing, the competition for deals with prime sponsors like Nike will likely drive the value of those deals down for most teams. Teams like the Cowboys and 49ers may be better off but most teams will lose, and many smaller-market teams could lose dramatically. Is the average NFL owner better off with a marketing monopoly and shared profits or with 30 marketing competitors? With apologies to Ben Franklin, NFL owners had better hang together or else competitive markets will hang them all separately.

CONCLUSIONS

What is the bottom line on revenue sharing? Revenue sharing can be simply an out-and-out attempt by small-market franchises to expropriate the wealth of richer teams. . . . If that is the case, for most of us it may be interesting theater but it is not interesting from either a finance or a sports perspective.

Revenue sharing does have a strong economic justification based upon the cooperation required between teams to generate league revenues. Since the game is a joint effort, economic theory can be employed to suggest how revenues can be split to provide positive rather than negative incentives. . . .

The system of taxes and revenue sharing presented here addresses a fundamental problem of sports: that owners are in it both as a business and as a hobby and the weights that different owners place on these two goals sometimes differ dramatically. Taxing both excess costs and excess losses should move owners to roughly the same page in the playbook and should reduce losses at competently managed small-market franchises. This system of taxes also has the potential to reduce tensions between players and owners. Owners would have an incentive to more carefully monitor all costs, including player payroll, because of the cost tax. But owners also would have an incentive to make sure they field a competitive team because of the loss tax.

Revenue Sharing and Agency Problems in Professional Team Sport: The Case of the National Football League

Daniel S. Mason

Although professional sports leagues have operated in North America since the 19th century, the industry has seen its most significant changes over the past three decades. Although all four of the major sports leagues have witnessed increased revenues and interest, several problems continue to plague league operations. These include: (a) the government regulation of franchise allocation; (b) inappropriate franchise relocation; (c) monopolistic business practices; (d) antitrust immunity; and (e) the plight of small-market franchises and the subsequent attempts to use revenue sharing to increase both overall league revenues and support these franchises. . . . Another continuing problem concerns the independent actions of owners that, while often initiated for increased gain to their particular franchise, may result in a decrease in the welfare of a league as a whole. . . . In addition, teams that independently seek lucrative marketing agreements may eventually use the increased revenues to gain a competitive advantage over other clubs that ultimately undermines interest in the league product as a whole.

These problems have become particularly discouraging over the past 35 years as a team's individual success has become more dependent on its cooperation with other teams in its league. This dependency can be directly attributed to the advent of revenue sharing. The most significant event that contributed to revenue sharing was the National Sports Broadcasting Act (1961), which provided leagues the opportunity to negotiate pooled rights with a growing television market. This event, combined with other revenue-sharing practices, such as pooled licensing monies and some gate-sharing arrangements, allows sports leagues to be viewed as single business entities, as teams as a whole unite to produce the league product — a series of sporting contests.

In order to understand the consequences of increased revenue sharing and the marketing production of a combined league product, a closer look at the operations of professional sports leagues is required. Of the four established major North American professional sports leagues, the best example of a sports league endorsing the concept of single entity is the operating structure of the National Football League (NFL). Following the hiring of Alvin "Pete" Rozelle as League Commissioner in 1960, the NFL enacted revenue-sharing practices that allowed it to reach unprecedented levels of popularity. These practices have continued since Rozelle's retirement in 1989.

54

The League itself is an unincorporated association, organized to produce a single product, a series of football games. Each team pays a franchise fee, which fluctuates according to League determination, and receives a nonassignable League-designated territory. In addition, each team becomes a voting member of the League Executive Committee (LEC) and agrees to abide by the NFL Constitution and By-laws or any other authorized League policy. A team is free to negotiate its own lease terms, select its form of business organization and staff, negotiate salary terms with its players, and set its own ticket prices.

As the league product is dependent on the collective action of all teams, a means of regulating and administering the conditions of such a relationship is required. . . . An institutional response to obtaining the collective action of diffused stakeholders, such as team owners, would be to create a structure that performs the coordination of such action. For the NFL, this structure is the League's Constitution and By-laws. In addition, NFL teams collectively hire a commissioner to oversee League operations and to temper any disputes that may arise among League stakeholders. Within this arrangement, the commissioner has no voting rights as a member of the LEC. Therefore, to administer operations, the cooperation of the owners is required.

As commissioner from 1960 to 1989, Rozelle recognized the potential that television had as both a revenue source and as a means of expanding its fan base, and he allowed professional football to become a television-viewing staple and a part of the greater entertainment market. . . . The commissioner saw operating as a single entity as a means of allowing smaller market teams the opportunity to compete, and by merging with any rival leagues, allow an expanded NFL to sustain its competitive advantage by reducing the opportunities for competitive duplication.

This advantage has continued. . .

The financial success of the National Football League over the past few decades has shown that enacting revenue-sharing practices and operating as a single-business entity have been beneficial to the operations of this specific league. . . . Although there are mechanisms created by the League . . . to forge the NFL into a single-business entity, the effectiveness of such mechanisms, like revenue sharing, are still undermined by opportunistic owner behavior.

. . . . *[The author's discussion of the theoretical framework underlying agency theory is omitted.]*

THE TRANSFORMATION FROM CARTEL TO SINGLE ENTITY

The NFL was already a well-established professional sports League prior to Rozelle's appointment to the position of NFL Commissioner in 1960. The League had begun operations in 1920, when it was called the American Professional Football Association, with franchise costs set at $25 each. The League was renamed the National Football League in 1922. While initially generating revenues solely through paid attendance and related concessions, the NFL slowly developed into a more powerful organization, moving into larger markets. Eventually, the League would sell its product to three distinct groups: (a) those who attend NFL games who could be spending their money on other entertainment options; (b) television networks purchasing broadcasting rights to games instead of other programming options; and (c) municipal stadium authorities who compete to be a tenant for NFL teams by offering the most lucrative leasing package. Today, corporate sponsorships and merchandising and licensing royalties provide additional revenues. . . .

After becoming commissioner, Rozelle promptly moved the NFL's League offices to New York and immediately began forming social relations with television executives. Rozelle recognized the potential revenue source and exposure that television could provide. In the past, television revenues had been obtained independently by the NFL teams. The potential for a greater total revenue gain through collective negotiation was witnessed through the contract agreement between the rival American Football League (AFL) and the American Broadcasting Company (ABC). Rozelle then proposed to sell a single-network package for the NFL. However, a previous court decision made pooled negotiations impossible. To overcome this obstacle, Rozelle sought and received from Congress a special statutory exemption that allowed the NFL to negotiate for pooled rights. Thus, on April 24, 1961, the NFL reached an agreement with Columbia Broadcast System (CBS), with the monies received divided evenly among the NFL clubs.

Some of the clubs had already arranged contracts with different television networks. The larger market clubs received about $500,000 per season, while teams in smaller centers received around $150,000. Rozelle had to persuade the larger centers that a greater leverage could be obtained in negotiating pooled rights. However, these markets might see an initial drop in revenue that would be redistributed to the smaller market clubs. The result was that the CBS deal generated $330,000 for each team. This amount jumped to more than $1 million per team when the League negotiated a new contract with CBS in 1964. This provides a strong example of how Rozelle was able to convince the team owners that the NFL, in the long term, would be more successful (and more profitable) if it recognized that it needed to operate more as a single entity. It also shows how the commissioner and League Executive Committee were able to implement a revenue-sharing practice that could reduce agency costs by decreasing the likelihood of opportunistic behavior.

Rozelle had persuaded the owners of the larger market clubs to receive $170,000 less per year in order to both help the smaller market teams and to increase the League's bargaining power with the television networks. However, this loss would be quickly recovered over the next few years. As interest in NFL games increased, the three major networks bid against one other for the rights to show the NFL's product; these contracts would eventually become the major source of revenue for the NFL. . . . Thus, the advent of sharing network television revenues in the early 1960s continues to be a lucrative source of revenue for all League teams and provides an ideal means through which the League can maintain competitive balance.

Another means in which the NFL has grown through revenue sharing and also made teams more interdependent, was the creation of NFL Properties, a privately held firm consisting of three divisions: retail licensing, marketing and promotions, and publishing. . . . While also used as a promotional tool, the League soon realized the profit-making potential that this arm had for the League. In creating a unified marketing and licensing group, the NFL could pool its resources, further act as a single-business entity, and generate significant revenues for all teams. . . .

Rozelle was a catalyst for increasing the League's revenues and also reducing opportunistic behavior of the teams by making the clubs more dependent on one another. The NFL had been operating for four decades prior to the appointment of Pete Rozelle as League Commissioner, but the League transformed quickly after his arrival in 1960. In negotiating pooled television rights and creating NFL Properties, the League was able to keep bidding high for contracts with broadcasting and other companies, while eliminating the potential for clubs to compete against one another for television and merchandising revenues. In doing so, the NFL would then emerge as a single entity that would produce, market, and sell its product as one unit.

. . . .

Although the NFL is comprised of individual teams, the League increased its profitability and popularity by operating as a single-business entity when making decisions beyond those concerning the independent day-to-day operations of the clubs. However, the appearance of independence among clubs is crucial to the appeal of the league product, as the uncertainty of game outcomes is paramount to retaining consumer interest. To maintain this appearance, Leagues allow teams to vie with each other in several areas. These include the hiring of coaching, scouting, and administrative staff, and other nonplayer personnel. These activities are necessary, as the public must be assured that the teams are independently controlled with regard to all activities that affect on-field performance. In addition, the teams also have a vested interest in the competitive success of the other franchises. A greater equality of playing strengths of the teams ensures a greater uncertainty of game outcomes, which maintains consumer interest in matches played.

As a result of the need to promote an image of independence and rivalries between the clubs (with regard to on-field performance), there are some tendencies for certain clubs to remain autonomous. In instances where teams and club owners create rivalries with one another in terms of competition, feuds may develop that spill over to issues and activities that do not involve the actual production of league games. . . .

At the same time, the league requires parity in the competition between clubs. The competitiveness of the weaker teams is crucial in sport to maintain the uncertainty of game outcomes. In an effort to overcome this and make all teams ideally equally competitive by not allowing any teams an unfair advantage, gate receipts, which comprise almost 28% of a team's total revenues, are shared along with licensing and network television revenues in the NFL. Unlike professional hockey and basketball, where the home team receives all gate revenues, the NFL divides gate receipts, using a 60-40, home–visitor split. Thus, the teams have a vested interest in the competitiveness of all clubs, as "sustained incompetence by a number of teams presumably would lead to lowered television revenues — a loss incurred by all teams."[1]

While the success of the revenue-sharing agreements among NFL clubs seemed to have an effect on increasing total League revenues, Rozelle sought to reduce owner conflicts through controlling who actually owned and operated NFL clubs. In this manner, Rozelle felt owners would be a more homogenous group, and this could reduce the likelihood of them acting opportunistically. . . . Thus, Rozelle determined that he could keep a greater control of the owners if he could ensure that no person or group purchased a team that might act in a manner different from the other, more similar owners. In addition, the likelihood of owners choosing to act opportunistically would be reduced, as they would have similar interests. . . . Rozelle could then foster a corporate identity for the NFL, while also allowing only those parties who espoused similar characteristics to become club owners. In this manner, Rozelle could pursue his vision of transforming the NFL into a single-business entity, with the interests of the owners more likely to be aligned and a single commissioner overseeing League operations.

The personality or corporate character of the NFL, which Rozelle had carefully implemented through revenue sharing, was called "Leaguethink". . . In order to control the types of owners in the League and, therefore, have a greater ability to control the decision-making processes, Rozelle proposed an ownership policy. With a more homogenous group of owners, Rozelle also sought to decrease the likelihood of conflict and opportunistic behavior. . . . The ownership policy contained four basic rules: (a) no corporate ownership; (b) no public ownership; (c) at least one person must own at least a majority (51%) of a team; and (d) no cross-ownership (no owners may have interests in other sporting teams, in any sport). The policy was fraught with problems, particularly Rule 4. However, in 1978, Rozelle finally convinced the Executive Committee to forbid cross-ownership.

Rozelle had hoped to maintain the image of football owners as a group of hobbyists who were interested in sport and not the profitability of ownership, which would be more evident if teams were corporately operated. In addition, corporate and public ownership might mean that a number of individuals would try to run each club, making the decision-making process more difficult. Public ownership would reveal the financial characteristics of team operations, which the League wanted to remain proprietary. Rozelle also rued cross-ownership, as he felt that skills in running the NFL should not be shared with other leagues.

Rozelle's scheme was partly successful; the NFL has the longest tenure of ownership (13.2 years) of any of the major professional sports in North America. This stability of ownership illustrates the success of his desire to unify the League owners through "Leaguethink." . . . Thus, the success of the NFL would hinge on the ability of the League owners to understand and accept Rozelle's vision of a modern combine. In positioning the League as a single-business entity, Rozelle sought to align the franchises to work in the best interests of the League as a whole.

. . . . *[The author's discussion of unwanted opportunistic behavior and barriers to enforcing league governance mechanisms is omitted.]*

DISCUSSION

. . . Opportunistic activity has reached the point where disputes within the NFL must be decided in the courts, and not through the NFL's Constitution and By-laws, or voting by the LEC. Thus, it is the threat of legal intervention that has led to the reduced success of "Leaguethink." However, the problems faced by the NFL are only compounded by legal intervention. . . . The NFL has failed to align owner interests to an extent that opportunistic behavior is minimized. In effect, the ability of the League to forge itself into a single-business entity has not been completely successful, which explains why the League continues to have problems of opportunistic behavior that, while increasing the welfare of the individual team . . . results in a decrease in the welfare of the League as a whole and, ultimately, the remaining NFL teams.

. . . From an agency perspective, the NFL (as principal), governed by its League Executive Committee, should act entrepreneurially to maximize wealth for the entire League and subsequently all its member clubs. In order to act entrepreneurially in this manner, the independent owners must then agree to a contractual relationship with one another. This contract specifies what the principal (the NFL) expects from the agent (the team) and what the agent will receive in return. However, an agency problem arises when the entrepreneur is the agent and not the principal. Thus, although NFL teams are aware of the governance mechanisms, they continue to act opportunistically by moving their franchises or seeking marketing opportunities that undermine league-wide agreements.

While the solution to typical agency problems is achieved through contracting on the outcome of the agent's behavior or by creating information systems to monitor agent behavior, the unique structure of professional sports leagues which require seemingly autonomous clubs to unite to produce a single-league product suggests that revenue sharing would be an ideal means through which the interests of the principal and agents could be converged. In addition, the creation of various governance mechanisms should also result in the increased ability of the principal (the NFL) to monitor the behavior of the agent and reduce the likelihood of opportunistic behavior. However, in any principal–agent relationship, complete information is difficult to achieve; therefore, there are always going to be incidents of opportunistic agent behavior.

. . . . While revenue sharing would seem to be an effective means to align agent interests, this can only occur when the agent is a profit-maximizer. Thus, a mechanism such as revenue sharing will be undermined when an agent is a wealth-maximizer and not an exclusive profit-maximizer, which may serve to explain the behavior of certain agents in certain situations. In this manner, a team owner might raise players' salaries by paying too much to assemble a winning team. The owner then achieves wealth through the competitive successes of the team, rather than its profitability. The result damages the profits of the leagues as a whole by escalating salary costs that increase as a result of the precedent set by the original, wealth-maximizing owner. Thus, revenue sharing would not reduce the opportunistic behavior of an owner whose sole reason for owning a club was winning, which would bring that owner significant wealth. Therefore, the implicit or explicit contract between the principal and agent must try to determine what rewards are sought by both parties within the principal–agent relationship. Not only are there potential contract problems concerning an inadequate amount of reward to the agent (the amount of compensation), there is also the potential for the wrong type of reward (the form of compensation) being used to govern the relationship.

Thus, the failure of League governance mechanisms may have less to do with the competence of the LEC and its commissioner, or the actions of maverick agents; rather, it lies in the determination of the contract between principal and agent in the professional sports industry. . . . The non-monetary benefits sought by the owners of teams may mitigate the effectiveness of revenue sharing. Thus, the problem was further exacerbated when considering what motivated the owners into acting against the wishes of the other league teams. . . . Owners and managers were motivated by different types of benefits. Thus, Rozelle and the LEC could not succeed in aligning owner interests through revenue sharing if the acquisition of revenue was not the sole purpose of operation for some owners. . . . The prestige and publicity associated with club ownership often motivate involvement in professional sports. . . . Many own teams for fun, attention, and ego fulfillment. Thus, Rozelle's quest for the owners to endorse a greater unity of interest would prove far more difficult. . .

Thus, the leagues need to look more closely at the contract that governs the relationship between the principal and agent. However, opportunistic behavior will continue until some of the wealthier owners of the independent clubs are willing to sacrifice some of their own personal gain, be it financial or other, for the greater good of the league. In order for the NFL to continue to thrive, the owners must agree to and abide by the Constitution and By-laws of the League, without which the team would have little, if any, function. . . . Thus, the agency problems associated with the National Football League may have costs that will ultimately harm both individual teams and the League as a whole.

The success of the NFL and other professional sports leagues with similar structures may be more dependent on the voluntary acceptance of league governance mechanisms, in addition to the creation of more efficient revenue sharing or other practices. . . . In the context of the NFL, the Constitution and By-laws then have little value or power unless the owners understand and accept the principles that underpin the need for such regulations. Therefore, the ability of the League Executive Committee to align owner interests will only be effective if members restrain personal opportunistic activity.

Unfortunately, such compliance by the teams is unlikely. . . It seems as though the NFL owners of today are even less likely to buy into "Leaguethink." It is also apparent . . . that both the League and its clubs are still likely to pursue court action as an alternative to League governance mechanisms to settle League conflicts. This has severely undermined the governance capabilities of the LEC and its policies. . . . This divergent behavior reduces the welfare of the league and can be viewed as a residual loss, as the league as a whole will collectively lose profits. . . .

. . . . The need for the league to project the image of autonomy among teams would suggest that it is unlikely that teams could or should become more interdependent through practices such as revenue sharing. This is because if all revenues were shared equally, there would be less incentive for teams to produce winning clubs and/or more profits. This behavior is described . . . as moral hazard, which exists due to a lack of effort, or shirking on the part of the agent.

If it is impossible to get the agents to mutually agree to not act opportunistically, then the remaining option for the NFL would be to try to alter its existing mechanisms to try to reduce the unwanted behavior of some agents. Perhaps what the NFL needs is a revenue-sharing agreement that does not increase the amount of revenues shared but the methods in which they are distributed. This could be done by rewarding on-the-field performance (giving the incentive to field-competitive teams, while allowing owners to pursue other sources of wealth such as the prestige of owning a winning team), and clubs that pursue marketing opportunities. . . .

A revised revenue-sharing agreement will allow teams who are able to generate more revenues to benefit from their position but, at the same time, allow smaller market clubs the opportunity to compete for playing talent. Obviously, the NFL needs to be able to reward certain clubs (such as the Dallas Cowboys) in positions who can gain marketing revenues greater than those in smaller markets. However, if the Cowboys continue to generate revenues that are far greater than that of the other clubs, there will ultimately be a disparity in the competitiveness of certain clubs that results in a loss of consumer interest in the League product as a whole. Thus, agency theory has shown how owners like Jerry Jones have put their self-interest ahead of the remainder of the League. However, without the other NFL teams, Jones has no product in which to promote, own, and market, and without the existence of competitive clubs interest in his club will eventually wane.

CONCLUSION

. . . .

While not exclusively responsible for the success of the NFL over the past four decades, revenue sharing and "Leaguethink" allowed Rozelle to transform the League from a group of independent owners into a single-business entity that produces and markets a single League product. However . . . interests will diverge within the principal–agent relationship unless they are reduced by appropriate governance mechanisms; the NFL can contract on the relationship through clubs agreeing to abide by the League's Constitution and By-laws. The League has only been partially successful in doing so, as recent legal intervention has reduced the governing power of the LEC. Clubs that do not want to abide by League policies can defy the LEC and wait for the dispute to be settled in court. In addition, it is also unlikely that the interests of the League clubs can be converged any further. The need for the perception of competition between League clubs with respect to on-the-field performance — to retain consumer interest — will require that clubs remain separate legal entities. It is also unlikely that, during this time of relative prosperity, League clubs would consider relinquishing further autonomy for the greater good of the League as a whole.

REFERENCES

1. Kurlantzick, L. S. (1983). Thoughts on professional sports and antitrust laws: Los Angeles Memorial Coliseum Commission vs. National Football League. 15 *Connecticut Law Review* 183, 190 (1983).

THE REPORT OF THE INDEPENDENT MEMBERS OF THE COMMISSIONER'S BLUE RIBBON PANEL ON BASEBALL ECONOMICS

Richard C. Levin, George J. Mitchell,
Paul A. Volcker, and George F. Will

SUMMARY OF FINDINGS, CONCLUSIONS, AND RECOMMENDATIONS

Overall Conclusions

The Commissioner's Blue Ribbon Panel on Baseball Economics . . . was formed to study whether revenue disparities among clubs are seriously damaging competitive balance, and, if so, to recommend structural reforms to ameliorate the problem. After 18 months of extensive investigation, we conclude:

a. Large and growing revenue disparities exist and are causing problems of chronic competitive imbalance.

b. These problems have become substantially worse during the five complete seasons since the strike-shortened season of 1994, and seem likely to remain severe unless Major League Baseball ("MLB") undertakes remedial actions proportional to the problem.

c. The limited revenue sharing and payroll tax that were approved as part of MLB's 1996 Collective Bargaining Agreement with the Major League Baseball Players Association ("MLBPA") have produced neither the intended moderating of payroll disparities nor improved competitive balance. Some low-revenue clubs, believing the amount of their proceeds from revenue sharing insufficient to enable them to become competitive, used those proceeds to become modestly profitable.

d. In a majority of MLB markets, the cost to clubs of trying to be competitive is causing escalation of ticket and concession prices, jeopardizing MLB's traditional position as the affordable family spectator sport.

Revenue Disparities

Measured simply in terms of gross revenues, which almost doubled during the five complete seasons (1995–1999) since 1994, MLB is prospering. But that simple measurement is a highly inadequate gauge of MLB's economic health. Because of anachronistic aspects of MLB's economic arrangements, the prosperity of some clubs is having perverse effects that pose a threat to the game's long-term vitality. Here are a few of the facts about revenue imbalances:

a. What are called local revenues (including gate receipts, local television, radio and cable rights fees, ballpark concessions, advertising and publications, parking, suite rentals, post-season and spring training) are the largest single component of most clubs' annual revenues. The ratio between the highest and lowest club's local revenues has more than doubled in just five years. . .

b. Since 1995, local revenues have increased an average of $54 million for clubs in revenue Quartile I (the highest-revenue clubs), but local revenues have increased an average of only $8 million for clubs in Quartile IV.

c. In 1999, one club's local revenues exceeded by approximately $11 million the combined local revenues of six other clubs.

. . . .

e. Between 1995 and 1999, clubs in revenue Quartile I increased their total annual revenues (which includes local revenue, Central Fund revenue and revenue sharing) by an average of $55 million, while the total annual revenues of Quartile IV clubs increased only by an average [of] $32 million.

. . . .

h. Between 1995 and 1999, the difference between the highest and lowest club's total revenues rose from $74 million to $129 million.

i. In 1999, the total revenue of the highest revenue club exceeded by $14 million the combined revenues of the three lowest revenue clubs.

. . . .

Payroll Disparities

Not surprisingly, widening revenue disparities have been accompanied by widening payroll disparities:

a. In 1999, one club had a payroll approximately equal to the sum of the payrolls of the lowest five payroll clubs.

. . . .

c. In 2000, the salary of the game's highest paid player is equal to the entire Opening Day player payroll of one club (Minnesota).

. . . .

e. Between 1995 and 1999, the average payroll of clubs in the top revenue quartile increased $28 million, while the average payroll of clubs in the bottom revenue quartile increased only $4 million.

. . . .

h. The average payroll of clubs in payroll Quartile I was $32 million (70 percent) larger in 1999 than in 1995, but the average payroll in Quartile IV increased only $2 million (13 percent).

i. In 1995, payroll Quartile I clubs spent two and one half times more on payrolls than the Quartile IV clubs. By 1999, Quartile I clubs spent four times more.

. . . .

Payroll and Competitiveness

Not surprisingly, there is a strong correlation between high payrolls and success on the field. Although a high payroll is not always sufficient to produce a club capable of reaching postseason play — there are instances of competitive failures by high payroll clubs — a high payroll has become an increasingly necessary ingredient of on-field success:

a. From 1995 through 1999, every World Series winner was from payroll Quartile I and no club outside payroll Quartile I won even a single game in the Series. Indeed, the winner each year was among the five clubs with the largest payrolls.

. . . .

Other Findings and Conclusions

Sports leagues do not function as free markets. If they did, the clubs would be clustered in a few large markets. Rather, sports leagues are blends of cooperation and competition — cooperation for the sake of producing satisfactory competitiveness.

MLB has enjoyed a long-standing exemption from antitrust laws that govern other industries. MLB and other professional sports leagues operate under rules which have withstood legal scrutiny. These rules are intended to protect the public interest by enabling franchises in communities of varying sizes and with different market conditions to compete against each other with a reasonable opportunity to succeed.

The goal of a well-designed league is to produce adequate competitive balance. By this standard, MLB is not now well designed.

In the context of baseball, proper competitive balance should be understood to exist when there are no clubs chronically weak because of MLB's structural features. Proper competitive balance will not exist until every well-run club has a regularly recurring reasonable hope of reaching postseason play.

Granted, competitive balance as here defined has been an elusive goal, when it has been a goal at all, throughout MLB's history. However, the fact that baseball's structural flaws are historic is not an argument for continuing acceptance of them. This is particularly so when they are producing revenue disparities with unhealthy consequences for competitive balance.

What has made baseball's recent seasons disturbing, and what makes its current economic structure untenable in the long run, is that, year after year, too many clubs know in spring training that they have no realistic prospect of reaching postseason play. Too many clubs in low-revenue markets can only expect to compete for postseason berths if ownership is willing to incur staggering operating losses to subsidize a competitive player payroll.

Furthermore, baseball fans are not, and should not be asked to be, as stoical about competitive imbalance as they have been in the past. Competition for the sports entertainment dollar, and for the sport fan's attention, is increasingly intense. There was a time when baseball had the almost undivided attention of sports fans from April to October. Now, however, there are just six weeks between the last National Basketball Association ("NBA") championship game and the first National Football League ("NFL") preseason game. MLB must improve its competitive balance if it is to remain competitive with other sports attractions.

Unfortunately, one of MLB's strengths — its long tradition, with roots running deep into 19th century America — currently has a debilitating cost. Baseball operates under an anachronistic economic model, unlike the NFL and NBA. Forty years ago, those leagues were soft wax that could be given shapes appropriate to the exigencies of the modern market for professional sports. But forty years ago, MLB was operating, as it still is, under many fundamental arrangements that even then were more than sixty years old. These arrangements long predate the advent of, to cite just one example, broadcasting.

The NFL and NBA have thrived with structures that allow franchises in widely different kinds of markets . . . to succeed. To ensure baseball's broad and enduring popularity, and to guarantee its future growth, MLB needs a structure under which clubs in smaller markets can have regularly recurring chances to contend for championships.

Solutions to baseball's competitive imbalance should flow from the following postulates:

a. Baseball should vigorously develop new ways to increase revenues, but that alone will not solve baseball's problem of competitive imbalance.

b. The heart of the problem is the large and growing disparity of what are called "local" revenues.

c. Although most of baseball's revenues are these local revenues, none of the revenues really result exclusively from the sale of a local product. It takes two clubs to have a game and 30 clubs to have today's divisional races. All clubs are selling — indeed, all are elements of — a single product, MLB.

d. Therefore, to reform baseball's structure to produce reasonable competitive balance, substantially more of the industry's revenues should be treated as just that — the industry's revenues — and should be distributed in ways that cause all clubs to operate within a much narrower band of unequal economic resources. The band should be broad enough to allow baseball entrepreneurship to be rewarded, but narrow enough that intractable differences between local markets do not produce a baseball underclass of chronically uncompetitive clubs.

e. The fundamental objective of reform should be an industry in which each team's success on the field, over time, will be determined by the skill of the players and the baseball acumen of the men and women who conduct the team's business — scouting, player development, baseball management, marketing, etc.

f. Any reform of MLB should protect and balance the interests of players, clubs and fans. These three constituencies should cooperate to create an economic structure that promotes a reasonable rate of growth of player salaries, produces competitive balance, and preserves baseball as affordable family entertainment.

Our mission has been to consider the relevant economic data, indicators, and variables. We have concluded that a majority of MLB clubs today are not reasonably competitive, that the problem of competitive balance is a product of MLB's economic structure, and that this structure is adversely affecting the ability of most clubs to increase revenues and achieve operating stability.

. . . . *[The authors' discussion of recommendations for reform to MLB's economic structure is omitted.]*

THE ECONOMIC CONDITION OF THE GAME

Overview

Despite impressive industry-wide revenue growth over the past five years, MLB has an outdated economic structure that has created an unacceptable level of revenue disparity and competitive imbalance over the same period. The growing gap between the "have" and the "have not" clubs — which is to say the minority that have a realistic chance of succeeding in postseason play and the majority of clubs that have poor prospects of reaching the postseason — is a serious and imminent threat to the popularity, health, stability, and growth of the game.

. . . .

The introduction of limited revenue sharing and a "luxury tax" on payrolls for a trial period under the 1996 Collective Bargaining Agreement (known as the "Basic Agreement") apparently did not create any significant "drag" on player salaries and has not significantly enhanced competitive balance. In fact, a number of low revenue clubs, realizing that they had no realistic chance to compete for the postseason, opted instead for marginal profitability from revenue sharing proceeds and did not increase their player payrolls. This grim fact of modern baseball life has frustrated fans in low-revenue markets.

Baseball's flawed economic structure also has contributed to a surge in ticket and concession prices, a trend that threatens to compromise baseball's traditional role as the "national pastime" and its important niche as affordable family entertainment in the professional sports marketplace. . . .

The combination of competitive imbalance and rising prices eventually could alienate MLB's core fan base and make the development of new generations of fans problematic, even as the global market for baseball expands and golden opportunities abound to make the game more popular and prosperous.

In recent years, there has been a rapidly accelerating disparity in revenues and, consequently, payrolls between clubs in high- and low-revenue markets. There also has been a stronger correlation between club revenues/payrolls and on-field competitiveness in the years since the issue of competitive balance was studied by the Joint Economic Study Committee which issued its report in 1992. The inescapable conclusion is that major structural problems exist in the economics of professional baseball. If these flaws are not addressed by MLB promptly, decisively, and ultimately in conjunction with the MLBPA, the future of the game as we have known it will be imperiled.

A reasonably level playing field, on which clubs representing markets that are quite diverse geographically, demographically, and economically can compete with at least periodic opportunities for success, is fundamental to MLB's continued growth and popular appeal. Yet, from 1995 through 1999, a total of 158 MLB postseason games were played. During this period, no club whose payroll fell in the lower half of the industry won even a single postseason game. Only one has even qualified for the postseason.

MLB is now essentially divided into three groups of unequal size: 1) clubs that expect to perform well in the postseason; 2) clubs that hope for an occasional "dream season" to reach the postseason; and 3) clubs that know going to spring training that they will not make the playoffs.

Also distressing from an ownership standpoint are several other facts that are of less concern to fans: 1) only three MLB clubs have operated profitably over the past five years, despite the industry's revenue growth; 2) club debt nearly quadrupled over seven years, from $604 million in 1993 to $2.08 billion in 1999; and 3) appreciation in MLB franchise values has not matched that in other major professional sports leagues.

In short, it should be apparent that the time for tinkering with MLB's existing, flawed economic structure has passed and that sweeping changes in the game's economic landscape are necessary. . . .
. . . .

Industry Revenues

. . . .

Revenue to clubs comes primarily from three sources: 1) so-called local revenues include ticket sales, local television, radio and cable rights, ballpark concessions, parking, and team sponsorships; 2) Central Fund revenues are generated by industry-wide contracts, such as national television contracts and licensing arrangements, and historically have been distributed evenly to all clubs; and 3) revenue sharing, introduced in 1996, transfers locally generated money from high-revenue clubs to low-revenue clubs.

Revenues, in all likelihood, will continue to grow during the next decade as new ballparks are opened. . . .

The new generation of ballparks that began with the 1992 opening of Oriole Park at Camden Yards in Baltimore includes design and programming features and modern amenities that have proved to be enormously popular with the public. These ballparks have dramatically increased the attendance and revenues of the clubs that play in them. In addition to Baltimore, the franchises with new ballparks that opened in the 1990s include Arizona, Atlanta, Chicago White Sox, Cleveland, Colorado, Seattle, and Texas. St. Louis and Anaheim undertook major renovations that transformed dual-purpose stadiums (football and baseball) into baseball oriented facilities. New ballpark construction and renovation has made a significant contribution to revenue growth in the second half of the past decade.

In fact, the construction or renovation of facilities to add modern amenities has been effective in increasing the revenue — and therefore the player payroll and competitiveness — of some clubs. In many cases, the ballparks themselves have become attractions, dramatically increasing attendance and revenues and providing the club the financial resources to field teams with payrolls high enough to have a chance to be competitive.

It is reasonable to expect that new ballparks will continue to fuel industry revenue growth for the foreseeable future, and this is a positive trend for the industry. However, revenue growth alone does not provide a long-term solution for the structural flaws in MLB's economic system. Eventually, most clubs will have attractive, baseball-oriented facilities with modern amenities, and then the revenue/payroll disparities that breed competitive imbalance will be magnified because the clubs in large media markets have revenue opportunities from new ballparks that are greater than those of their counterparts in smaller markets. They can command more for naming rights, ballpark signage, team sponsorships, etc. They can charge more for tickets, sell more suites and club seats than their small market competitors, as well as receive substantially more for local television and radio rights. The level of public investment in new ballparks also varies dramatically from community to community, which means that some clubs need to devote much more of their newly generated revenue to private financing and debt service than others.

New ballparks are vitally important for expanding the game's prosperity. Baseball is best enjoyed in intimate, charming venues that become attractions themselves, regardless of whether the home team is winning or losing. However, they are not in and of themselves the answer to solving the competitive balance and economic problems that plague MLB.

Local Revenues

. . . Local revenue is the single fastest growing component of industry revenues. . . .

Local revenue grew 87 percent from 1995 to 1999, adding some one billion dollars (or roughly $200 million each year) to the industry's total revenues. From 1996 through 1999, local revenue constituted approximately 79 percent of total industry revenue.

In 1999, the range of local revenues was enormous, from $12 million for Montreal to $176 million for the New York Yankees. This begs the obvious question: How can a club like Montreal expect to compete with the New York Mets, whose local revenues are ten times greater? The inescapable answer is: They cannot, even with a productive scouting and player development system and sound baseball management. Several low-revenue clubs in the 1990s have tried to remain competitive on the field with a strategy of devoting their modest resources to scouting and player development and fielding teams of young, talented players who likely would have had more minor-league seasoning with higher-revenue, higher payroll clubs. The theory under which these lower-revenue clubs have operated is that their fans would appreciate seeing young, aggressive, "hungry and hustling" teams and that they would be able to retain a nucleus of these young stars long enough to contend periodically for the postseason. Unfortunately, doing so has become increasingly problematic, and fans in those markets have become progressively frustrated, disillusioned, and resigned to also-ran status as a seemingly endless succession of their home-grown talent has moved on, via free agency or financially motivated trades, to help high-revenue, high-payroll clubs to championships.

. . . .

Local revenues generally are the largest component of most clubs' annual revenue. Unlike other professional sports, in which a much larger portion of television rights fees are pooled and distributed equally among all teams, most MLB television and radio rights are negotiated and sold locally, in each individual market. Only the rights to network television and radio (essentially the rights to postseason games) and a national cable package are sold by MLB, with the revenue going to the Central Fund. Because local markets vary greatly in size, the local TV and radio revenues flowing to each club vary in size by large amounts. The local radio and TV rights received by some clubs exceed the total revenues of other clubs.

Media market rank also affects other local revenues available to clubs, including the amount they can charge for ballpark naming rights, signage, sponsorships, etc. No matter how well managed a club might be, it cannot change its media market rank, a factor in the revenue disparity that translates to payroll disparity and competitive imbalance.

. . . .

The seemingly unbridgeable — and ultimately unacceptable — chasm between the "haves" and "have-nots" has grown wider.

Central Fund Revenues

Central Fund revenue historically has been distributed equally to all clubs. . . . Central Fund distributions have risen each year, but not as fast as the local revenues of some of the highest revenue clubs. The lowest revenue clubs, however, find that their Central Fund distribution is now larger than their local revenues.

. . . .

Club Payrolls

The amount of each club's player payroll generally is related to its revenue. That is, the greater the club's revenue, the higher its payroll.

. . . .

Quite simply, the higher revenue clubs have the financial resources to: 1) sign high-salaried free agents from other clubs; 2) retain their own high-salaried players; and 3) sign top prospects from the Rule 4 draft, where signing bonuses for highly sought-after players have risen dramatically in recent years, and from foreign countries, where players are exempt from the draft and can be signed as free agents. The rich clubs become richer in talent, stockpiling expensive players, while poor teams cannot afford to bid on premium players either at the entry level or on the veteran free agent market.

. . . .

The difference between the highest and lowest club player payrolls increased from $45 million in 1995 to $77 million in 1999. *[The difference was $148 million in 2003.]*

The payroll disparity in MLB is in stark contrast to the situation in professional football and basketball. . . .

Club Competitiveness

The total number of games won is generally closely related to the club's payroll. That is, the higher the payroll, the more games the club is likely to win. This is clearly not a foolproof correlation or an exact science. Occasionally, a low-payroll club does well on the field. High-payroll clubs also have flopped on the field. Team chemistry, skillful player evaluation, and baseball management make a difference. But while it is evident that a high payroll is not the only element in fielding a winning club, it is an increasingly important element. Put another way, a high payroll does not automatically guarantee a good win–loss record and a contending season, but a low payroll usually means that a club cannot contend for a postseason berth or a championship.

. . . .

Conclusions Regarding Competitive Balance

. . . .

While most fans do not demand or expect that their team will reach postseason play each year, some have ample reason to believe that the club they root for will remain chronically uncompetitive. . . . Many fans have come to believe that it is unlikely these clubs will reverse that fate in the next few years. The presence in the game of clubs, perhaps a majority, that are chronically uncompetitive, alongside clubs that routinely dominate the postseason, undermines the public's interest and confidence in the sport.

Remedies for Competitive Imbalance

The objective of competitive balance in baseball should be taken to mean a reasonable opportunity for all clubs, not equal outcome. Clubs should expect to be rewarded for good management, on and off the field, as well as by periodic good fortune.

The internal market arrangements for professional baseball, as in all professional sports, are cooperative arrangements necessary for the maintenance of on-the-field competitiveness between teams representing unequal markets.

Baseball's economic system has never been, is not, and should not be a wholly unregulated market. Baseball, like all professional sports, has recognized that the drive for unbridled competition on the field must be harnessed or tempered by regulations designed to ensure fairness and the inherent need for cooperation among clubs with unequal economic resources to preserve the "league" as an institution. All professional sports regulate issues such as roster size, late season trades, and access to new talent (via a draft) in ways that would not be tolerated in an unregulated environment.

Whatever their other differences, both owners and players have supported market regulations as a necessary component of MLB's economic landscape. Owners, even those who have suffered significant economic losses, have agreed to limits on franchise relocation because they recognize that teams are a civic asset and too many franchises in the most fertile markets would be bad for fans and the game. Players have recognized that unlimited free agency is unacceptable because too much player movement could destroy the fabric of the game.

Even the courts and Congress have recognized the unique economic structure of Baseball by creating and upholding MLB's long-time exemption from the antitrust laws. The exemption is founded on the notion that it is in the public's interest to have MLB as a national enterprise with orderly operations and a reasonable degree of cooperation among the clubs, even if that cooperation is not strictly in compliance with the pro-competitive policies that underlie the antitrust laws. (See Table 1 for MLB team financial data and Table 2 for NFL team financial data.)

DISCUSSION QUESTIONS

1. Describe the revenue-sharing agreements in each of the four major professional sports leagues.
2. How are the current revenue-sharing arrangements in each league optimal or suboptimal?
3. What is the ideal amount of revenue sharing for a league to engage in? Explain.

4. With the current economics of Major League Baseball, will it be possible for teams in small markets to be competitive for a sustained period of years or to win a championship?

5. Why do owners seek to undermine league welfare by not complying with league policies?

6. How much revenue is shared in each league?

7. Why should any revenue be shared?

8. Is there an economic justification underlying revenue sharing? How can the problems associated with revenue sharing be overcome?

9. Sheehan's tax plan calls for the taxing of those teams that are not competitive. What are the reasons for doing this? Would this be effective? Why or why not?

10. What is the major problem that Major League Baseball has uncovered about itself? How should this problem be solved?

11. How do the results of the 2002 and 2003 seasons — in which the Anaheim Angels and the Florida Marlins won the World Series and fellow low-revenue clubs such as the Minnesota Twins and Oakland A's made the postseason — impact the validity of the conclusions of the Blue Ribbon Panel?

12. How did Commissioner Rozelle ensure a stable ownership of NFL franchises? Is this still effective today? Why or why not?

13. In each professional sports league, where does the majority of team revenue come from? Will it continue to grow? Why or why not?

TABLE 1.

MLB 2001 TEAM-BY-TEAM REVENUES AND EXPENSES FORECAST (IN THOUSANDS)							
	Operating revenue						
	Regular-season game receipts	*Local TV, radio, and cable*	*Post-season*	*All other local operating revenue*	*Local operating revenue*	*National revenue*	*Total operating revenue*
Anaheim	$30,208	$10,927	—	$26,195	$67,330	$24,401	$91,731
Arizona	46,509	14,174	13,000	32,970	106,653	18,479	125,132
Atlanta	62,141	19,988	2,629	37,692	122,450	24,401	146,851
Baltimore	53,216	20,994	—	29,691	103,901	24,401	128,302
Boston	89,743	33,353	—	29,485	152,581	24,401	176,982
Chic. Cubs	51,189	23,559	−17	30,642	105,373	24,401	129,774
Chic. White Sox	30,898	30,092	—	26,291	87,281	24,401	111,682
Cincinnati	32,102	7,861	—	6,523	46,486	24,401	70,887
Cleveland	69,470	21,076	2,000	45,295	137,841	24,401	162,242
Colorado	54,015	18,200	—	35,197	107,412	24,401	131,813
Detroit	42,299	19,073	—	21,018	82,390	24,401	106,791
Florida	16,756	15,353	—	4,037	36,146	24,401	60,547
Houston	49,161	13,722	519	36,826	100,228	24,401	124,629
Kansas City	19,520	6,505	—	13,270	39,295	24,401	63,696
Los Angeles	50,764	27,342	—	41,100	119,206	24,401	143,607
Milwaukee	46,021	5,918	—	37,010	88,949	24,401	113,350
Minnesota	17,605	7,273	—	6,987	31,865	24,401	56,266
Montreal	6,405	536	—	2,829	9,770	24,401	34,171
N.Y. Mets	73,971	46,251	−154	38,162	158,230	24,401	182,631
N.Y. Yankees	98,000	56,750	16,000	47,057	217,807	24,401	242,208
Oakland	24,992	9,458	2,686	13,932	51,068	24,401	75,469
Philadelphia	30,435	18,940	—	7,739	57,114	24,401	81,515
Pittsburgh	48,610	9,097	—	26,598	84,305	24,401	108,706
St. Louis	67,084	11,905	1,488	27,581	108,058	24,401	132,459
San Diego	34,381	12,436	—	8,504	55,321	24,401	79,722
San Francisco	67,173	17,197	—	61,524	145,894	24,401	170,295
Seattle	76,570	37,860	7,392	56,211	178,033	24,401	202,434
Tampa Bay	18,193	15,511	—	28,633	62,337	18,258	80,595
Texas	50,664	25,284	—	34,561	110,509	24,401	134,910
Toronto	25,363	14,460	—	14,255	54,078	24,401	78,479
Consolidation	1,383,458	571,095	45,543	827,815	2,827,911	719,965	3,547,876

Note: Player compensation includes 40-man roster costs and termination pay.
The consolidated loss, when $174,234,000 of nonoperational charges such as amortization of debt are added in, comes to $518,966,000.
Source: Major League Baseball.

| Operating expenses | | | Income | | Income (loss) | Income (loss) |
Player com-pensation & benefit plan	National and other local expenses	Total op-erating expenses	(loss) from baseball operations	2001 revenue sharing	from baseball operations after revenue sharing	from baseball operations after interest
$52,239	$49,061	$101,300	−$9,569	$9,594	$25	−$4,953
99,434	57,850	157,284	−32,152	−4,432	−36,584	−44,358
99,671	61,540	161,211	−14,360	−10,647	−25,007	−23,868
79,783	47,059	126,842	1,460	−6,807	−5,347	−13,732
118,471	55,799	174,270	2,712	−16,438	−13,726	−13,675
78,091	46,886	124,977	4,797	−6,568	−1,771	2,894
66,721	50,648	117,369	−5,687	−4,201	−9,888	−7,625
45,410	36,533	81,943	−11,056	13,404	2,348	−285
102,491	57,870	160,361	1,881	−13,254	−11,373	−14,242
69,983	65,245	135,228	−3,415	−6,029	−9,444	−11,522
57,184	49,074	106,258	533	5,127	5,660	−10,694
42,084	46,204	88,288	−27,741	18,561	−9,180	−10,820
71,577	54,266	125,843	−1,214	−5,185	−6,399	−9,455
42,704	37,126	79,830	−16,134	15,997	−137	1,474
116,077	72,873	188,950	−45,343	−9,107	−54,450	−68,887
51,164	47,801	98,965	14,385	1,744	16,129	9,001
30,494	44,305	74,799	−18,533	19,089	536	−3,791
37,676	35,014	72,690	−38,519	28,517	−10,002	−12,837
99,144	75,195	174,339	8,292	−15,669	−7,337	−5,225
117,936	83,413	201,349	40,859	−26,540	14,319	8,230
43,821	38,761	82,582	−7,113	10,520	3,407	−532
49,384	52,996	102,380	−20,865	11,752	−9,113	−9,352
53,227	58,463	111,690	−2,984	1,782	−1,202	−5,879
80,148	50,442	130,590	1,869	−8,229	−6,360	−7,322
46,089	49,784	95,873	−16,151	8,668	−7,483	−10,298
72,185	79,110	151,295	19,000	−6,308	12,692	−139
83,946	84,222	168,168	34,266	−18,791	15,475	14,793
57,000	46,438	103,438	−22,843	12,384	−10,459	−17,880
92,793	57,806	150,599	−15,689	−8,744	−24,433	−31,248
83,801	47,605	131,406	−52,927	9,830	−43,097	−42,504
2,140,728	1,639,389	3,780,117	−232,241	—	−232,241	−344,732

TABLE 2.

NFL Profit by Team (in 1999)	
Rank/NFL team	*Operating profit*
1. Cleveland	$36.5 million
2. Washington	$32.4 million
3. Tennessee	$32.1 million
4. Jacksonville	$27.7 million
5. Dallas	$25.8 million
6. Tampa Bay	$24.6 million
7. St. Louis	$20.0 million
8. N.Y. Giants	$18.4 million
9. Pittsburgh	$12.2 million
10. Buffalo	$11.6 million
11. Philadelphia	$10.8 million
12. Carolina	$10.5 million
13. Minnesota	$9.8 million
14. N.Y. Jets	$9.8 million
15. Miami	$9.7 million
16. Baltimore	$9.4 million
17. Kansas City	$9.0 million
18. Cincinnati	$8.6 million
19. San Francisco	$8.3 million
20. Chicago	$7.9 million
21. San Diego	$6.9 million
22. Indianapolis	$4.2 million
23. Detroit	$4.1 million
24. Denver	$3.2 million
25. Atlanta	$2.9 million
26. Oakland	$1.9 million
27. Arizona	$1.5 million
28. Seattle	$544,000
29. New England	$354,000
30. Green Bay	$288,000
31. New Orleans	−$849,000

Source: NFL documents.

CHAPTER 4

ACCOUNTING, TAXATION, AND BANKRUPTCY

INTRODUCTION

Though often difficult to grasp, it is important for sports industry leaders to understand many basic concepts of accounting, taxation, and bankruptcy. Despite the numerous differences between sports and other industries that are highlighted throughout this book, there are many similarities in the application of the principles of accounting, taxation, and bankruptcy. Nonetheless, differences remain. Thus, rather than restate the basics of this subject matter, this chapter sets forth the areas in which sports are different from other industries.

Like many other industries, the operations and financial results of professional sports franchises are highly seasonal in nature. Likewise, sports organizations are entities with inventories, production functions, research and development functions, and very high fixed costs that require significant capital. However, unlike other industries, there is a significant amount of variation in the accounting practices of professional sports franchises.

One common accounting issue for professional sports franchises involves the use of related-party transactions. The ownership of sports franchises by nonsports-related businesses and the nature of the sports industry have created numerous opportunities for these types of transactions. Typically, the presence of the nonsports business is used to lower the apparent profitability of the sports franchise in favor of improving the situation of the other, related businesses. This is problematic in that the tax liability of the sports franchise is lowered, and the financial outlook is distorted. Paul Beeston, a former Toronto Blue Jays vice president of business operations, summed up how the use of related-party transactions can dramatically affect the book profits of a professional sports franchise: "Anyone who quotes profits of a baseball club is missing the point. Under generally accepted accounting principles, I can turn a $4 million profit into a $2 million loss and get every national accounting firm to agree with me."[1] A professional sports franchise with an operating profit may be able to claim a book loss. This distortion has been the cause of much controversy, as the misleading financial picture has been relied upon by professional sports franchises in pursuit of new, publicly funded stadia and by professional sports leagues when negotiating collective bargaining agreements with the athletes. Teams and leagues have argued that their dire financial status requires that other stakeholders make significant concessions in negotiations. While the use of related-party transactions is not an illegal practice per se, it has created animosity and mistrust and, consequently, has harmed the long-term relationship between the negotiating parties. As a result, there exists the perception among other stakeholders that the financial statements of sports franchises cannot be relied upon whether related-party transactions are being used or not. Given the recent spate of accounting scandals in the United States that have depleted consumer and investor confidence in big businesses across numerous sectors of the economy, it is imperative that the sports industry avoid a similar fate. These and other accounting issues are described in the first selection by Stein and Gorman.

There are also taxation issues that are particular to the sports industry. These issues arise primarily upon the transfer of a sports franchise and involve the accounting concepts of amortization and depreciation. A significant part of the acquisition of a professional sports franchise involves intangible assets such as the league membership agreement, facility lease, contracts with season ticketholders, media contracts, and player contracts. These intangible assets are exempted from the tax rules that apply to the sale of a normal business. The preferential treatment that professional sports franchises receive under the tax code — especially with respect to player contracts — is controversial, as it provides their already wealthy owners with a lucrative tax shelter for a period of years after the purchase transaction.

The resulting tax benefits associated with ownership of a professional sports franchise help to keep the marketplace robust. Along with the consumption value of team ownership and the opportunity for operating profits and overall capital appreciation, the generous tax treatment of professional sports franchises is a primary reason for investment in this industry. Thus, it is very important for prospective and current owners to understand the applicable taxation principles. In the second excerpt, McKenney and Nemeth provide an excellent overview of these tax issues. In the third article, Robert Reilly delves into some of the details of tax law as he explains the numerous challenges associated with the allocation of the purchase price of a professional sports franchise.

Despite the relative financial strength of the professional sports industry compared to other industries, recently there have been several franchises whose financial failures have led them to seek financial reorganizations. Such a reorganization can be done either privately between the franchise and its creditors, or publicly through Chapter 11 of the Bankruptcy Code. While hardly a desirable outcome, it is important for sports industry leaders to understand the process of financial reorganization. In the final selection, Ralph Anzivino gives a comprehensive explanation of this process.

REFERENCES

1. Larry Millson, *Ballpark Figures: The Blue Jays and the Business of Baseball.* Toronto: McClelland & Stewart, 1987, 137.

ACCOUNTING PRINCIPLES

KEEPING THE FINANCIAL SCORECARD: ACCOUNTING FOR A SPORTS FRANCHISE

Richard Stein and Jerry Gorman

ACCOUNTING CONSIDERATIONS OF A SPORTS FRANCHISE

. . . All investment decisions regarding sports franchises will revolve around a franchisee's financial statements and projections. But even with teams in the same sport that play in the same league, the financial statements can be quite different. Financial statements of a sports franchisee are often clouded by related party transactions, differences in accounting policies, varying levels of vertical integration, variations in accounting for uncertainties and contingencies, and the effects of purchase accounting adjustments. To fully understand the financial statements of a sports franchisee, it is important to understand the breadth of franchised operations, become familiar with its accounting practices, and read the financial statements very carefully.

Related Party Transactions

The existence of related party contractual arrangements on stadium leases, concession agreements, and local television contracts are common within the sports industry. It is not uncommon to have the ownership of a franchise as part of the marketing strategy of an owner's unrelated business. With the prices being sought by owners today, rarely can the purchase of a sports franchise be justified on its own separate-entity merits. Having a sports franchise connection usually has a significant benefit to nonsports businesses that directly or indirectly benefit from the sports investment. . . .

. . . .

A reviewer of the financial statements of sports franchises with related party arrangements must assess if the agreements among an owner's businesses were entered into on terms equivalent to an arm's-length basis and, therefore, whether the financial statements are truly reflective of prevailing market conditions. This is not easy. Transactions involving related parties cannot be presumed to be carried out on an arm's-length basis. SFAS 57, Related Party Disclosures, does require that the nature of related party transactions be disclosed in financial statements along with 1) information deemed necessary to an understanding of the effects of the related party transactions on the financial statements, 2) the dollar amount of related party transactions for each of the periods for which income statements are presented and the effects of any change in the method of establishing the terms from that used in the preceding period, and 3) amounts due to or from related parties as of the date of each balance sheet and their terms and manner of settlement. However, while financial statement disclosure requirements may be met, the level of disclosure supplied by a franchisee in its financial statements may not be sufficient for a reader intent on making an investment decision.

Readers beware! Ownership may have motivations for making one segment of its business look better than another. Because each related party arrangement will likely be unique in its marketplace, an extensive analysis is required to determine what an independent contractual arrangement would be. It is often difficult to project what is likely to happen if a new arrangement were to be negotiated with a third party. Such analysis is highly judgmental in nature and may require significant industry expertise. As an example, the cash flow statement for a team owned by a large conglomerate may be different from a team not so owned. Intercompany borrowing and centralized cash management procedures put in place by the parent company can distort the actual availability and funds flow for a franchisee to the point where cash flows would not be comparable with teams that have to rely on independent lenders for financing. Interest expense, cash balances, and the current ratio are likely to be markedly different between the two teams.

There is a lack of uniformity in the accounting policies used by sports franchisees. One complex area of accounting, which results in one of the most diverse in accounting practice, is player contracts. . . . Consideration must also be given to league guidelines. . . . Player contracts today are often structured to include significant signing bonuses and deferred compensation arrangements. Most teams capitalize signing bonuses and amortize them over the contract term, but certain franchises expense bonuses when paid.

Certain franchisees will establish players' contract assets and liabilities upon signing. Such contract assets are written off over their terms while liabilities will be reduced when paid. This practice has a tendency to inflate the level of assets and liabilities of a franchisee, and the effect could be significant if a franchisee has many players signed to long-term agreements. While the amount of the liabilities committed under such contracts could be significant, such information could be disclosed in the footnotes, without "grossing up" the franchisee's assets and liabilities.

There is also diversity in the recording of compensation agreements which defer payments to future years. While GAAP [generally accepted accounting principles] suggests recording the expense for deferred compensation at its present value during the period that the amounts are earned (i.e., when the player plays), certain teams historically expense the compensation when paid or record the compensation at its nominal amount rather than at its present value. Such diversity of accounting practices can take the comparability out of compensation expense and reported results.

Vertical Integration

To help meet the industry's skyrocketing payrolls, many teams have undertaken various forms of vertical integration to enhance revenues. . . . The ability of each franchisee to take advantage of these opportunities will vary depending on the team's on-field performance and the size of the market in which they play. Few teams own their stadium, but usually franchisees are often tenants under generous long-term leases with municipal landlords.

. . . First, a franchisee that owns its facility will have significantly more employees and payroll expense than one which does not. Its tangible assets and charges for depreciation will be greater. It will not have a large rent expense but will probably pay significant property taxes. Overall, its financial statements will look markedly different from those that do not own their facilities. Wherever possible, such franchisees today are making the capital expenditures required to build luxury suites and take in the premium revenues these suites command. In doing so, they will be further increasing the tangible asset amount on their balance sheet and likely increasing their debt capitalization. The suites are often subject to long-term leases, which are usually accounted for as operating leases. Franchisee tenants seem to be using their political leverage or making other arrangements with their landlord to capitalize on the trend toward luxury suites. Such leasehold improvements will be amortized over the life of the stadium lease, or their useful life, whichever is shorter.

. . . .

The extent to which franchisees make the investment required to obtain these new lucrative revenue streams will significantly affect the types of revenue and expenses they report and their level of debt and capital assets.

The Importance of Winning

. . . Perhaps no industry is subject to more uncertainties and contingencies than sports. Even if an organization plans its budget, signs its players, and manages its operations flawlessly, in most cases its bottom line results will hinge on the on-field performance of the team. The public loves a winner and is willing to pay to see them. There is no amount of financial or accounting skills that can substitute for success between the lines, on the court, or on the ice.

. . . Fans' fickle behavior cannot be accounted for. Attendance can fluctuate markedly from year to year. Gate revenue must be recorded in the period in which the fans attend games, even if tickets are purchased well in advance in accordance with a season ticket plan, and matched against such period's costs. In addition, revenues from concessions will fluctuate with attendance. In certain leagues, the visiting team shares in the gate receipts of the home team; this practice will tend to have a smoothing effect on the bottom line as well.

. . . Broadcasting revenues, which typically are under long-term contracts (which may include an up-front "bonus" payment) are usually recognized as games are played. This has a smoothing effect, thereby assuring some teams of a steady stream of income year-to-year despite what may be a poor on-field performance. It is not unusual, however, to incorporate provisions of a broadcasting transaction so as to justify the immediate recognition of advances made at the beginning of the contract period. Such contracts further complicate comparibility of financial reporting among teams.

The Risks of Losing

The road has been far from smooth when it comes to accounting for uncertainties and contingencies in the sports world. . . .

Accounting for contingencies is governed by SAS 5. The pronouncement requires that a charge to income be made if 1) information available prior to the issuance of the financial statements indicates that it is probable that an asset had been impaired or a liability had been incurred at the date of the financial statements, and 2) that the amount of the loss can be reasonably estimated. If no accrual is made because both conditions (1) and (2) are not met, or if exposure to a loss exists in excess of the amount accrued, disclosure should be made when there is at least a reasonable possibility that a loss or an additional loss may have occurred.

As a result of this pronouncement accounting for uncertainties will always be subject to significant judgment. Most sports franchises are independent organizations operating within their league. Not only will franchisees view the underlying issues necessary to do the accounting differently, but each will likely differ with other members of the league as to what is probable and can be reasonably estimated. With different year ends, franchisees in the same league can be forced to make accounting decisions at different points in time, causing further lack of uniformity. To appropriately prepare financial statements, industry issues and uncertainties of the day must be understood. Those who are to rely on the financial statements must obtain an understanding as to how such issues were handled to get the true picture of financial position and results of operations.

TAXATION PRINCIPLES

THE PURCHASE AND SALE OF A SPORTS TEAM: TAX ISSUES AND RULES

Paul L. B. McKenney and Eric M. Nemeth

Given the rising values of American professional franchises, as well as league expansions and more sale transactions, the Internal Revenue Service has taken interest in this growing industry. The service has established a sports franchise office in Plantation, Florida. Unlike years past where a local revenue agent was "star struck" because the taxpayer was the local team, and the agent had no experience in this complicated tax arena, the examination is now quarter-backed by exceedingly competent IRS personnel in Florida who are also knowledgeable about the business and tax issues. In short, the government has greatly enhanced its audit game.

BASIC TAX BATTLEGROUNDS

The government tends to allocate purchase price first to the franchise and broadcast contracts, which are arguably not amortizable, second, to amortizable items such as the lease, season ticket holders, and skybox leases, and third, to player contracts. "Aren't those professional athletes grossly overpaid anyway? How can player contracts have any value?" seems to be one school of thought, though of those who have never read a collective bargaining agreement with a players association. A sports franchise is specifically excluded from "section 197 intangible" status. See IRC 197(e)(6). *[See relevant IRS code sections in Figure 1.]*

Club owners are keenly aware, not only that player contracts are amortizable under IRC 1056, but also that each such contract is amortizable over its remaining term rather than the IRC 197(a) 15-year period. Club owners will next allocate what is left after player contracts to the lease, ticket holders, skybox leases, etc., and view the nonamortizable franchise as of little value. There is also a dispute whether television contracts are eligible for amortization.

IRC 1060's residual method of allocation will apply to an asset acquisition. Allocation of the purchase/sale amounts to component assets is obviously of concern for cost basis/amortization purposes and the seller will be concerned about recapture. The IRS is generally not bound by allocation of costs if the allocation does not reflect relative fair market value of asset components or economic reality.

Generally, the parties are bound by the allocation within the agreement. There are, however, exceptions to this principle. . . .

PLAYER CONTRACTS

Before the 1976 adoption of current IRC 1056, player contracts were allocated among the purchased assets according to fair market value. The purchaser amortized player contracts under IRC 167 prior to adoption of IRC 1056. IRC 167 case law had allowed what the government perceived as very generous allocations to player contracts. IRC 1056 provides the general rule that in connection with a sale or exchange of "a franchise to conduct any sports enterprise" transfer of the contract for services in an athlete shall not exceed the sum of (a) adjusted basis of contract in the hands of the transferor immediately prior to the transfer, plus (b) any gain recognized by the transferor on the transfer. There are exceptions for IRC 1031: like-kind exchange (player trades routinely chronicled in the sports sections of newspapers), as well as property acquired from a decedent within the meaning of IRC 1014(a). . . . There is a rebuttable presumption, according to IRC 1056(d), that "not more than 50 percent of the consideration is allocable to contracts for services of athletes unless it is established to the satisfaction of the secretary that a specified amount in excess of 50 percent is properly allocable to such contracts. Nothing in the proceeding sentence shall give rise to a presumption that the allocation of less than 50 percent of the consideration to contracts for services of athletes is a proper allocation." The 50 percent presumption has given rise to considerable controversy. However, it is not permissible to arbitrarily allocate up to 50 percent to the player contracts. That may have been done in some situations many years ago, but it will be vigorously challenged today. Competent appraisals are a practical necessity.

Likewise, just because less than 50 percent is allocated to player contracts does not mean that the service either cannot or will not challenge the allocation. . . . A question is "50 percent of what consideration?" . . . There is an allocation to each player contract. Player contracts tend to have relatively short lives, usually one to six years. Option years are generally included.

One must consider all facts and circumstances in establishing the value of each player contract. The Collective Bargaining Agreement (CBA) with the players association is perhaps the most influential factor in determining fair market value in the relevant league. . . .

. . . .

IRC 197 governs many intangible assets in the acquisition and sale of many businesses, but it does not either (a) apply to any item in connection with the sale of a sports franchise or (b) supersede IRC 1056.

IRC 1245(a)(4) applies recapture treatment to gain on the sale or exchange of player contracts. PLR [Private Letter Ruling] 9617001 suggests [that] IRC 1056 applies to a new expansion franchise's acquisition of players.

Player trades generally constitute an IRC 1031 like-kind exchange of standard player contracts. Rev. Rul. 67-380, 1967-2 C.B. 291. . . . The Sports MSSP [Market Segment Specialization Program] concludes Chapter 12 stating, "It appears that future draft picks of a sports franchise are inseparable from its franchise intangible asset. Accordingly, it appears that future draft picks and existing player contracts do not constitute like-kind property for purposes of IRC section 1031." Many tax lawyers simply disagree with the government's interpretation of the statute.

STADIUM LEASE

The lease of the stadium, where the team plays their home games, is often assigned as part of the sale of a team, such stadiums being often built solely at taxpayer expense. It is a special use facility expressly designed to comply with the league's specific requirements for playing area, seating capacity, press boxes, parking, etc. . . .

Chapter 8 of the Sports MSSP opines that "Numerous cities have proven their willingness to mortgage their futures through taxes and the sale of bonds to attract or keep a sports franchise." In valuing the stadium lease, conventional wisdom would point to a comparison of other leases throughout the league to determine if this lease has any terms that make it more or less favorable to the club than other leases. . . .

A new football or basketball facility with state-of-the-art sky boxes and other amenities costs at least $250m. Some stadiums are now in the $350m price range. A modern basketball or hockey custom facility with the now standard amenities represents an expenditure in excess of $200m. . . .

A question of the lease value is a large dollar issue. The MSSP is silent regarding this issue, leaving several questions: Is the value of this lease of a special use facility

a. The nine-figure replacement cost?
b. Any financially determined value representing a premium over the "league average?" (Note that under this approach a lease could possibly be allocated a negative value.) The service has argued this for years. . . .
c. A very large sum, but less than (a) above?

The tax court stated the proper standard — a stadium lease represents two distinct values that may be calculated using conventional financial analysis models:

a. Bargain element of the lease. The sports team pays a fraction of the nightly usage fee charged to other multi-event users, such as the circus, ice shows, etc. That daily usage savings must be refined to reflect what (or more accurately who) is included. For example, NBA and NHL leases typically require the stadium authority to provide all ushers, ticket takers, security (including both locker rooms), traffic control personnel, first aid, maintenance, and myriad other personnel . . . at the landlord's expense. Also, normally, the multi-night user who is not a pro sports team will not receive parking revenues or concessions. Some users bring their own merchandise sellers and retain all associated revenues. Some deals are hybrids.
b. Revenue streams from signage, concessions, and parking. With new stadiums there is also revenue from naming rights. Unlike conventional leases for the tenant, net occupancy costs are not expenses, but rather, significant annual revenue streams. This is akin to conventional appraisal of cash flows with appropriate growth factors. Even with probably unrealistically

low growth projections, these cash flows typically represent in the aggregate a very large value in the acquisition of any sports franchise.

ECONOMIC ISSUES/INTANGIBLE ASSETS

As the service economy and information age trends continue, the impact and value of intangible assets continue to increase. Most value in the entertainment industry, including the professional sports subset, is intangible in nature. In a typical nonservice business, the economics are that the fair market value of the balance sheet assets, net of liabilities, may be $100X. However, the fair market value of the business may be $150X to $200X, as now adjusted for nonbalance sheet intangible assets. Many service businesses are worth many times their book value. You should think of a sports team as a marketing operation.

The economic question is: "What does that spread represent and how should the components of that spread be treated for income taxation purposes?" In terms of raw dollars, intangibles disputes are the second biggest area of controversy between taxpayers and the service. The cases inherently focus upon the "facts and circumstances" of a given situation.

Under longstanding Treas. Reg. Sec. 1.167(a)-3, intangible assets, except for going concern value and goodwill value, could be amortized if certain criteria are satisfied. Neither goodwill nor going concern value are amortizable. Goodwill and going concern value are different from each other. The service defines goodwill as follows: "In the final analysis, goodwill is based upon earnings capacity. The presence of goodwill and its value, therefore, rests upon the excess of net earnings over and above a fair return on the net tangible assets." Rev. Rul. 1959-1 C.B. 237, 59-60, Sec. 4.02(f). Going concern value, on the other hand, has been described as an ongoing business's ability "to continue to function and generate income without interruption as a consequence of [a] change in ownership." *VGS Corp v Commissioner,* 68 T.C. 563, 592 (1977). In *UFE, Inc, v Commissioner,* the tax court distinguished goodwill from going concern value: "going concern value has been described as related less to business reputation and the strength of customer loyalty, than to the ongoing relationship of assets and personnel in an ongoing business."

If both are present, the purchaser should separately allocate between these two items.* Under Treas. Reg. Sec. 1.167(a)(3), an intangible asset cannot be amortized unless it does not represent either goodwill or going concern value and the two following requirements are satisfied: the intangible asset must have an ascertainable cost basis aside from goodwill or going concern value and it must also have had a limited useful life the "length of which can be estimated with reasonable accuracy." The useful life requirement was typically the focal point of disputes between the service and taxpayers.

These tests inevitably resulted in numerous factual controversies and some fine-line distinctions. Some cases have allowed professional baseball and football teams to amortize player contracts over the remaining lives of the respective contracts, while others have consistently refused to allow any amortization of consideration paid for the acquisition of television rights in connection with purchasing professional athletic teams. Such rights are viewed as effectually perpetual, despite the stated term of a given contract. Intangibles assets and other tax advantaged assets commonly encountered are not ordinarily balance sheet items. Accordingly, these frequently valuable assets are sometimes overlooked in smaller transactions. . . .

---

* Amortization criteria prior to IRC 197.

. . . .

IRC 197(e)(6) specifically excludes from 15-year amortization "a franchise to engage in professional football, basketball, baseball, or other professional sport, and any item acquired in connection with such a franchise." Treas. Reg. Sec. 1.197-2(c)(10) specifically excludes from IRC 197 "any item (even though otherwise qualifying as a section 197 intangible) acquired in connection with such a franchise." (Emphasis added.) Previously proposed legislation during the last Congress would have extended the scope of IRC 197 to professional sports franchises. One major league has reacted favorably to this proposal.

. . . .

SEASON TICKET HOLDERS, SKY-BOX LEASES, AND SPONSORSHIPS

A typical factual scenario for an existing team is that there are a substantial number of annually renewable season ticket holders and a lesser number of long-term sky-box lessees. These season ticket holders/sky-box leases represent critical income streams to any club. . . . There are also myriad corporate sponsorship agreements. Such agreements typically provide for a corporate sponsor to purchase certain TV and radio advertising spots, team media advertising, stadium signage, and special promotions. . . . Thus, to any potential purchaser, these represent significant revenue sources, and resultant intangible assets. There is an ebb and flow to who is, and is not, in the income stream.

Since the burden of proof to substantiate any deduction is always upon the taxpayer, it is imperative that the taxpayer have proper appraisals of these valuable rights, documents the same, and claims and substantiates appropriate deductions. Such appraisals should review factors such as with the annual season ticket renewal rates, is there a waiting list? When do sky-box leases expire? At what pricing? Renewal prospects and similar information on major corporate sponsors are likewise important.

COVENANTS NOT TO COMPETE

The 15-year level amortization rule of IRC 197 applies generally to a covenant not to compete or similar arrangement entered into in connection with an acquisition, directly or indirectly, of an interest in a trade or business, or a substantial portion thereof. However, IRC 197 does not apply to any intangible assets acquired in connection with a sports franchise. Thus, the pre-IRC 197 caselaw applies.

The tax question today is both simple and complex. Is the allocation to the covenant reflective of fair market values?

The grantor of the covenant recognizes ordinary income. It has long been established that covenant income is ordinary income to the recipient. Additionally, covenant income is not passive income for the IRC 469 purposes, but rather it is in the nature of compensation income although covenant payments are for doing nothing, rather than providing services. Since in a sports franchise situation IRC 197 is inapplicable, payments should be amortized over the life of the covenant.

. . . .

INCOME RECOGNITION — WHICH PARTY? WHEN?

When teams are sold, often between seasons, the seller has already collected prepaid income for items such as season tickets, television, and broadcast rights. There is always extensive work to be done between the execution of a binding purchase agreement and closing. There are myriad third-party approvals that must be obtained, such as assignments of the lease, sponsorship agreements, and numerous other contractual rights, as well as the all-important league investigation of the new owner and approval.

If such revenues are received between seasons by the seller, but the games will be played under the new owner, which party is taxable on the revenues? What does the purchase agreement provide? Even when there is no change of ownership, there are timing issues if prepaid items are received in tax year one, but the games, or some of the games, are not played until tax year two.

The service's position is that the income has to be recognized in the tax year received, rather than when the games are played. . . .

. . . .

OTHER TAX ISSUES

You should also be aware of the following income tax issues:

1. Consulting Agreements — Is the allocation of purchase price proper?
2. Strike fund payments — *INDOPCO* [INDOPCO v. Commissioner, a U.S. Supreme Court ruling that a taxpayer's realization of significant future benefits from a transaction must be capitilized rather than deducted as a current expense.] lives in sports! See Chapter 7 of the Sports MSSP for the government perspective. This will be important to baseball and hockey clubs as work stoppages are expected at the end of their CBAs.
3. Fines and penalties.
4. Sponsorship/Advertising Revenues — Do they fit within Rev. Proc. 71- 21? Caselaw treats advertising as a service.
5. Private Seat License (PSL) issues: Can the subscribers deduct the cost of the PSLs? Do the PSLs have a definite life? Indefinite?
6. An expansion team generally pays the existing teams in installments. The existing teams report the revenues as a combination of ordinary income and capital gain items for the player contracts and the sale of other assets. How does the existing team calculate its adjusted bases as offsets to gain?
7. Disability and life insurance payments on key players — Are the premiums deductible to the franchise that would receive any benefits under the policy?
8. Barter income to the club. Often automobiles, airline tickets, etc., are given to the club in exchange for seats, luxury boxes, or special promotions.
9. Relocation inducements by a new city. . . .
10. Signing bonuses.
11. Application of IRC 1060 allocation regulations.

Sec. 197. Amortization of goodwill and certain other intangibles

(a) General rule

A taxpayer shall be entitled to an amortization deduction with respect to any amortizable section 197 intangible. The amount of such deduction shall be determined by amortizing the adjusted basis (for purposes of determining gain) of such intangible ratably over the 15-year period beginning with the month in which such intangible was acquired.

(b) No other depreciation or amortization deduction allowable

Except as provided in subsection (a), no depreciation or amortization deduction shall be allowable with respect to any amortizable section 197 intangible.

(c) Amortizable section 197 intangible

For purposes of this section—

(1) In general

Except as otherwise provided in this section, the term "amortizable section 197 intangible" means any section 197 intangible—

(A) which is acquired by the taxpayer after the date of the enactment of this section, and

(B) which is held in connection with the conduct of a trade or business or an activity described in section 212.

(2) Exclusion of self-created intangibles, etc.

The term "amortizable section 197 intangible" shall not include any section 197 intangible—

(A) which is not described in subparagraph (D), (E), or (F) of subsection (d)(1), and

(B) which is created by the taxpayer.

This paragraph shall not apply if the intangible is created in connection with a transaction (or series of related transactions) involving the acquisition of assets constituting a trade or business or substantial portion thereof.

(3) Anti-churning rules for exclusion of intangibles

For exclusion of intangibles acquired in certain transactions, see subsection (f)(9).

(d) Section 197 intangible

For purposes of this section—

(1) In general

Except as otherwise provided in this section, the term "section 197 intangible" means—

(A) goodwill,

(B) going concern value,

(C) any of the following intangible items:

    (i) workforce in place including its composition and terms and conditions (contractual or otherwise) of its employment,

    (ii) business books and records, operating systems, or any other information base (including lists or other information with respect to current or prospective customers),

    (iii) any patent, copyright, formula, process, design, pattern, knowhow, format, or other similar item,

    (iv) any customer-based intangible,

    (v) any supplier-based intangible, and

    (vi) any other similar item,

(D) any license, permit, or other right granted by a governmental unit or an agency or instrumentality thereof,

(E) any covenant not to compete (or other arrangement to the extent such arrangement has substantially the same effect as a covenant not to compete) entered into in connection with an acquisition (directly or indirectly) of an interest in a trade or business or substantial portion thereof, and

(F) any franchise, trademark, or trade name.

(2) Customer-based intangible

(A) In general

The term "customer-based intangible" means—

    (i) composition of market,

    (ii) market share, and

    (iii) any other value resulting from future provision of goods or services pursuant to relationships (contractual or otherwise) in the ordinary course of business with customers.

(Continued)

Figure 1 Relevant IRS code sections.

(*Continued*)

(B) Special rule for financial institutions

In the case of a financial institution, the term "customer-based intangible" includes deposit base and similar items.

(3) Supplier-based intangible

The term "supplier-based intangible" means any value resulting from future acquisitions of goods or services pursuant to relationships (contractual or otherwise) in the ordinary course of business with suppliers of goods or services to be used or sold by the taxpayer.

(e) Exceptions

For purposes of this section, the term "section 197 intangible" shall not include any of the following:

(1) Financial interests

Any interest—

(A) in a corporation, partnership, trust, or estate, or

(B) under an existing futures contract, foreign currency contract, notional principal contract, or other similar financial contract.

(2) Land

Any interest in land.

(3) Computer software

(A) In general

Any—

(i) computer software which is readily available for purchase by the general public, is subject to a nonexclusive license, and has not been substantially modified, and

(ii) other computer software which is not acquired in a transaction (or series of related transactions) involving the acquisition of assets constituting a trade or business or substantial portion thereof.

(B) Computer software defined

For purposes of subparagraph (A), the term "computer software" means any program designed to cause a computer to perform a desired function. Such term shall not include any data base or similar item unless the data base or item is in the public domain and is incidental to the operation of otherwise qualifying computer software.

(4) Certain interests or rights acquired separately

Any of the following not acquired in a transaction (or series of related transactions) involving the acquisition of assets constituting a trade business or substantial portion thereof:

(A) Any interest in a film, sound recording, video tape, book, or similar property.

(B) Any right to receive tangible property or services under a contract or granted by a governmental unit or agency or instrumentality thereof.

(C) Any interest in a patent or copyright.

(D) To the extent provided in regulations, any right under a contract (or granted by a governmental unit or an agency or instrumentality thereof) if such right—

(i) has a fixed duration of less than 15 years, or

(ii) is fixed as to amount and, without regard to this section, would be recoverable under a method similar to the unit-of-production method.

(5) Interests under leases and debt instruments

Any interest under—

(A) an existing lease of tangible property, or

(B) except as provided in subsection (d)(2)(B), any existing indebtedness.

(6) Treatment of sports franchises

A franchise to engage in professional football, basketball, baseball, or other professional sport, and any item acquired in connection with such a franchise.

Sec. 1056. Basis limitation for player contracts transferred in connection with the sale of a franchise

(a) General rule

If a franchise to conduct any sports enterprise is sold or exchanged, and if, in connection with such sale or exchange, there is a transfer of a contract for the services of an athlete, the basis of such contract in the hands of the transferee shall not exceed the sum of—

(1) the adjusted basis of such contract in the hands of the transferor immediately before the transfer, plus

(2) the gain (if any) recognized by the transferor on the transfer of such contract.

Figure 1 Relevant IRS code sections.

(b) Exceptions

Subsection (a) shall not apply—

(1) to an exchange described in section 1031 (relating to exchange of property held for productive use or investment), and

(2) to property in the hands of a person acquiring the property from a decedent or to whom the property passed from a decedent (within the meaning of section 1014(a)).

(c) Transferor required to furnish certain information

Under regulations prescribed by the Secretary, the transfer shall, at the times and in the manner provided in such regulations, furnish to the Secretary and to the transferee the following information:

(1) the amount which the transferor believes to be the adjusted basis referred to in paragraph (1) of subsection (a),

(2) the amount which the transferor believes to be the gain referred to in paragraph (2) of subsection (a), and

(3) any subsequent modification of either such amount.

To the extent provided in such regulations, the amounts furnished pursuant to the preceding sentence shall be binding on the transferor and on the transferee.

(d) Presumption as to amount allocable to player contracts

In the case of any sale or exchange described in subsection (a), it shall be presumed that not more than 50 percent of the consideration is allocable to contracts for the services of athletes unless it is established to the satisfaction of the Secretary that a specified amount in excess of 50 percent is properly allocable to such contracts. Nothing in the preceding sentence shall give rise to a presumption that an allocation of less than 50 percent of the consideration to contracts for the services of athletes is a proper allocation.

Sec. 1031. Exchange of property held for productive use or investment

(a) Nonrecognition of gain or loss from exchanges solely in kind

(1) In general

No gain or loss shall be recognized on the exchange of property held for productive use in a trade or business or for investment if such property is exchanged solely for property of like kind which is to be held either for productive use in a trade or business or for investment.

(2) Exception

This subsection shall not apply to any exchange of—

(A) stock in trade or other property held primarily for sale,

(B) stocks, bonds, or notes,

(C) other securities or evidences of indebtedness or interest,

(D) interests in a partnership,

(E) certificates of trust or beneficial interests, or

(F) choses in action.

For purposes of this section, an interest in a partnership which has in effect a valid election under section 761(a) to be excluded from the application of all of subchapter K shall be treated as an interest in each of the assets of such partnership and not as an interest in a partnership.

(3) Requirement that property be identified and that exchange be completed not more than 180 days after transfer of exchanged property

For purposes of this subsection, any property received by the taxpayer shall be treated as property which is not like-kind property if—

(A) such property is not identified as property to be received in the exchange on or before the day which is 45 days after the date on which the taxpayer transfers the property relinquished in the exchange, or

(B) such property is received after the earlier of—

(i) the day which is 180 days after the date on which the taxpayer transfers the property relinquished in the exchange, or

(ii) the due date (determined with regard to extension) for the transferor's return of the tax imposed by this chapter for the taxable year in which the transfer of the relinquished property occurs.

(b) Gain from exchanges not solely in kind

(Continued)

Figure 1   Relevant IRS code sections.

(*Continued*)

If an exchange would be within the provisions of subsection (a), of section 1035(a), of section 1036(a), or of section 1037(a), if it were not for the fact that the property received in exchange consists not only of property permitted by such provisions to be received without the recognition of gain, but also of other property or money, then the gain, if any, to the recipient shall be recognized, but in an amount not in excess of the sum of such money and the fair market value of such other property.

(c) Loss from exchanges not solely in kind

If an exchange would be within the provisions of subsection (a), of section 1035(a), of section 1036(a), or of section 1037(a), if it were not for the fact that the property received in exchange consists not only of property permitted by such provisions to be received without the recognition of gain or loss, but also of other property or money, then no loss from the exchange shall be recognized.

(d) Basis

If property was acquired on an exchange described in this section, section 1035(a), section 1036(a), or section 1037(a), then the basis shall be the same as that of the property exchanged, decreased in the amount of any money received by the taxpayer and increased in the amount of gain or decreased in the amount of loss to the taxpayer that was recognized on such exchange. If the property so acquired consisted in part of the type of property permitted by this section, section 1035(a), section 1036(a), or section 1037(a), to be received without the recognition of gain or loss, and in part of other property, the basis provided in this subsection shall be allocated between the properties (other than money) received, and for the purpose of the allocation there shall be assigned to such other property an amount equivalent to its fair market value at the date of the exchange. For purposes of this section, section 1035(a), and section 1036(a), where as part of the consideration to the taxpayer another party to the exchange assumed (as determined under section 357(d)) a liability of the taxpayer, such assumption shall be considered as money received by the taxpayer on the exchange.

(e) Exchanges of livestock of different sexes

For purposes of this section, livestock of different sexes are not property of a like kind.

(f) Special rules for exchanges between related persons

(1) In general

If—

(A) a taxpayer exchanges property with a related person,

(B) there is nonrecognition of gain or loss to the taxpayer under this section with respect to the exchange of such property (determined without regard to this subsection), and

(C) before the date 2 years after the date of the last transfer which was part of such exchange—

(i) the related person disposes of such property, or

(ii) the taxpayer disposes of the property received in the exchange from the related person which was of like kind to the property transferred by the taxpayer, there shall be no nonrecognition of gain or loss under this section to the taxpayer with respect to such exchange; except that any gain or loss recognized by the taxpayer by reason of this subsection shall be taken into account as of the date on which the disposition referred to in subparagraph (C) occurs.

(2) Certain dispositions not taken into account

For purposes of paragraph (1)(C), there shall not be taken into account any disposition—

(A) after the earlier of the death of the taxpayer or the death of the related person,

(B) in a compulsory or involuntary conversion (within the meaning of section 1033) if the exchange occurred before the threat or imminence of such conversion, or

(C) with respect to which it is established to the satisfaction of the Secretary that neither the exchange nor such disposition had as one of its principal purposes the avoidance of Federal income tax.

(3) Related person

For purposes of this subsection, the term "related person" means any person bearing a relationship to the taxpayer described in section 267(b) or 707(b)(1).

(4) Treatment of certain transactions

This section shall not apply to any exchange which is part of a transaction (or series of transactions) structured to avoid the purposes of this subsection.

(g) Special rule where substantial diminution of risk

(1) In general

Figure 1   Relevant IRS code sections.

If paragraph (2) applies to any property for any period, the running of the period set forth in subsection (f)(1)(C) with respect to such property shall be suspended during such period.

(2) Property to which subsection applies

This paragraph shall apply to any property for any period during which the holder's risk of loss with respect to the property is substantially diminished by—

(A) the holding of a put with respect to such property,

(B) the holding by another person of a right to acquire such property, or

(C) a short sale or any other transaction.

(h) Special rules for foreign real and personal property

For purposes of this section—

(1) Real property

Real property located in the United States and real property located outside the United States are not property of a like kind.

(2) Personal property

(A) In general

Personal property used predominantly within the United States and personal property used predominantly outside the United States are not property of a like kind.

(B) Predominant use

Except as provided in subparagraph [1] (C) and (D), the predominant use of any property shall be determined based on "subparagraphs."

(i) in the case of the property relinquished in the exchange, the 2-year period ending on the date of such relinquishment, and

(ii) in the case of the property acquired in the exchange, the 2-year period beginning on the date of such acquisition.

(C) Property held for less than 2 years

Except in the case of an exchange which is part of a transaction (or series of transactions) structured to avoid the purposes of this subsection—

(i) only the periods the property was held by the person relinquishing the property (or any related person) shall be taken into account under subparagraph (B)(i), and

(ii) only the periods the property was held by the person acquiring the property (or any related person) shall be taken into account under subparagraph (B)(ii).

(D) Special rule for certain property

Property described in any subparagraph of section 168(g)(4) shall be treated as used predominantly in the United States

Sec. 1060. Special allocation rules for certain asset acquisitions

(a) General rule

In the case of any applicable asset acquisition, for purposes of determining both—

(1) the transferee's basis in such assets, and

(2) the gain or loss of the transferor with respect to such acquisition,

the consideration received for such assets shall be allocated among such assets acquired in such acquisition in the same manner as amounts are allocated to assets under section 338(b)(5). If in connection with an applicable asset acquisition, the transferee and transferor agree in writing as to the allocation of any consideration, or as to the fair market value of any of the assets, such agreement shall be binding on both the transferee and transferor unless the Secretary determines that such allocation (or fair market value) is not appropriate.

(b) Information required to be furnished to Secretary

Under regulations, the transferor and transferee in an applicable asset acquisition shall, at such times and in such manner as may be provided in such regulations, furnish to the Secretary the following information:

(1) The amount of the consideration received for the assets which is allocated to section 197 intangibles.

(2) Any modification of the amount described in paragraph (1).

(3) Any other information with respect to other assets transferred in such acquisition as the Secretary deems necessary to carry out the provisions of this section.

(c) Applicable asset acquisition

(Continued)

Figure 1   Relevant IRS code sections.

(Continued)

For purposes of this section, the term "applicable asset acquisition" means any transfer (whether directly or indirectly)—

(1) of assets which constitute a trade or business, and

(2) with respect to which the transferee's basis in such assets is determined wholly by reference to the consideration paid for such assets.

A transfer shall not be treated as failing to be an applicable asset acquisition merely because section 1031 applies to a portion of the assets transferred.

(d) Treatment of certain partnership transactions

In the case of a distribution of partnership property or a transfer of an interest in a partnership—

(1) the rules of subsection (a) shall apply but only for purposes of determining the value of section 197 intangibles for purposes of applying section 755, and

(2) if section 755 applies, such distribution or transfer (as the case may be) shall be treated as an applicable asset acquisition for purposes of subsection (b).

(e) Information required in case of certain transfers of interests in entities

(1) In general

If—

(A) a person who is a 10-percent owner with respect to any entity transfers an interest in such entity, and

(B) in connection with such transfer, such owner (or a related person) enters into an employment contract, covenant not to compete, royalty or lease agreement, or other agreement with the transferee, such owner and the transferee shall, at such time and in such manner as the Secretary may prescribe, furnish such information as the Secretary may require.

(2) 10-percent owner

For purposes of this subsection—

(A) In general

The term "10-percent owner" means, with respect to any entity, any person who holds 10 percent or more (by value) of the interests in such entity immediately before the transfer.

(B) Constructive ownership

Section 318 shall apply in determining ownership of stock in a corporation. Similar principles shall apply in determining the ownership of interests in any other entity.

(3) Related person

For purposes of this subsection, the term "related person" means any person who is related (within the meaning of section 267(b) or 707(b)(1)) to the 10-percent owner.

(f) Cross reference

For provisions relating to penalties for failure to file a return required by this section, see section 6721

Sec. 1245. Gain from dispositions of certain depreciable property

(a) General rule

(1) Ordinary income

Except as otherwise provided in this section, if section 1245 property is disposed of the amount by which the lower of—

(A) the recomputed basis of the property, or

(B)

(i) in the case of a sale, exchange, or involuntary conversion, the amount realized, or

(ii) in the case of any other disposition, the fair market value of such property,

exceeds the adjusted basis of such property shall be treated as ordinary income. Such gain shall be recognized notwithstanding any other provision of this subtitle.

(2) Recomputed basis

For purposes of this section—

(A) In general

The term "recomputed basis" means, with respect to any property, its adjusted basis recomputed by adding thereto all adjustments reflected in such adjusted basis on account of deductions (whether in respect of the same or other property) allowed or allowable to the taxpayer or to any other person for depreciation or amortization.

Figure 1 Relevant IRS code sections.

(B) Taxpayer may establish amount allowed

For purposes of subparagraph (A), if the taxpayer can establish by adequate records or other sufficient evidence that the amount allowed for depreciation or amortization for any period was less than the amount allowable, the amount added for such period shall be the amount allowed.

(C) Certain deductions treated as amortization

Any deduction allowable under section 179, 179A, 190, or 193 shall be treated as if it were a deduction allowable for amortization.

(3) Section 1245 property

For purposes of this section, the term "section 1245 property" means any property which is or has been property of a character subject to the allowance for depreciation provided in section 167 and is either—

(A) personal property,

(B) other property (not including a building or its structural components) but only if such other property is tangible and has an adjusted basis in which there are reflected adjustments described in paragraph (2) for a period in which such property (or other property)—

  (i) was used as an integral part of manufacturing, production, or extraction or of furnishing transportation, communications, electrical energy, gas, water, or sewage disposal services,

  (ii) constituted a research facility used in connection with any of the activities referred to in clause (i), or

  (iii) constituted a facility used in connection with any of the activities referred to in clause (i) for the bulk storage of fungible commodities (including commodities in a liquid or gaseous state),

(C) so much of any real property (other than any property described in subparagraph (B)) which has an adjusted basis in which there are reflected adjustments for amortization under section 169, 179, 179A, 185, [1] 188 (as in effect before its repeal by the Revenue Reconciliation Act of 1990), 190, 193, or 194.

(D) a single purpose agricultural or horticultural structure (as defined in section 168(i)(13)),

(E) a storage facility (not including a building or its structural components) used in connection with the distribution of petroleum or any primary product of petroleum, or

(F) any railroad grading or tunnel bore (as defined in section 168(e)(4)).

(4) Special rule for player contracts

(A) In general

For purposes of this section, if a franchise to conduct any sports enterprise is sold or exchanged, and if, in connection with such sale or exchange, there is a transfer of any player contracts, the recomputed basis of such player contracts in the hands of the transferor shall be the adjusted basis of such contracts increased by the greater of—

  (i) the previously unrecaptured depreciation with respect to player contracts acquired by the transferor at the time of acquisition of such franchise, or

  (ii) the previously unrecaptured depreciation with respect to the player contracts involved in such transfer.

(B) Previously unrecaptured depreciation with respect to initial contracts

For purposes of subparagraph (A)(i), the term "previously unrecaptured depreciation" means the excess (if any) of—

  (i) the sum of the deduction allowed or allowable to the taxpayer transferor for the depreciation attributable to periods after December 31, 1975, of any player contracts acquired by him at the time of acquisition of such franchise, plus the deduction allowed or allowable for losses incurred after December 31, 1975, with respect to such player contracts acquired at the time of such acquisition, over

  (ii) the aggregate of the amounts described in clause (i) treated as ordinary income by reason of this section with respect to prior dispositions of such player contracts acquired upon acquisition of the franchise.

(C) Previously unrecaptured depreciation with respect to contracts transferred

For purposes of subparagraph (A)(ii), the term "previously unrecaptured depreciation" means the amount of any deduction allowed or allowable to the taxpayer transferor for the depreciation of any contracts involved in such transfer.

(D) Player contract

(Continued)

Figure 1   Relevant IRS code sections.

(*Continued*)

    For purposes of this paragraph, the term "player contract" means any contract for the services of an athlete which, in the hands of the taxpayer, is of a character subject to the allowance for depreciation provided in section 167.

(b) Exceptions and limitations

    (1) Gifts

        Subsection (a) shall not apply to a disposition by gift.

    (2) Transfers at death

        Except as provided in section 691 (relating to income in respect of a decedent), subsection (a) shall not apply to a transfer at death.

    (3) Certain tax-free transactions

        If the basis of property in the hands of a transferee is determined by reference to its basis in the hands of the transferor by reason of the application of section 332, 351, 361, 721, or 731, then the amount of gain taken into account by the transferor under subsection (a)(1) shall not exceed the amount of gain recognized to the transferor on the transfer of such property (determined without regard to this section). Except as provided in paragraph (7), this paragraph shall not apply to a disposition to an organization (other than a cooperative described in section 521) which is exempt from the tax imposed by this chapter.

    (4) Like kind exchanges; involuntary conversions, etc.

        If property is disposed of and gain (determined without regard to this section) is not recognized in whole or in part under section 1031 or 1033, then the amount of gain taken into account by the transferor under subsection (a)(1) shall not exceed the sum of—

        (A) the amount of gain recognized on such disposition (determined without regard to this section), plus

        (B) the fair market value of property acquired which is not section 1245 property and which is not taken into account under subparagraph (A).

    (5) Section 1081 transactions

        Under regulations prescribed by the Secretary, rules consistent with paragraphs (3) and (4) of this subsection shall apply in the case of transactions described in section 1081 (relating to exchanges in obedience to SEC orders).

    (6) Property distributed by a partnership to a partner

        (A) In general

            For purposes of this section, the basis of section 1245 property distributed by a partnership to a partner shall be deemed to be determined by reference to the adjusted basis of such property to the partnership.

        (B) Adjustments added back

            In the case of any property described in subparagraph (A), for purposes of computing the recomputed basis of such property the amount of the adjustments added back for periods before the distribution by the partnership shall be—

            (i) the amount of the gain to which subsection (a) would have applied if such property had been sold by the partnership immediately before the distribution at its fair market value at such time, reduced by

            (ii) the amount of such gain to which section 751(b) applied.

    (7) Transfers to tax-exempt organization where property will be used in unrelated business

        (A) In general

            The second sentence of paragraph (3) shall not apply to a disposition of section 1245 property to an organization described in section 511(a)(2) or 511(b)(2) if, immediately after such disposition, such organization uses such property in an unrelated trade or business (as defined in section 513).

        (B) Later change in use

            If any property with respect to the disposition of which gain is not recognized by reason of subparagraph (A) ceases to be used in an unrelated trade or business of the organization acquiring such property, such organization shall be treated for purposes of this section as having disposed of such property on the date of such cessation.

    (8) Timber property

Figure 1   Relevant IRS code sections.

> In determining, under subsection (a)(2), the recomputed basis of property with respect to which a deduction under section 194 was allowed for any taxable year, the taxpayer shall not take into account adjustments under section 194 to the extent such adjustments are attributable to the amortizable basis of the taxpayer acquired before the 10th taxable year preceding the taxable year in which gain with respect to the property is recognized.
>
> **(c)** Adjustments to basis
>
> The Secretary shall prescribe such regulations as he may deem necessary to provide for adjustments to the basis of property to reflect gain recognized under subsection (a).
>
> **(d)** Application of section
>
> This section shall apply notwithstanding any other provision of this subtitle

Figure 1 Relevant IRS code sections.

The Challenges of Professional Sports Franchise Purchase Price Allocations

Robert F. Reilly

INTRODUCTION

. . . The sales/purchases of professional sports franchises generally receive a great deal of publicity and media attention. This attention is usually welcome by the new team owner, the national franchise association, and the existing team owners.

And, the allocation of the franchise sale/purchase price often receives a great deal of attention from the Internal Revenue Service and from other taxing authorities. . . .

. . . It is often difficult to economically justify the prices paid for professional sports franchises based on traditional pricing metrics — such as price/earnings multiples. This is because many sports franchises do not generate positive accounting earnings.

Nonetheless, sports franchises are regularly bought and sold by sophisticated investors at increasing transaction prices. Accordingly, the actual marketplace of willing buyers/willing sellers does recognize the increasing value of sports franchises. The function of the valuation analyst is to emulate (and predict) actual marketplace mechanics. Therefore, the use of traditional pricing metrics (e.g., price/earnings multiples) and traditional income measures (e.g., accounting-based earnings) may not be applicable to sports franchise valuations.

. . . .

TAXING AUTHORITY INTEREST IN SPORTS FRANCHISE TRANSACTIONS

In addition to team and player fans, taxing authorities are interested in sports franchise transactions for several reasons. The Internal Revenue Service pays particular attention to franchise sale/purchase transactions. . . . Compared to the typical closely held business sale, professional sports franchise sales involve fairly large prices. Therefore, these transactions often result in fairly large taxable gains or losses to the seller.

. . . .

With regard to transaction purchase price allocations, sports franchises are generally subject to different basis/amortization tax rules than most other businesses. . . .

State and local taxing authorities are also interested in sports franchise sales. These transactions may provide the justification for a revaluation of the franchise arena/stadium for ad valorem property tax purposes.

While the Service often concludes that the franchise purchase price principally relates to non-amortizable franchise value, local taxing officials often conclude that the same purchase price relates principally to the arena/stadium leased fee interest/leasehold interest. In these cases, the new franchise owner is caught in the valuation equivalent of a "Catch-22."

PURCHASE PRICE ALLOCATION FINANCIAL ACCOUNTING

Virtually all professional sports franchises are closely held businesses. The individual franchises do not publicly report their financial statements. Accordingly, franchise buyers/owners may not be overly concerned with how they allocate the franchise lump sum purchase price for financial reporting purposes. However, many franchises have minority owners who receive periodic financial statements. And, even single owner franchises typically prepare financial statements in compliance with generally accepted accounting principles (GAAP). And, the GAAP provisions for purchase accounting affect these financial statements.

. . . . *[The author's discussion of SFAS no. 141 and no. 142 is omitted.]*

PURCHASE PRICE ALLOCATION INCOME TAX REPORTING

Like all other taxpayers, sports franchise acquirers allocate the acquisition purchase price under either (1) Internal Revenue Code Section 338 (if the deal structure is a qualified stock purchase) or (2) Section 1060 (if the deal structure is a qualified asset purchase).

. . . .

. . . In summary, the regulations under both Sections 338 and 1060 first require the taxpayer to determine the total purchase price paid for the acquisition.

Specific rules determine (1) what acquisition-related expenses should be capitalized and (2) what tax liabilities (assumed or created by the transaction) should be included in the total purchase price. It is noteworthy that due to (1) capitalized acquisition expenses and (2) income tax liabilities, the income tax purchase price is typically much greater than the financial accounting purchase price for the same sports franchise.

. . . . *[The author's discussion of asset class allocations under Sections 338 and 1060 is omitted.]*

In terms of (1) determining the total purchase price paid and (2) allocating that purchase price to individual acquired assets, the process for sports franchise owners is pretty much the same as for any other acquisitive taxpayer. However, the process of amortization deductions for the acquired intangible assets is distinctly different for sports franchise owners compared to virtually all other acquisitive taxpayers.

This is because most taxpayers claim amortization deductions for the allocated cost of all acquired intangible assets (including acquired goodwill) over a 15-year period under the provisions of Section 197. Section 197 amortization deductions are not allowed for professional sports franchises, however.

. . . .

Section 197 Sports Franchise Exception

However, Section 197(e) provides a short list of specified assets that are exceptions to Section 197. Exception number 6 is:

(6) Treatment of Sports Franchises. A franchise to engage in professional football, basketball, baseball, or other professional sport, and any item acquired in connection with such a franchise.

Due to this Section 197(e) exception, a sports franchise purchase price allocation is different from most acquisitions in two ways:

1. In order to claim amortization deductions, fair market value and a remaining useful life (RUL) must be estimated for each identified intangible asset.
2. No amortization deduction is allowed for purchased goodwill (i.e., the amount of residual, unallocated purchase price) — as it would otherwise be under Section 197.

So, in order to claim amortization deductions for acquired intangible assets, sports franchise owners need to substantiate (1) a separate fair market value and (2) a separate RUL for each identified intangible.

The list of intangible assets in Section 197(d) is a good starting point to identify acquired sports franchise intangibles. Of course . . . acquired goodwill is not amortizable for sports franchise owners.

REORGANIZATION OF THE PROFESSIONAL SPORTS FRANCHISE

Ralph C. Anzivino

The financial viability of a sports franchise is driven by a combination of factors: (1) gate receipts, (2) media revenue, (3) venue revenues, (4) player costs, and (5) operating expenses. As in any business, once the expenses begin to exceed the revenues, a financial reorganization becomes a reality. . . .

Financial reorganizations fall into two categories — private or public reorganizations. A private reorganization is an agreement between the debtor and its creditors to restructure the debtor's obligations. A public reorganization is a restructuring through Chapter 11 of the Bankruptcy Code. Any reorganization, whether private or public, generally focuses on improving the debtor's net income. Since net income is a factor of income minus expenses, the means by which a financially distressed debtor is able to reorganize, either formally or informally, is by some form of debt relief. In fact, the primary means to successfully reorganize is to substantially reduce the debtor's expenses. The debt reduction normally occurs as a result of either debt forgiveness, or converting the outstanding debt to an equity position in the reorganized entity. . . .

Most business reorganizations are private reorganizations. . . . At the time of the creation of Chapter 11, Congress indicated that the first and best solution for a financial reorganization was a private reorganization, and the use of Chapter 11 should be the last resort. . . . (See Table 1 for a list of sports bankruptcies.)

. . . .

II. PRIVATE REORGANIZATION

Once a sports franchise finds itself in financial trouble, a private reorganization may be the best solution to its problems. . . .

TABLE 1.

LIST OF SPORTS BANKRUPTCIES
Major sports team bankruptcies since 1969

2003	Buffalo Sabres (Hockey)
2003	Ottawa Senators (Hockey)
1998	Pittsburgh Penguins (Hockey)
1995	Los Angeles Kings (Hockey)
1993	Baltimore Orioles (Baseball)
1975	Pittsburgh Penguins (Hockey)
1970	Seattle Pilots (Baseball)
1969	Philadelphia Eagles (Football)

Source: http://money.cnn.com/2003/01/01/commentary/column_sportsbiz/bankruptcies/.

In addition to the reasons noted by Congress, there are a number of other significant advantages to a private reorganization. First, a private reorganization has no public stigma associated with it, as compared to a public declaration of bankruptcy via Chapter 11. . . . Second, a Chapter 11 reorganization is a very public process. Chapter 11 reorganization requires the bankrupt to make sensitive disclosures about its financial operations through court documents. Any papers filed in a bankruptcy case, including the docket, are public records. . . The franchise, however, does have the means to protect itself. On request of a party in interest, the bankruptcy court does . . . [allow] filing documents with the court under seal. . . . Third, in Chapter 11, the officers and executives of the sports franchise are required to be examined under oath in a public hearing. . . . Fourth, a private reorganization generally poses no risk of turnover of current management. In Chapter 11, "any party in interest" can petition the court to replace current management. . . . Fifth, and perhaps most important, the "ownership" of the franchise is likely to remain intact in a private reorganization. On the other hand, in a Chapter 11, the current "ownership" will likely not continue in the reorganized debtor without the contribution of "new value" by the current owners.

There are a number of factors, however, that militate against a private reorganization. First, a private reorganization requires the agreement of substantially all of the creditors of the sports franchise. The threat of a Chapter 11 process, however, will cause some of the creditors to become more flexible. . . . Nevertheless, it is a difficult task to get substantially all the creditors to agree to a private plan of reorganization. Second, the debtor may need certain bankruptcy powers in order to successfully reorganize. There are many powers that are available only in bankruptcy and are not available in a private reorganization. Third, if the private reorganization results in any cancellation of debt, such cancellation or forgiveness of debt is considered income to the debtor. In Chapter 11, cancellation of debt is not income. Fourth, if the sports franchise wishes to issue securities to secure additional funds, the Chapter 11 process provides exemptions from securities law compliance, which are not available through a private organization.

Finally, there may be certain factors present, which indicate that Chapter 11 is the only choice available. For example, the sports franchise may need immediate relief from aggressive, creditor activity. The filing of a bankruptcy petition automatically protects the franchise from any creditor activity including lawsuits, foreclosure actions or any other kind of collection activity. In addition, filing a Chapter 11 permits the sports franchise to stop making payments on virtually all of its pre-petition unsecured debts. This practice will immediately improve the cash flow of the franchise. However, there is a downside to not paying the pre-petition debts. Current employees will not be happy about not getting their paychecks for the work they performed pre-petition. . . . Further, Chapter 11 will permit the sports franchise to more easily obtain credit because of the favorable bankruptcy provisions facilitating the extension of post-petition credit. Finally, the sports franchise may need certain avoidance or other powers to successfully reorganize which are only available under federal bankruptcy law and not state law. . . .

. . . In most circumstances, the sports franchise should initially pursue a private reorganization. Failing that, Chapter 11 will be its fall-back position. There is a caveat, however, if the sports franchise reaches agreement on a private reorganization and subsequently wishes to convert to a Chapter 11 reorganization. An unsuccessful private reorganization may preclude a subsequent Chapter 11 filing. . . .

III. PREPACKAGED CHAPTER 11'S

In the event a private reorganization is not feasible, there is an expedited Chapter 11 process available that is the next-best solution. This process is called a prepackaged Chapter 11. Oftentimes, an out-of-court attempt at financial restructuring leads to the filing of a prepackaged Chapter 11. Normally, in a prepackaged Chapter 11 case, the solicitation of the creditor's votes in favor or against the plan occurs in advance of filing the case. This will be a normal byproduct of the attempt to achieve a private reorganization. Once the requisite percentages and amounts to approve the plan are reached, the franchise's plan of reorganization is filed with the bankruptcy petition. At the same time, a request is made for an expedited hearing. . . . The time period from filing to confirmation can be less than thirty days. . . .

There are a number of advantages to the prepackaged Chapter 11. First, the prototype for a prepackaged Chapter 11 is the over-leveraged debtor with a relatively limited number of creditors. A financially stressed professional sports franchise fits that prototype and would be an ideal candidate for a prepackaged Chapter 11. Second, and a very significant advantage for a prepackaged Chapter 11, is that the nonconsenting creditors who refused to cooperate in the private organization will be bound by the confirmed plan of reorganization. Third, the prepackaged Chapter 11 is quicker and less expensive than the conventional Chapter 11. In a conventional Chapter 11 case, the debtor files a bankruptcy petition, negotiates a reorganization plan with its creditors, seeks court approval of a disclosure statement, solicits acceptances, and seeks confirmation of its plan of reorganization. The prepackaged Chapter 11 anticipates a streamlined bankruptcy process, which involves substantially less time and costs. Fourth, the prepackaged Chapter 11 permits the sports franchise to utilize the many advantages of Chapter 11. . . .

. . . .

Prepackaged Chapter 11 cases are also subject to the same infirmities as a conventional Chapter 11 case. Prepackaged Chapter 11 cases have been unsuccessful when the debtor was unable to prepare an acceptable disclosure statement, current management was deemed unacceptable to operate the debtor during the bankruptcy case, final agreement was not reached with the "owners" prior to filing the bankruptcy petition, and the solicitation process contained irregularities. In addition, prepackaged Chapter 11 cases will not be successful where one of the secured creditors is aggressively pursuing lift stay actions to pursue state foreclosure and otherwise not being agreeable with the franchise. . . .

IV. FINANCING THE CHAPTER 11 REORGANIZATION

The success of a Chapter 11 reorganization will depend on the ability of the franchise to be able to obtain post-petition financing. The franchise must be able to pay its current operating expenses in order to be able to reorganize its affairs. The franchise is generally prohibited from enforcing any loan agreements or other financial commitments that existed prior to the filing of the case. In addition, the franchise is prohibited from using any cash that is a secured creditor's collateral unless the secured creditor consents to the use of the cash or the franchise is able to secure court approval to use the cash. As a result of these bankruptcy protections for lenders, in virtually every reorganization, the franchise will be exceedingly cash-poor at inception. It is essential, therefore, to secure post-petition financing. Oftentimes, post-petition financing is arranged prior to filing the bankruptcy petition through negotiations with a pre-petition lender. Failing a pre-petition agreement, there are two post-petition means to secure financing — cash collateral financing and/or post-petition credit.

A. Cash Collateral Financing

Upon the filing of the bankruptcy petition, the sports franchise may have cash in its possession or its bank accounts. The cash will most likely be "cash collateral." Cash collateral is cash or cash equivalents that are claimed by a secured creditor as collateral. . . . For a sports franchise, the cash in its possession will be generated from some form of ticket sales, advertising, or concession sales. In most cases, these revenue streams will be used by the sports franchise as collateral. If so, the cash is cash collateral, and its use is restricted. . . . The debtor may use cash collateral to finance its reorganization, but only if the debtor obtains the consent of the secured party or court approval. Cash collateral financing is preferred over post-petition credit because it avoids the payment of interest and other charges that are associated with the four types of post-petition credit.

In order to obtain court approval to use cash collateral, the sports franchise will be required to provide "adequate protection" to the secured claimant. . . . The purpose of providing adequate protection is to protect the secured party against any diminution in the value of its collateral during the reorganization process. The courts will generally authorize the use of cash collateral where the sports franchise has an equity cushion or is able to provide one of the other means of adequate protection.

. . .

B. Post-petition Credit

The franchise may need to borrow money or obtain credit in order to undertake any rehabilitation efforts under Chapter 11. The need for the infusion of working capital is usually prompted by the severe financial situation that prompted the bankruptcy filing. The Bankruptcy Code provides four levels of authorized financing. The first level is unsecured credit incurred in the ordinary course of the franchise's business. The second level is unsecured debt outside the ordinary course of the franchise's business. The first two levels are accorded administrative expense treatment, which means they are required to be paid in full on the effective date of the plan. The third level, which is only available if credit cannot be obtained with the administrative expense priority, is debt that is given priority over administrative expenses, is secured by a lien on unencumbered property, or is secured by a junior lien on encumbered property. The fourth level, again which is only available if credit cannot be obtained at the third level, is a debt secured by a senior or equal lien on encumbered property of the estate.

There are two options to obtain credit on an unsecured basis. First, the sports franchise is permitted to incur unsecured debt in the ordinary course of its business without court approval. Any creditor who extends credit to the sports franchise in the ordinary course of its business will receive administrative expense treatment. . . . If court approval is required and not obtained, the post-petition extension of credit will not be accorded administrative expense status. In addition, the extension of credit may be denied the status of a general unsecured claim. . . . Second, after notice and a hearing, the bankruptcy court may authorize the sports franchise to incur unsecured debt outside the ordinary course of its business. This debt is also accorded administrative expense treatment.

If the sports franchise is unable to obtain unsecured credit with the promise of administrative expense treatment, the second level to obtain post-petition credit has three options available. After notice and a hearing, the court may authorize the sports franchise to obtain credit or incur debt (1) "with priority over all administrative expenses," (2) "secured by a lien on property that is not otherwise subject to a lien," or (3) "secured by a junior lien on property of the estate that is subject to a lien." The three methods are not mutually exclusive and can be used in conjunction with each other. This type of post-petition financing is generally only available when the debtor has assets or equity in the estate sufficient to pay the requested credit extension. Unsecured creditors will normally object to such an extension of credit because it encumbers what otherwise would be unencumbered assets in the estate. . . .

Finally, if neither of the foregoing methods is sufficient to obtain post-petition financing, the sports franchise may be able to obtain credit secured by a prime or equal lien on currently encumbered property. . . . Thus, if the court is satisfied that the sports franchise has made a reasonable effort to seek alternative sources of financing, and the current secured creditor's position is adequately protected, the court may relegate the lien of an existing secured creditor to a position equal to or junior to the lien afforded to the post-petition lender.

. . . .

V. THE AUTOMATIC STAY

A. Scope

Upon the filing of the bankruptcy petition, an automatic stay arises. The automatic stay provides the franchise with relief from creditor activity. In a Chapter 11 case, it protects property that may be necessary for the franchise's fresh start and provides breathing space to permit the franchise to focus on its reorganization efforts. Without the automatic stay, the creditors would dismember the franchise's assets. Any action taken in violation of the stay is ineffective even if the creditor has no actual knowledge of the bankruptcy.

The scope of the automatic stay is extremely broad. It applies to virtually every type of formal or informal action against the franchise or property in the estate. . . . Although the automatic stay protects the franchise against a broad range of actions and creditor activities, it does not protect related entities such as corporate affiliates, partners, or co-defendants in pending litigation. . . . Similarly, an action can be brought against guarantors of the franchise. The bankruptcy court, however, does have the authority to stay actions against related entities if the creditor's action would substantially interfere with the franchise's reorganization.

The automatic stay protects the sports franchise's property as of the moment of filing the bankruptcy petition. The primary property of a sports franchise is its contract rights and leases. . . .

One area of immediate concern under the automatic stay is administrative freezes. An administrative freeze occurs when a bank freezes a debtor's bank account upon filing for bankruptcy relief. . . . The franchise will need to contact the bank immediately after filing, if it did not do so in advance, to arrange for the continuation of banking. The continuation will be on behalf of the franchise as debtor-in-possession. An alternative approach is for the franchise to file an emergency motion with the court seeking an order to unfreeze the bank accounts and honor all checks presented. . . .

. . . .

VI. THE FRANCHISE OR MEMBERSHIP AGREEMENT

Membership in a professional sports league is the most valuable asset of the sports franchise. Membership is recognized through a franchise or membership agreement. As part of the Chapter 11 reorganization, the franchise is authorized to assume or reject most executory contracts. A debtor's ability to assume and reject executory contracts is vital to a Chapter 11 reorganization. It is imperative for the sports franchise to maintain its membership in the league by assuming the franchise agreement. Once assumed, the franchise can decide whether it is in its best interest to reorganize itself or assign the franchise agreement to a third party. . . .

A professional sports franchise agreement is an executory contract. . . Therefore, it can be assumed in the reorganization.

The franchise agreement must not be terminated at the time of the filing of the bankruptcy petition. The events that would justify a league terminating a franchise's membership are contained in each league's Constitution and Bylaws. . . . However, if the franchise files its petition before the league vote, the automatic stay will enjoin any further action by the league, including the vote. On the other hand, if the vote occurs before the petition is filed, the franchise agreement will be validly terminated under state law.

. . . .

The franchise must assume or reject any executory contract in its entirety. In other words, the franchise may not assume favorable provisions while eliminating unfavorable ones. The Code, however, does not provide any standard for the court when addressing the assumption or rejection request. The primary standard used by the courts is the business-judgment rule. Under the business-judgment rule, the assumption or rejection will be approved upon a showing that the action will benefit the franchise. . . . Rejection of an executory contract results in the claim being treated as a pre-petition breach. Any provision in a contract whereby the franchise agrees not to reject an agreement in the event of bankruptcy is unenforceable.

. . . .

The effect of an incurable default is to render the franchise agreement nonassumable in the reorganization. The practical effect is the death knell for the franchise. It is also important to note that a default cannot be declared because of the franchise's insolvency or filing of a bankruptcy petition. In addition, there can be no forfeiture or loss of any rights under the franchise agreement as a result of the franchise's insolvency or the filing of its bankruptcy petition.

. . . .

Pre-petition loan contracts, credit contracts, and other forms of financial accommodations are also not assumable in bankruptcy. Lenders are not required to make financial advances or loans pursuant to a pre-petition credit agreement because of the franchise's changed financial status. Rather, the franchise needs to arrange for post-petition financing. However, a pre-petition contract to extend credit or to make a financial accommodation that is entered into in anticipation of bankruptcy is assumable post-petition. . . .

Finally, ipso facto clauses are not enforceable in bankruptcy. An ipso facto clause is one that causes a contract to terminate upon the franchise's insolvency or bankruptcy. A franchise's insolvency or bankruptcy is a common ground for termination of the franchise's membership in the league. Such a contract clause or provision in the league's membership agreement, Constitution, or Bylaws is unenforceable in the franchise's bankruptcy. In conjunction with such a clause, it is also commonly provided that the member agrees not to contest the automatic termination in any court proceeding. This kind of a provision would also be unenforceable in bankruptcy to the extent it seeks to validate an ipso facto violation. Interestingly, it has also been suggested that working capital requirements or minimums may also violate the ipso facto prohibition.

VII. THE LEASE OR SPORTS FACILITY AGREEMENT

A typical condition of league membership is that the sports franchise has a facility to play its home games. . . . For bankruptcy purposes, however, the sports facility agreement is still a lease.

. . . .

As part of the Chapter 11 reorganization, the franchise is authorized to assume or reject unexpired leases. . . .

The franchise has sixty days following the filing of the petition to decide whether to assume or reject its lease. . . .

Based on the economics of the lease, the franchise will reject the lease, assume the lease for itself or, if able, assume and assign the lease to a new entity. If the franchise believes it can secure more favorable lease terms, it should reject the lease. The franchise's ability to reject an unexpired lease is considered essential to relieve its estate of burdensome obligations. . . . Any contractual provision in a lease whereby the franchise agrees not to reject the lease in bankruptcy is unenforceable. Rejection of the lease will be treated as a pre-petition claim, and the lessor's claim for the remaining rents due under the lease will be subject to a statutory maximum. There is, however, a detrimental side effect to rejecting the lease with the sports facility. A rejection in which the franchise is the lessee under a primary lease and sublessor under a sublease causes the subleases to be rejected as well. The franchise has almost certainly entered into many subleases with its patrons and may not wish to cause those subleases to be rejected.

If the franchise decides to assume the lease, the franchise must assume the unexpired lease in its entirety and may not assume favorable provisions while eliminating unfavorable ones. . . .

. . . .

. . . The sports franchise's insolvency or bankruptcy filing will not be recognized as a valid ground for termination of the sports facility lease. . . . It will be critical to determine whether the sports facility lease has been terminated prior to the filing of the bankruptcy petition. In order for a lease to be properly terminated under state law, all actions required under state law for termination of the lease must be completed before the petition is filed. If the lease has been validly terminated under state law, the lease cannot be assumed or assigned in the Chapter 11 case. In addition, the debtor may not revive the terminated lease by alternative means. A terminated lease will have a very deleterious effect on the franchise's reorganization if the lease was a favorable one that the franchise wished to maintain either for itself or to assume and assign to a new entity.

. . . .

VIII. CONTRACTS WITH PLAYERS

. . . . Understandably, an area of potential cost savings for the franchise will be the player's salary. Upon filing the bankruptcy petition, each player's contract becomes property of the bankruptcy estate. Each player's contract will be treated as an executory contract since performance is due to a material extent on both sides. It will be important for the franchise to review each individual player's contract. As part of the reorganization, the franchise will need to decide whether to reject or assume each one of the player contracts. The decision can be made in the proposed plan of reorganization, unless the player requests the court to set an earlier time for the decision. . . .

If it's in the franchise's best interest, the franchise can selectively reject certain players' contracts. Upon rejection, the franchise is no longer required to comply with the contract terms. The rejection is deemed a breach of contract, and the player is relegated to a pre-petition claim for the breach. If the player's contract has a remaining term for greater than a year beyond the filing date, the player's claim is capped at one year's salary, plus any delinquent compensation due under the contract. . . .

For those players' contracts the franchise wishes to maintain, the franchise will need to assume those contracts. The contracts must meet the business-judgment test, and any defaults must be cured before the court will approve the assumption. . . .

IX. CONTRACTS WITH PATRONS, ADVERTISERS, AND VENDORS

. . . .

A. Luxury Suites

. . . .

The luxury suite agreements are either in a license or lease format. As with the sports facility agreement, it will again be very important to determine whether the luxury suite agreement is a lease or a license. . . . It is important to note that for the luxury suite agreements, the sports franchise is now the lessor, as contrasted with its position as lessee in the sports facility agreement. The tenant is the lessee under the luxury suite agreement. In the event the luxury suite agreement is rejected, either by the franchise's volitional rejection or automatically by its rejection of the primary lease, the tenant has two options available. First, the tenant can accept the rejection and assert a claim in the bankruptcy for the damages associated with the termination of the sublease. Second, the tenant can choose to remain in possession and retain all rights under the sublease agreement, plus any renewal periods. If the tenant chooses to retain its rights under the sublease agreement, the lessee is permitted to set-off against the rent due under the sublease any damages for breach of the sublease caused by the franchise's nonperformance. Set-off is the tenant's sole remedy. . . .

. . . In the event the luxury suite agreement is rejected, either by the franchise's volitional rejection or by its rejection of the primary license, the licensee does not have the option to remain in possession. The licensee's only choice is to file a claim in the reorganization for the damages associated with the rejection. Upon rejection, the franchise would be able to enter into new sublicense agreements to increase the revenue for the reorganized entity.

. . . .

D. Current Season Ticket Sales

. . . . These categories are distinct from the ticket holders for future seasons. . . For those patrons who have paid for their tickets, under the material breach test, the contracts are not executory. Therefore, the franchise cannot reject the sales and must perform. For those patrons who have exercised their option to purchase the tickets, but have not paid for them, those contracts are executory and can be rejected by the franchise. Under the functional analysis test, both categories of ticket holders could be executory contracts, and thereby able to be rejected.

E. Naming Rights

. . . .

. . . The naming rights agreement is an ongoing relationship between the naming rights sponsor and the sports franchise/facility. The naming rights agreement likely qualifies as an executory contract under both the material breach and functional analysis tests. Therefore, the naming rights agreement will be subject to the rejection/assumption analysis. The revenue stream flowing from the naming rights agreement is often utilized as collateral by the franchise. There is significant disagreement among the courts on the legal effect of rejecting an agreement that is used as collateral, and whether the secured creditor has a claim to the replacement naming rights agreement, if any.

. . . .

XI. REORGANIZATION PLANS

The plan of reorganization for a sports franchise will either be one that seeks to reorganize through an ongoing plan that allows current ownership to retain its equity or one that intends to reorganize the sports franchise by having new ownership through a liquidating plan. Liquidating plans are expressly authorized by the Code. Since a liquidating plan anticipates transferring the franchise's assets, it will be imperative to be able to assume and assign to the new owner the league membership agreement. Also, the sports facility agreement will need to be assumed and assigned to the new owner or rejected, depending on the attractiveness of its financial terms. Finally, the favorable players' contracts will need to be assumed and assigned to the new owner and the unfavorable ones rejected. . . . Sometimes, the prospect for a successful reorganization is so remote, the court cannot let the case proceed. In that event, a complete liquidation is the only available choice. . . .

The Bankruptcy Code, however, has a built-in bias favoring reorganization over complete liquidation. . . . Universally, the owner's first choice is to seek to reorganize by preserving its equity in the sports franchise. This, however, is a difficult task and fraught with legal uncertainties. A basic principle in reorganization is that all creditors must be paid 100% of their claim before the current owners can receive any interest in the reorganized entity. This is called the absolute priority rule. Since it is exceedingly rare that creditors will receive payment on 100% of their claims in bankruptcy, the current owners cannot retain an equity position in the reorganized debtor without contributing "new value." This is called the new value exception to the absolute priority rule. In essence, the current owners are repurchasing their interest in the reorganized entity and not retaining an equity position on account of their prior ownership. . . .

Another issue surrounding the new value exception is how to measure the "new value." There are four requirements to the new value exception. The value must be (1) new, (2) necessary, (3) substantial, and (4) equal to or in excess of the value of the interest purchased. The current owners must satisfy all four requirements in order to be the new owners of the reorganized entity. A very significant risk is that an outside bidder may submit a competing plan that contains new value and thereby become the new owner of the reorganized franchise. When there are competing plans, the creditors will ultimately select the final plan confirmed by the court. The Chapter 11 process, however, has exposed the franchise to a takeover situation. . . .

. . . .

DISCUSSION QUESTIONS

1. Why are book profits not a necessary reflection of true profitability when dealing with sports franchises?

2. How are teams owned by individuals taxed differently than the more common corporate owned teams? What are the pros and cons of each?

3. Discuss the ethics surrounding the use of related-party transactions by professional sports franchises.

4. How do franchises that own stadia differ from those that do not?

5. What are the factors that lead to the large discrepancies and the lack of uniformity one sees when looking at the books of various franchises both in the same and different leagues?

6. What are the differences between goodwill and the going concern principle both in theory and in practice?

7. How does one establish the value of a player's contract? What are the main factors that play a role in establishing the value of a player's contract?

8. The author makes the point that it is sometimes common to see a franchise sold during the course of a season. What are some of the major issues that arise when a franchise is sold in the course of the season? How are these issues dealt with?

9. What are some of the reasons why a sports franchise would choose to reorganize privately rather than publicly? Why then are there times when a franchise will reorganize publicly?

10. What are some of the pros and cons of filing Chapter 11?

11. If you were the owner of a sports franchise that found itself in major financial trouble, how would you go about dealing with reorganizing your franchise so as to minimize your losses?

12. How significant do you believe the "ego premium" associated with sports franchise ownership to be?

13. Discuss the unique aspects of accounting for professional sports franchises.

14. Why should franchises be thought of as marketing operations?

15. What are the unique issues surrounding the filing of Chapter 11 by a professional sports franchise?

CHAPTER 5

STADIUMS AND ARENAS

INTRODUCTION

A major income generator for sports enterprises is the facility where teams play or events are held. This is also often a major revenue factor on the budgets of cities. It can be a huge expenditure for the parties involved as well. The importance of a quality facility to the financial success of a sports franchise is now clearly appreciated by all parties involved. More on this will be discussed in Chapter 12, "Sports Franchise Valuation." The focus here is on the major sources of income and the major political issues associated with sports facilities.

From a leadership perspective, the broad scope of the successful sports venue is not complex. The first priority is to make sure the facilities generate revenues, and the second is to make sure a substantial portion of that revenue stream goes to the sports owner or promoter. That is, of course, unless you represent the city. The direction of revenue streams is the main focus of complex negotiations between teams and the venue owners.

The understanding of this formula has evolved as the burden of the construction of facilities has shifted from initially being a largely private task, to a predominantly public expenditure, to the current mix that exists today where there are various forms of public and private partnerships. The taxpayers in these cities are seeking a clearer understanding of the return they receive on their sports facility investments. (See Table 1 for recent stadium costs.)

Franchises often pursue new facilities or renegotiate leases in pursuit of additional revenues. The revenues that have increased most dramatically in importance are those that are not shared with other teams via league-wide revenue-sharing plans. These important revenue sources include luxury boxes, naming rights, and signage.

The excerpts from *The Stadium Game* lay out the major revenue-generating streams these facilities create. Here we highlight some of the major sources. All are the subject of the stadium lease negotiations previously noted.

"The Name is the Game in Facility Naming Rights" focuses on one of the most important revenue streams, facility naming rights deals. We highlight this source separately because of the dominant role this revenue source plays. Facilities with names like Enron, Adelphia, CMGI, PSINET, and TWA, companies that no longer exist or toil in bankruptcy, add an additional element that both sports and corporate leadership should be aware of in marrying the two sectors.

TABLE 1.

SELECTED RECENT STADIUM CONSTRUCTION				
City	*Sport*	*Year opened*	*Total cost*	*Public subsidy*
Cincinnati	Baseball	2003	$334 million	$30 million
Detroit	Football	2002	$325 million	$115 million
Houston	Football	2002	$367 million	$252 million
Seattle	Football	2002	$400 million	$100 million
Milwaukee	Baseball	2001	$394 million	$304 million
Denver	Football	2001	$400 million	$300 million
Pittsburgh	Football	2001	$252 million	$176 million
Pittsburgh	Baseball	2001	$262 million	$222 million
San Francisco	Baseball	2000	$330 million	$10 million
Houston	Baseball	2000	$248 million	$169 million
Detroit	Baseball	2000	$300 million	$100 million
Cincinnati	Football	2000	$450 million	$450 million
Denver	Basketball/Hockey	1999	$170 million	$9 million
Seattle	Baseball	1999	$534 million	$372 million
Los Angeles	Basketball/Hockey	1999	$375 million	$12 million
Baltimore	Football	1998	$223 million	$200 million
Tampa	Football	1998	$169 million	$169 million

Source: http://www.forbes.com/2002/03/28/0327allstarowners_print.html.

The chapter closes with a description of the policy dilemma the stakeholders confront in the "who should build it" decision-making process. The excerpt from *The Sports Franchise Game* provides this overview.

THE STADIUM GAME

Martin J. Greenberg

FINANCING OVERVIEW

The financing of sports facilities has recently garnered considerable attention. Sports facilities have become increasingly important components in the public finance marketplace with many state and local governments aggressively trying to keep or lure sports franchises into their communities. Over the last five years, there has been an explosion in the number of financing projects for stadiums and arenas, as communities have made plans to build state-of-the-art facilities to attract and retain professional franchises and draw major sporting events.

Fueling this development explosion is league expansion, facility obsolescence and a demand for increased franchise revenue. Since 1990, there have been seventy-seven major league facility lease re-negotiations, stadium renovations, or new venues built for professional football, baseball, basketball, and hockey at an approximate cost of $12 billion.

Since 1990, thirty-seven new stadiums and arenas — worth more than $6.5 billion in construction costs — have opened. By 2000, more than half of the country's major professional sports franchises were either getting new or renovated facilities, or had requested them. This increase in sports facility construction is expected to continue throughout the decade as league expansion and the underlying economics of the sports industry evolve.

The evolution of stadium and arena financing can be divided into four distinct periods: the Prehistoric Era dating back before 1965; the Renaissance Era carrying through 1983; the Revolution Era occurring between 1984 and 1986; and finally the New Frontier Era, from 1987 until today. . . .

The Prehistoric Era: Prior to 1965, the sports industry was not quite the big business that it is today. Government financing was the only source of funding. The most common funding instrument was general obligation bonds. *[Wholly privately financed stadiums could be found in this era as well.]*

The Renaissance Era: From 1966 to 1983, the popularity of professional sports grew tremendously in terms of both live attendance and television viewership. Franchise owners saw the values of their sports investments grow dramatically. The financial performance of arenas and stadiums improved through increased utilization by other events, such as concerts and family shows. Financing for the facilities continued to be dominated by the public sector.

During this era, bonds secured by taxes were the most traditional approach to stadium and arena financing taken by the public sector. In this situation, the municipality (city, county, state, or other government entity) backs a bond issue with a general obligation pledge, annual appropriations, or the revenues from a specific tax.

The Revolution Era: The Deficit Reduction Act of 1984 and the Tax Reform Act of 1986 both had large implications on stadium and arena financing. Many of today's older facilities were financed on a tax-exempt basis prior to the Tax Reform Act of 1986.

The Deficit Reduction Act lowered the priority of constructing public assembly facilities using funds from the public sector in light of the need to lower the national deficit. The Tax Reform Act made it much more difficult to finance stadiums and arenas with tax-exempt bonds. As a result, financing structures became more complex as revenue streams are often segregated to support multiple issues of debt in both taxable and tax-exempt markets.

New Frontier Era: Since 1987, stadium and arena financing has embarked upon a fascinating new path. The days of "vanilla" financings are over, giving way to greater complexity in financing arrangements. In addition, the planning and construction period has been stretched to a five to ten year time horizon. "Typical" construction risks, voter approval, and political "red tape" associated with the public's participation in stadium and arena financing projects have caused significant delays and have put the financial feasibility of some new facilities in doubt.

Most deals now involve partnerships between multiple parties from the public and private sectors. These mutually beneficial public/private partnerships are dictated by what each party can bring to the table. The public sector may be able to provide any combination of land, public capital/revenue streams, condemnation, infrastructure improvements, and tax abatement. The private sector may likewise provide any or all of the following: land, investment capital in the form of debt or equity, acceptance of risk, operating knowledge, and tenants.

Private sector participation in financing structures has typically been through taxable debt secured by the facility's operations and/or corporate guarantees. This is a relatively expensive source of funding that has generally required a higher debt coverage ratio and significant equity contributions. Thus, the private sector has sought other nontraditional sources. Those can include luxury suites, club seats, personal seat licenses (PSLs), concessionaire fees, and naming rights, among others.

The unique background and political environment surrounding the financing and construction of professional sports facilities plays a critical role in shaping the appropriate financing structure. The changing economics of professional sports has led franchises to demand a greater share of facility-generated revenue. As a result, reliance solely on public bond financing has become increasingly difficult and a combination of both public and private participation is often the cornerstone of current financing structures.

FINANCING INSTRUMENTS

Stadiums and arenas have been financed through a variety of public and private financial instruments. Because sports facilities represent a significant capital investment and provide benefits, both economic and social, to the public, financing structures typically rely on a combination of public and private financing instruments. These structures can become complex, particularly when traditional landlords and tenants form partnerships to provide capital for the facility. The appropriate financial instruments depend significantly on the unique circumstances surrounding the particular project.

Defined Instruments

Municipal notes and bonds are publicly traded securities. Congress exempted municipal securities from the registration requirements of the Securities Act of 1933 and the reporting requirements of the Securities Exchange Act of 1934. However, anti-fraud provisions remain in effect for any offering circulars issued to prospective investors.

Congress has not regulated issuers of municipal securities nor required that they issue a registration statement for several reasons. Among these reasons are the desire for government comity, the absence of recurrent abuses, the greater level of sophistication of marketplace investors, and few defaults. Municipal bonds are often analyzed by rating agencies such as Fitch, Moodys, and Standard & Poors. The key factors considered by rating agencies, credit enhancers, and investors in analyzing tax-secured debt include:

- Level of coverage;
- Broadness, stability, and reliability of tax base;
- Historic performance of revenue stream;
- Appropriation risk;
- Underlying economic strength;
- Political risk; [and]
- Financial viability of the project.

[See Chapter 12 for further discussion of the credit rating process.]

The following are descriptions of common financial instruments used to fund sports facilities.

General Obligation Bonds: General obligation (G.O.) bonds are secured by the general taxing power of the issuer and are called *full faith and credit obligations.* States, counties, and cities are common issuers of this form of debt. Repayment of the debt comes from the entity's general fund revenue, which typically includes property, income, profits, capital gains, sales, and use taxes. The full faith and credit pledge is typically supported by a commitment from the government issuer to repay the principal and interest through whatever means necessary, including levying additional taxes. In addition, double-barreled bonds are issued and secured not only by taxing power, but also by fee income that is outside the issuer's general fund. G.O. bonds secured by limited revenue sources such as property taxes alone are called *limited-tax general obligation bonds.* This type of bond typically requires legislative or voter approval.

Since G.O. bonds are backed by the general revenue fund of the issuing instrumentality, they usually represent the issuer's lowest cost of capital. General obligation bonds, however, are becoming increasingly difficult to issue for sports facilities with a growing demand on government for other capital projects and services.

Special Tax Bonds: These bonds are payable from a specifically pledged source of revenue — such as a specific tax — rather than from the full faith and credit of the municipality or state. *Tax and Revenue Anticipation Notes* (TRANs) are issued for periods from three months to three years in anticipation of the collection of tax or other revenue. Similarly, TRANs are issued in anticipation of a bond issue. *Tax-exempt commercial paper* is issued for thirty to 270 days, and typically is backed by a letter of credit from a bank or a bank line of credit. These are all used to even out cash flows when revenues will soon be forthcoming from taxes, revenues, or bond sales.

Revenue Bonds: Revenue bonds are more complex and less secure than general obligation bonds. Revenue bonds are typically project specific and are secured by the project's revenue, income, and one or more other defined revenue sources, such as hotel occupancy taxes, sales taxes, admission taxes, or other public/private revenue streams. The debt service (principal and interest) is paid for with dedicated revenue.

Since revenue bonds limit the financial risk to the municipality, they typically have a lower credit rating. The more stable and predictable the source of revenue, the more creditworthy the bond issue. Naturally, revenue sources with an existing collection history are preferable to underwriters and rating agencies, but revenue bonds do not offer that predictability.

Lease-Backed Financing (Lease Revenue Bonds): This financial instrument still benefits from the credit strength of a state or local government. An "authority" typically issues bonds with a facility lease arrangement with the governmental entity. The government leases the facility from the authority and leases the facility back to the authority pursuant to a sublease. The lease typically requires the government to make annual rental payments sufficient to allow payment of the debt service on the authority's bonds. There are several related lease structures including Sale/Leaseback and True Lease arrangements.

Certificate of Participation: Certificates of Participation (COPs) have become an increasingly common financial instrument used to finance sports facilities. COP holders are repaid through an annual lease appropriation by a sponsoring government agency. COPs do not legally commit the governmental entity to repay the COP holder, and therefore generally do not require voter approval. In addition, COPs are not subject to many of the limitations and restrictions associated with bonds.

Although COPs offer the issuing authority less financial risk and more flexibility, they tend to be more cumbersome due to the reliance on the trustee. In addition, COPs carry a higher coupon rate relative to traditional revenue bonds.

. . . . *[The author's examples of applications of the financial instruments described are omitted.]*

Economic Generators

The creation and expansion of sports facility revenue generators has been one of the driving forces behind the sports facility boom in the 1990s. These new revenue generators are joining traditional income sources such as concessions, parking, and advertising in determining whether the lessor or the lessee will earn a profit at the facility. Thus, the allocation of revenues derived from items such as club seats, seat licenses, corporate naming rights, restaurants, luxury suites, and retail stores is quickly becoming an important part of every sports facility lease agreement.

This . . . is an examination of the primary revenue generators and how these items are currently being addressed in major and minor league sports facility lease agreements.

Club Seats

Club seats were the invention of former Miami Dolphins' owner Joe Robbie who created a new level of premium seating in hopes of securing enough funding to privately finance a new home for the Dolphins. Robbie placed 10,214 wide, contour-backed seats in the middle tier of the three-tiered facility and dubbed them, "individual club seats." The seats, which cost from $600 to $1,400 annually, had to be leased on a ten-year basis. In return, club seat patrons received twenty-one-inch-wide seats, overhead blowers puffing cool air on them during hot days or nights, and access to an exclusive series of lounge areas that were finely decorated and serviced by wait-staff ready to handle the patrons' concessionary needs. With the guaranteed revenues from the ten-year leases for the club seats and luxury suites in hand, Robbie was able to secure the financing necessary to build the facility that was later named in his honor and assumed a place in the stadium financing annals.

Since its inception in the mid-1980s, club seating has become one of the largest revenue producers for stadiums. And since 1991, the number of leased club seats has risen by more than 500 percent, producing a significant and steady revenue stream for the four major league professional sports teams. . . .

Luxury Suites

In 1883, Albert Spalding's new baseball stadium for the Chicago White Stockings catered to the upscale fan by offering eighteen private boxes furnished with drapes and armchairs. Since then, professional sports franchises have continued their race to install luxury suites in their playing facilities.

Luxury suites have entrenched themselves as the second-most important revenue stream for professional sports franchises behind television revenues. . . .

. . . .

Personal Seat Licenses

In Tampa Bay, Buccaneers owners used it to finance the National Football League team's sparkling new stadium. On campus at the University of Wisconsin, Badgers' officials are using it to help fund the school's athletics program. And in Green Bay, Packers management intend to use a variation to pay for much-needed renovations to Lambeau Field and thereby join ten other NFL teams (Baltimore, Carolina, Cincinnati, Cleveland, Dallas, Oakland, Pittsburgh, St. Louis, Tampa Bay, and Tennessee) that have variations of them.

It is a personal seat license, or PSL, one of the most important — and often misunderstood — of the legal and financial vehicles available for sports stadium funding.

Although there has been a greater increase in private sector contributions to sports stadium and arena development, teams and communities continue to seek new ways to finance stadiums. Personal seat licenses have provided, at least in some instances, another means of contributing to the private equation in the facilities partnership formed between private financiers and public funding.

In addition to providing private sector funds for the construction of sports facilities, personal seat licenses also have generated season ticket sales and facility revenues, and have been used as a means to attract teams contemplating relocation.

The expanded use of seat licenses seems beneficial for all parties involved [in the] financing process of sports facilities. Teams receive upgraded facilities and guaranteed tickets bases, which should allow them to remain competitive on and off the field for many years. Fans receive property rights in their personal seat licenses, which can become valuable items on the open market. And governmental entities receive the benefits of upgraded or new sports facilities at reduced costs to taxpayers, theoretically allowing these entities to allocate tax monies for essential governmental services.

The stadium financing effort in the Carolinas for the home of the Carolina Panthers is an example of the interaction between seat licensing revenues and governmental interests. Ericsson Stadium, the $248-million home for the NFL's expansion Carolina Panthers opened in 1996, was built at a cost to taxpayers of $55 million, while the rest of the financing for the facility was derived from seat license revenues. The Panthers were projected to have a $200- to $300-million impact on the Carolina economy, easily generating enough of a return to cover the initial taxpayer investment.

. . . .

Funds for the bulk of the Panthers' development costs — $162 million (about $100 million after taxes) — came from private seat licenses priced from $700 to $5,400 for season tickets and club seats. Nearly 62,000 private seat licenses were sold by the time the stadium opened, including 49,724 seat licenses and 104 suites (valued at nearly $113 million) a month before the franchise was awarded. Today, 156 of 158 suites (price: $50,000 to $296,000) are leased for six- to 10-year periods.

. . . .

Understanding the PSL

A personal seat license is defined as a contractual agreement between a team (the PSL licensor) and the purchaser (the PSL licensee) in which the licensee pays the team a fee in exchange for the team guaranteeing the licensee a right to purchase season tickets at a specified seat location for a designated period of time (such as five years, ten years, or even the life of the facility) as long as the license holder does not violate the terms of the license agreement. Should the licensee violate these terms, the team automatically gets the personal seat license back, or has the ability to exercise a right to buy back the license at the original selling price and then resell it on the open market.

A personal seat license, which can be resold on the open market, generally offers the purchaser no guarantee of a return on the initial investment — none, of course, except for the benefits of enjoying use of a seat at a game. The main variables in legal constructions of modern personal seat licenses — which also have been called permanent seat licenses — are (1) the cost and (2) the time period of the license.

Variations on the Personal Seat License Theme

Tampa Bay employed a variation of the personal seat license to raise money for constructing Raymond James Stadium, home of the Buccaneers. Fans were asked to pay a deposit for the right to buy tickets for the next ten years. The deposit, which was equal to the price of a season ticket for one year, is to be refunded at the rate of 5 percent per year for nine years, with the balance paid at the 10th season.

The Kohl Center — home of University of Wisconsin hockey and the men's and women's basketball teams — has a plan called the Annual Scholarship Seating Program. It calls for season ticket holders to donate to the University Scholarship Fund in exchange for the right to purchase prime seats.

Recently, the Green Bay Packers announced a $295 million plan to renovate Lambeau Field, which would be paid for through a public/private split of 57/43 percent. The team, through a one-time user fee on paid season ticket holders, would raise a total of $92.5 million. Lambeau Field season ticketholders would pay $1,400 per seat and Milwaukee package season ticket holders would be asked to pay $600 per seat.

A one-time user fee differs from a PSL. In Green Bay, the fee paid only entitles the season ticket holder to obtain tickets to renovated Lambeau Field. It does not guarantee the season ticket seat beyond the first season in renovated Lambeau, nor is the right transferable. The Packers are discussing, however, implementing a policy that, if season ticketholders ever surrendered their tickets, the next person on the team's waiting list would be required to reimburse the user fee to the original ticket holder before any tickets actually changed hands.

In December of 1999, Robert McNair's Houston NFL Holdings, Inc. unveiled its plan to sell fewer personal seat licenses at a lower price than has been fashionable recently in financing new NFL stadiums. Its goal is to attract a broader demographic to games.

. . . .

Comparatively, 80 percent of the seats in Cleveland Browns Stadium and 85 percent of the seats at Adelphia Coliseum, home of the Tennessee Titans, were subject to licenses. The Steelers sold 50,000 PSLs for Pittsburgh's new 64,000-seat stadium.

. . . .

Naming Rights *[For a more extensive discussion of naming rights, see the following reading.]*

One of the most recent additions — and the most lucrative — to the list of stadium revenue generators is the selling of naming rights. Naming rights are currently sold for not only the right to rename an entire stadium, but also to name entryways into the stadium, the field, breezeways, etc.

In 1987, the Los Angeles Forum, then home to the Lakers and Kings, became the Great Western Forum when Great Western Bank became the first corporation to purchase the rights to name any professional sports facility. Since then, it has become the rule rather than the exception for a facility to bear the name of a company.

Historically, stadiums and arenas have been named either for a geographic region (Milwaukee County Stadium), in honor of a renowned individual (RFK Stadium), or after the name of the home team (Giants Stadium). Today, the increasing need for capital has resulted in most new facilities bearing the name of an individual company. In fact, the naming rights deals have grown so lucrative, that even storied stadiums such as Lambeau Field in Green Bay are considering the sale of its naming rights in some fashion or another.

The selling of naming rights is a trend that will continue because as time goes on, the revenue it produces is vital to financing venue development and renovations. Jerry Colangelo, owner of the Arizona Diamondbacks and Arizona Cardinals, has stated that, "I think you're going to see more and more corporate involvement in terms of naming rights and major involvements with large companies. In order to deliver that product, the game itself, you need to build venues that have the opportunity to pay for it. Our group is indicative of that trend."[74]

. . . .

Beyond Stadium Naming Rights

There are times when a facility chooses not to sell the name of [the] facility itself, but rather sell the rights to name the field, breezeways, or portals into the stadium. This is a very new concept that began in 1999 when the Cleveland Browns christened its new stadium without a corporate naming rights sponsor — by choice. The club chose instead to sell only the rights to name the stadium's portals at $2 million a year for ten years.

One such company is National City Bank, who receives other benefits with their deal, including:

- The right to call themselves the "Official Bank of the Cleveland Browns" for five years while serving as the team's sole bank provider;
- The right to use the Cleveland Browns logo in conjunction with various advertising and promotional activities;
- Maintains the right for product merchandising for several unnamed existing products, as well as several new products;
- Name identification in the southeast quadrant (presumably the gate with the most public exposure) of the new stadium, including logos on all turnstiles, entranceways, directional signage, tickets, and seat cup holders;
- A 65′×15′ permanent presence in the west end zone scoreboard; [and]
- Numerous other signage rights throughout the stadium.

The selling of auxiliary stadium areas is the model that likely will be followed when Soldier Field undergoes renovations. In the case of Soldier Field, selling naming rights to auxiliary areas will be the only option to generate this type of revenue because the overall naming rights of the stadium are not for sale. Chicago Mayor Richard Daley recently stated publicly, "(The stadium) will always be known as Soldier's Field. That is dedicated to the veterans here in Chicago. It will always be that."[165]

But selling the rights to the auxiliary facility areas is not limited only to those facilities that choose not to sell their overall naming rights. When the Patriots sold the naming rights to their new field for $114 million-plus over fifteen years to CMGI — an Internet holding company with affiliations and financial interests with 70 Internet companies — the Patriots reserved the right to additionally sell the rights to the stadium's entrances, which is expected to earn the team millions more on an annual basis, based on the Cleveland deal.

These auxiliary areas can even include seating sections. At Bank One Ballpark, for example, Nissan struck a deal with the Arizona Diamondbacks to name the premium seating level the Infiniti Level. Nissan's annual price tag for that right actually exceeds the $2.3 million paid annually by Bank One for the facility's naming rights deal, although Bank One's deal included several other options bringing its annual commitment to $4.6 million per year.

And naming rights are not limited to the game-day field only. The Indianapolis Colts recently announced that they sold the rights to their practice facility to Union Federal Bank. The venue will be known as Union Federal Football Center. Although no price was announced, team officials said it was the largest sponsorship deal in the team's history. The package includes radio spots, sponsorship of the team's fan club, signage in the RCA Dome, and print advertising.

. . . .

In the most recent Houston deal with Reliant Energy, the deal also called for Reliant to maintain the naming rights to the Astrodome Complex, which includes the Astrodome, the AstroArena, and a new convention center.

Parking

Of the main economic generators discussed . . . parking revenue, continues to remain the smallest revenue generator of this group. As a result, parking — in a strictly financial sense — is not usually the most significant issue during lease negotiations between teams and sports facilities.

. . . .

Advertising

It may appear as though sports teams have a new interest in advertisements and sponsorships. As recently as 10 years ago, nearly all stadiums bore the names of famous people or cities. These days all but a handful carry the names of companies willing to pay millions to have a corporate logo identified with a team and its hometown stadium.

It is not so much that it is a new revenue source, however. Instead, it is the ability of teams to keep this revenue that is making advertising the goose that laid the golden egg. In the NFL, for instance, advertising and signage revenue is exempt from the league's revenue-sharing program.

The demand for advertising has turned every square inch of a sports facility into a potential source of advertising income. Advertising consists of everything from signage on the outside of arenas to sleeves that cover the turnstiles to posters above the urinal.

For the Washington Wizards, the new MCI Center will earn more than $6 million from signs alone, a 100 percent increase over US Airways Arena. The Washington Redskins earned approximately $250,000 in advertising income during the team's final season at RFK Stadium, a figure ranked near the bottom of the NFL. When the team moved in to Jack Kent Cooke Stadium, the new home of the Redskins, advertising industry specialists believe advertising revenue climbed to between $6 million and $8 million a year from sponsorships alone.[222] That number grew even larger when new owner Daniel Snyder sold the naming rights for the stadium to Federal Express.

These examples of the boost advertising can give to team revenue are not uncommon. Generating revenue that a team can keep for itself has become a necessity for teams to keep up with climbing player salaries.

Stadium advertising has become necessary to maintain a profitable franchise. . .

. . . .

Concessions

Concession rights are rights transferred to a concessionaire for the sale and dispensing of food, snacks, refreshments, alcoholic and nonalcoholic beverages, merchandise, souvenirs, clothing, novelties, publications, and other articles in the stadium or arena, pursuant to a concession agreement. The concession agreements set aside sales spaces which include, concession stands, condiment areas, vending machines, hawker's station, the press room, the stadium club, cafeterias, executive clubs, executive suites, food courts, outdoor cafés, and waitress service for club seats, among others. Either a team or facility owner hires the concessionaire. The concession agreement will normally grant a concessionaire the exclusive right to exercise concession rights in concession spaces throughout a facility.

Wes Westley, President and CEO of SMG, has said:

"In the past, facilities relied solely on the success of concession stands. With 'state of the art' arenas and stadiums being built, emphasis is now placed on luxury box and club seating, catering, restaurants, hospitality suites, and other nontraditional concessionaire sales. In addition, branded foods and franchising has also impacted the amount of gross sales being generated. Simply stated, there's now a much greater pie of revenue to share."[388]

This shift has dramatically increased total gross sales at all new venues. Today's concession contracts include commission payments on specific types of sales rather than on total sales. New contracts may have as many as 15 different sales categories in which various commission rates are paid.

. . . .

Other Economic Generator Provisions

At a time when sports teams are looking to meet the demands of increasing player salaries and still provide a growing income stream to owners, alternative sources of revenue are becoming increasingly important and popular.

Everything from restaurant operations to sports amusement parks are developed to create excitement about the team and generate revenue in the process. While stadium tours and team retail stores may only provide a few thousand dollars to the annual income statement, they often go a lot further in keeping teams at the top of the mind of fans.

The more interesting development is that there appears to be little or no uniformity among how these programs are developed or how they are implemented. While most restaurants, for instance, are operated by a concessionaire, some leases send the revenue to the team, while others give it to the district.

The same is true of tours. Some new stadiums are offering them and raking in revenue, while others never even opened the doors to paying tour groups. And then there is the Grand Dame of stadiums, The Louisiana Superdome, which is expanding its tours even though it is more than two decades old.

What is clear, however, is that ancillary revenue is increasingly important, whether it goes to the teams or the stadium districts.

Restaurants

Restaurants are becoming an important part of making stadiums a constant attraction, even when there are no games scheduled. The Southeast Wisconsin Professional Baseball Park District proved this when it allowed for the completion of the Klements Sausage Haus, a freestanding restaurant, even after the opening of Miller Park for the Milwaukee Brewers was delayed for a year because of a construction accident.

The Milwaukee Brewers have started using the Sausage Haus, which is currently open during games, for press events. The team, for instance, introduced its new skipper at the restaurant. The restaurant stands adjacent to Miller Park.

The District's lease agreement with the Brewers calls for the facility to be operated by an outside vendor, with revenue from the restaurant to go to the Brewers.[445]

Like many new stadiums, the Brewers' Miller Park also features several restaurants, all of which will be operated by SportService, Inc.

In addition to the Klements Sausage Haus, Miller Park will have a sports bar and restaurant, which is scheduled to be open all year. It will also have a high-end restaurant near the luxury boxes, which will be open only during games and for special events.

The goal is to allow fans to use baseball games for all sorts of entertaining. The restaurant facilities are capable of hosting everything from a business meeting to birthday party.

The Brewers retain all of the revenue from the restaurants.

The St. Louis Rams also collect all of the revenue from the restaurant at the TransWorld Dome [Now known as the Edward Jones Dome].[448] The only time the Rams do not collect the revenue from the restaurant is when the St. Louis Convention and Visitors Commission, which operates the TransWorld Dome, hosts an event at the restaurant. That money goes to the commission.

The Rams, however, are also responsible for all the costs associated with the restaurant.

The Miami Heat have yet another arrangement. The team gets all revenue from the restaurants during its games and 47.5 percent of the revenue from all other concessionaires operated during Heat games.

The Colorado Rockies' lease gives the team 97 percent of year round bar and restaurant revenue if the team uses the facility's approved concessionaire. If the team chooses another operator, its percentage drops to 95 percent.[450] The District collects the remainder of the revenue.

Revenue, however, is not the only concern of a team when it comes to food served at stadiums. Teams have started specializing in regional delicacies in an effort to make the food more interesting and thus increase sales.

The Baltimore Ravens offer Maryland's famous crab cakes, Latin food is common at Pro Player Stadium in Miami, and sushi is a regular offering in San Francisco at Pacific Bell Park.

The theory is that improved gastronomy will increase the amount of money spent at the ballpark. . .[451]

Along with local specialties, however, some ballparks are favoring national chains that will bring in diners all year. Both Bank One Ballpark, home of the Arizona Diamondbacks, and the Texas Rangers' Arlington ballpark are home to TGI Friday's restaurants.

Reservations at the Rangers' Friday's restaurant include the price of a ticket to the game and offers seating on three levels, with pool tables and darts serving as a diversion from the baseball game.

Freestanding restaurants, whether as part of a national chain or with a local flair, are almost a requirement for a new ballpark intended to keep the interest of fans, according to Stan Kasten, chairman of Philips Arena in Atlanta.

Facility Tours

Enron Field *[the former name of Minute Maid Park],* the home of the Houston Astros, has a fancy coal-fired train, but no tours. Neither does the shiny new Cleveland Browns Stadium. In San Francisco, however, Pacific Bell Park charges $10 a head for tours. The revenue from the tours goes to the team.

The two stalwart stadiums of the NFL still lead the league in tour revenue.

Lambeau Field, which only offers tours from June to August, takes an average of 12,500 fans from the press box to the field each summer. The tours begin at the Packers Hall of Fame on the same grounds as the stadium and take upwards of 90 minutes. Brown County operates the tours and collects about $6 per person. The Green Bay Packers collect the revenue, according to the team.

The Louisiana Superdome collects $7.50 per person for tours and all of the revenue goes to the stadium district. The Superdome, however, developed a special tour of the engineering marvels of the stadium in 1999. Those tours are only offered for groups and prices vary depending on the size of the group and the amount of interest the group has in seeing the underbelly of the stadium.

The Maricopa County Stadium District collects all of the revenue from tours of Bank One Ballpark in Phoenix. Tickets to the BOB tour are $7.50.

What makes the Superdome and Lambeau Field unique, however, is that most stadium districts find enough demand to justify having a tour staff for up to five years. After that, few fans are interested in touring the stadiums. It is the uniqueness and history of these two facilities that continue to draw the interest of fans.

While younger facilities eventually lose the allure that makes a tour operation successful, older teams continue to look for new ways to generate both revenue and fan interest.

The Green Bay Packers, with the help of the Brown County Convention & Visitors Bureau, created the Packers Experience, which it runs from June to August. The Packers Experience allows fans to get involved in every facet of the game, mimicking the now familiar Lambeau Leap and practicing the punt, pass, and kick.

Fun and Games

The facility is open during the training camp season and serves, along with the Green Bay Packers Hall of Fame, as part of a destination package for football fanatics.

The revenue for the Packers Experience is divided evenly between the team and the Brown County Convention & Visitors Bureau. The indoor amusement park drew an average of 65,000 visitors each summer in the first two years it was open.

After its first year, attendance at The Packers Experience dropped from 73,000 to 54,000. All of the revenue from the Packers Hall of Fame goes to the Packers. It is open year round and takes in as many as 75,000 visitors a year.

In Denver, the Colorado Rockies and Denver Metropolitan Major League Baseball Stadium District split the revenue equally from the baseball museum at Coors Field. The District gives its portion of the revenue from the museum to the Rockies Youth Foundation.

The real fun, however, is coming from the newest stadiums.

For $4,000, fans can watch a game at Phoenix's . . . Bank One Ballpark from the outfield swimming pool.

The Texas Rangers have a running track, Six Flags water park, children's center, and baseball museum, all of which are busier when there is no game at the ballpark than when the Rangers are in town.

Perhaps the most controversial of the entertainment venues is the Coca-Cola-sponsored playground at . . . Pacific Bell Park in San Francisco, shaped like a Coke bottle. Some argue it is a symbol of commercialism finally going too far.

Baseball purists worry that the game is being overwhelmed by all the other attractions at the stadiums, but teams counter that they are only giving fans what they want: a destination rather than just a ball game.

Retail Stores

While teams have always sold their merchandise and retained the revenue from it — t-shirts, puffy fingers, and the like — many teams are now negotiating for retail stores that are open year round at the stadiums. This is all part of making the venue a constant tourist destination.

The Baltimore Orioles, Anaheim Mighty Ducks, and St. Louis Rams all have exclusive rights to revenue from their retail stores. The management company that operates The Pond gives the Mighty Ducks retail space. The team is allowed to retain 100 percent of the revenue from the sale of merchandise at the store.

The Orioles are one of the teams that have their retail store open all year, even when the team is not playing at Camden Yards, or when it is not baseball season. Like the Mighty Ducks, the Orioles retain all revenue from the store.

The Tampa Bay Devil Rays embarked on the most aggressive retail strategy in professional sports when the team designed a full-scale mall with several restaurants into the renovated Tropicana Field in 1997.[467]

The team paid a portion of the costs for the $85 million renovation, which also included a reconfiguration of the ball field. In return, the Devil Rays collect the revenue from the shopping and dining center.

The mall remains open year round, providing a constant revenue stream for the Devil Rays. The team designed the park so that fans would treat Tropicana Field as a place to spend a day or a weekend, rather than just a game-time destination.

The granddaddy of this concept, of course, is Toronto's Skydome, which was built more as a destination than a ballpark.

The stadium features a 350-room hotel, the largest McDonald's in North America, a Hard Rock Café, a health club, movie theater, meeting rooms, and shopping mall.[469]

Skydome has established itself as a destination regardless of the time or year or the events on the field. Revenue from the various businesses associated with Skydome is divided between the team and the stadium district. The profits are divided at different rates depending on which venture is contributing to the revenue stream.

CONCLUSION

What has become obvious through alternate forms of revenue generation is that teams are seeking ways to get fans to the stadium as much as they are seeking outside forms of revenue.

Few teams, if any, will say that revenue from restaurants, museums, retail stores, and the like, have saved their budget. What teams are likely to say, however, is that the additional revenue from these ventures allows the team to capture a larger portion of the fan's wallet. That is what makes sports good business.

REFERENCES

74. Don Ketchum, "D-Backs Go to the Bank (One) for Stadium Name: 30-Year Deal Continues Trend to Sponsorship," *Phoenix Gazette,* April 6, 1995, at C1, and Eric Miller, "Million-Dollar Name: Bank One Ballpark," *Arizona Republic,* April 6, 1995, at A1.

165. Mark J. Konkol, "Daley Says Soldier Field Has Right Ring," *Daily Southtown,* June 16, 2000.

222. "Clear and Visible Signs of the Times," *The Washington Post,* Aug. 24, 1997.

388. Presentation, National Sports Law Institute, "Stadium Revenues, Venues and Values," October 1995.

445. Southeast Wisconsin Professional Baseball Park lease, p. 12.

448. Amended and restated St. Louis NFL lease by and among the Los Angeles Rams Football Club, the Regional Convention and Visitors Commission, and the St. Louis NFL Corp., Jan 17, 1995, Annex 3, at O.

450. Amended and restated lease and management agreement by and between the Denver Metropolitan Major League Baseball Stadium District and Colorado Rockies Baseball Club Ltd., March 30, 1995, at 18,19.

451. Alexander F. Grau, "Where Have You Gone, Joe DiMaggio? And Where Are the Stadiums You Played In?" *Georgetown Science, Technology & International Affairs,* Fall 1998, p. 5.

467. Tampa Bay Devil Ray Internet site: http://www.devilrays.com/thetrop/thetrop.php3.

469. Grau, p. 4.

THE NAME IS THE GAME IN FACILITY NAMING RIGHTS

Martin J. Greenberg and April R. Anderson

WHY THE BOOM?

The growth of naming rights deals did not occur in a vacuum; rather, they increased in tandem with the recent boom of new sports venues. The bottom line, of course, has been money. Corporate naming of stadia and arenas provides significant revenue for sports facilities and a positive attempt to defray public sector building costs.

It has really only been in the last decade when the use of corporate names for sports venues has gained widespread acceptance. The first corporate naming rights agreement was negotiated in 1973 between Rich Products Corporation and the County of Erie, New York, under which the new stadium for the NFL's Buffalo Bills would be called Rich Stadium at a cost of $1.5 million over 25 years. Fourteen years later, in 1987, the contemporary use of corporate naming rights began in earnest when the naming rights to the Los Angeles Forum were purchased by Great Western Bank. Prior to 1990, only two of the NBA's twenty-seven teams (7.4%) had sold naming rights. Compare that with post-1990 figures: fourteen of twenty-nine NBA teams (48.3%) have sold naming rights to their facilities in the last eight years. *[As of January 1, 2004, 22 of 29 NBA teams had sold naming rights to their playing facilities. Overall, 82 of 121 teams in the NBA, NFL, NHL, and MLB have sold naming rights to their facilities.]*

Since that time, corporate naming rights for stadia and arenas have become the norm. This has occurred for two reasons. First, as more facilities take on corporate names, the public acceptance for such a practice has grown. Whatever initial reluctance there may have been toward what some experts have called the "corporatization" of stadia and arenas has largely dissipated to the point where naming rights deals are now status quo; an expectation that comes with obtaining a new facility.

Second, the increasing costs of building these facilities and the reluctance of public officials to raise taxes in order to fund them, make it necessary to maximize facility revenues. Thus, the selling of corporate naming rights creates an additional funding vehicle to recover, or reduce, initial sports facility costs and debt payments, which would otherwise be subsidized by taxpayers. As the trend toward building new facilities continues, so too will the use of naming rights, especially in light of the fact that if a new facility is to be built, it must carry with it some opportunity to pay for itself.

WHY CORPORATE AMERICA BUYS NAMING RIGHTS

A variety of corporations, representing a myriad of industries, purchase stadium naming rights. Airlines, automobile manufacturers, beverage producers, telecommunication companies, financial services, computer manufacturers, and consumer product producers all are currently represented by facilities bearing their names.

Corporate entities generally purchase the naming rights of sports facilities for seven reasons.

First, buying an arena's naming rights is a highly cost effective way for companies to advertise. Television, radio, and the media all use the company name when reporting on events held at the facility, while visibility is also attained by the signage on the facility itself. Consider the following examples: In 1991, America West Airlines purchased the naming rights for the new arena being built for the Phoenix Suns at a cost of $550,000 for the first year with a three percent annual increase to this initial fee. During the 1993 NBA Finals, when the Suns hosted the Chicago Bulls, one thirty-second television commercial spot on NBC cost $300,000. Because the company purchased the naming rights to the facility, America West's name and logo were seen countless times throughout the series at a mere cost of $583,495 — less than a single one-minute television commercial.

Meanwhile, 3Com, a computer company in Santa Clara, California, paid $500,000 for the naming rights to San Francisco's Candlestick Park for a six month period. Company spokesmen have publicly stated that 3Com has been featured in at least 180 articles, that the company has received forty percent more resumes since the naming, and that the volume of trading on the company's stock has increased dramatically in that time.

This cost-effectiveness theory was recently buttressed by a study conducted by Joyce Julius and Associates of Ann Arbor, Michigan, which determined the gross value of "impressions" generated by naming rights deals. By studying twelve sports venues (in markets averaging 2.16 million television households), and counting the number of impressions made on the site itself, print media, and national, regional, and local television and radio, analysts were able to calculate the financial impact of the impressions and the amount that it would have cost the companies to generate the same degree of impressions through traditional national and local television advertising. The results were quite impressive. Stadium naming right packages generated an average of $31.7 million worth of "impressions" in 1997, and arena naming rights packages generated an average of $69.9 million of "impressions." Had the sponsors of those sports facilities purchased the same degree of traditional media advertising, the costs would have been ten times those amounts.

Second, the purchase of corporate naming rights represents a unique opportunity for corporate entities. Sports facilities are relatively few in number, making imitation or duplication by competitors nearly impossible. The exclusivity in purchasing external signage that cannot be used by anyone else is extraordinarily valuable.

Third, the purchase of naming rights allows a company to project a positive image and create goodwill into the community in which the facility is located. For example, General Motors of Canada and Fleet Financial Group, purchasers of naming rights to sports facilities in Vancouver and Boston, respectively, have announced new community service programs coinciding with the purchase of those arena naming rights.

Fourth, companies may use naming rights to establish a presence in regions where they may not have previously conducted business, or in areas where they are seeking to expand operations. Key Bank adopted this approach when it purchased the naming rights to the newly refurbished Seattle Coliseum. The bank had recently purchased new branches in Washington and wanted to expand its name recognition throughout the state.

Fifth, naming rights agreements usually allow for cross-promotion through on-site product tie-ins. For instance, sports facilities in Boston, Seattle, and Grand Rapids, Michigan have automated teller machines placed by the banks which have purchased the naming rights to those buildings. Arenas in Chicago and Phoenix have ticket booths for their airline namesakes. General Motors plans on capitalizing on its purchase of naming rights to the new home of the Canucks and Grizzlies in Vancouver by tying in vehicle promotions with events at the stadium. Finally, Anaheim Arena suites and concession stands offer bottled water from Arrowhead Water Company, the corporation which purchased the naming rights to the home of the Mighty Ducks of Anaheim.

Sixth, corporate entities usually receive, or purchase, a skybox or suite at the facility as a part of the naming rights contract. Bringing prospective clients or sought-after prospective employees to a sports facility with the company name on the building offers considerable corporate prestige.

Finally, there may be tax advantages associated with purchasing naming rights to a sports facility, in that such expenditures may be taken as a business expense deduction pursuant to the Internal Revenue Code. . . .

Anatomy of the Deal

Any naming rights agreement is comprised of important contractual provisions, such as ownership rights, cost, time payments and escalators, term and renewal options, exclusive rights and noncompete covenants, first options and rights of first refusal, and intellectual property related clauses. All of these issues may become a part of the contract and may ultimately impact the value of the deal to the corporate sponsor.

Generally, naming rights are achieved by making an initial, up-front payment, followed by annual payments for a specified term, typically 15 to 30 years. Additionally, the corporate sponsor may be permitted to extend the term of the agreement by holding an option to renew, a right of first option to negotiate, or a right of first refusal. For example, CoreStates agreed to pay $1.5 million up-front and $2 million per year for 29 years for the naming rights to Philadelphia's sports arena. CoreStates owns these rights exclusively for the first ten years, and holds the opportunity to renew the terms and conditions of the contract. In contrast, Continental Airlines' deal to name the Meadowlands arena in northern New Jersey is for 12 years, $29 million, and contains no option to renew.

Naming rights agreements, like other contracts, also include other contractual concerns such as trademark ownership rights and termination, indemnification, default, and force majeure clauses.

While the phrase "naming rights deal" often connotes merely signage, the total deal package actually is often much more extensive. Understanding the extent of amenities to be included in the package is a significant consideration in the economic valuation of the deal. In addition to the corporate signage associated with the facility, purchasers of naming rights also tend to negotiate deals related to luxury box suites, television and radio advertising, uniforms for facility personnel, use of the facility, and the incorporation of the sponsor's product as a part of the total package.

. . . . [The authors' discussion of the Indianapolis Colts deal with RCA and Thomson Consumer Electronics is omitted.]

VIABILITY AND PRICING

The viability and pricing of sports facility naming rights agreements are determined by four factors. The first factor is the number of events to be held at the facility. The presence of a professional or collegiate team playing its home games at the facility is a basic requirement for a naming rights agreement because it guarantees a minimum number of dates that a particular facility will be in operation.

The presence of an anchor tenant team also can lead to a facility's hosting of other sports related events, such as All-Star and championship games, bowl games, league meetings, and camps. Camps can range from the RCA Dome's hosting of the NFL's annual February prospect combine to fantasy camps allowing fans to compete with their childhood heroes. Concerts, conventions, conferences, or other community events also can generate considerable exposure. For instance, Chicago's United Center hosted the Democratic National Convention in 1996. By combining sports and non-sports related events, a facility can generate the number of events necessary to make naming rights attractive to potential buyers.

The second factor is the type of events which take place at the facility. The presence of a professional or amateur team again is a basic requirement because teams usually generate the high-profile exposure events necessary to satisfy the needs of naming rights purchasers. The hosting of special events at the facility — such as the Super Bowl, the NCAA Final Four, college bowl games, All-Star games, or political conventions — also increases the facility's visibility, creating more demand for that arena's naming rights.

The third factor determining the viability and pricing of naming rights agreements is the presence of corporate entities in the city or region where the facility is located. Because companies usually are more willing to buy naming rights for facilities in their home cities or regions, stadia and arenas in cities or regions with a concentration of corporate entities are likely to have an easier time selling their rights.

Keep in mind that the final factor affecting viability and pricing of naming rights is the composition of the package purchased by the company from the facility. As indicated earlier, the trend in this area is towards the purchase of naming rights as part of a larger, more extensive package, which also may include items such as team sponsorship or media rights.

TRENDS FOR THE FUTURE

The one certainty in this area is that highly lucrative naming rights deals will continue to proliferate, evidenced by the $50 million deals signed for the naming of Anaheim's Edison International Field and San Francisco's Pacific Bell Park, Bank One's $66 million deal to name the Arizona Diamondback's baseball stadium, and the landmark $100 million deal signed by Staples for the rights to name Los Angeles's new arena. Now, new trends are emerging in the structure of these complex deals.

First, the terms of the deals are becoming shorter in length. As previously noted, naming rights deals typically run for a term of 15 to 30 years. Recently, however, deals with terms of ten years or less are becoming popular. For example, Cinergy Field in Cincinnati has a six year term, ARCO Arena in Sacramento has a seven year term, and Ericsson Stadium in Charlotte has a ten year deal.

Second, smaller markets, which are typically home to minor league or collegiate teams, also are selling naming rights in order to reduce costs and increase revenues. For example, Knickerbocker Arena in Albany, New York, which is home to the American Hockey League's River Rats, the Arena Football League's Firebirds, and the Siena College men's basketball team, was renamed Pepsi Arena. Additionally, Oldsmobile Park in Lansing, Michigan is the new home for the Class A minor league baseball Lugnuts. What was once a phenomenon reserved for elite leagues in major cities has filtered down to lower tiers, allowing smaller markets to benefit.

Third, naming rights deals are emerging for nonsports related facilities such as convention centers and amphitheaters. In Milwaukee, Wisconsin, for example, Midwest Express Airlines entered into a 15-year, $9.25 million deal to purchase the naming rights to the city's downtown convention center. Other examples include the Nissan Pavilion in Stone Ridge, Virginia, and the PNC Arts Center in Holmdel, New Jersey.

Finally, consulting organizations are continually reassessing how naming rights deals can be better structured to effectively benefit both parties. Such analysis includes, for example, exploring the tax ramifications of such deals. As a result, some experts agree that it is likely that future deals may routinely involve loans or equity partnerships instead of standard annual payments, which may be taxable to the recipient as ordinary income.

The cost of sports venues continues to increase as demand for state-of-the-art sports and entertainment facilities proliferates. To help meet these construction needs in tenuous economic climates, corporate America has again demonstrated its ingenuity by providing relief to taxpayers and facility owners alike through the purchase of naming rights. And with deals such as Staples' $100 million Los Angeles arena naming rights agreement hovering over the industry, it appears certain that the days of naming a facility for an honored individual or government locality are long past. The name is the game, and it is one which only corporations can afford to play. (See Table 2 for selected naming rights deals.)

TABLE 2.

STADIUM NAMING RIGHTS

Stadium name	Sponsor	Home teams	Avg. $/Year	Expires
Air Canada Centre	Air Canada	Toronto Maple Leafs, Raptors	$1.5 million	2019
Alltel Stadium	Alltel Corp.	Jacksonville Jaguars	$620,000	2007
American Airlines Arena	American Airlines	Miami Heat	$2.1 million	2019
American Airlines Center	American Airlines	Dallas Mavericks, Stars	$6.5 million	2031
America West Arena	America West	Phoenix Suns, Coyotes, Mercury	$866,667	2019
Arco Arena	Atlantic Richfield	Sacramento Kings, Monarchs	$750,000	2007
Bank One Ballpark	Bank One	Arizona Diamondbacks	$2.2 million	2028
Bell Centre	Bell Canada	Montreal Candiens	N/A	N/A
Cinergy Field	Cinergy	Cincinnati Reds	$1 million	2002
Citizens Bank Park	Citizens Bank	Philadelphia Phillies	$2.3 million	2028
Comerica Park	Comerica	Detroit Tigers	$2.2 million	2030
Compaq Center	Compaq Computer	Houston Rockets, Comets	$900,000	2003
Compaq Center at San Jose	Compaq Computer	San Jose Sharks	$3.1 million	2016
Conseco Fieldhouse	Conseco	Indiana Pacers, Fever	$2 million	2019
Continental Airlines Arena	Continental Airlines	New Jersey Nets, Devils	$1.4 million	2011
Coors Field	Coors Brewing	Colorado Rockies	N/A	INDEFINITE
Corel Center	Corel	Ottawa Senators	$878,142	2016
Delta Center	Delta Airlines	Utah Jazz, Starzz	$1.3 million	2011
Edison International Field	Edison Intl.	Anaheim Angels	$2.5 million	2018
Edward Jones Dome	Edward Jones	St. Louis Rams	$2.65 million	2013
Ericsson Stadium	Ericsson	Carolina Panthers	$2 million	2006
FedEx Field	Federal Express	Washington Redskins	$7.6 million	2025
FedEx Forum	Federal Express	Memphis Grizzlies	$4.5 million	2023
Wachovia Center	Wachovia Bank	Philadelphia 76ers, Flyers	$1.4 million	2023
Fleetcenter	Fleet Bank	Boston Celtics, Bruins	$2 million	2010

TABLE 2. (Continued)

STADIUM NAMING RIGHTS

Stadium name	Sponsor	Home teams	Avg. $/Year	Expires
Ford Field	Ford Motor Co.	Detroit Lions	$1 million	2042
Gaylord Entertainment Center	Gaylord Entertainment	Nashville Predators	$4 million	2018
General Motors Place	General Motors	Vancouver Canucks	$844,366	2015
Gillette Stadium	Gillette	New England Patriots	N/A	2017
Great American Ball Park	Great American Insur.	Cincinnati Reds	$2.5 million	2033
Gund Arena	Owners	Cleveland Cavs, Rockers	$700,000	2014
Heinz Field	H.J. Heinz	Pittsburgh Steelers	$2.9 million	2021
HSBC Arena	HSBC Bank	Buffalo Sabres	$800,000	2026
Invesco Field at Mile High	Invesco Funds	Denver Broncos	$6 million	2021
Jacobs Field	Richard Jacobs	Cleveland Indians	$695,000	2014
Key Arena	Key Corp.	Seattle Supersonics, Storm	$1 million	2010
Lincoln Financial Field	Lincoln Financial Group	Philadelphia Eagles	$6.7 million	2022
M & T Bank Stadium	M & T Bank	Baltimore Ravens	$5 million	2018
MCI Center	MCI	Wash. Wizards, Caps, Mystics	$2.2 million	2017
Mellon Arena	Mellon Financial	Pittsburgh Penguins	$1.8 million	2009
Miller Park	Miller Brewing	Milwaukee Brewers	$2.1 million	2020
Minute Maid Park	Coca Cola	Houston Astros	$6 million	2030
Nationwide Arena	Nationwide Insurance	Columbus BlueJackets	N/A	INDEFINITE
Network Associates Coliseum	Network Associates	Oakland A's	$1.2 million	2003
Office Depot Center	Office Depot	Florida Panthers	$1.4 million	2013
Pacific Bell Park	Pacific Telesis	San Francisco Giants	$2.1 million	2024
Pengrowth Saddledome	Pengrowth Mgmt.	Calgary Flames	$1 million	2016
Pepsi Center	PepsiCo	Denver Nuggets, Colorado Avalanche	$3.4 million	2019
Phillips Arena	Royal Phillips Electronics	Atlanta Hawks, Thrashers	$9.3 million	2019

(Continued)

TABLE 2.   (Continued)

STADIUM NAMING RIGHTS

Stadium name	Sponsor	Home teams	Avg. $/Year	Expires
PNC Park	PNC Bank	Pittsburgh Pirates	$2 million	2020
Pro Player Stadium	Fruit of the Loom	Miami Dolphins, Florida Marlins	COMPANY BANKRUPT	N/A
Qualcomm Stadium	Qualcomm	San Diego Padres, Chargers	$900,000	2017
Raymond James Stadium	Raymond James Financial	Tampa Bay Buccaneers	$3.1 million	2026
RBC Center	RBC Centura Banks	Carolina Hurricanes	$4 million	2022
RCA Dome	RCA	Indianapolis Colts	$1 million	2004
Reliant Stadium	Reliant Energy	Houston Texans	$10 million	2032
Safeco Field	Safeco Corp.	Seattle Mariners	$2 million	2019
Savvis Center	Savvis Communications	St. Louis Blues	N/A	DEFAULTED
SBC Center	SBC Communications	San Antonio Spurs	$2.1 million	2022
Skyreach Center	Skyreach Equipment	Edmonton Oilers	$675,493	2003
Staples Center	Staples	Los Angeles Lakers, Kings, Clippers, Sparks	$5.8 million	2019
St. Pete Times Forum	St. Petersburg Times	Tampa Bay Lightning	$2.1 million	2014
Target Center	Target	Minnesota Timberwolves, Lynx	$1.3 million	2005
TD Waterhouse Centre	TD Waterhouse Group	Orlando Magic, Miracle	$1.6 million	2003
Toyota Center	Toyota	Houston Rockets	N/A	N/A
Tropicana Field	Tropicana	Tampa Bay Devil Rays	$1.5 million	2026
United Center	United Airlines	Chicago Blackhawks, Bulls	$1.8 million	2014
U.S. Cellular Field	U.S. Cellular	Chicago White Sox	$3.4 million	2025
Xcel Energy Center	Xcel Energy	Minnesota Wild	$3 million	2024

Source: ESPN.com.
Copyright © 2003 ESPN Internet Ventures.

POLITICS

THE SPORTS FRANCHISE GAME: CITIES IN PURSUIT OF SPORTS FRANCHISES, EVENTS, STADIUMS, AND ARENAS

Kenneth L. Shropshire

Why do teams move? The obvious and most accepted reason is financial survival. . . But financial survival is not the sole motivation. Sport is a unique business. Moving a sports franchise is not an easy thing to do, even when a franchise is in dire financial straits and good business acumen would dictate a move to a fresh venue. However, a move by a franchise can be delayed, or even prevented, by other players in the sports franchise game. If the owner is an Al Davis, Charlie Finley, or Bill Veeck he may have trouble gaining league approval for a move not for business reasons but merely because the commissioner or a fellow owner or two does not like him.

A sports franchise owner has limited options compared with the proprietors of other businesses. Like operators of fast-food franchises such as McDonald's, a sports franchise owner usually cannot just pack up and relocate when such a move makes good economic sense to the owner. The guidelines for successful relocation of a sports franchise are not the same as those of a privately owned dry cleaning business, where the sole proprietor may choose to move to a site where customers may more fully appreciate the business. Sports franchises belong to a bigger entity, a professional sports league. The National Football League, National Basketball Association, Major League Baseball, and National Hockey League operate in much the same way as does a partnership. The individual teams within a league share profits but usually not individual franchise financial losses.

Several key parties affect the sports franchise business, and to varying degrees, each party looks out for his or her own self-interest. Apart from the owner and the league, the sports franchise business involves fellow owners, the athletes, the competing cities, politicians, and the fans. . . More so in the past but sometimes even today, these fans forget they are taxpayers and do not always realize the consequences of urging their politicians to do "whatever it takes" to convince a team to stay, to attract a new team, or in some cases, to coax a team back home. More frequently, some sports fans and politicians now show signs of decreasing zeal. A major portion of the 1990 Oakland mayoral campaign that saw longtime mayor Lionel Wilson voted from office focused on whether the city should make the investment to bring the Raiders professional football franchise back "home" from Los Angeles. Voters have refused to spend on sports in such diverse communities as Phoenix, San Francisco, Santa Clara, and San Jose. But this trend is not absolute. The voters in Denver, for example, said yes to a tax increase to finance stadium construction. They wanted a Major League Baseball expansion franchise and thought that building a stadium was the only way to get one. . .

Although money constitutes the main reason cities fight over sports franchises, cities also admit that their civic image is almost as important a factor. Today, sports pages constantly mention incidents of cities trying to entice a team or of a team trying to move to a new area. Direct and indirect economic benefits such as increased tourism, arena or stadium rental income, sports franchise expenditures in the city, taxes, and employment are often mythically thought to be guaranteed by the acquisition of a professional sports franchise. Such is the proverbial carrot at the end of a stick that cities chase. In reality, the only reward a city that successfully attracts a sports franchise may receive is the public perception that their metropolis has been thrust into that class of cities nebulously described as "big league."

The value of that big league label to a city defies accurate accounting. Some may perceive overhauling a city's image to be priceless. When the sports franchise game revs up in high gear, it certainly seems that virtual pricelessness is the value a team acquires. When the Los Angeles Rams deserted the inner city for suburban Anaheim, many civic leaders, headed by the late City Councilman Gilbert Lindsay, asserted that the situation must be remedied. Their position was that an expansion franchise was not enough. The "great" city of Los Angeles (and particularly the feisty councilman's downtown inner-city district) deserved a team with a "name" — certainly if Oakland and Anaheim had name franchises, Los Angeles should have one, too. That was part of the hyperbole that eventually brought the Raiders to Los Angeles from Oakland.

Sports franchises and American cities are not alone in their pursuit of sports. Nagano, Japan, spent between $11 million and $14.3 million on public relations alone in its successful efforts to host the 1998 Winter Olympics. And planners estimate that the cost of constructing facilities for the Winter Olympics in Nagano will exceed $2 billion. In an unsuccessful effort to land these same Olympics, the Utah state legislature approved expenditures of $56 million for the development of a site in Salt Lake City. In its bid to host the 2000 Summer Olympics, the Berlin bid committee announced that tickets to all events would be free. This policy represented the forfeiture of $68 million in potential ticket revenue.

The factor that seems to trigger most relocations today is the desire of an owner to make *more* money. The public reasons have ranged from complaints about the quality of the stadium or arena or having to share it with another tenant, to poor fan support or too small of a fan base. General complaints about the terms of the stadium or arena lease are often raised as the major point of contention as well. . . One key area of revenue that some owners began to tap in the 1970s is the luxury box, luxury suite, sky box, or executive suite. These seats, which are often elaborate suites, vary from facility to facility. Generally, such a suite is an enclosed area, approximately the same size as a living room, with a plexiglass front and great sight lines for the event. The suite may include elevator access, private bar, private restrooms, catering service, and customized decor. Generally, corporate entities purchase the suites at a price that includes enough tickets to fill the box with clients or potential clients or as an incentive or reward for employees. The revenue from these boxes, which can be worth millions per year to an owner, are generally retained by the home team. Unlike other game ticket revenues, this income is not likely to be shared with fellow league members. From an owner's viewpoint, a stadium with luxury boxes is far more valuable than one without them. . .

. . . . *[The author's discussion of revenue sharing is omitted. See discussion in Chapter 3.]*

A vivid example of the price a city may pay when competing for a franchise is instructive. St. Petersburg, Florida, has long publicly expressed the desire to be the home of a Major League Baseball franchise. In 1988, St. Petersburg spent tax dollars to build a 43,000-seat baseball stadium, the Florida Suncoast Dome, purely on speculation. No team had committed to move to St. Petersburg, and no expansion franchise was guaranteed. Without a commitment in place, even *more* money had to be spent to attempt to attract a franchise. An initial prime candidate for the new stadium was the Chicago White Sox, who played in what was the oldest stadium in baseball, Comiskey Park. St. Petersburg officials, via Lear jet, flew in a group of White Sox executives to present a sales pitch on the city and facility. The city further promised White Sox owner Jerry Reinsdorf a $10 million loan if the team would move south. A city official highlighted the recruitment with the statement, "If there is something else the White Sox need, I hope they tell us."

Motivations in the negotiation process are never fully revealed. The interest that the White Sox had in St. Petersburg may have been sincere. Once the St. Petersburg offer was received, however, Reinsdorf headed back for further negotiations in Chicago. In Chicago he was not only aided by the St. Petersburg offer but by the statement of Illinois Governor James Thompson, who said, "I'll bleed and die before I let the Sox leave Chicago."[29] In 1991 the new Comiskey Park opened in Chicago. The old Comiskey Park is now a parking lot. The state financed $150 million in construction and also paid for the construction-dictated demolition of one hundred family homes. The displaced residents were also paid $25,000 per household for their trouble. The $150-million deal followed an initial $120-million offer that St. Petersburg knocked out of contention. The funding for the new Comiskey Park came from a 2 percent tax on hotel and motel rooms in Chicago. The team will pay rent on the stadium only if the attendance at games exceeds 1.2 million fans per year. The deal was approved by the Illinois State Legislature in a midnight session and passed by only one vote.

. . . .

Spending by cities that are courting franchises generally represents the largest sports expenditure a city can make. Other expenditures, such as bids for Olympic Games or lesser sporting events, can have a major impact as well.

REFERENCES

29. "White Sox Incentive Deal Striking Out in Legislature," *Chicago Tribune,* May 29, 1988, p. 2.

DISCUSSION QUESTIONS

1. What is the relationship between player salaries and new stadium construction?
2. Why do the residents of many cities fight to keep sports franchises? Why do others "let" them go?
3. What is the likely reaction of a mayor to a franchise owner who threatens to relocate to another city?
4. Why do sports franchise owners often desire to relocate?

5. What types of business enterprises are most likely to enter into naming rights deals?

6. What are the seven reasons companies enter into naming rights deals?

7. Describe the basic structure of a naming rights deal.

8. What are the most important lease provisions related to stadium revenue generation?

9. What role do lease provisions play in sports franchise relocations? What role do they play in demands for new facilities?

10. Describe luxury suites, personal seat licenses, and club seats.

CHAPTER 6

MEDIA

INTRODUCTION

In most industries, a revenue stream periodically appears that ultimately leads to a fundamental change in the way that the industry conducts its business. The sports industry is no exception. Revenue sources for sports franchises have evolved over time, with owners continuously searching for new ways to profit from their investments. In sports, the sea change was fueled by television. Sports teams were able to generate significant amounts of revenue from the sale of the rights to televise their games to broadcasters. Broadcasters found that sports could attract an audience with significant buying power that was otherwise hard to reach in large numbers because of its inconsistent viewing habits — young male viewers in their 20s and 30s.

This demographically strong audience was quite attractive to companies searching for an effective medium through which they could advertise their products to their intended buyers. With this demographic in place, broadcasters were able to sell advertising spots on sports programs for a higher rate than on other programs. Thus was born the symbiotic relationship between sports, television, and advertisers that endures to this day. Though the relationship between these stakeholders has become increasingly complex with the passage of time and the introduction of both new broadcasting mediums and methods of distribution, today it is the rare sports business model that does not begin and end with television as the main financial driver. This is the case in all major successful sports enterprises around the globe. Whether it be a single pay-per-view or a multiyear broadcasting contract, there are few structural decisions that are made without first considering the impact on broadcast revenues.

This was not always the case. When television emerged as a role player in sports in the 1950s, the initial concern was about the negative impact broadcasting an event would have on live attendance at the gate. The logic of the owners of the day made sense. Why would fans pay to see a game in person when television would allow them to see the game for free? Those concerns were short-lived as the experiment with television proved to be both a financial engine and a fan base builder. Rather than leading to depletion in attendance as feared, television instead led to the creation of new fans who ultimately attended the games. In the 1960s television started to become the financial engine that it is today.

Many of the early concerns about the effect of television on gate attendance were addressed by establishing home game local broadcast and blackout rules. At the heart of the rules was the view by league leaders that "if the game is sold out, let's find a way to allow local fans to see the game." With the evolution of cable, satellite, and pay-per-view, the effect of television on the local gate has become even less of a concern.

Broadcasting of league games occurs at both the national and regional levels. All sports leagues collectively pool and sell their television rights on a league-wide level, with the resulting rights fee divided equally among all of the teams. These national television contracts are considered to be essential for the long-term success of a sports league, as leagues are provided with the broad exposure that is necessary to build spectator interest in the sport, as well as the revenues that are required for survival. Traditionally, national television contracts have been executed with networks that are available on free television nationwide. Whereas there were only three bona fide networks in the United States until the early 1990s, there are now six networks: long-time incumbents ABC, CBS, NBC, and relative newcomers Fox, WB, and UPN. In addition to the networks, over 80% of U.S. homes currently pay a monthly fee to subscribe to cable television. Technological innovations have led to the creation of hundreds of channels that are broadcast on cable television. Beginning with the advent of ESPN in 1979, a number of these cable channels searching for attractive content have broadcast sports programming because of its aforementioned appeal. There are now over 90,000 hours of sports programming broadcast in the United States each year, four times the amount shown in 1994.

The proliferation of general and sports-related programming options that are available to viewers has been the primary cause of the decrease in the ratings of televised sports. The ratings decrease has slowed down the growth of what was once rapidly increasing advertising rates, which has in turn contributed to a slowdown in the increases that the networks are willing to pay in rights fees to the leagues. Networks have lost significant amounts of money on their sports programming due to the enormous rights fees that they have paid and their inability to recoup their investment through advertising sales. Most notably, Fox has predicted that it will lose over $900 million on its existing rights deals with the NFL, MLB, and Nascar. Nonetheless, the networks are still interested in sports programming because of the ancillary benefits that it provides — namely, the promotional opportunities that it offers to its other, nonsports shows, and an important branding opportunity. The promotion of a network's prime-time lineup during its sports programming exposes this programming to an audience that would not otherwise be as likely to be aware of it. If this increased awareness leads some of the sports audience to watch these other offerings, then the network could see a ratings increase in its other programming and allow it to reap additional advertising revenues as a result. Thus, sports could be seen as an overall ratings driver for the network.

Sports programming also offers a network a significant branding opportunity. Fox established itself as a legitimate network when it acquired the broadcasting rights to the NFL and NHL in 1994. The network was able to use its acquisitions to add a number of affiliates in NFL markets that previously had balked at the opportunity to associate themselves with the fledgling network. With the leagues in tow, Fox had instant credibility. Thus, networks may be willing to view sports programming as a loss leader to a certain degree. Recently, NBC has been reluctant to pay the huge rights fees demanded by sports leagues and has turned to an array of niche sports instead. *[See Chapter 11 for a discussion of NBC's deal with the Arena Football League.]* This may be an indication of what the future holds for major sports properties on network television.

If this proves to be the case, cable television is likely to dominate the national broadcasting agreements entered into by major sports properties. As leagues seek out rights fee increases, cable television networks will be most able to bear the additional costs of doing so. This is a function of the fact that whereas broadcast networks receive revenues primarily from advertising, cable television networks have dual revenue streams — advertising and subscriber fees that they charge cable system operators for the right to carry their channels on their systems. This will enable them to better afford the high cost of sports programming. Carriage of sports programming is important for cable system operators despite the increasing subscriber fees sought by the cable networks because of subscriber demand for the programming and the need to differentiate themselves from their competitors, including direct satellite subscription providers such as DirecTV. However, some cable systems operators have negotiated fiercely with cable networks over proposed increases in subscriber fees. They feel that they must absorb some of this increase themselves rather than pass all of it along to their subscribers, many of whom have no interest in sports and do not want to pay higher cable bills in order to pay for the networks that carry this programming. This has led some cable systems operators to place many regional sports networks on a pay-tier where subscribers have to pay an additional monthly sum for access to the network instead of on an expanded basic cable package, where all subscribers have access to the channel. However, this is unlikely to occur for established national cable networks such as ESPN and TNT.

Despite a continued difference in penetration between network and cable television of approximately 15% of U.S. homes, the line between the two broadcasting universes is becoming increasingly blurred. Popular cable programming garners ratings that are competitive with network shows. Cross-ownership of network and cable broadcasters such as Disney's ownership of ABC and the ESPN channels, and News Corporation's ownership of Fox and Fox Sports Net has contributed to the distinction between cable and network being even less important. Thus, cable is likely to be the new national rights model for sports programming. This raises a significant transitional issue confronting sports leagues today, as they consider whether they should move away from the original network model and to what degree. The NBA led the way in this thinking by entering into a 6-year, $4.6 billion deal with ESPN, TNT, and ABC. Most analysts concluded that it is too early to tell whether this route is more beneficial to the relevant stakeholders than the league's single network focused model, but a few differences are clear. Although there are fewer viewers, there is an opportunity for the sports property to receive an increase in its rights fees. The NBA will earn more money over the length of this agreement than in its previous broadcasting contract with NBC and TNT, but these cable outlets only reach 80% of the households that network television reaches. But even with this, all of the broadcasters are experiencing better ratings than they did with the programming they had in place the year before.

In addition to the league-wide national agreements in place with network and cable broadcasters, sports franchises in the NBA, NHL, and MLB have individual deals in place with broadcasters in their home territories. These deals can be quite important, for the vast majority of each team's games are broadcast on this basis. It should be noted that in the NFL, the rights to all regular and postseason games are controlled by the national broadcast partners, with only preseason games shown on a local basis. The value of the local broadcasting agreement varies according to a number of factors, the most important of which is the size of the market in which the team plays. Prior to the advent of cable television, most of the local broadcasting agreements were with independent, over-the-air stations that had limited geographic reach. Cable television created the opportunity for teams to expand their presence on a more regional basis. The aforementioned proliferation of cable networks included a number of distinct regional sports networks (RSNs) whose programming is built around the home teams. Ultimately, there was a consolidation of many of these RSNs, and Fox Sports Net emerged as the dominant player in the marketplace with its ownership of 11 RSNs nationwide and an affiliation with 10 others. The majority of NBA, NHL, and MLB teams are broadcast partners with Fox Sports Net. The ratings for sports programming on RSNs is still strong, reflecting fans' continued interest in their home teams. Recognizing an opportunity to exploit its revenue potential, cable system operators, individual teams, and even leagues have started their own RSNs. In addition, a number of niche channels focusing on a single sport such as football, tennis, golf, auto racing, and nonrevenue college sports have either been launched or are in the planning stages. While the programming content on the RSN must be attractive to viewers or no one will watch it, it is apparent that distribution of the regional sports network to a large number of subscribers is a key to its success. There must be enough people who have access to the channel to allow advertising rates and subscription fees to sustain the RSN. Thus, it is vital for the RSN to be carried by a large number of cable systems. Without sufficient carriage, the RSN will fail. The RSN concept is still evolving and thus far has been met with varying degrees of success across the country. It clearly has not been the answer for every team. The Portland Trail Blazers, Seattle SuperSonics, and Dallas Stars all unsuccessfully attempted to launch a regional sports network. Notably, Trail Blazers owner and Microsoft cofounder Paul Allen's Action Sports Network lost a reported $25 million when the RSN failed after it could not get sufficient distribution in the Pacific Northwest. This embodies the significant risk that teams face when attempting to launch an RSN. While the potential payoff to sports teams that own their own RSN is huge, it is very difficult to do so. Carriage and distribution are difficult obstacles to overcome, especially for sports teams that are newcomers to this aspect of the television business. Even Disney was unsuccessful in its attempt to launch ESPNWest, a proposed regional sports channel that would have carried the games of both the Disney-owned Anaheim Angels and Mighty Ducks. This should send a cautionary note to any team attempting to launch its own RSN. It may be that the team is better off using the possibility of starting its own RSN as leverage in negotiating new rights fees deals with its local cable networks.

In the first article, Stanley Baran traces the history of the relationship between sports and television and provides a good starting point for the analysis that follows. In the second selection, Jere Longman examines the decrease in the popularity of televised sports in "Pro Leagues Ratings Drop; Nobody Is Quite Sure Why." This article provides a solid perspective on the importance of television and the nervousness that emerges from sports business leaders when ratings decline.

This is followed by a description of one league's strategy in television exposure, "The NBA Strategy of Broadcast Television Exposure: A Legal Application." This basketball-specific analysis is applicable to other sports as well.

Next, the structure of vertically integrated sports organizations is discussed in "Vertical Integration in Sports."

Sports properties have exerted considerable efforts to find other technological revenue streams beyond television. The "new media" certainly encompasses analog and digital cable, satellite, high definition television (HDTV), and other broadcast vehicles. The largest focus in this new media realm, however, has been the Internet. There is not a sector in the sports business that did not dabble in some way in cyberspace seeking to find a way to add the Internet to their business model. From ticket sales, to athletic apparel, to athletes chatting, the initial influx was huge.

The next article provides some nuts and bolts in Internet usage. The except from "Toward a Scheme for Football Clubs Seeking an Effective Presence on the Internet" suggests how a sports enterprise should contemplate incorporating the Internet into its business model.

The global nature of sports is clear in this context of broadcasting and new media. The excerpt from "Japanese Spectator Sport Industry: Cultural Changes Creating New Opportunities" focuses on the role of new media in the spread of sports. The Japanese market is the model here.

HISTORY

SPORTS AND TELEVISION

Stanley J. Baran

The history of sports on U.S. television is the history of sports on *network* television. Indeed, that history is closely related to the development and success of the major television networks. "Television got off the ground because of sports," reminisced pioneering television sports director Harry Coyle. He continued, "Today, maybe, sports need television to survive, but it was just the opposite when it first started. When we (NBC) put on the World Series in 1947, heavyweight fights, the Army–Navy football game, the sales of television sets just spurted."

With only 190,000 sets in use in 1948, the attraction of sports to the networks in its early period was not advertising dollars. Instead, broadcasters were looking toward the future of the medium, and aired sports as a means of boosting demand for television as a medium. They believed their strategy would eventually pay off in advertising revenues. But because NBC, CBS, and DuMont manufactured and sold receiver sets, their more immediate goal was to sell more of them. Sports did indeed draw viewers, and although the stunning acceptance and diffusion of television cannot be attributed solely to sports, the number of sets in use in the United States reached ten and a half million by 1950.

Technical and economic factors made sports attractive to the fledgling medium. Early television cameras were heavy and cumbersome and needed bright light to produce even a passable picture. Boxing and wrestling, contested in confined, very well-lit arenas and baseball and football, well-lit by the sun and played out in familiar, well-defined spaces, were perfect subjects for the lens. Equally important, because sporting events already existed there were no sets to build, no writers and actors to hire. This made sports inexpensive to produce, a primary concern when the audience was small and not yet generating large advertising revenues.

The first televised sporting event was a college baseball game between Columbia and Princeton in 1939, covered by one camera providing a point of view along the third base line. But the first network sports broadcast was NBC's *Gillette Cavalcade of Sports,* which premiered in 1944 with the Willie Pep vs. Chalky White Featherweight Championship bout. Sports soon became a fixture on prime-time network programming, often accounting for one-third of the networks' total evening fare. But in the 1950s, as television's other genres matured and developed their own large and loyal (and approximately 50% female) followings, sports began to disappear from network prime-time, settling into a very profitable and successful niche on weekends. This, too, would change, like so much else in television, with alterations in the technology and economics of the medium.

Gillette Cavalcade of Sports stayed on the network air for 20 years, a prime example of sporting events presented by a single sponsor. By the mid-1960s, however, televised sports had become so expensive that individual advertisers found it increasingly difficult to pay for sponsorship of major events by themselves. Still, the number of hours of sports on network television exploded as the audience grew and the multiplying ranks of spot-buying advertisers coveted these valuable minutes. This mutually beneficial situation persisted until well into the 1980s when the historically increasing amounts of advertising dollars began to decline, and networks experienced diminishing profit margins on sports.

But the economics of televised sports had begun to unravel earlier. In 1970, for example, the networks paid $50 million to broadcast the National Football League (NFL), $2 million for the National Basketball Association (NBA), and $18 million for major league baseball. In 1985 those figures had risen to $450 million, $45 million, and $160 million respectively. These large increases were fueled by growing public interest in professional sports, in part as a result of more and better television coverage. But equally important, the networks saw the broadcasting of big time sports as the hallmark of institutional supremacy in broadcasting. Major league sports meant major league broadcasting — not an unimportant issue for the networks now challenged by VCR, the newly empowered independent stations, and cable. Many of these cable channels were themselves carrying sports (WGN, WTBS, and HBO, for example), and one, ESPN, offered nothing but sports. Seemingly unconcerned, the CBS, NBC, and ABC attitude could be described as "Who cares about Australian Rules Football?" (a high point of early ESPN programming). (See Table 1 for the evolution of television rights fees.)

But rising fees for rights to major sporting events were not, in themselves, bad for the networks. They could afford them, and the cable and independent channels could not. But increasing rights fees, accompanied by falling ratings, proved to be disastrous. From 1980 to 1984, broadcasts of professional football lost 7% of their viewership (12% among men 18 to 34 years old) and baseball lost 26% of its viewers, showing a 63% decline among young males. Nonsports programming on cable, home video use, and the independents took many of these viewers. In addition, sports on the competing channels further diluted the remaining sports audience. To make up for falling revenues on all its programming as they began to lose audience, the networks began to raise the price of advertising time on sports shows to cover the huge rights fees contractually owed to the sports leagues.

Advertisers balked. Not only were they unwilling to pay higher prices for smaller audiences, but the once attractive male audience was becoming less desirable as working women came to control even larger amounts of consumer capital. Rather than pay what they saw as inflated rates for a smaller and now less prized set of viewers, many advertisers bought commercial time away from sports altogether, feeling they could reach their target audiences more efficiently through other types of shows. Car manufacturers turned to prime-time drama to reach women, who were increasingly making car-buying decisions; beer makers were turning to MTV to get young women and young men.

Finally, in order to make the most of their expensive contracts with the major sports leagues, the networks began broadcasting more sports. But spots on sports shows would have been easier to sell had there been fewer of them on the market. The three networks together showed 1,500 hours of sports in 1985, double what they programmed in 1960. With about 8 minutes of commercials an hour,

TABLE 1.

RECENT TELEVISION RIGHTS DEALS			
Contract period	Rights holder(s)	Total rights fee	Avg. annual value/league
NFL			
1994–1997	ABC, Fox, NBC, ESPN/TNT	$4.3 billion	$1.1 billion
1998–2005	ABC, Fox, CBS, ESPN	$17.6 billion	$2.2 billion
MLB			
1996–2000	Fox, NBC, ESPN	$1.7 billion	$340 million
2000–2005*	ESPN	$851 million	$141.8 million
2001–2006	Fox	$2.5 billion	$416.7 million
NBA			
1994–1998	NBC, TNT	$1.1 billion	$275 million
1998–2002	NBC, TNT/TBS	$2.64 billion	$660 million
2002–2008	ABC/ESPN, AOL Time Warner	$4.6 billion	$766.7 million
NHL			
1994–1999	Fox	$155 million	$31 million
1999–2004	ABC/ESPN	$600 million	$120 million
NASCAR			
2001–2008**	Fox/NBC, Turner	$2.4 billion	$400 million

*Terms of the deal replaced the terms of the previous MLB deal for ESPN for the 2000 season.
**Represents a six-year, $2.4 billion deal, plus two additional years for Fox. Under the terms of NASCAR's previous television contract, individual tracks made their own TV deals and Winston Cup races were spread across CBS, ABC, ESPN, TNN, TBS, and NBC for about $100 million in total rights fees paid.
Sources: Street & Smith's SportsBusiness Journal research, Gould Media, NFLPA.

the addition of even relatively few hours of programming had a noticeable effect on the supply-and-demand balance of the commercial spot market.

It was during this same period that superstations WTBS and WGN, and premium channel HBO, began national, cable-fed sports programming. ESPN was launched in 1979 and by mid-1980 reached 4 million homes. By 1986, 37 million households subscribed. The glut of sports on television was abetted even more by crucial court decisions affecting intercollegiate competition. Universities, desirous of their own access to broadcast riches, successfully challenged the National Collegiate Athletic Association (NCAA) and, at times their own regional athletic conferences, to be free of what they considered restrictive television contracts and broadcast revenue-sharing agreements. College basketball and football, once local or regional in appeal, began appearing on the television dial in a complex array of syndication packages and school-centered or conference-centered television networks.

While the history of televised sports may have been directly related to network television, the current and future states of the genre certainly are not. There are more televised sports today than ever before and they continue to draw a large total audience, but it is an audience fragmented among many available choices. Sports on television, then, is decreasingly likely to originate on a national network. Despite the Super Bowl's annually growing audience and increases in the price of a 30-second spot . . . it remains a television anomaly, unique as a television and cultural event. Ratings for individual television sports programs generally continue to decline . . .

. . . . *[The author's discussion of the industrial benefits, appeal, aesthetics, and reality of television is omitted.]*

Current Status

Pro Leagues' Ratings Drop; Nobody Is Quite Sure Why

Jere Longman

There has never been a more uncertain moment in the recent history of America's $250-billion-a-year sports industry.

Broadcast television ratings for the four major professional sports — baseball, basketball, football, and hockey — have been generally decreasing for more than a decade. (See Table 2 for a list of the top-rated television sports events.) With the exception of the National Football League, average attendance at games in the most established pro sports has been static or diminishing. No one is certain why this is happening. Some experts contend that declining ratings and static attendance do not mean that Americans are losing interest in sports. They note that the fees paid by television networks to broadcast major professional sports continue to rise, as does the value of most franchises.

But others think that there are signs of a fundamental change in the golden age of American sports, which began in the last quarter of the 19th century.

"Sport just doesn't carry the central metaphoric position in our culture that it did in 1935," said Robert Thompson, a professor of pop culture and television at Syracuse University. "When Richard Hatch can become a reluctant American hero on 'Survivor,' then the question of 'Where have you gone, Joe DiMaggio?' becomes very relevant."

America's interest in sports has become as fragmented as its interest in television, many experts say. Golf has its own cable channel. Women's professional leagues now exist in basketball, soccer, and softball. Extreme sports like snowboarding, mountain biking, and windsurfing have become mainstream. Figure skating and stock car racing have developed such broad appeal that over the past seven years, only the National Football League has drawn consistently higher ratings.

The way Americans experience sports has changed dramatically. There are now more cable versions of ESPN (four) than there were broadcast networks (three) a decade ago. The proliferation of the Internet and of regional cable networks and satellite packages have further diluted the broadcast networks' television ratings.

TABLE 2.

2001–2002 Top Rated TV Sports Events			
	Date	*Net*	*Rtg/Sh*
1 Super Bowl XXXVI (Patriots vs Rams)	2/3/2002	FOX	40.4/61
2 Winter Olympics (Women's figure skating long program, men's GS)	2/21/2002	NBC	26.8/41
3 MLB World Series — Game 7 (Yankees at D'backs)	11/4/2001	FOX	23.5/34
4 NFC Championship Game (Eagles at Rams)	1/27/2002	FOX	22.7/40
5 Winter Olympics (Women's figure skating short program, women's b'sled final)	2/19/2002	NBC	22.3/34
6 AFC Championship Game (Patriots at Steelers)	1/27/2002	CBS	21.2/46
7 Winter Olympics (Pairs figure skating long program, men's singles luge final; men's halfpipe)	2/11/2002	NBC	19.6/30
8 NFC Playoff Game (Packers at Rams)	1/20/2002	FOX	19.5/36
9 Winter Olympics (Women's slalom, men's/women's skeleton final; men's 1500 short track)	2/20/2002	NBC	19.5/31
10 Winter Olympics (Men's figure skating short program, ski jumping)	2/12/2002	NBC	18.5/29

Final 2001–2002 network television ratings for nationally telecast sports events, according to Nielsen Media Research. Covers period from Sept. 1, 2001, through Aug. 31, 2002. Events are listed with ratings points and audience share; each ratings point represents 1,055,000 households and shares indicate percentage of TV sets in use.
Source: http://www.infoplease.com/ipsa/A0884496.html.

Some people speculate that mainstream professional sports might be following the life cycle of any other product, meaning that baseball, football, basketball, and hockey could be in a period of late growth, or in some cases, early decline.

The concerns of sports leagues and television networks are apparent in cold, hard numbers:

- Ratings for the World Series sank to record lows in two of the last three years. Attendance for Major League Baseball reached a high last season at 72 million, but the average attendance was a thousand fewer than before the player strike in 1994. The sport is considering reducing the number of franchises.

- While the National Football League has continued to set attendance records, its television ratings hit a low in the 2000 regular season; this season, it will move some playoff games into prime time in an attempt to improve ratings.
- The 2001 National Basketball Association finals tied for the third-lowest rated ever. The N.B.A.'s regular-season ratings are down 40 percent since 1995–96. Attendance has dropped in three of the past four seasons.
- The National Hockey League's attempt to expand from regional to national appeal was blunted by poor television ratings this season. While revenues are up, the league is drawing only 500 more fans a game than five years ago.

(See Figure 1 for a list of television ratings and advertising costs for the Super Bowl.)

"There is always concern when ratings decline," said Sean McManus, president of CBS Sports. "I think we're kind of in a series of crossroads. It's an evolving industry, and one that hopefully will make sense economically for the networks. If it stops making sense, somebody will say, 'Enough is enough; we'd rather put on old movies instead of golf or football or basketball.' "

THE EROSION OF TRADITION

There seems to be a growing dislocation between fans and traditional sports, as players, coaches, and teams move frequently, as athletes misbehave publicly, as salaries skyrocket, and as ticket prices become prohibitive, many experts said. When Jerry Buss bought the Los Angeles Lakers in 1979, a courtside seat cost $15 a game. Next season, it will cost $1,500.

"We've become unhinged as traditional fans," said Richard Lapchick, director of the Center for the Study of Sport in Society at Northeastern University.

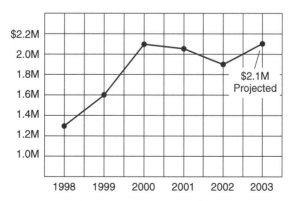

Rates are the estimated average cost for a 30 second commercial.

Source: Advertising Age.

Figure 1 Super Bowl ad rates.

Once, sports made heroes of the common man. As athletes become multimillionaires, that becomes much more difficult. Asked why fans resented the astronomical salaries of athletes but not of movie stars, Sharon Treacy of Fawn Grove, Pa., said at an NBA playoff game last May, "Because we don't have to pay $113 to get into a movie."

There may also be a racial component to dwindling television and attendance figures, as predominantly white audiences are faced with the growing diversity of sports teams. "To market a game that's played increasingly by young African-Americans, not hiding their history and heritage, to upper middle-class white guys getting their companies to buy tickets is a continuing challenge," said Jay Coakley, a sports sociologist at the University of Colorado at Colorado Springs.

America's thirst for a different sporting experience can be seen in the explosion of youth soccer. It can be seen in the construction of more than 100 minor league baseball parks, with their intimate atmosphere and inexpensive tickets, since 1990. It can be seen, too, in the fact that the most celebrated American athlete of the spring was a high school runner, Alan Webb, who broke the national schoolboy record for the mile.

Most visibly, this yearning could be seen during the 1999 Women's World Cup of soccer, an event that began off the public radar and, in three weeks, built itself with joyful, fierce team play into a galvanizing moment that attracted 90,000 people to the Rose Bowl and 40 million watching on American television.

Habits that once led youngsters to become fans at an early age are also changing. Children are more likely to be home mastering video games than roaming the neighborhood looking for sandlot ball games, said Thompson, the Syracuse University professor. Team sports have become so structured that individual sports like skateboarding and inline skating have become popular alternatives, a form of rebellion from strict youth sports organizations and overbearing parents.

Americans are also growing increasingly numb to spectacle and are seeking a more personal, simple, and direct connection with the world around them, said Charles Hess, managing director of Inferential Focus, a New York consulting firm that monitors societal change. That might help explain why so many more people are participating in the solitary pursuit of road racing. In 1999, 7.1 million Americans finished a road race, as against 3 million in 1985, according to the United States Track and Field Federation.

"Professional sports have been so successful at marketing and packaging, they've created a product which is a little too remote from the fans," said Craig Masback, chief executive officer of the Track and Field Federation. "I think people want to participate or attend where they feel like they have some connection.

"Participation in running and golf has gone up. Look at minor league sports, track meets, women's events. It's for regular people. It doesn't cost as much. You can take your family and get near the athletes, whether it's the women soccer players or Marion Jones signing autographs until everyone leaves."

SPONSORSHIP SPENDING RISES

Although the signs of change are everywhere, the broadcast television networks are not about to give up their investment in professional sports. The big leagues are still big business.

Not only is the value of franchises and broadcast fees continuing to rise, but spending on athletic sponsorship rights by corporations increased to $5.9 billion in 2000 from $5.1 billion in 1999, according to industry estimates. *[It is estimated that this spending increased to $7 billion in 2003.]*

Broadcasting major professional sporting events still gives networks an aura of major league status. It also enables them to promote their entertainment programs, all the while keeping big-ticket events like the Super Bowl or World Series away from their competitors.

"The fan base can even be growing while TV ratings decline," said Nadine Gelberg, executive director of sports and entertainment for Harris Interactive, the market research and polling firm. "It's not that sports no longer are reflective of our cultural values. How we experience sports has changed."

The splintering of the television audience can be seen in statistics compiled by CBS, based on data from Nielsen Media Research. In 1990, the three broadcast networks at the time televised 1,572 hours of sports programming. In 2000, with Fox added to the network sports lineup, the hours climbed to 2,453. Meanwhile, the average television sports audience dipped from 8.7 million viewers to 6.8 million. That 22 percent decline, however, is less than the 30 percent decline of overall network viewing since the mid-1980s, which gives television sports their cachet.

It might seem logical that the exorbitant fees the networks pay to sports leagues to broadcast their games would also decline. Not necessarily, network and league executives say. While the exponential growth of fees paid for television rights might level off, an actual decrease will most likely occur only if all the networks begin losing hundreds of millions of dollars on their sports deals, said Dick Ebersol, the chairman of NBC Sports.

In other words, the more difficult it becomes to attract a broad audience in these fragmented times, the more attractive major sporting events become to networks and corporate sponsors. Even with declining ratings, NBC remains sanguine about its contracts worth $3.5 billion to broadcast the Olympics through 2008, because this is the only event that gets the entire family in front of the television set.

"It makes the big events probably even more appealing than they were 10 to 15 years ago," said Chuck Fruit, marketing chief for Coca-Cola.

CBS's loss, after three decades, of its National Football Conference contract in 1993 was like "trying to play the game with one arm," said Leslie Moonves, president of CBS Television. So CBS was more than willing to shell out $500 million a year for the American Football Conference contract in 1998. CBS has also agreed to pay $6 billion over 11 years for the NCAA men's basketball tournament, an arrangement that includes Internet rights and other collegiate championships.

"When CBS lost the NFL, it was a devastating loss," McManus, the president of CBS Sports, said. "We're the No. 1 network now in terms of having the largest audience watching our programming. I don't think anyone would argue that we would be in that position without the NFL. We can promote our prime-time lineup from August through January. It's possible for a network to survive without the NFL, but it's difficult to survive long-term without that programming.

"But if the deals start becoming economic disasters, then a network may make that decision. Hopefully, we manage our business well enough so that we never reach that point."

Still, the new television climate has produced evident tension among sports leagues, broadcast networks, their affiliates, and advertisers. NBC has opted out of the NFL, projecting that it would lose $150 million a year, an amount Ebersol calls "obscene." Against his advice, NBC's West Coast affiliates plan to show the 2002 Winter Olympics from Salt Lake City on videotape instead of live, in an effort to maximize ratings.

Ebersol said he was more concerned about a weakening economy than soft ratings. Fewer dollars from corporate sponsorships would mean fewer dollars for networks to pay in fees to professional leagues, which would then have fewer dollars to pay athletes.

"And then," Ebersol said, "you get to the point of, does a shortstop batting .220 have a fundamental right to make $2 million or $3 million a year?"

THE NBA STRATEGY OF BROADCAST TELEVISION EXPOSURE: A LEGAL APPLICATION

John A. Fortunato

I. INTRODUCTION

Sports television is a unique form of broadcasting compared to other programming genres because of the relationship between a professional sports league and a broadcast network. The most unique characteristic of sports television is that a league and a television network sign a multi-year contract for broadcasting rights. Television networks pay large sums of money to a sports league for the rights to broadcast a certain number of games over a certain number of years. The television network then sells the commercial time during these games to advertisers. This unique relationship exists because a sports league is granted permission by the federal government through the Sports Broadcasting Act (hereinafter "SBA"), to act as a cartel and collectively package and sell the broadcast rights of its games to television networks. Professional sports leagues reap their greatest economic rewards and gain their most significant exposure source through network television contracts.

. . . . *[The author's discussion of literature review and antitrust issues is omitted.]*

B. Sports Broadcasting Act

. . . The leagues and the networks petitioned Congress for permission to pool and sell the broadcast rights to television networks. The result of hearings before the House of Representatives was the SBA, which was approved by Congress on September 30, 1961. The new law simply granted clubs in professional sports leagues an antitrust exemption allowing them to pool their broadcast rights for the purpose of selling those rights to the highest bidder. The purpose of the SBA is different from that of the Sherman Anti-Trust Act (hereinafter "Sherman Act"), which is designed to ensure free market competition and prevent restriction of trade.

The SBA established the legality of the professional sports leagues' practice of packaging league games to a network and not allowing teams to individually sell their rights, which would otherwise be an unlawful restraint on competition. The SBA is, however, a "special interest legislation, a single-industry exception to a law designed for the protection of the public."[37] Section 1291 of the SBA amended antitrust laws so that they "shall not apply to any joint agreement by or among persons engaging in or conducting the organized professional team sports of football, baseball, basketball, or hockey, by which any league of clubs . . . sells or otherwise transfers all right or any part of the right of such league's member clubs in the sponsored telecasting of the games."[38]

The SBA facilitates the acquisition of network television money by professional sports leagues, entitling the leagues to their greatest source of revenue. In its current television broadcast contract signed on November 12, 1997, and beginning with the 1998–1999 season, the NBA once again substantially increased its broadcast rights revenues to a total of $2.64 billion. NBC doubled its payments to a total of $1.75 billion (up from $750 million) and Turner more than doubled its payments to a total of $890 million (up from $350 million) for a four-year contract through the 2001–2002 season. *[The NBA subsequently agreed to a 6-year, $4.6 billion television deal with ABC/ESPN and Turner beginning in the 2002–2003 season. ABC/ESPN will pay $2.4 million and Turner will pay $2.2 million in a deal that runs through the 2007–2008 season.]* Tommy Roy, Co-Executive Producer for the NBA on NBC, describes the professional sports league and television network partnership as a cycle where if the NBA does well, more people watch the games, which provides higher ratings and advertising, and eventually leads to rights fees for the league.

C. Exposure: The "Less is More" Strategy

. . . .

While the SBA permits a league as a collective to sell broadcast rights for its games to networks, it does not prohibit individual teams from entering into their own national television contracts. These individual team broadcast contracts hinder the league's control and maintenance over national television exposure. The NBA took several measures, including litigation, to limit the rights of individual teams to sell games so the league could maximize the value of the television rights it sells to the national networks.

During the late 1970s and through the mid-1980s broadcast exposure was a major problem for the NBA: few regular season games were being broadcast, some playoff games were not being broadcast on television, and even some games of the NBA Finals were being broadcast on tape delay. This exposure problem is highlighted by the 1981 NBA Finals between the Boston Celtics and the Houston Rockets when four of the six games were broadcast on tape delay at 11:30 p.m. One of the first initiatives the NBA implemented during these years to increase the league's finances and marketability was for the league as a whole to take greater control of its television exposure. Specifically, the league exerted more control over the independent franchises that had the capability to get their games broadcast on national television superstations. The NBA defined a superstation as "any commercial over-the-air television station whose broadcast signal is received outside of the local Designated Market Area." The Atlanta Hawks, Chicago Bulls, and New Jersey Nets were three franchises who were able to get their games broadcast on the three NBA-recognized superstations: TBS, WGN, and WOR respectively. The league, along with its broadcast partners, can control exposure by creating a programming schedule that carefully selects days and times of games and also the players and teams who will appear on network television broadcasts.

The NBA adopted a "less is more" strategy where the league would better attempt to control the positioning of the NBA on television and not saturate the market with games. Regarding the "less is more" strategy, NBA Commissioner David Stern states, "when your ratings are not strong, and your product is not secure in its identity, a lot of exposure is not a good thing because the worst thing for a bad product is a lot of exposure, and so we were trying to shape up our product at the same time that we were trying to define exposure."[52] . . .

. . . .

D. Exposure: Superstations and the WGN Lawsuit

In 1979, the NBA made its initial attempt to legislate the exposure of its game telecasts. The NBA's Board of Governors adopted a resolution that all future television contracts entered into by individual teams would be made "subject to the Constitution, Bylaws and all other rules and regulations" of the league, "as they present ly exist and as they may from time to time be amended," subject to "the terms of any existing or future" television contracts entered into by the league and subject to review by the Commissioner to guarantee compliance.[54] The Board of Governors also passed a resolution providing the league with "the exclusive right to enter into contracts for the direct telecasting of NBA games by cable systems located outside the territory of all members."[55]

The new resolution voided a national contract the New York Knicks had signed with the USA Network, which was to pay the Knicks $1.5 million for the broadcast rights to their games for three seasons from 1979–80 to 1981–82. The NBA continued with their "less is more" strategy restricting exposure, and for the 1980–81 season teams were limited to forty-one over-the-air telecasts because, for example, the Atlanta Hawks for the 1979–80 season had broadcast all eighty-two of their regular season games on TBS. At the time, the NBA was not receiving revenue from independent individual team broadcast rights contracts — only the Hawks profited from their contract with TBS.

Teams were still permitted to sell the other forty-one nonnetwork games (if they were not on CBS — the national television network for the NBA from 1974 to 1990) to a local cable outlet only, and keep all of the revenue from whatever contracts they signed. The NBA agreed to broadcast its games on national cable outlets, signing contracts for the 1982–83 and 1983–84 seasons with both ESPN and USA for forty games with ESPN televising on Sunday night and USA televising on Thursday night. The NBA would not allow any of these forty-one nonnetwork games to be nationally broadcast opposite its new cable partners.

The NBA continued to impose restraints on its teams' ability to broadcast independently on a national network by limiting the superstation games to twenty-five for the 1985–86 season. In October 1989, the NBA passed a resolution "'blacking out' superstation games on nights when an NBA game is shown nationally on cable as part of the league's national cable package." While individual teams are not permitted to broadcast a game on a superstation opposite a TNT or TBS game, teams can air a game head to head with a TNT or TBS game, but strictly on a local over-the-air or local cable channel. For example, if the New York Knicks are playing the Chicago Bulls on TNT, the game could not be broadcast nationally on WGN because it is a superstation, but could be televised on the Madison Square Garden Network (hereinafter "MSG"), the local carrier for the Knicks. Games that are televised on NBC are not permitted to be broadcast by an individual team carrier at all, not even on tape delay. For example, if the New York Knicks are playing the Chicago Bulls on NBC, neither WGN nor MSG would be permitted to broadcast that game live or at any other later moment.

In 1990, WGN and the Chicago Bulls challenged the NBA's attempt to control the television packaging of its product by reducing the number of games on superstations from twenty-five to twenty. WGN and the Bulls sued the NBA to have the number remain at twenty-five, arguing that the antitrust exemption provided in the SBA of 1961 did not apply, and this limit was an unreasonable restraint of trade. The Bulls had approved the Board of Governors' resolutions for earlier reductions to forty-one and subsequently twenty-five games, but moved to block this further restriction. At the time WGN reached 34% of all of the television households nationwide, and 31% of those homes were outside of the Chicago area. WGN received no money from cable subscription, and relying on advertising sales for 98% of its revenues, was losing money by not having the Bulls games broadcast to the entire nation. The Bulls and WGN also had a successful ratings and advertising commodity with the broadcast rights to the most talented and marketable player — Michael Jordan.

In the early 1990s, WGN and the Bulls also failed to take advantage of a tremendous advertising opportunity. Due to microwave transmission technology, a superstation could generate two signals, one for local over-the-air, and another to send out to the rest of the nation. Ted Turner had been using this technology of splitting the feed with TBS in Atlanta and thus, for one program, had the ability to double the advertising revenues with two feeds to sell two different sets of advertising: (1) local spots for Atlanta viewers only, and (2) national spots which would be seen throughout the country. While WGN had not been splitting the feed for its Bulls telecasts, the superstation had been using this transmission technology for its broadcasts of Cubs baseball games. For its baseball telecasts, WGN offered advertisers three possibilities: (1) over-the-air Chicago only, (2) national cable only, or (3) both.

E. NBA Position on WGN and Exposure

The positioning of the NBA in this legal matter and its rationale behind the need to limit the number of national broadcasts on superstations refers directly back to the main benefits a league achieves when it signs a national television contract: revenue and the proper exposure. The NBA was not receiving any revenue or exposure from the contract between the Bulls and WGN. The beliefs of the NBA were clearly spelled out in the Proposed Findings of Fact and the Proposed Findings of Law that were filed by the NBA and cited in the case. The extensive rationale of the NBA's argument is:

The reduction protects the teams' grant of exclusivity in their local markets, and enhances the value of the teams' local television contracts by protecting the exclusivity of those contracts from dilution caused by the importation of games from other NBA cities by reason of superstation telecasts. It also promotes the teams' media and sponsor relationships. It protects the value of the market extension agreements pursuant to which cable systems pay a fee shared equally by all NBA teams for the right to telecast local cable games in a team's extended market. It enhances the ability of the NBA to grant exclusive and lucrative national broadcast contracts and protects the value of those contracts. It ensures the league is compensated for all national exposure of its games. It preserves the price sponsors pay for national exposure on NBA national cablecasts and broadcasts. It promotes the NBA's relationship with the national broadcast and cable networks. It enhances the perception in the marketplace that the NBA offers a unique product and has control over that product. It fosters the development by the NBA of new technologies. It improves the level of competition in the television market and benefits consumers by making the NBA a stronger competitor and by providing greater national network coverage of NBA games. And in the long run, if the NBA as a league has no right to regulate the national distribution of NBA games by individual teams, the attractiveness of the league's national television product will be undermined, its national and local revenues will decline, the weaker teams will face financial difficulties, and the league's future will be threatened. The NBA also believed that its position was viable under the Sherman Act because the reduction of games actually promotes competition "between the NBA's network packages and other network programming and between local NBA broadcasts by the teams and other local programming."

. . . . *[The author's discussion of the ruling in the WGN case in favor of WGN and the Chicago Bulls is omitted.]*

G. NBA Exposure Strategy

As a result of the NBA efforts through the *WGN* case, the league, and not individual teams, has control over all of its national television exposure. Once the league has permission granted by the government for economic and exposure control over its product, the NBA along with its broadcast partners can determine how to best present the league in terms of placement of the schedule and which teams and players to televise. . . . All NBA broadcast partners increase the number of game telecasts during the playoffs. The preference of network television in scheduling league games is still a prevalent strategy employed by the NBA. As the largest revenue source for the NBA and to preserve the lucrative broadcast income, television networks need to broadcast the best games that will achieve the highest audience ratings and advertising dollars. To demonstrate the importance of the network television schedule, the overall NBA game schedule is composed after the national television schedule is arranged.

The broadcast partners are always involved in formulating the NBA season and television schedule. . . . This negotiation of the program schedule is where the strength of the relationship between the NBA and its broadcast partners can easily be recognized; the national television broadcasts are the best opportunity to showcase the league from the NBA perspective, and the networks simply want the most popular game. Commissioner Stern explains that "we used to be much more insistent that every team be represented a certain amount, and frankly we have been more open to the networks' strategic view, which is the way to grow the sport is to focus on those teams that people want to see."[86] . . .

. . . .

Through this scenario, the networks are receiving the most desirable NBA product for their broadcasts: competitive teams featuring the top players in the league. Problems could arise between franchises as certain teams are obviously on national television more than others. Teams such as New York, Los Angeles, and Chicago might receive national exposure often, but through the NBA broadcast agreements, each team receives the same amount of national television revenue. Dave Checketts, former President and CEO of Madison Square Garden, explains the situation:

"We don't forget about the fact that we get a major share of the national revenue. [However] . . . we get 1/29th of the national revenue and our marketplace probably accounts for 1/7th of the watching audience. . . . If we were to really argue that case, we would say we deserve much more than 1/29th and so you shouldn't put the Knicks on national television any more than you do anyone else. . . . The truth is they put the Knicks on . . . as many times as they possibly can, because we do have such interest in New York."[89]

The rights fees from the league's broadcast partners represent the single largest source of shared revenue among the twenty-nine NBA franchises. These franchises, in essence, have agreed not to compete with one another in the area of broadcasting. In a free open market and each team having permission to negotiate their own national television contract, strong franchises from large media markets such as the New York Knicks or Los Angeles Lakers would easily earn more money than franchises in smaller markets such as the Sacramento Kings or the Memphis Grizzlies. The greater revenue could easily alter the scales of competitive balance between all of the teams with large market teams being able to sign more high-priced talent. The rationale for the revenue sharing of the NBA is commented on in *Chicago Prof'l Sports Ltd. P'ship and WGN Cont'l Broad. Co. v. NBA:*

"It is not disputed, and it is plain from the financial figures, that the prosperity of the league currently depends on the volume of the shared revenues generated by the league's economic activity on behalf of the teams and particularly on the revenues generated by the broadcast contracts with the national networks."[90]

Ed Desser comments on the league revenue sharing ideas and the importance of these objectives in the overall operation of the NBA, stating how the revenue aspects of this play into issues of competitive balance:

"There are a whole variety of systems that are designed to help maintain the integrity and quality of the product. It goes beyond just how it is televised or how it is presented. . . . Milwaukee and San Antonio collect the same amount of network television revenue as the Knicks and the Lakers [in order to give] them the same number of chips, or close to the same number of chips, to play with as they compete for talent."[91]

IV. CONCLUSION

The purpose of this paper is to demonstrate that the federal government permits the NBA, at the expense of individual teams, to systematically maintain control over national television exposure of its games. The philosophy of the federal government is clear: professional sports leagues are unique and deserving of special legislation like the SBA of 1961, which allows the league to pool the broadcast rights to their games to the highest television network bidder. Once this right to collectively package and sell the rights to games has been granted, sports leagues now have their greatest source of revenue.

In addition to unmatched revenue, television provides unmatched exposure. The NBA policy of television exposure is, if not dictated by, at least permissible through, both legislative and judicial government guidelines. . . . The NBA, and not individual teams, must have the ability to control the overall television exposure of its games in order to maintain the value of national television rights contracts. The NBA's extensive litigation in the *WGN* case, particularly since it essentially focused on five games of the Chicago Bulls, was illustrative of the league exerting its right to maintain economic value and control exposure of national television. Once league-wide control is permitted, the NBA and its broadcast partners can then create a schedule of teams and games that is the most appealing to the national television audience.

REFERENCES

37. *Chicago Prof'l Sports Ltd. P'ship v. Nat'l Basketball Ass'n,* 961 F.2d 667, 671 (7th Cir. 1992).
38. 15 U.S.C. § 1291 (1961).
52. Interview with David Stern, commissioner, NBA (Apr. 14, 1999).

54. *Chicago Prof'l Sports Ltd. P'ship v. Nat'l Basketball Ass'n,* 754 F. Supp. 1336, 1342 (N.D. Ill. 1991).

55. Id.

86. Interview with David Stern, commissioner, NBA (Apr. 14, 1999).

89. Interview with Dave Checketts, former president & CEO, Madison Square Garden (Oct. 16, 1998).

90. *Chicago Prof'l Sports Ltd. P'ship v. Nat'l Basketball Ass'n,* 754 F. Supp. 1336, 1340 (N.D. Ill. 1991).

91. Interview with Ed Desser, president, NBA Television (Aug. 26, 1998).

Structural Considerations

Vertical Integration in Sport

David K. Stotlar

Traditionally, vertical integration has been defined as a strategy wherein a corporation extends its scope of operations either backward toward suppliers or forward toward retailers and consumers. . . . Risks of vertical integration exist in both cases. In backward vertical integration, a company is exposed to increased risks as capital investment demands typically increase. This is clearly visible in sport where integrating backward exposes the firm to the continued escalation in player salaries. The risks of forward integration exist through fluctuations in consumer demand. If demand falters, producers are left with inventory that no one wants. Thus far in sport, consumer demand has continued to rise, although in some sports, spectator attendance has declined.

The benefits of vertical integration include cost savings realized through a reduction of redundant services and personnel . . . Disney provides the best example of this advantage. With ownership of the Anaheim Angels and the Mighty Ducks, Disney personnel can provide services to both operations at critical times during their respective seasons. While some season overlap is unavoidable, the winter-summer dichotomy does provide economies of labor for Disney . . .

One of the drawbacks of vertical integration is that some business units of the integrated corporation resent having to purchase from mandated suppliers . . . This was one of the key elements that prompted Disney Sport to change its name to Anaheim Sport. Under the Disney moniker, the purchase and supplier requirements were deemed by management to be too restrictive.

In 1995, when Disney acquired Capital Cities/ABC, it consolidated its cable, pay TV, and Buena Vista Television production operations under Capital Cities/ABC management. This demonstrates the efficiencies that were gained through the acquisition. . . .

Primary players in the vertical integration game (Disney, News Corp., and Time-Warner) are essentially distribution entities for an array of sport program content. Every distributor knows that the supply of product and material is critical to success in any industry. Backward vertical integration is performed, in part, to assure sources of supply. It presents a classic "make vs. buy" dilemma. The sport industry . . . introduces three ingredients: sport production, sport performance, and sport promotion. Disney, News Corp., and Time-Warner operate primarily in the performance and promotion segments of sport. Yet, if we take a broader view of the industry and envision these companies operating in an industry called sport and entertainment, they may actually participate in production, distribution, and retail sales of properties in the industry.

. . . The following is a partial listing of the sport and entertainment properties *[at various times]* owned or controlled by Disney:

- A&E Network (minority position)
- ABC Sports
- ABC Television
- Anaheim Angels (MLB)
- Buena Vista Pictures
- Disney Channel (43 million households)
- Disney's Wide World of Sports
- E! Entertainment (minority position, reaching 24% of all US households)
- ESPN (75 million households)
- ESPN2 (61 million households)
- ESPN Classic (15 million households)
- ESPN International (150 million households, 20 languages)
- ESPNEWS (10 million households)
- History Channel (minority position)
- Hollywood Records
- Lifetime Television (50%)
- Lyric Street Records
- Mammoth Records
- Mighty Ducks of Anaheim (NHL)
- Miramax (film)
- Ownership of 10 Broadcast Stations[1]

Rupert Murdoch acknowledged that much of News Corp.'s success was attributable to the formation of a "vertically integrated global media company." He also stated that "it is true that Disney and ABC form an immense and powerful vertically integrated company," but he added, "we built the prototype." Central to the issue of content is television programming. . . .

Murdoch's attempt to purchase England's Manchester United soccer team (through subsidiary BSkyB) for 627 million pounds (1.05 billion U.S. dollars) was centered on "providing content for his media empire." News Corp.'s attempt to purchase the team was eventually thwarted by the Monopolies and Merger Commission as anticompetitive. However, the Manchester United deal is not the only source for content. Murdoch was also able to negotiate a deal in early 1999 with Tele-Communications, Inc. (TCI) through their joint Fox Liberty Networks to buy 40% of Cablevision's sport assets (multiple regional Fox Sport stations, the Madison Square Garden Network, and 40% of the Knicks and Rangers) for $850 million to add to the regional coverage for Fox Sports Network.

. . . . .

The Manchester United tactic also was predicated, in part, to allow Murdoch to sit at both sides of the negotiating table. As the current rights holder for the league, BSkyB would be looking to extend their contractual rights to televise Premier League matches. Yet, as the primary shareholder of Manchester United, Murdoch would also be entitled to a seat on the League side of the negotiations. Ownership of the team would provide access to the team's players, team highlights, videos, and international pay TV around the globe, as well. Manchester United is, perhaps, the most popular sports team in the world, and Murdoch's publishing arm, Harper-Collins, would be sure to profit handsomely.

Murdoch's purchase of the Los Angeles Dodgers ($311 million, which included Dodger Stadium and the surrounding land) and Liberty Media ($1.4 billion) provided the same benefits. Through these acquisitions, Murdoch gained both product (sport programming) and distribution (shares in Madison Square Garden Network and control over several regional sport channels). This appears to mirror Disney's move to develop sport properties (Mighty Ducks of Anaheim and Anaheim Angels), sport facilities (The Arrowhead Pond and Disney's Wide World of Sports), and media outlets (ESPN, ESPN2, ABC Sports).

Disney's purchase of 43% of Infoseek in 1998 and ultimate creation of their own Internet portal (GO.com) also provide Disney with the capacity to promote their properties across the spectrum of telecommunication. If you doubt that this is happening, just tune into ABC or ESPN or visit any Web site currently under Disney control and view the multiplicity of links between their holdings. In early 1998, Disney emailed previous customers about an upcoming Beanie Baby offer and sold out in four hours. News Corp. and Time-Warner were reportedly searching for Web-based properties.

Time-Warner's arsenal includes the venerable Warner Brothers studios, the WB Network, HBO, and Turner's media holdings (CNN, WTBS, TNT). The sport properties comprise the MLB Atlanta Braves, NBA Atlanta Hawks, NHL Atlanta Thrashers (1999), and *Sports Illustrated*. Turner was adamant with other MLB owners that Murdoch's purchase of the Dodgers be blocked. His arguments failed, as the purchase was approved 27–2. *[Time-Warner subsequently merged with AOL to form AOL Time Warner. The merged company then sold most of its sports franchises while maintaining its other sports holdings.]*

The U.S. courts always have had an interest in reviewing vertical integration in light of the anticompetitive schemes that occurred in the 1920s. Morse noted that while the U.S. government issued guidelines on vertical mergers in the 1980s, the revised guidelines of 1992 and 1997 fail to provide direction to the Department of Justice and the Federal Trade Commission on vertical integration. Consequently, few recent court cases have been heard on this topic. The most recent Supreme Court case on vertical integration is over 25 years old; however, high profile hearings such as those involving giant corporations like Microsoft have resulted in a rise in the collection of fines. . .

The Department of Justice (DOJ) challenged the proposed 1994 merger between Tele-Communications, Inc. (TCI) and Liberty Cable on the grounds that the vertical merger would result in the ability of TCI to restrict competition for programming. This test would fail if applied to the situations subject to review in this paper. The sport programming involved is part of arrangements through various sport leagues; therefore, other carriers have ample opportunity to purchase and air similar programming. In fact, ESPN (Disney), WTBS (the Time-Warner–owned Turner Superstation), and Fox Sport (Murdoch's News Corp.) are available to over 75 million households. Therefore, competition clearly exists, and program access has not been restricted by vertical integration. The Federal Trade Commission (FTC) also intervened in Time-Warner's purchase of Turner Networks because TCI held 7.5% of Turner stock. The FTC required TCI to divest itself of that stock to prevent possible collusion. Additionally, the FTC ordered the dissolution of a 20-year contract that required TCI to carry Turner networks. Lastly, the FTC prohibited Time-Warner from bundling "marquee" channels with less desirable programming that could coerce cable carriers into accepting unwanted programming.

[News Corp. sold the Dodgers and related properties to Frank McCourt for $430 million in 2004. Disney sold the Angels to Arte Moreno for $180 million in 2003.]

The lack of action of the DOJ and the FTC seems grounded in the fact that these vertical mergers do not raise prices to consumers. Rather, the net effect has been that consumers have benefited from reduced costs and greater variety of programming through diminished programming costs realized through the vertical merger. Because an adequate supply of programming is available, at least for the present time, inadequate legal grounds could be found to block these actions as being detrimental to market entry. This situation brings to light the environment of the 1980s when the Supreme Court ruled that the NCAA's control over college football did constitute a restraint of trade and reinforced the colleges' right to control their own broadcasts. Could it be that individual teams may eventually block leagues from selling packaged broadcast rights? A similar controversy is brewing in Europe over the legality of sport leagues' collective broadcast agreements.

One of the issues that remains to be investigated is the effect of vertical integration on salary policies in the professional leagues. All of the U.S. professional sport leagues have formulas established through the collective bargaining agreements concerning the percentage of club revenues which must be available for distribution as salary to players. If the parent corporation were to purchase the TV rights to the team for $1.00, the receipts that constitute "defined gross revenues" would be diminished. The parent corporation naturally would be the beneficiary with significantly enhanced revenue-to-expense ratios, but the overall profit picture would not have changed. The opposite situation could also occur. The parent corporation could provide a TV payment far in excess of industry standards, which would supply clubs with additional dollars for player salaries. Major League Baseball has rarely enforced its 60-40 rule enacted in 1982, which mandates that franchises maintain a ratio of assets to liabilities of a least 60% to 40%. In 1998, ten teams were in violation of that ratio. To the surprise of many, they were not the big spenders like the Yankees and the Dodgers. These teams have significant assets in their TV contracts, and, in the case of the Dodgers, their land holdings surrounding the stadium.

The time-tested business strategy known as vertical integration appears to be running rampant in the sport industry. Disney, News Corp., and Time-Warner collectively own or control a substantial portion of the world's sport and entertainment complex. . . From satellite services, cable channels, production facilities, sport teams, and content sources, these vertically integrated, divisionalized multinational corporations may well represent the future of sport.

REFERENCES

1. Walt Disney Company, 1998 Annual Report.

TOWARD A SCHEME FOR FOOTBALL CLUBS SEEKING AN EFFECTIVE PRESENCE ON THE INTERNET

John Beech, Simon Chadwick, and Alan Tapp

INTRODUCTION

The emergence of the internet represents one of the most significant technological developments of all time. As a result, there is a wealth of literature that claims the medium is still in its infancy but that the use and development of the net is set to grow and revolutionize whole societies, communities, and organizations. This paper examines a more specific area of web activity and focuses on sport, specifically football, as a basis for exploring developments (and the need for development) in the provision and design of websites. In particular, the paper works towards providing a schema for practitioners seeking to develop and manage sports club websites. As a basis for this, it draws upon previous work by the authors as part of an ongoing examination of the nature and content of English Premier League football club websites. . . .

. . . . *[The authors' broad discussions of "Business and the Internet" and "Sports and the Internet" are omitted.]*

FOOTBALL AND INTERNET

. . . .
Football websites . . . warrant further analysis for the following reasons:

- The Internet is an emerging and rapidly changing medium that has commercial and communications implications for football clubs and their supporters;
- Following an initial survey undertaken by the authors of this paper, many Premier League clubs have, thus far, not made the best use of the Internet;

- From the same research, it is apparent that English football clubs have yet to reconcile the global opportunities presented by the web with the global popularity of the game;
- There is an increasing emphasis being placed on the need for some clubs to deliver financial returns;
- A number of football clubs have formal marketing functions intended to develop and enhance relationships with supporters; [and]
- Many football supporters want to engage actively with their "chosen" team and will seek information and merchandise related to this team.

. . . . [The authors' discussion of "Research Method" is omitted.]

RESEARCH FINDINGS

The following observations were made. The twenty-eight items used in the pro-forma [the survey conducted by the authors] have been grouped, according to their focus, into the following categories:

- Selling features;
- Information features;
- Promotional features;
- Communication features;
- Data collection features; [and]
- Design features.

SELLING FEATURE

The most notable feature of Premier League websites is the strong emphasis placed upon sales. In the light of commercial pressures this is hardly surprising, although the practice is premised on a largely unsophisticated use of technology. A majority of clubs provides ticketing information on-line, relating primarily to home games, but a significant minority of clubs gives no such information. Only two of the clubs surveyed actually allow the user to purchase tickets on-line.

Despite the importance of ticket sales to most clubs . . . there was a much stronger emphasis placed on the sale of merchandise. Only one club in the sample failed to include information about merchandise on its site. Typically, most clubs offered little more than a catalogue facility where pictures and prices of the items available were shown. Although sites were supported by mail order services, on-line ordering and payment were not used by any of the clubs in the sample.

Information about corporate hospitality arrangements was available on most of the sites. Interestingly, this related to match-day activities only and failed to indicate the facilities available on days other than those available for matches.

A range of other products was available from some club sites. These included the provision of screen savers and wallpapers, and a limited service entitling supporters to use the domain name of the club as part of their e-mail address. These services tended to be quite complicated to access and required users to be competent in the use of information technology.

INFORMATION FEATURE

All of the clubs surveyed contained a section relating to club news. This tended to be both formal and factual, detailing actual events and giving information on, for example, player transfers that had been completed. This contrasts with many unofficial football club sites where the emphasis is on speculation and anecdotal information about the club. For some supporters, the opportunity to engage in the latter is often more important than "the facts."

Allied to this feature, all sites provided information on players. These generally focused on providing statistical data and career biographies for team members. The information was characterized by an absence of dialogue between club, player, and supporter. Information flowed in one direction, from club to supporter, and there were no opportunities for the latter to interact with players.

Sites were generally very good at reporting details of previous games although there was a strong bias towards the coverage of home games. A similar bias existed in the provision of information for away games. Although detailed information was often available on home games, such as ticketing arrangements and travel details, information on traveling to away games was sparse. This places the onus of responsibility on the supporter to gather this information from elsewhere.

Information about club history was widely available from most sites. This tended to be characterized by information relating to the last eight to ten years. Information about the clubs prior to the formation of the Premier League was generally absent, and sites failed to add value in providing this type of service given the availability of this information elsewhere.

PROMOTIONAL FEATURES

A minority of clubs in the sample devoted space on their websites to community activities. Indeed, there was generally little evidence of attempts to forge meaningful links or dialogue with supporters or supporters' communities. In contrast to the experience of some American sports websites, there were no facilities in place for supporters to engage with "their" team (for example, by allowing supporters to build unofficial club websites linked to the official club server). Club efforts to engage with junior supporters were more evident although this tended to be sales rather than community focused, with an emphasis placed on the sale of merchandise.

Increasingly, clubs appear to be using their websites to provide links to sponsors and to other products. Once more, this was characterized by a commercial motivation that more often had a national and not a local focus. For example, there was little evidence of attempts to link to websites of local interest such as local tourist information centers or to city information sites. Despite the impact that many clubs have on their local economies, there was also a general failure to promote local businesses.

COMMUNICATION FEATURES

All of the sites visited during the period of the research developed the content of their sites although, in one notable case, the club site remained empty for a considerable length of time. It is to their credit that most clubs now have professionally developed and presented sites. Nevertheless, the predominant motivation for most clubs appears to be the need to sell.

Approximately half of the sites surveyed contained information about the relevant supporters' club. This information tended to relate to the sale of tickets, particularly season tickets, and failed to offer anything to interested surfers that they could not find elsewhere. There were no serious attempts to add value, and no moves to engage supporters in a dialogue with the clubs concerned.

Similar failures to add value were apparent in the provision of audio-visual site content. A small number of clubs offers live audio broadcasts of games and no clubs have yet begun to broadcast pictures via the web. A number of American sports clubs have used the web to show edited highlights of games, and some show highlights of great games on the net. The negotiation of television rights may be one reason why clubs have hesitated to explore opportunities in this area, but they are even failing to advertise club videos using selective highlights.

A majority of the clubs have on-line chat facilities on their websites, despite one club having to suspend the service due to the use of offensive language. The services generally involved unregulated discussions between supporters, and so effectively duplicated channels of communication available elsewhere. In this sense, there were no attempts to add value or to eliminate the barriers that traditionally exist between Premier League clubs and their supporters, that is, by holding on-line discussions between owners, managers, players, and supporters.

DATA COLLECTION FEATURES

There were various attempts to use the ability of the web to gather information about supporters and their behavior. The use of "cookies" by clubs in the sample is widespread and clubs are obviously keen to capture technical information such as the user's domain name. A number of clubs also required supporters to complete on-line forms when making purchases of merchandise although it is unclear how the clubs intend to use this information. None of the sites surveyed required users to register to use a site. Consequently, most users, unless they chose to buy merchandise, could move anonymously around a site.

DESIGN FEATURES

It is generally apparent that a majority of the sites surveyed utilize the services of the same website development company, and there is a significant degree of homogeneity between different sites. . . .

CONCLUDING OBSERVATIONS

From the evidence of the first and the second surveys carried out by the authors, it is clear that the football club websites examined are still not taking full advantage of available technology. It has not been the purpose of this paper to explore the reasons for this although it is likely that resources, technical competence, and a lack of understanding of the medium are all contributory factors. . . .

. . . The following schema is proposed, although the reader is asked to note that the items included are not necessarily mutually exclusive, and that the observations made under each item are not necessarily exhaustive.

A football club website should:

- Address supporter access in the context of football-related emotions;
- Promote global opportunities for leveraging brand value;
- Connect with the changing technological environment;
- Establish innovative opportunities for delivering products and services;
- Attract and monitor new and existing supporters;
- Perpetuate "fan culture";
- Synergize with and add value to existing activities; [and]
- Forge new relationships with supporters.

1. Addressing supporter access in the context of football-related emotions

Many of the clubs in the research sample provide supporters with the opportunity to communicate directly with the club and with one another. The most common forms of enabling such access are via bulletin boards and chat fora. In one notable case this provision had to be temporarily suspended when "football chat" degenerated into little more than abuse and vulgarities.

For football supporters who regularly attend matches there is likely to be grudging acceptance of such behavior. But the Internet allows unrestricted access to children and to others who are likely to be more concerned about the content of websites. At a moral or social level, clubs should therefore be aware of the possible ramifications that unregulated fora can have. More specifically, if the site is being used for marketing purposes, the failure to monitor and regulate supporter communications could lead to a multitude of difficulties. These may include negative perceptions about club brands and, ultimately, a potential decline in the number of times supporters access the site.

It is therefore imperative that clubs reconcile the needs of supporters seeking website access to "their team" with those of younger users, the less abusive, and with prospective clients (corporate or otherwise). The task of managing the multiple expectations of users is a significant one. Decency and taste may dictate control and regulation, but there is already an established culture of accessing unofficial football club sites. If clubs are not to lose users to such sites they should address this issue as a priority, particularly where marketing opportunities may be lost.

2. Promoting global opportunities for leveraging brand value

It should be recognized that the Internet is a global medium and a number of Premier League football club brands are amongst some of the strongest brand names in the world. In this context, the opportunity to leverage brand value on a global basis is indisputable. The sole use of the English language on club websites in the survey nevertheless implies that most clubs are still not taking the commercial implications of the net as seriously as they might. Manchester United, for example, is currently engaged in developing retail facilities in the Far East. There is currently no evidence to indicate that the club is planning to address specifically this segment of the market through its official site.

However, this is not an isolated case. Another club regularly receives ticket requests from the United States and Canada. But the site in question offers the user only price information and a simple two-dimensional plan of the stadium. For infrequent or geographically remote supporters, there is generally little to induce attendance at games. This is in marked contrast to many American sports sites that have on-line seat viewing and stadium tours, and secure on-line purchasing. Similarly, although a majority of Premier League club sites provides detailed information about merchandise, there is less evidence that moves towards on-line buying are taking place.

As a signal of intent, clubs should at least provide users with the option to view sites in languages other than English. Beyond this, sites should acknowledge the global nature of club support as the basis for a more sophisticated approach to site development. It is important that clubs not only recognize the esteem in which supporters hold their teams but also their expectations as consumers and the segmentation opportunities that this will generate. Sites should therefore aim to reflect user needs more accurately such that people seeking more detailed information about ticketing arrangements, those wanting to buy replica strips on-line, or supporters wanting regular e-mail updates of club news are targeted more effectively.

3. Connect with the changing technological environment

Despite the hype, the club websites currently offer little to supporters that is not available elsewhere. Many of the sites that were surveyed appeared to exist in a basic form compared to other industrial sectors such as retailing and American sports sites. Thus far they have not taken full advantage of technology which currently allows radio broadcasts, on-line discussions, and picture coverage (live or edited) of games. At a less sophisticated, but no less important, level the use of cookies and supporter monitoring (noted below) was not apparent.

If sites are to offer more than the replication of information and services available elsewhere, then clubs need to address why they have a website and what they are seeking to use it for. For clubs that are serious about the role of the net in club marketing, an appreciation of technology at both the strategic and the operational levels is needed. To an extent, users will drive the need to keep abreast with web development, although, unlike on-line book services or e-travel companies, the reverence in which supporters hold clubs and their unquestioning brand loyalty will serve as a buffer to change.

What clubs should remember, however, is the proliferation of Internet technology and the impact that this is predicted to have on the media rights market and sports broadcasting. The use of the web as a medium of communication is thus likely to extend beyond providing basic club information into providing users with a multimedia experience. At an industry level this will impact upon the balance and allocation of revenues and, for smaller clubs or the technically less competent, may have serious long-term consequences.

4. Establishing innovative opportunities for delivering products and services

In many other industrial sectors, organizations are starting to use the net as the basis for developing new product or delivery concepts. For example, in food retailing several major chains of supermarkets now allow consumers to buy goods from home via the web which are then delivered to the purchaser's house. Logistical issues aside, this is helping to open up new segments of the food retail market. It is unlikely that virtual football matches could ever replace the live experience of a game. But there will be opportunities to develop the use of Internet technology in creative ways, particularly where the physical experience of consuming a good or service is less significant.

Of particular significance will be the impact of compact discs onto which information can be downloaded. In the music industry this is already set to revolutionize how people buy their music. In the same way, there will be scope to offer football supporters a similar service, particularly with the proliferation of the Internet and broadcast media. Clubs should be able to provide audio-visual materials such as highlights from games and interviews with players which supporters can download to disk and view off-line.

Such developments may be some distance away but current technology could still be used in more creative ways than is currently the case in most clubs. A number of American websites allow supporters to take on-line tours of their stadium facilities. Linked to this, there is also growing evidence of sites that allow supporters to access the view from each section of a ground. On-line ticket purchases can then be made using this information and the supporter can decide the payment method and mode of delivery for the ticket. At present, most football club sites do not approach this level of sophistication. For clubs operating at maximum seat utilization this is understandable although for larger grounds, major games, or in the event of unsold tickets, American provision provides a useful benchmark.

5. Attracting and monitoring new and existing supporters

There appear to be two key factors that dictate the club that a supporter will follow. The first is geographical proximity; if a supporter is born and brought up in an area, there is a strong likelihood that the person will identify with the local team. Secondly, many supporters ally themselves to the most successful team at a particular time (regardless of geographical proximity). In common, it is likely that the two sets of supporters will both want up-to-date information about "their" club, will want to make a contribution to discussions about the club, and may want to purchase club-related merchandise.

For the geographically remote, the Internet is a significant development that spans the boundaries of time and place. The challenge for website developers in this context is that of how to attract and engage users. For example, for supporters in the Far East (where a significant number of supporters follow Premier League football), how to make them aware of the existence of a site and then to ensure that they access it are key challenges. Although search engines can be used to locate official sites, supporters can also find rival, unofficial sites using this technology. If clubs are to target such groups effectively it is important to establish a direct relationship with the supporter. This can be achieved by using traditional media such as supporters' club newsletters or club-related publicity such as match-day programs. Alternatively, clubs could offer virtual inducements by providing free club-branded Internet access discs, by making e-mail addresses containing the name of the club available or by allowing supporters to set up their own club sites within the club website.

Once the existence of the site has been established in the minds of supporters, the challenge then becomes the conversion of initial users into more active browsers and then active users of the site. This is not just a geographical issue but also relates to teams that may currently be successful, particularly if this is not enduring and the club gets relegated. In such circumstances, attracting and retaining users becomes as challenging as motivating them to access the site in the first instance.

One of the best ways to attract users and to keep them coming back is to find out what particular segments of supporters want from a website and then to make offers that will lead them to revisit. A fundamental question in this context, is how do you find out what supporters want? It is clear that many Premier League websites underutilize browser cookie technology. That is, users are generally not asked to register to use a site, or to provide anything other than basic information when engaging in a transaction. Should clubs decide to collect this type of information, there are a number of benefits that may accrue. At the very least, clubs would be able to identify first visitors and repeat users. But available technology allows a level of sophistication beyond this. Browser cookies can indicate which parts of a website have been accessed and how the supporter has used them once there. This potentially allows the site manager to build up a profile of users and their areas of interest. In turn, this can facilitate the provision of other supporter services. For those who use websites to buy tickets on-line, cookie technology enables clubs to target them with e-mail offers.

6. Perpetuating "fan culture"

The social role of Premier League football clubs is an important one that creates a strong sense of community and loyalty, and provides an opportunity to engage in bravado. The implication is that, in any contact with "their" club, supporters will want to feel a sense of belonging, to express views and opinions, and to be recognized as a supporter of the team. The "remoteness" of web access and the general absence of physical prompts in its use mean that it cannot currently simulate the experience felt at a ground during a game or at a bar in discussion after a game.

The web can perpetuate fan culture through the non-exclusiveness that it offers. Supporters can voice opinions on an equal basis on-line, something they may be unable to do when using other media. The disintermediating impact of the net also enables users to span boundaries. For example, a letter about the team sent to a local newspaper or a fanzine may not be published. A chat room or a bulletin board on a club website generally avoids such exclusion.

The clubs surveyed appear to be making use of these facilities although it is not clear whether supporters expect to see a tangible link between their comments and the decisions being taken at a team or club level. What is encouraging, though, is the amount of space being allocated to young supporters' groups and to community areas on club sites. This could be taken further, as the American experience demonstrates. Team sites such as the Houston Astros actually provide fans with space to set up their own Astros websites. There is also some evidence of "buddying" between specific groups of fans. This is interesting and suggests that people's affiliations can be expressed in many ways. Rather than giving an opinion, they may simply want to make the statement "I am a supporter; this is my club." Others may want to communicate with like-minded fans who have similar aspirations and views. The sub-cultural and segmentation issues for website managers are therefore likely to be complex.

7. Synergizing with and adding value to existing activities

There are numerous ways in which football clubs engage with supporters: at a game, at supporters' group meetings, via the sale of merchandise. There is already some progress towards enhancing these via the web. Radio broadcasts can be accessed (with video highlights being available in some North American sites), the role of supporters' clubs appears to be have been acknowledged on many Premier League club sites, and merchandise can be purchased on-line in a number of instances.

The immediate task for any club seeking to develop their site is to get supporters to use the site in the first instance. It is therefore important that references are made to the site in match-day programs, on perimeter hoardings, during match-day announcements, and through links from the sites of sponsors. The second challenge is then to induce supporters to make return visits to the site. By comparison with rival, unofficial sites, football clubs enjoy a competitive advantage because of their direct access to the players and manager. Clubs could therefore extend the experience of watching players during a game by promoting regulated on-line discussions between supporters and players through on-line chat facilities. This is something that happens already in English football through supporters' meetings and club open days. These are nevertheless characterized by the constraints of time and distance. Not only is football a global game, but many of those people loyal to a particular team are geographically dispersed and may be unable to attend such meetings.

It is evident from the research undertaken that many Premier League clubs are unclear about the role and purpose of their websites. The homogenous nature and level of sophistication of many of the sites surveyed indicates that clubs think they have to have a website but do not really know why. In one sense, this reflects a general failure to understand the strategic context of the web. This is amply illustrated in the provision of on-line merchandising facilities. Most club sites allow supporters to view available merchandise on-line; many give information about the prices and specifications of their products and services; some detail the arrangements for buying merchandise. However, at the time of this research, no club gave the option to engage in secure transactions on-line, and this typifies a failure to understand the medium. Clubs could derive value from the disintermediating effects of the web. That is, the net can eliminate intermediaries from the process of buying and selling, thus delivering cost savings and opportunities for enhanced customer services.

8. Forging new relationships with supporters

The emergence of the "supporter as stakeholder" perspective is largely a response to the growth of commercialism in football. But supporters have always sought to claim a stake in "their" team, be it through match attendance, involvement in a supporters' club, or in more informal ways such as an argument in a bar. With the growth of the web, it is likely that supporters will seek to replicate their experiences on-line.

Whilst it has already been noted that the physical experience of supporting a team at a game can not currently be duplicated by technology, there are new ways in which supporters can engage with both their club and other supporters. Examples of this are already evident on some Premier League websites, including the prominence of community space and the use of supporter discussion fora. In America, there are instances of supporters being allowed to develop team-related websites, on the servers of baseball teams. What is clear for official website developers is that, if they cannot offer the experience being generated by the multitude of unofficial sites and the sub-cultural context of their developers, then it is likely that clubs will not realize the full potential of the medium.

In the Premier League, there are still a number of unexplored opportunities. Most clubs use a registered domain name, for example www.arsenal.co.uk, www.lcfc.co.uk (Leicester City) and www.saintsfc.co.uk (Southampton). Clubs could begin to offer a service whereby supporters developing their own websites, or selecting an e-mail address, could include the club name as a component of their address. Clubs could also use data that, thus far, they are failing to collect. Using browser cookies as the foundation, personal messages could be sent to particular users with very little time or expense involved. For instance, it would be relatively easy for a star player to send a birthday greeting to supporters who have been asked about their birth date and favorite player when they initially registered to use the site.

The eight-point schema above is offered as a blueprint for those clubs which wish to use the Internet and the various facilities it can offer in order to promote themselves, their products, and their brands more effectively. The authors' research indicates that all Premiership clubs have begun to follow some form of Internet strategy, but that there are still many opportunities which have yet

TABLE 3.

Top Sports Websites						
Brand or channel	*Unique audience (000)*	*Active reach (%)*	*Web page views (000)*	*Sessions per person*	*Web pages per person*	*Time per person (hh:mm:ss)*
ESPN	14,727	10.93	1,051,941	7.4	71	0:54:09
Yahoo! Sports	7,354	5.46	828,631	7.43	113	0:56:48
Sportsline.com	7,217	5.36	255,641	4.43	35	0:27:56
SI.com	6,059	4.5	85,313	2.58	14	0:11:39
AOL Sports	4,648	3.45	22,601	4.11	11	0:26:52
MLB.com	4,297	3.19	102,088	3.49	24	0:16:05
nascar.com	3,976	2.95	108,194	4.87	27	0:22:11
OCSN	3,465	2.57	62,633	2.93	18	0:12:23
NBA Internet Network	3,228	2.4	64,786	3.47	20	0:14:47
NFL Internet Network	3,183	2.36	69,185	4.26	22	0:16:34
NCAA	2,829	2.1	31,366	2.03	11	0:07:49
Lycos Fox Sports	2,486	1.84	50,255	2.6	20	0:12:32
sportingnews.com	1,658	1.23	52,689	2.87	32	0:17:26
USATODAY.com Sports	1,625	1.21	30,807	3.93	19	0:18:41
NHL.com	1,614	1.2	37,862	3.87	23	0:13:57

Source: http://espn.go.com/mediakit/research/competitive.html.

to be seized. Future research will include both continued monitoring of the English Premiership clubs' websites and surveys of the clubs which constitute other major European soccer leagues. (See Table 3.)

NEW MEDIA

JAPANESE SPECTATOR SPORT INDUSTRY: CULTURAL CHANGES CREATING NEW OPPORTUNITIES

Mark McDonald, Toru Mihara, and Jinbae Hong

The development of sport is influenced by the cultural and social characteristics of a country. Changes in Japanese culture are creating an environment supportive to the continued emergence and professionalization of the spectator sport industry. For example, the gradual change in Japanese corporate culture from traditional human resource management based on Confucianism and emphasizing harmony, unity, and cooperation to a performance based evaluation and reward system, has helped spark the trend of agents signing professional athletes to contracts. The launch of the new broadcasting satellite . . . has been influenced by the importance of mass media in Japanese daily life, the growth of the fame phenomenon in Japanese society, and the creation of celebrities through mass media, and the internationalization of Japanese TV. Japanese response to the interaction between the global and local has been to continue to develop local sports such as Sumo, to adapt foreign sports to Japanese culture, and to co-host one of the world's largest sport events, the 2002 World Cup.

. . . . *[The authors' additional discussion of cultural trends is omitted.]*

GLOBAL-LOCAL NEXUS

. . . Globalization has dissolved the old structures and boundaries of national states and communities, introducing new international economies and cultures. As always, when new meets old, the result has been confrontation and conflict. Therefore, the global–local nexus, establishing new and complex relations between global and local spaces is of significance to a number of endeavors, including sport.

Since the late 1960s, American sports and American sport cultures have spread throughout the world. However, in this process of "sportization," there has been continuous debate on whether this process should be interpreted as globalization or Americanization. Of the four most significant "American" sports, football and baseball are not widely played. Also, the international basis of sports such as tennis, golf, cycling, boxing, soccer, and track and field are indicative of a process of globalization, not Americanization. However, one cannot ignore that adopting American marketing, promotional, and presentational techniques have Americanized sport. The globalization or Americanization of sport has significantly influenced national sport policy or cultures. Japan has been able to protect local sports (e.g. Sumo wrestling), while adopting American marketing and promotions. On the other hand, Japan imported professional sports such as baseball and soccer from the United States, Europe, and South America. However, it is noteworthy that both the Japanese Baseball League and the J-League adapted these sports based on unique Japanese cultural and social patterns. For example, in Japanese professional baseball, teamwork and cooperation are emphasized over individualism and egotism to achieve the collective goal of winning the pennant. Teams and managers ask for players' devotion to the collectivity, and self-discipline for team harmony. These characteristics of Japanese professional baseball are a direct reflection of Japanese culture.

When the local emerges with significant influence either through economic or cultural success, the local can attract more global attention and receive many benefits. In sport, the appearance of countries and cities in global society by hosting of world sport events and other cultural activities, including the summer and winter Olympics, soccer World Cup, Motor Car and Cycle Grand Prix, world fairs, "expos," festivals, and exhibitions, can significantly help them to re-imagine themselves and reinvigorate their local economies. There are increasingly intense competitions between countries and cities to host world sport events in order to generate significant economic activity, facilitate urban redevelopment, attract national and international media attention, and signify global status. Therefore, in global society, hosting world sport events will help the locale to renew its economy, create civic pride through success, and assist in re-imagining and culturally repositioning itself. Japan and the Japanese cities hosting 2002 World Cup soccer games will have opportunities to attract global attention and lasting benefits.

GLOBAL MEDIA AND JAPANESE MASS CULTURE

The emergence of new global media, including the Internet and satellite broadcasting, has significantly influenced the speed and quality of sending local information to the world, and receiving global transmissions. Global media developed because national media are not able to satisfy the information and entertainment needs of an increasingly complex and interdependent world. Most importantly, the global media have helped integrate people from different cultures and societies into global perspectives. By importing foreign culture and social phenomenon, and exporting local perspectives, global media has helped cross-cultural understanding and reduced social conflict.

Reflecting the significant impact of global media on current society, sport media has also significantly influenced culture and society, and increased opportunities in the sport related market. . . . By broadcasting world sport events such as the Olympics and World Cup that have contributed to harmony and understanding of people of the world, the sport media is playing an integrating role. Furthermore, the global sport media has created a large and important business environment for corporations. It provides opportunities for television advertising, merchandising and the sale of exclusive rights to specific events, leagues or tournaments. Also, it helps to package and market American sports, including football, baseball, and basketball. Sport superstars like Michael Jordan and Tiger Woods become global figures and their images are merchandised globally. The continuous development of new media technologies will accelerate the phenomenon of global integration and business opportunities related to global sport.

The growing influence of the media is readily apparent in local cultures. In Japan, newspapers and television have significantly influenced daily life. As a result of the combination of the development of mass publication and the high literacy rate of the people, reading daily newspapers including sport newspapers has become indispensable to life in Japan. Television, however, is the undisputed number one medium in Japan, with a wide variety of programming.

In Japanese mass culture, one notices a kind of layer-cake structure consisting of three cultures. One of them is the folk culture that originated in old agricultural society and still survives in rural communities. The second layer is the popular culture and public arts founded in the eighteenth century. Ukiyoe in the field of painting, kabuki in drama, haiku in literature, and those forms of arts are rooted in the popular culture. After the Meiji restoration in 1868, Japan very rapidly imported all kinds of Western cultural products. Public entertainment was no exception, and this westernized entertainment, in turn, forms the third layer of Japanese mass culture. Balancing three characteristics, Japan has developed its own mass culture and absorbed Western mass cultures. Based on the three layers of mass culture, programming includes a variety of dramas, traditional cultures such as kabuki and samurai shows, cartoons, sports, and foreign programs.

Given the importance of media and the characteristics of mass culture, it is not surprising that the development of new media technology such as satellite broadcasting and the Internet has rapidly become significant to the Japanese way of life. For example, the number of consumer satellite broadcast contracts exceeded 10 million in 1997. In this same year, the number of host computers in Japan that were connected to the Internet numbered 730,000. With a 4.5% share of the global market, this was second only to the United States. This well-developed infrastructure will help Japan to fully participate in the global media industry and develop its local mass media. Additionally, Japanese sport media will be continuously developed to import international sports and export its local sports such as Sumo wrestling to global society.

With the development of mass media, there has been growth of the fame phenomenon in Japanese society. The regular publication of newspapers necessitates the ongoing creation of "news." Moreover, stories of human greatness are what sell the news, and the need for such heroes and heroic acts outstrips their supply in the real world. With hundreds of hours of programming time to fill, Japanese television has come to rely on personalities. In order to attract and hold large audiences, television turns "everyday events into celebrated performances." Thus, television requires famous people to fill its hours and these individuals need television to create and maintain their fame. Japanese society's fascination with fame is accelerating the presentation of celebrities to the public through television, movies, and sport. This aspect of Japanese popular culture provides an inviting business environment for the field of sport marketing.

As to be expected, Japanese high technology will accelerate the development of global media, especially in the field of sport broadcasting. More Japanese and foreign sport will be introduced through rapidly expanding television channels. Simultaneously, Japanese and foreign sport celebrities will get more airtime to satisfy the public's fascination with fame.

. . . . *[The authors' discussion of the Japanese spectator sport industry is omitted.]*

DISCUSSION QUESTIONS

1. Why is there an apparent move by leagues away from network television deals to deals led by cable networks?

2. What do football Web sites do well?

3. What could football Web sites do better?

4. Describe the eight-point Internet schema.

5. How applicable is this schema to Major League Baseball? The NBA? A major university? A high school?

6. Why has there been significant new media growth in Japan?

7. What does this say for global new media growth?

8. What has the success rate been for other regional sports networks, those without the multinationals like News Corp. and Disney behind them?

9. How does the European television model differ from the U.S. model? Which appears to be most successful? What can the leaders of each learn from one another?

10. What are the benefits of vertical integration for a sports franchise owner? What are the benefits for a media mogul?

11. Do you anticipate that the vertical integration business model will begin to dominate the industry?

LICENSED PRODUCTS

INTRODUCTION

In addition to revenues generated directly from the playing facility and through the sale of media rights, professional sports franchises, leagues, and other sports properties realize significant monies through the sale of officially licensed products bearing their names, logos, and marks. In 2001, the NFL sold $2.5 billion of licensed products, while MLB had sales of $2.3 billion, and Nascar's sales were $1.2 billion. The NBA generated $1.0 billion, and the NHL sold $900 million of its goods. Collectively, the sale of sports-related products represented 14.9% of all licensed goods sold in the United States in 2001. Though this is an impressive figure, the overall sales of sports-related licensed goods has decreased from previous years. This is likely attributable to both a shift in fashion trends and a downturn in the economy. The fickle nature of fashion trends creates a fluctuation in revenues that can present a problem to professional sports leagues and franchises, as the uncertainty in the revenue stream can dissuade the entity from relying on the sale of licensed products in its budgeting process.

Licensees — the manufacturers of these products — typically pay the sports property a royalty fee of approximately 8.5% of the wholesale selling price of the goods in exchange for the right to sell products containing league and team names, logos, and marks. These monies are paid by the licensees to each league's properties division. The respective properties division then pools the funds and distributes them equally across all league teams, similar to the manner in which revenues generated from the sale of national media rights are apportioned. Thus, while all teams benefit from the increased royalties generated from an increase in the sales of licensed products, there would appear to be little incentive for any individual club to incur a significant amount of the cost of doing so and yet reap little of the benefit in the form of increased revenue. To overcome this obstacle, leagues have carved out exceptions to this general revenue-sharing rule and typically allow teams to keep a disproportionate share of the proceeds generated from the sale of their licensed products in their playing facilities or within a specific mile radius of this facility. Despite these efforts, the general sentiment among popular clubs with strong licensed product sales such as the Dallas Cowboys is that they should not be forced to share the value of their brands with other, less popular clubs that have a lower brand value. Thus, the manner in which revenues generated by the sale of licensed products are

TABLE 1.

TOP ATHLETE ENDORSERS OF THE 20TH CENTURY
1) Michael Jordan
2) Tiger Woods
3) Arnold Palmer
4) Muhammad Ali
5) Babe Ruth
6) Bruce Jenner
7) Jeff Gordon
8) Jack Nicklaus
9) Bo Jackson
10) Mia Hamm

Source: Burns Sports and Celebrities, Inc.

allocated is likely to remain a matter of intraleague dispute. Though the net revenues received by each club from the sale of licensed products are approximated to be only several million dollars per year, the resolution of this debate may serve as an important indicator of the future of revenue sharing in each league.

An overview of the sale of sports-related licensed products is provided in the first selection from Masteralexis, Barr, and Hums, including a brief historical perspective and a review of current issues in sport licensing. In the second excerpt, Brandon Grusd reviews various leagues' licensing programs, analyzes the goodwill that is sold through these programs, and presents several reasons why league-wide licensing programs are suboptimal.

In the next selection, Gladden and Milne introduce the reader to the importance of brand equity in professional sports. A discussion of the impact of a team's logo, name, and playing facility on its brand equity is followed by an examination of the relationship between brand equity, winning, and licensed product sales in the NHL, NBA, and MLB. The article concludes with a discussion of the implications of their findings for sports industry leaders.

In the final article, Gladden and Funk explain the concept of brand management by examining the relationship between brand loyalty and brand associations among highly loyal followers of professional sports franchises. The authors offer insights into the importance of a brand-oriented approach for a sports franchise and suggest strategies for sports franchises to follow in maintaining long-term fan loyalty. (See Table 1 for the top athlete endorsers of the 20th century.)

PRINCIPLES AND PRACTICE OF SPORT MANAGEMENT

Lisa Pike Masteralexis, Carol A. Barr, and Mary A. Hums

LICENSING

A quick glance at the crowd at a sporting event, or shoppers at the mall, or students in a classroom, will reveal that many are wearing an item of clothing bearing the name or logo of a popular collegiate or professional sport team. In addition, it is likely that most of these fans own a pen, notebook, poster, or pennant also displaying the name and colors of their favorite sport teams. These are all licensed products. The manufacturers of these products, the licensees, include well-known sport-product companies such as Nike, Champion, and Reebok; prominent electronics manufacturers Nintendo, Sega, and Sony; and smaller firms . . . Licensees pay teams and leagues, the licensors, for the right to manufacture products bearing team and school names, nicknames, colors, and logos. . . .

Those who own such items are among the millions of consumers who purchase licensed product items to show support for and demonstrate affiliation with sport entities. Revenues from licensed product sales have become a big part of the sport industry in a relatively short period of time. . . .

Licensing enables schools and teams to generate brand recognition and interest and to increase revenues with very little financial risk. . . . The licensees assume the risk by manufacturing the product, then pay a fee to the licensor, called a royalty, for the use of specific trademarks on specific products. Royalty fees generally range from 6 to 10% and are based on gross sales at wholesale costs. . . . Licensees use the established images and popularity of sport teams to boost their sales. . . .

History of Licensing Programs

Professional Sport. The licensing programs in professional sport leagues are administered by a for-profit branch of the league, generally referred to as a properties division. Properties divisions approve licensees, police trademark infringement, and distribute licensing revenues equally among league franchises. Properties divisions usually handle marketing and sponsorship efforts as well. The NFL was the first professional league to develop a properties component in 1963, under the leadership of Pete Rozelle, the commissioner at the time. . . .

Player unions also administer licensing programs, such as the National Football League Players Association's (NFLPA's) Players Inc., which represents agreements with nearly 3,000 current and former NFL players. Union properties divisions such as this establish separate licensee agreements, and also jointly license and share revenue with leagues, for trading cards, electronics and video games, and associated memorabilia sales. The Major League Baseball Players Association (MLBPA) was the first to enter into such an agreement in the late 1960s when then-Executive Director Marvin Miller entered into a two-year, $120,000 pact with Coca-Cola to permit the beverage manufacturer to put players' likenesses on bottle caps. Such royalties helped fund the emerging union's organizing activities. Miller also negotiated a comprehensive agreement with trading card manufacturer Topps Company in 1968. Topps was permitted to continue manufacturing trading cards bearing player likenesses for double the players' previous yearly fees (from $125 to $250), and it paid the union 80% on annual sales up to $4 million and 10% on all subsequent sales. The first year the contract earned the MLBPA $320,000. . . .

Some smaller professional leagues hire independent companies to run their licensing operations. . . . These firms serve as "middle persons" for smaller leagues lacking the resources to maintain effective licensing operations, and work for a percentage (as high as 35%) of gross revenues from retail sales.

The strengths of league-based licensing programs are the ability to coordinate efforts among many licensees, the ability for increased quality control over approved merchandise, the ability for easier national distribution of product, and an increased and effectively coordinated enforcement of trademark infringement by nonlicensed manufacturers. The ownership of team trademarks by the league also provides greater value to licensees, who need only go to one source to access all league marks, and provides potential product licensing exclusivity. League programs also effectively segment the national market for licensed sport products by emphasizing the varied colors, logos, and uniforms of league teams in specific local markets. The major weakness of league-based programs . . . is that popular and successful clubs . . . have the leverage to strike up their own deals and are loathe to share any revenues with other clubs. The same holds true for merchandise sales. . . [Some owners maintain] that they should be able to make full use of their respective clubs' earning potential. If they sell more merchandise, these . . . owners feel they should be entitled to keep their teams' percentage of the sales revenue in proportion to unit sales and should not be forced to subsidize less desirable properties through the equal division of sales revenues.

. . . .

Branded Apparel

Many sport fans also wear apparel items bearing only the logo, mark, or name of the manufacturer . . . referred to as branded products. The popularity of branded merchandise is a relatively recent phenomenon, as manufacturers who established their brand awareness as licensees have now established their own brand identity independent of professional or college team marks.

. . . .

Established branded nonsport apparel manufacturers have also begun to enter the sport market. Fashion apparel companies with strong label recognition . . . have delved into the licensing and sporting goods market to further entrench their brand awareness. . . . In addition, new companies are forming with the intent to create branded lines with associated licensed tie-ins. . . .

. . . .

Current Issues

. . . .

International Sales.   As growth diminishes in the domestic market, licensors and licensees alike are looking toward international markets to boost sales. Licensees are purchasing foreign companies not only to market U.S. products overseas but also to capitalize on the growth of indigenous sales as well. . . .

Leagues see foreign markets as ripe for sales expansion as well. Foreign exhibition and regular season games have been used successfully to prompt local interest in league games and merchandise. . .

Manufacturer and Licensee Conduct.   Although licensors demonstrate quality control over the images on licensed products, they do not control all operations of the licensees. Licensees are independent businesses, and as such conduct their businesses as they see fit. . . . Sometimes, however, the business practices of licensees reflect back on the licensors. . . .

. . . .

Logos: Expansion and Redesign.   . . . Although teams that win tend to sell the most merchandise, teams, leagues, colleges, and manufacturers realized that sales could be increased through logo introduction and redesign, as well as through uniform redesign and diversification and secondary and commemorative logos and marks. . . . Minor league baseball teams . . . enjoy high national sales and distribution due to innovative logos and color schemes. The introduction of alternate logos and uniform components, such as jerseys, hats, and patches, has also served to increase sales. . . .

. . . .

Retail Trends.   Retailers are looking to keep sales from lagging in the coming years by fine-tuning their selling efforts. Here are a few things retailers, licensors, and licensees will be working on together to ensure continued growth:

- Popular product segments such as children's apparel (gearing associated promotional efforts to coincide with holiday and back-to-school purchase windows), electronics and video games, authentics and sideline/courtside merchandise, including alternate uniforms.
- Continued product expansion, such as commemorative "throwback" items that celebrate tradition and history, casual-wear lines (as many older fans want a more understated look and won't buy authentics or replicas), and items specifically for women. . . .
- A continued development of specialty stores and purchasing areas. Such outlets and space allocations are used to reinforce brand awareness and affiliation for licensees, licensors, and retailers. . . .

. . . .

Sponsorship and Licensing Synergy.   As relationships between sport entities become more fully integrated, the lines that formerly separated sponsors and licensees have begun to blur. Licensees with significant marketing clout and experience are looking to use sport as a promotional vehicle in many ways, including advertising at contests, at venues, during broadcasts, and at associated events. Leagues, teams, and colleges no longer restrict licensing agreements to merchandise production but look to create marketing partnerships with licensees to increase not only merchandise sales but also sponsorship revenues and overall brand awareness.

THE ANTITRUST IMPLICATIONS OF PROFESSIONAL SPORTS' LEAGUEWIDE LICENSING AND MERCHANDISING ARRANGEMENTS

Brandon L. Grusd

II. SELLING GOODWILL

Sports merchandising is big business. . . . The enormous merchandise licensing revenue that each league receives is the product of the background legal rules concerning a team's intellectual property rights and the economics concerning the sale of such property rights.

In the sports merchandising business, the property that is of value to a team is . . . the teams' logos and names (e.g., the stylized "NY" on the hat of Yankees players, or the name "Yankees" as seen on the uniform), which are used to sell team merchandise and promote team allegiances.

The goodwill value of these logos is extracted by the owner through the sale of the property or, more commonly, by licensing the use of it to others through sponsorship and merchandising agreements. Merchandise licensing agreements entitle the licensee to manufacture goods with the logos, trademarks, and trade names of the team. The licensor (i.e., the team) receives a royalty upon each sale of the licensed product. The licensee (e.g., Reebok, Champion, adidas) enters into these agreements on the belief that the team's goodwill will enhance the appeal and perceived value of the licensee's goods.

In addition, sponsorship agreements typically allow licensees to use the sporting event as a means for advertising and promotion. Again, licensees believe that the goodwill the fans and consumers associate with a particular team will carry over to the sponsor's products or services. This belief is not unfounded. . . .

An individual team's ability to profit from its logo in the aforementioned manner would be lost without the protections granted by intellectual property laws, which reward the creator of the intangible property (i.e., the logo or team name) with a limited monopoly. This limited monopoly creates incentives for persons to produce works of intangible property by adding value to the property that the owner would have been otherwise unable to capture. The law creates the value of these trademarks and trade names by designating the owners of such logos as the exclusive owners. In the trademark setting, one commentator has stated, "[Such exclusivity] encourages businesses to invest in symbolic representation of their goods and services by prohibiting competitors from using the same symbol on their wares."[38] This symbolic representation of the goods and services embodies the goodwill built by the team.

. . . .

III. LEAGUE-WIDE MERCHANDISING AND LICENSING

While the major professional sports leagues vary in how they collect merchandise and sponsorship licensing revenues, each league utilizes a similar organizational structure to negotiate merchandising and licensing agreements with third parties, such as Nike or Reebok. Rather than having its teams negotiate separately with different companies, each league has created an entity to act as the teams' exclusive negotiating agent. Within such a structure, each NFL, NHL, NBA, and MLB team is owned and operated independently, and remains individually responsible for its own profits, losses, and capital expenditures. The details of two of the leagues' marketing arms (NFL Properties and MLB Properties) are elaborated below.

In 1984, the MLB teams established MLB Properties, a subsidiary of MLB Enterprises. Via an agency agreement, MLB Properties controls (1) marketing and licensing of the marks of all . . . teams, (2) the marks of the league and its events, and (3) the marks of the American and National Leagues. This agreement includes a provision whereby a three-fourths vote of the teams is required to bind all teams. Furthermore, the agreement mandates that MLB Properties must act as the exclusive negotiating agent with respect to the marks for teams newly admitted to the league. The geographic coverage of the agency agreement extends beyond the North American market to the entire world. Individual teams retain certain rights to license and exploit their marks for limited purposes within limited geographic areas. These retained rights are generally limited to the promotion of the teams' baseball games through local advertising, team programs, and other team publications.

The MLB agency agreement was renewed and amended on January 1, 1991 and again on December 1, 1995. The latest agreement designates MLB Properties as the exclusive agent for the marketing and licensing of the marks of all the league teams. For example, MLB Properties entered into a contract with Pepsi that made Pepsi the official soft drink of MLB and gave Pepsi exclusive rights to use MLB's marks in advertising, merchandising, packaging, and promotions. . . . Furthermore, the agency agreement dictates that MLB Properties is to distribute domestic promotional and retail licensing income in equal amounts to each team, regardless of the actual income generated by a particular's marks. International promotional and retail licensing income, and income from other sources are not distributed to any team. In addition to its role as the exclusive agent for negotiating these licensing deals, MLB Properties also enforces and protects all team and league marks. MLB Properties subtracts fees for this service from the gross income received before distributing it to the teams.

Similarly, NFL teams have created NFL Properties to act as the exclusive agent for negotiating and entering merchandise licensing and sponsorship agreements. This arrangement was organized in

1981, when twenty-six of the then twenty-eight teams entered a Trust Agreement. Under this agreement, the teams transferred the exclusive commercial rights of their marks to the trustees of the NFL Trust. The NFL Trust then entered into a licensing agreement with NFL Properties, whereby NFL Properties would act as the exclusive licensee of all the NFL and team marks. NFL Properties negotiates with third-party companies such as Pepsi, Nike, and Reebok. The income derived from these licensing deals is passed on to the NFL Trust and then to the teams on an equal share basis, regardless of the amount earned by any particular team's marks.

As in MLB, each NFL team retains some control over the licensing of its marks. The rights retained by each team include: (1) the exclusive right to use its team marks in connection with the presentation of a football game; (2) the nonexclusive right to use its team marks in local advertising to promote football games; (3) the nonexclusive right to allow third parties to use its team marks in advertisements in local sections of the team's program; and (4) the nonexclusive right to use its marks in its own publications. . . .

. . . According to industry analysts, the NFL and the other professional sports leagues are able to enter such lucrative contracts because sporting events "achieve a broad penetration of the adult male market that advertisers want to reach."

Like the NFL and MLB, the NHL and the NBA have a single entity that acts as the exclusive agent for each league and its teams in conducting merchandise licensing and sponsorship negotiations. For example, NBA Properties acts as the league's licensing arm. Through NBA Properties, the league controls the trademarks and logos of all the teams outside each team's own area. In addition, all . . . teams have granted NBA Properties the exclusive right to license and use their marks internationally. Income collected from such deals is pooled and shared evenly among the teams.

NHL Enterprises is that league's marketing division. As in the other three leagues, all teams have granted NHL Enterprises the exclusive right to license and use their marks. In exchange, all . . . teams receive an equal share of income from those marketing, licensing, and sponsorship deals. Like in the other leagues, NHL teams retain limited rights to sell and license their marks. NHL teams are allowed to license their own marks within a seventy-five mile radius of their respective arenas.

The overall effect of these league-wide structures is to reduce the level of competition in the merchandise license and sponsorship markets between teams within the same league. Competition between leagues in the merchandising market still exists, but the concentration of economic actors in sports merchandising has been increased. As a result, the aforementioned league structures are prototypical examples of collusion. . . .

. . . .

The cartel described above is inherently unstable because each team will find it profitable to increase its own output. For example, successful teams like the Yankees would find it in their interests to increase their market share by licensing their logos to a greater number of third parties than the league would allow. . . .

The incentives to cheat in the sports setting are even greater than those described for the stylized cartel model. This is because teams like the Yankees receive only 1/30th of the pooled licensing income, but the Yankees's marks generate more than 1/30th of the income. The same problem exists in football. In 1994, Jerry Jones's Cowboys lead the NFL with 30% of the merchandise sales, yet Jones only received 3.6% (1/28th) of the income. In response, Jones "cheated" on the NFL merchandise licensing structure by signing deals with Nike and Pepsi. Cheating of this type can lead to the unraveling of the entire cartel. As an increasing number of teams find it in their best interests to cheat, the entire league-wide merchandising system may fail.

Even if cheating does not cause the cartel to unravel, it may undermine its effectiveness to extract monopoly profits. . . .

While such cheating may undermine the effectiveness of the league-wide merchandising cartel, it does not necessarily lead to its complete failure. Although Steinbrenner and Jones have cheated, their cheating has not gone unpunished by their respective leagues. MLB has thrown Steinbrenner off its ruling executive committee for his cheating, and the NFL has sued Jones for trademark infringement. . . .

. . . .

The Individual Team argues that the league-wide merchandising structure lacks a substantial connection to the attainment of the leagues' legitimate goal. The leagues' goal is the production of an interrelated series of competitive games (the league product). The league-wide merchandising plan works against this goal by creating incentives that diminish the level of competitiveness. When games are less competitive, the value of the league product decreases, and most teams make less money.

The league plan fails to increase competitiveness in four ways: (1) sharing merchandise revenue creates disincentives for owners to pay to create competitive teams; (2) instead of eliminating the free-rider problem, the league plan exacerbates it; (3) the league plan provides no incentive for those teams who are inefficient and lower the value of the league product to exit the market; and (4) the teams would promote the league product better individually than they do when acting through the league.

i. Disincentive to Win

The problem with the league-wide restraints on individual merchandise licensing deals is that they create a disincentive to win. Under the league-wide plan, revenues from merchandising sales are shared equally among all teams. Without such a plan, teams would seek to maximize the value of their franchises because on-the-field performance would correlate with financial success. Under league-sharing arrangements, teams do not reap the full value of their on-the-field success. Instead, each team receives only 1/nth (where n is equal to the number of teams in the league) of the income generated. This creates an incentive for every team to lower its costs because all costs accrue to the team, while the team receives only 1/nth of the income it generates. Accordingly, teams would seek to sign cheaper, less competitive players. This would in turn would lead to less competitive teams. Since consumers value a high level of competition in addition to a certain parity of competition, the league-wide structure actually harms consumers. Without the league plan, each team would get all the benefits of its actions and all the losses. Teams would then seek to enter into lucrative endorsement deals, so as to purchase the better players. This type of bidding in the free market would make each team and the league as a whole more competitive.

ii. Exacerbates Free-Riding

The revenue sharing aspect of the league plan also exacerbates free-riding by smaller market teams. In the merchandising market, consumers buy a disproportionately large amount of merchandise licensed with the marks of popular or larger market teams. Nevertheless, all teams share equally in this income regardless of the amount of merchandise that was actually sold with any particular team's logo. Under this system, smaller market teams have no incentive to market their merchandise or the league product because they receive, for example, 95% of their merchandise and sponsorship revenue from the other teams. Thus rather than curing the free-rider problem, the league plan exacerbates it. If, however, teams were free to enter the market individually and license their logos and get sponsorship deals, this free-rider problem would disappear. This free market approach is better for the league product because in competition for merchandising revenues and sponsorships, all teams would have the incentive to promote their team and league.

Evidence of the free-rider problem abounds. . . . The league-wide plan actually creates disparity in competitiveness among teams, decreasing the league's overall value to consumers.

iii. Inefficient Subsidies

The league-wide plan creates a system that subsidizes inefficient teams by re-distributing revenue. This allows teams that contribute less to the league product to survive. There is no reason to assume that the current number of teams in each league is efficient. . . . The league might be better off without teams that cannot survive without subsidies.

iv. Individual Teams Are Better Promoters

Individual teams are better able to assess their local demographics, consumers, and sponsorship bases. This informational advantage is useful when teams are seeking sponsors or seeking to license their marks. The league cannot have better information about the local team than that local team. The informational cost for the league to investigate the markets of each individual team is greater than having the respective teams investigate their local markets. In part, it is this informational cost that makes the decentralized handling of team finances, player signings, and management more efficient than a singular entity. It is rather ironic that in these other areas the league has chosen to use a decentralized approach, but in the merchandising realm they have not, in spite of the advantages local teams would have in this area. In summary, the league's restriction adversely impacts the merchandising market itself and fails to stimulate competition in league games.

REFERENCES

38. Balaram Gupta, Names and Logos: Protection Under Intellectual Property Laws and Consequences, 2 Sports Law. J. 245, 246 (1995).

BRANDING

EXAMINING THE IMPORTANCE OF BRAND EQUITY IN PROFESSIONAL SPORT

James M. Gladden and George R. Milne

INTRODUCTION

Strategic brand management is an important focus of both marketing academics and practitioners. A brand is a name or symbol attached to a product that allows for differentiation from similar product offerings. . . . Management of brands is important because consumers base purchase decisions on their awareness, perception, and attachment to brands. . . . Specifically, brand equity represents positive or negative associations with a particular brand name (or logo/mark) that adds to (or subtracts from) the value provided by the product. . . .

Brand equity is also a vitally important tool for sport managers. Examples of sport-related businesses employing brand management strategies to grow revenues are increasingly evident. . . .

Such a strategic focus is not limited to corporately owned sport business entities. Executives of professional sport teams are turning to long-term strategic brand management as the overriding philosophy for their marketing efforts. . . .

A long-term focus on brand management strategies is warranted given the volatility of success in team sport. . . . In the past, substandard revenue generation has usually been blamed on a lack of on-field success. In response, sport managers have largely resorted to short-term tactics such as firing a head coach or signing a free agent to a multimillion-dollar contract. Although winning is vitally important, implementing short-term tactics does not necessarily guarantee long-term and consistent revenue streams. Further, sport managers have realized that winning is only part of the consumer's experience. . . .

. . . .

The conceptual framework . . . suggests antecedent conditions (team related, organization related, and market related) lead to the creation of brand equity (perceived quality, brand awareness, brand associations, and brand loyalty). Based on a team's brand equity, six forms of marketplace consequences result: national media exposure, merchandise sales, individual donations, corporate support, atmosphere, and ticket sales. The product of the antecedents, brand equity, and consequences then creates a marketplace perception. . . .

. . . The conceptual framework . . . can be expanded to provide for an understanding in the broader context of team sport. . . . Such changes allow for application of the framework to professional sport, both in North America and abroad. With the changes, two additional antecedents need to be recognized: the design of a team's logo and the stadium/arena in which the team plays are included as antecedents of brand equity. In addition, the consequence donations is expanded to "additional revenues" in order to better capture the abundance of miscellaneous marketing outcomes that result from brand equity. . . .

LOGO DESIGN

In recent years, professional sports teams have proven that brand equity can be created based on the logo and name of the team. By 1991, the San Jose Sharks of the National Hockey League (NHL) built up brand equity using logoed merchandise sales prior to the team's playing its first game. Through extensive research, San Jose developed a nickname (the Sharks) and a fashionable logo that created equity prior to ever playing a game. . . . The use of a logo to introduce a team has become a common tactic in both major and minor professional sport. In addition, teams with low brand equity are now turning to logo redesigns and color changes as a means of changing their image. . . .

STADIUM/ARENA

The building in which a sport team plays may significantly impact the development of brand equity. This may occur for two reasons. First, the relationship between the stadium and the organization varies across the sport industry. Some team owners own their stadiums/arenas and benefit greatly from complete control over the stadium's ancillary activities and revenue sources. However, often teams do not own their stadium/arena and are forced to negotiate lease arrangements. In some cases, these lease agreements allow for little control by the team. . . . Overall, those teams that have more control over the stadium are likely to generate more revenues from the stadium-related extensions such as concessions, parking, and luxury suites. . . . Such enhanced control also allows for increased marketing activity and consequently increased brand equity. . . .

Second, the stadium tradition and design may play an important part in the development of brand equity. Certain stadiums possess significant histories . . . whereas others are more generic. In addition, many new stadiums are being designed with nostalgic themes in mind . . . thus emphasizing the aesthetic qualities of the stadium or arena. A sport consumer's brand associations may be enhanced when the stadium itself plays a part in the attending or viewing experience. Extending this reasoning, the area in which the stadium or arena exists can also enhance the associations with the team sport product. . .

ADDITIONAL REVENUES

. . . This consequence is expanded to include all other marketing activities (aside from corporate support, ticket sales, and merchandise sales) that may benefit or suffer depending on the creation of brand equity. If a team possesses high brand equity, its ability to create revenue-generating marketing extensions will increase. Such extensions would include, but not be limited to . . . team-owned or licensed restaurants, practice facilities, and merchandise stores. . . .

IMPLICATIONS OF THE BRAND EQUITY FRAMEWORK

. . . . Building the brand requires a long term vision, thus implying brand equity is developed over time. Although specific antecedents to brand equity may not occur in a given year, the existence of brand equity from past development may suffice to produce positive marketplace outcomes. The conceptual framework for brand equity in the team sport setting reflects this view.

Given the framework, the next logical step is to assess the importance of brand equity in the realization of marketplace outcomes. If sport managers can predict which consequences result from brand equity (even in the absence of specific antecedents), they will be better able to manage their team's brand and realize positive marketplace consequences. Historically, winning has been consistently linked to increased team revenues and increased attendance. . . . Such knowledge largely justifies a short-term marketing approach that is geared around the success of the team. Therefore, in an effort to establish the utility of brand equity for sport managers, this study examines the importance of brand equity as compared to winning in the realization of a selected marketplace outcome (merchandise sales) over time.

. . . .

. . . The ability to license one's marks provides an excellent example of the strength of a brand name. Sport consumers purchase team-logoed merchandise in an effort to be affiliated with a given team. . . . Such affiliation, or "fan identification," may be largely the result of the brand loyalty and brand associations possessed by sport consumers. Because a team's logoed merchandise is sold outside of the home market, merchandise sales would provide a national indicator of brand equity. Unfortunately, the professional sport leagues do not release the team-by-team sales figures. However, rankings by team are published every year. . . .

. . . .

COMPARISONS OF THE IMPORTANCE OF
BRAND EQUITY AND WINNING

Interesting differences occurred in the relationship between brand equity and winning percentage and merchandise sales across the three professional sport leagues [examined]. In general, brand equity was more important to the sales of merchandise in the NHL and in MLB whereas winning percentage was more important in the NBA. Such findings have significant implications for sport managers.

There were positive relationships between both brand equity and winning percentage with the sales of team-logoed merchandise in the NHL. . . .

. . . Teams that have developed brand equity over time sell more team-logoed merchandise than do teams that experience short-term success or reap the benefits of recent entry into the league. Expansion teams such as the Mighty Ducks of Anaheim and San Jose Sharks experience high merchandise sales after unveiling their logos. However, this finding suggests the realization of such an outcome is only short-term. An analysis . . . reveals that established teams with long histories in the league . . . are annually the leaders in merchandise sales for the NHL.

Brand equity was more important to the attainment of merchandise sales in MLB. Across both definitions, only brand equity exhibited a positive relationship with merchandise sales. Again, the long-term development of brand equity was more important than short-term success. This is not surprising given the rich and lengthy history of Major League Baseball. The heritage and popularity of baseball stretch back more than 100 years. No other sport league in North America has been around for nearly this long. As a result, MLB teams have had the longest history of forging relationships and associations with sport consumers. Teams such as the Chicago Cubs, Los Angeles Dodgers, and New York Yankees were leaders in merchandise sales in the years studied despite not always having winning records.

These findings suggest NHL and MLB sport managers should focus their efforts toward building their team brand in addition to putting a winning team on the ice or field. Therefore, efforts should be made to increase the brand associations and brand loyalty for each team in these leagues. Particularly in the days of eight-figure annual salaries, it becomes even more important to focus on building the bond with the sport consumer. Given such high salaries, it is easier than ever for fans to feel disassociated with a professional sports team. . . .

These findings also have implications for managerial action specifically with respect to team-logoed merchandise. Teams with established and consistent levels of brand equity should definitely consider owning and operating a merchandise store. Because each of the leagues equally shares the royalties from the cumulative sales of logoed merchandise with all league members, teams that sell more merchandise do not receive a disproportionate payout. Therefore, to capitalize on high consumer demand and identification with the team, the sport team should open a merchandise store in which they will reap all of the profits. Such stores are now commonplace in most professional sport arenas. However, teams should also consider separate locations in high-traffic shopping areas. Along these lines, teams should explore creating their own catalogs and opening cyberstores at each of their individual Web site locations. Increased sales of logoed merchandise also serves to build brand awareness as the people purchasing the logoed merchandise then serve as walking billboards.

Winning percentage was a more important predictor of merchandise sales in the NBA. . . . This suggests that team-operated merchandise stores may be more reliant on success for sales, and are thus riskier ventures. Further, it also suggests apparel licensees of the NBA must be prepared to capitalize mostly on a short-term basis associated with winning seasons.

Overall, winning was a significant predictor of merchandise sales in two of the three professional sport leagues examined. Based on these results, teams should consider implementing logo redesigns when their team is winning rather than when their team is losing (as is so often the case in today's marketplace). Logo redesigns should be employed to change or enhance the image of a team. If a losing team redesigns its logo and changes its colors, the new brand associations developed by the consumer will still be attached to a losing team. Therefore, sport managers should wait until their team begins to improve (or has a better chance of improving) before they attempt to make image modifications through their logo. In addition, the sport manager should manipulate other antecedents to brand equity concurrent with attempts to maximize marketplace outcomes. For example, when a team experiences moderate success and introduces a new logo, it may also want to sign a highly acclaimed

TABLE 2.

Top Team Merchandise Sales, 2002–2003: NBA and NFL	
NBA	*NFL*
1) Los Angeles Lakers	Oakland Raiders
2) New York Knicks	Tampa Bay Buccaneers
3) Philadelphia 76ers	Dallas Cowboys
4) Boston Celtics	Green Bay Packers
5) New Jersey Nets	Pittsburgh Steelers
6) Washington Wizards	Philadelphia Eagles
7) Chicago Bulls	Chicago Bears
8) Sacramento Kings	St. Louis Rams
9) Orlando Magic	New England Patriots
10) Dallas Mavericks	San Francisco 49ers

Source: ESPN.com.

TABLE 3.

Top Jersey Sales, 2002–2003: NBA and NFL	
NBA	*NFL*
1) Kobe Bryant	Brian Urlacher
2) Allen Iverson	Ricky Williams
3) Tracy McGrady	Michael Vick
4) Michael Jordan	Warren Sapp
5) Paul Pierce	Donovan McNabb
6) Jason Kidd	Tom Brady
7) Shaquille O'Neal	Jerry Rice
8) Latrell Sprewell	Jeff Garcia
9) Dirk Nowitzki	Jeremy Shockey
10) Michael Finley	Brett Favre

Source: NBA.

free agent to further fuel the development of brand equity. Clearly, this suggests that the adaptation of a strategic brand management focus requires commitment from the top of the organization such that the marketing, business, and player personnel divisions of the team work together.

. . . .

TABLE 4.

Top Athlete Shoe and Apparel Deals		
Athlete	*Shoe company*	*Value*
Tiger Woods	Nike	$100M/5 yrs.
LeBron James	Nike	$90M/7 yrs.
Allen Iverson	Reebok	$10M/1 yr.
Michael Jordan	Nike	$47M/5 yrs.
Kobe Bryant	Nike	$40M/5 yrs.
Venus Williams	Reebok	$40M/5 yrs.
[*Serena Williams*]	[*Nike*]	[*$55M/8 yrs.*]

Source: http://money.cnn.com/2003/07/21/news/companies/kobe_impact/index.htm.

CONCLUSION AND FUTURE DIRECTIONS

This study has established that, in addition to winning, a focus on strategic brand management is also warranted in professional sport. Sport is unique in the way that it impacts its customers and fan base. . . . The core product, performance in competition, is inconsistent and very difficult for the sport manager to control. In addition, there are cases where winning occurs but positive marketplace outcomes do not result. . . . By expanding the focus of strategic marketing to include efforts to increase brand awareness, brand associations, and brand loyalty, the sport manager can improve the frequency and degree to which positive marketplace consequences are realized.

. . . .

Finally, it would be instructive to begin evaluating the development of brand equity by professional athletes competing in individual, rather than team, sports. Professional tennis players, golfers, and even extreme athletes develop brand equity associated with their names and images. . . . (See Tables 2 and 3 for a list of top merchandise sales by league and by player, respectively, and Table 4 for a list of top athlete shoe/apparel deals.)

Understanding Brand Loyalty in Professional Sport: Examining the Link Between Brand Associations and Brand Loyalty

James M. Gladden and Daniel C. Funk

Brand loyalty is important to sport teams for two broad reasons. First, brand loyalty ensures a more stable following even when the core product's performance falters (i.e. the team has a losing season). As a result of such loyalty, a price premium can be charged. . . . In many cases, teams have been able to leverage this price premium to increase revenues and help offset areas where expenses are increasing (e.g. player salaries and debt obligation on new stadiums or arenas). Brand loyalty also ensures a more stable following through the broadcast media. . . .

Second, brand loyalty creates opportunities for product extensions beyond the core product. . . . New products such as team-related merchandise stores and restaurants in close proximity to the venue enable the team to create additional revenue streams by owning and operating the ventures or sharing in profits through licensing agreements. Similarly, admission is now being charged to practice facilities of professional teams. High brand loyalty also allows the team to offer these brand extensions across geographic boundaries. . . .

. . . .

BRAND MANAGEMENT

. . . .

. . . Brand associations are anything in a consumer's memory linked to a specific brand. Such associations form networks ultimately creating an overall brand image. . . . In team sport a wide variety of associations are formed, most of which are intangible and experiential. . . . Some might see the game as an opportunity to watch their favorite team, while others might view it as a social outing. Collectively, some audiences (e.g. Los Angeles Lakers' spectators) are very focused on the social experience and peripheral activities, while others (e.g. Cleveland Browns' spectators) are

194

solely focused on the actual game. Therefore, it is important for sport marketers to understand the type of associations consumers have when consuming (in person or through the various forms of media) a team sport product. If the sport marketer understands what creates brand associations, then marketing activities can be geared toward creating new, favorable brand associations and reinforcing the positive brand associations that exist. . . .

. . . .

BRAND LOYALTY

. . . .

The Link Between Brand Associations and Brand Loyalty

. . . .

As a starting point in examining the link between brand associations and brand loyalty, this study examines one segment of consumers, those already exhibiting a propensity to follow a particular team. Loyal followers ensure a more stable following, and consequently a more stable revenue stream over time. Whereas it is also important to understand casual followers, or those people exhibiting spurious loyalty, this segment does not provide consistent revenues to the team in the long term. By understanding loyal followers, team marketers would be more able to design programs and communications tailored to nurturing and reinforcing the key brand associations related to loyalty. Therefore, it can be argued that it is logical to begin with the segment that is most important to the organization — those people that are already committed followers.

. . . .

DISCUSSION

. . . This research begins to provide insights into what aspects of the professional sport team brand should be focal points when devising marketing efforts targeted to highly loyal fans.

. . . .

It is interesting to note that only three of the eight association dimensions classified as attributes were significant predictors of brand loyalty (i.e. tradition, product delivery, and star player). Meanwhile, four of the five benefit dimensions were predictive of team loyalty (i.e. identification, nostalgia, peer group acceptance, and escape). These results suggest that efforts to nurture and maintain long-term brand loyalty may be augmented by understanding the role the team plays in consumers' daily lives. That is, the sport marketer should ask: "what benefits does the team provide my core consumers?" For example, sport marketers should begin asking how identification with the sport team can be more effectively enhanced. Strategies such as heightened communications through a variety of mediums (email, mail, and special "limited access" events) may serve to enhance and reinforce the degree to which committed consumers feel like they are treated special and truly part of a team.

This research also brings into question the importance of success in fostering brand loyalty. Certainly, winning leads to short-term positive marketplace outcomes. However, this research indicates that the success of the team is not a significant predictor of long-term brand loyalty. In one sense, this is good news for sport marketers because it suggests that winning is not related to (i.e. predictive of) team loyalty among committed consumers. In another sense, this finding presents a significant challenge. . . . : understanding what brand associations can be used to transition a casual follower (or someone whose loyalty is spurious) into a loyal follower. . . . Nevertheless, this research suggests it may be foolhardy to hinge all marketing energies on whether a team wins or loses. . . . Furthermore, attributes of the sport product often identified to be integral in attracting fans (e.g. a new stadium, a charismatic head coach), were not found to be significant predictors of team loyalty among highly loyal consumers. Rather, there was a much stronger link between team loyalty and satisfying specific consumer needs. . . .

. . . Among the 13 association dimensions, identification . . . was most predictive of team loyalty. . . . This relationship suggests efforts toward reinforcing identification among highly committed fans are advisable. To do so, the sport organization must adopt a customer-oriented focus. . . . This suggests teams should strive to provide an optimal experience every time the loyal consumer comes into contact with the team brand. This might also include special access to players, coaches, and other team executives as a means of making the highly identified fan feel like a part of the team. For example, special chat rooms with players could be created for those belonging to a special fan club. Similarly, teams could send daily emails to fans updating them on practices, injuries, and other interesting tidbits.

Sport teams also evoke fond memories from the past as evidenced by the strong positive relationship between nostalgia and brand loyalty. . . . The challenge for team marketers is to determine what team aspects evoke memories of the past in the minds of loyal fans. . . . Once these catalysts of nostalgia are identified, marketing communications can be tailored to remind the consumer of the team's ability to satisfy that need by priming nostalgic associations. . . .

The benefit of escape was observed to be a significant predictor of team loyalty. . . . This suggests that the sport team's ability to provide an escape is an important part of the committed fan's everyday life. To capitalize on the relationship between escape and team loyalty, team marketers should strive to increase the frequency with which the team provides an escape for the fan. Witness the fact that player drafts have turned into nationally televised events and the number of people participating in fantasy sports and leagues are at an all-time high as evidence of people's desire to escape into their favorite team's management. A team's Web site provides an excellent tool to increase the frequency with which someone escapes through the team. For example, video clips from past games and on-going or current press conferences allow the fan to be involved with the team more frequently. . . .

The negative relationship found between peer group acceptance and team loyalty . . . is understandable. The highly-committed fan might be offended by the suggestion that they follow a particular team *only* because their friends do. Rather, the construct of peer group acceptance may be more important to individuals who possess a slight or mild interest in a particular team. For these individuals, the ability to achieve social acceptance may be more highly associated with outcomes related to the team. . . .

In terms of attribute dimensions, negative relationships were observed between team loyalty and tradition and star players. At first glance, the negative relationship between tradition and brand loyalty . . . was perplexing. It is more likely the case that fans of perennial losing teams do not associate tradition with their team since a rich, winning tradition has never existed. Another explanation may rest in the history of North American professional sport. As recently as 30 years ago, there were less than 20 teams in each of the North American professional sport leagues. Today, each league is at or above 30 teams. Thus, in each instance, nearly half of the league's teams have not had time to develop a "rich history" or a "tradition of winning," as the items were worded. The implication of this suggestion is that loyalty can be created in the absence of a strong history. . . .

Given the amount of sport promotion that revolves around the athlete, and in particular, star athletes, one might expect there to be a positive relationship between star players and team loyalty. However, as the results demonstrate, there is actually a significant negative relationship. . . . Given the highly-committed nature of respondents, the presence of star players may have little impact on the loyal fan. Alternatively, the highly-mobile nature of today's North American professional athlete may have decreased the importance of the player to the highly-committed fan. This suggests that while building marketing campaigns around star players may succeed in encouraging product trial, there is no evidence to suggest this will also be effective in reinforcing long-term loyalty. Therefore, in a time of open markets and frequent player movement (even among the most talented players), building a branding strategy based on a player or players may not be the most advisable strategy for communicating with highly-committed fans.

Instead, this research suggests the sport marketer should focus on providing an entertaining experience for the highly committed fan. Consistent with past research efforts . . . that suggest the consumer of sport has a need to be entertained, there was a significant positive relationship between product delivery and team loyalty. . . . Thus, while winning was not a significant predictor of team loyalty among highly-committed fans, the ability of a team to entertain was. . . . Further, this finding brings into question recent pay-per-view strategies employed by teams. Rather than charging people to follow the team through the media, the team should focus on continually expanding its reach as a means of reaching highly-committed fans that do not attend games.

DISCUSSION QUESTIONS

1. What incentives do leagues provide for owners to offer greater cooperation with league licensing rules?

2. Why are teams tempted to defy league rules regarding the sale of licensed goods?

3. How can a sports franchise maintain long-term loyalty among its fans?

4. Why is a brand-oriented approach important to a sports franchise?

5. How can professional sports teams enhance their brand equity?

6. How is a professional sports team's development of brand equity affected by its league's revenue-sharing mechanisms?

7. Should the licensing agreements of professional sports leagues be amended to better balance the goals of the leagues with the individual teams' ability to market themselves? How would you restructure these agreements?

8. How are the licensing agreements of professional sports leagues optimal or suboptimal?

CHAPTER 8

LABOR MATTERS: UNIONS

INTRODUCTION

The agreement between management and labor and how they will conduct business between themselves as well as resolve disputes is set forth in their collective bargaining agreement (CBA). This agreement is hammered out in the collective bargaining process, a process that in sports, as in other industries, is often bounded by the economic weapons of a lockout or strike.

The framework for this relationship for U.S. based sports leagues is established by the National Labor Relations Act (NLRA). The first selection, "Blue-Collar Law and Basketball," focuses on the technical and cultural applicability of the labor–management legal and business regime on sports. The focus in this excerpt is basketball, but the substance is applicable to all sports. The key business lesson highlights the dilemma of facing labor strife with high-profile unions often peopled by multimillionaires.

As with any business enterprise utilizing workers, the union issues must be fully contemplated. Sports business leaders should have a clear vision of how to address union matters. It is important, too, that union leaders and members understand how their organization fits into the sports business model.

A unique aspect of both the sports and entertainment industries is that the unions allow the individual employees to negotiate their salaries on their own. In contrast to the steelworkers and other unions that establish salaries along with the other collectively negotiated terms and conditions of employment, the salary negotiation in professional sports is typically in the hands of the athlete. The collective bargaining agreement establishes only a minimum floor for negotiations in most sports leagues. In the case of the NBA, the collective bargaining agreement sets a ceiling as well. Thus, collective bargaining agreements in professional sports merely set general salary parameters instead of the actual salaries. The next chapter fully explores this compensation issue.

The Major League Baseball Players Association is considered by many to be one of the strongest unions in existence in any industry. "Major League Baseball's Labor Turmoil: The Failure of the Counter-Revolution," written by noted baseball agent Jeff Moorad, provides a good foundation of the union basics and sets forth the framework for collective bargaining. From this reading a firmer grasp of the labor–management history in sports should be obtained.

"Creating a Win–Win Situation Through Collective Bargaining: The NFL Salary Cap" looks at one of the tools created in recent years in the collective bargaining process, the salary cap. Although the focus of this article is the NFL, a salary containment mechanism is now a staple of virtually every sports league labor negotiation. This excerpt is valuable, not only for looking at some of the specifics of a selected salary cap, but also for understanding how a league and union might deal with any single issue such as drug testing, the number of preseason games, or roster sizes. (See Table 1 for a time-line of labor relations in professional sports.)

TABLE 1.

TIME LINE OF LABOR RELATIONS IN PROFESSIONAL SPORTS

MLB

1885: National Brotherhood of Professional Ball Players founded
1890: Players' League founded
1900: League Protective Players' Association founded
1912: Baseball Players Fraternity founded
1946: American Baseball Guild founded
1954: Major League Baseball Players Association founded
1966: Marvin Miller named executive director of MLBPA
1972: Strike, 13 days
1973: Lockout, 17 days
1976: Lockout, 17 days
1981: Strike, 50 days
1985: Strike, 2 days
1990: Lockout, 32 days
1994–1995: Strike, 232 days

NFL

1956: NFLPA formed
1968: Strike/lockout, 10 days
1971: Strike/lockout, 20 days
1974: Strike, 42 days
1982: Strike, 57 days
1987: Strike, 24 days
1988: NFLPA decertified
1993: NFLPA recertified

NHL

1958: NHLPA formed
1992: Strike, 10 days
1994: Lockout, 103 days

NBA

1954: NBPA formed
1995: Lockout, 77 days
1998: Lockout, 191 days

BLUE-COLLAR LAW AND BASKETBALL

Mark Conrad

Maybe you don't see a connection between those men and women who risked everything they had to ask for minimum wage, overtime, and safe working conditions, and . . . basketball players . . . especially given the rather substantial wages some of them receive. The connection is there, however, and it is as real as the . . . NBA finals . . . What is at stake when professional athletes strike is a principle, and a protection for every working man and woman, a protection once fought for in the streets of our nation, with fists and guns, and lynching and mass arrest.

— Commentator Howard Cosell

. . . . [The author's introduction is omitted.]

THE LABOR LAW MODEL

American labor law concepts — conceived to protect blue-collar workers in their quest to improve working conditions — have been injected into the world of professional basketball as well as other sports, over the last quarter of the twentieth century. Although basketball fans may hate to admit it, labor law in sports is here to stay.

In one sense, it is incongruous. Professional basketball employs personnel to represent elite, skilled practitioners of a sport barely a century old. Their working conditions (about six or seven months per year, arguably less than thirty-five hours per week) and their compensation scales are beyond the hopes and aspirations of the ordinary or even not-so-ordinary American worker. With an average salary of $1.5 million per season in 1998, players in the National Basketball Association surpassed the averages for partners in the nation's largest law firms and all but the very top surgeons; some salaries even exceeded those of many CEOs of Fortune 500 corporations. *[The average salary in the NBA was $4.5 million in 2002–2003 season.]*

Also, unlike the automobile and steel industries, professional basketball is a relatively new business, which came to fruition well after New York Senator Robert Wagner drafted the National Labor Relations Act in 1935. At the time of the law, Senator Wagner most likely did not consider it applicable to the weak professional basketball leagues of his day, which could not compete with the successful college basketball game of the 1930s. At Wagner's death in 1951, the modern NBA — conceived from the merger of the Basketball Association of America and the National Basketball League — was just two years old.

The passage of the National Labor Relations Act (NLRA) in 1935 marked a milestone in American labor. Called the "Magna Carta of Labor," the NLRA was intended to protect auto workers, printers, and clerical employees in their quest to unionize and bargain collectively with management without the fear of retaliation. The enactment of this law changed the nature of labor–management relations.

. . . .

The NLRA guarantees workers the right to be represented by a union and provides for specific methods to attain union representation and employer recognition of a particular "collective bargaining unit" to negotiate on behalf of a group of workers. Elections are held, and if the National Labor Relations Board certifies the results, the union is recognized. Usually, if union recognition is granted, individual employees lose their right to negotiate on such subjects as "wages, hours or working conditions."

The NLRA also gives employees the right to strike. Most strikes occur when a satisfactory collective bargaining agreement, usually an attempt to secure better wages, hours, or working conditions, cannot be reached. This pits the collective economic power of the unionized workers against the employer's attempts to go on without the aid of their labor. Employers may replace striking workers with temporary or permanent replacements or get by with managerial employees who are not part of the collective-bargaining unit. (This was done in the 1987 National Football League strike.)

The flip side of the strike is the lockout, a tactical measure taken in blue-collar law and basketball by employers to prevent the union members from working. Just as the strike is an economic pressure tactic taken by the union, the lockout is a similar strategy for management. With the expiration of a collective-bargaining agreement, management may prefer to "call the shots" in determining the shutdown of an operation, rather than wait for the union to seize the opportunity. This tactic was employed by the National Hockey League (NHL) in 1994, resulting in a disruption of almost half the season. In 1998 the NBA owners, possibly taking their cue from the NHL outcome, declared a lockout in basketball.

One of the central components to the NLRA involves a series of actions known as "unfair labor practices." Both employers and employees may be liable for these violations, which include interference with the unionization process, discriminatory treatment against employees for union-related activities, and most important, the refusal by either side to bargain in good faith. The last condition requires both sides to negotiate on the "mandatory" subjects — wages, hours, and working conditions. The law also established the National Labor Relations Board as the administrative agency to enforce the mandates of the NLRA.

APPLICATION TO BASKETBALL

To keep operating costs down, the NBA originally copied the system employed in professional baseball and football to restrain player salaries. That device, the use of a "reserve" system to hitch players to their respective teams, severely restricted players' right to test their talents on the open market. This de facto monopolization achieved its effect and resulted in considerably lower player salaries, due to the lack of a free market for the players. The use of a contractual limitation on the right to secure employment remains a unique element of sports law and one of the most hotly contested issues in labor–management relations to this very day.

Yet trade unionism in the NBA came slowly. The National Basketball Players Association (NBPA) was formed in 1954, with Boston Celtics great Bob Cousy as its leader. Taking a cue from the nineteenth-century captains of industry, the NBA at first refused to recognize the association. In 1957, Commissioner Maurice Podoloff reluctantly conceded its validity, in part because he feared the NBPA would affiliate itself with a larger and stronger union, such as the steelworkers or teamsters. But the union's mettle was not seriously tested until 1964, when the NBPA threatened a strike at the 1964 All-Star Game.

In the 1950s, most professional sports "unions" were more like medieval guilds than modern labor organizations. The idea of collective bargaining between the union representatives and basketball owners did not begin in earnest until the 1960s, at just about the time that the percentage of unionized American workers began to shrink. Union membership in the United States peaked in 1953 to 37 percent of nonagricultural workers and has dropped steadily since. By 1991, the figure was 16 percent.[10] Though sports unions, including the NBPA, were late bloomers, in recent years they have crafted a singular position among American labor.

It was during the regime of union executive director Larry Fleisher that the NBPA began to think of itself in the same mold as other trade unions. Fleisher, called "the most successful labor leader of the 20th century"[11] by former New Jersey senator Bill Bradley, served as the head of the union until 1988 and negotiated the groundbreaking 1983 and 1988 collective bargaining agreements (CBAs), which created the salary-cap structure but also guaranteed the players a percentage of league revenues in either salary or benefits. In 1967, the average salary of an NBA player was $9,400; when Fleisher retired, it was $600,000. Not as well known as his compatriots Marvin Miller in baseball and Ed Garvey in football, Fleisher ably guided his players gradually, without protracted litigation and strikes.

In those days, the NBPA's representation dovetailed some of their experiences with those of other unions. Some thought their labor battles were a central component to trade unionism, as was stated by the late sports commentator Howard Cosell, in the epigraph to this chapter.[12] In the 1960s, Cosell's assessment accurately reflected the kinship between sports unions and unions at large. Today it serves as cant, glossing over major differences between the American labor experience on the one hand and the NBA and its players on the other. The differences far outweigh the similarities, legally, economically, and practically.

THE PECULIARITIES OF BASKETBALL LABOR LAW

As *New York Times* sportswriter Murray Chass has noted, collective bargaining in professional sports has been described less as negotiating over working conditions than as "two mega-corporations talking to each other about mergers or splits or sales."[13] In the recently expired 1995 NBA collective bargaining agreement are sections that would be unheard of in a typical CBA.

First, much space was devoted to revenue sharing between the employer teams and the players. Players shared 59 percent of "gross defined revenues" and were guaranteed 48 percent of all NBA revenues — a staggering $700 million in 1994–95. *[The players shared nearly 65% of the approximately $2.5 billion in NBA revenues in the 2002–2003 season.]* Such revenues included fees from arena signage, sponsorships, parking, concessions, and luxury boxes. Players were entitled to share in the moneys generated from licensing and merchandising. True, some indications of a traditional labor contract exist, such as the minimum salary. But that amount, which began at $225,000 per season and rose to $272,500, towers over the $500-per-week minimum one frequently finds in the general labor force. And we are not even considering the complicated salary-cap structure.

The very nature of this agreement is more akin to a European Social Democratic partnership between labor and management than to the typical American model. It is both an irony and a success story that such sharing of the wealth has the potential to make both the employers and the employees very rich.

This brings us to the nature of the services and the public loyalty to the services provided. Brand loyalty occupies a sacred place in the dreams of a marketer. If a company's brand name exudes stature and quality, it will retain a following among consumers of that type of product. And that will be the case even if the actual quality of the brand suffers. To paraphrase that often-stated theme from the 1992 presidential campaign: "It's the perception, stupid."

Most buyers do not care who makes the cars they drive, as long as the vehicles run dependably, are well designed, and have reasonable comfort and performance. Even in a service industry, one doesn't care about who the individual employees are but rather about the service itself. So, while the employee is a cog in the overall scheme, the replacement of that person with another will not necessarily cause consumer discomfort (unless the service declines in quality).

Contrast this with professional basketball players. The fan loyalty to a star player may be of incalculable value. Only a very small number of athletes play professional basketball in the United States; they make up an elite group by definition, especially considering the millions who play the game. Only a select few make the cut through high school, college, and the draft to get in and stay in the NBA and to occupy an exalted place there. And unlike other industries, where a choice of products abounds, basketball has one — the NBA. Without any rival, the NBA is the ultimate brand, and its employees are the ultimate makers of that brand.

The athletes' clout is a function not only of their unique skills but also of the unique relationship consumers have with the service they deliver. The players' agents and their union leaders know this all too well. With the value of the individual players far from being equal, basketball stars such as Michael Jordan, Patrick Ewing, Kevin Garnett, and Shaquille O'Neal can command huge salaries, bonuses, and other contractual perks negotiated through a position of tremendous strength. They and the other elites who dominate their franchise get the top marquee billing. The less-talented players, good enough to play but not to star in the NBA, do the job but are not irreplaceable. The wide disparity in value of the talent makes the NBA players a widely diverse union, a group of employees with great differences of wages. Consequently, it is a union that is very hard to hold together. Fleisher could do so; things have become more difficult since.

In the 1980s, the union and the NBA negotiated novel CBAs that dramatically changed the landscape of professional sports. In 1981, sixteen of the then twenty-three teams lost money. Rumors of rampant drug use and escalating salaries resulted in declines in game attendance, television ratings, and league revenues.[14] Sensing the desperate situation, both the NBA and NBPA concluded the 1983 CBA, the first to include revenue sharing (53 percent of gross revenues, including the national TV contract, local gate profits, playoff profits) in return for a team cap on salaries. This CBA was further refined in 1988.

The league and the union became victims of their success. As professional basketball attained new heights of popularity both in the United States and worldwide, the marquee value of teams and players increased. Today, a great disparity in salaries exists. In 1998, 40 players made over $5 million per season and 120 made the league minimum. *[In the 2002–2003 season, 101 players made over $5 million and 28 made the league rookie minimum of $349,458.]* Free-agency rights apply only to certain veteran players. The salary-cap structure is porous, permitting the elites to command whatever the market will bear as long as they stay with their teams. While the union negotiates many working conditions on behalf of all the players, it does not mandate the actual money individual players make. The resulting disparity adversely affects union solidarity — difficult in many situations but far more challenging for the leader of the NBPA.

UNION RULES?

Tensions exist in many unions. But the kinds of tension that now exist at the NBPA reflect the huge differences between castes of players. For the best and the brightest, the union may be a hindrance and can put them in a weaker position than if they were "on their own." As the CBA does not involve individual salary negotiation, the impact that player agents have on the process is not insignificant. The major agents representing the big-time players do not have any built-in loyalty to the NBPA or to its continued existence. Indeed, attempts at decertification of the NBPA were seriously considered in 1995, during a period of contentious negotiations. Michael Jordan, Patrick Ewing, and Reggie Miller signed decertification notices because they were dissatisfied with the leadership of the union. They feared that the union would capitulate into accepting a "harder" salary cap. A tentative agreement exacerbated the issue. Ultimately, the union prevailed by a 226–134 vote, or 63 percent against decertification. The union accepted a final collective bargaining agreement the next year. Yet the issue of player "haves" versus player "have-nots" will not go away, and decertification may be revisited. . . .

These problems represent an inner weakness in a union of such disparate members and a systematic weakness of individual (both in the performance sense and in the negotiating sense) employees attempting to band together. The greater the salary disparities, the more untenable the NBPA is. The structure of these labor–management relations also has led to use of a legal tactic that has probably done as much or more to accomplish union goals than collective bargaining: invocation of antitrust laws.

THE ANTITRUST TANGO

As every law student knows, antitrust law ranks as one of those subjects full of theorists, long on explanation, and brimming with complex judicial determinations. Most unions do not partake of antitrust theory in their dealings with employers. The NBPA (along with the National Football League Players Association) has made antitrust application a virtual art form.

The basic antitrust laws — the Sherman Antitrust Act and the Clayton Act — date from 1890 and 1914 respectively and apply to concerted activities that restrain trade in interstate commerce. The intentions of these laws were to stop monopolistic activities that often resulted in large "trusts" in such industries as oil, sugar, and tobacco. To avoid the argument that union activity may constitute restraint of trade, section 6 of the Clayton Act states that "the labor or commerce of a human being is not subject to antitrust laws." The scope of that provision has been a matter of considerable academic debate and practical application in the field of sports law.

Ostensibly, section 6 protects unions and employers from engaging in concerted activities such as strikes and lockouts. But what if there are sections in a collective bargaining agreement that may have antitrust implications? For example, does a salary cap or a limitation of free agency become a restraint of trade under antitrust laws? Because of the history of free-agency limitations and salary restrictions in all professional sports, including basketball, this issue has occupied the time of a number of courts over the last two decades of the twentieth century.

In the NBA, the issue has been the continuing validity of the exemption during and after the expiration of a collective bargaining agreement. In the case of *Wood v. NBA,*[19] Leon Wood, a point guard on the 1984 gold-medal U.S. Olympic team, was picked by the Philadelphia 76ers in the first round. Because of salary-cap constraints, Wood was offered a $75,000 one-year contract, well below his true market value. Ultimately, when cap room became available, his contract was amended to a four-year $1 million deal. Nevertheless, he sued the NBA, claiming that the cap violated antitrust laws. Wood was still in college at the ratification of the 1983 CBA that created the system and alleged that he should be a party to its provisions. The court rejected his claims, as the agreement was subject to the labor exemption. Otherwise, the court noted, federal labor policy would be subverted.

Also in 1987, a lower federal court, ruling in *Bridgeman v. NBA,*[20] concluded that the labor exemption continues to apply after the conclusion of a CBA during an impasse stage, if the employer "reasonably believes that the practice or a close variant of it will be incorporated in the next collective bargaining agreement." Junior Bridgeman challenged the cap rules but also lost. Shortly afterward, the 1988 CBA was concluded. . . .

The results of the *Bridgeman* case demonstrate how the NBPA turned a defeat into a victory. Even though the NBA won, the union, in a daring and ingenious move, threatened to decertify itself — meaning that no collective bargaining process would be in place and the owners would be wide open to antitrust suits. The plan worked; the NBA capitulated, not wanting anything to do with negotiating individual contracts with players in a free market, subject to antitrust laws. Shortly afterward, the parties concluded the 1988 agreement.

The ingenious tête-a-tête between labor and antitrust has benefited the NBPA. It is difficult to conceive of a nonsports union working the legal realm in such a way. Given the recent vintage of the NBPA, the disparity of talents and of payments made to its members, and the power of the player agents, it is ironic that the basketball players union could utilize the labor laws — especially the decertification threat — as a negotiating tactic to get its way. Or maybe, because of these attributes, the decertification sword had to be utilized to make the union's point.

In fact, a strong possibility for decertification exists in the not-too-distant future. The elite twenty-five players who help establish the worldwide recognition of the NBA don't need a union. They could thrive in a nonunion market because their services are in demand. But the lesser stars and journeymen would suffer in an environment where the gulf among the players may be as wide as the disparities between the players and the owners.

A FEW LAST WORDS

Despite the fissures in the union, the disparate interests, the pressures from the agents, and the difficulties of bargaining with a league composed of twenty-nine separate entities, the NBA players have done exceedingly well. And for most of the 1980s and 1990s, management has also done well in this fascinating industrial partnership. . . .

. . . .

But when all is said and done, the fact remains that in a splintered union of six-figure employees, millionaires, and multimillionaires using the labor and antitrust laws to win concessions from multiparty employers who are multimillionaires or billionaires themselves, something is askew. Is this what Robert Wagner had in mind when he drafted the landmark National Labor Relations Act? That's hard to believe.

REFERENCES

10. See also Melvyn Dubofsky, *The State and Labor in Modern America* (Chapel Hill: University of North Carolina Press, 1994), 130, cited in Deborah A. Ballam, "The Law as a Constitutive Force for Change, Part II: The Impact of the National Labor Relations Act on the U.S. Labor Movement," *American Business Law Journal* 123, 126 (1995).

11. "Fleisher Is Eulogized," *New York Times,* May 9, 1989, D3.

12. Howard Cosell, *What's Wrong with Sports* (New York: Pocketbooks, 1991).

13. See Murray Chass, "As Trade Unions Struggle, Their Sports Cousins Thrive," *New York Times,* September 5, 1994, i; Kenneth A. Kovach, Patrizia Ricci, and Aladino Robles, "Is Nothing Sacred? Labor Strife in Professional Sports," *Business Horizons* (January 11, 1998): 34.

14. Martin Greenberg, *Sports Law Practice* (Charlottesville, Va.: Michie, 1993), vol. 1, 210.

19. 809 F. 2d 954 (2d Cir. 1987).

20. 675 F. Supp. 960 (D.N.J. 1987).

MICRO: LEAGUE PERSPECTIVES

MAJOR LEAGUE BASEBALL'S LABOR TURMOIL: THE FAILURE OF THE COUNTER-REVOLUTION

Jeffrey S. Moorad

I. THE HISTORY OF LABOR RELATIONS IN BASEBALL

To understand the current tenor of labor relations in baseball, it is important to analyze their history. This history reveals patterns of owner behavior that readily explain the atmosphere of mistrust and animosity that pervades the sport to this day.

A. The Reserve Clause

Although the official position of baseball's first governing body, the National Association of Baseball Players, was that paying players for their services was "reprehensible and not in the best interests of the game," it was not uncommon for teams to pay talented players. Many players began to move from team to team during the season, allowing for greater compensation, a practice called "revolving."

Revolving continued as regular professional play began. Talented players found that "contract jumping" created competition for their services and thus increased their compensation. This practice proved financially ruinous for the nascent National League clubs, however, and as a result more than one-half of the League's teams collapsed under the economic strain caused by competition for players.

The owners of the remaining National League clubs, determined to halt contract jumping, reached a secret "gentlemen's agreement" under which each team could "reserve" five players. Other teams agreed not to court players on the reserve lists. These lists proved so successful in stifling increases in player salaries that by the 1890s every professional baseball contract included a reserve clause.

The reserve clause allowed a team to renew a player's contract for one year unilaterally upon its expiration, even if the player refused to re-sign with the team. Because the new contract would also include a reserve clause, players found themselves in a contractual hall of mirrors, with endlessly repeating obligations and no reasonable way out. Players could not seek employment with other teams; those that did, found themselves permanently barred from the sport. Thus, players remained bound to their original team, absent retirement or the team's decision to trade or cut them. These conditions led one judge to liken the practice to indentured servitude. . . .

The owners' purported rationale for the maintenance of the reserve system was the necessity of maintaining healthy and robust competition between teams, a dynamic referred to as "competitive balance." Competitive balance was indeed an issue at times during the early years of professional baseball. However, the reserve system was hardly a panacea. At the same time owners were prohibiting players from choosing to switch teams on their own, they often promoted competitive imbalance. Poor clubs would literally sell the contracts of their talented players to richer teams. As has frequently been the case, owner justification for policies limiting player freedom were disingenuous at best.

. . . . *[The author's discussion of the development of baseball's exemption from the antitrust laws and the additional leverage this provides management in labor negotiations is omitted.]*

C. The Rise of the Player Association

Players' efforts to gain bargaining strength through the formation of a collective bargaining unit date back more than a century. In 1885, John Montgomery Ward, a shortstop with the New York Giants, formed the Brotherhood of Professional Baseball Players. The Brotherhood's goal was to fight the reserve clause and the $2,500 salary cap imposed by owners. After the failure of its Players League, the Brotherhood collapsed in 1891.

Over the next five decades, two additional attempts at organization were made. First came the Players Fraternity, which enjoyed some success as a result of the concurrent establishment of the Federal League in 1914. The additional league provided players with leverage, and collectively they had a measure of power. Because the Players Fraternity's fortunes were intertwined with those of the Federal League, however, the union dissolved along with the Federal League in 1915.

In 1946, Robert Murphy, a Boston attorney, made another attempt at unionization. Murphy hoped his organization, the American Baseball Guild, would give players the leverage they needed to increase their salaries at a time when star players were dying in poverty. Unfortunately, the decidedly anti-union environment of the mid-1940s doomed Murphy's efforts. Finally, in 1954 the players voted to establish the Major League Baseball Players Association (MLBPA). . .

. . . [Eventually], the players hired Marvin Miller, a negotiator for the United Steelworkers Union. Within a year, the MLBPA, under Miller's leadership, had settled upon a pension plan and virtually doubled players' benefits. After years of stagnation, the MLBPA became so effective under Miller's stewardship that MLB was compelled to form its own collective bargaining unit, the Player Relations Committee (PRC).

In 1968, the MLBPA and the PRC settled on the first collective bargaining agreement in professional sports called the Basic Agreement. The Basic Agreement was unique in that it was the first time players and owners negotiated items such as minimum salaries, benefits, pension payments, and the like. Significantly, the first Basic Agreement included a grievance process, which allowed players to file complaints against owners who violated their contractual rights. The grievance process gave the players the ability to enforce the rights for which they had fought at the bargaining table.

The second Basic Agreement emerged two years later, in 1970. While the new Basic Agreement involved increases in minimum salaries and restricted salary cuts to twenty percent, the provision which would have the most impact on player/owner relations was one which established the right to binding impartial arbitration. This provision laid the foundation for today's player compensation system.

In 1972, the third Basic Agreement was concluded after a thirteen day players' strike during spring training and the scheduled start of the regular season. This was the first league-wide work stoppage in baseball history. The 1972 Basic Agreement took the grievance-arbitration process one step further, establishing the mechanism which facilitated the loss of the reserve clause: players were now permitted to arbitrate grievances.

D. The Evisceration of the Reserve Clause

After the 1974 season, Andy Messersmith, a pitcher for the Los Angeles Dodgers, and Dave McNally, a pitcher for the Montreal Expos, were dissatisfied with their clubs' respective contract offers. Unable to reach agreement on terms, the two were "renewed" by their clubs pursuant to the renewal clause in their 1974 contracts, and they both played the 1975 season without ever signing new contracts for that season. Following the conclusion of the 1975 season, Messersmith and McNally were in a position to test whether the renewal clause governed a player's rights in perpetuity, as clubs contended, or expired after one season, as the clause's plain language seemed to indicate.

The arbitration panel consisting of Marvin Miller, John Gaherin (the PRC's director), and Peter Seitz, MLB's arbitrator, heard Messersmith and McNally's challenge to the reserve system. Free agency for major league baseball players was at stake for the first time since the introduction of the reserve system. Because Miller and Gaherin were split along obvious lines, the decision fell to Seitz.

One month before Seitz released his scholarly decision, he wrote a letter to Bowie Kuhn, the MLB Commissioner at the time, warning him about the likely outcome of the arbitration. Kuhn, either because he did not understand the implications of the arbitration or because he simply was foolhardy, ignored Seitz's warning. On December 23, 1975, Seitz released the panel's decision that the reserve clause allowed unilateral renewal for one season only, and not, as the owners had believed for nearly a century, for successive seasons beyond the first renewal. Consequently, Andy Messersmith and Dave McNally became free agents.

Seitz was fired within hours of the decision, and the owners immediately appealed to the courts. A federal district court found no impropriety on Seitz's part and upheld the arbitration, which survived an appeal to the federal appellate court. All that remained of the reserve system was its shell, because it no longer allowed owners to enslave players for their entire careers.

E. The 1976 Basic Agreement and Successors

The fourth Basic Agreement was negotiated in the wake of the Messersmith/McNally arbitration, following a spring training lockout in 1976. The destruction of the reserve clause gave players negotiating leverage: owners were haunted by images of runaway free agency. Owners apparently did not understand the implications of free agency, and they were concerned that the MLBPA would demand immediate free agency for all players. Miller, however, was smarter than that. He understood a basic economic theory: the smaller the supply of free agents, the greater the demand for them, and the more clubs would be willing to pay for them. Miller did not want wholesale free agency.

The Basic Agreement established the basic three-tiered compensation structure in use today. Players became free agents after six seasons of major league service. Those with less than six years' experience but at least two years in the majors could submit their contracts to salary arbitration, which had been in effect since 1974. Clubs had renewal rights for players not yet eligible for arbitration, limited only by rules defining the minimum salary and maximum salary reductions.

Immediately following the establishment of free agency in 1976, baseball salaries skyrocketed: the average salary jumped from $51,501 in 1975 to $76,066 in 1976, and on to $143,756 by 1980. Despite the owners' instinctive fear of free agency, their aggressive, and sometimes ill-advised, signing of free agents was the principal cause of the dramatic salary increases.

The next Basic Agreement, scheduled to take effect for the 1980 season, was only concluded after a midseason strike was narrowly averted. Nevertheless, a fifty day mid-season strike occurred in 1981, resulting in 719 canceled games. The 1980 agreement, which saw few substantive changes to the revolutionary new player compensation system established in 1976, promoted the escalation of major league salaries. In just six seasons, from 1980 to 1985, the average salary rose from $143,756 to $371,157, an increase of 158%. Predictably, baseball's overlords were determined to stunt this tremendous growth.

Baseball's labor talks in 1985 were no more free of acrimony than any previous round. In terms of the player compensation system, management's stated goals were to impose a salary cap, limit the raises that could be awarded players in arbitration, and raise the threshold of eligibility for arbitration from two to three years of major league service. In support of their oft-asserted contention that player salaries had risen beyond the capacity of the sport's revenues to maintain MLB's economic viability, the clubs agreed to disclose their financial records to the union. When Professor Roger Noll, a Stanford University economist, analyzed the books on the players' behalf, however, he concluded that MLB clubs collectively had earned a profit of $25,000,000 in 1984, notwithstanding the clubs' proclamations of a $41,000,000 loss. After another season-interrupting strike, this time for only two days, the parties agreed to a deal that increased the threshold for salary arbitration eligibility to three years of service but otherwise left substantially intact the player compensation system.

F. Collusion

Dissatisfied by the relatively minor inroads into player gains won through negotiation, the owners decided to try other tactics in order to halt the growth in player compensation. Immediately upon ratification of the 1985 Basic Agreement, owners set about undercutting its provisions via collusion.

After the 1965 season, Los Angeles Dodgers star pitchers Sandy Koufax and Don Drysdale teamed up to attempt to increase their salaries through quasi-collective bargaining. This gambit so enraged owners that during negotiations for the first Basic Agreement they insisted that an anti-collusion provision be inserted into the agreement. In its present form, that provision decrees in relevant part that "players shall not act in concert with other Players and Clubs shall not act in concert with other Clubs." Ironically, this provision proved instrumental in an entirely unintended context.

Taking a page from baseball's early days, owners entered into a "gentlemen's agreement" following the 1985 season to restrict free agent movement. Cowed by constant pressure from new MLB Commissioner Peter Ueberroth to act with "fiscal responsibility," the owners collectively refused to sign any free agents whose previous clubs were interested in retaining their services. The existence, nature, and extent of the agreement did not remain a secret for long.

The owners made little effort to disguise their collusive behavior; rather, they flaunted their unwillingness to compete with each other for the services of free agents. A conspiracy to bypass mediocre free agents could have gone undetected, or at least unproven. However, when a player such as the 1984 American League Most Valuable Player Kirk Gibson was unable to attract any interest on the free agent market, and a mega-star like the Chicago Cubs' Andre Dawson was forced to sign for substantially less than he had earned in the previous year, suspicions quickly grew to near certainties.

Shortly after the extent of the restrictions on free agent signings became clear in 1985, the Players Association filed a grievance against the clubs claiming collusion ("Collusion I"). After the free agent crop available following the 1986 season was similarly spurned, the MLBPA filed a second grievance, alleging that owners had not altered their behavior and again had colluded to restrict the free agent market ("Collusion II"). Following the 1987 season, club owners tried a different tactic, bidding for free agents but using an "information bank" in which they shared information about offers made to free agents. The MLBPA challenged this practice as well ("Collusion III").

The owners' concerted effort to lower player costs was certainly effective: the average player salary for the 1987 season, $412,454, actually represented a decline from the 1986 average of $412,520. The information bank in use following the 1987 season was almost as effective, limiting the average salary increase in 1988 to about six percent ($438,729).

While providing temporary respite from the large annual increases in player costs, collusion ultimately carried a very large price tag. In Collusion I, the arbitrator rejected the owners' claims that there could be no collusion without a formal agreement, and eventually held that the dramatic changes in the free agent market could not have occurred without some form of agreement. In Collusion II, the arbitrator found that the clubs' claims of the existence of a free agent market were untenable and that the owners had again acted in concert to eliminate the free agent market. After the MLBPA's challenge to the information bank, Collusion III, was also upheld, it was clear that the industry-wide effort to control labor costs through "fiscal restraint" was a complete failure. Determination of damages was a challenge since estimates of the degree to which the free agent and even arbitration markets were depressed by collusion were highly speculative. Ultimately, the three cases were settled for $280,000,000, to be distributed to individual players by the MLBPA.

Collusion proved costly in another way as well. The owners' collusive behavior reinforced suspicions held by MLBPA veterans that owners could not be trusted to abide by their agreements. For younger players, who may have been only vaguely aware of the "bad old days" prior to 1976, collusion was an education and an affirmation of the need for vigilance.

G. The 1990 Basic Agreement

Following the end of collusion, player salaries surged to an extent never-before experienced by professional athletes. The 1989 average salary of $497,254 shot to $597,537 in 1990 and to $851,492 in 1991. Owners were alarmed by the rapid growth. These increases, however, represented an appropriate correction after collusion created a huge imbalance between MLB revenues and player salaries. For example, in 1985, the last year prior to collusion, MLB's total revenues were $717,813,000. While collusion held salaries relatively flat for the next three seasons, revenues continued to climb, reaching $1,007,519,000 in 1988 and $1,241,059,000 the following season. Further, clubs were flush with national television broadcast rights money; CBS agreed to pay $1,060,000,000 for the rights to televise baseball's 1990–1993 seasons, double the previous network contract. Former salary standards fell quickly.

In this setting, the PRC and MLBPA sat down to discuss a new Basic Agreement. As had become standard in the industry, an agreement came only after a 32 day work stoppage, in this case a spring training lockout in 1990. The major point of contention in the negotiations was salary arbitration. Players desired to return to the two year threshold for arbitration eligibility that had been obtained prior to the 1985 Basic Agreement. Owners, on the other hand, wanted to eliminate the arbitration process entirely, which they blamed for dramatic salary increases. They also demanded a salary cap.

The lockout was ended and an agreement was reached only through the intervention of MLB Commissioner Fay Vincent. The owners agreed to set the threshold for salary arbitration back below the three year level. In addition, players received an increase in management's pension contributions from $39,000,000 to $55,000,000, and the major league minimum salary was increased from $68,000 to $100,000. The owners' victories included a lower pension plan amount and a change in the rules concerning collusion.

II. THE PLAYER COMPENSATION SYSTEM

As noted above, the three-tiered player compensation system has been in place, with few changes, since free agency emerged twenty years ago. Players with six years of major league service are unrestricted free agents; they can offer their services to any team. Players with less than six but more than two-plus years of service may arbitrate their salaries, but will remain the sole property of their club unless the club refuses to participate in arbitration and permits the player to become a free agent. Finally, players not yet eligible for arbitration are subject to the clubs' renewal rights.

Although this structure is far more favorable to players than the old reserve system that prevailed for the first three-quarters of [last] century, owners retain a great degree of discretion over the size and allocation of their payrolls. Obviously, owners are in complete control of salaries for all players who fall into the third tier, as they are not able to seek employment independently, nor are they eligible for salary arbitration. In 1995, while the average player salary was $1,110,766, the average for those players not yet eligible for salary arbitration was $170,778, only $61,778 more than the major league minimum salary. *[In 2002, the average player salary was $2,383,000, and the average for those players not yet eligible for salary arbitration was $324,562.]* As exactly one half of the major league players surveyed, 412 out of 824 total players, fell into this grouping, the average club has near-total discretion over the salaries paid roughly half the players on its roster. *[In 2002, the numbers represented 365 out of 895 total players.]* Under current rules, players must participate in at least three major league seasons before arbitration becomes an option, giving clubs a reasonable period during which they can obtain a player's services very cheaply.

The arbitration process forces clubs to pay players a market price that is determined by similarly situated players on other clubs. Arbitration hearings are relatively rare, as most filed cases settle prior to hearing. Nevertheless, even players who compromise prior to hearing or who actually lose their arbitration cases tend to receive substantial raises.

Increasingly, clubs have elected to avoid the arbitration process, either by signing younger players to long term contracts that preempt arbitration or by nontendering players. In the off-season prior to 1995, of the 194 players with at least three but less than six years of major league service, only seventy actually filed for arbitration, of which only nine proceeded to hearing. *[In the off-*

season prior to the 2003 season, only 72 of these players filed for arbitration and only 7 proceeded to hearing.] Of the 210 players entering 1995 with adequate service time for arbitration eligibility (including super-two's), whether they were actually afforded the opportunity to file for arbitration, the average salary for that season of $1,580,044 was considerably higher than even the average for all players ($1,110,766). *[In 2002, these 245 players earned an average of $2,333,442. The average salary for all players was $2,383,000.]*

The third group of players, the free agents with at least six years of service, are the most highly compensated. In 1995, the 202 players in this category earned an average of $2,542,186. *[In 2002, these 285 players earned an average of $4,796,992.]* Because pure market forces drive the contracts signed by players in this grouping, there can be no argument but that the owners are ultimately in control of the salaries paid this group.

The three-tiered approach to player compensation under the Basic Agreements leaves MLB ownership in virtually complete control of player salaries for the bulk of the players on the roster. Of 824 major league players in 1995, only seventy-six filed for arbitration and only ten had their salaries set by an arbitrator. The rest signed as free agents, re-signed with clubs who already held their rights, were bound to multi-year deals signed in 1994 or earlier, or were renewed by their clubs pursuant to paragraph 10a of their 1994 contracts.

III. THE FAILURE OF THE OWNERS' COUNTER-REVOLUTION

The foregoing history should illuminate two recurrent themes in labor–management relations in baseball. First, it should be clear that owners have resisted player attempts at emancipation at every turn. Second, it should be clear that owners have acted in what may be uncharitably termed "bad faith" in their attempts to regain what they perceive to be lost ground. While owners were able to forestall efforts at player advancement from the beginning of professional baseball well up to the mid-1970s, the revolutionary system established in 1976 has survived all serious challenges.

. . . . *[The author's recounting of the details of the 1994–95 collective bargaining negotiations is omitted.]*

D. The Cost of the Strike

. . . .

As the 1996 season began, estimates placed the total cost of the strike to both parties in the area of $1,000,000,000. Players were reported to have lost $243,000,000 in wages due to canceled games, while owners lost $376,000,000 in reduced attendance and television revenues in 1994 and $326,000,000 in lost attendance in 1995. Almost incalculable are the lost opportunities for all involved in the sport, including endorsement and other marketing opportunities and ancillary revenue sources. Attendance in 1996 was noticeably below pre-strike levels, and television ratings were positively anemic, raising the specter of lost revenue for years to come. Fan cynicism and disillusionment must be at an all-time high.

To the extent that the owners' destructive efforts to overthrow the sport's player compensation system were truly motivated by a straightforward desire to control costs, the irony is that the average salary of MLB players has remained static for most of [the 1990s] following the post-collusion market correction previously discussed. In 1992, the average salary was $1,028,667. In 1993, after the owners voted to reopen the Basic Agreement but before any substantive negotiations occurred, the average salary was $1,076,089, less than five percent higher. In 1994, the first strike year, the average salary (not adjusted for wages lost to the strike) was $1,168,263, an increase of less than nine percent. Salaries the following year, in 1995, averaged $1,110,766, a five percent decline. Thus, over a four-year period, the average salary of a major league baseball player increased only eight percent from 1992 to 1995. Even without the strike, the rapid salary growth of the post-collusion years was finished. *[The average salary increased to $1,560,000 in 1999 and to $2,383,000 in 2003.]*

Further, it has been clear from the start that any financial difficulties that some franchises face could be eliminated or at least alleviated through more extensive revenue sharing. In a very real sense, the root cause of many owners' dissatisfaction with their clubs' bottom lines was not that too great a share of the industry's revenues were flowing to the players, but that too great a share of the industry's revenues were flowing to other owners.

It seems clear, then, that the owners' counter-revolution has been a dismal failure. It was launched from the disingenuous premise that the extant player compensation system was in need of overhaul, or that the players could be forced to dismantle their hard won gains. The counter-revolution was neither subtle in its tactics — eviscerating the Office of the Commissioner, failing to make contractually required benefits payments, declaring impasse and imposing a new compensation system when bargaining clearly remained available, misleading the NLRB concerning their intent to reinstate the old rules, refusing to accept the President's offer of binding mediation, foisting the replacement player debacle upon the public — nor effective in attaining its goals. As it stands now, salary arbitration and free agency will not be eliminated. There will be no salary cap. When a new Basic Agreement is ratified, it seems more than likely that business will continue as before.

IV. THE FUTURE

Of the many features of major league baseball that set it apart from other professional sports in America, one of its most troubling is its lengthy history of virulent antagonism between labor and management. Buoyed by the fortuitous protection of the special antitrust exemption, baseball owners held their athlete employees in virtual bondage throughout their professional careers. When negotiations and litigation compelled changes in the way ownership has run its industry over the past 20 years, all such changes, and indeed even agreements to maintain the status quo, have come only after continued acrimony and "hardball" measures.

In recent years, owners' twin desires to gain greater authority over players' freedom and redistribute a greater portion of industry revenues from players to clubs have, if anything, exacerbated the historic tension between the two camps. Like the boy who cried "wolf," owners have destroyed their own credibility when it comes to assertions of heavy financial losses. Further, their naked efforts to crush union loyalty, whether through the deprivation of benefits, the retention of replacement players, the arbitrary refusal to negotiate in good faith, and even the advancement of spurious legal positions have done little to suggest that baseball's ownership has emerged from the feudal (and therefore futile) model of management–labor relations.

Baseball players and owners have a mutual stake in the economic health of the game. Clearly, the most economically advantageous relationship for both sides would be one that permitted the formation of a true partnership in the celebration and promotion of baseball. Unfortunately, relations between the two sides have been so poor that collective bargaining negotiations tend to take on the character of a sporting contest themselves, with owners scoring wins or losses depending upon the degree to which they can roll back player rights or impede their exercise. When restoration of hegemony is the primary goal for owners, there is no chance that the sides can progress to the point of understanding and evaluating each other's needs and interests in the negotiation setting.

. . . Until ownership is willing to put the good of the game over individual desire for authority and ever-increasing shares of the revenues, there is no hope that a fully productive and efficient bond can be formed with players.

CREATING A WIN-WIN SITUATION THROUGH COLLECTIVE BARGAINING: THE NFL SALARY CAP

Adam Heller

[The author's overview of the collective bargaining that led to the development of the NFL salary cap is omitted.]

II. THE SALARY CAP

Since 1994, NFL player salaries have been negotiated under a Salary Cap. This Cap was one of the main features of the 1993 Collective Bargaining Agreement between players and owners. In 1998, the CBA was extended through the 2004 season. . . *[The CBA has since been extended through the 2007 season.]*

The Cap is determined through a complicated calculation system. To set the stage for those calculations, the initial section . . . addresses key definitions used throughout the Cap system.

A. Revenues — Definitions

The first definition group deals with the revenue structure upon which the Cap is built. The Cap is based on income that the teams earn during a League Year. A percentage of that income, termed Defined Gross Revenues (DGR), is allocated for player expenditures. Those expenditures fall into two categories: collectively bargained benefits and negotiated player salaries.

Both owners and players have a common interest in striving to achieve the highest possible revenues. Depending upon the percentage utilized, as DGR grows, so too does the cap and players' salaries. However, since not all revenues are contained in DGR, players seek means of increasing those income streams which are part of DGR, while owners aim to maximize revenues not covered by the system.

There are three distinct revenue categories:

(1) DGR revenues, those completely included in Salary Cap calculations;
(2) Revenues considered within DGR but excluded from Salary Cap calculations (Excluded DGR); [and]
(3) Revenues NOT considered part of DGR for Salary Cap purposes (Not DGR).

A nationally-recognized accounting firm resolves disputes over fair market value and determines whether or not revenues should be included in DGR. If a dispute is for $10 million or more, either party can appeal the result to the Special Master.

1. DGR.   All revenues generated by the performance of players during games are included in DGR. That includes:

(1) All gate receipts from preseason, postseason, and regular season games;
(2) Income from luxury box and premium seating as long as those funds are subject to NFL revenue sharing;
(3) Revenue from the sale of NFL radio and television broadcast rights. Covered television broadcasts include network, local, cable, pay television, satellite encryption, international broadcasts, and all other distribution means. Income generated from delayed broadcasts is also included if the game is shown within seventy-two hours of the already played actual contest, or if the broadcast is the first showing in any market; [and]
(4) Revenues from sale of any right to receive revenue from sources contained within DGR definitions.

Furthermore, transactions between related entities (i.e., from NFL Properties to NFL Attractions) must be at reasonable or fair market values.

2. Not DGR.   Owners also receive revenues from sources not directly related to on-the-field performance. These items are termed Not DGR and include income from:

(1) Trading players;
(2) Selling existing NFL franchises;
(3) Granting NFL expansion franchises;
(4) Dues;
(5) Capital contributions;
(6) Fines;
(7) Revenue sharing;
(8) Interest income;
(9) Insurance recoveries; and
(10) Sale of interest in real estate or other property.

. . . .

3. Excluded DGR.   The third revenue group, Excluded DGR, consists of income generated from:

(1) Concessions;

(2) Parking;

(3) Program and novelty sales;

(4) Local advertising and promotions;

(5) Signage;

(6) Magazine advertising;

(7) Local sponsorship agreements;

(8) Stadium teams;

(9) Luxury box income (other than actual gate receipts); and

(10) Any revenue categories currently derived from NFL Films, NFL Properties, Inc., and their subsidiaries (unless that income is already included in DGR).

The NFL and NFLPA have agreed to exclude certain network television revenue from DGR if that revenue is used to fund stadium construction or renovations that will, over time, increase DGR or Excluded DGR. . . .

B. Benefits

The second set of definitions concerns player benefits covered by the Salary Cap. The wide array of benefits that have been collectively bargained for include:

(1) Pension funding for the Bert Bell/Pete Rozelle NFL Player Retirement Plan, the National Football League Pre-59er Special Benefit Program, and the Second Career Savings Plan;

(2) The Supplemental Disability Plan and Group Insurance Programs which comprise life, medical, and dental coverage;

(3) Injury protection, workers compensation, payroll, unemployment compensation, and social security taxes;

(4) Preseason per diem amounts and regular season meal allowances;

(5) Moving and travel expenses;

(6) Postseason pay;

(7) Player medical costs including fees to doctors, hospitals, and other healthcare providers and the cost of drugs and medical supplies for the treatment of injuries; excluded are the salaries of trainers, other related team personnel, or costs of team medical or training equipment. Medical costs covered by the Salary Cap cannot increase more than 10% each season;

(8) Severance Pay; and

(9) The new Player Annuity Program.

C. Salary

The final set of definitions concerns player salary terms. Salary means all compensation paid to a player, including money, property, investments, loans, or anything else of value. Salary, however, does not include benefits. Furthermore, a player's salary will also include compensation for nonfootball-related services if such payment does not seem to represent an approximate fair market value. This broad definition of salary becomes complicated because it is affected by numerous rules which are used in computing the precise nature of the system.

III. THE BEGINNING OF THE CAP

A. How the Salary Cap Was Triggered

Starting in 1993, once player costs (i.e., the total salaries and benefits, but excluding loans, loan guarantees, unearned incentive values, and the value of unarbitrated grievances) for all teams equaled or exceeded 67% of that season's actual DGR, the Salary Cap would begin operating the next season. That condition was met when player costs for the 1993 season reached nearly 70%. The Salary Cap then went into effect for the 1994 season and has remained in place since.

B. Guaranteed Leaguewide Salary

Players are guaranteed to receive at least 58% of actual DGR in any capped season. If player costs for all NFL teams fall below 58% of DGR in a capped season, owners must pay the difference directly to the players that played during that season by April 15 of the next League Year. If such payment occurs, the owners and the union must determine the way those funds will be distributed.

IV. HOW THE SALARY CAP IS CALCULATED

A. Mathematical Calculation

The basic formulas for determining the Salary Cap are as follows:

(1) (Projected DGR × CBA Percentage) = Players Share of DGR;
(2) Players Share − Projected Leaguewide Benefits = Amount Available for Player Salaries;
(3) Amount Available for Player Salaries / Number of Teams = Unadjusted Salary Cap per Team; and
(4) Projected Leaguewide Benefits / Number of Teams = Equal Allocation per Team for Benefits.

This process begins many months before a season is played, however, and involves a group of accountants that establish the likely level of income the League will earn. Then, in February, three days before the beginning of each NFL League Year, the accountants generate what is termed an "Initial Special Purpose Letter." This document offers an early analysis of the previous year's DGR, Excluded DGR, each team's player costs and benefits, as well as relevant costs of NFL operations. From the Initial Special Purpose Letter, the Salary Cap for the upcoming season, the minimum team salary amounts, and the increases in required tenders and qualifying offers are then determined.

To determine the Salary Cap and minimum team salary for an upcoming season, the accountants calculate the projected DGR by anticipating the revenue growth from new stadiums, expansion teams, and provisions in television contracts. The projected DGR must be as accurate as possible. If, for example, a new television contract is signed, the new contract must be included to determine projected DGR. If the actual DGR for a season is different than the projected DGR, that difference will be added or subtracted accordingly from the projected DGR for the next season. For example, if the actual DGR is less than the projected DGR for a particular season, the difference will be deducted from projected DGR for the next season.

Projected benefits are also used in the calculation of the Salary Cap and minimum team salary. Projected benefits estimate benefits paid to players for an upcoming year. If actual benefits for any season are less than the projected benefits, the difference will be subtracted from the projected benefits for the next season. If actual benefits are greater than the projected benefits for a particular season, the difference will be added to projected benefits for the next season.

The accountants then review the estimates of the team's DGR reports for the year, and make changes in the estimates where appropriate. Expenses deducted from television, cable, and radio broadcast revenue must be reasonable. The accountants will resolve disputes over the amount of revenues, expenses, or player costs that are included in DGR after meeting with the NFL and the NFLPA. However, if the dispute is for more than $5 million, either party can contest the adjustments made by the accountants in a Special Master Proceeding.

The 1998 CBA extension calls for these DGR Salary Cap percentages:

1998–2001   63%
2002   63.5%

[A recent extension of the CBA through 2007 sets the percentages at 64.25% in 2003, 64.75% in 2004, 65.5% in 2005, and 64.5% in 2006. 2007 is an uncapped year.]
. . . .

Furthermore, the Salary Cap carries certain restrictions. For example, the Salary Cap cannot fall below the Salary Cap level of the previous year. Moreover, the projected benefits, when added to the amount of the Salary Cap multiplied by the number of teams, can never be greater than 70% of projected DGR. Finally, if total player costs of all teams during a season fall below a certain percentage, then the Salary Cap percentage for the next season will be increased by a percentage of DGR.

B. The Use of Excluded DGR in Determining the Salary Cap

To determine if any Excluded DGR is included in the current season Salary Cap calculation, use the following formula:

(Excluded DGR) / (Excluded DGR + DGR from all sources except network TV revenues) = x;
(1992 Excluded DGR) / (1992 Excluded DGR + 1992 DGR from all sources except network TV revenues) = y.

If x is greater than y, that excess amount of Excluded DGR will be included in the current season's DGR.

C. Minimum Salary for Individual Teams

For all capped years, each team must have a minimum team salary that equals 54% of the projected DGR minus the projected benefits divided by the number of teams ([projected DGR − Projected Leaguewide Benefits] / number of teams). *[The minimum team salary is now set at 56% of projected DGR less projected benefits.]* Each team must have a total salary above this amount at the end of each season. Any team that does not meet this minimum salary must pay the difference directly to the players who were on its roster at any time during the season. If the team fails to pay the difference to the players, the NFL is then forced to make the payment.

D. Computing Team Salary

Several different amounts must be included when computing team salary. Team salary includes the amount a team must pay its current or former players under their player contracts. Team salary also includes the Rookie Minimum Active Salary as of the day of the draft for all drafted rookies. The salary for drafted rookies will stay at this amount until the player is signed, the team's rights are relinquished through waivers, or until the Tuesday following the tenth week of the regular season if the player is unsigned. . . .

 . . . .

V. TREATMENT OF PERSONAL SEAT LICENSE REVENUES

Personal Seat License revenues are included in DGR. However, the CBA provides teams with a credit against DGR attributable to PSL or premium seat amounts spent on stadium construction or renovation, but only those revenues that lead to an increase in DGR and are not shared by owners. These provisions encourage construction/renovation of stadiums through the use of PSLs and the sale of premium seats and thus promote increases in DGR and available funds to be spent on player salaries.

When determining increased DGR from a new stadium, accountants compare DGR generated by the old stadium with DGR generated by the new stadium. For stadium renovations, increased DGR is determined by comparing DGR generated by the specific area of the stadium renovated before and after renovation. However, if the players and owners agree that such renovation is substantial enough to increase revenues throughout the stadium, then accountants will consider DGR increased for the entire facility.

 . . . . *[The author's discussion of salary grievances and the salary cap is omitted.]*

VII. VALUATION OF PLAYER CONTRACTS

The following items are included in player salary, which counts toward team salary for Salary Cap purposes.

A. Paragraph 5 Salary

Paragraph 5 salary is the base salary of a player contract and is not guaranteed. The highest possible salary in Paragraph 5 of the player contract is included in team salary in the year the salary was earned. However, there is an exception to this rule regarding players who are not among the team's fifty-one highest valued player contracts. . . .

Salary that is paid in a different year than it is earned is called "deferred salary." Deferred salary is included in Team Salary in the year that it is earned (not paid) at its present value. If a player switches teams and his contract provides for a bonus for the switch, the bonus is included in the player's salary and is charged to the team paying the bonus.

B. Signing Bonuses

Signing Bonuses are paid to players for coming to terms with their respective teams. Signing bonus money is usually guaranteed and can be paid up front or in installments agreed to by the player and team.

When determining team and player salary, the signing bonus will be prorated over the length of the contract. For example, if a player signs a four-year deal with a $1 million signing bonus, $250,000 of that bonus will count toward team salary for each contract year ($1 million divided into the four-year contract is $250,000 per year). Contracts containing signing bonuses agreed to in a capped year may not be prorated more than three years after the Final Capped Year. Also, signing bonuses that are agreed to in the 1999 or 2000 Seasons cannot be prorated more than seven years. *[The proration period was shortened to six years in 2004, five years in 2005, and four years in 2006 as part of the 2002 CBA extension.]*

. . . .

1. Allocating Signing Bonuses in Contracts with Voidable Years. Since signing bonuses can be allocated over the length of the contract, teams can save Salary Cap room by negotiating longer player contracts (i.e., the longer the contract, the lower the signing bonus allocation in each year). While players benefit from the increased guaranteed money that comes with higher signing bonuses, it is not normally in the best interest of the player to be bound to a long-term deal. Therefore, the teams and players have creatively constructed contracts that extend for many seasons for Salary Cap allocation purposes, but contain clauses that "void" years off the deal if certain performance levels are attained by the player.

However, if a player can void years of his contract based on actions that he takes under his own control, then the voided years are not counted as contract years when prorating a signing bonus. This same rule applies to rookie contracts unless the right to void the contract is conditioned upon certain playtime requirements.

2. The Deion Sanders Rule. The Salary Cap system is set up to give owners an incentive to pay high signing bonuses over a long term of years instead of having high base salaries. However, owners started taking advantage of the uncapped years at the end of the CBA by extending player contracts and back-loading the base salaries in those uncapped years. The players and owners agreed to address these types of contracts by adopting a set of guidelines that essentially reallocate money from the uncapped years back into the capped years of the contract.

The "Deion Sanders Rule" affects contracts that extend into uncapped years *[currently 2007]* . . . The first step in applying the rule is to determine if the contract is one that is affected by the rule. The league looks at the total of the base salaries in the capped years and the total of the signing bonus allocations in the capped years. If the total signing bonus allocation is greater than the total base salaries in the capped years, then the league takes 50% of the total signing bonus allocations in the uncapped years and reallocates it equally over the capped years. Then the team receives a cap credit for the reallocated amounts in the uncapped years if those years eventually become capped.

For example, Player X signs a seven-year deal in 1999 for the minimum salaries ($175K in 1999, $250K in 2000, $325K in 2001, $350K in 2002, $375K in 2003, $400K in 2004, and $400K in 2005) and a $7 million signing bonus. The signing bonus is allocated at $1 million per year over the seven years. The total base salary in the capped years is $1,475,000 (175K + 250K + 325K + 350K + 375K). The total signing bonus allocation in capped years is $5 million ($1 million per year in the five capped years). The total of $5 million is obviously greater than $1,475,000. Therefore, the league takes 50% of the total signing bonus allocations in the uncapped years, which is $1 million (50% of $2 million), then allocates the $1 million over the five capped years. This adds $200,000 to the team's cap in the first five years of the contract (1999–2003). If years 2004 and 2005 eventually become capped, the team would receive a $500K cap credit in each year (the $1 million divided equally between the two years).

3. Signing Bonuses with Contract Extensions.   In order to save cap room and keep star players, owners will often renegotiate player contracts during a season. By renegotiating base salary into signing bonus money the player gets more guaranteed cash, and the owner gets more cap room as well as the services of the player for a longer period of time if the term of years is extended. However, a problem can arise when dealing with the allocation of the original signing bonus and the new signing bonus at the time of renegotiation.

If a player renegotiates his contract and gets a new signing bonus, the new signing bonus is pro-rated over the remaining years of the original contract and also over the extension. The allocation of the original signing bonus remains unchanged. For example, Player X is currently in the third year of a four-year deal (1997–2000) that paid him a $1 million signing bonus. In 1999, Player X renegotiates his deal extending his contract to the 2002 season while getting a $2 million signing bonus. The original $1 million signing bonus is allocated at $250,000 per year over 1999 and 2000 just as it would be if there were no renegotiations. However, the new $2 million signing bonus is allocated at $500,000 per year over the remaining two years of the original contract (1999–2000) and the extended two years (2001–2002).

4. Salary Cap Acceleration.   If a player is waived on or before June 1, the remaining signing bonus that has not been included in salary "accelerates" and is included in that year's team salary. For example, assume Player X signs a four-year deal in 1998 with a $4 million signing bonus. The bonus is allocated toward the cap over the four years at $1 million per year. However, if Player X is cut before June 1 in 1999, the remaining cap money that was allocated for 2000 and 2001 "accelerates" and counts against the team's cap for the 1999 season. However, if a player is waived after June 1, the remaining portion of his signing bonus can be divided over the next two seasons instead of one. During a season prior to an uncapped year, the rules that apply to players being waived on or before June 1 will also apply after June 1.

Acceleration also occurs when a player is traded or waived and picked up by another team. The new team is not responsible for any of the original signing bonus. The team that waived or traded the player is responsible for the accelerated signing bonus (in the same manner as described above).

Voidable years can be included when determining the term of years for signing bonus proration. However, if the player meets the goal that voids the year or years of the contract, any amount of the signing bonus that was allocated to the voided year or years will be accelerated and added immediately to team salary. If the accelerated signing bonus puts the team over the Salary Cap, the amount that the team is over the cap will be deducted from the team's Salary Cap for the next year. If a player can void a contract based on a "likely to be earned incentive," and the player is on the roster at a later time, there will be no acceleration. If a contract is renegotiated to reduce the number of years of the contract, the portion of the signing bonus that has not been allocated is included in team salary at the time of the renegotiation.

5. Payments Treated as Signing Bonuses. For the purpose of determining team salary, signing bonuses include the amount specifically described in a player contract as a signing bonus. Also included in the "signing bonus" are guaranteed reporting bonuses and guaranteed workout bonuses. Roster or reporting bonuses earned or paid before preseason training camp are also considered signing bonuses. Guaranteed salary advances or advances that do not have to be repaid are treated as signing bonuses. Money guaranteed or paid for option years, contract extensions, contract modifications, individually negotiated rights of first refusal, and option buyouts are considered signing bonuses. Reporting bonuses are treated as signing bonuses if the contract is signed after the start of training camp. Roster bonuses are also considered signing bonuses if the contract was signed after the last preseason game. Finally, individually negotiated relocation bonuses are treated as signing bonuses.

The nonguaranteed amount of any salary advance, off-season workout bonus, off-season roster bonus, or off-season reporting bonus is included in the team's salary in the year it was earned. These bonuses cannot be prorated. "Guaranteed" refers to those bonuses that are fully guaranteed — regardless of skill, injury, or termination of the contract.

Contracts signed, renegotiated, or extended in the final capped year are governed by a somewhat special set of rules if the signing bonus is to be paid to the player in the final capped season. In this situation, a salary advance that the player is not obligated to repay is considered a signing bonus. Any off-season workout bonus that calls for a player to participate in less than thirty-two days of the team's program is also considered a signing bonus. Finally, all off-season reporting and roster bonuses are considered signing bonuses.

6. Payback of Signing Bonuses. Due to the Salary Cap, owners are now investing a greater amount of money up front for players in the form of guaranteed signing bonuses. Thus, the owners must try to protect their investments by including language in the contract that calls for a player to return a portion of the signing bonus to the team if the player "fails or refuses" to practice or play with the team. In certain situations, a team will be repaid some of the signing bonus it paid to a player (i.e., a refund), or a team will fail to pay part of a signing bonus that was already allocated toward team salary. If this happens, the amount previously included in team salary will be added to the team's Salary Cap in the next year.

C. Incentives

All incentives are included in team salary if they are likely to be earned (LTBE). LTBE incentives are performance levels that the player or team has reached in the previous year. For example, if a quarterback threw twenty touchdowns last year and his incentive clause for this year is set at fifteen touchdowns, then this incentive is "likely to be earned." Also, incentives that are in the sole control of the player, like nonguaranteed reporting bonuses and off-season workout and weight bonuses, are considered LTBE. An impartial arbitrator will hear disputes between the owners and the players concerning what should be considered LTBE (especially for rookies or veterans who did not play in the prior year). A list of accepted performance incentives for veterans and rookies is included in Exhibits A & B of the CBA. Conversely, if a player did not reach the performance incentive in the previous year, the incentive is deemed not likely to be earned (NLTBE) and is not included in team salary.

To determine whether a clause is LTBE or NLTBE for Salary Cap purposes (i.e., not whether the player actually earned the incentive), it is necessary to look at the performance of the team in the prior season, not the current season. For example, assume Player X receives an incentive bonus if he participates in 50% of the team's offensive plays this season. Assume further that last season the team had 1,000 offensive plays. Therefore, as soon as Player X plays in 500 plays in the current season (or 50% of last year's 1,000 plays), the incentive will be considered earned for Salary Cap purposes. The same incentive is considered not earned if the same player in the current year only participated in one of the team's first 502 offensive plays. In this situation, it would be impossible for the player to achieve the 50% incentive based on last year's performance of 1,000 plays. It is important to remember that looking to last year's performance level is only for Salary Cap purposes and will not affect the players right to receive a bonus for his performance in the current year.

1. Actual Performance Incentives Paid vs. Performance Incentives Allocated.   At the end of the season, the teams must pay the actual performance bonuses earned by their players. If the actual amount of performance bonuses paid to players puts the team over the Salary Cap, the team must make up for the excess in the following year. Any amount paid above the Salary Cap in performance bonuses will be subtracted from the team's Salary Cap in the next year.

However, if the opposite occurs, and a team has included performance bonuses in their team salary, but these bonuses were not actually earned, then the team can earn a credit towards their Salary Cap number for the following year. The credit is determined by considering whether the included but not earned bonuses exceeded the earned but not included benefits. This excess amount will be added to the team's cap in the following year only up to the amount that the excess exceeds the team's room under the Salary Cap at the end of a season.

2. Entering Player Pool (Rookie) Incentives.   For rookies, most incentives awarded for leading the team in any official statistical category will not be included in team salary. However, incentives given for any other ranking will be included in team salary. If the incentive concerns leading the team in kick or punt returns, and the player qualifies for the statistical categories, then a certain portion of the bonus will be included in team salary.

A noncumulative incentive clause involves a player that can earn a certain amount of money for a lower level of performance, or more money for better performance, but not both. For example, a running back might receive $10,000 for rushing up to 150 yards or $20,000 for rushing 151–350 yards, etc. In this situation, only the highest amount is counted toward team salary.

Some rookie incentives only partially count toward the Salary Cap. For example, if a rookie receiver drafted in the first round has an incentive for getting thirty-three total receptions, only 50% of the incentive bonus is counted toward team salary. However, if the same receiver has an incentive for catching ten passes, 100% of the bonus will count toward team salary. Bonuses based on team statistics achieved in the prior season, incentives controlled solely by the player (nonguaranteed reporting bonuses, workouts, weight clauses, etc.), and relocation or completion bonuses all count 100% toward salary. Incentives not measured by official NFL statistics (i.e., hurries, tackles, and assists), or incentives based on subjective standards, each count 100% toward team salary. Bonuses for preseason or off-season statistics, bonuses based on another player's performance, and bonuses based on leading a team in punting or kicking also count 100% toward team salary. Finally, any guaranteed salary or guaranteed bonus is counted 100% toward team salary.

. . . .

The CBA also outlines certain honors and recognized media that can be used for player incentives. For example, a player can earn a bonus for making the Pro Bowl, being named Defensive Player of the Year, or being recognized by the Associated Press, the Sporting News, or other accepted media.

3. Additional Incentives for Veterans, Rookies, Individuals, and Teams.   Any team performance bonus is automatically considered LTBE if the team met or exceeded the performance level in the previous year. Alternatively, the team performance is NLTBE if the team did not meet the performance in the previous year. Team and individual performance incentives based on categories not listed in either Exhibit A or B of the CBA are also considered LTBE. Individual performance incentives are considered LTBE if the incentive is based on a category other than those used to assess performance at the player's primary position. For example, if a running back has an incentive clause for touchdown passes, this bonus is LTBE.

When a player is traded or waived and picked up by another team, any performance incentive will be revalued under the LTBE rules for the new team. For example, if Player X is traded and his contract contains a bonus if the team gains 1,000 rushing yards, it is necessary to look at the new team's (the one the player was traded to) statistics for the prior season to determine whether it is LTBE.

Renegotiated contracts will be revalued at the time of the renegotiation. Therefore, if the player has already reached the incentive bonus level at the time of the renegotiation, this bonus will be considered LTBE. If a new or changed incentive bonus is renegotiated into a preexisting contract after the start of the regular season it is considered LTBE. Further, any incentive based on another player's performance is considered LTBE. This also includes incentives for offensive players that are based on defensive or special teams performance, and incentives for defensive players that are based on offensive or special teams performance.

. . . .

D. Guaranteed Contracts

Any part of salary that is guaranteed is included in team salary in the year that it is earned. However, there are four exceptions to this rule. First, teams might enter into a contract that does not include guaranteed money during a capped year but includes guaranteed money after the final capped year. This guaranteed money will be included in team salary in the capped years in any manner the team chooses. For example, assume the Salary Cap is in effect for 2002 and 2003. A player signs a four-year contract in 2002. The salary in 2002 and 2003 is not guaranteed but the salary for 2004 and 2005 (uncapped years) is fully guaranteed. The 2004 and 2005 guaranteed salary will be included in the team's salary amount for 2002 and 2003 in any proportion determined by the team.

Second, 50% of salary guaranteed beyond three years after the last capped year is included in team salary during the capped years of the contract. Third, salary that is guaranteed after a player is released is counted immediately toward team salary at the time of the release. The player still has the option of being paid the guaranteed amount immediately at the present value or in the schedule determined by the contract. Finally, teams might enter into a contract in the last capped year or later that is fully guaranteed, unguaranteed, and then fully guaranteed again. The amount that is fully guaranteed following the unguaranteed year is counted in the capped years in any manner decided by the team.

E. Loans, Salary Advances, and Noncash Provisions

The principle amount of a loan made to a player is included in team salary. However, when a player repays all or part of the loan, that portion is added back to the team's Salary Cap. Also, a loan which is used only as a way to move cap credit to a future year is improper. . . . As per salary advances, those that are directly paid to a player are immediately included in team salary. Furthermore, if the salary advance does not have to be repaid, it is treated as a signing bonus.

Noncash items like cars, houses, or insurance policies are included in team salary at their fair market value. If a fair market value cannot be agreed upon, the dispute will go to the impartial arbitrator. . . .

The compensation that players receive for participating in the off-season workout or classroom programs is included in team salary on the first day of the programs. This amount is calculated by multiplying the minimum amount paid for these programs, the number of players scheduled to participate in the programs, the number of days per week of the programs, and the number of weeks scheduled for the programs.

. . . .

F. Traded and Mid-Season Contracts

If a player is traded or waived and picked up by another team, the new team will only count what is remaining on the contract toward its team salary. The old team will count what it already paid or is obligated to pay the player as team salary. Also, team performance incentives will automatically be considered LTBE if a player is assigned to a new team through trade or waiver. If a player signs with a team after the start of the regular season, the player's salary that the team actually pays or is obligated to pay will count toward team salary.

G. Thirty Percent Rule

The 30% rule governs veteran contracts that are entered into in a capped year and extend into the final year of the CBA. The rule states that these contracts cannot have an annual increase of more than 30% of the salary, excluding amounts treated as a signing bonus, provided for in the final capped year.

H. Renegotiations and Extensions

The first renegotiation of a veteran contract can take place at any time. However, a veteran may not renegotiate to raise his salary for twelve months after the most recent renegotiation. Additionally, no player or team can agree to renegotiate a term of a previously signed contract for a prior year. No contract can be negotiated for a current season after the last regular season game. Furthermore, rookie contracts cannot be renegotiated for one year after the signing date or the following August 1, whichever is later.

No player can agree to a contract, renegotiation, or extension that expires before the last day of a season. If a player wants to terminate his contract, he must do so before the first day of any season. Moreover, renegotiated contracts are revalued for Salary Cap purposes at the time of the renegotiation. If at the time of the renegotiation an incentive bonus has already been reached, that bonus is considered LTBE. Also, any new or changed incentive bonuses renegotiated after the start of the regular season are automatically considered LTBE. . . .

VIII. CONCLUSION

The NFL has created a win-win system through collective bargaining that benefits all parties involved. Through their partnership, the players and owners have developed a wealth distribution model aligning their respective goals — increasing team value and salaries. The statistics support the conclusion that the salary cap system is indeed successful. Over the life of the current collective bargaining agreement, player salaries have shown marked growth. The average salary has increased 61.5%, the minimum salary has risen 75% and there are nearly twice as many millionaires in 1999 as there were in 1993. *[The number of millionaires increased from 516 in 1999 to 649 in 2002, and average salary increased to $1,258,800 in 2003.]* On the other side, team values have also exploded, which is demonstrated by the hefty price tag placed on the expansion teams in Cleveland and Houston, and the recent sale of the Washington Redskins.

Creating a system that works for both labor and management is an accomplishment in collective bargaining. However, in professional sports, the agreement must do more than merely satisfy the wants and needs of the respective parties. The system must allow for the league to thrive and compete in the competitive entertainment industry in order to attract a sizeable customer base. Thus, another goal, as expressed by Commissioner Tagliabue in the 2000 State of the League Address, is to create competitive balance throughout the league. To this end, the success of the NFL system was evident throughout the 1999–2000 season, as each game day embodied the purpose of the current collective bargaining agreement. League-wide parity creates close exciting contests with little predictability from week to week. Furthermore, if a fan is disgruntled with the performance of the hometown squad one season, there is hope for a quick turn around. Through free agency, the amateur draft, and strategic player signing and development, every team has the ability to field or quickly develop a championship caliber squad. All of these factors result in an exciting product for fans to enjoy.

. . . . This outcome is symbolic of the goals of the win-win system created by the owners and the players. Instead of being able to buy championships and maintain dominance because of deep pockets, the NFL chose to have its winners decided by successful front office decisions, quality coaching, and the ability of the athletes to persevere when matched on an even playing field.

While salaries and team value increase, the real test for the success of the NFL system lies with the fans. If people continue to buy tickets to the games and watch them on television, the win-win system will allow the players and owners to share in the ever-increasing revenue pie. Judging by the statistics, fan support for the NFL has never been stronger. NFL attendance for the 1999–2000 season was 16,206,640, which averages out to 65,349 spectators per game. *[NFL total attendance in 2003 was 17,081,873. The average attendance in 2003 was 66,726.]* This represented an all-time high for the NFL. . . . These statistics prove that football fans around the globe embrace the initiative of achieving leaguewide competitive balance. Greater fan support leads to increased revenues for the NFL. And thus, the question arises: how to share the profits? By aligning the goals of the players and owners, and developing a wealth distribution system through collective bargaining, the NFL has created a win-win situation that is the model for sports leagues in the twenty-first century.

DISCUSSION QUESTIONS

1. Why and how has it become more difficult for union leadership to maintain the cohesiveness of the membership?

2. What arguments can you make to explain why sports labor unions should be viewed and treated as any other union?

3. What is the benefit of a salary cap to management? Does that differ from the benefit to labor?

4. What lessons should Major League Baseball management learn from past labor disputes? What about the players?

CHAPTER 9

LABOR MATTERS: ATHLETE COMPENSATION

INTRODUCTION

It is well known that professional athletes competing in each of the four major North American sports leagues receive lucrative compensation. In 2002 and 2003, average salaries across these leagues were $4.546 million in the NBA, $2.555 million in Major League Baseball, $1.642 million in the NHL, and $1.173 million in the NFL. What is not well known is how these salaries are determined. Professional athletes are often perceived to be overpaid instead of merely well paid. This reflects a misunderstanding of the relevant marketplace for athlete compensation. A comparison of athlete salaries to those of the average person is misleading. Instead, athletes should be regarded as entertainers. When considered in this manner, athlete compensation is quite reasonable. Much like entertainers, there is a limited supply of highly skilled athletes who the average person desires to watch either live or on television. This is a significant reason why athletes (and entertainers) are able to earn such high salaries.

There is, however, an area in which it is fair to compare an athlete's salary to the average worker's — the economic justification for how much one is paid. Individuals who are employed in a free and open marketplace are compensated based on their marginal revenue product (MRP); that is, how much the individual employee contributes to the employer's revenues. Conversely, individuals who are employed in a restricted, uncompetitive marketplace are not compensated based on their MRP. Instead, the employer retains most of the MRP and the individual is compensated (and some would say *exploited*) at a more conservative rate.

The MRP concept explains why the salaries of professional athletes typically increase with the athletes' years of experience. A truncated version of the reserve system that set athlete salaries in each league at artificially low rates until the mid-1970s in MLB (and later in other leagues) still exists. Similar to the reserve system that perpetually bound a player to a team at the team's discretion, each league limits player access to a competitive marketplace for a period of years at the beginning of a player's career. Not surprisingly, most studies indicate that athletes tend to earn close to the minimum salary established in the league's collective bargaining agreement during this monopsonistic period. The team captures most of the athlete's MRP at this stage of his career. After this initial period, the player in each league gains increased but still restricted access to the marketplace (and the full value of the MRP) for a period of years as a result of restricted free agency or salary arbitration or both. Upon completing this stage, the athlete gains access to the open marketplace via unrestricted free agency. This allows the player to realize close to the full value of his MRP.

In professional sports leagues, the salary of an individual athlete is determined pursuant to the athlete compensation framework established by collective bargaining between the union and management. This determination is typically accomplished through a negotiation between a team and the athlete's representative. While the collective bargaining agreement establishes the parameters for this negotiation, the salary for any particular athlete depends on a number of factors both internal and external to that athlete. First, of course, are the factors that are internal to the athlete that exist outside of the context of the collective bargaining agreement. The athlete's skill level, position, experience, injury history, drawing power, and league all impact the compensation that is earned. A highly-skilled, experienced, and seldom injured athlete playing a "glamour" position in a thriving league will be better compensated than one lacking any of these qualities. In addition, there are several external factors that are products of the collective bargaining agreement that can either increase or decrease athlete salaries. Free agency, salary arbitration, and the presence of a competitor league can all increase athlete salaries, while a salary cap, luxury tax, and the presence of a reserve system can all decrease athlete salaries. These external factors require further elaboration.

As previously mentioned, free agency grants athletes access to a more open marketplace for their services. There are two basic types of free agency — restricted and unrestricted. An athlete is granted restricted free agency after completion of the initial reservation period at the beginning of his career. Restricted free agency provides the athlete whose contract has expired the ability to receive employment offers from other teams in the same league. The athlete's movement to other teams is restricted, however, as the current employer typically has a right to match the outside offer and maintain the athlete's services under those exact terms. Alternatively, the team can choose to allow the player to defect and may receive compensation from the new team in exchange for this player. Restricted free agency, then, allows the athlete to obtain a salary increase through the introduction of a quasi-open marketplace. The salary effect is lower if a compensation mechanism is in place, as this places a cost on outside teams that solicit new players. Conversely, the less restrictive the compensation mechanism, the greater the effect of restricted free agency on player salaries.

Unrestricted free agency provides more experienced athletes whose contracts have expired with the opportunity to receive offers from all league teams in an open marketplace. This allows players to receive fair market value for their services. Athlete compensation increases significantly with the arrival of free agent eligibility. It should not be surprising, then, that owners are generally opposed to free agency because of the effects that it has on player salaries. Though now accepted as an essential characteristic of the athlete compensation framework, owners still attempt to impose as limited a system of free agency as possible. However, free agency itself is not necessarily bad for owners. Rather, it is the intersection of free agency with the laws of supply and demand that negatively impacts owners. Unrestricted free agency is not available to every athlete every year. Instead, only those athletes with a particular level of experience whose playing contracts have expired are eligible for free agency. By limiting the number of athletes who are eligible for free agency each year, the supply of players entering the free agent marketplace is artificially lowered. This allows free agents to receive higher salaries than they would in a truly open marketplace where every player is a free agent every year. Doing so would flood the marketplace and depress salaries. Interestingly, then, athletes have an interest in limiting their access to free agency in order to reap its maximum benefits.

Salary arbitration provides owners and athletes with a method of resolving disputes over the athlete's salary for the upcoming season while ensuring that the athlete will continue his employment with the team uninterrupted by a holdout over salary. Salary arbitration allows athletes who have completed the initial phase of their careers to compare themselves to other similarly situated athletes in the marketplace in order to obtain salary increases. Athletes have been quite successful in doing so, especially because of the intersection that has occurred between free agency and salary arbitration. The free market effects of free agency have trickled down to the salary arbitration process.

The presence of a competitor league provides athletes with an attractive employment alternative. A new league needs players, the most talented and well known of whom are employed in the established league. These leagues do not abide by their rivals' collective bargaining agreements. Thus, unencumbered by the established league's reserve system, all athletes whose contracts have expired are able to gain access to an open marketplace regardless of experience. Historically, the introduction of another bidder for their services has lead to a dramatic increase in players' salaries. Similar to other industries, competition among employers in the labor marketplace benefits the employees — in this case, the athletes.

Over the years, owners have devised various tactics that attempt to depress athlete compensation below competitive levels. The reserve system accomplished this very effectively by perpetually binding a player to a team, thereby preventing him from obtaining a market-level salary. Since the evisceration of the reserve system nearly a generation ago, the collective bargaining process has yielded the development of salary caps and luxury taxes.

The presence of a salary cap provides a team with a degree of cost certainty in addressing their single highest expenditure — athlete salaries. A salary cap is actually a revenue-sharing device for owners and athletes, with the owners guaranteeing the players a significant percentage of certain revenue streams. A hard cap places an absolute limit on this percentage and allows for few exceptions to this limit. A soft cap sets a limit but allows for a number of exceptions.

Another type of cost containment mechanism is a luxury tax. Rather than limit the amount that each team can pay its players, a luxury tax gives a team a disincentive to exceed paying its players beyond certain salary levels by penalizing them for their excessive spending. This penalty is set at a percentage of the dollar amount of the excess. The higher the percentage and the lower the tax threshold, the greater the disincentive on the team.

The excerpts chosen for this chapter describe all of the aforementioned issues and ideas in great detail. In the first article, Quirk and Fort establish the broad framework for the discussion of athlete compensation. In the next selection, Kahn explains the impact of reserve systems, rival leagues, free agency, and incentives on the labor market for professional athletes. In the third excerpt, Aubut provides a description and analysis of salary arbitration in the NHL and MLB and salary caps in the NFL and NBA. In the next excerpt, Conti also reviews the impact of salary arbitration on Major League Baseball.

In the fifth article, Duffy reviews the *Bosman* decision that led to the demise of the reserve system in European soccer and analyzes its impact on the sport throughout the continent. In the sixth excerpt, Frick examines the impact of the soft salary cap on the NBA. In the penultimate selection, Ahlstrom, Si, and Kennelly review the impact of free agency on Major League Baseball.

Finally, as the outtake from *The Business of Sports Agents* discusses, the athlete has for years generally hired a sports agent to handle the task of negotiating the playing contract with the team.

TABLE 1.

LEAGUE SALARY INCREASES FROM **1990–1991** TO **2002–2003**				
Year	*MLB*	*NFL*	*NBA*	*NHL*
2002–2003	$2,555,476	$1,316,000	$4,540,000	$1,640,000
1999–2000	$1,938,849	$996,000	$3,170,000	$1,350,000
1997–1998	$1,341,000	$751,000	$2,600,000	$1,200,000
1993–1994	$1,012,424	$645,000	$1,350,000	$430,000
1990–1991	$597,537	$351,800	$990,000	$320,000

Sources: National Football League Players Association, National Basketball Players Association, National Hockey League Players Association, Associated Press.

Thus, the agent must have a sound knowledge of all of the aforementioned matters. In the best instances the sports agent too is a valuable sports business professional. This excerpt focuses on the role of the agent and the parties that have taken on this responsibility. (See Table 1 for a list of the average salary growth in each league.)

FRAMEWORK

PAY DIRT: THE BUSINESS OF PROFESSIONAL TEAM SPORTS

James Quirk and Rodney D. Fort

PRO ATHLETES AS ENTERTAINERS

. . . . Unlike unions in most industries, players' unions do not negotiate "standard wage" policies binding on most or all members. Instead, individual player salaries are determined by direct negotiation between the player and the team owner. Unions do bargain for league-wide minimum salaries, so the changes over time in minimum salaries reflect in part changes in the bargaining power of unions. . . .

While average salary levels are much lower for football and hockey, football (and, to a lesser extent, hockey) also showed marked increases in real salary levels in the 1980s, despite the restrictions on player mobility (free agency) for NFL football relative to baseball and basketball. Thus, in rounding up the usual suspects to explain the real growth in player compensation in all sports, free agency is not the only candidate. Other factors must be at work as well, including the impressive increase in demand for pro team sports tickets, and the striking increase in value of pro sports television rights for all pro team sports. . .

But the common perception of fans is that pro athletes are wildly overpaid, and that free agency is the culprit. Every red-blooded American boy wants to grow up to be a major leaguer in some sport, and most red-blooded American adult males would toss their careers in a minute if they thought they had a chance to make it in the pros. One example of this sports idolatry can be found in the vastly overinflated assessments that high school athletes make about their chances of turning pro, and, in turn, the similar mistaken perceptions that possess college athletes. Given that many fans would pay for the privilege of playing in the majors (and some actually do pay for the major league experience at adult major league baseball fantasy camps), fans find it a little difficult to accept the fact that pro athletes demand and get salaries in the six- or seven-figure range.

One way to add some perspective to the rise in real salaries for pro athletes is to look at the compensation paid to other entertainers. Perhaps Norby Walters put it best during his 1988 trial for signing college athletes to pro contracts prior to expiration of their college eligibility: "No difference. A sports star is a rock star. They're all the same."[1] Walters' insight is right on the mark — star pro athletes are entertainment stars every bit as much as movie and rock stars. The same factors are at work determining the sizes of the big incomes in sports as in other areas of entertainment. These factors are demand by the public for tickets to see stars, the rarity of skilled and/or charismatic individuals with star qualities (in the economist's jargon, an inelastic supply of talent), and the bargaining power of stars relative to that of the promoters who hire them (team owners in the case of pro sports). In explaining the rise in salaries for sports stars, both increases in the demand for their output and changes in their bargaining power (for example, free agency's replacing a reserve system) are relevant.

. . . .

. . . . In an interesting analogy to the elimination of the reserve clause in baseball, movie entertainers' earnings skyrocketed with the breakdown of the "contract player" mode of operation in place in the motion picture industry until the 1950s. Studio owners of that era, much as sports team owners today, argued vigorously that the runaway growth in star salaries spelled disaster for their industry. True to predictions, the earnings of movie stars did go up dramatically, but the U.S. motion picture industry remains quite healthy even up to the present time, and is one of the few American industries that has retained its competitive edge in an international setting.

It is interesting that the public perception of the importance of rising salaries for entertainers is so different between movie stars and pro athletes. That star salaries in pop music or the movies cause little public concern is borne out by where news on salaries can be found. . . . If the level of discussion about salaries in movies and in popular music is a murmur, then it is a high-pitched scream in pro sports. . . .

To fans, the answer to why pro sports are different from other entertainment endeavors is obvious. Other mass entertainment media do not bring philosophers to their defense, lead presidents of the United States to throw out first pitches, or give poets pause to reflect. Whatever the reason, pro team sports are viewed differently from the other mass entertainment industries by almost everyone — fans, sportswriters, players, and owners. But there are some fundamental economic facts of life that apply across the board to all labor markets, including the market for rock stars and pro sports players.

THE WORKINGS OF THE PLAYER MARKET

The market for any labor service, such as the market for the services of pro athletes, follows the good old law of supply and demand and operates on the basis of bids and offers by teams and players. Looking at things from the point of view of any team, we can calculate the *most* that a profit-oriented team would offer a player; it is the amount that the player would add to the team's revenue if he were signed. In the jargon of economists, as noted earlier, this is the player's *marginal revenue product,* which we will refer to as his *MRP.* The player's MRP is the most a team would pay a player because paying a player more than this would decrease team profits; on the other hand, signing a player for anything less than his MRP means that adding the player increases profits for the team.

. . . George Steinbrenner . . . . was asked once how he decided how much to pay a player. He said, "It depends on how many fannies he puts in the seats." That was George's way of saying it depends on the player's MRP. . . .

From the player's point of view, the least he would be willing to accept as a salary offer to sign with a team is what he could earn in his next-best employment opportunity (taking into account locational and other nonmonetary considerations). We hesitate to push our luck, but economists refer to this next-highest employment value as the player's *reservation wage.* If a team offers a player less than his reservation wage, the player would simply reject the offer and remain employed in his next-best opportunity.

The player's MRP and reservation wage give the maximum and minimum limits on the salary that a player can be expected to earn. Just where the player's salary will end up within these limits depends on a number of considerations. Union activities have an impact, especially on players whose reservation wage would have been below the league-wide minimum salary resulting from collective bargaining. The most important consideration is the bargaining power of the player relative to that of the owner. Generally, the more close substitutes there are (that is, the easier he is to replace), the more bargaining power the team has, and the salary will be closer to the player's reservation wage than to his MRP. The more unique are the skills and drawing power of the player (that is, the tougher he is to replace), the more bargaining power the player has, and the closer the salary will be to the player's MRP.

Just how far apart the reservation wage and MRP limits on a player's salary will be depends critically on the negotiating rights for players and owners, built into the player market by the rules of the sport. At one extreme is complete free agency, where the ability of players and owners to negotiate with whomever they choose is unrestricted. At the other extreme is the reserve clause system that operated in baseball until 1976. Under the reserve clause, . . . a player can negotiate only with the team owning his contract. Generally speaking, the more freedom there is for players and owners to negotiate, the closer the minimum (reservation wage) and maximum (MRP) limits on a player's salary will be. However, there can be substantial remaining bargaining room even under unrestricted free agency.

Suppose first that there is unrestricted free agency, with players and owners free to negotiate with whomever they choose. Under such circumstances, if we ignore locational and other nonmonetary considerations, each player will end up signing with the team to which he is most valuable (the team for which the player has the highest MRP). He will be paid a salary that lies between his MRP with that team, and his MRP with the team to which he is second most valuable (the team to which he has the second-highest MRP). The reason for this is that the team to which the player is most valuable can outbid any other team for the player's services, and still increase its profits by hiring him. But the team can sign the player only if it offers him at least as much as the player can earn elsewhere (the player's reservation wage), and the most the player can earn elsewhere is clearly his MRP with the team to which he is second most valuable. In a market with completely unrestricted free agency, if we ignore nonmonetary considerations, the grand conclusion is that the highest salary offered to the player will capture at least his second-highest value in the league, and can be up to (but not exceeding) his *highest* value in the league.

Under a reserve clause system, the team owning a player's contract has exclusive negotiating rights to the player. Similarly, the college draft gives the team holding a player's draft rights exclusive rights to negotiate with him (in baseball, for up to six years, and longer in football and hockey). Instead of a competitive market for the player's services, under a reserve clause system, there is only one bidder for the player's services. The highest salary the team holding the player's contract would be willing to pay the player still is the MRP of the player for that team; but under the reserve clause, there is no competitive pressure on the owner of the contract. As a result, the player's reservation wage is not bid up to his second-highest MRP in the league. Instead, the player's reservation wage under a reserve clause system is what the player can earn *outside* of the league, or the league minimum salary, whichever is higher.

Needless to say, for most athletes, the reservation wage calculated in this way lies far below the player's value to *any* team in the league. Under the reserve clause system, a player's wage will end up some place between his reservation wage and his MRP with the team owning his contract. The reserve clause system lowers the value of the player's reservation wage by eliminating competing offers by other teams, and, unless the player happens to be under contract with the team in the league to which he is most valuable, the upper bargaining limit has been reduced as well. Predictably, the overall effect of a reserve clause system is to lower player salaries relative to what they would earn under free agency.

Put another way, a reserve clause system acts to direct more of the revenue that a player produces to the team owner than to the player. The effect of unrestricted free agency on a league that previously was under a reserve clause system, as in the case of baseball since 1976, would be a bidding up of player salaries to the point where most of the revenue that is linked to the performance of the team ends up in player salaries. Under a reserve clause system, the team can capture a significant fraction of the revenue linked to a team's performance, as well as revenue that is not so linked.

For both players and owners, the issue of free agency is critical to their economic well-being. While claims that free agency will destroy pro sports thus far are clearly exaggerated, the division of the monopoly rents created by pro sports certainly is at stake. It should come as no surprise, then, that free agency is the central issue in pro team sports collective bargaining. A secondary collective bargaining concern is the league minimum salary, which under a reserve clause system becomes the reservation wage for most players. Under free agency, the league minimum salary is no longer relevant to regulars, but it remains an important bargaining element for other players not yet eligible for free agency.

The point of all this is that the sports labor market has the same fundamental driving forces as any other labor market, that is, the value produced by an employee and his or her bargaining power, with the wage rate ending up somewhere between the reservation wage and the player's MRP, and with the player's MRP depending upon the demand by the public for the sport. Interestingly, what goes on in the player market is often portrayed in the press in exactly the opposite fashion, as though it were changes in player salaries that controlled ticket prices and TV revenues.

TICKET PRICE AND PLAYER SALARIES

Owners of sports teams understandably are concerned about escalating salaries for players. After all, they have to pay the bills. But when owners and league commissioners express their opinions about the level of player salaries in public, they like to come on in their self-appointed role of protectors of the fans. Owners are fond of pointing out that if player salaries increase, they (the owners) will be forced to raise ticket prices, or turn to pay-per-view alternatives, in order to obtain the revenues to pay those salaries. The owners' line would have it that putting a brake on salary increases really is in the interest of fans, who prefer low ticket prices to high ones. This argument seems to be very effective, because fans typically side with the owners in salary disputes with players and in labor negotiations with player unions. . . .

While the owners get effective mileage from this line, it makes very little economic sense. With some rare classic exceptions, such as Phil Wrigley and Tom Yawkey, owners of sports teams are in the business to make money, or at least not lose money. Nobody has to force an owner to raise ticket prices if he or she is fielding a successful team with lots of popular support and a sold-out stadium. Put another way, even if player costs did not rise, one would expect that ticket prices and TV contract values would rise in the face of increasing fan demand. On the other hand, if the team already is having trouble selling tickets, only sheer folly would dictate raising ticket prices.

Given a team's roster of players, the simple economic fact of life is that the ticket pricing decision by a profit-oriented owner is completely independent of the salaries paid to those players. Profit-oriented ticket-pricing decisions depend solely on the demand by fans for tickets to the team's games. The demand for the inputs used to produce the games, including players, is derived from this profit-oriented decision, not the other way around. Ticket prices rise when fan demand rises, which in turn increases player MRPs, which spills over into higher salaries for players.

Nowhere is this logic more clearly evident than in the case of baseball in the period just after the beginning of free agency. Free agency acted immediately to raise player salaries. . . . But fans would not pay more to watch the same players just because they started earning more. The initial effect of free agency was to lower team profits with little impact on ticket prices. . . . With few exceptions, ticket prices *fell* in real terms during the very first years of free agency! Indeed, only the Boston Red Sox and New York Yankees had ticket prices in excess of their 1971 levels as late as 1980, four years after free agency. Thus, salaries rose, but ticket prices did not. Ticket prices prior to free agency were already set by owners at levels representing their best guesses as to what would maximize revenue for their teams. Free agency shifted the bargaining power in the direction of players, and player salaries went up. But changes in player salaries per se had no effect on the demand for tickets and no effect on ticket prices.

. . . . This has been a period of rising demand by the public for the major pro team sports. Rising demand led to increases in both ticket prices and TV contract revenues. In turn, the increased demand for pro sports tickets and TV coverage acted to increase the value of skilled players to teams, that is, their MRPs rose. Then, the bargaining process translated the increased value of player skills into higher player salaries. Salaries continued to grow through the 1980s for all pro sports, spurred on by the growth in team revenues. Under free agency, as in baseball and basketball, more of the increased revenue goes to players than under a reserve clause system, such as that in football and hockey. But salaries go up in either case when demand for the sport increases, and, contrary to the argument of owners, they are the effect and not the cause of higher ticket prices.

It might be that the mistaken perception about the link between player salaries and ticket prices comes from a confusion of two different sources of salary escalation. If a team's salary bill rises because the team has acquired more expensive talent, then the owner can and undoubtedly will raise ticket prices, not because he or she is paying more in salaries, but because he or she is fielding a more attractive team. That was certainly the case with the Yankees in the early days of free agency. . . . But looking at the league as a whole, the same group of players was around right after free agency as before, so for an average team, the quality of players didn't change. Consequently, there was no way that the average owner could pass on to fans the increase in salaries that came with free agency; the salary cost increase came directly out of profits, instead.

THE WINNER'S CURSE

Things are not quite as simple as we have been making them, of course — general managers and scouts really do earn the money they are paid. It is no easy task to predict how a player will perform next season, what his contribution to the team will be, and the size of the crowds the team will draw. . . .

We do not pretend to any such skills. Instead, we assume that the market for players "works" in the sense that, on average, bids by skilled general managers and offers by skilled player agents lead to a situation in which players get paid pretty much according to what we have outlined, that is, what they would be worth in their second-best employment in the league.

Well, actually, they may get a little more than that, and maybe even more than their MRPs to the teams that sign them. There is a well-known phenomenon in bidding theory known as "the winner's curse," which might be operative in the player markets of the free agency period. . . .

In a sealed-bid auction, say, for league TV rights, the prospective bidders (the networks and cable systems) each evaluate the revenue potential of the TV rights and then, at a specified time, each in effect submits a dollar bid in a sealed envelope. The "lucky" winner is the individual submitting the highest bid. "Lucky" is in quotes, because, by definition, the winning bidder ends up paying more for the right to televise games, and occasionally much more, than any other bidder was willing to offer. Given that all bidders had access to pretty much the same information about the potential market for TV, this suggests that the winner might well have made a mistake in overvaluing the revenue potential of the contract. This is the "winner's curse" — winning in a sealed-bid auction means the winner might very well have bid too much, and maybe far too much, for the property. In particular, a measure of how much the winner has overbid is the difference between the winner's bid and the second-highest bid. In the jargon of the field, this difference is what is "left on the table."

The free agent market in baseball is not as formal as a sealed-bid auction, but there are problems for a general manager in determining how much a player will be worth to his team and in guessing how much other teams will be willing to offer the player. Ideally, a general manager would like to pay any player just $1 more than the player's best offer anywhere else, but this option is only available in cases where the team has "right of first refusal," that is, the right to match any outside offer.

With lots of teams out there operating in the free agent market (and assuming no collusion), there will be vigorous competitive bidding for players. Clearly, teams underestimating the MRPs of free agents will typically not be the teams signing them; instead, there is better chance that the "winners" in the free agent market will be teams overestimating player MRPs, and these are the teams stuck with the "winner's curse." And, in turn, the presence of the winner's curse means that players get paid on average even more than their value in their second-best employment opportunities in the league. This cannot be too surprising. Sportswriters, each year, are fond of rubbing owners' noses in the winner's curse by pointing out how overpaid many (some would say most) free agents are, relative to their subsequent performance.

SALARY DETERMINATION IN BASEBALL

Assuming that the baseball player market operates to generate salary offers that correlate roughly with player MRPs, we can identify factors that can be said to "determine" baseball player salaries in the sense that these factors are highly correlated with market-determined salary levels, and thus do a good job of predicting the level of baseball player salaries. . . . The equation is a "best fit" model of salary determination in the sense that (1) it explains a large portion of the total variation in player salaries, and (2) adding other factors to the equation would not significantly improve its predictive power. Models . . . are used both by players and by owners in justifying their positions on salary demands in the baseball salary arbitration process. . . .

. . . The clear conclusion is that income inequality in the rest of the U.S. economy, although high relative to other countries, pales in comparison to the inequality in recent years in baseball salaries.

It is also clear that baseball salaries have become less equally distributed over time, and skewed toward the top of the salary scale, with a noticeable jump between the reserve clause and free agency periods. . . Overall, from the baseball salary data, we can conclude that while all players benefited from free agency, a disproportionate share of the benefits went to the top players, who were the big gainers from free agency. Players at the lower end of the distribution, still held captive by united mobility for their first six years, lost ground relative to their star teammates.

. . . .

REFERENCES

1. Quoted in Rick Telander, The Hundred Yard Lie, New York: Simon & Schuster 1989, at 41.

THE SPORTS BUSINESS AS A
LABOR MARKET LABORATORY

Lawrence M. Kahn

Professional sports offers a unique opportunity for labor market research. There is no research setting other than sports where we know the name, face, and life history of every production worker and supervisor in the industry. Total compensation packages and performance statistics for each individual are widely available, and we have a complete data set of worker–employer matches over the career of each production worker and supervisor in the industry. These statistics are much more detailed and accurate than typical microdata samples such as the Census or the Current Population Survey. Moreover, professional sports leagues have experienced major changes in labor market rules and structure — like the advent of new leagues or rules about free agency — creating interesting natural experiments that offer opportunities for analysis.

. . . .

Of course, it is wise to be hesitant before generalizing from the results of sports research to the population as a whole. The four major team sports employ a total of 3,000 to 4,000 athletes who, in the mid-1990s, earned . . . far above the 1997 median earnings of full-time, full-year equivalent workers of $25,000–$26,000. But at a minimum, sports labor markets can be seen as a laboratory for observing whether economic propositions at least have a chance of being true. . . .

MONOPSONY AND PLAYER SALARIES

Sports owners are a small and interconnected group, which suggests that they have some ability to band together and act as monopsonists in paying players. The result is that player pay is held below marginal revenue product. I discuss three sources of evidence on monopsony in sports: evidence from the rise and fall of rival leagues, evidence from changes in rules about player free agency, and studies comparing the marginal revenue product of players with their pay. Sports owners have often had monopsony power over players in the sense that in many instances players have the option of negotiating only with one team. Here, salaries are determined by individual team–player bargaining in which marginal revenue product, and the outside options available to teams and players, will affect the outcome. Rules changes and the rise and fall of rival leagues have their effects by changing players' and teams' outside options.

RIVAL LEAGUES

There have been two time periods in which rival leagues posed a substantial threat to existing professional sports. The first is the period from 1876 to 1920, when there was a scramble of professional baseball leagues forming, merging, and dissolving. The second is the period from the late 1960s into the early 1980s, when new leagues were born in basketball, hockey, and football.

. . . Baseball is the oldest major league sport in the United States, beginning with the birth of the National League in 1876. In this early period, there was competition for player services from other baseball leagues. To protect itself against the competition of rival leagues and improve the team owners' balance sheets, the National League introduced the "reserve clause" in 1879, which meant that players were bound to the team that originally acquired the rights to contract with them. Owners now had additional monopsony power over players, and player salaries dropped.

However, the lower salaries may have contributed to the birth of a new league in 1882, the American Association. . . . Average nominal National League salaries rose from $1,375 in 1882 to $3,500 in 1891, which would be equivalent to about $63,000 in 1998.

This increase in salaries is not conclusive evidence that monopsony power of owners decreased; after all, salaries could have risen for other reasons, like the growth of baseball's popularity. However, in 1891, four of the American Association teams were absorbed into the National League, and five dissolved AA franchises were bought out by the survivors. . . . [which coincided with] an abrupt, massive decline in National League player salaries starting in the first season of the merger: player pay fell from $3,500 in 1891 (before the merger) to $2,400 in 1892 to $1,800 in 1893. This pay cut was accomplished as the outcome of the National League owners announcement in 1893 of a new salary policy: the maximum pay for a player was to be $2,400. Indeed, some teams imposed lower caps: eight top players on the Philadelphia Phillies who were all paid more than $3,000 in 1892 found that they were all paid exactly $1,800 in 1893. The sharp decline in player salaries does not appear to reflect a major decline in the demand for baseball entertainment, as attendance climbed through the 1895 season.

The success of the National League waned somewhat in the late 1890s, partly due to a lack of competitive balance, but the baseball market was growing. A new rival league, the American League, began in 1901 with eight teams. It successfully lured many star players from the older league and actually outdrew it in attendance in 1902 by 2.2 million to 1.7 million. In response, the National League attempted to have its reserve clause enforced by state courts to prevent players from jumping leagues; however, because state courts have no jurisdiction for player movements outside a given state, it was ultimately unsuccessful in this effort.

A familiar pattern then emerges. The huge success of the American League brought with it a dramatic rise in player salaries. In fact the salary increase appears to begin in 1900, perhaps reflecting anticipation of the new league. The two leagues merged during the 1903 season, at the end of which the first World Series was played. Then in 1903, salaries in Major League Baseball fell immediately by about 15 percent. . . . Again, this decline does not seem to reflect any fall in baseball's popularity that year.

Major League Baseball prospered for the rest of the first decade of the twentieth century, with player costs under control and attendance on the rise. However, attendance fell beginning in 1910, and owners kept a tight lid on salaries. Player discontent resulted in the formation of a union, the Fraternity of Professional Baseball Players of America, at the end of the 1912 season. The owners were under no legal obligation to bargain with a union and reacted to it with some hostility.

This dissatisfaction among players helped pave the way for the Federal League, which was able to recruit to long-term contracts several well-known Major League ballplayers beginning in 1913. The pay cycle began again. While the Federal League was in existence from 1913 through 1915, many players jumped leagues, and major league salaries went from about $3,000 in 1913 to $5,000 in 1915. After the 1915 season, most of the Federal League's owners were "bought out" in December 1915 by the major leagues, and nominal salaries plummeted back to $4,000 by 1917, a fall that was even larger in real terms due to the inflation of the World War I period.

The Federal League owners who were not part of the settlement pursued an antitrust suit against the settling parties for creating a monopoly; however, this suit was lost in 1922, when the U.S. Supreme Court declared that baseball was not a business.[1] This decision began baseball's antitrust exemption, which was upheld several times, most notably in an unsuccessful attempt by a player named Curt Flood to become a free agent in 1969.[2] While Flood lost his case, it may have set the stage for baseball players' ultimately successful quest for free agency. However, this goal was not achieved through the antitrust laws; in fact, baseball's exemption lasted with respect to player relations until legislation ending it was passed in 1998. Rather, collective bargaining brought free agency to baseball, as discussed below.

The early experiences of Major League Baseball provide some compelling evidence for the potential impact of monopsony in this labor market. However, the comparisons just discussed all concern baseball, and thus have no real control group. In the modern period, we can use salaries in some sports as control groups for other sports.

From the late 1960s into the 1970s, highly credible rival leagues were born in basketball and hockey. The American Basketball Association (ABA), which lasted from 1967 to 1976, was able to field some very good teams. In 1976, four of its teams were absorbed into the NBA, and these all made the NBA playoffs in several seasons after the merger. The NBA Players Association (NBPA) challenged the merger on antitrust grounds, but then withdrew its lawsuit as the result of a settlement which granted free agency rights to NBA players. The World Hockey Association (WHA), which lasted from 1971 to 1979, also had several excellent teams which were absorbed into the NHL starting in 1979.

The rise and fall of these two rival leagues offer another opportunity to test how monopsony might affect salaries since the other two major team sports — baseball and football — had no such competition in their labor markets until the advent of free agency in baseball in 1976 and the birth of the United States Football League (USFL) in 1982.

. . . . In 1967, there were no rival leagues in baseball, football, or hockey, and the ABA was just getting started. Further, there was no free agency, and players unions had not yet negotiated their first agreements. Thus, the 1967 salaries can be viewed as representing common initial conditions with respect to negotiating rules, although not necessarily with respect to demand conditions.*

---

* The higher NFL salary level may have represented the lingering effects of the bidding war between the National Football League and the American Football League earlier in the 1960s. The two leagues agreed to merge in 1966, a merger that required congressional approval. This episode is not discussed here because NFL salary level information is not available before 1967. However, there is strong anecdotal evidence of bidding wars between the two leagues over college stars such as Joe Namath.

By 1970 and 1972, the ABA had been in existence for several years, and NBA players rapidly became the highest paid of the major team sports. The World Hockey Association started in 1971, and by 1972, NHL players outearned football and baseball players by similar margins. These upward movements in the relative salaries of basketball and hockey players, while consistent with effects of the new competition, need to be judged against the changing popularity of these two sports. For example, in the NBA, total attendance rose by 120 percent between 1966–67 and 1971–72, while television revenues went from $1.5 million to $5.5 million during the same period, rises that were much, much greater than the increases for football or baseball during this time. . . . The shock of higher salaries may also have spurred the teams to market themselves better. Moreover, NBA salaries as a percentage of gross basketball revenues rose from 30 percent in 1967 to 66 percent in 1972, which suggests a structural shift in salary determination that goes beyond a rise in revenues. In the NHL, attendance growth was actually much faster in the five years before the birth of the WHA (135 percent) than while the WHA was in business (7 percent). Thus, the acceleration of NHL salaries after 1971 is telling indeed.

There is one more important example of the impact of a rival league on player salaries, the United States Football League (USFL). Like some of the baseball experiences earlier in the century, the USFL was born out of labor strife in the established league; in this case, it was a seven-week NFL strike in 1982, in which the players had failed to gain any significant ground in their fight for free agency or a share of revenues. From 1982 to 1985, the USFL posed a challenge to the established NFL. The USFL had strong financial backing from such owners as Donald Trump; many NFL players switched leagues; and the USFL was able to sign some high-profile college players such as Anthony Carter and Herschel Walker. However, poor television ratings for the USFL ultimately signaled its demise.

The pattern of football player salaries during the USFL years follows that set by the example of other rival leagues. Real salary increases for NFL players averaged 4 percent per year from 1977–1982, before the USFL, and 5 percent per year from 1985–1989, just after the USFL. In between, real player salary increases were 20 percent per year from 1982–1985. Changes in the popularity of football do not seem sufficient to explain the explosion of salaries during the USFL years. From 1977 to 1981, NFL attendance rose 23 percent, but attendance was actually 2 percent lower in 1985 than in 1981; further, NFL television revenues rose by similar rates before and during the USFL years. Overall, NFL salaries during the USFL period were much higher than could have been predicted on the basis of revenues during that time.*

If one uses other sports as a control group for the experience of football salaries in the USFL years, the same lesson emerges. The salary growth for football players from 1982 to 1985 was 8–10 percentage points per year higher than baseball and basketball, and 17 percentage points per year higher than for hockey players. However, during the 1981–85 period, attendance grew 5 percent in baseball, 11 percent in the NBA, 11 percent in the NHL, and, as noted, fell 2 percent in the NFL; television revenues grew 211 percent in baseball and 35 percent in the NBA, compared to 29 percent in the NFL. The faster growth of NFL salaries during the 1982–85 period despite worse attendance and television revenue increases again suggests the importance of the USFL.

---

* Deceleration of the growth of NFL television revenues from nearly 30 percent per year from 1981 to 1985 to just 2.6 percent annual growth from 1985 to 1988 could also have explained the deceleration of salaries after 1985. However, it is also true that attendance in the NFL picked up from 1985 to 1988, rising 1.5 percent, in contrast to the 2 percent fall from 1981 to 1985. Quirk, James and Rodney D. Fort. 1997. *Pay Dirt: The Business of Professional Team Sports.* Princeton, NJ: Princeton University Press.

FREE AGENCY

Until 1976, players in each of the four major sports were bound by the reserve clause to remain with their original team, unless that team decided to trade or sell them to another team. They were not allowed to become free agents, who could sell their services to any team.

The path toward free agency started in baseball. The Major League Baseball Players Association (MLBPA) was started in 1952, but it didn't become a modern union until the former United Steelworkers negotiator, Marvin Miller, took over in 1966. The MLBPA achieved a collective bargaining agreement in 1968, and in 1970 the National Labor Relations Board ordered the parties to use outside arbitrators for resolving grievances. In a farsighted decision, Miller obtained management's agreement to incorporate the standard player contract, which included the reserve clause, into the collective bargaining agreement. This meant that grievances about the interpretation of this clause were a proper subject for arbitration. In December 1975, an arbitrator ruled that the reserve clause meant that the team could reserve a player for only one year beyond the expiration of any current contract. With the reserve clause in place, almost all teams signed players exclusively to one-year contracts, and so this ruling would have freed virtually all of the veteran players after the 1976 season. The teams, threatened with this possibility, were thus moved to negotiate a formal system of free agency with the union in 1976, calling for free agency (with some relatively minor compensation to any team losing a free agent) for players with at least six years of Major League Baseball service. This provision remains basically in place. In 1994, about 33 percent of players had at least six years' service. *[This number remained almost the same — 32% — in 2002.]*

The rise of free agency in the 1976–77 period had a powerful impact on the salaries of baseball players. The average real increase in baseball salaries was from 0–2 percent per year from 1973–75. In 1976 the average real salary increase was almost 10 percent; in 1977, the first year under the new collective bargaining agreement, 38 percent (!); in 1978, 22 percent, before falling back into single digits growth in 1979. Moreover, baseball salaries as a percentage of team revenues rose from 17.6 percent in 1974 to 20.5 percent in 1977 to 41.1 percent in 1982, further suggesting that free agency has had a structural effect on baseball salary determination.* A final point to note about baseball salary determination is that in a series of grievance arbitration decisions in the 1980s, the owners were found guilty of colluding by not making offers to free agents. This reassertion of cartel wage-setting behavior appeared to be successful in restraining salary growth. Real annual growth in baseball salaries fell from 11 percent in the 1982–85 time period to 3 percent from 1985–87. Moreover, salaries as a percent of revenues fell from about 40 percent in 1985 to 32 percent in 1989 during the collusion period. In 1989, arbitrators levied a $280 million back pay penalty on the owners to be paid out over the 1989–91 period as compensation for the losses imposed by collusion, and salaries as a percent of revenue bounced back to 43 percent by 1991. The collusion episode provides a further illustration of the potential impact of monopsony on salaries.

Basketball players also won free agency in 1976, but by a different route, through the settlement of the players' antitrust suit challenging the ABA–NBA merger. As a result, free agency in the NBA came on the heels of the ABA–NBA salary war period of 1967–76. Possibly as a result, average salaries

---

* In the 1974 and 1975 seasons, many players were eligible for salary arbitration, but without free agency, arbitration alone seemed to have little impact on average salaries. However, salary arbitration, in combination with free agency, can have an effect on players' average salaries, because arbitrators are often entitled to compare players' demands and team offers to the salary levels of free agents. Using fixed effects methods on panel data for individual players for the late 1980s, I found that, other things equal, being eligible for salary arbitration increased players' salary by about 30–45 percent. See Kahn, Lawrence M. "Free Agency, Long-Term Contracts and Compensation in Major League Baseball: Estimates from Panel Data." *The Review of Economics and Statistics.* 75:1, pp. 157–64.

grew more slowly in the NBA in the 1977–82 period than in football or baseball, a comparison which does not suggest a major impact of free agency in the NBA in addition to the impact of competition from the ABA. On the other hand, NBA salaries amounted to about 70 percent of revenue in 1977 and "nearly three quarters" in 1983, suggesting some further increase in basketball players' relative power after the coming of free agency even without the benefit of an alternative league.[3] Finally, basketball imposed a salary cap in 1983, and salaries did indeed decelerate after 1985. However, there were many exceptions to the salary cap, and it may ultimately have had little effect on salaries during this period.

EVIDENCE ON THE DEGREE OF MONOPSONISTIC EXPLOITATION

To this point, the argument has relied on presenting abrupt shifts in salaries that are difficult to explain without appealing to the theory of monopsony. An alternative mode of research on salary determination is to compare estimates of players' marginal revenue products to salaries, and in this way to approximate the degree of monopsonistic exploitation. . . .

. . . . Scully found that star players in 1987 were paid 29–45 percent of marginal revenue product; even though this was the height of the collusion period, the percentage was still much higher than the 15 percent he found for the reserve clause days.[4] Zimbalist's approach compares the players eligible and not eligible for free agency.[5] In 1989, for those players with less than three years service, and thus not eligible for salary arbitration or free agency, the ratio of salary to marginal revenue product was just .38 times what it was for those eligible for salary arbitration only and .18 times that for those eligible for free agency.*

These measures of monopsonistic exploitation must be interpreted cautiously since (as noted by the authors of the studies) they do not control for a player's effects on revenue other than through his own playing statistics' effects on winning.† However, taken as a whole, this line of research produces additional evidence that making the labor market more competitive leads to higher salaries than would be the case under monopsony. Nonetheless, during the 1980s there still appeared to be widespread monopsonistic exploitation in baseball, and research from this period also showed similar results for basketball.

. . . . *[The author's discussion of the Coase theorem and sports and racial discrimination is omitted. See Chapter 19 for a discussion of the latter topic.]*

INCENTIVES, SUPERVISION, AND PERFORMANCE

Some of the most intriguing evidence on the links from incentives to performance comes from sports that have not been much discussed to this point, like golf and marathon running. Ehrenberg and

---

* The low relative levels of exploitation for the free agency eligible suggest that in the free agent market, teams may have been affected by the "winner's curse." . . . .

† As an extreme example of such effects not captured by the revenues of the player's home team, Hausman and Leonard estimate Michael Jordan's value to other NBA teams during the 1991–92 season to be roughly $53 million. This consisted of effects on attendance at away games, television ratings, and merchandise sales. Hausman, Jerry A. and Gregory K. Leonard. 1997. "Superstars in the National Basketball Association: Economic Value and Policy." *Journal of Labor Economics.* 15:4, pp. 586–624.

Bognanno used data from the 1984 U.S.-based Professional Golf Association (PGA) and 1987 European PGA tours to estimate the impact of incentives on player performance.[6] Because the prize structure of a given tournament is known in advance, one can compute the dollar gain to improving one's finishing position in a tournament. Ehrenberg and Bognanno found that a greater dollar gain to a better finish had a statistically significant favorable effect on a player's performance, controlling for the player's ability, his opponents' ability, and the difficulty of the course. In addition, golfers appear to perform better when it matters more, particularly in the later rounds of a tournament. Finally, golfers' labor supply, as measured by their propensity to enter a given tournament, is positively affected by the expected gain to participating, implying an upward-sloping labor supply schedule.* However, a more recent replication study, using 1992 PGA data, found that monetary incentives had small and statistically insignificant effects on player performance and that results were sensitive with respect to who rated the weather that prevailed during a tournament.[7]

The framework devised by Ehrenberg and Bognanno has been used to examine the incentive impact of prize money in two additional sports: marathon running and auto racing.[8] In auto racing, Becker and Huselid found that larger monetary rewards to better finishes lowered individual racers' finishing times and raised the incidence of accidents, presumably due to a greater effort to go fast.[9] In marathon races, Frick found that better prize money and performance bonuses for setting records lowered racing times.[10]

In the major team sports that have been the primary focus of this paper, free agency has brought with it an increased incidence of long-term contracts, a finding Lehn argued was consistent with wealth effects, as players in essence buy long-term income insurance.[11] He noted that as the incidence of long-term contracts went from virtually zero during the days of the reserve clause to 42 percent of baseball players with at least two years pay guaranteed as of 1980, the share of baseball players who spent time on the disabled list rose from an average of 14.8 percent from 1974 to 1976 (before free agency) up to 20.8 percent from 1977 to 1980 (the early years of free agency). Lehn surmised that this increase was a moral hazard response by players on guaranteed long-term contract. In this instance, moral hazard refers to a player's impact on the decision to go or stay on injured reserve.

To perform a sharper test of this hypothesis, he compared players in 1980 who had long-term contracts of three years or more with those who had short-term contracts of two years or less. Prior to signing these contracts, those with long-term contracts were almost two years younger and had 2.2 days per season less disability than those who signed short-term contracts. Thus, those with long-term contracts do not appear to be an especially injury-prone group. Nonetheless, after signing their agreements, those with long-term contracts averaged 12.6 disabled days per season, compared to only 5.2 days for those with 0–2 years. Lehn confirms in a regression setting that this effect is highly statistically significant.[12] The finding is strongly suggestive of a moral hazard effect, although one

---

* Labor supply effects also appear in men's professional tennis. The Association of Tennis Professionals (the governing body of the men's pro tour) decided several years ago to consider just a player's results in the most recent 14 events in which [he has] competed in computing his ranking, which affects his seeding and therefore success probability in future tournaments. For example, in 1999, one player was ranked first in the world for part of the year, despite a string of first round tournament losses. These did not count in his ranking point total, and observers surmised that he would have entered fewer tournaments (and thus conserved his energy) if the costs of losing were higher. Because of these poor incentives, the Association of Tennis Professionals (the ruling body of men's tennis) has instituted a new system which will count in a player's ranking a core set of tournaments, whether the player plays in the tournament or not, and then some other tournaments as well. See the ATP's Web site at (http://www.atptour.com).

cannot completely rule out that players who had private information that they were fragile were more likely to sign long-term contracts, in which case the results could also reflect adverse selection.

Of course, one way for a team to reduce the moral hazard response is to reward players for not being injured. Lehn notes that 38 out of 155 players with contracts of three or more years, or about 25 percent, had incentive clauses in their contracts.[13] These clauses sometimes rewarded either being available to play for most of the season or postseason awards won (such awards typically require being active for all or most of the year). Before signing such long-term contracts, those who ended up with incentive bonuses had virtually identical average propensities to be injured as those without such incentive bonuses. However, after signing, the injured time of players without incentive bonuses was 2.4 times that of those with bonuses. Again, a strong moral hazard response is suggested, although as before, we cannot rule out the adverse selection possibility that players who suspected that they were likely to be fragile have turned down the opportunity to sign a contract with an incentive bonus.

Hiring better quality management is an alternative route, along with contract incentives, for eliciting desired performance levels. In a study of the impact of baseball managers, I estimated the effect of better managers on team and individual player performance.[14] Managerial quality was measured by first running a 1987 regression with manager salary as the dependent variable and managerial experience, career winning percentage, and a National League dummy variable as the explanatory variables. Then, using the coefficients from the regression, I plugged in each manager's actual experience and winning percentage to get a predicted salary level. I then calculated that during the 1969–86 period, hiring a better quality manager significantly raised the team's winning percentage relative to its past level — even if one also controls for team scoring and runs allowed, suggesting that good managers win the close games. The effect of good managers was even larger when I didn't control for offense and defense. The latter effect could indicate that better managers are superior judges of talent, or motivate their players, and thus indirectly contribute to offense and defense.

I also studied individual player performance relative to established career levels when the team was taken over by a new manager. The better the quality of the new manager, the better a player's future performance relative to his past performance. In related calculations, I found an increase in managerial quality more than pays for itself based on Scully's results for the effect of winning on revenue.[15] Because of this, one might have expected the salaries of highly talented managers to be bid up. The fact that they weren't as measured in the 1987 salary data used in this study may be further indirect evidence of collusion between baseball owners during this time period.

FINAL THOUGHTS

Labor issues in sports may seem distant from the rest of the economy, since they often seem to pit millionaire players against billionaire owners. But while it would be unwise to extrapolate too strongly from the labor market experience of sports, evidence on a particular labor market should not be discounted just because the market has a high profile, either. The strong evidence for monopsony in sports has some parallels to a similar effect that has been found among groups such as public school teachers, nurses, and university professors.[16] The evidence from these areas suggests that the phenomenon of employer monopsony power could be more widespread than is commonly acknowledged by economists. The presence of customer discrimination in sports reminds us that there are many sectors in the economy with producer–customer contact where discrimination could persist.

The results on player performance suggest that athletes are motivated by similar forces that affect workers in general.

While this paper has concentrated on sports in North America, many of the same economic issues arise in the sports industry elsewhere. Professional soccer leagues in Europe are tremendously lucrative and also must be concerned with player movement and competitive balance. For example, television contracts for soccer in the United Kingdom, France, Italy, Spain, and Germany had a combined annual value of roughly $1 billion in 1997; this compares favorably to the 1996 total media revenues of roughly $1.3 billion for the most lucrative league in North America, the NFL. In fact, European soccer draws more TV revenue than the NBA, Major League Baseball, or the NHL. The promotion and demotion of individual teams to and from a new European superleague involving teams from several countries raise fascinating questions about the role of competitive balance.

Recent developments in North American sports will provide some additional opportunities to observe economic theories at work. For example, the NBA and the NFL have adopted explicit revenue sharing rules between labor and management so that salaries are supposed to comprise a certain share of total revenue. Major League Baseball has adopted revenue sharing and a "luxury tax" on payrolls over a particular amount. While explicit revenue sharing can promote cooperation between labor and management by automatically joining each side's economic success together, the 1998 basketball lockout suggests that agreeing on an appropriate sharing rule can be difficult. (See Table 2 for salary cap growth in the NBA and the NFL.)

REFERENCES

1. Federal Baseball Club of Baltimore, Inc. vs. National League of Baseball Clubs, et al., 259 U.S. 200 (1922).

2. Flood vs. Kuhn, 407 U.S. 258 (1972).

3. Staudohar, Paul D. 1996. *Playing for Dollars: Labor Relations and the Sports Business.* Ithaca, NY: Cornell University Press, at 108.

4. Scully, Gerald W. 1989. *The Business of Major League Baseball.* Chicago: University of Chicago Press.

5. Zimbalist, Andrew. 1992. *Baseball and Billions.* New York: Basic Books.

6. Ehrenberg, Ronald G. and Michael L. Bognanno. 1990. "Do Tournaments Have Incentive Effects?" *Journal of Political Economy.* 98:6, pp. 1307–1324; Ehrenberg, Ronald G. and Michael L. Bognanno. 1990. "The Incentive Effects of Tournaments Revisited: Evidence from the European PGA Tour." *Industrial & Labor Relations Review.* 43:3, pp. 74–88.

7. Orszag, Jonathan M. 1994. "A New Look at Incentive Effects and Golf Tournaments." *Economics Letters.* 46:1, pp. 77–88.

8. Ehrenberg, Ronald G. and Michael L. Bognanno. 1990. "Do Tournaments Have Incentive Effects?" *Journal of Political Economy.* 98:6, pp. 1307–1324; Ehrenberg, Ronald G. and Michael L. Bognanno. 1990. "The Incentive Effects of Tournaments Revisited: Evidence from the European PGA Tour." *Industrial & Labor Relations Review.* 43:3, pp. 74–88.

9. Becker, Brian E. and Mark A. Huselid. 1992. "The Incentive Effects of Tournament Compensation Systems." *Administrative Science Quarterly.* 37:2, pp. 336–50.

10. Frick, Bernd. 1998. "Lohn und Leistung im Professionellen Sport: Das Beispiel Stadt-Marathon." *Konjunkturpolitik.* 44:2, pp. 114–40.

TABLE 2.

SALARY CAP GROWTH IN **NBA** AND **NFL**			
NBA		NFL	
Year	Value	Year	Value
1984–1985	$3.6 million	1994	$34.6 million; Average club salary expenditures of $36.6 million
1985–1986	$4.2 million	1995	$37.1 million; Average club salary expenditures of $41.9 million
1986–1987	$4.9 million	1996	$40.7 million; Average club salary expenditures of $44.9 million
1987–1988	$6.2 million	1997	$41.5 million; Average club salary expenditures of $42.7 million
1988–1989	$7.2 million	1998	$52.4 million; Average club salary expenditures of $61.4 million
1989–1990	$9.8 million	1999	$57.3 million; Average club salary expenditures of $64.7 million
1990–1991	$11.9 million	2000	$62.2 million; Average club salary expenditures of $68.3 million
1991–1992	$12.5 million	2001	$67.4 million; Average club salary expenditures of $66.8 million
1992–1993	$14.0 million	2002	$71.1 million; Average club salary expenditures of $64.5 million
1993–1994	$15.1 million	2003	$75.007 million; Average club salary expenditures of $77.4 million
1995–1996	$23.0 million		
1996–1997	$24.4 million		
1997–1998	$26.9 million		
1998–1999	$30.0 million		
1999–2000	$34.0 million		
2000–2001	$35.5 million		
2002–2003	$40.3 million		
2003–2004	$43.9 million		

Source: ESPN.com. http://espn.go.com/nba/s/2000/0801/663417.html, NFLPA documents.

11. Lehn, Kenneth, 1990. "Property Rights, Risk Sharing and Player Disability in Major League Baseball," in *Sportometrics.* B. Goff and R. Tollison, eds. College Station, Texas: Texas A&M Press, pp. 35–58.
12. Id.
13. Id.
14. Kahn, Lawrence M. 1993. "Managerial Quality, Team Success and Individual Player Performance in Major League Baseball." *Industrial & Labor Relations Review.* 46:3, pp. 531–47.
15. Scully, Gerald W. 1989. *The Business of Major League Baseball.* Chicago: University of Chicago Press.
16. Ehrenberg, Ronald G. and Robert S. Smith, 2000. *Modern Labor Economics,* 7th ed. Reading, Mass.: Addison-Wesley.

WHEN NEGOTIATIONS FAIL:
AN ANALYSIS OF SALARY ARBITRATION AND SALARY CAP SYSTEMS

Melanie Aubut

I. INTRODUCTION

Irreconcilable differences between owners' and players' interests have changed professional sports over the last few decades, from a pillar of North American culture to the big business machine we now know. On the one hand, the owners have a vested interest in their teams' financial success, and in the event that teams fail in this respect, their owners may consider the option of moving their teams to more lucrative markets or selling them to richer investors. On the other hand, players' interests lie in earning the highest salary possible during their relatively short professional careers. They are thus constantly searching for ways to market themselves in order to secure more lucrative contracts.

Players believe that by being restricted to negotiating with only one team, they lose leverage in negotiating their salaries and therefore the potential to make more money. Therein lies the raison d'etre for free agency: granting the opportunity to players who fulfill certain requirements to market themselves in order to enter into lucrative agreements with the highest bidding team. In professional sports leagues, the free agency concept has helped to create a vastly different society from that which has traditionally existed in sports. To name but one of these differences, before the option clause . . . was successfully challenged by the players, a player could conceivably spend his entire career with the same team, a concept that today is the exception rather than the rule.

These opposing interests frequently give rise to strained labor relations, culminating at times in strikes, lock-outs, team relocations, or more commonly, the movement of players between teams. Over the last three decades (particularly the 1990s) professional sports has experienced the most troubled employee–employer relations of any industry in America. Salary arbitration and the salary cap are two important concepts borne out of these heated disputes, and they are now integral elements of collective bargaining agreements (CBAs) between professional leagues and their players' association. Together with free agency, these concepts have transformed sports into a business world where the employees hold seemingly more leverage than the employers.

. . . .

II. SALARY ARBITRATION IN GENERAL

In a professional sports context, salary arbitration is the system implemented to settle salary disputes between a team and a player when negotiations for new terms regarding compensation fail. Accordingly, such disputes are submitted to neutral arbitrators who weigh evidence of a player's performance, ability, and leadership, in comparison with other players, and then render a binding decision with respect to the precise amount of compensation to which a player shall be entitled.

. . . .

In the sports world, the word "association" is used instead of the common designation "union." When the players' unions were first created, it was determined that "the latter term was considered appropriate only for the teams' concession vendors or maintenance crew, not for elite athletes."[9] A professional league players' association acts as the exclusive collective bargaining representative for all of the league's players. The association assists players in grievance and salary arbitration matters and works closely with the league to ensure that playing conditions meet safety guidelines.

Parties who agree to submit to arbitration usually do so to substitute for the predetermined setting of wages in CBAs. When negotiating arbitration agreements, parties are able to tailor the arbitration structure to respond to their specific needs. An arbitrator derives his jurisdiction from that which the parties provide in their CBA. For example, as expressed in the NHL/NHLPA CBA, when an NHL player submits a request to an arbitrator, this alone vests jurisdiction of the dispute in the arbitrator. However, the advantages of parties tailoring the arbitration structure as they see fit does not mean that the process is any less complex.

It is important to differentiate between a grievance and salary arbitration, which are both provided for in the CBA. In a salary arbitration, the player's case is presented by his or her agent or lawyer, and the players' association usually has a representative present at the hearing to assist the agent or lawyer. Salary arbitration is limited to issues of compensation and results in the creation of new terms (the salary) and rights for a player and the club for which he plays. Grievance arbitration, on the other hand, "interprets and enforces rights already created by the CBA."[14]

III. THE HISTORY OF SALARY ARBITRATION SYSTEMS

Prior to the 1970s, the concepts of salary caps, salary arbitration, and free agency did not exist. During that time, owners set the players' salaries. When players' associations came onto the sports scene in the late 1960s, players began to feel that they were being taken advantage of by the owners in the negotiation of their contracts and wanted their terms of employment changed, particularly regarding their salaries. The "perceived unfairness of this traditional practice" resulted in many changes in the terms of employment for these athletes. One of the most significant was the implementation of the salary arbitration system. Hockey was the first major professional sport to adopt such a system in 1970 and baseball followed suit in 1973.

. . . .

B. MLB

. . . . *[The author's discussion of the history of and legal challenges to the reserve system is omitted.]*

The players were finally successful in challenging the option clause in 1976 in the Messersmith–McNally case. The arbitration panel concluded that "players were free to bargain with other clubs once their [option year] contracts expired."[55] This meant that the clubs no longer had the right to automatically renew a contract at the end of the option year and the reserve system was brought to an end. In deciding that the specific language in the contract provided clubs with only a single, one-year renewal right, the arbitrator granted the players free agency.

The decision quickly led to an agreement between owners and players on a free agency system that began following the 1976 season. Thereby, MLB was the first major professional sport to secure a broad free agency system enabling players to gain substantial leverage over the owners. When the salary arbitration system was first agreed to, free agency did not exist. Salary arbitration was not troublesome then, because it only forced less generous owners to grant salaries equivalent to those offered by other owners. During this period, salary inflation was nearly nonexistent as there was no bidding for players. This situation changed dramatically when free agency was thrown into the mix. The result has been that MLB players have since enjoyed the best market setting for salary negotiations in professional sports. The co-existence of free agency and salary arbitration without a salary cap resulted in substantial salary increases that continued for nearly two decades. Additionally, it provided players greater leverage with which to maintain their free agency and salary arbitration systems.

Since then, owners have tried to regain some of their powers lost through free agency, salary arbitration, and "freedom of industry-wide salary controls."[63] . . .

. . . .

IV. SALARY ARBITRATION SYSTEMS

A. Arbitration Eligibility

1. NHL.   In the NHL, players elect to submit their salary issue to arbitration. In order to do so, players must meet two requirements. First, the player must not have signed an offer sheet after the expiration of his current contract. Second, a player must be a Group II player (restricted free agent), pursuant to article 10.2 of the CBA. Players are grouped depending on their age and the number of years of experience they have accumulated in the NHL. A year of professional experience is acquired by playing a number of NHL games, depending, once again, on the player's age.

If a player falls into Group II and has the right to elect arbitration, a club must tender a qualifying offer to the player before June 30th following the completion of a given season if it wants to maintain its right to the player. The offer must be equal to at least ten percent of the league's average salary at that time. However, in the event that the player's salary was already above the league's average salary, the club can then offer the same salary the player earned the previous season.

When a player is offered a contract, he is then faced with three options. First, he can accept the offer as is and play for the team under the terms the contract provides. Second, he can accept the offer but not the salary, in which case the parties will go to arbitration to determine the salary. In this case, the club has the right to elect a one- or two-year contract unless the player will qualify as a Group III player (free agent without compensation) after one year, in which case the club cannot elect a two-year contract. Third, a player can simply reject the offer and become a holdout.

2. MLB. . . . .

Salary arbitration is available for baseball players in three situations. It is available when both the player and the club agree to submit the issue to an arbitrator or if the player has three or more, but less than six, years of service in MLB. Alternatively, if a player has between two and three years of service at the major league level he may be eligible if: (1) he has performed at least 86 days of service during the preceding season, and (2) his statistical performance ranks in the top seventeen percent of the players who could be eligible for arbitration for the same reasons. These players are known as "super-two" players. . . .

B. Procedure

1. NHL. . . . .

The arbitrators are not bound by any evidentiary rule and can therefore determine the weight given to each piece of evidence. The parties can offer any of the following evidence: the player's overall experience, the number of games he has played, his injuries or illnesses, the length of his service in the league and/or for the club, his overall contribution to the club's success or failure, special leadership qualities or public appeal, and the performance and/or compensation of comparable players.[111] However, the arbitrator can only take into consideration the performance and compensation of players in similar situations as the player who elected arbitration. . . .

The following factors are not admissible as evidence: terms of the contract entered into when the player was not a Group II restricted free agent; a contract entered into when the player was an unrestricted free agent; qualifying offers made by the club; prior offers during negotiations; testimonials, videotapes, and similar material; reference to actual or potential walk-away rights; any award issued by an arbitrator as to which a club exercises its walk-away right; and the financial condition of the club or the league.[115]

The arbitrator's decision must be sent to each of the parties by fax within forty-eight hours of the end of the hearing (or seventy-two hours if the hearing closes on Friday). This procedure replaces a previous practice which did not provide for a timetable, and the rendering of decisions could take between three to four weeks. The decision establishes the terms of the player's new contract, including whether it is for one or two years (as specified by the club in its brief), the player's base salary, any bonuses, a possible minor league clause, the salary the player would be paid in the minor leagues, and an explanation of the reasons on which the arbitrator based his/her decision, including which comparables were relied on. The salary can be either one of the two offers made by the parties or an amount ranging anywhere between the two. . . .

The decision of the arbitrator is final and binding on the parties. Once the arbitrator's decision is rendered, the club and the player must enter into a player's contract, pursuant to the terms of the arbitrator's decision. . . .

To settle the labor dispute which resulted in a lock-out in 1995, players conceded to the owners a walk-away right, i.e., the right to reject an award within restrictions provided for in the CBA. Each club can exercise this right up to three times in two continuous years and no more than twice in the same year. In this scenario, in the event that the owner elects to reject the award, the player becomes a free agent. If the player is unable to obtain a better offer from another team, he can then return to his previous team and accept the offer that was last on the table prior to his becoming a free agent. To this day, this procedure has been used once, by the Boston Bruins, five years after its inception. The Bruins walked away from a $2.8 million arbitration award to Dimitri Kristich, who then signed with the Toronto Maple Leafs. *[The Bruins also walked away from a $2.51 million arbitration award to Bryan Berard in 2003, the only other time that the procedure has been used.]*

. . . .

3. MLB. . . . .

Since 2000, the hearings have been assigned to a panel of three arbitrators during a three-week period in February. The player has the right to be present during the entire hearing. The arbitrators are chosen annually by the players' association and the PRC [Player Relations Committee]. . . .

At the hearing, each party has one hour to make its presentation. Statistical analysis is the key to these presentations. Once both parties have made their representations, they are granted an additional half-hour to make their rebuttal arguments and summations. These time limits can be extended if the arbitrator deems it appropriate.

Article VI(F)(12) of the Basic Agreement provides the arbitrator with guidance as to which [party's] final offer is more reasonable. Guidance includes criteria such as the quality of the player's contribution during the previous season (including but not limited to his overall performance, special qualities of leadership, and public appeal), the length and consistency of his career contribution, the record of his past compensation, competitive baseball salaries (salary tabulation), physical or mental defects, and the recent performance of the player's team, such as attendance figures and position in the standings, as a measure of public acceptance.[163] *[The salary arbitration provisions remain the same in the 2003–2006 Basic Agreement.]* The parties must therefore present statistical evidence of the player's performance and compare them with the performance and salaries of players in comparable situations. Any evidence can be submitted to prove the criteria mentioned above. The arbitrators have complete discretion in the weighing of the evidence.

The following evidence is not admissible: the financial position of the player and the club; press comments, testimonials, or similar material regarding the player's performance produced by the club or the player himself (except if it refers to the player's awards for playing excellence); offers made by either party prior to arbitration; the cost to the parties of their attorneys, representatives, etc; and salaries in other sports or occupations.[166] Also, the parties cannot make reference to, and the arbitrator cannot take into consideration, the luxury tax. . . .[167]

Unlike the forty-eight hours provided for in the NHL arbitration system, the panel renders its decision within twenty-four hours of the closing of the arguments. The arbitrators are restricted to selecting the offer of either the club or the player. The arbitrators cannot select an amount between the two offers or any amount they might deem more appropriate. A distinctive characteristic of the

MLB arbitration system is that arbitrators cannot reveal the grounds on which they based their selection. The arbitration award is final and binding on the parties.

C. The Distinction Between the NHL and MLB Systems

As previously mentioned, MLB arbitrators are limited to selecting one of the salary figures submitted by the parties. Also, MLB arbitration decisions do not provide reasons for the award, while the NHL arbitrators must justify their decisions. Thus, the NHL provides for a system of precedents on which the parties can rely in future cases.

Another major difference is that the NHL requires parties to exchange briefs forty-eight hours prior to the hearing. Parties to a MLB salary arbitration hearing only exchange their briefs at the hearing itself and therefore have no time to prepare rebuttals.

. . . .

V. SALARY CAP SYSTEMS

A. NFL

As opposed to the NHL and MLB, the NFL has always interpreted its reserve/option clause as being renewable only for one year, instead of perpetually. In the NFL, once the option year expires, the players become free agents, i.e., they no longer have any contractual obligations to their respective teams. Moreover, the CBA expressly states that the option clause is discontinued, unless a player and a club negotiate otherwise. In the event that an option clause is included in a player's contract, it must state the amount the player will be paid for the option year.

In the early 1960s, NFL Commissioner Pete Rozelle instituted the rule that any team signing a free agent had to "compensate" the player's previous team for the loss of the player's services. This became known as the "Rozelle Rule" and it was incorporated by reference in the 1968 CBA. The compensation required was in the form of players and/or draft picks. In the event that the parties could not agree on the compensation, the Commissioner would decide and his decision was final. Because the rule deterred the signing of free agents, players challenged it in Mackey v. NFL in which the Eighth Circuit Court of Appeals found that the Rozelle Rule violated the Sherman Act because it unreasonably restrained trade.[177] Shortly after winning this case, the players and the League agreed to a new CBA.

In 1993, . . . they signed a new seven-year CBA, which provided for a new system of free agency, a salary cap, and a salary floor.

To better understand how the NFL system deals with player movement and salaries, the basis of the free agency system must be explained. In 1993, a CBA was finally reached, providing for a floor and a ceiling on the total payroll permitted by each team. The following paints a broad picture of how free agency is established in the NFL and, then, how salaries are attributed to the athletes, in light of the salary cap.

FREE AGENCY: Veteran players with the required years of service are either restricted or unrestricted free agents; within these categories, there are also "transition" and "franchise" players.

RESTRICTED FREE AGENT: When the contract of a veteran with less than four "accrued seasons" (seasons in which a player had full pay status for six or more regular-season games) expires, he becomes a restricted free agent. This means that he cannot negotiate or sign a contract with any team other than his prior team if that team tenders him an offer on or before a set date. This offer must include a salary predetermined by the CBA. On the other hand, if the club fails to tender such an offer before the due date, the player is free to negotiate and sign a contract with any other team.

UNRESTRICTED FREE AGENCY: When the contract of a player who has played four or more accrued seasons expires, he becomes an unrestricted free agent. He can then negotiate and sign with other teams, until a specified date. After this date, the rights to the player revert to his prior club if it tenders him an offer consisting of at least 110% of his previous salary. The club has until the tenth week of the regular season to sign the player. If it does not, the player is required to sit out the season. Furthermore, if the club does not tender another contract by June 1st, the player can be signed by any other team at anytime throughout the season.

TRANSITION PLAYER: Each team can designate . . . "transitional" players if it offers them the greater of: the average of the previous season top ten salaries at the player's position or, 120% of the player's previous year salary. The transition player designation gives the prior club the right to match offers from any other team made to that player within seven days of the offer. If no offer is received, the prior club must pay the player the average of the ten highest paid players in the league at his position, or 120% of his previous year salary. If an offer is received and the club matches it, the player is forced to remain with his team. However, if the team does not match the offer, the player can sign with the second team and the prior team does not receive any compensation.

FRANCHISE PLAYER: Every year, each club can designate one of its unrestricted free agents as a "franchise player." There are two categories of franchise player: exclusive and nonexclusive. Designation of either category depends on the salary offered by the player's club. If it offers the greater of the minimum of the average top five salaries at the player's position as of April 16th of that year, or 120% of the player's previous year salary, the player becomes an "exclusive" franchise player. In that case, he cannot negotiate nor sign with any other club. If the player is offered the minimum of the average top five salaries of the last season at his position, he becomes a "nonexclusive" franchise player and can thus negotiate with other clubs, but his prior club can match any offer from another team or receive two first-round draft choices if it decides not to match the offer.

. . . .

ROOKIE SALARIES: The NFL established the "Entering Player Pool," a system which signifies "the league-wide limit on the total amount of salary to which all of the NFL clubs may contract for in signing drafted rookies" every year. . . . [213]

SALARY CAP: NFLPA Executive Director Ed Garvey first proposed the introduction of a salary cap in 1982. In January 1993, after six years of strikes and litigation following the expiration of the previous CBA, a settlement was finally reached in which the NFL and NFLPA agreed to the players' demand to an overall cap on teams' payrolls. In effect since 1994, the salary cap is the absolute maximum each club can spend on players' salaries in a given year. The NFL's salary cap is designated as a "hard" salary cap because it does not permit exceptions (as opposed to the one in place in the NBA, which is referred to as a "soft" cap). Working within the structure of a hard cap, a team must plan and manage its payroll carefully in order to ensure that it is financially accountable and to avoid having to cut or trade its players. . . .

In the calculation of the salary cap, a player's signing bonus is prorated over the number of years for which a contract is signed, regardless whether the bonus is entirely paid in the first year of the contract. As for a performance bonus, it is included depending on whether the player is likely to earn the particular bonus. If the player is not likely to receive it, such as if it is conditional on running for thirty or more touchdowns in a given season, the bonus is not included in the first year the contract provides for such a bonus. In the event the player is awarded the bonus, it is calculated in the salary cap for the following year. On the other hand, if the bonus is easily attainable (for example, if it is conditional on the player being on the roster by or on a certain date), it will be included in the year he should fulfill the requirements to receive the bonus. If the player does not receive the bonus, it is credited in the calculation of the following year's salary cap.

A loophole was found in the NFL system which resulted in a controversy, referred to today as the "Deion exception." For the 1995 season, the Dallas Cowboys offered Deion Sanders a seven-year, $35 million contract with a $13 million bonus. This bonus was to be prorated to $1.87 million a year for the seven years of the contract, as per the requirements of the CBA, even though the $13 million was paid immediately to Sanders. The parties had worked out the terms so that a large portion of the salary would be pushed into the uncapped "out years." Following Commissioner Tagliabue's disapproval of the contract and a settlement of a grievance filed by the NFLPA, the NFL and NFLPA agreed to revise the CBA "to bar more than a 50% gap between the size of the prorated signing bonus and the lower base salary for that year."[228]

As previously discussed, the salary cap also includes a limit on the amount that can be paid by each team to all its rookies. However, no limit is fixed for the amount that can be granted to one specific rookie, which means that a team can actually spend the maximum amount on only one rookie (and thus not be able to pay any others). Therefore, in the NFL system, players are granted free agency early in their careers, but are limited by "firm overall size of team payrolls and a separate limit on rookie payrolls which applies to the entire rookie payroll, not to individual salaries."[230]

The NFL and NFLPA also agreed on a minimum payroll each team must respect....

. . . .

The fact that salary restraints are a matter of collective bargaining, i.e., a matter which must be negotiated, cannot be overlooked....

B. NBA

The NBA was the first professional sports league to establish a salary cap. In 1983, the majority of NBA teams experienced financial difficulties and others were both spending and losing a lot of money. The Commissioner and the NBPA decided to develop a salary structure "designed to accommodate the interests of both sides."[245] They created a salary cap on the amount teams can pay new players, regardless of whether they are free agents or rookies. The parties agreed not only on a ceiling but also on a floor, i.e., a minimum for a team's total payroll, as well as on a cap for rookie salaries, in which their salaries are predetermined. According to this rookie salaries system, a player's salary for his first four years in the NBA is not based on his performance but rather on the position he was selected in the draft. Because a player's performance in college is not necessarily representative of his potential for success in the NBA, this system may result in unfairness regarding a player's true market value.

The Larry Bird exception was also included in the same 1983 CBA. "This exception allows a team to exceed the salary cap when it re-signs its own free agents, up to the player's maximum salary. [The player] must have played three seasons without being waived or changing teams as a free agent."[251] In that case, the team can offer up to 12.5% more of the player's salary per season. A new team signing such a player can also use the exception, however, it can only offer up to ten percent of the player's previous salary. This major exception to the salary cap explains the reason why the

NBA salary cap is described as "soft" (as opposed to the NFL's "hard" salary cap). This exception thus permits the teams' total payrolls to exceed the salary cap in order to sign their own free agents. This led to contracts evaluated at $100 million. To avoid such contracts being granted to players, a luxury tax was created to prevent teams from going substantially over the salary cap. This luxury tax does not bar teams from exceeding the salary cap but presents strong monetary incentives to avoid doing so.

The teams' salary cap for each year is determined in the CBA. . . .

. . . .

The NBA and NBPA have also negotiated a minimum team salary in the CBA, equal to 75% of the salary cap in a given year, that does not prevent teams from granting higher salaries, as long as the total of the salaries does not exceed the salary cap. On the other hand, a team cannot have a lower team payroll than the prescribed 75% of the salary cap. In the event that a team has a lower team payroll, the NBA has the power to force that team to pay the players the amount equal to the shortfall. The minimum and the maximum salary budgets can be spent by each team when signing new players, whether rookies or veterans. What constitutes a salary is also determined in the CBA, by rules regarding calculation of deferred compensation, signing bonuses, loans to players, incentive compensation, foreign player payments, one-year minimum contracts, and existing contracts entered into before the Agreement was made.

. . . .

VI. AN EVALUATION OF THE NHL AND MLB SYSTEMS

Because the option clause in both the NHL and MLB was interpreted for a long time as being perpetually renewable, it brought about a dilemma regarding who should decide on players' salaries and how their market value should be determined. In many situations, it seemed quite unfair for the option year's salary to be decided by the owners. It is mainly in response to this problem that free agency and salary arbitration systems were created. . . .

A. NHL

. . . .

The most important factor that results in such salary augmentation is the free agency system. It enables players to "shop" their services around the league and enter into a deal with the highest bidding team. In so doing, the player raises the stakes and is able to secure a very lucrative contract.

It is these and other factors that cause the salary market to increase substantially. It is not merely the existence of salary arbitration itself. Indeed, salary arbitration is seen as an extension of negotiations between the parties. Statistics on players' compensations, which are negotiated voluntarily between players and their teams, are used in order to prove the market value of a player. Hence, if a club grants a high salary to one player, there is a good chance that the arbitrator will follow the trend and grant a comparable player a salary in the same range. Therefore, it is fair to say that salary arbitration "follows" the individually negotiated contracts existing in the market place and is not the sole cause for increasing salaries.

Regarding the salary arbitration procedure itself, its conventional design did not have a "chilling or narcotic effect on salary negotiations." In effect, in 1991, 77 of 100 players who filed for salary arbitration settled their cases prior to the hearing. In 1999, 12 out of 36 filings went to the hearing, while it was 13 out of 32 in 2000 and 17 out of 44 in 2001. *[In 2003, 6 of 31 filings proceeded to a hearing.]* This demonstrates that, even though parties use salary arbitration as a negotiation tool and even though some cases get very close to the hearing itself, most cases are settled without an arbitrator's involvement. Negotiation is still very much a part of players–owners relationship.

Because the arbitrator can decide on any figure between the parties' submissions (as opposed to one or the other in MLB), the arbitrator can take into account circumstances specific to a player in determining the most reasonable salary. This procedure also has its disadvantages. Knowing that the arbitrator will most likely choose a figure close to the midpoint between the two offers submitted, parties are less likely to submit reasonable offers. Indeed, the parties will tend to make extreme offers instead of reasonable ones, to provide the arbitrator with a great deal of leeway in which to reach a decision. The rules of the game simply do not provide any incentive for parties to make reasonable offers. However, it is important to note that offers made during negotiations are not admissible as evidence during the arbitration hearing. Parties can thus make reasonable offers during this period up to the arbitration hearing, where they can then resort to extreme positions.

Regarding the presentation of evidence, the best way to establish that an offer should be awarded is by presenting statistics on performance and compensation of comparable players. As previously mentioned, a club's financial position is not admissible evidence. This rule brings together two views that are hardly reconcilable.

On the one hand, each team operates under its own economic situations, which enable some teams to pay players more than others. Obviously, smaller market teams cannot support the same payrolls as those in larger markets. To ensure the viability of the teams evolving in smaller markets, it would seem only fair to take their financial situations into account. It would also seem logical from a league-wide competitive balance point of view to help smaller market teams gain access to the best available talent in order to ensure that the sport remains competitive and attractive for fans, sponsors, and players alike. What if a team is unable to afford a salary awarded by an arbitrator? It must either walk away from the arbitral award or trade the player, two options that result in the loss of the player.

On the other hand, it is also logical not to hold a certain player responsible for the financial health of the club for which he plays. One could argue that players do not choose the teams they play for and should therefore not be made to bear the burden of the choice others make for them. However, one could also argue that players being transferred from one team to another without their consent is merely "part of the game." Players are well aware of this reality before they enter the professional game.

Taking financial situations of the teams into account raises the complex question of how this can be conceptually achieved. In the event a team alleges that it has budgeted $5 million for a player because that is his "market value," no problem is apparent. However, if a team claims it has budgeted $5 million because it is unable to pay more, the issue of proving this claim comes into play, which seems nearly impossible. That is to say, clubs would be forced to open their books, which would result in a "second trial," i.e., a trial of the club's financial situation.

The reverse situation is also possible, i.e., when a team, as opposed to being unable to pay, has a very stable financial situation. Indeed, a player could argue that even though his market value is $2 million, his team has the financial ability to pay him more and therefore should do so. This, once again, raises the potential problem of putting the club's financial situation on trial. The fact that a club's financial situation should be taken into consideration (because salary arbitration is a continuation of the negotiations between the parties, negotiations in which the club's financial situation is taken into consideration) seems hardly reconcilable with how this can be applied in practice.

It appears that failing to take this factor into consideration in determining a player's salary can have extremely negative effects upon the club while being quite advantageous for the player. Players' salaries do not fail to increase at the rate of the market even though the team they play for is not doing well financially. In failing to take this into consideration, however, the arbitration system negates the fact that some teams are in, or can fall into, very difficult financial positions and that large arbitration awards can spell their demise. The NHL salary arbitration system, therefore, elects to consider the players' concerns and well being, regardless of the team they play for.

. . . .

The NHL/NHLPA CBA expires in June 2004, when issues such as free agency and salary arbitration will be reopened. It will be interesting to evaluate how the parties have worked within the current system and how they seek to modify it to better suit their collective needs. More interesting will be the power struggle between players and owners raising the question of which side has more leverage.

B. MLB

As previously mentioned, players have gained substantial negotiation leverage since the current salary arbitration and free agency systems were created. Baseball's union has been very successful in securing advantageous employment conditions for its players and in increasing the share of league revenues players receive from 20% in 1967, to over 60% in 1999. The result of such leverage is most evident in the average player's salary, which, since 1976, has risen from $51,000 to $2.15 million, while baseball's revenue has grown from $182 million, to approximately $3.4 billion. By 1994, the average salary was $1.15 million, up 600% from $197,000 in 1981. Moreover, in the year 2000, the average player's salary was $1,894,216 and the minimum salary was $200,000. *[The minimum salary increased to $300,000 in 2003.]* While players seek to protect the important rights they have secured regarding salary arbitration and free agency, their owners are trying to restrict the players' privileges by, for example, establishing a salary cap in the name of "leveling the playing field."

. . . .

Looking back to the evaluation of salary arbitration itself, the advantages that players draw from using salary arbitration as a tool are significant. Arbitration decisions award salary increases ranging on average, from 75% to 150% from the players' previous salary. Between 1974 and 2001, arbitrators ruled on behalf of the players one hundred ninety-one times, while ruling for the owners two hundred fifty times. However, even when the owners win their case, players' salaries still increase from between 50% to 75%, resulting in a raise of a half million dollars or more. Moreover, in 2001, the salaries determined by arbitration increased by 144% of the players' previous salaries. However, like the NHL, negotiations between owners and players are still the primary tool used to conclude an agreement on compensation. During the mid-1990s, only five of sixty to eighty players who entered the salary arbitration process did in fact go through with the arbitration hearing. For the 2001 "arbitration season," while 102 players filed for arbitration, only fourteen cases proceeded to an arbitration hearing, eight of which were won by the owners. Since 1990, nearly 87% of the disputes over salaries were settled prior to hearing the case.

The procedure set out to decide on an award provides a great incentive to settle salary disputes without salary arbitration since it permits parties to make reasonable offers. Both parties must be careful not to create significant gaps between the two salary figures submitted. For example, if the arbitrators think that a player is worth just over the middle point between the two offers, they will award the highest offer, even though they might think that it is too high.

Regarding the procedure of arbitration itself, MLB's Basic Agreement stipulates, as does that of the NHL, that a team's financial resources are not admissible as evidence. Therefore, the above comments regarding this issue also apply to MLB.

. . . .

. . . . Revenue disparity between teams means that owners have very different interests and goals in addition to very different ways to go about achieving them. Existing revenue disparity results in owners having much different views, economic perspectives, and interests from one another. In this sense, the owners are not a unified group battling for the best interest of the league, but rather a collection of businessmen fighting among themselves to preserve and/or reach their individual goals and expectations.

Because of this huge disparity in team revenues, the possibility of the owners agreeing on a fair and reasonable league-wide salary cap seems most improbable. A salary cap that takes into consideration teams such as the Montreal Expos would mean that a richer team, like the Yankees, could make up to 150% profit. This is obviously a result the union would not agree to without even considering the fact that the owners' consent to such a system would be almost impossible to obtain. To the contrary, if a salary cap is established, taking into account the financial position of the Yankees, many teams evolving in smaller markets will not be able to survive economically. Even more importantly, an even greater imbalance would be created in the competition between teams.

Another factor that prohibited the owners from getting a salary cap is that, while on strike, baseball players have been more loyal to their players' association than any other professional sports athletes. . . . It could be said that it is mainly due to this loyalty that the players and the union were able to secure the substantial rights of free agency and salary arbitration they have today without securing a salary cap.

. . . .

VII. EVALUATION OF THE NFL AND NBA SYSTEMS

A. NFL

The NFL has designed a system providing that for every dollar the league generates, approximately sixty cents is divided equally among its teams. This amount then becomes the salary cap. There exists a strong incentive for the players and the owners to work collectively towards the financial health of the league as the amount that the teams stand to make is directly proportionate to the amount generated by the league as a whole. In turn, the financial success of the players is dependent on the success of their teams. Of course, this amount also sets a cap, or a limit, on how much players are paid, but more importantly, this amount guarantees the players that they will be paid. This commercial venture between the players' union and the owners appears to be working quite well from a theoretical standpoint since both the league and the players are working together to achieve the same goal: the profitability of the league. . . .

Also, in the NFL, the league granted the players a system of free agency which enables players to benefit from it at a relatively early stage of their careers (restricted free agency after three years of service and unrestricted free agency after four years). In doing so, a player can "market" himself and thus earn higher salaries, while playing in the city, and for the coach, he chooses. In return for these advantages, the players conceded the implementation of a salary cap which limits players' salaries and consequently player movement. It is therefore fair to say that the NFL has enjoyed a certain degree of success in creating a system which allows players to be granted substantial salaries while at the same time avoiding placing their teams in financial jeopardy. As a matter of fact, the system established in the NFL has been somewhat successful in controlling the rate at which players' salaries have increased. . . .

B. NBA

. . . .

The NBA's salary scale has a very different basis than the salary arbitration systems found in the NHL and MLB. While the NHL and MLB base their salary figures on player performance compared to the performance of comparable players, the NBA bases players' compensation on the number of years the player has been in the league or, in the case of rookies, the position they were selected in the draft.

. . . .

VIII. CONCLUSION: A NEW REALITY

As is evident from the history behind the salary arbitration system in the NHL and MLB, the majority of labor–management disputes have arisen primarily as a result of the option clause. The following question can be posed: were the owners, who agreed to put an end to this turmoil by giving in to the demands of the players, not sufficiently strong, or were the NFL and NBA team owners simply more creative in their approach at granting concessions to players? The creativity of the NFL and NBA systems lies in the fact that players are seen as "partners" with their teams, mainly because they share the league's revenue by having a salary cap and floor, which serve the interests of both the players and the owners. This fosters sharing between the league and the players, and resembles more of a partnership between the two sides than an actual employer–employee relationship. Clearly, in the NHL and MLB, the employees are constantly trying to get a bigger piece of the owners' pie while in the NFL and NBA systems, both parties appear, in theory, to be trying to make the pie grow bigger with the goal of sharing more of it.

With respect to the procedure employed in the NHL and MLB salary arbitration systems, both have their benefits. The NHL system enables the arbitrator to hear both parties' points of view and, from these positions, is able to come to a reasonable compromise in regards to the specific circumstances surrounding a certain player. MLB's system encourages the parties to submit offers that are sufficiently reasonable so as to persuade the arbitrator to select them. One might argue that in doing so, negotiations are more effective since the difference between the two offers might not be as large as in the NHL (where both parties tend to take extreme positions to leave room for the arbitrator to decide on a figure somewhere in the middle). This is likely the reason why such a small percentage of the cases filed actually reach the stage of an arbitration hearing.

As previously discussed, an important characteristic of both the NHL and MLB systems is that the arbitrators cannot consider a club's budget in deciding on the appropriate salary for one of its players. Rather, the arbitrators can only compare the player to others in the same position with similar playing abilities. The wealth of the club, the market in which it operates, its revenues, and whether or not the club can in fact afford to pay the salary determined, are not taken into consideration. This forces small market teams with correspondingly small budgets to lose some of their players as they cannot afford to pay their salaries; the player is then traded to a team that can. The end result is wealthy teams securing more talented players on their rosters simply because they can pay them. Unfortunately, the success of an NHL or MLB franchise does not depend on scouting, development, or management decisions anymore: it rather depends on the size of the team's bank account. As a result of this reality, large market teams have an immeasurable competitive advantage over those in smaller markets and a competitive imbalance is created.

. . . .

Since players' unions were established in the 1960s, the sports world has experienced astronomical increases in the salaries paid to their players. As previously discussed, many factors are at the origin of the skyrocketing salaries. Yet, further factors contributing to this situation include the enormous sums of money the leagues receive from broadcasting contracts with networks and cable companies. Adding to this are the increasingly large revenues derived from licensing fees. Another factor comes directly from the heart of the team itself: some wealthy owners are incapable of restraining themselves and allow huge contracts to be signed with players. As well, some owners, fearing the possibility of losing some players, have entered into long-term deals with them which can prove costly as the player's skills diminish over time or if he is unable to perform consistently at a high level of excellence on the field.

This demonstrates that, as previously explained, salary arbitration does not set up the players' market but rather follows it. In basing their salary awards on comparable players' salaries, the arbitrators are merely following the trend set by individually negotiated contracts between players and owners. Therefore, if an owner grants a very lucrative contract to a player, the next salary arbitration awards will reflect this decision. It is the result of a limited number of owners, fearless of granting high salaries that the market value of players rises at such a tremendously fast pace.

All this goes to show that salary arbitration and free agency are not the only factors which have contributed to the soaring of salaries in professional sports. One cannot lose sight of the fact that before it was made part of CBAs, salary arbitration was freely negotiated and accepted by both the owners and the players.

REFERENCES

9. Paul C. Weiler & Gary R. Roberts, Sports and the Law, 239 (West Group 2d ed. 1998).

14. Id. at 336.

55. Nat'l & Am. League Prof'l Baseball Clubs v. MLBPA, 66 Lab. Arb. 101 (1976) (Seitz, Arb.).

63. Jeffrey S. Moorad, Major League Baseball's Labor Turmoil: The Failure of the Counter-Revolution, 4 Vill. Sports & Ent. L.J. 53, 54 (1997).

111. 1995 Collective Bargaining Agreement between the NHL and the NHLPA, as extended July 1997, art. 12.5(f)(ii). [hereinafter NHL/NHLPA CBA].

115. NHL/NHLPA CBA 12.5(f)(iii).

163. Basic Agreement between the American League of Professional Baseball Clubs, the National League of Professional Baseball Clubs, and the Major League Baseball Players Association (1997–2000) (MLB Basic Agreement) article VI(F)(12)(a).

166. Id. art. VI(F)(12)(b).

167. Id. art. VI(F)(14).

177. See Mackey v. NFL 543 F.2d 606 (8th Cir. 1976).

213. 1993 Collective Bargaining Agreement between the NFL Management Council and the NFL Players' Association, as amended February 25, 1998, art. XVII, 1(a). [hereinafter NFL/NFLPA CBA].

228. Paul C. Weiler & Gary R. Roberts, Sports and the Law, 330 (West Group 2d ed. 1998).

230. Paul C. Weiler, Leveling the Playing Field, 208 (Harvard Univ. Press 2000).

245. Paul C. Weiler & Gary R. Roberts, Sports and the Law, 315 (West Group 2d ed. 1998).

251. Larry Coon, NBA Salary Cap/Collective Bargaining Agreement FAQ, at http://members.cox.net/lmcoon/salarycap.htm (last visited Mar. 10, 2003); see also 1999 Collective Bargaining Agreement between the NBA and the NBPA, art. VII, 5(a).

THE EFFECT OF SALARY ARBITRATION ON MAJOR LEAGUE BASEBALL

Jonathan M. Conti

. . . Baseball has long experienced fierce struggles between the players and the owners over the splitting of the economic pie of America's national pastime. One issue which has been controversial since its inception is salary arbitration. Salary arbitration was collectively bargained for in 1973. This type of arbitration determines salaries for those players with between three and six years of service. It helps set their salaries for the upcoming season. Once either the player or the team has filed for salary arbitration, both sides submit salary figures to an impartial arbitrator. The arbitrator must then choose one figure or the other, but may not compromise and choose a figure that he may find preferable to the two submitted.

The owners of baseball teams have opposed the system of salary arbitration for over twenty years, citing the massive increases in salaries from such arbitration awards as one of the primary reasons for the economic crisis allegedly facing the sport today. Owners of small market, and accordingly less prosperous, teams claim that they cannot compete with the larger market teams because they cannot afford to pay the players astronomical salaries. The owners despise salary arbitration to the point that they attempted, unsuccessfully, to unilaterally eliminate it during the 1994 strike.

There is no doubt that salary arbitration awards result in a substantial increase for players over their previous year's salaries. Salaries for all players have risen dramatically over the last three decades. . . While salary arbitration has and always will be the target of the owners' wrath, there has not been enough discussion concerning the intricacies of the system and how it can be improved. Rather than simply calling for its removal, there should be an in depth look into both its pros and cons.

While the salary arbitration system has some flaws, this Article will illustrate why the owners' cries for the system's banishment are misplaced and counterproductive. Arbitration is an effective compromise between the reserve system and free agency, one in which players with between three and six years of service are given the opportunity to attain a salary closer to their market value. At the same time, arbitration allows a player's original team to hold onto his services for the first six years of that player's career so that it may, at the very least, recoup the expenses it has invested in the training of that player. Salary arbitration is not a perfect system, but it is, despite its flaws, a fair compromise between the owners and players.

II. HISTORICAL PERSPECTIVE

. . . . *[The author's discussion of the history of and various legal challenges to the reserve system is omitted.]*

In 1975, with the reserve system clause still present in individual player's contracts, Andy Messersmith, a successful pitcher for the Los Angeles Dodgers, decided to challenge the clause through grievance arbitration. . . .

With this one decision, baseball changed dramatically. After the owners unsuccessfully challenged the arbitrator's ruling in federal court, the 1976 collective bargaining agreement was formulated. Although the players were now in an unprecedented position of power, the Players' Association feared that complete free agency, after only one year, would result in a flooding of the market and, consequently, a depressing of salaries. Therefore, they agreed to a free agency system in which a player would be eligible for free agency upon the completion of six years in the major leagues. The 1976 collective bargaining agreement also included the salary arbitration system which had been in effect in 1974 and 1975. No arbitration cases were held in 1976 and 1977 because there was no signed collective bargaining agreement.

Salary arbitration and free agency had been separately negotiated provisions, the former in 1973 and the latter in 1976. However, interaction between the two was never really seriously considered by either side during the 1976 collective bargaining negotiations. Salary arbitration had been established prior to free agency, when the reserve clause was still in effect. At the time, it was a minor concession by the owners, in hope that the players would not again seriously question the reserve system. What neither side realized, however, was that free agency and salary arbitration would become undeniably linked, combining to form the bane of the owners' existence.

. . . . *[The author's discussion of the salary arbitration process is omitted.]*

IV. FINAL OFFER ARBITRATION

One of the major factors which makes salary arbitration in baseball so unique is that it is a final offer, or high/low, format. It differs from conventional arbitration in that final offer arbitration gives the arbitrator very little discretion. Each side submits a figure, and the arbitrator is required to select one offer or the other. The arbitrator cannot formulate a compromise figure, or even choose the exact midpoint between the two, which is an option in conventional arbitration.

In the nonsports context, final offer arbitration takes on two forms. There is "issue-by-issue" arbitration, in which the arbitrator selects one party's final proposal for each issue separately.[66] Operating in a collective bargaining context, the arbitrator has some discretion to trade one issue for another, so that the total package is a balanced one. The other type of final offer arbitration employed is "by package," in which the arbitrator must select either the union's or management's entire final proposal.[67] While such a format removes almost all of the arbitrator's discretion in formulating a resolution, the discretion is replaced by a higher degree of risk among the parties. That risk is that one's entire package of proposals may be eliminated.

Salary arbitration in baseball is a kind of hybrid of the issue-by-issue arbitration and package style arbitration. There is obviously only one issue in question, but there is the high element of risk similar to that which exists in the package style.

The theory behind final offer arbitration is the promotion of a convergence in the final salary positions of the two parties. The idea is that each party, conscious of the risk that an unreasonable proposal will have little chance of acceptance by the arbitrator, will make concessions in order to submit what it believes is a reasonable offer. If one of the two proposals is too extreme, the other side essentially wins by default. The two sides are more likely to bargain in good faith in hopes of reaching a settlement if they fear that the arbitrator may view the other side's offer as more reasonable.

One of the theoretical reasons for not implementing a more conventional style of arbitration, in which the arbitrator is free to compromise the two proposals, is that it will have "a chilling or deterrent effect on the parties' incentives to bargain in good faith as both sides hold back in anticipation of handing the dispute to an arbitrator."[72] Conventional arbitration allows the parties to posture while bargaining and establish more extreme positions knowing that the arbitrator, at worst, will arrive at a compromise somewhere between the two proposals. In essence, the fear of losing, which presumably encourages the parties to reach a settlement, is missing in conventional arbitration. Thus, the limited risk in going to arbitration may undercut serious negotiations between the parties and discourage the exchange of realistic proposals prior to the arbitration hearing. Good labor relations demand that arbitration serve not as a replacement for negotiated settlement, but rather as a means of last resort.

Despite the noted advantages of final offer arbitration, the real disadvantage, the lack of flexibility in the arbitrator's decision-making process, can become problematic. In some instances, it is an easy choice. If the final offers are close together, it may not really matter which of the two proposals the arbitrator chooses. Similarly, if the offers are far apart but one side has submitted a ridiculous offer, the arbitrator once again is faced with an easy decision. If the offers are far apart and equally ludicrous, however, then the arbitrator's decision becomes much more difficult. Possibly wanting to compromise by settling somewhere in the middle, the arbitrator's hands are tied by not having the option to make fine distinctions in his judgments.

V. THE CONTROVERSY

One of the major questions regarding salary arbitration in baseball today is whether it truly accomplishes a narrowing of salary disputes and the encouragement of settlements among the parties. The owners' major justification for the abolition of salary arbitration is that it is a win-win proposition for the players. The players always come out better than they were before. Whichever figure is chosen results in an increase in the player's salary, as the team does not want to submit too low a figure, for fear that it be dismissed out of hand, let alone submit a figure that is below or even equal to the player's previous year's salary.

In approaching this issue, there are several ways to look at the question of whether final offer arbitration has indeed accomplished what its creators envisioned. The statistics support the premise that the salary arbitration system encourages settlement between the parties (presumably because of the fear factor previously mentioned). . . . The rate of filings, however, has continually increased. . . . Despite this massive upswing in the initial use of the process, the trend can generally be attributed to the fact that many players feel it is necessary to have the threat of arbitration as a way to force their clubs to negotiate with them in good faith.

While arbitration filings have indeed increased, good faith negotiation does appear to occur once such a filing has been made. . . . Results indicate that only approximately one out of ten arbitration filings will ever result in a hearing. . . . What the figures seem to indicate is that final offer salary arbitration is encouraging parties to bargain in good faith and reach mutually acceptable settlements prior to the use of an outside arbitrator. In this regard, final offer arbitration has achieved its primary goal.

Theoretically, final offer arbitration should also promote convergence in the disparities between the two offers given to the arbitrator. This is linked to the previously expressed notion that the risk of the no-compromise environment of an arbitration hearing will compel the two parties to submit reasonable figures that are fairly close together. There are two ways to approach this issue. The first is to look at the average spread between the player's final offer and the club's final offer. The average spread has increased. . . . These figures appear to discredit the theory that final offer arbitration in baseball encourages a convergence between the two offers. In actuality, when one considers inflation, increased attendance, and increased television revenue, all of which combine to raise the market value of the players, such a statistic is not truly indicative of the situation.

A better indicator of the convergence or divergence between the team's offer and the player's demand is the relative spread between these two offers. In 1974, the relative spread of 1.20 means that on average, the players' salary requests were 20% higher than the clubs' salary offers. Salary offers and demands since that time have not shown a significant convergence or divergence using relative spread. . . . Thus, while there has not been a reduction in the gap between the clubs' offers and the players' requests, the system has not significantly widened the gap either.

. . . . What one can surmise . . . is that although the players' demands and the clubs' offers are not remarkably close, they are also not extremely divergent. One does not see a consistent effort on the part of the players to massively inflate their demands, nor is there a consistent level of low-ball offers from the clubs. With the threat that the arbitrator can only pick one of the two figures, the parties realize that they cannot risk significantly inflating or deflating their offers. Unable to rely on an arbitrator to settle the dispute somewhere in the middle, the parties are forced to negotiate within reason. Thus, it appears as though final offer arbitration has achieved its goal, at least to a degree, of getting the parties to either settle their cases prior to arbitration, or at least to submit figures that are within the same ballpark.

VI. SALARY ARBITRATION'S EFFECT ON SALARIES

Whatever the merits of a final offer arbitration system are, most owners are of the opinion that salary arbitration is destroying the game by facilitating a substantial rise in salaries. They would much rather see its abolishment than debate the merits of the final offer procedure in bringing about a convergence of proposals or settlements prior to a hearing. In order to defend or reject salary arbitration as a means of setting salaries for a certain group of players, it is necessary to examine the current protests and relevant statistical data.

The owners have always been understandably concerned with the escalating costs of labor. From the late 1960s, when the union first began to make strides, to the current collective bargaining situation, the owners have been waging a generally losing battle against the increase in player salaries. Within the last decade, salary arbitration has taken a large amount of the blame for the current economic crisis enveloping the game. What makes this criticism especially interesting is the fact that the salary arbitration clause only covers about 25% of the employees in the bargaining unit. With only a small percentage of the players eligible to even invoke the process, and far fewer who actually follow through with a hearing, the attack appears, at first glance, to be misdirected. . . .

Nonetheless, the reason behind the owners' distaste for salary arbitration is their belief that the practice inflates the level of salaries so that the wages paid out to many players exceed their true market value. Furthermore, the owners argue that the actual win–loss record of arbitration hearings is misleading because players are essentially in a win-win situation. . . . A vast majority of arbitration-eligible players who file, not just those who follow through with a hearing, see significant increases in their salaries. Thus, while final offer salary arbitration may encourage settlements, these settlements also result in considerable gains for players. The average annual negotiated settlement between 1974 and 1993 resulted in a gain ranging from 33% to 110% over the previous year's salary while the average annual winner received increases ranging from 44%–174%. Even the losers in arbitration "won." Furthermore, between 1974 and 1993, only nine cases resulted in the reduction of a player's salary. It is these kinds of statistics that the owners cite when they claim salary arbitration is a "win-win" proposition for the players.

Facially, the numbers appear to support the owners' claims that salary arbitration is unfair because a player, whether he wins or loses, is almost guaranteed to achieve an increase, often substantial, from his previous year's salary. While it is true that a player invariably makes gains on his previous year's salary, it is imperative that one remember the system that was in place prior to the institution of salary arbitration in 1973.

As was indicated earlier, prior to the union's triumphant securing of salary arbitration during the 1973 collective bargaining negotiations, baseball operated under a complete reserve system. The clubs who originally signed the player owned his contractual rights for his entire career. Obviously, in comparison to the way things used to be, salary arbitration is immeasurably more burdensome to the owners. Marvin Miller, the undisputed leader of baseball's labor movement, due to his successful reign as union president, illustrated this point quite well when he stated: "There is not an employer in the world who would not prefer baseball's prior system of salary determination solely by the employer and enforced by the hammer of a life-long blacklist of recalcitrant employees. Accordingly, any other method of salary determination understandably is considered objectionable by baseball officialdom."[104] When free market forces and impartial adjudication become the key factors in salary determination, as opposed to owner fiat, the backlash from those whose power has been greatly diminished is quite understandable. Nonetheless, the fact that a shift in bargaining power has occurred is not in itself a legitimate reason for condemning salary arbitration as an utter failure. Furthermore, from an economic standpoint, salary arbitration has resulted in the demise of the monopsony situation from which the owners had so unfairly benefited.* Whenever there is a movement from such a monopsony to a competitive labor market, there is bound to be salary escalation, regardless of whether the process for determining such salaries is salary arbitration, unrestricted free agency, a combination of the two, or any other salary system operating in a competitive market.

While it is true that salaries have increased considerably ever since the introduction of salary arbitration, another way to view the situation is that the salaries under the reserve system were artificially low, as a result of the owners having the luxury of being the only employer able to negotiate with a player. The one-sidedness of that process is further illustrated by the fact that under the old reserve system, if the player were to reject the club's offer, his only leverage was to hold out. If the club considered the player valuable enough, it might increase the offer, but if not, then the player could either accept the team's original offer, or retire.

---

* A monopsony situation exists where one employer has the benefit of being the only employer allowed to negotiate with a particular employee over the salary amount at which he will be paid for his services.

Another argument for salary arbitration is that the club is not required to renew a player's contract once a player decides to file for arbitration. While the club has the option to participate in the process and thus retain the player for a one-year commitment, the club also has the option to nontender, or refrain from offering a contract to that player. Thus, the club does have the option of cutting a player rather than paying him the salary he might receive in arbitration. The owners, therefore, unlike the players during the era of the old reserve system, are not left without an option. If the club does decide to take its chances at the arbitration hearing but loses, it can still trade that player if it does not feel the player is worth the award he received from the arbitrator. Thus, assuming the team is not economically irrational, the team will keep the player if it feels the player's worth to the team is greater or equal to the arbitration award.

In examining the owners' claims that there is an inherent unfairness in the arbitration system, what appears to be overlooked amidst the numerous statistics and claims of impending economic ruin, is that players' salaries during their first three years are kept artificially low. The reserve system has not been totally eradicated because players still belong to the team that signed or drafted them for the first six years of their careers. For the first three years, when many play at or near the minimum wage set forth in the Basic Agreement, it can be argued that they are being underpaid, as their salaries are artificially kept down because they are unable to offer their services in the free agent market. After having one's salary held down for three years, it is only natural that one achieves a sizable increase once eligible for arbitration. Such an increase makes up for the utter lack of bargaining power during the previous three years of the player's career.

VII. ASSESSING THE ADMISSIBLE CRITERIA

Although salary arbitration has taken the brunt of the owners' criticism for the escalating salaries in Major League Baseball, it is unrealistic and misleading to consider the salary arbitration process as the sole cause. Since the Messersmith ruling in 1975, free agency and salary arbitration have been inextricably entwined. While salary arbitration determines the setting of salaries for players who have three to six years of service, free agency applies to players who have completed six years of major league service. Such players, provided they have not signed a multiyear contract, are free to offer their services on the open market.

The intermingling between free agency and salary arbitration is illustrated in the current collective bargaining agreement. The Agreement states, when discussing the criteria that is admissible for the arbitrator to consider in his decision, that "the arbitrator or arbitration panel shall, except for a player with five or more years of major league service, give particular attention, for comparative salary purposes, to the contracts of players with major league service not exceeding one annual service group above the player's annual service group."[117] Thus, it appears as though arbitrators should only be concerned, for comparative purposes, with the salaries of similarly situated ballplayers who have related skill and service time. The Agreement goes on to state, however, that "this shall not limit the ability of a player or his representative, because of special accomplishment, to argue the equal relevance of salaries of players without regard to service, and the arbitrator or arbitration panel shall give whatever weight to such argument as is deemed appropriate."[118] The Agreement does not specifically limit the player from comparing himself, for salary purposes, to a player with considerably more years of service. This situation, in which a free agent's contract can be considered for comparative salary purposes during an arbitration hearing, has come under the most criticism from the owners.

The free agency era has brought many positives and negatives to the game of baseball, depending on one's perspective. For ballplayers, free agency represents the same opportunity possessed by most workers in America — the ability to change jobs if one is unhappy or dissatisfied with one's current position. No longer tied up in a master–slave type of relationship with his original team, a player is free, albeit after six years, to choose a new employer. For the teams and owners, however, free agency results in a lack of control over those players on whom they have spent considerable time and money cultivating in both the minor and major leagues. Nothing hurts a team more than to lose a valuable player to another team.

Yet, free agency has its obvious upside for owners who are able to sign away such a free agent, as a signing can translate into a quick fix, or the final piece of the puzzle for a near-championship team, or a marquee attraction to fill the seats. Due to the enticing prospect of signing a star player for one's team, owners often cannot help themselves in believing that a particular free agent will be the one to get the team over the hump in the standings or at the gate. . . . The other teams come to the realization that the team signing the free agent has improved its team, while they have done nothing. The previously complacent team starts to panic, and it consequently tries to keep up with its competitors by signing a free agent of its own. The result is that the price for the remaining (and often less desirable) free agents escalates according to the law of supply and demand, instead of in relation to the player's talent and usefulness. Press and fan anticipation in turn further fuel this desperation, as they are eager to see their team become better over the off-season, especially if a rival team has signed a big-name free agent. . . .

. . . . As was indicated earlier, a player is not prohibited from comparing his ability and contract to that of a player not within his own service group. Thus, when a player signs a large free agent contract, that contract immediately becomes a yardstick by which many players will base their demands. When an owner lavishes millions of dollars on a free agent, especially in cases where such money does not seem appropriate, then the team's hard line stance on an equally talented player who is eligible for salary arbitration is difficult to justify. The higher the free agent salaries, the greater likelihood that there will be an increase in salary arbitration demands.

Despite these ironies, there are legitimate grounds for preventing arbitrators from considering free agent salaries for comparative purposes. The major argument is that it is extremely difficult to compare a free agent salary to a one-year contract submitted to arbitration. Often cited in this argument is the notion that free agency negotiations are based on criteria not applicable to the negotiations involving players eligible for salary arbitration, such as future performance and fan interest. Furthermore, most free agency deals are multiyear pacts, often consisting of bonuses and incentives which give the club and the player flexibility in adopting a total compensation package. Salary arbitration, however, involves a one-year deal for the upcoming season.

[A] free agent's salary, when translated into annual compensation, can be misleading. Comparing the one-year wage of a free agent who signed a multiyear pact with a comparable player in salary arbitration is too speculative. Since salary arbitration covers only one year, it is merely a single snapshot in the total picture of a player's career.[127]

Another difference between free agent negotiations and salary arbitration is that the circumstances surrounding an offer to a free agent are not the same as those surrounding an arbitration award. It is argued that free agency is based on what the team hopes the player will provide in the upcoming season. Free agent salary offers, however, are "lures" to entice players to change teams and are buoyed by competitive bidding and the perceived urgency of the team's need. Salary arbitration awards, however, operate as an award for past excellence.

A particularly interesting argument on this matter is that because salary arbitration is essentially a compromise between free agency and a strict reserve clause, it thereby creates a "hybrid labor market without the traditional operation of supply and demand."[131] As a result, this market simultaneously maintains elements of a competitive marketplace and the essential characteristics of the reserve clause. Salary arbitration can be seen as an attempt to construct a "fictional labor market . . . especially on the demand side."[132] The Agreement emphasizes comparability among player salaries from which a going rate for the class of players can be derived, yet the criteria is vague regarding how the free agent market, with its myriad of differences, mingles with the salary arbitration market to determine player salaries. When one considers the aforementioned notion of comparing multiyear contracts with one-year salary arbitration demands, there is a definite problem.

Critics of this so-called artificial market argue that another problem that surfaces is the disregard of the true supply of labor at a particular position throughout the league. For example, a team might have three great starting outfielders and a very capable fourth, reserve outfielder who only receives minimal playing time. Even though this reserve might be able to start for many other teams were he a free agent, this short supply of league-wide outfielders is not reflected in the artificial market. Lack of playing time cannot be considered because it is pure conjecture as to how the player would perform were he a member of another team. Thus, salary arbitration only takes into account the supply of labor on a team, as opposed to the total supply of a particular position in both leagues.

The players look at the salary arbitration process in a considerably different light. They argue that free agent salaries are legitimate for comparison in salary arbitration because they directly reflect the combined judgment of the parties as to the appropriate salary. Free agency negotiation is based on the player's performance record, career consistency, and past compensation, to name a few. These are the same criteria that are considered during the salary arbitration process. Furthermore, without free agent salaries as a comparison, the market will become artificially depressed. This is based on the notion that the clubs, by being able to hold onto a player for the first years of his career, can keep salaries down because there is no competitive bidding for his services. Thus, by ignoring the actual free agent market, those players eligible for salary arbitration whose ability is comparable to that of many free agents would be prevented from asking for salaries that they undoubtedly could get if they were free agents.

While the players argue that the reserve/salary arbitration system artificially keeps salaries below market value during the players' first five years, there are some inequities in allowing players to compare themselves to free agents. A free agent salary negotiation encompasses a number of factors that do not go into a one-year arbitration figure and involves a player who has more years of service and who is courted by many teams out on the market. Therefore, the notion that comparative salary analyses be relegated to players with "comparable statistics and comparable contracts"[139] seems a logical one. Nonetheless, there is no escaping the fact that, absent a change in the criteria in the next collective bargaining agreement, it is in the owners' power to curtail salary arbitration awards. This can be accomplished to a degree if the owners show a bit more restraint in their free agent bids. A decrease in the number of ridiculous contracts lavished on free agents . . . would result in a curtailing of monstrous salary arbitration awards. The owners do not have to collude, as they once did, but rather just show better judgment regarding the amounts of money paid to free agents. Thus, rather than bemoaning the fact that an impartial third party sets their payrolls in salary arbitration, they can attempt to minimize such awards by showing more control in their free agent dealings.

. . . . *[The author's discussion of large market versus small market teams and possible alternatives and procedural changes to salary arbitration is omitted.]*

[See Table 3 for a list of salary arbitration results and data from MLB.]

TABLE 3.

SALARY ARBITRATION RESULTS AND DATA, MLB		
Arbitration year-by-year		
Year	Players	Owners
2003	2	5
2002	1	4
2001	6	8
2000	4	6
1999	2	9
1998	3	5
1997	1	4
1996	7	3
1995	2	6
1994	6	10
1993	6	12
1992	9	11
1991	6	11
1990	14	10
1989	7	5
1988	7	11
1987	10	16
1986	15	20
1985	6	7
1984	4	6
1983	13	7
1982	8	14
1981	11	10
1980	15	11
1979	8	5
1978	2	7
1977	No arbitration	
1976	No arbitration	
1975	6	10
1974	13	16
Total	194	259

Source: The Associated Press.

REFERENCES

66. Jeffrey Chicoine, A Critical Review of Collective Bargaining Dispute Resolution under the PECBA and Alternative Models, 13 LERC Monograph Ser. 53, 68 (1994).

67. Id.

72. James B. Dworkin, Salary Arbitration in Baseball: An Impartial Assessment After Ten Years, Arb. J., Mar. 1986, at 65 (quoting Peter Feuille, Final Offer Arbitration 8, Chicago: International Personnel Management Ass'n 1975).

104. Marvin V. Miller, Arbitration of Baseball Salaries: Impartial Adjudication in Place of Management Fiat, 38 Arb. J. 31, 33 (1986).

117. Basic Agreement art. VI(F)(12)(a) (1997).

118. Id.

127. John B. LaRocco, Reforming Salary Arbitration, Arbitration 1994, Proceedings of the 47th Annual Meeting, National Academy of Arbitrators 224 (Gladys W. Gruenberg ed.).

131. Id. at 223.

132. Id.

139. Id. at 234.

FREE AGENCY

FOOTBALL MAY BE ILL, BUT DON'T BLAME BOSMAN

William Duffy

I. INTRODUCTION

In the past five years, European football (soccer) has experienced a fundamental shift in the employment relationships between players and their clubs. Traditionally, the power of employment resided firmly with the national associations and private clubs, with the players having a relatively weak union and (with very few exceptions) little to say about their careers. That balance of power began to shift when Jean-Marc Bosman, a midfielder from the Belgium team RC Liege, attempted to transfer to the French team US Dunkerque in July of 1990. Although Bosman was no longer under contract, his Belgian employer demanded compensation (a so-called "transfer fee") from the French club with which he wished to sign, and refused to allow Bosman to play until payment was received.

Bosman subsequently sued RC Liege, the Belgian Football Association (URBSFA), and the Union of European Football Associations (UEFA), alleging that the rules governing the transfer of players among clubs in the Union were unfairly restrictive. . . . The specific issue was whether the rules regarding the movement of players from between clubs and the rules governing the number of foreign players allowed to play for a team during a match were in violation of the European Community Treaty.

After a protracted and complex legal battle that effectively ended Bosman's playing career, the E.C.J. [European Court of Justice] agreed with Bosman and found the transfer rules to be in violation of the European Treaty. The Court ordered the Federation Internationale de Football Associations (FIFA), UEFA, and the national football organizations of every member state to implement fundamental changes in the way they administer the movement of players between clubs within the European Union. As a result of Bosman's lawsuit and the ruling that bears his name, football players in Europe today enjoy a great deal of professional freedom. . . .

. . . .

II. THE FACTS OF MR. BOSMAN'S CASE

A. The Structure of Football: Organization, Transfer of Players, Restrictions on Foreign Players

1. The Organization of Football.   The structure of football clubs, leagues, and associations is basically the same world-wide. Organized amateur and professional football is played under a structure called an "association." In order to participate in international competition, clubs and leagues, as well as the national associations that govern them, are required to conform to certain guidelines prescribed by regional international confederations (in the case of Europe, the UEFA). Each level of the structure is afforded a certain amount of responsibility for the administration of the game. At the base, each club is responsible for its players. In order to be eligible for a match played by his club, each professional player must be registered as a professional with his national association. As a registered professional, the player is considered an employee of the club which holds his registration.

National associations are comprised of clubs playing organized competitions within the nation's borders. These associations organize league competitions and national knock-out cup competitions, and administer the national team. The associations also draft the regulations by which the game functions. . . .

The regional confederations comprise the membership of the international organizational body known as FIFA. The regulations of the regional confederations are subject to the approval of FIFA. . . .

2. The Transfer Rules: Belgium, UEFA, and FIFA.   . . . .

The FIFA rules were important to Bosman, in that they expressly stated that the registration of players in national associations (which made the player eligible for competition) was dependent on the release and receipt of the player's professional registration certificate. While the rules stated that the out-of-contract player could not play until his certificate was received, they did not state that the former club would be required to release the player's certificate once a new contract had been reached between the player and the new club. Thus, the former club effectively retained control over the player's career. This issue led Bosman to sue RC Liege.

3. Restrictions on Foreign Players.   . . . . The rules regarding participation in national competitions by foreign players were, until the Bosman ruling, deliberately restrictive. As stated in Advocate General Lenz's opinion, "(f)rom the 1960s on, many — but not all — football associations introduced rules restricting the possibility of engaging players of foreign nationality."[31] . . . UEFA introduced a rule in 1991 that fixed the number of foreign players allowed to play in a UEFA sanctioned match. The rule, which became known as the "3+2 Rule," required that teams limit the number of foreign players included on the team sheet for any one match to three, plus two additional foreign players who had played professionally in the host country for a period of five uninterrupted years, including three years in junior teams.

The abolition of the 3+2 rule by the European Court of Justice in the *Bosman* decision has impacted football at least as much as the abolition of transfer fees. Its impact is seen in the increased availability of movement for all players within UEFA. It is curious that the abolition of the foreign player restriction does not receive as much attention as the transfer fees rules. . . .

. . . .

III. THE OPINION OF THE ADVOCATE GENERAL AND THE RULING BY THE EUROPEAN COURT OF JUSTICE

A. The Opinion of the Advocate General

1. The Transfer Rules.   In his advisory opinion to the European Court of Justice, Advocate General Lenz found the transfer rules to be "a *direct* restriction on access to the employment market." The Advocate General stated, "the transfer rules are in breach of Article 48, and would be lawful only if they were justified by imperative reasons in the general interest and did not go beyond what is necessary for attaining those objectives (emphasis included in original text)."[47] One such "imperative reason in the general interest" that was advanced during litigation, according to the Advocate General, was the protection of the financial and sporting equilibrium necessary to preserve the balance between competing clubs.[48] It was argued that because clubs are compensated for players moving from club to club, money remains circulating within the game, and that it is more efficient for teams to exchange cash for players, rather than players for players (i.e., a barter system, as exists in the United States professional sports leagues). This compensation was alleged to be necessary for the survival of small clubs, who reap big rewards for selling their prized assets.

For the purpose of maintaining the financial and sporting equilibrium, the Advocate General found the transfer rules to be an inadequate measure, and therefore still unlawful under Article 48. The transfer rules, he said, often force small clubs to sell their best players to generate income for their survival as entities.[51] While this certainly generates revenue for the club, it significantly weakens the club on the playing field. The movement of the best players was decidedly one way, as the small clubs were not in the financial position to lure players from the wealthiest clubs. Finally, since only the wealthiest clubs could afford the transfer fee to begin with, less wealthy clubs could seldom enjoy the benefit of the transfer fee arrangement. This further weakens the argument that it was necessary to maintain the sporting and financial equilibrium.

. . . .

Besides maintaining the sporting equilibrium among clubs, Advocate General Lenz addressed (and refuted) the argument that transfer fees were necessary to compensate clubs for the cost of training players that are eventually sold to other clubs. The Advocate General found this argument invalid based on two main points: the fee is not calculated according to the club's investment in the player, and applies to all players.[59]

The transfer fee's calculation, by its nature, does not account for the amount invested by a club in training a player, but is instead tied to the player's salary. . . .

Second, the clubs demand a transfer fee when selling established professional players as well as new players. . . .

2. The Restrictions on Foreign Players.   In his opinion, the Advocate General stated,

> No deep cogitation is required to reach the conclusion that the rules on foreign players are of a discriminatory nature. They represent an absolutely classic case of discrimination on the ground of nationality. . . . The rules on foreign players are therefore incompatible with the prohibition of discrimination under Article 48(2), in so far as they relate to nationals of other Member States.[62]

UEFA tried to argue that the rule was not actually in violation of the Article, however, because the restriction was only against the number of foreigners who could play in a match, and not against the number that could be employed by a particular club. The Advocate General was not persuaded by this argument, because the purpose of employing a football player is to actually play him in a match. He reasoned, therefore, that because a club would be limited in the number of foreign players it could use in any one match, the club would not hire more foreign players than it needed, thus restricting the opportunities for players to move freely about the European Union.

This is a rather important part of the decision, but it receives far less attention than the transfer rules, though it arguably has a similarly prominent place in the economics of the sport following the ruling. This part of the decision effectively deepened the pool of football talent available to clubs. In effect, the shopping market for all clubs became exponentially larger than it had been before Bosman. As such, the clubs with money to spend could buy foreign players that they may have previously refrained from buying because they did not have space in their starting eleven. As a result of the Court's decision, the supply of players increased. Along with the increase in supply, should a decrease in the amount clubs are willing to pay for players be expected? Whether or not that is the expectation, it clearly has not happened. Although the supply of players increased, demand for their services also increased. From the player's point of view, the number of potential employers also increased following the Bosman decision. For the best players, that means more suitors who might view them as attractive investments. As such, the clubs who can afford to pay out large sums of cash have driven the cost of the best players higher, taking them out of the reach of more modest clubs. At the same time the clubs increased the value of merely mediocre players. The effect of this has been to concentrate the quality of players at the top of the economic pyramid. . . .

B. The Ruling by the European Court of Justice

1. The Transfer Rules.   The ruling of the European Court of Justice, with regard to Article 48 and the transfer rules, states:

> Article 48 EEC precludes the application of the rules laid down by sporting associations, under which a professional footballer who is a national of one Member State may not, on the expiry of his contract with a club, be employed by a club of another Member State unless the latter club has paid to the former club a transfer, training, or development fee.[64]

In its brief discussion, the court essentially agreed with the points made by the Advocate General, namely that no justification put forward by UEFA, URBSFA, or any national association would allow the existence of the restriction on the movement of football players within the European Union.

2. The Restrictions on Foreign Players.   With regard to the restrictions on the number of foreign players allowed to play in any given match between clubs sanctioned by UEFA, the European Court of Justice ruled that those rules were also precluded by Article 48.[65] As such, the restrictions on the limitations regarding foreign players were abolished.

IV. THE EFFECTS OF THE BOSMAN RULING

A. The Lawsuit Within the Economics of the Game

It would be inaccurate to describe the Bosman case as the only economic turning point in football since 1996. In reality, the Bosman ruling exists within a larger context. Football's explosive growth began in the early 1990s, when some of the bigger leagues in Europe aggressively began to sell television rights as a commodity. The traditional source of revenue for clubs, gate receipts, was becoming marginalized even as early as the 1980s. Television rights, sponsorship deals, and savvy marketing were on their way to replacing gates as the main source of income. . . . The gap between rich clubs and poor clubs, part of the argument in favor of transfer fees, was demonstrated by the distribution of this income: three-quarters to the first division clubs, one-eighth to the third and fourth divisions combined. By 1997, these television rights were sold to BskyB in a deal worth £647 million over four years. This year, 2002, BskyB and the Premier League agreed to a £1.6 billion deal, which will be shared exclusively within the Premiership, meaning that none of this money will go to the lower divisions. Clearly, football was changing, whether Bosman brought his lawsuit or not.

B. Arguments Against the Lawsuit

In their 1998 article, The Impact of the Bosman Ruling,[69] Gardiner and Welch addressed concerns that Bosman, fairly or unfairly, could become "a scapegoat, for all the perceived ills in the game, such as the problems that some club managers report in exerting discipline over star players who earn more than they do even when not being selected for first team football."[70] Although they acknowledge that Bosman may or may not have been the actual cause of "the big money circulating in the upper echelons of the game,"[71] . . . they argue that Bosman's lawsuit effectively attacks the co-dependent nature of the football leagues, and furthers the commercialization of the game. They further argue that the lawsuit broke down an invisible barrier between sport and society by needlessly introducing the societal instrument of law into what amounted to an internal disagreement between an employee and employer. In their own words:

> There is a need for competition and although this may be keen on the field, the clubs are dependent on each other to a much greater extent than in other businesses. Therefore, until now, there have been collective interests between clubs not to allow free market principles to operate so that the top clubs buy all the best players. An issue of ongoing major concern for football clubs and supporters alike which has been facilitated, if not created, by Bosman is the way that the top clubs no longer appear to regard themselves bound by the collective interest as they look for ever greener pastures anew, such as the European Super League. . . . The attack on the transfer system in football can be seen as a classic battle concerning the legitimacy of intervention in particular sectors of industry and employment. . . . The partial removal of the transfer system that Bosman represents increases the view that football is no longer intrinsically and essentially a sport, but merely a product to be consumed. . . . As football has increasingly become subject to this process of commodification, so juridification has operated as a concomitant process. The intervention of the law into new areas of social life, and in this case, "sporting arenas" modifies what are intrinsically social relationships between humans within a "social field. . . ."

The football industry has been adept in the past in insulating itself from the impact of legal regulation. However, Bosman exemplifies this process: the system of transfer of players has historically primarily been seen as determined by the football authorities; now it is one primarily determined by law.[72]

There are two general points upon which I disagree. First, the commodification of the game, which the authors claim was exacerbated by Bosman's lawsuit, was happening regardless of the lawsuit. This was evidenced by the influx of money into the game via television rights deals. Second, in linking the commodification and juridification of the game, the authors seem to suggest that Bosman was somehow wrong to go outside of the authorities of the game for relief from his employer, as if he should have considered the deleterious effects upon football that his personal relief would have brought.

These are the primary anecdotal arguments used against the Bosman ruling in general, and against Bosman himself, by his and the ruling's detractors. The arguments suggest that Bosman is to blame for dragging football down to the same level as society and that his lawsuit helped entrench the sharp claws of capitalist and consumerist power into the game. The commodification argument is particularly ironic, since Bosman's lawsuit was arguably the classic worker's struggle against a repressive system of employment. The transfer system, after all, was designed by a cartel of employers living off the exploitation of the working class.

To place Bosman in the same category as television rights and kit sponsorships, and to call him equally responsible for the disproportionately large sums of money being traded between rich clubs and an elite mix of mercenary-like players places blame where it simply does not belong. There are serious issues of causation to consider: did Bosman start the trend, or was the trend towards commodifications well underway before he brought suit? Gardiner and Welch claim that Bosman was a reflection of the financial pressures of the game. They say that clubs were looking for legal ways to purchase the greatest number of the most highly skilled players available.[73] They assert that players were seeking to increase their bargaining power before the Bosman decision. To include Bosman in this category of players is fundamentally wrong. Bosman was not trying to increase his bargaining power; he was trying to earn a living in his chosen profession. Bosman simply argued that he was being prevented from doing so by his former employer, in direct violation of European law.

C. Ramifications of the Lawsuit on the Game

Without the restrictions of transfer fees or limitations on the number of foreign players that a team may have, players are more free to move from club to club and league to league. Clubs are now more inclined to offer longer contracts, thus making it more likely that they will be able to secure a fee of some kind when it comes time to sell a player. As a result, players are in a much stronger bargaining position when negotiating their contracts with clubs. All players are free agents once their contracts have expired. However, a select few players are effectively free agents even while under contract, because their exceptional skills are in such demand.

Since the Bosman decision took effect, players have acquired the power to demand and extract transfers in a way that would have been unthinkable before the lawsuit. Players who are unhappy with a club's management, who think that their club does not have a realistic chance of winning a title or trophy, or players who are simply bored or petulant, now have the leverage to demand to be transferred without fear of repercussion as long as they are skilled enough as players.

. . . .

Not surprisingly, the national footballing organizations of Europe have come together to solve what they view as a problem that could undermine the game. . . . The organizations agreed in December 2001, to set up two transfer "windows" per year, one each in summer and winter, to limit when clubs may buy and sell players. The hope is that the windows will add some stability to a system that is perceived to be out of control. By making it impossible for all players to move outside of the windows, clubs hope to remove the incentive for players to demand transfers in the middle of a season. An obvious flaw in that reasoning, however, is that players who demand transfers may simply . . . sit out until the next window allows them to leave.

With regard to the second half of the Bosman ruling, an interesting result of the abolition of foreign players has been what I call the "cosmopolitization" of clubs. Before Bosman, eight (sometimes six because of the "3+2 Rule") of the eleven players on the pitch were of the club's nationality. So, for example, a German team would have eight Germans. The rules defining a "foreign player," however, were set by the national associations. In England, for example, a player from any of the "Home Countries" counted as "domestic." An English team could include any British citizen, as well as those of the Republic of Ireland. Today, however, clubs can, and do, field any combination of players, from all over Europe and the world. Some complain that the importation of foreign players into the highest leagues in their respective countries inhibits the development of youth talent to the detriment of their national team. They blame this on the limitation of first team action for citizens of the home country.

Whether this is true or not should be the subject of another study. . . .

V. WHY BOSMAN IS NOT TO BLAME FOR THE POOR STATE OF THE GAME

The timing of Bosman's case was particularly important, given the fact that football began an economic boom at about the time he initiated his litigation. Despite the apparent economic rebirth of the game, however, all is not well. There is legitimate criticism that only a very few of the hundreds of clubs in Europe have actually benefited from the explosive growth in the game, and that the money now flowing freely has caused the game to lose touch with its working class roots. Bosman is frequently faced with criticism that his personal greed resulted in the explosive growth in players' salaries and that he has changed the game forever. Although Bosman makes an attractive target, especially for club owners and chairpersons, this attack on him is disingenuous in that it seeks to shift the blame for the current rot in the administration of the game.

For example, take the case of the English Football League and ITV Digital television. The Football League (the bottom three divisions of England's professional league, seventy-two teams in total) entered into a television rights deal with ITV Digital in June 2000. For £315 million, the League sold the rights to broadcast its matches in Great Britain on a pay-per-view basis. The purpose of the deal was to enable the clubs in the Football League to cash in on the success that the Premiership had enjoyed through its own television deal with BskyB. ITV Digital, owned by media companies Granada and Carlton, had not yet paid the full £315 million to the League, but that did not stop many clubs from spending the money before they had it. Clubs who invested what they were due in contract spent their money on debts, buying new players, and ground improvements, but were sorely disappointed when ITV Digital went bankrupt in February 2002, just seven months into its inaugural season.

The clubs of the Football League were further disappointed in August 2002, when a British high court ruled that Granada and Carlton were not liable for ITV Digital's debts, totaling nearly £200 million, because the contract that ITV Digital had with the Football League made no guarantees about the project's viability. As a result of the ITV Digital fiasco, many professional clubs in England are now in financial crisis. In fact, of the seventy-two teams that comprise Divisions 1 through 3 in England, fifteen teams have been placed into administration. Many other clubs are in precipitous financial positions and could have their seasons ended before they have played all their matches. While one exceptionally bad deal does not necessarily represent the entirety of the business, it does illustrate the point that Jean-Marc Bosman's impact upon football in Europe must be examined in a larger context.

Bosman represents an opportunity for those in positions of authority to deflect criticism from where it really belongs — on them. Bosman never made a policy decision that had wide ranging implications for the game. Bosman never negotiated a television rights deal, a kit sponsorship deal, or even a player transfer (his own transfer was voided when RC Liege failed to release his player's certificate). Bosman never offered an inflated contract to a young player (or a highly skilled player for that matter), nor did he refuse to field a skilled player under contract without explanation. Bosman never had the opportunity to exercise complete control over an entire group of young men's careers. Bosman was not responsible for the decline in conditions at the football stadia, nor for any other reason that the supporters left the game in droves in the 1980s.

REFERENCES

31. 1 CMLR 645, P 37, at 662.
47. Id. P 212, at 728.
48. Id. P 218, at 730.
51. Id. P 226, at 733.
59. Id. P 237, at 737.
62. Id. P 135, at 693.
64. Id. Ruling 1, at 778.
65. Id. Ruling 2, at 778.
69. 3 [1998] CIL, no. 4, 289–312.
70. Id. at 309.
71. Id.
72. Id. at 307–08.
73. Id. at 303.

MANAGEMENT ABILITIES, PLAYER SALARIES, AND TEAM PERFORMANCE

Bernd Frick

1. INTRODUCTION

Competition among professional sports teams — which are assumed to maximize their respective win percentage (or, in other words, the quality of their services to be delivered to their audiences) while retaining their financial viability[1] — is twofold: Before entering into the competition on the playing field, the teams enter into a bidding process for the services of the best players (and coaches) available. Most likely this bidding process has two consequences: First, escalating player salaries will threaten the financial viability of the teams that are engaged in what has been termed a "rat race."[2] Second, since in practically all existing leagues the member teams are located in cities of widely varying revenue potentials, teams from weak drawing cities are in an inferior position, i.e. they will not be able to sign the best players available, because the "big city teams" can always offer better financial conditions to the players they want to sign. These differences in the financial situation of the member teams of a league constitute the basis for what Neale[3] termed "the peculiar economics of professional sports": Since sports leagues sell competition on the playing field, they must find ways to preserve and maintain competitive balance, because otherwise teams from small-city markets would lack the incentives to field teams that can compete at the level that would maximize league revenues. Most leagues, therefore, have developed a variety of devices to cross-subsidize teams from weak drawing markets, with the announced objective of promoting their economic survival and enhancing competitive balance. These subsidies, however, must be paid in ways that preserve public confidence in the legitimacy of the competition on the playing field, because otherwise fan interest will vanish as it would if one or two teams dominated the championship for a long time. Thus, the two main problems of the teams are the result of the same underlying phenomenon: the competition for players combined with fixed costs for teams can lead some or most of the teams to be unprofitable, a situation that can be corrected by shifting rents from players to owners. Therefore, a large number of different institutional arrangements, such as player reservation clauses and salary caps, have been developed that are thought to generate competitive balance within a league and to control spiraling player salaries. Under a salary cap such as the one used in the "National Basketball Association" (NBA) the league agrees to set aside some fixed percentage of total league-wide revenues for player salaries. Each league team is required to spend a specified minimum amount on salaries and is banned from spending more than a specified amount, subject to certain exceptions. . . . The question, whether and to what extent a salary cap equalizes the differences in the financial situation of the teams of any given league, has been and still is debated by economists and sports fans alike: On the one hand, it has been argued that "an enforceable salary cap is the only one of the cross-subsidization schemes currently in use that can be expected to accomplish this (to maintain financial viability for teams located in weak-drawing markets, B.F.) while improving competitive balance in a league"[4] On the other hand, salary caps have been identified as "a unique form of cost-sharing collusion. . . . If NBA teams collusively behave as the firm, the profit maximization is reduced to revenue maximization for the league. . . . The imposition of a payroll cap allows a cartel of teams to collusively behave as the firm, and the capping of team payrolls leads to the increased exploitation of players and decreased competitive balance within the league."[5]

The purpose of the following paper is to test whether the rather "soft" salary cap that has been imposed in the NBA in 1984/85 has led to a more equal distribution of player talent and, consequently, of the "service qualities" delivered by the teams. Such an equalization, in turn, should have led to an increase in competitive balance. . . . If the cap was binding for all teams to the same extent and if it was strictly enforced by the league, it should not be possible to "buy" a championship team, i.e. the (spurious) correlation between team payroll and team performance that has been observed by a number of economists should have become weaker over the past decade (and should finally disappear).

2. PAY, MONITORING, AND PERFORMANCE IN PROFESSIONAL BASKETBALL

. . . .

2.2. PLAYER SKILLS, PLAYER SALARIES, AND COACHING PERFORMANCE

The constraint set facing professional teams in either basketball, football, or ice hockey is constant across clubs and is time invariant. The teams are identical in many respects: they produce an identical output, use the same units of input skills, compete under the same rules, employ the same production function, and share a common technology. More specifically, it is player quality on the one hand and the quality of managers/head coaches on the other that is crucial to the performance of teams: First, the degree of interaction among player skills determines the nature of the production function. Since the production technology is not additive, but exhibits complementarities among inputs, the individual player's contribution to output (wins and/or revenues) cannot be measured accurately even though his "productivity" (scoring and defensive behavior) can be easily assessed. Second, managers and head coaches share the responsibility for the coordination of player skills and the transformation of these skills into output. In the classic principal–agent model the principal (the team owner) observes the output of the agent (the player) precisely, but cannot tell to what extent that output reflects effort (which reduces worker utility) and random factors (which do not directly affect the player's utility). In the case of professional athletes, an important source of uncertainty is just how productive the player will turn out to be; but once that is known, those with productive draws have an incentive to court outside offers, which is certainly to the disadvantage of those with less favorable draws. One solution to this problem is to underpay young players and overpay older ones.[6] Another source of uncertainty for the players is the errors made by their head coaches in assessing performance, in situations where precise measurement is either too costly or even impossible. Here again, [the more] the relationship between pay and either true or measured performance is reduced the less reliable is the performance assessment.[7]

Moreover, risk-averse players prefer to be compensated for effort which they control, rather than output or performance evaluations that are subject to random shocks or measurement errors. In many cases these sources of uncertainty can be reduced by using relative comparisons in setting compensation. In team sports, however, this is a problematic strategy insofar as the ability of the players to affect their teammates performance is rather large: a player can adversely influence the performance of one or more of his teammates and he can fail to provide assistance that would otherwise be desirable.

A large number of empirical studies model the incomes of professional basketball players as a function of their individual "productivity" on the one hand and their ability and willingness to cooperate with their teammates on the other.[8] Most of the studies . . . find a concave relationship between experience (either measured as career length in years or as years with the current team) and individual earnings: salaries increase by about 7 1/2 percent per year in the early stages of a player's career, reaching a maximum after six to eight seasons and declining thereafter. The resulting age-earnings-profile not only reflects the accumulation of human capital (knowledge of the game and of the team's opponents) and the pay-off to better player–team matches (more able players stay in the league longer than less able ones), but also the ability and the willingness of a player to act as a team member — a characteristic that is crucial for the performance of the team, but not visible to outsiders, i.e. it is private information of the player's current team. Moreover, the evidence suggests that the more productive players earn significantly more than the less productive ones: the higher the number of points per minute/per game and the higher a player's "nonscoring" performance (rebounds, assists, steals, and blocks — again per minute or per game), the higher is his salary.

Thus, although higher individual salaries and higher team payrolls signal a higher player and team potential, this potential is not automatically translated into a better win–loss record. In a world of asymmetric information and self-interested individuals, the manager's task is to monitor inputs and meter rewards, thereby reducing the incentive to shirk and raising each player's productivity.[9] The more dependence there is in the marginal products of the team members, the more important is the role of the head coach. His objective is to win as many games as possible with the relative offensive and defensive playing skills at hand. This goal is achieved by maximizing scoring, minimizing opponent scoring, and transforming that relative scoring production into wins. Controlling for team payrolls and team potential, successful teams are most likely to retain their managers while teams that win less games than expected will terminate their head coaches more frequently.

3. TEAM SALARIES AND TEAM PERFORMANCE: EMPIRICAL EVIDENCE FROM THE NBA

. . . .

If the salary cap was enforced, we should observe the following developments:

- A reduction in the standard deviation of team salaries over time;
- A reduction in the standard deviation of the teams' win–loss records over time;
- A declining influence of team salaries on the teams' winning percentages; and
- A declining influence of team salaries on the teams' championship records (divisional, conference, and national championship titles).

. . . It appears that neither team salaries nor the teams' winning percentages have converged since the mid-1980s. In the case of team salaries, the expected development occurred in the early 1990s, when the so-called "grandfathering effects" dissipated.[10] Since the mid-1990s, however, the trend has been reversed. . . .

This development was by and large accompanied by a similar pattern in the development of competitive balance within the league: in the second half of the 1980s the teams became more unequal with regard to their win–loss records, a development that came to a preliminary stop in the early 1990s, but was intensified in the second half of that decade. This finding is in line with Fort and Quirk[11] who examine the effect of the NBA's salary cap on competitive balance by comparing the standard deviations of the win percentage over a period of eighteen years (the pre- and post-cap seasons 1975/76–1983/84 vs. 1984/85–1992/93). They find that — even after controlling for the possible effects of league expansions that occurred during the period under consideration — no significant change in the standard deviation occurred after the salary cap became operational. They conclude that until the early 1990s the cap had failed to equalize spending on player talent and player quality.

. . . .

4. SUMMARY AND CONCLUSIONS

The finding that in professional team sports player quality and management quality are equally important for success in the playing field is no surprise, neither to economists nor to sports fans. Therefore, players and head coaches are (immediately) replaced and/or terminated if their performance is too low.[12]

Given the peculiarities of the product market in professional team sports, "market failure" is likely to occur if no action is taken to compensate small-market teams for their inferior financial position which, in turn, leads to an "unhealthy" distribution of player talent. One possible instrument to correct for this failure is a "salary cap," that attempts to equalize player quality across teams by restricting the large-market teams' possibilities to sign additional (star) players. The results presented above, however, show that the salary cap as it is currently used in the NBA does not at all foster the equalization of player talent among the teams. Thus, the NBA's "soft" salary cap is not an instrument to increase competitive balance. To the contrary: after one and a half decades in which the salary cap was in operation, the NBA teams are less equal with regard to their payrolls and their win percentages (the service quality they deliver to their respective audiences) than they were in the early 1980s. This does not mean, however, that a salary cap is a generally ineffective instrument: whether a cap that allows no exceptions and that is strictly enforced, works in the intended direction remains to be seen.

REFERENCES

1. Kesenne, S.: League Management in Professional Team Sports with Win Maximizing Clubs. European Journal for Sport Management, 2 (1995), 14–22.
2. Akerlof, G.A.: The Economics of Caste and of the Rat Race and other Woeful Tales. Quarterly Journal of Economics, 90 (1976), 599–617.
3. Neale, W.E.: The Peculiar Economics of Professional Sports. Quarterly Journal of Economics, 78 (1964), 1–14.
4. Fort, R., Quirk, J.: Cross-subsidization, Incentives, and Outcomes in Professional Team Sports Leagues. Journal of Economic Literature, 33 (1995), 1265–1299, at 1296.
5. Vrooman, J.: A General Theory of Professional Sports Leagues. Southern Economic Journal, 61 (1995), 971–990, at 989.
6. Milgrom, P., Roberts, J.: Economics, Organization and Management, Englewood Cliffs, NJ: Prentice Hall 1992, at 336.
7. Milgrom, P., Roberts, J.: Economics, Organization and Management, Englewood Cliffs, NJ: Prentice Hall 1992, at 221–223.
8. Wallace, M.: Labor Market Structure and Salary Determination among Professional Basketball Players. Work and Occupations, 15 (1988), 294–312; Hamilton, B.H.: Racial Discrimination and Professional Basketball Salaries in the 1990s. Applied Economics, 29 (1997), 287–296; Brown, E., Spiro, R., Keenan, D.: Wage and Nonwage Discrimination in Professional Basketball: Do Fans Affect It? American Journal of Economics and Sociology, 50 (1991), 333–345; Kahn, L.M., Sherer, P.O.: Racial Differences in Professional Basketball Players' Compensation. Journal of Labor Economics, 6 (1988), 40–61; Koch, J.V., Vander Hill, C.W.: Is There Discrimination in the "Black Man's Game"? Social Science Quarterly, (1988), 83–94; Harder, J.W.: Play for Pay: Effects of Inequity in a Pay-for-Performance Context. Administrative Science Quarterly, 37 (1992), 321–333; Frick, B.: Personal-Controlling und Unternehmenserfolg in: Egger, A., Grtin, O., Moser, R. (eds.): Managementinstrumente und -konzepte. Entstehung, Verbreitung und Bedeutung für die Betriebswirtschaftslehre, Stuttgart: Schaffer-Poeschel 1999.
9. Alchian, A.A., Demsetz, H.: Production, Information Costs and Economic Organization. American Economic Review, 62 (1972), 777–795.
10. Fort, R., Quirk, J.: Cross-subsidization, Incentives, and Outcomes in Professional Team Sports Leagues. Journal of Economic Literature, 33 (1995), 1265–1299.
11. Fort, R., Quirk, J.: Cross-subsidization, Incentives, and Outcomes in Professional Team Sports Leagues. Journal of Economic Literature, 33 (1995), 1265–1299.
12. Staw, B.M., Hoang, H.: Sunk Costs in the NBA: Why Draft Order Affects Playing Time and Survival in Professional Basketball. Administrative Science Quarterly, 40 (1995), 474–494; Scully, G.W.: Coaching Quality, Turnover and Longevity in Professional Team Sports. Advances in the Economics of Sport, 1 (1992), 53–65; Scully, G.W.: Managerial Efficiency and Survivability in Professional Team Sports. Managerial and Decision Economics, 15 (1994), 403–411.

FREE AGENT PERFORMANCE IN MAJOR LEAGUE BASEBALL: DO TEAMS GET WHAT THEY EXPECT?

David Ahlstrom, Steven Si, and James Kennelly

Professional sport has become a large and competitive industry. Given the vast amounts that teams now spend on player salaries, it has grown increasingly important for professional sports organizations to understand whether this money is being well spent. The apportionment of rewards in organizations is an important focus of research in management. . . . Research is thus needed to determine what effect compensation has on employee performance, particularly given the challenges associated with motivating highly paid professionals. This paper contributes by examining the performance of free-agent players in Major League Baseball (MLB).

MLB salaries have been escalating rapidly in recent years. In 1976 the average salary was $51,500,[1] and by 1997 it had risen to about $1.33 million, representing an increase of roughly 2,500%. *[The average salary was $2,555,476 on opening day in 2003. This corresponds to nearly a 100% increase since 1997 and a 5,000% increase since 1976.]* This escalation is partly the result of a contractual change in late 1975 that permitted veteran players not under contract to sell their services to the highest bidders. The new free-agency system has helped increase player salaries while creating rather large salary differences among players.[2] The situation of rapidly growing salaries coupled with large pay differentials among similarly skilled players raises a number of questions concerning motivation and the link between pay and performance.

. . . .

Although the environment of Major League Baseball is good for studying motivational predictions, MLB's system of free agency presents a motivational paradox. On one hand, free agents might feel relatively undercompensated as they approach the end of their old contracts.[3] It is common for players to experience acrimonious negotiations with their team owners over pay.[4] Players who feel relatively undercompensated have been known to reduce their effort levels,[5] which is consistent with the predictions of equity theory. On the other hand, players who are at the end of their existing contracts might also be expected to "go all out" to improve their bargaining positions,[6] which would be consistent with the predictions of expectancy theory.[7] Both arguments have been used in MLB circles and in the motivational literature to explain player performance, despite their apparent contradiction. . . .

PAY AND PERFORMANCE IN MAJOR LEAGUE BASEBALL

Baseball players' salaries have traditionally generated much curiosity and controversy. The 1869 Cincinnati Red Stockings were the first all-salaried baseball team, and they thoroughly outperformed all their opponents. Seeing the Red Stockings outclass all other teams led owners of rival clubs to start paying their players as well. To prevent top players from jumping from team to team, team owners soon included in contracts a reserve clause that bound players to their teams in perpetuity. After signing a contract to play professional baseball, a player had to play for that team until he was traded, sold, or released. Only released players could negotiate in a free market with several teams, although migration because of player releases was uncommon.[8]

The reserve clause restricted players' freedom of negotiation and mobility because the owners of their contracts exercised much power over the them.[9] Player bargaining rights had been virtually eliminated except for the level of their annual financial compensation. A player could only choose between accepting whatever contract his owner offered or retiring. Other than holding out, players had little recourse to increase their salaries. Once a final offer was made, a player would have to either sign or quit and seek a different career.

By limiting player mobility, the reserve clause severely depressed salaries and created a monopsony whereby a single buyer (an MLB team owner) faced many small suppliers (the players). The players recognized this in the earliest days of the reserve clause, and many sought out new teams in other professional leagues. In 1890 the short-lived Players League was formed, and a number of National League players joined it. A decade later the American League was formed, and after raiding the National League for several top players, its management also recognized the monopsonistic benefits of the reserve clause and joined the National League in adopting it. In 1922, the U.S. Supreme Court upheld an earlier ruling maintaining MLB's reserve clause and the right of the clubs to, in the words of Justice Oliver Wendell Holmes, "retain the services of sufficient players." The owners' monopsonistic control over their players would not be seriously challenged again for another 50 years.

The Age of Free Agency

In the mid-1970s, baseball experienced a major institutional change. In 1972 outfielder Curt Flood challenged baseball's reserve clause in the U.S. Supreme Court. Although Flood lost his suit, shortly thereafter, in December 1975, baseball arbitrator Peter Seitz ruled that all players without contracts at the end of the 1976 season would be declared free agents. The subsequent basic agreement between team owners and players stipulated that any player with 6 or more years of major league service and not under contract could negotiate with almost any team. The system of free agency in MLB is essentially the same today.

As microeconomic theory predicts, the reserve clause's demise, coupled with a new salary arbitration system, removed the artificial ceiling imposed on baseball player salaries. In the 25 years before 1976, average salaries had increased at an annual rate of 5.6%. From 1976 to 1997, average salaries increased roughly 17% annually.[10] The rapid increase in salaries created some very large pay differentials among players with similar performance histories, because salaries paid to the top free agents often rose rapidly.[11]

This salary escalation could have two simultaneous effects: (a) creating perceptions of inequity in players who have older contracts and have fallen behind the salary curve and (b) creating strong motivation in those players to improve their performances in order to enhance their bargaining positions as they vied for new contracts. This dual effect has interesting motivational implications in the context of MLB free agency.

. . . . *[The authors' discussion of equity and expectancy theories is omitted.]*

Results

. . . . Some of the expectancy theory predictions were upheld, whereas none of the equity theory predictions were. . . . The equity hypothesis . . . suggested that performances would decline in the free-agent years compared with the previous years' performances, whereas the expectancy hypothesis . . . predicted that players' free-agent-year performances would improve. Although average performances did improve slightly in three of four performance measures in the free-agent year, the differences were not statistically significant. Thus, neither hypothesis was supported, because players did not significantly improve their performances. This suggests that imminent free agency had little motivational impact one way or the other. Similarly, hypotheses . . . compared the free-agent years with career averages. Once again, neither the equity nor the expectancy hypothesis was supported, because players' performances in their free-agent years did not differ significantly from their career averages.

Concerning the last two pairs of hypotheses, the expectancy predictions received some support. . . . In three out of four hitting performance measures, as well as ABs, [at-bats] mean player performance in the 1st year of the new contract was significantly lower than in the previous (free-agent) year. . . .

Players' mean BAs [batting averages] declined by 14 points, SAs [slugging averages] declined by 24 points, RBIs [runs batted in] went down by 5, and ABs declined by 35. HRs [home runs] also went down slightly, although the difference was not significant and could be attributed to the 35 fewer ABs. This drop in player performance in the 1st year of a new contract is contrary to equity theory predictions and is consistent with expectancy theory predictions.

Hypotheses . . . compared player performance in the 1st year new contract with the career average for BA and SA. Expectancy predictions were upheld — player BAs and SAs in the 1st years of the new contract were significantly lower than career averages. This further reinforces the observation that players suffer performance declines after signing new free-agent contracts, possibly as a result of the demotivating effect of a guaranteed contract.

CONCLUSIONS

It is commonly believed in baseball circles that multiyear, guaranteed contracts harm player motivation, ostensibly by weakening the link between pay and performance, and particularly in the 1st year or two of a contract. This study provided additional evidence to support that belief. The effects that aspects of North American Major League Baseball's current free-agent system can have on player performance were tested. In doing so, this study tested opposite predictions made by equity and expectancy theories in this context. The results presented here indicate that free-agent player performances rose slightly in the players' free-agent years as they anticipated signing new contracts, only to decline significantly in the 1st year of their new contracts in three out of four offensive performance categories and in times at-bat. Large declines occurred in two important performance categories: BA and SA.

In contrast to some past research on MLB free agency, this study, based on a larger sample of MLB free agents from 1976 to 1992, did not support equity theory predictions that MLB players would experience a decline in performance in their free-agent years because of underpayment. Nor did it support equity theory predictions that player performance would subsequently improve after signing new contracts. This suggests that player perceptions of inequity, if present, have no impact on hitting performance. Rather, the results suggested that expectancy effects might work to dampen the motivation of free agents that sign new contracts. Some declines were also found in RBIs and HRs, but these were the result of the 35 fewer ABs that each player had on average in the 1st year of his new contract as compared with his free-agent year. HR averages and RBI averages were quite stable for the sample.

Empirical studies have also shown that players with multiyear contracts spend 50% more time on the disabled list, largely with minor injuries, than players with 1-year contracts do.[12] Indeed, time spent on the disabled list often reflects minor injuries that players in days past would play through for fear of losing their jobs — a nonnecessity in the current age of guaranteed contracts. The results presented here are consistent with that evidence — the free agents in this sample batted less often in the 1st year of their new contracts than in the year before. This represents a significantly lower amount of playing time and might further reflect the reduced motivation often associated with new free-agent contracts.

Since the start of the free-agent era in 1976, baseball teams that signed free agents away from other teams might not have gotten the levels of performance and playing time that they expected from those players. The results of this study suggest that if teams give free agents contracts based on their free-agent-year performances, the teams (and their fans) are liable to be somewhat disappointed. The substantial decline in performance and playing time that free-agent players tended to suffer after signing contracts with new teams also raises questions concerning the value of long-term, guaranteed contracts that are not tied to current performance. In MLB, teams have started to respond to this problem by granting fewer long-term contracts and adding more performance and playing-time incentives than they did early in the free-agent era.[13] Players have also recognized that their salaries can quickly become obsolete. . . .

This study suggests the possibility that guaranteed contracts not substantially linked to performance might harm motivation, which reinforces a parallel argument in human resource management that pay for performance is a significant motivating tool, and its absence can harm productivity.[14] In terms of external applications, one might ask whether highly paid professionals with contracts not linked to performance also suffer performance decrements, especially in the early period of their contracts, when performance-outcome instrumentality is weakest. The issue of motivating employees whose compensation is both high and guaranteed represents a major concern for management in many professions, from professional sports to medicine.

REFERENCES

1. Scully, G.W. (1989). *The business of Major League Baseball.* Chicago: University of Chicago Press.

2. Zimbalist, A. (1992). "Salaries and performance: Beyond the Scully model." In P. Sommers (Ed.), *Diamonds are forever: The business of baseball* (pp. 109–133). Washington, DC: Brookings Institution.

3. Lord, R.G., & Hohenfeld, J. (1979). Longitudinal field of assessment of equity effects on the performance of Major League Baseball players. *Journal of Applied Psychology, 64*(1), 19–26.

4. (Jim Bouton, Ball Four, John Wiley and Sons, 1971).

5. Lyle, S., & Golenbock, P. (1979). The Bronx zoo. New York: Crown Publishers.

6. Harder, J.W. (1991). Equity theory versus expectancy theory: The case of Major League Baseball free agents. *Journal of Applied Psychology, 76*(3), 458–464.

7. Duchon, D., & Jago, A. (1981). Equity and the performance of Major League Baseball players; An extension of Lord and Hohenfeld. *Journal of Applied Psychology, 66*(6), 728–732; Vroom, H. (1964). *Work and motivation.* New York: Wiley & Sons.

8. Cymrot, D.J., & Dunlevy, J. (1987). Are free agents perspicacious peregrinators? *Review of Economics and Statistics, 69*(1), 50–58.

9. Scully, G.W. (1974). Pay and performance in Major League Baseball. *The American Economic Review, 64*(6), 915–930.

10. Scully, G.W. (1989). *The business of Major League Baseball.* Chicago: University of Chicago Press; Star News Services. (1997, December 3). *The Kansas City Star* (Metropolitan ed.), p. D6.

11. Zimbalist, A. (1992). "Salaries and performance: Beyond the Scully model." In P. Sommers (Ed.), *Diamonds are forever: The business of baseball* (pp. 109–133). Washington, DC: Brookings Institution.

12. Helyar, J. (1991, May 20). How Peter Ueberroth led the major leagues in the 'Collusion Era.' *Wall Street Journal,* p. A1; Lehn, K. (1990). Property rights, risk-sharing and player disability in Major League Baseball. In B. Goff & R. Tollison (Eds.), *Sportometrics* (pp. 35–38). College Station: Texas A&M Press.

13. Zimbalist, A. (1992). "Salaries and performance: Beyond the Scully model." In P. Sommers (Ed.), *Diamonds are forever: The business of baseball* (pp. 109–133). Washington, DC: Brookings Institution.

14. Schuler, R., & Jackson, S. (1996). *Human resource management: Positioning for the 21st century* (6th ed.). Minneapolis/St. Paul: West Publishing.

Role of Agents

The Business of Sports Agents

Kenneth L. Shropshire and Timothy Davis

The agent concept in sports is similar to that which has long existed in the motion picture, theatrical, television, and music sectors of the entertainment industry, as exemplified by the influential William Morris Agency. The duties that agents undertake in the entertainment industry, however, are often more specific than those of the agent in sports. In the entertainment industry, traditionally it is common for a performer to employ a group of advisers, including an agent, a personal manager, a business manager, and an attorney, in contrast with the athlete who may employ *an* agent.

   . . . .

Increasingly, sports agents provide services beyond the negotiation of the professional contract. These additional services may include the following: providing advice regarding financial matters such as tax, investment, insurance, and money management; obtaining and negotiating endorsement contracts; medical and physical health and training consultations; legal (including criminal) consultation; post-playing career counseling; counseling players regarding their particular sport; counseling players regarding their media image; and counseling players on matters pertaining to everyday life. All of these services and more are certainly required, in varying degrees, by today's professional athletes. Once the player signs a contract, the agent may continue to have ongoing obligations, depending on the nature of the specific athlete/agent agreement. Some agents are finished with their duties once the player contract is negotiated and simply receive their fee. Others maintain an ongoing relationship, providing certain of the laundry list of functions described above, particularly financial, endorsement, and counseling services.

   . . . .

Not all sports agents can provide all the services an athlete may require. That too causes some confusion in the business. Most people today accept that professionals such as doctors or lawyers specialize in particular areas. You may go to a general practitioner who will refer you to a surgeon to take care of the actual problem you are enduring. Likewise, your tax attorney may refer you to a trial lawyer. There are agents, however, who will attempt to provide services they are not qualified to perform for fear that they will lose their athlete clients by referring them to an expert. This is especially true when the expert is (or is secretly anxious to become) a rival agent.

FULL-SERVICE FIRMS

Some agents maintain that athletes not only want their contract negotiated but want to have the agent manage their income as well. Obviously, this is appropriate when the agent is qualified. In other cases, however, the agent may not provide adequate service in this capacity. In fact, the agent may be violating state or federal laws or relevant codes of ethics if not properly licensed to perform this duty. To remedy this and similar problems, agents have recognized that special steps must be taken if they want to provide more than contract negotiation services. One solution is the full-service sports management firm, the largest and most prominent being Cleveland-based IMG. There are mega newcomers as well, such as SFX Sports, Octagon Professional Athlete Representation, and Assante. These full-service firms provide, under one roof, individuals who negotiate contracts and deal with financial issues, endorsements, and whatever else athletes might encounter during and even after their careers. In addition, these firms possess the resources that allowed IMG to plow millions of dollars into the development of a controversial 190-acre sports academy. The facility gives it a competitive advantage not only against smaller agencies but also against larger rivals SFX, Octagon, and Assante, which send their clients to independent training sites with which they have forged relationships. The newer firms also promise entree to the entertainment industry. Many of the most successfully marketed athletes, such as basketball's Michael Jordan and golf's Arnold Palmer and Tiger Woods, are clients of these firms. Jordan even remained a client of SFX during his retirement from the NBA.

The key benefits of a full-service agency are twofold. First, the athlete is presumably able to receive the best service possible without having to shop around for various specialists. Second, the agent does not lose any part of the client's business. In fact, the athlete often pays an additional fee for any services beyond the initial contract negotiation. Where the cost of a contract negotiation may range anywhere from a low of 2 percent to a typical high of 5 percent of the total value of a contract, often an endorsement will cost the athlete as much as 30 percent of the value of the contract negotiated.

The marketing service a sports agent provides is not just a matter of pairing an athlete with some product that will pay the price. Although there is no special license required to be involved in product endorsements, an athlete can be harmed by an inexperienced representative. . . .

Not only is the product choice important, but so is the type of relationship the athlete has with the product. The athlete/product relationship may range from a one-day appearance at a local automobile dealership to what Falk calls the "autograph relationship" with a product. The autograph relationship is one where a product is named for a particular athlete, such as the Air Jordan athletic shoe manufactured by Nike and named after NBA star Michael Jordan, a long-time Falk client.

The agent must be particularly conscious of client overexposure. There is a view in the sports and entertainment industry that a client who is overexposed, or who appears in the public eye too frequently, will not be able to demand high endorsement dollars. The full-service sports marketing firms pay particular attention to this issue. By way of example, Octagon used the in-house resources available to its clients in devising a comprehensive marketing plan for the NFL's top pick in 2001, Michael Vick. Octagon's director of media and business development created pre- and post-draft strategies for shaping and marketing Vick's image. These strategies included creating a series of comedic commercials that revolved around Vick and the Heisman Trophy, developing a plan to broaden the scope and extent of public service announcements that Vick would make, controlling media access to Vick, and working with the Atlanta Falcons (the team with which Vick signed) to develop and implement marketing plans for Vick.

. . . .

Another alternative available to the athlete who wants agent services that go beyond contract negotiations is to pull together his or her own team of professionals. If the athlete is able to retain the appropriate mix of professionals, a natural check-and-balance system is established. Each professional necessarily has some overlap with the others as well as the opportunity to review portions of their work in an unbiased manner. The athlete in this situation may, for example, hire an attorney to negotiate the player contract, an accountant to handle finances, an investment firm to handle investments, and one of the sports marketing firms to handle endorsements.

DISCUSSION QUESTIONS

1. Why does the public tend to support management over labor during sports work stoppages?

2. What are the inflators and deflators of player salaries?

3. Why do athletes hire sports agents to negotiate their wages? Why is there rarely a party playing a similar role in other industries?

4. Are professional athletes overpaid? Explain.

5. Explain the relationship between ticket prices and player salaries.

6. Why should more cases proceed to a salary arbitration hearing in the NHL than in MLB?

7. Is there any utility to the walk-away provision in NHL salary arbitration since teams have only used it once?

8. What league has the most restrictive system of free agency? The least?

9. If the offers that a party makes during negotiations are an indication of its belief of the player's value, why are they inadmissible as evidence during the salary arbitration hearing?

10. How are small-market clubs disadvantaged by salary arbitration?

11. Should a party be able to discuss its financial situation in a salary arbitration hearing? Why or why not?

12. Should athlete compensation be tied more closely to performance or experience? What are the advantages of each philosophy?

13. What does your knowledge of the reserve system, salary arbitration, and the performance of free agents in MLB tell you about the optimal method of building a club?

14. Design an athlete compensation framework that best balances the interests of both owners and athletes.

CHAPTER 10

INDIVIDUAL SPORTS

INTRODUCTION

There are a number of professional sports involving individual athletes that operate outside of a league structure. Competition in these sports is generally organized around a professional tour of events, matches, races, or meets held in disparate geographic locations. Within this structure, there are a number of stakeholders that must be accounted for, including governing bodies, event owners and operators, athletes, and agents. An individual sport generally has a central governing body that, at a minimum, establishes playing and eligibility rules, sanctions events, and serves as an administrative body for the sport, similar to league offices in team sports. The governing body may generate revenues from sources such as the sale of media rights, sponsorships, tickets, and athlete fees. Examples of governing bodies are the PGA Tour (men's golf), LPGA Tour (women's golf), ATP Tour (men's tennis), WTA Tour (women's tennis), and NASCAR (stock car racing).

The governing body's need for a strong leader is perhaps more important in individual sports than in team sports because of the number of stakeholders in individual sports and their vastly divergent interests. A governing body that lacks strong leadership is, not surprisingly, likely to be under-monetized and fractious. A comparison of NASCAR and the WTA Tour is instructive in this area. NASCAR's governance of stock car racing is unparalleled among individual sports. As a closely held organization controlled by the France family since its inception, NASCAR's revenues surpass those of any other individual sport. Juxtaposed to NASCAR is the WTA Tour, which has an unwieldy structure and transient leadership. Despite the presence of several immensely popular athletes that has led the sport to all-time high levels of both fan attendance and television ratings, women's tennis lags behind other popular sports in revenue generation.

Event owners and operators are responsible for the staging of the competition in their particular geographic location. Depending on the sport, an event owner may generate revenues from ticket sales, concessions, local and national sponsorships, and, in the case of the WTA Tour, the sale of media rights. Stock racing and most golf events are owned by their governing bodies, while tennis events are sanctioned by the governing body but owned by third parties.* In addition, the marquee events

---

* The exceptions are the WTA and ATP end-of-season tour championship events, which are owned and operated by the governing bodies.

in golf and tennis are the four major championships, yet the majors are neither owned nor operated — and thus not controlled — by the governing bodies. This is roughly the equivalent of a professional sports league not controlling the most important games of its season, the playoffs. This is untenable to a professional sports league, yet de rigueur to the governing bodies of golf and tennis. Gate receipts are a significant revenue stream for event owners, and the presence or absence of one or more marquee athletes can have a significant impact on attendance. Thus, it is very important for the event owner to secure a commitment from the marquee athlete(s) as far in advance of the event as possible to maximize ticket sales. In tennis, the IMG and Octagon agencies control approximately 80% of the events, yet they also represent nearly 75% of the athletes competing in those events. While this allows the event owner to secure the participation of the marquee athletes, it also creates a conflict of interest — sometimes perceived, sometimes genuine — for the event owner.

The final stakeholder, albeit the most visible, is the individual athlete. Unlike team sport athletes who are salaried employees of their teams, individual sport athletes are independent contractors who may be able to generate income through prize money won in competitions, endorsements, and appearance fees in some sports. Though the prize money available to be won by individual sport athletes is far less than the collective salaries paid to athletes by the professional leagues, individual athletes may earn significant income from endorsements. Collectively, individual sport athletes are less powerful than team sport athletes because they are not unionized, and thus they do not deal with owners and governing bodies in a singular fashion. This is a reason why the average individual athlete earns less money than the average team sport athlete. However, it is possible that the top athletes in individual sports are more powerful than those in team sports, because they are more visible, since they do not share attention with any teammates, and they are not limited by the presence of a union — specifically, the lower-runged union members. Tiger Woods and the Williams sisters are prime examples of this. Another important difference between the two groups of athletes is that as independent contractors, individual sport athletes are responsible for many of their own expenses. Thus, individual sport athletes must pay for their own travel, lodging, and coaching expenses, while these costs are absorbed by the employer team in a league setting.

The initial readings in this chapter describe two successful structures for individual sports: NASCAR's race series and the PGA Tour's tournament model. In the first article, Michael Cokley offers an overview of the history, growth, and revenue sources of NASCAR and its athletes, as well as the challenges it faces in attempting to become more inclusive of minority groups. Indeed, the attraction of minority fans and participants is a major issue for virtually all individual sports. The discussion of this highly successful structure is followed by Charles Daniel's presentation of the tournament model embraced by the PGA Tour. The next selection contains highlights from the annual report of World Wrestling Entertainment (WWE). Though the outcome of matches are preordained and hence not truly sport, WWE's entrepreneurial use of individual athletes for entertainment purposes is worthy of investigation, as it has proven to be a strong business venture. The review of NASCAR, the PGA Tour, and WWE, is followed by a discussion of two ineffectively structured — and thus undermonetized — individual sports at central moments in their histories: women's tennis and professional boxing. Bruce Schoenfeld's critique of the WTA offers a glimpse of a sport that boasts star athletes yet is unable to fulfill its revenue potential. Scott Baglio's article on the boxing industry provides telling insight into a sport that is in danger of becoming marginalized because of its poorly conceived structure.

SUCCESSFUL MODELS

IN THE FAST LANE TO BIG BUCKS: THE GROWTH OF NASCAR

Michael A. Cokley

Over the past fifty-two years, NASCAR has evolved from a sport that was once raced on dirt tracks, sandy beaches, and short tracks, to a sport where speedways and superspeedways are the primary venues for racing events. . . . During this time, the one constant has been its leadership. NASCAR started out as a small, privately owned family business and has remained in the hands of its "first-family" since its inception. It has grown from a regional attraction . . . to a sport embraced by corporate America. NASCAR is truly one of the rags to riches stories in the professional sports world.

. . . .

II. GREEN FLAG: HISTORY OF NASCAR

On December 14, 1947, at the Ebony Bar atop the Streamline Hotel in Daytona Beach, Florida, William Henry Getty "Bill" France, Sr. called the first organizational meeting of what would be called the National Association For Stock Car Auto Racing, bringing together thirty-five racing promoters throughout the southeast for a four-day summit. . . . He knew the sport needed a central racing organization whose authority outranked all drivers, car owners, and track owners. Without a central racing organization, participants were forced to deal with different rules at different tracks. France envisioned a set of rules that would keep the cars and competition uniform. His vision included instituting a point system so drivers could compete for a driving championship. . . . He envisioned races being moved from the outdated dirt tracks that were the "backbone" of the sport to bigger tracks, speedways, and superspeedways, including a 2.5-mile speedway in Daytona Beach.

At that meeting, "Big Bill" France was elected president of the yet to be named central racing organization. The organizers of NASCAR established races that were to be run on the beach/road courses in Daytona Beach, Florida. On February 15, 1948, NASCAR officially incorporated, and on that day the first modified stockcar race took place in Daytona Beach. . . .

From that initial race, NASCAR has shared in auto racing's success in becoming a $2 billion a year industry. . . .

. . . .

IV. TURN TWO: GROWTH OF NASCAR

From its early days of holding races on dirt tracks, short tracks, and sandy beaches in small towns throughout the country, NASCAR has found its way to large metropolitan areas. . . Auto racing in general, and stock car racing in particular, has experienced tremendous growth over the last decade. It has gone from drawing crowds as small as fifty people to having an average attendance of more than 190,000 people and hosting the third-largest sporting event in the nation. Part of what has made NASCAR "the hottest commodity in sports" is the changing demographics of its fan base. The sport has gone from one that only "good ol' boys" attended, to a family event. Today, nearly thirty percent of race fans have an annual income of over $50,000. . . .

NASCAR's popularity may be seen in its television ratings . . . which topped those of Major League Baseball, the National Basketball Association, and the National Hockey League. . . . Television ratings for NASCAR have risen more than any other "major" sport. Capitalizing on its growing popularity, in November 1999, NASCAR signed a new six-year, $400 million deal with FOX, NBC, and TBS. . . To put this deal in perspective, in 1985, NASCAR received just $3 million for television rights to twenty-eight races. In 1999, the total revenue from TV was estimated at $100 million. This new television deal enables NASCAR to earn more money annually than baseball and hockey do from their TV deals.

V. TURN THREE: LICENSING AND SPONSORSHIP AGREEMENTS

A by-product of this growth is the revenue that NASCAR generates by way of sale of NASCAR-licensed merchandise. Its growth and popularity can be measured at the cash register in terms of sales of NASCAR-licensed merchandise. In 1990, sales of NASCAR-licensed goods were $80 million. By 1995, sales of NASCAR-licensed merchandise topped $600 million. In 1999, estimated gross retail sales of NASCAR-licensed merchandise were expected to top $1 billion.

In conjunction with what is made through licensing of its merchandise, NASCAR also benefits from corporate America buying into the sport. Whereas team owners annually budget $9 to $10 million a year for approximately twelve cars for the driver and salaries for employees, corporate sponsorship covers most, if not all of these costs. The combined income sources of licensing and sponsorship revenue have made for a successful formula. The team owners receive the bulk of their revenue from sponsorships, with licensing revenue representing a nice supplement.*

---

* Licensing revenue is generally split between the driver, the owner, and the sponsors. . . . Another way a company can take advantage of sponsorship opportunities is by purchasing advertising in the race event program. This marketing strategy delivers the company's message to the fans in an inexpensive way. This is not sponsorship in the strict sense of the word, but it has the same effect, in that the company's name is being associated with a particular race event.

A. Licensing

. . . In NASCAR, the licensing program is designed to benefit the drivers, teams, and tracks by growing business opportunities for the sport's corporate sponsors. In the merchandising game there are four major players: the drivers, the race team, the sponsors, and the licensees that make the goods. With the sale of each die-cast car, pack of trading cards, piece of apparel, or any other miscellaneous product, each of the four groups earns a share of the revenue.

The licensing scheme in NASCAR is complex, involving NASCAR, individual teams/ drivers, manufacturers, and vendors. Between NASCAR and the vendors, the majority of the souvenirs and merchandise are licensed by NASCAR, the speedway, or the sponsor associated with any particular name, trademark, image, or likeness represented on the item. The licensing scheme works this way: the licensee pays NASCAR a percentage of the gross receipts from sales of the licensed merchandise. In order for vendors to sell souvenirs and merchandise at NASCAR races, each must obtain a license from the speedway and pay a fee for each NASCAR event, along with a percentage of its gross sales. The speedway, in turn, pays a percentage of its gross receipts to NASCAR.

As for the drivers, NASCAR has cross-licensing agreements with each driver whereby NASCAR can package the drivers, race teams, and events in an integrated merchandising program. This cross-licensing agreement was the result of NASCAR controlling much of the licensing of merchandise. In the past, vendors worked independent of NASCAR, cutting individual deals that created distribution problems and were hard for NASCAR to monitor. In 1996, NASCAR sought to alleviate these problems by getting drivers, teams, and merchandisers to cross-license the products with NASCAR. However, not all merchandise is cross-licensed.

Each driver is an independent contractor. Either the driver controls the licensing of each of his/her likenesses or the team negotiates licensing matters for him/her. This allows teams to have a choice of how they want to handle the licensing of their driver's merchandise. They may either contract out to a marketing company or they may handle licensing matters internally. In fact, some drivers, like Jeff Gordon, incorporate and handle licensing matters in-house. However, other drivers . . . incorporate but have a marketing company to handle licensing. Some smaller teams may contract out to larger, more successful teams for all of their licensing matters. While the lion's share of team owners' revenue comes from sponsorship, this is supplemented handsomely by the sale of licensed products bearing the likeness of the team, car, and driver.

With the success realized from the increased revenue from the sale of NASCAR-licensed merchandise, NASCAR has sought to improve upon what it has done with its licensing arrangements. NASCAR has sought to expand consumer awareness beyond its traditional market, to reach those who would not ordinarily attend an event. NASCAR has done this by establishing NASCAR Thunder, the official NASCAR store, which specializes in apparel. It has also established NASCAR Cafes, NASCAR Speed Parks, and NASCAR Silicon, an entertainment motor speedway.

NASCAR differs from other sports when it comes to licensing. The drivers hold a significant financial advantage over athletes in other sports, as they are able to control their own licensing and souvenir sales. In all other professional sports leagues, property divisions control the licensing.

While the teams and leagues profit from the popularity of their biggest stars, these profits are split equally among the teams and athletes. . . . In NASCAR, however, the royalties from the sale of merchandise are only split between the driver, team owner, and sponsors.

The licensing scheme, which included NASCAR covering about eighty percent of the drivers, teams, and in-house merchandisers, resulted in everyone being treated fairly, and the problems that once existed with renegade vendors supposedly became nonexistent. . . .

. . . .

B. Sponsorship

. . . .

. . . Drivers are quick to praise corporate sponsors after winning a race, apologize to them after losing a race or wrecking a car, and to thank them for their continued support.

. . . The corporate sponsors and team owners/drivers view sponsorship differently. For team owners/drivers, corporate sponsorship is their lifeline, a necessary component in order for the team to remain competitive. Corporations get involved with sponsorship in order to get their product valuable exposure. Exposure increases the impression consumers have towards the product. This is parlayed into sales. . . . Companies, in fact, sometimes use NASCAR as a springboard to jumpstart sagging sales.

Other companies use NASCAR to bolster already huge revenue numbers. . . . Sponsorship is nothing new to NASCAR, as it has always been a large part of NASCAR, and it is the backbone of the sport. In 1938, prior to the formation of NASCAR, France, understanding the necessity of sponsorship, solicited the aid of businesses. . . . France knew that in order for the sport to survive it needed the financial support of big business.

Today, the largest part of a team's revenue comes from sponsors. In exchange for providing financial backing for a particular driver, corporate sponsors advertise their products on the cars and on the uniforms worn by the drivers and their pit crew. In this respect, NASCAR differs from all the other major sports. In other sports, television rights fees and ticket sales make up the majority of the revenue, with less emphasis placed on sponsorship. From its inception, NASCAR differed from other sports when it came to generating revenue. Because NASCAR was mostly regional, it relied heavily on corporate sponsorship. It had no choice, because it was not able to charge a lot for television rights or tickets.

The look of the corporate sponsor has changed dramatically since NASCAR's early days. As recently as the late 1980s, the sport's top sponsors consisted of companies selling products that you could drink (e.g., Miller-Lite), smoke (e.g., KOOL), or chew (e.g., SKOAL). Today, NASCAR is moving away from its image of being too regional. The list of "official" sponsors includes a diverse group of businesses. . .

Not only has the look of the corporate sponsor changed, but the number of sponsors has changed as well. Today there are over 250 corporate sponsors associated with stock car racing, including seventy Fortune 500 companies. NASCAR has several different types of sponsorship programs that companies may choose from.* Team sponsorship is considered the most valuable of all of the sponsorship

---

* NASCAR has four types of sponsorship programs for those companies wanting to spread its marketing dollars over the widest area. Those programs are: (1) Official Status Program, (2) Series Sponsorship Program, (3) Special Awards Program, and (4) NASCAR online. The Official Status Program is for those companies with large budgets. They can become "official" sponsors for approximately $1.5 million a year. For example, Pepsi is the "Official Soft Drink of NASCAR," and Raybestos is the "Official Brake of NASCAR." Under the Series Sponsorship Program, a company's name can be used to identify one of the thirteen NASCAR racing series. For example, Anheuser-Busch is the corporate sponsor of the Busch Grand National Series and is the most expensive of the sponsorship programs. RJR Nabisco, the corporate sponsor of the premier series in NASCAR, pays $30 million annually for the privilege

opportunities because it allows a company to take direct equity participation in the sport. A team sponsor is allowed to put the company's name, logo, or brand directly on the car and the uniforms of the driver and crewmembers. This is, however, an expensive proposition. The race car is treated like a side of beef; each part is a choice cut, and it is identified by name and a specific value is attached to it. There are two types of sponsors: the primary sponsor and the associate (or contingency) sponsor.

The primary sponsor is the sponsor most identified with the driver because it is the sponsor that is most visible. The primary sponsor can usually expect to pay anywhere from $3 million to $9 million dollars a season and grants the primary sponsor the exclusive right to advertise on the hood and rear quarter panel areas. This may include the trunk lid, called the TV panel, which itself may cost between $500,000 and $1 million.

Associate sponsors usually advertise on smaller decals and may advertise on a number of different places on the car for approximately $500,000 to $2.5 million. Advertising on the B-Post costs approximately $200,000. For $250,000 to $750,000, a sponsor can advertise either behind the back tires or on the C-Post. For a little less, sponsors may pay approximately $64,000 for a twenty-six inch decal and advertise on the sides of the car or, for approximately $84,000, the company can buy a thirty-two inch decal and advertise on either side of the car. The lower quarter panels go for $25,000 to $100,000, and the front fender costs approximately $30,000 to $150,000 a season.

VI. TURN FOUR: MINORITY PARTICIPATION

Despite its growing popularity, there has been a segment of society that NASCAR has yet to tap. Minority groups, particularly African-Americans, have yet to share in NASCAR's growth. African-Americans and other minority groups are nearly nonexistent in every facet of the sport: drivers, pit crew, ownership, and spectators. NASCAR has 250 corporate employees in its Daytona Beach, New York, Charlotte, and Southern California offices. Of these, the number of minorities is imperceptible. Is this changing, or more importantly, is there a desire for change? Those associated with NASCAR hope that it does change. But just as NASCAR's evolution from a southern redneck pastime into the fastest growing spectator sport has taken over fifty years, early indications are that this may be wishful thinking. That being said, many have recognized the need for diversity.

Market executives have speculated that in order for NASCAR to capitalize on its fast-growing popularity, it needs to tap into minority markets. Minority groups have in the past expressed an interest in participating in stock car racing. While this interest had been small, those who have tried their hand at breaking into the field found limited success. This has paved the way for a new gener-

---

of having the premier series named after one of its cigarette brands (Winston Cup Series). *[NASCAR renamed its premier series the Nextel Cup pursuant to a 10-year, $750 million sponsorship agreement with the wireless company that will expire in 2013.]* The Special Awards Program is a program in which cash awards are represented to the race fans, which are linked to the drivers' performance. NASCAR online is NASCAR's Internet site on the World Wide Web. For $15,000 per month, or $120,000 per year, a sponsor gets exclusive full-page coverage on NASCAR's website, www.NASCAR.com. Within the series sponsorship, there are other sponsorship opportunities. There is event sponsorship, which is when a company sponsors one specific race in a particular series. For example, Coca-Cola sponsors the Coca-Cola 600 at Lowe's Motor Speedway in Charlotte, North Carolina; Pepsi sponsors the Pepsi 400 at the Daytona International Speedway in Daytona Beach, Florida; and Mountain Dew sponsors the Mountain Dew Southern 500 at the Darlington Raceway in Darlington, South Carolina. Sponsoring one of the NASCAR Winston Cup series will cost at a minimum $1 million and often exceeds that amount by several million dollars.

ation of minorities to build on what those who have come before them have done. Spurred by the renewed interest among minority groups, NASCAR, along with the governing bodies of the other racing leagues, has instituted different types of minority participation programs to take advantage of segments of society that have, now more than ever, sought to participate in what has historically been an all-white venture. Success has been slow in coming, but those minorities who have ventured into the sport are determined to remain.

. . . .

B. Team Ownership

Breaking into NASCAR is not easy. It takes a lot of capital. That being said, several high profile African-Americans have sought to gain entry into NASCAR, in one form or another. While no African-American currently owns a NASCAR Winston Cup team, there are minority owners at the lower levels. . . .

C. Driver Developmental Programs

Brian France, whose main job is to oversee the business deals of NASCAR, formed a diversity management council in 1999 within NASCAR. France's goal is to address the needs of minority race drivers, mechanics, and support staff who say they have been overlooked by the white structure for decades. . . .

THE PGA TOUR: SUCCESSFUL SELF-REGULATION OR UNREASONABLY RESTRAINING TRADE?

Charles R. Daniel II

II. PGA TOUR HISTORY AND MEMBERSHIP

The PGA Tour was formed in 1968 as a nonprofit organization doing business as a business league or trade association. The purpose of the PGA Tour is to regulate, promote, and improve the business of professional tournament golf. The PGA Tour strives to achieve this purpose through its tournament regulations. . . These regulations were created and enacted by the players. Amendments to the tournament regulations require the affirmative vote of at least three of the four player directors of the PGA Tour tournament policy board, who are also PGA Tour members.

Currently, there are 254 members of the PGA Tour. *[There are 258 members in 2004.]* . . . To qualify for membership, players must satisfy reasonable performance criteria as tournament-playing professionals as set out for each particular Tour. . . .

. . . . A typical PGA Tour tournament is set up as follows:

(1) The PGA Tour contracts with a local sponsor. The local sponsor is generally a local non-profit organization that donates the net receipts from the tournament to charity. . . . Charities that receive contributions range from family and youth services to athletic programs for children, to medical facilities for adults and children. Approximately 900 charities benefit from the PGA Tour every year.

(2) After a local sponsor is found to act on behalf of these charities, the local sponsor must then arrange for the use of a golf course and ensure that the course meets PGA Tour specifications. The sponsor is also responsible for staffing the event. The average spectator draw for a PGA Tour event is 80,000–160,000 people. As a result, staffing for a tournament can involve as many as 1,000–1,500 people to direct traffic, operate shuttle buses from parking areas, direct spectators, keep spectators quiet on and off the course, collect admission tickets, clean

up the grounds, and otherwise perform all administrative functions necessary for operation of a golf tournament. Most of the staff are volunteers who support the local charity which will benefit from the tournament.

(3) In addition to choosing a course and coordinating staffing arrangements, the local sponsor is also responsible for paying the tournament purse (prize money). Usually, the purse is divided among the top seventy finishers in the Tournament. . . . It is obvious in light of the combined responsibilities mentioned above that the ultimate financial responsibility of the event lies with the local sponsor.

(4) The PGA Tour's major responsibility is to contract with a television or cable network. The network pays a rights fee to the PGA Tour for the right to broadcast the tournament. . . .

In the late 70s and early 80s, networks showed an unwillingness to televise tournaments unless local sponsors, in cooperation with the PGA Tour, could ensure a substantial portion of television advertising. Professional golf faced the prospect of losing what little television contracts it had, and fans of the sport would lose the opportunity to see and root for their favorite golfers on network television. The PGA Tour, under the direction of former Commissioner Deane Beman, devised a two-part strategy:

First, the PGA Tour, in cooperation with local sponsors, sold advertisers and the networks a package of tournaments rather than single tournaments. This allowed advertising messages to be spread over several tournament telecasts, reducing the risk to advertisers and the networks, who often are asked to compensate advertisers if programming fails to reach anticipated audiences.

Second, the PGA Tour embarked on a strategy of using title sponsors to purchase large portions of network advertising and to underwrite most or all of the tournament purses. Title sponsors would benefit from the returns on advertising as well as from their presence at the site of an event through celebrity events and a host of other tournament activity. But, sponsors were reluctant to bear the cost of sponsorship if competing golf events were broadcast on another network. These competing broadcasts would fragment both the field of golfers and an already-small viewer base.

In order to guarantee quality players for televised events and exclusivity of professional golf telecasts as requested by advertisers and title sponsors, the PGA Tour adopted the Conflicting Events Rule and the Media Rights Rule. These rules, enacted and supported by PGA Tour members, limited but did not prohibit PGA Tour members from competing at non-PGA Tour tournaments. These rules were critical to the recruitment and retention of title sponsors, for whom the corporate exposure associated with a major tournament is one of the primary reasons for sponsorship.

. . . .

III. THE CONFLICTING EVENTS AND MEDIA RIGHTS RULES

The Conflicting Events Rule states that, in order to contribute to the success of PGA Tour events and to fulfill its obligations concerning representative fields, no PGA Tour member shall participate in any other golf event on a date when a PGA Tour co-sponsored regular event, for which the member is exempt, is scheduled. . . .

. . . .

Under the Media Rights Rule, players assign their media rights to the PGA Tour in return for the benefits of membership in the PGA Tour, including television coverage of virtually all PGA Tour events. As a part of the assignment, players agree to limit their appearances on other live or recorded television golf programs without the prior approval of the PGA Tour commissioner. Wholly instructional golf programs and personal appearances are exempted from the rule.

ENTREPRENEURIAL MODEL

ANNUAL REPORT FOR THE FISCAL YEAR ENDED APRIL 30, 2002

World Wrestling Entertainment, Inc.

PART I

Item 1. Business

We are an integrated media and entertainment company, principally engaged in the development, production, and marketing of television programming, pay-per-view programming and live events, and the licensing and sale of branded consumer products featuring our successful World Wrestling Entertainment brand. . . .

The key economic drivers of our business are live event attendance, pay-per-view buys, and television ratings. While these drivers have continued to be soft in recent months relative to their previous highs, they nonetheless continue to reflect our strong presence in the marketplace and the loyalty of our fan base. This marketplace strength and loyal fan base have been monetized across our many revenue streams within our live and televised and branded merchandise segments. . . .

. . . We have deepened our talent pool through our acquisition of certain assets of World Championship Wrestling, and as a result of a contraction in the number of competing sports entertainment companies. In an effort to further exploit and bolster our business, we launched a brand extension, creating two separate and distinct brands, *Raw* and *SmackDown!,* which each have their own distinct storylines, thus enabling us to have two separate live event tours. The two tours will allow us to visit domestic markets that we have been unable to visit and will also allow us to tour internationally on a more frequent basis.

. . . .

World Wrestling Entertainment, Inc., formerly known as World Wrestling Federation Entertainment, Inc., was incorporated in Delaware in 1987, and in 1988 we merged with our predecessor company, which had existed since 1980. In October 1999, we sold 11,500,000 shares of Class A common stock to the public at an initial offering price of $17.00 per share. To further broaden our exposure in the financial marketplace, in October 2000, we began trading our Class A common stock on the New York Stock Exchange (NYSE symbol: "WWE"). . . .

. . . .

Creative Development and Production.   Our creative team, headed by Vincent McMahon, develops soap opera–like storylines employing the same techniques that are used by many successful television series. We create compelling and complex characters and weave them into interactive entertainment that combines social satire, action adventure, drama, mystery, athleticism, and humor. The interactions among the characters reflect a wide variety of contemporary topics, often depicting exaggerated versions of real life situations and typically containing "good versus evil" or "settling the score" themes. Story lines are usually played out in the wrestling ring, our main stage, and typically unfold on our weekly television shows and monthly pay-per-view events. Woven into the story lines is the ongoing competition for the various World Wrestling Entertainment championship titles.

Our creative team also develops a character for each performer. Once a character's basic traits have been formulated, we work to define and emphasize those traits through various accessories, including costumes and entrance music. We own the rights to substantially all of our characters, and we exclusively license the rights we do not own through agreements with our performers.

Our success is, in large part, due to the continuing popularity of our performers. We currently have exclusive contracts with approximately 150 performers, ranging from development contracts with prospective performers to long-term guaranteed contracts with established performers. These contracts vary depending upon a number of factors, including the performers' popularity with our audience, their skill level, and prior experience. Our performers are independent contractors who are highly trained and motivated and portray popular characters. . . . We constantly seek to identify, recruit, and develop additional performers for our business. Once recruited, established performers are immediately incorporated into our story lines, while less experienced performers participate in our own extensive developmental training programs. Under agreements with regional promoters of wrestling events, promising candidates are often "loaned" to the regional promoters allowing these new performers to hone their skills by working in front of live audiences and appearing on local television programs. The most successful and popular performers are then incorporated into our television programming and pay-per-view events where their characters are more fully developed.

With limited exceptions, we retain all rights in perpetuity to any intellectual property that is developed in connection with the characters portrayed by our performers. This includes the character and any associated costumes, names, props, story lines, and merchandise. Our performers share in a portion of the revenues that we receive. . . .

Live and Televised Entertainment.   Live events, television programming, and pay-per-view programming are our principal creative and production activities. Revenues from these activities were approximately *[$295.4 million]* $323.5 million, $335.7 million, and $265.5 million in fiscal *[2003]* 2002, 2001, and 2000, respectively.

Live Events.   Live events are the cornerstone of our business, providing the content for our television and pay-per-view programming. Each event is a highly theatrical production, which involves a significant degree of audience participation and employs various special effects, including lighting, pyrotechnics, powerful entrance music, and a variety of props.

In fiscal 2002, we held 237 live events in approximately 100 cities in North America, including 18 of the 20 largest metropolitan areas in the United States, as well as several international locations. . . *[In fiscal 2003, 327 live events were held in 193 North American cities.]*

With the increase and depth of our talent pool and the introduction of two separate tours, we expect to hold approximately 350 live events in fiscal 2003. In an effort to meet strong international demand, we have increased our ability to tour internationally on a more frequent basis. . . . *[Approximately 30 international events were planned in 2003.]*

We promote our live events through a variety of media, including television, radio, print, and the Internet. Our revenues from live events are primarily derived from ticket sales, with prices for our live events averaging approximately $36 per ticket. *[Ticket prices increased to $39 in 2003.]* The operator of a venue at which our live event is held typically receives a fixed fee or a percentage of the revenues from ticket and merchandise sales. . . .

Revenues from live events were approximately *[$72.2 million,]* $74.1 million, $81.9 million, and $68.9 million for the fiscal years ended April 30, *[2003,]* 2002, 2001, and 2000, respectively.

Television Programming.   We are an independent producer of television programming. Relying primarily on our in-house production capabilities, we produce seven shows consisting of nine hours of original programming 52 weeks per year. On a weekly basis, our nine hours of programming deliver approximately 24 million television impressions each week. In addition to our television programming, we also produce on an annual basis 12 domestic pay-per-views, which are also distributed through certain international pay-per-view providers and 2 international pay-per-views which are produced in the U.K.

Seven hours of our programming air domestically on cable and broadcast networks owned by Viacom Inc., and two hours air in syndication. . . .

    . . . .

In connection with our TNN and MTV programming, we receive a rights fee totaling $572,000 per week. *[In 2003, rights fees from TNN and UPN totaled $0.9 million per week.]*

    . . . .

Domestic television rights fee revenues were *[$38.8 million,]* $35.0 million, $20.9 million, and $7.1 million for the fiscal years ended April 30, *[2003,]* 2002, 2001, and 2000, respectively.

Due to the density of certain key demographics that our programming reaches, we are an attractive and efficient buy for our advertisers. Our programming is principally directed to audiences aged 12 to 34. Since our programming appeals to such a wide spectrum of age groups, we voluntarily designate the suitability of each of our shows using standard television industry ratings.

We sell a substantial portion of the advertising time on our domestic and Canadian television programs to over 110 major advertisers and sponsors. We advertise products from some of the leading companies in the food and beverage, video game, toy, movie and television studio, and telecommunications industries, among others. In addition to the sale of our advertising time, we also package sponsorships to meet the needs of our advertisers. . . . Through these sponsorships, we offer advertisers a full range of our promotional vehicles, including television, Internet, and print advertising, arena signage, on-air announcements, and special appearances by our performers. Additionally, as part of certain sponsorship packages, we produce commercials featuring our performers.

Advertising time and customized sponsorship programs are sold directly by our New York . . . and Toronto-based sales forces. Our arrangement with our television network partners provides that we pay the network the greater of a fixed percentage of our net advertising revenues less certain adjustments or a minimum guaranteed amount. . . .

Advertising revenues were *[$72.9 million,]* $83.6 million, $90.2 million, and $77.9 million for the fiscal years ended April 30, *[2003,]* 2002, 2001, and 2000, respectively.

. . . .

Pay-Per-View Programming.   On a monthly basis, our story lines either culminate or change direction at each pay-per-view. We intensively market and promote the story lines that are associated with our upcoming pay-per-view event through our television shows, our Internet sites, and a variety of other promotional campaigns. We produce 12 domestic pay-per-view programs and two international pay-per-view programs annually, which consistently rank among the pay-per-view programs achieving the highest number of buys. Pay-per-view buys of our domestic events over the past three fiscal years were *[5.4 million,]* 7.1 million, 8.0 million, and 6.9 million in fiscal *[2003,]* 2002, 2001, and 2000, respectively. . . .

. . . We also distribute our pay-per-view programs to commercial locations for public viewing. Consistent with industry practices, we share the revenues with the cable systems and satellite providers and pay fees to inDemand.

. . . .

Domestic and International pay-per-view revenues were *[$91.1 million,]* $112.0 million, $128.2 million, and $106.4 million for the fiscal years ended April 30, *[2003,]* 2002, 2001, and 2000, respectively.

International.   In an effort to meet strong international demand, we have expanded our international live event tours and the distribution of our television programming. Our television programming is currently broadcast in over 130 countries and 13 *[12]* different languages. . . .

Television rights fee revenues outside of North America were *[$19.7 million,]* $18.3 million, $14.3 million, and $5.1 million for the fiscal years ended April 30, *[2003,]* 2002, 2001, and 2000, respectively.

. . . .

Branded Merchandise.   We offer a wide variety of branded merchandise through a licensing program and an integrated direct sales effort. Our revenues from the sale of our branded merchandise were approximately *[$78.9 million,]* $86.1 million, $102.5 million, and $112.4 million in fiscal *[2003,]* 2002, 2001, and 2000, respectively.

Licensing and Direct Sales.   We have an established licensing program using our World Wrestling Entertainment mark and logo, copyrighted works and characters on thousands of retail products, including toys, video games, apparel, and a wide assortment of other items. In all of our licensing agreements, we retain creative approval over the design, packaging, advertising, and promotional material associated with all licensed products to maintain the distinctive style, look, and quality of our intellectual property and brand. Our licensing agreements provide that we receive a percentage of the wholesale revenues as a royalty and require minimum guarantees.

Our direct merchandise operations consist of the design, marketing, and sale of various products, such as shirts, caps, and other items, all of which feature our characters and/or our scratch logo. All of these products are designed by our in-house creative staff and manufactured by third parties. The merchandise is sold at our live events under arrangements with the arenas, which receive a percentage of the revenues. Our merchandise is also sold through internally developed catalogs . . . our television shows, our *wweshopzone.com* Internet site, and our retail store in New York. *[The retail store ceased operations in 2003.]*

. . . .

New Media.   We utilize the Internet to promote our brand, create a community experience among our fans, and to market and distribute our various products. Through our network of Internet sites, our fans can purchase our branded merchandise online, obtain our latest news and information, including content that is accessible only online, stay abreast of our evolving story lines, tap into interactive chat rooms to communicate with each other and our performers, and experience archived video and audio clips of performers and previous media events. . . . In addition to *wwe.com,* our network of sites includes, among others, *wweshopzone.com, therock.com, wwedivas.com, undertaker.com,* and *wwecorpbiz.com.*

WWE.com continues to maintain a strong base in the number of people visiting our sites and purchasing our products via the Internet. In April 2002, our Internet sites generated approximately 330 million page views as compared to approximately 300 million page views in April 2001 and approximately 200 million page views in April 2000. *[In April 2003, the sites generated approximately 210 million page views worldwide and approximately 5.8 million unique visitors worldwide.]* According to Net Score, we had approximately 7.3 million, 8.7 million, and 4.4 million unique visitors in April 2002, 2001, and 2000, respectively. The 7.3 million visitors spent an average of 45 minutes on our site.

. . . .

Competition.   We compete for advertising dollars with other media companies. For our live, television, and pay-per-view audiences we face competition from professional and college sports as well as from other forms of live, film and televised entertainment, and other leisure activities. We compete with entertainment companies, professional and college sports leagues, and other makers of branded apparel and merchandise for the sale of our branded merchandise. . . .

. . . .

Item 7. Management's Discussion and Analysis of Financial Condition and Results of Operations

. . . .

Background.   . . . .

Over the past year, we believe that the audience for sports entertainment has contracted and/or moved to other forms of entertainment. As a result, a number of competitors within this industry are no longer operating. For fiscal 2002, we experienced a softening in the key drivers of our business: television ratings, average attendance at our live events, and pay-per-view buys. *[This softening continued in fiscal 2003.]* Nevertheless we have retained our distinction as consistently being the #1 regularly scheduled program on cable with *Raw* which airs Monday nights on TNN, and we are the highest-rated show on network television on Thursday nights among male teens with our UPN program, *SmackDown!*

As the industry contracted, we were able to sign additional performers, thus deepening our talent pool. At the same time, we have broadened our story lines. As a result, we created two separate brands under the WWE umbrella: *Raw* and *SmackDown!* Through our separate branded tours, we now deliver two unique story lines with two distinct groups of talent to our fans around the world. We now have two live event tours and as a result, have increased the number of live events and are playing markets that heretofore we could not visit given the size of our talent pool and logistical constraints on our television shoots.

. . . .

Our operations are organized around two principal activities:

Live and televised entertainment, which consists of live events, television programming, and pay-per-view programming. Revenues consist principally of attendance at live events, sale of television advertising time and sponsorships, domestic and international television rights fees, and pay-per-view buys.

Branded merchandise, which consists of licensing and direct sale of merchandise. Revenues include the marketing and sale of merchandise, magazines and home videos, consumer products sold through third party licensees, and the operations of our entertainment complex located in New York City. *[The complex discontinued operations in 2003.]*

. . . .

Fiscal Year Ended April 30, 2002 compared to Fiscal Year Ended April 30, 2001—*[and FY 2003 compared to 2002]*.

Net Revenues. Net revenues were $425.0 million for the fiscal year ended April 30, 2002 *[later revised to $409.6 million]* as compared to $456.0 million for the fiscal year ended April 30, 2001, *[revised to $438.2 million]* a decrease of $31.0 million, or 7%. Of this decrease, $12.2 million was from our live and televised entertainment activities and $18.8 million was from our branded merchandise activities. *[Net revenues for FY 2003 were $374.3 million, a 9% decrease. This reflected a $28.1 decrease in live and televised activities and a $7.2 million decrease in branded merchandise activities.]*

Live and Televised Entertainment. Net revenues were $323.5 million for the year ended April 30, 2002 as compared to $335.7 million for the year ended April 30, 2001, a decrease of $12.2 million, or 4%. Pay-per-view revenues decreased by $16.2 million in the year ended April 30, 2002. Pay-per-view buys for the twelve events held in fiscal 2002 decreased by 0.7 million to approximately 6.1 million. Additionally, prior year buys decreased by 0.2 million from 1.2 million in fiscal 2001 to 1.0 million in fiscal 2002. During fiscal 2002, we lost carriage from one of our satellite providers for four months. Revenues from live events decreased by $7.8 million primarily due to lower average attendance in the fiscal year ended April 30, 2002, partially offset by an increase in the number of events and a higher average ticket price. Revenues from the sale of advertising time and sponsorships decreased by $6.7 million to $83.6 million in the fiscal year ended April 30, 2002 as a result of lower sell-thru of inventory within our TNN programming due to a significant contraction in the advertising market and our decreased ratings. These decreases were partially offset by increased revenues from our television rights fees of $18.1 million, which resulted from the full year impact of our agreement with Viacom which became effective September 2000 and new and renewed international television agreements. *[Net revenues were $295.4 million in FY 2003, a $28.1 million decrease, or 9%. Pay-per-view revenues decreased by $20.9 million, as pay-per-view buys decreased by 1.7 million to approximately 5.4 million. Revenues from live events decreased by $1.9 million primarily due to decreased average attendance, despite more events and higher ticket prices. Advertising and sponsorship revenues decreased by $10.7 million to $72.9 million, which were partially offset by a $5.2 million increase in television rights fees.]*

Branded Merchandise. Net revenues were $101.5 million *[revised to $86.1 million]* for the fiscal year ended April 30, 2002 as compared to $120.3 million *[revised to $102.5 million]* for the fiscal year ended April 30, 2001, a decrease of $18.8 million *[$16.4 million, revised]*, or 16%. Licensing revenues decreased by $8.7 million primarily due to lower royalties within the video game and book categories. As a result of lower attendance at our live events, merchandise revenues decreased by

$2.7 million. Revenues from our entertainment complex, *The World,* decreased by $2.5 million due to the decrease in tourism in New York City. *SmackDown! Records* revenues decreased by $2.5 million due to the timing of the release of our albums. New media revenues decreased by $1.2 million due primarily to decreased advertising on our Web site. Publishing revenues decreased by $0.8 million due primarily to a decrease in circulation, offset partially by a price increase for *Raw Magazine.* Offsetting the decreases noted above was an increase in home video revenues of $1.4 million due to an increase in DVD units sold. . . . *[Net revenues were $78.9 million in FY 2003, a $7.2 million decrease. Licensing revenues decreased by $2.6 million, merchandise revenues decreased by $3.8 million, publishing revenues decreased by $1.1 million, while home video revenues increased by $0.2 million, and Internet advertising revenues increased by $0.5 million.]*

Cost of Revenues.   Cost of revenues was $260.2 million for the fiscal year ended April 30, 2002 as compared to $259.0 million for the fiscal year ended April 30, 2001, an increase of $1.2 million. Of this increase, $6.5 million was from our live and televised entertainment activities offset by a decrease of $5.3 million from our branded merchandise activities. Gross profit as a percentage of net revenues was 39% for the fiscal year ended April 30, 2002 as compared to 43% for the fiscal year ended April 30, 2001. . . . *[Loss of revenues was $237.3 million for the fiscal year ended April 30, 2003, and gross profit as a percentage of net revenues was 37%.]*

Live and Televised Entertainment.   The cost of revenues to create and distribute our live and televised entertainment was $194.2 million for the fiscal year ended April 30, 2002 as compared to $187.7 million for the fiscal year ended April 30, 2001, an increase of $6.5 million, or 3%. *[This cost decreased to $190.6 million in 2003.]* This increase was primarily due to an $8.0 million increase in television production costs, resulting in part from *Sunday Night Heat* which had been broadcasted live from *The World* from October 2000 through February 10, 2002. Our television costs include, among other things, production costs, staff related expenses, and freelance crews. Additionally, travel costs increased by $2.9 million due primarily to the full year impact of our leased corporate jet and the added number of performers in our live events. These increases were partially offset by a $1.9 million decrease in participation fees to venues for our live events and a $2.2 million decrease in participation fees paid to our television partners due primarily to lower advertising revenues. Gross profit as a percentage of net revenues was 40% for the fiscal year ended April 30, 2002 as compared to 44% for the fiscal year ended April 30, 2001. The decreased pay-per-view revenues substantially accounted for the majority of the margin decline in this segment.

Branded Merchandise.   The cost of revenues of our branded merchandise was $66.0 million for the fiscal year ended April 30, 2002 as compared to $71.3 million for the fiscal year ended April 30, 2001, a decrease of $5.3 million, or 7%. *[This cost decreased to $46.7 million in 2003.]* Talent royalties decreased by $3.6 million, which was directly related to our lower licensing, merchandise, appearance, and *SmackDown!* records revenues. In addition, the decrease was due in part to lower cost of revenues at *The World* of $1.3 million which was directly related to the decreased revenues in this business. In December 2001, the Company's agreement to sponsor an NHRA racing team lapsed, resulting in a decrease in such costs of $1.7 million compared to fiscal 2001. These decreases were partially offset by distribution fees related to the sale of our home videos through Sony Music Video. Gross profit as a percentage of net revenues was 35% for the fiscal year ended April 30, 2002 as compared to 41% for the fiscal year ended April 30, 2001. The decrease in gross profit as a percentage of net revenues was due to the mix of product within the segment.

Troubled Models

WTA: The League That Wasn't There

Bruce Schoenfeld

Today's WTA Tour is as hollow as an empty can of tennis balls. It consists of a new action logo, a set of rules and regulations, and a board of directors whose members represent a paralyzing array of constituencies.

In its current incarnation, it is part player union, part marketing arm, part governing body, and deficient in all three. It has no title sponsor, no CEO, and no juice. *[Larry Scott has since been appointed CEO.]*

As opposed to, say, the PGA Tour, the WTA doesn't own its tournaments, other than its year-end championship, which has in recent years been cast adrift like an unwanted orphan. Unlike almost every pro league, it doesn't control the domestic television rights to its events.

Perhaps because it has almost nothing to sell, it attracts scant loyalty from its players, who feel a stronger affiliation with their country, their agents, and their coaches than with their governing body. Even the organization's name is hollow. The words behind the acronym, the Women's Tennis Association, officially disappeared several years ago.

"It's a service and governing organization, and that's about it," admitted Dave Larson, the WTA's vice president for marketing and communications. "Right now, our value is, we do the rules and we answer questions."

In the past four years, the WTA has shifted from Corel to Sanex to nobody as its title sponsor, altering its name, its look, and its Web site each time. Since Virginia Slims pulled out in 1994, no title sponsor has renewed a deal. It relocated its season-ending $3 million championship event out of Madison Square Garden to Munich two years ago, then hastily sent it back to North America, where it was met with indifference last November at Los Angeles' Staples Center. Some afternoon sessions were seen by as few as 200 fans.

WTA executives abandon ship with distressing regularity, giving the organization an institutional memory that rarely reaches back more than a year or two. . . .

. . . .

"We're certainly in a weird bind losing our CEO again so soon," said former world No. 1 Lindsay Davenport. "The players feel like we've done everything possible to make the women's tour more popular and keep it the elite women's sport in the world. We really feel like if we had the right leadership, that our sport could dominate most women's sports. I think the players are a little frustrated that more hasn't really happened."

Women's tennis has the story lines, and it has the name recognition. "I defy you to name five athletes on a first-name basis whose worldwide recognition is greater than the top five names in women's tennis," said Arlen Kantarian, the U.S. Tennis Association's chief executive for professional tennis. Yet television coverage is spotty, and accounts of matches are usually buried deep in the nether regions of America's sports sections, hard by the agate type.

. . . .

The WTA's media relations staff, a revolving door of its own, has been upgraded recently with some smart new hires, but it still has little, if any, leverage in getting players to talk about topics that don't strike their fancy. And, really, why should a player do more than the bare minimum in the service of growing the sport, especially if she has her endorsements set?

Up against the desire of agencies like IMG and Octagon to control the flow of information about their players, the toothless WTA doesn't have a chance.

For years, the Virginia Slims Tour gave women's tennis one of the most organized and professional organizational bodies in sports. Since 1994, when Philip Morris withdrew its support, that situation has deteriorated. One mistake has been the frantic search for a title sponsor to replace Virginia Slims. Several times in recent years, the WTA has hired IMG to find a company willing to put its name on the tour. At the end of 1999, with the deadline on its commission fast approaching, IMG signed Sanex, a European personal products company that doesn't even distribute its brands in the United States.

The deal was worth an approximate $1 million a year to IMG in a finder's fee, but it provided little other than a quick cash infusion to the WTA.

. . . . The current idea is to leave the WTA name unadorned and sell a series of regional sponsorships in the ATP model. The first is Porsche, which begins a four-year deal this year.

Like Mercedes, which has had a successful long-term partnership with the ATP, Porsche carries an impressive name that may well help attract other sponsors. But if the next CEO arrives with a different vision, the WTA will find itself back at the beginning yet again, with a fractured constituency heading off in several directions at once.

The continuing tumult makes choosing the right CEO that much more important. But because the organization is all but bereft of major revenue streams, it may be unable to pay the kind of salary that a top-level CEO commands in today's marketplace . . . . far less than the commissioner of any major sport. . . .

"They need a combination of diplomat and promoter," Kantarian said. "A combination of Jimmy Carter and P.T. Barnum — with a little Tony Soprano thrown in."

. . . .

A compelling figure would help alleviate the dissatisfaction expressed by many of the players, who can't understand why magazine covers with Serena Williams and Anna Kournikova haven't translated into greater exposure for the sport, including equal prize money. . . .

. . . .

. . . . But the organization would be well served to heed the words of Jack Kramer, who pulled tennis into the professional era by the force of his own personality. "Tennis cannot possibly ever be run by somebody neutral outside the sport," Kramer once wrote. "Tennis is . . . entirely too complicated, so it must be run by the ones who have been involved in it and know how it works. The obvious trouble . . . is that the people of authority in tennis are bound to have some conflicts of interest."

Those intertwined conflicts have scuttled the good intentions of more than one chief executive. Even as the players push for more prize money, for example, the tournaments look to decrease it so they can remain profitable. Yet most of the tournaments are owned by the same agencies that represent the players.

Between them, IMG and Octagon control 75 percent of the players and 80 percent of the tournaments, as well as several seats on the WTA board. By the time they finish sorting out their vested interests, what's best for the sport usually hasn't been considered.

It doesn't help that the individual tournaments, not the WTA, are able to sell television rights, preventing women's tennis from establishing a consistent presence on any U.S. network. U.S. Open telecasts are shown on one network, . . . Nasdaq-100 championships on another, occasional Tier II WTA events on whichever entity buys the rights.

"I still think the hallmark of any successful sports property is a consistent television package," Kantarian said. "That's what creates more money for athletes, more exposure for sponsors, more value for fans. The current system does not allow that."

Kantarian is attempting to unite the North American WTA and ATP tournaments leading up to the U.S. Open as a series, bundling the television rights to complement those of the U.S. Open. It is telling that he is not required to pay the WTA — or even consult with it, for that matter — in order to do so. To put that in context, imagine buying the television rights to all the Philadelphia Eagles games in November and December without doing business with the NFL.

The WTA also has ceded on-site sponsorship rights to its 2003 tournaments to the owners of the individual events, mostly IMG and Octagon. That's who will stand to prosper even if the economy improves and more local corporate money becomes available.

In essence, the WTA has become the equivalent of a renter in its own home.

"Unless they change the current structure of the board, I don't know how much can be accomplished," said Ilana Kloss, a former player and WTA board member and the commissioner of World Team Tennis. "Everybody is trying to protect their piece of the territory. When you have three player votes, three tournament votes, three outside business advisers, the ITF, and then the CEO, it's very hard to get much done."

One day, perhaps, the WTA will have a CEO with the clout to disentangle the conflicts inherent in the way the organization is governed. Then he or she will negotiate a vested interest in the sport for the WTA — say, 25 percent ownership of every tournament in exchange for continued sanction.

One day a WTA CEO will have the heft to convince players that more media access is in everyone's best interest, and the new era of glasnost that results will spread compelling features about these athletes across the pages of America's magazines and newspapers.

One day women's tennis will be on the same television network all year long, at predictable times.

Until that day comes, however, this nominal organization will continue to operate from the shadows, going nowhere, signifying nothing.

THE MUHAMMAD ALI BOXING REFORM ACT:
THE FIRST JAB AT ESTABLISHING
CREDIBILITY IN PROFESSIONAL BOXING

Scott Baglio

The boxing industry is comprised of many parties who influence and direct a boxer's career. Generally, before a bout can take place, several business transactions must be completed. A boxer must first hire a manager, who then represents the boxer in all business negotiations in exchange for a percentage of the boxer's purse for each bout. The boxer and manager must then negotiate with a promoter, who agrees to provide a certain number of bouts and compensation for each bout, in exchange for exclusive promotional rights to the boxer. Each bout in which a boxer participates is regulated by the boxing commission of the state in which the bout takes place. State commissions are responsible for establishing and enforcing health and safety procedures, and for selecting the judges for nonchampionship bouts. As a boxer advances through his career and becomes successful, his goal is to be ranked as a contender in his weight class, and eventually to be recognized as world champion. Rankings are determined by numerous sanctioning organizations that are responsible for recognizing a world champion and the ten leading contenders in each weight class. Thus, before a bout can successfully take place, numerous interactions take place between the aforementioned parties.

A manager is responsible for handling all of the boxer's business affairs, including the selection of a promoter, the negotiating of contractual terms with that promoter, the selection of a trainer, and approving the opponents for the fighter. Early in a boxer's career, the manager is also usually responsible for paying the training expenses and providing a stipend on which the boxer lives. The manager and trainer are generally compensated by receiving a combined 33.3% of the boxer's purse for each fight. The boxer's purse is contractually guaranteed prior to each bout and is not altered by the outcome of the match. The manager's compensation arrangement provides a major incentive to negotiate shrewdly with the promoter, because more money paid to the boxer translates into more money for the manager.

A promoter contracts with a boxer and agrees to provide a certain number of fights each year at a minimum compensation in exchange for exclusive promotional rights to the boxer. The promoter is the party who assumes the financial risk for the promotion of each match by guaranteeing each fighter a certain purse, and by paying all of the expenses of the promotion. The promoter is not supposed to receive a percentage of the boxer's purse, but rather is compensated by the difference between the total revenues and total expenses for the promotion of a bout. The revenue generated from a boxing match generally comes from three sources. The first is the fight's live gate, which results from either the renting of an arena and sale of tickets, or for major fights that take place in a casino setting, from a site fee paid to the promoter, with the casino maintaining responsibility for the distribution of tickets. The second and most significant source of revenue is the sale of domestic and foreign television rights to the fight. The third source of income is derived from the sale of advertising rights, videocassettes, and fight programs.

A promoter's interests are in direct conflict with those of the boxer, because the less money a boxer accepts for a particular bout, the more profits are available for the promoter. Because this conflict of interest exists, it is essential that the manager negotiate vigorously on behalf of the boxer, and that both parties have relatively equal bargaining power so that one side is not forced to accede to unconscionable contractual terms.

. . . .

Sanctioning organizations are involved only with championship and title-elimination matches. The three major sanctioning bodies are the International Boxing Federation (IBF), the World Boxing Association (WBA), and the World Boxing Council (WBC). Each of these organizations designates a world champion in each weight division, and also ranks the top ten to twenty contenders per division. The power of these organizations is derived from the fact that without their official sanction, a fight cannot be recognized as a "championship bout," and thus is less attractive to both television and the viewing public. For each bout sanctioned by one of these organizations, there is a sanction fee charged that is usually 3% of each fighter's purse. Boxers are also charged specific fees for the selection of officials, including judges and referees. Each organization has its own variation of rules, but generally a champion is required to face the top contender at least once every nine months, and can only defend his title against the top 15 contenders. The designation as number one contender is a very important distinction because only that boxer is guaranteed an opportunity to fight for the title.

For nonchampionship bouts, judges are selected by the state athletic commission responsible for supervising the bout. Although state commission rules make no exception for championship bouts, judges for title bouts are usually named by the sanctioning organization, sometimes subject to the approval of the state commission. Judges are paid by promoters and are provided a specific fee for the bout, along with reimbursement for travel, food, and entertainment. The compensation for each judge is sometimes distributed by the sanctioning organization, and other times by the promoter himself.

A boxer can achieve a successful career only if all of these parties perform their obligations. Because this does not always occur, a boxer can be very successful inside the ring, but have little to show financially if the manager has not vigorously negotiated for his interests. In addition, victories inside the ring can be meaningless if the promoter does not supply the boxer with frequent bouts against respected competition. Boxers are also at the mercy of sanctioning organizations, because without their recognition of a boxer as a top contender, the boxer may never get an opportunity to fight for a championship. Thus, no matter how talented a particular boxer may be, he can only be guaranteed a fair opportunity at success if all parties fulfill their roles in an honest and faithful manner.

DISCUSSION QUESTIONS

1. Compare and contrast the structure of NASCAR with those of the professional sports leagues that you have read about.

2. Why has the growth of the business of NASCAR outpaced the major professional sports leagues?

3. What lessons can the other professional sports leagues learn from NASCAR? What can NASCAR learn from other professional sports?

4. Describe the structure of the PGA Tour.

5. Why do auto racing and golf suffer from a lack of minority participation and fan interest?

6. Describe the athlete development system used by the WWE.

7. Could this program be used in other sports?

8. What potential difficulties could the WWE face as it tries to expand its international operations?

9. How does the manager's role in boxing differ from that of the agent in team sports? What similarities are there?

10. Are the sanctioning bodies in boxing the equivalent of sports leagues? Why or why not?

11. How is the business structure of professional boxing suboptimal? How might it be improved?

CHAPTER 11

STORY-UP LEAGUES AND NICHE SPORTS

START-UP LEAGUES AND NICHE SPORTS

INTRODUCTION

Beyond the four major professional sports leagues and individual sports such as NASCAR, golf, and tennis, there are a number of start-up leagues and niche sports competing for a space on the professional sports landscape. A recent count of those entities attempting to do so found baseball teams competing in 19 affiliated and independent minor leagues, four basketball leagues, four football leagues, six hockey leagues, five soccer leagues, two lacrosse leagues, and softball, team tennis, and volleyball leagues. In addition to those disparate leagues are athletes competing in individual sports such as horseracing, rodeo, various motor sports, fishing, billiards, bowling, and, perhaps most importantly, action sports, embodied largely in festival-type atmospheres such as the X Games and Gravity Games.

The varying sports discussed in this chapter can be described as belonging to at least one of four categories, with some accurately described by multiple categories. The first of these categories is Minor Leagues, with the league not representing the top level of competition in its sport. Minor leagues may serve three functions: player development, entertainment, and grassroots marketing. In a player development function, athletes are trained for a potential future career at the sport's top level of competition. Examples of leagues serving in this capacity are the affiliated minor leagues in baseball, with Major League Baseball teams involved in a relationship with teams at the AAA, AA, A, and Rookie levels, which form a major league team's player development system. In the sport of indoor football, the Arena Football 2 (af2) league serves in a similar capacity.

Second, a minor league may serve an entertainment function, with a focus on providing fans with low-cost, family entertainment at the stadium. While af2 and affiliated minor league baseball both serve in this capacity as well, independently owned and operated minor league baseball leagues act purely in this function instead of also serving as a vertically integrated player development system. The proliferation of unaffiliated independent minor leagues over the past decade indicates that entrepreneurs believe that the demand for low-cost, family entertainment outstrips the available supply of these entertainment options.

Third, minor leagues may serve as a grassroots marketing function. Primarily located in smaller markets, affiliated minor leagues have historically provided large segments of the population located in secondary and tertiary markets with access to professional sports that would be otherwise unavailable. Thus, along with television, they help allow interest in the sport of baseball to continue in these markets. Recently, independent minor league franchises have been established in close proximity to major media markets, providing a lower-cost alternative to the Major Leagues and allowing segments of the population to have increased access to a sport that may be available geographically but not economically.

Leagues in the remaining categories of emerging and niche sports often aspire to become the next major professional sports league in the United States. The second category that these leagues fall into is those emerging and niche sports that represent the top level of competition in their respective sport. In addition, these sports often have large numbers of recreational participants. This combination of high level competition and participation would seem to bode quite well for the future of professional competition in these sports. However, this has yet to translate into financial success in anything but action sports. Examples of leagues fitting into this category are Major League Soccer (MLS), the now defunct Women's United Soccer Associaton (WUSA), the Major League Lacrosse, World Team Tennis, the Women's National Basketball Association (WNBA), and professional softball and volleyball leagues. The challenge for sports industry leaders is to convert the large number of participants in these sports into commercial users. It remains to be seen whether this can be accomplished, or whether the popularity of these sports is limited to participation rather than spectating.

A third category of emerging and niche sports involves leagues that are indoor variations of traditionally outdoor sports. Seeking to capitalize on the popularity of established outdoor leagues, entrepreneurs have created separate indoor leagues that utilize a different (and usually less-talented) pool of athletes than the outdoor leagues, and adopt modified playing rules to tailor the sport to a smaller playing field. Typically played in hockey and basketball arenas, these leagues allow the operators of these facilities to host events when the facility otherwise would have been unused, thereby generating additional revenues in the forms of rental payments and ancillary activities. Examples of these leagues include the Arena Football League (AFL), Major Indoor Soccer League (MISL), and the National Lacrosse League. Though it is possible for these leagues to achieve financial success, it is unlikely that they will ever eclipse their outdoor counterparts in revenues or popularity.

The fourth category of emerging sports is the gender-specific leagues that offer women the opportunity to participate in their own league in a sport in which there is a separate men's league. These leagues are attempting to take advantage of an opportunity created by the increased buying power of women resulting from societal changes and the increased female participation rate and interest in sports resulting from Title IX. None of the women's leagues that have been established — including the WNBA, WUSA, World Team Tennis, and various women's football leagues — have been profitable thus far, and most have mounted substantial losses. The future viability of these sports on the professional level is dependent upon a change in the financial status of the leagues, which must translate women's increased buying power, participation, and interest in sports into involvement in their products as paying spectators, television viewers, and consumers of league sponsors.

In general, emerging sports are monetized from three different sources: gate receipts and concessions, broadcast-related revenues, and sponsorships. The importance of these revenue sources varies according to the sport. For example, minor league baseball teams rely very heavily on gate receipts and concessions sales, while many action sports such as the X Games do not charge an admission fee. Correspondingly, broadcast-related revenues are important to action sports and the Arena League and insignificant to most minor league baseball teams. Sponsorships may impact an emerging sport in several ways. At both the national and local levels, sponsorships can serve two roles: They provide the revenues and/or products-in-kind that are necessary to support team and league operations, allowing teams and leagues to conserve their valuable resources. In addition, sponsorships can provide emerging and niche leagues with invaluable exposure when activation of the sponsorships occurs, allowing the sport to receive broad distribution at little cost. For sponsors, relationships with emerging and niche sports allow them to attempt to reach a particular demographic in a cost-effective manner. The appeal of these sports is their lower cost and the quality of the individuals reached rather than the quantity reached, because the overall audience is generally small compared to established sports. Emerging sports can thus prove to be a good value for sponsors.

Similar to other businesses, start-up costs for emerging sports leagues can be substantial, with expenditures reaching well into the millions of dollars. Once initiated, the primary operating costs for emerging sports are the playing facility, administration, and athletic talent. In recent years, many start-up leagues have adopted a unique, single-entity structure in order to help them control costs. While the single-entity structure has been somewhat effective in doing so (particularly with respect to expenditures on athletic talent), thereby allowing sports to survive the start-up phase, it is sufficiently flawed such that it may be an ineffective long-term structure. *[See Chapter 2 for further discussion of the single-entity structure.]*

For an emerging sport to achieve long-term financial success, it must possess several characteristics. First, the sport must be appealing to an audience. While it seems obvious that a sport lacking audience appeal is likely to fail, the determination of what makes a sport attractive to an audience is quite unclear. At a minimum, it must be interesting to watch highly skilled participants compete in the sport, and the general population must have a significant participation rate in the sport. In other words, the sport must be fun to watch and people must be interested in playing it to allow for a large enough following. While the presence of both of these elements does not guarantee success, the absence of either one will ensure long-term failure. Second, a television presence is very important to emerging sports. Television provides a sport with the exposure needed to grow interest. This exposure drives attendance figures upward. The increased attendance, in turn, can lead to increases in both local and national sponsorship revenues and ancillary, facility-driven revenues such as concessions and parking. Sponsorship revenues can be increased, because a larger audience is reached, making an affiliation with the sport more valuable. Facility-driven revenues can be increased because a larger audience size will lead to an increasing consumption of concessions and parking spaces.

Continuous improvements in technology have led to a dramatic increase in the number of cable television networks. The increased size of the cable universe has created broadcasting opportunities for sports that were previously unavailable, as these networks need programming content. Sports are attractive to them because of the potentially strong demographics, even if the overall audience size is small. Thus, the opportunity for emerging sports leagues to receive broad television exposure is greater than ever.

A third important trait for emerging sports to possess is deep-pocketed ownership. Not unlike other entrepreneurs, owners in emerging sports must be both willing and able to withstand substantial start-up costs and significant operating losses in at least the first several years of business. Unwilling or undercapitalized ownership leads to franchise instability or suboptimal management practices, either of which can lead to the ultimate failure of the entire league enterprise. It is important that the league consider this issue when selecting ownership. It is perhaps better for the league to begin play with a smaller number of well-financed franchises than with a larger number of thinly capitalized ones. In addition, the sport must consider the amount of the entrance fee that it will charge to prospective owners. The franchise fee must be sufficient to support league operations yet not lead to owners becoming overleveraged.

Fourth, the sport must access appropriate markets. This is dictated by the desire to be located in major markets, the regional popularity of the sport, and ownership preferences. These determinants of franchise location often conflict. Location in major markets historically has been the primary determinant of franchises in emerging sports leagues. The impetus behind this idea is the notion that media outlets are only interested in broadcasting sports with broad audience appeal, which is more likely in large population centers. Having placed itself in these centers, the league would thus be able to sign a lucrative national television contract. In addition, attendance is likely to be higher in larger markets. Location in major markets also allows for increased attention from both the national media and potential advertisers, as it lends a sense of cultural relevance to the sport that makes it worthier. However, there is a hubris associated with locating an emerging sport in major markets. Operational costs are likely to be significantly higher in major markets, and there is increased competition for fan and media attention in the form of other sports franchises. This may render the emerging sport irrelevant on the landscape of the large markets.

Location that is driven by the regional popularity of an emerging sport may allow the sport to have large attendance revenues and local sponsorship revenues. Operational costs are likely to be lower in smaller markets, and the existing interest will allow the sport to avoid many of the costs associated with developing a fan base. This is the equivalent of "fishing where the fish are." In addition, there is likely to be less competition for fan and media attention in the local marketplace. Yet location that is based on a sport's regional popularity will likely place it in smaller markets where it is unattractive to national broadcasters. This could relegate the sport to fringe status, with revenue growth limited because of the regional nature of the sport. This could also make the sport less appealing to investors.

A final determinant of franchise location in emerging sports leagues is investor preference. An owner may choose to eschew major markets or regions where a sport is popular in favor of another location. Sports ownership has a high consumption value, and factors such as an individual's ego, desire to foster civic pride in the city of residence, or an opportunity to exploit the potential synergies available through the existing ownership of other investments may dictate location in a particular market. However, an owner's preferences may conflict with the best interests of the sport. An emerging sport requires investors, but it must consider the long-term impact of its decisions. The short-term investment in the league by a willing and able individual may have negative repercussions in the long term if the sport is located in inappropriate markets.

Finally, an emerging sport must have strong leadership. While it is desirable to have an independent leader free from any involvement with any individual team or athlete that could create a conflict of interest, it is just as important that the leadership possess other characteristics. The leadership must have the vision to guide the long-term direction of the league. The leadership must also be able to build consensus among the entity's ownership interests while addressing their conflicting agendas; coordinate and negotiate leaguewide broadcasting, marketing, and sponsorships; and generate enthusiasm for the sport.

While the aforementioned elements are necessary for an emerging sport to be successful, the athletes participating in these sports remain an essential component. Unlike many of the athletes competing in established sports, the athletes competing in emerging sports typically earn low salaries. There are several reasons for this disparity. First, emerging sports do not generate sufficient revenues to justify significant expenditures by ownership on athlete compensation. Second, athletes competing in emerging sports typically do not unionize. There are some exceptions to this rule, as athletes competing in the WNBA, MLS, Arena Football League, and minor league hockey and baseball have done so. These efforts to seek increased bargaining power through a collective voice may be short-sighted, however. While unionization may result in increased compensation for athletes, it may lead owners to incur increased operating losses. Ultimately, those increased operating losses may lead to the market failure of the emerging sport, which would render the union members unemployed. Third, the organization of emerging sports into single-entity structures decreases athlete compensation. Since athletes are signed by the league itself and then allocated to a particular franchise, this precludes competition for athlete services among league teams. Thus, single-entity leagues are a monopsony, as there is only one purchaser of athletic talent. This prevents athlete compensation from reaching competitive levels.

The Arena Football League (AFL) is an emerging sports league that was founded in 1987 but only recently has seen an improvement in its financial situation. Most AFL clubs have struggled financially since the league's inception, with numerous teams sold after suffering staggering losses, including the Orlando Predators, a franchise that lost nearly $6 million in 2002 before its sale in 2003. Many other teams that were poorly managed or undercapitalized were either folded or relocated, with a migration to larger markets from second-tier cities. The AFL's financial situation first began to improve in 1999, when the National Football League purchased a three-year option to buy a 49% stake in the AFL. Though the option to buy was not exercised, three individual NFL owners purchased AFL expansion teams at a 50% discount, and three others possess options to buy AFL expansion teams in the future. This lent the AFL a sense of credibility that has proven quite valuable. The revenue sources for AFL teams are similar to other emerging sports. Beginning in 2003, the AFL entered into a three-year television deal with NBC that is the first of its kind in professional sports and could bring the AFL the exposure that it needs to become the fifth major league. The agreement requires NBC to rebroadcast 70 regular-season AFL games and five playoff games. The financial aspect of the deal is unique. NBC does not pay the AFL a rights fee in the initial three-year contract, which it has the right to renew in perpetuity. The parties agreed to a revenue-sharing partnership in which NBC receives the first $8–$10 million in revenues to offset its production costs. After NBC's production costs are covered, the AFL receives the next $3 million in revenues, after which the parties share all advertising revenues equally. In its first year, the advertising revenue stream was sufficient to allow the parties to reach this final level of revenue sharing. The contract offers little risk to NBC, and allows it to avoid the untoward situation of developing the AFL into a valuable property and then having to pay an inflated rights fee in the future as a result of the league's increased value. The AFL deal also provides NBC with a near-guarantee that it will not lose money on the deal and potentially high returns if the league becomes popular with viewers. While this is unlikely to occur, the potential upside cannot be ignored. For the AFL, the NBC exposure should lead to an increase in attendance, which would increase the value of local sponsorships. Combined with the additional revenues yielded by the television contract, this should lead to an increase in franchise values. This strategy seems to be working already. Franchise values for expansion teams have increased from $500,000 in 1998 to approximately $12 million in 2003. The AFL is conceding its long-term television revenues for short-to-medium term growth and exposure. This will benefit both franchise owners and NBC, as the network will reap 5 percent of the sale price for any franchise that is sold for more than $12 million. While, as to be expected, television ratings for AFL games on NBC are low, AFL per game attendance increased from 9,155 in 2001 to 9,957 in 2002. This 9% increase has been followed by a 20% increase in 2003, to 11,945, or 77.7% of capacity. Finally, AFL sponsorships have also increased, with four league-wide sponsors paying fees in the mid-six-figure range. It will certainly be interesting to see how the AFL grows in the future, as its ownership of its minor league af2 in small markets provides it with a grassroots marketing effort and the possibility of expansion. The AFL could potentially achieve international growth, with Europe and the Pacific Rim as targets for future expansion.

In the aftermath of the 1999 Women's World Cup, WUSA initiated play in 2001 with an initial $40 million commitment to the venture. WUSA's investors were seeking to exploit the opportunity created by the combination of this highly successful event, the high participation in the sport for girls, the increased interest in sports by women, and the substantial buying power of women. Similar to other start-up leagues, WUSA was organized as a single-entity structure with teams located in eight cities. With revenues derived from attendance, sponsorships, and television, WUSA struggled financially, losing $80 million since its inception. Spurred by a 30% decrease in costs, the league's losses decreased 45% from 2001 to 2002, yet WUSA remained far from profitability. In 2003, the players agreed to cooperate with WUSA's cost-saving measures. The league's financial situation was considered dire enough that WUSA's top players accepted a 25% pay cut from $80,000–$85,000 to $60,000. They were not alone in their sacrifice, as the league's average salary decreased approximately 20% to $37,000 and roster sizes were decreased by two. Including complimentary tickets, league attendance decreased from 8,103 in 2001 to 6,957 in 2002, a 14% decrease. While these figures exceeded league expectations, attendance needed to improve for the WUSA to survive. League-wide sponsorship revenues were between $5.5 million and $12 million, with two charter sponsors paying between $1 million and $2.5 million each, and seven league sponsors paying between $500,000 and $1 million each, depending on the sponsorship category and details. The league's television revenues and ratings were below expectations. After the 2001 season, in which games broadcast on the highly visible cable networks TNT and CNN/SI resulted in 0.3 Nielsen ratings, WUSA's shift to the better time slots offered by the relatively obscure PAX network yielded a 0.1 rating in 2002, as it competed head-to-head with MLS broadcasts on ESPN on a weekly basis. While it is debatable whether WUSA partnered with the appropriate channels, these moribund ratings had to improve if WUSA games were to continue to be broadcast on broadly distributed cable networks. Several league games were broadcast on ESPN2 in 2003. Perhaps an even greater challenge for WUSA was to differentiate itself from two other competitors — MLS and the WNBA. Though WUSA and MLS competed in the same sport during the same calendar months and their games were often broadcast at the same time, they targeted largely different audiences. MLS consumers are primarily young men of various ethnic heritages, while WUSA targeted families and specifically younger females. In this sense, the WNBA seemed to be the most significant competition for WUSA. With both leagues competing for the same consumers during the same time of year, the marketplace could not support both the deeper-pocketed WNBA and WUSA.

Action sports have emerged as the most significant of all of the sports described in this chapter. These sports, which include snowboarding, skateboarding, BMX biking, in-line skating, and aerial skiing, as well as their various subdisciplines, have entered the sporting mainstream but have been the subject of little academic research. Exciting, fast-paced, and dangerous, action sports are particularly appealing to the lifestyle of 12 to 34-year-old males, a target market that is highly desirable to advertisers. Thus, it should not be surprising that skateboarding and snowboarding are the fastest-growing sports among 7 to 17-year-olds. Not coincidentally, youth participation and interest in most team sports is slowly declining. In addition, television ratings for action sports are steadily increasing, while the opposite is occurring in team sports. While the overall audience for action sports is still smaller, its desirable demographics and increasing participation rates and interest levels should concern the leaders of the traditional "stick and ball" sports. Faced with a potential long-term erosion of their fan bases as these youths mature into adults, the traditional sports cannot merely hope that there will be a migration back to them when they become adults or that action sports will fade away. Recognizing this, each of the "big four" sports leagues has responded to the threat posed by action sports by adopting grassroots marketing programs aimed at youths.

Long participated in on an informal basis and considered to be part of the counterculture, action sports began to enter the mainstream in 1995 with the creation of the Extreme Games by ESPN. An amalgamation of competition in nine different sports, the 8-day, Olympic-style event provided ESPN with its own low-cost programming during a lull in professional sports, when only baseball is playing its regular season. Simultaneously, the Extreme Games introduced an organized platform for action sports. Largely ignored and mocked by both broadcasters and leaders of mainstream sport, ratings were surprisingly strong, resulting in a 1.0 Nielsen rating on ESPN and 0.5 on ESPN2. In 1996, ESPN changed the name to "X Games" in order to gain greater audience appeal and allow for easier international marketing. As the popularity of the summer event increased, the Winter X Games were added in 1997 to fill a similar void in ESPN's programming and to further exploit the increasing demand in the marketplace. The X Games are monetized though television advertising and sponsorships. ESPN's ownership of its programming inventory allows it to reap directly the revenues generated from the sales of advertising and sponsorships. Top-level sponsors pay $3 million and second-tier sponsors pay $1 million for the Summer X Games. ESPN regularly sells out all of its sponsorship packages, and generated $30 million in sponsorship revenues in 2001, along with an additional $10 million in advertising revenues. Despite total event attendance that regularly exceeds 200,000 in the summer and approximately half of that in the winter, ESPN currently does not charge an admission fee and thus does not generate revenue from ticket sales. Nonetheless, the X Games have generated annual profits of approximately $12 million over the past several years. ESPN has expanded the X Games, brand globally by adding competitions in Latin America, Asia, and Europe. It has also added global team competitions, as well as qualifying events for all X Games competitions, Junior X Games, and touring skatepark events.

Given its extraordinary success, it should not be surprising that competitors to ESPN's X Games have emerged. Founded in 1999, the Gravity Games are jointly owned by Octagon and Primedia and offer action sports in an Olympic-style competition that is similar to the X Games. Unlike the X Games, the Gravity Games charge an admission fee of $12, and generated $1 million in ticket sales in 2002. Other entities have focused on presenting action sports tours, with live music acts joining in with the athletic demonstrations in festival-like events. NBC plans to start its own action sports property. Despite these efforts, the X Games remain the dominant brand in action sports.

Athletes competing in action sports receive compensation primarily in the form of endorsements, with top athletes earning over $1 million a year and very good athletes earning between $250,000 and $500,000. Athletes also receive income in the form of prize money earned in competitions, with the X Games offering $1 million and the Gravity Games offering $900,000 in prize money in 2002. However, this pales in comparison to the profits generated by the owners of these events.

Action sports now appear to be a permanent part of the sports landscape, but the genre has not yet achieved first-tier status. Action sports have strong demographics that attract top-tier sponsors, an increasing participation rate, a year-round presence, and strong product extensions such as video games, music, and toys. Its lifestyle appeal is undeniable. However, the lifestyle that action sports embraces has strong anti-corporate roots. Its notoriously fickle fans and athletes have traditionally shunned the mainstream and could abandon the mass presentation and media coverage of action sports as the genre becomes further embraced by the corporate world. In addition, action sports are unlikely to generate revenues comparable to established sports properties until this occurs. The irony is that the same corporate embrace that could send revenues skyrocketing could also lead to the demise of action sports. Thus, leaders of the action sports properties face an interesting dilemma: how is big business made out of a sport whose fan base, participants, and athletes have traditionally avoided big businesses. In addition, it is likely that the various individual sports that comprise the action sports genre will attempt to survive independently of one another. This may lead to a fragmentation of the marketplace that could cause the failure of several individual sports. It may be that the marketplace is sufficiently sized such that it can only support these sports when consumed collectively.

This chapter looks at various start-up leagues and niche sports in detail. In the first selection, Arthur Johnson provides a broad perspective of the business of minor league baseball, reviewing the structure of minor league baseball, league and team operations, and the relationship between the minor leagues and Major League Baseball. The next excerpt takes the reader from a sport with a long history to a relative newcomer, the Arena Football League. Insight into this emerging sport is gained by reviewing the annual report of a publicly traded member franchise, the Orlando Predators. In the next selection, a helpful explanation of the structure that is typical of many of the emerging sports leagues is given by the United States Court of Appeals for the First Circuit in its consideration of litigation involving Major League Soccer, a league that has adopted the controversial single-entity structure. In the final article, Elyachar and Moag describe the history of the growth of women's sports and explain the financial models of the WNBA and WUSA, before its demise.

MINOR LEAGUES

MINOR LEAGUE BASEBALL AND LOCAL ECONOMIC DEVELOPMENT

Arthur T. Johnson

THE BUSINESS OF MINOR LEAGUE BASEBALL, THE MAJOR LEAGUES, AND COMMUNITY OWNERSHIP OF STADIUMS

Governance and Structure of Minor League Baseball

The National Association of Professional Baseball Leagues governs . . . professional baseball leagues that are popularly referred to as the minor leagues. Each league has its own officers, who manage their league's affairs under the jurisdiction of their league's bylaws, the National Association Agreement, and the Professional Baseball Agreement (PBA). The PBA governs the relationship between the major leagues and the minor leagues as well as certain specified actions of minor league clubs, the minor leagues, and their governing body. . . .

The minor leagues are organized according to the level of the players' skills. Leagues are classified, from highest to lowest: AAA ([three] leagues, including the Mexican League), AA (three leagues), A (seven leagues), and Rookie (five leagues. . .). Single A-level leagues are subclassified . . . as A-Advanced (three leagues), A (two leagues), and short-season A (two leagues). Rookie leagues also are subclassified as Rookie-Advanced . . . and Rookie. . .

. . . Cities hosting minor league teams vary greatly in size. This diversity in size exists within leagues and within each level of play. With the exception of the AAA leagues . . . minor leagues tend to be geographically compact. This reduces the travel costs of league members.

. . . .

Nearly all minor league games are played in the evening, except those played on Sundays. The weather is extremely important financially to minor league teams. Rained-out games are difficult to make up because there are few open dates in the teams' schedules. As a result, many teams do not play their full schedule of revenue-producing home games in a season.

The Renewed Popularity of Minor League Baseball

Interest in minor league baseball on the part of fans, prospective owners, and local governments was rekindled in the 1980s. . . .

Minor league baseball suffered severe financial problems and loss of fan interest in the 1950s. . . . This was a consequence of several factors, including more telecasts of major league games into minor league territories, relocation of major league franchises into minor league territories, and increased leisure-time options for the public. The number of minor league teams declined from 448 teams (in fifty-nine leagues) in 1949 to 152 teams in 1960. Since 1960, the total number of teams remained stable for two decades but in 1982 began to increase slowly.

. . . .

Renewed fan interest in minor league baseball is largely due to the . . . team owners' emphasis on the entertainment aspects of the business. It was not surprising, therefore, that team representatives . . . described their business as entertainment, not baseball, when asked what business they were in. . . . They do not scout, draft, or sign players. A team's managers and coaching staff are assigned by the major league club and take their instructions from that organization, not from the minor league team's owner or general manager. In fact, the latter have little to do with what happens on the field of play. Team representatives stated uniformly that they provide family entertainment — "good clean fun." This is exemplified by the variety of promotions used to attract fans. Virtually every club uses promotions of some sort. These include performances by the San Diego Chicken . . . fireworks displays, cow milking contests, concerts after the games, and innumerable giveaways (e.g., bats, balls, batting gloves, helmets, seat cushions, and coffee mugs).

Attendance at minor league games, especially in the lower-level leagues, is not necessarily related to the quality of team play. Most team representatives agreed that if a team is not competitive, attendance will be hurt, but a winning team is not necessary to attract large crowds. One owner estimated that fewer than half the fans attended a game for the contest itself.

Team representatives identified their competition not solely as other sports activities, but as any opportunity that competes for the individual's leisure time, whether it be major league games on television; participant sports, such as softball or hiking; or more passive entertainment, such as movies and concerts.

In the 1940s and 1950s, the major league teams were the principal owners of minor league teams, especially at the AAA, AA, and A levels. For example, major league teams owned or controlled through working agreements 79 percent of the AAA teams, 88 percent of the AA teams, and 80 percent of the A teams in 1952. Overall, "independent" owners owned 46 percent of the minor league teams, concentrated mainly in the lower-level leagues, which were then classified B, C, and D.

There is evidence that the financial success of minor league teams helped subsidize the major league owners before the 1950s. This changed in the 1950s, and by the 1970s, tired of losing money, the major league clubs were selling their minor league teams. Combined income statements of the major league clubs show that the minor league teams sustained annual operating losses ranging from $459,746 to $954,050 per team, beyond other player development expenses, during the period of 1974–79.

Franchises, which were virtually given away or sold for no more than a few thousand dollars only a few years ago, are . . . attracting offers of . . . several million dollars for AA-level and AAA-level teams.

Communities are pursuing franchises just as eagerly as team owners are seeking communities to host their teams. . . .

. . . This portends a significant restructuring of the minor leagues and offers the potential for cities without a franchise to obtain one and for cities with an A-level or AA-level franchise to host a team at the AAA level. . . .

Sports entrepreneurs periodically propose the creation of new minor leagues. Investors and communities express interest, even though these leagues would lack affiliation with the National Association and would be without any major league team affiliations.

Franchise Ownership

A team owner must be awarded a franchise from a league for a team to operate and compete as a minor league team. The franchise prevents another team from operating within the team's "home territory." . . .

If an owner of a franchise in a higher-level league wants to operate within another team's home territory, that encroaching owner's league can "draft" the territory for its use. This effectively forces the original lower-level franchise from the territory, but with "just and reasonable" compensation.

Minor league teams are owned by private individuals, major league teams, nonprofit organizations, community residents organized as stockholders, and local governments. As interest in minor league baseball has increased, new owners have appeared, ranging from . . . celebrities . . . to small investment groups and Japanese corporate interests. Several individuals and ownership groups own and operate more than one team. Minor league teams owned by major league teams tend to be at the lower levels. . . .

To ensure financial stability of franchises, the Professional Baseball Agreement [PBA] imposes formal requirements on new owners. It requires that they demonstrate "financial viability" by possessing, and having the ability to maintain, an equity-to-liabilities ratio of at least 55 to 45 and "a ratio of current assets to current liabilities of at least 1.0 after any injection of new capital by the new owner." New owners also are required to submit to the league a three-year operating budget and business plan for the franchise. The PBA also requires that the franchise "be owned and/or managed by individuals with strong ties to the local community" and that new owners have "a strong interest in maintaining the stability of the franchise in its existing location." Any intent to relocate a franchise after a purchase must be revealed to the league.

The Player Development Contract

A standard Player Development Contract (PDC) is negotiated between the National Association and the major leagues as part of the Professional Baseball Agreement. The PDC details the relationship (or "working agreement") between the major league teams and their minor league affiliates. Although there are slight variations between league levels, the PDC applies uniformly to all minor league teams. No PDC can be negotiated individually by a team owner or modified by a major league team or minor league team. . . .

In nearly all cases, major league teams provide their minor league affiliates with players. It is possible, however, for a minor league franchise owner to operate without a PDC. This occurs only in A-level and Rookie-level leagues. In such instances, owners will stock their team with players from a number of major league teams or sign their own players, including foreign players. . . These teams are referred to as cooperatives in the former case and independent clubs in the latter case. It is diffi-cult to operate profitably as a cooperative club or as an independent club because the owner must cover a significantly higher percentage of the team's expenses and because the quality of the team's players is not likely to be as high as that of the teams with which it competes. . . .

. . . .

. . . The new PBA forces minor league teams and their leagues to assume greater financial responsibility for the National Association's operating expenses. The major league clubs, however, are obligated by the new PBA to pay all players' salaries (including those of AAA players) and players' meal money for away games. The major league clubs also must purchase . . . equipment for the minor league teams. The National Association and its members will also receive [revenue] from a joint licensing program with Major League Baseball Properties (MLBP), which controls trading card and logo rights. Since this is the estimated value of trading card revenue that minor league teams are capable of generating, some thought it represented no new income. Others believed that MLBP's access to national and international markets would produce much more revenue than individual clubs could produce by themselves.

Minor league team representatives projected that these changes in the PDC would cost minor league teams an estimated $25,000 to $100,000 per season, depending on the league level, how much each club previously invested in equipment, and how the National Association distributes its financial obligations. Whatever the amount, the new PBA and PDC have imposed greater costs on minor league teams.

Team Finances

A minor league team depends on several sources for its revenues. . . In general, it is difficult to assess the profitability of minor league teams, but it is fair to conclude that although not all teams are profitable, it is possible to make a significant profit operating a minor league franchise.

Revenue sources include the sale of season tickets and luxury boxes (if a stadium has such), out-field fence signs advertising a product or business, advertisements in a team program, and a broad-casting package (and telecasting, in a few cases). These sales take place before the season begins and provide the owner with a pool of cash with which to begin the season's operations. . . . Typically, two dozen or more signs will be on a stadium's outfield fence. Parking revenues also can be appreciable, if a stadium has parking facilities and if a team retains the parking fees.

Another source of revenues is ticket sales during the season. . . .

A park will frequently be "bought out" for a night by a community organization or business, and tickets will be given at no charge or minimal charge to customers, clients, employees, or community residents. This occurs more frequently at the lower-league levels than at the AAA or AA levels. There is a difference of opinion among team operators as to whether giving tickets away in this manner or in other ways devalues the product and hurts attendance in the long run. Some are afraid that if "buyouts" are too frequent, fans will not buy tickets but will wait for the free ones.

High attendance is desirable not only for the ticket revenue, but also for the revenue from the sale of concessions and novelties. The size of concession revenues greatly influences whether a team is profitable. In many cases, concessions account for more than 25 percent of a team's revenues. In some circumstances, tickets can therefore be given away, and a profit will still be realized.

As noted, much of a minor league team's operation is subsidized by its major league affili-ate. . . . A minor league team's labor expenses are principally for office staff and part-time stadium help (e.g., vendors, ticket takers, and clean-up crews). Many team employees work on a commission basis, earning income from advertising and ticket sales. Travel expenses are a significant portion of a team's operating expenses, as are advertising and promotion expenditures.

The ownership or lease of a stadium is a critical factor in a team's financial equation because many of a team's expenditures, other than rent, are mandated by the PDC. To the extent that the new PBA threatens the profitability of minor league teams, team owners will look to their local government-landlords to improve stadium rental terms, because rent is one of the few expense factors that can be reduced without undermining revenue potential.

Arrangements for a playing facility, therefore, are the crux of the relationship between a local government and a minor league team and are a critical factor in determining a team's profitability.

Stadiums, Leases, and Community–Team Relations

. . . .

Minor league stadium leases tend to be short-term. . . .

There is no typical minor league stadium lease. Some communities subsidize the cost of operating a stadium for the team (e.g., utilities, water, field maintenance). Other communities seek to recover the stadium's operating costs [and] impose a rental fee, which is often a flat fee or a percentage of revenues derived from ticket sales.

Communities tend not to share directly in revenues that are produced by minor league teams at the stadiums. . . .

Very few communities, regardless of the league level of their team, reported generating sufficient revenues from professional baseball to cover the operational costs of the stadium. . . .

Lease negotiations offer the opportune time for a team to make demands on its host community. . . . The most frequent demands centered on improved lease terms . . . and stadium improvements or stadium expansion. . .

. . . .

There is evidence that team demands for stadium improvements are both justified and effective. Communities that reported renovating their stadiums most frequently cited facility deterioration . . . and team demands . . . as the reasons renovation was undertaken. . . .

Although team demands were not always accompanied by a threat to relocate . . . 40 percent of seventy communities that reported being the target of team demands said they were threatened with relocation. . . .

Franchise relocation is a reality in minor league baseball; no league level is immune. . . .

Communities . . . overwhelmingly asserted that maintaining professional baseball is a priority . . . in spite of the financial costs of hosting a minor league team and team demands for additional public expenditures. Respondents reported a general agreement among local government officials that the presence of minor league baseball in their communities is important. . .

A majority . . . of the reporting communities were without other professional or college sports activities (i.e., no major league sports, no other minor league sports, no training facilities for major league teams, and no college or university sports). Nearly a third . . . of the communities reported being without a community theater, a symphony orchestra, and a zoo. . . . Minor league baseball, therefore, offers many communities, especially smaller communities, a significant entertainment opportunity. . . . Historically, the minor leagues made baseball the *national* pastime. The place of minor league baseball in the nation's small communities, however, became threatened when the minor leagues declined and local economies weakened. . . .

. . . The ability of small communities to retain their teams continues to be threatened by the economics of minor league baseball. . . .

The Major League–Minor League Nexus

The ability of local officials to determine the degree of risk entailed in investing in a minor league baseball facility is complicated by the fact that minor league baseball's financial health is dependent on major league baseball and by the fact that minor league baseball does not have independent decision-making authority for many issues.

. . . The major league affiliate heavily subsidizes a minor league team's operations. This subsidy was reduced by the new PBA because major league team owners believed that minor league teams had become very profitable businesses at their expense and minor league team owners no longer needed subsidies. . . .

If the economic health of Major League Baseball suffers, the consequences will be felt at the minor league level. A consolidation of a major league team's minor league system would be an obvious way to reduce costs. . . . Whether a minor league team can be financially viable over the long term without a PDC is debatable.

Another issue is one of control. The new PBA recognizes the right of the commissioner of Major League Baseball to intervene in decisions of the National Association and to reverse a decision if it is deemed to be not in "the best interests of baseball." All proposed franchise sales and transfers must be registered with the commissioner, who in certain instances can reject a sale or transfer. Minor league clubs must submit an audited financial statement to the commissioner upon request. Eighteen months notice must be given to the commissioner if a minor league intends to expand or reduce the number of its teams. The commissioner can overturn the National Association's approval of such expansion or reduction, as he can any approval of a proposed franchise relocation. The commissioner also must approve any grant of protected territory . . . to a minor league club.

It is unclear how this power will be used by the major leagues . . . but history does not provide reasons to be optimistic. . . .

. . . .

Approvals of franchise relocations will not be withheld at the major league level if such relocations promise improved playing facilities, better player accommodations, or more fans in front of whom to play. In fact, major league clubs are likely to pressure their minor league teams to relocate if they are unable to acquire modern facilities from their host communities. . . .

Finally, local officials should be aware that the increased number of televised Major League Baseball games has an impact on minor league baseball. Minor league baseball's popularity declined after World War II, partly because major league games were televised in the minor leagues' territories. . . .

CONCLUSION

This analysis makes clear that the governance structure and the economics of minor league baseball are responsible for making stadiums, and the arrangements through which minor league teams occupy them, the essence of the relationship between a team and its host community. The conditions that influence franchises' financial viability and the supply and stability of franchises not only fix attention on stadiums and the terms of their rental but also warn against long-term assumptions about such arrangements.

Limited revenue sources and expenditures mandated by the . . . PBA focus team owners' attention on stadiums and negotiated lease terms as an obvious means to increase revenues and decrease operating costs. Team owners identify their options as the reduction or elimination of rent, acquisition of a new stadium that will attract more fans and permit more revenue streams, or relocation to a larger market within the region where the league operates. As current owners sell their franchises either to take advantage of inflated value or to avoid the less favorable economics . . . , new owners must seek ways to recoup their investment. These owners justify their stadium demands by citing their large investments in their teams.

The history of the minor leagues is not one of stability. Local officials who understand the history, structure, and economics of minor league baseball, especially of its lower-level leagues, will view skeptically stadium proposals based on assumptions about the long term. The relatively large number of minor league teams does not imply greater franchise availability for cities without teams, because minor league teams relocate within specific regions, not nationally as major league teams do. At the same time, the short term of minor league leases suggests the potential for greater franchise instability.

This analysis also suggests why minor league teams are not significant economic forces within communities. In nearly all cases, the economic impact of a minor league team will be minimal, given attendance levels, payroll size, number of employees, media interest, and other factors. The fact is minor league teams have relatively small operating budgets . . . especially in the lower-level leagues, and best fit the analogy of a small business. Also, it is reasonable to assume that smaller communities may not be able to capture all of the potential economic benefits that a sports operation produces; leakage (i.e., expending or investing money earned or generated within a local economy beyond local boundaries) is probably greater in communities with minor league teams than in those with major league teams.

This is not to deny that minor league teams contribute to local economies, but it is to warn against expecting them to have the same impact that major league teams have. . .

NICHE LEAGUES

ANNUAL REPORT FOR THE FISCAL YEAR ENDED SEPTEMBER 30, 2002

The Orlando Predators Entertainment, Inc.

PART I

Item 1. Description of Business

. . . .

History of the AFL.   The AFL governs the arena football teams that comprise the League and sell team memberships ("Memberships"). The AFL's first season commenced in 1987. Between 1987 and 2002, the League grew from four teams to 16 teams. For the 2003 season, 16 teams will play including an expansion team in Denver, Colorado. Since 1992, announced League attendance has grown from 736,000 to over 1,228,000 (including playoff games). Game broadcasts during this period have included local, regional, ESPN, ESPN2, TNN, and ABC coverage. In the 2002 season, 25 games were broadcast on national cable television stations, including ABC's live broadcast of Arena Bowl XVI. From 11 million television households in 1994, the AFL reached over 27.5 million households in 2002.

In March 2002, the League entered into a broadcasting agreement with NBC under which NBC will broadcast 71 AFL games, including four regional games each Sunday, the AFL playoff games and the Arena Bowl. NBC and the League will divide the advertising revenue equally after payment to NBC of its production costs for the broadcasts. Broadcast begins in the 2003 season, which the AFL agreed to reschedule to run from February through June each year. NBC (i) became a revenue-sharing partner of the AFL, (ii) has the rights to renew the broadcasts in perpetuity, and (iii) is entitled to share in any increased value from the sale of an AFL team, including the Predators, for more than $12 million.

Arena Football and the Arena Football League.   . . . .

Four teams were fielded for the League's inaugural 1987 season. By 1991, the League had eight teams and had played exhibition games in London and Paris. In 1992 and 1993, the League fielded 12 teams and 10 teams, respectively, with some games televised on the ESPN cable network. For 2002, 16 teams played in the League.

AFL games are generally played in an indoor basketball/hockey sports arena which offers fans climate-controlled conditions and a more intimate view of the game. As a result of the smaller playing field, the rebound nets, and a general emphasis on offensive play, Arena Football games are generally high scoring, fast-paced action contests.

AFL game attendance has risen over the years with total fan attendance exceeding 1,228,000 in the 2002 season. Per game announced attendance averaged approximately 10,000 during the 2002 season. . . . League research indicates that approximately 66% of AFL viewers are male and 34% are female with 60% of such viewers under the age of 35. In terms of education, we believe that 47% have college or graduate degrees, 28% have some college attendance, and 87% hold at least high school diplomas.

AFL player salaries are subject to a collective bargaining agreement between the League, its member teams and the Arena Football League Players' Association (AFLPA). . . . For the 2002 season, the Predators' players' total compensation was approximately $1,398,000 in the aggregate.

The Predators provide a $250,000 occupational health, accidental death, and disability insurance policy. Each team is required to pay the first $35,000 of claims for an injured player up to an aggregate of $356,000 for the two Florida based AFL teams provided through a carrier.

Rules of Arena Football.   . . . . There are eight players on the field for each team as part of a 24-man active roster. Players play both offense and defense with the exception of the kicker, quarterback, an offensive specialist, two defensive specialists, and a kick returner.

. . . The average AFL football game is played in approximately two hours and 30 minutes compared to over three hours for an NFL game.

. . . .

Regular Season and Playoffs.   Prior to the 2003 season, following two pre-season games, the regular AFL season extended from April to August, with each team playing a total of 14 regular season games against teams from both conferences. . . .

. . . .

Gate Receipts, AFL Assessments, and Distributions.   AFL teams are entitled to keep all gate receipts from preseason home games, regular season home games, and playoff home games. Teams do not receive any gate receipts from away games except that visiting teams are reimbursed for hotel expenses by the home team. Each team is required to pay an annual assessment to the AFL which is generally equal to the team's share of the League's annual operating costs and each team is contingently liable for other team membership purchases, team repurchases by the League, and League litigation. During the 2002 and 2001 seasons, League assessments were $466,092 and $419,000, respectively. . . . Each team's assessment is generally funded by its share of revenue derived from the League's national television contracts, from the sale of AFL licensed merchandise, and from revenues generated by the League's sale of expansion team memberships. Each visiting team participating in the playoffs is reimbursed for hotel expenses and receives a fixed payment of $45,000 for each playoff game and $50,000 for the Arena Bowl.

AFL Licensing.   The AFL operates a League licensing program on behalf of its teams. Under the program, product manufacturers sign agreements allowing them to use the names and logos of all AFL teams, the AFL itself, and AFL's special events (including playoffs and the Arena Bowl) in exchange for royalty and guarantee payments. OPE [Orlando Predators Entertainment] did not receive any licensing revenue in 2002. For the year ended September 30, 2001, OPE's share of net revenues from licensing was $80,000. In 2002 our share of net revenue from the League (the "Team Share") was equal to 1/24 of the AFL's net revenue. . . . League assessments are also based upon the Team Share. Each team is also permitted to license its club identified products locally for sale at its arena, at team owned and operated stores, and through team catalogs. We purchased two nonvoting equity interests in 1998, and in 2002 our Team Share was 4% together with an additional 8% net revenue interest earned from our two nonvoting interests. Our Team Share and net revenue interest for 2003 is 4.5% and 9%, respectively.

League Governance.   The AFL is generally responsible for regulating the conduct of its member teams. The AFL establishes the regular season and playoff schedules of the teams, and negotiates, on behalf of its members, the League's national and network broadcast contracts. Each of the AFL's members is, in general, liable on a pro rata basis for the AFL's liabilities and obligations and shares pro rata in its profits. Under the Bylaws of the AFL, League approval is required to complete a public offering of any team's securities and for the sale or relocation of a team.

The AFL is governed by a Board of Directors, which consists of one representative from each team. The Board of Directors selects the AFL Commissioner, who administers the daily affairs of the AFL including interpretation of playing rules and arbitration of conflicts among member teams. The Commissioner also has the power to impose sanctions, including fines and suspensions, for violations of League rules. David Baker has been the Commissioner of the AFL since 1996. . . .

arenafootball2 League.   In August 1999 the AFL established the arenafootball2 League ("af2") to be comprised of smaller market teams playing under an 18-week, 120-game schedule. af2 teams are primarily located in the midwest and southeast and consist of 28 teams expected to play in the 2003 season, down from 34 teams in the 2002 season.

In October 2000 the af2 acquired substantially all of the assets of the Indoor Football League. . .

Restrictions on Ownership.   The AFL Charter and Bylaws contain provisions which may prohibit a person from acquiring the Common Stock and affect the value of the Common Stock. In general, any acquisition of shares of Common Stock which will result in a person or a group of persons holding 5% or more of our outstanding Common Stock will require the prior approval of the AFL, which may be granted or withheld in the sole discretion of the AFL. The prospective purchaser would be required to submit an AFL application, in form prescribed by the AFL, providing certain information relating to that person's background. Upon receipt of such application, the AFL has the right to conduct an investigation of the prospective purchaser. In addition, the AFL may condition its approval upon the execution, delivery, and performance by the prospective purchaser of such documents as the Charter or Bylaws shall prescribe. If a prospective purchaser obtains the AFL's consent to acquire a 5% or more interest in OPE, such prospective purchaser will be required to acknowledge that the purchaser will be bound by the applicable provisions of the AFL Charter and Bylaws. AFL approval is not required for private placements of our securities.

In addition, no person who directly or indirectly owns any interest in an AFL team, may own, directly or indirectly, a 5% or more interest in any other team, without the prior approval of the AFL. The AFL Bylaws also contain provisions which prohibit team owners from engaging in certain activities, such as wagering on any game in which an AFL team participates. AFL players and referees and employees of the AFL and its member clubs (other than OPE) are not eligible to purchase or hold Common Stock. . . .

The grant of a security interest in any of the assets of OPE or the Predators or any direct or indirect ownership interest in OPE, of 5% or more, requires the prior approval of the AFL, which may be withheld in the AFL's sole discretion. AFL rules limit the amount of debt that may be secured by the assets of, or ownership interests in, an AFL team and require that the parties to any secured loan that is approved execute an agreement limiting the rights of the lenders and the team (or stockholder) under certain circumstances, including upon an event of default or foreclosure. . . .

. . . .

Current Operations of OPE.   . . . Revenue from the Teams' operations results from the sale of tickets to the Teams' home games, the sale of advertising and promotions to sponsors, the sale of local and regional broadcast rights to Predators' games, the sale of merchandise carrying the Teams' logos, and concession sales at Predators' home games. Revenue from our League ownership results from our share of all League revenue, primarily consisting of League contracts with national media organizations, expansion team Membership fees, national corporate sponsorships and League merchandising sales.

In March 1998, we entered into an agreement with the AFL pursuant to which we agreed to purchase two additional Team Shares in the League (which then represented 2/19 of the League's revenue) for $6,000,000. Under the terms of the agreement (which was amended in March 2000), we receive a minimum of $480,000 per year of distributions from the League including principal and interest until total distributions reach $6,000,000. Distributions from our two additional Team Shares are accounted as a reduction of debt until paid in full. When the debt is repaid in full, then the Team Shares will be recognized as revenue.

Ticket Sales.   . . . . Under the AFL Bylaws, OPE receives all revenue from the sale of tickets to regular season and preseason home games and no revenue from the sale of tickets to regular season and preseason away games. . . .

. . . .

Advertising and Promotion.   OPE generates revenue from the sale of advertising displayed on signs located throughout the arenas in which our teams play, and through other promotions utilizing the teams' name or logos. In addition, we market team sponsorships to local and regional businesses which provide a combination of advertising rights, promotional rights, and VIP ticket privileges. Advertising rights include the use of corporate logos within the arenas, commercials on radio and television, advertisements in fan magazines, display of the sponsor's name on signs in the arena, public address announcements, the inclusion of customer names on team posters, and the like. Promotional rights include banners displayed in the teams' VIP rooms at the arenas, availability of blocks of seats for specific games, the use of the teams' logos, and autographed helmets. VIP privileges include high priority seating selections, parking passes, VIP room passes, and travel packages, which include attendance at team away games.

Local and Regional Television, Cable, and Radio Broadcasts.   We contract with local and regional media to cover our teams' games. Most of the revenue we receive from these contracts is in the form of barter credits and the amounts of such revenue are negligible.

. . . .

Sale of Merchandise.   We generate a small amount of revenue from the sale of merchandise carrying our teams' logos (primarily athletic clothing such as sweatshirts, T-shirts, jackets, and caps).

Telemarketing.   From time to time we use telemarketing techniques to improve our teams' ticket sales.

. . . .

The Collective Bargaining Agreement.   In 2002 the League entered into a Collective Bargaining Agreement ("CBA") with its players. Under the terms of the CBA, the League has agreed with the NFLPA (the players' bargaining unit) to a salary cap equal to the greater of $1,643,000 per team, or 50% of defined gross revenue ("DGR") as defined in the CBA, increasing to the greater of $1,921,633 or 63% of DGR by 2007. Minimum per player salaries are $1,484 per game.

. . . .

The af2 does not have a collective bargaining agreement with its players. af2 player payroll, which is paid through the league, is limited to $87,000 per season.

TD Waterhouse Center.   The Predators have played in the TD Waterhouse Center, which has a seating capacity of approximately 16,000, since 1991. In March 1998, OPE signed a five-year lease (with an additional five-year option) with the TD Waterhouse Center commencing in the 1998 season at approximately the same per game rental (approximately $15,000 per game) as its previous lease, but which provides OPE with an approximately 20% share of revenue generated from food and beverage concessions in exchange for OPE reducing ticket prices by approximately 10% to 20%, depending upon seat location. OPE also receives a rebate against rent of $3 per person (up to $10,000) for games in which attendance exceeds 9,000 persons.

. . . .

Competition.   Our teams compete for sports entertainment dollars with other professional sports teams and with college athletics, high school athletics, and other sports-related entertainment. Our teams also compete for attendance and advertising revenue with a wide range of other entertainment and recreational activities available in their market areas.

. . . .

Risk Factors.   . . . .

The League's new game schedule may reduce our ticket sales and sponsorships.

Under the terms of the League's new broadcast contract with NBC, most AFL games will be played on Sunday afternoons rather than Friday or Saturday nights, and the season will be played between February and May, rather than between April and July. Arena football fans may prefer Friday and Saturday night games to Sunday afternoon games, thereby reducing game attendance. Moreover, our corporate sponsors may prefer the April to July schedule, rather than the new February to May schedule which puts arena football games in direct competition with NBA basketball games. In such event, corporate sponsors may reduce their sponsorships and advertising expenditures.

We did not receive any League distributions in 2002 and may not receive any distributions in the future.

In 2002 we were entitled to receive an aggregate of 12% of all distributions made by the League to its teams and other share owners. However, due to increased League expense, and costs of litigation, the League did not make any distribution in 2002 and may not make distributions in future years.

. . . .

Our teams compete for sports entertainment dollars with other professional sports teams and with college teams and with other sports-related entertainment.

We are subject to League obligations.

The membership agreements with the Arena Football League generally make the Predators and other teams of the AFL liable on a pro rata basis for the debts and obligations of the AFL. Any failure of other members of the AFL to pay their pro rata share of any such debts or obligations could adversely affect the Predators by requiring us to make additional payments on behalf of failing or defaulting teams. To date, we have not been required to pay any material debts or obligations of the AFL. The success of the AFL and its members depends in part on the competitiveness of the teams in the AFL and their ability to maintain fiscally sound operations. Certain AFL teams have encountered financial difficulties in the past, and there can be no assurance that the AFL and its teams will continue to operate. If the AFL is unable to continue operations, the Predators and the other teams forming the AFL would be unable to continue their own operations. In addition, the Predators and their personnel, as well as our af2 teams, are bound by a number of rules, regulations, and agreements imposed upon them by their Leagues as well as by national television contracts. Any change in these rules, regulations, and agreements will be binding upon our teams and their personnel, regardless of whether they agree with such changes, and it is possible that any such change could adversely affect them.

We will be subject to increased competition as a result of AFL and af2 expansion.

The AFL and af2 may add additional teams in the future. While such expansion affords the AFL the opportunity to enter new markets and increase revenue, it also increases the competition for talented players among AFL teams. Expansion teams are permitted to select in an expansion draft designated unprotected players playing for existing AFL teams. There can be no assurance that the teams will be able to retain all of the team's key players during an expansion draft or that the rules regarding the expansion draft will not change to the detriment of the teams. In addition, we may receive less revenue from the AFL as the result of League expansion since AFL teams share equally in the revenue generated from national television contracts and sale of AFL merchandise.

. . . .

We depend upon the competitive success of our teams for ticket and merchandise sales. Our financial results depend in part upon our teams achieving game winning success. By achieving and maintaining such success, we expect to (1) generate greater fan enthusiasm, resulting in higher ticket and merchandise sales throughout the regular season and (2) capture a greater share of local television and radio audiences. Failure to participate in the playoff games would deprive our teams of additional revenue that may result from sales of tickets for home playoff games and from media contracts. Revenue is, therefore, significantly adversely affected by a poor game winning performance, especially involving losses of home games.

. . . .

The success of our teams depends, in part, upon the teams' ability to attract and retain talented players. There can be no assurance that our teams will be able to retain players upon expiration of their contracts or obtain new players of adequate talent to replace players who retire or are injured, traded, or released. Even if our teams are able to obtain and retain players who have had previously successful football careers, there can be no assurance of the quality of their future performance.

Fraser v. Major League Soccer

United States Court of Appeals for the First Circuit

In the wake of a successful World Cup USA, MLS was officially formed in February 1995 as a limited liability company ("LLC") under Delaware law. The league is owned by a number of independent investors (a mix of corporations, partnerships, and one individual) and is governed by a management committee known as the board of governors. Some of the investors are passive; others are also team operators as explained below.

MLS has, to say the least, a unique structure, even for a sports league. MLS retains significant centralized control over both league and individual team operations. MLS owns all of the teams that play in the league (a total of 12 prior to the start of 2002), as well as all intellectual property rights, tickets, supplied equipment, and broadcast rights. MLS sets the teams' schedules; negotiates all stadium leases and assumes all related liabilities; pays the salaries of referees and other league personnel; and supplies certain equipment.

MLS has the "sole responsibility for negotiating and entering into agreements with, and for compensating, Players." In a nutshell, MLS recruits the players, negotiates their salaries, pays them from league funds, and, to a large extent, determines where each of them will play. For example, to balance talent among teams, it decides, with the nonbinding input of team operators, where certain of the league's "marquee" players will play.

However, MLS has also relinquished some control over team operations to certain investors. MLS contracts with these investors to operate nine of the league's teams (the league runs the other three). These investors are referred to as operator/investors. . . . Each operator/investor has the "exclusive right and obligation to provide Management Services for a Team within its Home Territory" and is given some leeway in running the team and reaping the potential benefits therefrom.

Specifically, the operator/investors hire, at their own expense and discretion, local staff (including the general managers and coaches of their respective teams), and are responsible for local office expenses, local promotional costs for home games, and one-half the stadium rent (the same portion as MLS). In addition, they license local broadcast rights, sell home tickets, and conduct all local marketing on behalf of MLS; agreements regarding these matters do not require the prior approval of

MLS. And they control a majority of the seats on MLS's board, the very same body which runs the league's operations. Among other things, the board is responsible for hiring the commissioner and approving national television contracts and marketing decisions, league rules and policies (including team player budgets), and sales of interests.

The operator/investors also play a limited role in selecting players for their respective teams. While the operating agreements provide that the operator/investors will not bid independently for players against MLS, they may trade players with other MLS teams and select players in the league's draft. Such transactions, however, must follow strict rules established by the league. Most importantly, no team may exceed the maximum player budget established by the management committee.

In return for the services of the operator/investors, MLS pays each of them a "management fee" that corresponds (in large part) to the performance of their respective team. The management fee equals the sum of one-half of local ticket receipts and concessions; the first $1,125,000 of local broadcast revenues, increasing annually by a percentage rate, plus a 30% share (declining to 10% by 2006) of any amount above the base amount; all revenues from overseas tours; a share of one-half the net revenues from the MLS Championship Game and a share of revenues from other exhibition games.

The remaining revenues of the league are distributed in equal portions to all investors. Thus, while the investors qua investors share equally in the league's profits and losses, the individual team operators qua operators fare differently depending at least in part on the financial performance of their respective teams. It bears mentioning, however, that neither the league nor, apparently, any of its teams has yet made a profit. *[In 2002 the Columbus Crew became the first MLS team to earn a profit.]*

Although the league retains legal title to the teams, the operator/investors may transfer their operating rights, within certain limits, and retain much of the value created by their individual efforts and investments. Investors may transfer their ownership stakes and operating rights to other current investors without obtaining prior consent; transfers to outside investors, however, require a two-thirds majority vote of the board. For its part, MLS may terminate any operating agreement on its own initiative if, by a two-thirds vote of the board, an operator/investor is determined to have failed to act in the best interests of the league. If so, it must still pay such operator/investor fair market value for its operating rights and ownership interest.

THE GROWTH OF WOMEN'S SPORTS

Rachel Elyachar and Lauren Moag

OVERVIEW

. . . The growth of women's sports has manifested itself in the form of "big" dollars being spent on/earned in women's individual sports, such as tennis, and a raised profile for women's professional sports leagues, such as the WNBA and the WUSA.

History

. . . .

Historically, there have been few sports leagues for women, and fewer still that were considered even mildly successful. One league in particular, created before Title IX, paved the way for future women's professional sports leagues. The All-American Girls Professional Baseball League was created in 1943 in order to cover the costs of maintaining ballparks when minor league teams discontinued play due to World War II. Philip K. Wrigley devised the league's original plan, which was to maximize the use of major league parks that, by definition, were used only 50% of the season. However, the league eventually would begin play in vacant minor league parks in Kenosha (Wisconsin), Racine (Wisconsin), Rockford (Illinois), and South Bend (Indiana). The idea of a women's sports league was initially not well received and did not get off the ground until Wrigley agreed to fund half the cost of operating each team and all cost overruns. The host cities agreed to pay the other half of projected operating costs.

The league's initial success led to a round of expansion before its second season. At that point, the league was so popular among fans that civic groups in each of four expansion cities chose to finance their own franchises rather than have Wrigley pay half of the expenses as he did with the original teams. In addition, Wrigley, along with Paul Harper and Branch Rickey, helped finance two teams that would play in major league parks, in accordance with Wrigley's initial plan. However, the larger size of the parks and the lack of local support resulted in these teams being not nearly as successful as the teams that played in the minor league parks.

As a reflection of the times, the league emphasized femininity and beauty, making charm school and cosmetics lessons mandatory for all players. Initially, the league's creators believed that it was necessary for the players to be physically attractive in order to attract fans. However, fans quickly recognized the talent of the players, and the beauty factor became less relevant to the success of the league.

Interest in the AAGPBL peaked in 1948, though the end of World War II and the return of the men who played major and minor league baseball foreshadowed the end of the first professional women's sports league. The All-American Girls Professional Baseball League folded in 1954. . . .

. . . . *[The authors' discussion of Title IX is omitted. This topic is addressed in Chapter 17.]*

. . . In 1973, a year after Title IX was passed, Billie Jean King started the Women's Tennis Association (WTA). King was the first woman to earn more than $100,000 as a professional athlete, a feat she accomplished in 1971. The following year, she won the U.S. Open, but received about $15,000 less than the men's winner did that year. Angered by this disparity, she said she would refuse to participate in future tournaments if the men's and women's prize money was not equal. As a result, in 1973, the U.S. Open became the first major tennis tournament to award equal prize money to male and female players. Shortly thereafter . . . King defeated Bobby Riggs in the "Battle of the Sexes" in September of 1973.

Women's Individual Sports

. . . Today, tennis remains one of the only professional sports in which women can earn more than men. To that end, in 2002, Serena Williams . . . earned more than any other athlete in the sport. . . In terms of sponsorship dollars, women and men generally receive comparable compensation. In some instances, women are paid more by their sponsors than are men. For example, Venus Williams signed a five-year contract with Reebok worth $40 million; Pete Sampras, whose contract with Nike was recently terminated, received an estimated $40 million over 8 years.

. . . .

Women's Team Sports

In contrast to women's individual sports, and women's tennis in particular, women's professional team sports endeavors have been largely unspectacular at best, and failures at worst. To date, women's professional team sports have not captured the attention of the mainstream sports fan — neither at the box office nor on television. Recently, however, there are indications that the tide may be turning. Bolstered by growing interest at the grassroots/amateur levels — for instance, women's college basketball, women's World Cup soccer, women's Olympic ice hockey — leagues such as the Women's National Basketball Association and the Women's United Soccer Association have begun to establish a foothold on the professional team sports landscape.

BASKETBALL AND THE WOMEN'S NATIONAL BASKETBALL ASSOCIATION (WNBA)

Encouraged by the success of professional women's tennis in the 1970s, professional women's basketball made its initial foray into the sports universe. The Women's Basketball League (WBL), which operated from 1978 to 1981, was the pioneer basketball league for women. The league initially featured 8 teams, and expanded to 14 teams before its second season, a move that proved in retrospect to be too aggressive. The WBL barely finished its third and final season before collapsing under the weight of this premature expansion.

It would not be until fifteen years later that women's professional basketball would reemerge in the form of the American Basketball League (ABL), which played from 1996 to 1999. Alas, the ABL folded after four seasons due in large part to escalating player salaries that the league could not support.

The WNBA also originated in 1996, and was more cautious than the ABL with regard to player salaries and other expenses. . . .

The WNBA differs from its male counterpart, the NBA, in many ways, beginning with its appeal to typical sports sponsors. The NBA is a well-established league that generates significant income from sponsors, while the WNBA is thus far largely without its own sponsors and primarily dependent upon NBA sponsors . . . for its national income. An additional, positive differentiating factor for the WNBA is its fan base. The gender breakdown of attendees of WNBA games is approximately 70-30 female–male, and the television audience is about 50-50 female–male, with a large number of non-adult viewers. The WNBA fan base allows advertisers to focus on a different, more female-oriented audience . . . Contributing to the differentiation between the leagues' respective fan bases are ticket prices. The average ticket price for a WNBA game (about $15), is designed to keep fans interested and willing to pay to see games. The relatively inexpensive ticket price also encourages entire families to come to games, whereas families are much less likely to go to NBA games, for which the average ticket price is more than $50.

Television rights fees, however, are perhaps the most significant difference between the leagues. The NBA has recently signed a $4.6 billion deal with ABC and ESPN, whereas the WNBA has recently signed a revenue-sharing deal with ABC, ESPN, ESPN2, and Oxygen. Whereas television rights fees account for a considerable portion of the NBA's revenues, the lack of a lucrative deal leaves the WNBA with much less financial flexibility. WNBA Commissioner Val Ackerman has indicated that the WNBA pays the broadcasting and production costs for its games, and has explained that sponsorship sales are the main source of revenue for the league.

The WNBA has estimated collective annual revenues of $85 million. Each team's revenue comes primarily from concessions, local sponsorships and ticket sales. The teams must pay the salaries of coaches and staff, traveling expenses, promotion and advertising. Each franchise must also contribute to the league to cover league expenses, such as players' salaries.

The WNBA has reportedly lost money in its first six seasons, and is continually referred to as an "investment" by Ackerman and David Stern, the commissioner of the NBA. The NBA assists the WNBA financially by giving a reported $8 million annually to subsidize the league, and will continue to do so according to Stern . . . Ackerman claims that "some teams have made a small profit over the years," and she has expressed confidence that, in the future, the league will be a successful, moneymaking entity. Maloof Sports and Entertainment, the owner of the Sacramento Monarchs, has reportedly experienced six figure losses every year of the team's existence. . .

. . . .

. . . The NBA Board of Governors has recently elected to reorganize the ownership structure of the WNBA. Specifically, the Board of Governors approved the transition of WNBA teams away from centralized ownership and local operating agreements to local ownership. Following the reorganization, the NBA owner who has previously operated each WNBA team will also own that team. Two NBA team owners, however, have declined the right to own the WNBA team in their markets. A third WNBA team, the Utah Starzz, will be relocated to San Antonio for the 2003 season.

The reorganization also calls for WNBA teams to be located in non-NBA markets. In conjunction with this decision, non-NBA team owners will be permitted to pursue ownership of WNBA teams in both NBA and non-NBA markets. . . .

THE WOMEN'S UNITED SOCCER ASSOCIATION (WUSA) *[WRITTEN PRIOR TO THE LEAGUE'S DEMISE.]*

Inspired by the U.S. National Team's successful runs at the 1996 Olympics and the 1999 Women's World Cup, which was played in the United States and drew more than 90,000 to the championship game at the Rose Bowl, John Hendricks, Chairman and CEO of Discovery Communications, founded the WUSA in early 2000. The WUSA consists of eight teams — the rights to each were acquired by an individual or a media company for $5,000,000 in February 2000. Investors include such companies as Cox Enterprises (Atlanta) and Cox Communications (San Diego), Time Warner (New York and North Carolina), and Comcast (Philadelphia). P.H. Soccer, Inc. owns the Boston team and half of the San Jose team. John Hendricks owns the Washington, D.C. team and half of the San Jose team. . . .

The $40 million invested was intended to sustain the league through its first five seasons, though the WUSA — only two years old — has already lost more than the initial $40 million. It should be noted that Major League Soccer (MLS), the WUSA's male counterpart, has not fared much better, losing $250 million between 1996 and 2001. Despite the losses, the WUSA has no plans to suspend play. . .

. . . .

The WUSA's revenue comes from ticket sales, television rights, and sponsors. Initially, the WUSA signed a four-year television contract with TNT and CNN/SI, though the contract was terminated after the 2001 season. The WUSA subsequently signed a two-year contract with PAX TV (financial terms were not disclosed). Despite relatively low ratings, the WUSA has indicated that it is not particularly concerned due to the financial support it receives from its well-known investors and sponsors. . . .

Valuing a Women's Sports League Franchise

Neither the WNBA nor the WUSA has generated enough revenue to earn a profit in its short history, though both leagues remain confident that they will be financially successful in the future. Absent a better measure, perhaps the most telling factor in determining the leagues' values is their revenue. Whereas the WUSA has declined to reveal league revenue, the WNBA's revenue is reported to be $85 million; if that number is divided by the sixteen teams in the league, then revenue per team is approximately $5.3 million. For illustrative purposes, using a revenue multiple range of 2.0× to 2.5×, the implied valuation range of a WNBA team is approximately $10.6 million to $13.3 million.

CONCLUSION

Given the similarities between the attendance and revenues of teams in the WNBA and the WUSA and those in leagues such as the Arena Football League and minor league baseball, it is not unreasonable to think that WNBA and WUSA franchise transactions could occur within the valuation ranges implied by those men's leagues. *[The Connecticut Sun of the WNBA were purchased for $10 million in 2003.]*

That said, the valuation analysis herein is based on 2.0× to 2.5× revenue multiples — multiples that are not based on an examination of comparable transactions as such comparables do not yet exist. To the extent that a 2.0× to 2.5× revenue multiple is not appropriate, or that a revenue multiple in general is not the most accurate measure of WNBA (or WUSA) franchise values, our valuation and conclusions may be premature.

DISCUSSION QUESTIONS

1. What are the advantages and disadvantages of a single-entity league structure?

2. Does a single-entity structure make sense for an established league? Why? Does it make sense for a start-up league? Why?

3. How might MLS and WUSA have partnered to grow the sport of soccer in the United States?

4. What obstacles do you see to this growth occurring?

5. What can major league professional sports learn from the minor leagues and start-up leagues?

6. How are the outside forms of competition for major league teams similar to and different from those faced by minor league teams? Explain.

7. How do revenue sources of minor league teams differ from those of major league teams?

8. What dynamics have allowed Arena Football to be successful while other niche sports have failed?

9. What can other emerging and niche leagues learn from the AFL–NBC deal?

10. What are the various risk factors faced by AFL franchises?

11. What will it take for action sports to achieve first-tier status?

CHAPTER 12

SPORTS FRANCHISE VALUATION

INTRODUCTION

Whether for a prospective sale, a bankruptcy, or leveraging debt, at various times it is imperative to place an accurate value on a sports franchise. As this chapter reveals, valuation in sports is no simple task. As evidenced by the numerous sales of both established and expansion teams in the four major North American sports leagues for ever-increasing amounts of money, the market for professional sports franchises continues to be robust. While the study of firm and asset valuation has been a common area of research in finance, there has been little application of these principles to professional sports franchises. Valuation of professional sports franchises is much different than valuations of most other assets. This is likely because of the idiosyncratic nature of sports franchises, which are somewhat comparable to the valuation of art in that, ultimately, beauty is in the eye of the beholder. Thus, there is significant volatility in the marketplace. The total financial return to owners of professional sports franchises is determined by calculating a team's profitability and capital appreciation. While the franchise's ability to earn a profit and its likelihood of increasing in value in the long term play important roles in determining a team's present value, there are numerous other factors that impact franchise value.

The nature and quality of a team's facility arrangement is one factor. Given the increase in the number of new, revenue-generating facilities in the last 15 years, it is important to gauge the impact that these stadia and arenas have on franchise values. The building boom that has occurred since the late 1980s has resulted in new stadia for approximately three-fourths of the teams in the four major North American sports leagues. The presence of a playing facility with a lease arrangement that allows the team to generate and retain significant revenues from luxury boxes, club seats, signage, naming rights concessions, parking, and outside events at a low cost (i.e., little rent) will drive franchise values upward. The absence of such an agreement will have the opposite effect.

In addition, a team's media contracts impact its value. The size of the league-wide television contract provides guaranteed revenues to each team and indicates the nationwide popularity of the sport; the size of the local television contract secured by a club varies greatly, provides a team with revenue that is largely unshared and is an indicator of a team's popularity in its home market. The increased involvement of teams in the ownership of regional sports networks not only provides the opportunity for the team to dramatically increase the revenues earned from local broadcasting but also provides the team owner with a valuable asset against which capital can be raised. Therefore, the size of a team's national and local television contracts will be factors in determining its value.

The league in which a franchise plays impacts its value in several ways. As previously mentioned, the league's national broadcasting contract guarantees revenue to the franchise. Second, the league's revenue-sharing agreement can either enhance or hinder the value of its franchises. A league with a high degree of revenue sharing can ensure the long-term viability of its franchises by guaranteeing them monies every year and protecting them against a shortfall in nonshared revenues in any particular year. However, this may harm the short-term value of franchises that generate significant amounts of revenue by redistributing their wealth to other franchises. Third, a league's collective bargaining agreement with its athletes can affect the value of its franchises. A settled labor situation with a mechanism for control over player compensation benefits owners by providing them with an assurance that their revenue-generating games will continue to be played. A mechanism for controlling player compensation is vital in that, similar to most businesses, a sports franchise's ability to predict and control its costs is a very important aspect of its operations. The single greatest cost to professional sports franchises is player salaries; a salary cap provides a team with a degree of cost certainty by dictating the amount of money that it can spend on athlete compensation. Though loopholes and exceptions to these compensation containment systems have somewhat eroded their benefits, they still enhance team values.

There are several other factors that can impact franchise value. The debt accumulated by a team requires consideration. Team debt typically arises when an owner purchases a team and when the team must pay for part, or all, of the construction costs of a new facility; this obligation may be onerous and can ultimately cause transferal of a team for a lower cost. It is for this reason that it is often better for a sports franchise to lease rather than own its playing facility, especially if the lease terms are advantageous. A team's debt is often guaranteed by a revenue stream accruing from its facility. This negatively affects a team's cash flow, as the revenues that would otherwise be used for team operations must be utilized to service the debt. In an attempt to protect its members, each league has enacted rules that limit the amount of debt that can be accumulated by a team. However, there are numerous exceptions to these debt limitation rules, and they are rarely enforced.

The tax benefits associated with ownership of professional sports franchises have an impact on value, as well. *[See Chapter 4 for further discussion of this topic.]* The real estate value of the sports franchise must also be considered. A real estate developer may purchase a sports franchise as part of a larger development scheme upon which profits can be realized, even if the team itself may suffer operating losses. This will increase the transfer price of the franchise. The nature of the seller will affect team value as well. A corporate owner typically must sell the franchise fairly quickly in order to appease analysts or shareholders, while an individual owner, realizing the significant consumption value associated with team ownership, must be compensated for the loss of the psychological premium that team ownership brings. Consequently, an individual owner is less likely to sell the team with any degree of urgency and can thus afford to "hold out" until obtaining the desired price. Thus, the purchase price of a team sold by a corporation may be lower than a comparable franchise sold by an individual.

The quality or reputation of a team as measured in terms of its win–loss record also may impact value. Though seemingly irrational due to the cyclical nature of sports, a team's recent performance record may factor into the valuation equation.

The market size of the city in which a team is located may be important because of its potential effect on the size of the team's fan base, local television contract, local sponsorship and advertising agreements, and the number of large corporations and wealthy individuals in the city with the ability to afford luxury seating. In addition, the degree to which the market is saturated by the presence of other professional sports franchises may impact a team's value. Despite this, market size is generally not considered to be a major driver of franchise values because of the impact of the other aforementioned factors.

It is for all of these reasons that valuation of professional sports franchises is considered more of an art than a science. The selections used in this chapter shed additional light on the valuation process. In the first article, Leeds and von Allmen establish the background for the discussion that ensues in the remainder of the chapter. In the second excerpt, Eric Thornton offers an in-depth analysis of the valuation of the sports franchise's intangible assets. This is followed by Scott Levine's insights on how the playing facility affects the franchise's value. In the fourth excerpt, Gerald Scully discusses the impact of reputation on team value and the operating profits, capital appreciation, and length of ownership of sports franchises. The chapter concludes with a Moody's research publication that provides an overview of the rating process for sports-related transactions. (See Table 1 for a list of Forbes Franchise Valuations, Table 2 for a list of franchise sales before, during, and after bear markets, and Table 3 for a list of average league franchise valuations.)

TABLE 1.

FORBES FRANCHISE VALUES AS OF FEBRUARY 2004			
Team	*League*	*Owner*	*Value*
Washington Redskins	NFL	Daniel Snyder	$952 million
Dallas Cowboys	NFL	Jerry Jones	$851 million
Houston Texans	NFL	Bob McNair	$791 million
New England Patriots	NFL	Robert Kraft	$756 million
New York Yankees	MLB	George Steinbrenner	$730 million
Cleveland Browns	NFL	Randy Lerner	$695 million
Denver Broncos	NFL	Pat Bowlen	$683 million
Tampa Bay Buccaneers	NFL	Malcolm Glazer	$671 million
Baltimore Ravens	NFL	Art Modell	$649 million
Carolina Panthers	NFL	Jerry Richardson	$642 million
Miami Dolphins	NFL	Wayne Huizenga	$638 million
Detroit Lions	NFL	William Ford	$635 million
Chicago Bears	NFL	Virginia McCaskey	$621 million
Tennessee Titans	NFL	Ken Adams	$620 million
Philadelphia Eagles	NFL	Jeffrey Lurie	$617 million
Seattle Seahawks	NFL	Paul Allen	$610 million
Green Bay Packers	NFL	Public	$609 million
Pittsburgh Steelers	NFL	Dan Rooney	$608 million *(Continued)*

TABLE 1. **(Continued)**

FORBES FRANCHISE VALUES			
Team	*League*	*Owner*	*Value*
St. Louis Rams	NFL	Georgia Frontiere	$602 million
Kansas City Chiefs	NFL	Lamar Hunt	$601 million
New Orleans Saints	NFL	Tom Benson	$585 million
Oakland Raiders	NFL	Al Davis	$576 million
New York Giants	NFL	W. Mara/P. Tisch	$573 million
Jacksonville Jaguars	NFL	Wayne Weaver	$569 million
San Francisco 49ers	NFL	Denise DeBartolo York	$568 million
New York Jets	NFL	Woody Johnson	$567 million
Buffalo Bills	NFL	Ralph Wilson	$564 million
Cincinnati Bengals	NFL	Mike Brown	$562 million
San Diego Chargers	NFL	Alex Spanos	$561 million
Indianapolis Colts	NFL	Jim Irsay	$547 million
Minnesota Vikings	NFL	Red McCombs	$542 million
Atlanta Falcons	NFL	Arthur Blank	$534 million
Arizona Cardinals	NFL	Bill Bidwell	$505 million
New York Mets	MLB	Fred Wilpon	$482 million
Los Angeles Lakers	NBA	Jerry Buss	$447 million
Los Angeles Dodgers	MLB	Frank McCourt	$435 million
Boston Red Sox	MLB	John Henry	$426 million
Atlanta Braves	MLB	AOL/Time Warner	$424 million
New York Knicks	NBA	C. Dolan/J. Dolan	$401 million
Seattle Mariners	MLB	Hiroshi Yamaguchi	$373 million
Cleveland Indians	MLB	Larry Dolan	$360 million
Chicago Bulls	NBA	Jerry Reinsdorf	$356 million
Texas Rangers	MLB	Tom Hicks	$356 million
San Francisco Giants	MLB	Peter Magowan	$355 million
Colorado Rockets	MLB	Jerry McMorris	$347 million
Dallas Mavericks	NBA	Mark Cuban	$338 million
Houston Astros	MLB	Drayton McLane	$337 million
Philadelphia 76ers	NBA	Comcast Corp.	$328 million
Baltimore Orioles	MLB	Peter Angelos	$319 million
Boston Celtics	NBA	W. Grousbeck/S. Pagliuca	$290 million
Chicago Cubs	MLB	Tribune Co.	$287 million
Detroit Pistons	NBA	William Davidson	$284 million
Phoenix Suns	NBA	Jerry Colangelo	$283 million

(Continued)

TABLE 1. (Continued)

FORBES FRANCHISE VALUES			
Team	*League*	*Owner*	*Value*
San Antonio Spurs	NBA	Peter Holt	$283 million
Arizona Diamondbacks	MLB	Jerry Colangelo	$280 million
Indiana Pacers	NBA	H. Simon/M. Simon	$280 million
Houston Rockets	NBA	Les Alexander	$278 million
Sacramento Kings	NBA	G. Maloof/J. Maloof	$275 million
Washington Wizards	NBA	Abe Pollin	$274 million
New York Rangers	NHL	C. Dolan/J. Dolan	$272 million
Portland Trail Blazers	NBA	Paul Allen	$272 million
St. Louis Cardinals	MLB	B. DeWitt/F. Hanser	$271 million
Dallas Stars	NHL	Tom Hicks	$270 million
Toronto Maple Leafs	NHL	Larry Tanenbaum	$263 million
Detroit Tigers	MLB	Michael Ilitch	$262 million
Cleveland Cavaliers	NBA	G. Gund/G. Gund	$258 million
Philadelphia Flyers	NHL	Comcast Corp.	$252 million
Toronto Raptors	NBA	Maple Leaf Sports & Ent.	$249 million
Detroit Red Wings	NHL	Michael Ilitch	$245 million
New Jersey Nets	NBA	Bruce Ratner	$244 million
Pittsburgh Pirates	MLB	Kevin McClatchy	$242 million
Utah Jazz	NBA	Larry Miller	$239 million
Milwaukee Brewers	MLB	Bud Selig Trust	$238 million
Miami Heat	NBA	Micky Arison	$236 million
Philadelphia Phillies	MLB	B. Giles/D. Montgomery	$231 million
Minnesota Timberwolves	NBA	Glen Taylor	$230 million
Colorado Avalanche	NHL	Stanley Kroenke	$229 million
Memphis Grizzlies	NBA	Michael Heisley	$227 million
Boston Bruins	NHL	Jeremy Jacobs	$223 million
Chicago White Sox	MLB	Jerry Reinsdorf	$223 million
Denver Nuggets	NBA	Stanley Kroenke	$218 million
New Orleans Hornets	NBA	G. Shinn/R. Wooldridge	$216 million
Los Angeles Clippers	NBA	Donald Sterling	$208 million
San Diego Padres	MLB	John Moores	$207 million
Cincinnati Reds	MLB	Carl Lindner	$204 million
Atlanta Hawks	NBA	Atlanta Spirit LLC	$202 million
Orlando Magic	NBA	Rich DeVos	$199 million
Seattle SuperSonics	NBA	Howard Schultz	$196 million

(Continued)

TABLE 1.   (Continued)

FORBES FRANCHISE VALUES			
Team	*League*	*Owner*	*Value*
Anaheim Angels	MLB	Arturo Moreno	$195 million
Chicago Blackhawks	NHL	Bill Wirtz	$192 million
Golden State Warriors	NBA	Chris Cohan	$188 million
Los Angeles Kings	NHL	P. Anschutz/E. Roski	$183 million
Toronto Blue Jays	MLB	Rogers Communications	$182 million
Milwaukee Bucks	NBA	Herb Kohl	$174 million
Montreal Canadiens	NHL	George Gillett Jr.	$170 million
Minnesota Wild	NHL	Robert Naegele Jr.	$166 million
Oakland Athletics	MLB	S. Schott/K. Hofman	$157 million
Kansas City Royals	MLB	David Glass	$152 million
New York Islanders	NHL	C. Wang/S. Kumar	$151 million
St. Louis Blues	NHL	Bill Laurie	$147 million
New Jersey Devils	NHL	YankeeNets	$145 million
Columbus Blue Jackets	NHL	John McConnell	$144 million
Tampa Bay Devil Rays	MLB	Vincent Naimoli	$142 million
Florida Marlins	MLB	Jeffrey Loria	$137 million
San Jose Sharks	NHL	K. Compton/G. Reyes	$137 million
Tampa Bay Lightning	NHL	William Davidson	$136 million
Washington Capitals	NHL	Ted Leonsis	$130 million
Minnesota Twins	MLB	Carl Pohlad	$127 million
Vancouver Canucks	NHL	John McCaw Jr.	$125 million
Phoenix Coyotes	NHL	S. Ellman/W. Gretzky	$120 million
Ottawa Senators	NHL	Eugene Melnyk	$117 million
Pittsburgh Penguins	NHL	Mario Lemieux	$114 million
Florida Panthers	NHL	Alan Cohen	$113 million
Anaheim Mighty Ducks	NHL	Walt Disney Co.	$112 million
Atlanta Thrashers	NHL	Atlanta Spirit LLC	$110 million
Carolina Hurricanes	NHL	Peter Karmanos Jr.	$109 million
Montreal Expos	MLB	Major League Baseball	$108 million
Nashville Predators	NHL	Craig Leipold	$101 million
Calgary Flames	NHL	Limited Partnership	$97 million
Buffalo Sabres	NHL	Tom Galisano	$95 million
Edmonton Oilers	NHL	Edmonton Investors Group	$91 million

Source: ESPN.com. Copyright ©2003 ESPN Internet Ventures.

TABLE 2.

357 *Chapter 12 Sports Franchise Valuation*

FRANCHISE SALES BEFORE, DURING, AND AFTER BEAR MARKETS

Years before & after	Team	Sale price	Sale year	Previous purchase price	Previous purchase year	Franchise % change	S&P 500 % change*	Return multiple: franchise % change/ S&P 500 % change
1972	Boston Celtics	$ 4,000,000	1972	$ 6,000,000	1970	-33%	39%	NEG
	Chicago Bulls	5,100,000	1972	1,300,000**	1966	292%	27%	10.8 ×
	St. Louis Rams	19,000,000	1972	7,100,000	1962	168%	71%	2.3
Bear market Jan-73 to Dec-74	Vancouver Canucks	$ 8,500,000	1974	$ 6,000,000	1970	42%	-19%	NEG
	San Diego Padres	12,000,000	1974	12,500,000	1968	-4%	-26%	N/A
1975	Pittsburgh Penguins	$ 3,800,000	1975	$ 7,000,000	1971	-46%	-6%	7.7
	Chicago White Sox	10,700,000	1975	7,800,000	1961	37%	46%	0.8
1980	Cleveland Cavaliers	$ 7,000,000	1980	$ 3,700,000	1970	89%	60%	1.5 ×
	Calgary Flames	16,000,000	1980	6,000,000	1972	167%	31%	5.4
	Oakland Athletics	12,700,000	1980	3,800,000	1960	234%	144%	1.6
	New York Mets	21,000,000	1980	1,800,000**	1960	1067%	144%	7.4
Bear market Mar-81 to Aug-82	Houston Rockets	$ 11,000,000	1982	$ 2,000,000	1973	450%	21%	21.2
	New Jersey Devils	30,000,000	1982	6,000,000**	1974	400%	46%	8.8
	Seattle Mariners	13,000,000	1981	6,250,000**	1976	108%	22%	5.0 •
	Chicago White Sox	20,000,000	1981	10,700,000	1975	87%	59%	1.5
1983	Kansas City Royals	$ 22,000,000	1983	$ 5,550,000**	1968	296%	79%	3.8
1986	Utah Jazz	$ 20,000,000	1986	$ 6,150,000**	1974	225%	151%	1.5 ×
	New York Mets	80,750,000	1986	21,000,000	1980	285%	112%	2.5

(Continued)

*Except for sales occurring in 2001, represents the % change from last close in January in the year of the prior sale to the last close in December of the sale year.
**Expansion Fee.
Source: Moag and Company Research; Pay Dirt.

TABLE 2. **(Continued)**

FRANCHISE SALES BEFORE, DURING, AND AFTER BEAR MARKETS

Years before & after	Team	Sale price	Sale year	Previous purchase price	Previous purchase year	Franchise % change	S&P 500 % change*	Return multiple: franchise % change/ S&P 500 % change
Bear market Aug-87 to Nov-87	Phoenix Suns	$ 52,000,000	1987	$ 2,000,000	1968	2500%	168%	14.9
1988	Portland Trailblazers	$ 70,000,000	1988	$ 3,700,000**	1970	1792%	227%	7.9
	Dallas Cowboys	95,000,000	1988	60,000,000	1984	58%	70%	0.8
	Seattle Seahawks	80,000,000	1988	16,000,000**	1974	400%	188%	2.1
	Los Angeles Kings	39,000,000	1988	2,000,000**	1967	1850%	221%	8.4
	Quebec Nordiques	16,500,000	1988	6,000,000**	1979	175%	178%	1.0
	Baltimore Orioles	70,000,000	1988	13,100,000	1979	434%	178%	2.4
1989	Denver Nuggets	$ 54,000,000	1989	$ 19,000,000	1985	184%	97%	1.9 x
	Toronto Maple Leafs	104,000,000	1989	2,000,000	1961	5100%	472%	10.8
	Seattle Mariners	80,000,000	1989	13,000,000	1981	515%	173%	3.0
	Texas Rangers	80,000,000	1989	11,100,000	1971	621%	269%	2.3
Bear market Jul-90 to Oct-90	Dallas Stars	$ 31,500,000	1990	$ 5,300,000	1977	494%	224%	2.2
	Montreal Expos	86,000,000	1990	12,500,000**	1968	588%	258%	2.3
	San Diego Padres	75,000,000	1990	12,000,000	1974	525%	242%	2.2
1991	Denver Nuggets	$ 70,000,000	1991	$ 54,000,000	1989	30%	40%	0.7
	Orlando Magic	110,000,000	1991	32,500,000**	1989	238%	40%	5.9
	Minnesota Vikings	102,000,000	1991	54,300,000	1985	88%	132%	0.7
	Toronto Blue Jays	134,000,000	1991	7,000,000**	1976	1814%	314%	5.8

(Continued)

*Except for sales occurring in 2001, represents the % change from last close in January in the year of the prior sale to the last close in December of the sale year.
**Expansion Fee.
Source: Moag and Company Research; Pay Dirt.

TABLE 2. (Continued)

FRANCHISE SALES BEFORE, DURING, AND AFTER BEAR MARKETS

Years before & after		Team	Sale price	Sale year	Previous purchase price	Previous purchase year	Franchise % change	S&P 500 % change*	Return multiple: franchise % change/ S&P 500 % change
1999		Pittsburgh Penguins	$ 70,000,000	1999	$ 3,800,000	1975	1742%	1809%	1.0 ×
		St. Louis Blues	96,000,000	1999	2,000,000**	1967	4700%	1596%	2.9
		Tampa Bay Lightning	115,000,000	1999	45,000,000***	1991	156%	327%	0.5
		Washington Capitals	85,000,000	1999	6,000,000	1975	1317%	1809%	0.7
		Montreal Expos	214,000,000	1999	86,000,000	1990	149%	346%	0.4
		Cleveland Indians	323,000,000	1999	4,000,000	1956	7975%	3253%	2.5
		Florida Marlins	150,000,000	1999	95,000,000**	1991	58%	327%	0.2
		Cincinnati Reds	186,000,000	1999	24,000,000	1984	675%	799%	0.8
Bear	Jan-00 to	Dallas Mavericks	$195,000,000	2000	$ 12,000,000**	1980	1525%	1057%	1.4
market	Present	Seattle SuperSonics	200,000,000	2001	21,000,000	1984	852%	649%	1.3
		Vancouver Grizzlies	170,000,000	2000	125,000,000**	1994	36%	174%	0.2
		Atlanta Falcons	545,000,000	2001	8,500,000***	1965	6312%	1201%	5.3
		New Jersey Devils	175,000,000	2000	30,000,000	1982	483%	997%	0.5
		New York Islanders	190,000,000	2000	6,000,000**	1972	3067%	1170%	2.6
		Boston Red Sox	700,000,000	2001***	22,500,000	1978	3011%	1183%	2.5

*Except for sales occurring in 2001, represents the % change from last close in January in the year of the prior sale to the last close in December of the sale year.
**Expansion Fee.
***Purchase price includes 100% of team (including $40 million in team debt), 80% of New England Sports Network, and Fenway Park.
Source: Moag and Company Research; Pay Dirt.

TABLE 3.

AVERAGE LEAGUE FRANCHISE VALUES (IN MILLIONS)				
	NHL	*NFL*	*NBA*	*MLB*
2004	$159	N/A	$265	N/A
High	272	N/A	447	N/A
Low	91	N/A	174	N/A
2003	$164	$628	$248	$295
High	266	952	426	849
Low	86	505	168	113
2002	157	530.5	223	286
High	277	845	403	730
Low	79	374	135	108
2001	148	466	207	263
High	263	796	395	635
Low	77	338	118	92
2000	135	423	183	N/A
High	235	741	334	N/A
Low	73	305	103	N/A
1999	125	385	167	220
High	195	663	303	491
Low	67	293	94	84
1998	N/A	288	N/A	194
High	N/A	413	N/A	362
Low	N/A	227	N/A	87
1997	90	205	148	134
High	151	320	250	241
Low	43	170	95	71
1996	74	174	127	115
High	126	272	205	209
Low	34	133	88	62
1994	61	153	99	107
High	104	190	168	166
Low	35	138	67	75

Source: Forbes.

OVERVIEW

THE ECONOMICS OF SPORTS

Michael Leeds and Peter von Allmen

SPORTS FRANCHISES AS PROFIT-MAXIMIZING FIRMS

. . . .

. . . Most, if not all, owners of professional sports teams have made substantial fortunes in other industries. . . . Owners are some of America's wealthiest individuals. It seems unlikely that individuals so successful in other areas would suddenly take leave of their business senses.

When team owners minimize the importance of profits they may simply be telling the fans what they want to hear. Because fans are the source of revenue, it is poor politics — and hence poor business — for an owner to announce that his primary objective is to make a big profit. Thus, contrary to appearances, standard profit maximization may still be the appropriate frame of analysis for sports.

It is also possible that the owners are telling the truth. A team owner may regard owning a franchise as a hobby, considering any losses to be simply consumption expenditures. . . . A common joke among owners in the 1930s and 1940s was that the best way to make a small fortune was to start with a large fortune and buy a professional sports team. Owners may also be motivated by a sense of civic pride that inspires them to help their hometown attract or retain a franchise.

In addition to money, owning a team brings its owner recognition. . . . If owning a team involves both ego maximization and profit maximization, then models based on profits alone fail to predict the owners' behavior.

Richard Sheehan notes, for example, that the owners of MLB and NBA franchises pay an average of $40 million more than their teams are worth from a strictly financial perspective and that NFL owners overpay by roughly $70 million for their franchises. . . . [1]

WHAT ARE PROFITS AND HOW ARE THEY MAXIMIZED?

Economists define profits as total revenue minus total cost . . . Total revenue is the sum of all revenues that the firm receives per period. In a typical product market, total revenue is simply the price of the product times quantity sold . . . There is no single, clear-cut definition of output in the professional sports market. This difficulty stems from the fact that teams have numerous sources of revenue, not all of them directly related to attendance. Thus, total revenue . . . is actually the sum of several types of revenue: ticket sales, television rights, stadium revenues other than tickets (such as concessions and stadium naming rights), licensing sales (jerseys, hats, etc.), shared or redistributed revenue from other teams, and subsidies from governments. An additional challenge for the study of team profits in professional sports is that profits — at least those profits reported using standard accounting rules — are easily manipulated. . . .

Economists break down total costs into fixed costs . . . and variable costs. . . . Fixed costs are those costs that remain the same regardless of changes in output, such as mortgage payments that the firm must pay regardless of how much it produces. Sports franchises frequently pay a fixed fee to the city for the use of a publicly funded stadium.

. . . As with revenue, the nature of costs for professional sports teams is quite different from that of a typical firm. For a professional team, most costs, including labor costs, are fixed, or at least are variable only within a relatively narrow range over the course of a single season. . . .

A DETAILED LOOK AT REVENUE

Professional teams generate revenue from four principal sources: ticket sales or gate receipts, local and national broadcasting rights, licensing income, and other stadium-related revenues including luxury boxes, concessions, and stadium naming rights. . . The proportion of total revenue generated from each source varies substantially from sport to sport, and it is determined by the level of demand for each. The sources of revenue have also changed dramatically over time. . .

. . . .

. . . Whereas gate receipts used to be an owner's sole source of revenue, they are now outweighed by other sources, such as national and local media contracts. . . . In addition, gate receipts now make up only about 75 percent of the total revenue earned from the use of the facility. Venue revenues, which include suite rentals, parking, concessions, venue advertising, and naming rights, and sometimes revenue earned from other venue events make up the other 25 percent. Pro teams typically earn several million dollars per year through merchandising and licensing fees, which include revenue from official apparel sales and use of logos.

GATE RECEIPTS

Before the advent of television, all professional sports lived and died by gate revenue. Concession revenue was limited, and luxury suites were nonexistent. In such an environment, teams maximized profits by attracting as many fans as possible. If teams do not share gate revenue, as is the case with the NHL and NBA, then they do not profit from attendance at away games. . . . When teams do not share ticket revenue, gate receipts equal the price of a "typical" ticket times the number of tickets sold. If they do share gate receipts, then a team's revenue from ticket sales equals the sum of its share of revenue from home games plus its share of revenue from away games. . . . Our simple model of profit maximization can explain why an owner wants to field a good team — or why he or she may be content with a bad one. If teams must pay more for good players than for bad ones, and fans want to see a good team more than they want to see a bad one, the team faces a trade-off. Fielding a better team increases the demand for tickets, shifting the demand curve to the right. Prices and revenues both rise as a result. Higher revenues, however, do not necessarily mean higher profits. Fielding a better team is also more expensive, and so both costs and revenues rise. The team must decide whether it is better to be a bad team with low costs and low revenues, or a good team with high costs and high revenues.

 . . . .

The NHL, like the NBA, does not share gate revenue. Unlike the NBA, the NHL does not have a substantial TV contract to even out total revenues. More than any other sport, teams in the NHL depend on their own home attendance for their revenue. . . .

. . . Revenue sharing in all sports generally shifts money from teams that spend a lot on good players to teams that do not. This helps to explain why "small market" teams like baseball's Milwaukee Brewers favor revenue sharing so strongly while "big market" teams like the New York Yankees or Mets do not. The reasons for revenue sharing, however, go deeper than that.

Sharing revenue can help bring a league financial stability. Most franchises struggle in the early years of any league. The early years of the NFL were perhaps the most precarious. Teams moved, entered, and left the league with alarming regularity. Founded in 1920, the league could not field the same set of teams for two consecutive years until 1936. The extreme financial weakness of the NFL led it to adopt a more radical version of revenue sharing than other leagues. Teams saw that they could not survive without a stable set of opposing teams. Even the financially strongest teams saw that their long-term financial success depended on propping up the financially weakest franchises.

Owners have another — less benevolent — reason for sharing revenues. . . . Sharing revenues reduces the value of fielding a good team. As a result, teams are less willing to spend large sums for talented players, reducing the salaries they are willing to pay. Revenue sharing may thus provide financial stability to teams in part by artificially depressing the pay of their players. . . .

TELEVISION REVENUE

No single event has changed the finances of professional sports as much as the advent of television. All four major sports currently enjoy huge revenue streams from both local and national broadcasting rights. . . .

National broadcasting rights are the lifeblood of professional football. . . . Not surprisingly, media revenues account for nearly half of all football revenues. . . . The NFL would not be much more profitable than the NHL without its mega-contract.

In baseball, local revenues are far more important than in football. In the New York market, the Yankees and Mets generate huge media revenues. . . By contrast, teams in small markets . . . receive only a small fraction of what the Yankees and Mets receive . . . The inequality in local TV revenues created by the vast difference in the size of media markets defines large- and small-market teams in baseball much more so than the actual size of the city. . . . The impact of the media, however, is more pervasive than simple lump sum additions to profits.

When a network or a local station broadcasts a game, it receives no revenue from the viewers. The bulk of its revenue comes from advertisers. When a game is broadcast over a cable outlet such as ESPN, the station receives a monthly premium from the viewer in addition to advertising revenue. Neither broadcast allows the team to calculate a per-viewer charge. Payments to teams from broadcasters come from the fixed fees for broadcast rights that leagues and networks negotiate at the national level, and individual teams and stations negotiate at the local level.

Like fixed costs in a profit equation, fixed revenues like broadcast fees have no impact on how revenues or costs change with output. Ignoring for the moment the possible impact of televising games on gate receipts, a fixed revenue payment for broadcast rights enters the profit function as a constant.

TELEVISION AND GATE RECEIPTS — EXPOSURE VERSUS SUBSTITUTION

Broadcasting games is a double-edged sword to teams. To the extent that fans prefer to watch games on television rather than go to the stadium, televising home games reduces gate receipts. . . . This is why the NFL "blacks out" (forbids networks from showing in the local market) games that are not sold out. . . . On the other hand, if television stimulates fans' interest in the game, more broadcasts may increase attendance at the gate. The NFL owes a good deal of its popularity to its focus on nationally broadcast games and the "Sunday doubleheader," which allows fans to watch popular teams from other cities.

Networks televise games when they profit from doing so. The demand by networks or local stations to televise games is a derived demand. The demand for a good or service is derived from the demand for another when the amount people are willing and able to buy depends on the market for a different product. . . . In the case of broadcasting rights, the demand by TV networks for sporting events depends on — is derived from — the demand by sponsors for advertising time. A network's willingness to pay a league or team for the right to broadcast a game stems from its ability to sell advertising during the game. . . .

A network might pursue broadcast rights even though it knows that it will lose money as a result. . . . The broadcast itself might lose money, but if it attracts viewers to other shows on the network, it may still be consistent with overall profit maximization. In the case of new entrants to the market like Fox, a contract with a major sport gives the network an air of credibility with sponsors and potential affiliates. . . .

. . . .

STADIUM AGREEMENTS

. . . .

Venue revenues, or nonticket revenues from stadia, include revenue from parking and concessions, and especially revenue from luxury suites and other special seating. Luxury seating has become particularly valuable in the NFL, which shares other sources of revenue so equally. While teams share a substantial portion of ticket revenue with each other . . . only a small portion of the price of a luxury suite counts as ticket revenue. . . . Again, much of this revenue enters as a lump sum per season, because luxury boxes are typically leased on a per-season basis. Other attendance-related revenue such as parking and concession revenue is directly connected to attendance at the games.

. . . .

PROBLEMS CREATED BY STADIUM DEALS

In recent years several NFL teams have moved in apparently illogical directions. . . . On the surface, all these moves seem unprofitable, as they limit both the fan base and the media exposure for the teams. Why, then, do the teams move?

The answer can be found in the peculiar interaction of revenue sharing and stadium deals. Since the teams in the NFL split their national TV contract equally and their gate receipts almost equally, the consequences of a team's moving to a smaller city are spread over all the other teams. In baseball, where teams depend so heavily on local media revenue, a team in a media market the size of Los Angeles would never leave for a much smaller city. . . . The moves to smaller cities, however, may hurt the NFL's ratings in the nation's second largest media market. This, in turn, could lead to worse TV contracts for the NFL — and less revenue for all teams, including the teams that moved — in the future.

. . . NFL teams do not worry about the consequences of leaving major media markets uncovered if they can get a better individual deal elsewhere. . . .

. . . As long as municipalities continue to try to outbid one another for the right to host an NFL franchise, the league may suffer continued instability as teams pursue better stadium arrangements. . . .

. . . . *[The authors' discussion of revenue sharing is omitted. See Chapter 3 for a treatment of this issue.]*

COST

When considering the cost side of the profit equation, we again see substantial differences between what costs mean to a professional sports franchise and what they mean to most other industries. With one important exception, the difference between operating cost and total cost, . . . cost is relatively straightforward.

. . . Not surprisingly, players' salaries figure prominently in the total costs of professional franchises. Salaries, which include deferred payments, bonuses, workers' compensation expenses, and pension contributions, make up over half a team's costs in every major sport. With a few exceptions, player costs are generally fixed from year to year.

The remaining expenses include travel, marketing, administrative (both team and league), and venue expenses. For baseball and hockey, expenses also include player development. Travel expenses increase as the size of the team increases, with the number of away games, and with the distances traveled. Teams incur marketing and administrative costs at two levels. Each team does its own marketing specific to its own club and market, and each team has its own administrative costs, which include everything from office supplies to the salaries of the team executives. Marketing and administrative costs are also incurred at the league level. These costs include broad-based marketing campaigns designed to increase demand for the sport, and administrative costs such as the cost of paying a commissioner and maintaining league offices.

. . . .

Both the NHL and MLB endure substantial player development costs because they both maintain extensive minor league systems. In exchange for the minor league team's developing talent and providing players, the major league team subsidizes a major portion of the minor league team's labor and operating expenses. . . . These costs seem even greater when one considers that each minor league system generates only a few major league players per year. . . .

TAXES, PROFIT, OWNER BEHAVIOR, AND VERTICAL INTEGRATION

. . . Fans of all sports look back fondly to owners who had nurtured the game and viewed it as more than a profit center or ego boost. Unfortunately, that image is largely fiction. As early as the 19th century, commentators were complaining that the spirit of sport had been lost in the clamor for profit. . . .

One change has occurred, however, in the pattern of sports ownership. As the prices of franchises have risen to stratospheric levels, the prices of franchises have risen beyond the means of most individual bidders. Media-related individuals . . . or corporations . . . now own more and more franchises. The joint ownership of sports franchises and media outlets for the teams suggests that businesses see efficiency gains from vertical integration and cross subsidization (the ability to move profits and expenses from one firm to another).

. . . .

At first glance, a media outlet's purchase of a sports franchise looks like a losing proposition for the consumer with little or no net gain for the producer. Alone, both the team and the broadcaster have monopoly power. Bringing the two together seems to create a "super monopoly" with even greater power to exploit consumers. Economic theory shows, however, that vertical integration of a team and a media outlet may actually improve the well-being of consumers.

. . . .

From the owner's perspective, when an individual or group owns two vertically integrated firms, it will seek to maximize total profits of the two combined enterprises. From a purely financial standpoint, the owner does not worry whether one firm shows a larger profit than the other. The price at which the upstream firm sells to the downstream firm is called the transfer price. Changes in transfer prices change accounting profits (those reported to the IRS), but not the overall profitability of the combined enterprises. Thus, the joint owner of a franchise and the cable network that broadcasts the franchise's games will set a low transfer price (i.e., broadcast rights fee) if tax or political considerations make it advantageous to do so. For example, if a team did not want to show high profits while seeking a public subsidy, or if the players were entitled to a given percentage of team profits, then the owner could keep more of the profits by having them transferred to his cable company through a low broadcast rights fee. Conversely, if the profits of the cable company were regulated, the owner may want to minimize earnings by charging a high broadcast rights fee. The moral of the story is that when firms are vertically integrated, as is becoming more and more common in the sports industry, one must view accounting profits with a skeptical eye.

. . . . *[The authors' discussions of accounting and sports leagues are omitted. See Chapters 2 and 4 for the coverage of these issues.]*

REFERENCES

1. Richard G. Sheehan, *Keeping Score: The Economics of Big-Time Sports* (South Bend, Ind.: Diamond Press, 1996), pp. 75 and 90.

Intangible Assets

How to Value Professional Sports Franchise Intangible Assets

Eric A. Thornton

INTRODUCTION

Transactions involving the acquisition of a professional sports team are often the subject of considerable scrutiny by the Internal Revenue Service. Much of the Service's scrutiny involves Internal Revenue Code Section 197 ("Section 197"), which presents rules regarding the amortization of acquired intangible assets for income tax purposes.

Section 197 provides that the franchise agreement intangible asset acquired in the purchase of a professional sports team is not amortizable for income tax purposes. However, other intangible assets acquired with the purchase of a sports team (but not components of the national franchise agreement) may be amortizable for income tax purposes. These acquired intangible assets may be amortized if the intangibles (1) have an identifiable value separate from any acquired goodwill, going-concern value, and the franchise agreement intangible asset and (2) have a determinable remaining useful life ("RUL").

A professional sports team's intangible assets typically account for the greatest percentage of all of the team assets. And, as indicated above, not all of the professional sports team intangible assets are amortizable for federal income tax purposes.

Accordingly, the Service often carefully scrutinizes the valuation analysis of separately identified professional sports team intangible assets as part of a purchase price allocation. Therefore, it is important to use the appropriate methodology to estimate the fair market value of these acquired intangibles.

. . . .

PROFESSIONAL SPORTS TEAM INTANGIBLE ASSETS

Professional sports franchises are comprised of a number of different tangible and intangible assets. Some of the most common types of professional sports team intangible assets include the following: player contracts, local cable television, broadcast television, and broadcast radio contracts, stadium lease, advertising and/or sponsorship agreements, concession agreements, luxury suite agreements, season ticketholder relationships, coach and management employment contracts, draft rights, national franchise agreement, and goodwill and going-concern value.

SPORTS FRANCHISE INTANGIBLE ASSET VALUATION PROCEDURES

As with commercial intangibles acquired in most business acquisitions, sports franchise intangible assets are valued using cost, sales comparison, and income valuation approaches. A valuation approach represents a category of related economic analysis methods. Therefore, each approach includes a number of independent valuation methods. And, within each valuation method, there are a number of applicable specific procedures. Such specific procedures may be either qualitative or quantitative in nature. So, valuation procedures build up to valuation methods. And, valuation methods aggregate to valuation approaches.

However, many sports franchise intangible assets are specific to this industry. Therefore, many of the data sources that analysts refer to in order to estimate valuation variables are also specific to this industry. . . . And, the applications of otherwise generalized valuation procedures are often tailored to this industry. . . .

It is noteworthy that the sales comparison approach is also called the market approach in the valuation vernacular. Regardless of this terminology, sports franchise owners and their advisors should understand that all valuation approaches can be used to estimate market value. And, all valuation variables (as used in each valuation approach) should be empirically based and market-derived.

It is also noteworthy that valuation analysts only "estimate" market values for sports industry intangible assets. It is the marketplace of actual sports industry franchise buyers and sellers that actually "determines" market values for sports industry intangible assets.

Cost Approach Methods

The cost approach is based on the economic principles of substitution and utility. The conceptual premise of this approach is that a sports franchise buyer will pay no more for an intangible asset than the cost of a substitute intangible that provides the same utility as the subject intangible.

Most cost approach methods estimate cost in current dollars as of the valuation (e.g., franchise acquisition) date. The two most common measures of cost are replacement cost and reproduction cost.

Replacement cost estimates the current dollar amount necessary to provide the same level of utility as the subject. Reproduction cost estimates the current dollar amount necessary to recreate an exact duplicate of the subject. For an intangible, replacement cost is typically not the same as (and is usually much lower than) reproduction cost.

The cost of an intangible, whether measured by either the replacement or reproduction model, is not the value of the intangible. Cost has to be adjusted for all forms of obsolescence in order to arrive at an estimate of value. The four common forms of obsolescence include (1) physical deterioration, (2) functional obsolescence, (3) technological obsolescence, and (4) external obsolescence.

While physical deterioration usually does affect the value of commercial intangible assets, it may affect the valuation of sports intangibles — such as player contracts. Of course, the contracts themselves do not become physically obsolete, but the professional athletes do become older and/or injured. In any event, analysts should identify and quantify all forms of obsolescence associated with each intangible.

The total cost measure less allowances for all forms of obsolescence results in a value indication for the subject intangible. And, the allowances for obsolescence are a function of (1) the condition of the subject, (2) the expected RUL of the subject, and (3) the measure of cost selected. . . .

Sales Comparison Approach

The sales comparison (or market) approach is based on the economic principles of efficient markets and rational behavior. The market approach relies on transactional data regarding arm's-length, third-party sales or licenses of discrete intangible assets. Empirical transactional data are extracted from the willing buyer/willing seller marketplace.

These transactional data are analyzed in order to conclude cash equivalency prices for the intangible sales and/or licenses. Both the transactional intangibles and the subject intangible are analyzed on common quantitative fundamentals, such as growth rates, profit margins, returns on investment, and so on.

Pricing metrics are calculated for the transactional intangibles based on common units of comparison. . . Based on the comparative analysis of quantitative fundamentals, subject-specific pricing metrics are selected from the range of transactional pricing metrics. The selected pricing metrics are then applied to the subject intangible's quantitative fundamentals, resulting in a value estimate.

The market approach considers both sales and licenses/leases of comparative intangible assets. Accordingly, the market approach examines market-derived license fees, royalty rates, profit split percentages, and other intangible asset transfer price arrangements in addition to fee simple sales of intangibles. However, all valuation methods within the market approach rely on commercial transfers of naked (i.e., individual or unbundled) intangibles.

For this reason, other methods such as (1) the guideline sales method, (2) the guideline license method, and (3) the market rental income method often are not applicable to sports franchise intangibles. This is because individual intangible assets are not often sold/licensed between sports franchise owners. Nonetheless, when sufficient transactional data exist so that the market approach can be used to value stadium leases, concession agreements, trademark licenses, and so on, the approach does provide a convincing valuation analysis.

Income Approach Methods

The income approach is based on the economic principles of anticipation and rational expectations. The income approach relies on the present value of a future economic income stream to provide a value indication. There are two principal valuation methods within the income approach: (1) direct capitalization and (2) yield capitalization.

Direct capitalization is used when the intangible is expected to generate a normalized amount of income, changing at a constant rate over time. The constant rate of change can be a positive rate (i.e., increasing income), a negative rate (i.e., decreasing income), or a zero rate (i.e., constant income). Yield capitalization is used when the intangible is expected to generate uneven (and unrelated) amounts of income over discrete periods of time.

Economic income can be measured many different ways within the income approach methods. Economic income can result from any expected increase in revenues, decrease in operating costs or expense, decrease in incremental investments, decrease in costs of capital, acceleration of a cash receipt, or deferral of a cash disbursement.

Accordingly, economic income is not the same concept as accounting income. Economic income can be measured by operating income, net income, operating cash flow, or net cash flow. It can also be measured before income taxes or after income taxes. Because many sports franchises do not earn positive accounting income, cash flow-based measures of economic income are commonly used in franchise intangible asset analyses.

The value of an intangible is the present value of the income it is expected to generate for its owner/operator/lessor. The present value is calculated by (1) multiplying a projection of periodic income amounts by a corresponding series of present value discount rates or (2) dividing a normalized single period income projection by a direct capitalization rate.

While various measures of economic income can be used in the analysis, the selected discount/capitalization rates should be calculated on a consistent basis with the projected income. . . .

The selected discount/capitalization rate is a function of two factors: (1) the market's expected rate of return on the intangible asset investment and (2) the expected duration of the intangible's income generation. Since it is difficult to extract the market's expected return on investment, analysts typically use market-derived costs of capital. This procedure is based on the economic theorem that (in the long run) an investor's expected rate of return will equal the investor's cost of capital. Due to limitations of publicly available data in the professional sports industry, analysts often use an individual franchise owner's cost of capital as a proxy for the market cost of capital.

The term of the income projection depends on the intangible's expected RUL. For most sports franchise intangibles, RUL is a function of either: (1) legal/contract life or (2) actuarial/analytical life. Many sports franchise intangibles have finite contractual lives, such as leases, licenses, permits, contracts, agreements, and so on. However, the expected RUL of some contract-related intangibles is greater than the current term to maturity. This is because of expected contract renewals. . . .

An actuarial analysis is performed on the historical "placements," "retirements," and turnover rates on these intangibles in order to estimate the expected number of renewals of each acquired contract/subscription. Accordingly, the appropriate discount/capitalization factor for each intangible is a function of (1) the expected rate of return (i.e., investor's cost of capital) and (2) the intangible's RUL.

Premise of Value

The selected discount/capitalization rate is also influenced by the premise of value appropriate to the valuation assignment. The premise of value means: (1) is the individual intangible to be valued separate from all other assets? or (2) is the individual intangible to be valued as part of a going-concern sports franchise operation?

For purchase price allocation purposes, the premise of value as part of a going-concern sports franchise is the most applicable premise. Accordingly, analysts typically derive discount/capitalization rates related to the sports franchise business when valuing intangibles for purchase price allocation purposes.

Expected Remaining Useful Life

The analysis of the sports franchise intangible's RUL is an important procedure in the valuation process. This procedure is an integral component of each valuation approach.

In the income approach, the RUL directly affects the selection of the income projection period. In the sales comparison approach, the RUL affects the selection and/or adjustment of comparative sale/license transactions. And, in the cost approach, the RUL affects the quantification of any obsolescence allowances.

Valuation Synthesis and Conclusion

The value synthesis and conclusion is the final procedure in the intangible asset valuation process. If two or more approaches were used (or, if two or more methods were used within one approach), the analyst has to conclude a final value estimate based on alternative value indications. There are two categories of steps in the synthesis and conclusion procedure.

First, the analyst reviews each analysis. . .

Second, the analyst assigns a weighting to each value indication based on: (1) the quantity and quality of available data, (2) the relative applicability of the selected approaches/methods to the subject intangible, (3) any applicable statistical tests of data/analysis reliability, (4) the degree of dispersion of the value indications, (5) the professional judgment of the analyst, and (6) the accumulated experience of the analyst in performing sports franchise valuations.

The synthesis of alternative value indications can be based on either a quantitative or a qualitative weighting. Ultimately, regardless of the weighting mathematics, the final value estimate is a product of the individual analyst's reasoned judgment and professional experience.

In the case of sports franchise intangibles, it is often the case that only one valuation approach is applicable. . . .

Common Valuation Methods for Individual Sports Franchise Intangible Assets

This discussion will present common intangible asset valuation methods. Analysts should consider all reasonable valuation approaches/methods in the analysis of sports franchise intangibles. Particularly with regard to sports franchise intangibles, the ultimate selection of the appropriate valuation methods should be based on the facts and circumstances of the actual assignment.

Player Contracts

Player contracts often represent the largest acquired intangible asset of a professional sports team. Additionally, because player contract values are amortized over the remaining useful lives of the individual player contracts, this results in significant income tax savings.

The player contracts related to the team's professional athletes are often valued using a cost approach method. The multiyear player development process is much more complicated than the process to train, say, the franchise customer relations manager.

. . . However, the analytical procedure of estimating the current cost to replace a seasoned player is still applicable to the valuation of player contracts.

The replacement cost analysis of a contract athlete is very complicated. The analysis involves a detailed examination of the procedures the franchise would use to hypothetically replace its current roster. This analysis involves consideration of the costs and player development activities of farm teams, minor leagues, and other professional training programs. The valuation also involves a detailed analysis of each player, in terms of position, statistics, quantitative and qualitative rankings, age, experience, current physical condition, and so forth.

And, the analysis involves a detailed analysis of each contract, including compensation, term to maturity, expected renewals (based on a rigorous RUL analysis), and any contract-specific conditions. Coaches, franchise officials, sports writers, industry experts, and other industry authorities are often consulted as part of the replacement cost analysis.

The result of the replacement cost analysis may be (1) a unique value estimate and (2) a unique RUL estimate for each acquired player contract.

The market approach is often used to corroborate the cost approach when valuing player contracts of a professional sports team. The most common variation of the market approach is to find a qualified independent industry expert in that particular sport who would give an independent assessment of the value of each player contract based upon his/her personal experience in the sport. However, there are difficulties with this methodology in that these estimates of value can be deemed very subjective and considered anecdotal evidence by the Service.

. . . .

Franchise Agreement

Membership in a professional sports league provides the member franchise with certain privileges and rights. Among these privileges and rights is the right to share in revenue generated by the national league.

. . . .

. . . A critical question in the franchise agreement valuation analysis is: "To what revenue is the professional sports team entitled because of its ownership of the franchise intangible asset?"

. . . .

The national franchise agreement is typically valued using the income approach. The income approach analysis is based on projections of the economic income specifically attributable to the franchise agreement. Projected economic income from the franchise agreement is then discounted at an appropriate present value discount rate in order to estimate the value of the franchise intangible asset.

The national franchise agreement can be valued several different ways. The franchise is sometimes valued based on the present value of a projection of future (1) ticket sales net income and (2) any other income not assigned to other intangibles. This projection is made over the term of the franchise expected RUL.

Another method used to value the franchise is to project the total economic income expected to be generated from all sources over the franchise expected RUL. From this "gross" projection of economic income, an economic rent or capital charge (i.e., a fair rate of return) on each of the other identified intangibles is subtracted. The present value of this "net" economic income projection (i.e., total annual income less the annual economic rent/capital charge on all other intangibles) over the franchise expected RUL provides a value indication for the national franchise agreement.

Stadium Lease

The venue in which a professional sports team plays is an increasingly important factor in its financial success. As such, stadium leases have become core assets of professional sports franchises.

A professional sports team will either own or lease its stadium. In the event that a professional sports team leases its stadium (typically from the local stadium authority), the stadium lease may be a significant intangible asset.

To estimate the value of a lease agreement, traditional analyses compare (1) the terms of the subject lease to (2) the terms of other leases for similar properties. This "market-based" analysis allows the analyst to determine whether rent paid by the subject lessee is favorable or unfavorable to that paid under leases for comparable property. For "favorable" lease agreements, value is estimated based on the present value of future rent savings.

It may be difficult to show that a particular stadium lease agreement is favorable. This is because the specific terms of stadium lease agreements are usually confidential. Moreover, even if lease terms are available, the level of revenue generated and the expenses incurred vary significantly by team. The substantial variance in revenues and expenses makes direct comparisons of rent payments among professional sports teams difficult.

The difficulty of performing a traditional valuation analysis for stadium lease agreements is compounded by the fact that lease "comparables" generally do not exist in the professional sports industry. . . .

In some cases, however, it is possible to estimate the value of a stadium lease using the income approach. This analysis involves the projection of future economic income attributable to the lease agreement itself. . . .

In addition to the stadium, many sports franchises either own or lease training facilities and other specialized real estate properties. Obviously, owned stadiums and training facilities are substantial components of the overall value of the franchise. Real estate-related contracts are also important intangible assets to franchise holders. The real estate-related intangibles may include:

1. leasehold interest to the primary arena/stadium property,
2. leasehold interest to training or other specialized facilities,
3. sub-lease agreements with event promoters to present concerts and other events at the arena/stadium,
4. contracts with advertisers to display/broadcast advertisements within the arena/stadium,
5. leases of skyboxes and other premium seating, and
6. sub-leases with restaurants, retailers, and other vendors.

. . . .

Trained and Assembled Workforce

Several sports franchise intangible assets relate to employees. First, there is a trained and assembled administrative workforce. This workforce includes management, marketing, public relations, customer relations, accounting, and other "front office" and "back office" personnel. Other than a few senior executives, it is unlikely that these employees will be under contract.

Second, there is the coaching and player development staff. This workforce includes scouts, recruiting agents, special team and assistant coaches, physical therapy and medical personnel, and senior coaches. Many, but not all, of these employees are likely to be under contract.

And, third, there are the team players. Typically, all of the team players will be under some type of contract.

For human capital-related intangibles, the cost approach is often used. For sports franchise administrative personnel, value is often a function of the cost to recruit, hire, and train an assembled workforce of equivalent experience and expertise as the subject workforce. For the coaching and player development staff, the replacement cost method may also be used.

Because of (1) the relatively limited pool of employment candidates and (2) the strategic importance of head/specialty coaches to the franchise, the recruitment costs for these employees can be quite large (compared to, say, similarly compensated marketing franchise executives).

. . . .

Intellectual Property

There are four legal categories of intellectual property: patents, copyrights, trademarks, and trade secrets. The value of the franchise workforce generally encompasses the value of the organization's trade secrets. The franchise may have developed some specialized systems and procedures related to accounting, administration, player therapeutic procedures, and even player development. These trade secrets may be documented in written standards and manuals. If such manuals exist, they are also intangible assets. However, most of the trade secrets of a sports franchise are encompassed in the collective knowledge and experience of its employees.

Some franchises may hold copyrights on team songs, team brochures, team slogans, and so forth. If these copyrights exist, they are also acquired intangible assets.

Typically more valuable than copyrights, most sports franchises have trademarks and trade names (and services marks, associated trade dress, etc.). This intangible asset category may include the team name. Related to the team name and logo, there may be national and/or local product licenses. These name-related product licenses are a secondary, but important, source of income to the franchise.

Contracts

In addition to product licenses (and to the national franchise agreement and stadium lease), many sports franchises have numerous contract-related intangible assets. . . .

For contract-related intangibles (other than player contracts), the income approach is often used. These analyses typically involve estimating the present value of the economic income projected to and earned by the franchise over the contract RUL (including expected renewals). The specific type of economic income depends on the type of contract. . .

Favorable vendor/supplier contracts may be valued using a cost savings method, where the reduction in operating costs/expenses (compared to noncontract market rates) is (1) projected and (2) present valued over the RUL of the current contract.

Season Ticketholder Subscriptions

Clearly, an important intangible asset for many sports franchises is the customer-related intangible. This intangible typically includes recurring customer relationships with both (1) corporate/institutional season ticketholders and (2) individual season ticketholders.

Season ticketholders are often valued using the income approach. This analysis considers: (1) the expected coverage RUL of the season ticketholder relationships, (2) current and future ticket prices, and (3) the cost of servicing (providing sports entertainment to) the season ticketholder fan. The present value of the expected future net income from season subscriptions provides a value indication for this intangible.

Acquired Goodwill

Lastly, buyers sometimes pay for intangible goodwill in their acquisitions of professional sports franchises. With regard to sports franchises, goodwill is often considered to be the portion of the franchise purchase price that cannot be associated with any of the identified tangible or intangible assets. Under this definition, goodwill is the residual (i.e., remaining) purchase price premium that is not allocated to any other acquired tangible or intangible asset.

Goodwill is typically valued based on a residual analysis for purchase price allocation purposes. That is, the residual value assigned to the acquired intangible value in the nature of goodwill is:

total purchase price paid for the sports franchise
less: value of transferred net working capital (if any)
less: value of transferred tangible personal property (if any)
less: value of tangible real estate (if any)
less: value of acquired individual intangible assets
equals: value assigned to acquired goodwill

. . . . *[The authors' example of a simplified purchase price allocation is omitted.]*

THE IMPACT OF STADIUM ECONOMICS ON THE VALUE OF THE PROFESSIONAL SPORTS FRANCHISE

Scott Levine

The economics of professional sports franchises have changed dramatically over the last few years. Sports franchises have increased in value throughout the history of sports. Recently, due primarily to changes in the value of franchises' stadium/arena assets, this franchise value increase has been exponential.

. . . .

PRÉCIS

. . . The value of a professional sports franchise is increasingly tied to the venue in which it plays.
. . . Changing stadium economics and . . . the development of new stadiums/the renovation of existing stadiums have resulted in increased revenue streams that accrue to the sports teams — rather than to the city where the team plays.

The increasing value of professional sports franchises has resulted in greater regulatory scrutiny on the valuation of these organizations and, specifically, on the valuation of their intangible assets. . . .

. . . .

THE RECENT INCREASE IN CONSTRUCTION OF NEW STADIUMS

Historically, a sports stadium was simply a venue where games were played. Professional sports franchises typically earned little revenue from the facility, other than (perhaps) sharing in concession and parking revenue. Currently, however, new stadiums are state-of-the-art entertainment facilities. And, professional sports team owners have seized on the opportunities provided by new stadiums to maximize stadium revenue and increase team value.

Accordingly, the construction of new stadiums or the renovation of existing stadiums is prevalent throughout the professional sports industry. This is due principally to demands made by the team owners. Many teams have suggested that survival in their current market depends on the construction of a new stadium. Franchise owners in each of the four major sports leagues complain that team economic losses continue to accumulate even as player salaries increase. Therefore, the stadium is increasingly being used as a resource to generate greater revenue and offset higher player salaries.

The basic economic principles of supply and demand explain (1) why there is an increase in stadium construction and (2) why cities are willing to acquiesce to the demands of the professional sports franchise. The number of cities interested in being home to a professional sports franchise far exceeds the supply of such franchises. . . .

Many other professional sports franchise owners have successfully used the threat of relocation as leverage to obtain new stadium deals. These stadium deals are often financed indirectly by taxpayers — and not by the franchise owner. Favorable lease terms also allow the professional sports franchise to receive most of the revenue associated with the team's stadium without having to incur the costs related to the construction of the stadium.

. . . .

Therefore, it is not surprising that the construction of new stadiums has increased exponentially in recent years. . . .

. . . .

Those teams without new stadium deals will be on the wrong end of the increasing gap in the values of professional sports franchises.

STADIUM ECONOMICS AND VALUE OF PROFESSIONAL SPORTS FRANCHISES

Each of the four major sports leagues has some type of revenue sharing arrangement that is, at least in theory, designed to lead to economic parity. Each league shares licensing revenue, merchandise sales, and national television revenues without regard to (1) a team's win–loss record or (2) the number of appearances on network television.

With the exception of gate receipts, all stadium-related revenues may be subject to negotiated sharing arrangements. Revenues related to luxury suites, club suites, naming rights, advertising, parking, and concessions can be shared between the team and the municipal/private stadium owner/lessor. The revenue-sharing arrangements are spelled out in the stadium lease agreement.

Cities are competing more aggressively to retain existing franchises or to persuade franchises to relocate. Therefore, franchises are increasingly able (1) to negotiate favorable lease terms and (2) to control all facility-related events (games, concerts, etc.).

. . . .

Approximately two-thirds of the 120 teams in the four major sports leagues play or will play in facilities that have sold naming rights. Those teams that haven't sold naming rights — or are not in a position to control the use of naming rights — are finding it more difficult to compete both on and off the playing field.

. . . .

The phenomena of (1) new stadium-related revenue streams and (2) increasing team value attributable to stadiums have resulted in a greater focus on the valuation of the stadium lease asset.

WHY A VALUATION ANALYSIS IS NECESSARY

Generally, a valuation of a professional sports franchise is required for one of the following purposes:

1. the purchase or sale of the franchise,
2. gifting of a block of the franchise stock, or
3. corporate strategic planning for the franchise owners.

The value of the franchise can be estimated without a separate valuation of all of the franchise tangible and intangible assets. However, the most credible valuation typically includes an independent analysis of each franchise asset, including the stadium asset. In the event of a purchase or sale of the franchise, accounting standards require a discrete valuation of each franchise asset.

GENERALLY ACCEPTED VALUATION APPROACHES

There are three generally accepted approaches to value any asset, including a sports franchise asset: (1) the cost approach, (2) the market approach, and (3) the income approach.

The cost approach is based upon the economic principle of substitution. This basic economic principle asserts that an investor will pay no more for an asset than the cost to obtain an asset of equal utility.

The market (or sales comparison) approach is based upon the related economic principles of competition and equilibrium. These economic principles conclude that, in a free and unrestricted market, supply and demand factors will drive the price of an investment to equilibrium.

The income approach is based upon the economic principle of anticipation. In this approach, the value of an asset is the present value of the expected economic income to be earned from the ownership of that asset.

VALUATION OF THE STADIUM LEASE ASSET

The traditional valuation approaches with regard to the stadium lease asset may need to be reevaluated. This is because these traditional valuation approaches may not reflect the changing environment of sports stadium economics.

The cost approach is not often used to value a sports stadium lease. This is because the cost approach does not account for [the] projected future income generating capacity of the stadium. For older stadiums, the cost approach may result in an understated value.

Historically, a market approach analysis was typically used to value the stadium lease asset. This was because the terms of lease agreements were homogenous, and that fact allowed for a market-based rental comparison. The market approach was based primarily on a comparison of the favorability of the subject stadium lease compared to other stadium leases.

For favorable lease agreements, the value of the stadium lease asset was estimated based on the present value of future rent savings. However, the intricacy and variability of stadium leases (as well as the diversity of revenue streams generated by each stadium) makes a valuation analysis based on favorability more difficult.

. . . The amount of additional income generated by a new stadium . . . depends on (1) the circumstances under which the stadium is constructed, (2) the allocation of stadium construction costs, and (3) the provisions of the stadium lease. Of course, these are all variables that are individual (1) to each franchise and (2) to each franchise stadium lease.

In addition, the contractual terms of most stadium leases are kept confidential between the municipal lessor and the franchise owner lessee. Accordingly, due to these data limitations, the market approach is not always relevant in the valuation of the stadium lease asset.

As the professional sports stadium has become more of an income producing asset with predictable revenue streams, income approach methods are used to a greater extent. The revenue and expenses directly related to the stadium are estimated over a discrete time period into the future. This projection of economic income is converted into a present value by the use of the present value discount rate.

The present value discount rate is the investor's required rate of return over the expected term of the economic income projection. The term of the income projection period depends on the expected remaining useful life ("RUL") of the stadium. The stadium lease asset RUL is generally measured based on the remaining term of the lease agreement.

CONCLUSION

The owner of a professional sports team, though still focused on winning championships, is increasingly concerned with profitability. As a result of efforts to identify and maximize new revenue streams, the professional sports stadium now serves as a core asset of a professional sports franchise.

New state-of-the-art stadium facilities have successfully generated greater revenue for the resident teams. Ultimately these stadium leases have contributed to higher franchise values for many franchise organizations.

The number of new stadiums currently under construction or planned for development should extend this franchise value enhancement trend well into the future.

As the professional sports team operations focus more attention on aspects related to the economics of the franchise, the stadium asset will be used (1) as a tool to increase franchise value as well as (2) a mechanism to reduce the franchise income tax obligations.

THE MARKET STRUCTURE OF SPORTS

Gerald W. Scully

REPUTATIONAL CAPITAL AND THE SALE OF FRANCHISES

In theory the sales price of a going enterprise is the cost of replicating its assets. A buyer will pay no more than it would cost to start a comparable enterprise from scratch. A seller will take no less than the market value of the assets. Yet firms have reputations as well as assets, and business reputations may be good or bad. The most obvious instances of a bad reputation are bankruptcy and managerial ineptitude that lead to poor returns on assets. Firms with poor reputations sell at prices below the cost of replicating the assets, and have a higher probability of being sold, because new owners with average business skills can earn at least the competitive return on the assets. Some firms have good reputations, and they may sell at prices greater than the cost of replicating their assets. The theory of why reputable firms exchange at a price above the cost of replicating their assets is not well developed. One possibility is that reputable firms have a larger market share (sales per unit of assets) and more loyal (repeat) customers than firms with average or poor reputations. Another argument rests on the notion of the "winner's curse." In an auction the winner (the one paying the highest price for the asset) is the person with the greatest expectation of making a return on the investment. Winners . . . paid more than the expected value . . . and hence were losers.

Sports provide a good opportunity for modeling and measuring the effect of reputation. . . . Teams do not have win percents (outputs) that randomly fluctuate around the mean; rather, they have long cycles of momentum. Over some period, a club's record improves serially, perhaps culminating in a championship. This is followed by a period of serial decline, perhaps culminating in a cellar finish. Over this momentum cycle teams acquire reputations as winners or losers. Reputation affects the value and the timing of the sale of sport franchises.

. . . .

REPUTATIONS AND ASSET VALUES

. . . .

. . . Brand names, trademarks, and business reputations are specific intangible assets whose value is peculiar to the firm. . . . Such investments are like physical investments and are capitalized in the value of the firm. Beyond these tangible and intangible assets, firms may have good or bad reputations. These intangible assets are reputational capital that affect the exchange price of physical capital (both general and specific).

Bankruptcy is bad reputation. It has been observed that the assets of bankrupt firms exchange at a lower price than those of nonbankrupt firms, and that the prices of foreclosed houses or commercial property and automobiles are lower than the prices of nonforeclosed assets. . . . Part of the price differential, however, may be due to bad reputation. . . . In the case of bankrupt firms, particularly those that rely on repeat business, there may be a perception of unreliability and potential malfeasance (cost-cutting during start-up by the new owner) that results in previous customers switching their business to competing firms. The bad reputational capital of bankrupt firms implies that the physical assets of such firms will exchange at lower prices than their replication cost for reasons beyond thinness of the market or creditor pressure.

Some firms have good reputations. These firms make products or provide services that are perceived by customers to be of particularly high quality. Where product or service quality is due entirely to capital (physical and human) investment, assets of high-quality firms exchange at their replication cost, no more and no less. In equilibrium the increased cost of production is reflected in a price differential for the product or service. Where price differentials do not exist for products or services that differ by quality, pure reputational rents (positive or negative) are earned by firms. . . . The prospective new owner has some assurance that customers will continue to deal with the firm with an established reputation for quality. This stream of net revenue from customer satisfaction is capitalized in the exchange price of the franchise. The argument, mutatis mutandis, holds for firms with bad reputations. The bad reputation (negative rents) is capitalized in the exchange value of the assets.

. . . .

REPUTATIONS AND THE VALUE AND TIMING OF THE SALE OF FRANCHISES

. . . .

. . . The demand for wins depends on the size of the franchise market, which is measured conventionally by SMSA or MSA population, and on the elasticity of demand for winning, which includes such factors as per capita income and number of competing sports. . . . Conventionally, clubs in big cities or with fickle fans win more games than small-city clubs or clubs with loyal fans.

. . . .

The value of a franchise is the discounted net cash flow of the club. Over some range in the win percent . . . the value of a franchise is a constant. The value . . . is an empirical matter. In other words good and bad luck, as random events, do not affect the market perception of the value of the franchise. However if the club win percent is . . . not a random event, the market value of the franchise is affected. A club that is sustaining a record of say two or three standard deviations above . . . is perceived as a winner (good reputation), while a club that is sustaining a record of two or three standard deviations below . . . is perceived as a loser (bad reputation). These reputational effects are theorized to affect the price at which the franchise will exchange. . .

. . . .

. . . All clubs in all sports go through periods of rising performance and then periods of decline . . . A club's search for and development of playing talent takes considerable time. As players are developed, their skills and performance increase, and these net increments to the stock of club playing talent increase the win percent. Player skills reach a peak and then decline. Veteran star players attract fans for reasons beyond their playing skills (recognition and reputation). Because roster size is fixed, and aging veterans' skills are in decline, the retention of these star players leads to a decline in club standing. Eventually, the stars are replaced with rookies, and the club's fortunes on the playing field decline until the new rookie talent matures.

This momentum in club win percent mimics a pattern of good and bad reputation. As the team declines over a long period of time, its reputation declines. Losing in sports is equivalent to bankruptcy. A long pattern of decline and a level of decline that leads to severe financial distress can bankrupt a franchise and induce a distress sale. A number of clubs have been bankrupt or have been near bankruptcy because of long stays in the cellar. . .

. . . Bankrupt or cellar teams are sold for reasons of financial distress. Because of a bad reputation, the club's assets exchange for less than the assets of a club in a market of similar size with an average reputation. There exists a market of specialists who believe that they can take over a club's playing assets and transform the bad reputation into an average reputation. . . . Thus the probability of a sale is high for clubs with bad reputations.

Clubs with good reputations (e.g., those with positive momentum that culminates in a league championship) will exchange at a price above the price of a club in a market of similar size with an average reputation. Thus the probability of a sale also is high for franchises with good reputations. Because the evidence on momentum suggests that there are cycles in reputations, the payment of a premium for a winning franchise would seem irrational. Such sales are partly due to the "winner's curse" and partly to asymmetrical information between the buyer and seller. The buyer purchases the team for his own use, and he and other potential buyers have different estimates of their ability to run the team. As in a common-value auction, the winning bid is from the buyer with the highest regard for his abilities to run the club. Furthermore the information between the seller and the potential bidders may be asymmetric and not very dense. The seller is likely to know with more certainty than potential buyers the path of future team performance, given the stock of playing talent. Potential buyers may overestimate their ability to maintain the team's momentum with acquisitions in the players' market. . . .

As an empirical matter, franchise sales at the bottom of the market occur with about twice the frequency of sales at the top of the market. Finally, a club with an average reputation will have a lower probability of sale. Average assets exchange at a fair market value; all that a new owner can expect is the average rate of return.

. . . . *[The author's discussion of the empirical evidence of the timing of sales is omitted.]*

PROFITS, CAPITAL APPRECIATION, AND THE DURATION OF OWNERSHIP

Several decades ago sport was more sport than business. The press reported the games, players played for small wages, owners were from the sport and ran the front offices indifferently, and the fans paid a few dollars to see their favorite team beat the visiting club. Nothing in the front office was of any concern except player trades and acquisitions. Now sport is a big business. Many players earn millions of dollars and are celebrities. . . .

For several decades public policy concerns have been raised about professional sports: Does the restriction on the number of clubs in a league lead to "excess" profits? Do league rules on revenue sharing and exclusivity of franchise territory affect the bottom line sufficiently to preclude small-city clubs from being competitive? Is the fading of family ownership of clubs and the tax-shelter feature of franchises responsible for a more rapid turnover of clubs?

OPERATING PROFITS IN SPORTS

As with any business, there are two dimensions to the financial returns of club ownership: annual net cash flow from operations and capital gains from the appreciation of the business. The historical evidence on profitability in team sports is scant. The conventional wisdom is that, except for football, clubs located in small markets are marginal operations that cannot effectively compete with big-city clubs. Given the wide disparity in franchise market size, the view is that big-city clubs earn large monopoly profits, while small-city clubs hang by a thread to survive another day.

. . . .

It is difficult to separate fact from fancy about operational profits in professional team sports for several reasons. As privately owned entities, the clubs have no obligation to reveal their finances. Fearing political scrutiny of their business practices, the teams tend to overstate expenses and understate operating profits in public pronouncements. Stated losses from operations are often a figment of creative accounting. It is not unusual for a club, even one with a losing record located in a small market, to generate a positive cash flow while the books show red ink. This is due in part to the way clubs are purchased. A common method of purchasing a club is for investors to form a separate corporation that owns the club. The investors lend the money for the purchase and receive interest payments. These payments are a cost on the club's books, but are in fact a method of taking a cash flow from its operations. Further, an owner (managing partner) may take a large salary, a generous expense account, insurance, and other benefits. These are operational costs to a club, but may in part represent a profit withdrawal. . . . These are but a few of the accounting issues in sports that cause skepticism about statements of financial duress in professional team sports.

. . . .

. . . The effect of winning on the club's bottom line is 2.9 times that of franchise market size and is comparable to the effect on team revenue. Winning in team sports not only generates revenue for a club but greatly affects the profit margin. Is it any wonder that baseball and basketball owners bid aggressively for star-caliber free agents?

CAPITAL APPRECIATION OF SPORTS FRANCHISES

Generally, the profit margin in professional team sports is quite good, and for some clubs it is extraordinary. What of capital gains? Casual empiricism suggests that the value of a typical franchise rises over time. Historically, owners have been able to count on substantial capital gains at the time of sale. . . . Multi-million-dollar gains in the value of sports franchises have been the rule in all sports in recent times.

What has been the historical rate of appreciation of sport franchises? Are there differences in capital appreciation rates by sport? Are the appreciation rates skewed among clubs based on franchise market size? . . .

. . . .

While inspection . . . reveals that franchise values are correlated with franchise market size, we might ask if the rate of capital appreciation is related to the type of sport or to the franchise market size. Owning a sport franchise is more risky than owning treasury bonds, but the risks across sports should be the same. Efficient capital-market theory would suggest that no significant differences should exist in returns by sport or by size of the market.

. . . It is fair to conclude that there are no differences in the rates of return by sport or by market size.

TOTAL RETURN TO FRANCHISE OWNERSHIP

The total return to franchise ownership is annual profit plus capital gain. . . . For all sports the total return during the early 1990s was 27 percent per year. Big-city clubs had higher total returns than small-city clubs (33.3 percent versus 20.5 percent). . . .

Can we conclude that monopoly profit exists in professional sports? An annual rate of return of 27 percent for an average club is very attractive. The median profit as a percent of sales (revenue) for the 500 largest industrial corporations typically ranged from 3.9 to 5.5 percent over the period 1975–89. Investors in the stock market obtain gains in stock prices and dividends of about 10 percent per year. Thus, compared to profits in large corporations or the risky alternative of the stock market, the return to franchise ownership is much larger.

. . . .

. . . It would be fair to conclude that a number of clubs do evidence a monopoly return. If a 30-percent or greater return to franchise ownership is taken as evidence of monopoly, then about half of the clubs in professional team sports earn a monopoly return.

THE DURATION OF OWNERSHIP

For how long are clubs held before they are sold to other investors? Are there differences in the tenure of ownership among the sports? I was able to construct a sample of 387 franchise sales in the history of the four team sports. . . . While the distributions in all of the sports are skewed, there are apparent differences among them. Football has the longest average tenure of ownership at 13.2 years. . . Baseball has a mean tenure of 11.2 years. . . Hockey has a mean tenure of 11.8 years. . . Tenure of ownership is shortest in basketball, with a mean of 7.6 years. . .

The change in type of ownership from family to corporate or syndicate ownership and the rise of sports as a tax shelter have been identified as sources of a greater turnover of franchises. The conventional wisdom is that the new corporate and syndicate investors in sports are more concerned with financial return than with bringing a championship to the hometown fans.

. . . . *[The author's discussion of taxation and accounting of professional sports franchises is omitted. See Chapter 4 for a discussion of this topic.]*

MOODY'S METHODOLOGY FOR RATING SPORTS-RELATED ENTERPRISES

Neil Begley, David Hamburger, and Robert Konefal

THE RELATIONSHIP BETWEEN ENTERTAINMENT, MEDIA, AND SPORTS

. . . Sports provide broadcasters and advertisers with: 1) attractive demographics; 2) strong lead-ins to promote other properties; 3) a strong national and local branding strategy; and 4) a loyal viewer base. On a stand-alone basis, . . . the ownership of sports franchises is not a major direct source of cash flow relative to its asset value. However, some franchises provide significant indirect benefits as a programming asset that has been used to develop cable networks. . . . Therefore . . . sports franchises will continue to be important to media entertainment content and distribution companies, whether directly owned or not, for the foreseeable future.

. . . The media industry will have an increasing impact on both sports and the credit ratings of sports transactions as rights fees for both local and national broadcasting contracts have become larger percentages of team revenues. Over the last decade, the monetary value of these contracts has grown at a tremendous rate. However . . . economic downturns make these contracts less profitable to the media outlets (i.e. broadcast networks), and extended challenging economic periods will temper their values. The other threats to contract growth come from: 1) the fragmentation of television audiences resulting from the increase in the number of cable channels and the rise in the number of alternate entertainment sources, such as the Internet, and 2) also from potential consolidation of broadcast networks and stations if the FCC [Federal Communications Commission] relaxes current regulations which could reduce the number of independent bidders for broadcast rights. As a result . . . media companies will strain to turn a material profit, if any, on their sports investments, and the rising rights fees could affect the profits of broadcast and cable distributors with adverse consequences for their credit quality, and the credit quality of the sports leagues they support.

METHODOLOGY FOR RATING SPORTS-RELATED ENTERPRISES

Top-Down Analytical Approach

Moody's believes in using a top-down analytical approach to rating all sports-related transactions. The four primary areas of analytical focus include:

1. Strength of the league, trade association, or sanctioning body and its impact and ultimate control on the sports franchises,
2. Characteristics of the individual company or franchise, the ownership and age of the playing facility, the stability of the revenue base, and market size,
3. Specific transaction, the organization and capital structure, indenture terms and conditions for the financing,
4. Revenue (particularly COD analysis, credit metrics, and asset coverage).

Sports Leagues and Sanctioning Bodies

. . . .

Degree of implicit support from the league and history of governance.   . . . Sports leagues/sanctioning bodies play a significant role in the rating of a sports team. In addition to assessing the financial quality of the league, including the amount of league debt (which very likely is senior to even secured franchise debt in terms of priority of claim on some of the most creditworthy revenue streams, though if divided among all teams it often represents a very minor portion of the capital structure and, therefore, would not likely have an impact on the rating at the secured team debt level) and its impact on the profitability of the individual teams, Moody's assesses the degree to which the league provides implicit support to the teams. Moody's measures implicit support by judging the league on three criteria: 1) ability to limit franchise indebtedness; 2) socialistic nature, including framework for revenue sharing and maintaining competitive balance; and 3) ability and history of governance and assessment of teams for financial needs and default cures for distressed franchises.

1. League can help limit franchise indebtedness.   The strength of the league's constitution and by-laws helps restrain a team's propensity for higher credit risk by limiting the amount of secured debt at individual teams. They also define the degree to which the league can step in to assist a team that is in financial distress within the commissioner's unilateral rights. The league or sanctioning body can enforce the by laws because a significant portion of revenues flow through them to the teams (such as national media rights and licensing in contrast to local media and advertising rights), assuming that the league controls those revenues and can withhold or offset a team's share against unpaid assessments or other violations.

While these debt restrictions limit the amount of debt that can be secured by the assets of the team, they generally do not restrict unsecured or subordinated (structurally or contractually) debt, or, sometimes, debt incurred by the stadium or arena if not owned directly by the franchise or franchise owners. The league's ability to limit overall indebtedness, not just debt secured by the assets, is an important rating factor as it helps strengthen the individual franchise's credit metrics. However, Moody's is concerned that team owners will succeed in pressuring the leagues to increase these debt limits (and they generally have), especially given the increase in both players' salaries expenses and media contract revenues, as was the case with the NFL when they raised the secured debt limit to $125 million from $100 million. Moody's takes all consolidated enterprise debt into consideration when arriving at a rating assessment. This includes double and triple leverage such as debt at the partnership or stadium levels, which can cause overhang on the assessment if there is recourse to the franchise or its revenues, or if the franchise is servicing this debt in any fashion. As well, another one of the several important criteria for attaining a better high-yield or investment grade rating, is if asset coverage of total enterprise debt is well over 3.0×.

In order to skirt around secured debt limits, there is a growing interest in the securitization of specific contractually obligated revenue streams, such as the Major League Baseball deal and as stadium companies often do with COI [contractually obligated income] streams. . . . Securitization of teams and arenas may possess the same risks as "whole business securitizations" as significant cash flows are stripped from the franchise, and its ability to service its debt and operate as a going concern can be questioned from the outset. Also, separation of the arena and the franchise is difficult, and the arena on its own may be worth very little without the franchise continuing to operate in the venue as intended and as a going concern. That aside, securitizations can have a negative impact on corporate ratings, even though they are usually secured by revenue streams and are not secured by "team" assets, since they often siphon off some of the strongest and most predictable revenue streams.

2. Socialistic nature can help ensure economic viability. . . . Leagues that maintain a socialistic view regarding revenue sharing and competitive balance ensure a greater degree of economic viability. Ratings decisions incorporate an analysis of which revenues streams are shared and what sharing agreements are firmly in place. While revenue sharing may reduce the short-term profitability of the most profitable teams, it helps ensure the long-term stability of the whole league. . . . The NFL and NASCAR are models of the most progressive and socialistic of the major sports because of their strong revenue-sharing provisions.

3. Ability to assess teams for financial needs and default cures for distressed franchises. . . . A league's unilateral and unconditional ability to assess individual teams for its own financial needs or to cure defaults for distressed franchises is an important credit factor for both league and individual franchise debt. Moody's A3 senior unsecured rating for the NFL is predicated on the NFL Commissioner's power to assess the teams in order to meet debt service requirements or cure default. There have been few instances when a major sports team has filed for bankruptcy protection. . . . In order for a league/team to obtain a strong debt rating, Moody's would look to the league or sanctioning body's willingness to step in prior to default and bridge the default with a cure or repayment until the team is sold. This would only likely serve the secured creditors as unsecured creditors above the franchise level who are structurally subordinated have generally little or no recourse until the team is sold (assuming they are covered by the asset value). Therefore, unsecured or structurally subordinated creditors benefit little from the league's direct implicit support but do benefit if the result is a timely ownership change at reasonable resale levels. Moody's looks for language in the debt indentures, league bylaws or constitution allowing the league to cure any teams before they default or need to make a public bankruptcy filing, even if it means assessing other teams or borrowing to do so. . . .

Player salary controls and labor relationship. An important influence the leagues have over the teams stems from the overall quality of the leagues' relationship with labor and, specifically, the leagues' ability to cap or contain player salary costs in the event that the team owner's history of financial discipline in containing player costs relative to the revenues generated is very weak. Over the past several years, player salary costs have increased dramatically, outpacing overall team revenue growth. As a result, we have seen an increase in the percentage of revenues that goes to player salaries. . . . Adequate control of payroll costs is essential to ensuring league-wide financial health and a league-wide competitive environment. Moody's focuses on the collective bargaining agreements (CBA's), especially on the following factors:

1. The strength and reach of the salary caps ("hard" or "soft" caps): A "hard" cap, like that of the NFL, can enhance the credit characteristics of a franchise since it fixes salaries as a percentage of total revenues so that operating margins do not compress during times of revenue decline. A "soft" cap, like that of the NBA, which provides cap exemptions, such as a one-time exemption for signing veteran free agents, could pressure margins given revenue volatility. Moody's views the salary caps instituted by the NFL and the NBA as positive for the credit profile of the two leagues while the lack of significant controls at MLB, even with the new CBA, and NHL could be detrimental to the overall credit quality of those leagues.

2. Luxury taxes or player fines, through escrow arrangements, to force salary controls: Moody's views these structural cap controls as beneficial since they help instill financial discipline (though they do not enforce absolute discipline) and help towards rationalizing the league's cost structure.

3. Tenor of the CBA: In order to achieve a Ba or investment grade rating, Moody's prefers to see the expiration of the CBA extend beyond the maturity of franchise or league debt. In some cases, a franchise can establish a work stoppage reserve that could mitigate the impact of a strike on debt service. However, these reserves are not generally funded sufficiently to weather a protracted work stoppage or to comfort lenders sufficiently enough to refinance maturing debt. In addition, the CBA ideally should extend beyond the maturity of the national broadcasting contract in order to ensure fewer obstacles for the renewal of the media rights.

4. Manner in which players are paid (i.e. salary vs. up front bonus) and the existence of guaranteed contracts: . . . Up front bonuses essentially put capital at risk should that player underperform or be injured. As well, the prevalence of long-term guaranteed contracts increases the risk of uncontrolled player costs when a hard cap does not exist and under performance by the team when hard caps do exist. Without a salary cap, to the extent that teams sign players to long-term guaranteed agreements and then either trade or release them, this practice could lead to high player costs, reflecting both the costs of present players and the costs of players no longer on that team.

5. Deferred compensation clauses and pre-funding: Just as important as controlling present salary costs is the ability of the leagues to control future expenses. Many athletes sign long-term contracts with deferred compensation clauses. . . . An important factor in assessing the financial health of a team is the amount of deferred compensation it has and, if the league mandates pre-funding of such contracts, what, if any, impact does it have on the team's liquidity. . . . A conservative approach is necessary to ensure proper coverage of the obligations. The NFL, for instance, requires teams to allocate the present value of their deferred compensation when the contract is signed. That money is placed in a separate escrow account, which is controlled by the league.

. . . .

National broadcast contracts.   One of the most important influences the leagues have on the teams, particularly in the NFL, NASCAR, and in the NBA, is the national broadcasting contract, which has become a critical source of income for the smaller market teams. . . . Analysis of these contracts focuses on the ability of the broadcasters to make timely payments and to continue those payments in the event of a stoppage of play. Essentially, Moody's looks for an unconditional guarantee to make the timely payments and then to work out any give-backs at a later date. . . . Moody's factors in the credit quality of the broadcasting partners, using a weighted average rating (assuming the counterparty is equivalent in credit quality to the rated entity), into our analysis. The ratings of the individual counterparties are not a ceiling on our rating of the sports transaction.

Financial assessment of member franchises.   The value of a sports franchise is dependent, in part, on the exploitation of the franchise. Moody's views a moderate level of exploitation as positive for the league. Moody's assesses the potential for league expansion and the degree to which past expansion teams have succeeded financially. We also assess the stability of the current franchises, how many are financially viable, how many are up for sale or are seeking to move to another city or to a new facility. . . . Analysis also focuses on whether the sporting event is being diluted through increased competition or over-saturation. Finally, Moody's examines how the event is marketed and exposed to its intended audience, through free or cable television or through pay-per-view, which could affect the ability of the event to expand.

Ranking the Traditional U.S. Sports Leagues

. . . The assessed credit strength of a franchise generally correlates with that of its sanctioning body, or league, when compared to the credit of sports franchises broadly. However, the team with the strongest credit profile in a lower ranked league could be stronger than a weak credit profile team in a higher credit ranked league. The league credit rating doesn't necessarily act as a cap on franchise ratings. Of course, the rating of any specific team or organization is dependent on the specifics of each transaction.

1. The National Football League (NFL).   . . . .

2. National Association for Stock Car Auto Racing (NASCAR).   . . . .

3. The National Basketball Association (NBA).   . . . .

4. Major League Baseball (MLB).   . . . .

5. The National Hockey League (NHL).   . . . .

THE SPORTS FRANCHISE

. . . .

Moody's evaluates the credit quality of the team to establish a framework for the rating of the transaction. Moody's examines the company's sources and uses of cash, with specific emphasis on the key factors listed above.

Diversity, predictability, and quality of revenues. Moody's assesses the diversity and predictability of the company's revenue streams with particular attention to the characteristics of COI. COI generally includes revenues generated from long-term contracts, with at least 2-years remaining in the contract, for broadcast rights, advertising signage, stadium and arena naming rights, and luxury suite leases. . . . COI analysis takes into consideration the length and staggering of the contracts along with guarantees, default terms, renewal and strike risk, and timely payment terms. This also entails a consideration of debt maturity relative to COI turnover risk. We assess the strength or the risk to these cash flow streams by assessing that a reasonably high percentage of COI counterparties are investment grade. Because of the existence of long-term COIs, Moody's rates to the overall financial strength and history of the individual franchises without prejudice to the strong or weak performance of the teams on the field of play. As for very general thresholds, and again only when considered in concert with other main credit drivers, a Ba-rated credit should possess COI representing a minimum of 50% of total revenues while an investment grade rating assumes a minimum of 75%. In the absence of significant levels of COI, Moody's assumes average performance and looks to explicit safety nets, such as operating support agreements, to support the rating during under-performing years. Without adequate safety nets, we would rate to weak on-field/court/ice/track performance. Like any business enterprise, we recognize the strengths of those teams with a deep and long historical financial performance, while newer franchises lack predictability and stability.

Moody's also assesses the effect of economic cycles and the degree of fan loyalty by examining the stability of general admission ticket sales, ticket pricing trends, the percentage of season ticket holders, the size of the season ticket waiting list, recent seating expansion, and the accounting convention used to recognize revenue from season tickets sales.

Free cash flow generation and leverage. Unlike most business enterprises, most sports asset valuations do not closely reflect the cash flow generating ability of the enterprise. As a result, a fairly strong $2.0\times$ asset coverage of debt will only result in a high single-B rating but will not push the credit rating to the Ba level without positive free cash flow generation or very strong explicit operating support or guarantees. Generally, a franchise will not receive an investment grade rating unless they are generating free cash flow available for debt amortization, unless the debt has an unconditional guarantee from a strong guarantor. On the other hand, an enterprise with negative cash flow and no explicit operating support could result in a weak B or lower rating.

Free cash flow generation is generally supported by the existence of a diversified revenue stream. The franchise's ability to secure or consolidate the revenues from nonfranchise events, either through the playing facility or through the existence of a multi-franchise enterprise, is a significant credit enhancement characteristic of investment grade ratings. Single franchise enterprises lack a diversified cash flow stream because of the seasonality of revenues including ticket sales and broadcasting contracts. In some sports, such as MLB, revenues from the local broadcasting contract can be significantly larger than the national contract. Multi-franchise enterprises smooth out the revenue streams over the course of the year and diversify the revenues. This reduces some of the risk to bond holders that a downturn or weak performance in one sport or sometimes even in one economic region will affect the ability of the company to fulfill its debt obligations.

In addition to the other significant qualitative, quantitative, and structural strengths, an enterprise should possess leverage (as measured by total debt-to-EBITDA [earnings before interest, taxation, depreciation, and amortization], assuming no material capital spending and normal working capital requirements) well under 5.0× in order to be considered investment grade. This metric also presumes the existence of stable free cash flow available for debt amortization. Without meaningful debt amortization there is often a significant balloon refinancing risk that is generally not a risk faced by investment grade debt issuers.

Financial wherewithal of owners and quality of management.   . . . Assessment of the financial wherewithal of the team's ownership and quality of management includes the willingness and ability to contribute additional capital to fund cash flow shortfalls, or even the existence of an explicit operating support agreement, guarantees, or letters of credit. Because many sports franchises do not generate significant free cash flow, the existence of an unconditional operating support agreement from high net worth owners can supplement cash flow resulting in a Ba rating. However, if all of the owner's wealth is tied up in the franchise, the value of an operating support agreement or the ability to shoulder a large debt burden, for that matter, would be severely limited (and could have an adverse impact on the rating assessment). This analysis also incorporates the professionalism and fiscal sophistication of ownership, the net worth of both the majority and minority owners, the stability of management, the degree of fiscal conservatism of both the owners and management, and the ability of management to control expenses. Analysis of net worth is important to assess both the ability of ownership to contribute additional equity to the team and the likelihood that ownership may need to dividend cash out of the team to cover personal expenses. Audited and certified financial statements are the most reliable for judging net worth since it takes into consideration encumbrances of assets by debt. Fair market value [FMV] assessments including a judgment regarding liquidity of the assets and a sensitization of the FMV are performed to arrive at net worth.

Condition of the stadium or arena.   Moody's examines the terms and conditions surrounding the relationship between the franchise and the arena or stadium. If the team or ownership enterprise owns the venue, Moody's assesses the mortgage on the property, looking at what revenues are secured by the mortgage. If the stadium construction was partially financed through a municipality, Moody's examines the nature of the agreement between the team and the municipality, what subsidies are involved and what constraints, if any, exist, especially those relating to moving (such as liquidated damages provisions), upgrading/refurbishing the arena, and new construction. . . . Generally presume that the debt at the team or against any individual team related revenue stream are linked. So for example, analysis of debt financing backed by luxury suite revenues or media rights will be significantly impacted by the highly leveraged team that is the foundation for those revenue streams. However, a highly leveraged stadium or other facility, if there is no common ownership, may have less impact on debt ratings for the franchise. If the stadium is leased to the team, Moody's examines the terms of the lease, seeing if it is an annual fixed contract or a percentage of revenues, who owns the revenue streams coming from the luxury boxes/suites, advertising, naming rights, parking, concessions, etc. . . . Calculate a capitalization of the lease cost and any other fixed or minimum payments, and add it to arrive at total debt on the enterprise.

In examining each venue, Moody's judges the state of the facility, the number of suites and club seats, when will the venue need to be upgraded, when will it need to be replaced. We measure the facility's ability to generate additional revenues, through franchise and, especially, non-franchise events. In doing so, we determine what other venues in the area would compete for events. Finally, Moody's assesses management's marketing and pricing strategies, that is, what is the team's plan to draw fans.

CREDIT ENHANCEMENTS VS. SAFETY NETS

Moody's views credit enhancements as those structural elements of a transaction that provide for better than expected financial results and balance sheet strength. On the other hand, safety nets merely guard against any significant deterioration in the credit or risk of default. Some examples of credit enhancements that could result in a higher rating include:

- Excess cash flow (assuming that it is highly likely to be generated) recapture prevents cash leakage that occurs with dividends paid to owners. While this might not weaken the enterprise's credit profile, the retention of that cash could strengthen the balance sheet providing additional financial flexibility.
- Diverse revenue streams from multiple franchises or nonfranchise arena or stadium events. Diverse revenue streams mitigate potential volatility and usually support greater cash flow generation.
- Targeted debt amortization backed by a posted letter of credit ensures a path towards deleveraging and mitigates refinance risk.
- Unconditional debt guarantees from guarantors with significant financial wherewithal.
- League imposed debt limitations.
- Pledged asset sales or equity infusions.

Safety nets provide Moody's with comfort that financial projections will be met ensuring that the enterprise's credit profile will not deteriorate, they do not enhance the credit in any way. Some examples of safety nets that help insure the enterprise against potential credit deterioration include:

- Operating support agreement from high net worth individuals.
- 12-month principal and interest debt service reserves.
- Work stoppage reserves.
- Appropriate financial covenants such as minimum EBITDA and minimum debt service coverage.

CONCLUSION — 10 CHARACTERISTICS MOODY'S LIKES TO SEE IN RATED SPORTS TRANSACTIONS

While Moody's does not advise on structuring specific transactions, here's our wish list of items that would be viewed as strengths in making our rating decision:

1. Transactions that include cross-collateral/guarantees from multiple assets or franchises. This allows for diversification of cash flows and reduces the risk of distress from one franchise defaulting.
2. Predictable revenue streams and expense structure. Revenues derived from long-term COI and salary caps for players' salaries.
3. League's ability and desire to cure distressed franchises in a debtholder friendly manner. Either through financial intervention or curing the franchise through a sale.

4. Term of transaction within the length of the Collective Bargaining Agreement and/or broadcasting contract. Lowers the risk that a work stoppage could occur or that a new television contract could result in lower annual revenues.

5. Low enterprise leverage and strong interest coverage. Partly through conservative operations and league imposed debt limits. In addition to other significant qualitative and structural strengths, an enterprise must possess leverage well under $5.0\times$ total debt-to-EBITDA and generate material free cash flow to amortize debt in order to be considered investment grade.

6. Significant asset coverage. Minimum asset coverage of $2.0\times$ in order to achieve a high single-B rating with potentially higher ratings achieved for coverage above this minimum.

7. First security interest on all assets. Where capital structure is multi-layered, Moody's will derive a senior implied rating that reflects the credit quality of the entire business enterprise as if there was one class of debt, and notch up and down accordingly for priority of claim and capital weighting at each layer. But, Moody's will notch more severely for unsecured debt above the team level given differential league treatment.

8. Limitations on further indebtedness, unfunded deferred compensation, and dividends. Limiting the ability to put on too much leverage, dividend up excess cash to the owners ahead of servicing the debt, or create potential contingent liabilities.

9. Excess cash flow recapture and P&I and work stoppage reserve funds.

10. Operating support agreements from high net worth owners for negative cash flowing enterprises. Posting a letter of credit (from a highly rated financial institution) or cash deposit to back-up the operating support agreement provides credit enhancement, particularly if the franchise budget anticipates cash flow shortfalls in the ensuing 2–4 quarters.

DISCUSSION QUESTIONS

1. From a valuation perspective, what are the advantages and disadvantages of revenue sharing in professional sports leagues?

2. What is a team's "reputation" and how does it impact a team's value? Why is this relationship irrational?

3. What is the impact of reputation on the frequency of team sales?

4. How does Scully calculate total return to franchise ownership?

5. How could the NFL's ownership rules impact the duration of ownership in the league?

6. What are the pros and cons of an NFL team securing a new stadium deal just outside of the major city in which they currently play?

7. Compare and contrast the advantages and disadvantages of using each of the three valuation approaches for sports franchise intangible assets.

8. How does the impact of asymmetric information between buyers and sellers of sports franchises on the sales price of professional sports franchises differ from the impact it has on sales of nonsports businesses?

9. Why do large-market clubs have higher revenues than small-market clubs?

10. Given the choice, would you rather pay a premium for a winning franchise or get a discount on a team with a lesser reputation? Why?

PART II

OLYMPIC SPORTS

CHAPTER 13

OLYMPIC SPORTS

INTRODUCTION

Whereas the professional sports discussed previously are all about business and the bottom line, at least in a relative sense, there is a greater sense of pageantry, politics, and global goodwill associated with the Olympic Games. These added elements do not necessarily mesh with the goals of an enterprise striving for black ink.

The entity in the Olympic alphabet stew that has the clearest charge to reach for financial success is the organizing committee for a given Olympiad. The formally labeled Organizing Committee for the Olympic Games (OCOG) will be the primary focus of this chapter. However, before that focus, this introduction will describe the positioning of the various organizing committees in the overall Olympic world.

The business of the Olympics is a combination of organizations, referred to in the industry by their abbreviations. Each wields a certain degree of power and all must, sometimes with difficulty, work together to stage the Olympics in both their winter and summer forms. Figures 1 and 2 depict the organizational structure of the Olympics.

The rights to the Olympic Games and all of the intellectual property associated with them — including the five rings, their colors, the flag, and the words Olympics, Olympiad, and Olympic Games — are held by the International Olympic Committee (IOC) based in Lausanne, Switzerland. The primary sources of revenue for the IOC are broadcast rights, sponsorships, ticket sales, and licensing-related revenues. The financial driver for the Olympics, just as is the case at the professional level, is television. The numbers are truly staggering in this arena. The sale of worldwide broadcast rights will provide the IOC with $2.236 billion — half of its total revenues — from 2001 to 2004. The IOC relies heavily on the United States broadcast networks, with nearly 75% of these revenues coming from NBC, 16% from Europe, and the remainder from the rest of the world. This situation is unlikely to change in the near future, with NBC paying $4.5 billion for the right to broadcast in the United States the Olympic Games of 2004 in Athens, Greece; 2006 in Turin, Italy; 2008 in Beijing; 2010 in Vancouver; and 2012, the site of which will be determined in 2005. The IOC distributes half of the broadcast rights fees of each Olympics to the OCOG responsible for the respective Olympic Games, and half to the Olympic Movement. A broader discussion of television and the business of sports appears in Chapter 6.

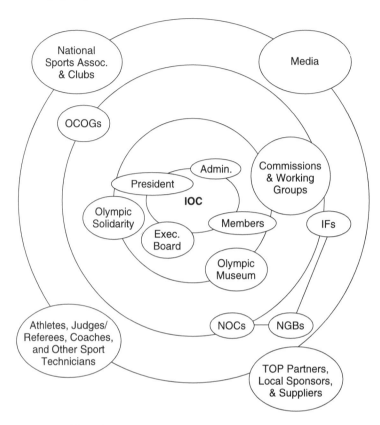

Figure 1. Structure of the Olympic Movement.
Source: http://www.olympic.org/organisation/index_uk.asp.

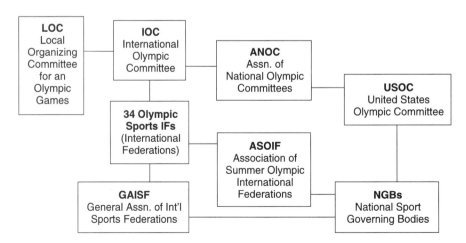

Figure 2. International sports organizational relationships.
Source: United States Olympic Committee.

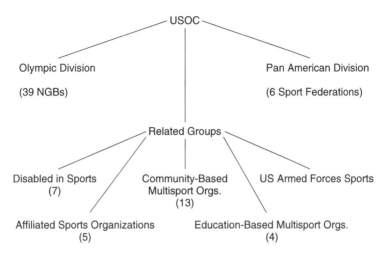

Figure 3. Organization of the U.S. Olympic Movement.

Sponsorships established by the IOC sponsorship program, formally called The Olympic Program (TOP), are a vital source of revenue for the IOC, accounting for 40% of its revenues from 2001 to 2004. Comprised of 10 global companies that receive broad category exclusivity, the TOP program generated $1.815 billion during this quadrennial. Again, the IOC is heavily dependent on the United States for its sponsorships, with eight TOP sponsors based in this country. Ticket sales to Olympic opening and closing ceremonies and events provided $380 million for the IOC, or 8% of its revenues. The sale of Olympic-related licensed products, coins, and stamps complete the IOC financial picture, generating $100 million (or 2%) of the organization's revenues.

The IOC distributes over 90% of its revenues to OCOGs, National Olympic Committees (NOCs) and international federations (IFs). For example, the Salt Lake Organizing Committee (SLOC) received $443 million in broadcast rights and $130 million from the TOP program. This $573 million represented 40% of SLOC's operating budget. The IOC will provide the Athens Organizing Committee (ATHOC) with $960 million, or 60% of its operating budget, for the 2004 Games. In addition, the IOC distributed $305 million to the NOCs that sent teams to the 2002 and 2004 Olympic Games, $190 million to the 28 summer sports IFs for the 2000 Olympic Games, and $92.4 million to the 7 winter sports IFs for the 2002 Olympic Games. The IOC retains nearly 10% of its revenues to pay its administrative and operating expenses.

Each of the 199 countries that are a part of the Olympic family has its own national Olympic committee. NOCs are the prime organizations that run the business of fielding Olympic teams. The United States Olympic Committee (USOC) shoulders this responsibility in the United States. Figure 3 depicts the organization of the U.S. Olympic Movement. Empowered by the Amateur Sports Act, the USOC derives much of its revenue from the IOC. The USOC receives royalty payments from the IOC and broadcast networks for the U.S. Olympic broadcast rights. Approximately 25% of the IOC's broadcast revenues ultimately are delivered to the USOC, with NBC providing the USOC with $418 million for the Olympic Games from 2000 to 2008. This bounty is not limited to television. The USOC also receives a substantial amount of IOC sponsorship revenues — more than all of the other 198 NOCs combined. The USOC also generates significant revenues from its own domestic sponsorships, joint ventures, and fundraising and licensing efforts and earns annual revenues approaching $200 million.

Despite its not-for-profit status, the USOC has struggled to avoid red ink in recent years. The USOC has a staggering amount of overhead expenses and also provides American athletes and various national governing bodies (NGBs) with over $80 million of financial support each year. However, it should be noted that, unlike almost every other country's NOC, the USOC does not receive any direct government support. The fact that the IOC and USOC are so mutually dependent is thought to have generated significant resentment of the United States in the European-controlled IOC.

The next layer of governance is among the individual sports. Each sport is governed at its highest level by an international federation. There are 28 IFs involved in the Summer Olympics and 7 in the Winter Olympics. For example, the International Amateur Athletics Federation governs "athletics," popularly referred to as track and field. This organization sets the rules and holds the rights to various championships and other competitions around the globe. Each country that has athletes involved in that sport at the international level has a domestic national governing body. In the United States the NGB for athletics is USA Track & Field (USATF), formerly The Athletics Congress (TAC). Overall, there are 39 recognized Olympic NGBs in the United States.

All of these various enterprises are permanent and often extremely political. The perks for leadership within these organizations include global travel, gifts, and important political and business relationships.

The most unique of the Olympic-related organizations are the organizing committees noted initially. In the United States, the OCOGs that people are most familiar with are the Los Angeles Olympic Organizing Committee (LAOOC), which planned and operated the 1984 Olympics and the more recent U.S. committees at Atlanta in 1996 (ACOG) and Salt Lake City in 2002 (SLOC). The uniqueness comes primarily from the fact that once the games are complete, the OCOGs disband. The OCOGs are also heavily dependent on the IOC, which provides the OCOG with revenues from its broadcasting and sponsorship rights. An OCOG generates its own revenues through the sale of local sponsorships, tickets, and licensed products. For example, SLOC earned $575 million in sponsorship revenues, $180 million in ticket sales, and an additional $25 million in sales of licensed products. The OCOG also retains 95% of its local sponsorship, ticketing, and licensing revenues, and gives 5% to the IOC.

A number of other chapters are of interest in conjunction with the readings on the Olympics. Certainly the chapter on ethics has relevance, given the number of scandals associated with the Olympic Games. Those issues range from the votes of judges to the influencing of IOC members in their site selections for the games. The chapter on amateurism highlights the thinking behind the creation of a class of athletes characterized as amateur. Ironically, though the concept is most often associated with the Olympic Games, there are essentially no longer any "pure" amateurs participating. Many, including members of the United States Olympic basketball squads, are professionals in their sports. Many others receive payment from their countries, with the highest rewards given for gold medals or the breaking of world records.

In the first reading, "Management of the Olympic Games: The Lessons of Sydney," Chappelet focuses on the key management elements of running an Olympics: time, money, human resources, and information.

In the second selection, *The Future of the Olympic Games,* Lucas focuses on the two major revenue sources for an OCOG, television and sponsorships.

In the final reading, *Economics of the Olympic Games: Hosting the Games 1972–2000,* Preuss provides an overview of the dominant expenditures the OCOG must make on facilities. Preuss also focuses on how expenses are determined in calculating a given Olympiad's profitability in terms of "Games-related," versus "non-Games-related" expenses.

MANAGEMENT OF THE OLYMPIC GAMES: THE LESSONS OF SYDNEY

Jean-Loup Chappelet

. . . We shall define management as the optimization of the resources available to managers. These resources can be divided into four main categories: time, money, human resources, and information. The main features of the management of each of these resources for the Sydney Games will be examined below. Comments will then be made on the organizational structures put in place to manage these resources.

TIME

Time is the rarest resource of any major event-type project as, by definition, such an event cannot be postponed, even by a single day. The Games of the new millennium were scheduled to open on 15 September 2000, and this date had been virtually carved in stone over six years earlier. For an OCOG, every additional day is a day less. . . In this respect it is important to note that SOCOG [Sydney Organizing Committee for the Olympic Games] was very quickly set up by virtue of a law enacted by the Parliament of New South Wales on 12 November 1993, less than two months after the IOC's decision to award the Games to Australia's biggest city. A new record for diligence had been set!

One and a half years later the OCA (Olympic Coordination Authority) was created, with the principal task of building most of the sports facilities that were required, including the Olympic Park in Homebush, which would host fifteen of the twenty-eight sports on the program. All of the sports venues for the Sydney Games were thus ready around one year before the Games, except for the temporary beach volleyball stadium on Bondi Beach. This meant that test events could be organized well in advance, and provided the opportunity to correct *in situ* all manner of unanticipated organizational problems.

These dress rehearsals undoubtedly contributed to the success of the sports management of the Games. They did away with the need for last-minute fixes, which are a source of stress and additional expense. In Atlanta, the Olympic stadium was opened just three months before the Games, and work began on fitting out the Main Press Centre just three days before the Games opened. The contrast is striking: The time spent on preparation in Sydney in a sense resulted in time saved during the Games. The daily coordination meetings with the IOC each morning became progressively shorter. One was even canceled.

MONEY

Although it is still too early to draw any definitive conclusions, initial figures suggest that SOCOG's budget will balance at around A$ 2.5 billion. (In September 2000, the exchange rates were approximately A$ 1 = CHF 0.97, US$ 0.56.) This certainly owes something to the limitations placed on operating expenditure, but also and above all to the optimization of the Games revenues themselves.

After the disappointment — an understatement — that greeted the announcement of the total figure negotiated by the IOC for television rights to the Games in the United States (which were sold to NBC rather than Fox Network), SOCOG turned to other possible sources of revenue, mainly sponsoring and the sale of tickets for the competitions.

Nearly A$ 700 million were obtained from the 24 *Team Millennium* sponsors (including the 11 partners of the IOC's TOP program), the 19 Sydney 2000 Supporters, and the 60 official providers (including 23 sports equipment companies).

To this sum was added some A$ 70 million in royalties from the three thousand or so products manufactured with SOCOG's emblems by around a hundred licensed businesses. This licensing program remained within the bounds of good taste and was a considerable success. Even during the Games, long queues formed outside various "Olympic Stores" set up specially to sell these products.

A total of A$ 770 million in revenue was therefore attributable to commercialization in the strict sense of the word, compared with the A$ 1,039 million SOCOG received for the television rights. This represents approximately A$ 40 for each inhabitant of Australia, or thirteen times more than the commercial revenue from Atlanta, in terms of population. As far as tickets were concerned, SOCOG beat the sales records set by previous OCOGs despite the major difficulties caused by a multi-tiered distribution program that proved to be needlessly complicated. While over two million tickets remained unsold three months out from the Games, an average of 50,000 tickets were sold each day during the Games. For the first time in Olympic history, SOCOG's Internet site was also made to pay its way, through sales of tickets as well as licensed merchandise. The sight of the 110,000-seat Olympic stadium being filled almost to capacity during the athletics heats was particularly impressive. Approximately 87% of the Olympic tickets were finally sold, almost meeting the budgetary objective of A$ 566 million. The tickets for the cultural program also sold well.

The success of the commercial program, built up over the years of preparation and boosted towards the end by the ticketing program, enabled SOCOG to avoid digging too deeply into the A$ 140 million reserve allocated in June 2000 by the government of New South Wales to enable SOCOG to balance its budget. This reserve also undoubtedly had a psychological effect. It helped to avoid a situation in the final months where SOCOG had to base its operational decisions solely on financial criteria, as was the case in Atlanta in 1996. We now know that, in order to avoid the slightest hint of a deficit, the organizers of the Centennial Games economized as much as possible during the final year leading up to the Games, to the point of jeopardizing the transport and information systems.

The icing on the cake in terms of optimizing financial resources came when SOCOG had the good fortune of seeing the Australian dollar decline sharply against the U.S. dollar as the Games approached, contrary to the historical tendency of host country currencies to appreciate during the Olympic year. Although the television rights negotiated in U.S. dollars had been prudently hedged against exchange rate fluctuations, this stroke of luck nevertheless provided additional revenues of the order of A$ 50 million. *[Table 1 shows the cost of the Sydney Olympic Games and others.]*

HUMAN RESOURCES

Preparations for the Games require putting in place an organization that in six years grows from a handful of personnel to several thousand (2,500 in Sydney), only to drop one month after the Closing Ceremony to a few hundred staff, who virtually all disappear in the year following the Games. During the Olympic period, the core staff is augmented by an army of volunteers (47,000 in Sydney). It is not difficult to imagine the enormous challenge of managing the human resources of such a business, which has virtually no past, and no future at all as soon as the Games are over.

SOCOG encountered major difficulties in this area. It went through two presidents before the appointment, after the Atlanta Games, of Michael Knight, who was already the Olympics Minister for New South Wales. The controversial management style of the last president led over the years to the voluntary and involuntary departure of several staff members, including one chief executive. Evidently, however, SOCOG's second chief executive, Sandy Hollway, was able to maintain the motivation of the majority of his troops right up to the end. This was to the detriment of his relationship with

TABLE 1.

Olympic Costs			
City (year)	*Bid cost*	*Games cost*	*Results*
Barcelona (1992)	$10 million	$10.7 billion	$3 million profit for the Olympic organizing committee, $6.1 billion in debt for government and public entities
Albertville (1992)	$2 million–$3 million	$2 billion	$57 million loss
Lillehammer (1994)	$3 million	$1.6 billion	$40 million–$50 million profit
Atlanta (1996)	$7 million	$1.7 billion	Broke even
Nagano (1998)	$11 million	$14 billion	$28 million profit for organizing committee, $11 billion debt to various government groups
Sydney (2000)	$12.6 million	$3.24 billion	Broke even
Salt Lake City (2002)	$7 million	$1.3 billion	$100 million profit

Sources: Street & Smith's SportsBusiness Journal research, International Olympic Committee, USA Today, Associated Press, Snow Country Magazine.
Originally published November 11, 2002.

the president, who withdrew a large part of his prerogatives one month before the Games and sought to limit public recognition of the man he had appointed as his "number two."

In contrast, the volunteer program was perfectly conducted, and most certainly contributed to the success of the Games. Word quickly spread among the Olympic family, the media, and the spectators about the spontaneous friendliness of the thousands of young and less young Australians (and foreign nationals) who had volunteered their services. The volunteers were the shop window of the Games, and the main point of contact between the organization and its "clients."

Planning began almost three years before the Opening Ceremony (compared with 18 months before in Atlanta), and volunteers were recruited through a national campaign in October 1998. A complete training program was set up by the public training agency TAFE NSW, based on manuals, videos, and an Internet site. The program began in June 2000 and enabled Sydney's volunteers to fill the majority of posts during the Games, unlike in Atlanta, where the volunteers had often not been trained for the tasks they were performing. Some of the drivers even used their own leisure time to familiarize themselves with the Olympic routes. The volunteer leaders, often volunteers themselves, were also given leadership courses.

The low drop-out rate for volunteers during the Games, far lower than in Atlanta, is an indication that this fundamental human resource was well managed. Although it was not announced in advance, most of the volunteers were compensated with tickets for sports competitions or rehearsals for the Opening Ceremony. Five thousand of them were also able to attend the Closing Ceremony free of charge. They also had free use of public transport. One of Sydney's daily newspapers even published all of their names, from Naseem Aadil to Warren Zylstra, in a special section entitled: *"47,000 heroes."*

INFORMATION

Information is still all too seldom identified as a managerial resource on a par with human and financial resources. And yet it is a vital resource in today's postindustrial society, which is a service society whose main raw material is information. It is such information, in the broad sense, that the media broadcast during the Games in the form of text, images, and sound, and, which, after the Games, constitutes the only tangible trace of the Games apart from the Olympic facilities.

Information management proved particularly disastrous at the beginning of the Centennial Games: the results sent out to the Olympic Family and the media by the information system were full of errors, which meant that the press agencies were obliged to re-enter them manually for transmission around the world. Unsatisfactory transport and accommodation conditions for the journalists only increased their recriminations which, in a few short days, irretrievably damaged the reputation of Atlanta and its Games. Rightly or wrongly, IBM was held responsible. Not wishing to see a repeat of the fiasco, IBM proposed to SOCOG that it would take charge of systems integration, a role that had been filled in Atlanta by the OCOG itself.

The information system for the Sydney Games comprised four sub-systems: 1) for generating the competition results; 2) for broadcasting information on the Games to the Internet; 3) for communication within the Olympic Family through two thousand "INFO" terminals; 4) for management of SOCOG services (accreditation, accommodation, ticketing, transport, recruitment, etc.). These systems included some systems provided by other technology partners, such as Xerox for data printouts, Swatch Timing for competition timekeeping, Kodak for 200,000 accreditation photographs, and Panasonic for broadcasting text and images on giant screens. Overall, the information system for SOCOG and the Games was implemented through the efforts of 850 experts, and was accessed by nearly seven thousand networked personal computers.

We should not omit to mention the great success of the official Sydney 2000 website, managed for SOCOG by IBM (www.olympics.com). The site welcomed some 8.7 million visitors from the day before the opening until the Closing Ceremony of the Games, most of them from the United States (38%), Australia (17%), Canada (7%), Great Britain (5%), Japan (3%), and 136 further countries. These visitors — the great majority of them women — spent an average of 17 minutes on the site, and downloaded a total of 230 million pageviews. Fans from 199 countries sent 371,654 emails to the participating athletes, over four thousand of whom created a personal page on the computers available in the Olympic Village.

The site of the TV network NBC (www.nbcolympics.com), the only site, along with Australia's Channel 7, authorized to webcast short video sequences of the Games, attracted 2.2 million Americans during the Olympic fortnight. In comparison, 59 million people saw NBC's recorded coverage of the competitions. (Television viewing figures were lower than usual because of the time difference.) These statistics are particularly impressive considering that the first Internet browser became available the same year that the Games were awarded to Sydney. Thanks to the Internet, results, sound, still and moving images of the Olympic festival undoubtedly constitute a mine of new rights to be exploited by the IOC and the OCOGs, while respecting the public's right to information.

This very brief overview of information management by SOCOG would not be complete without a mention of the TOK program (Transfer of Olympic Knowledge), which was launched one year before the Games to synthesize the bulk of information essential to their organization. This work, in the form of around 100 manuals drafted during the year 2000 by SOCOG's managers, was financed by the IOC, and will be used by the OCOGs of Athens and Turin before being updated and passed on to future OCOGs. These TOK manuals will provide a useful supplement to the official report of the Sydney Games, work on which was begun very intelligently well in advance. For the first time, all of the organizational information, all of the tacit knowledge of a complete edition of the Games, will be turned into formalized knowledge for the following Games, in line with the new theories of knowledge management.

ORGANIZATION

This overview of the management of the Sydney Games would not be complete without a brief comment on their structural organization, that is, the political and administrative arrangement of the various bodies involved in organizing the Games. In addition to SOCOG, these were mainly: the OCA (Olympic Coordination Authority), responsible for building most of the sports facilities since 1995; SOBO (Sydney Olympic Broadcast Organization), founded in 1996 and responsible for producing the sound and image signal for the Games (host broadcaster); ORTA (Olympic Roads & Transport Authority), created in 1997; and the OSCC (Olympic Security Command Center), set up in 1998.

Like SOCOG, the OCA, ORTA, and OSCC were agencies belonging to the state of New South Wales. SOBO was officially a commission of SOCOG's board of directors. Apart from the OSCC, which was chaired by the state police commissioner, all of these bodies were chaired by Michael Knight, who was also New South Wales Minister for the Olympics and president of the DHA (Darling Harbour Authority), which manages the area where six of the Olympic sports were held.

The Sydney Games thus benefited from a highly decentralized structure, unlike that of Atlanta. Every organization mentioned above was responsible for one of the essential organizational tasks: general operations (SOCOG), construction and management of the facilities (OCA), production of televised images of the Games (SOBO), road and rail transport (ORTA), and public security (OSCC). It is perhaps surprising to see how, over the years of preparation, SOCOG was little by little divested of major responsibilities. Although for operational reasons the minister/president felt the need, a few months before the Games, to bring together the various bodies he chaired under a single central deci-sion-making structure called "Sydney 2000," it is highly likely that their original autonomy — which guaranteed that they were completely focused on their mission — contributed greatly to the ultimate success of the Games.

Moreover, one can see to what extent the organizing of the Games in Sydney was state-controlled, from both a legal point of view and a personnel point of view, since the main leaders were senior government officials and civil servants. This is particularly striking as the Atlanta OCOG was entirely private (though a non-profit organization). The lack of coordination with the authorities of the state capital and the state of Georgia contributed to the various problems, particularly in terms of sponsorship, traffic, and security. These problems were naturally resolved in Sydney thanks to the active participation of elected government officials and the local and regional administrations con-cerned, which ended up spending over A$ 2 billion on the Games, over and above SOCOG's budget. Added to this was the coordinated contribution of some thirty agencies of the Australian Federal Government, estimated at A$ 484 million, including, for the record, the first "official poet" of the Games since Pindar.

Is Sydney's managerial model preferable to that of Atlanta? Yes, probably, because the Games have become an event that affects an entire country. Whatever their legal status, the OCOGs have to work very closely with the public authorities, with whom they have to share their goals of public ser-vice, and the harmonious development of the managerial objective should no longer be to stage bigger Games, because "gigantism" is an ever-present threat, but to stage Games that are unique and special, that leave a lasting mark in the collective history of the nation and the human race.

THE FUTURE OF THE OLYMPIC GAMES

John A. Lucas

OLYMPIC ENTREPRENEURSHIP: THE SEARCH FOR THE GOLDEN MEAN

The IOC and Television Entrepreneurship, 1988 to 1994

Amid the blizzard of IOC enterprises, but not necessarily at its center, is the serious business of making money through contracts with television networks around the world. IOC agreements with corporations in Europe, Africa, South America, Canada, the Soviet Union, Australia, and Japan are worth millions of dollars and represent a potential source of revenue for the IOC. Yet their combined monies do not approach the sums received from the United States and its . . . major networks . . . *[See Table 2, which shows U.S. television ratings and rights fees.]* ABC's agreement with the IOC for the Calgary '88 Winter Olympic Games was $326 million (Canadian), and NBC finally agreed to pay the IOC a guaranteed $300 million with an additional $200 million on a risk-sharing basis, a total of $500 million for the Summer Games in Seoul.

. . . .

CBS outbid NBC "by a lot" to win the broadcasting rights to the 1992 Winter Olympic Games in Albertville, France. Because of its failing popularity ratings compared to those of ABC and NBC, CBS paid the IOC $243 million and was back in Olympic TV business for the first time since Rome 1960. NBC moguls blasted CBS for paying such an "absurdly high sum." Annoyed NBC sports president Arthur Watson said, "You always want to be a winner. But you don't want to commit suicide at the same time."[14] When the dust settled, and the IOC found itself richer by nearly half a billion dollars for the two Olympic Games in 1992 (thanks to CBS and NBC), it was the IOC that expressed "high spirits" — not the television executives. Michael Janofsky of the *New York Times* was there and described IOC senior officials as "almost giddy with satisfaction and relief." "I never expected to get so much money," said President Samaranch. "So the contract we got is a very good one, no?" he asked rhetorically.[15]

TABLE 2.

THE GAMES ON TV: NETWORK RATINGS, RIGHTS FEES, AND RELATED INFORMATION SINCE THE OLYMPICS WERE FIRST TELEVISED

Year	Games	Location	Network	Average prime time rating	Total network hours*	Number of nations	Number of events	U.S. rights fee (adjusted**)
1960	Winter	Squaw Valley, Calif.	CBS	NA	NA	30	27	$50,000 ($299,160)
1960	Summer	Rome	CBS	NA	20	84	150	$390,000 ($2.3 million)
1964	Winter	Innsbruck, Austria	ABC	NA	17.5	36	34	$600,000 ($3.4 million)
1964	Summer	Tokyo	NBC	NA	14	94	163	$1.5 million ($8.6 million)
1968	Winter	Grenoble, France	ABC	13.5	20	37	35	$2.5 million ($12.7 million)
1968	Summer	Mexico City	ABC	NA	43.75	113	172	$4.5 million ($22.9 million)
1972	Winter	Sapporo, Japan	NBC	17.2	26	36	35	$6.4 million ($27.1 million)
1972	Summer	Munich, Germany	ABC	24.4	62.75	122	195	$7.5 million ($31.8 million)
1976	Winter	Innsbruck, Austria	ABC	21.5	27.5	37	37	$10 million ($31.1 million)
1976	Summer	Montreal	ABC	23.9	76.5	93	198	$25 million ($77.8 million)
1980	Winter	Lake Placid, N.Y.	ABC	23.6	35	37	39	$15.5 million ($33.3 million)
1980	Summer	Moscow	NBC	None***	None***	81	203	$87 million ($187.0 million)
1984	Winter	Sarajevo, Yugoslavia	ABC	18.4	41.5	49	40	$91.6 million ($156.1 million)
1984	Summer	Los Angeles	ABC	23.2	180	140	221	$225 million ($383.5 million)
1988	Winter	Calgary	ABC	19.3	95	57	46	$309 million ($462.6 million)
1988	Summer	Seoul, Korea	NBC	17.9	176	160	237	$309 million ($462.6 million)
1992	Winter	Albertville, France	CBS	18.7	107	64	57	$243 million ($306.7 million)
1992	Summer	Barcelona, Spain	NBC	17.5	148	171	257	$409 million ($516.3 million)
1994	Winter	Lillehammer, Norway	CBS	27.8	110	67	61	$295 million ($352.5 million)
1996	Summer	Atlanta	NBC	21.6	164	196	271	$456 million ($514.7 million)
1998	Winter	Nagano, Japan	CBS	16.3	124	80	68	$375 million ($407.4 million)
2000	Summer	Sydney, Australia	NBC	13.8	162.5	199	300	$705 million ($725.1 million)
2002	Winter	Salt Lake City	NBC	16.9^	168.5	80	78	$545 million

(Continued)

TABLE 2.   (Continued)

The Games on TV: Network Ratings, Rights Fees, and Related Information Since the Olympics Were First Televised

Year	Games	Location	Network	Average prime time rating	Total network hours*	Number of nations	Number of events	U.S. rights fee (adjusted**)
2004	Summer	Athens, Greece	NBC	TBD	TBD	TBD	TBD	$793 million^^
2006	Winter	Turin, Italy	NBC	TBD	TBD	TBD	TBD	$613 million^^
2008	Summer	Beijing	NBC	TBD	TBD	TBD	TBD	$894 million^^
2010	Winter	Vancouver, Canada	NBC	TBD	TBD	TBD	TBD	$820 million
2012	Summer	TBD	NBC	TBD	TBD	TBD	TBD	$1.18 billion

Note: For the 2002 Winter Games in Salt Lake City, a total of 375.5 hours of programming was scheduled across NBC, MSNBC (13 hours), and CNBC (76 hours).
NA: Not available; no television ratings system was in place at the time.
TBD: To be determined.
*Total hours listed for the Winter Olympics from 1960 to 1984 are for prime time only.
**Fee converted to 2001 value using U.S. Department of Labor Bureau of Labor Statistics formula. Figure represents 2001 buying power.
***The United States boycotted the 1980 Summer Games; NBC's coverage was limited to highlights and two anthology-style specials after the Games were completed, though the network still paid the full rights fee.
^Projected rating below which NBC indicated it would provide make-good advertising for major advertisers. Subsequent posted actual rating: 19.2.
^^Part of a $2.3 billion three-Olympic bid.
Sources: Street & Smith's SportsBusiness Journal research, U.S. Olympic Committee, Nielsen Media Research, the networks.
Originally published February 4, 2002.

ABC got out of the business of televising Olympic Games in March 1989, having broadcast 10 Olympic Games since 1964. "We do not intend to bid for the 1994 Winter Games in Lillehammer," was how they put it. (There had been "stunned silence" at the IOC meeting on 15 September 1988 in Seoul when it was announced that the little Norwegian resort town of Lillehammer had won the coveted prize — until the usually taciturn Scandinavians "erupted with joy and flag-waving, pinched themselves and began to celebrate.")[16] The two remaining American television giants began serious bidding, and on 24 October 1989, CBS again won the contract, this time for $300 million. Mark Harrington of CBS began plans to send 1,500 technicians to Lillehammer "in groups of 500 at a time."[17] On 23 April 1990, the Norwegian Parliament gave its full political, moral, and financial support to the Lillehammer Olympic Organization Committee (LOOC), their collective voice "Norway is proud" supported by the allocation of 7 billion Norwegian kroner ($1 billion). "This will be the largest sporting event Norway has ever organized, but we have the resources," said Prime Minister Gro Harlem Brundtland. The president of the LOOC, Gerhard Heiberg, said the money would be well spent, repeating the litany of previous organizing leaders, "Our winter Olympic Games will be the best ever."[18] It was comforting to the IOC that the collective brain power of the whole, mammoth Olympic family seemed to have everything well in hand: the imminent Olympic Games in 1992; a national mandate for a successful 1994 Winter Games; powerful social, cultural, political, and multi-billion dollar support for the 1996 Summer Olympic Games in Atlanta; and another dozen cities clamoring for the privilege of hosting either the 1998 festival or the Olympic Games in the millennial year 2000. For the IOC it seemed that, to parrot Dickens, "it was the best of times." Only a natural catastrophe or, more likely, some human global cataclysm can put an immediate end to these best-laid plans.

Corporate Sponsorship Provides More Balance

There was a time not so long ago when the IOC depended on television for 95% of its income. No longer. The international Coca-Cola Company spent $22 million at the Seoul Olympic Games to guarantee that no competitive soft drink be allowed to display the Olympic rings or to sell their products at any Olympic stadia. The Olympic Program (TOP) is the worldwide sponsoring agent of the IOC. . . TOP was first discussed at the New Delhi meeting of the IOC in 1982, and the Swiss-based company ISL was created the same year, following the soccer World Cup in Madrid. Slowly, discreetly, small numbers of billion-dollar corporations have been invited into the TOP-ISL-IOC inner circle, and by 1991, the sums of money earned by the IOC began to approach 50-50, or equal amounts of IOC income earned from television and other corporations.[19] Diversity had nearly been achieved, because the IOC hierarchy anticipated a possible decrease of television monies in the second half of the 1990s.

There seemed to be no crisis at the 1990 meeting of the IOC in Tokyo, where some of the world's richest corporations lined up and signed up with the TOP-ISL-IOC, all for the privilege of Olympic five-rings exclusivity. There were new wrinkles, but it was a very old game. Older than Coca-Cola at the 1928 Olympic Games and Kodak film at the first modern Games in Athens 1896, was the first automobile sporting event in 1887, supported by the French magazine *Velocipéde*. The British journal *Investor's Chronicle* recently chirped, "There is a new professionalism in the air and sponsorship is seen as a part of the promotional package."[20]

Some of France's biggest and best corporations (the SNCF French National Railways; Renault; AGF Assurance Générales de France; IBM; and others) formed a consortium, called Club Coubertin, and nearly 2 billion French francs (FF) are anticipated, with the Albertville organizing committee, the corporations, and the IOC to share the wealth.[21] Not far away, Barcelona's organizing committee (COOB '92) was working hard on a projected final $140 million profit from services rendered, ticket sales, accommodations, lotteries, stamp, medal, and coin sales, and, of course, the great "double dip" — television and corporate sponsorship.[22] Professionalism in the packaging and selling of the Olympic Games is a new phenomenon and the Olympic Movement has entered this entrepreneurial arena with all — possibly more — of the enthusiasm and skill of older and more experienced competitors. The IOC and its affiliated NOCs and sport federations have made the decision to go this direction, because, as their leaders say, they are inexorably drawn there, and the entire future of the international Olympic Movement lies in the direction of *shared* funding from most of the world's governments and from some of the biggest and best business corporations.

The IOC Climbs into the Marketplace

During the Winter and Summer Olympic Games at St. Moritz and Amsterdam (1928), at Lake Placid and Los Angeles (1932), and the double German Games of 1936 in Gannisch and Berlin, 95 to 98% of the thousands of competitors made no money from their participation, not a franc, dollar, or mark. In other words, only a small, smart-looking cadre of superstars profited at all from their dearly-won gold medals. We know them well: Paavo Nurmi, Charley Paddock, Sonja Heine, Maribel Vinson, Eleanor Holm, Buster Crabbe, Glenn Morris, Ray Barbuti, Willy Ritola, and several other marketable Olympic champions. Two generations later, nothing has changed, except the sums of money involved. In the 1980s and 1990s, 90% of Olympic athletes came away with memories, good and bad, but absolutely nothing more. To be sure, there were those in North America, Asia, and Europe who became "as rich as Croesus." That hasn't changed in 60 years — and yet almost everything else is different in the Olympic story.

The single, biggest development has been the democratization of the Olympic Movement today and with it, the attendant bedfellow, capitalism. In the old days of elitist Olympic administration, that athletes should profit monetarily was anathema. Even today, the mounting profits being made by the Olympic Tripartite and by some highly visible Olympic champions have roused a far louder criticism than in the past — and in the 1920s and 1930s, there were legions of Olympic Games critics. The nature and intensity of today's faultfinding is different from yesteryear's.

Nowhere in the world is it well known that most of the money earned by the Olympic network reverts back to the athletes. What is better understood by the media and the public is that there is very big money out there in the Olympic world, that a great many Olympic-related people are living well, and that a relatively small number of superathletes are being treated in an idolatrous manner, that is, they are allowed to make a great deal of money. There is some public disenchantment with this in Europe and North America, and . . . more criticism of national Olympic committees, domestic and international sport federations, and the IOC itself will occur. This last company . . . has made an effort to counter this poor publicity by underscoring the importance of the Pierre de Coubertin-created movement, *Sport-for-All.* Every third or fourth speech of IOC President Samaranch has emphasized the moral urgency of the Olympic family moving in this direction of mass sport, school physical education, and healthy, safe recreational activities for the millions. There seems to be a blind spot in many societies, however, when it comes to providing modest financial assistance to aspiring Olympic athletes not yet ranked in the "Top Ten" in their event. Almost no NOC or sport federation is giving much real help to these very talented young men and women.

The drumbeat of concern, questioning, constructive criticism, and plain written and verbal censure, directed at the IOC especially, continues in regard to a perceived unapologetic preoccupation of the Olympics with high finance. It is not enough that these critics are told (perhaps too infrequently) that they do not fully understand that this money is returned in an honest and efficient manner to those people and institutions that need it most. The Olympic family talks to itself, through blizzards of letters, notes, telegrams, and . . . fax sheets when it needs to talk to the world and explain the disposition of these monies. It needs a better system by which to better inform all branches of the media, perhaps requesting that they in turn write interesting, even provocative features about Solidarity monies, grants to NOCs and ISFs, and the hundred imaginative ways in which deserving athletes around the world are given tiny but still helpful financial grants. . . . For example, there seemed to be no visible support or condemnation from the IOC when American tycoon Ted Turner bought 50 hours of television time for $50 million, in order to sell cable "pay-per-view" of the Barcelona Games. In fact, NBC sold 600 hours of Olympic Games events for $500 million to three simultaneous-broadcast pay channels. These were exciting, extraordinary, and honest business deals. And yet, because it is a nonprofit sporting organization, the IOC must be ever responsive to the all-too-frequent criticism that, since the days of its previous presidents, Brundage and Killanin, it has moved like a shot in the direction of a monopolistic, international business syndicate.

TOP-I was the successful ISL-IOC marketing plan for the 1988 Olympic Games. An even more ambitious TOP-II plan for the double games of 1992, involving Coca-Cola, Eastman Kodak, 3M, Ricoh, Matsushita, *Sports Illustrated,* Visa, and the U.S. Postal Service's international express mail service, brought in "more than $120 million" to the IOC coffers.[24] British television historian, Steven Barnett, warned the IOC to resist what he saw to be an ever-growing American demand for their Olympic pound of flesh. If we are not careful, the Olympic Games could be hijacked by an obsessively competitive American television industry, whose money will eventually corrupt completely the original [Olympic] spirit.[25]

Similarly, Steven Aris's acid article in the *London Financial Times* supplement said that Baron de Coubertin would have found fault as "the lordly IOC climbed down into the market place."[26] "Money and the IOC are synonymous in this growing commercialism of the Games" was the overstated comment in the *New York Times.*[27]

There have been a hundred warnings and many harsh words leveled against the Olympic committee, but John Rodda, the veteran Olympic Games journalist from the *London–Manchester Guardian,* possibly summed it up best when he said that "although the enormous new wealth enjoyed by the IOC has the capacity to erode Olympic democracy, impartiality, and independence, this has not yet happened." And because the benefits to athletes everywhere are enormous, Rodda concluded, the perilous experiment with big business should be allowed to continue.[29]

During the titanic years of money-making in American history (1880–1910), men like John D. Rockefeller, J.P. Morgan, Charles Schwab, Andrew Mellon, George Pullman, and Andrew Carnegie spent their vigorous years accumulating wealth, rose in power almost equal to that of the federal government, and then, without exception, moved to unprecedented generosity. The Olympic Movement, especially the IOC, is bedazzled by its newfound avenues of financial opportunity and will continue exploring them for some years to come. By the millennial year 2000, the IOC will have accumulated in properties, investments, credits, and cash sufficient billions of dollars so that it can "ease off." It will pull back appreciably from this financial focus and be able at last to devote nearly all of its vast power, influence, and new wealth to educational and altruistic efforts at an even higher level and through a more universal presence than are now possible. Jacques Rogge . . . voiced the concern of many: "The Olympic Movement should control this financial [preoccupation] and keep its soul."[30] Balance, control, and historic perspective are everything in this blending of the Olympic past, present, and future.

REFERENCES

14. Watson's quote is in the *Wall Street Journal,* 26 May 1988, 32. Much more literature exists. See *Sports Illustrated,* 68, 6 June 1988, 30–32; *Dallas Morning News,* 25 May 1988, Sport section; *Sports Inc., f,* 20 June 1988, 49; *Advertising Age,* 59, 30 May 1988, 3, 70; *Broadcasting,* 114, 30 May 1988, 24; and the *New York Times,* 30 May 1988, 32.

15. *New York Times,* 6 December 1988, B22.

16. See "ABC Will Stop Being Olympic Torchbearer," *USA Today,* 24 March 1989. Norwegians celebrate: see *New York Times,* 16 September 1988, 19, 21; *International Herald Tribune,* 16 September 1988, 17; the *Christian Science Monitor,* 16 September 1988, 18; Randy Harvey: in "Longshot Lillehammer" quotes IOC Vice President Richard Pound: "One thing I've learned in 10 years on the IOC is that nothing is a surprise." See *Los Angeles Times,* 16 September 1988, part 3, 3; and; the *Korea Herald,* 17 September 1988, 3.

17. *Newsflash 1,* April 1990, newsletter for the XVIIth Olympic Winter Games; also the *London Times,* 25 October 1989, 52.

18. *Frankfurter Allgemeine,* 27 November 1989, 32; *Lillehammer* 1994, *Budget Facts and Figures* (LOOC: August 1990), 5; *Newsflash 2,* June 1990, 2–3; Status Report address by LOOC President Heiberg to the 96th Session of the IOC, Tokyo, September 1990.

19. Several helpful articles (from a cache of several hundred references) are: "IOC-ISL: The TOP," *Review,* 213, July 1985, 384; *Advertising Age,* 59, 30 May 1988, 48–49; *Olympic Message,* 24, July 1989, special issue on marketing and Olympism; *Marketing Communications,* January 1989, 18–26; Richard W. Pound, "The International Olympic Marketing Programme," *Olympic Review,* 220, February 1986, 84–86; Randy Harvey, "IOC Chief Hurdles Financial Bag," *International Herald Tribune,* 13 September 1989, 18; " 'Ambush' Marketing," *Journal of Advertising Research,* 29, August–September 1989, 9–14; *Olympic Review,* 263–264, September–October 1989, 445; TOP *Worldwide Sponsorship of the Olympic Movement* (23-page brochure, International Olympic Committee, Lausanne, Switzerland, 1990).

20. *Investor's Chronicle,* 14 July 1989, 14.

21. "Club Coubertin '92," Olympic Review, 257, March 1989, 75–77, and "Club Coubertin: L'Important c'est de Parrainer," *Le Magazine du Comite d'Organisation Des XVIes Jeux Olympiques D'Hiver D'Albertville,* June 1989, 10–11. In October 1990, Alcatel, France Telecom, and Thomson joined the "club"; *Flash Cojo,* 37, 30 October 1990.

22. Mary Beth Double, "Barcelona Olympics Will Open Doors for U.S. Business," *Business America,* 110, 28 August 1989, 2–5; *Press Dossier 1990* (COOB '92, S.A.).

24. *Advertising Age,* 61, 30 April 1990, 23. General Motors and McDonald's joined in late 1990, paying very big money. Also *Advertising Age,* 61, 29 October 1990, 3, 62; *USA Today,* 16 November 1989, 16c (for postal service full-page ad).

25. Steven Barnett, *Games and Sets. The Changing Face of Sport on Television* (London: BFI, 1990), 134.

26. "The Great Olympic Soap Sell," *London Financial Times Supplement,* 11 June 1988, 1.

27. *New York Times,* 12 September 1988, sec. 6.

29. Rodda, in the *Olympic Message,* 23, March 1988, 6–15.

30. Jacques Rogge "Editorial," *Sport Europe. AENOC Official Magazine,* 3, 1990, 3.

ORGANIZING COMMITTEE EXPENDITURES

ECONOMICS OF THE OLYMPIC GAMES: HOSTING THE GAMES IN 1972–2000

Holger Preuss

ASPECTS OF BUSINESS ECONOMY

An OCOG can be called a corporation with limited life which has the task of organizing, planning, and decision-making processes related to the Olympic Games. Primarily, it must provide the funds necessary to stage the Games and close without a deficit. In other words the OCOG objective is to at least cover the required expenditures with adequate revenues or, if possible, to achieve a surplus. Therefore, an investigation of which areas and to what amount revenues and expenditures are generated must be made. The possibilities that an OCOG has to influence these figures as well as the system-related constraints must also be analyzed. It is difficult to determine expenditures since sources state figures as a balance or do not mention certain types of expenditure at all. Therefore, the investigations often only determine the quantities of resources to be provided. . . .

REVENUES OF AN ORGANIZING COMMITTEE

The OCOG is responsible for the entire organization of the Olympics and must also ensure that the sports venues comply with IF requirements. In the past, OCOG revenues covered most of the capital funds. However, the size of today's Olympics increasingly calls for host cities to finance the required urban infrastructure, in particular sports facilities, by themselves in order to enable the staging of the Games. The investments of the city can only, if at all, pay off in the long run by the follow-up benefits of the Olympics.

. . . .

It is striking that between Munich '72 and Los Angeles '84, the real OCOG revenues increased very little. . . . The surplus of the Los Angeles '84 Olympics, for example, was due to low expenditures and not to increased revenues, as was generally assumed. None of the OCOGs achieved an excessive surplus. The large growth of the Games and the related costs for organization and infrastructure are reflected in the development of the overall OCOG revenues. The OCOGs even had to open new financing sources and/or expand existing ones in order not to run the Games at a deficit. From Los Angeles '84 to Atlanta '96, the financial means at an OCOG's disposal increased considerably.

. . . The revenue structure completely changed with Los Angeles '84. Revenues of private financing sources . . . [now] outweigh public financing sources . . . In the seventies, the OCOG revenues almost exclusively depended on special financing means. Consequently, they depended on the favorable attitude and financial power of the host country. In contrast to this, since Los Angeles '84, private financing sources have increasingly come to the foreground.

. . . .

GAMES-RELATED AND NON-GAMES-RELATED EXPENDITURES

In order to stage the Games, an OCOG requires more than just a number of sports facilities. It is also necessary, by the time the Games take place, for the host city to feature an adequate infrastructure for traffic, telecommunications, an athletes' village, a media village, an MPC [Main Press Center], and an IBC [International Broadcast Center] — all of which have steadily increased in number and size as a result of the corresponding increases to the number of athletes, disciplines, and types of sports being included at the Olympic Games. In view of the ever more complicated requirements for Olympic venues, already Coubertin stated: "As for the construction of the stadium which, in its completed state, would cost in the neighbourhood of a million, it was a permanent building to be helped by subsidies from the state and the town. Stockholm stood to gain whichever way you looked at it."[1] Later the former IOC President M. Killanin said after the Montreal '76 Games: "Who forces the cities to take on excessive costs? They use the Olympic Games to redevelop their city and to create new sports facilities. . . . Mexico City, Tokyo, Munich, and also Montreal used the Games as an occasion to develop their cities. Sport is not guilty for this."[2] Similarly, IOC Vice president U.-J. Kim made the following remark regarding the ever rising costs for the sports facilities and attempted to shift the responsibility for them to the city: "Instead of having one facility per sport, the city could build a sports complex."[3] The assertion that staging the Olympic Games leads to redevelopment within a host city is entirely valid. However, it is also possible to understand the IOC's position that the funding for this redevelopment must come from the city and not from the accounts of the OCOG. The redevelopment of a city and the construction of permanent facilities should strictly be an undertaking of the public sector alone. Thus, an OCOG would only have to then bear the location costs — which are separated from investments in the following discussion.

Investments are "deliberate, generally long-term capital tie-ups to gain future autonomous profit."[5] This includes all expenditures for new constructions, as well as all those that are incurred for extensions, modernization, and the redevelopment of sports venues, the installation of infrastructures, and Olympic villages. If locations are defined as "places of industrial . . . settlement,"[6] then location costs include all those expenditures which are caused by the settlement at a certain place, such as those expenditures which are not investments. On the following pages, location costs include the construction of temporary installations, the costs for providing the money for pulled forward construction activities, maintenance costs, and rents, to name but a few examples.

Before dealing with the location costs in detail, a clear distinction shall be made between the costs for "Games-related" and "non-Games-related" facilities. By making use of this clear categorization for the facilities, the discussions that take place in the host cities regarding the allocation of expenditures for the "Olympic" facilities could be quickly brought to a conclusion. Furthermore, the chance to manipulate cost-benefit analyses will be weakened. . . .

. . . All the sports venues which are built because there is a general need for them, even without the Games, are classified as "non-Games-related." Thus, in these instances, the facilities that are built are not a financial burden for the OCOG. However, passing along the financial burden to others is not always so straightforward for an OCOG since the costs for any building that is deemed to be "Games-related" must be covered by the OCOG. A direct example of this is seen in the many problems that arise for potential host cities when an Olympic hall or stadium does not exist and there is no follow-up demand for such a facility within the city at the conclusion of the Games. In this situation, an OCOG would be forced to erect the facility as a temporary structure, thereby risking the possibility of quickly surpassing the financial limits of an OCOG. This example clearly demonstrates the issue of whether a city is at all suited to serve as the host of an Olympic celebration. Cities that do not have adequate sports facilities or an appropriate follow-up demand should seriously discuss the question of whether a bid to host the Olympics should even be made at all. If only one or two sports facilities are missing and there is no follow-up demand, then these missing facilities could be erected temporarily. The related expenditures would then be allocated to the location costs. The location costs which correspond to the Games-related expenditures . . . include the following items:

Rents: A considerable part of the location costs consists of the fees that must be paid for using existing or newly constructed facilities. In addition to the fees for sports venues, the OCOGs have also been required to pay rent for the use of Olympic villages, accreditation centers, offices, storage rooms, parking spaces, trade fair halls, and convention centers. The Atlanta '96 OCOG, for example, spent US$ 7.9 million just to rent the convention center and the Georgia Dome.

Costs of pulling forward: If there is a follow-up demand for a newly erected sports facility that has been built earlier than planned because of the Olympic Games, the OCOG must bear all the costs caused by the pulling forward. These so-called costs of pulling forward include both the costs incurred by the provision of funding and the increased construction costs that can be incurred by the need for a more rapid building process.

Additional buildings and extensions: If additional construction work that does not, in turn, cause follow-up costs is carried out in order to make Olympic-specific changes to the sports facilities then it is the responsibility of the OCOG to pay the costs incurred for this work. However, the OCOG does not also incur the costs if the changes are subsequently removed. It is a matter of agreement between the owner of the sports facility and the OCOG as to whether the organizers will still be expected to pay a rental fee after the improvements have been carried out.* The IOC has even gone so far as to have required all the bidders for the 2002 Olympics to show all additional construction as "short-term investments."[7]

Construction and removal of temporary facilities: In the instances when there is no follow-up demand for a facility or an extension, it becomes the responsibility of the OCOG to oversee both the construction of these types of structures before the Games and their subsequent removal after the

---

* This arrangement was made for Los Angeles '84. . . .

celebration is over. In addition to the costs that are incurred from installing and dismantling any necessary temporary structures, there is also the possibility that an OCOG might be required to pay rental fees for the real estate space that is used for these structures.

As an alternative to erecting a temporary facility, an OCOG could offer the host city the money required to, instead, build the facility as a permanent structure. By adopting this strategy, the host city would then be able to build facilities that were more expensive, permanent, and had no follow-up usage in the sports sector and provide it at first for the Olympic usage. A possibility could also be to make the facilities smaller after the Games as was the case with the Atlanta '96 Olympic stadium. Here, the OCOG would have to pay the costs for the extension and the removal of the extension while the city would have to pay for erecting the "basic" facility.

Today, almost all sports venues can be erected temporarily on an economically safe basis but this certainly does not apply to the Olympic village. Even the construction of the relatively small youth camp as a temporary facility in Munich '72 caused many problems. The new construction of an entire Olympic village surpasses by far the financial capabilities of an OCOG. So far the construction of villages has been mostly financed privately, in a few cases by the public sector (social housing schemes) to be sold after the Games. The only alternative for the OCOG is to rent the villages. In addition to rents, an OCOG must cover the furnishing, temporary security facilities, and other changes in the construction.*

TYPES OF SPORTS FACILITIES

In the early 70s, the requirements placed on the sports facilities strongly increased. The fact that many sports were shifted from outdoors into halls changed the demand for sports venues in the host city both in terms of quantity and structure. In addition, there has been an evolution in the type of facilities that have been available for staging the Games. This evolution has progressed from a need for stadia at the very early Games to the additional need for halls in the 60s to the present day need for special facilities such as velodromes. For special venues, however, the follow-up usage frequently causes problems with the consequence that more of these facilities and/or stands will have to be built temporarily. If the IOC should push through its demand that the OCOG revenues must no longer be invested in constructing permanent sports facilities (as long as this counts as urban development) this would reinforce the demand for temporary facilities. This, in turn, would increase the operational costs of an OCOG since the costs of the temporary facilities are included in the location costs. . . .

REFERENCES

1. Baron Pierre de Coubertin, 1936, Olympische Erinnerungen, Berlin: Limpert, p.137.
2. Humberty, E. and Wange, W. B., 1976, Die Olympischen Spiele. Montreal Innsbruck. Munich, citing Killanin, M., My Olympic Years. London, p. 11–12.
3. Kim U.-J., 1990, The Greatest Olympics — From Baden Baden to Seoul. Seoul. (transcript).
5. Sellien R. and H. Sellien, 1997, Gablers Wirtschaftslexikon, 14th ed., Wiesbaden, (transcript).

---

* "'88 Games to Cost 7 times as much as L.A. Olympics," *The Korean Herald,* Aug. 25, 1984.

6. Ibid.

7. International Olympic Committee, 1995, Manual for Candidate Cities for the Games of the XXVIII Olympiad. Lausanne, p. 102 (transcript).

DISCUSSION QUESTIONS

1. What is the major revenue source for the Olympics?

2. What entity is charged with running the Olympic Games?

3. What strategies might an OCOG use to make a given Olympiad more profitable?

4. What role do volunteers play in putting on the Olympic Games?

5. How are the different expenditures related to an Olympiad categorized for the determination of profit?

6. Why do corporations, such as Coca-Cola, pay such large sums for sponsorship rights?

7. What problems do people perceive with the commercialization of the Olympic Games?

8. What are the positive aspects of Olympic commercialization?

9. Why did CBS outbid all of the other major U.S. networks by so much for the broadcasting rights to the 1992 Winter Olympic Games? Was this a prudent move?

10. How has the IOC's reliance on the television networks and those contracts that are formed with these networks changed over time?

11. What is the surplus realized by the 1984 Los Angeles Olympics attributable to?

12. What are the necessary prerequisites for a city in order to be considered an adequate host?

13. How are the facilities that are built with the purpose of follow-up usage different than those that are built without any purpose of follow-up usage?

PART III

COLLEGE SPORTS

HISTORY AND STRUCTURE

INTRODUCTION

The National Collegiate Athletic Association (NCAA) is the dominant organization in the United States governing college sports. There have been other organizations playing various roles over the years, including the National Association of Intercollegiate Athletics (NAIA), but the NCAA is the most prominent. The most important business issues related to collegiate sports are largely confined to the NCAA, which is the focus of this chapter.

The key distinction between collegiate sports and the professional sports, discussed previously, is the role of profit. College sports are focused, in theory and practice, on more than just the bottom line. Collegiate athletics are tied to interests as diverse as student morale, campus public relations, institutional profile, fundraising, and student physical fitness. Athletic directors and college presidents arguably have a much more complicated business juggling act than the professional sports team general manager or team owner.

The overview presented in this chapter will provide much of the background of the NCAA. It is most important to note that when the organization was originally formed at the turn of the last century it was focused on promoting safety, specifically to end the deaths that had been occurring in the sport of football. The excerpted Smith article, "A Brief History of the National Collegiate Athletic Association's Role in Regulating Intercollegiate Athletics," will provide much of this background, as will the material from Masteralexis, Barr, and Hums, excerpted from *Principles and Practice of Sport Management.*

What most informal critics miss when contemplating collegiate sports is the actual governing structure of the NCAA. Those who understand college athletics point out that the NCAA is not a monolithic organization that dictates what occurs in the governance of collegiate sports. The NCAA is, in fact, governed by over 1,000 member institutions. Via numerous representative paths, it is these member organizations that determine how collegiate sports will operate. These governing rules range from eligibility to the operation of championships. The selection from Yasser, McCurdy, Goplerud, and Weston, *Sports Law: Cases and Materials,* provides a textbook overview of the organization.

The rules of the NCAA are set forth in the organization's constitution and bylaws, which are available in the NCAA manual. Governing information may be found at http://www.NCAA.org. There are numerous violations of these rules. The selection from Mahony, Fink, and Pastore, "Ethics in Intercollegiate Athletics: An Examination of NCAA Violations and Penalties — 1952–1997," focuses on the types of violations made against these rules and who tends to violate them.

A BRIEF HISTORY OF THE NATIONAL COLLEGIATE ATHLETIC ASSOCIATION'S ROLE IN REGULATING INTERCOLLEGIATE ATHLETICS

Rodney K. Smith

II. A BRIEF HISTORY OF THE NATIONAL COLLEGIATE ATHLETIC ASSOCIATION

A. 1840–1910

The need for regulation of intercollegiate athletics in the United States has existed for at least a century and a half. One of the earliest interschool athletic events was a highbrow regatta between Harvard and Yale Universities, which was commercially sponsored by the then powerful Elkins Railroad Line. Harvard University sought to gain an undue advantage over its academic rival Yale by obtaining the services of a coxswain who was not a student. Thus, the commercialization and propensity to seek unfair advantages existed virtually from the beginning of organized intercollegiate athletics in the United States. The problem of cheating, which was no doubt compounded by the increasing commercialization of sport, was a matter of concern.* Initially, these concerns led institutions to move the athletic teams from student control to faculty oversight. Nevertheless, by the latter part of the nineteenth century, two leading university presidents were voicing their fears that intercollegiate

---

* The commercialization of intercollegiate athletics, with the payment of star athletes, was rather firmly entrenched by the latter part of the 19th century. For example, it is reported that Hogan, a successful student-athlete at Yale at that time, was compensated with: (1) a suite of rooms in the dorm; (2) free meals at the University club; (3) a one-hundred dollar scholarship; (4) the profits from the sale of programs; (5) an agency arrangement with the American Tobacco Company, under which he received a commission on cigarettes sold in New Haven; and (6) a ten-day paid vacation to Cuba. Rodney K. Smith, "The National Collegiate Athletic Association's Death Penalty: How Educators Punish Themselves and Others," 62 Ind. L.J. 985, 989 (1987).

athletics were out of control. President Eliot at Harvard was very concerned about the impact that commercialization of intercollegiate athletics was having, and charged that "lofty gate receipts from college athletics had turned amateur contests into major commercial spectacles."[10] In the same year, President Walker of the Massachusetts Institute of Technology bemoaned the fact that intercollegiate athletics had lost its academic moorings and opined that "[i]f the movement shall continue at the same rate, it will soon be fairly a question whether the letters B.A. stand more for Bachelor of Arts or Bachelor of Athletics."[11] In turn, recognizing the difficulty of overseeing intercollegiate athletics at the institutional level, whether through the faculty or the student governance, conferences were being created both to facilitate the playing of a schedule of games and to provide a modicum of regulation at a broader level.

Despite the shift from student control to faculty oversight and some conference regulation, intercollegiate athletics remained under-regulated and a source of substantial concern. Rising concerns regarding the need to control the excesses of intercollegiate athletics were compounded by the fact that in 1905 alone, there were over eighteen deaths and one hundred major injuries in intercollegiate football. National attention was turned to intercollegiate athletics when President [Theodore] Roosevelt called for a White House conference to review football rules. President Roosevelt invited officials from the major football programs to participate. Deaths and injuries in football persisted, however, and Chancellor Henry MacCracken of New York University called for a national meeting of representatives of the nation's major intercollegiate football programs to determine whether football could be regulated or had to be abolished at the intercollegiate level. Representatives of many major intercollegiate football programs accepted Chancellor MacCracken's invitation and ultimately formed a Rules Committee. President Roosevelt then sought to have participants in the White House conference meet with the new Rules Committee. This combined effort on the part of educators and the White House eventually led to a concerted effort to reform intercollegiate football rules, resulting in the formation of the Intercollegiate Athletic Association (hereinafter IAA), with sixty-two original members. In 1910, the IAA was renamed the NCAA. Initially, the NCAA was formed to formulate rules that could be applied to the various intercollegiate sports. *[The NCAA's current stated purposes are shown in Figure 1.]*

In the years prior to the formation of the NCAA, schools wrestled with the same issues that we face today: the extreme pressure to win, which is compounded by the commercialization of sport, and the need for regulations and a regulatory body to ensure fairness and safety. In terms of regulation, between 1840 and 1910, there was a movement from loose student control of athletics to faculty oversight, from faculty oversight to the creation of conferences, and, ultimately, to the development of a national entity for governance purposes.

B. 1910–1970

In its early years, the NCAA did not play a major role in governing intercollegiate athletics. It did begin to stretch beyond merely making rules for football and other games played, to the creation of a national championship event in various sports. Indeed, students, with some faculty oversight, continued to be the major force in running intercollegiate athletics. By the 1920s, however, intercollegiate athletics were quickly becoming an integral part of higher education in the United States. Public interest in sport at the intercollegiate level, which had always been high, continued to increase in intensity, particularly as successful and entertaining programs developed, and also with increasing access to higher education on the part of students from all segments of society.

The purposes of this Association are:

(a) To initiate, stimulate and improve intercollegiate athletics programs for student-athletes and to promote and develop educational leadership, physical fitness, athletics excellence and athletics participation as a recreational pursuit;

(b) To uphold the principles of institutional control of, and responsibility for, all intercollegiate sports in conformity with the constitution and bylaws of this Association;

(c) To encourage its members to adopt eligibility rules to comply with satisfactory standards of scholarship, sportsmanship and amateurism;

(d) To formulate, copyright and publish rules of play governing intercollegiate athletics;

(e) To preserve intercollegiate athletics records;

(f) To supervise the conduct of, and to establish eligibility standards for, regional and national athletics events under the auspices of this Association;

(g) To cooperate with other amateur athletics organizations in promoting and conducting national and international athletics events;

(h) To legislate, through bylaws or by resolutions of a Convention, upon any subject of general concern to the members related to the administration of intercollegiate athletics; and

(i) To study in general all phases of competitive intercollegiate athletics and establish standards whereby the colleges and universities of the United States can maintain their athletics programs on a high level.

Figure 1.   NCAA Constitution, Article 1.2: Purposes. (Source: 2003–04 NCAA Division I Manual, p. 1.)

With this growing interest in intercollegiate sports and attendant increases in commercialization, outside attention again focused on governance and related issues. In 1929, the highly respected Carnegie Foundation for the Advancement of Education issued a significant report regarding intercollegiate athletics and made the following finding:

> [A] change of values is needed in a field that is sodden with the commercial and the material and the vested interests that these forces have created. Commercialism in college athletics must be diminished and college sport must rise to a point where it is esteemed primarily and sincerely for the opportunities it affords to mature youth.[31]

The Carnegie Report, echoing themes that appear ever so relevant in the year 2000, concluded that college presidents could reclaim the integrity of sport.[32] College administrators "could change the policies permitting commercialized and professionalized athletics that boards of trustees had previously sanctioned."[33]

While the NCAA made some minor attempts to restructure rules to increase integrity in the governance of intercollegiate athletics, those efforts were insufficient to keep pace with the growing commercialization of, and interest in, intercollegiate athletics. Recruitment of athletes was not new, but the rising desire to win, with all its commercial ramifications, contributed to recruitment being raised to new heights. Red Grange, for example, is often given credit for "starting the competition for football talent through . . . recruiting."[36] Public interest in intercollegiate athletics continued to increase with support from the federal government during the 1930s. The capacity of the NCAA to regulate excesses was not equal to the daunting task presented by the growth of, interest in, and commercialization of sport.

After World War II, with a dramatic increase in access to higher education on the part of all segments of society, largely through government support for returning military personnel to attend college, public interest expanded even more dramatically than it had in the past. Increased interest, not surprisingly, led to even greater commercialization of intercollegiate athletics. With the advent of television, the presence of radios in the vast majority of homes in the United States, and the broadcasting of major sporting events, these pressures further intensified. More colleges and universities started athletic programs, while others expanded existing programs, in an effort to respond to increasing interest in intercollegiate athletics. These factors, coupled with a series of gambling scandals and recruiting excesses, caused the NCAA to promulgate additional rules, resulting in an expansion of its governance authority.

In 1948, the NCAA enacted the so-called "Sanity Code," which was designed to "alleviate the proliferation of exploitive practices in the recruitment of student-athletes."[41] To enforce the rules in the Sanity Code, the NCAA created the Constitutional Compliance Committee to interpret rules and investigate possible violations. Neither the Sanity Code with its rules, nor the Constitutional Compliance Committee with its enforcement responsibility, were successful because their only sanction was expulsion, which was so severe that it rendered the committee impotent and the rules ineffectual. Recognizing this, the NCAA repealed the Sanity Code in 1951, replacing the Constitutional Compliance Committee with the Committee on Infractions, which was given broader sanctioning authority. Thus, in 1951, the NCAA began to exercise more earnestly the authority which it had been given by its members.

Two other factors are worth noting in the 1950s: (1) Walter Byers became Executive Director of the NCAA, and contributed to strengthening the NCAA, and its enforcement division, over the coming years to televise intercollegiate football; and (2) the NCAA negotiated its first contract valued in excess of one million dollars, opening the door to increasingly lucrative television contracts in the future. The NCAA was entering a new era, in which its enforcement authority had been increased, a strong individual had been hired as executive director, and revenues from television were beginning to provide it with the wherewithal to strengthen its capacity in enforcing the rules that were being promulgated. Through the 1950s and 1960s, the NCAA's enforcement capacity increased annually.

C. 1971–1983

By 1971, as its enforcement capacity had grown yearly in response to new excesses arising from increased interest and commercialization, the NCAA was beginning to be criticized for alleged unfairness in the exercise of its enhanced enforcement authority. Responding to these criticisms, the NCAA formed a committee to study the enforcement process, and ultimately, in 1973, adopted recommendations developed by that committee designed to divide the prosecutorial and investigative roles of the Committee on Infractions. In the early 1970s, as well, the membership of the NCAA decided to create divisions, whereby schools would be placed in divisions that would better reflect their competitive capacity. Despite these efforts, however, by 1976, when the NCAA was given additional authority to enforce the rules by penalizing schools directly, and, as a result, athletes, coaches, and administrators indirectly, criticism of the NCAA's enforcement authority grew even more widespread. Indeed, in 1978, the United States House of Representatives Subcommittee on Oversight and Investigation held hearings to investigate the alleged unfairness of the NCAA's enforcement processes. Once again, the NCAA responded by adopting changes in its rules designed to address many of the criticisms made during the course of the hearings. While concerns were somewhat abated, the NCAA's enforcement processes continued to be the source of substantial criticism through the 1970s and 1980s.

The NCAA found itself caught between two critiques. On the one hand, it was criticized for responding inadequately to the increased commercialization of intercollegiate athletics, with all its attendant excesses; while on the other hand, it was criticized for unfairly exercising its regulatory authority. Another factor began to have a major impact as well. University and college presidents were becoming more directly concerned with the operation of the NCAA for two major reasons: (1) as enrollments were beginning to drop, and expenses were increasing in athletics and elsewhere, presidents began, with some ambivalence, to see athletics as an expense, and as a potential revenue and public relations source; and (2) they personally came to understand that their reputations as presidents were often tied to the success of the athletic program and they were, therefore, becoming even more fearful of the NCAA's enforcement authority.

D. 1984–1999

In difficult economic times for higher education in the 1980s, university presidents increasingly found themselves caught between the pressures applied by influential members of boards of trustees and alumni, who often demanded winning athletic programs, and faculty and educators, who feared the rising commercialization of athletics and its impact on academic values. Many presidents were determined to take an active, collective role in the governance of the NCAA, so they formed the influential Presidents Commission in response to these pressures. In 1984, the Presidents Commission began to assert its authority, and by 1985, it took dramatic action by exercising their authority to call a special convention to be held in June of 1985. This quick assertion of power led one sports writer to conclude that "There is no doubt who is running college sports. It's the college presidents."[61]

The presidents initially were involved in a number of efforts to change the rules, particularly in the interest of cost containment. These efforts were not all successful. Over time, however, the presidents were gaining a better understanding of the workings of the NCAA, and they were beginning to take far more interest in the actual governance of intercollegiate athletics. A little over a decade later, the presidents' involvement grew to the extent that they had changed the very governance structure of the NCAA, with the addition of an Executive Committee and a Board of Directors for the various divisions, both of which are made up of presidents or chief executive officers.

. . . .

During this time period, there were a number of additional developments that had an impact on the role of the NCAA in fulfilling its enforcement and governance of responsibilities. Even in a short history, like this one, a few of those developments are noteworthy.

As the role of television and the revenue it brings to intercollegiate athletics [have] grown in magnitude, the desire for an increasing share of those dollars has become intense. The first television event in the 1950s was a college football game, and the televising of college football games remained under the NCAA's control for a number of years. In time, however, a group of powerful intercollegiate football programs were determined to challenge the NCAA's handling of the televising of games involving their schools. In *NCAA v. Board of Regents*,[85] the United States Supreme Court held that the NCAA had violated antitrust laws.[86] This provided an opening for those schools, and the bowls that would ultimately court them, to directly reap the revenues from the televising of their football games. . . . Because these schools have been able to funnel more television revenues in their direction, which has led to increases in other forms of revenue, they have gained access to resources that have unbalanced the playing field in football and other sports.

Another matter that has dramatically impacted intercollegiate athletics during the past two decades is Title IX, with its call for gender equity in intercollegiate athletics. With some emphasis on proportionality in opportunities and equity in expenditures for coaches and other purposes in women's sports, new opportunities have been made available for women in intercollegiate athletics. The cost of these expanded opportunities has been high, however, particularly given that few institutions have women's teams that generate sufficient revenue to cover the cost of these added programs. This increase in net expenses has placed significant pressure on intercollegiate athletic programs, particularly given that the presidents are cost-containment conscious, desiring that athletic programs be self-sufficient. Revenue producing male sports, therefore, have to bear the weight of funding women's sports. This, in turn, raises racial equity concerns because most of the revenue producing male sports are made up predominantly of male student-athletes of color, who are expected to deliver a product that will not only produce sufficient revenue to cover its own expenses, but also a substantial portion of the costs of gender equity and male sports that are not revenue producing.

The gender equity and television issues have been largely economic in their impact, but they do indirectly impact the role of the NCAA in governance. Since football funding has been diverted from the NCAA to the football powerhouses, the NCAA for the most part has had to rely even more heavily on its revenue from the lucrative television contract for the Division I basketball championship. Heavy reliance on this funding source raises racial equity issues, since student-athletes of color, particularly African-American athletes, are the source of those revenues. Thus, the very governance costs of the NCAA are covered predominantly by the efforts of these student-athletes of color. This inequity is exacerbated by the fact that schools and conferences rely heavily on revenues from the basketball tournament to fund their own institutional and conference needs.

Generally, developments during the past two decades have focused on governance and economic issues. There have been some efforts, however, to enhance academic integrity and revitalize the role of faculty and students in overseeing intercollegiate athletics. Of particular note in this regard has been the implementation of the certification process for intercollegiate athletic programs. The certification process involves faculty, students (particularly student-athletes), and staff from an institution in preparing an in-depth self-study, including substantial institutional data in the form of required appendices. The study covers the following areas: Governance and Rules Compliance, Academic Integrity, Fiscal Integrity, and Commitment to Equity. This process helps institutions focus on academic values and related issues. These efforts also provide the chief executive officers with additional information and a potentially enhanced role in intercollegiate athletics at the campus level.

The past two decades have been active ones for the NCAA. With meteoric rises in television and related revenues, the commercialization of intercollegiate athletics has continued to grow at a pace that places significant strain on institutions and the NCAA. These commercial pressures, together with increasing costs related to non-revenue producing sports, costly gender equity requirements, and other resource demands (e.g., new facilities), make it challenging to maintain a viable enforcement process and a balanced playing field.

III. THE FUTURE

Over the past 150 years, the desire to win at virtually any cost, combined with the increases in public interest in intercollegiate athletics, in a consumer sense, have led inexorably to a highly commercialized world of intercollegiate athletics. These factors have created new incentives for universities and conferences to find new ways to obtain an advantage over their competitors. This desire to gain an unfair competitive advantage has necessarily led to an expansion in rules and regulations. This proliferation of rules and the development of increasingly sophisticated regulatory systems necessary to enforce those rules, together with the importance that attaches to enforcement decisions, both economically and in terms of an institution's reputation (and derivatively its chief executive officer's career), places great strain on the capacity of the NCAA to govern intercollegiate athletics. This strain is unlikely to dissipate in the future because the pressures that have created the strain do not appear to be susceptible, in a practical sense, to amelioration. Indeed, the one certainty in the future of the NCAA is the likelihood that big-time intercollegiate athletics will be engaged in the same point–counterpoint that has characterized its history; increased commercialization and public pressure leading to more sophisticated rules and regulatory systems.

As rules and regulatory systems continue along the road of increased sophistication, the NCAA will more closely resemble its industry counterparts. It will develop an enforcement system that is more legalistic in its nature, as regulatory proliferation leads to increasing demands for fairness. In such a milieu, chief executive officers will have to take their responsibilities for intercollegiate athletics even more seriously. It can be hoped, as well, that their involvement, and the increased involvement on the part of faculty and staff, through the certification process and otherwise, will lead to a more responsible system in terms of the maintenance of academic values. If the NCAA and those who lead at the institutional and conference levels are unable to maintain academic values in the face of economics and related pressures, the government may be less than a proverbial step away.

REFERENCES

10. Rodney K. Smith, "Little Ado About Something: Playing Games With the Reform of Big-Time Athletics," 20 Cap. U. L. Rev. 567, 570 (1991).
11. Id.
31. Rodney K. Smith, "The National Collegiate Athletic Association's Death Penalty: How Educators Punish Themselves and Others," 62 Ind. L.J. 985, 991 (1987).
32. Id.
33. Id.
36. Id. at 992.
41. Id.
61. Id. at 997.
85. 468 U.S. 85 (1984).
86. Id. at 113, 120.

Structure

Principles and Practice of Sport Management

Lisa Pike Masteralexis, Carol A. Barr, and Mary A. Hums

INTRODUCTION

Intercollegiate athletics is a major segment of the sport industry. It garners increasingly more television air time as network and cable companies increase coverage of sporting events, receives substantial coverage within the sport section of local and national newspapers, and attracts attention from corporations seeking potential sponsorship opportunities. The business aspect of collegiate athletics has grown immensely as administrators and coaches at all levels have become more involved in budgeting, finding revenue sources, controlling expense items, and participating in fund development activities. The administrative aspects of collegiate athletics have changed as well. With more rules and regulations to be followed, there is more paperwork in such areas as recruiting and academics. . . .

. . . .

ORGANIZATIONAL STRUCTURE AND GOVERNANCE

The NCAA

The primary rule-making body for college athletics in the United States is the NCAA. Other college athletic organizations include the National Association of Intercollegiate Athletics (NAIA), founded in 1940 and having approximately 280 member institutions, and the National Junior College Athletic Association (NJCAA), founded in 1937 and having approximately 550 member institutions. The NCAA is a voluntary association with more than 1,000 institutions, conferences, organizations, and individual members. All collegiate athletics teams, conferences, coaches, administrators, and athletes participating in NCAA-sponsored sports must abide by its rules. The basic purpose of the NCAA as dictated in its constitution is to "maintain intercollegiate athletics as an integral part of the educational program and the athlete as an integral part of the student body and, by so doing, retain a clear line of demarcation between intercollegiate athletics and professional sports."[1] *[The fully stated basic purpose is show in Figure 2.]* Important to this basic purpose are the cornerstones of the NCAA's philosophy that college athletics are amateur competitions and athletics are an important component of the institution's educational mission.

The NCAA has undergone organizational changes throughout its history in an attempt to improve the efficiency of its service to member institutions. In 1956, the NCAA split its membership into a University Division, for larger schools, and a College Division, for smaller schools, in an effort to address competitive inequities. In 1973, the current three-division system, made up of Division I, Division II, and Division III, was created to increase the flexibility of the NCAA in addressing the needs and interests of schools of varying size. This NCAA organizational structure involved all member schools and conferences voting on legislation once every year at the NCAA Annual Convention. Every member school and conference had one vote assigned to the institution's president or CEO, a structure called "one-school, one-vote." The NCAA established support groups and committees made up of member school presidents, athletic directors, and NCAA staff members to handle business affairs and policy between conventions.

In 1995, the NCAA recognized that Divisions I, II, and III still faced "issues and needs unique to its member institutions," leading the NCAA to pass Proposal 7, "Restructuring," at the 1996 NCAA Convention.[2] The restructuring plan, which gives the NCAA divisions more responsibility for conduct within their division, took effect in August 1997. Restructuring includes the elimination of the "one-school, one-vote" structure. The annual convention was replaced by division-specific mini-conventions, or meetings. In addition, each division has an overseeing body called either the Board of Directors or Presidents Council, as well as a Management Council made up of presidents, CEOs, and athletic directors from member schools who meet and dictate policy and legislation within that division. The NCAA Executive Committee, consisting of representatives from each division as well as the NCAA Executive Director and chairs of each divisional Management Council, oversees the Presidential Boards and Management Councils for each division.

The unique governance of the NCAA involves the membership's overseeing legislation regarding the conduct of intercollegiate athletics. Member institutions and conferences vote on proposed legislation, thus dictating the rules they need to follow. The NCAA National Office . . . merely enforces the rules the membership passes. . . . The NCAA National Office currently employs approximately 250 people who administer the policies, decisions, and legislation passed by the membership, as well as providing administrative services to all NCAA committees, member institutions, and conferences. The NCAA National Office is organized into departments, including administration, business, championships, communications, compliance, enforcement, educational resources, publishing, legislative services, and visitors center/special projects.

The competitive athletics programs of member institutions are designed to be a vital part of the educational system. A basic purpose of this Association is to maintain intercollegiate athletics as an integral part of the educational program and the athlete as an integral part of the student body and, by so doing, retain a clear line of demarcation between intercollegiate athletics and professional sports.

Figure 2.   NCAA Constitution, Article 1.3.1: Basic Purpose. (Source: 2003–04 NCAA Division I Manual, p. 1.)

Two of the more prominent departments within the NCAA administrative structure are Legislative Services and Enforcement and Eligibility Appeals. These two departments are pivotal because they deal with interpreting and enforcing NCAA rules and regulations. The Legislative Services department has . . . legislative assistants responsible for answering inquiries from member institutions and conferences regarding the interpretation of particular rules. The majority of legislative assistants have a legal background. A member school or conference office can contact the Legislative Services department and speak to a legislative assistant, who provides an interpretation regarding a particular rule. The Enforcement and Eligibility Appeals department staff members are responsible for investigating possible rule violations by member institutions and restoring eligibility to student-athletes who may have been involved in possible NCAA rules violations. It is important to note that although the NCAA National Office staff members collect information and conduct investigations on possible rule violations, the matter still goes before the Committee on Infractions, a committee of peers (representatives of member institutions), which determines responsibility and assesses penalties.

Institutions are taking a more proactive approach regarding potential violations by conducting their own investigations rather than waiting for the NCAA enforcement staff members to perform an investigation and uncover the facts. In 1996, the NCAA estimated that of 1,200 cases involving secondary or minor violations, 90% were self-reported by the institution. Schools also initiate 30% to 40% of the 15 to 20 cases that arise during the year that involve major violations. This proactive approach is encouraged by the NCAA through the endorsement of institutional control, the concept that the individual university is responsible for conduct within its athletic department. Through this principle of institutional control the institution's administrators must oversee and monitor the activities of the athletic department, making sure that NCAA and conference rules and regulations are being followed.

Divisions I, II, and III

As the latest NCAA restructuring calls for divisions to take more responsibility and control over their activities, it is important to look at similarities and differences among these divisions. A few of the more prominent differences among divisions are highlighted in this section. . . . Each institution has its own philosophy regarding the structure and governance of its athletic department. This section concentrates on the differences between Division I and Division III philosophies as these two divisions represent the two extremes. Division II institutions can be categorized as a hybrid of the other two, with some Division II institutions following a Division I philosophy and some following a Division III philosophy. Keep in mind, though, that some Division III institutions, although not offering any athletic scholarships, can be described as following a nationally competitive, revenue-producing philosophy that is more in line with a Division I philosophy. Thus, generalizations regarding divisions are not applicable to all institutions within that division. . . .

Division I of the NCAA is further divided into two subdivisions: Division I-A is the category for institutions that are the somewhat larger football-playing schools in Division I, and Division I-AA is the category for institutions playing football at the next level down from I-A. *[There is a third subcategory, Division I-AAA, comprised of the schools that compete at the Division I level in all sports but do not sponsor a football team.]* In order to be a member of the NCAA within Division I, II, or III, an institution must sponsor a minimum number of sport programs and is held to certain restrictions in terms of athletic scholarship funding to student-athletes. Additional membership requirements include football stadium size, attendance at home football contests, and scheduling of competitions against other division member schools, to name a few. Each division also has its own philosophy statement providing operational guidelines to the member institutions within that division.

It is important to note some of the differences that exist among the divisions. Division I athletic departments are usually larger in terms of number of sport programs sponsored, number of coaches, and number of administrators. Division I athletic departments also have larger budgets due to the number of athletic scholarships allowed, the operational budgets needed for the larger number of sport programs sponsored, and the salary costs associated with the larger number of coaches and administrators. The philosophy statements of the divisions further define some differences that exist. For example, Division I institutions (1) strive for regional and national prominence, (2) sponsor at the highest feasible level the spectator-oriented, income-producing sports of football and basketball, and (3) strive to finance their athletics program from revenues generated by the program itself. *[See Figure 3.]* Division II and, to a greater extent, Division III institutions (1) strive and encourage broad participation, (2) serve the participants rather than the spectators or general public, and (3) do not mention revenue at all within their philosophy statements. *[Division III's philosophy statement appears in Figure 4.]*

In addition to the purposes and fundamental policy of the National Collegiate Athletic Association, as set forth in Constitution 1, members of Division I support the following principles in the belief that these statements assist in defining the nature and purposes of the division. These statements are not binding on member institutions but serve as a guide for the preparation of legislation by the division and for planning and implementation of programs by institutions and conferences. A member of Division I:

(a) Subscribes to high standards of academic quality, as well as breadth of academic opportunity;

(b) Strives in its athletics program for regional and national excellence and prominence. Accordingly, its recruitment of student-athletes and its emphasis on and support of its athletics program are, in most cases, regional and national in scope;

(c) Recognizes the dual objective in its athletics program of serving both the university or college community (participants, student body, faculty-staff, alumni) and the general public (community, area, state, nation);

(d) Believes in offering extensive opportunities for participation in varsity intercollegiate athletics for both men and women;

(e) Sponsors at the highest feasible level of intercollegiate competition one or both of the traditional spectator-oriented, income-producing sports of football and basketball. In doing so, members of Division I recognize the differences in institutional objectives in support of football; therefore, the division provides competition in that sport in Division I-A and Division I-AA;

(f) Believes in scheduling its athletics contests primarily with other members of Division I, especially in the emphasized, spectator-oriented sports, as a reflection of its goal of maintaining an appropriate competitive level in its sports program;

(g) Strives to finance its athletics program insofar as possible from revenues generated by the program itself. All funds supporting athletics should be controlled by the institution; and

(h) Understands, respects and supports the programs and philosophies of other divisions. Occasionally, institutions from other divisions or athletics associations will seek membership in Division I. In such cases, the applicants should be required to meet, over a period of time, prescribed criteria for Division I membership in order to assure that such institutions agree and comply with the principles and program objectives embodied in this statement.

Figure 3. NCAA Division I Philosophy Statement. (Source: 2003–04 NCAA Division I Manual, p. 351.)

Colleges and universities in Division III place highest priority on the overall quality of the educational experience and on the successful completion of all students' academic programs. They seek to establish and maintain an environment in which a student-athlete's athletics activities are conducted as an integral part of the student-athlete's educational experience. They also seek to establish and maintain an environment that values cultural diversity and gender equity among their student-athletes and athletics staff. *(Revised: 1/10/95)*

To achieve this end, Division III institutions:

(a) Place special importance on the impact of athletics on the participants rather than on the spectators and place greater emphasis on the internal constituency (students, alumni, institutional personnel) than on the general public and its entertainment needs;

(b) Award no athletically related financial aid to any student;

(c) Encourage the development of sportsmanship and positive societal attitudes in all constituents, including student-athletes, coaches, administrative personnel and spectators;

(d) Encourage participation by maximizing the number and variety of athletics opportunities for their students;

(e) Assure that the actions of coaches and administrators exhibit fairness, openness and honesty in their relationships with student-athletes;

(f) Assure that athletics participants are not treated differently from other members of the student body;

(g) Assure that athletics programs support the institution's educational mission by financing, staffing and controlling the programs through the same general procedures as other departments of the institution;

(h) Provide equitable athletics opportunities for males and females and give equal emphasis to men's and women's sports;

(i) Support ethnic and gender diversity for all constituents; *(Adopted: 1/12/99)*

(j) Give primary emphasis to regional in-season competition and conference championships; and

(k) Support student-athletes in their efforts to reach high levels of athletics performance, which may include opportunities for participation in national championships, by providing all teams with adequate facilities, competent coaching and appropriate competitive opportunities.

The purpose of the NCAA is to assist its members in developing the basis for consistent, equitable competition while minimizing infringement on the freedom of individual institutions to determine their own special objectives and programs. The above statement articulates principles that represent a commitment to Division III membership and shall serve as a guide for the preparation of legislation by the division and for planning and implementation of programs by institutions and conferences.

Figure 4.   NCAA Division III Philosophy Statement. (Source: 2003–04 NCAA Division I Manual, p. 216.)

Conferences

The organizational structure of intercollegiate athletics also involves member conferences of the NCAA. Member conferences must have a minimum of six member institutions within a single division in order to be recognized as a voting member conference of the NCAA.[3] Conferences provide many benefits and services to their member institutions. For example, conferences run seminars regarding NCAA rules and regulations in an effort to better educate member schools' coaches and administrators. Many conferences also have specific staff members identified to assist member institutions with questions regarding NCAA rules. Thus, the member school can contact the conference office for a rule interpretation rather than contacting the NCAA National Office. The conference staff member is in contact with the NCAA National Office through usage of a computer database that assists the conference with NCAA rule questions.

Conferences also have legislative power over their member institutions in the running of championship events and the formulation of conference rules and regulations. Conferences sponsor championships in sports sponsored by the member institutions within the conference. The conference member institutions vote on the conference guidelines to determine the organization of these conference championships. Member institutions of a particular conference must adhere to conference rules in addition to NCAA rules. It is important to note, though, that while a conference can never be less restrictive than an NCAA rule, many conferences maintain additional rules that hold member institutions to stricter standards. For example, the Ivy League is a Division I NCAA member conference, but it prohibits its member institutions from providing athletic scholarships to student-athletes. Therefore, the Ivy League schools, while competing against other Division I schools that allow athletic scholarships, do not allow their athletic departments to award athletic scholarships.

Conference realignment is one of the current issues affecting collegiate athletic departments. . . . Some of the reasons for a school's wanting to join a conference or change conference affiliation are (1) exposure from television contracts with existing conferences, (2) potential for more revenue from television and corporate sponsorships through conference revenue sharing, (3) the difficulty independent schools were experiencing in scheduling games and generating revenue, and (4) the ability of a conference to hold a championship game in football, which can generate millions of dollars in revenue for the conference schools if the conference possesses at least 12 member institutions.

REFERENCES

1. Article 1.3.1, 1996–97 *NCAA Manual,* p. 1.
2. (Joseph N. Crowley, 1995, p. 4) History Demonstrates That Change Is Good, *The NCAA News,* December 18.
3. National Collegiate Athletic Association, 1996–97 NCAA Manual, Bylaw 3.3.2.2.2.1.

Sports Law: Cases and Materials

Ray Yasser, James R. McCurdy,
C. Peter Goplerud, and Maureen A. Weston

B. NATIONAL COLLEGIATE ATHLETIC ASSOCIATION— AUTHORITY AND RULES

1. Overview of the Association and Its Structure

The NCAA is an unincorporated, voluntary, private association, consisting of nearly one thousand members. Members are predominantly colleges and universities, both public and private. Athletic conferences are also members of the NCAA. Public universities constitute approximately 55 percent of the membership. All member schools and conferences are required to pay dues, the amounts varying depending upon the division in which membership is held. The association is divided into three divisions: Division I, Division II, and Division III. Division I is itself divided into Division I-A, I-AA, and I-AAA. The organization has a large permanent professional staff, with discrete departments for administration, business, championships, communications, compliance services, enforcement, legislative services, and publishing. The association is headquartered in Indianapolis.

The membership governs the organization, and since 1997, it is essentially a federation system, with each division governing itself on nearly all issues. *[The NCAA governance structure is shown in Figure 5.]* There is, however, an Executive Committee which presides over the entire organization. It consists of 20 members. The Executive Director and the chairs of the three divisional Management Councils serve as ex officio nonvoting members. The other sixteen members include 8 Division I-A CEO's from the Division I Board of Directors, 2 Division I-AA CEO's from the Board, 2 Division I-AAA CEO's from the Board, 2 Division II CEO's from the Division II Presidents Council, and 2 Division III CEO's from the Division III Presidents Council.

The Executive Committee is to:

(a) Provide final approval and oversight of the Association's budget;

I.

EXECUTIVE COMMITTEE

Responsibilities
A. Approval/oversight of budget.
B. Appointment/evaluation of Association's CEO.
C. Strategic planning for Association.
D. Identification of Association's core issues.
E. To resolve issues/litigation.
F. To convene joint meeting of groups within boxes II, III and IV.
G. To convene same-site meeting of groups within boxes V, VI and VII.
H. Authority to call for constitutional votes.
I. Authority to call for vote of entire membership when division action is contrary to Association's basic principles.
J. Authority to call special/annual Conventions.

Members
A. Eight I-A members from box II.
B. Two I-AA members from box II.
C. Two I-AAA members from box II.
D. Two members from box III.
E. Two members from box IV.
F. Ex officio—President.[1]
G. Ex officio/nonvoting—Chairs of boxes V, VI and VII.

[1]May vote in case of tie.

ASSOCIATION-WIDE COMMITTEES

A. Committee on Competitive Safeguards and Medical Aspects of Sports.
B. Honors Committee.
C. Minority Opportunities and Interests Committee.
D. Olympic Sports Liaison Committee.
E. Postgraduate Scholarship Committee.
F. Research Committee.
G. Committee on Sportsmanship and Ethical Conduct.
H. Walter Byers Scholarship Committee.
I. Committee on Women's Athletics.
J. Foreign Student Records (Divisions I and II).
K. Core-Course Review Committee (Divisions I and II).
L. NCAA Committees that have playing rules.

II.

**DIVISION I
BOARD OF DIRECTORS**

Responsibilities
A. Set policy and direction of division.
B. Adopt bylaws for division.
C. Delegate responsibilities to Management Council.

Members
A. Institutional CEOs.

III.

**DIVISION II
PRESIDENTS COUNCIL**

Responsibilities
A. Set policy and direction of division.
B. Delegate responsibilities to Management Council.

Members
A. Institutional CEOs.

IV.

**DIVISION III
PRESIDENTS COUNCIL**

Responsibilities
A. Set policy and direction of division.
B. Delegate responsibilities to Management Council.

Members
A. Institutional CEOs.

V.

**DIVISION I
MANAGEMENT COUNCIL**

Responsibilities
A. Recommendations to primary governing body.
B. Handle responsibilities delegated by primary governing body.

Members
A. Athletics administrators.
B. Faculty athletics representatives.

VI.

**DIVISION II
MANAGEMENT COUNCIL**

Responsibilities
A. Recommendations to primary governing body.
B. Handle responsibilities delegated by primary governing body.

Members
A. Athletics administrators.
B. Faculty athletics representatives.

VII.

**DIVISION III
MANAGEMENT COUNCIL**

Responsibilities
A. Recommendations to primary governing body.
B. Handle responsibilities delegated by primary governing body.

Members
A. Institutional CEOs.
B. Athletics administrators.
C. Faculty athletics representatives.
D. Student-athletes.

Figure 5. NCAA governance structure. (Source: 2003–04 NCAA Division I Manual, Figure 4-2, p. 216.)

(b) Employ the Association's chief executive officer (e.g. executive director), who shall be administratively responsible to the Executive Committee and who shall be authorized to employ such other persons as may be necessary to conduct efficiently the business of the Association;

(c) Provide strategic planning for the Association as a whole;

(d) Identify core issues that affect the Association as a whole;

(e) Act on behalf of the Association to resolve core issues and other Association-wide matters;

(f) Initiate and settle litigation;

(g) Convene at least one combined meeting per year of the divisional presidential governing bodies;

(h) Convene at least one same-site meeting per year of the three divisional Management Councils;

(i) Forward proposed amendments to Constitutions 1 and 2 and other dominant legislation to the entire membership for a vote;

(j) Call for a vote of the entire membership on the action of any division that it determines to be contrary to the basic purposes, fundamental policies, and general principles set forth in the Association's Constitution. This action may be overridden by the Association's entire membership by a two-thirds majority vote of those institutions voting; and

(k) Call for an annual or special Convention of the Association.[1]

Division I is composed of the schools which are the most visible athletic competitors, the so-called "big time programs." For Division I, the primary rule making body in the new NCAA structure is a Board of Directors, made up of fifteen CEO's from Division I member institutions. *[The Division I governance structure is shown in Figure 6.]* The following eight conferences have one representative each on the Board: Atlantic Coast Conference, Big East, Big 12, Big 10, Pac-10, Southeastern, Western Athletic Conference, and Conference USA. One member must come from either the Big West or Mid-American Conferences. The remaining six members come from Division I-AA and I-AAA (Division I schools which do not play Division I football). Each conference in the latter divisions must be represented on either the Board or the Management Council.

The primary duties of the Board are: 1) to establish and direct general policy; 2) to adopt bylaws and other operating provisions; 3) approve an annual budget for Division I; and 4) to ensure gender and ethnic diversity among the members of the governance structure. Members of the Board are elected by the constituencies they represent and serve four year terms, with no immediate re-election. The terms are staggered to provide continuity and stability.

The next body in the organizational structure of Division I is the Management Council. This group consists of athletic administrators and faculty athletic representatives. The Council has 34 members. There are two members of the Council from each of the following conferences: Atlantic Coast Conference, Big East, Big 12, Big Ten, Conference USA, Pacific-10, Southeastern, and Western Athletic Conference. There are two members from among the members of the following two conferences: Big West and Mid-American. Sixteen members of the Council are from among 9 Division I-AA conferences, 11 Division I-AAA conferences, and 2 at-large positions. There are requirements that each Division I-AA and I-AAA conference must be represented either on the Board or the Council.[2]

The Management Council has the responsibility to:

(a) Adopt operating bylaws and rules to govern Division I . . . ;

(b) Take final action on matters delegated to it by the Board . . . ;

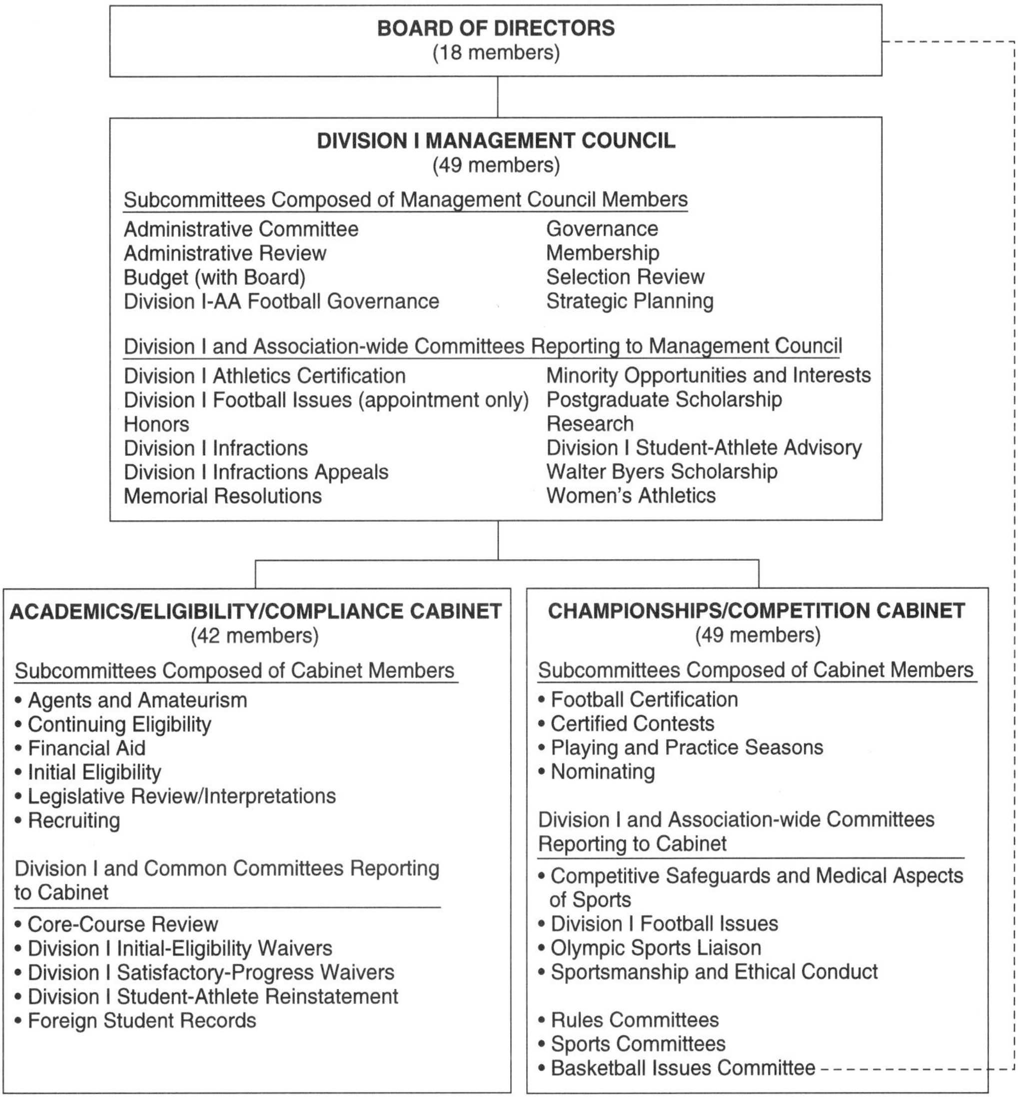

Figure 6. NCAA Division I governance structure. (Source: 2003–04 NCAA Division I Manual, Figure 4-1, p. 31.)

(c) Make recommendations to the Board of Directors on matters it deems appropriate;

(d) Make interpretations of the bylaws of Division I;

(e) Suggest policies to the Board of Directors that are necessary to ensure the proper management of Division I;

(f) Review the recommendations of the substructure of Division I;

(g) Appoint the members of the substructure (e.g., cabinets and committees) of Division I;

(h) Review and approve policies and procedures governing the enforcement program of Division I;

(i) Recommend Division I championship policies, and fiscal, competitive, and academic policies to the Board . . . ;

(j) Develop and administer the annual budget of Division I with the approval of the Board of Directors; and

(k) Advise the Board of Directors on the performance of the Association's chief executive director.[3]

Cabinets and committees provide for the governance substructure of Division I. Division I cabinets include: the Academics/Eligibility/Compliance Cabinet; the Championships/Competition Cabinet; the Strategic Planning Cabinet; and the Business Finance Cabinet.[4] The Cabinets each have committees that report directly to the Cabinet. In addition, Division I committees on athletics certification, infractions, infractions appeals, and student-athlete advisory report directly to the Management Council.[5]

The NCAA openly states that one of its primary purposes is to promote the concept of amateurism. Related to this is the idea that athletics are an integral part of the educational experience at the intercollegiate level. The NCAA, of course, is big business, with a 1999–2000 operating budget of nearly $300 million. It includes a huge television contract for collegiate basketball, smaller contracts for other sports, and an extensive scholarship program. In short, the Association is the governing body, and to a great extent, business agent and primary entity for intercollegiate sports.

In order to understand the more difficult issues faced by the NCAA and its individual member schools, it is necessary to have an understanding of the critical portions of the NCAA Constitution and Bylaws. These are contained in the NCAA Manual, for the appropriate division, which is updated annually. The following is a summary of the key provisions of the Division I Manual.

A basic purpose of the Association is to ensure that intercollegiate athletics are maintained as "an integral part of the educational program and that the athlete [is] an integral part of the student body."[6] Theoretically, this should promote a clear cut delineation between amateur sports and professional sports. The athletes who make up the program at a school are to be amateurs. Amateur is defined as one whose participation is "motivated primarily by education and by the physical, mental, and social benefits to be derived."[7] Ironically, the Association also urges that its *student-athletes,* and that is the operative term, "should be protected from exploitation by professional and commercial enterprises."[8]

The rules on amateurism are a major focal point of the Association. As noted, only an amateur student-athlete is eligible for participation in a particular sport.[9] An athlete may be a professional in one sport and still retain eligibility in other sports, however. An athlete will be deemed a professional, and thus lose his or her eligibility if the individual:

(a) Uses his or her athletics skill (directly or indirectly) for pay in any form in that sport;

(b) Accepts a promise of pay even if such pay is to be received following completion of intercollegiate athletics participation;

(c) Signs a contract or commitment of any kind to play professional athletics, regardless of its legal enforceability or any consideration received;

(d) Receives, directly or indirectly, a salary, reimbursement of expenses, or any other form of financial assistance from a professional sports organization based upon athletic skill or participation, except as permitted by NCAA rules and regulations;

(e) Competes on any professional athletics team and knows (or had reason to know) that the team is a professional athletics team . . . , even if no pay or remuneration for expenses was received; or

(f) Enters into a professional draft or an agreement with an agent or other entity to negotiate a professional contract.[10]

The NCAA defines "pay" to include the following items and concepts: salaries, extra educational expenses beyond that allowed by the NCAA, expenses for parents, payment based upon performance, prizes, and preferential treatment or benefits.[11] An individual also becomes a professional in a sport if he or she signs a professional contract, regardless of its enforceability or a delayed start date. Participation on a professional sports team makes one a professional. As noted, an athlete may be a professional in one sport and retain eligibility in other NCAA sports. That individual, however, may not accept institutional financial aid while involved in professional sports or receiving remuneration from a professional sports organization.[12] An athlete's eligibility may be impacted by activity associated with a professional sports draft. A football player who declares himself available for the draft immediately loses his eligibility, regardless of whether he is actually drafted or eventually signs a contract.[13] That player may, however, make inquiry about his market value prior to declaring without jeopardizing his eligibility. A basketball player may enter a draft and, if not drafted, she has thirty days following the draft to make a decision to play professionally. The athlete may return to collegiate competition if she indicates that intention in writing to the athletic director within thirty days of the draft.[14] A college baseball player is in a different situation in that the baseball draft is conducted without the players having to declare themselves eligible. Thus, if a player meets age or collegiate progress requirements he is eligible to be drafted. A player who is drafted does not have his eligibility affected until he signs a contract. However, in all of the situations noted, the player immediately loses his or her eligibility if [he or she retains] an agent. The eligibility is lost even if the contract is for services to be rendered subsequent to completion of eligibility. In addition, an athlete may not receive benefits of any kind from an agent.[15] The only exception is for the athlete who is a professional in one sport, but continues to compete at the collegiate level in other sports. He may have an agent for the sport in which he is a professional, but the agreement with that agent must be limited, *in writing*, to that particular sport. If it is not so limited it will be deemed applicable to all sports, thus rendering the athlete ineligible. Finally, an athlete may secure advice from an attorney concerning a proposed contract, so long as the attorney does not become involved in negotiating the contract.

The NCAA has also historically been concerned about athletes becoming involved in promotional activities which benefit them solely because of their athletic abilities. The most absurd example of previously stringent policies occurred when a University of Indiana basketball player was suspended for one game because he appeared on a sorority calendar, the proceeds from which went to charity. This rule has been relaxed somewhat. Athletes may now appear or have their picture used for charitable or educational purposes if written permission is secured, no class time is missed, and there is no cosponsorship by a commercial entity.[16]

The NCAA also has restrictions on employment for student athletes. The Association limits the scholarship of an athlete on full scholarship to tuition, fees, room, board, and books. Within limits, an athlete on full scholarship may also receive Pell Grant funds. A Division I athlete on full scholarship may work for compensation during the semester but may only earn $2,000 per year.[17] Any work obtained must be for a fair, prevailing wage, and must not be based on the athlete's athletic reputation.

The Association regulations also govern the educational status and progress of the student athlete. This area has been extremely controversial in recent years, particularly as it relates to the initial eligibility of entering student athletes. The student athlete has four years of eligibility for athletic competition for any one sport. [These] four years must be completed within five years of the time the athlete first registers for a minimum full time program of studies in a collegiate institution.[18] "To be eligible to represent an institution in intercollegiate athletics competition, a student-athlete shall be enrolled in at least a minimum full time program of studies, be in good academic standing and maintain satisfactory progress toward a baccalaureate degree."[19]

The initial eligibility rules have been the target of much criticism, tinkering and litigation. In 1983 the NCAA enacted the so-called Proposition 48 which became effective in 1986. It was intended to regulate the eligibility of incoming freshman athletes in an era when questions had arisen as to admissions practices at some institutions. This rule initially set up minimum grade point averages and college entrance examination scores which had to be attained. Failure to attain these minimal standards cost the athlete eligibility or scholarship funds or both. These rules have been amended several times since 1986 and are now even more stringent. To be eligible as a freshman for competition and scholarship funds, an incoming athlete must have a minimum grade point average in thirteen core courses in high school and a corresponding minimum test score on either the ACT or SAT test. The scale slides depending upon the level of grade point average or test score. If the athlete does not satisfy the standards, he will either be labeled a nonqualifier or a partial qualifier. The specific categorization will again depend on where the test scores and grades fall. If the athlete is a nonqualifier, she will not be able to receive athletic based financial aid, cannot practice or compete as a freshman, and retains only three years of eligibility. A partial qualifier may practice, can receive an athletic scholarship, but cannot compete as a freshman and will have only three years of eligibility left.[20] *[A nonqualifier may receive non-athletics based financial aid as a freshman. Both nonqualifiers and partial qualifiers may regain a fourth year of eligibility if they graduate in four years.]*

All initial eligibility matters are now handled by the NCAA Clearinghouse, a bureau set up through a contractual arrangement in 1993 with American College Testing in Iowa City, Iowa. Any athlete wishing to compete in NCAA athletics must, prior to entering college, be reviewed by the Clearinghouse. [Athletes'] transcripts and test scores are reviewed for discrepancies and for satisfaction of the core course requirements. Particularly troublesome for many athletes in recent years has been the determination of just what courses satisfy the core course requirement. There has been some question regarding consistency on the determinations and many instances of athletes receiving advice and counsel from high school counselors and administrators which is at odds with the ultimate determination by the Clearinghouse. The matter has been further complicated by the lack of adequate staff at the Clearinghouse and insufficient telephone lines to handle all of the inevitable questions arising during middle to late August as athletes are preparing to enroll as freshmen. Yet another aspect of the controversy is the manner in which the Clearinghouse and the NCAA have responded to cases involving athletes with learning disabilities.

An athlete who has been declared ineligible by the Clearinghouse may appeal this determination to the Subcommittee on Initial Eligibility of the NCAA. Until recently, however, this committee had only been meeting every other week, adding to the frustrations of athletes, parents, and coaches. If that avenue does not produce eligibility the athlete may appeal to the NCAA Council. The only other option available to the athlete is litigation. This has occurred on numerous occasions since 1995. . . .

The NCAA also has extensive and complex rules governing the recruitment of prospective student-athletes by schools. These include a prohibition on involvement in the process by supporters of the institution. They also include the number of visits a recruit may make to member schools, the number of recruits a particular school may bring to its campus, and elaborate restrictions on when coaches may talk to recruits, see them play, and bring them to campus.[21] There are also detailed restrictions and requirements concerning competition and practice, including length and time of season, limitations on numbers of contests, and number of hours of practice per week during the season. Finally, the Association conducts and regulates postseason championship events in more than two dozen sports.[22]

Another linchpin of the Association is the concept of institutional control of intercollegiate athletics.[23] Each member institution is to control its program in a manner consistent with the rules and regulations of the Association. The CEO of the institution is ultimately responsible for the program at a given school. This responsibility extends to the conduct of administrators, coaches, athletes, and supporters of the program. When the conduct of the program transgresses the rules, the enforcement arm of the NCAA goes to work, as do the administrators and coaches of the program under investigation. *[Figure 7 outlines the enforcement process.]*

The Association has a large full time enforcement staff which handles investigations. An investigation may begin either as a result of information being given to the enforcement staff by some outside source, on the initiation of the enforcement staff itself, or as a result of a self-reported violation of the rules by the school itself. All investigations are treated as confidential until announcements are made according to the prescribed procedures.[24] The initial step in the investigative process is the evaluation of the information received concerning possible violations by the enforcement staff. If the information is not substantiated, the case will be closed. If it is determined to be reasonably substantial, the institution will be notified that a preliminary investigation is under way. This notice will provide the school with information regarding the charges, the persons allegedly involved, the time frame of the violations, and will notify the school and involved individuals that they may be represented by counsel throughout the process. Following the preliminary investigation, the process can go in one of three directions: the case may be closed for lack of evidence; a major violation may be found and summary disposal discussions begin with the school; or a lesser or secondary violation may be found and appropriate penalties are then discussed and imposed.

If the alleged violations are determined to be major and summary disposition is not possible, the NCAA then serves an Official Inquiry on the CEO of the institution. This OI will detail the allegations with perhaps even more specificity than the notice of preliminary investigation. The institution will then conduct its own investigation, often utilizing outside counsel and investigators. Individual coaches and athletes may also have their own legal representation. The rules of the Association require the institution to cooperate fully with the NCAA enforcement staff, the Committee on Infractions, Infractions Appeals Committee, and the Council. Failure to cooperate is itself a violation of the rules. (Another significant violation, frequently found in these matters, is lack of institutional control of the program.) Theoretically, then, it is not an adversarial process.

Following the investigation the Committee on Infractions will conduct a hearing to determine findings and any penalties deemed appropriate. This hearing will involve the institution's representatives, involved parties, the enforcement staff, and, where appropriate, the report of an independent hearing officer. Following the hearing the Committee on Infractions will issue its report, which will include penalties. Potential penalties range from public censure and reprimand to the "death penalty," the total shut-down of a program or particular sport for a set period of time. In between are such sanctions as reduction in scholarships allowed, forfeiture of tournament money, ineligibility for championship events, limitations on recruitment activities by certain personnel, and ineligibility for appearance on television. The school has the opportunity to appeal the ruling to the Infractions Appeals

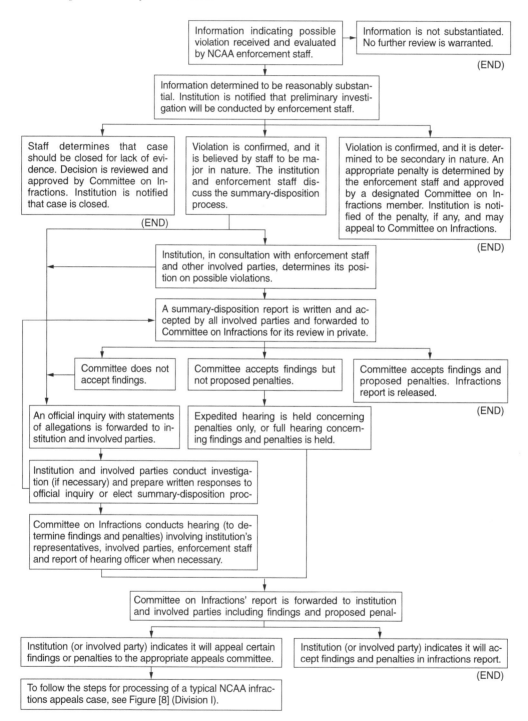

Figure 7. Processing of a typical NCAA infractions case. (Source: 2003–04 NCAA Division I Manual, Figure 32-1, p. 449.)

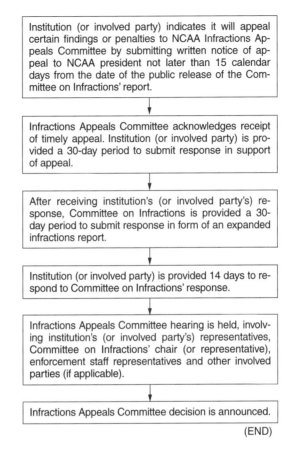

Institution (or involved party) indicates it will appeal certain findings or penalties to NCAA Infractions Appeals Committee by submitting written notice of appeal to NCAA president not later than 15 calendar days from the date of the public release of the Committee on Infractions' report.

Infractions Appeals Committee acknowledges receipt of timely appeal. Institution (or involved party) is provided a 30-day period to submit response in support of appeal.

After receiving institution's (or involved party's) response, Committee on Infractions is provided a 30-day period to submit response in form of an expanded infractions report.

Institution (or involved party) is provided 14 days to respond to Committee on Infractions' response.

Infractions Appeals Committee hearing is held, involving institution's (or involved party's) representatives, Committee on Infractions' chair (or representative), enforcement staff representatives and other involved parties (if applicable).

Infractions Appeals Committee decision is announced.

(END)

Figure 8. Processing of a typical NCAA infractions appeals case. (Source: 2003–04 NCAA Division I Manual, Figure 32-2, p. 450.)

Committee. *[The appeals process is outlined in Figure 8.]* This appellate body will receive written "briefs" from the institution and from the Committee on Infractions. It will also hold a hearing involving all interested parties. Unlike earlier appeals to the NCAA Council, the Infractions Appeals Committee has actually modified or partially reversed findings of the Committee on Infractions.

The enforcement process, as set out above, has been substantially modified in the last several years. Prior to 1993 there were major concerns regarding fairness and due process raised by schools and individuals within the membership.

REFERENCES

1. NCAA Division I Manual, 4.1.2 (1999–2000).

2. Division I Manual 4.5.

3. Division I Manual, 4.5.2.

4. Division I Manual, 21.6.

5. Division I Manual, 21.6.7.

6. Division I Manual, 1.3.1.

7. Division I Manual, 2.9.

8. Id.

9. Division I Manual, 12.01.1.

10. Division I Manual, 12.1.1.

11. Division I Manual, 12.1.1.

12. Division I Manual, 12.1.2.

13. Division I Manual, 12.2.4.

14. Division I Manual, 12.2.4.2.1.

15. Division I Manual, 12.3.

16. Division I Manual, 12.5.1.

17. Division I Manual, 15.2.6.1.

18. Division I Manual, 14.2.1.

19. Division I Manual, 14.01.2 (1996).

20. *See generally* Division I Manual, 14.

21. Division I Manual, 13.

22. Division I Manual, 17, 18.

23. Division I Manual, 2.1.

24. Division I Manual, 32.1.1 (1996).

ETHICS IN INTERCOLLEGIATE ATHLETICS: AN EXAMINATION OF NCAA VIOLATIONS AND PENALTIES — 1952–1997

Daniel F. Mahony, Janet S. Fink, and Donna L. Pastore

The notion that sport teaches participants the importance of fair play has received little support in recent years. . . . Prior to much of the research on ethics in athletics, research in business settings had already found unethical behavior increased when competition increased and when the rewards for cheating were higher. Sport is, by its very nature, highly competitive. Moreover, sport places a heavy emphasis on winning, and the rewards for winning are great.

. . . .

. . . Thus, the current study attempted to answer a number of questions related to NCAA violations by men's and women's college sport teams to determine whether such incidences of cheating had, indeed, increased through the years and whether the incidences of cheating were related to the level of competition:

1. Do violations in men's and women's sports occur more often at the Division I level? Has this changed over time?
2. Do violations in men's and women's sports occur more often in the more prestigious sports (football, men's basketball, and women's basketball)? Has this changed over time?
3. Has there been an increase in the number of violations found in men's and women's intercollegiate sports during recent years?
4. Has there been a change in the types of violations and the severity of violations in men's and women's intercollegiate sports in recent years?
5. Has there been a change in the types of penalties and the severity of penalties in men's and women's intercollegiate sports in recent years?

It is logical to surmise that programs that violate the rules do so because they are trying to gain a competitive advantage. Therefore, one would suspect that programs that violate the rules would improve during the period of the violations. Thus, the study also attempted to answer the following question:

    6. Do violations by men's and women's sport teams have a positive impact on team performance?

The goal of NCAA enforcement program is to decrease the incentive to violate the rules and to discourage other institutions from committing similar violations. Prior research has suggested when the penalties for cheating are higher, the incidences of cheating tend to decrease. If the NCAA's program has been successful, one would expect to see a decrease in team performance in the years after the program has been penalized. Thus, the study attempted to answer the following question:

    7. Do the penalties given to men's and women's sport teams have a negative impact on team performance?

Finally, many researchers have suggested the large increase in men coaching women's sport teams would result in the "male model" of intercollegiate athletics used in women's sports. Traditionally, the male model has been based on a "win at all costs" attitude that is contradictory to the female model which traditionally focused more on the process than the outcome. Based on the heavier focus on winning in the "male" model, one might guess that male coaches would be more likely to violate the rules than female coaches. Thus, the study attempted to answer the following question:

    8. Do male coaches of women's sport teams violate the rules more often than female coaches of women's sport teams?

  . . . .

RESULTS AND DISCUSSION

Violations in Men's Sport Programs

    Table 1 presents a summary of data related to men's sport teams that have violated NCAA rules from 1952 to 1997. . . .

    Violations by Division. When examining violations by division, the data indicates that most violations occurred at the Division I level. Although only about 34% of NCAA institutions compete at this level, 81% of the men's programs that have been penalized for violating the rules were at the Division I level. Moreover, this ratio did not change significantly over time. The percentage of violators that were Division I schools has remained relatively consistent, ranging from a low of 78% in the 1970s to a high of 87% in the 1980s.

    . . . . Perhaps, as Stoll and Beller[1] suggest, athletes at both levels are willing to cheat to win; yet, due to the glamour, money, and prestige that comes along with being a winning Division I intercollegiate athletic program, the increased opportunity and "payoff" of immoral behavior serves as a strong impetus for those involved in such a system to act immorally. A second explanation is that Division I institutions, because of their stature, receive more scrutiny in terms of compliance than do Division III institutions. Thus, cheating may occur at similar rates at the two levels, but, because of closer scrutiny of the Division I programs, more of them are caught.

TABLE 1.

Means for Men's Programs That Violated NCAA Regulations by Decade						
	1950s	*1960s*	*1970s*	*1980s*	*1990s*	*Total*
Division I	86%	85%	78%	87%	83%	81%
Revenue sports	100%	93%	82%	82%	58%	79%
Violations						
Academic	2%	0%	14%	13%	34%	15%
Recruiting	72%	70%	60%	77%	60%	67%
Benefits	72%	77%	75%	88%	84%	81%
Eligibility	7%	7%	47%	32%	57%	36%
Illegal participation	12%	30%	29%	15%	9%	19%
Unethical conduct	2%	7%	28%	42%	48%	30%
Institutional control	0%	3%	19%	24%	78%	32%
Penalties						
Probation (years)	1.20	1.12	1.35	1.39	2.56	1.63
Postseason (years)	0.79	0.85	0.94	0.55	0.62	0.72
TV ban (years)	0.48	0.38	0.77	0.28	0.16	0.40
Scholarships	0%	0%	14%	35%	60%	28%
Forfeit contests	0%	0%	1%	13%	40%	14%
Penalize coach	0%	1%	14%	24%	36%	20%
Reduced comp	2%	4%	2%	4%	9%	5%
Recruiting restrictions	0%	3%	6%	22%	41%	18%
Reduce association	20%	0%	12%	26%	18%	15%
Public reprimand	23%	26%	18%	21%	22%	21%
Programs per year	7.1	7.3	13.9	16.4	18.5	12.6

Violations by Sport. When examining violations by sport, it is clear most of the violations have been in football and men's basketball. Although the average school offers more than seven men's sports, 79% of the violations occurred in these two sports alone. However, this ratio has decreased significantly over time. It appears that investigations and violations have become much more common in non-revenue men's sports than they were in the past. In the 1950s (100%) and the 1960s (93%) almost all of the violations were in the two revenue producing sports. In the 1990s, the percentage of violations that were in revenue sports dropped to 58%.

It is an interesting phenomena that the percentage of violations in revenue sports dropped significantly through the years. It may be that because of the close scrutiny given to the revenue producing sports and the increased size of the NCAA enforcement staff, they are less likely to attempt to engage in rules violations due to a fear of being caught. Or, revenue producing sports may commit the same amount of violations but because the NCAA enforcement staff has grown, more non-revenue sports are caught cheating, thus lowering the percentage of revenue sports found in violation. Finally, the change may be a result of a changing approach in men's non-revenue sports. The heavy emphasis on winning and the incentives to cheat may have become stronger in the men's non-revenue sports in recent years, which could explain the increase in violations in these sports.

Violations by Year. When examining trends in violations, there does appear to have been some significant changes in the number and severity of the violations in men's sport programs. The number of men's programs that have been penalized for violating the rules has increased significantly from 7.1 per year in the 1950s to 18.5 per year in the 1990s. While it appears cheating is occurring with greater frequency in the 1990s, it should be noted that this increase could be related to the increased size of the NCAA enforcement staff during this time and may not necessarily indicate the frequency of rules violations has increased.

In order to determine if the NCAA violations were changing in nature over time, the current study also examined the severity of the violations. Although there was no significant difference in the percentage of schools penalized for committing violations related to recruiting and excessive benefits, there were a number of significant changes in other categories. Illegal participation penalties have actually decreased significantly over time. This may be related to the fact that games are given much more media attention today, so it would be more difficult to compete without the NCAA learning of the contest. In the past, schools may have believed they could play an extra game or have some extra practices without the NCAA knowing; because this is less likely today, fewer schools are likely to take that risk.

There were significant increases in the number of academic related violations and eligibility related violations. These results indicate that more programs have attempted to circumvent academic rules (i.e., initial eligibility rules, satisfactory progress rules) to get players eligible. Some of these violations have been very severe and one led to a federal court case for academic cheating and transcript altering. Because most of the increases in violations in this area have taken place in the last decade, the increases may be related to stricter academic and eligibility requirements passed during the 1980s. There would have been little need to violate these rules when the eligibility requirements were much easier to satisfy.

Finally, a clear indication of the increasing severity of the violations in men's sport programs is the significant increase in the percentage of violations that have included charges of unethical conduct and a lack of institutional control. According to the *1997–98 NCAA Division I Manual,* unethical conduct includes: "(a) refusal to furnish information relevant to an (NCAA investigation) . . . ; (b) knowing involvement in arranging for fraudulent academic credit or false transcripts . . . ; (c) knowing involvement in offering or providing a . . . student-athlete an improper inducement or extra benefit . . . ; (d) knowingly furnishing the NCAA or the individual's institution false or misleading information concerning . . . a possible violation of an NCAA regulation; or (e) receipt of benefits by an institutional staff member for facilitating or arranging a meeting between a student-athlete and an agent. . . ."[2] A charge of unethical conduct would appear to be an indication the NCAA believes the violation is significant and an individual at the institution intentionally and knowingly violated the rules.

. . . . While a charge of unethical conduct indicates an individual failed to live up to their responsibility to act in an ethical manner, a finding of a lack of institutional control indicates the NCAA does not believe the University did enough to prevent violations resulting from the unethical behavior of their employees, or the NCAA believes they failed to provide enough instruction regarding the rules to prevent the violations. Therefore, this would be considered a serious charge against the University.

. . . . It is interesting to note that while these accounts involve athletes, both violations revolve around those in charge of the athletes indicating a problem within the athletic system, institutional structure, or both. It appears that cheating in intercollegiate athletics is becoming more systemic and, thus, more difficult to contain.

Penalties by Year. While there has been no significant change in the percentage of programs publicly reprimanded or the percentage of programs forced to reduce association with an individual outside of the athletic department, there has been a significant change in some of the other penalty areas. The number of years of probation given to each men's program has increased significantly from 1.2 years per institution in the 1950s to 2.56 years per institution in the 1990s, with the biggest change occurring during the last 10 years. Moreover, there have been significant increases in the percentages of programs forced to forfeit contests and reduce competitive opportunities in the future. In addition, these penalties generally result in a reduction of income because the institutions that forfeit games are often required to return related revenue and the reduction of future competitions provides less opportunities to earn money in the future. Reduction in competitive opportunities can also be damaging to player development and can decrease the university's and team's chances to garner positive public relations through the success of the team.

The NCAA has also increased the use of reduced scholarships and reduced recruiting opportunities to penalize men's programs that violate the rules. Although these increases may be related to the increasing severity of violations discussed earlier, there are other possible explanations for these changes. The NCAA appears to believe that taking away scholarships and, consequently, the institution's chances for obtaining the best athletes, will have a greater impact than a reduction in television appearances or a post-season ban. Moreover, these penalties appear to make sense considering the type of violations that are escalating (e.g., use of ineligible players, academic fraud). Taking away scholarships and reducing recruiting privileges would appear to be appropriate penalties for a program that has used an ineligible player(s) or engaged in academic fraud to get an athlete into [the] program.

In contrast, both the number of years of post-season suspension and the number of years of a television ban have decreased significantly over time. . . . Moreover, these decreases do not appear to be a result of a decrease in the severity of the violations. The NCAA appears to be decreasing the use of these penalties slightly, while substantially increasing the use of other penalties (e.g., scholarship reductions, recruiting restrictions, penalizing coaches) that the NCAA believes will have more of an impact or are more appropriate given the violations.

Finally, there has been a significant increase in the percentage of coaches being personally penalized for the involvement with the violations. This increase may be related to a couple of factors. First, it is possible the NCAA believes this type of penalty will have more of an impact. Penalties that only focus on the school allow the coach to leave the institution and avoid suffering from any of the penalties. Penalties specific to the coach often follow the coach to another institution so those who are responsible for breaking the rules are penalized. Second, it is possible an increase in charges of unethical behavior by coaches, discussed earlier, has led to the increase in this type of penalty.

The Impact of Violations and Penalties on Team Records. An analysis of the team records before and after institutions were penalized by the NCAA . . . indicates that the violations committed by the programs did not significantly improve their performance. In other words, cheating did not seem to help team performance. *[See Table 2.]* It should be noted, however, that the average record for teams that were penalized was consistently above .500 before the penalties were enacted. This may suggest the teams which were violating the rules were already doing this well before the violations occurred and their willingness to break the rules was more related to the pressure to pursue a superior record

TABLE 2.

MEAN WINNING PERCENTAGES OF MEN'S AND WOMEN'S PROGRAMS BEFORE AND AFTER NCAA PENALTIES		
	Men	*Women*
Before Penalties		
5 years before	.540	.430
4 years before	.576	.439
3 years before	.590	.576
2 years before	.534	.600
1 year before	.554	.557
After Penalties		
1 year after	.536	.419
2 years after	.541	.490
3 years after	.540	.562
4 years after	.577	.600
5 years after	.583	.596

or a championship, instead of a desire to turn around a traditionally unsuccessful program. Additionally, it could also suggest that these teams had been engaging in unethical behavior for several years before being caught, thus giving them an unfair advantage and the increased ability to sustain a winning program.

Moreover, the penalties given to schools by the NCAA did not have a significant impact on team records. This would suggest the penalties given by the NCAA in recent years are not severe enough to actually decrease a program's chances for success. Even after the penalties, the average records were consistently above .500 and even increased during the five year "after penalization" period. Perhaps the recent changes in the types of penalties being used by the NCAA are a result of the NCAA realizing the former penalties had few negative consequences. It will be interesting to see if these changes in penalties result in any differences in team performance in the upcoming years.

Violations in Women's Sport Programs

. . . .

Violations by Division. Similar to the results for the men's programs, approximately 82% of the violations in women's sport programs occurred at the Division I level and this percentage was relatively consistent over time. *[See Table 3.]* Again, this is clearly greater than the percentage of institutions at the Division I level (34%). Based on this difference by division, one must conclude that either the NCAA is focusing most of its attention and investigations on the highest division or that violations are more likely to occur at the level where the pressure to win is the greatest.

TABLE 3.

MEANS FOR WOMEN'S PROGRAMS THAT VIOLATED NCAA REGULATIONS BY DECADE			
	1980s	*1990s*	*Total*
Division I	85%	81%	82%
Revenue sports	35%	35%	35%
Violations			
Academic	0%	48%	34%
Recruiting	65%	50%	54%
Benefits	90%	83%	85%
Eligibility	35%	67%	57%
Illegal participation	10%	10%	10%
Unethical conduct	35%	50%	46%
Institutional control	20%	73%	57%
Penalties			
Probation (years)	0.95	2.67	2.16
Postseason (years)	0.15	0.67	0.51
TV ban (years)	0.00	0.04	0.03
Scholarships	15%	58%	46%
Forfeit contests	20%	50%	41%
Penalize coach	10%	38%	29%
Reduced comp	15%	15%	15%
Recruiting restrictions	20%	13%	15%
Reduce association	20%	7%	10%
Public reprimand	35%	29%	31%
Programs per year	3.3	6.0	4.7

Violations by Sport. When examining violations by sport, it was expected that the sport with the most violations would be women's basketball because it is the most frequently offered sport and it is usually the women's sport with the greatest fan base and subsequent pressure to win. An examination of the data reveals that 35% of the violations in both the 1980s and the 1990s occurred in women's basketball, more than any other sport. It is interesting to note there were almost no violations in many of the other frequently offered sports, such as volleyball and softball. However, there were an unusually high number of violations in track and cross-country (slightly less than 30%). Although it is not clear why there are more violations in these sports, it is possible that it is related in part to the high number of international athletes in these sport programs which present some unique problems related to eligibility and recruiting benefits.

Violations by Year. Similar to the men's sport program violations, there were some significant changes in the number and severity of the violations in women's sport programs. The number of women's programs that have been penalized for violating the rules has increased significantly from 3.3 per year in the 1980s to 6.0 per year in the 1990s. In other words, the average number of programs violating the rules has almost doubled in a very short period of time. We were particularly interested in whether this increase was related to an increasing emphasis on enforcement by the NCAA, in which case violations in men's and women's programs should increase at the same rate, or whether violations in women's sport programs were increasing at a faster rate than violations in men's sport programs. An analysis of the data appears to indicate the latter is true. In the 1980s, 14% of the total violations (approximately 1 in 7) occurred in women's sport programs. In the 1990s, this ratio jumped to 24%; thus, nearly 1 in 4 violations in recent years have occurred in women's programs. Although the percentage of violations in women's sport programs is still well behind the men, they have increased at a faster rate in recent years. . . . Additionally, this provides further evidence that as teams are provided more media attention, prestige, and glamour (as women's sports have in recent years), the pressure to win may, in turn, lead to an increase in incidences of cheating.

Although there have been no significant changes in violations related to illegal participation, recruiting, and excessive benefits (already consistently high), there have been significant changes in four violation categories. Similar to the men's programs, there has been a significant increase in academic related violations and a significant increase in eligibility related violations. Again, this may be related in part to stricter rules related to initial eligibility and satisfactory progress. However, it should be noted that the percentage of programs violating academic rules was greater for the women (48%) than for the men (34%) and the percentage of eligibility violations was greater for women (67%) than for men (58%). In addition, an analysis of the data indicated there was a significant increase in lack of institutional control charges in women's sports. These results would indicate that like the men's programs, many of the violations of rules in women's sports are related to an inability or unwillingness of universities to control unethical behavior. Although the change was not significant, unethical behavior violations also increased, from 35% in the 1980s to 50% in the 1990s. Overall, these results would suggest that while there are still fewer violations found by the NCAA in women's sports, the severity of the violations in women's programs is equal to or greater than the severity of violations in men's programs.

Penalties by Year. There have been no significant changes in the number of years of a television ban, the percentage of programs penalized using recruiting restrictions, the percentage of programs given restrictions related to future competition, the percentage of programs publicly reprimanded, and the percentage of programs forced to reduce association with an individual outside of the athletic department. However, there have been significant changes in some of the other penalty areas. The number of years of probation given to each women's program has increased significantly from .95 years per institution in the 1980s to 2.67 years per institution in the 1990s. This sharp escalation in probation length, almost 3 times the initial length, in such a short period of time may indicate the NCAA is trying to send a stronger message to women's programs that violate the rules. The NCAA may believe the severity of the violations has increased and, thus, hope to prevent any further onslaught of cheating with stiff penalties.

Similar to the men's programs, there was a significant increase in the percentage of programs penalized through scholarship reductions and the percentage of programs forced to forfeit games. The increase in these penalties was consistent with the increase in academic related violations and eligibility violations. While scholarship reductions appear focused on impacting the future performance of the program on the field, forfeiting contests takes away both the financial and public relations benefits of past success. Also similar to the men's programs, there was a significant increase between the 1980s and the 1990s in penalizing coaches. Again, this is consistent with the increase in unethical conduct charges and with an apparent desire by the NCAA to hold the coaches responsible for violations in their programs. Finally, in contrast to the men, there was a significant increase in the number of years of postseason suspension given to programs that violate the rules. However, the number of years is still fairly low, an average of .67 year per school in the 1990s, which suggests this is not a penalty the NCAA often utilizes to penalize women's sport programs.

The Impact of Violations and Penalties on Team Records. An analysis of the women's team records before and after institutions were penalized by the NCAA . . . indicates the average program's performance increased during the period in which the violations occurred. Also in contrast to the men's programs, the average record of women's sport programs that violated the rules was below .500 five years before the penalty (.430). Team performance then increased to a high of .600 two seasons before being penalized. Thus, it appears that cheating helped the women's programs gain a competitive advantage.

The penalties given to women's sport programs also appeared to have a negative impact on performance, which seemed to fade away over time. Although the average winning percentage of teams penalized for violations dropped from .557 the year before the penalties to .419 the year after the penalties, the average records the fourth (.600) and fifth year (.596) after the penalties were quite high and a significant improvement over their performance five years prior to the penalties (.430). These results would indicate that although the severity of the penalties is increasing for women's sport programs, they have only a short-term effect and most of the programs appear able to reach high levels of performance just a few years after the penalties.

The Impact of the Gender of the Coach. It should be noted before examining the impact of the gender of the coach that recent data suggest the percentage of women's sport programs with a female coach is approximately 47–48%.[3] Analysis of the programs penalized by the NCAA for violations in women's sport programs found that 48% percent of these programs had a female coach. Moreover, of the coaches of women's sport teams who were penalized personally, 47% were female. In other words, gender of the coach had no significant impact on the likelihood that a program or coach would be penalized by the NCAA for rules violations in women's sports. Male and female coaches of women's sport teams violated the rules at the same rate. If, as has been suggested, the NCAA takeover of women's athletics has brought the "male model" (traditionally focusing on a "win at all costs" attitude) to women's sports, the female coaches appear to follow this model as often as the male coaches. Perhaps this is a result of the fact that most athletic administrators in hiring positions are male, and thus, when hiring a coach, whether male or female, the administrator hires "like" candidates in terms of values, priorities, and/or ideologies resulting in more coaches who have adopted the "male model." Or, it may be that the current system of intercollegiate athletics somehow serves to encourage incidences of cheating whether it be due to the manner in which competition is currently viewed or due to the positive consequences and high stakes involved in creating and maintaining winning programs.

CONCLUSIONS

Many espouse the belief that "sport builds character"; yet nearly every week we are bombarded with incidences of corruption in sport, particularly in intercollegiate athletics. From recruiting violations, to academic record tampering, to institutional cover-up of athletic dishonesty, many argue that the arena of intercollegiate athletics appears to be more about "tipping the scales" to one's favor than providing an opportunity for building character and improving sportsmanship. . .

The current study appears to support these contentions. In both men's and women's intercollegiate athletics, the number of violations has increased significantly over time and unethical conduct occurs more frequently at the higher levels of play (Division I). Further, the most severe violations, such as charges of unethical conduct and lack of institutional control, have increased significantly. And while a number of specific penalties have also increased (i.e., the reduction of scholarships and recruiting opportunities), the current study indicates that these penalties provide very few negative consequences in terms of a penalized team's winning percentages. These light penalties are in contrast to penalties for ethical violations in other professions, such as law, medicine, and business, which may include prison sentences, substantial fines, and losing one's license to practice.

Moreover, many of the rule violators in college athletics are probably never caught. The NCAA spends only about 1.4% of their budget on rule enforcement, less than is spent on public relations.[4] Consequently, the "payoff" for cheating to obtain a winning program in college athletics and the windfall of money and prestige that accompanies it are far greater than the fear of punishment. Thus, as the unethical behavior appears to become more and more endemic in intercollegiate athletics, the NCAA's attempts to punish and thwart such behavior seems to fail. This finding is consistent with Frey's[5] suggestion that the NCAA is not an effective rule enforcer. Although the NCAA compliance manual becomes thicker each year with rules that attempt to put an end to innovative ways of cheating or various loopholes in the current rules, the NCAA appears to be falling further and further behind in the race to establish a sense of sportsmanship and ethical conduct throughout the sport management profession.

For many years, scholars and journalists alike have pointed to the incidences of corruption in sport and called for significant changes to the current structure of intercollegiate athletics. These suggestions have included (a) structural reform to allow more presidents, faculty, and lower division representation on NCAA decision-making committees, (b) a reconfiguration of the NCAA that allows student-athletes a stronger voice in procedures, (c) a complete reconstruction of intercollegiate athletics which would measure success by student-athlete development rather than by wins and losses, (d) an increase in NCAA enforcement efforts, and (e) stricter penalties for professionals and institutions that violate the rules. While not providing an answer as to the "best" way to change the structure in order to curb unethical behavior, our findings tend to corroborate the view that the current structure is not working. As Frey[6] suggested, the combination of loose supervision and heavy rewards for ethical violations that lead to more victories has led to an increasing amount of cheating in both women's and men's programs. Further, the increase in certain types of violations indicates the cheating is more systemic. That is, not only are athletes and coaches engaging in unethical behavior, but athletic administrators and institutional leaders are also being caught in the midst of corruption indicating an endemic, complex, and burgeoning problem that current efforts do little to contain.

REFERENCES

1. Stoll, S.K., & Beller, J.M. (1995). *Moral reasoning of Division I and Division III athletes: Is there a difference?* Paper presented at the American Alliance of Health, Physical Education, Recreation, and Dance. Portland, OR.

2. *1997–98 NCAA Division I Manual,* 51 (1997). Overland Park, KS: National Collegiate Athletic Association.

3. Acosta, R.V., & Carpenter, L.J. (1992). As the years go by — Coaching opportunities in the 1990s. *Journal of Physical Education, Recreation, and Dance,* 63 (3), 36, 41. Acosta, R. V., & Carpenter, L. J. (1996). Women in intercollegiate sport: A longitudinal study — Nineteen year update, 1977–1996. Brooklyn, NY: Photocopied report.

4. Wong, G. M. (1994). *Essentials of amateur sports law* (2nd ed.). Westport, CT: Praeger.

5. Frey, J. H. (1994). Deviance of organizational subunits: The case of college athletic departments. *Journal of Sport and Social Issues,* 18, 110–122.

6. Id.

DISCUSSION QUESTIONS

1. What were some of the early complaints voiced about the growing commercialism of intercollegiate athletics? Have these complaints endured?

2. Why was the NCAA formed?

3. Describe the structural evolution of the NCAA.

4. How did the NCAA react to the critics who stated that it exercised its enforcement authority unfairly?

5. Describe the present management structure of the NCAA.

6. Is the current structure the ideal governing structure for collegiate sports?

7. Describe an alternative governing structure that might operate more effectively.

8. Give some examples of the rule violations that predominantly occur in both women's and men's sports.

9. What is the Sanity Code?

10. Why was the Sanity Code repealed?

The NCAA and Conference Affiliation

INTRODUCTION

It is now clear that intercollegiate athletics has been infused with a degree of commercialization since its outset. What is not as apparent, however, is the size of the college sports industry. This chapter and the one that follows explain the business of intercollegiate athletics from the perspective of the NCAA as a collective, its member conferences, and its individual member institutions.

The first three selections in this chapter by Koch, Noll, and Fort and Quirk provide a comprehensive overview of the financial aspects of intercollegiate athletics. As shown in Table 1, the primary asset of the NCAA is the Division I men's basketball tournament. The NCAA budget was $422 million in the 2002–2003 season. Nearly 88%, or $370 million, of this amount was generated by the NCAA's new, 11-year, $6.2 billion contract with CBS to broadcast what has become widely known as "March Madness." Another 6%, or $25.4 million, was earned in ticket sales for this tournament. The organization's remaining revenues (6%) were the result of gate receipts from all of its other tournaments across all three divisions ($12.8 million combined), licensing efforts ($3.3 million), and other investments, sales, fees, and services ($10.7 million).

It is important to note that the NCAA is not involved in Division I-A football, despite the fact that its revenue potential is much greater than that of basketball. Thus, individual conferences and schools (namely, Notre Dame) negotiate separate broadcast agreements for regular-season football; a separate coalition of top conferences and Notre Dame control the postseason through the Bowl Championship Series (BCS). All other postseason games are controlled by the promoters of the various independent bowl games that have entered into individual agreements with broadcast networks and cable channels to televise their contests. They typically have arrangements with conferences to send predetermined place teams to play in the games.

The NCAA distributes the majority of its revenues to the members of Division I through various mechanisms. These distributions totaled $245 million, or 58% of the NCAA's expenses in 2002–2003. (The details of these distributions are provided in the NCAA's *2002–03 Revenue Distribution Plan.*)

TABLE 1.

NCAA Budget, 2002–2003		
The National Collegiate Athletic Association Proposed Budget for Fiscal Year Ended August 31, 2003		
	Proposed 2002–2003 budget	*Percentage of total operating revenue/exp.*
Revenue		
Television	370,000,000	87.63%
Championships revenue		
Division I men's basketball	25,400,000	6.02%
Other Division I championships	12,128,000	2.87%
Division II championships	440,000	0.10%
Division III championships	265,000	0.06%
Total championships revenue	38,233,000	9.05%
Licensing and royalties	3,300,000	0.78%
Investments	7,240,000	1.71%
Sales, fees, and services	3,460,000	0.82%
TOTAL NCAA OPERATING REVENUE	**422,233,000**	**100.00%**
Division Specific Expenses		
Division I Expense & Allocation		
Distribution to Division I members		
Dist. to institutions' athletic programs (note 1)	195,000,000	46.18%
Dist. to student-athlete programs (note 2)	44,209,000	10.47%
Distribution to conference programs	5,817,000	1.38%
Total distribution to Division I members	245,026,000	58.03%
Championships		
Men's basketball		
Game expense	5,460,000	1.29%
Travel	10,411,000	2.47%
Other Division I championships		
Game expense	8,160,500	1.93%
Travel	26,860,500	6.36%
Total Division I championships	50,892,000	12.05%
Other Division I programs		
Basketball mentoring	550,000	0.13%
Championships promotions	910,000	0.22%
Total other Division I programs	1,460,000	0.35%
TOTAL DIVISION I EXP. & ALLOCATION	**297,378,000**	**70.43%**
		(Continued)

TABLE 1. **(Continued)**

NCAA BUDGET, 2002–2003		
THE NATIONAL COLLEGIATE ATHLETIC ASSOCIATION PROPOSED BUDGET FOR FISCAL YEAR ENDED AUGUST 31, 2003		
	Proposed 2002–2003 budget	*Percentage of total operating revenue/exp.*
Division Specific Expenses (Continued)		
Division II Exp. & Allocation (Note 4):		
Championship game expense	2,232,000	0.53%
Championship travel	9,925,000	2.35%
Distribution of enhancement fund	3,900,000	0.92%
Programs and other expenses	2,407,000	0.57%
Championships and program support	214,200	0.05%
Funding from D II reserves	(226,200)	−0.05%
TOTAL DIVISION II EXP. & ALLOCATION	**18,452,000**	**4.37%**
Division III Expense & Allocation (Note 4)		
Championship game expense	2,365,000	0.56%
Championship travel	8,215,000	1.95%
Programs and other expenses	3,019,000	0.72%
Championships and program support	563,530	0.13%
Funding from D III reserves	(735,530)	−0.17%
TOTAL DIVISION III EXPENSE & ALLOCATION	**13,427,000**	**3.18%**
Association-Wide Expense		
Program and Services Expense		
Student-athlete welfare and youth programs and services (note 5)		
Catastrophic insurance	10,000,000	2.37%
Sports sciences	3,969,000	0.94%
Initial eligibility	965,000	0.23%
Youth programs	2,308,000	0.55%
Award ceremonies	486,000	0.12%
Scholarships	362,000	0.09%
NCAA Foundation—Student-athlete programs	386,000	0.09%
Sports agents/gambling and basketball certification	263,000	0.06%
Total student-athlete welfare and youth programs and services	18,739,000	4.44%
	(Continued)	

TABLE 1.   (Continued)

NCAA BUDGET, 2002–2003		
THE NATIONAL COLLEGIATE ATHLETIC ASSOCIATION PROPOSED BUDGET FOR FISCAL YEAR ENDED AUGUST 31, 2003		
	Proposed 2002–2003 budget	*Percentage of total operating revenue/exp.*
Association-Wide Expense (Continued)		
Program and Services Expense (Continued)		
Membership programs and services		
Public affairs	1,859,000	0.44%
Branding, broadcasting, and promotions	8,900,000	2.11%
Convention and seminars	975,000	0.23%
Education outreach and professional development	2,784,000	0.66%
Liability insurance	3,110,000	0.74%
Officiating improvement programs	785,000	0.19%
Research	941,000	0.22%
Athletics certification and education	759,000	0.18%
Grants and other services	151,000	0.04%
Other program services		
Membership services (note 7)	4,181,000	0.99%
Enforcement services and basketball certification (note 7)	3,852,000	0.91%
Championships (note 7)	4,349,500	1.03%
Education services (note 7)	3,559,000	0.84%
Total membership programs and services	36,205,500	8.57%
TOTAL PROGRAM AND SERVICES	**54,944,500**	**13.01%**
LEGAL SERVICE AND CONTINGENCIES	7,000,000	1.66%
GOVERNANCE/COMMITTEES	4,032,000	0.95%
Association-wide Expenses		
Administrative Services		
General and administrative expenses (note 6)	11,016,000	2.61%
Executive and governance staff (note 7)	5,438,000	1.29%
Public affairs (note 7)	3,588,500	0.85%
Finance and information services (note 7)	4,135,000	0.98%
Contingency-administrative services	400,000	0.09%
TOTAL ADMINISTRATIVE SERVICES	**24,577,500**	**5.82%**
		(Continued)

TABLE 1. (Continued)

NCAA BUDGET, 2002–2003

<table>
<tr><td colspan="3">THE NATIONAL COLLEGIATE ATHLETIC ASSOCIATION PROPOSED BUDGET
FOR FISCAL YEAR ENDED AUGUST 31, 2003</td></tr>
<tr><td></td><td>*Proposed
2002–2003
budget*</td><td>*Percentage of
total operating
revenue/exp.*</td></tr>
<tr><td colspan="3">*Association-wide Expenses (Continued)*</td></tr>
<tr><td colspan="3">*Administrative Services (Continued)*</td></tr>
<tr><td>Division II and III championships and program support</td><td>(778,000)</td><td>−0.18%</td></tr>
<tr><td>**TOTAL ASSOCIATION-WIDE EXPENSES**</td><td>**89,776,000**</td><td>**21.26%**</td></tr>
<tr><td>Unallocated funds</td><td>–</td><td>0.00%</td></tr>
<tr><td>**TOTAL NCAA OPERATING EXPENSES**</td><td>**419,033,000**</td><td>**99.24%**</td></tr>
<tr><td>NCAA presidential transition reserve</td><td>600,000</td><td>0.14%</td></tr>
<tr><td>Association-wide reserve (note 3)</td><td>2,300,000</td><td>0.54%</td></tr>
<tr><td>Repair and replacement reserve</td><td>300,000</td><td>0.07%</td></tr>
<tr><td>Funded operating/furniture and equipment reserve</td><td>–</td><td>–</td></tr>
<tr><td>**TOTAL**</td><td>**422,233,000**</td><td>**100.00%**</td></tr>
</table>

Note 1: Amount sent to institutions and conferences to subsidize student-athletes' grants-in-aid and sports programs.

Note 2: Distribution to student-athlete programs includes the academic enhancement fund, special assistance fund, and student-athlete opportunity fund.

Note 3: The membership trust/association-wide reserve is money allocated by each respective Division for future use for that respective Division.

Note 4: Division II and III allocations are calculated at 4.37% and 3.18%, respectively, of NCAA operating revenue.

Note 5: 'Student-Athlete Welfare and Youth Programs and Services' does not include the distribution to student-athlete programs.

Note 6: General and administrative expenses include facilities costs, employee procurement, computer services, furniture and equipment, depreciation, and other general office expenses.

Note 7: Includes salaries, payroll taxes, pension contributions, insurance, travel & entertainment expenses, postage, telephone, printing, and duplicating for each functional area.

Source: NCAA.

Another $31.9 million, or 7.5%, of the NCAA's revenues was distributed to the members of Divisions II and III, as is mandated by the NCAA constitution. The NCAA pays for all of the game and travel expenses for the schools participating in its 87 postseason tournaments, totaling nearly $51 million in 2002–2003, or 12% of its budgeted expenses. The NCAA also provides a number of programs and services for its members and athletes and spent nearly $55 million in a wide range of areas in 2002–2003, or 13% of its budget. Finally, the NCAA's expenditures on attorney's fees, lobbyists, its internal governance and committees, staff salaries, and general and administrative services totaled over $35 million, or 8% of its budget in 2002–2003.

Though there are more than 30 conferences in Division I, it is not surprising that the NCAA's revenue-sharing system favors the members of the "Big Six" athletic conferences that dominate Division I — the ACC, Big East, Big Ten, Big 12, Pac-10, and SEC. The NCAA's distribution to athletic programs is based on three factors. First, the number of NCAA sports that the institution offers affects the amount of money that it receives from the association. With the funds distributed being directly proportionate to the number of teams fielded, the more comprehensive athletic programs receive larger amounts of NCAA monies. Only the Ivy League received more money than the Big East, Big Ten, Pac-10, and ACC in 2001–2002. Second, the number of athletic scholarships that a school offers to its students impacts its receipt of NCAA funds; the more athletic scholarships offered, the greater the amount of money received. The Big Six conferences occupied six of the top seven spots on this distribution list in 2001–2002. The third distribution is based on each conference's performance in the men's basketball tournament over the previous 6 years. Each of the Big Six conferences received more from this distribution than any other conference. This should be expected given the depth and strength of these conferences and their dominance of college basketball. No school from outside of this power base has won a national championship in the sport since 1990. The dominance of these conferences is not limited to basketball. Overall, institutions from Big Six conferences won 25 of the 34 Division I NCAA championships in which they competed in 2002–2003.

Though the other distributions to Division I institutions are divided far more equitably, via the academic enhancement fund, special assistance fund for student-athletes, and conference grants, they represent a much smaller amount of money — approximately one-quarter of the amount that is dispersed through the aforementioned athletic scholarships, sports sponsorship, and basketball funds.

While the ACC, Big East, Big Ten, Big 12, Pac-10, and SEC receive favorable NCAA distributions, a far greater advantage is gained from the revenue sources that the NCAA does not control: the negotiation of television agreements by these elite conferences for regular season and postseason conference basketball and football contests and the participation in postseason BCS bowl games by members of these conferences. College conferences operate quite similarly to professional sports leagues in the negotiation of television agreements for football and basketball. Each conference pools certain rights of its member schools and enters into its own conference-wide broadcasting agreement, with the revenues divided equally among the member institutions. These contracts are lucrative. As Table 2 shows, in 2001–2002, the SEC, Big Ten, ACC, Big 12, Pac-10, and Big East received television revenues of $51 million, $50 million, $49.1 million, $43 million, $37.8 million, and $28 million, respectively. These contracts indicate the popularity of big-time college football and basketball. The importance of television in the landscape of college sports is discussed in the selections from Fizel and Bennett as well as Zimbalist, who also provides a review of bowl games and conference revenue sharing. In addition, each of these conferences stages a profit-generating postseason basketball tournament, with revenues ranging from $3.5 million (SEC) to $5.8 million (ACC) in 2001–2002. Further, the presence of 12 schools in both the Big 12 and SEC (and the ACC beginning in 2005) allows these conferences to hold a postseason championship football game, as per current NCAA rules. These games generated $12 million for the SEC and $5 million for the Big 12 in 2001–2002.

Football is the most important source of revenue for the elite conferences. Beyond the aforementioned television contracts and championship games, membership in a Big Six conference (aside from Notre Dame) is nearly a prerequisite for participation in the Bowl Championship Series. The

TABLE 2.

BIG SIX CONFERENCE FINANCIAL SNAPSHOT, 2001–2002	
SEC	
Total distribution	$95.7 million
TV	$51.0 million
SEC basketball tourn.	$3.5 million
NCAA basketball tourn.	$7.9 million
Bowl games	$30.7 million
SEC football champ. game	$12.0 million
TV households	6.6 million
	(11 markets)
Big 12	
Total distribution	$84.0 million
TV	$43.0 million
Big 12 basketball tourn.	$4.0 million
NCAA basketball tourn.	$8.4 million
Bowl games	$26.6 million
Big 12 football champ. game	$5.0 million
TV households	6.5 million
	(10 markets)
Big Ten	
Total distribution	$97.8 million
TV	$50.0 million
Big Ten basketball tourn.	$3.9 million
NCAA basketball tourn.	$8.9 million
Bowl games	$24.7 million
TV households	10.8 million
	(11 markets)

(Continued)

TABLE 2.   (Continued)

Big Six Conference Financial Snapshot, 2001–2002	
PAC-10	
Total distribution	$84.0 million
TV	$37.8 million
Pac-10 basketball tourn.	$4.0 million
NCAA basketball tourn.	$6.9 million
Bowl games	$19.3 million
TV households	11.9 million
	(7 markets)
ACC	
Total distribution	$87.6 million
TV	$49.1 million
ACC basketball tourn.	$5.8 million
NCAA basketball tourn.	$7.6 million
Bowl games	$20.5 million
TV households	6.1 million
	(7 markets)
Big East	
Total distribution	$55.4 million
TV	$28.0 million*
Big East basketball tourn.	NA
NCAA basketball tourn.	$7.8 million
Bowl games	$18.7 million
TV households	20.0 million
	(11 markets)

*Includes radio-broadcast rights revenues.
NA: Not available.
Sources: Street & Smith's SportsBusiness Journal research, NCAA,
the conferences, IRS Form 990s, and Nielsen Media Research.

BCS is a coalition of the Fiesta, Orange, Rose, and Sugar Bowls, which doled out over $109 million to the Big Six conferences in 2002–2003. The five other Division I-A conferences, combined, shared approximately $4 million. There were 24 other, non-BCS bowl games in 2002–2003 that played host to a collection of lesser teams, most of which still came from the Big Six conferences. The non-BCS bowl games distributed $67 million in 2002–2003, approximately $52.6 million of which went to the elite conferences. Thus, while none of the Big Six conferences earned total bowl revenues of less than the Big East's $20 million, no other Division I-A conference earned bowl revenues greater than $6 million (Conference USA). Overall, the Big Six conferences collected $161.9 million from bowl games played in 2002–2003, and the other five conferences reaped $19.8 million.

However, in addition to the substantial amount of revenue that is generated by participation in bowl games, there is also a significant expense associated with playing in these contests. Each institution must pay for the transportation, meals, housing, entertainment, awards, and per diem allowances for its team and coaching staff, marching band, cheerleaders, and official traveling party, many of whom arrive in the host city at least several days prior to the game. The participating schools also must sell an allotment of tickets to the game and are responsible for the cost of any unsold tickets. These expenses are much higher for the BCS bowls than the non-BCS games. However, they are more than offset by the revenues generated in the BCS games. The average net distribution to conferences and institutions in each of the BCS bowls was $12.7 million in 2002–2003. The non-BCS bowls are quite different, as their lower revenues resulted in an average net distribution of approximately $421,000 in 2002–2003. Thus, the average profit margin for BCS bowls was 89%, while it was only 30% for the non-BCS bowls in 2002–2003.

Each conference has a different formula for sharing the revenues that its institutions receive from bowl games and NCAA tournaments. Similar to professional sports leagues, a revenue-sharing system that gives participating teams a disproportionate amount of the monies creates profit-maximizing behavior, including cheating, while one that is too generous to nonparticipating schools encourages free-riding among lesser teams and creates a disincentive for self-improvement. The key for each conference is to find the appropriate level of revenue sharing. These systems are discussed in the excerpt from DeSchriver and Stotlar.

While the Big Six conferences generate substantial revenues, an existence in Division I outside of these conferences is much more difficult. There are presently 25 other conferences that play Division I basketball, 5 other conferences that play Division I-A football, and 8 additional conferences that play Division I-AA football. These "have-not" conferences generally struggle both competitively on the field and financially off of it. The 25 other Division I basketball conferences lag in total NCAA distributed revenues, with only 4 conferences (Atlantic 10, Conference USA, Mid-American, and Western Athletic) receiving even half of what was received by any of the Big Six conferences in 2001–2002 and most receiving less than one-quarter. For the 5 other conferences participating in Division I-A football (Conference USA, Mid-American, Mountain West, Sunbelt, and Western Athletic), the situation is even more daunting. The problem facing these football programs is that they have a cost structure that is similar to the Big Six conference programs (athletic scholarships, coaching staff, facility costs, etc.), but lack the popularity — that is, the fan demand for tickets and television — to generate comparable revenues during the regular season. In addition, these schools receive a fraction of the revenues from bowl games that are earned by the Big Six conferences, as previously noted. Finally, the 8 conferences that participate in Division I-AA football are financially troubled. Though the cost structure is lower than it is in Division I-A because of the lower scholarship total (63), and smaller coaching staffs and infrastructure, it remains quite high in comparison to the paltry revenues generated. With its small attendance, little television coverage, and largely ignored NCAA playoff in lieu of bowl games, Division I-AA football conferences have little hope for profitability.

THE ECONOMIC REALITIES OF AMATEUR SPORTS ORGANIZATION

James V. Koch

It is not the raw economic size of amateur athletics, then, that should garner our attention. Rather, it is the fact that amateur athletics constitutes an industry that can be analyzed much like any other industry that should be of interest to us. Far from being an exception to economic analysis, amateur athletics, especially big-time intercollegiate athletics, has exhibited surprisingly predictable behavior and development. . . .

I. INTERCOLLEGIATE ATHLETICS AS AN INDUSTRY

A rough, but usable, definition of an industry is that it is a collection of firms, each of which is supplying products that have considerable substitutability to the same potential buyers. The firms in the intercollegiate athletic industry are the individual colleges and universities that field athletic teams. From an economic standpoint, these "university-firms" are primarily involved in the selling of athletic entertainment to potential fans and ticket purchasers. In addition, there exists the belief that the university-firms are supplying, via their athletic teams, intangibles such as pride and identification to alumni, legislators, and friends of the institution who might reward or support the institution. In addition, the university-firms in recent years have also been actively engaged in selling to radio and television networks the rights to broadcast or televise the intercollegiate athletic contests in which their teams compete.

Some of the inputs to this multiproduct productive process involve capital: stadiums, equipment, and the like. But the most crucial inputs to the production of intercollegiate athletics are people: the coaches, athletic directors, and especially the student-athletes who play on the teams that the university-firms field. The key to understanding the development of modern intercollegiate athletics is an understanding of the competition for, and use of, inputs such as student-athletes. The development of the NCAA as the largest regulatory body in intercollegiate athletics has primarily come about because most university-firms have desired to limit competition between themselves concerning how they may hire and utilize their student-athlete inputs. The NCAA has written hundreds of detailed rules and regulations that circumscribe the conditions under which an individual university-firm may contact, visit, compete for, hire, and eventually use student-athlete inputs. The genesis of these rules has nearly always been a desire on the part of the university-firms to restrict the competition for, and use of, student-athlete inputs. A review of the development of the NCAA demonstrates how and why this has taken place.

II. THE DEVELOPMENT OF THE NCAA

The NCAA is the most powerful organization concerned with intercollegiate athletics. The NCAA currently has almost 800 individual university-firms as members in addition to almost 175 other organizations and conferences as institutional members. *[There are currently 1,039 individual members of the NCAA and 226 other members.]*

The NCAA has traditionally had two major rivals, the Amateur Athletic Union (AAU) and the National Association for Intercollegiate Athletics (NAIA). The AAU is a nonprofit, volunteer organization that is no longer as strong a rival to the NCAA as it once was. The AAU once sponsored a host of athletic meets that were competitive substitutes for NCAA-sponsored events. Both the NCAA and the AAU seemingly delighted in disqualifying each other's athletes from their meets. But the NCAA emerged victorious in most of these jousts for two reasons. First, the NCAA has effectively controlled the fountain source of post-high school athletic talent — the colleges and universities. Second, the NCAA has been far better heeled financially than the AAU and has been able to outspend the AAU in critical areas. Today, the AAU's major efforts are confined to its Junior Olympics and its Masters sports and fitness programs.

The NCAA's only legitimate collegiate rival, the NAIA, is a much smaller and economically less significant entity that caters to institutions that are typically small in size and which do not seek to compete in "big-time" intercollegiate athletics. Since 1981 the NCAA has extended its dominance to include women's intercollegiate athletics, resulting in the demise of the one-time capstone organization in women's intercollegiate athletics, the Association of Intercollegiate Athletics for Women (AIAW).

The NCAA was founded in 1906 as a consequence of the efforts of President Theodore Roosevelt and others to reduce the unsavory violence and mayhem that characterized intercollegiate football contests at the time. An additional concern of Roosevelt and others was the preservation of amateurism. One means of doing that was to define athlete eligibility; another was to develop common rules for conducting games and competition. These rules were used by the NCAA when it began to sponsor regional and national championships in a growing number of sports.

The post–World War I years were boom years for intercollegiate athletics. Rising consumer disposable incomes, along with increased public interest in intercollegiate athletic competition, spurred developments such as the designation of "All-American" teams by the media, the national ranking of teams by the press, and the desire of radio networks to broadcast key intercollegiate athletic contests. This led many university-firms to utilize intercollegiate athletics both as a means to attract enrollment and in some cases as a means to augment their revenues.

Then, as now, most fans were not interested in paying to see losing teams compete. This led to increasingly fierce struggles between and among university-firms for the best student-athlete inputs.

Already at this time some colleges and universities concluded that they would not compete and pay for student-athletes. Thus, the 1920s and 1930s saw the beginning of the membership dichotomy between smaller institutions (for example, Rhode Island College) that chose not to compete to purchase student-athletes and larger institutions (for example, the University of Notre Dame) that decided to operate "big-time" intercollegiate athletic programs and to compete both for student-athletes and ticket-purchasing fans.

The end of World War II in 1945 brought with it a flood of military veterans into colleges and universities across the United States. This threatened to upset the status quo in intercollegiate athletics, at least partially because some university-firms fielded teams composed of individuals who were superb athletes, but indifferent or totally uninvolved students. A series of scandals concerning unethical practices, payoffs to student-athletes, altered grades, and the like brought with it many cries for reform. The result was the NCAA-sponsored "Sanity Code," which sought to bring to a halt the many abuses occurring. However, compliance with the Sanity Code was voluntary, and the financial incentives to violate it were too great. The code was abandoned by the NCAA in 1951.

Simultaneously, a new technological innovation, television, threatened to alter the intercollegiate athletic landscape even further. Many colleges and universities became convinced that the televising of intercollegiate athletic football contests reduced gate attendance at their own games. The combination of adverse public attention concerning the abuses noted above and the desire of most NCAA members to limit the effects of television upon their gate attendance led to dramatic increases in the power and control of the central NCAA organization. Within a few years, the NCAA was transformed from a coordinating organization that was largely confined to rule-making and sponsoring championships, to one that had considerable financial clout. This transformation occurred for two reasons: (1) the NCAA negotiated lucrative television contracts for its members; and, (2) the NCAA undertook punitive actions that often carried with them significant financial penalties in order to enforce its rules. It is generally conceded that individual NCAA members approved of these trends because the anticipated effect was to equalize competition and to harness what would have otherwise been a free market for televising intercollegiate football contests. The typical NCAA member institution exhibited a much greater interest in protecting its share of the intercollegiate athletic financial pie than it did in promoting either amateurism in general or the academic progress of student-athletes in particular.

The NCAA has always controlled the television rights to its own annually sponsored championships such as men's basketball and, until 1984, also controlled the right to negotiate on behalf of its members the right to televise any intercollegiate football contest. These television rights turned out to be a gold mine for the NCAA. . . . A 1984 United States Supreme Court decision forced the NCAA to allow the individual university-firms to negotiate their own football television contracts in the same fashion that they had always been able to do in other sports such as basketball. This threatened the financial stability of the NCAA and at the same time accentuated the existing inequality among the various university-firms. Institutions like the University of Oklahoma had much greater ability to sell the television rights to their contests than did others like McNeese State University.

In sum, the history of intercollegiate athletics and its dominant organization, the NCAA, is one in which the financial bases for every decision and development have become increasingly obvious. The NCAA has consistently reacted to the commercialization of intercollegiate athletics in two ways. First, it has attempted to minimize costs of competition between and among its members by legislating rules that restrict competition, particularly for student-athlete inputs. Second, it has attempted to retain and control the most significant source of intercollegiate athletic revenue, the televising of contests between its members. Unfortunately for the NCAA, the basic structure of the intercollegiate athletic market has made these two goals exceedingly difficult to attain. A look at the actual operation of the NCAA will reveal why this is so.

III. THE NCAA AS A CARTEL

The NCAA euphemistically talks about "the amateur student-athlete . . . who engages in a particular sport for the educational, physical, mental, and social benefits derived therefrom and to whom participation in that sport is an avocation."[15] This view of the intercollegiate athletic world would no doubt come as a surprise to the members of the men's basketball team at a prominent southwestern public university, for not one of the individuals who competed on this university's powerhouse teams between 1968 and 1982 ever received a baccalaureate degree from the university.

It is an easy task to provide other glaring examples of the gross discrepancy between what is actually true in intercollegiate athletics and the innocent rhetoric that the NCAA says typifies its activities. In fact, the NCAA has in recent years operated primarily as an economic entity and has supported activities that have led to cartelization. *[See Figure 1 for the stated economic policy of the NCAA.]* This assertion requires further examination.

A cartel is an organization of firms that agrees to pursue joint policies with respect to key aspects of the environment in which the firms operate. The most common subjects of agreement are pricing policies, levels of output, market territories, sales quotas, use of inputs, and advertising expenditures. The NCAA is a reasonably effective, though somewhat unstable, cartel because it: (1) sets the maximum price that can be paid for intercollegiate athletes; (2) regulates the quantity of athletes that can be purchased in a given time period; (3) regulates the duration and intensity of usage of those athletes; (4) occasionally fixes the price at which sports outputs can be sold; (5) periodically informs its members about transactions, costs, market conditions, and sales techniques; (6) occasionally pools and distributes portions of the organization's profits; and, (7) polices the behavior of its members and assesses penalties upon those deemed to have broken the organization's rules.

A. What Motivates the NCAA?

Insofar as the university-firms are concerned, the NCAA exists to suppress and equalize competition between and among its members. Few, if any, NCAA members would admit openly to this motive. However, athletic competition works best and is most profitable when competition is relatively equal. It is worth noting that the major spurts of "reform" in the NCAA's history have typically occurred when there has been significant evidence of competitive imbalance between members. The effect of these and other "reforms" has nearly always been to suppress and equalize competition. Indeed, there is little evidence that in the long run the NCAA is truly interested in reforms that have

---

Intercollegiate athletics programs shall be administered in keeping with prudent management and fiscal practices to assure the financial stability necessary for providing student-athletes with adequate opportunities for athletics competition as an integral part of a quality educational experience.

Figure 1.   NCAA Constitution, Article 2.16: The Principle Governing the Economy of Athletics Program Operation. (Source: 2003–04 NCAA Division I Manual, p. 5.)

the effect of enhancing academic standards. The NCAA and its members have seldom supported academic initiatives that would result in competitive imbalance or reduce the profitability of intercollegiate athletics. As one observer has put it, the NCAA and its members "recognize only two things — money and bad publicity."[19] As a consequence, "big-time college sports programs are notorious for shortchanging athletes who are supposed to be receiving educational opportunities."[20]

It is important to differentiate between the motivation of the university-firms and the NCAA central organization. Whereas the members typically are interested in some form of joint profit-maximization designed to wring maximum revenues out of intercollegiate athletics, the NCAA central organization, like a typical bureaucracy, gives strong evidence of being interested in its own power, size, and permanence. Concern for abstract ideals such as amateurism and academic standards has seldom been in evidence among the NCAA leadership. . . . Given the financial incentives that confront the NCAA's members, and given the structure of the intercollegiate athletics industry, different behavior on the part of the NCAA and its members could hardly be expected.

B. The NCAA's Structure as a Source of Success and Problems

Cartels succeed or fail primarily on the basis of the structure of the cartel and the environment in which the cartel operates. Generally, the most important facets of cartel structure and environment are: (1) the number of firms in the cartel; (2) the number of points of initiative in the cartel; (3) the knowledge that cartel members and outsiders have of the cartel's transactions; (4) the existence of barriers to entry; (5) the similarity of the interests of the cartel members, particularly where revenues and costs are concerned; and, (6) demand conditions in the cartel's markets. Each of these facets will be examined in turn.

1. Number of Firms. Successful cartels seldom have large numbers of member firms. A small membership allows the cartel to police member behavior more easily and to impose effective discipline upon wayward cartel members. Since the NCAA now has almost 800 *[1,039 in 2003]* individual members, it has severe difficulties monitoring the behavior of its members. If the NCAA's enforcement division were to visit one NCAA member daily on each day of a five-day work week, and do so fifty-two weeks per year, it would take the enforcers over three years simply to visit each member. . . .

No magic number can be deduced relative to whether or not a cartel has too many members to be effective. . . . Hence, a small membership assists, but does not guarantee, the success of a cartel.

2. Number of Points of Initiative. A point of initiative, in cartel jargon, is a place where one can buy, sell, exchange, or otherwise utilize the property rights to a resource. Successful cartels seldom have large numbers of points of initiative. The probability of cartel success increases if the cartel can restrict its members to undertaking their economic actions only at certain times and places.

The number of points of initiative are almost unlimited insofar as the NCAA and its membership are concerned. Approximately 10,000 football players and 1,000 coaches exist in the NCAA's highest competitive division in football. In men's and women's basketball, the comparable numbers are approximately 45,000 players and 1,200 coaches. The number of alumni and camp followers of a team who might intrude are virtually infinite in number. Add to this the antics of professional agents who seek to represent highly skilled players in their negotiations with professional sports teams.

The large number of points of initiative militates against the NCAA's effectiveness; however, when the NCAA can determine that a rule has been violated, it can impose truly impressive penalties upon violators. . . .

The NCAA has in recent years changed its internal governance several times in order to reduce the disparity between and among members and at the same time reduce the number of points of initiative. . . . This has had the effect of increasing homogeneity of university-firms inside a given division, but increasing the heterogeneity between the divisions. . . .

3. Knowledge of Cartel Transactions. In effective cartels, members immediately learn of a transaction undertaken by a member, but noncartel members are kept in a state of ignorance about such transactions, as well as the operation of the cartel as a whole. Individual cartel members find it difficult to cheat when other cartel members are quickly apprised of the cheater's actions. . . .

Much the same situation exists in the case of the NCAA. Some of its members' actions, for example, the signing of a blue-chip athlete, are widely publicized. Other actions, for example, procuring a lush summer job for an athlete, are largely hidden from the view of other NCAA members as well as the public. Indeed, when Mike Rozier, the Heisman Trophy winning running back for the University of Nebraska, revealed in 1984 that he had received a steady series of cash payments from a professional agent while playing football for the Cornhuskers, this activity had not been detected by the NCAA, or by the University of Nebraska's competitors, or even, the University argued, by itself.

Industries and markets that are characterized by competition are typically ones in which any given competitor finds it extremely difficult to hide its actions from its competitors. . . . Yet, quite the opposite circumstances often exist in intercollegiate athletics. How can the NCAA keep track of all of the perquisites and concessions that might be offered to the parents and girl- or boyfriends of athletes being courted in locations far removed from the campus? How can the NCAA monitor the actual prices that supporters of a university-firm's basketball team pay the members of that team for the complimentary tickets that each player typically receives for each game? The answer, of course, is that the NCAA cannot do so effectively, and that is one of the most important reasons why the NCAA receives a relatively low grade when this aspect of cartelization is considered. . . .

4. Barriers to Entry. A typical cartel strategy is to attempt to limit entry into its market in order to enhance the chances of cartel members to earn economic rents. The NCAA has done so, but only in a limited sense. In theory, the NCAA is a voluntary organization with only minimal barriers to entry. Any college or university that subscribes to the NCAA's stated purposes, and which agrees to abide by the NCAA's rules, may join the NCAA. Nonetheless, the NCAA has established strict requirements for admission into several of its divisions, for example, the "big-time" Division I-A in football. In order to be classified in Division I-A, a university-firm must sponsor a given number of intercollegiate sports, and then satisfy requirements that relate to the size of the university's football stadium and the attendance at the university's football games. . . . This criterion immediately eliminates from consideration well over eighty percent of all university-firms in the NCAA.

The major reason why the Division I-A institutions wish to limit entry into their division is so that they may fashion rules and regulations more to their own tastes. This desire typically translates into rules and regulations that recognize the profound economic basis and competition involved in big-time intercollegiate athletics. . . .

Until 1984, one of the significant incentives for Division I-A institutions to limit membership in their division was the apparent correlation of Division I-A status with increased access to the millions of dollars of football television revenues connected to the NCAA's contract with the television networks. The United States Supreme Court decision on that subject ended the NCAA's practice of preventing Division I-A members from negotiating their own football television contracts. Several different coalitions of NCAA members now negotiate their own football television contracts.

. . . .

5. Similarity of Interests.   Successful cartels are characterized by general similarity of the interests of their members. The most important aspects of similarity relate to classic economic variables: revenues, costs, levels of production, and the like. . . .

The amoeba-like division of the NCAA into more and more subdivisions has been a clear attempt to group together members who have similar revenues, costs, and output characteristics. Some view these actions as presaging the imminent dissolution of the NCAA as an organization. However, dissolution is not likely to occur. The NCAA, or some other organization of a different name but similar objectives, will almost surely continue to exist. There are two major reasons why this is so. First, even the NCAA's most vocal opponents admit to a need for some form of a national organization that undertakes the regulatory and primarily noneconomic functions of the NCAA like rule-making and the sponsoring of championships. Second, there are significant financial disincentives that are associated with any movement out of the NCAA by a single institution, or even a group of such institutions, operating a big-time program. This latter point is worthy of additional discussion.

A successful secession movement from the NCAA would require a large number of homogeneous university-firms to leave the NCAA at the same time. Only then could this group negotiate its own television contracts, conduct its own championships, and provide the considerable services that the NCAA currently provides its members. The NCAA's only visible competitor, the NAIA, is simply not a viable option in this regard if the university-firm wishes to field nationally prominent teams that attract media attention and ticket-purchasing fans. . . .

. . . .

Most likely, then, the NCAA or a similar organization will continue to exist, but even more segmentation of the NCAA's membership will take place. The degree of dissimilarity of members' interests will be the most important determinant of any new divisions that develop. . . .

6. Demand Conditions.   The economic success of a cartel is enhanced when the cartel purchases its inputs from sellers who are small and unorganized. This is quite evidently the case with respect to most intercollegiate athletes, whose ability to bargain is constrained by collusion between and among university-firms, and whose ability to unite and organize is severely damaged by their ages and geographic dispersion. The result is that the university-firms often earn rents because they possess an input that is relatively limited in supply, but which is unable to negotiate a price for itself that approximates its market value.

. . . .There are two options open to an athlete of this skill who wishes to realize some or all of his marginal revenue product. First, he can accept illicit, under-the-table benefits and payments, as discussed previously in the Rozier situation. Second, he can leave the university-firm and sign with a professional team for whatever financial rewards his skills will command. . . .

When the NCAA sells its ouputs, it confronts some customers who are unorganized (fans who purchase tickets to contests) and some who definitely possess some oligopsony power (television networks). In the latter case, the NCAA has exhibited considerable skill in getting the television networks to bid against each other for the privilege of televising events such as the Division I men's national basketball championship. . . .

. . . . *[The author's discussion of current industry issues is omitted.]*

CONCLUSION

The National Collegiate Athletic Association is the dominant organization in modern big-time intercollegiate athletics. Unbeknownst to most of its members, the NCAA has in recent decades acted as an economic cartel. Prices have been fixed, outputs controlled, and extensive rules and regulations have been promulgated concerning the use of the primary input to intercollegiate athletics, the student-athletes.

The cartelized behavior of the NCAA was never a matter of great import either to its own members or to the public until the dollar magnitude of the NCAA's actions became large. . . .

In 1950, big-time intercollegiate athletics was substantially non-cartelized, and the plethora of rules and regulations that now exist in the industry was unknown. Many of the most important actions and decisions of the day were made in a nonmarket context. There was much less reference to purchasing inputs and selling outputs. Rather, intercollegiate athletics was often sponsored by a university without reference to market acceptance, or lack thereof.

The . . . decades since 1950 have seen the obvious emergence of economic motives in intercollegiate athletes. An identifiable industry now exists in big-time intercollegiate athletics . . . Women's intercollegiate athletics, particularly women's basketball, increasingly evidences the same evolution. The NCAA has accelerated the emergence of these developments by cartelizing the industry and consistently advocating policies that have increased economic incentives. The NCAA, then, is both a cause and a reflection of powerful forces that have resulted in the emergence of big-time intercollegiate athletics as an industry.

REFERENCES

15. National Collegiate Athletic Association, 1983–1984 Manual of the National Collegiate Athletic Association, 9 (1983).
19. Dan Stormer, as quoted in *New Day for Athletes?,* The Sporting News, Aug. 8, 1984, at 6.
20. Id.

THE BUSINESS OF COLLEGE SPORTS AND THE HIGH COST OF WINNING

Roger C. Noll

Intercollegiate athletics is a strange business — one whose profits end up in the most unlikely pockets. But I'm getting ahead of the story.

For some 50 colleges and universities, football and men's basketball are modest enterprises that generate enough revenues to cover full scholarships for about 100 athletes — and, in a good year, to yield a profit of a few million dollars. At a few universities, women's basketball is also profitable, and baseball is more or less a break-even operation. For all other sports, and for major sports outside the top group of colleges, intercollegiate athletics is a financial drain. Yet almost all American colleges and universities field an impressive array of men's and women's teams across a variety of sports that have few players and virtually no spectators.

What's more, intercollegiate sports chronically generate serious controversy that leaves college administrators cringing behind their desks. The media regularly report scandals about drug use, criminal activity, excessive financial aid, and poor academic performance punctuated by low graduation rates. No less important, big-time sports cause friction among faculty and university administrators. Some see sports as diverting resources and attention to an unimportant — even frivolous — non-academic activity. Explicit favoritism to athletics also is controversial. If coaches are paid more than Nobel Prize winners, if athletes have larger scholarships and better dorms than academic superstars, are colleges transmitting the wrong lessons to students and society at large? And if college sports cast so dark a shadow, why do they endure?

WHY AMERICAN UNIVERSITIES SUPPORT SPORTS

To the rest of the world, American intercollegiate athletics seem like pagan rituals. Universities rarely sponsor athletics teams — let alone encourage them to play before thousands or to appear on television.

The popularity of intercollegiate sports in the United States is not driven by Americans' greater interest in sports. Professional soccer in most high-income nations is more popular — and even more successful financially — than any American sport. In Europe, average revenues per soccer team are . . . below American football, roughly equal to baseball, and above American basketball. Several English soccer teams are publicly traded companies with market caps between $500 million and $1 billion, putting their market value in the range of NFL teams and above teams in other American sports.

Nor are intercollegiate sports popular because more Americans follow sports that first interested them as students. Intercollegiate athletics in the United States has been a popular entertainment since the beginning of the century, when the fraction of Americans who had gone to college was far lower than the proportion of college-educated Europeans and Japanese today.

Finally, the special prominence of American intercollegiate athletics is not explained by television exposure. College sports were popular before radio and long before television. Moreover, since Europe has liberalized broadcasting by allowing cable television, sports on cable has proliferated — but not intercollegiate sports.

So why do American colleges devote so much effort to sports? Primarily, because their students demand it as athletes, not as spectators. Public enthusiasm focuses on the so-called revenue sports — basketball and football. But the vast majority of college athletes play other, minor sports, for which no significant demand exists other than from the athletes themselves. The inescapable conclusion: universities have comprehensive varsity athletics programs largely because students want to be athletes. And they compete to enable students to follow their interests, whether in physics or field hockey, linguistics or lacrosse.

THE FINANCIAL STAKE IN SPORTS

Colleges and universities follow diverse policies regarding intercollegiate athletics. The vast majority sponsor teams with no expectation of generating revenues. Indeed, the typical intercollegiate sports program is based on the traditional amateur model.

But focusing on the typical ignores the big-time sports schools with multimillion dollar profit centers in basketball and football, and the many other schools that dabble in the so-called revenue sports. The NCAA divides colleges and universities into three divisions according to the depth of their financial commitment. The top group, Division I, is further subdivided into I-A and I-AA for football. And even this categorization understates the extent of diversity.

In Divisions II and III, sports are relatively low-cost activities. Most schools use part-time coaches, play only nearby competitors and give few athletic scholarships. These schools can field most teams for $50,000 per year; football, the most expensive, can be had for $200,000. Thus, a college can run a comprehensive intercollegiate program for $1 million a year, not counting capital investments in facilities. This sum is not large compared to a university budget. But a small liberal arts college with 1,000 students may end up spending 5 to 10 percent of tuition on a comprehensive sports program.

At the top of the heap are about three dozen Division I-A schools that compete for national championships in several sports including football and both men's and women's basketball. Just below are another dozen mostly small, Catholic colleges that have the same ambitions in all but football. At these schools, game attendance for the trophy sports approaches the numbers for professional sports. They expect to be in the NCAA championship basketball tournament and, if they play Division I football, in a postseason bowl.

PUNTING ON FOOTBALL

[Tables 3 through 6 show revenues generated by bowl games.]

The financial returns from football can be very large for top teams. Typically, they play six or seven games at home, bribing weaker schools to be cannon fodder against far superior opponents in front of large crowds. For the best of the best, season stadium revenues of $15 million are feasible.

The top teams also expect to appear on television almost every week, with two or three games per season broadcast nationwide. Television generates $2 to 3 million for these teams and sometimes

TABLE 3.

2002–2003 POSTSEASON FOOTBALL SUMMARY OF OPERATIONAL EXPENSES		
	2002–2003 *BCS*	*2002–2003* *Non-BCS*
Bowl payout	$114,724,842	$66,997,114
Expenses		
Transportation		
Team and staff	1,583,685	7,119,304
Band and cheerleaders	1,167,199	2,644,181
Official party	423,781	858,096
Total transportation expense	3,174,665	10,621,582
Meals/lodging/per diem		
Team and staff	3,212,293	9,375,362
Band and cheerleaders	824,538	2,070,119
Official party	633,294	1,078,242
Total meals, lodging, and per diem expense	4,670,125	12,523,723
Entertainment	238,866	536,505
Promotion	141,025	562,044
Awards	535,205	2,921,159
Equipment and supplies	331,135	1,189,103
Tickets absorbed by conference and participating team	2,191,855	11,947,060
Administrative	640,656	3,506,086
Other	836,717	2,996,107
Conference sponsorship fee		
Total game expense	4,915,458	23,658,063
Total expenses	12,760,249	46,803,368
Net income (Loss)	$101,964,593	$20,193,746

Note 1: Bowl Championship Series payout includes Rose Bowl distribution.
Source: The National Collegiate Athletic Association, March 28, 2002.

TABLE 4.

2002–2003 DISTRIBUTION OF BCS REVENUE	
Total BCS revenue	*$114,724,842*
Distributions:	
Pacific 10 (Note 1)	21,477,977
Big 10	21,062,222
Southeastern	16,562,222
Atlantic Coast	16,562,222
Big East	16,562,222
Big 12 (Note 1)	16,977,977
Western Athletic	960,000
Mountain West	960,000
Conference USA	960,000
Mid-American	960,000
Big Sky	180,000
Atlantic 10	180,000
Mid-Eastern	180,000
Gateway	180,000
Ohio Valley	180,000
Southwestern Athletic	180,000
Southland	180,000
Southern	180,000
Sunbelt	240,000
Total BCS distribution	$114,724,842

Note 1: Includes Rose Bowl distribution.
Source: The National Collegiate Athletic Association,
April 14, 2003.

much more, although in most conferences the money must be shared with other conference members. Notre Dame does even better since it sells national television rights to all its home games and does not belong to a conference.

In addition, bowl games guarantee a payoff of about $1 million per team. For teams picked for a top bowl game . . . the payoff is several million dollars — although, for most schools, bowl income, too, must be shared with conference members. The dozen schools with the best football teams in the Midwest and South bring in $30 million or more, while other successful schools take in $20 million.

For the rest of the Division I-A football teams and all of the ones in Division I-AA, television exposure is unusual and total ticket receipts rarely top $2 million. Thus, these teams must get by on revenues about one-tenth that of their superpower brethren — a reality that explains why most jump at the chance to earn a few hundred thousand dollars to be drubbed by Penn State or Michigan.

TABLE 5.

2002–2003 POSTSEASON BOWL AVERAGE INFORMATION	
Average bowl payout	
Average bowl payout: non-BCS bowls	$1,395,773
Average bowl payout: BCS bowls	14,340,605
Average expenses	
Non-BCS bowls	975,070
BCS bowls	1,595,031
Average net receipts	
Average net to conferences and institutions: non-BCS bowls	420,703
Average net to conferences and institutions: BCS bowls	12,745,574

Source: The National Collegiate Athletic Association, April 18, 2003.

TABLE 6.

2002–2003 POSTSEASON FOOTBALL ANALYSIS OF EXCESS BOWL REVENUE AND EXPENSE BY CONFERENCE				
Conference	Institution's bowl revenue	Participating institution's expense	Excess of revenue over expenses	Percentage of excess revenue/expenses per conference
ACC totals	$24,368,078	$7,230,060	$17,138,018	14%
Big East totals	20,355,043	6,641,532	13,713,511	11%
Big Ten totals	31,948,036	8,454,771	23,493,265	20%
Big Twelve totals	26,741,849	9,379,226	17,362,623	14%
Pac-10 totals	27,542,709	8,869,462	18,673,247	15%
SEC totals	30,954,882	6,967,962	23,986,920	20%

Source: The National Collegiate Athletic Association, April 16, 2003.

Football team operating costs are driven by the school's business strategy. Does it try to field a ranked team that will go to a major bowl? If so, the team must play interregional foes, running up travel costs of hundreds of thousands per trip. And it must hire a top coach at salaries ranging from $400,000 to $1 million for a head coach.

Management costs typically are attributed to something other than salary — endorsements, in-kind payments (e.g., a mansion, a Cadillac) — in order to keep compensation in line with that of top faculty. But this practice is mainly a public-relations device: competition for top coaches insures that, one way or another, they are paid according to their ability to generate revenue. By contrast, a team that does not aspire to national ranking can minimize travel costs and rely on mediocre veterans for coaching.

Stadium operation costs are roughly proportional to attendance, and range from $100,000 annually at the bottom of the heap to $2 million at the top. . . .

The major source of differences among teams' financial aid budgets is tuition. Tuition depends on the quality, reputation, and scope of activities of the school as well as whether it is public or private. All athletic scholarships include about $12,000 for room and board so that 85 scholarships (the Division I-A ceiling for football) cost about $1 million plus tuition. At leading private universities, tuition runs $20,000 or more, so 85 football scholarships cost about $1.7 million.

Scholarship costs explain why two-thirds of Division I basketball schools do not play in Division I-A football. Athletics departments at private schools need to dish out two or three times more in aid to play Division I-A football as do most public schools. Thus for nearly all private schools in Division I, football revenues can't come close to covering the costs of scholarships, coaches, travel, equipment, and stadium operations. So very few opt in.

Tuition does not necessarily reflect actual costs to the university. A key consideration is whether the school is at its enrollment ceiling. At highly rated academic schools — California, Duke, Michigan, Northwestern, Stanford, U.C.L.A., Wisconsin — many applicants are rejected who would be willing to pay all of the university's charges. So the decision to subsidize another athlete is a decision not to admit someone who might pay full tuition.

But where an extra athlete does not displace a tuition-payer, the cost of admitting 85 football players is very small compared to the average cost of providing the education. Thus, if an under-enrolled private school can generate enough revenue from football to pay the tuition of its players, the tuition payments are gravy for the university.

Capital facilities are a very important cost of football. In theory, a university could go into debt to build a stadium, and then cover the debt from its operating budget. But, in practice, capital investments are covered by special fundraising drives or, for public universities, by separate appropriations. The reason is simple: no university generates a large enough surplus to justify the capital expenditures necessary to field a football team.

Profits (neglecting capital costs) from football can exceed $10 million for Division I-A teams that play in an "alliance" bowl game. But returns this large are only possible if football generates substantial donations for both scholarships and facilities. In the bottom two-thirds of Division I, losses typically run $1 million to $2 million per year.

MARCH MADNESS

Basketball operates on a smaller gross, but with disproportionately lower costs. Like football, the best basketball schools play more home games than the worst, with cash changing hands to arrange unbalanced schedules. A dozen Division I men's teams have a home attendance of around 300,000 per season, while some 50 draw more than 100,000.

Colleges ration student attendance to sell more tickets at higher prices. The best men's basketball teams have game revenues of over $5 million per year, plus television revenues of $1 to 2 million more. A few top women's teams take in over $1 million. But most of the 50 or so schools that try to field a ranked team and usually make the NCAA championship tournament have revenues below this.

The NCAA has a complex formula, based on past success, for dividing the profits from the NCAA tournament. Nearly all payments go to conferences that share revenues, so a school's tournament revenue depends more on the success of its conference than its own record. *[Tables 7 and 8 show distribution amounts to Division I conferences.]*

For conferences that routinely place multiple teams in the men's tournament and typically have two or three teams that go through several rounds of play, the payments amount to several million dollars a year. A men's team from a top conference expects a profit of between $100,000 and $500,000 per year from the NCAA championship tournament, depending on the league's revenue-sharing rules. Revenues derived from women's teams are lower, but in the top conferences can run to $100,000 or more per team. So, all told, the best men's teams generate $10 million revenue, the top women's teams about $2 million.

Over 300 schools play Division I basketball, compared to over 100 in Division I-A football and about 80 more in Division I-AA. And for the majority, revenues from all sources are usually under $1 million for the men's and women's teams combined.

Basketball is far less expensive than football because teams need pay only 15 scholarships and travel with fewer than 15 players. Coaches are paid about the same as in football, but staffs are smaller. Thus, a modest Division I team can pay as little as $150,000 for coaching, while the big time schools fork out $1 million.

As in football, the cost of a scholarship to the athletics department can run from $12,000 to over $30,000. But even in the latter case, the total team cost is under $500,000. Thus revenue of $1 million is more than sufficient to pay the out-of-pocket costs of a team at a private school, and half that can do the job at an inexpensive public school. The doormats in Division I basketball lose $200,000 at most while the top schools can earn several million dollars from the men and $1 million from the women.

WHAT'S IN IT FOR SPORTS U?

Schools not well known outside their home region can benefit indirectly from a successful Division I team by increasing applications for admission. Whether this actually helps the school, though, depends upon its circumstances. A school at its enrollment ceiling will gain only to the extent that it can be more selective in admissions. But a private school that has trouble filling its dorms can admit more students and collect more tuition. Even an extra 100 students at $20,000 each represents a serious piece of change for the average university.

Some claim that big-time sports can increase donations to academic programs. But several studies have concluded that athletics has essentially no effect on contributions to the school outside the athletics programs. The only plausible source of an indirect financial benefit is through the enrollment effect: if more and better students attend, the university might receive more alumni gifts a few decades later.

The vast majority of departments of athletics do not make a profit, even from the two revenue sports. Indeed, a majority of Division I schools lose substantial amounts on football and, at best, break even on basketball. Thus, for all schools outside (and most in) Division I, intercollegiate athletics is a financial drain — commonly hundreds of dollars annually per student enrolled.

For the top schools that do profit from their revenue sports, the profits are significant. But the money rarely accrues to the academic side of the university. Competition is fierce for high-end coaches — as well as for people who can run big-time athletics departments efficiently. Thus, much of the surplus from revenue sports is spent on salaries.

TABLE 7.

2001–2002 NCAA Total Distribution to Members	
Conference	*2001–2002*
America East	$4,104,128
Atlantic 10	7,833,805
Atlantic Coast	13,278,199
Atlantic Sun	2,913,008
Big 12	13,492,911
Big East	14,193,904
Big Sky	3,028,397
Big South	2,031,928
Big Ten	17,727,922
Big West	3,047,030
Colonial	3,237,359
Conference USA	9,157,744
Horizon League	2,682,626
Ivy Group	3,708,302
Metro Atlantic	2,643,054
Mid-American	7,712,677
Mid-Continent	2,421,228
Mid-Eastern	3,227,561
Missouri Valley	4,409,032
Mountain West	4,288,230
Northeast	3,122,280
Ohio Valley	2,859,492
Pacific-10	13,435,200
Patriot League	3,030,091
Southeastern	15,025,301
Southern	3,272,103
Southland	3,085,162
Southwestern	3,184,985
Sun Belt	3,642,988
West Coast	2,893,899
Western	7,433,299
Independents	504,724
Total	$186,628,629

Source: The National Collegiate Athletic Association.

TABLE 8.

2001–2002 DIVISION I BASKETBALL FUND	
Conference	*2001–2002*
America East	$704,698
Atlantic 10	4,429,530
Atlantic Coast	7,550,336
Atlantic Sun	805,369
Big 12	6,442,953
Big East	7,348,993
Big Sky	704,698
Big South	604,027
Big Ten	8,859,060
Big West	704,698
Colonial	704,698
Conference USA	4,127,517
Horizon League	1,208,054
Ivy Group	805,369
Metro Atlantic	604,027
Mid-American	1,308,725
Mid-Continent	805,369
Mid-Eastern	805,369
Missouri Valley	1,610,738
Mountain West	402,685
Northeast	604,027
Ohio Valley	604,027
Pacific-10	6,854,638
Patriot League	604,027
Southeastern	7,852,349
Southern	805,369
Southland	604,027
Southwestern	604,027
Sun Belt	604,027
West Coast	1,711,409
Western	3,624,161
Total	$75,000,001

Source: The National Collegiate Athletic Associaton.

What's more, universities are inclined to spend anything left on unremunerative sports. This phenomenon has been boosted by the requirement for gender equality in varsity athletics. Women have no counterpart to football with its 85 scholarships. So in the wake of legal requirements to balance gender participation in varsity sports, football schools have been forced either to drop some men's sports or to add women's. Schools that make a lot of money on football pursue the second strategy. After all — returning to the earlier theme — men and women students alike want more women's sports, not fewer men's sports.

"CHEATING" AND THE ROLE OF THE NCAA

Athletics scandals typically arise from violations of the NCAA's rules, and thus are commonly labeled as "cheating" to emphasize the idea that the offending institutions are attempting to gain advantages unfairly. These scandals fall into three categories. The first is excessive financial assistance to student-athletes — under-the-table payments or no-show jobs. The second is toleration of antisocial behavior that does not directly affect athletic performance — drug use, theft, violence, or simply low academic performance that would not be tolerated for nonathletes. The third is toleration of performance-enhancing drugs or training regimes that consume most of a student's time. All of these rules violations follow from the financial incentives facing universities and, especially, coaches.

Top coaches' salaries are comparable to top pay in law and medicine. To obtain a job at one of the 30 or so universities that aspire to the first tier in revenue sports, a coach must first win consistently at a lower level. Then, to keep a plum job or move on to the pros, a coach must win consistently against quality opponents. At the very top schools, winning seasons without major bowl victories in football or a shot at the quarterfinals in [the] NCAA basketball tournament will lead to dismissal.

The basic principle behind the NCAA's rules regarding competition for athletes is that it must be limited to two dimensions: the overall college environment and the skills of the coach. Many highly skilled athletes are in college to prepare for professional sports careers. They seek scholarships for one purpose: to obtain experience and training needed to advance to the pros with the least possible disruption to what they do off the playing field. And like other adolescents, some athletes cut class, take drugs, beat up other students and, on occasion, knock off a liquor store if they think they can get away with it.

For a coach, success assures a decades-long career with a salary of hundreds of thousands of dollars. And with few exceptions, coaches have no alternative employment opportunities anywhere near as lucrative. Consequently, a coach facing an athlete who wants extra money (or a free pass on school rules) has compelling reasons to succumb.

Persistent rule breaking by coaches is not likely to go unnoticed by vigilant university administrators. But the incentive to cheat spills over if they regard athletic performance as a way of attracting students or encouraging the generosity of alumni and state legislators. All that is needed to let cheating persist is inattention.

The cheating label is a device for generating adverse publicity that might pressure universities to adhere to the NCAA's rules. But looking behind the public relations, much of what the NCAA and the press call cheating is not ethically questionable.

The NCAA's financial rules are incredibly detailed, frequently picayune, and vigorously enforced. Isolated minor infractions usually lead to minor penalties: While at Stanford, Tiger Woods regained eligibility when he reimbursed Arnold Palmer for dinner. But repeated minor violations are interpreted as a sign of laxity in a university's enforcement efforts. When U.C.L.A. was placed on probation in basketball, the documented crimes were repeated gifts of T-shirts and Thanksgiving dinners.

THE NCAA CARTEL

Economists who have studied intercollegiate sports unanimously agree that the NCAA is the harshest price-fixing cartel in all athletics, amateur or professional. Recall that an athletic scholarship actually covers only about $10,000 in basic living costs. The rest goes for tuition, books, and other fees. For an athlete who has no interest in the educational aspects of being a college athlete, the part of a scholarship that covers academics has no value. If attending college were regarded as more or less a full-time job, the student-athlete could do better working an equivalent number of hours at a fast-food restaurant. The problem from the athlete's perspective is that McDonalds does not field a football team.

Financial cheating arises because an athlete is worth more to a university and its fans than the NCAA scholarship limit. If five good players can increase the revenue of a men's basketball team from $1 million to $3 million — still a modest amount — these players are worth $400,000 each. Thus if schools were to bid competitively for these athletes, the winning bids would be ten times more than the list price of a year at Stanford.

Where would this money come from? Some, presumably, from subsidies now going to minor sports. Some would come from coaches' salaries, because recruiting superstar athletes would no longer be as profitable. And for a handful of top sports schools, some would come out of profits now used to cover academic expenditures.

The beneficiaries of the NCAA scholarship rules are thus athletes in other sports, the very best coaches, and, in rare cases, academic programs. For the most part, these beneficiaries are either highly paid or from families with above-average incomes. By contrast, NCAA financial rules harm the star athletes in football, men's basketball, and, to a lesser degree, women's basketball — athletes who disproportionately come from lower-income families. Thus, the NCAA financial rules are primarily a means of redistributing income regressively.

The overall impact of the financial rules varies enormously among schools and students. For a minority of college athletes, including some in minor sports, the main benefit of intercollegiate athletics is preparation for a professional sports career. For those who do become pros, the payoffs are very large and college life is a far more pleasant way to gain experience and acquire training than playing in minor leagues. In this sense, college athletes are not exploited because their alternatives are less attractive.

Nevertheless, the prospects for a pro career are poor in every sport. Each year, about 1,500 men receive Division I basketball scholarships, while 2,000 receive Division I-A football scholarships. Of these, about 150 will ever play an N.B.A. game, and about 250 will ever play in the N.F.L. Moreover, most of the athletes who succeed as pros will come from the elite athletics programs. For players from the bottom half of Division I, the odds against a pro career are about 25:1.

For scholarship athletes who never become pros, intercollegiate sports can provide two other benefits. One benefit — competition itself — is frequently overlooked because of the focus on preparing athletes for pro careers. Nevertheless, this benefit is not trivial.

Then, too, a college degree has a big effect on lifetime income. The return to the investment in college is very high and has increased sharply in the last two decades. Thus for a serious student, a free education at a private university is worth not just the $100,000-plus scholarship, but another $200,000 in the "present value" of the extra income the student will earn over a lifetime.

At the other end of the spectrum, if a school has no academic standards or graduates few athletes, restrictions on scholarships are just an instrument for taking advantage of the NCAA price-fixing cartel. In the trophy sports, many scholarship athletes do not take academics seriously and very few graduate, so that they do not enjoy the post-graduation benefits of higher education.

For these, the majority of Division I scholarship athletes, college is nothing more than an opportunity to play organized sports for a few more years before facing the reality of adulthood. The nub of the issue about the place of sports on campus is whether these athletes, numbering a few thousand in all sports combined, are better off in college than out. For the most part, they enjoy their college experiences — but not for anything having to do with academics.

PLAYING BY THE RULES

On paper, the NCAA's rules seem to say that college is for athletes ready to benefit from the academic side of school. For the most part, however, the NCAA's rules [that are] unrelated to money or the games themselves are minimal and rarely enforced. The NCAA does maintain eligibility rules for both admissions and grades. But these requirements are actually very low — well below the formal admissions requirements for universities and colleges with well-regarded academic programs, including many schools that compete in Division I athletics. Indeed, in the trophy sports only a small fraction of athletes who could play regularly for a top team satisfy the normal admissions requirements of the academically oriented colleges.

To maintain eligibility, the NCAA insists that athletes be registered as full-time students, remain in good academic standing, and make normal progress toward a degree. But since schools are extremely heterogeneous in their academic standards, these requirements boil down to very little. Good standing means whatever the university decides. Normal progress toward a degree means almost nothing, since progress is not judged retrospectively by actual graduation results. Most schools graduate a third or fewer of scholarship athletes in the trophy sports and some graduate none.

With respect to antisocial behavior, the NCAA's basic rule is that athletes should be treated like other students. As a result, if a school does not expel other students for felonies, they need not expel athletes. In most cases, universities' disciplinary actions are taken on a case-by-case basis. And some schools are perfectly happy to field a team of alleged perpetrators who, when they behave the same way in the pros, are suspended.

In theory, the NCAA also limits the time athletes can spend on sports. But these rules have no bite. If coaches and universities want a longer season, the NCAA accepts extended time limits. And for some sports, the "season" is the academic year.

The hours-per-week limit is more an accounting formality than a strict constraint. The norm is to practice far more than the limits allow, so that each athlete "voluntarily" decides to commit extra time to training in order to compete effectively against others who devote extra time to training.

By contrast, the prohibition against performance-enhancing drugs is rigidly enforced. Student-athletes sometimes are declared ineligible to compete in NCAA events after taking prescription drugs for an illness. While athletes often protest the NCAA's testing protocols, the strict rules against steroids, painkillers, and stimulants definitely serve their long-term interests.

THE TRUE IMPACT OF THE NCAA CARTEL

Step back, and the picture is clear: the NCAA is mostly a device for "cartelizing" universities while doing little to enforce standards of academic performance and social behavior among student-athletes. With the exception of the prohibition against performance enhancing drugs, the only rules that are both strict and vigorously enforced pertain to limiting financial aid. Thus, to judge solely by cause and effect, the NCAA is mostly interested in suppressing payments to athletes in a way that benefits coaches and the athletes who play minor sports.

The NCAA's inclinations are also revealed by its other business activities. Until the mid-1980s, the organization required all colleges and universities to give the NCAA a monopoly in television rights for daytime Saturday football games. The practice ended only after the rule was declared a violation of antitrust law. This court decision led to the proliferation of football telecasts on cable channels, which reduced the total fees collected by colleges, increased the disparity in television revenues among colleges (favoring the strongest football programs) and substantially increased the total number of Saturday games available to viewers.

The NCAA's current practice with respect to extra-season games parallels the old practice with telecasts. With minor exceptions, NCAA teams cannot play more than 11 games. Additional games are only permitted if the game has received advance approval from the NCAA, and the NCAA controls the number of such games, along with which teams can be invited to play and what financial guarantees must be provided by game sponsors. As with the old TV arrangements and the present scholarship limits, the NCAA is acting as a classic cartel: restricting output to maximize profits.

The NCAA's rules on the number of games go far beyond what is necessary to limit the demands on athletes. That objective could be achieved by a much simpler rule — say, by entitling every college football team to play 11 regular-season games, one preseason special event, one postseason bowl game, and one league championship game. But schools and sponsors could determine through the market how many extra-season games would be played, and how much sponsors pay colleges to participate. The main effect, if not purpose, of the differences between the simple rule and existing practice is to increase revenues to colleges.

This cynical conclusion is not intuitively obvious, and to some seems to deny the organization's history. Early in the [last] century, football came very close to being banned because it had become so violent and dangerous. The NCAA rewrote the rules of play to solve this problem, and hardly anyone would dispute the legitimacy of this role.

A few decades later, as intercollegiate football became more important many schools abandoned the principle of a student-athlete, and became professional operations. The NCAA's present limits on the number and value of scholarships and its academic requirements arose to combat this professionalization.

But the NCAA's rules do not prevent professionalization among universities that seek to pursue it. Indeed, by making certain that coaches and schools — not athletes — are the main beneficiaries, the NCAA makes the problem worse by giving them a reason to abandon academic values in pursuit of athletic glory.

ARE INTERCOLLEGIATE SPORTS A DESTRUCTIVE INFLUENCE?

Perhaps 50 colleges and universities participate in trophy sports to generate revenues, with the benefits going in part to coaches and athletic administrators, in part to other sports, and, in a few cases, to academic programs. For all other sports, and even for trophy sports at all but the top programs, intercollegiate sports exist not to make money but to please important constituencies — primarily students. If all universities collectively banned intercollegiate sports or athletic scholarships, higher education as a whole probably would be stronger financially than it is.

But this is far from the complete story. Most colleges and universities also would be better off financially if they agreed to eliminate comparative literature and advanced mathematics. The difficult question is whether varsity sports bring enough value to universities to offset their costs. And part of the answer revolves around the scandals that surround athletics.

Scandals embarrass universities and undermine their moral authority as transmitters of social values. But scandals are not intrinsic to intercollegiate sports. Intercollegiate athletics create scandals only in schools that are powers in trophy sports — or seek to become powers.

The incentive of coaches to win is a necessary component of the incentive to break the rules. And much of this is created by the cartel aspects of the NCAA's rules, which limit the cost of all programs and substantially increases the profitability of trophy sports at top schools.

If the NCAA behaved less like a cartel, the financial benefit of on-field success would be smaller. In turn, salaries for top coaches would fall, and schools would have less reason to recruit athletes who seek only a pro career and not an education. Moreover, relaxed rules would lead to fewer violations and fewer scandals. Cutting to the chase, if colleges had to pay something closer to market value for top athletes, they would admit fewer of them and be less interested in athletes who are likely to be behavioral problems.

The economics of intercollegiate athletics is not a story of administrators willfully perverting academic values for the fast buck. Such things do happen, but this is not an accurate characterization of the vast majority of intercollegiate sports programs. The more fundamental force driving college sports is the intense interest that so many students and alums have in sports. And the idea that colleges would abandon something as universally popular as intercollegiate athletics is a fantasy.

But things could be far better. Higher education and society at large would be better served if the NCAA did not limit scholarships or set the price for postseason events in trophy sports.

OPTIONS

Breaking up the NCAA cartel is probably as unrealistic a goal as banning intercollegiate athletics. Any effort to eliminate the cartel aspect of the NCAA would probably lead many Division I schools to set up a rival organization that adopted the practices the NCAA now follows. If the schools that value athletics most highly all joined the new cartel, reforming the NCAA would have little effect.

So what, if anything, can be done? Perhaps, not much.

Too many people currently involved in sports, from coaches to athletes in non-trophy sports to the commercial interests that cohabit with [the] best college sports programs, would fight hard to preserve the business as usual. Moreover, as the demand for revenue sports rises along with affluence and leisure time in America, the financial incentives to do well in trophy sports will only grow. The future is likely to be a larger version of the past.

But for optimists in the crowd, there are a couple of plausible routes to reform. The first is to attack the NCAA through antitrust laws. The NCAA has already lost its television monopoly this way. And an unrelated antitrust suit forced a consortium of elite universities to abandon collusion on need-based financial aid. But an antitrust suit would be slow and expensive. And it would probably require the active involvement of the Antitrust Division of the Department of Justice, which is notably uninterested.

The Justice Department's reluctance is understandable: The Federal Trade Commission was barred from attacking the NCAA on the ground that it is only allowed to enforce competition in for-profit markets. Moreover, unlike the television case in which some universities had financial incentives to break the NCAA's control, private parties are unlikely to pursue the antitrust route on scholarships or postseason play.

Another way to castrate the cartel would be to alter the existing rules in ways that change the universities' incentives. One might base the number of scholarships a school can offer on the academic success of its scholarship athletes. I can imagine a system in which a university is allowed the full limit of scholarships in a sport if its graduation rate over the past few years exceeded, say, 30 percent. For each five percentage-point shortfall, schools would lose 5 percent of their scholarships in that sport.

A more radical possibility is to convert the current limit on the value of an athletic scholarship to a budget ceiling on all payments to athletes — much like the salary caps in some professional sports. For example, if a school presently awards 15 basketball scholarships worth $20,000 each, the new rule would allow it to spend up to $300,000 in financial aid for basketball on as many students as it sees fit. A school could decide to "hire" Kobe Bryant for $300,000 (to give him an attractive option to playing in the N.B.A. after high school) and use walk-ons for the rest of the roster.

The key to change in all these proposals parallels the general drift of economic policy reform in the past three decades: rely more on incentives and less on rules. The practical way to make the values of intercollegiate sports more closely parallel the academic values of universities is to give universities less incentive to abandon academic values.

THE COLLEGE FOOTBALL INDUSTRY

Rodney Fort and James Quirk

INTRODUCTION

The analysis of college sports has proceeded without any comprehensive, rigorous theoretical foundation. Seeking a remedy, we derive many well-known, but heretofore casual, observations about the players' and coaches' markets, examine the effects of play-for-pay on profits and competitive balance, and profile cheating by coaches and athletic departments. The analysis sheds light on arguments that paying college players will only benefit large-revenue colleges. No new empirical investigation is undertaken, but our results are related to past findings by other researchers. . . .

THE MODEL

Major college football production is comprised of three components. Players choose between different scholarship offers. The level of coaching talent chosen is based upon its contribution to winning programs. Player and coaching talent markets also are distinguished by their relative level of competitiveness, in the economic sense of that word.

We model college football programs as profit-maximizers. There are two reasons why this is justified. The first argument follows the same logic that Fleisher, Goff, and Tollison offer concerning the NCAA: The fact that the NCAA is a nonprofit organization simply changes the balance sheet item which is maximized. Instead of "profits" or returns to shareholders, it may be implicit subsidies to the University general operating expenses, coaches' salaries, office facilities, and so on which are maximized. The accounting practices of colleges and universities merely mask the recipients of cartel rents.[1] The same can be said for individual athletic departments. Even though athletic departments are nonprofit organizations, accounting practices simply show the flow of rents as administrative and coaches' salaries and operating budgets. . . .

Finally, we assume that the college football industry is organized as a cartel. . . .

... The idea seems so well-entrenched that economists in the popular press simply take it for granted and Noll[2] does not even pause to discuss it on his way to a full characterization of NCAA cartel behavior. Given all of this, plus the fact that a major argument against the monopsony power of colleges simply holds no water (detailed later), we go with the cartel view.

The model only treats the upper level of college football teams. We are well aware that most college players are playing for the joy of it without any unrealistic dreams of an NFL career. On the other hand, it is the small group of premiere players with NFL potential who are most important in determining the success or failure of a top-level college team. The decision making of those players, their coaches, and athletic departments is the focus of this chapter.

Players

Just like other students, players have their eye on income after college. They are assumed to be rational economic actors, choosing among different colleges to maximize their "permanent income." ...

. . . .

Coaches

. . . .

In stark contrast to the players' market, where NCAA rules are highly restrictive and market imperfections abound, the coaches' market is relatively free from economic restriction. There are rules limiting the number and earnings of some assistant coaches. However, head coaches operate in a market that is close to the competitive ideal since colleges are free to make whatever dollar and fringe benefit offers they wish to coaches. The existence of NFL assistant and head coaching jobs serves to intensify college-level competition over coaches.

. . . .

Athletic Department

The athletic department is constrained to obey the academic requirements of its college. . . .

Each college . . . belongs to its football conference. . . . Because of competitive balance considerations, football conferences tend to consist of colleges with roughly the same level of academic standards as well as roughly the same level of revenue potential, as discussed later.

There are some major differences between the athletic department of a college and the college's academic departments. Coaches, in general, and football coaches, in particular, are paid much more than professors but coaches typically are signed to relatively short-term contracts and are not covered by tenure and promotion rules. Moreover, as with many academic departments, athletic departments, on average, barely break even. . . . However, football gate receipts, TV income, postseason earnings, and booster contributions typically are in excess of athletic department spending on football.

So, why do colleges typically support athletic departments with direct budget appropriations? If the typical athletic department generates any value to the typical college at large, it is through endowments and gifts from boosters that may be tied to football success, any sort of increase in the application pool derived from football success, plus any other spillovers to the rest of the college due to its affiliation with a "major conference." In many ways, the athletic department and its football program perform a development function for the college. The few extremely successful programs also provide direct revenues to their fortunate (but few) colleges.

It is well established that winning enhances giving to the athletic department itself. But the value to the college, at large, is less well settled. Brooker and Klastorin[3] and Grimes and Chressan- this[4] find that winning boosts general giving to colleges. On the other hand, Sigelman and Bookheimer,[5] Gaski and Etzel,[6] and Sack and Watkins[7] did not find such a relationship. Sigelman and Carter[8] present sort of an intermediate finding; giving to the college, at large, only rises with dramatic program turnarounds. On other dimensions of interest to the college, athletic success has been found to increase the quality of the student body[9] and enhance the size of the applicant pool.[10]

It is commonly believed that college football programs are operated with little concern for net operating revenue generated for the college at large.[11] However, within the constraints imposed by a college's ethical framework and academic standards, we cast college football programs as profit maximizers. The rationalization for this modeling choice was discussed at the beginning of this chapter. The forces of stable equilibrium and competitive balance require the development to which we now turn.

Padilla and Baumer[12] have established that revenues clearly go up with winning. Successful teams have larger direct revenues, as well as gifts and endowments to the athletic department, than less successful teams. To see how a stable equilibrium with competitive balance depends on profit maximization, suppose that all colleges in a given conference operate football programs that do not fully exploit profit opportunities. Such a situation cannot be stable since there are incentives for each college in the league to improve its team, hire a better coach, recruit better athletes, and gain a higher winning percent. Since, within a league, changes in winning percents are zero-sum, the improved team's revenues rise and all other teams' revenues fall. Unless they are willing to live with this reduced situation, other teams must respond by moving in the direction of profit maximization. Their only other alternative is to move to another league with lower revenue and profit potential. Thus, the only stable equilibrium is one where all athletic departments are pursuing something approximating profit maximization. That football programs often carry the other intercollegiate sports within the department only serves to reinforce this observation.

Ultimately, through the administrative branch of the college, athletic department budgets are sub- ject to approval by external monitors of the college, usually some type of board of regents that serves at the state governor's discretion. Formally, then, individual coaches attempt to maximize winning percent subject to the athletic department allocation to the football program. While this does not nec- essarily imply a simple one-to-one relation to the profits generated in the department, in fact, athletic budgets and coaches' salaries are clearly directly related to the success of the team and the revenues that follow such success.

. . . .

. . . Additional coaching input increases winning percent directly (for any level of playing strength) and indirectly by increasing the playing strength of the team through both recruiting a better class of player and improving the skills of players that are recruited. Because coaching inputs are acquired in a competitive market, coaches capture their marginal revenue product, including increases in athletic department revenue resulting from both direct and indirect coaching impacts on winning percent.

The NCAA does not allow athletic departments to offer more than a full-ride scholarship (although athletes in some sports do receive partial scholarships) and recruiting rules restrict the number of full-ride scholarships that can be offered in any given sport. Thus, scholarship offers are not determined on the basis of their cost to the athletic department, or the value to players. Further, it is a meta-fact of college sports that athletic departments always allocate all of their full-ride equivalent scholarships. As Noll points out, "Hence, recruiting three or four additional first-rate athletes per year can move a school from being marginally profitable to being very successful, generating an additional million dollars a year or more in net revenues."[13] . . .

. . . . Under NCAA rules limiting the number of scholarships, every scholarship player at Division I-A colleges (except, perhaps, at the skill-level margin) is exploited in the sense that his marginal revenue product exceeds the tuition grant in Division I-A schools.

. . . .

Under NCAA rules limiting the number of scholarships, the higher is a player's probability of an NFL career, the greater is the degree of exploitation of that player.

. . . .

. . . . Arguments like those by Goff, Shugart, and Tollison[14] are supported. They argued that amateurism both redirects wealth from athletes to their organizations and lessens competition for the athletes' positions (by erecting low pay as an entry barrier).

However, we hasten to point out that there is some evidence that the returns to this exploitation may end up being spent in net socially wasteful ways. While tuition, room and board, books, and the chance at a higher expected future income represent the monopsony payment to athletes, recruiting costs are competitively determined. Unlike professional sports, there is no "draft" for new talent entering the college ranks. While the NCAA limits some types of recruiting spending, clearly large amounts are spent during the process. Rent-seeking ideas of the Tullock[15] variety may mean that athletic departments already spend up to and including the added value of the recruit during the recruiting process. But, since only one school gets the recruit, and a cheaper way for talent to enter the Division I ranks is easy to envision, such expenditures by the other schools represent social waste.

Rushin[16] cites an instructive example. George Raveling, USC basketball coach at the time, wrote around 100 letters per week to a potential recruit. As long as it was on two-color letterhead, this practice was within NCAA rules, but surely wasteful. Thus, exploitation in the presence of rent-seeking incentives may mean that coaches and athletic department administrators do not keep the difference between marginal revenue product and scholarships.

. . . .

. . . . Thus, just as in professional team sports, college football leagues face a problem of lack of competitive balance. Colleges in the strongest-drawing locations will field stronger teams, on average, than colleges in weaker-drawing locations.

One consequence of the imbalance is that if there is a great disparity in drawing potential between two conference colleges, either the weaker or the stronger, or both, will be under both internal and external pressure to leave the conference. Conferences thus tend to end up with members of similar drawing potential, just as they tend to end up with colleges of roughly similar academic standards. The University of Chicago, which dropped football and left the Big 10 in the late 1930s, is one historical example. A more recent example is Northwestern University; only the recent resurgence of its football fortunes have silenced rumors that the Wildcats would be leaving the Big 10 Conference.

THE IMPLICATIONS OF PLAY-FOR-PAY

One of the most controversial issues currently confronting college football is paying cash to college athletes, over and above the usual scholarship and expected higher income after graduation. Our model generates the following insights into the consequences of replacing the present set of NCAA amateur standing rules with a freely competitive market for player services.

Under a competitive market, players would receive money/tuition offers, as well as expected later income, that would reflect the skill levels of individual players. This is in stark contrast to the present system where, at any given college, all players receive the same scholarship regardless of skill levels. Because colleges differ from one another in the value of scholarships, schools with lower academic standards (and lower discounted present value of income for players who choose to enroll there) would have to offer higher cash payments to offset the differential in scholarship value. Also, since colleges differ in coaching inputs, which affect the probability of an NFL career, offers to players under play-for-pay would have to reflect this differential as well. Under a perfectly competitive market for players, with complete information, players would be completely indifferent between colleges, just as would be the case with coaches under the present system of NCAA rules.

. . . .

. . . . On the one hand, NCAA rules do not permit colleges with low marginal revenue products for players and coaches to offset the coaching input advantage that colleges with higher marginal revenue products have under the rules. This generates part of the competitive imbalance result; better recruits are attracted to higher marginal revenue product colleges. On the other hand, high marginal revenue product colleges have a wider gap between player marginal revenue product and tuition cost and, hence, a larger unsatisfied demand for players. Just how these two forces balance out is problematic. . . .

. . . .

CHEATING ON NCAA RULES

We turn to the other important college football problem, cheating on the rules. . . .

Colleges most likely to gain substantially from cheating are colleges with high marginal revenues from winning. These would be colleges with low winning percents, large unused stadium capacity, and a large potential TV and gate audience.

Similarly, losses from NCAA penalties if a college is caught cheating are largest for the most successful football programs, that is, programs with lucrative TV earnings, wealthy donors, and perennial postseason play. Looking at things from a coach's point of view, older established coaches have made their reputation and figure to lose most if caught cheating while young unknowns have little in the way of reputation to lose and much to gain from establishing themselves as winning coaches. Thus, assuming that [the probability of being caught in a violation of NCAA rules] is the same for all colleges, one would predict that a college with a currently weak football record, a high potential for financial gain if its team is a success, and headed by a young coach, is most likely to engage in cheating.

Further, coaches and boosters almost never bear the penalties imposed by the NCAA. Even if the coach is caught, the winning percent reward to cheating stays on his record and only seldom is a coach ever sanctioned for cheating. As Noll states, "Cheating against the NCAA rules will continue — indeed, increase — because it is the profit-maximizing strategy for nearly all universities and the income-maximizing strategy for coaches."[17]

There is evidence to this point. Padilla and Baumer[18] analyze cheating at both the athletic program level and for individual sports. Programs with a history of NCAA violations tended to generate greater revenues and profits, while the short-run impacts of recent sanctions were negligible or zero. For football, sanctions did not affect revenues. They did for basketball, but only for a short time. Fleisher, Goff, and Tollison[19] also found that "crime pays." Winning percents of violators were much different than others before they were caught even though there was a reduction in their winning percent after NCAA sanctions. It appears that Noll was correct.

But there are mitigating factors. The NCAA must surely be aware of these facts, which means that it should allocate its scrutiny heavily toward just such programs; the probability . . . of being caught would be higher for the teams most likely to cheat. Fleisher, Goff, and Tollison[20] note the usual cheating incentives force cartel members to carefully monitor each other's output levels; the NCAA would be on the lookout for dramatic changes in winning percent, success in recruiting, and changes in conference affiliation.

There also appear to be incentives for schools to monitor cheating by their own athletic departments. Grimes and Chressanthis[21] find evidence that NCAA sanctions reduce giving to the academic portion of the college. Such losses, if large enough, should bring the college's own watchdogs sniffing after the athletic department.

Also, there shouldn't be much cheating by colleges with high academic standards. . . . They already have the advantage in recruiting the only type of players that they are willing to admit by virtue of the higher value of their scholarship. In a sense, these colleges are competing for different players than are other colleges.

Finally, Noll[22] points out that conference revenue sharing blunts the incentive to cheat. If each conference member only earns a portion of the reward to cheating and must share the rest with other conference members, cheating should be reduced. Further, teams in conferences with more extensive revenue sharing should cheat less. We summarize these ideas as follows:

. . . NCAA rules provide incentives for under-the-counter payments to highly skilled players, and for cheating on SAT and other entrance requirements, for players with low academic credentials at weak programs, with high potential payoffs, a young coach, low academic standards, and low revenue sharing imposed by its conference.

PAST EMPIRICAL WORK

. . . .

Turning first to the evidence on monopsony exploitation of college athletes; . . . compensation to college football players will be less than their contribution to athletic department revenues and more so for star players. Past empirical work by others supports both of these propositions. Leonard and Prinzinger . . . found monopsony exploitation in the 90% range.[23] Brown[24] put the level of exploitation at about $500,000 for college football stars, with the rate at 90%. In a related area, Brown[25] puts the estimate of marginal revenue product near $1 million for college basketball.

Noll[26] provides an instructive example. Noting that quarterback John Paye was the only major roster difference in 1987 versus 1986, Noll finds about a $200,000 increase to Stanford's football program. The value of a scholarship that year was about $17,000. Without adjustment for Paye's future value as a pro (after the fact, it was not extensive), the exploitation rate in this example matches the 90% level found in other work.

There also are some interesting findings by others . . . which [dictate] competitive imbalance based on different relative values of college football by fans at different colleges. Padilla and Baumer[27] find no strong relationship between coaches' salaries and profits. But . . . higher marginal revenue products should drive higher salaries and higher returns to athletic departments. After noting that the data may have let them down, Padilla and Baumer add, "Another interpretation is that there is also room here for cost-cutting, as spending for salaries is not strongly related to profitability in many cases."[28] But . . . [there is] yet another explanation. They simply may have taken an empirical snapshot of an equilibrium among similarly situated teams, from the marginal revenue product perspective.

Fleisher, Goff, and Tollison[29] investigate some of the implications. . . They find that variability in winning percent and conference switching both increase the chances for NCAA enforcement actions. In addition, the easier it is to monitor recruiting by other rivals, the less the chance of enforcement action by the NCAA. Further, they conclude that perennial winners and teams that never win are less likely to face such actions.

In summary, it appears that the empirical work of others offers some important verification of the theory in the last section. The three areas of significant past work concern . . . college athlete monopsony exploitation, . . . success and marginal revenue product, and . . . cheating. This leaves substantial room for suggestions for future work.

REFERENCES

1. Fleisher, Arthur A. III, Brian L. Goff, and Robert D. Tollison. 1992. *The National Collegiate Athletic Association.* Chicago: University of Chicago Press, p. 21.
2. Noll, Roger G. 1991. "The Economics of Intercollegiate Sports." In Judith Andre and David N. James (eds.), *Rethinking College Athletics.* Philadelphia: Temple University Press, 1991.
3. Brooker, George and T. D. Klastorin. 1981. "To the Victors Belong the Spoils? College Athletics and Alumni Giving." *Social Science Quarterly,* December, 62, 744–750.
4. Grimes, Paul W. and George A. Chressanthis. 1994. "Alumni Contributions to Academics: The Role of Intercollegiate Sports and NCAA Sanctions." *American Journal of Economics and Sociology,* January, 53, 27–40.
5. Sigelman, Lee and Samual Bookheimer. 1983. "Is It Whether You Win or Lose? Monetary Contributions to Big-Time College Athletic Programs." *Social Science Quarterly,* June, 64, 347–359.
6. Gaski, John F. and Michael J. Etzel. 1984. "Collegiate Athletic Success and Alumni Generosity: Dispelling the Myth." *Social Behavior and Personality,* 12, 1, 29–38.
7. Sack, Allen L. and Charles Watkins. 1985. "Winning and Giving." In Donald Chu, Jeffrey Segrave, and Beverly J. Becker (eds.), *Sport and Higher Education.* Champaign, IL: Human Kinetics Publishers, Inc.
8. Sigelman, Lee and Robert Carter. 1979. "Win One for the Giver? Alumni Giving and Big-Time College Sports." *Social Science Quarterly,* September, 60, 284–294.
9. McCormick, Robert E. and Maurice Tinsley. 1990. "Athletics and Academics: A Model of University Contributions." In Brian Goff and Robert Tollison (eds.), *Sportometrics.* College Station, TX: Texas A&M University Press.
10. Murphy, Robert G. and Gregpru A. Trandel. 1994. "The Relation Between a University's Football Record and the Size of Its Applicant Pool." *Economics of Education Review,* September, 13, 265–270.
11. For example, see Sperber, Murray. 1990. *College Sports, Inc.: The Athletic Department vs. the University.* New York: Henry Holt.

12. Padilla, Arthur and David Baumer. 1994. "Big-Time College Sports: Management and Economic Issues." *Journal of Sport and Social Issues,* May, 18, 123–143.

13. Noll, Roger G. 1991. "The Economics of Intercollegiate Sports." In Judith Andre and David N. James (eds.), *Rethinking College Athletics.* Philadelphia: Temple University Press, p. 205.

14. Goff, Brian L., William F. Shugart, III, and Robert D. Tollison. 1988. "Disqualification by Decree: Amateur Rules as Barriers to Entry." *Journal of Institutional and Theoretical Economics,* June, 144, 515–523.

15. Tullock, Gordon. 1967. "Welfare Costs of Tariffs, Monopoly, and Theft." *Western Economic Journal,* June, 224–232.

16. Rushin, Steve. 1993. "The Wooing Game." *Sports Illustrated,* November, 29, 96.

17. Noll, Roger G. 1991. "The Economics of Intercollegiate Sports." In Judith Andre and David N. James (eds.), *Rethinking College Athletics.* Philadelphia: Temple University Press, p. 198.

18. Padilla, Arthur and David Baumer. 1994. "Big-Time College Sports: Management and Economic Issues." *Journal of Sport and Social Issues,* May, 18, 123–143.

19. Fleisher, Arthur A., III, Brian L. Goff, and Robert D. Tollison. 1992. *The National Collegiate Athletic Association.* Chicago: University of Chicago Press.

20. Id.

21. Grimes, Paul W. and George A. Chressanthis. 1994. "Alumni Contributions to Academics: The Role of Intercollegiate Sports and NCAA Sanctions." *American Journal of Economics and Sociology,* January, 53, 27–40.

22. Noll, Roger G. 1991. "The Economics of Intercollegiate Sports." In Judith Andre and David N. James (eds.), *Rethinking College Athletics.* Philadelphia: Temple University Press, p. 207.

23. Leonard, John and Joseph Prinzinger. 1984. "An Investigation into the Monopsonistic Market Structure of Division One NCAA Football and Its Effect on College Football Players." *Eastern Economic Journal,* October–November, 10, 455–467.

24. Brown, Robert W. 1993. "An Estimate of the Rent Generated by a Premium College Football Player." *Economic Inquiry,* October, 31, 671–684.

25. Brown, Robert W. 1994. "Measuring Cartel Rents in the College Basketball Player Recruitment Market." *Applied Economics,* January, 26, 27–34.

26. Noll, Roger G. 1991. "The Economics of Intercollegiate Sports." In Judith Andre and David N. James (eds.), *Rethinking College Athletics.* Philadelphia: Temple University Press.

27. Padilla, Arthur and David Baumer. 1994. "Big-Time College Sports: Management and Economic Issues." *Journal of Sport and Social Issues,* May, 18, 123–143.

28. Padilla, Arthur and David Baumer. 1994. "Big-Time College Sports: Management and Economic Issues." *Journal of Sport and Social Issues,* May, 18, 136.

29. Fleisher, Arthur A., III, Brian L. Goff, and Robert D. Tollison. 1992. *The National Collegiate Athletic Association.* Chicago: University of Chicago Press.

TELECASTS AND RECRUITING IN NCAA DIVISION I FOOTBALL: THE IMPACT OF ALTERED PROPERTY RIGHTS

John L. Fizel and Randall W. Bennett

For three decades the National Collegiate Athletic Association (NCAA), through its Television Plan, exercised complete jurisdiction over all aspects of contract negotiations for college football telecasts. The NCAA Television Plan consisted of exclusive contracts with the television networks that limited the number of appearances by any one member over a specified time period, stipulated the times at which games could be televised, required the airing of a certain number of Division I-AA, II, and III games, and set a single price to be paid to any university team that appeared on a telecast. The final NCAA Television Plan allowed two networks, ABC and CBS, to each air 14 exposures annually. These exposures could be made up of a mixture of national and regional games, but each network was required to telecast at least 82 different teams over a 2-year period. Also, ABC and CBS together had to show at least 115 different teams on television over the 2 years of the plan. The NCAA also set a maximum number of four national and six total appearances for any team during this period. Finally, all teams involved in a telecast received equal remuneration, regardless of the attractiveness of the game to consumers or the number of stations that broadcast the game. In the fall of 1982, . . . Oklahoma, the University of Southern California, Appalachian State, and the Citadel each received the same compensation even though the Oklahoma–USC game was broadcast over 200 stations and the Appalachian State–Citadel game was broadcast over only 4.

The NCAA insisted that its continued control of the rights to football telecasts was necessary to achieve competitive balance among collegiate teams. If instead universities were given the right to negotiate their own telecast contracts, a proliferation of telecasts would ensue, with most appearances being awarded to conference leaders and nationally ranked teams. Because television appearances are a marketing and financial tool for recruiting top athletes, a distribution of appearances skewed toward traditional football powers would increase the talent pool of the traditional football powers relative to the struggling football programs and only accentuate the existing inequality among football programs. Existing powers would prosper; nonpowers would face further decline.

In the case of the *National Collegiate Athletic Association v. Regents of the University of Oklahoma and University of Georgia Athletic Association* (468 U.S. 85), the Court ruled that the NCAA Football Television Plan restricted output and fixed price in violation of the Sherman Antitrust Act. So, on June 27, 1984, the Supreme Court eliminated the NCAA's control over college football telecasts by reassigning the property rights of telecasts to the individual universities. As predicted by the NCAA, a frenzy of activity soon followed as schools, conferences, and select organizations of schools frenetically pursued local, regional, national, and cable outlets to televise their games. However, an empirical analysis of recruiting during the time period of expanded television coverage of college football has yet to be done. . . . This paper analyzes the pattern of recruiting that has occurred during the period of changed property rights. We examine both the short- and long-run effects for Division I football teams.

ANALYSIS

The recruiting success of teams in all nine NCAA Division I football conferences are assessed in this study. . . . *[There are currently 11 Division I-A football conferences.]*

. . . .

The power of the time variables can be addressed in a discussion of other structural changes developing concurrently with the change in telecast property rights. During the period of this study only one other major structural change affecting football recruiting occurred. Beginning in 1989, the NCAA reduced the maximum number of scholarships that major colleges could award prospective football players from 30 to 25 per year. This policy change was to reduce the recruiting prowess of traditional football powers. Yet, as will be seen, the results of this study indicate that the recruiting success of traditional football powers increased during this time. In effect, the results indicate that the recruiting success bestowed upon football powers by the 1984 Supreme Court decision overwhelmed the dampening of the football powers' recruiting success due to the scholarship reduction. . . .

. . . .

SUMMARY

Multiple measures and techniques were used to determine if the recruiting equity of college football was altered after the Supreme Court decision transferred telecast property rights from the NCAA to individual institutions. The results are as follows. First, the recruiting rankings within conferences changed little when measured by rank correlations between pre- and postdecision periods. Only the Big Eight and Southwestern conferences seemed to show turnover in recruiting rankings, generated, however, by abrupt changes for only one team in each of the two conferences. Second, changes in the disparity between the recruiting success of the top and bottom teams in each conference were addressed. Analyses included top and bottom teams identified on the basis of past recruiting success and then on past winning percentages. . . . The net result of both of these analyses indicated reductions in recruiting equity. The conference "powers" improved their recruiting after the Supreme Court decision. Finally, a regression analysis was used to determine if the recruiting success of traditional powers in Division I football was transformed after the change in telecast property rights. The evidence indicates a statistically significant improvement in recruiting success of traditional powers relative to nonpowers. The magnitude of the improvement, 30% for 1985–1991 and 41% for 1988–1991, is substantial. The marginal increase in recruiting disparity within conferences and the dramatic increase in recruiting disparity between traditional football powers and nonpowers gives credence to the NCAA's argument that control over telecast property rights may have been an aid to recruiting equity among Division I football programs.

UNPAID PROFESSIONALS

Andrew Zimbalist

THE MEDIA: COMMERCIALIZATION AND STRATIFICATION

Throughout the three decades of NCAA control of football telecasting, then, there was an abiding tension between general overexposure and underexposure of particular schools. NCAA policy varied a bit through the years, but the basic plan after 1951 was to permit one national and several regional telecasts each week. Each particular school was limited to two television appearances per year, and the only schools receiving television revenue directly were those that appeared in broadcast contests.

The NCAA skimmed between 4 and 12 percent off the top, and the rest was distributed to the colleges whose games were televised, with appearances in the national game bringing around 30 percent more than regional games. However effective this policy may have been in the aggregate, it left few satisfied customers. The big-time football programs wanted more exposure and the small programs wanted greater revenue sharing.

At a special summer convention in 1973, the Association moved to placate the big-time colleges by breaking into three divisions. Each division would operate with significant autonomy, setting its own policies with regard to scholarship limits or number of coaches per sport. The NCAA Council would now have eight representatives from Division I and only three each from Divisions II and III. The Association attempted to mollify Divisions II and III by giving each its own football championship, each of which would be televised by ABC. In recognition of this, the two lower divisions would be allocated $500,000 of the new $16 million TV contract.

. . . . *[The author's discussion of the Supreme Court's ruling in* NCAA v. Bd. of Regents *that the NCAA's television policy violated the antitrust laws is omitted.]*

With the NCAA's TV product struck down, schools and conferences were left to fend for themselves. The NCAA television cartel was broken. The leading football colleges and conferences were cut free and the weaker football colleges lost the protection of the NCAA plan. Meanwhile, the NCAA was left without football television revenue and with a legal bill of over $2.2 million.

503

More Product, Greater Inequality, and Intensified Commercialism

What did happen in the wake of the Supreme Court decision was predictable. In the short run, disorder reigned. Oklahoma, Georgia, Nebraska, and USC put their football contests up for sale, but they were disappointed with the networks' offers. Notre Dame got the largest offer, $20 million, but turned it down. Scurrying about to arrange a deal in time for the 1984 season, the CFA [College Football Association] managed to ink one-year deals with ABC and ESPN worth $35 million. In addition to the CFA pact, the Big Ten and Pac-10 signed their own contract with CBS for around $10 million. The combined value of the CFA and Big Ten/Pac-10 deals was still well below the value of the NCAA's 1983 contracts despite the fact that it involved roughly twice as many network games. Some economists have viewed this outcome as a confirmation of monopoly theory: monopolists artificially lower output below and raise price above competitive levels. Thus, when the NCAA monopoly power in the television market was broken up, the resulting output was higher (almost double the number of televised games) and the price (TV revenue per game) was lower. While this dynamic probably explains part of the price drop in 1984, it is likely that a substantial portion of the drop is attributable to the inexperience and disorganization of the Division I football colleges in negotiating television deals as well as the shortness of time before the 1984 season. Indeed, for 1984 it was not only the revenue per game but the overall revenue from television that had fallen. There was not, after all, very much competition in 1984 — only two groups, the CFA and the Big Ten/Pac-10, existed. The CFA, which had instigated and supported the suit against the NCAA's monopoly, was now part of a duopoly — and that was more competition than it wanted. The CFA had attempted to persuade the Big Ten/Pac-10 to join its elite group. When this effort proved futile, the CFA then refused to allow CBS to broadcast "crossover" games, involving contests between CFA and Big Ten/Pac-10 schools. CBS went to court in 1984 claiming restraint of trade (group boycott and price fixing) and won.

Ironically, it was not until the duopoly of the 1980s gave way to more competition in the 1990s that television revenue from college football began its next rapid ascent. In 1990, Notre Dame broke from the CFA and signed its own 5-year deal with NBC, worth $38 million. The new 5-year deal that the CFA had inked with ABC and ESPN was promptly reduced by $35 million, down to $300 million, which was still $25 million more per year than its previous 1987–90 contract.

Notre Dame's bolting from the CFA, however, had a larger significance. It revealed the fragility of the CFA cartel and the potential attractiveness for other schools or conferences to do their own negotiating. Conferences took this message to heart and began discussions with the networks. They were given a basic lesson in television economics. Their rights fees would grow in proportion to the size of their market. Further, the larger each conference, the fewer the number of conferences in Division I-A and the lesser the competition. Not surprisingly, the conferences began to realign and expand to extend their market coverage. The first step was taken by the Big Ten which voted in June 1990 to admit Penn State into its conference. The Atlantic Coast Conference (ACC) added previously independent Florida State. The Southeastern Conference (SEC) expanded to twelve teams, and the Big 8 annexed four teams from the Southwest Conference. Cosmetically enhanced, the conferences one by one broke off from the CFA cartel and signed their own TV deals. In February 1994 the SEC led the way with an $85 million deal with CBS, commencing after the last year (1995–96) of the CFA contract with ABC and ESPN. Three days later the ACC signed up with ABC and ESPN; the next day the Big East inked a deal with CBS and three weeks later the Big 8 entered into a contract with ABC and Liberty Sports.

The revenue bonanza did not stop here, however. Network rights fees for postseason bowl games roughly doubled between 1985 and 1995. The payout to each team participating in the Rose Bowl, for instance, rose from $925,000 in 1969, to $1.42 million in 1974, $2.9 million in 1983, $5.75 million in 1992, $8.25 million in 1996, $9.5 million in 1997, and . . . $11 million in 1998. These payouts come from all revenues generated by the game (TV rights, ticket and concession sales, sponsorship fees, etc.). The bowl with the largest payout in 1996 was the Tostito Fiesta Bowl. Aided by a $12 million, 3-year sponsorship/naming rights deal with Frito-Lay, the minimum Fiesta Bowl payout in 1996 was reported at between $8.6 million and $13 million per team. The Orange and Sugar Bowls also had per team payouts in excess of $8.2 million.

Meanwhile, corporate advertisers were tripping over each other trying to buy spots for the 1996 Fiesta Bowl. Thirty-second spots sold for $500,000, or 122 percent of the rate for the "national championship" game (at the Orange Bowl) in 1995. This spot rate was approximately half the going rate for NFL Super Bowl spots the same month. The 1996 Super Bowl was the top-rated sports event during the 1995–96 season, with a 46.0 rating (where each rating point represented 959,000 households watching the game), while the 1996 Fiesta Bowl tied for 29th place with game 6 of the NBA Finals and an 18.8 rating. These were heady times for college football.

The Bowl Alliance and Antitrust

Like the rest of college football, bowl revenues have grown increasingly stratified . . . Bowl TV ratings had been lagging and network executives began to carp that quality control was next to impossible.

College bowl games generally are organized and controlled by local chambers of commerce, convention and tourist bureaus, and assorted businesses. The games' understood purpose is to generate business for the local economy, which they usually do to some extent because the majority of attendees come from out of town. The bowls have contracts with individual conferences that provide for conference champions, runner-ups, or other designated teams to participate in the bowl each year. On behalf of the conference, the participating school gets a share of the bowl revenue and, in turn, is obligated to purchase a substantial block of tickets for the game which it attempts to resell to its alumni, students, boosters, and others.

Under this system, each bowl did not know the quality of the teams it would be getting until the end of the season. The conference champion associated with a particular bowl may have had a relatively low national ranking and the opposing team may be no better. TV networks found themselves in the uncomfortable position of reserving a prime spot for a bowl and paying top rights fees, yet facing the possible prospect of two teams ranked below the top ten going against each other. In the best of circumstances, only one or at most two bowl games were relevant to determining the national champion; the audience for the other games was small.

David Downs, senior vice president of ABC Sports, explained: "All of the networks were souring on the bowl business. We couldn't go one more cycle where we wake up on the 1st of December and find out that we have a bad matchup and that we were going to get hammered in the ratings. How can we sell a college football game [to advertisers] when we don't know if we are going to have a 19 [in ratings points] or if we are going to have a 4?"[24]

The first step to rectifying this commercially threatening situation was taken in 1991 when the Atlantic Coast (ACC), Big East, Big Eight, Southeastern (SEC), and Southwestern conferences, along with Notre Dame, formed a bowl coalition with the prestigious college bowl committees of the

IBM Fiesta Bowl, the Mobil Cotton Bowl, the USF&G Sugar Bowl, and the Federal Express Orange Bowl. Under the agreement, the Orange, Sugar, and Cotton Bowls continued to be hosted by their affiliated conference champions, while the Fiesta Bowl had two open slots. These four bowls agreed to choose teams in order and to fill their open slots from among the champions of the ACC and Big East, Notre Dame, and other highly ranked schools.

Although this coalition improved the chances of top, competitive matchups, it precluded contests between the teams ranked number one and two if they came from the Big East (champion obligated to play in the Orange Bowl), the SEC (obligated to play in the Sugar Bowl), or the Southwest (obligated to play in the Cotton Bowl). Nonetheless, this arrangement did manage to produce "national championships" between the teams ranked numbers one and two in both 1992 and 1993. The other problem from the networks' point of view was that there was no guarantee that any of the individual bowls would be host to the top matchup. Selling advertising under these circumstances remained problematic.

The next step was taken in 1994 with the formation of the Bowl Alliance. The Big East, ACC, Big 12 (a merger of the Big 8 with 4 teams from the Southwest), the SEC, and Notre Dame agreed to the following terms with the Orange, Sugar, and Fiesta Bowls: the champions of the four conferences plus Notre Dame (unless the team had a losing season) and one other top-ranked school either from within or outside the Alliance would play in these three bowls; the traditional conference bowl ties would be severed in the interest of maximizing the possibility of having a national championship; and, the highest ranked game each year would rotate among the Orange, Sugar, and Fiesta Bowls. Since the bowls would share the championship game, advertisers were assured of the top matchup at least one out of every three years.

From the perspective of the Bowl Alliance conferences, there was still one missing piece. The champions of the Big Ten and Pac-10 conferences had been matched in the Rose Bowl for over fifty years. Moreover, teams from these conferences were often ranked either first or second in the nation. Without the Big Ten and Pac-10, the Alliance goal to offer a national championship game every year was elusive. In 1994, for instance, the No. 2 team was Penn State, from the Big Ten.

In June 1996, the Alliance struck a deal with the Big Ten, the Pac-10, the Rose Bowl, and ABC (which had broadcasting rights to the Rose Bowl). Beginning with the 1998–99 season, the national championship game would rotate among the four bowls and ABC would have broadcast rights for all four games over a seven-year period (for which the network paid the estimated modest sum of $700 million, or $25 million per game, which was roughly 2.5 times the average 1996 rights fees for the four games).[25] The teams for the national championship will be picked according to a new, computer-driven formula, which will include the team record, difficulty of schedule, the average of the *USA Today*/ESPN coaches' poll and the AP media poll, and the average of three computer rankings (*Seattle Times, New York Times,* and Jeff Sagarin). *[This formula has since been modified.]*

Of course, what was good news for the Super Bowl Alliance or the Bowl Championship Series, as it is now called with the Rose Bowl brought into the fold, was bad news for virtually all the other bowl games. As these four bowl games came increasingly to be associated with a national championship, interest in the other bowls waned. Accordingly, TV ratings and attendance for the other bowl games have suffered. With one anointed championship game, ABC may even have difficulty sustaining interest in the three nonchampionship, runner-up games each year.

Although many fans welcomed the heightened prospect of a national championship game in college football, the Bowl Championship Series came under sharp attack and close scrutiny from many observers. Senator Mitch McConnell of Kentucky, for instance, was concerned that his home state school, the University of Louisville, was being excluded from a reasonable opportunity to participate in the most prestigious and lucrative bowl games. The University of Louisville belonged to the Conference USA (C-USA) which, along with three other Division I-A conferences and eleven independents, were not invited to join the Bowl Alliance. Senator McConnell first raised the issue in 1993 when Louisville had a 7–1 record and a top ranking, but was automatically excluded from the leading bowls. The U.S. Justice Department commenced an inquiry and the Alliance agreed to open up two of the six Alliance bowl slots "to any team in the country with a minimum of eight wins or ranked higher than the lowest-ranked conference champion from among the champions of the ACC, Big East, Big 12 and SEC."

. . . .

The Alliance, instead of promoting the highest level of postseason competition, seemed to be promoting the economic fortunes of its members and the college bowls, to the exclusion and detriment of other Division I-A schools. The bowls themselves were originated in the 1930s to promote tourism in the host cities. The bowl committees continue to prefer to host universities with large, spendthrift student and alumni bodies. BYU is from the sparsely populated state of Utah (bad for TV ratings), and its students and alumni have the reputation of frugality and sobriety. Utah Senator Bob Bennett stated before the May 1997 U.S. Senate hearing on the Bowl Alliance: "BYU does not travel well. I'll be very blunt. There is a perception out there, and it may be true, that [BYU fans] do not drink and party the way the host city would prefer. Our football coach has been quoted as saying that BYU fans travel with a $50 bill and the Ten Commandments in their pocket, and they leave without breaking either one." Bowl host committees preferred teams from larger, wealthier, and wilder states.

The overall picture of bowl access in Division I-A almost makes the income distribution in Haiti look equitable. The Big 12 is guaranteed an appearance in an Alliance bowl plus 5 additional bowls; the SEC is guaranteed an Alliance bowl plus 4 additional bowls; the Big Ten, an Alliance bowl plus 4 other bowls; the Pac-10, an Alliance bowl plus 3 bowls; the ACC an Alliance bowl plus 3 others; the Big East, an Alliance bowl plus 3 others; the WAC, 3 bowls; C-USA, 1 bowl; the Big West, 0 bowls; the Mid-American, 0 bowls; and 11 independents, 0 bowls.

. . . .

The Alliance bowls, then, distributed approximately $68 million to its member conferences after the 1995–96 season. The new ABC contract promises that this figure will far exceed $100 million in 1998–99. *[See Table 4 on page 480 for the 2002–03 distribution of BCS revenue.]* This gives the six commissioners of the Alliance conferences an enormous amount of influence in the world of college sports. These commissioners, unlike athletic directors, coaches, or university presidents, are not college employees, are not located on campus, and operate with a thicker veil of secrecy than the NCAA.

Schools with access only to the minor bowl games find that there is little, if any, financial payoff to bowl participation. Participating teams [may earn] $750,000 or $1 million from the bowl, but out of this they have to cover expenses, sometimes revenue-share with their conference, and must cover any shortfall in their obligation to sell a specified, large number of tickets. For instance, the Hall of Fame Bowl requires each school to sell 15,000 tickets and the Carquest Bowl requires 12,500 each, which at a minimum price of $30 a pop can set a school back hundreds of thousands of dollars. Expenses include hauling approximately one hundred players, coaches, administrators, the school band, and cheerleaders, among others, considerable distances to warmer climes, then housing and wining and dining them for several days. In some cases, the free-ride contingent has risen to nearly five hundred people. Stories about schools having to eat a large share of their tickets and losing money from their minor bowl participation are legion.

Especially with the advent of the Alliance Bowl games, the eighteen minor bowls have less and less significance. Fan interest in these games has plummeted, affecting both television rights fees and ticket sales. Nonetheless, the NCAA has increased the number of sanctioned bowl games by five over the last two years. Now 44 of the 112 Division I-A schools play in postseason bowl games. *[56 of the 118 schools in Division I-A played in bowl games in 2002–2003.]*

 . . . . The practical effect of the Alliance is to create (or rigidify) two tiers within Division I-A football (already a subdivision within Division I, itself the top of three NCAA athletic divisions). The bottom tier is effectively precluded from participating in the most prestigious, highest revenue bowls. The fans of the forty-nine football teams left out of the Alliance are thus deprived of the potential excitement associated with these bowls, and the schools are excluded from the revenue source and advertising value of playing in the top tier. This exclusion, many maintain, constitutes a restraint of trade and a group boycott.

 . . . .

But the politics of change are not encouraging. The bowl committees would lose control if a playoff format were adopted, and, hence, resist such a change. The Alliance members would lose privileged access to their self-proclaimed championship games and they would be forced to share their postseason revenues with dozens, if not hundreds, of other NCAA schools. They too would also resist the change. Conference commissioners, ADs [athletic directors], coaches, and sometimes college presidents and trustees from the Alliance would lose the enticing perquisites provided by the bowl committees. Conference commissioners may also prefer to defer to the NFL wishes to have no intrusion of competition during its playoffs and Super Bowl.

Unfortunately, these groups are already sufficiently powerful to make such a reform unlikely. They seemed, for instance, to have been able to pull the necessary strings in 1996 to dislodge an investigation into the Alliance by the Antitrust Division of the Justice Department.

The Alliance is also cunning. In the aftermath of the Senate Judiciary Committee's hearings, the Alliance held out a carrot to the other Division I-A conferences. It would pay the WAC $1.6 million annually for making its sixteen teams available to play in an Alliance bowl; similarly, C-USA would receive $800,000 for its eight teams. Also, the Alliance would donate a total of $900,000 to the Big West and Mid-American Conferences and $150,000 to the six Division I-AA football conferences whose members offer the maximum number of scholarships permitted by the NCAA.

 . . . .

Testifying before the Senate hearings on the Super Bowl Alliance, Tulane University Law School professor (as well as Tulane Athletic Representative and a member of the Sugar Bowl Committee) Gary Roberts argued that the real problem with the Alliance goes beyond legalistic matters of antitrust:

> Intercollegiate athletics is supposed to be about education and amateur student-athletes. We should run our programs with the primary emphasis on optimizing the welfare of the young men and women who play sports while they are getting their education. We should try to preserve the amateur nature of this enterprise and be always vigilant of the need to preserve the academic and moral integrity of the institutions of higher learning upon which our nation's future depends. To turn this amateur athletic enterprise designed to give students an extracurricular activity through which to broaden their horizons into a purely revenue driven commercial business that caters to the welfare of consumers is a perversion of the values for which it was founded and should stand. This is why the Alliance is so offensive — it accelerates and magnifies the perverse commercial motivations and values that have all too much corrupted intercollegiate athletics.

Ratings, Attendance, and the Future

Television rights fees for sports have experienced a protracted boom. But few industries rise forever and no industries rise without cycles. The 1980s and 1990s have witnessed unprecedented competition among the traditional and newer networks, as cable sport networks have been formed and over-the-air networks (FOX, WB, UPN) have been created. This competition has helped to bid up the rights fees.

But as rights fees and opportunities for television coverage have grown, new sports have appeared (e.g., professional soccer, women's professional basketball, beach volleyball) and others have augmented their visibility and popularity (e.g., car racing and golf). The proliferation of televised sports inevitably results in lower ratings. And lower ratings, especially once the network shakeout occurs and the economy slows down, will bring either stagnation or diminution in rights fees.

This danger is particularly problematic for college football because (a) the number of telecasts has skyrocketed since the 1984 Supreme Court decision and (b) the networks overbid in their initial effort to pry conferences loose from the CFA. The ratings trend for college football is not promising. Games televised on ABC had a rating of 9.9 in 1983 before the Court decision, falling to 8.3 in 1984 and continuing to decrease to an average 6.6 between 1991 and 1995, and an average of 5.1 during 1996 and 1997. Notre Dame's ratings on NBC averaged only 5.1 between 1991 and 1995, and 3.2 during 1996 and 1997. The combined ratings points for all New Year's Day bowl games fell from 92.1 in 1975, to 69.8 in 1994, and 50.7 in 1997.

Likewise, supersaturation of the airwaves with college football and other sporting events seems to have cut into the live fan base for intercollegiate games. Average attendance at Division I-A games peaked in 1982 at 43,689, after which it has trailed off steadily to 41,471 in 1995 and to 41,337 in 1996 before recovering somewhat. . . This decrease of 1,179 over the last sixteen years is hardly alarming, but it feeds an overall concern about rights and gate fees in the future, particularly for schools which find themselves outside the self-designated football elite.

Television and College Basketball

Men's basketball has always played second fiddle to football as a revenue generator for colleges. In 1995, football accounted for 66 percent of all athletic revenues at Division I-A schools while men's basketball accounted for 25 percent. Basketball, however, has been catching up; that sport's contribution to total athletic revenues rose from 8 percent in 1960, to 9 percent in 1969, 12 percent in 1977, 13 percent in 1981, 15 percent in 1985, 18 percent in 1989, and 22 percent in 1993.

And the fastest growing component of big-time basketball revenues has been income from the end-of-the-year NCAA Final Tournament. Between 1985 and 1995 while postseason football TV revenues approximately doubled, postseason basketball TV revenues increased four and a half times.

The NCAA basketball tournament began in 1939 with eight teams, expanded to 24 teams in 1952, 32 teams in 1953, 48 teams in 1979, and to its present 64-team format in 1985. The NCAA lost $2,531 on the 1939 tournament. The following year the tournament champion was awarded $750. Prize money was modest for the next two decades.

As tournament hours televised more than quintupled from the late sixties to the mid-nineties, the television rights fees grew from $140,000 in 1966, to $28.3 million in 1985, and to $166.2 million in 1995 (accounting for 90 percent of total tournament receipts in 1995).

One of the NCAA's motives for expanding its tournament was competition with the National Invitational Tournament (NIT), which until the early 1960s was the preeminent postseason basketball championship. In 1960, the NCAA Executive Committee instructed its member schools and conferences that they had to prioritize participation in the NCAA tournament over the NIT. With the NCAA's increased television revenues and exposure, the NIT gradually receded in importance.

In 1990 the NCAA signed a monster-contract with CBS for $1 billion over seven years to broadcast the tournament, almost double the annual value of the existing contract. The investment paid off for CBS, as ratings for the final game rose from 18.8 in 1988 to 22.7 in 1992, and then steadied at 22.2 in 1993 and 21.6 in 1994. In this latter year, CBS locked in the NCAA tournament by renegotiating its contract, this time for eight years (1995–2002) for $1.75 billion. Ratings have trailed off a bit, averaging 18.8 during 1995–97 (still considerably above the 15.1 average ratings for the NBA final game during 1991–96), but in the strong advertising market spot fees have continued to skyrocket, reaching a reported $600,000 for thirty seconds during the 1997 final game.

The NCAA has gone out of its way to help CBS get a good return on its investment. During the first half of the 1997 final men's game there were 8 minutes of commercials and 20 minutes of playing time. "Coaches run out of advice to give players as timeout breaks drag past 2-1/2 minutes. Teams like Kentucky and Kansas, noted for benches deep enough to wear down exhausted opponents, lose that advantage."[39] Not even the NBA allows commercial breaks to so disrupt the game's tempo and strategy.

Basketball's meteoric success created something of an embarrassment for the NCAA. Prior to the 1990 CBS contract, which took effect in 1991, the NCAA distributed 60 percent of the tournament revenues to the participating teams. For each round a team advanced in the tournament up to the Final Four, their school would receive an additional share of that year's tournament income.

The payout was increasingly handsome. Some worried that the incremental sums involved had grown too large and placed excessive pressure on the players to perform. The favorite metaphor was the $300,000 foul shot. Then, with television rights fees about to double in 1991, the NCAA decided to modify its revenue distribution practices in a way that putatively placed less emphasis on winning.

Here's what the NCAA did. First, they reduced the share of tournament receipts going to participants from approximately 60 percent down to 30 percent. The remaining 70 percent would now be distributed irrespective of a team's or a conference's performance. In 1990–91, the first year of the new CBS contract, the NCAA received $117 million; of this, $47 million covered NCAA costs and financed NCAA programs, such as catastrophic injury insurance for athletes, academic enhancement for athletes, emergency financial assistance for athletes, and the Division II and III national championships. The balance of $70 million was divided in half, with equal parts going to performance awards to the tournament teams and to broad-based distribution to schools according to the number of athletic teams and scholarships they sponsor. This was certainly a step away from performance incentives and toward a more equal sharing of the television booty.

Second, the NCAA changed the basis for the performance awards. Prior to the 1990–91 season, team awards were proportional to the number of tournament games they played up to the Final Four. With the March 1991 tournament the awards were made proportional to the number of wins a team had over the previous six years in the postseason tournament. Thus, a tournament win in a particular year was worth only one-sixth as much as it had been in that year. That win, however, now would also be paid off in the subsequent five years and, hence, the present value of the win would be equal to roughly six times the first-year payoff. For example, in 1996–97 each tournament game played was worth $74,000 that year, so over the six-year period the present value of that game would be

$74,000 × 6, or $444,000 (the payoff per game grew each year at roughly the same percentage as the discount rate).

If a team made it to the Final Four in 1996–97, it would receive a payoff of $2.22 million. The payoff for making it to the Final Four in 1988–89 was $1.37 million. In both cases, the NCAA sends the payment to the team's conference where it is then subjected to redistribution among all conference schools, generally with the participating school receiving a larger share (see below).

The bottom line, then, is that the NCAA in stretching out payments over six years has done nothing whatsoever to lower the value of a foul shot; on the contrary, as the television package has grown richer, the foul shot has greater value than ever before. Even with the diminished share of TV revenues going to tournament participants (in 1996–97, participants shared $50 million out of total CBS and ESPN revenues of $191.1 million), the monetary incentive to win is greater than it has ever been. Overall, the distribution of the NCAA basketball fund among the major Division I conferences in 1997 (based on tournament success from 1991 through 1996) displayed the pattern of inequality. . .

The spread between the maximum and minimum conference distributions from the basketball fund has widened from $3.96 million in 1991 to $6.06 million in 1997, while the spread for the total distribution increased from $7.16 million in 1991 to $12.86 million in 1997. *[The spread between the distributions from the basketball fund was $8.25 million in the 2001–2002 season, and the spread for the total distribution was $89.4 million.]* The conferences receiving more from the basketball fund are also receiving more from the other distributions.

The NCAA does not arrange TV packages for regular season games; those are handled by the individual schools and conferences. There has been a veritable explosion of TV coverage of regular season games in the 1990s. In 1988–89, there were 2,078 college basketball games shown on cable or broadcast television; in 1995–96, there were 3,854. Ratings for regular season games have dropped 10 to 20 percent, depending on the carrier, but the number of televised games has increased 85 percent. Thus, the number of people watching the games has grown appreciably, and so have the TV rights fees.

Along with the glut of televised games, attendance at men's basketball contests fell from 29.4 million in 1991–92 to 27.7 million in 1996–97. Meanwhile, attendance at Division I women's games has increased from 3.1 million in 1991–92 to 4.9 million in 1996–97, compensating for the entire men's decrease. . . .

. . . .

Revenue Redistribution Within Conferences

When the NCAA stumbled upon its basketball gold mine with the $1 billion CBS contract commencing in 1991, idealism ran wild. Many believed that part of the funds would find their way into academic programs and others saw an opportunity to lift the financial fortunes of the low-revenue sports programs.

Neal Pilson, president of CBS sports when the NCAA deal was signed, offered some thoughts on how the NCAA might use its newfound riches.[46]

> Besides being a television executive, I am a citizen, a taxpayer, and a father of three children, two currently in college. I would like to see this money used for broad educational purposes as well as athletic purposes.

Pilson went on to suggest one way such a balance of purposes might be achieved. He proposed that the television dollars be distributed to the NCAA schools in proportion to the graduation rate of their athletes rather than their success in the basketball tournament. Pilson reported that he had discussed his idea with Dick Schultz, NCAA Executive Director at the time, and that Schultz fully supported it.

Roy Kramer, longstanding and powerful commissioner of the Southeast Conference, also articulated some magnanimous ideals back in 1990:[47]

> I believe that we can make a major statement in intercollegiate athletics by the way we distribute this money, if it is properly handled. I think that for the first time, we're really looking at positive ways to distribute the money, based not on the concept of winning in order to balance your budget, but from the standpoint of a commitment to student-athletes across the board in your program.

> We're making the statement that "We're going to play for the trophy." That's the real purpose of the types of championships we sponsor in the NCAA. We're not doing it in order to enhance the paycheck or the coach's position at the end of the year.

A few years later Roy Kramer was defending the elitism of the Bowl Alliance and the right of six Division I-A conferences to share the TV rights of $25 million per premiere bowl game among themselves. In fact, as television rights fees have skyrocketed, intercollegiate athletic revenues have become more stratified, not more equal. The NCAA does not publish a detailed breakdown of revenue distribution among athletic programs, but a reasonably clear picture of growing inequality can be assembled from the scant data they do produce. *[The NCAA Revenue Distribution Plan is presented in the next article.]* For instance, if one considers the ratio of reported revenue from the top revenue program in the country to the average revenue of roughly the top 150 programs, one can discern a pattern for this ratio to grow consistently through 1985 and then to stabilize. Overall, by this measure, revenue inequality increased by 92.3 percent between 1962 and 1997 among the nation's top athletic colleges. A trend toward growing inequality is also apparent in the 1990s.

Yet, it is axiomatic in the world of sports that in order to sustain fan interest a sports league must maintain a certain degree of competitive balance, meaning that there has to be substantial uncertainty as to the outcome of each contest as well as to the ultimate league or conference champion each year. If there was not such uncertainty, then, one presumes, fans would quickly lose interest.

. . . .

In professional sports, it is clear that the profit-maximizing degree of competitive balance is not one where all the teams are of equal strength. A league will generate the most revenue when teams from larger metropolitan areas, with more modern stadiums or arenas, or where fans are willing and able to pay more to see their team win, are relatively stronger.

The same dynamic will apply, *mutatis mutandis,* for NCAA conferences. Most significantly, schools with historically strong teams will have an incentive to build larger and fancier facilities, and, once built, the same schools will experience a larger payoff to athletic success. For instance, the University of Tennessee plays in a stadium with a capacity of 102,544, while the University of Michigan stadium has a capacity of 107,501, UCLA's has 102,083, USC's 94,159, Penn State's 94,159, and Ohio State's 89,800. These schools are more likely to spend the largest sums on recruitment, coaching, training programs, academic tutoring, and so on, in order to attract the best athletes to matriculate. Other things being equal, these schools will also have sharper incentives to stretch NCAA rules.

To support competitive balance and deter rampant commercialism, then, conferences have cause to distribute their revenues in relatively equal fashion among member institutions. At the same time, for conferences to retain their stronger members they cannot be overly zealous in redistributing earnings from top bowl games, television appearances, the NCAA basketball tournament, and gate revenues.

Each conference is allowed to develop its own revenue distribution formula. Although the details differ most conferences follow broadly similar patterns, and these patterns have not changed much over time. Interestingly, though most conferences are composed largely of public, tax-supported institutions, many hold the specifics of their revenue distribution policies as closely guarded secrets. The tendency to regard such information as proprietary reinforces the view of big-time athletic programs as commercial enterprises, rather than as part of universities whose mission it is to promote open, intellectual discourse in pursuit of the truth.

From the information which is available, actual revenue distribution practices vary widely. The Big Ten appears to be the only major conference that shares gate revenues, with 35 percent going to the visiting conference team. The former Big 8 used to share the gate 50/50, but when it expanded into the Big 12 all ticket revenue sharing was terminated. Regular season television income sharing varies from 80 percent to participating team(s) and 20 percent to the conference in the Big 8 and Big East (for non-conference games), to 100 percent to the conference for subsequent equal distribution. Of course, some teams also have their own deal with a local television station, and most have such deals with local radio stations. Revenue from the NCAA basketball tournament is shared relatively equally by most big-time conferences, with the participating school often receiving from one to several extra shares (roughly, an additional 10–30 percent). The Atlantic 10 is an exception to the rule: in 1995–96 a conference team going to the semifinals would have earned the conference $336,925 in that year and would have received nearly half of that ($160,000) in conference revenue-sharing payments. There appears to have been a modest tendency for revenue sharing within conferences from postseason competition to have grown more equal over the last fifteen years.

The largest payoffs come from participation in the postseason football bowl games, particularly the Orange, Sugar, Fiesta, and Rose Bowl games associated with the Bowl Championship Series. When Notre Dame plays in one of these games, since it does not belong to any conference, the school retains the entire payoff plus any subsidiary income generated. When a school from a Bowl Championship Series conference plays, it has to share its payoff with the other members of the conference. Most conferences today allow the participating school an expense budget in the neighborhood of $1.2 to $1.6 million and then divide the balance of the $8 to $12 million payoff to the participant in the Orange, Sugar, Fiesta, or Rose Bowl among the conference schools. The expense budget provides for team, band, cheerleader squad, top administrators, boosters, local politicians, and invited guests travel to and from the bowl as well as generous per diem and entertainment expenses. For instance, back in January 1996 the Pac-10 allocated $902,000 to crosstown USC to participate in the Rose Bowl. On this generous sum, the Trojans housed and fed about 150 players, coaches, trainers, equipment personnel, and others for about two weeks (school was out of session); bought Rose Bowl watches and rings for them; housed and fed the Trojan band for a week; shuttled everybody about for various bowl functions and practices; dealt with the cost of selling some 41,000 Rose Bowl tickets and bought a few extras for VIPs as well as for the players to give to their families or whomever; and threw elaborate parties for alumni and financial supporters.

The expense budget always provides ample perquisites for those associated with the program and helps to set a basis for deepening the athletic department's endowment. Often, the "expense" budget is purposefully inflated to provide a bonus to the participating school. Other times, the idiosyncrasies of bowl management actually leave the school at a financial disadvantage for participating in the game. Consider, for instance, the case of the University of Nebraska and the Big 12 Conference in January 1997.

The Big 12 held its first conference championship game in December 1996. The game between the favored Nebraska Cornhuskers and the Texas Longhorns was certainly a financial bonanza for the conference, generating about $7.5 million in revenue. The Longhorns unexpectedly beat the Cornhuskers, so Nebraska went to the Orange Bowl, the second-ranked bowl game in January 1997, while Texas went to the "national championship" game at the Sugar Bowl. The Orange Bowl, however, required that each participating school purchase and resell 15,000 tickets at an average price of $80 each. The Cornhuskers fans already had spent money traveling to the St. Louis Trans World Dome for the Big 12 Championship and were disappointed that the team was no longer playing for the national championship. Further, it was estimated that some 10,000 Nebraska fans had purchased nonrefundable packages to the Sugar Bowl in New Orleans. The Orange Bowl in Miami was a tough sell, so tough that the university only sold 3,600 of the 15,000 tickets, taking a loss on the required seat sale of $912,000. They did receive $1.5 million in expense money for the Orange Bowl, but 60 percent of that was eaten up by the ticket deficit alone. Thus, other members of the Big 12 received $600,000 apiece from the Cornhuskers' appearance in the Orange Bowl, but the Cornhuskers, it seems, may have lost money.

Similarly, Michigan State seems to have generated some red ink by participating in the 1997–98 Aloha Bowl in Honolulu. They received a guarantee of $750,000, but the school chartered a plane to Hawaii for 97 players, 85 band members, the coaches and their families, and administrators and trustees which alone cost $300,000. Add to this the healthy per diem expense for this entourage and the school was $150,000 out of pocket. John Lewandowski, Michigan State's sports information director, claimed that the short-run cash drain would be more than made up for by the favorable publicity the school received: ". . . In terms of rebuilding our program, you can't assess the value of being in a bowl game just by the bottom line. It's a way to keep up our recruiting. It's great exposure for the program. There's no better marketing tool."[53] If any prospective students were among the few who were watching the Aloha Bowl on television, one wonders whether they might rather go to the University of Washington, which demolished Michigan State 51–23 in the game. Of course, Lewandowski and his bosses (and families) enjoyed an all-expenses-paid week in Hawaii, and nobody doubts that the bowl trip was worth it to these decision makers.

In the case of the Big East conference, the charade of the bowl "expense" allowance is magnified beyond all credibility as the $3.5 million expense allotment to Virginia Tech in 1995 makes manifest. In general, it appears that the expense category is a rather transparent subterfuge for providing a financial incentive to the school, or at least the school's top academic and athletic administrators as well as its benefactors, to perform at a top competitive level.

Bookkeeping legerdemain notwithstanding, the practices of conference revenue sharing are substantial and do support at least two worthy objectives of the athletic programs. First, revenue sharing guarantees a certain minimal revenue stream each year to allow for more even expenditures and more accurate budgeting. The Big Ten Conference, for instance, has contracts for appearances with five different bowl games and the possibility of additional invitations that guarantee a certain annual income flow. Second, revenue sharing supports competitive balance within conferences. Although most big-time conferences tend to have perennially dominant teams, this imbalance would presumably be more acute without revenue sharing. As conference revenue sharing has tended to become more nearly equal since the mid-1980s, there has been a modest, attendant equalization of win percentages of teams within most big-time conferences.[54]

Many, of course, would like to see the financial incentive to win entirely eradicated from college sports. Winning teams, however, benefit from larger sponsorship revenues, more largesse from the sneaker companies, greater ticket and concessions sales, and usually higher booster contributions. Coaches, athletic directors, and school administrators stand to gain financially as well as in perquisites if their team wins. The importance of these revenue sources, financial incentives, and centrifugal tendencies within the NCAA . . . makes it unlikely that further revenue equalization will occur.

REFERENCES

24. Cited in Jim Naughton, "Debate Over the Championship Game in Football Reflects Larger Tensions in College Sports," Chronicle of Higher Education, Sept. 19, 1997.
25. Id.
39. Mike McGraw, Steven Rock, and Karen Dillon, "Revenues Dominate College Sports," Kansas City Star, Oct. 5, 1997, p. 3.
46. Quoted in New York Times, April 1, 1990, p. S10.
47. Quoted in New York Times, June 14, 1990, p. D27.
53. Richard Sandomir, "Big Bowl Payouts Don't Always Offset Teams' Expenses," New York Times, Dec. 30, 1997.
54. R. Fort & J. Quirk, "Introducing a Competitive Environment into Professional Sports," in Wallace Hendricks, ed., Advances in the Economics of Sport, vol. 2, Greenwich, Connecticut: JAI Press, 1997.

2002–03 REVENUE DISTRIBUTION PLAN

NCAA

1. ACADEMIC ENHANCEMENT FUND

A total of $16.78 million is allocated for enhancement of academic-support programs for student-athletes at Division I institutions. A payment of approximately $51,000 is sent in late June to each Division I institution. There are no specific guidelines for the use of these academic-enhancement moneys, other than the funds may not be used for scholarships for fifth-year student-athletes who have exhausted eligibility, for summer school tuition, or for the purchase of course books. Institutions can utilize the funds for new or existing student-athlete academic programs and services. For research purposes only, institutions report on how the funds were used to enhance their academic programs and services for student-athletes. Among the common uses are tutorial services, equipment (e.g., computer), supplies, and additional personnel.

2. SPECIAL ASSISTANCE FUND FOR STUDENT-ATHLETES

A total of $10,425,000 is sent to conference offices in late July to assist student-athletes in Division I with special financial needs. The guiding principles of the fund are to meet the student-athletes' needs of an emergency or essential nature for which financial assistance otherwise is not available. *[See Table 9 for examples of eligibility.]* Conference interpretations not addressed by the Executive Committee should stay within this intended purpose.

The following student-athletes are eligible to apply for funds:

1. Pell-eligible student-athletes, including student-athletes who have exhausted their athletics eligibility or no longer are able to participate because of medical reasons.

TABLE 9.

Special Assistance Fund Eligible Student-Athletes Chart	
Aid and need status	*Eligible for fund including $500 clothing*
Countable aid and Pell-eligible.	Yes
Countable aid, not eligible for Pell, and demonstrates need.	Yes
Countable aid, not eligible for Pell, and no demonstrated need.	No
No countable aid and Pell-eligible.	Yes
Countable aid, Pell-eligible, and exhausted eligibility or no longer able to compete due to medical reasons.	Yes
No countable aid, Pell-eligible, and exhausted eligibility or no longer able to compete due to medical reasons.	Yes
No countable aid, not eligible for Pell, and demonstrates need.	No
Nonqualifiers in their initial year of residence.	No

Source: NCAA.

2. Student-athletes who are receiving countable aid and who have demonstrated financial need, including student-athletes who have exhausted their athletics eligibility or no longer are able to participate because of medical reasons.

    a. Demonstrated financial need is defined as the cost of attendance minus expected family contribution prior to any athletics related aid or other aid being awarded.

    b. Domestic student-athletes will have demonstrated financial need if they qualify for a Pell Grant or have demonstrated financial need determined annually by the institution's financial aid department using the federal methodology or the needs analysis methodology used to award institutional need-based funds to all students.

    c. Demonstrated financial need for foreign student-athletes must be determined and certified annually in writing by the official foreign student entity of the institution outside of the department of athletics.

The following student-athletes are not eligible to apply for the funds:

1. Student-athletes (domestic or foreign) who receive countable aid (i.e., aid that counts against team limits) and are not Pell-eligible and do not demonstrate financial need.
2. Student-athletes (domestic or foreign) who do not receive any countable aid (i.e., aid that counts against team limits) and are not Pell-eligible.
3. Nonqualifiers in their initial year of residence.

A student-athlete must qualify for the fund on an annual basis.

The following are permissible uses of the fund:

1. Cost of clothing, travel from campus to home and other essential expenses (not entertainment) up to $500.
2. Cost of expendable academic course supplies (e.g., notebook and pens) and rental of nonexpendable supplies (e.g., computer equipment and cameras) that are required for all students enrolled in the course.
3. Medical and dental costs not covered by another insurance (e.g., premiums for optional medical insurance, hearing aids, vision therapy, and off-campus psychological counseling).
4. Costs associated with student-athlete or family emergencies.

The following are restrictions on the use of the funds:

1. Financing any portion of an institutional grant-in-aid that could have been awarded to the student-athlete is prohibited.
2. Entertainment expenses for student-athletes are not permissible.
3. The purchase of disability, illness, or injury insurance to protect the loss of potential future professional sports earnings is not permissible.
4. The funds may not be used for administrative purposes (conferences may not charge an administrative fee nor may salary or staff expenses for administration of the funds [be] paid from these moneys). [sic]

The responsibility for oversight and administration of the fund, including interpretations, rests solely with the conferences. The guiding principles of the fund are to meet the student-athletes' needs of an emergency or essential nature for which financial assistance otherwise is not available. Conference interpretations not addressed by the Division I Management Council should stay within this intended purpose.

A conference may accumulate not more than the total allocation received over the previous two years. The conference will not receive any additional dollars if it has exceeded the two-year cap amount.

Independent institutions' funds have [been] assigned to a conference office for administrative purposes. . .

Conferences annually will be required to report to the NCAA national office the number of Special Assistance Fund recipients by sport, purposes for which the moneys were used, and the specific amounts for each purpose.

3. CONFERENCE GRANTS

A total of $5.8 million is allocated for grants to Division I men's and women's basketball-playing conferences. Grants of approximately $187,000 will be made to each Division I conference that employs a full-time administrator and that [is] eligible for automatic qualification into the Division I men's and women's basketball championships, regardless of whether the conference is granted automatic qualification.

These grant funds must be used to maintain, enhance, or implement programs and services in each of the following areas:

a. Improvement of men's and women's basketball officiating.
b. Enhancement of conference compliance and enforcement programs.
c. Heightening the awareness of athletics staffs and student-athletes to programs associated with drug use, and assisting coaches, athletics administrators, and student-athletes in this regard.
d. Enhancement of opportunities — employment, professional development, career advancement, and leadership/management training — in intercollegiate athletics for ethnic minorities.
e. Enhancement of opportunities — employment, professional development, career advancement, and leadership/management training — in intercollegiate athletics for women.
f. Development of conference gambling education programs.

A conference may determine the specific amount it wishes to allocate to these six areas, but it must spend at least some portion of its grant in all six.

4. BROAD-BASED DISTRIBUTION

The broad-based distribution is made to all Division I institutions on the basis of the number of varsity sports sponsored (weighted one-third, totaling $32.5 million) and the number of athletics grants-in-aid awarded (weighted two-thirds, totaling $65.0 million).

The sports-sponsorship payment is sent to institutions in mid-August; the grants-in-aid payment is sent in late August. If a conference so desires, the moneys may be sent to the conference office (rather than to individual institutions) upon the unanimous approval and authorization of the chief executive officer of each institution in that conference. . . .

The annual distribution is based on sports-sponsorship and grants-in-aid data from the preceding academic year (e.g., the 2002–03 distribution is based on 2001–02 data). The grants-in-aid distribution is based on previously submitted squad lists, and the number of athletics grants-in-aid is calculated from those lists.

The NCAA Committee on Infractions may consider withholding all or a portion of an institution's share of the broad-based distribution moneys as a penalty in infractions cases.

a. **Sports-sponsorship fund.** An institution receives a unit for each sport sponsored beginning with the 14th sport (the minimum requirement for Division I membership). Only sports in which the NCAA conducts championships competition (which meet the minimum contests and participants requirements of Bylaw 20.9.3.3) and emerging sports for women are counted. In the 2001–02 distribution, for sports sponsored beginning with the 14th, an institution received approximately $13,827 per sport (i.e., an institution sponsoring 16 total sports received $41,482; an institution sponsoring 24 sports received $152,102). *[Even though the association does not conduct a Division I-A football championship, that sport and athletics grants awarded in it will be counted in the broad-based distribution.]*
b. **Grants-in-aid fund.** The grants-in-aid component is based on the number of athletics grants awarded by each institution (based on full-time equivalencies), beginning with one grant and

progressing in value in increments of 50. Grants awarded above 150 are valued at the same amount. The value of each basis point in the 2001–02 distribution was $144.05. *[See Table 10 for grant values.]*

As examples, an institution that awarded 82.77 grants-in-aid received a check for $16,644; an institution awarding 165.74 grants-in-aids received $138,979, and an institution awarding 245.42 received $368,538.

As with sports sponsorship, athletics grants are counted only in sports in which the NCAA conducts championships competition, emerging sports for women and Division I-A football. However, sports that do not meet the minimum contests and participants requirements of Bylaw 20.9.3.3 are included in the grants-in-aid component. Institutions also receive credit in the grants-in-aid component for grants awarded to fifth-year student-athletes who have exhausted eligibility and for students who, for medical reasons, do not count on the squad list but are receiving aid. Credit is not given for Proposition 48 student-athletes.

5. BASKETBALL FUND

The basketball fund provides for moneys to be distributed to Division I conferences based on their performance in the Division I Men's Basketball Championship over a six-year rolling period (for the period 1997–2002 for the 2002–03 distribution). Independent institutions receive a full unit share based on its tournament participation over the same rolling six-year period. The basketball fund payments are sent to conferences and independent institutions in mid-April each year.

One unit is awarded to each institution participating in each game, except the championship game. In 2001–02, each basketball unit was worth approximately $100,671 for a total distribution of $75 million.

In 2002–03 each basketball unit will be worth approximately $130,697 for a total distribution of $97.5 million.

For the purpose of distributing the basketball fund, a conference is defined as one that comprises at least six member institutions that have been classified in Division I for the eight preceding

TABLE 10.

GRANTS-IN-AID FUND VALUES		
No. of grants	*Valuation points*	*Grant value*
1–50	1 point each × $144.05	$144.05
51–100	2 points each × $144.05	$288.10
101–150	10 points each × $144.05	$1,440.50
151 and above	20 points each × $144.05	$2,881.00

academic years. If a conference falls below the six-member requirement, the basketball fund moneys are retained by the conference for a one-year period only.

The following policies also apply when a conference's membership changes or realignment occurs:

a. If an institution leaves a conference and realigns with another and its original conference remains in operation, the units it earned remain with the conference that it left.

. . . .

No conference will lose all of its units if it is represented in the tournament by an institution that later is declared ineligible. In this situation, the number of units in the basketball pool would be reduced to one. [By way of example, assume that Conference A is represented in the tournament by only one institution (the automatic qualifier), and that it advances to the Final Four, thereby earning five units. If the institution subsequently is declared ineligible, the number of units will be reduced to one. In another scenario, assume that the conference is represented by two teams (one automatic qualifier and an at-large team), and one of the teams subsequently is declared ineligible. Its units will be completely vacated; the units earned by the other team will be unaffected.] *[The preceding bracketed material is from the original text.]*

Conferences are urged, but not required, to distribute moneys from the basketball fund equally among all their member institutions.

7. DIVISION II ENHANCEMENT FUND

A total of $3.9 million is distributed among Division II members in late May, according to a formula developed by the Division II Championships Committee.

One-third of this fund is divided evenly among all Division II members, excluding those institutions that chose to compete in one or more NAIA team championship.

One-third of the fund is distributed to conference offices and independent institutions based upon their participation in the Division II Men's and Women's Basketball Championship in accordance with the same procedures that have been implemented for the Division I basketball fund (i.e., using a rolling six-year average).

One-third of the fund is distributed to conference offices based on the number of championships the conference sponsors.

In order to receive moneys from the enhancement fund, an institution must be active and eligible for championships competition and have declared its intention to participate in all NCAA championships competition in sports in which both NCAA and NAIA championships are conducted. Exception may be granted in extenuating circumstances.

AN ECONOMIC ANALYSIS OF CARTEL BEHAVIOR WITHIN THE NCAA

Timothy D. DeSchriver and David K. Stotlar

FINANCIAL DISBURSEMENT POLICIES

To build a model estimating the expected costs and benefits of committing an NCAA rules violation with respect to NCAA tournament revenues, the manner in which these revenues were disbursed must be discussed. Prior to 1991, the NCAA distributed payouts directly to tournament participants based on playing success. However, most conferences had revenue-sharing plans that distributed the payouts to all conference members. In this section, the researchers reviewed the conference policies regarding revenue sharing for teams in six conferences as well as the manner in which these conferences distributed revenues to teams that were on NCAA probation. . . .

There was no standard procedure that conferences followed in disbursing revenues. Discussion will center on the policies of six conferences: the Atlantic Coast Conference (ACC), the Big East, the Big 10, the Big 8, the Southeastern Conference (SEC), and the Pacific 10. The amount of revenue distributed through these plans was quite large; in 1990, over $35 million was disbursed to the 64 qualifying teams. *[In 2003, $97.5 million was distributed to the various conferences.]*

Since 1985, the NCAA basketball tournament has had a 64-team single elimination format with competition occurring on three successive weekends in March and April. *[The tournament expanded to 65 teams in 2002.]* There have been six rounds with two rounds played per weekend. As a team advanced further in the tournament, the amount of revenue it received increased. For example, all 64 teams that qualified in 1989 received a minimum of $250,200. However, a team that advanced to the Final Four received $1,251,000. This policy was altered in 1991 with the signing of a new television contract between the NCAA and CBS.

The contract, which gave CBS the exclusive right to televise the 1991 through 1997 tournaments, has resulted in over $1 billion for the NCAA and its members. After the signing of the television contract, the NCAA implemented a new revenue disbursement plan that decreased the importance of individual team success in the tournament. First, a portion of the revenues has been disbursed to conferences, not qualifiers, as was the policy before 1991. Second, there have been three basic criteria for revenue distribution to the conferences and institutions. The first criteria has been the success of the conference in the tournament during the previous 6 years; over $40 million was distributed to conferences through this process in 1995. However, the amount of these revenues disbursed to individual institutions was determined by the conferences. Another $40 million was disbursed to institutions based on the number of sports in which they competed and the number of athletes that received scholarships. Last, $12 million was given to universities to finance academic support programs for student-athletes.

Revenue disbursements prior to the 1991 contract differed substantially from the new plan and varied considerably among conferences. Of all the conferences, the ACC allowed its members to retain the highest percentage of their payout. They retained the full amount of revenue obtained by competing in the first round and 70% of the additional revenues gained after the first round. The remaining 30% of the post-first round dollars was split among all eight conference members. Of the six conferences studied, ACC teams had the greatest financial incentive to be successful in the tournament.

The Big East and Big 10 allowed qualifiers to retain 50% of the revenues generated by participation in the tournament. The other 50% was split equally among all conference members. Members of the Pacific 10 and the Big 8 kept the lowest percentage of their payout. These conferences pooled all revenues generated by member teams and divided them equally among all conference members. Therefore, in 1988 when the University of Arizona, a Pacific 10 member, advanced to the Final Four, it received the same amount of tournament revenue as the University of Oregon, which did not qualify for the tournament. This same policy was in effect for the SEC and the Big 8. The only variation was that the SEC, which had 10 members throughout the 1980s, divided the revenues into 11 equal shares. Each school received one share, and the conference headquarters also retained one share to pay for administrative costs.

The policies for some conferences have been altered because of the new NCAA disbursement policy effective in 1991. However, the policies of the Pacific 10, the Big 8, and the SEC have remained the same. The total tournament revenue has been divided equally among the conference members. However, the SEC has added two new schools: the University of South Carolina and the University of Arkansas. They have divided the revenues into 13 shares, with the conference office retaining one share.

The Big East has initiated a new policy since 1991. A Big East team has received $120,000 for every round in which [it has] competed. A team that advances to the championship game has played six games and receives $720,000 from the conference. The conference has used the money disbursed from the NCAA to make these payouts. In addition, after disbursing this money to members that qualify for the tournament, the remainder of the NCAA disbursement has been divided equally among the 10 conference members. This plan has maintained the incentive for Big East teams to qualify and advance deep into the tournament.

The Big 10 and the ACC have developed new policies since the inception of the CBS contract, patterning their plans on the Pacific 10's policies. The NCAA's disbursement to the Big 10 and the ACC has been divided equally among all conference members. For conferences with this policy it has appeared that the incentive has been to get the largest possible number of teams in the tournament per year, since one of the NCAA disbursement criteria has been the number of tournament qualifiers over the past 6 years.

Another important feature of the disbursement of tournament revenue has been the different conference policies regarding distribution to teams on NCAA probation. A team can be placed on probation for violating any of the NCAA rules pertaining to collegiate athletic competition. . . . Examples of penalties levied against teams have included probation, a ban on postseason competition, limitation of television appearances, and suspension. An important question that must be asked is, Can a team barred from competing in the postseason or on television share in the revenues generated from these sources? For example, Syracuse University was placed on NCAA probation and banned from participating in the 1993 basketball tournament. The obvious financial effect on Syracuse was that it did not have an opportunity to earn the $120,000 per round that the Big East disburses to tournament participants. However, would Syracuse be permitted to share in the revenues that the conference distributes to all members regardless of tournament success? Conferences differ in how they handle such cases.

The Big 8 stated that a team that has been penalized by the NCAA was not permitted to share in revenues generated from competition for which the team has been barred. For example, if a Big 8 team was barred from competing in the NCAA tournament, that team would not share in Big 8 tournament revenues. However, the penalized team was permitted to share in all other disbursements, such as NCAA tournament and television revenues.

SEC teams found in violation of NCAA regulations have been punished more severely than violators in any of the other five conferences. The conference has not allowed a team on probation to share in any revenues generated by that sport. Thus, if the University of Tennessee basketball team was not permitted to compete in the postseason tournament, it did not share in the revenues generated from this source or any television contracts that cover basketball. Tennessee would have been permitted to share in revenues generated from all other sports, primarily bowl and football television revenue.

The ACC policy regarding the revenue sharing privileges of its teams varies depending on the seriousness of the violations. When a team has been placed on probation by the NCAA, the member institutions have decided by majority vote whether the team was allowed to share in revenues. . . . In general, teams on probation for serious rules violations have not been permitted to share in revenues for that sport. However, the schools have been permitted to share in revenues from other sports.

The Big East and Big 10 policies regarding violators have been the most lenient. In these conferences, violators have been permitted to maintain their full share of revenues. So, to answer our earlier question — yes, Syracuse *would* receive its full share of the NCAA basketball tournament disbursement. Syracuse would also receive its full share from all other revenue sources. However, there is still an expected loss in revenue for Syracuse. As stated earlier, the Big East pays its members $120,000 for every round they play in the tournament. Syracuse would have missed the opportunity to earn this revenue.

The Pacific 10 policy regarding teams found in violation has not been strictly defined. In general, the Pacific 10 has handled this situation on a case-by-case basis . . . . [but] teams on probation usually have been permitted to remain in the revenue-sharing plan.

DISCUSSION QUESTIONS

1. Explain the dichotomy that formed between different universities, in terms of their membership, during the post–World War I era. How does this relate to intercollegiate athletics? How did this lead to the rise of big-time teams?

2. How does the NCAA act as a cartel? Is the cartel effective?

3. Describe each facet of a successful cartel and how it applies to the NCAA.

4. Compare and contrast the motivations driving the NCAA versus those driving university-firms.

5. Compare and contrast those NCAA institutions that are typical versus those that profit from their athletic programs.

6. Describe how the profits are divided among teams that compete in the NCAA Men's Basketball Tournament.

7. According to Noll, how do schools benefit, or not benefit, from having large athletic programs (namely large football and men's basketball programs)? Do you agree?

8. According to Noll, what are some plausible reforms the NCAA might consider implementing? Do you have any other suggestions that might help reform the NCAA?

9. What is the rationale for casting college football programs as profit maximizers? Do you agree with this characterization?

10. What reason did the NCAA give to justify its continued control over the rights to football telecasts? Was this argument logical?

11. Discuss the outcome of *NCAA v. Regents of the Univ. of Oklahoma and University of Georgia Athletic Association* and its impact on intercollegiate athletics.

12. Describe the significance of Notre Dame's leaving the CFA to sign its own TV contract with NBC.

13. How did the NCAA modify its revenue distribution practices in order to place less emphasis on winning in men's basketball? Did it accomplish its goal?

14. Although the NCAA does not publicize a detailed breakdown of revenue distribution among athletic programs, how can one identify the inequality in the way the revenues are distributed?

15. Why do conferences distribute revenues in a relatively equal fashion? Do you agree with this type of distribution?

CHAPTER 16

MEMBER INSTITUTIONS

INTRODUCTION

The vast majority of the over 1,000 NCAA member institutions find sports to be a money-losing endeavor. These losses are expected at each of the nearly 300 Division II and over 400 Division III member institutions, where the athletic department is viewed as an integral part of the university, as indicated by the Division II and Division III philosophy statements. The financial expectations for the members of Division I are typically quite different, with intercollegiate athletics viewed as a potential money-maker. However, as indicated by the NCAA's most recent financial survey, published in 2001, the results are usually the same. Only 9 of the 124 members of Division I-AA and 6 of the 84 members of Division I-AAA operated profitable athletic departments in 2001, excluding institutional support. The average I-AA institution lost $3.4 million and the average I-AAA member lost $2.8 million that year. Even the few schools that did profit did so only marginally, with average operating surpluses of $520,000 in Division I-AA and $1.08 million in Division I-AAA.

The financial expectations are much greater for the 117 members of the big-time world of college sports that is NCAA Division I-A. Forty universities — most of whom were assuredly members of the Big Six conferences — had profitable athletic programs, and averaged $5.26 million net revenues over expenses in 2001, excluding institutional support. The rest of the schools in Division I-A lost money, at an average of $3.8 million per school, excluding institutional support. Overall, the average member of NCAA Division I-A lost $600,000 in 2001. A closer look behind these numbers is warranted.

The average institution in Divisions I-A and I-AA fields 19 teams, and 16 teams in Division I-AAA, where there are no football teams. However, the only sports that generate net revenues over expenses at almost all of these schools are football and men's basketball, with a handful of schools also able to run profitable programs in regionally popular sports such as ice hockey, women's basketball, and wrestling. All of the other sports lose money. Thus, the football and men's basketball programs must generate significant net revenues in order for the entire athletic program to operate profitably. Despite generating far less revenues than football programs, men's basketball programs have a greater likelihood of profitability than football programs in both Division I-A and I-AA. Seventy-five Division I-A men's basketball programs made money in 2001, with an average profit of $2.71 million. Thirty-five teams lost money, with an average loss of $370,000. Another four broke even. Overall, the average Division I-A men's basketball program earned revenues of $3.67 million against expenses of $1.95 million, and thus profited $1.72 million in 2001.

Nearly 70% of Division I-AA men's basketball programs lost money in 2001, with an average loss of $300,000 at these 77 institutions. Twenty-nine other Division I-AA men's basketball programs made money, with an average profit of $430,000. Seven schools broke even. Overall, the average Division I-AA men's basketball team lost $138,000. In Division I-AAA, 48 schools had an average loss of $340,000 in 2001, while 30 teams made an average of $390,000. Eight schools broke even. In total, the average I-AAA basketball program lost $52,000 in 2001.

As noted in the previous chapter, big-time college football is a potentially lucrative business. In 2001, nearly 70% of Division I-A institutions realized this potential, earning an average profit of $7.4 million. It is safe to say that many of these 79 institutions were among the 62 members of the Big Six conferences. Conversely, 32 Division I-A football programs lost money, with an average deficit of $1.3 million. Overall, the average Division I-A football team profited by $4.75 million in 2001. The financial story is much different in the off-Broadway world of Division I-AA football, where only 22 football programs were profitable in 2001, with an average gain of $280,000. Another 10 schools managed to break even. However, 81 Division I-AA football programs lost money, with an average deficit of $780,000. Overall, the average football program in Division I-AA lost $514,000 in 2001.

Across all three levels of Division I athletics, there are several items that are worth noting. First, average revenues and average expenses are both increasing, with expenses growing faster than revenues. Second, there is a continually increasing separation between the "haves" and "have-nots" of college sports. The schools that are making money are making more of it, and those that are losing money are losing more of it. Finally, approximately 55 to 65 of the 325 Division I institutions are profitable in any given year. The remainder lose money.

Although Division I-A, I-AA, and I-AAA institutions compete against each other for NCAA championships in all sports other than football, it is this one-sport distinction that marks the difference between these levels of competition. In reality, Division I-A occupies an entirely different financial strata than the others, with the average institution having approximately 4 to 5 times the amount of both revenues and expenses. A brief discussion of the sources of revenues and operating expenses in college sports sheds additional light on these differences. Ticket sales are the single largest source of revenue for Division I-A institutions, with the average school collecting $6.5 million in 2001. This is approximately 15 times the amount earned in I-AA and I-AAA. Fundraising is the second most important revenue source, with the average I-A member bringing in $4.6 million in 2001, or approximately 9 times the amount of the other subdivisions. The average athletic department in Division I-A receives $2.5 million per year from the institution despite the fact that most are supposed to be auxiliary enterprises that are financially self-supporting. While the athletic departments in Divisions I-AA and I-AAA receive slightly less institutional support (approximately $2.3 million in 2001), it constitutes over 40% of the total revenues at these schools. When looking at the overall profits or losses at any one NCAA member, it is appropriate to exclude institutional support from the revenue equation. Although it does represent the transfer of administrative funds to the athletic department from the institution, it does not represent monies that are otherwise earned by the institution because of the athletic department. Similarly, student activity fees provide Division I-A athletic departments with slightly more revenue than in I-AA or I-AAA ($1.4 million versus $1.1 million), but constitute approximately 20% of the revenues of the latter groups. Thus, the average Division I-AA and I-AAA schools receive over 60% of their revenue from their institutions and students, and are hardly self-sufficient. Table 1 shows net operating results excluding instituional support.

TABLE 1.

NET OPERATING RESULTS	
	2001 excluding institutional support (in thousands of dollars)
Division I-A	
Total revenues	22,600
Total expenses	23,200
Profit (deficit)	(600)
Division I-AA	
Total revenues	3,400
Total expenses	6,800
Profit (deficit)	(3,400)
Division I-AAA	
Total revenues	2,700
Total expenses	5,500
Profit (deficit)	(2,800)
Division II — with football	
Total revenues	1,000
Total expenses	2,300
Profit (deficit)	(1,300)
Division II — w/o football	
Total revenues	500
Total expenses	1,600
Profit (deficit)	(1,100)

Note: Total expenses do not include debt service or capital expenditures.
Source: Daniel Fulks, NCAA.

The various NCAA and conference distributions discussed in the previous chapter bring in much more revenue in Division I-A ($2.2 million in 2001) than in Divisions I-AA and I-AAA ($200,000 to $300,000), as does postseason compensation from participation in bowl games and tournaments ($905,000 versus $10,000 to $20,000). Again, this is largely due to the dominance of the six power conferences. Finally, the average Division I-A school earns much more from radio and television ($1.8 million in 2001), signage and sponsorships ($1.1 million), and miscellaneous items including licensing ($2 million) than does the average school in I-AA and I-AAA (approximately $225,000 for all of these items combined). Overall, Division I-A schools averaged revenues of $25.2 million in 2001 (or $22.7 million when excluding institutional support), while Division I-AA and I-AAA institutions averaged $5.4 million and $5.1 million, respectively (or $3.2 million and $2.7 million when excluding institutional support).

On the expense side of the ledger, the single greatest cost at all three levels of Division I is staff salaries and benefits ($7.2 million in I-A, $2.4 million in I-AA, and $1.9 million in I-AAA). The second largest expense at all three levels is funding for athletic scholarships, on which the average Division I-A school spent $3.9 million and the average I-AA and I-AAA school spent approximately half of that amount. Other average operating expenses which differed significantly between Division I-A and Divisions I-AA and I-AAA include team travel ($1.8 million versus $500,000 to $600,000); guarantees and options to visiting teams ($1 million versus $60,000); equipment, uniforms, and supplies ($1 million versus $300,000); and recruiting ($530,000 versus $150,000). In addition to these differences in operating expenses, Division I-A institutions spend more on capital expenditures ($1.5 million) and debt service ($950,000) than Division I-AA or I-AAA institutions ($100,000 to $200,000 combined). This reflects the recent and still ongoing $4 billion spending spree on athletic facilities, an increase of nearly 260% since 1993. Overall, Division I-A athletic departments averaged costs of $25.5 million in 2001, while the average costs were $6.8 million in Division I-AA and $5.8 million in I-AAA.

While the above analysis is certainly important, it must nonetheless be taken with a requisite grain of salt. This is necessary because there is a lack of standard accounting techniques across NCAA institutions, with related party transactions involving other departments within the university used prevalently and some revenues and costs improperly allocated across sports within the athletic department.

The aforementioned topics are discussed in the excerpt from Sperber's *Beer and Circus: How Big-Time College Sports Is Crippling Undergraduate Education* and Goff's "Effects of University Athletics on the University: A Review and Extension of Empirical Assessment," as well as in Litan, Orszag, and Orszag's "The Empirical Effects of Collegiate Athletics: An Interim Report." Former University of Michigan president James Duderstadt addresses these topics from both a macro and micro perspective, with a focus on Michigan's athletic department in *Intercollegiate Athletics and the American Unversity: A university president's perspective.* The review of the business of sports at the University of Michigan, one of the powerhouses of the industry and a member of the Big Ten conference, continues with a look at the athletic department's internal budget documents for 2003–2004.

As previously noted, both licensing and fundraising have become important revenue sources in college sports. The $2.5 billion college licensing industry is elaborated upon in Lattinville's "Logo Cops: The Law and Business of Collegiate Licensing." A second selection from Sperber's *Beer and Circus* and Stier and Schneider's "how-to" article, "Fundraising: An Essential Competency for the Sport Manager in the 21st Century" provide a solid background on this topic.

The economics of college sports often results in institutions making strategic decisions to change either their goals or the breadth and depth of their athletic programs. These decisions have broad consequences. The addition or subtraction of a team from an institution's athletic offerings is usually spurred by programmatic, gender equity, and/or financial considerations. In the past decade, a number of institutions in pursuit of increased media attention and the big-money potential of college sports have upgraded their athletic departments to a higher NCAA division. The article by Wahl and Dohrmann entitled "Welcome to the Big Time" investigates this often foolish endeavor.

As per the Internal Revenue Code, universities are non-profit entities that are generally tax-exempt. As a consequence, the revenues that university athletic departments receive are not taxed either, despite the profit-motive of Division I members. Another important consequence of this favorable tax treatment is that institutions that build or renovate athletic facilities are usually eligible for tax-exempt bonds to help fund these projects, and the lower interest rate allows them to maintain substantially lower debt service than if they were otherwise ineligible for this treatment. Finally, this not-for-profit status is quite favorable for alumni and boosters making contributions to the athletic department, as their donations are fully tax-deductible. When the donation is a prerequisite to the purchase of season tickets or luxury seating, it is still 80% tax-deductible. This makes donating to colleges and universities an even more attractive option for alumni and boosters, and allows athletic departments to generate substantial amounts of revenues from fundraising. The average member of Division I-A brought in $4.625 million in cash donations in 2001, while the average Division I-AA and I-AAA institutions collected $497,000 and $434,000, respectively. Collectively, the members of Division I received nearly $640 million in tax-free donations in 2001, most of which was tax-deductible for the donors. As this represents forsaken taxable income, it is fair to conclude that the federal government lost at least $100 million in 2001 in uncollected taxes — and thus implicitly subsidizes the college sports industry. The tax issues surrounding college athletics are further discussed in Musselman's "Recent Federal Income Tax Issues Regarding Professional and Amateur Sports."

BEER AND CIRCUS: HOW BIG-TIME COLLEGE SPORTS IS CRIPPLING UNDERGRADUATE EDUCATION

Murray Sperber

More than 110 schools play Division I-A football; however, unless they reside within the BCS fold, they remain at home during the bowl season or collect spare change in such marginal contests as the Motor City Bowl and the Las Vegas Bowl. In addition, although more than 300 schools play Division I basketball, the six BCS conferences hog the largest proportion of payout dollars from March Madness. According to a recent analysis of the finances of big-time college sports, the average annual revenue of the BCS conferences was $63 million, whereas the amount for the other twenty-three leagues in Division I averaged less than $3 million per year.

Those are the revenue totals in big-time intercollegiate athletics. But the expenses numbers are higher, resulting in the amazing fact that *most college sports programs lose money*. Most extraordinary of all, the losers include many schools in the BCS conferences, including those playing in the most lucrative bowl games and advancing deep into the final rounds of the NCAA basketball tournaments. In late 1999, the athletic director of the University of Michigan — a school with an always full 110,000-seat stadium and 20,000-seat basketball arena — acknowledged that "the Wolverines intercollegiate sports program . . . last year ran a deficit," more than $2 million dollars of red ink. If Big Blue loses money in college sports, what hope is there for smaller programs?

Historically, and contrary to popular myth, almost all colleges and universities have always lost money on their intercollegiate athletics programs. Moreover, athletic departments ran deficits long before the federal government's Title IX mandated equality for women's intercollegiate athletics, and male athletic directors seized upon their Title IX costs to excuse their overall money losses. Historically, the main causes of athletic department red ink were waste, mismanagement, and fraud, and this situation continues today.

Of course, these annual deficits preclude paying the players: journalists . . . have logic and ethics on their side when they demand that the athletes receive their fair "share" of the TV payouts

— except, after the athletic directors, coaches, and athletic department staff spend the revenue, nothing remains for the players. Before the athletes can obtain their share, the entire athletic department finance system must be overhauled. But the people who run intercollegiate athletics, and benefit so handsomely from the corrupt system in place, will not willingly overturn the red ink trough.

The NCAA, in its regular financial reports, provides an indication of the profit-and-loss situation in big-time college sports. The most recent edition revealed that a majority of Division I athletic departments lost money in the 1990s, running larger deficits at the end of the decade than at the beginning, even though their revenue increased every year. However, because of the accounting tricks used by almost all athletic departments, the NCAA reports are only partially accurate, and the actual annual deficit numbers are much higher than the NCAA and member schools admit publicly.

Some accounting experts multiply the NCAA's deficit numbers by a factor of three. They point out that almost all athletic departments routinely move many legitimate costs from their ledgers and place them on their universities' financial books. These items include the utilities, maintenance, and debt-servicing bills on their intercollegiate athletic facilities — multimillion-dollar annual expenses for most big-time programs. . . .

Athletic department deficits impact on host universities in many negative ways. Not only are millions of dollars siphoned from schools when athletic departments move expenditures onto university books, but more millions depart when schools cover the annual athletic department deficits. At the end of each fiscal year, universities "zero out" athletic department books; to do so they divert money from their General Operating Funds and other financial resources to cover the college sports losses. Money that could go to academic programs, student scholarships and loans, and many other educational purposes annually disappears down the athletic department financial hole.

The bottom line is clear: Big-time intercollegiate athletics financially hurts NCAA Division I schools more than it helps them. For every dollar that a few of these institutions acquire through college sports phenomena like the Flutie Factor, many more Division I members annually lose millions of dollars as a result of their athletic department deficits and other negative college sports factors. One inescapable conclusion appears: *College Sports MegaInc. is the most dysfunctional business in America.*

. . . .

The myth of college sports profitability not only masks the deficits of intercollegiate athletic programs, but it generates other negative financial consequences:

> The public hears about the millions that universities rake in from the NCAA basketball tournaments and bowl games, and people conclude that higher education doesn't need their tax dollars or private contributions. They believe that universities are doing great from their big-time college sports teams. . . . At Illinois, it couldn't be further from the truth, and that's also the situation at most other schools.
>
> — Howard Schein, professor at the University of Illinois, Urbana-Champaign

During the last two decades, legislative and taxpayer support for higher education has declined considerably. The role of big-time intercollegiate athletics in this decline is difficult to ascertain, but some observers believe that the never-ending college sports recruiting and academic scandals have made the public cynical about intercollegiate athletics, and stingy toward the universities that promote it. . . . Common sense suggests that the myth of college sports profitability is a factor, possibly an important one, in the decline of public support for higher education. . .

Not only is the public unaware of the financial reality of college sports, but it knows even less about the causes of this situation. The media trumpets the huge payouts from bowl games and the NCAA basketball tournaments, and the public sees the high dollar numbers, but rarely does the media go beyond the myths and explore the financial facts.

A discussion of the following myths and realities helps explain why College Sports MegaInc. is the most dysfunctional business in America. It also explains how and why the men and women who administer universities and supposedly control their schools' athletic departments are totally complicit in the deficit financing of College Sports MegaInc.

* * *

Myth: Schools make millions of dollars when their teams play in football bowl games.

Reality: Most universities lose money when their football teams appear in bowl games. In a typical case, the University of Wisconsin received $1.8 million for participating in the 1999 Rose Bowl, but racked up almost $2.1 million in expenses on this event, close to $300,000 of rose-colored ink. The Rose Bowl payout could have helped the UW athletic department balance its books — its announced deficit at the end of the 1998–99 fiscal year was $1.1 million — but its excessive spending on this trip turned potential profit into real loss. The cost of flying the football team, the coaches, and the team's support staff to and from Los Angeles, and housing and feeding them while there came to $831,400. In addition to this cost, like all schools going to bowl games, Wisconsin took along the families of the coaches, as well as babysitters (six) for the coaches' kids. Also a large number of other athletic department personnel and their spouses made the junket. Also on the "gravy plane" were members of the University of Wisconsin Board of Regents and spouses, school administrators and spouses, plus the so-called Faculty Board of Control of Intercollegiate Athletics and their spouses, and many hangers-on (termed "friends of the program") and their spouses. Then there was the marching band and cheerleaders, and not one but *three Bucky Badger mascots* — possibly in case the school-sponsored New Year's Eve celebration, costing $34,400, incapacitated one or two Buckys and the third one had to suit up on January 1.

The official Wisconsin traveling party numbered 832 people, including well over one hundred university officials and spouses. The Wisconsin group journeyed in the usual athletic department deluxe-class-for-all style, staying at a very expensive Beverly Hills hotel, wining and dining in an extravagant manner. After the UW athletic department paid all the bills from the trip, the expenses totaled $2,093,500. . . .

. . . .

In the amazing world of college sports finances, Wisconsin's losses were not an anomaly: most athletic departments lose money on their bowl game excursions, and often they incur greater losses than Wisconsin's because few payouts equal or top the $1.8 million the Badgers received from the Rose Bowl Corporation.

With bowl paydays so fat, why do athletic directors pass up these excellent opportunities to help balance their books? The answer is twofold: despite all the corporate jargon that ADs spout, their management style has never been lean and mean. Because Big-time U's always sop up the red ink at the end of the fiscal year, most ADs spend in an extravagant and wasteful manner and allow many of their employees, particularly their football and men's basketball coaches, to do the same.

The other reason ADs sanction lavish bowl trips is self-protection: long ago, they learned that by spending money on university officials and faculty boards of control, taking them and their spouses to bowl games and on other junkets (as well as providing them with free skyboxes or excellent seats to all home football and basketball games), athletic departments obtained insurance policies — they persuaded the people within the university who have direct oversight over inter-collegiate athletics to back it enthusiastically. The potential critics of the financial and other abuses of big-time college sports climb onto the gravy planes and become complicit in the wasting of large sums of money. As a result, these university officials rarely question the specific expenses or the general financial operations of their athletic departments, nor do they hesitate to cover the annual deficits.

Not only are most university officials intimidated by powerful ADs and coaches and fear dis-pleasing them, but, in the current era, many administrators seem to believe the NCAA and athletic department propaganda about the wonderful benefits that College Sports MegaInc. bestows upon the university. . .

Is this the total explanation? It accounts for athletic department behavior — ADs and coaches are merely doing what comes naturally — but beyond the obvious causes of administrative complicity in the deficit spending, a more complex reason for their official conduct exists. Many Big-time U offi-cials, knowing that their schools cannot provide the vast majority of undergraduates with meaning-ful educations, try to distract and please these consumers with ongoing entertainment in the form of big-time college sports. For all of its high expenses, an intercollegiate athletics program costs far less than a quality undergraduate education program. University officials deny employing this strategy, but their denials are less important than the current reality: many Big-time U's supply their students with an abundance of college sports events and accept the drinking culture that accompanies the fun and games; meanwhile, these schools offer their undergraduates few quality educational opportunities, reserving those for the honors students (usually a single-digit percentage of the student body).

An administrator of a Sunbelt university, when presented with this thesis, replied:

> There's certainly no plot or conspiracy by school officials on this. You have to remember that most universities are always in a money bind. We sure as hell can't get enough money out of our state leg-islature or anyone else to turn our undergraduate education program into one big honors college. But we need every undergraduate tuition dollar we can get . . . and we can swallow the million bucks a year that the athletic department costs us. . . . Maybe that's how it all happens. I can assure you that we never thought any of this out beforehand, nor did any other school.

He also mentioned, somewhat defensively:

> Yes, I've been to bowl games and the NCAA tourney with our teams, and I'm not going to apologize for enjoying those trips. I see them as rewards for me working hard on behalf of the athletic department. . . .

He concluded:

> I don't know how it all happened, how our athletic department never stops growing, and how this school always rates high on the "party school" lists in the college guides, but I'm not going to carry the can for it, and my president sure wouldn't. Anyway, he's mainly concerned with our research and graduate programs which have really improved under his leadership.

Finally, in an age of accepting personal responsibility, college presidents and administrators at beer-and-circus schools should assume some of the blame for the current situation. They make fre-quent pronouncements on "refocusing student life" and "curtailing drinking" on their campuses, but they sanction, promote, and sometimes even participate in the beer-and-circus culture out of which student sports fandom and partying come. Remarkably, they never acknowledge their hypocrisy, even when they tailgate with alums before and after college sports events.

In the 1960s, rebel students often accused university administrators of "selling out" undergraduate education to gain power and perks for themselves, and to keep their institutions running efficiently. Thirty-plus years later, the activities of university officials in charge of beer-and-circus schools add a new dimension to the term *selling out.*

Another illustration of presidential and administrative misconduct concerns their dealings with the NCAA. Deconstructing a popular myth about the March Madness money provides a way into this subject.

* * *

Myth: Thanks to the NCAA's billion-dollar TV contract for its Division I basketball tournaments, schools make millions when their teams participate in March Madness, and college officials put this money into academic programs.

Reality: the association distributes the tournament revenue through a complicated formula that sends most of it to the conferences of the participating schools. Because the BCS football conferences also form the big-time college basketball leagues and dominate the NCAA tourney, they receive the highest percentage of the money. As a result, when a school in a minor conference makes a brief appearance in the men's tourney — thirty-two of sixty-four teams lose in the first round — it receives a low-six-figure check.

On the other hand, if several teams from the same conference enter and reach the final rounds, they and their fellow conference members gain low-seven-figure payouts. With more than three hundred schools in NCAA Division I men's basketball, the minority who receive the million-dollar checks resemble lottery winners. But, like addicted gamblers, all three-hundred-plus schools spend big bucks to enter the Division I basketball season lottery, and most end up holding losing tickets. Athletic directors and coaches drive this process, and university presidents and administrators approve it.

But financial reality never deters fanatic lottery players, especially when they are playing with other people's — in this case, their school's — money. After the announcement of the recent NCAA/CBS television deal, a national newspaper predicted that the increased payout will prompt "a continued migration of schools from lower divisions into the NCAA's Division I to more fully share the wealth." Probably the migration will occur, but the NCAA wealth is a mirage. Economist Andrew Zimbalist states bluntly: the new "CBS contract will have precious little impact on the economics of college sports."[1] According to this expert, of the three-hundred-plus athletic departments in Division I basketball operating under the current multimillion-dollar CBS contract, a tiny percentage "generate black ink in any given year. The prudent bet is that college sports will be in the same financial mess or worse in 2003,"[2] when the new NCAA/CBS deal begins, and that the red ink will continue to flow for the length of the contract until 2013.

But, thanks to the media, the public only hears about the NCAA's fabulous deals with CBS, and it considers March Madness a financial bonanza for American higher education. The public also believes that the colleges and universities who belong to the NCAA run the association, and they use the TV money to help their academic missions. In reality, the NCAA is a large, autonomous bureaucracy acting primarily out of self-interest, and because almost all members lose money on their college sports programs, they rarely have excess revenue to put into academic programs.

Finally, the March Madness money is not an NCAA share-the-wealth plan with higher education, but trickle-down economics in a slow-drip phase. The bottom line for almost all NCAA members is simple: *Belonging to the NCAA costs much more money annually than they receive from the association.*

Every year, the largest financial drain on NCAA members results from the association's requirement that schools field a minimum number of teams to remain in good standing — for Division I, at least fourteen teams in seven sports. *[This requirement will rise to 16 teams in 2004.]* This is a compulsory stake in a very expensive poker game. The motive behind this rule is self-interest: NCAA executives, mainly former athletic directors and coaches, regard the NCAA as a trade association, in business to promote college sports; they are empire-builders, they want athletic programs to be as large as possible, and to employ as many athletic administrators and coaches as possible.

Because, throughout Division I, almost all of a school's fourteen teams lose money every year, the minimum team requirement locks athletic departments and universities into huge annual expenses. Within the context of American higher education, this NCAA rule is an anomaly — no other outside agency forces universities to spend money in this way. Only the NCAA, with its minimum team requirements, totally ignores the financial autonomy of colleges and universities. Currently, this situation occurs during a period of severe financial constraints within higher education, when many parts of the university are experiencing drastic cutbacks.

Ironically, the presidents and administrators who wield the sharpest financial axes at their schools, slashing undergraduate programs and services, are often the men and women on the gravy planes to NCAA events. When these administrators cut academic programs, and then underwrite ever-escalating athletic department costs, they weaken the educational fabric of their schools and increase the beer-and-circus aspects. Furthermore, in the last decade, not one of these officials asked the NCAA to consider changing its team minimum rules, allowing schools to spend less money on their college sports programs. This sends a signal to people inside and out of the university system that, at any Big-time Us, intercollegiate athletics comes before undergraduate education.

Beyond the NCAA minimum team requirements, a huge part of the stake in the association's poker game concerns facilities, not only stadiums and arenas but training structures and state-of-the-art equipment. For a school to remain in Division I-A, the NCAA requires it to have large stadiums and arenas, and to meet attendance levels. . . . In the 1990s, many athletic departments either upgraded their facilities or built new ones, often moving the expenses, including the debt-servicing, off their books and onto university ledgers. As always, athletic directors and coaches pressured presidents and administrators to approve the construction — whether the institution could afford the costs or not. Often the ADs and coaches enlisted the sports media and fans in their campaigns.

In 1999, University of Minnesota football coach Glen Mason lobbied for a new stadium for his team, arguing that his program needed to keep up with the recent stadium upgrades at Penn State and Ohio State ($100 million each), and new structures at other schools: "When you look at what is happening nationally with the amount of investments these great academic institutions are making in athletics and football, it's mind-boggling." It is particularly mind-boggling when these investments are compared to the proportionally lower ones that these supposedly "great academic institutions" put into their undergraduate education programs.

Virginia Tech AD Jim Weaver was more honest than Glen Mason about his department's construction spree, not bothering to put academic ribbons on it: "If you are not upgrading your facilities, you are going backward. In college athletics today . . . we're in the game of keeping up with the Joneses. I don't like it, but it's a fact."

Sociologist Harry Edwards calls this the "Athletics Arms Race," and although the Cold War competition ended, College Sports MegaInc. has intensified its version. According to ADs, coaches, and the executives who run their trade association, the NCAA, athletic departments must never stop expanding, and should never reach a spending equilibrium — even though they run continual deficits. A former athletic official at the University of Nebraska explained:

> When we won the national [football] championship at Nebraska in 1994, what we did instantly was continue to expand. That's when we started the project to build skyboxes and expand the stadium and continue to improve facilities.

Colossal new football stadiums and basketball arenas, as well as luxury skyboxes, are the most visible symbols of College Sports MegaInc. In addition, in many college towns, big-name coaches build enormous mansions, part of the harvest from their million-dollar annual incomes. . . .

The only consistent financial losers are the schools that belong to the NCAA and furnish the stadiums, arenas, and facilities for its operations. Contrary to one of the most tenacious myths in American society, *the vast majority of colleges and universities do not make money in big-time intercollegiate athletics.* But the myth will never die as long as university officials use it to justify their affection and need for beer-and-circus, particularly as a substitute for quality undergraduate education.

REFERENCES

1. Andrew Zimbalist, Sports Business Journal, Dec. 27, 1999.
2. Id.

Effects of University Athletics on the University: A Review and Extension of Empirical Assessment

Brian Goff

Many factors may influence strategic decisions concerning athletic programs. Certainly university executives responsible for these decisions ought to take into consideration a wider spectrum of information than can be obtained solely from analyzing the impact of athletics on financial and other quantitative variables. For example, other relevant benefits are the positive influence of intercollegiate athletics on issues such as institutional unity and loyalty and on an institution's reputation. Nonetheless, carefully scrutinized empirical data about quantitative impacts of intercollegiate athletics are very important decision making considerations.

. . . .

DIRECT FINANCIAL IMPACTS

The importance of accurately assessing the direct financial impact of university athletics hardly requires justification. The "profitability issue" has attracted considerable attention in the popular media in books such as *College Sports, Inc.*[1] and *Keeping Score*[2] and in newspapers and magazines such as *USA Today,* the *Chicago Tribune, U.S. News and World Report, Academe,* and the *Chronicle of Higher Education.* The studies reported in these outlets challenge the "myth," allegedly held by many, that college athletics is a significant net contributor to university treasuries. Instead, these reports have estimated that even some of the giants of college sports operate in the red. For instance, the University of Michigan, Auburn University, and even Notre Dame University have been estimated to be losing up to $3 million per year on their athletics programs. As discussed below, such claims are muddled by the not-for-profit setting of universities and related accounting practices.

The denial that big-time college athletics is a net revenue generator runs counter to intuition and to evidence based on simple economic insights. Athletic programs such as those of Michigan and Notre Dame generate revenues . . . approaching professional team revenues . . . while avoiding the $30 million dollar payrolls which professional teams must meet. The NCAA earns hundreds of millions of dollars every year from its contract with CBS to televise its basketball tournament. Brown[3] has estimated that better college football players could earn $600,000 or more per year if paid market-based salaries, while basketball players could earn even more. The kinds of revenues available to major NCAA programs, restrictions on payments to players, and avoidance of antitrust regulation, seemingly signal a very profitable enterprise. From this viewpoint, reported losses for programs are more likely due to misleading accounting methods and university budgetary practices than to a lack of economic viability.

A basic issue that we address is whether intuition based on principles of economics or published reports alleging college sports' losses are correct. Only two detailed, peer-reviewed studies of college sport finances, which fully utilize appropriate economic/managerial accounting methods, have been published. These are studies of athletics at Utah State University[4] and Western Kentucky University.[5] Rather than relying on institutional figures reported at high levels of aggregation, these studies use detailed information from university accounts to determine the flow of dollars into and out of universities because of athletics programs. The widely circulated reports of losses among college sports programs utilize much less detailed data usually drawn from aggregate university budget figures.

Key questions that were asked in these two studies are important for an assessment of an athletic program's financial situation: What revenues would be lost if a sport is dropped, and what expenses would be saved if a sport is dropped? Although these questions are simple, arriving at accurate answers is not. Because of complex organizational arrangements, accompanying inter-unit transfers, noneconomic valuation methods, and university-specific accounting conventions, merely taking data about revenues and expenses reported by institutions at a high level of aggregation leads to the errors and to wide variances in reported estimates. Attention here is centered on football and basketball because, for most universities, these are the sports that raise significant revenues and that often subsidize the other "non-revenue" sports.

Adjustments are necessary to arrive at accurate assessments:

1. Valuing grant-in-aid expenses at their true incremental expense to the university. Most universities value athletic grant-in-aid expenses at their "list price" (full tuition price, full housing price, full book price). This can account for $1 million to $5 million of athletic expenses, depending on tuition at a specific university. However, the amount of money that a university actually spends to instruct and house 100 additional football and basketball players is only a fraction of the "list price." The incremental instructional expense is nearly zero because at universities, where even small amounts of excess capacity exists, few, if any, additional faculty or staff must be employed to accommodate the additional student-athletes.

2. Attributing athletics-produced revenues to non-athletic accounts. At most universities, all, or some of, merchandise sales, concession revenues, parking receipts, and related revenues, are attributed to the general fund or to a non-athletic unit of the university. Such revenues can be substantial. In many cases, even the revenues paid by athletic foundations for athlete tuition are credited directly to the general fund so that grant-in-aids deliver a "double blow" to athletics — overvaluation on the expense side and undervaluation on the revenue side.

3. Attributing athletics-produced expenses to non-athletic accounts. Items such as the custodial care and maintenance of sporting venues may be charged as an expense to units other than the athletic department. While occurring, the evidence in the studies cited above indicates that this is a relatively minor adjustment.

For Utah State and Western Kentucky, estimates of operating profits/losses differed widely from publicly reported estimates that were based on university figures. . . . Utah State's program, publicly reported to be experiencing a loss of almost $700,000, actually turned a $366,000 profit. Western Kentucky's program, publicly reported to be experiencing a $1.2 million loss, was losing money, but just over $300,000 per year. Neither of these studies incorporates athletics-induced merchandise sales that would increase adjusted revenue figures.

Because the data required to make the appropriate adjustments exists only in very detailed university accounts, and gathering it requires intimate knowledge of a university's accounting conventions, arriving at such detailed estimates for a few, or even for one, athletic department is a daunting challenge. However, if we take the two studies described above as indications of the average amount of adjustment necessary at public universities and adjust more recent estimates based on aggregate level data by this amount, we can gain a more realistic assessment than currently exists. In fact, the Skousen and Condie and the Borland et al. studies provide minimum adjustments because neither of the programs examined are near the top of college revenue producers. As a result, omitting revenues such as merchandise would not have as big as an effect as it would for a program such as Michigan's where merchandise sales attributable to athletics would run into the millions.

Sheehan is the most recent study of college football and basketball (i.e., not the entire athletic program) finances. He has gone to greater lengths than most studies in attempting to collect accurate figures. Yet, by his own admission, his figures do not adjust for accounting conventions at universities or take into account merchandise sales due to athletics. . . . According to his figures, 16% of the schools lose money and 29% earn less than a $1 million profit (a profit large enough, by his estimation, to compensate for state subsidies). Even though these results show that most programs contribute net revenues to the university, the results have been used to indicate the lack of financial health of college athletics.

In order to obtain more realistic estimates of the financial health of athletic programs, Sheehan's results are adjusted for the accounting problems discussed above. Without detailed accounting information from each school, a complete revision is not possible. However, revisions based on estimates of under-valuation of revenues and over-valuation of expenses are possible given the results of the Skousen and Condie and Borland et al. studies. Based on these studies which suggest adjustments of $1,040,000 and $870,000 respectively, we add a conservative amount, $800,000, to the profits of the athletic programs of public universities in Sheehan's study. No detailed study of necessary valuation adjustments for private universities exists; we add $1.5 million, which assumes tuition for athletes at the private schools is slightly less than double the tuition for athletes at public schools. . . . The results indicate that only 10% of the schools lost money. All but three of these are in the Mid-American Conference — universities whose football programs would rate at the lowest level of Division I-A schools and whose basketball programs would rate below the top seven or eight conferences. After the tuition adjustment, 79% of schools exceed $1 million in annual profits with 72% exceeding $2 million. Although used as evidence of faltering financial performance in college athletics, Sheehan's data show just the opposite, even without including further adjustments such as revenues for sales of merchandise.

In addition to the issues related to accurate accounting for university athletics discussed above, three others are worth noting. First, at universities where enrollments are relatively fixed (mainly selective private schools), admitting 100 athletes may or may not reduce admission of paying students so that tuition revenue may or may not be foregone due to athletics. Whether, and the extent to which, revenue is actually lost depends upon the admission and tuition practices of a specific school.

If a school were to admit 100 students paying full tuition (say $20,000 per student) in place of student athletes, the revenue foregone is substantial. If the school were to admit 100 students paying the average tuition among students (always less than full tuition), revenue foregone would be reduced. If the school were to admit 100 students with full tuition grants themselves, or if the school did not increase admissions of non-athletes after dropping athletics, then revenue foregone would be zero.

Second, the assessment of financial viability depends on whose perspective is taken. If it were the perspective of a university president, then any revenue from state treasuries that is received because of athletics would be included in financial calculations. If the perspective is that of the state legislature — the ultimate policy-making body for public universities — such revenues would be excluded.

Finally, the difference between for-profit environments and the not-for-profit setting of universities must be taken into account when interpreting profit/loss data. As in other not-for-profit settings, unit directors in universities (e.g., department chairs, deans, athletic directors) do not typically have an incentive to maximize profits (budget surpluses). If surpluses are experienced or anticipated, most unit directors increase expenditures in order to fully utilize their budgets. As a result, expenses rise to match, and often exceed, budgets regardless of revenue. So it should come as no surprise that expenses for even the largest revenue producers in college sports are frequently reported as equal to, or greater than, revenues, especially when relying on self-reported figures.

INDIRECT IMPACTS OF ATHLETICS

While much more could be said concerning inaccurate analyses of the direct revenues and expenses of major college athletics, other issues relevant to making strategic decisions concerning university athletics could also be quantitatively addressed. There are many anecdotal, or isolated, reports of indirect impacts (e.g., increased visibility, applications, donations) of newfound athletic success. A recent example is Northwestern University's turnaround football seasons in 1995–1996. There exists, however, minimal work concerning the extent of indirect impacts of such turnarounds across different campuses using rudimentary descriptive statistics, much less using sophisticated statistical analyses. Below, the empirical literature relating to these issues is summarized and then extended.

. . . .

UNIVERSITY EXPOSURE: THE MECHANISM FOR INDIRECT IMPACTS

The most common skepticism related to measurements of the indirect impacts of athletics pertains not to the statistical methods utilized, but to the credibility of sizable effects. The skepticism usually grows out of a misunderstanding of the mechanisms by which athletics influence seemingly unrelated behavior. A question arises in the minds of many, especially university faculty: Outside of hardcore fans, are there enough people who care so strongly about athletics to alter enrollments, giving, and other oft-touted outcomes?

This question presumes that the primary mechanism of athletics' influence is via sports fans and boosters. When 100,000 people attend a football game, as they do at places such as the Universities of Michigan and Tennessee, six or seven times per year, turning people into university boosters would appear to be a viable means by which athletics could influence indirect outcomes. The means to influence outcomes extends considerably more broadly, however. Athletics is an integral source of name exposure for almost every university and often the only frequent source of exposure for schools possessing little in the way of academic reputation. Even for institutions with highly regarded academic reputations, many potential donors and potential students are more likely to become aware of, and interested in, the institution due to its participating in a major bowl game or the NCAA "Sweet Sixteen" than they are due to the work of a Nobel prize-winning chemist. Also, athletic events provide opportunities for large numbers of prospective students and their parents — some of whom may have only a passing interest in the athletic event — to visit campuses they might not otherwise visit.

. . . . The evidence is the number of articles in which Northwestern University, a very selective private institution with a heavy orientation toward research and graduate education — and Western Kentucky University — a mid-sized, regional public institution with an undergraduate orientation — appear in eight leading newspapers over the period 1991–1996.

A review of this data leads to two noteworthy conclusions. First, athletic success translated into substantially increased exposure for both institutions. Articles about Northwestern jumped by 185% during 1995, the season leading to Northwestern's Rose Bowl visit, in comparison with the prior three-year average. Articles about Western Kentucky University jumped from about 2 or 3 in typical years to 13 and 30 in 1992 and 1993 when the men's and women's basketball programs enjoyed atypical successes, a final sixteen appearance for the men, and a final four appearance for the women. Second, even in years without special success, athletic articles were an important source of exposure. In 1992, for instance, Northwestern athletics accounted for almost 70% of the coverage of the university. In contrast, research-related stories accounted for less than 5%. For Western Kentucky, non-athletic stories were either 0 or 1 in each year.

Many factors contribute to the decisions of boosters and students. The evidence presented here about exposure from athletics is not intended to suggest that athletics is the only determinant of these decisions. However, the influence of such exposure may be very important.

GENERAL CONTRIBUTIONS TO UNIVERSITIES

One of the most contentious debates surrounding the indirect effects of athletics concerns its impact upon non-athletic gifts to universities. The major improvements of programs at Northwestern in 1995 and Georgia Tech in 1991 prompted speculation and some anecdotal evidence supporting the argument that athletic success contributes to additional general giving. However, this evidence, and the proposition behind it, has often met strong rebuttal.

The reasons behind the challenges are easy to understand; the likely impacts of athletics on general giving are much harder to unambiguously assess than are the types of effects we have discussed to date (athletic department revenues and expenses, media coverage). Moreover, the cause–effect relationships can be quite ambiguous. Some benefactors are interested in both athletics and general university welfare but have a fixed amount of money they are willing to donate. In such cases, increased athletic success may help steer these donors toward athletic giving and away from general gifts. On the other hand, greater exposure for a university — whatever its source, may help spur giving across many fronts. The effect that is expected to dominate (athletic vs. general giving) cannot be theoretically determined.

Comparisons across empirical studies are complicated by the use of different dependent variables, use of different variables to account for athletic success, different control variables, and a lack of investigation of lag relationships. For example, Baade and Sundberg[6] try to explain gifts per alumni for 167 schools over an eighteen-year period, Grimes and Chressanthis[7] consider annual gifts for one school over a thirty-year time frame, and McCormick and Tinsley[8] use individual-level contributor data for one school over 14 years. While Baade and Sundberg consider the effects of winning percentages in football and basketball along with postseason play, McCormick and Tinsley estimate the relationship between athletic gifts and general giving. Even if effects are determined using comparable methods for different institutions, the answer as to whether athletic success and athletic giving reduce or increase general giving may depend on the specific university in question as well as the specific circumstances surrounding its athletics success (e.g., how "big" and how novel the success was).

Existing Studies

. . . .

In what is likely the most comprehensive study, Baade and Sundberg use data from over 300 institutions of various types over the years 1973–1990. They find that general giving depends very little on [an] overall winning record. However, bowl appearances and basketball tournament appearances were found to raise general giving by 35 to 55%. Using data from Mississippi State covering 1962–1991, Grimes and Chressanthis find a positive effect of basketball winning percentage (an extra $200,000 to $1 million depending on the size of the increase in winning) as well as a $200,000 to $300,000 increase for television appearances, most directly related to College World Series appearances. Using data at the level of individual contributors over a 5-year period at Clemson University, McCormick and Tinsley find that general giving and athletic giving complement, rather than take away from, each other.

New Assessments

As an additional source of information on the relationship between athletics and contributions, we collected market value endowment data for Northwestern and Georgia Tech Universities to test whether the years of major football success translated into additional giving. These two schools were selected because of the rapid and significant degree of athletic success they recently enjoyed after many years of poor to moderate performance.

. . . .

Overall, the equation explains 76% of the endowment changes. The variable for Georgia Tech's athletic success is not statistically different from zero. Alternative formulations of this variable (to include more years) also did not show any effects. The variable for Northwestern's football success, however, indicates an increase of almost $200 million. In commenting on these results, however, Henry Bienen, President of Northwestern, indicated that a large part of this increase was due to his having moved a substantial amount from cash into long-term equity during the period we studied. Our assessment of the relationship between athletics and contributions, therefore, is more suggestive of the difficulty of conducting such research purely with secondary data than it is of the relationship of interest.

While the data used to generate this estimate are accurate with respect to publicly reported figures, consistent with arguments made elsewhere in this paper, assessing the indirect effects of intercollegiate athletics is fraught with methodological challenges. Among these that are relevant here are the necessity of considering complex organizational arrangements, including inter-unit transfers and university-specific accounting conventions, and the development of sound knowledge of a university's accounting conventions. In short, great care is necessary in conducting and reporting such research.

Student Interest

Athletic success may also have an effect on student interest measured by the number of students desiring to attend a university and/or the quality of those students. For public universities with relatively open enrollment policies and with funding being dependent on enrollment figures, enrollment might be the best gauge of the effect of athletics upon student interest. For universities with more selective admission policies where enrollments stay relatively fixed over time, application data and/or data on academic aptitude of incoming students (e.g., SAT scores) are more relevant measures for assessing the athletics-student interest link.

Existing Studies

Using time series methods on data covering 30 years, Borland et al. find substantial effects for basketball and smaller effects for football on enrollments at Western Kentucky University. A movement from a winning percentage of 0.50 to one of 0.75 in the prior two seasons resulted in estimated enrollment increases of about 430 students. Postseason play in football was estimated to increase enrollment by about 340 students, but the statistical significance of this result was marginal. . . . Mixon and Hsing[9] also find effects of athletic success on enrollments. In a statistical model explaining the percentage of out-of-state students across universities, they estimated that membership in the NCAA's highest division increased the percentage by 2–4 points after controlling for a number of other university characteristics.

If, in fact, enrollments increase due to athletic success, a closely related question follows: What kinds of students are being attracted? One might assume that students who focus excessively on sports and, therefore, are of questionable academic quality, are responsible for enrollment increases. Interest on the part of better students may also increase, however, as a result of the increased exposure due to athletic success. Theory does not provide an unambiguous answer.

. . . . Controlling for a number of factors associated with student quality, McCormick and Tinsley[10] use data from 150 schools to assess both relationships within a single year (1971) and changes across years (from 1981 to 1984). These researchers find a positive relationship between major athletic success and student quality for the single year but only marginally positive or no relationship for the changes across years. Using essentially the same control data used by McCormick and Tinsley for bowl game and basketball tournament appearances in the years 1989 and 1981–89, Bremmer and Kesserling[11] cannot find any SAT effects of athletic success. In an imitation of McCormick and Tinsley, Tucker and Amato[12] find effects of football success and no effects of the basketball success. At the average level of football success, SAT scores increased by about 3% relative to a school with very poor football performance. Using the number of games played in NCAA basketball tournaments over 1978–1992, Mixon[13] finds a positive impact of basketball success. His results indicate SAT scores increase by 30 points for a difference of 20 games played in the tournament.

New Assessments

We supplement existing evidence on the effects of athletic success on enrollment with data from three universities: Wichita State University (WSU) and The University of Texas–Arlington (UTA), both of which dropped football, and Georgia State University (GSU), which added football at the I-AA level. The value of examining the effects at these three schools is that the changes involved more than just incremental changes in athletic performance, which may or may not be the result of strategic decisions by university executives. Instead, the changes involved major strategic moves with respect to athletics.

. . . .

. . . . Although enrollment trends for these schools are highly correlated with U.S. enrollment trends, the annual changes that make up these trends are highly individualistic. The football/no football variable, however, . . . indicates that, on average, "no-football" years were associated with about a 550-student decline relative to years with football across the three universities. If the equation is re-estimated, including only the two schools that dropped football in the mid-1980s (Wichita State and UT–Arlington), the estimated impact is slightly larger — a decline of just over 600 students. Estimates for Georgia Southern alone indicate a 500-student increase from adding football with a big increase in overall explanatory power of the equation to 36%.

As mentioned earlier, for a university with more selective admission policies, the number of applicants is a more appropriate measure of student interest than is enrollment. Using freshman applications from Georgia Tech that enjoyed a share of the national football championship in 1990, a very simple estimate of the relationship between the dramatic athletic success and applications filed is generated based on applications to Georgia Tech from 1982 to 1996. . . .

A 28% (1,686 applicants) increase in applications occurred for 1991–93 in comparison with 1988–90. The average increase from 1991–94 was 34% higher than the average from 1983–90. . . .

Athletics as an Albatross

In this section we address whether athletics can have negative effects on the types of outcomes addressed above. . . . The evidence presented so far indicates that athletics has either positive or no indirect effect on a number of university outcomes. In several of the empirical studies, teams performing at high levels generated improved outcomes compared with teams performing at low levels; but this is a relative effect. The research does not indicate that poor performance leads to absolute declines in any of the outcomes studied.

. . . .

Existing Study

An important exception to the research limitations described just above is the study of Grimes and Chressanthis. These authors include a variable for NCAA sanctions in their equation estimating contributions to Mississippi State. While sanctions made no difference in their general equation, their equation [that] included only football-related variables and sanctions did find an effect. In particular, they found that football sanctions reduced contributions to the university by $1.6 million per year, a sizable reduction given average contribution levels.

New Assessments

The case of Southern Methodist University permits an estimation of negative publicity in an extreme case. SMU's athletic program had improved substantially in the late 1970s and early

1980s, earning a second place finish in football polls at the end of the 1982 season. Because of repeated violations of NCAA rules, however, the NCAA imposed a "death penalty" on SMU's football program for 1987 and 1988, banning their participation in these years and severely restricting football scholarships in following years. The severity of the penalty brought substantial publicity to the university. Using data from newspaper citations, one can observe the jump in (negative) publicity surrounding this event. The same eight leading newspapers referred to above devoted 133 stories to SMU between 1987 and 1988 compared with a range of 5 to 8 stories per year for 1991–1995.

. . . . Changes in the market value of SMU's endowment were available for 1980–1996. Examination of the data without controls for other factors highlights two points. First, SMU enjoyed large increases in its endowment from 1982 to 1986, following its highly successful 1982 campaign and its emergence as a national football power. Market value grew over 156% from 1982 to 1986. Second, although SMU's endowment did not fall in the post-penalty years, the increases fell back into line with those prior to its 1982 success.

. . . .

. . . . The years of marked improvement in football appear to have benefited SMU. However, it does not appear that the sanctions decreased SMU's ability to attract funds other than those funds that were attracted due to its becoming a national football power. Thus, while the "death penalty" did not result in endowment decreases, it did result in increases falling back to what they were prior to the 1982 and subsequent football successes.

Data on applications to SMU from 1985 to 1996 were also analyzed. As with the endowment data, because data in years prior to the sanctions are limited, conclusions must be tentative. The number of applications fell by 12% from 1985–86 to 1987–88. However, by 1989–90 applications jumped 30% over this low point. These data may indicate a decline due to the negative publicity followed by a boost due to positive exposure associated with reestablishing the program on a more reputable footing. On the other hand, these data may merely indicate variations due to other factors. Without additional data, the two conclusions cannot be distinguished.

CONCLUSIONS

The purpose of the evidence presented here is to provide a review and extension of empirical assessments of university-wide effects of intercollegiate athletics and to provide university personnel with improved information with which to formulate strategies with respect to intercollegiate athletics. The results presented above permit several conclusions to be drawn.

- For nearly all universities in major conferences (most Division I-A football and top tier Division I basketball), direct revenues from football and basketball are greater than direct expenses; for at least 70% of the schools, the difference is greater than $1 million.
- For universities below the major conferences (Division I-AA football and second tier Division I basketball), the difference between direct revenues and expenses may be negative but is likely less than $1 million.
- Athletic success, particularly significant improvement, can substantially increase national exposure for universities regardless of their academic reputation.

- Achievements in athletics (e.g., bowl trips, basketball tournament wins, college world series appearances) appear to substantially increase general giving to universities; these effects are present for both average and major improvements in athletics.
- Major achievements in athletics appear to spark additional interest from prospective students, even at schools with highly rated academic programs. Major achievements in athletics may lead to an improved pool of entering students (in terms of aptitude tests) at selective universities.
- Dropping football can have measurable, negative impacts on enrollments and possibly other indirect variables (e.g., giving), even for universities that do not have top tier programs.
- Negative exposure due to NCAA sanctions may offset the gains made by past athletic success, but the evidence to date does not show that such negative exposure does more than negate the positive influence of past success.

. . . .

. . . . As addressed earlier, idiosyncratic accounting conventions obscure accurate assessment of the financial status of programs and comparisons across programs. Such practices are not easily overcome even by extensive, detailed examination and review of university accounting procedures and records. The study of appropriate inter-unit (transfer) pricing mechanisms is another important, underdeveloped, and underappreciated area. Many of the opaque accounting conventions exist because university executives want to keep certain information confidential and to diminish scrutiny.

REFERENCES

1. Sperber, M. (1990). College Sports Inc. New York, NY: Henry Holt and Company.

2. Sheehan, R. G. (1996). Keeping Score. South Bend, IN: Diamond Communications.

3. Brown, R. W. (1993). The rent associated with college football players. Economic Inquiry, 31, 671–685.

4. Skousen, C. R. & Condie, F. A. (1988). Evaluating a sports program: Goalposts v. test tubes. Managerial Accounting, 60, 43–49.

5. Borland, M. V., Goff, B. L., & Pulsinelli, R. W. (1992). College athletics: Financial burden or boon? In G. Scully (Ed.), Advances in the Economics of Sport (pp. 215–235) Greenwich, CT: JAI Press.

6. Baade, R. A. & Sundberg, J. S. (1996). Fourth down and gold to go? Assessing the link between athletics and alumni giving. Social Science Quarterly, 77, 789–803.

7. Grimes, P. W. & Chressanthis, G. A. (1994). Collegiate Sports, NCAA sanctions, and alumni contributions to academics. American Journal of Economics and Sociology, 53, 27–38.

8. McCormick, R. E. & Tinsley, M. (1990). Athletics and academics: A model of university contributions. In B. L. Goff and R. D. Tollison (Eds.), Sportometrics (pp. 193–206).

9. Mixon, F. G. & Hsing, Y. (1994). The determinants of out-of-state enrollments in higher education: A Tobit analysis. Economics of Education Review, 13, 329–35.

10. McCormick, R. E. & Tinsley, M. (1987). Athletics versus academics: Evidence from SAT scores. Journal of Political Economy, 95, 1103–16.

11. Bremmer, D. S. & Kesserling, R. G. (1993). Advertising effects of university athletic success. Quarterly Review of Economics and Business, 33, 409–21

12. Tucker, I. B. & Amato, L. (1993). Does big-time success in football or basketball affect SAT scores? Economics of Education Review, 12, 177–81.

13. Mixon, F. G. (1995). Athletics v. academics: Rejoining evidence from SAT scores. Education Economics, 3, 277–83.

THE EMPIRICAL EFFECTS OF COLLEGIATE ATHLETICS: AN INTERIM REPORT

Robert Litan, Jonathan Orszag, and Peter Orszag

EXECUTIVE SUMMARY

Observers of college athletics hold dramatically different views regarding the empirical effects of athletics on institutions of higher education. One view, reflected in the so-called Flutie effect, suggests that athletic programs generate a variety of direct and indirect benefits for the school sponsoring them. Another view, reflected in two reports from the Knight Commission, suggests that college athletics [are] suffering from "a financial arms race" and college athletics "threaten to overwhelm the universities in whose name they were established." Unfortunately, the debate between these two schools of thought is often based more on assertions and anecdotes than on empirical evidence.

The purpose of this paper is to examine empirically the effects of college athletics, with a particular focus on the financial effects. In particular, the paper draws on evidence contained in previous academic studies; statistical analysis of a new, comprehensive database compiled from school-specific information collected as part of the Equity in Athletics Disclosure Act (EADA), merged with data from other sources (such as the Integrated Post-Secondary Education Data System managed by the Department of Education); and a detailed survey of chief financial officers from 17 Division I schools. These various sources of data have important limitations, especially in areas such as the treatment of capital expenditures, but they nonetheless represent a comprehensive empirical effort to shed light on key issues related to college athletics.

The paper specifically examines ten hypotheses about college athletics, focusing primarily on Division I-A schools. Using our data and the existing academic literature, we examine each of the hypotheses. Our analysis confirms five of the hypotheses; the other five are not proven and require further empirical analysis:

Hypothesis #1: Operating athletic expenditures are a relatively small share of overall academic spending.

- According to Department of Education data, reported athletic spending represented roughly three percent of total higher education spending for Division I-A schools in 1997 (the most recent comprehensive Department of Education data publicly available).
- In 2001, NCAA/EADA data suggest that operating athletic spending represented roughly 3.5 percent of total higher education spending for Division I-A schools.
- The share of operating athletic spending in a university's total budget is higher for smaller schools than for larger schools because of the fixed costs associated with an athletic department.
- The share of operating athletic spending in overall higher education spending has increased only slightly over time. In recent years, there is indirect evidence of a modest acceleration in athletic spending relative to total spending, but comprehensive data are not yet available to confirm such a trend.
- We conclude that operating athletic expenditures in the aggregate are a relatively small share of total higher education spending for Division I-A schools.

Hypothesis #2: The football and basketball markets exhibited increased levels of inequality in the 1990s.

- A common measure of inequality is the Gini coefficient, which would equal one if one school accounted for all spending and zero if spending were the same across schools. Increases in the Gini coefficient represent increased levels of inequality and vice versa.
- Between 1993 and 2001, the Gini coefficient for Division I-A football spending rose from 0.26 to 0.29. To put that increase in perspective, it is approximately equal to the increase in income inequality in the United States during the 1980s. The Gini coefficient for Division I-A basketball spending rose even more sharply, from 0.26 to 0.31.
- Inequality also increased among top-spending schools. The Gini coefficient for football spending among schools in the top 25 percent of the spending distribution, for example, rose from 0.08 in 1993 to 0.11 in 2001.
- We conclude that the football and basketball markets exhibited increased levels of inequality between 1993 and 2001.

Hypothesis #3: The football and basketball markets exhibit mobility in expenditure, revenue, and winning percentages.

- More than two-fifths of the schools that were in the top quintile of Division I-A football spending in 1993 were no longer in the top quintile by 2001. Nearly 60 percent of the schools in the middle quintile in 1993 were no longer there in 2001; more than one-third had moved up and more than one-fifth had moved down.
- Net revenue also exhibited some degree of mobility: Among the schools in the middle quintile of football net revenue in 1993, roughly two-thirds were no longer in the middle quintile in 2001.
- A school's winning percentage exhibits only modest levels of persistence. For example, the correlation of winning percentages from one year to the next is only about 50 percent. The

correlation dissipates over time: the correlation between winning percentages ten years apart is 20 to 30 percent.

- We conclude that the football and basketball markets exhibit some degree of mobility in expenditure, revenue, and winning percentages.

Hypothesis #4: Increased operating expenditures on football or basketball, on average, are not associated with any medium-term increase or decrease in operating net revenue.

- Our statistical analyses suggest that between 1993 and 2001, an increase in operating expenditures of $1 on football or men's basketball in Division I-A was associated with approximately $1 in additional operating revenue, on average. The implication is that spending an extra $1 was not associated with any increase or decrease in *net* revenue, on average, from these sports.
- These results, although based on better data than previous studies, nonetheless have limitations. For example, our database extends only from 1993 to 2001. It is possible that increased spending on athletics has long lags — that is, it produces significant benefits or costs after a long period of time. If this were the case, our database may be too short to capture the "true" effects of increased spending. In addition, the NCAA/EADA data do not adequately record capital expenditures; our analysis therefore focuses on operating spending. It is possible that the effects of operating spending differ from the effects of capital spending.
- We conclude that over the medium term (eight years), increases in operating expenditures on football or men's basketball are not associated with any change, on average, in operating net revenue.

Hypothesis #5: Increased operating expenditures on football or basketball are not associated with medium-term increases in winning percentages, and higher winning percentages are not associated with medium-term increases in operating revenue or operating net revenue.

- A variety of econometric exercises suggest no statistical relationship between changes in operating expenditures on football and changes in football winning percentages between 1993 and 2001.
- A variety of econometric exercises also suggest no statistical relationship between changes in winning percentages and changes in football operating revenue or net revenue between 1993 and 2001.
- We conclude that increased operating expenditures on football or basketball are not associated with medium-term increases in winning percentages, and higher winning percentages are not associated with medium-term increases in operating revenue or operating net revenue.

Hypothesis #6: The relationship between spending and revenue varies significantly by subgroups of schools (e.g., conferences, schools with high SAT scores, etc.).

- We examined the relationship between spending and revenue across various subsets of schools. We were not able to detect evidence of systematic differences when separating the schools by characteristics such as: public vs. private schools; schools with high SAT scores vs. schools with low SAT scores; large student populations vs. small student populations;

schools that were ever in the Associated Press (AP) rankings; and schools that were ranked in the top 25 in the AP poll in 1993.

- Some schools benefited from moving up to Division I-A, but the experience varied across schools. For example, two schools experienced significant increases in football net revenue after moving to Division I-A; one school experienced a decline in football net revenue after moving to Division I-A.

- In many cases, the sample sizes for the subsets of schools were quite small; given the paucity of data in some cases, it is difficult to reject the hypothesis outright. Instead, we conclude that the hypothesis that the relationships vary significantly by sub-groups of schools is not proven.

Hypothesis #7: Increased operating expenditures on big-time sports affect operating expenditures on other sports.

- Our statistical analysis suggests that each dollar increase in operating expenditures on football among Division I-A schools may be associated with a $0.21 increase in spending on women's sports excluding basketball and $0.35 including basketball, but the results are not robust to changes in the econometric specification. Such a potential spillover effect may be expected given Title IX and other pressures to ensure equity between men's and women's sports.

- Previous studies have found that increases in football spending are associated with increased spending on women's sports.

- Given the lack of robustness of the results, we conclude that the hypothesis that increased operating expenditures on big-time sports affect operating expenditures on other sports is not proven.

Hypothesis #8: Increased operating expenditures on sports affect measurable academic quality in the medium term.

- Our statistical analysis suggests no relationship — either positive or negative — between changes in operating expenditures on football or basketball among Division I-A schools and incoming SAT scores or the percentage of applicants accepted.

- The academic literature is divided on whether athletic programs affect academic quality. While our results suggest no statistical relationship one way or the other, our data are limited to eight years and such a relationship may exist over longer periods of time. In addition, the relationship between athletics and academic quality may manifest itself in ways other than the effect on SAT scores or other directly measurable indicators.

- We conclude that the hypothesis that changes in operating expenditures on big-time sports affect measurable academic quality in the medium term is not proven.

Hypothesis #9: Increased operating expenditures on sports affect other measurable indicators, including alumni giving.

- Econometric analysis using our database shows little or no robust relationship between changes in operating expenditures on football or basketball among Division I-A schools and alumni giving (either to the sports program or the university itself).

- The academic literature is again inconclusive on this issue. As with the previous hypothesis, our results suggest little or no statistical relationship — but our data are limited to eight years and such a relationship may exist over longer periods of time.
- We conclude that the hypothesis that increased operating expenditures on sports affect other measurable indicators, including alumni giving, is not proven.

Hypothesis #10: The football and basketball markets exhibit an "arms race" in which increased operating expenditures at one school are associated with increases at other schools.

- Analysts have used the term "arms race" to describe a variety of phenomena. We use the term to refer to a situation in which increased spending at one school [is] associated with increases at other schools.
- Some of our econometric analyses suggest that increased operating expenditures on football at one school may be associated with increases in operating expenditures at other schools within the same conference, but other specifications suggest no relationship.
- We conclude that the hypothesis that the football and basketball markets exhibit an "arms race" in which increased operating expenditures at one school are associated with increases at other schools is not proven.
- It is important to emphasize that the existence of an "arms race" may be concentrated in capital expenditures, which are not adequately recorded in the NCAA/EADA data, rather than in operating expenditures.

CONCLUSION

This interim report reflects an effort to advance the debate over college athletics by using data to assess the validity of different hypotheses. We find that many widely held perspectives about spending on big-time sports by colleges — by both proponents and opponents of such spending — are not supported by the statistical evidence.

Our results must be qualified, however. Although the data in this paper are more comprehensive than other datasets that have been used in the past, they are nonetheless imperfect: they are available only since 1993, and they fail to capture fully various components of athletic activities (especially total capital expenditures and staff compensation from all sources). Further efforts to improve and analyze the data are likely to provide additional insights into the effects of college athletics on institutions of higher education. Given the available data, neither the proponents of the Flutie effect nor those who argue that big-time college athletics are imposing directly measurable financial harm on higher education have proven their case.

TABLE 2.

TOTAL REVENUES, EXPENSES, AND OPERATING RESULTS, DIVISION I-A, 2001	2001 (in thousands of dollars)
Total Revenues	
Men's	15,800
Women's	1,400
Nongender	7,900
Total Revenues	
Average	25,100
Largest reported	79,600
Total Expenses	
Men's	10,900
Women's	4,600
Nongender	7,700
Total Expenses	
Average	23,200
Largest reported	52,100
Average Profit (Deficit)	
Men's	4,900
Women's	(3,200)
Nongender	200
Total Profit (Deficit)	1,900
Restated Without Institutional Support	
Average deficit	(600)

Notes: Only revenues and expenses specifically related to men's and women's programs are shown as such. Nongender-specific items are reported as Nongender.

The largest total revenue reported by a division member is reported, as is the largest total expense. All other amounts are division averages.

The average profits have been restated to reflect the deficit that results from the removal of institutional support from total revenues.

Source: Daniel Fulks, NCAA.

INTERCOLLEGIATE ATHLETICS AND THE AMERICAN UNIVERSITY: A UNIVERSITY PRESIDENT'S PERSPECTIVE

James J. Duderstadt

The sports media fuel the belief that money is the root of all evil in college athletics. And, indeed, the size of the broadcasting contracts for college football and basketball events, the compensation of celebrity coaches, and the professional contracts dangled in front of star athletes make it clear that money does govern many aspects of intercollegiate athletics.

For example, Michigan, along with many other universities with big-time athletics, claims that football is a major money-maker. In fact, Michigan boasted that it made a profit of $14 million from its football program in 1997, the year it won the national championship. Furthermore, Division I-A football programs reportedly averaged profits of $5 million in this year. Yet at the same time, most athletic departments plead poverty when confronted with demands that they increase varsity opportunities for women or financial aid for student-athletes. In fact, many athletic departments in Division I-A will actually admit that when all the revenues and expenses are totaled up, they actually lose money.

What is going on here? Could it be that those reporting about the economics of college sports have difficulty understanding the Byzantine financial statements of athletic departments? Are accounting tricks used to hide the true costs of intercollegiate athletics? Or perhaps those who lead and manage college sports have limited understanding of how financial management and business accounting works in the first place?

It is probably all of the above, combined with the many other myths about the financing of college sports, which confuse not only outsiders such as the press and the public, but even those insiders such as the university administration, athletic directors, and coaches. Before we dive into a discussion of how college athletics are financed these days, I want to straighten out several of the more common misperceptions.

STRIPPING AWAY THE MYTHS

First, most members of the public, the sports press, and even many faculty members believe that colleges make lots of money from sports. In reality, essentially all of the revenue generated by sports is used by athletic departments to finance their own operations. Indeed, very few intercollegiate athletics programs manage to balance their operating budgets. The revenue from gate receipts, broadcasting rights, postseason play, licensing, and other commercial ventures is rarely sufficient to cover the full costs of the programs. Most universities rely on additional subsidies from student fees, booster donations, or even state appropriations. Beyond that, college sports benefit from a tax-exempt status on operations and donations that represents a very considerable public subsidy.

The University of Michigan provides an interesting case study of the financing of intercollegiate athletics, since it is one of only a handful of institutions that usually manages to generate sufficient revenue to support the cost of operations (although not the full capital costs) for its intercollegiate athletics programs. Even for Michigan, financing intercollegiate athletics remains an ongoing challenge. For example, during the 1988–89 fiscal year, my first year as president, the University of Michigan won the Big Ten football championship, the Rose Bowl, and the NCAA basketball championship. The university also appeared in seven national football telecasts and dozens of basketball telecasts, played in a football stadium averaging 105,000 spectators a game, and sold out most of its basketball and hockey events. Yet it barely managed to break even that year, with a net profit on operations of about $1 million on $35 million of revenue. We should have been thankful for even this small operating "profit" since in more recent times, Michigan has begun to experience significant operating deficits.

Michigan's 1997–98 operating budget for intercollegiate athletics amounted to roughly $45 million based on revenues from gate receipts of $16 million; sponsorship, signage, and licensing revenue of $8 million; and private gifts of $7 million. This sounds like a large budget, but it is less than 2 percent of a total university budget of roughly $3 billion. When I was provost, football coach Bo Schembechler once complained to me about the enormous pressures to keep Michigan Stadium filled. He pointed to the losses that we would face if stadium attendance dropped 10 percent. I responded that, while this loss would be significant, it paled in comparison to the loss we would experience with a 10 percent drop in bed occupancy in the University of Michigan hospitals, which have an income more than twenty times larger than that of Michigan football ($1.2 billion in 1997). Even football revenue has to be placed in perspective.

The University of Michigan, as one of the nation's most successful athletics programs, generates one of the highest levels of gross revenue in intercollegiate athletics. Despite this fact, in some years, the expenditures of our athletic department actually exceed revenues. For example, in the 1998–99 fiscal year following the football team's national championship season, the athletic department actually ran an operating deficit of $2.8 million. This paradox is due, in part, to the unique "business culture" of intercollegiate athletics. The competitive nature of intercollegiate athletics leads most athletic departments to focus far more attention on generating revenue than on managing costs. There is a widespread belief in college sports that the team that spends the most wins the most, and that no expenses are unreasonable if they might enhance the success of a program. A fancy press box in the stadium? First-class travel and accommodations for the team? A million-dollar contract for the coach? Sure, if it will help us win! Furthermore, the financing of intercollegiate athletics is also complicated by the fact that while costs such as staff salaries, student-athlete financial aid, and facilities maintenance are usually fixed, revenues are highly variable. In fact, in a given year, only television revenue for regular events is predictable. All other revenue streams, such as gate receipts, bowl or NCAA tournament income, licensing revenue, and private gifts, are highly variable. While some revenues such as gate receipts can be accurately predicted, particularly when season tickets sales are significant, others such as licensing and private giving are quite volatile. Yet many athletic departments (including Michigan, of late) build these speculative revenues into annual budgets that sometimes crash and burn in serious deficits when these revenues fail to materialize.

Needless to say, this business philosophy would rapidly lead to bankruptcy in the corporate world. It has become increasingly clear that until athletic departments begin to operate with as much of an eye on expenditures as revenues, universities will continue to lose increasing amounts of money in their athletic activities, no matter how lucrative the television or licensing contracts they may negotiate.

Well, even if athletic departments essentially spend every dollar they generate, don't winning programs motivate alumni to make contributions to the university? To be sure, some alumni are certainly motivated to give money to the university while (and, perhaps, only when) basking in the glow of winning athletic programs. But, many of these loyal alumni and friends give only to athletic programs and not to the university more generally. And the amounts they give are relatively modest. For example, the total gifts to Michigan's athletics program amount to only about $5 million per year. By way of comparison, the annual gifts to the university more generally are currently about $180 million a year. In 1997 we finished a $1.4 billion fund-raising campaign, with less than $10 million of this amount given to intercollegiate athletics.

University fund-raising staff have known for many years that the most valuable support of a university generally comes from alumni and friends who identify with the *academic* programs of the university, not its athletic prowess. In fact, many of the university's most generous donors care little about its athletic success and are sometimes alienated by the attention given to winning athletics programs.

The staggering sums involved in television contracts, such as the $6 billion contract with CBS for televising the NCAA tournament, suggest that television revenue is the goose that lays the golden eggs for intercollegiate athletics. But for most institutions, ticket sales are still the primary source of revenue. Indeed, there is some evidence that television can have a negative impact on the overall revenues of many athletic programs by overexposing athletic events and eroding gate receipts. Lower game attendance brought on by television has been particularly harmful to those institutions and conferences whose sports programs are not broadcast as primetime or national events, since many of their fans stay home from university events in order to watch televised events involving major athletic powers.

The additional costs required to mount "TV quality" events tend to track increasing revenue in such a way that the more one is televised, the more one must spend. More and more institutions are beginning to realize that there is little financial incentive for excessive television coverage. While exposure can convey the good news of successful athletic programs and promote the university's visibility, it can also convey "bad news," particularly if there is a major scandal or a mishap with an event.

If the financial and publicity impact of television is not necessarily positive, why is there then such a mad rush on the part of athletics programs for more and more television exposure? Speaking from the perspective of one of the most heavily televised universities in the country, my suspicion is that the pressure for such excessive television coverage is not coming from the most successful and most heavily televised institutions — the Michigans, Ohio States, and UCLAs. It is, instead, coming from the "have-not" institutions, those who have chosen not to mount competitive programs but who have become heavily dependent on sharing the television revenue generated by the big box office events through conference or NCAA agreements.

Stated more bluntly, the television revenue-sharing policies of many conferences or broader associations, such as the NCAA, while implemented with the aim of achieving equity, are failing. They are, in reality, having the perverse effect of providing strong incentives for those institutions that are not attractive television draws to drive the system toward excessive commercialization or exposure of popular events. While the have-not universities share in the revenues, these institutions do not bear the financial burden or disruption of providing television-quality events. In a sense, the revenue-sharing system does not allow for negative feedback that might lead to more moderate approaches to television broadcasting.

What about the suggestion that student-athletes deserve some share of the spoils? The argument usually runs as follows: College sports is golden — witness, for example, the $550 million paid each year by CBS for the NCAA tournament or the $12 million payout per team for the football Bowl Championship Series games. And yet the athletes do not even get pocket money. Look at how much Chris Webber and Juwan Howard make in the pros. And what about college coaches, some of whom make over a million dollars a year? Shouldn't we pay the athletes who generate all this money? Late in his long tenure as executive director of the NCAA, Walter Byers argued that since colleges were exploiting the talents of their student-athletes, they deserved the same access to the free market as coaches. He suggested letting them endorse products, with the resulting income going into a trust fund that would become available only after they graduated or completed their eligibility.[2]

These myths are firmly entrenched not only in the public's mind but in the culture of the university. We need now to separate out the reality from the myth, to better understand the real nature of the financial issues facing college sports.

Reality 1: What Do Universities Really Make from Athletics?

As we noted earlier, in 1997, the University of Michigan generated $45 million from its athletics activities, of which only about $3 million came from television. Although the university actually generated far more than this from the broadcasting of events such as football and basketball games, the Rose Bowl, and the Big Ten and NCAA basketball tournaments, most of this revenue was shared with the other Big Ten and NCAA schools. How much of this revenue can we attribute to the efforts of students? This is hard to estimate. On the one hand, we might simply divide the entire revenue base by the number of varsity athletes (seven hundred) to arrive at about $45,000 per athlete. But, of course, coaches and staff also are responsible for generating revenue, by building winning sports programs or marketing or licensing sports apparel. Certain unusual assets, like Michigan Stadium, attract sizable crowds and generate significant revenue regardless of how successful the team is. Finally, we have not said anything yet about expenses. Operating expenditures at Michigan, as at every other university in the nation, are sometimes larger than revenues. As a result, the net revenues, the profit, is zero! While it is admittedly very difficult to estimate just how much income student-athletes bring to the university, it is clear that it is far less than most sportswriters believe.

Reality 2: What Do the Players Receive from the University?

At Michigan the typical instructional cost (not "price" or tuition) of our undergraduate programs is about $20,000 per student per year. When we add to this support for room and board and incidentals, it amounts to an investment of about $30,000 per year per fully tendered student-athlete, or between $120,000 to $150,000 per athlete over four or five years of studies. The actual value of this education is far higher, since it provides the student-athlete with an earning capacity far beyond that of a high school education (and even far beyond that of most professional sports careers, with the exception of only the greatest superstars). Of course, only a few student-athletes will ever achieve high-paying careers in professional sports. Most do not make the pros, and most of those who do are only modestly compensated for a few short years.

The real reward for student-athletes is, of course, a college education. Despite having somewhat poorer high school records, test scores, and preparation for college, athletes tended to graduate at rates quite comparable to those of other students. The reasons for their academic success involved both their strong financial support through scholarships and their academic support and encouragement through programs not available to students at large. Yet it is also the case that recruiting college athletes based entirely on physical skills rather than academic promise undermines this premise. As William Dowling, professor at Rutgers, has noted, "Problems will remain as long as players in the so-called revenue sports represent a bogus category of students, recruited on the basis of physical skills rather than for academic or intellectual ability."[4]

Those who call for professionalizing college athletics by paying student-athletes — and they are generally members of the sports media — are approaching college sports as show business, not as part of an academic enterprise. Only in show business do the stars make such grossly distorted amounts. In academics, the Nobel Prize winner does not make much more than any other faculty member. In the corporate world, the inventor of a device that earns a corporation millions of dollars will receive only a small incentive payment for her or his discovery. The moral of the story is that one simply cannot apply the perverse reward system of the entertainment industry to college sports — unless, of course, you believe college sports is, in reality, simply another form of show business.

A PRIMER ON COLLEGE SPORTS FINANCING

Most business executives would find the financial culture of intercollegiate athletics bizarre indeed. To be sure, there are considerable opportunities for revenue from college sports. . . . In terms of their revenue-generating capacity, three college football teams, Michigan, Notre Dame, and Florida, are more valuable than most professional football franchises.[5] Such statistics have lured college after college into big-time athletics, motivating them to make the investment in stadiums, coaching staffs, [and] scholarships, to join the big boys in NCAA's Division I-A.

Yet most intercollegiate athletics programs at most colleges and universities require some subsidy from general university resources such as tuition or state appropriation. Put another way, most college athletics programs actually lose money. . . . And, while football coaches might like to suggest that the costs of "nonrevenue" sports are the problem, particularly those women's sports programs mandated by Title IX, before blaming others, they should first look in a mirror. While football generates most of the revenue for intercollegiate athletics, it also is responsible for most of the growth in costs. More precisely, when college sports is transformed into an entertainment industry, and when its already intensely competitive ethos begins to equate expenditure with winning, one inevitably winds up with a culture that attempts to spend every dollar that it is generated, and then some.

Stated another way, the costs of intercollegiate athletics within a given institution are driven by decisions concerning the level of competition (e.g., NCAA Division, regional, or nationally competitive), the desire for competitive success, and the breadth of programs. Although football generates most of the revenue for big time athletic programs through gate receipts and broadcasting, it is also an extremely expensive sport. Not only does it involve an unusually large number of participants and attendant coaching and support staff, but the capital facilities costs of football stadiums, practice facilities, and training facilities are very high. Furthermore, many of the remaining costs of the athletic department, such as marketing staff, media relations, and business are driven, in reality, primarily by the needs of the football program rather than the other varsity sports. In this sense, football coaches to the contrary, big-time football programs are, in reality, cost drivers rather than revenue centers.

It is instructive to take a more detailed look at the various revenue streams and costs associated with intercollegiate athletics in order to get a sense of scale. *[Tables 3 and 4 show average revenues and expenditures for Division I institutions.]* The following are the principal sources of revenues and expenditures:

Revenues
- Ticket sales
- Guarantees
- Payouts from bowl games and tournaments
- Television
- Corporate sponsorships, advertising, licensing
- Unearned revenues
- Booster club donations
- Student fees and assessments
- State or other government support
- Hidden university subsidies

Expenditures
- Salaries
- Athletic scholarships
- Travel and recruiting
- Equipment, supplies, medicine
- Insurance
- Legal, public relations, administrative
- Capital expenditures (debt service and maintenance)

Furthermore, intercollegiate athletics is highly capital intensive, particularly at a big-time program such as Michigan. Few athletics programs amortize these capital costs in a realistic fashion. Including these imbedded capital costs on the balance sheet would quickly push even the most successful programs far into the red.

To illustrate, let us walk through the budget of the University of Michigan Department of Intercollegiate Athletics. First let me note that it is the practice of the university that intercollegiate athletics be a self-supporting enterprise, not consuming university resources. It receives neither state appropriation nor student tuition. Furthermore, this financial firewall works in both directions: any revenue balance earned by the athletic department cannot, under normal circumstances, be transferred to the academic side of the university. They must pay for what they cost the university, and they keep what they make. . . .

Not included in these figures were onetime expenditures of roughly $18 million to expand Michigan Stadium, to decorate it with a gaudy maize-and-blue halo designed by the noted architect Robert Venturi, complete with the ten-foot-high words to the Michigan fight song, "Hail to the Conquering Heroes"; to install $8 million worth of "Jumbo-tron" television scoreboards; and to build a sophisticated control room for Internet broadcasts. These onetime expenses were charged

TABLE 3.

SOURCES OF TOTAL REVENUES, DIVISION I-A, I-AA, I-AAA, 2001

	Division I-A		Division I-AA		Division I-AAA	
	Total division (in thousands of dollars)	Percentage of total	Total division (in thousands of dollars)	Percentage of total	Total division (in thousands of dollars)	Percentage of total
Ticket sales						
Public/faculty/staff	6,180	25	428	8	325	6
Students	283	1	5	0	15	0
Total ticket sales	6,463	26	433	8	340	7
Postseason compensation						
Bowl games	704	3	0	0	0	0
Tournaments	201	1	20	0	11	0
Total postseason	905	4	20	0	11	0
NCAA and conference distributions	2,231	9	273	5	196	4
Student activity fees	1,425	6	1,061	20	1,099	21
Guarantees and options	883	4	185	3	76	1
Cash contributions from alumni and others	4,625	18	497	9	434	8
Direct government support	371	1	224	4	128	3
Institutional support	2,525	10	2,206	41	2,390	47
Other						
Concessions	485	2	24	0	21	0
Radio/television	1,815	7	12	0	32	1
Program sales/advertising	137	1	26	0	42	1
Signage/sponsorship	1,129	4	142	3	103	2
Sports camps	234	1	73	1	90	2
Miscellaneous	1,955	8	184	3	154	3
Total other	5,755	23	461	9	442	9
Total	25,183	100	5,360	100	5,116	100

Source: Daniel Fulks, NCAA.

TABLE 4.

OPERATING EXPENSES BY OBJECT OF EXPENDITURE, DIVISION I-A, I-AA, I-AAA, 2001

	Division I-A		Division I-AA		Division I-AAA	
	Total division (in thousands of dollars)	Percentage of total	Total division (in thousands of dollars)	Percentage of total	Total division (in thousands of dollars)	Percentage of total
Grants-in-aid						
Men	2,229	9	1,170	17	814	14
Women	1,528	6	882	13	950	16
Administrative and non-gender	123	0	30	0	32	1
Total	3,880	15	2,082	31	1,796	31
Guarantees and options						
Men	991	4	49	1	36	1
Women	20	0	3	0	5	0
Administrative and non-gender	8	0	6	0	2	0
Total	1,019	4	58	1	43	1
Salaries and benefits						
Men	2,791	11	910	13	610	11
Women	1,258	5	527	8	505	9
Administrative and non-gender	3,232	13	920	14	791	14
Total	7,281	28	2,357	35	1,906	33
Team travel						
Men	1,147	4	356	5	260	5
Women	618	2	251	4	224	4
Administrative and non-gender	60	0	30	0	22	0
Total	1,825	7	637	9	506	9

(Continued)

TABLE 4. (Continued)

OPERATING EXPENSES BY OBJECT OF EXPENDITURE, DIVISION I-A, I-AA, I-AAA, 2001

	Division I-A		Division I-AA		Division I-AAA	
	Total division (in thousands of dollars)	*Percentage of total*	*Total division (in thousands of dollars)*	*Percentage of total*	*Total division (in thousands of dollars)*	*Percentage of total*
Recruiting						
Men	373	1	108	2	70	1
Women	153	1	56	1	53	1
Administrative and non-gender	4	0	3	0	5	0
Total	530	2	167	2	128	2
Equipment/uniforms/supplies						
Men	457	2	152	2	94	2
Women	178	1	71	1	73	1
Administrative and non-gender	363	1	94	1	99	2
Total	998	4	317	5	266	5
Fund-raising						
Men	50	0	9	0	10	0
Women	7	0	5	0	5	0
Administrative and non-gender	207	1	39	1	33	1
Total	264	1	53	1	48	1
Game officials						
Men	142	1	54	1	45	1
Women	73	0	33	0	36	1
Administrative and non-gender	3	0	4	0	1	0
Total	218	1	91	1	82	1

(Continued)

TABLE 4. (Continued)

OPERATING EXPENSES BY OBJECT OF EXPENDITURE, DIVISION I-A, I-AA, I-AAA, 2001

	Division I-A		Division I-AA		Division I-AAA	
	Total division (in thousands of dollars)	Percentage of total	Total division (in thousands of dollars)	Percentage of total	Total division (in thousands of dollars)	Percentage of total
Contract services						
Men	348	1	40	1	53	1
Women	82	0	14	0	15	0
Administrative and non-gender	514	2	99	1	59	1
Total	944	4	153	2	127	2
Sports camps						
Men	101	0	21	0	33	1
Women	60	0	14	0	20	0
Administrative and non-gender	200	1	21	0	18	0
Total	361	1	56	1	71	1
Other						
Men	2,277	9	193	3	129	2
Women	619	2	80	1	74	1
Administrative and non-gender	2,899	11	454	7	372	6
Total	5,795	23	727	11	575	10
Total operating expenses						
Men	10,906	43	3,041	45	2,154	37
Women	4,596	18	1,922	28	1,960	34
Administrative and non-gender	7,613	30	1,679	25	1,434	25
Total	22,754	89	6,642	98	5,548	96

(Continued)

TABLE 4. (Continued)

OPERATING EXPENSES BY OBJECT OF EXPENDITURE, DIVISION I-A, I-AA, I-AAA, 2001

	Division I-A		Division I-AA		Division I-AAA	
	Total division (in thousands of dollars)	Percentage of total	Total division (in thousands of dollars)	Percentage of total	Total division (in thousands of dollars)	Percentage of total
Debt service						
Men	226	1	25	0	0	0
Women	18	0	5	0	3	0
Administrative and non-gender	706	3	26	0	18	0
Total	950	4	56	1	21	0
Capital expenditures						
Men	625	2	21	0	81	1
Women	90	0	12	0	75	1
Administrative and non-gender	769	3	23	0	46	1
Total	1,484	6	56	1	202	4
Total expenditures						
Men	11,757	46	3,087	46	2,235	39
Women	4,704	18	1,939	29	2,038	35
Administrative and non-gender	9,088	36	1,728	26	1,498	26
Total	25,549	100	6,754	100	5,771	100

Source: Daniel Fulks, NCAA.

against (and largely decimated) the flexible reserve funds of the department. Lest you think these latter expenses were unusually extravagant, Ohio State is in the midst of several construction projects that will leave their athletic department saddled with a $277 million debt, to be paid over the next thirty years. (And you wonder why people believe that the financial culture of intercollegiate athletics is wacko?)

As I noted earlier, the financial strategy in intercollegiate athletics is strongly driven by competitive pressures. The belief that those who spend the most win the most drives institutions to generate and spend more and more dollars. The prosperous programs at institutions such as Michigan, Penn State, and Notre Dame set the pace for the entire intercollegiate athletics enterprise, no matter what the size of the school. As expenditures on athletics programs continue to spiral out of control, there have been increasing calls for action at both the national and conference level. Yet part of the problem is that many athletic departments hide the true nature of the financial operations not only from the prying eyes of the press and the public, but even from their own universities. Several years ago, the Big Ten Conference launched an effort to contain costs by restricting the growth of institutional expenditures on athletics to the rate of inflation. At that time, many universities were suffering as their athletics revenues were insufficient to cover costs. There were also concerns about competitiveness, since the wealthier schools tended to dominate most Big Ten sports, particularly football.

More specifically, Michigan and Ohio State, because of their very large stadiums, had considerably more gate receipt revenue than the other Big Ten members. Onetime football powers such as Wisconsin and Minnesota had fallen on hard times, with mediocre teams and low stadium attendance. Minnesota was in a particularly difficult bind since it had shifted its football games to the downtown Minneapolis Metrodome and torn down its on-campus stadium. Earlier attempts to address this discrepancy among institutions through revenue-sharing formulas had finally become burdensome enough to the larger stadium schools, particularly with the entry of Penn State, that the conference agreed to accept a more equitable formula.

Therefore, attempts to control expenditures rather than to redistribute revenues became the focus. But there was a big problem here. Nobody really knew how much the athletic departments in each university were spending. On top of that, no one seemed to know how much or where the revenue came from. And because most athletics programs were independent of the usual financial management and controls of their institutions, it was clear that this comparative information would be difficult if not impossible to obtain through the departments themselves.

Member institutions decided to form a special subcommittee to the Big Ten Council of Presidents comprised of the universities' chief financial officers. This CFO committee was charged with developing a system to obtain and compare annual athletics revenues and expenditures within the Big Ten. Needless to say, this decision to go outside of the athletic enterprise for supervision did not go down well in some schools where the athletic department had unusual autonomy. And while opening their books for examination was not particularly troublesome to most Big Ten universities, since as public institutions they frequently had to endure audits from state government, this was a very sensitive matter to the one private university in the Big Ten, Northwestern.

The first set of comparisons across all universities was eye opening.[8] Among the factors of particular note was the distribution of revenues.

Ticket sales	38 percent
Television and radio	13
Gift income	13

Subsidies	11
Licensing, concessions, etc.	9
Game settlements, guarantees	8
Bowls and NCAA revenue	4
Miscellaneous	4

Although broadcasting and bowl revenues were important — and are becoming more so — the largest single revenue source (38 percent) remained gate receipts. This explains why the three universities with very large stadiums (Michigan at 105,000, Ohio State at 98,000, and Penn State at 96,000) stand out in revenues. Among the public universities, there was great disparity in the capacity to generate private support for athletics (with Michigan ranking, surprisingly enough, toward the bottom of the range) and in their subsidies from state support.

The financial studies revealed that 72 percent of total athletic department revenue is attributable to football. Another 23 percent comes from men's basketball. In other words, 95 percent is generated by football and basketball combined. (Ice hockey contributes 4 percent and women's basketball 1 percent.) A further breakdown of revenue sources shows the difference between men's and women's sports.

Men's sports	71.1 percent
Women's sports	4.3
Administrative operations	24.6

In terms of expenditures, 57 percent was spent on football and men's basketball, while 24 percent was spent on women's sports, and 14 percent on all other men's sports. Despite the Big Ten Conference's efforts to achieve gender equity, women's programs amounted to only one-quarter of expenditures in the 1990s. Financial aid was distributed 67 percent to men, 33 percent to women, roughly in proportion to their representation among varsity athletes.

Two universities stood out in terms of the breadth and comprehensiveness of their programs: Ohio State, with thirty-five programs, and Penn State with thirty. Michigan's twenty-three programs were only in the middle of the pack, despite the fact that Michigan ranked number one in revenues ($45 million).

There was a factor-of-two difference in athletic department revenues and expenditures, ranging from Michigan and Ohio State at $45 million to Northwestern and Purdue at $25 million. The analysis also quickly made apparent why Northwestern had been so reluctant to share its financial data. In sharp contrast to the public universities, Northwestern was subsidizing its athletics programs from general academic resources to the tune of about $8 million per year (almost half their revenues). Although today, after two Big Ten football championships, faculty and students might believe it was worth the roughly eight hundred dollars per student of tuition (or other academic income) it cost to remain in the Big Ten, at the time of the first CFO surveys, this was highly sensitive information. While Northwestern's hidden subsidy was the largest among Big Ten universities, it was certainly not unique. Some institutions provided hidden subsidies by waiving tuition or granting instate tuition rates for student athletes. Others received direct subsidies for their athletics programs through state appropriations (e.g., Wisconsin received $634,000 per year).

There were a number of other significant differences among the expenditure patterns of the various universities. For example, several of the public universities charged only in-state tuition to athletes, even if they were out-of-state residents, thereby reducing very significantly their costs for athletic scholarships. In contrast, Michigan charged full out-of-state tuition levels, which were comparable to those of private institutions, thereby driving up the costs of athletic grants-in-aid programs considerably. Labor costs also varied widely among institutions, ranging from urban and unionized wage scales to rural and nonunionized wage scales.

It was finally concluded, after several years of effort, that the great diversity among institutions in terms of the manner in which revenue was generated, expenditures were managed, and accounting was performed made it almost impossible to attempt conference-wide cost containment. Hence, the Big Ten presidents adopted a policy encouraging rather than requiring cost containment. However, they also decided to continue the annual CFO comparative analysis of revenues and expenditures, if only to provide visibility for unusual practices.

SHOW ME THE MONEY!

Revenue flows into athletics departments from a number of sources and out again through a complex array of expenditures. . . . In this brief discussion, I will focus only on a few items of particular interest.

One of the most expensive elements of sports is the current grants-in-aid system for the financial support of student-athletes. In contrast to the need-based financial aid programs for regular students, colleges are allowed to provide student-athletes with sufficient support to meet "all commonly accepted educational expenses" — a full ride, regardless of financial need or academic ability. This policy, first implemented in football in the 1950s, has spread rapidly to all varsity sports. As the costs of a college education have rapidly increased over the past two decades, the costs of grants-in-aid have risen dramatically. For example, the University of Michigan currently spends about $8 million a year on grants-in-aid. But there is considerable variation among institutions, as the Big Ten financial data indicate.

Michigan	$7.6 million
Northwestern	5.7
Ohio State	4.6
Penn State	4.5
Michigan State	4.3
Indiana	4.1
Illinois	3.4
Minnesota	3.4
Purdue	3.4
Iowa	3.3
Wisconsin	1.8

In some cases, this discrepancy is due to institutions that choose to subsidize financial aid by granting all athletes in-state tuition levels, in effect hiding the subsidy of the difference between in-state and out-of-state levels. Although some universities restrict the number or types of grants-in-aid they provide in various sports, the University of Michigan has long had a policy of fully funding all allowable grants-in-aid in all sports in which it competes. Since most student-athletes are subject to out-of-state tuition levels, the resulting cost of athletically related student aid is unusually high at $8 million.

A second factor in the inflating costs was the rapid growth in size of football programs as coaches pushed through the unlimited-substitution rules in the 1960s. This system allowed college football to develop specialists for essentially every position and every situation in the game — offense and defense, blocking and tackling, kicking and passing. Although it was promoted as a way to make the game more exciting, it was not just a coincidence that it also made football far easier to play and to coach. More significantly, it transformed college football into a corporate and bureaucratic enterprise, with teams of over one hundred players, dozens of coaches, trainers, and equipment managers, and even technology experts in areas such as video production and computer analysis. Furthermore, unlimited substitution not only transformed college football into the professional football paradigm, but it also demanded that high school football follow the colleges and the pros down the same expensive path.

The third factor driving the rapid expansion of the program's cost and complexity has been the insatiable desire of football coaches for any additional gimmicks that might provide a competitive edge, either in play or competition. Special residences for football players became common, some resembling country clubs more than campus dormitories. Many football programs have built not only special training facilities but also even museums to display their winning traditions to prospective recruits. . . . Teams usually travel in high style, with charter jet service, four-star hotels, and even special travel clothing such as team blazers. And, of course, each time a coach at one university dreams up a new wrinkle, all of the other coaches at competing universities have to have it, no matter how extravagant or expensive.

This competitive pressure from coaches and fans — and even the media — has made it very difficult for athletic departments to control costs. Each time actions are proposed to slow the escalation of costs in the two main revenue sports, football and basketball, they are countered with the argument that the more one spends, the more one will win and hence the more one will make. The relative financial inexperience of those who manage athletic departments makes it even more difficult to resist these competitive forces. They tend to develop a one-dimensional financial culture, in which all attention is focused on revenue generation, and cost controls are essentially ignored.

A conversation with any athletic director soon reveals just how much of their attention is devoted to generating revenue to cover ever-increasing costs. This preoccupation with revenue generation propagates up through the hierarchy, to university presidents and governing boards, athletic conferences, and even the NCAA. Far more time is spent on negotiating broadcasting contracts or licensing agreements than on cost containment, much less concern about the welfare of student-athletes or the proper role of college sports in a university.

Though most of the revenue for college sports has traditionally come from revenue associated with football and basketball events, several of the most popular programs have generated very extensive licensing income from the use of institutional logos and insignia. A number of major athletics programs, Michigan among them, have signed lucrative contracts with sports apparel companies. Many athletic departments have also launched extensive fund-raising efforts involving alumni and fans, both for ongoing support and endowment. In fact, both athletic scholarship programs and key athletic department staff such as athletic directors and football coaches are supported by endowments in some universities.

Athletic departments go to great lengths and considerable creativity to find new sources of revenues. For example, when Michigan decided to replace its artificial turf in Michigan Stadium with natural turf in 1992, the athletic department got the bright idea that people might want to purchase a piece of the old carpet for nostalgic reasons. They chopped up the old artificial turf into an array of souvenirs, ranging from coasters to doormats to large rugs containing some of the lettering on the field. To their delight, these sold like hotcakes, and the department made over two hundred thousand dollars. . . .

Another example is the construction of an elegant new plaza and fence surrounding Michigan Stadium in 1995. The athletic department decided to sell paving bricks at a premium (one hundred to one thousand dollars apiece) and allow people to inscribe their names and perhaps even a brief message. Again, demand soared for the opportunity to become "a part of Michigan Stadium," and the department rapidly raised the several hundred thousand dollars required for the project.

Licensing provides a more standard means for generating revenue for the athletic department. Michigan moved early into a more direct merchandising effort, placing retail shops (the M-Go Blue Shops) in various athletics venues, so that it could participate directly in the profits from athletic or signature apparel. It was always a fascinating experience to browse through these shops to see what the fertile creativity of the marketing side of the athletic department had devised or approved for licensing: maize-and-blue toilet seats that play "The Victors" when raised, the Michigan football helmet chip-and-dip bowl, and hundreds upon hundreds of different sweatshirt designs. The catalog mail-order business became particularly lucrative.

. . . .

We have noted earlier the extreme volatility of most revenue sources for intercollegiate athletics. While a New Year's Day bowl appearance or success in the NCAA Basketball Tournament can provide a windfall, a poor season can trigger rapid declines in gate receipts, licensing income, and private gifts. Catastrophe awaits the naive athletic director who builds an expenditure budget based on such speculative income, since disaster awaits when the books are finally closed at year end. During my tenure as president, we not only required the athletic department to budget very conservatively, but it also was encouraged to build a reserve fund with sufficient investment income to compensate for any uncertainty in the operating budget. In fact, our athletic director generally measured financial performance in terms of the growth of the reserve fund from year to year.

FINANCIAL ACCOUNTABILITY

The athletic department at most NCAA Division I-A universities is treated as an auxiliary activity, separated by a financial firewall from the budgets of academic programs. This strategy allows athletic directors to offer up the excuse that the sometimes flamboyant expenditures of the department are not being made at the expense of the university. But it also creates major problems. It tends to focus most of the athletic department's energy (not to mention the conference's and NCAA's) on revenue generation rather than cost management. It subjects coaches and staff to extreme pressures to generate additional revenue in the mistaken belief that it will enhance the competitiveness of their programs. And, perhaps most significantly, it further widens the gap between the athletic department and the rest of the university.

Despite the boasts of athletic directors and football coaches to the contrary, intercollegiate athletics at most institutions — perhaps all institutions, if rigorous accounting principles were applied — is a net financial loser. All revenues go simply to support and in some cases expand the athletic empire, while many expenditures that amount to university subsidy are hidden by sloppy management or intricate accounting. Put more pointedly, college sports, including the celebrity compensation of coaches, the extravagant facilities, first-class travel and accommodations, VIP entertainment of the sports media, shoddy and wasteful management practices, all require subsidy by the university through devices such as student fees, hidden administrative overhead support, and student tuition waivers.

Yet our athletic departments not only tout their self-supporting status, but they vigorously seek and defend their administrative and financial independence. And well they should, since their primary activity is, increasingly, operating a commercial entertainment business. As college football and basketball become ever more commercial and professional, their claim on any subsidy from the university is diminished.

Of course, few of our sports problems are self-supporting. If we illuminate hidden costs and subsidies, we find that all intercollegiate athletics burden the university with considerable costs, some financial, some in terms of the attention required of university leadership, some in terms of the impact to the reputation and integrity of the university, and some measured only in the impact on students and staff. Experience has also shown that expenses always increase somewhat more rapidly than the revenues generated by college sports.

In conclusion, the mad race for fame and profits through intercollegiate athletics is clearly a fool's quest. Recognition on the athletic field or court has little relevance to academic reputation. Nebraska can win all the national championships it wishes, and it will never catch fair Harvard's eye. Indeed, fame in athletics is often paradoxical, since it can attract public scrutiny, which can then uncover violations and scandal. As the intensity and visibility of big-time athletics build, the university finds itself buffeted by the passion and energy of the media and the public, who identify with their athletics programs rather than their educational mission.

Yet every year, several more universities proudly proclaim they have decided to invest the resources to build sports programs that will earn them membership in NCAA's Division I-A. Sometimes lessons are never learned.

REFERENCES

2. Walter Byers with Charles Hammer, Unsportsmanlike Conduct: Exploiting College Athletes. Ann Arbor: University of Michigan Press, 1995.
4. William Dowling, "To Cleanse Colleges of Sports Corruption, End Recruiting Based on Physical Skills," Chronicle of Higher Education, July 9, 1999, B9.
5. Richard Sheehan, Keeping Score: The Economics of Big-Time Sports, New York: Diamond Communications, 1996, chaps. 11, 12.
8. Athletic Operations Survey, 1993–94, Big Ten Conference, Chicago, 1994.

University of Michigan Department of Athletics Operating Budgets, 2003–2004

For the proposed FY 2004 Operating Budget (described in detail on the following pages), we project an operating surplus of $1.7 million based on operating revenues of $58.9 million and operating expenses of $57.2 million. *[See Table 5.]* Highlights are as follows:

- The budget once again reflects a seven home-game schedule for football (as compared to six for a typical year).
- Revenue from sponsorship, licensing, and annual fund gifts continue to be budgeted at a conservative level and well below the projected results from FY 2003. These revenue sources are typically volatile and we will strive to achieve results more in line with FY 2003.
- In this year's budget, operating expenses again includes a $2.25 million transfer to a deferred maintenance fund established last year. The deferred maintenance fund is used as a means to provide for major repair and rehabilitation projects for our athletic facilities. We hope to continue to set aside additional funds in future years for this purpose.
- Expenditures other than compensation, financial aid, and University re-charges (including insurance), are budgeted at essentially flat levels from FY 03.

The budgeted operating surplus in FY 04 will be used to partially fund our capital needs for FY 04, which are budgeted at $2.4 million. Although we have stabilized our operating cash flow, our aging physical plant continues to require significant investment.

We are also pleased to report that based on preliminary results, we project that the operating surplus for FY 03 will be $5.0 million, $3.2 million more than budgeted. The favorable outcome is the result of greater than expected revenues from admissions, licensing, and annual gifts; offset by one-time expenses associated with our NCAA sanctions.

. . . .

2003–2004 BUDGET NOTES AND ASSUMPTIONS (ALL DOLLAR AMOUNTS IN 000'S)

Basis for Accounting

The University of Michigan Athletic Department manages its financial activity through the use of three different funds, the Operating Fund, the Endowment Fund, and the Plant Fund. The

Operating Fund budget is presented herein. (A consolidated financial statement is prepared annually and audited by PricewaterhouseCoopers.)

The Operating Fund budget includes most of the revenues and expenditures of the Athletic Department, with the exception of Endowment Fund gifts and associated market value adjustments (which are recorded in the Endowment Fund), and investments in the physical plant (with the associated debt, which are recorded in the Plant Fund).

Governmental Accounting Standards Board Statement No. 33 ("GASB 33") became effective for the University's 2001 reporting year. GASB 33 requires that the promises of private donations be recognized as receivables and revenues in the year the pledge was given, provided they are verifiable, measurable, and probable of collection. The Athletic Department Operating Fund budget presented herein records gifts when received (i.e., on a cash basis).

1. **Spectator admissions:** Spectator admissions are net of associated guarantee payments to visiting schools and consist of the following:

	Actual FY02	Projected FY03	Budget FY04
Football	21,815	27,467	28,190
Basketball	2,129	2,384	2,137
Hockey	1,429	1,501	1,438
Other	279	223	133
Total	25,652	31,575	31,898

Increased attendance revenue for football in FY 03 and FY 04 is primarily due to a seven home game football schedule in the 2002 and 2003 football season.

2. **Conference distributions:** Expected Big 10 conference distributions consist of the following:

	Actual FY02	Projected FY03	Budget FY04
Television (football and basketball)	5,647	5,721	6,053
Football bowl games	1,437	1,848	1,767
NCAA basketball based distributions	1,494	2,043	2,066
Other miscellaneous	350	441	350
	8,928	10,053	10,236

3. **Facilities:** Facility income includes the fee and rental revenue from the University of Michigan Golf Course, the Varsity Tennis Center, Yost Ice Arena, and the various other athletic department facilities.

4. **Investment income:** Investment income includes the return from the University Investment Pool (UIP) program as well as the quarterly distribution from Endowment and Quasi-Endowment Funds.

5. **Other income:** Other income consists of guarantees received for hockey and basketball away games, ticket handling fees, and other miscellaneous income.

6. **Compensation expense:** The athletic department has approximately 229 full time employees including those that have joint appointments with other University units, and various part time employees, interns, and graduate assistants. Compensation expense by area is as follows:

TABLE 5.

Michigan Budget 2003–2004

Michigan Athletic Department 2003/2004 Operating Budget (in thousands)

	FY 01/02 Actual	FY 02/03 Budget	FY 02/03 Projected	FY 03/04 Budget	% Change Budget	% Change Projected	$ Change Budget	$ Change Projected
Revenues								
Spectator admissions	25,652	29,458	31,575	31,898	8.3%	1.0%	2,440	323
Conference distributions	8,928	9,869	10,053	10,236	3.7%	1.8%	367	183
Corporate sponsorship	5,303	4,248	4,300	4,200	−1.1%	−2.3%	(48)	(100)
Licensing royalties	3,282	2,200	3,000	2,200	0.0%	−26.7%	—	(800)
Athletic scholarship fund and other gifts	4,017	2,805	3,805	2,900	3.4%	−23.8%	95	(905)
Radio	1,300	1,285	1,285	1,285	0.0%	0.0%	—	—
Facilities	2,008	1,995	1,900	1,900	−4.8%	0.0%	(95)	—
Concessions and parking	1,404	1,390	1,532	1,496	7.6%	−2.3%	106	(36)
Other income	1,152	809	1,140	828	2.3%	−27.4%	19	(312)
Investment income	2,378	2,000	2,100	2,000	0.0%	−4.8%	—	(100)
CURRENT FUND REVENUES	**55,424**	**56,059**	**60,690**	**58,943**	5.1%	−2.9%	**2,884**	**(1,747)**
Expenses								
Salaries, wages, & benefits	17,881	19,148	19,348	20,481	7.0%	5.9%	1,333	1,133
Financial aid to students	9,913	10,792	10,792	11,547	7.0%	7.0%	755	755
Team and game expense	9,361	9,830	9,830	10,528	7.1%	7.1%	698	698
Facilities	4,347	4,186	4,566	4,317	3.1%	−5.5%	131	(249)
Deferred Maintenance Fund transfer	—	2,250	2,250	2,250	NA	NA	—	—
Other operating and administrative expenses	6,092	6,078	6,893	6,463	6.3%	−6.2%	385	(430)
Debt service transfer to Plant Fund	1,945	1,950	1,950	1,680	−13.8%	−13.8%	(270)	(270)
CURRENT FUND EXPENSES	**49,539**	**54,234**	**55,629**	**57,266**	5.6%	2.9%	**3,032**	**1,637**

(Continued)

TABLE 5. (Continued)

MICHIGAN BUDGET 2003–2004

MICHIGAN ATHLETIC DEPARTMENT 2003/2004 OPERATING BUDGET (IN THOUSANDS)

	FY 01/02 Actual	FY 02/03 Budget	FY 02/03 Projected	FY 03/04 Budget	% Change Budget	% Change Projected	$ Change Budget	$ Change Projected
NET OPERATING SURPLUS (DEFICIT)	**5,885**	**1,825**	**5,061**	**1,677**				
Transfers and capital expenditures								
Capital expenditures from Current Funds and transfers to Plant Fund	(2,747)	(3,597)	(5,738)	(2,100)				
Transfers to Endowment Fund	(259)	(100)	(200)	(300)				
Transfer from Quasi-Endowment Fund	—	—	—	—				
Net transfers and capital expenditures	**(3,006)**	**(3,697)**	**(5,938)**	**(2,400)**				
INCREASE (DECREASE) IN CURRENT FUND BALANCES	**2,879**	**(1,872)**	**(877)**	**(723)**				

Source: University of Michigan.

	Actual FY02	Projected FY03	Budget FY04
Coaches and team staff	7,099	7,786	8,352
Compliance, sports information, and other administration	2,141	2,335	2,364
Athletic medicine, conditioning, academic support	1,870	2,049	2,132
Facilities	1,930	2,094	2,148
Sports marketing, development, & studio operations	791	876	831
Ticket and business office	615	641	618
Fringe benefits	3,435	3,567	4,036
Total	17,881	19,348	20,481

7. **Financial aid to students:** The athletic department grants the maximum allowable scholarships to all varsity sports (men's soccer and women's water polo, where varsity status started in 2001, phased in scholarships over a three-year period with full implementation in FY 03). Total grant-in-aid equivalencies are forecasted at 334 with an in-state to out-of-state ratio of 30% to 70%.

8. **Sports programs:** Sports program expense is comprised of the following:

	Actual FY02	Projected FY03	Budget FY04
Team travel expenses	3,035	2,970	3,179
Equipment	1,709	1,689	1,668
Home game, hosted events, & officials	1,352	1,629	1,744
Training and medical expenses	725	876	905
Recruiting	801	851	871
Vacation board	406	464	494
Post season expenses, net	413	465	575
Other sport program expenses	920	886	1,092
Total	9,361	9,830	10,528

Postseason expenses are estimated based on the likelihood of participation in postseason events for the majority of varsity sports. The postseason budget assumes that the football bowl expenditures will not exceed the bowl expense allowance received.

9. **Facility expenses:** Facility expenses consist of the following:

	Actual FY02	Projected FY03	Budget FY04
Repairs & maintenance	1,495	1,650	1,400
Utilities	1,591	1,698	1,760
Supplies & equipment	672	640	620
Other facility expenses	589	578	537
Total	4,347	4,566	4,317

10. **Deferred Maintenance Fund Transfer:** In FY 02 the department established a Deferred Maintenance Fund and $2.25 million was transferred from the Operating Fund to the Plant Fund as a means to provide for repair and rehabilitation projects for the athletic physical plant. The FY 03 operating expenses also include a $2.25 million transfer to the Deferred Maintenance Fund. Activity in the Fund is projected as follows:

	Actual FY02	Projected FY03	Budget FY04
Beginning balance	-	-	1,700
Transfers	-	2,250	2,250
Uses	-	(550)	(1,105)
Ending balance	-	1,700	2,845

11. **Other operating and administrative expenses:** Other operating and administrative expenses consist of the following:

	Actual FY02	Projected FY03	Budget FY04
Corporate sponsor and development expenses, including television production costs	1,950	1,963	2,075
University re-charges	869	901	1,009
Postage, office equipment, & supplies	428	627	594
Telephone	508	504	426
Publications & printing	402	393	371
Professional travel	245	292	287
Insurance	293	398	547
Band expenses, excluding postseason expenses	151	155	155
Big 10 conference and other dues	95	100	100
NCAA penalties	-	580	-
Other expenses	1,151	980	899
Total	6,092	6,893	6,463

12. **Debt service:** Debt service and associated debt is forecast as follows:

	Budgeted Interest	Budgeted Principal	Projected Balance
Canham Natatorium	160	685	3,040
Stadium expansion	143	595	2,650
Tennis center — phase 2*	-	-	-
1995 refinance (Yost & tennis center)*	-	-	-
Gymnastics practice facility	71	480	1,425
Rowing facility	51	45	995
Projected ending FY 2003 balance	425	1,805	8,110

Total debt service	2,230
Less amounts on deposit in Plant Fund	(550)
Net debt service for Operating Fund	1,680

*Bonds paid off in fiscal year 2003.

13. **Transfers to Plant Fund for capital expenditures:** Capital expenditures and estimated Plant Fund transfers are budgeted at $2.1 million and consist of various renovation projects. These amounts are based on transferring the full estimated construction cost to the Plant Fund or otherwise providing for full construction cost in the Operating Fund.

BUDGET PRINCIPLES

Self-Supporting

The University of Michigan is one of the few athletic programs in the country that is expected to be self-supporting from an economic perspective, as there are no tuition waivers, student fees, or state tax dollars that directly fund the Athletic Department operations. Historically, Athletics has managed to "stand on its own." More recently, however, the Department has been challenged to achieve a balanced budget. From fiscal year 1999 through 2001, Athletics accumulated three consecutive years of operating deficits totaling nearly $6 million. These deficits were funded by reserves which had been accumulated from prior budget surpluses in addition to a one-time transfer from the University in FY 2001. As of June 2003, the Athletic Department has a positive operating fund balance which includes expendable funds of approximately $5 million. In addition to these available funds, the Athletic Department also has approximately $5 million of expendable funds in the Quasi-Endowment Fund that have been accumulated from prior budget surpluses.

Sources of Revenue

The Athletic Department primarily relies on admission revenue and conference distributions to fund the department. (All television contract revenue and NCAA tournament revenues are directed to the conference office where it is shared equally with the Big 10 conference members.) While football admissions and other revenue related to the football and basketball programs provide substantial revenue (approximately 95% of revenues are tied directly or indirectly to football, men's basketball, and ice hockey; the balance is derived from investment income and other facility revenues), the athletic department is financially dependent on private support to fund the overall operations. (Without private support, the deficit for the three year period 1999–2001 would have been $8.5 million higher.) Energizing the development efforts of the Athletic Department has been a key initiative of the department.

Adequate Funding for All Sports

The Athletic Department has operated under a philosophy to generally provide adequate funding for all sports teams to compete successfully at a national level. Fundamental to this policy is that the Athletic Department grants the maximum allowable scholarships to all varsity sports. The combined NCAA maximum scholarship level for all Michigan varsity sports equates to over 300 full scholarships at a current cost of approximately $11.5 million. Although the department pays an out-of-state tuition rate to the University for those student-athletes from outside of Michigan who are on scholarship, there are no restrictions placed on our coaches to recruit in-state versus out-of-state prospective student-athletes (which allows our teams to be competitive at a national level).

Equity Goals

The Athletic Department has been a leader in the conference in terms of providing opportunities for women student-athletes. Approximately 50.5% of all participating student-athletes are female, and approximately $5.2 million will be spent on aid for female student-athletes for FY 2004. Overall direct expenses for women's sports are budgeted for approximately $11 million for FY 2004.

Corporate Partnerships

The financial pressures on the Athletic Department have grown significantly over the last two decades at Michigan as expenditures have risen and the opportunity for increased revenue streams have been limited. Many premier athletic programs are overcoming similar challenges by embracing the commercialization of all aspects of collegiate athletics. At Michigan, we have resisted most of these opportunities (e.g., stadium skyboxes, stadium advertising, etc.) as inconsistent with our traditions and values. We are one of the few major institutions that prohibit advertising and signage within the football stadium. Corporate solicitation efforts are carried out with respect and preservation of the Michigan values and traditions.

Facility Renewal

Financial pressures have led to an absence of regular budget revenues dedicated to major maintenance and repair that has led to episodic and uneven attention to the rehabilitation and renewal of the physical plant. The magnitude of necessary facility renovations is significant. An effective capital campaign that maintains the quality of the athletic campus is a main focus for the upcoming year.

Beginning in the 2003 fiscal year, the Athletic Department established a ***deferred maintenance fund.*** The deferred maintenance fund will be used as a means to provide for major repair and rehabilitation projects for our athletic facilities. Providing for additional funds in future years to fund the upkeep of the athletic facilities is a priority in Athletic Department long-term planning.

Balanced Budget

Delivering a consistent balanced budget each year is a prerequisite to the Athletic Department's maintenance of its excellence. For the 2003 fiscal year, the Athletic Department is projected to show an approximate $5 million surplus on an operating basis, and essentially breaking even after capital spending.

The Athletic Department's goal is to provide a "balanced budget" that consists of a reasonable surplus based on conservative assumptions. The budget will only be truly balanced after consideration of funds for the maintenance and improvement of the athletic facilities.

ANNUAL DETAIL BUDGET PROCESS

Background on Fund Accounting and Relationship to the University

The University of Michigan Athletic Department manages its financial activity through the use of three different funds, the Operating Fund, the Endowment Fund, and the Plant Fund.

The Operating Fund budget has grown from $35 million six years ago to approximately $60 million in the latest fiscal year. The operating fund includes most of the revenues and expenditures of the Athletic Department, with the exception of Endowment Fund gifts and associated market value adjustments (which are recorded in the Endowment Fund), and investments in the physical plant (with the associated debt, which are recorded in the Plant Fund).

While the Athletic Department uses University central accounting systems, the operations are managed in a decentralized fashion. Like other University units, Athletics is expected to develop [its] own budgeting tools to the extent it is necessary to ensure appropriate controls and to extract the level of detail desired. The University assists by providing a central data warehouse for standard financial information which may be queried and combined with local information.

Budget Development

The business office of the Athletic Department regularly analyzes current financial information and prepares periodic updates to both the annual forecasts and long-term financial projections. Information and assumptions for spectator admissions, conference distributions, licensing revenue, investment income, and other revenue items are reviewed on a monthly basis. The business office prepares detail budgets annually for spectator admissions, conference distributions, licensing revenues, investment income, salary and benefits expense, debt service, and financial aid expense based on current operating plans and review with the Athletic Director.

A department-wide detail budgeting process begins in the winter for each of the 25 sports, 20 facilities, and 12 administrative departments. These budgets are based on a "zero-based" budgeting approach whereby each cost center is required to justify and document its requested operating budget annually.

The sports teams typically have an operating budget request of approximately $10 million that consists of team travel, recruiting, equipment, and other team related expenses (not including salaries, benefits, and financial aid expense). These budgets are reviewed and approved by the appropriate sports administrator and the business office. Team expenditure requests that are outside of the standard operating budget, yet legitimate (e.g., extra away game, postseason banquets, etc.), are required to be funded by booster gifts or supplemental fundraising activities (see "Booster clubs and special accounts" below).

The facility cost centers typically have an operating budget request of approximately $5 million that would consist of utilities, repairs and maintenance, and other related facility expenses. These budgets are reviewed and approved by senior facility administration and the business office.

The Administrative cost centers typically have an operating budget request of approximately $6 million consisting of expenses for the ticket office, sports information, compliance, academic support, development, marketing, promotions, and other administration. These cost centers are reviewed and approved by the Chief Financial Officer.

Capital Budget

A department-wide detail capital budgeting process for each cost center also begins in the winter. In addition to an annual component, all department heads are encouraged to document their facility needs over the next three years. Each requested capital project requires justification before approval. Capital project requests are prioritized by senior facility administration, the Chief Financial Officer, and the Athletic Director and approved for the current year based on available funds.

Booster Clubs and "Special Accounts"

Booster clubs and special accounts are used as a means to fund team expenditures that are outside of the "standard" operating budget. A standard operating budget involves the judgment of the sports administrators in terms of a schedule, equipment, and other resources the department will support on an annual basis. Team expenditure requests that are outside of the standard operating budget, yet legitimate (e.g., extra away game, postseason banquets, etc.), are required to be funded by booster gifts or supplemental fundraising activities.

Booster club and special account transactions are processed in the same manner as other University transactions and require a similar approval process.

LOGO COPS:
THE LAW AND BUSINESS OF
COLLEGIATE LICENSING

Robert Lattinville

INTRODUCTION

.... Universities offering intercollegiate athletics have become wise to the virtues of properties licensing. The once fortuitous sale of a college sweatshirt at the campus bookstore has given way to a concerted, sophisticated, national (and increasingly global) endeavor by universities to harvest the bounty of its licensed products. College athletics is big business and the licensing of merchandise capitalizing on its popularity is its latest venture.

The undeniable success of collegiate licensing belies its contemporary advent. The debut of collegiate sports on television in the 1970s created fans, spawned an awareness of rivalries and rekindled loyalties among alumni. By the early to mid-1980s, an exponential increase in televising college sports inspired many colleges and universities to implement licensing programs in order to insure control over goods and services bearing collegiate marks. Concurrent with increased interest in their sports, universities experienced a decrease in governmental support. These circumstances cultivated a fertile atmosphere for collegiate licensing programs.

The most recent growth in the collegiate licensing industry is attributable to the tremendous popularity of prominent schools with highly visible athletic programs. At present, slightly over 10% of U.S. colleges and universities operate licensing programs. Thus, growth of the collegiate licensing industry should continue as established programs pursue different products and distribution channels and licensing neophytes implement new programs. . . .

. . . . *[The author's discussion of trademarks is omitted.]*

III. THE BUSINESS OF COLLEGIATE LICENSING

A. Two Forms of Licensing Programs

The sale of licensed merchandise yields universities tremendous rewards in terms of money, recognition, and status. Not surprisingly, most colleges and universities have implemented licensing programs which merchandise properties associated with their athletic teams. A number of universities, most notably Notre Dame, operate self-contained programs employing a full-time licensing department. The licensing departments of these independent programs act in concert with the university's general counsel's office to operate all aspects of the university's licensing effort. Other universities choose to contract with a licensing agent which, for a fee, can register the universities' marks, negotiate licensing agreements, evaluate quality control, police infringers and, if necessary, litigate. Finally, universities may opt for a hybrid program which permits independence in local or regional markets but may execute contracts for national programs or unique products via its licensing agent.

1. Independent Programs.   . . . The primary reason for operating an independent or hybrid program is control. Independent programs permit selection and control of trademark registration, licensees, artwork, overall product quality, and control of the program's manufacturers and retailers. This independence also offers flexibility. For example, an independent licensing program may vary its fees according to the type of product sold, the nature or volume of a licensee's sales, and the geographic market serviced by the licensor. Cost is also a factor. A university that contracts with a licensing agent may pay as much as 40% to 50% of the royalty revenues generated to the licensing agent. However, at least in the formative stages of a university's licensing program, the expenses of staffing and support for the program may cancel out any additional revenues derived from internal operations.

A university may also wish to exercise independent judgment with respect to the enforcement of the trademarks. . . . An independent program permits a "personal touch and attention to detail" which may only be found in an independent licensing program's singular purpose: generating revenue for and enhancing the image of its sponsor university. Although in the minority, independent licensing programs have proven to generate significant revenue for their sponsor universities.

2. Licensing Agents.   Licensing agents provide valuable services to new and established licensing programs. Their specialization and expertise afford their client universities with sage counsel in the registration of marks, negotiation of licensing agreements with manufacturers, policing of infringers and quality control among manufacturers and, when necessary, litigation. Policing marks against infringers is a costly process and one that bodes in favor of employing a licensing agent to share the burden, especially in a program's formative years when revenues cannot support such an effort. Even universities with successful independent programs . . . [contract] with licensing agents to take advantage of their national scope of business or lucrative manufacturer lists. Two agencies, the Collegiate Licensing Group (CLC) and the Licensing Resource Group, Inc. (LRG), represent the vast majority of universities which maintain a licensing program.

. . . .

The impressive resumes of CLC and LRG underscore the principal benefit to a university contracting with a licensing agent: economies of scale. . . . Irrespective of a university's decision to hire an agent or operate a licensing program, the licensing agreement will define its rights and obligations among its licensees.

. . . .

IV. THE FUTURE OF COLLEGIATE LICENSING

Collegiate licensing appears bounded only by the imagination of its constituents and technology. The prospects of new products, new channels of advertising and distribution, and new participants (licensors, manufacturers, and licensees) should stoke collegiate licensing's uninterrupted growth.

A. New Products

Anticipating the potential saturation of trademarked apparel, universities are adopting principles of collateral-licensing to expand into non-apparel markets. Paper towels, napkins, paper plates, utensils, table cloths, and stadium blankets are all logical mediums for capitalizing on the throng of tailgaters at a Saturday afternoon game. Some less obvious examples of collateral products which have been licensed by schools are toilet paper, fishing lures, coffins, and even an attempt to license condoms. Without exception, all participants in the collegiate licensing business recognize the enormous potential for electronics, video games, and CD-ROMs. . . .

Some universities re-create the market for existing apparel items by changing the style of their uniforms or logos. The Collegiate Licensing Company has commissioned a New York City designer to redesign the logos of highly-visible universities. Sales of merchandise bearing the redesigned logos have been tremendous. . . . On its face, this practice appears tantamount to churning a consumer's investment in collegiate licensed wear.

Another area of intense competition and growth is the market for authentics. Companies . . . spend millions of dollars each year to receive an "official" affiliation with schools which provide the company sweeping exposure through television and school name recognition. . . . This arrangement should pay handsome sums to both parties as . . . supporters across the United States and Canada rush out to purchase the uniforms of their favorite players. Additionally, universities have begun to license products in recognition of special events or accomplishments: 100 years of football, an NCAA tournament berth, or a national championship.

B. New Channels of Advertising and Distribution

The most popular advertising and publicity mediums for promoting consumer awareness of collegiate licensed products are event programs, broadcast media, and trade publications. Licensed product exposure also has been generated by providing licensed products for inclusion in television, movies, and public sales or auctions. Fashionably, the Internet is playing a role in the advertising and distribution of collegiate licensed products. Universities are establishing home pages on the World Wide Web which concurrently entreat customer interest and facilitate purchases. The NCAA has also implemented its own program on the Internet which will distribute merchandise through the program's electronic catalogs, on and off-campus retailers, and electronic kiosks. Geographically, the frontier of collegiate licensing is experiencing international expansion. In fact, licensing agents specializing in international business already possess sophisticated experience in the global marketing of collegiate licensed products.

C. New Participants

This section of the article could well be entitled New Combinations of Participants. Cross-licensing is the term used to define joint licensing of one school's mark with other schools' marks.

Collegiate licensing programs are actively pursuing joint-use agreements where two or more licensors allow their logos to appear together on merchandise. The Southeastern Conference's football championship, for example, is a fertile area for cross-licensing arrangements among the conference and its respective divisional winners. Outside of intercollegiate athletics, cartoon characters are commonly used as successful joint-use agreement sources. The Collegiate Licensing Company is currently preparing a cross-licensing program involving Olympic marks in conjunction with collegiate marks. Similarly, The Licensing Resource Group has established a cross-licensing project which licenses the NCAA's marks with those of its member institutions.

Although cross-licensing offers lucrative opportunities, licensors must be completely cognizant of their co-parties' affiliations. . . . From a legal perspective, the results are predictable. The manufacturers and or retailers participating in such national programs customarily execute non-exclusive agreements. The participating universities, as trademark owners, are uniformly entitled to render final approval of the manufacturer's artwork. Thus, a genuine legal conflict will rarely exist among retailers, but if it does, the university will have ultimate control over the product before it is introduced into commerce. The potential business conflict, however, should be recognized and addressed in the negotiation stage of these multi-party arrangements.

Some commentators suggest that the NCAA serve as the clearinghouse for cross-licensing arrangements, functioning similarly to the properties divisions of this country's professional sports leagues. Though logically appealing, this suggestion is untenable as each university owns the rights to its marks. Assigning the universities' marks to the NCAA would not solve the problem. In an analogous situation, the Supreme Court has previously held that the NCAA violated federal antitrust law in its negotiations on behalf of its members for the televising of football games.

The most obvious area of expansion for collegiate licensing is the addition of new licensors and licensees. As noted, just over 10% of this country's universities maintain a licensing program. Arguably, not every school is qualified to adopt one. However, many small schools such as Tuskegee University have implemented modest licensing programs which take advantage of a school's local, regional, or unique appeal. Likewise, scores of manufacturers could be added to the roles of licensees. Given the powerful market control exerted by established sports product manufacturers, however, the biggest opportunities for manufacturers are in the area of collateral goods.

V. CONCLUSIONS AND PRESCRIPTIONS

Collegiate licensing has become an integral part of the business of universities. As its operation becomes better understood, new licensors and licensees will be compelled to participate in its generous benefits. From a university's perspective, the recent trend in case law affecting collegiate licensing has been favorable and the global appreciation for collegiate sports is unparalleled by any other time in history. The issue for the industry remains how to cultivate the growth of this business.

In addition to the quantitative methods of expanding collegiate licensing discussed above, qualitative measures must also be considered. One of the most glaring omissions of collegiate licensing programs has been the lack of licensee/retailer programs. Such programs might include sales recognition awards, certificates of appreciation, and licensee/retailer social or merchandising functions. The Coalition to Advance the Protection of Sports Logos (CAPS) and the Association of Collegiate Licensing Administrators (ACLA) are two organizations established to advance the interests of licensees. CAPS is comprised of the properties divisions of the NFL, NHL, NBA, and MLB as well as . . . the Collegiate Licensing Company. This organization facilitates the flow of interleague information. Boasting over 250 members, ACLA provides collegiate licensing administrators with a forum for compiling, reviewing, and interpreting information on industry trends and contemporary business and legal issues. Bolstered by these organizations, licensors start farther out along the licensing industry's learning curve and gain experience at an accelerated pace.

The most rewarding but equally challenging operation of any university's licensing program is the distribution of royalty revenues. Among the alternatives to be considered are endowments for athletic scholarships and contributions to the general scholarship fund. This author posits the potentially unpopular position that without the existence of successful athletic teams and the media's chronicling of their accomplishments, a university would derive little or no revenue from its licensing program. Hence, directing licensing royalties to the university's athletic department should receive equal, if not priority, consideration. An immediate benefit would be realized by universities feeling the pressures of Title IX compliance. Many commentators submit that revenues generated by a university's athletic department should be deducted from university contributions for purposes of complying with Title IX.

Capitalizing on the insatiable interest in college athletics, collegiate licensing affords its participants significant opportunities for generating revenue and recognition. Universities can no longer afford to overlook or underappreciate the significance of collegiate licensing.

TABLE 6.

NCAA DIVISION I-A FOOTBALL AND BASKETBALL FACILITY NAMING-RIGHTS DEALS (RANKED BY TOTAL VALUE)

Facility	School	Sponsor	Total gift	No. of years	Expires	Avg. annual value
Save Mart Center (a) (b)	Fresno State University	Save Mart Supermarkets	$40 million	20	2023	$2 million
Comcast Center	University of Maryland	Comcast Corp.	$20 million (c)	25	2026	$800,000
Jones SBC Stadium	Texas Tech University	SBC Communications Inc.	$20 million	20	2019	$1 million
Value City Arena	Ohio State University	Value City Department Stores	$12.5 million (d)	Indefinite	NA	NA
Cox Arena at Aztec Bowl	San Diego State University	Cox Communications Inc.	$12 million	Indefinite	NA	NA
United Spirit Center	Texas Tech University	United Supermarkets Co.	$10 million	20	2015	$500,000
Bank of America Arena	University of Washington	Bank of America Corp.	$5.1 million (e)	10	2009	$510,000
Coors Events Center	University of Colorado	Adolph Coors Co.	$5 million	Indefinite	NA	NA
Cox Pavillion	University of Nevada–Las Vegas	Cox Communications Inc.	$5 million	10	2009	$500,000
Papa John's Cardinal Stadium	University of Louisville	Papa John's	$5 million	Indefinite	NA	NA
Wells Fargo Arena	Arizona State University	Wells Fargo & Co.	$5 million	Indefinite	NA	NA
Carrier Dome	Syracuse University	Carrier Corp.	$2.75 million	Indefinite	NA	NA
Alltel Pavillion	Virginia Commonwealth University	Alltel Corp.	$2 million	10	2008	$200,000

NA: Not applicable.
(a) Facility under construction, scheduled to open in fall 2003.
(b) PepsiCo acquired naming rights to the venue as part of a 23-year, $40 million sponsorship — the first three years of which have come while the arena is under construction — but passed the rights to Modesto, Calif.-based Save Mart Supermarkets while retaining campuswide pouring rights. Save Mart declined to disclose its contribution for the naming-rights portion of the deal.
(c) To be paid over 10 years; naming rights last 25 years. Comcast paid an additional $5 million for logo rights to the basketball floor.
(d) Value City Arena was part of the naming-rights deal for the Jerome Schottenstein Center.
(e) For renovations to existing facility.
Source: Street & Smith's SportsBusiness Journal research. Originally published November 18, 2002.

BEER AND CIRCUS: HOW BIG-TIME COLLEGE SPORTS IS CRIPPLING UNDERGRADUATE EDUCATION

Murray Sperber

Many myths about intercollegiate athletics endured through the twentieth century and beyond, but the one most deserving of a silver stake through its heart is the contention that universities need big-time college sports programs to attract alumni donations, and the more the teams win, the more money the alums give to old, now new Siwash.

* * *

Repeat after me: There is no empirical evidence demonstrating a correlation between athletic department achievement and [alumni] fund-raising success. A number of researchers have explored this putative relationship, and they all have concluded that it does not exist. The myth persists, however, aided by anecdotal evidence from sports reporters who apparently spend more time in bars than in development [fund-raising] offices.

— Richard W. Conklin, vice president of the University of Notre Dame

Many studies indicate that alumni giving is independent of college sports success or failure, and has no relation to whether a school has a big-time intercollegiate athletic program or not. Yet, the myth continues; central to its perpetuation are the University of Notre Dame Fighting Irish. Currently, many members of the sports media claim that because the famous Notre Dame football program is in a "down period," ND alumni are angry and closing their checkbooks to the school's fund-raisers. This is not true. Notre Dame alums feel intense loyalty to their university, in large part because of its historic emphasis on undergraduate education and the bonds that, as students, they established with faculty, staff, and fellow undergraduates. As a result, ND alums support their alma mater during good times and bad, and they give as much money — often more — during losing football seasons as during championship years. As Richard Conklin suggests, the sports media should exit the saloon and examine nonsports parts of the university.

A major element of Notre Dame's fund-raising success is its concept of "Notre Dame Family." The freshmen class, less than two thousand men and women, join it and remain within it for the rest of their lives. Many Big-time U's also try to use this concept of "family" but fail; they attempt to include legions of freshmen into a "family" of twenty-five thousand or more students on campus and a multitude of graduates. Freshmen at these schools cannot feel attached to more than a hundred thousand of their "closest friends." For many students at Big-time U's, alienation begins at entrance, continues through their undergraduate careers, and turns into indifferent, often hostile, alumni. The size and success of the school's intercollegiate athletic program rarely changes this attitude.

Contrary to the myth that big-time college sports equals alumni donations, the formula for extracting maximum dollars from alums involves education. In addition to establishing an authentic sense of university family, a school must provide undergraduates with a quality education. Subsequently, if its graduates are pleased with what they learned and proud of their degrees, they want "to give something back" to their alma mater and continue a lifetime relationship with it. The "Alumni giving" rankings in *U.S. News's* annual college issue indicate that schools using this formula raise much more money from their alums than do Big-time U's that neglect undergraduate education. For example, the magazine rates Notre Dame fourth in "Alumni giving." . . .

The proponents of the third New R should examine the *U.S. News* "Alumni giving" rankings. Other than Notre Dame and Duke, no other NCAA Division I-A football school makes the top-ten list. . . Instead, the usual suspects — institutions famous for their quality undergraduate education programs and relatively small student bodies — dominate the "Alumni giving" list. From Number 1 to 10 are: Princeton, Dartmouth, Yale, Notre Dame, Harvard, Cal Tech, Duke, MIT, Penn, and Brown.

The schools through the teens also feature non-big-time college football teams, and although several are in Division I-A, only one, Stanford, has had outstanding football success in recent years. From Number 11 down are: Rice, Lehigh, Wake Forest, Emory, Chicago, Cornell, Stanford, Washington of St. Louis, and Brandeis. Again, all of these universities have relatively small student bodies and provide their undergraduates with a first-rate education.

Undoubtedly, that education helps their graduates gain good jobs, earn lots of money, and give some of it back to their alma maters. Yet, if big-time college sports universities also provided quality educations to all of their students, wouldn't they head the "Alumni giving" list? After all, these institutions graduate thousands upon thousands of students every year, and simply by weight of numbers, they should bulldoze the smaller schools in "Alumni giving." Instead, such Big-time U's with top college sports teams as Wisconsin (Madison), Michigan, UCLA, Texas (Austin), and the University of Washington rank, respectively, 126, 128, 134, 136, and 144 on the *U.S. News* "Alumni giving" list.

These statistics contradict the myth that big-time college sports generates alumni dollars. One of the reasons for the reality is the fact that many successful alums of Big-time U's obtained their education *despite* these institutions, not because of them, and these men and women were alienated as students and remain so as graduates. . . .

. . . .

. . . . Nevertheless, the big-time college-sports-equals-alumni-giving myth continues, in part because athletic departments claim to raise millions of dollars in donations to the university every year, and the media never examines this money, or asks why it is given, or where it ends up in the institution. This money trail begins with the alumni and the boosters.

At Big-time U's, a small percentage, usually in single digits, of alumni contribute annually to the school's intercollegiate athletics program (a similarly low percentage donate to its educational programs). However, often the main contributors to athletic departments are boosters — rabid sports fans who, unlike alumni, never attended the institution and whose interest in it focuses almost exclusively on its college sports teams. Within the context of college sports finances, because of the constant deficits, every alum and booster dollar obtained by an athletic department remains in its cashbox, soaking up a bit of red ink.

These alumni and booster dollars are clearly not gifts to the academic parts of the university, but are they donations at all? Only if one accepts a College Sports MegaInc. tax scam. In reality, the majority of this alumni and booster money goes to purchase seats at football and basketball games. At schools where ticket demand outpaces supply, athletic departments call season tickets "priority" items, adding a large "priority" surcharge to the low face value of the seat and pricing the package as high as the market will bear. Because of the NCAA's lobbying power in Congress, 80 percent of the surcharge is now deemed a tax-deductible donation to higher education, and a similar deduction applies to the "priority" rental and purchase of skyboxes in college stadiums and arenas. No matter what the Congress, the NCAA, and member universities want to call this money, because Joe Alum and Booster Bob would not obtain their seats or boxes without paying the "priority" surcharge, their dollars are simply the cost of admission to a sports event — definitely not gifts to higher education.

Nevertheless, many Big-time U's claim these "priority" purchases as alumni donations and use them to inflate their fund-raising statistics. This ploy adds stadiums and arenas full of "priority" fans to the institution's "Alumni giving" totals. Yet, most of these Big-time U's still do not break into *U.S. News'* Top 100 in this category.

The final irony of the big-time college-sports-equals-alumni-giving myth is that, at many schools, the athletic department actively undermines efforts to raise money from alumni for educational programs. Often athletic department fund-raisers compete with regular university development (fund-raising) officers for dollars from the same alum. Because of the "Athletics Arms Race," intercollegiate athletic programs always need new and bigger facilities, and they try to get wealthy graduates to pay for them. After Joe Alum gives $250,000 for the "Joseph J. Alumnus Weight-Training Vestibule," usually he has no desire to donate $250,000 to the College of Arts and Sciences.

Big-time college sports hurts alumni fund-raising efforts in other ways. As many universities have discovered, publicity from intercollegiate athletics is a two-edged sword, generating attention and feel-good camaraderie when the teams are winning; but when a scandal occurs, the sword swings back, drawing buckets of negative media coverage and public scorn. During times of scandal, some alumni become embarrassed by and angry at their school; they blame its administrators for lack of control of the athletic department, and they close their checkbooks.

The alumni of Southern Methodist University, after enduring major football scandals in the mid-1980s, punished their alma mater for a number of years, contributing much less to its educational programs than they had during prescandal times. Moreover, the winning-while-cheating years at SMU had not produced an increase in alumni donations, but the scandals caused a significant decrease. (In addition, boosters, not alumni, caused the SMU debacle, and although athletic departments like to call these people "Friends of the University," boosters are usually the most dangerous and unreliable of associates, often causing scandals and other maladies, and doing nothing positive for the academic side of the university.)

All of these arguments should drive a silver stake into the heart of the big-time college-sports-equals-alumni-giving myth, but athletic department personnel and Big-time U administrators will not allow this to happen. Perpetuating the myth is in their self-interest — it provides one of the most popular justifications for big-time college sports. Its speciousness will never negate its power. As long as athletic directors want to grow their empires and university officials encourage them to do so, the myth will live on.

For all of College Sports MegaInc.'s endorsement of the myth, the real winners in alumni giving are those Division III and Division I institutions that provide undergraduates with quality educations and turn them into dependable and generous alumni. It never occurs to the proponents of College Sports MegaInc. that the Ivy League schools — the founders of intercollegiate athletics — had a reason for dropping out of big-time college sports, and that many wealthy Division III schools have a similar reason for not entering it. The officials of these institutions believe that a major sports entertainment enterprise on their campuses is incompatible with their academic missions.

But these schools, beyond their desire to give their students a first-rate education, also act out of self-interest: their institutional health depends upon their alumni, and they realize that if they provide mainly beer-and-circus to their undergraduates, this insubstantial diet will not build devoted alums, men and women whom the school can count on for ongoing contributions and support.

The most prominent alumni of a school often become members of its Board of Trustees, making general policy and guiding the institution through the present and into the future. In the 1950s, the trustees of Ivy League colleges and universities, in concert with a group of farsighted Ivy presidents, removed their schools from big-time intercollegiate athletics and, at the same time, committed them to excellence in undergraduate education. Unfortunately, both then and later, the trustees of public research universities allowed their schools to go in the opposite direction, enlarging their intercollegiate athletics programs and diminishing their undergraduate education ones. Indeed, many trustees of Big-time U's were (and are) rabid supporters of big-time college sports, not only condoning all of its sins but sometimes participating in them.

FUNDRAISING: AN ESSENTIAL COMPETENCY FOR THE SPORT MANAGER IN THE 21ST CENTURY

William F. Stier, Jr., and Robert Schneider

THE NEED FOR ADDITIONAL FUNDS FOR SPORT PROGRAMS

Inflation, increased popularity of sports, and an increase in the number of participants are three of the reasons for this financial challenge. Another reason is the fact that many central administrators are reluctant or unable to fully fund sport programs, such as school based athletic programs, via the normal budgetary level. Rather, sport administrators are expected, more than ever before, to generate the additional resources that are needed from outside the organization via external fundraising. In fact, there is an ever-growing expectation among some school administrators (at all levels) that athletic teams and programs should be somewhat financially self-supporting, if not totally so.

Consequently, more and more sport managers in the 21st century are going to be held accountable not only for managing and organizing their sport programs but for providing the necessary financial resources their programs require. Towards this end, there exists a body of knowledge that sport managers must be familiar with in terms of planning promotional activities and implementing fundraising events for sport programs, events that have the potential to provide the necessary resources, both financial and otherwise, needed by sport entities.

. . . .

Understanding the Concept of Fundraising

Fundraising is a process by which additional financial resources can be secured outside of the regular budgetary operation. These resources can be anything and everything that is of value, money, goods and services. . . . It is also important that sport managers recognize that fundraising is not an end in itself but a means to an end. The reason one engages in fundraising is to enhance and expand the financial base for the sport organization or program. Thus, the ultimate success is often as simple as counting the net money (resources) raised for the sport organization or program.

. . . .

The Art and Science of Fundraising

There is both an art and a science to being a successful sport fundraiser. Fundraising can be considered an art because individual creativity and ingenuity is involved in mapping out various strategies and deciding on tactics (based on basic fundraising principles, guidelines, and knowledge) in light of whatever unique situation one finds oneself in. On the other hand, fundraising may also be viewed as a science, because there are general principles and concepts that are applicable for all types of fundraising activities and efforts. Thus, a systematic application of these fundamental principles and guidelines coupled with the creativity and ingenuity exhibited by organizers and planners can make for a successful fundraising project or event, depending upon the circumstances and situation that exists at that particular time and place.

No Two Fundraisers Are Identical

Each fundraising project is somewhat different depending upon the situation, environment, and circumstances. Successful fundraisers follow the tactic of adapting ideas to suit their own situation and different needs rather than copying exactly what some other organization did. Circumstances might well be significantly different for any given organization or entity in terms of financial and political atmosphere as well as in terms of expectations by various constituencies.

An important element for successful fundraising is being able to adapt and adjust strategies and tactics to suit one's unique situation or the particular circumstances in which one finds oneself. There is nothing inherently wrong with imitating the successful fundraising efforts of others. After all, imitation is said to be the sincerest form of flattery. Nevertheless, one must remain cognizant of the necessity for some adaptations, changes, or alterations made in light of individual differences in terms of resources, varying financial and political environments, community expectations as well as a host of other pertinent factors.

Four Types of Fundraising

All fundraising efforts can be arbitrarily placed into four categories, (1) individual solicitations, (2) corporate partnerships or sponsorships, (3) profit centers, and (4) special projects or events.[1] Individual solicitation, as the phrase indicates, involves one person asking another for some type of donation. This can involve personal (face-to-face) contact, telephone solicitation, or requests made through the mail or over the WWW.

A corporate partnership or sponsorship usually involves a commitment by an outside entity in exchange for some type of service, product, or linkage from the sport organization and program. Such an association also involves mutual promotional, public relations, and publicity benefits accruing to both entities. The operational concept here is the mutual benefit or profit to the outside entity (the sponsor) *and* to the sport program or organization.

There are any number of different corporate sponsorships that might be established with a sport organization, at any level. But essentially they usually involve having the sport organization enjoy an infusion of financial assistance in exchange for allowing some type of association, connection, or linkage to exist in the eyes of the public between the two organizations. The possibilities are almost endless. The essentials and possibilities of such agreements are limited only by one's imagination and ingenuity.

This so-called *association* can involve many things. For example, [it may entail] display of advertising and promotional signage at the sport facility, publicity blurbs within various sport publications, use of a sponsor's products and services by the sport organization and personnel, and the sale of a sponsor's products at contests and/or at the sport organization's site. . .

Types of Sponsorship Agreements

Sport partnerships or sponsorships may be nonexclusive, semi-exclusive, or exclusive in nature. The nonexclusive sponsorship provides that there can be any number and type of organizations or businesses serving as sponsors of the sport entity. Thus, there are no restrictions in terms of who may be a sponsor. . . .

In the semi-exclusive partnership agreement, a sponsor in one line of business is guaranteed that no other entity in that specific line of business may become a sponsor during a specified time period. . . .

The third type of corporate partnership is identified by the total exclusivity of the sponsorship agreement. In the exclusive sponsorship agreement the corporate partner or business becomes the *only officially recognized sponsor* (regardless of what kind of business it is) of the sport entity or to a specific sport program.

Profit Centers

Any stand-alone money making activity (mini-business) directly or indirectly associated with or related to the sport entity may be considered a profit center, the third method of generating additional income. Concession stands, ticket sales, program sales, rental of facilities to outside groups, parking, vending machines, and the sale of apparel and souvenirs can all be individual profit centers.

Special Events

The last category of fundraising involves either stand-alone or combined fundraising projects associated with a special event, an event that does not easily fall under any of the above three categories. Typically, these special fundraising projects or events involve significant promotional activities in addition to extensive publicity and public relations on behalf of the sport organization.

. . . .

FUNDRAISING ACTIVITIES AND THE FACTOR OF *TIME*

When thinking about planning and organizing a fundraising effort one should do so within a framework of *time.* That is, some fundraisers can only be done once. For example, if the football team's artificial turf is being torn up because the team is converting to natural turf, the one-time fundraising project could include selling small sections of the artificial turf (encased in plastic) to fans. This is an example of a *one-time fundraiser* as it can only be done once for obvious reasons.

An *annual fundraiser,* on the other hand, can be implemented each and every year. For example, induction into an annual Hall of Fame may be an ideal annual fundraiser. So too is the annual golf tournament. The third type of fundraiser, when one considers the time factor, is the *repeatable project*. This is an event that can be repeated — but not necessarily each and every year. Perhaps the public or constituencies might grow tired of the event if it is held each year. Thus, a number of years (2, 3, or more) are interspersed between when the fundraising project is held. This keeps the fundraising event fresh and successful.

Difficulty of the Fundraising Event

One doesn't have to plan an overly complicated fundraising project to generate big bucks. In point of fact, one of the keys to successful fundraising is to keep everything as simple and succinct as one can. Overly complicating the event only creates a situation in which confusion and problems will more likely surface. Toward this end, it is advisable to keep the number of fundraising efforts each year to a minimum. Ideally, one fundraising project is all that should be done. If one can generate all of the needed resources with a single project, so much the better. A common fault of inexperienced sport managers and fundraisers is to be engaged in too many different fundraising efforts. It is far better to do fewer projects but to complete those that have a greater chance of generating big money than to be associated with a lot of nickel and dime fundraisers.

Determining the Need

When faced with the necessity of having to raise outside funds, one should decide, in advance, how much is really required — and then plan for a single fundraising effort that can meet that need. If that is not possible to do with a single fundraiser, then plan for two projects. And if two won't generate the needed resources, then implement three. But don't have 25 different fundraising projects within a given year. One's staff, fans, and the public will soon be turned off (burned out) by the constant barrage of fundraising requests.

. . . .

Determining the "Right" Fundraising Project

Once it has been determined that outside fundraising is necessary, the next step is to select an appropriate vehicle (project or event) that can generate the needed resources. There are innumerable fundraising projects that can be used in various settings and under different circumstances. The key is to select the right one for one's own sport organization or program.

Selecting the "correct" or "appropriate" fundraising project or effort depends upon the type of organization or program one represents. For some organizations gambling and alcohol related fundraising projects might well be taboo while other sport entities might welcome such projects. One should also look at the history of fundraising within the sport organization and the community, since past efforts (successes as well as failures) may dictate what to do and what not to do.

Even the political and financial environments must be considered — both inside the sport organization and within the community at large. Is the community in the middle of a recession? Is the largest employer within the community downsizing and laying off employees? Or, is the financial health of the community robust and growing? These factors would certainly have an impact on any serious fundraising on behalf of the sport organization.

It is also important to have an accurate understanding and appreciation of the experience and skill levels and competency areas of those paid and volunteer staff available to help plan, organize, and implement the fundraising project. For, in the final analysis, it will be the people involved in the planning and implementing of the fundraising project who will have a major impact upon the success or failure of the total fundraising effort.

Another factor to consider when planning a fundraising project is to determine, in advance, what other fundraising efforts are being conducted or will be conducted by others in the community that might interfere with or compete with one's own activities. Too many fundraising projects (especially similar ones) within the community within a given time frame only serve to dilute the income potential for all fundraising groups. Discretionary income within the general population is finite. Try not to be in direct competition with other groups in one's own fundraising efforts. [Alternatively,] attempt to piggyback onto the other group's efforts by going into partnership, if this is feasible and mutually beneficial to both groups.

A final factor to consider is the current relationship between the sport organization and the community. Is it one of mutual respect and admiration? Or, is it one of mistrust and suspicion? How the sport organization is viewed by the general public, especially by those individuals who are expected to contribute resources, has an important bearing on fundraising efforts sponsored by the sport organization.

One must be politically astute as well as knowledgeable in the strategies and tactics of fundraising, promoting, publicity, and public relation if one is to be successful as a sport manager in today's society. One also needs to be a wise decision-maker, effective and efficient problem solver, and a risk taker (within reason).

. . . .

RECOGNIZING RESOURCES (ASSETS) AVAILABLE TO THE SPORT MANAGER

Part of the challenge in conducting a suitable fundraising project is to recognize one's capabilities, one's potential, as well as one's limitations. Sport administrators need to take a hard, discerning look at one's assets or resources in terms of people (perhaps the most important tool), money, time, facilities, equipment, supplies, reputation/image, and past achievements. How can these assets help to generate additional resources? Are these assets sufficient to allow the implementation of a successful fundraiser? An accurate inventory of all assets currently available or which might be made available to the sport organization will help determine those fundraising projects that are possible (and successful) and those that might not be.

The axiom that "it takes money to earn money" is certainly true. However, don't assume that this means that one has to spend a great deal of money to be successful in raising money. How one utilizes the resources available is often the mark of a truly competent fundraiser. Almost anyone can raise money if the person has an unlimited cash reserve with which to operate. The challenge is to raise meaningful resources without having a great deal of cash on hand.

Thus, fundraisers should always attempt to conserve the cash on hand. Try never to pay full price for anything. Of course, this sounds easier than it really is in real life. Nevertheless, effective and efficient fundraisers are adept at using their initiative and creativity to secure needed goods and services at a discount, or at cost, or better yet, for free; the use of *trade-outs* can be an effective method of securing goods and services without having to pay for them. Trade-outs occur when the sport organization exchanges something of value — tickets to games, for example — to a vendor or business in exchange for something that the vendor or business has and is of value to the sport organization.

. . . .

PROSPECTIVE DONORS AND CENTERS OF INFLUENCE

The sport manager should identify individuals who are more likely to be prospective donors (of money, goods, and services). This involves prospecting to detect those individuals with a propensity and the ability to support the sport organization in some meaningful and material fashion. These people then become the population pool from which to solicit contributions and donations in one form or another.

A related task to identifying likely contributors is to use what is commonly called *centers of influence.* These are important and influential individuals who already support the sport organization and are willing to help further by "opening doors to other important and influential people" within the community, individuals who might be approached by representatives of the sport organization for contributions, etc.

All too frequently sport managers are limited in their ability to approach specific individuals in the community, people who are important, influential, and financially well off. Using the centers of influence is an excellent strategy to bridge the social, financial, and cultural barriers that might exist between the sport representatives and future contributors by borrowing the respectability and prestige of the center(s) of influence to open doors to people who otherwise might well be unapproachable.

WHY PEOPLE CONTRIBUTE TO AND SUPPORT SPORT ORGANIZATIONS

Donations are made for any number of reasons. But essentially, people contribute to or "buy" from fundraisers for three basic reasons.[2] First, the donors perceive that the group is deserving of support. That is, the individuals subscribe to the same philosophy as the soliciting organization. Second, if the money raised will go to a worthy cause there is a greater likelihood of people loosening their purse strings. Third, the item that is purchased is worth the money in terms of its inherent value and the convenience of being able to secure it direct from the representative of the sport organization. This is frequently referred to as the supermarket approach.[3]

Thus, it is vital that the purpose for which the fundraising project is being held is worthwhile and is thought to be worthwhile by potential supporters and contributors. No one likes to donate to an organization to pay for utilities. On the other hand, contributions that improve the lot of youngsters (or for some other worthy cause) are more readily obtained. Another factor that plays a role in motivating people to contribute includes having some current or past affiliation with the sport organization. It is this connection that should be exploited by the sport manager.

DEVELOPING A PLAN OF ATTACK IN SCHEDULING A SUCCESSFUL FUNDRAISER

Stier[4] provides a step-by-step approach to implementing specific fundraising projects or events. These steps, factors that should be considered by the would-be fundraiser prior to coming to any final decisions, are presented below.

(1) There should be a determination of the total amount of money needed by the organization prior to becoming involved in any fundraising effort.
(2) A careful analysis of potential and feasible fundraising projects should be made in light of what other fundraising efforts are being conducted in the community.
(3) Evaluate potential fundraisers in light of any restrictions or limitations that may exist on behalf of the sport organization.
(3) A realistic estimation should be made of the complexity of each fundraising project being considered.
(4) Write down all aspects of the proposed fundraising project so that others can read it and fully understand it.
(5) Come to a decision as to when the fundraising project may best be scheduled for maximum return on effort and resources expended.
(6) Identify the resources that are necessary and the source of each resource that is essential for the success of the project. These resources include, but are not limited to, facilities, equipment, supplies, money, [and] time. . .
(7) Identify those individuals who possess specific skills and experience that will be required for the success of the project.
(8) Decide how the fundraising event will be . . . promoted as well as publicized within the community.
(9) Specify the various risks, i.e., financial risks, public relations risks, and legal liability risks, that are associated with the selected fundraising project.
(10) Identify those licenses, permits, permissions, and authorizations that are necessary for the fundraiser to take place.
(11) Identify those regulations and requirements that govern or specify how specific elements of the fundraising effort shall be conducted.
(12) Identify those elements associated with the fundraising project that must be critically analyzed after the conclusion of the effort in order to determine what things to change and what to keep the same should the project be repeated in the future.

CONCLUSIONS

Since the goal of any fundraiser is to motivate people to contribute in some fashion to the organization, it is obvious that interpersonal relationships and communication links between the sport personnel (paid and volunteer) and potential or would-be donors or contributors become very, very critical to the overall success of the fundraising effort. Likewise, understanding where the potential contributions or support may be coming from is very important. Conveying an appropriate urgency and need on behalf of the sport organization is similarly essential. And finally, there must be a connection or linkage between the prospective donor and the worthy cause promoted by those engaged in the fundraising effort.

REFERENCES

1. Stier, Jr., W. F. (1994). *Successful sport fund-raising.* Madison, Wisconsin: Wm. C. Brown & Benchmark, p. 5.

2. Ostlund, C. & Brown, D. (1985, March). Predicting potential donors for intercollegiate athletics. *Athletic Business.* 9, 30–31.

3. Bronzan, R. T. (1984). Fund-raising today demands better ideas. *Athletic Business.* 8(5), 12–18.

4. Stier, Jr., W. F. (1994a). *Fundraising for sport and recreation.* Champaign, Illinois: Human Kinetics Publishers. Stier, Jr., W. F. (1997). *More fantastic fundraisers for sport and recreation.* Champaign, Illinois: Human Kinetics Publishers.

WELCOME TO THE BIG TIME

Grant Wahl and George Dohrmann

Morris Brown is among the dozens of colleges that have jumped to Division I in recent years, lured by the siren song of increased prestige and a chunk of the 11-year, $6 billion television contract the NCAA has signed with CBS. In the last two decades the number of Division I basketball teams has skyrocketed by 24%, from 261 in 1980 to 292 in 1990 to a record 324 this season. In the last four years alone 15 schools have joined, including such powerhouses as Elon, High Point, Sacred Heart, and Stony Brook. Waiting in the wings as provisional members — those whose applications to move to Division I have been accepted but are awaiting the NCAA's final seal of approval — are Birmingham Southern, Gardner Webb, Lipscomb, Savannah State, and Texas A&M–Corpus Christi. Every Division I newbie thinks it can be the next something ("the next Valpo," as Mike Strickland, the athletic director at Belmont University in Nashville, calls his Bruins, or "the next Stanford," the goal of University of Denver chancellor Daniel Ritchie) and a handful of programs have prospered competitively since making the move, most notably College of Charleston, Division I class of '91.

Yet the vast majority soldier away in obscurity, negotiating a treacherous landscape that features chronic losing, uninterested fans, wacky conference affiliations (or even worse, none at all) and, not least, crushing financial deficits. To make the jump in basketball, most schools have to add other sports because the NCAA mandates that Division I teams compete in a total of at least 14 men's and women's sports. *[This requirement will increase to 16 in 2004.]* Most of them are in the nonrevenue category. Facilities often must be built, scholarships added, and recruiting budgets introduced. Contrary to popular myth, most Division I athletic programs lose money.

"Schools get caught up in the idea that they can make money off athletics," says Jamie Pollard, president of Collegiate Financial Services, a Wisconsin firm that examines the financing of college sports. "They can generate revenue, but few actually make money. Athletic departments rarely fund themselves."

The NCAA certainly thinks too many schools are taking the plunge. By next year the Division I Management Council plans to make the leap more difficult. It will increase the waiting period for lower-division schools jumping to Division I from two years to five (and increase it from four years to seven for schools coming from outside the NCAA). Says Steve Mallonee, the NCAA director of membership services, "The concern is, are schools really prepared when they commit to going to Division I?"

The evidence says that many are not.

. . . .

Is there a correct way to move to Division I? Or more precisely, how did the College of Charleston make a seamless transition from the NAIA to Division I in 1991? The Cougars reached the NCAA tournament with an at-large bid in their third year of play, and their winning percentage during the 1990s (.847) was one of the highest in Division I.

Charleston coach John Kresse never thought it would go so smoothly. Before the start of the 1989–90 season, the Cougars' first provisional Division I year, Kresse met with school president Harry M. Lightsey, Jr., to discuss his manifold fears. "I was scared," says Kresse, now 57. "I knew going to Division I was going to be something like purgatory — near hell — and I was worried I wouldn't have a job for too long. The president ended up giving me tenure in the P.E. department. That way, at least, I would have a job teaching P.E. if I got fired as the coach."

Stability — Kresse's, the school's, and the community's — was ultimately the key to Charleston's rise. A former assistant to Lou Carnesecca with St. John's and the New Jersey Nets, Kresse had turned the Cougars into an NAIA powerhouse after taking over in 1979. Unlike most coaches, though, he had no aspirations of moving up the ladder to a bigger school. "I have seen the lights of Broadway," Kresse says, and Charleston suits him fine. "I am not a coach who is looking to play musical chairs. To be able to tell players you will be here is important."

That wasn't all. Because of its NAIA success, its sizable student body (11,620), and its location in South Carolina's largest city, Charleston was courted by several conferences, which allowed it to bypass the usual scheduling hassles for new Division I schools. During its two provisional seasons the Cougars played what amounted to a Big South conference schedule, cutting down on travel costs and boosting the number of home games. As a result Charleston could build on the loyal fan base Kresse had established during the school's NAIA days. Having traded up from the Trans America conference to the Southern in 1998, the Cougars routinely play to packed houses in the 3,500-seat, appropriately named John Kresse Arena, and plans are under way for a 6,000-seat facility. (Even with all its success, the athletic department still runs a deficit, though it's minimal.)

Yet Charleston's Division I fairy tale remains an anomaly, the result of felicitous circumstances that rarely occur at other schools. "I get calls all the time from schools asking what we did right," says Jerry Baker, Charleston's athletic director. "Certainly we did some things that were critical to our success, but we were successful long before we thought we'd be."

Or as Kresse advises the Morris Browns of the world, "Get used to the hills and the mountains. There are going to be plenty to climb, but hopefully you'll be one of the fortunate few who like us have done it almost overnight."

In other words, good luck. (You'll need it.)

It's hard not to root for Reggie Witherspoon, the affable, perpetually hamstrung coach at Buffalo. . . . He has a two-year record of 7–44, has yet to win a conference road game, and is trying to right a program that has been on NCAA probation twice since it jumped to Division I from Division II in 1991. "It's like running a race with a bag of rocks on your back; then you take some off and run a little faster," Witherspoon says. "We haven't gotten them all off yet."

Buffalo could have received the NCAA death penalty last spring for its latest violations — mainly involving improper evaluation of recruits — committed by Witherspoon's predecessor, Tim Cohane. (The Bulls were repeat offenders, because an assistant coach had been caught providing players with free airline tickets in 1989, before the move to Division I.) Instead the NCAA spared the Bulls, noting that the violations came under different staffs, and slapped them with a minor sanction. (Buffalo will have four fewer recruiting visits than the usual limit of 12 this season.)

On the other hand, Witherspoon had to deal with Buffalo's self-imposed sanctions last year, which reduced basketball scholarships from 13 to 12, permitted only one coach at a time on recruiting trips and delayed the start of practice two weeks until Nov. 1. "Last year we had eight new guys and two new assistant coaches," he says, "and while everyone else was doing Midnight Madness, we were doing our Midnight Darkness." Opening its season only 16 days after the start of practice, Buffalo lost 18 of its first 20 games and finished 4–24.

Still, the question isn't whether Buffalo is big enough to support Division I athletics. It is. With more than 23,000 students, Buffalo is the largest school in the State University of New York (SUNY) system. Since 1998 it has belonged to the Mid-American Conference, one of the nation's most respected mid-major leagues. The reason the Bulls spent 10 years in Division III, from 1978 to '88, was that SUNY prohibited athletic scholarships at the time. "We're not a small, private liberal arts college," says William Greiner, Buffalo's president since 1991. "We're the same size as the smaller Big Ten schools."

He also insists that Buffalo has not sold its soul to join the big time, noting that the first NCAA violation took place when the Bulls were in Division II. "We weren't happy about the latest situation," he says. "It happened on our watch, and we'll take our lumps for that. But it had nothing to do with the academic standing of the athletes. Nor were there any payoffs or financial chicanery."

Others, though, wax nostalgic for the days before Division I. Dan Bazzani coached the Bulls from 1983 to '93, from Division III to Division II to Division I, and his fondest memories are of Buffalo's electric series against crosstown rival Buffalo State. "Those games were wonderful," he says. "The students would go crazy, throwing toilet paper everywhere. But Buff State wanted nothing to do with us when we moved up to D-I."

. . . .

There was the typical assortment of "guarantee games" — so-called because they come with a guarantee of up to $50,000 for the visiting team — that the Bulls had to play to boost their rapidly depleting $2 million athletic budget. At one point before his second season in Division I, Bazzani's staff was on the road recruiting and got called back to Buffalo. "The athletic director [Nelson Townsend] called us all in," he recalls, "and said, 'Do not spend any more money and turn in any recruiting money you have. We're broke.' "

. . . .

To the people who run Northeastern Illinois, the notion that their 11,000-student commuter school on the northwest end of Chicago needs Division I athletics seems laughable. The majority of the school's students work full time. Most are the first members of their families to attend college; half are minorities. There is little time for watching sports, and a mandatory $48 student fee for athletics is money that is needed elsewhere. Yet only four years ago Northeastern Illinois competed at the Division I level, using student fees and state funds to finance a program that few cared about and even fewer have missed since the university scuttled the entire athletic department at the end of the 1997–98 season.

In the late 1980s Gordon H. Lamb, Northeastern Illinois's president, argued to the school's trustees that the way to promote the school nationally was through Division I sports. "My predecessor had a dream, that the jump to D-I would bring glory," says current president Salme H. Steinberg, who was an associate provost when the school left Division II for Division I in 1990.

The centerpiece of the move was the men's basketball program, the only one of Northeastern Illinois's 14 sports with the chance of making money or gaining exposure. The Golden Eagles hired

Rees Johnson, a successful NAIA coach at Wisconsin–Parkside, and Northeastern Illinois squeezed $10.5 million from its capital development budget to build the Physical Education Complex, which included a 5,000-seat gymnasium. "I thought it would work," Johnson says. "But money was tight. When we jumped to D-I, we had eight scholarships. It stayed at eight for four years, even though 15 was the max at the time."

It was certainly a strange environment for the athletes. The average age of the students at Northeastern Illinois is 26.3. Without any dorms on campus, the 170 scholarship athletes lived in an apartment complex a few blocks away. Yet Johnson's program gradually improved each year, from 2–25 as an independent in 1990–91 to 17–11 in 1993–94 as a member of the East Coast Conference.

The next year, shortly before Northeastern Illinois's first season in the Mid-Continent conference — a move that greatly reduced travel expenses — the Illinois Board of Higher Education sent a directive to its universities asking them to determine the "appropriate scope and size" of their athletic programs "in relation to institutional and academic priorities." The board was concerned about the increasing amount of state funds going to athletics, and in the Golden Eagles it had a perfect example. That year Northeastern Illinois's basketball team generated $92,965 in revenue, not enough to cover its own expenditures of $163,130, much less those of the nonrevenue sports that drove the athletic budget to $1.57 million.

Steinberg formed a task force to examine the issue, and in May 1996, following a season in which Johnson's team went 14–13 but drew only 500 fans a game, it recommended that Northeastern Illinois drop to Division II. Later, Northeastern Illinois's board of trustees voted to stop using state money for athletics and to develop a fund-raising plan instead.

A study which focused on the school's ability to raise $3 million over three years concluded in August 1997 that many of Northeastern Illinois's alumni "believe the University should focus more on improving the quality of its academic programs rather than promoting athletics." A month later, after seven years in Division I, the trustees voted to drop all sports. "It was like getting punched in the stomach," says Johnson, whose 1996–97 team had finished 16–12, with wins over Arizona State and Oregon State. "You work for almost 10 years at something, then it gets taken away. The kids were devastated; I was devastated. We had good players coming back, and I think we could have made the NCAA tournament."

. . . .

While sympathetic, Steinberg supports the decision to deep-six Northeastern Illinois's sports. The more than $1.5 million used annually for the athletic budget has been diverted to academic programs, renovations, scholarships, and opportunities to study abroad. The phys-ed building that was rarely open to regular students is now a hub for intramural and club teams. Students with children bring them to swim in the Olympic-sized pool.

"We've tried to do a lot of things to foster community, and it's sad that athletics is not available," Steinberg says. "But it's all about choices and priorities. This was a difficult decision, but I don't think there's any doubt that it was the right choice."

. . . .

NOT READY FOR PRIME TIME

The roster of Division I schools has swelled by 15 in only the last four years, and the world that awaits new members is full of harsh realities: big losses, small crowds at home games, and the resulting red ink on the bottom line. Occasionally a fledgling program can take a bite out of Goliath — as Oakland did, upsetting Michigan in November 2000 — but for the most part it's a dog-eat-underdog world. Just check the stats.

Year School Joined Division I		Conference	Record	Average Home Attendance
2001	Binghamton	America East	14–14	972
	Morris Brown	None	6–23	700
	UC Riverside	Big West	8–17	1,849
1999	Alabama A&M	SWAC	17–11	1,428
	Albany	America East	6–22	1,148
	Belmont	Atlantic Sun	13–15	648
	Elon	Big South	9–20	708
	High Point	Big South	8–20	1,170
	Oakland	Mid-Continent	12–16	1,664
	Stony Brook	America East	17–11	1,193
1998	Ark.–Pine Bluff	SWAC	2–25	1,405
	Denver	Sun Belt	10–18	1,184
	IUPUI	Mid-Continent	11–18	1,186
	Portland St.	Big Sky	9–18	790
	Quinnipiac	Northeast	6–21	1,003

TABLE 7.

GENERAL REQUIREMENTS FOR DIVISION MEMBERSHIP					
	Sports sponsorship: number of sports				
	All-male or mixed-team sports	*All-female sports*	*Minimum number of team sports*	*Football scheduling requirement*	*Football attendance requirement*
Division I	7	7	2-All male/mixed	According to football classification	According to football classification
			2-All female		
	OR				
	6	8			
Division I-A	7 including football	7	2-All male/mixed	At least 60% of all games must be against Division I-A members and at least 5 home games against members of Division I-A	17,000 average per home game (or 20,000 average all football games) over last four years; *or,*
			2-All female		30,000 permanent seat stadium and 17,000 average per home football game (or 20,000 average all football games) in one of last four years; *or,*
	OR				Member of conference in which at least six conference members sponsor football and more than half of football schools meet attendance criterion
	6 including football	8			
Division I-AA	7 including football	7	2-All male/mixed	More than 50% of all games must be against Division I-A or I-AA members	NONE
			2-All female		
	OR				
	6 including football	8			

(Continued)

TABLE 7. (Continued)

GENERAL REQUIREMENTS FOR DIVISION MEMBERSHIP

	Men's basketball scheduling requirement	*Women's basketball scheduling requirement*	*Scheduling requirement—sports other than football and basketball*
Provisional member:	All but two games against Division I teams, *and* except for the first two years of provisional membership, $1/3$ of all contests must be played in home arena	All but two games against Division I teams	Sports used to meet sports sponsorship criteria: Each contest against Division I team to meet minimum number of contests. 50% of remaining contests against Division I opponents
Active member:	All but four games against Division I teams, *and* $1/3$ of all contests in home arena	All but four games against Division I teams	
Provisional member:	All but two games against Division I teams	All but two games against Division I teams	Sports used to meet sports sponsorship criteria: Each contest against Division I team to meet minimum number of contests. 50% of remaining contests against Division I opponents
Active member:	All but four games against Division I teams *and* $1/3$ of all contests in home arena	All but four games against Division I teams	
Provisional member:	All but two games against Division I teams	All but two games against Division I teams	Sports used to meed sports sponsorship criteria: Each contest against Division I team to meet minimum number of contests. 50% of remaining contests against Division I opponents
Active member:	All but four games against Division I teams *and* $1/3$ of all contests in home arena	All but four games against Division I teams	

(Continued)

TABLE 7. (Continued)

General Requirements for Division Membership	
	*Financial aid requirement**
Division I	a) 50% of maximum allowable grants in each sport** *or;* b) Minimum aggregate expenditure of $771,000 (with at least $385,000 in women's sports in 02–03 (excluding football and men's and women's basketball). Grant value may not be less than 38 full grants (with at least 19 for women), *or;* c) Equivalent of 25 full grants in men's sports and 25 full grants in women's sports (exclusive of grants in football and men's and women's basketball)****
Division I-A	a) 50% of maximum allowable grants in each sport** *or;* b) Minimum aggregate expenditure of $771,000 (with at least $385,000 in women's sports) in 02–03 (excluding football and men's and women's basketball). Grant value may not be less than 38 full grants (with at least 19 for women),*** *or;* c) Equivalent of 25 full grants in men's sports and 25 full grants in women's sports (exclusive of grants in football and men's and women's basketball)****
Division I-AA	a) 50% of maximum allowable grants in each sport** *or;* b) Minimum aggregate expenditure of $771,000 (with at least $385,000 in women's sports) in 02–03 (excluding football and men's and women's basketball). Grants value may not be less than 38 full grants (with at least 19 for women), *or;* c) Equivalent of 25 full grants in men's sports and 25 full grants in women's sports (exclusive of grants in football and men's and women's basketball)****

*For institutions that depend on exceptional amounts of Federal assistance to meet students' financial needs, the institution must provide a minimum of one-half of the required grants or aggregate expenditures cited in (a), (b), or (c) above. This provision shall be applicable to an institution in a given year if the average per-student allotment of Pell Grant dollars for undergraduates reported to the U.S. Department of Education the previous September is more than one standard deviation above the mean for all reporting Division I member institutions that year. If an institution does not qualify under this provision after having been able to do so the previous year, the institution may continue to utilize this alternative for one year and shall not be required to meet the provisions of (a), (b), or (c) until the following year. This provision shall be applicable only to institutions that were members of Division I on September 1, 1990.

**If an institution uses indoor track and field, outdoor track and field, and cross country to meet the financial aid criterion, it must award the equivalent of at least 80% of the full grants for men and 80% of the full grants for women in these sports. If the institution counts two of those three sports to meet the financial aid criterion, it must award the equivalent of at least 70% of the full grants for men and 70% of the full grants for women. If the institution counts indoor and outdoor track and field as one sport, it must award the equivalent of at least 50% of the full grants for men and 50% of the full grants for women.

***If the institution does not sponsor men's or women's basketball, the minimum aggregate expenditure must be $509,000 in 2002–2003 for men or for women, but no fewer than the equivalent of 29 full grants for men or for women.

****If the institution does not sponsor men's or women's basketball, it must provide a minimum of 35 full grants in men's sports and 35 full grants in women's sports. Source: NCAA.

RECENT FEDERAL INCOME TAX ISSUES REGARDING PROFESSIONAL AND AMATEUR SPORTS

James L. Musselman

[The bracketed material that follows in this excerpt is from the original text.]

III. APPLICABILITY OF THE UNRELATED BUSINESS INCOME TAX TO THE FUNDING OF COLLEGE AND UNIVERSITY ATHLETIC PROGRAMS

A. Introduction

Congress enacted the Unrelated Business Income Tax (UBIT) as part of the Revenue Act of 1950.[56] Prior to the enactment of UBIT, colleges and universities had enjoyed, under their general tax exemption,[57] tax-free use of all funds regardless of the source from which the funds were received.[58] The law prior to the enactment of UBIT "recognized only two possibilities — an organization was either entirely taxable or entirely tax-exempt."[59] As a result, "the courts generally upheld the tax-exempt status of" activities conducted by colleges and universities, regardless of the relationship of those activities to the institution's exempt purpose. . . .[60] The UBIT was enacted out of concern that the Treasury was in need of protection from loss of tax revenue in these cases, and taxpaying entities were in need of protection from unfair competition from the colleges and universities.

B. The Mechanics of the Unrelated Business Income Tax

The UBIT imposes a tax, at rates applicable to taxable corporations,[65] on the "unrelated business taxable income"[66] (UBTI) of most tax-exempt organizations, including colleges and universities. "Unrelated business taxable income" is generally defined as the "gross income [of] any organization from any unrelated trade or business . . . regularly carried on by [such organization], less [certain] deductions allowed . . . which are directly connected with the carrying on of such trade or business."[68] This definition requires a determination of whether an activity is (a) a trade or business, (b) regularly carried on, and (c) an "unrelated trade or business."[69] An "unrelated trade or business" is generally defined as a "trade or business [of a tax-exempt organization,] the conduct of which is not substantially related . . . to the [organization's] exercise or performance . . . of its [exempt] . . . function" (i.e., education in the case of a college or university).[70]

   . . . .

C. Application to College and University Athletic Programs

It is generally assumed that many college and university athletic programs seek profit, and thus constitute the conduct by those organizations of a trade or business, as that term has been defined by the courts. Any individual athletic program must be analyzed with respect to this issue on the basis of its own particular facts. It is equally assumed that the activities conducted by those programs are "regularly carried on," within the meaning of the Treasury Regulations, even with respect to special postseason bowl games and tournaments that are conducted annually but only for a brief period each year. The most difficult to apply of these three statutory elements is that the questioned activities not be substantially related to the institution's exercise or performance of its exempt function.

When UBIT was being considered by Congress, the House Ways & Means Committee and the Senate Finance Committee both perfunctorily stated that "[a]thletic activities of schools are substantially related to [the] educational functions" of the institutions, and concluded that "income of an educational organization from [admission] to football games" is accordingly not subject to UBIT.[87] This legislative history has resulted in a wide berth being given to college athletics in this regard.[88] In 1977, the Internal Revenue Service "notified several universities and the Cotton Bowl Athletic Association, a tax-exempt entity that [organized and operated] the annual Cotton Bowl football game, that revenue from the broadcasting rights to the game would [be subject to UBIT]."[89] After significant negative public reaction, the Service reversed its position by issuing a series of unpublished 1978 National Office Technical Advice Memoranda.[90] The Service stated in several of these memoranda that "there is no meaningful distinction between exhibiting the game in person [(the income from admissions is not subject to UBIT, as discussed above)] and exhibiting the game on television to a much larger audience where both groups of people [include students and nonstudents]."[91] In addition, in several of these memoranda, the Service went to great lengths discussing the close relationship of college athletics and education. In 1980, the Service issued two Revenue Rulings of similar effect.[93] In one of those Revenue Rulings, the Service stated that "[a]n athletic program is considered to be an integral part of the educational process of a university, and activities providing necessary services to student athletes and coaches further the educational purposes of the university."[95] The legislative history, coupled with the Service's position on this issue described in the rulings identified above, would serve to indicate that this third statutory element will continue to be applied liberally to college and university athletic programs.

D. Sponsorship Payments

In 1991, the Internal Revenue Service issued a National Office Technical Advice Memorandum[97] dealing with the issue of whether a payment by Mobil Oil Corporation (Mobil) to the Cotton

Bowl Athletic Association (CBAA), a tax-exempt entity, constituted advertising revenue to CBAA subject to UBIT. Mobil and CBAA had entered into a contract whereby Mobil agreed to pay CBAA a substantial sponsorship fee (apparently well over $1 million) in return for CBAA's agreement to "change the name of the Cotton Bowl to the Mobil Cotton Bowl [;] . . . imprint the new logo in a prominent place on the field [;] . . . display Mobil's commercial messages on the electronic sign in the stadium[;] broadcast Mobil's commercial messages over the [stadium's] public address system[; permit] Mobil [to] cancel the contract [in the event the Cotton Bowl was not televised; and] . . . arrange for hospitality suites and hotel rooms, tickets to the game, and tickets to event-related activities [on behalf of Mobil]."[99]

The Service ruled that the payment by Mobil to CBAA under the contract provided Mobil with a substantial return benefit, and as a result the payment constituted advertising revenue to CBAA taxable under UBIT. Subsequent to its issuance of the memorandum, the Service issued proposed examination guidelines consistent with its position set forth in the memorandum. The guidelines stated that "where an exempt organization performs valuable advertising, marketing, and similar services, on a quid pro quo basis, for the corporate sponsor, payments made to an exempt organization are not contributions to the exempt organization, and questions of unrelated trade or business arise."[102]

After extensive protest by a wide array of exempt organizations, Congress responded to the Service's ruling and proposed examination guidelines by issuing proposed regulations designed to liberalize the Service's position.[104] The Service responded with a set of proposed regulations of its own which were not as generous as those proposed by Congress, but represented a complete diversion from its earlier position.[105]

The Taxpayer Relief Act of 1997[106] enacted section 513(i) of the Code,[107] adopting in large part the Service's proposed regulations. Section 513(i) creates and defines a new term, "qualified sponsorship payments."[108] The activity of "soliciting and receiving qualified sponsorship payments" is now specifically excluded from the definition of "unrelated trade or business,"[109] thereby precluding such payments from being subject to UBIT.

A qualified sponsorship payment is defined as "any payment . . . with respect to which there is no arrangement or expectation . . . [of] any substantial return benefit other than use or acknowledgment of the [donor's] name or logo (or product lines)" by the organization receiving the payment.[111] This definition excludes advertising the donor's products or services, but does not define the meaning of "advertising."[112] Certain specific limitations to this definition are provided, including a provision excluding from the definition any payment which "is contingent upon the level of attendance . . . , broadcast ratings, or other [similar] factors."[113] In addition, section 513(i) provides for allocation of a single payment into two separate payments in cases where a portion of a payment constitutes a qualified sponsorship payment and the remainder does not. This allocation rule effectively eliminates that portion of the Service's proposed regulations which became known as the "tainting rule."[115] That rule had provided that "[i]f any activities, messages or programming material constitute advertising with respect to a sponsorship payment, then all related activities, messages or programming material that might otherwise be acknowledgments are considered advertising."[116] The tainting rule had received substantial negative public reaction.

Although section 513(i) leaves some key terms undefined and thus open to differing interpretations, it at least provides substantial guidance to institutions and organizations interested in entering into agreements like the one described above between Mobil and CBAA. By carefully structuring their agreement under section 513(i), any such institution that is a tax-exempt entity should be able to avoid taxation of payments received pursuant to such agreement under UBIT.

IV. DEDUCTIBILITY OF CONTRIBUTIONS TO COLLEGES AND UNIVERSITIES IN EXCHANGE FOR THE USE OF STADIUM SKYBOXES

Section 170(l) of the Code[119] allows donors to educational organizations to deduct as a charitable contribution 80% of amounts contributed for the "right to purchase tickets for seating at an athletic event in an athletic stadium of such [organization]."[121] A deduction is not allowed for the actual cost of purchasing the tickets for any such event.[122]

In 1996, an Iowa State University booster deducted as a charitable contribution 80% of a large donation for which he received a ten-year skybox lease at Iowa State University's renovated stadium. The taxpayer's 1996 tax return was audited and his deduction was challenged by the field agent conducting the audit. This issue caused significant concern among colleges and universities, several of which have added, or are in the process of adding, skyboxes to their stadiums. As a result, the National Collegiate Athletic Association, along with two athletic directors' associations, requested clarification on this issue from the Service.

In 1999, the Service issued a National Office Technical Advice Memorandum upholding the taxpayer's deduction.[128] The field agent had denied the taxpayer's deduction on the basis of section 274(l) of the Code,[129] which provides that the amount allowable as a deduction, where a skybox or other luxury box is leased for more than one event, "shall not exceed the sum of the face value of non-luxury box seat tickets for the seats in such box covered by the lease."[130] Section 274(f), however, provides that section 274 is not applicable to "any deduction allowable to the taxpayer without regard to its connection with his trade or business."[132] The Service correctly held that section 274 is therefore not applicable in determining whether charitable contributions are deductible under section 170 of the Code. As a result, the taxpayer was permitted to deduct that portion of his donation to the University allowable by section 170(l) of the Code.

REFERENCES

56. See Richard L. Kaplan, Intercollegiate Athletics and the Unrelated Business Income Tax, 80 Colum. L. Rev. 1430, 1434 (1980) (citing Revenue Act of 1950, Pub. L. No. 81-814, §§ 301, 331, 64 Stat. 906, 947, 957 (1950)).

57. "I.R.C. § 501(a) (1982) provides generally that certain organizations are exempt from federal income tax." Erik M. Jensen, Taxation, the Student Athlete, and the Professionalization of College Athletics, 1987 Utah L. Rev. 35, 44 n.41 (1987). Section 501(c)(3) includes colleges and universities within that list of organizations, subject to certain conditions stated therein. Id. In addition to receiving tax-exempt status, an organization described in section 501(c)(3) will enjoy the benefits of section 170, which will result in deductibility of contributions to such an organization, subject to certain limitations stated in that section. Id. One requirement for qualification under section 501(c)(3) is that a substantial portion of the organization's revenue must not be derived from sources unrelated to its exempt purpose. Id. Unrelated income would likely be substantial if it constituted more than one-half of the organization's annual revenue. Id.

58. Kaplan, supra note 56, at 1433.

59. Id.

60. Id.

65. See I.R.C. § 511(a)(1).

66. Id.

68. Id. I.R.C. § 512(a)(1). Gross income and deductions are both computed with the modifications provided in section 512(b). Id.

69. Id.

70. Id. § 513(a). This definition is subject to certain narrow exceptions. See I.R.C. § 513(a)(1)–(3).

87. Jensen, supra note 57, at 51 (quoting H.R. Rep. No. 2319, 81st Cong., 2d Sess. (1950), reprinted in 1950–2 C.B. 380, 409; and S. Rep. No. 2375, 81st Cong., 2d Sess. (1950), reprinted in 1950–2 C.B. 483, 505).

88. Id. at 51.

89. Id. at 51 n.68 (citing Bruce R. Hopkins, The Law of Tax-Exempt Organizations 615, 637 (4th ed. 1983)).

90. Id. at 51 n.69 (citing Tech. Adv. Mem. 78-51-002 (1978), 78-51-005 (1978), 78-51-006 (1978), 78-51-003 (1978), and 78-51-004 (Aug. 21, 1978)).

91. Id. at 51 (quoting Tech. Adv. Mem. 78-51-002 (1978), 78-51-004 (Aug. 21, 1978), and 78-51-006 (1978)).

93. Id. at 52 (citing Rev. Rul. 80-295, 1980–2 C.B. 194; Rev. Rul. 80-296, 1980–2 C.B. 195).

95. Id. (quoting Rev. Rul. 80-296, 1980–2 C.B. 195)(emphasis omitted).

97. Tech. Adv. Mem. 91-47-007 (Nov. 22, 1991).

99. Cynthia G. Farbman, Forced to Be a Fan: An Analysis and History of the IRS's Proposed Regulations Regarding Corporate Sponsorship, 2 Sports Law. J. 53, 54 (1995) (quoting Paul Streckfus, A Glimpse of Mobil–Cotton Bowl Contract Provisions, 55 Tax Notes 447 (April 27, 1992)).

102. I.R.S. Announcement 92-15, 1992–5 I.R.B. 51.

104. 138 Cong. Rec. H6637 (1992).

105. Prop. Treas. Reg. § 1.513-4, 58 Fed. Reg. 5687 (Jan. 22, 1993).

106. Tax Payer Relief Act of 1997, Pub. L. No. 105-34, § 965(a), 111 Stat. 788, 893–94 (1997).

107. I.R.C. § 513(i).

108. Id. § 513(i)(2).

109. Id. § 513(i)(1).

111. Id. § 513(i)(2)(A).

112. Id.

113. Id. § 513(i)(2)(B)(i).

115. Prop. Treas. Reg. § 1.513-4(c)(2), 58 Fed. Reg. 5687, 5690 (Jan. 22, 1993).

116. Prop. Treas. Reg. § 1.513-4(c)(2), 58 Fed. Reg. 5687. 5690 (Jan. 22, 1993).

119. I.R.C. § 170(l).

121. Id.§ 170(l)(2)(B).

122. Id.§ 170(l).

128. Tech. Adv. Mem. 00-04-001 (Jan. 28, 2000).

129. I.R.C. § 274(l).

130. Id. § 274(l)(2)(A).

132. Id. § 274(f).

DISCUSSION QUESTIONS

1. What are the main causes of the annual deficits that most athletic departments face each year?

2. Are the NCAA deficit numbers actually accurate? Why or why not? How could one get an accurate figure?

3. How has the myth of college sports profitability factored into the decline in legislative and taxpayer support for higher education?

4. Discuss the reality behind the myth that schools make money when their football teams play in bowl games. Give specific examples.

5. Why does the myth that most universities make money from their athletic departments persist?

6. What specific adjustments must be made in order for one to arrive at an accurate assessment of the amount a university makes or loses each year on its athletic programs? Explain each of these adjustments.

7. What are some of the positive effects that large football programs and men's basketball programs have on the publicity of an institution? Is there evidence of this? If so, what is it?

8. Does athletic success have an effect on student interest in an institution?

9. What led to the attempt by institutions to control expenditures rather than to distribute revenues? Was it successful? How so, or how not?

10. How does treating an athletic department as an auxiliary activity affect an institution?

11. How is the financial situation at Michigan likely to be different than at other Big Ten institutions? How about at Division I-A institutions not affiliated with the BCS?

12. What were the reasons that enabled the College of Charleston to make the move to Division I so seamlessly?

GENDER EQUITY

INTRODUCTION

One of the major issues that directors of collegiate athletics must factor into their operations are the elements that allow an institution to attain gender equity. The end concept of gender equity is often accomplished by the means of Title IX, the federal law that requires equal opportunity in school-related athletics. Title IX establishes that: "No person in the United States shall, on the basis of sex, be excluded from participation in, be denied the benefits of, or be subjected to discrimination under any education program or activity receiving Federal financial assistance." The articles and documents contained in this chapter explain what gender equity means, highlight the difficulties managers encounter in achieving it, and discuss the issues the athletics administrator must confront in order to comply.

Title IX is "Exhibit A" for the unique issues that collegiate administrators must grapple with that draw them away from the traditional professional sports and business goals of focusing on the bottom line or even exclusively upon winning. Federal law mandates that gender equity be an essential element in the operational equation. This priority, particularly during transitional phases, can have short- and long-term monetary impacts.

The first three documents provide the U.S. government's interpretation of the law. Insight is gained by looking at various letters interpreting the rules as issued by the United States Department of Education's Office for Civil Rights (OCR). Arguably these documents are the best place to start in attempting to understand the complexities of Title IX. The first is "Clarification of Intercollegiate Athletics Policy Guidance: The Three-Part Test." It is this three-part test that determines whether an academic institution is in compliance with Title IX. The OCR later issued additional clarification related to financial aid in a document referred to as the "Letter Clarifying Apportionment of Financial Aid in Intercollegiate Athletics." The next OCR-produced document is a letter that was designed to provide "Further Clarification of Intercollegiate Athletics Policy Guidance Regarding Title IX Compliance." This provides the most recent "final word" and guidance to the athletics administrator for Title IX. This letter was issued following contemplation of a report titled "Open to All: Title IX at Thirty," which was issued by a special commission created by the secretary of education to study Title IX. The Secretary's Commission on Opportunities in Athletics was charged to investigate and report back with "recommendations on how to improve the application of the current standards for measuring equal opportunity to participate in athletics under Title IX." The report was issued on February 26, 2003. The letter included in this chapter from U.S. assistant secretary of education for civil rights Gerald A. Reynolds essentially calls for no radical changes. However, it is clear that the guidelines and requirements — although now much more clearly defined — continue to evolve.

A broad overview of the law related to Title IX is set forth in Rosner's "The Growth of NCAA Women's Rowing: A Financial, Ethical and Legal Analysis." Rosner also provides the specifics of the applicability of Title IX in relation to rowing. Rowing is referred to by some as the equivalent of football in terms of the numbers of athletes that participate and the difficulty that it causes in efforts to insure equality.

The final excerpt, from Weistart's article "Can Gender Equity Find a Place in Commercialized College Sports?" focuses on the specific budgetary issues colleges must confront in dealing with these compliance issues. This article provides an excellent roadmap for the administrator to follow in making budgetary decisions in this environment.

Clarification of Intercollegiate Athletics Policy Guidance: The Three-Part Test (January 16, 1996)

United States Department of Education, Office for Civil Rights

The Office for Civil Rights (OCR) enforces Title IX of the Education Amendments of 1972, 20 U.S.C. § 1681 et seq. (Title IX), which prohibits discrimination on the basis of sex in education programs and activities by recipients of federal funds. The regulation implementing Title IX, at 34 C.F.R. Part 106, effective July 21, 1975, contains specific provisions governing athletic programs, at 34 C.F.R. § 106.41, and the awarding of athletic scholarships, at 34 C.F.R. § 106.37(c). Further clarification of the Title IX regulatory requirements is provided by the Intercollegiate Athletics Policy Interpretation, issued December 11, 1979 (44 Fed. Reg. 71413 et seq. (1979)).*

The Title IX regulation provides that if an institution sponsors an athletic program it must provide equal athletic opportunities for members of both sexes. Among other factors, the regulation requires that an institution must effectively accommodate the athletic interests and abilities of students of both sexes to the extent necessary to provide equal athletic opportunity.

The 1979 Policy Interpretation provides that as part of this determination OCR will apply the following three-part test to assess whether an institution is providing nondiscriminatory participation opportunities for individuals of both sexes:

1. Whether intercollegiate level participation opportunities for male and female students are provided in numbers substantially proportionate to their respective enrollments; or

2. Where the members of one sex have been and are underrepresented among intercollegiate athletes, whether the institution can show a history and continuing practice of program expansion which is demonstrably responsive to the developing interests and abilities of the members of that sex; or

---

* The Policy Interpretation is designed for intercollegiate athletics. However, its general principles, and those of this Clarification, often will apply to elementary and secondary interscholastic athletic programs, which are also covered by the regulation. *See* 44 Fed. Reg. 71413.

3. Where the members of one sex are underrepresented among intercollegiate athletes, and the institution cannot show a history and continuing practice of program expansion, as described above, whether it can be demonstrated that the interests and abilities of the members of that sex have been fully and effectively accommodated by the present program.

Thus, the three-part test furnishes an institution with three individual avenues to choose from when determining how it will provide individuals of each sex with nondiscriminatory opportunities to participate in intercollegiate athletics. If an institution has met any part of the three-part test, OCR will determine that the institution is meeting this requirement.

It is important to note that under the Policy Interpretation the requirement to provide nondiscriminatory participation opportunities is only one of many factors that OCR examines to determine if an institution is in compliance with the athletics provision of Title IX. OCR also considers the quality of competition offered to members of both sexes in order to determine whether an institution effectively accommodates the interests and abilities of its students.

In addition, when an "overall determination of compliance" is made by OCR, 44 Fed. Reg. 71417, 71418, OCR examines the institution's program as a whole. Thus, OCR considers the effective accommodation of interests and abilities in conjunction with equivalence in the availability, quality, and kinds of other athletic benefits and opportunities provided male and female athletes to determine whether an institution provides equal athletic opportunity as required by Title IX. These other benefits include coaching, equipment, practice and competitive facilities, recruitment, scheduling of games, and publicity, among others. An institution's failure to provide nondiscriminatory participation opportunities usually amounts to a denial of equal athletic opportunity because these opportunities provide access to all other athletic benefits, treatment, and services.

This Clarification provides specific factors that guide an analysis of each part of the three-part test. In addition, it provides examples to demonstrate, in concrete terms, how these factors will be considered. These examples are intended to be illustrative, and the conclusions drawn in each example are based solely on the facts included in the example.

THREE-PART TEST — PART ONE: ARE PARTICIPATION OPPORTUNITIES SUBSTANTIALLY PROPORTIONATE TO ENROLLMENT?

Under part one of the three-part test (part one), where an institution provides intercollegiate level athletic participation opportunities for male and female students in numbers substantially proportionate to their respective full-time undergraduate enrollments, OCR will find that the institution is providing nondiscriminatory participation opportunities for individuals of both sexes.

OCR's analysis begins with a determination of the number of participation opportunities afforded to male and female athletes in the intercollegiate athletic program. The Policy Interpretation defines participants as those athletes:

a. Who are receiving the institutionally-sponsored support normally provided to athletes competing at the institution involved, e.g., coaching, equipment, medical and training room services, on a regular basis during a sport's season; and

    b. Who are participating in organized practice sessions and other team meetings and activities on a regular basis during a sport's season; and

    c. Who are listed on the eligibility or squad lists maintained for each sport, or

    d. Who, because of injury, cannot meet a, b, or c above but continue to receive financial aid on the basis of athletic ability.

OCR uses this definition of a participant to determine the number of participation opportunities provided by an institution for purposes of the three-part test.

Under this definition, OCR considers a sport's season to commence on the date of a team's first intercollegiate competitive event and to conclude on the date of the team's final intercollegiate competitive event. As a general rule, all athletes who are listed on a team's squad or eligibility list and are on the team as of the team's first competitive event are counted as participants by OCR. In determining the number of participation opportunities for the purposes of the interests and abilities analysis, an athlete who participates in more than one sport will be counted as a participant in each sport in which he or she participates.

In determining participation opportunities, OCR includes, among others, those athletes who do not receive scholarships (e.g., walk-ons), those athletes who compete on teams sponsored by the institution even though the team may be required to raise some or all of its operating funds, and those athletes who practice but may not compete. OCR's investigations reveal that these athletes receive numerous benefits and services, such as training and practice time, coaching, tutoring services, locker room facilities, and equipment, as well as important non-tangible benefits derived from being a member of an intercollegiate athletic team. Because these are significant benefits, and because receipt of these benefits does not depend on their cost to the institution [or] whether the athlete competes, it is necessary to count all athletes who receive such benefits when determining the number of athletic opportunities provided to men and women.

OCR's analysis next determines whether athletic opportunities are substantially proportionate. The Title IX regulation allows institutions to operate separate athletic programs for men and women. Accordingly, the regulation allows an institution to control the respective number of participation opportunities offered men and women. Thus, it could be argued that to satisfy part one there should be no difference between the participation rate in an institution's intercollegiate athletic program and its full-time undergraduate student enrollment.

However, because in some circumstances it may be unreasonable to expect an institution to achieve exact proportionality — for instance, because of natural fluctuations in enrollment and participation rates or because it would be unreasonable to expect an institution to add athletic opportunities in light of the small number of students that would have to be accommodated to achieve exact proportionality — the Policy Interpretation examines whether participation opportunities are "substantially" proportionate to enrollment rates. Because this determination depends on the institution's specific circumstances and the size of its athletic program, OCR makes this determination on a case-by-case basis, rather than through use of a statistical test.

As an example of a determination under part one: If an institution's enrollment is 52 percent male and 48 percent female and 52 percent of the participants in the athletic program are male and 48 percent female, then the institution would clearly satisfy part one. However OCR recognizes that natural fluctuations in an institution's enrollment and/or participation rates may affect the percentages in a subsequent year. For instance, if the institution's admissions the following year resulted in an enrollment rate of 51 percent males and 49 percent females, while the participation rates of males and females in the athletic program remained constant the institution would continue to satisfy part one because it would be unreasonable to expect the institution to fine tune its program in response to this change in enrollment.

As another example, over the past five years an institution has had a consistent enrollment rate for women of 50 percent. During this time period, it has been expanding its program for women in order to reach proportionality. In the year that the institution reaches its goal — i.e., 50 percent of the participants in its athletic program are female — its enrollment rate for women increases to 52 percent. Under these circumstances, the institution would satisfy part one.

OCR would also consider opportunities to be substantially proportionate when the number of opportunities that would be required to achieve proportionality would not be sufficient to sustain a viable team, i.e., a team for which there is a sufficient number of interested and able students and enough available competition to sustain an intercollegiate team. As a frame of reference in assessing this situation, OCR may consider the average size of teams offered for the underrepresented sex, a number which would vary by institution.

For instance, Institution A is a university with a total of 600 athletes. While women make up 52 percent of the university's enrollment, they only represent 47 percent of its athletes. If the university provided women with 52 percent of athletic opportunities, approximately 62 additional women would be able to participate. Because this is a significant number of unaccommodated women, it is likely that a viable sport could be added. If so, Institution A has not met part one.

As another example, at Institution B women also make up 52 percent of the university's enrollment and represent 47 percent of Institution B's athletes. Institution B's athletic program consists of only 60 participants. If the University provided women with 52 percent of athletic opportunities, approximately 6 additional women would be able to participate. Since 6 participants are unlikely to support a viable team, Institution B would meet part one.

THREE-PART TEST — PART TWO: IS THERE A HISTORY AND CONTINUING PRACTICE OF PROGRAM EXPANSION FOR THE UNDERREPRESENTED SEX?

Under part two of the three-part test (part two), an institution can show that it has a history and continuing practice of program expansion which is demonstrably responsive to the developing interests and abilities of the underrepresented sex. In effect, part two looks at an institution's past and continuing remedial efforts to provide nondiscriminatory participation opportunities through program expansion.*

OCR will review the entire history of the athletic program, focusing on the participation opportunities provided for the underrepresented sex. First, OCR will assess whether past actions of the institution have expanded participation opportunities for the underrepresented sex in a manner that was demonstrably responsive to their developing interests and abilities. Developing interests include inter-

---

* Part two focuses on whether an institution has expanded the number of intercollegiate participation opportunities provided to the underrepresented sex. Improvements in the quality of competition, and of other athletic benefits provided to women athletes, while not considered under the three-part test, can be considered by OCR in making an overall determination of compliance with the athletics provision of Title IX.

ests that already exist at the institution.† There are no fixed intervals of time within which an institution must have added participation opportunities. Neither is a particular number of sports dispositive. Rather, the focus is on whether the program expansion was responsive to developing interests and abilities of the underrepresented sex. In addition, the institution must demonstrate a continuing (i.e., present) practice of program expansion as warranted by developing interests and abilities.

OCR will consider the following factors, among others, as evidence that may indicate a history of program expansion that is demonstrably responsive to the developing interests and abilities of the underrepresented sex.

- An institution's record of adding intercollegiate teams, or upgrading teams to intercollegiate status, for the underrepresented sex;
- An institution's record of increasing the numbers of participants in intercollegiate athletics who are members of the underrepresented sex; and
- An institution's affirmative responses to requests by students or others for addition or elevation of sports.

OCR will consider the following factors, among others, as evidence that may indicate a continuing practice of program expansion that is demonstrably responsive to the developing interests and abilities of the underrepresented sex:

- An institution's current implementation of a nondiscriminatory policy or procedure for requesting the addition of sports (including the elevation of club or intramural teams) and the effective communication of the policy or procedure to students; and
- An institution's current implementation of a plan of program expansion that is responsive to developing interests and abilities.

OCR would also find persuasive an institution's efforts to monitor developing interests and abilities of the underrepresented sex, for example, by conducting periodic nondiscriminatory assessments of developing interests and abilities and taking timely actions in response to the results.

In the event that an institution eliminated any team for the underrepresented sex, OCR would evaluate the circumstances surrounding this action in assessing whether the institution could satisfy part two of the test. However, OCR will not find a history and continuing practice of program expansion where an institution increases the proportional participation opportunities for the underrepresented sex by reducing opportunities for the overrepresented sex alone or by reducing participation opportunities for the overrepresented sex to a proportionately greater degree than for the underrepresented sex. This is because part two considers an institution's good faith remedial efforts through actual program expansion. It is only necessary to examine part two if one sex is overrepresented in the athletic program. Cuts in the program for the underrepresented sex, even when coupled with cuts in the program for the overrepresented sex, cannot be considered remedial because they burden members of the sex already disadvantaged by the present program. However, an institution that has

---

† However, under this part of the test an institution is not required, as it is under part three, to accommodate all interests and abilities of the underrepresented sex. Moreover, under part two an institution has flexibility in choosing which teams it adds for the underrepresented sex, as long as it can show overall history and continuing practice of program expansion for members of that sex.

eliminated some participation opportunities for the underrepresented sex can still meet part two if, overall, it can show a history and continuing practice of program expansion for that sex.

In addition, OCR will not find that an institution satisfies part two where it established teams for the underrepresented sex only at the initiation of its program for the underrepresented sex or where it merely promises to expand its program for the underrepresented sex at some time in the future.

The following examples are intended to illustrate the principles discussed above. At the inception of its women's program in the mid-1970s, Institution C established seven teams for women. In 1984 it added a women's varsity team at the request of students and coaches. In 1990 it upgraded a women's club sport to varsity team status based on a request by the club members and an NCAA survey that showed a significant increase in girls high school participation in that sport. Institution C is currently implementing a plan to add a varsity women's team in the spring of 1996 that has been identified by a regional study as an emerging women's sport in the region. The addition of these teams resulted in an increased percentage of women participating in varsity athletics at the institution. Based on these facts, OCR would find Institution C in compliance with part two because it has a history of program expansion and is continuing to expand its program for women in response to their developing interests and abilities.

By 1980, Institution D established seven teams for women. Institution D added a women's varsity team in 1983 based on the requests of students and coaches. In 1991 it added a women's varsity team after an NCAA survey showed a significant increase in girls' high school participation in that sport. In 1993 Institution D eliminated a viable women's team and a viable men's team in an effort to reduce its athletic budget. It has taken no action relating to the underrepresented sex since 1993. Based on these facts, OCR would not find Institution D in compliance with part two. Institution D cannot show a continuing practice of program expansion that is responsive to the developing interests and abilities of the underrepresented sex where its only action since 1991 with regard to the underrepresented sex was to eliminate a team for which there was interest, ability, and available competition.

In the mid-1970s, Institution E established five teams for women. In 1979 it added a women's varsity team. In 1984 it upgraded a women's club sport with twenty-five participants to varsity team status. At that time it eliminated a women's varsity team that had eight members. In 1987 and 1989 Institution E added women's varsity teams that were identified by a significant number of its enrolled and incoming female students when surveyed regarding their athletic interests and abilities. During this time it also increased the size of an existing women's team to provide opportunities for women who expressed interest in playing that sport. Within the past year, it added a women's varsity team based on a nationwide survey of the most popular girls high school teams. Based on the addition of these teams, the percentage of women participating in varsity athletics at the institution has increased. Based on these facts, OCR would find Institution E in compliance with part two because it has a history of program expansion and the elimination of the team in 1984 took place within the context of continuing program expansion for the underrepresented sex that is responsive to their developing interests.

Institution F started its women's program in the early 1970s with four teams. It did not add to its women's program until 1987 when, based on requests of students and coaches, it upgraded a women's club sport to varsity team status and expanded the size of several existing women's teams to accommodate significant expressed interest by students. In 1990 it surveyed its enrolled and incoming female students; based on that survey and a survey of the most popular sports played by women in the region, Institution F agreed to add three new women's teams by 1997. It added a women's team by 1991 and 1994. Institution F is implementing a plan to add a women's team by the spring of 1997. Based on these facts, OCR would find Institution F in compliance with part two. Institution F's program history since 1987 shows that it is committed to program expansion for the underrepresented sex and it is continuing to expand its women's program in light of women's developing interests and abilities.

THREE-PART TEST — PART THREE: IS THE INSTITUTION FULLY AND EFFECTIVELY ACCOMMODATING THE INTERESTS AND ABILITIES OF THE UNDERREPRESENTED SEX?

Under part three of the three-part test (part three) OCR determines whether an institution is fully and effectively accommodating the interests and abilities of its students who are members of the underrepresented sex — including students who are admitted to the institution though not yet enrolled. Title IX provides that a recipient must provide equal athletic opportunity to its students. Accordingly, the Policy Interpretation does not require an institution to accommodate the interests and abilities of potential students.*

While disproportionately high athletic participation rates by an institution's students of the overrepresented sex (as compared to their enrollment rates) may indicate that an institution is not providing equal athletic opportunities to its students of the underrepresented sex, an institution can satisfy part three where there is evidence that the imbalance does not reflect discrimination, i.e., where it can be demonstrated that, notwithstanding disproportionately low participation rates by the institution's students of the underrepresented sex, the interests and abilities of these students are, in fact, being fully and effectively accommodated.

In making this determination, OCR will consider whether there is (a) unmet interest in a particular sport; (b) sufficient ability to sustain a team in the sport; and (c) a reasonable expectation of competition for the team. If all three conditions are present OCR will find that an institution has not fully and effectively accommodated the interests and abilities of the underrepresented sex.

If an institution has recently eliminated a viable team from the intercollegiate program, OCR will find that there is sufficient interest, ability, and available competition to sustain an intercollegiate team in that sport unless an institution can provide strong evidence that interest, ability, or available competition no longer exists.

a) Is there sufficient unmet interest to support an intercollegiate team?

[First,] OCR will determine whether there is sufficient unmet interest among the institution's students who are members of the underrepresented sex to sustain an intercollegiate team. OCR will look for interest by the underrepresented sex as expressed through the following indicators, among others:

---

* However, OCR does examine an institution's recruitment practices under another part of the Policy Interpretation. See 44 Fed. Reg. 71417. Accordingly, where an institution recruits potential student athletes for its men's teams, it must ensure that women's teams are provided with substantially equal opportunities to recruit potential student athletes.

- Requests by students and admitted students that a particular sport be added;
- Requests that an existing club sport be elevated to intercollegiate team status;
- Participation in particular club or intramural sports;
- Interviews with students, admitted students, coaches, administrators, and others regarding interest in particular sports;
- Results of questionnaires of students and admitted students regarding interests in particular sports; and
- Participation in particular interscholastic sports by admitted students.

In addition, OCR will look at participation rates in sports in high schools amateur athletic associations, and community sports leagues that operate in areas from which the institution draws its students in order to ascertain likely interest and ability of its students and admitted students in particular sport(s).* For example, where OCR's investigation finds that a substantial number of high schools from the relevant region offer a particular sport which the institution does not offer for the underrepresented sex, OCR will ask the institution to provide a basis for any assertion that its students and admitted students are not interested in playing that sport. OCR may also interview students, admitted students, coaches, and others regarding interest in that sport.

An institution may evaluate its athletic program to assess the athletic interest of its students of the underrepresented sex using nondiscriminatory methods of its choosing. Accordingly, institutions have flexibility in choosing a nondiscriminatory method of determining athletic interests and abilities provided they meet certain requirements. These assessments may use straightforward and inexpensive techniques, such as a student questionnaire or an open forum, to identify students' interests and abilities. Thus, while OCR expects that an institution's assessment should reach a wide audience of students and should be open-ended regarding the sports students can express interest in, OCR does not require elaborate scientific validation of assessment.

An institution's evaluation of interest should be done periodically so that the institution can identify in a timely and responsive manner any developing interests and abilities of the underrepresented sex. The evaluation should also take into account sports played in the high schools and communities from which the institution draws its students both as an indication of possible interest on campus and to permit the institution to plan to meet the interests of admitted students of the underrepresented sex.

b) Is there sufficient ability to sustain an intercollegiate team?

Second, OCR will determine whether there is sufficient ability among interested students of the underrepresented sex to sustain an intercollegiate team. OCR will examine indications of ability such as:

- The athletic experience and accomplishments — in interscholastic, club, or intramural competition — of students and admitted students interested in playing the sport;

---

* While these indications of interest may be helpful to OCR in ascertaining likely interest on campus, particularly in the absence of more direct indications, the institution is expected to meet the actual interests and abilities of its students.

- Opinions of coaches, administrators, and athletes at the institution regarding whether interested students and admitted students have the potential to sustain a varsity team; and
- If the team has previously competed at the club or intramural level, whether the competitive experience of the team indicates that it has the potential to sustain an intercollegiate team.

Neither a poor competitive record nor the inability of interested students or admitted students to play at the same level of competition engaged in by the institution's other athletes is conclusive evidence of lack of ability. It is sufficient that interested students and admitted students have the potential to sustain an intercollegiate team.

c) Is there a reasonable expectation of competition for the team?

Finally, OCR determines whether there is a reasonable expectation of intercollegiate competition for a particular sport in the institution's normal competitive region. In evaluating available competition, OCR will look at available competitive opportunities in the geographic area in which the institution's athletes primarily compete, including:

- Competitive opportunities offered by other schools against which the institution competes; and
- Competitive opportunities offered by other schools in the institution's geographic area, including those offered by schools against which the institution does not now compete.

Under the Policy Interpretation, the institution may also be required to actively encourage the development of intercollegiate competition for a sport for members of the underrepresented sex when overall athletic opportunities within its competitive region have been historically limited for members of that sex.

CONCLUSION

This discussion clarifies that institutions have three distinct ways to provide individuals of each sex with nondiscriminatory participation opportunities. The three-part test gives institutions flexibility and control over their athletics programs. For instance, the test allows institutions to respond to different levels of the interest by its male and female students. Moreover, nothing in the three-part test requires an institution to eliminate participation opportunities for men.

At the same time, this flexibility must be used by institutions consistent with Title IX's requirement that they not discriminate on the basis of sex. OCR recognizes that institutions face challenges in providing nondiscriminatory participation opportunities for their students and will continue to assist institutions in finding ways to meet these challenges.

Letter Clarifying Apportionment of Financial Aid in Intercollegiate Athletics Programs (July 23, 1998)

United States Department of Education, Office for Civil Rights

Ms. Nancy S. Footer
General Counsel
Bowling Green State University
308 McFall Center
Bowling Green, Ohio 43403-0010

Dear Ms. Footer:

This is in response to your letter requesting guidance in meeting the requirements of Title IX specifically as it relates to the equitable apportionment of athletic financial aid. Please accept my apology for the delay in responding. As you know, the Office for Civil Rights (OCR) enforces Title IX of the Education Amendments of 1972, 20 U.S.C. § 1682, which prohibits discrimination on the basis of sex in education programs and activities. The regulation implementing Title IX and the Department's Intercollegiate Athletics Policy Interpretation published in 1979 — both of which followed publication for notice and the receipt, review, and consideration of extensive comments — specifically address intercollegiate athletics. You have asked us to provide clarification regarding how educational institutions can provide intercollegiate athletes with nondiscriminatory opportunities to receive athletic financial aid. Under the Policy Interpretation, the equitable apportioning of a college's intercollegiate athletics scholarship fund for the separate budgets of its men's and women's programs — which Title IX permits to be segregated — requires that the total amounts of scholarship aid made available to the two budgets are "substantially proportionate" to the participation rates of male and female athletes. 44 Fed. Reg. 71413, 71415 (1979).

In responding, I wish (1) to clarify the coverage of Title IX and its regulations as they apply to both academic and athletic programs, and (2) to provide specific guidance about the existing standards that have guided the enforcement of Title IX in the area of athletic financial aid, particularly the Policy Interpretation's "substantially proportionate" provision as it relates to a college's funding of the athletic scholarships budgets for its men's and women's teams. At the outset, I want to clarify that, wholly apart from any obligation with respect to scholarships, an institution with an intercollegiate athletics program has an independent Title IX obligation to provide its students with nondiscriminatory athletic participation opportunities. The scope of that separate obligation is not addressed in this letter, but was addressed in a Clarification issued on January 16, 1996.

TITLE IX COVERAGE: ATHLETICS VERSUS ACADEMIC PROGRAMS

Title IX is an anti-discrimination statute that prohibits discrimination on the basis of sex in any education program or activity receiving federal financial assistance, including athletic programs. Thus, in both academics and athletics, Title IX guarantees that all students, regardless of gender, have equitable opportunities to participate in the education program. This guarantee does not impose quotas based on gender, either in classrooms or in athletic programs. Indeed, the imposition of any such strict numerical requirement concerning students would be inconsistent with Title IX itself, which is designed to protect the rights of all students and to provide equitable opportunities for all students.

Additionally, Title IX recognizes the uniqueness of intercollegiate athletics by permitting a college or university to have separate athletic programs, and teams, for men and women. This allows colleges and universities to allocate athletic opportunities and benefits on the basis of sex. Because of this unique circumstance, arguments that OCR's athletics compliance standards create quotas are misplaced. In contrast to other antidiscriminatory statutes, Title IX compliance cannot be determined simply on the basis of whether an institution makes sex-specific decisions, because invariably they do. Accordingly, the statute instead requires institutions to provide equitable opportunities to both male and female athletes in all aspects of its two separate athletic programs. As the court in the Brown University case stated, "[i]n this unique context Title IX operates to ensure that the gender-segregated allocation of athletic opportunities does not disadvantage either gender. Rather than create a quota or preference, this unavoidable gender-conscious comparison merely provides for the allocation of athletic resources and participation opportunities between the sexes in a non-discriminatory manner." *Cohen v. Brown University,* 101 F.3d 155, 177 (1st Cir. 1996), cert. denied, 117 S. Ct. 1469 (1997). The remainder of this letter addresses the application of Title IX only to athletic scholarships.

Athletics: Scholarship Requirements

With regard to athletic financial assistance, the regulations promulgated under Title IX provide that, when a college or university awards athletic scholarships, these scholarship awards must be granted to "members of each sex in proportion to the number of students of each sex participating in . . . intercollegiate athletics." Since 1979, OCR has interpreted this regulation in conformity with its published "Policy Interpretation: Title IX and Intercollegiate Athletics." The Policy Interpretation does not require colleges to grant the same number of scholarships to men and women, nor does it require that individual scholarships be of equal value. What it does require is that, at a particular college or university, "the total amount of scholarship aid made available to men and women must be substantially proportionate to their [overall] participation rates" at that institution. It is important to note that the Policy Interpretation only applies to teams that regularly compete in varsity competition.

Under the Policy Interpretation, OCR conducts a "financial comparison to determine whether proportionately equal amounts of financial assistance (scholarship aid) are available to men's and women's athletic programs." The Policy Interpretation goes on to state that "[i]nstitutions may be found in compliance if this comparison results in substantially equal amounts or if a disparity can be explained by adjustments to take into account legitimate nondiscriminatory factors."

A "disparity" in awarding athletic, financial assistance refers to the difference between the aggregate amount of money athletes of one sex received in one year, and the amount they would have received if their share of the entire annual budget for athletic scholarships had been awarded in proportion to their participation rates. Thus, for example, if men account for 60% of a school's intercollegiate athletes, the Policy Interpretation presumes that — absent legitimate nondiscriminating factors that may cause a disparity — the men's athletic program will receive approximately 60% of the entire annual scholarship budget, and the women's athletic program will receive approximately 40% of those funds. This presumption reflects the fact that colleges typically allocate scholarship funds among their athletic teams, and that such teams are expressly segregated by sex. Colleges' allocation of the scholarship budget among teams, therefore, is invariably sex-based, in the sense that an allocation to a particular team necessarily benefits one sex to the exclusion of the other. Where, as here, disparate treatment is inevitable and a college's allocation of scholarship funds is "at the discretion of the institution," the statute nondiscrimination requirements obliges colleges to ensure that men's and women's *separate* activities receive equitable treatment.

Nevertheless, in keeping with the Policy Interpretation allowance for disparities from "substantially proportionate" awards to the men's and women's programs based on legitimate nondiscriminatory factors, OCR judges each matter on a case-by-case basis with due regard for the unique factual situation presented by each case. For example, OCR recognizes that disparities may be explained by actions taken to promote athletic program development, and by differences between in-state and out-of-state tuition at public colleges, 44 Fed. Reg, at 71415. Disparities might also be explained, for example, by legitimate efforts undertaken to comply with Title IX requirements, such as participation requirements. See, e.g., *Gonyo v. Drake Univ.* 879 F. Supp. 1000, 1005–06 (S.D. Iowa 1995). Similarly, disparities may be explained by unexpected fluctuations in the participation rates of males and females. For example, a disparity may be explained if an athlete who had accepted an athletic scholarship decided at the last minute to enroll at another school. It is important to note it is not enough for a college or university merely to assert a nondiscriminatory justification. Instead, it will be required to demonstrate that its asserted rationale is in fact reasonable and does not reflect underlying discrimination. For instance, if a college consistently awards a greater number of out-of-state scholarships to men, it may be required to demonstrate that this does not reflect discriminatory recruitment practices. Similarly, if a university asserts the phase-in of scholarships for a new team as a justification for a disparity, the university may be required to demonstrate that the time frame for phasing-in of scholarships is reasonable in light of college sports practices to aggressively recruit athletes to build start-up teams quickly.

In order to ensure equity for athletes of both sexes, the test for determining whether the two scholarship budgets are "substantially proportionate" to the respective participation rates of athletes of each sex necessarily has a high threshold. The Policy Interpretation does not, however, require colleges to achieve exact proportionality down to the last dollar. The "substantially proportionate" test permits a small variance from exact proportionality. OCR recognizes that, in practice, some leeway is necessary to avoid requiring colleges to unreasonably fine-tune their scholarship budgets.

When evaluating each scholarship program on a case-by-case basis, OCR's first step will be to adjust any disparity to take into account all the legitimate nondiscriminatory reasons provided by the college, such as the extra costs for out-of-state tuition discussed earlier. If any unexplained disparity in the scholarship budget for athletes of either gender is 1% or less for the entire budget for athletic scholarships, there will be a strong presumption that such a disparity is reasonable and based on legitimate and nondiscriminatory factors. Conversely, there will be a strong presumption that an unexplained disparity of more than 1% is in violation of the "substantially proportionate" requirements.

Thus, for example, if men are 60% of the athletes, OCR would expect that the men's athletic scholarship budget would be within 59–61% of the total budget for athletic scholarships for all athletes, after accounting for legitimate nondiscriminatory reasons for any larger disparity. Of course, OCR will continue to judge each case in terms of its particular facts. For example, at those colleges where 1% of the entire athletic scholarship budget is less than the value of one full scholarship, OCR will presume that a disparity of up to the value of one full scholarship is equitable and nondiscriminatory. On the other hand, even if an institution consistently has less than a 1% disparity, the presumption of compliance with Title IX might still be rebutted if, for example, there is direct evidence of discriminatory intent.

OCR recognizes that there has been some confusion in the past with respect to the Title IX compliance standards for scholarships. OCR's 1990 Title IX Investigator's Manual correctly stated that one would expect proportionality in the awarding of scholarships, absent a legitimate, nondiscriminatory justification. But that Manual also indicated that compliance with the "substantially proportionate" test could depend, in part, upon certain statistical tests. In some cases, application of such a statistical test would result in a determination of compliance despite the existence of a disparity as large as 3–5%.

We would like to clarify that use of such statistical tests is not appropriate in these circumstances. Those tests, which are used in some other discrimination contexts to determine whether the disparities in the allocation of benefits to different groups are the result of chance, are inapposite in the athletic scholarship context because a college has direct control over its allocation of financial aid to men's and women's teams, and because such decisions necessarily are sex-based in the sense that an allocation to a particular team will affect only one sex. See *Brown,* 101 F.3d at 176–78 (explaining why college athletics "presents a distinctly different situation from admissions and employment," and why athletics requires a different analysis than that used in such other contexts "in order to determine the existence vel non of discrimination"). In the typical case where aid is expressly allocated among sex-segregated teams, chance simply is not a possible explanation for disproportionate aid to one sex. Where a college does not make a substantially proportionate allocation to sex-segregated teams, the burden should be on the college to provide legitimate, nondiscriminatory reasons for the disproportionate allocation. Therefore, the use of statistical tests will not be helpful in determining whether a disparity in the allocations for the two separate athletic scholarship budgets is nondiscriminatory.

While a statistical test is not relevant in determining discrimination, the confusion caused by the manual's inclusion of a statistical test resulted in misunderstandings. Therefore, OCR is providing this clarification regarding the substantial proportionality provision found in the 1979 Policy Interpretation to confirm the substance of a longstanding standard. In order to ensure full understanding, OCR will apply the presumptions and case-by-case analysis described in this letter for the 1998–99 academic year. OCR strongly encourages recipients to award athletic financial assistance to women athletes in the 1997–98 academic year consistent with this policy clarification, both as a matter of fairness and in order to ensure that they are moving towards the policy clarification stated in this letter.

I trust that this letter responds to the questions the University has regarding the "substantially proportionate" provision of the Policy interpretation in the context of the funding for an institution's two separate athletic scholarship budgets for male and female athletes. . . .

Sincerely yours,

Dr. Mary Frances O'Shea
National Coordinator for Title IX Athletics

FURTHER CLARIFICATION OF INTERCOLLEGIATE ATHLETICS POLICY GUIDANCE REGARDING TITLE IX COMPLIANCE

United States Department of Education, Office for Civil Rights

July 11, 2003

Dear Colleague:

It is my pleasure to provide you with this Further Clarification of Intercollegiate Athletics Policy Guidance Regarding Title IX Compliance.

Since its enactment in 1972, Title IX has produced significant advancement in athletic opportunities for women and girls across the nation. Recognizing that more remains to be done, the Bush Administration is firmly committed to building on this legacy and continuing the progress that Title IX has brought toward true equality of opportunity for male and female student-athletes in America.

In response to numerous requests for additional guidance on the Department of Education's (Department) enforcement standards since its last written guidance on Title IX in 1996, the Department's Office for Civil Rights (OCR) began looking into whether additional guidance on Title IX requirements regarding intercollegiate athletics was needed. On June 27, 2002, Secretary of Education Rod Paige created the Secretary's Commission on Opportunities in Athletics to investigate this matter further, and to report back with recommendations on how to improve the application of the current standards for measuring equal opportunity to participate in athletics under Title IX. On February 26, 2003, the Commission presented Secretary Paige with its final report, "Open to All: Title IX at Thirty," and in addition, individual members expressed their views.

After eight months of discussion and an extensive and inclusive fact-finding process, the Commission found very broad support throughout the country for the goals and spirit of Title IX. With that in mind, OCR today issues this Further Clarification in order to strengthen Title IX's promise of non-discrimination in the athletic programs of our nation's schools.

Title IX establishes that: "No person in the United States shall, on the basis of sex, be excluded from participation in, be denied the benefits of, or be subjected to discrimination under any education program or activity receiving Federal financial assistance."

. . . .

In its 1979 Policy Interpretation, the Department established a three-prong test for compliance with Title IX, which it later amplified and clarified in its 1996 Clarification. . . . .

First, with respect to the three-prong test, which has worked well, OCR encourages schools to take advantage of its flexibility, and to consider which of the three prongs best satisfy the three-prong test if it maintains a history and continuing practice of program expansion for the underrepresented sex, or if "the interests and abilities of the members of [the underrepresented] sex have been fully and effectively accommodated by the present program." Each of the three prongs is thus a valid, alternative way for schools to comply with Title IX.

The transmittal letter accompanying the 1996 Clarification issued by the Department described only one of these three separate prongs — substantial proportionality — as a "safe harbor" for Title IX compliance. This led many schools to believe, erroneously, that they must take measures to ensure strict proportionality between the sexes. In fact, each of the three prongs of the test is an equally sufficient means of complying with Title IX, and no one prong is favored. The Department will continue to make clear, as it did in its 1996 Clarification, that "[i]nstitutions have flexibility in providing nondiscriminatory participation opportunities to their students, and OCR does not require quotas."

In order to ensure that schools have a clear understanding of their options for compliance with Title IX, OCR will undertake an education campaign to help educational institutions appreciate the flexibility of the law, to explain that each prong of the test is a viable and separate means of compliance, to give practical examples of the ways in which schools can comply, and to provide schools with technical assistance as they try to comply with Title IX.

In the 1996 Clarification, the Department provided schools with a broad range of specific factors, as well as illustrative examples, to help schools understand the flexibility of the three-prong test. OCR reincorporates those factors, as well as those illustrative examples, into this Further Clarification, and OCR will continue to assist schools on a case-by-case basis and address any questions they have about Title IX compliance. Indeed, OCR encourages schools to request individualized assistance from OCR as they consider ways to meet the requirements of Title IX. As OCR works with schools on Title IX compliance, OCR will share information on successful approaches with the broader scholastic community.

Second, OCR hereby clarifies that nothing in Title IX requires the cutting or reduction of teams in order to demonstrate compliance with Title IX, and that the elimination of teams is a disfavored practice. Because the elimination of teams diminishes opportunities for students who are interested in participating in athletics instead of enhancing opportunities for students who have suffered from discrimination, it is contrary to the spirit of Title IX for the government to require or encourage an institution to eliminate athletic teams. Therefore, in negotiating compliance agreements, OCR's policy will be to seek remedies that do not involve the elimination of teams.

Third, OCR hereby advises schools that it will aggressively enforce Title IX standards, including implementing sanctions for institutions that do not comply. At the same time, OCR will also work with schools to assist them in avoiding such sanctions by achieving Title IX compliance.

Fourth, private sponsorship of athletic teams will continue to be allowed. Of course, private sponsorship does not in any way change or diminish a school's obligations under Title IX.

Finally, OCR recognizes that schools will benefit from clear and consistent implementation of Title IX. Accordingly, OCR will ensure that its enforcement practices do not vary from region to region.

OCR recognizes that the question of how to comply with Title IX and to provide equal athletic opportunities for all students is a challenge for many academic institutions. But OCR believes that the three-prong test has provided, and will continue to provide, schools with the flexibility to provide greater athletic opportunities for students of both sexes.

OCR is strongly reaffirming today its commitment to equal opportunity for girls and boys, women and men. To that end, OCR is committed to continuing to work in partnership with educational institutions to ensure that the promise of Title IX becomes a reality for all students.

Thank you for your continuing interest in this subject.

Sincerely,

Gerald Reynolds
Assistant Secretary for Civil Rights

THE GROWTH OF NCAA WOMEN'S ROWING: A FINANCIAL, ETHICAL, AND LEGAL ANALYSIS

Scott R. Rosner

III. LEGAL ASPECTS

A. History of Title IX

Title IX of the Education Amendments of 1972 is a federal law prohibiting sex discrimination in education programs and activities receiving or benefiting from federal funding. While not specifically mentioned in the law itself, athletics are covered by Title IX. Consequently, this law has been the primary method by which women have achieved equal opportunity in high school and college athletics, and it has played a vital role in opening competition to female athletes. Though signed into law on June 23, 1972, the Department of Health, Education and Welfare's final Title IX regulations did not go into effect until July 21, 1975, and were not enforced until the three-year compliance period expired in 1978. In order to clarify the requirements of Title IX and to provide schools with guidance on their obligations under the law, the Office for Civil Rights (OCR) issued its final Policy Interpretation on December 11, 1979.[76] This outlines a detailed set of standards to be adhered to in three separate areas: student interests and abilities, athletic benefits and opportunities, and athletic financial assistance.

Though the Policy Interpretation is not a rule of law, it has been given substantial deference by courts determining the rights of female athletes. After the period of enforcement that followed the issuance of the Policy Interpretation, female athletes suffered a setback when athletic programs were removed from coverage under Title IX by *Grove City v. Bell.** As a result of this judicial setback,

---

* 465 U.S. 555 (1984). The Supreme Court limited the application of Title IX to programs or activities that received direct federal financial assistance. See id. As most athletic departments do not receive such direct funding, they were removed from coverage under Title IX.

OCR immediately cancelled all forty of its ongoing Title IX athletics investigations and ignored any new complaints regarding athletics. Congress acted rather quickly to correct the narrowing of Title IX that *Grove City* had accomplished and enacted the Civil Rights Restoration Act in 1988, overriding a veto by President Reagan. The Act served the purpose of reversing the Supreme Court's decision in *Grove City* by stipulating that Title IX applies to all programs of an educational institution that receive any federal financial assistance. The revitalization of Title IX was fortified by the Supreme Court's decision in *Franklin v. Gwinnett County Public Schools,*[84] which allowed private plaintiffs to receive monetary damages and attorney fees for an intentional violation of Title IX.[85]

In addition to these agency regulations and legislative and judicial statements, Title IX has been shaped by three other policy documents issued by OCR: the Title IX Investigator's Manual; the Clarification of Intercollegiate Athletics Policy Guidance: The Three-Part Test; and a letter offering guidance regarding the issuance of athletics scholarships. . . . *[See these two latter documents beginning on p. 619.]*

B. Analysis & Application of Title IX to Women's Rowing

1. Student Interests and Abilities. As previously mentioned, compliance with Title IX is measured in three separate areas: student interests and abilities, athletic benefits and opportunities, and athletic financial assistance. Under Title IX, the athletic interests and abilities of male and female students must be equally and effectively accommodated. OCR will assess whether an institution is in compliance with this aspect of Title IX through the application of the following three-part test:

(1) Whether intercollegiate level participation opportunities for male and female students are provided in numbers substantially proportionate to their respective enrollments; or

(2) Where the members of one sex have been and are underrepresented among intercollegiate athletes, whether the institution can show a history and continuing practice of program expansion which is demonstrably responsive to the developing interest and abilities of the members of that sex; or

(3) Where the members of one sex are underrepresented among intercollegiate athletes, and the institution cannot show a continuing practice of program expansion such as that cited above, whether it can be demonstrated that the interests and abilities of the members of that sex have been fully and effectively accommodated by the present program.

An institution may choose any one of the three benchmarks established by this test in order to satisfy the accommodation requirement. OCR also considers the quality of competition available to members of both sexes, but it is this three-part test that has been the most litigated aspect of Title IX in determining whether the interests and abilities of an institution's students are effectively accommodated.

Under part one of the three-part test, OCR looks at whether an institution's participation opportunities for its male and female students are substantially proportionate to their full-time undergraduate enrollments. Although OCR will find that an institution with a closely mirrored image between these two figures is effectively accommodating the interests and abilities of its students, very few institutions have been able to take advantage of this "safe harbor." In 1997, only fifty-one institutions in NCAA Division I were within even five percentage points of achieving substantial proportionality. For many institutions, this is due to the presence of football. The number of participation opportunities in football is unmatched by any other sport. An institution would typically have to sponsor at least three women's teams in order to match the number of athletes on a football team. Thus, it becomes extremely difficult for an institution sponsoring a Division I-A football team to comply with the first benchmark.

The growth of women's rowing in the NCAA is primarily attributable to its positive impact on institutions attempting to comply with the interests and abilities aspect of Title IX via the substantial proportionality test. The large roster size of a women's rowing team has made it an extremely attractive alternative for athletic administrators looking to increase the number of participation opportunities afforded to an institution's female students. The average roster size of a women's rowing team is the largest of any NCAA women's sport — nearly twice that of outdoor track and field, which has the second largest roster of any women's sport. It is not uncommon for a crew to have 100 rowers. Therefore, rowing is "women's football" in terms of roster size. It is a "quick fix" for institutions looking to offer substantially proportionate athletic opportunities to its female students.

While the first benchmark has been the focus of both litigants and courts, the dearth of institutions satisfying this test requires that attention be given to part two of the three-part test of Title IX compliance — whether an institution has a history and continuing practice of program expansion for the underrepresented sex. OCR reviews an institution's previous and ongoing remedial efforts to determine its compliance with this benchmark.* Of primary importance is ascertaining whether an institution has expanded its program over time in a manner that is demonstrably responsive to the developing interests of the underrepresented sex. To do so, OCR will review if the school has added or elevated women's teams to intercollegiate status, added participation opportunities for female athletes, and its responses to female students' requests to add or elevate sports. In determining whether an institution has a continuing practice of program expansion that is demonstrably responsive to the developing interests of the underrepresented sex, OCR looks to whether the institution has effectively communicated to students a procedure for requesting the addition or upgrading of a sport. In addition, the current implementation of an institution's plan to expand an underrepresented program is viewed favorably by OCR. In *Boucher v. Syracuse University,*[111] the court held that the institution's addition of women's lacrosse, soccer, and softball between 1996 and 1999 was evidence that it had a history and continuing practice of program expansion for its female athletes.[112] Syracuse University is the first . . . institution to successfully rely on this benchmark in proving its compliance with Title IX.

Women's rowing is beneficial to those institutions choosing to comply with the second benchmark. The tremendous growth of the sport at the intercollegiate level allows those schools that have recently begun to sponsor it to claim a history of program expansion. The addition or elevation of a women's rowing team, and the numerous participation opportunities added for female athletes via the sport, will be evaluated positively by OCR. At those institutions that have added or elevated the sport upon the request of its students, the affirmative response will receive similar approval from OCR. The large number of NCAA institutions that are able to make these claims because of women's rowing is reflected in the sport becoming the first to move from Emerging to Championship status. In addition,

---

* Office for Civil Rights, Clarification of Intercollegiate Athletics Policy Guidance: The Three-Part Test, January 16, 1996, available at www.ncaa.org/library/general/achieving_gender_equity/, at II-27. An institution cannot meet the requirements of part two simply by cutting men's teams or participation opportunities. Id. Nor can a school cut women's teams or participation opportunities without replacing them with additional teams or opportunities. Id. "Part two considers an institution's good-faith remedial efforts through actual program expansion." Id.

there are several institutions that have announced plans to add or elevate a women's rowing team in the near future. These institutions may claim a continuing practice of program expansion through their implementation of a plan to add the sport.

In part three of the three-part test, an institution may claim that it is fully and effectively accommodating the interests and abilities of its female students even though it has neither achieved substantial proportionality nor demonstrated a history and continuing practice of program expansion. In reviewing this claim, OCR evaluates whether there is unmet interest in a particular sport, sufficient ability to sustain a team in the sport, and a reasonable expectation of competition for a team. First, OCR looks at several indicators to determine whether there is unmet interest in a particular sport at an institution. These indicators include whether the institution has been requested to add or elevate a particular sport by its current or admitted students; participation in a particular club or intramural sport at the institution; participation in certain interscholastic sports by admitted students; and sports participation rates in the high schools, amateur athletic groups, and community sports leagues in the areas from which an institution draws most of its students. Second, OCR looks at the potential ability of either an existing club team or interested students to evaluate if there exists a sufficient ability to sustain an intercollegiate team in the sport. Third, OCR reviews if there is a reasonable expectation of intercollegiate competition available for a team in both the institution's conference and surrounding geographic area. If there is unmet interest in a particular sport, sufficient ability to sustain a team in the sport, and a reasonable expectation of competition for a team, then the institution has not fully and effectively accommodated the interests and abilities of its female students.

Women's rowing may or may not help an institution satisfy the third benchmark of Title IX compliance. There are many strong club teams at the college level. If one of them requests elevation to the intercollegiate level, and the institution is located in an area with a high participation rate at both the high school and intercollegiate levels, then the institution could not refuse to elevate the women's rowing team and still claim that it is fully and effectively accommodating the interests and abilities of its female students. This is due to the fact that all three compliance requirements would have been met by the women's rowing team. However, there are several potential problems with this analysis that may allow an institution faced with a request to add a women's rowing team to refuse to do so with no Title IX impunity. There is likely to be a paucity of feeder rowing programs in many institutions' normal recruiting area, as there are so few club and high school programs throughout the country. Depending on the geographic location of the institution and its conference affiliation, there may not be a reasonable expectation of intercollegiate competition in the institution's vicinity. Thus, there would be no unmet interest or reasonable expectation of competition. Under these circumstances, the institution could claim that it is fully and effectively accommodating the interests and abilities of its female students without adding a rowing team.

2. Athletic Benefits and Opportunities. The second area of concern for Title IX compliance is the parity of athletic benefits and opportunities between male and female students. Though only one court has issued a decision addressing these requirements at the intercollegiate level thus far, they are an important aspect of Title IX compliance that are likely to be the future focus of the courts. In addition to looking at student interests and abilities, the law specifies that OCR examine other factors in determining whether there is equal opportunity in athletics. The Policy Interpretation requires the following factors to be considered in determining whether an institution is providing equality in athletic benefits and opportunities: provision and maintenance of equipment and supplies; scheduling of games and practice times; travel and per diem expenses; opportunity to receive coaching and academic tutoring; assignment and compensation of coaches and tutors; provision of locker rooms and practice and competitive facilities; provision of medical and training services and facilities; provision of housing and dining services and facilities; publicity; provision of support services; and recruitment of student athletes. Each of these factors is evaluated by comparing an institution's entire male and female athletic program with respect to the availability, quality and kinds of benefits, opportunities, and treatment afforded. While identical benefits, opportunities and treatments are not required, the effects of any differences must be negligible.

The impact of women's rowing on any one particular aspect of this area of Title IX compliance is relatively small. However, any inequity in the women's rowing program is magnified because of the large number of participation opportunities provided by the sport.* Because a significant percentage of the female athletes at an institution may be rowers, the impact of women's rowing on this area may be considerable. Of primary concern is the effect of women's rowing on the provision and maintenance of equipment and supplies, scheduling of games, and the construction of practice and competitive facilities.[139]

Perhaps the most compelling of these components are equipment and supplies. The quality of equipment offered to both male and female athletes must be similar. However, the cost of the equipment used in women's rowing is quite high. As a result, many institutions opt to purchase used equipment to lower their expenses, especially when beginning a program. If a women's rowing program is using inferior equipment for a sustained period of time, the institution may encounter difficulty establishing compliance with this component. The amount of equipment provided to male and female athletes also must be similar. It seems logical to expect that there should be enough equipment to ensure that all members of a team will be able to practice at the same time. Providing enough boats for the entire team to be on the water at the same time becomes an expensive proposition for a rowing team. Due to this expense, many institutions have opted not to purchase a sufficient number of rowing shells; the rowers must "take turns" on the water. Institutions engaging in this practice may find it similarly difficult to prove compliance with this component.

One of the ways in which the maintenance of equipment and supplies is measured is by how equipment is repaired. Men's and women's teams should have their equipment repaired in the same manner. If there is a professional equipment manager, repairs should be done for a similar number of men's and women's teams. The specialized nature of rowing requires a trained individual to repair and maintain the equipment. While some institutions employ either a part-time or full-time rigger, in

---

* This is especially important given that the analysis of compliance with Title IX often focuses on whether the equivalent quality and quantities of benefits and services are provided to equivalent percentages of female and male athletes. See Valerie Bonnette, Title IX Basics, available at www.ncaa.org/library/general/achieving_gender_equity/ (n.d.). Many athletic administrators focus on comparing similar sports with each other for the purpose of this area of analysis, as they find that it is the easiest method by which to ensure compliance. See id. at II-2. Football creates a problem for these administrators because it is usually afforded better benefits than any other sport, yet does not have a similar women's sport to provide a basis for comparison. See id. at II-3. Thus, the administrators must provide "football-like" benefits to several sports in order to be in compliance with this area. See id.

Although the sports are dissimilar in nature, football and women's rowing are similar in the number of participation opportunities that they provide; this allows for an easier comparison between men's and women's athletes and, therefore, facilitates compliance with this area of Title IX. See generally id. at II-9-24. Even this comparison is not flawless; it is likely that football will still receive greater benefits in areas such as compensation of coaches, medical and training services, publicity, recruitment, and support services. However, the institution has available numerous justifications for the differences in the provisions of these services. Id.

many cases these repair duties are the responsibility of the coach. This may be a compliance problem for an institution, because its equipment repair policy may result in inequality between the men's and women's teams. Replacement of equipment typically must be done on the same schedule for men's and women's teams unless there is a difference justified by the nature of the sport. While rowing may be of a sufficiently unique nature to justify a different replacement schedule, this difference must not cause an inequity between male and female athletes if the institution wishes to remain in compliance with Title IX. The expense of purchasing new rowing equipment is likely to make it tempting for athletic administrators to delay this transaction. Nevertheless, administrators must not shy away from replacing old rowing equipment because of the expense involved if it results in inequitable treatment of female athletes.

Compliance with Title IX also implicates the procedures adopted by an institution for scheduling games and practice time for the women's rowing team.* The time of day during which competitive events and practices are scheduled should be equally convenient for the men's and women's teams.[153] Since most regattas are scheduled on weekends, the women's rowing team facilitates an institution's compliance with this component.

Women's rowing impacts upon the provision of practice and competitive facilities as well. Practice and competitive facilities must be of equivalent quality and availability. The assignment of a women's team to a poorer quality facility is a common compliance problem. This is manifested in the sport of women's rowing by the type of boathouse facility used by many crews. Construction or renovation of a boathouse is a very expensive proposition. Instead of engaging in such a project when adding or elevating a women's rowing team, many institutions choose to look at alternatives to incurring these large capital expenses. The institution may enter into a rental agreement with an existing boathouse or utilize an older boathouse that was previously used by the institution's men's or women's club rowing team. If these options prove unattractive, the institution may store equipment in a semi-trailer in close proximity to the practice water or simply transport equipment to and from the institution to the practice water on boat trailers every day. Engaging in these practices may make it extremely difficult for an institution to comply with this component; the poor quality of many of these facilities likely creates an inequity between male and female athletes. The availability of practice facilities involves the scheduling and location of these facilities. The location of the practice facility is of concern if the facility for a team of one sex is off campus and in an inconvenient location. Most boathouses fit this description, as they tend to be located some distance from campus. While the nature of the sport may justify some inconvenience in the availability of the practice facility, the institution should attempt to minimize this burden as much as possible so as to reduce any inequities between male and female athletes.

3. Athletic Financial Assistance. The final area of concern for Title IX compliance is athletic financial assistance. Though only 46 institutions are in compliance,[163] this area has also received little judicial attention. None of the three courts that have reviewed cases involving athletic financial assistance has found a violation of Title IX. OCR presumes compliance in this area if the total amount of athletic scholarship dollars awarded to male and female athletes is within one percent of their respec-

---

* See 44 Fed. Reg. 71416 (1979). "Compliance will be assessed by examining, among other factors, the equivalence for men and women of: (1) the number of competitive events per sport; (2) the number and length of practice opportunities; (3) the time of day competitive events are scheduled; (3) the time of day practice opportunities are scheduled; and (5) the opportunities to engage in available pre-season and post-season competition." Id.

tive participation rates in intercollegiate athletics at the institution. Women's rowing may play an important role in an institution's compliance with this standard due to the large number of athletic scholarships that can be awarded. The NCAA allows for the equivalent of twenty full athletic scholarships to be awarded in women's rowing. This is the largest of any women's sport. When all sports are taken into consideration, only football offers more scholarships. Thus, the presence of a women's rowing team is the single greatest ally to an institution hoping to comply with the athletic financial assistance standard established by OCR.

REFERENCES

76. The Office for Civil Rights within the U.S. Department of Education is responsible for the enforcement of Title IX. Letter from Dr. Mary Francis O'Shea, National Coordinator for Title IX Athletics, Office for Civil Rights, to Nancy Foster, General Counsel, Bowling Green State University (July 23, 1998), available at bailiwick.lib.uiowa.edu/ge/.
84. 503 U.S. 60 (1992).
85. Id.
111. 164 F.3d 113 (2d Cir. 1999).
112. Id. at 119.
139. See 44 Fed. Reg. 71414 (1979). See also Fed. Reg. 71416 (1979).
153. See Valerie Bonnette, Title IX Basics, available at www.neaa.org/library/general/achieving_gender_equity/ (n.d.) at II-11.
163. Chronicle of Higher Education, Participation: Proportion of Female Students on Athletic Teams, at http://www.chronicle.com/search97cgi/s97_cgi (last visited Jan. 19, 2001).

CAN GENDER EQUITY FIND A PLACE IN COMMERCIALIZED COLLEGE SPORTS?

John C. Weistart

I. THE STRUCTURE OF ATHLETIC DECISION-MAKING

. . . .

B. Budgetary Structure and Gender Equity

. . . .

2. The Implications of Present Budgetary Arrangements of Major Athletic Programs. The budgetary structure of major athletic programs has rather ominous implications for women's sports. Indeed, the interaction of the policy of rough self-sufficiency and the pressures to meet competitors' expenditures may go a long way in explaining why progress toward gender equity has been so slow. It may explain the intensity of the anger towards women's sports, especially that expressed by football partisans. The traditional budgetary arrangement inevitably relegates non-revenue sports to a secondary, contingent position. The position of these sports is secondary in the sense that the needs of football and basketball will come first. Indeed, the explanation for the primacy of these sports is nearly tautological: football and basketball must be preferred ahead of other sports because if they are not preferred there might not be any other sports. A weakening of the commitment to keep football and basketball competitive would affect the income stream upon which other sports depend and thus threaten their very existence. Thus, the revenue sports must be supported and they are supported at a level at which they are "competitive," a condition that is largely defined by many factors not within the immediate control of the school's budget makers.

The Padilla–Baumer study confirms these observations. Major athletic programs spend large amounts of money and receive significant financial returns. Only a small portion of that money is used to fund nonrevenue sports, however. The authors' analysis suggests that "for every additional $1 spent on athletic programs, between three and seven cents were spent on nonrevenue sports."[76] Thus, if an additional $1 million becomes available because the revenue sports win on the field, only about $50,000 of this will be spent on non-revenue sports.

This disparity explains why coaches and athletic directors can say, presumably with a straight face, that women's sports are expensive. Two hundred thousand dollars spent to establish a new women's team at a Big-Time school does not look like much compared to the $10 million spent on football. On the other hand, in the perspective of the athletic director, if an increased expenditure of $50,000 is regarded as "appropriate," then the prospect of spending $200,000 for a new women's sport is likely to be viewed as extraordinary. Stated another way, if one has been trained to think of non-revenue sports as nonessential and secondary, then any request beyond some very low minimum may seem like an unreasonable demand, even though in the larger perspective of the budget, it is quite modest.

Implicit in the budgetary structure is the further assumption that the claims of non-revenue sports will necessarily be contingent. They will be fully and generously funded only if the fortunes of the revenue sports prove bountiful. If revenues are not what was expected, then other sports should expect less. And in the event of a true crisis in one of the revenue sports, non-revenue sports should expect severe consequences. Their existence, after all, is derivative, and if truly significant adjustments have to be made, the contingency that underlies non-revenue sports will have to be realized in the form of severe budgetary cuts.

This secondary, contingent status that is described here extends to all non-revenue sports, men's and women's. It should be clear, though, that in the present environment women's sports are going to be more severely affected than men's. Men's non-revenue sports are already established and presumably have assumed a place that presents no threat to the existing balance that clearly prefers the two expensive men's sports. The claims of equality for women's sports represent a new long and potentially quite damaging demand. The money that would go to women's sports is a new expenditure and one that is potentially quite large if women's sports were funded at the levels of parity that Title IX demands. A school that unilaterally decided to divert significant sums of money to women's sports would be laying the seeds of its rather immediate self-destruction in the race for broadcast and attendance revenues. Thus, the incentives to step up and be the first to establish a well-supported women's program are few. Indeed, a path of quiet collective resistance to a full-scale implementation of Title IX will do the most to preserve the existing balance of power among major schools and seems to explain why progress under Title IX has been so limited.

. . . .

Some might argue that Title IX was intended to accept the traditional mechanisms for athletic funding and thus also accept that the advancement of non-revenue sports is dependent upon the availability of sufficient receipts from revenue sports. Under this view, the speed of the movement toward gender equity would accelerate or slow down depending on the flow of money from the on-the-field successes of football and men's basketball. After all, there is no evidence that Title IX was intended to mandate that schools spend more money on athletics, a policy choice that is highly dubious because of its potential drain on academic programs.

The suggestion that the hierarchical structure of athletic spending was intended to be approved by Title IX is refuted by both the statute and its legislative history. The language of the statute mandates gender-blind equal opportunity. No qualification is made based on the availability of funding. Thus, any suggestion that funds from a particular source were understood as a prerequisite to compliance finds no hint of plausibility in the text. The correctness of this conclusion would appear to be fully confirmed by Congress's refusal to adopt the Tower Amendment, a measure that would have exempted revenue sports from the coverage of the statute. One of the arguments made for exempting revenue sports was that they needed special protection because they were the source of funding for other sports. Rejection of the Tower Amendment rather strongly implies that Congress did not embrace the notion that women's sports were entitled to *only* a contingent status. With the proposed amendment defeated, the statutory commitment to equal opportunity remained unqualified.

3. Budgetary Arrangements in Other Competitive Programs.

. . . .

The revenue-generating potential of football reinforces its ability to command first attention in budgetary decisions. The revenues from football are both very welcome and somewhat fickle. A scaled-down version of the Arms Race will occur, for the question will be constantly presented whether hiring a better, but more expensive, coach or improving the locker room or spending more on recruiting will significantly improve the revenue picture. Similarly, on-the-field reversals — losing too many games — hold a real prospect for upsetting budget projections, an event which will ensure that the football program receives careful attention.

What is said about football is also true to a lesser extent for men's basketball. The revenues from basketball are attractive and are thus likely to be nurtured. Women's basketball is also a significant expense item, a fact that will ensure that it receives due attention in departmental decision-making. While it does not generate significant revenues in the budget presented here, there has been a rapid ascendancy in the popularity of women's basketball generally, and the dynamic forces that influence decision-making for the preferred men's sports may soon be seen in this women's counterpart.

The point of the above analysis is to underscore again that the predominant positions of football and basketball are likely to sway decision-making within the department, even in less competitive leagues. The numbers here serve to confirm that these sports command a level of attention that is not equaled by most women's sports. And in the face of the deficits already present, it is unlikely that not-yet-offered women's sports will command a high priority. The reality of this budget is that no sport pays for itself, and some sports, especially football, represent a significant budgetary risk; in this environment, there is no strong internal incentive to add additional sports. Absent such an incentive, a firm external control is necessary if gender equity is to be achieved.

A third perspective on athletic spending can be drawn from the factual in *Cohen v. Brown University*.[92] The case has produced selected data about the relative cost of sports at that school. . . .

When unrelated events prompted a trimming of the overall athletic budget, the department chose to eliminate two men's sports and two women's sports. This decision was made at a time when women were underrepresented among the school's athletes. The amount the University saved by eliminating the two women's sports was only $62,000. There is no evidence of a significant redirection in the more than $1.9 million allocated to the three expensive men's sports.

. . . . Not only do these sports have a long tradition at the school, they also have greater public appeal than other offerings. While the revenue potential of sports is not enough to cover their costs, the fact that money can be generated at all by these endeavors is thought to warrant their special treatment.

II. THE STANDARD FOR REVIEWING ATHLETIC DEPARTMENT DECISION-MAKING

A. The Demands of the Present Sports Context

We will eventually turn to the issue of whether this three-part test is appropriate for the task of securing compliance with Title IX. Before addressing that question, we must examine more closely the particular realities that any compliance measure will face in the modern sports context. A successful compliance standard must be sensitive to these. Three elements warrant particular attention. One is the apparent bias in favor of men's sports that is embedded in the present decision-making structure. A second is the reality that there can be no absolutes in predicting the extent of women's eventual interest in sports and in judging the relative appeal of men's and women's sports in the future. A particular effort must be made to avoid building new biases into the statute, whether in favor of particular sports or in the form of assumptions about the degree of women's interests. Third, any set of rules used in the present context should be seen as transitional. A major goal for such rules will be to guide the massive transition between a prior state of affairs that was almost exclusively male to a future in which the only certainty is uncertainty. Thus, a delicate balance must be achieved between firm prompting — necessary to achieve movement — and flexibility, which is necessary to deal with the uncertainty inherent in the future development of men's and women's sports.

1. Responding to the Structural Bias of Athletic Decision-Making.   The first section of this paper, discussing the structure of athletic decision-making, supports a conclusion that has very important implications for Title IX enforcement. The conclusion to be reached is that the commercial realities of college sports create a very strong bias against women's sports. Because of the financing arrangement that has been selected, revenue sports, particularly football and men's basketball, are strongly favored in budgetary allocations. Indeed, not to favor them would be to opt out of the most financially lucrative opportunities that are available, a choice that few schools are prepared to make.

This financial environment creates a strong incentive to give women's sports a very low priority in budgetary decision-making. Those sports are a net drain on the budget and, in the near term, hold a limited prospect of new revenues. In short, the demand for new women's sports creates a direct challenge to the primacy of the preferred men's sports. The nurturing of these latter sports requires flexibility. Adding women's sports has the potential of severely limiting a school's capacity to meet enhancements by competitors that may yield an athletic advantage.

The implication of this budgetary structure for Title IX is apparent: Title IX is not self-enforcing; a strong external mandate is needed to achieve the statute's goal. The task confronted by any regulation in this area will be to overcome the weak to non-existent internal incentives that a department has to expand women's offerings. This lack of internal incentives suggests that wide deference to internal decision-making is inappropriate. Rather, the emphasis of any regulation should be on clarity and directness. Phrasing that invites softened enforcement will be readily embraced and, thus, opportunities for avoidance should be carefully circumscribed.

The perspective developed here may provide some insight into the strong and vitriolic attacks on Title IX that have come from football partisans. When they suggest that Title IX represents a direct assault on football, there is a sense in which they are correct. The athletic financial pie is limited, and thus there cannot be both new expenditures for women's sports and a continuing commitment to match competitors' spending. Implementation of the former has undeniable implications for the latter. But the statute, and especially the rejection of the Tower Amendment, answers the question of which is to have priority. Title IX's commitment to women's sports is not qualified, by competitive needs or otherwise. It does not follow, however, that a full embrace of Title IX necessarily makes college football significantly less competitive or less attractive. To the extent that is the critics' fear, it is misdirected. There are mechanisms for accommodation of both interests, but these involve financing arrangements different from those now used by schools. A profitable alternative outlet for the energy of the critics of Title IX is to begin working on financial structures that permit effective and durable limits on program expenditures. . .

2. Challenging What We Think We Know About Women's Sports. The public discussion of Title IX reveals a surprising tendency toward firm statements about what women do and do not want in sports, and what they will and will not achieve. For example, one fan interviewed by the *Los Angeles Times* confidently surmised that "[it] is unrealistic to believe that under any circumstance the number of women interested in participating in a sports program in high school or college will ever approach the percentage of males that are doing so."[112] This comment was specifically intended as a refutation of the wisdom of a legal standard that requires substantial proportionality between women athletes and women in the student body. A columnist in the *Chicago Tribune* was certain that the court in the *Brown University* case was wrong in approving the substantial proportionality test. In his view, the real reason why women were underrepresented in athletics at Brown was clear: "[f]or better or worse, young women are generally less interested in sports than young men."[113]

Another set of "inherent truths" concerns the continuing primacy of football and men's basketball. Some people believe that these two sports will always be the most popular sports at the college level because they have professional counterparts. Or because men play sports better than women play theirs. Or just because these men's sports are more interesting.

A careful look at the developing landscape reveals why such assertions are much more confident than they should be. For example, in recent years, the women's basketball teams at Stanford University and the University of Colorado have outdrawn their men's counterparts in attendance. In addition, the 1995–96 basketball season saw a surge in the televised coverage of women's games, a decent gauge of whether fan interest is evolving. Moreover, the raw numbers on women's participation in sports can hardly leave one confident that we already know all that we can know. In 1971, before there was any significant activity under Title IX, approximately 290,000 girls were participating in high school sports. In just six years, the number rose to more than 2 million. Participation rates have been greatly affected by budgetary changes and shifts in total enrollment, but the number today is still 2.1 million. The obvious unanswered question is what this number would be after a couple of decades of adequate funding and vigorous enforcement of Title IX. Sobering implications can be found in the experience of one independent school in the Southeast. Several years ago it made a commitment to fund, and to find appropriate competition for, any group of students interested in forming any interscholastic team. For the last several years, 80 percent of the girls, as well as a similar percentage of the boys, have chosen to participate in interscholastic sports.

Those who contend that there never will be enough interest among women make another fatal analytical error as far as college athletics is concerned. The standard of substantial proportionality does not require, for example, that 50 percent of an evenly balanced student body actually participate in athletics. The number of women athletes needed to meet this standard is quite small at most schools. To take one example, at the University of Illinois, a school with a student body of 25,000, only 325 women athletes would be needed to meet the proportionality standard. And since the assumption at schools such as the University of Illinois is that athletes will be recruited, and not drawn from students who have independently decided to attend the school, women athletes will in fact be drawn from a pool that is much larger than 25,000. Hence, with an appropriate commitment from the school administration to encourage recruiting and to support women's teams, a sufficient number of athletes most likely can be found.

Another common assumption is that we already know what sports interest women and how relatively popular they will be. Again, however, recent history has taught us that we ought not to embrace any conventional wisdom. A few years ago, only a couple of thousand fans attended the women's Final Four basketball tournament. Last year the event sold out at over 18,000 fans. Fourteen cities vied to host the event in 1999 and 2000. Similar errors in judging popularity have been made with respect to sports other than basketball. For many years, it was assumed that soccer was mainly a men's sport. Indeed, in 1972 only about 300 women played collegiate soccer. But in 1992, there were over 8,000 participants in soccer at the three levels of NCAA competition. *[In 2001–02, there were over 19,000 paticipants in women's soccer across all three NCAA levels.]*

A further reason for reserving judgment about the long-term future of women's sports is the potential for major changes in the Big-Time football and basketball markets. At their highest level of competition, these sports are heavily commercialized. Many, if not most, of the successful programs operate at a significant distance from the notions of amateurism and academic primacy that were their origins. For example, graduation rates at many schools continue to be low, despite much publicized "reforms" promulgated by the NCAA. In recent years, the basketball programs at Kentucky, Arizona, Syracuse, and Oklahoma State had graduation rates of 20 percent, 20 percent, 21 percent, and 17 percent, respectively. For African-American basketball players at Kansas, Massachusetts, and Missouri, the graduation rates were 17 percent, 0 percent, and 0 percent. Results are not significantly more encouraging for Big-Time football programs. A national publication recently proposed that the University of Miami should shut down its highly successful football program because of a long series of academic, NCAA, and civil infractions. The athletic products of the top programs are extremely popular on television, and the flow of large broadcast dollars is not necessarily dependent on these sports having a university affiliation. Although there is no purely commercial alternative on the immediate horizon, it is not inconceivable that market forces will coalesce to give rise to new versions of pre-professional sports that are delinked from the present requirements for a four-year degree. Part-time enrollment of athletes or a loose or non-existent affiliation with colleges may eventually be seen as creating a larger labor pool and a more interesting product.

Such a development would be something of a mixed blessing for women's sports. A major source of funding would be adversely affected. On the other hand, a lessening of the role of Big-Time sports would allow for a reorientation of college sports toward less commercialized versions. The notion that the only good sports are those that have a professional counterpart may lose its present hold and permit a new emphasis on broader scale participation, albeit at less glamorous levels. In this environment, the relative acceptance of women's sports would likely increase, perhaps significantly so.

The basic point again is that any legal standard should accept the dynamic nature of women's sports at the college level. Our knowledge of women's sports at present is roughly at the level that our understanding of men's sports was in 1920. It clearly would have been a mistake to have frozen our assumptions about men's offerings at that point in time. We would probably still have college boxing programs and a curiously awkward version of basketball. Independent forces, including the desire to protect the preferred men's sports, create pressures to keep women's sports at their current levels. One function of the standard for legal review, therefore, should be to both allow for and encourage further development of women's sports. Sensitivity to this goal will accept that judges and administrative agencies will have to make decisions in the face of a good deal of uncertainty. Thus, remedies to expand women's opportunities should not be judged against a standard of scientific certainty as to future viability. A more suitable measure is one that asks whether there are plausible grounds to support an expansion that would further the broad goals of Title IX.

3. The Special Pressures of a Transitional Rule. As suggested, any legal standard used to judge compliance with Title IX in college sports should be sensitive to the fact that it is an area of endeavor that is very much in transition. Whatever the legal standard, it should not be defined by firm assumptions about what women's sports will look like in forty or fifty years. Indeed, a strong case can be made that whatever test for compliance we have now should not be the rule that applies several decades from now. The base of knowledge about the progress of women's sports will most likely be quite different at that future point. Perhaps we *can* eventually embrace a rule that assumes that athletic administrators will make neutral budgetary allocations. As previously suggested, however, there is little reason to be confident on that score. For now, our legal standard must deal with the known of the departmental resistance to the expansion of women's sports and the unknown of what women's sports will look like in the future.

A transitional rule should accept the fact that the historical context of college sports has been very male oriented. Clearly the adoption of Title IX was to change this. An effective transitional rule should have a significant element of urging and prompting built into it, as excessive deference to existing methods of decision-making is not likely to yield meaningful results. Given the continuing pervasive effects of the historical bias, a firm and clear method of judging progress may be necessary.

On the other hand, a transitional rule should avoid any specific direction as to the type of sports to be offered or the levels of funding to be provided. In a very concrete sense, the most useful rule for the present will be one that accepts a level of experimentation in women's athletics. New sports should not be rejected because they have no track record or an unproven one, nor should they be rejected because they might eventually fail. While universities should not be required to spend money foolishly, by the same token, schools cannot demand that new women's sports irrefutably prove their viability. Because women's sports are in transition, there cannot be exquisite certainty that all choices made now will become permanent. In short, transitional rules should embrace a procedure for change and resist any effort to codify a particular model for women's sports.

. . . . *[The author's analysis of the Department of Education's three-part test to determine whether a school is effectively accommodating the interests of men and women in athletics is omitted. The three-part test is presented on pages 619 to 627.]*

IV. CONCLUSION

In a very real sense, the present state of affairs of gender integration in college sports is not satisfactory. Supporters of expanded women's sports can properly claim that progress toward gender equity has been slow. Indeed, the fact that the equalization of sports programs lags well behind advances in other aspects of higher education understandably raises suspicions about the sincerity of the efforts that have been made to date. On the other hand, advocates for men's sports feel deeply wronged. After several instances in which schools have dropped men's non-revenue sports and explained their actions on the basis of the need to shift money to women's sports, questions have been raised about the fairness of an interpretation of Title IX that advances the interest of one group by denying opportunities to another. Adding to the debate are the proponents of men's revenue sports, especially football, who believe that Title IX requires the dismantling of their commercially successful ventures. Indeed, what may be most remarkable about the present Title IX debate is the absence of any voice that suggests that the existing trends are acceptable.

A number of different futures for Title IX and college sports can be foreseen. It is quite possible that the recent history of acrimony and slow progress will continue for some time. The present course is particularly subject to the uncertainties of outside forces. Changes in the political trends in the federal government will speed or retard forward movement as the then-current perception of ideological advantage dictates. By the same token, as long as women's sports are kept in a secondary, contingent relationship with men's revenue sports, a variety of other, seemingly distant events will move the fortunes of women's teams forward or backwards. These include changes in television viewing habits with respect to football and basketball, the development of new forms of nonsports entertainment products, and the revelation of evermore dismaying scandals in Big-Time sports.

To the extent that colleges continue to use a model of economic competition to dictate funding levels in men's revenue sports, the present atmosphere of suspicion and political maneuvering will be encouraged. Moreover, there will be a continuing need for strong external enforcement of Title IX. The economic competition model creates a selfishness in men's revenue sports and offers negative incentives for gender integration. Firm outside regulation is thus necessary to correct the distortions that are created.

While the present state of gender integration is not satisfactory, it is important to note that it is not inevitable either. Just as the existing tensions between genders in sports are the product of choice, they can be unchosen. There is an obvious decision that lies ahead and that is whether the economic engine that drives revenue sports will be restrained. The reasons for doing so are immensely attractive. A long-standing source of budgetary distress will be tempered, if not quieted. The attractiveness and variety of sports opportunities will be increased, with relatively little change in the versions that are presently popular. The intensity of external oversight will be reduced. And most importantly, a source of long simmering distrust will be removed. It may even be that universities are able to fulfill their educational function in a more effective way.

REFERENCES

76. Arthur Padilla & David Baumer, "Big Time College Sports: Management and Economic Issues," J. Sport & Soc. Issues, May 1994, at 139.

92. 809 F. Supp. 978 (D.R.I. 1992), *aff'd,* 991 F.2d 888 (1st Cir. 1993).

112. Bob Rohwer, An Even Field? *L.A. Times,* Nov. 1, 1994, at V1 (quoting Arlyn F. Obert).

113. Stephen Chapman, *Opinions: Title IX Debate Is a Matter of Interest,* NCAA News, May 10, 1995, at 4.

DISCUSSION QUESTIONS

1. What is the purpose of Title IX?

2. How does a college president know whether the institution is in compliance with Title IX?

3. How do the operational strategies of the athletic director differ from that of the general manager of a Major League Baseball franchise?

4. Could and should any form of gender equity guidelines apply to professional sports franchises?

5. Describe the various budgetary impacts of Title IX.

6. To comply with Title IX, do colleges and universities ever have no choice but to drop men's sports?

7. What steps could be taken in relation to football to move schools closer to gender equity?

8. Should football be exempted from the Title IX equation?

CHAPTER 18

AMATEURISM AND REFORM

INTRODUCTION

At the heart of the push for reforming collegiate sports are changing views of amateurism. As the readings that follow highlight, for most of the period organized collegiate sports have existed, Americans have believed that there should be a class of athletes that participate in sports for the glory of the games alone. Even as the Olympic Games have moved away from this view, collegiate sports, under the governance of the NCAA, continue to hold fast.

The excerpt from Kenneth L. Shropshire's "Legislation for the Glory of Sport: Amateurism and Compensation" provides an historic overview of amateurism and the mythology and misconceptions associated with its lofty status. The article briefly traces the history that provides the foundation for the lingering beliefs of the righteousness of what are arguably outdated concepts of amateurism. Once the reality of amateurism is grasped, the important question becomes whether any reforms recognizing this reality will improve college sports.

Peter Goplerud III then provides an examination of the possibilities of "pay for play." The logical extension of moving beyond pure concepts of amateurism is to pay student athletes based on their athletic abilities. His article "Symposium: Sports Law as a Reflection of Society's Laws and Values: Pay for Play for College Athletes: Now, More Than Ever" provides the evolution of his thinking on the topic. The concept of paying college athletes some level of compensation beyond room, board, tuition, and educational fees has been an ongoing debate in the NCAA, particularly from its critics.

We conclude with two entries focused on reform in collegiate sports. The first is an excerpt from James L. Shulman and William G. Bowen's *The Game of Life*. The chapter we excerpt focuses on the findings of their extensive study of the role of athletics in America's colleges and universities and, particularly, insight on the participating athletes.

The final entry in this chapter is the Report of the Knight Foundation Commission on Intercollegiate Athletics entitled "A Call to Action: Reconnecting College Sports and Higher Education." This document, published in June 2001, is probably the best-known effort focused on the reform of collegiate sports. Many individuals believe that this commission's ongoing efforts led to college presidents taking greater control of their athletic programs.

THE IDEAL

LEGISLATION FOR THE GLORY OF SPORT: AMATEURISM AND COMPENSATION

Kenneth L. Shropshire

B. ORIGIN OF THE RULES AGAINST COMPENSATION

1. Ancient Greeks

A common misconception held by many people today is that the foundation of collegiate amateurism had its genesis in the Olympic model of the ancient Greeks. . . . The "myth" of ancient amateurism held that there was some society, presumably the Greeks, that took part in sport solely for the associated glory while receiving no compensation for either participating or winning. In his book, *The Olympic Myth of Greek Amateur Athletics,*[11] classicist David C. Young reported finding "no mention of amateurism in Greek sources, no reference to amateur athletes, and no evidence that the concept of 'amateurism' was even known in antiquity. The truth is that 'amateur' is one thing for which the ancient Greeks never even had a word."[12] Young further traces the various levels of compensation that were awarded in these ancient times including a monstrous prize in one event that was the equivalent of ten years worth of wages.

The absence of compensation was not an essential element of Greek athletics. Specifically, the ancient Greeks "had no known restrictions on granting awards to athletes."[15] Many athletes were generously rewarded. Professor Young asserts that the only real disagreement among classical scholars is not whether payments were made to the athletes but only when such payments began.

The myth concerning ancient Greek athletics was apparently developed and perpetuated by the very same individuals that would ultimately benefit from the implementation of such a system. The scholars most often cited for espousing these views of Greek amateurism were those who sought to promote an athletic system they supported as being derived from ancient precedent. In his work, Professor Young systematically proves these theories false by countering with direct evidence and an analysis of the motivation for presenting inaccurate information. Similar faults by other scholars led to the inevitable development of fallacious cross-citations with each relying upon the other for authority. One scholar is believed to have actually created a detailed account of an ancient Greek athlete which Professor Young concluded was a "sham" and "outright historical fiction."[19] The reasoning behind such deliberate falsehoods was apparently designed to serve as "a moral lesson to modern man."*

In simplest terms, these scholars were part of a justification process for an elite British athletic system destined to find its way into American collegiate athletics. "They represent examples of a far-flung and amazingly successful deception, a kind of historical hoax, in which scholar[s] joined hands with sportsm[e]n and administrator[s] so as to mislead the public and influence modern sporting life."[21] With amateurism widely proclaimed by the scholars of the day, the natural tendency was for non-scholars to join in and heed the cry as well.

The leading voice in the United States espousing the strict segregation of pay and amateurism was Avery Brundage, former President of both the United States Olympic Committee (USOC) and the International Olympic Committee (IOC). Brundage believed that the ancient Olympic games, which for centuries blossomed as amateur competition, eventually degenerated as excesses and abuses developed attributable to professionalism.[23] "What was originally fun, recreation, a diversion, and a pastime became a business. . . . The Games . . . lost their purity and high idealism, and were finally abolished. . . . Sport must be for sport's sake."[24] Brundage was firmly against amateurs receiving any remuneration, justifying his belief upon the Greek amateur athletic fallacy. Brundage took extraordinary action during his tenure as president of the USOC and the IOC to ensure such a prohibition. . . .

Professor Young and other like-minded scholars contend that the development of the present day system of collegiate amateurism is not modeled after the ancient Greeks. Rather, today's amateurism is a direct descendant of the Avery Brundages of the world and is actually much more reflective of the practices developed in Victorian England than those originated in ancient Greece.

2. England

In 1866, the Amateur Athletic Club of England published a definition of the term "amateur."[26] Although the term had been in use for many years, this was, perhaps, the first official definition of the word. The definition which was provided by that particular sports organization required an amateur to be one who had never engaged in open competition for money or prizes, never taught athletics as a profession, and one who was not a "mechanic, artisan or laborer."[27]

The Amateur Athletic Club of England was established to give English gentlemen the opportunity to compete against each other without having to involve and compete against professionals. However, the term "professional" in Victorian England did not merely connote one who engaged in athletics for profit, but was primarily indicative of one's social class. It was the dominant view in the latter half of the nineteenth century that not only were those who competed for money basically inferior in nature, but that they were "also a person of questionable character."† The social distinction of amateurism, attributable to the prevailing aristocratic attitude at the time, provided the incentive for victory. "When an amateur lost a contest to a working man he lost more than the race. . . He lost his

---

* Young, supra note 1, at 13. The lesson is apparently somewhat self-serving and designed to present in a favorable light the values of the gentlemen amateur athletes of Victorian England. Id.

† Glader, supra note 26, at 15. The title "amateur" became a badge for upper class gentlemen seeking to evidence their good social standing. Young, supra note 1, at 18.

identity. . . . His life's premise disappeared; namely that he was innately superior to the working man in all ways."[31] Thus, concepts of British amateurism developed along class lines, and were reinforced by the "mechanics clauses" that existed in amateur definitions. These clauses typically prevented mechanics, artisans, and laborers from participation in amateur sport. The reasoning behind the "mechanics clause" was the belief that the use of muscles as part of one's employment offered an unfair competitive advantage.[32] Eventually, under the guise of bringing order to athletic competition, private athletic clubs were formed that effectively restricted competition "on the basis of ability and social position" and not on the basis of money.* Over the years this distinction has been used to identify those athletes who are ineligible for amateur competition, because their ability to support themselves based solely on their athletic prowess has given them a special competitive advantage. It is from these antiquated rules that the modern eligibility rules of the NCAA evolved. Any remaining negative connotations regarding professionalism owe their continued existence to these distinctions.

3. United States

The amateur/professional dilemma confronting today's American universities is based on the presumption that if a college competes at a purely amateur level it will lose prestige and revenue, as it loses contests. However, open acknowledgement of the adoption of professional athleticism would result in a loss of respectability for the university as a bastion of academia. The present solution to this dilemma has been for collegiate athletic departments to "claim amateurism to the world, while in fact accepting a professional mode of operation."†

Two sports, baseball and rowing, were the first to entertain the questions of professionalism versus amateurism in the United States. Initially, the norm for organized sports in this country was professionalism. Baseball was played at semiprofessional levels as early as 1860, and the first professional team, the Cincinnati Red Stockings, was formed in 1868. The first amateur organization, the New York Athletic Club, was established in the United States in 1868.

In 1909, the NCAA (which had successfully evolved from the Intercollegiate Athletic Association, established in 1905) recommended the creation of particular amateur/professional distinctions. With the subsequent adoption of these proposals, England's Victorian amateur and professional delineations were incorporated into American intercollegiate athletics. *[See Figures 1 and 2.]*

Prior to the adoption of the NCAA proposals, "professionalism" abounded. For example, in the 1850s Harvard University students rowed in a meet offering a $100 first prize purse, and a decade later they raced for as much as $500. Amateurism, at least as historically conceived, was largely absent from college sports in the beginning of the twentieth century. Competition for cash and prizes, collection of gate revenue, provisions for recruiting, training, and tutoring of athletes, as well as the payment of athletes and hiring of professional coaches had invaded the arena of intercollegiate athletics. . . . The sheer number of competing American educational institutions was, in itself, a major reason that athletics in the United States developed far beyond the amateurism still displayed [by their] learned British counterparts. In England, an upper level education meant one of two places,

---

* Glader, *supra* note 26, at 17. The laborer was classified as a professional due to his unfair physical advantage. Id.

† Smith, *supra* note 32, at 166. Although the reference is made to a "professional mode of operation," university scholarship athletes are not allowed to receive compensation above what amounts to tuition, room, board, and educational fees. Id.

Student-athletes shall be amateurs in an intercollegiate sport, and their participation should be motivated primarily by education and by the physical, mental and social benefits to be derived. Student participation in intercollegiate athletics is an avocation, and student-athletes should be protected from exploitation by professional and commercial enterprises.

Figure 1. NCAA Constitution, Article 2.9: The Principle of Amateurism.

Only an amateur student-athlete is eligible for intercollegiate athletics participation in a particular sport.

Figure 2. NCAA Bylaw 12.01.1: Eligibility for Intercollegiate Athletics.

either Oxford or Cambridge. With each institution policing the other, the odds of breaching the established standards of amateurism were not high. In the United States, while the Ivy League schools competed strongly amongst themselves, there was also the rapid emergence of many fine public colleges and universities. Freedom of opportunity, a pervasive factor in the genesis of American collegiate athletics, made it increasingly more difficult for the Harvards and Yales to maintain themselves as both the athletic and the intellectual elite within the United States.

According to some scholars, the English system of amateurism, "loosely" derived from the Greeks, simply did not have a chance of success in the United States. As noted above, one factor contributing to its demise was increased competition among a larger number of institutions. Another was the difference in egalitarian beliefs between the two nations:

> The English amateur system, based upon participation by the social and economic elite . . . would never gain a foothold in American college athletics. There was too much competition, too strong a belief in merit over heredity, too abundant an ideology of freedom of opportunity for the amateur ideal to succeed. . . . It may be that amateur athletics at a high level of expertise can only exist in a society dominated by upper-class elitists.[44]

In spite of the ideological conflicts, the early post-formative years of the NCAA were spent attempting to enforce the various amateur standards. The first eligibility code sought only to insure that those who participated in collegiate athletics were actually full-time registered students who were not being paid for their participation.* This initial set of amateur guidelines was largely ignored by the NCAA member institutions. After establishing this initial code, the NCAA

---

* NCAA Constitution, art. VII, Eligibility Rules (1906). The first NCAA Eligibility Code is set forth below:
The following rules . . . are suggested as a minimum:

1. No student shall represent a college or university in any intercollegiate game or contest, who is not taking a full schedule of work as prescribed in the catalogue of the institution.

Member institutions' athletics programs are designed to be an integral part of the educational program. The student-athlete is considered an integral part of the student body, thus maintaining a clear line of demarcation between college athletics and professional sports.

Figure 3.   NCAA Bylaw 12.01.2: Clear Line of Demarcation.

sought on numerous occasions to further define its views on amateurism. An intermediate step was the formal adoption of the Amateur Code into the NCAA constitution.[46] The impetus behind the adoption was "to enunciate more clearly the NCAA's purpose; to incorporate the amateur definition and principles of amateur spirit; and to widen the scope of government."[47] As the monetary resources of the NCAA grew, so too did its enforcement power. The prime targets of those enhanced enforcement powers were the principles of amateurism as incorporated into the NCAA constitution. *[See Figure 3.]*

The motivation to cheat existed even in the formative years of collegiate sports. Winning athletic programs had the potential to return high revenues to the institution. In its early years as a national football power, Yale University made $105,000 from its successful 1903 football program.[48] Thus, the financial incentive to succeed existed even then, and has continued to serve as a strong incentive for many schools to break the rules in order to obtain the best talent.

. . . . *[The author's discussion of the Sanity Code is omitted. See discussion of the Sanity Code in Chapter 14.]*

The NCAA was an organization formed to promote safety in collegiate sports. It later adopted the prevailing views of amateurism and is currently the largest sports organization to prohibit member athletes from receiving compensation. *[See Figures 4 and 5.]* The lack of compensation for the student participant permeates virtually all decisions in collegiate athletics today. Although the NCAA does not deliberately promote or associate itself with the tales of Greek amateurism, nothing has been done to correct popular misconceptions.

---

2. No student shall represent a college or university . . . who has at any time received, either directly or indirectly, money, or any other consideration, to play on any team, or . . . who has competed for a money prize or portion of gate money in any contest, or who has competed for any prize against a professional.

3. No student shall represent a college or university . . . who is paid or received, directly or indirectly, any money, or financial concession, or emolument as past or present compensation for, or as prior consideration or inducement to play in, or enter any athletic contest, whether the said remuneration be received from, or paid by, or at the instance of any organization, committee or faculty of such college or university, or any individual whatever.

4. No student shall represent a college or university . . . who has participated in intercollegiate games or contests during four previous years.

5. No student who has been registered as a member of any other college or university shall participate in any intercollegiate game or contest until he shall have been a student of the institution which he represents for at least one college year.

6. Candidates for positions on athletic teams shall be required to fill out cards, which shall be placed on file, giving a full statement of their previous athletic records.

Id.

An individual loses amateur status and thus shall not be eligible for intercollegiate competition in a particular sport if the individual:

(a) Uses his or her athletics skill (directly or indirectly) for pay in any form in that sport; *(Revised: 4/25/02 effective 8/1/02)*

(b) Accepts a promise of pay even if such pay is to be received following completion of intercollegiate athletics participation;

(c) Signs a contract or commitment of any kind to play professional athletics, regardless of its legal enforceability or any consideration received;

(d) Receives, directly or indirectly, a salary, reimbursement of expenses or any other form of financial assistance from a professional sports organization based upon athletics skill or participation, except as permitted by NCAA rules and regulations;

(e) Competes on any professional athletics team (per Bylaw 12.02.4), even if no pay or remuneration for expenses was received; *(Revised: 4/25/02 effective 8/1/02)*

(f) Subsequent to initial full-time collegiate enrollment, enters into a professional draft (see also Bylaws 12.2.4.2.1 and 12.2.4.2.3); or *(Revised: 4/25/02 effective 8/1/02; 4/24/03 effective 8/1/03 for student-athletes entering a collegiate institution on or after 8/1/03)*

(g) Enters into an agreement with an agent. *(Adopted: 4/25/02 effective 8/1/02)*

Figure 4.   NCAA Bylaw 12.1.1: Amateur Status.

A student-athlete may receive athletically related financial aid administered by the institution without violating the principle of amateurism, provided the amount does not exceed the cost of education authorized by the Association; however, such aid as defined by the Association shall not exceed the cost of attendance as published by each institution. Any other financial assistance, except that received from one upon whom the student-athlete is naturally or legally dependent, shall be prohibited unless specifically authorized by the Association.

Figure 5.   NCAA Constitution, Article 2.13: The Principle Governing Financial Aid.

REFERENCES

11. David C. Young, The Olympic Myth of Greek Amateur Athletics 7 Ares Publishers (1985).

12. Id.

15. Eugene Glader, Amateurism and Athletics 54 Human Kinetics (1978).

19. Young at 12, 13. See Harold Harris, Greek Athletes and Athletics Greenwood (1964).

21. Id. at 14.

23. Avery Brundage, USOC Report of the Games of the XIV Olympiad (1948).

24. Id.

26. Glader, Amateurism and Athletics 100 (1978).

27. Id. at 100. See also H. Hewitt Griffin, Athletics 13–14 (1891); H.F. Wilkinson, Modern Athletics 16 (1868).

31. Young, supra note 11, at 18 n. 17.

32. Glader, supra note 26 at 17. See also Ronald A. Smith, Sports & Freedom: The Rise of Big Time College Athletics 166 Oxford University Press (1998) (stating that the eligibility rules of the British Amateur Rowing Assoc. in 1870 contained a similar clause).

44. Smith at 174.

46. Paul Lawrence, Unsportsmanlike Conduct: The National Collegiate Athletic Association and the Business of College Football 24 Praeger (1987).

47. Id. (citing 1922 NCAA Proceedings at 10.)

48. Benjamin G. Rader, American Sports from the Age of Folk Games to the Age of Spectators 268–269 Prentice-Hall (1983).

Reform

Symposium: Sports Law as a Reflection of Society's Laws and Values: Pay for Play for College Athletes: Now, More Than Ever

Peter Goplerud III

I. INTRODUCTION

Imagine a large group of employees in a company working long hours, some of them far from home, going to school full-time, and helping bring in millions of dollars to their employer. Does this sound like a sweat shop . . . ? Actually, this describes the typical athlete in a revenue producing sport at a National Collegiate Athletic Association (NCAA) member institution.

Approximately one year ago this author wrote an article advocating a change in the Constitution and Bylaws of the NCAA to provide for the payment of stipends to some athletes at some of its member institutions. Specifically, the article proposed the payment of $150 per month to scholarship athletes in the revenue-producing sports of football and men's basketball and to a comparable number of scholarship athletes in women's sports. The stipend rule would have applied only to Division I member schools. An underlying premise of the article was that the concept of amateurism, a cornerstone of the NCAA, is essentially a sham due to the commercial nature of the end product. The athletes are used, abused, and then thrown out, while the schools make millions on television money, gate receipts, and sales of licensed products, many directly tied to particular players. The article suggested several legal, political, and financial hurdles that must be considered prior to implementing a policy of providing stipends for players. Included were legal concerns associated with employees, which the athletes would become under the proposal; among these would be workers' compensation, labor, taxation, antitrust, and gender equity issues. The article also noted the internal politics of the NCAA would be an obstacle, but also opined that the new restructuring might facilitate movement towards the concept of paying players. It also attempted to calculate the costs of providing stipends to approximately 200 athletes at each Division I school. Finally, sources of revenue to pay for the proposal were suggested, notably corporate sponsors and the possibility of a Division I football playoff.

In the intervening time numerous other voices have been heard on the subject and the NCAA itself has considered several alternatives and even adopted what its membership believes to be a compromise between the status quo and the instant proposal. However, no substantial or significant progress has been made to this point. The purpose of this article is to renew the call for a change in the rules. At this point, however, a slightly different proposal will be presented. Since this author now believes the current structure and the former proposal both present serious antitrust issues, the proposal will focus on a market-based approach to awarding stipends. It will still be limited to those athletes in revenue-producing sports and proportionate numbers of women athletes.

While there was much talk on the subject of athletes' rights and the creation of a special task force during the remainder of 1996, the NCAA did very little at the recently completed final convention prior to restructuring. Only a modest change and an arguably ill-conceived concession to costs of attendance was approved with regard to restrictions on work during the school year by athletes on scholarship.

It thus becomes relevant . . . to revisit the issue. . . . The basic premise will remain the same as before: the athletes at Division I schools, particularly those in revenue-producing sports, are exploited on a regular basis and must be compensated beyond the scholarship and beyond the cost of attendance.

II. INTERCOLLEGIATE ATHLETICS AND COMMERCIALISM

. . . . [The author's discussion of NCAA regulations and commercialism is omitted.]

C. The Proposal

It is time to give more serious consideration than ever before to stipends for collegiate athletes. As noted above, the proposal developed a year ago has flaws, mostly legal, which require modification. A market component must be inserted in the stipend, but the proposal must also provide for a certain amount of restraint and competitive balance in keeping with the NCAA's long-standing concerns for both factors within collegiate athletics. Therefore, the NCAA should develop legislation providing for stipends for athletes in major revenue-producing sports at the Division I level. The stipends should be available to men in football and basketball, and women in basketball, volleyball, and other sports in sufficient numbers to satisfy gender equity requirements. The exact amount of the stipend to an individual athlete would be within the discretion of the individual school. However, the schools should have a limit on the total amount of money allocated to student-athletes. This "salary cap" would be set at an average of $300 per month per scholarship athlete, with half of the money going into a trust fund to be paid to those athletes receiving degrees within five years of matriculation. Those schools with football programs would calculate their football amounts separately with the total amount varying depending upon whether a school is Division I-A or I-AA. These athletes would also be able to work, as under the new rule, with the stipend not counting against the cost of attendance. Schools may, of course, spend less than the cap or may choose not to pay the stipend to any athletes. In addition, scholarship athletes in the non-revenue sports would be allowed to be employed during the school year, even in campus settings, and would have no cap on their earnings. The only stipulation would be that the jobs must be available to non-athlete students as well as athletes.

III. LEGAL ISSUES WHICH ARISE FROM THE PROPOSAL

A. Antitrust Questions

An issue which could arise should the association choose to enact legislation allowing for the payment of players would be a question of price-fixing. The proposal made a year ago is flawed in this respect. It is quite believable that an athlete in a revenue-producing sport would become disgruntled with only receiving $150 per month while competing, and find a resourceful attorney willing to bring an action under the antitrust laws. For reasons discussed below, it is likely that such an action would be successful. Thus, the more prudent legislative action would be the salary cap approach which allows for individual decision-making based upon market determinations developed by the member institutions.

The NCAA has found itself as a defendant in antitrust actions on numerous occasions, with mixed results. Section 1 of the Sherman Antitrust Act provides that: "every contract, combination in the form of trust or otherwise, or conspiracy, in restraint of trade or commerce among the several States, or with foreign nations, is hereby declared to be illegal."[31] The Supreme Court has long held that only unreasonable restraints of trade are proscribed by the act. Some restraints on economic activity are viewed by the Court as so inherently anti-competitive that they are deemed per se illegal. Examples of this type of conduct would be group boycotts, market divisions, tying arrangements, and price-fixing.

It is arguable that most of the regulatory activity in which the NCAA engages is per se illegal. Actions such as the establishment of limits on the type and amount of financial aid appear to be price-fixing. Certainly a fixed stipend such as proposed previously appears to be price-fixing. However, in the context of intercollegiate athletics the Supreme Court has recognized that certain types of restrictive activity by the NCAA may, under appropriate circumstances, be allowed under the act. The very nature of competitive sports is such that in order to promote competition, some actions which would normally be viewed as restraints will be allowed to exist. The Court has said that "what the NCAA and its member institutions market . . . is competition itself — contests between competing institutions" and thus, it is "an industry in which horizontal restraints on competition are essential if the product is to be available at all."[35] Any number of rules relating to the size of playing fields, squad size, length of seasons, number of scholarships, academic standards, and the like must be agreed upon in order to market a product, collegiate sports, which might not otherwise be available. The Court, therefore, in reviewing a challenge to the NCAA's actions in entering into a television contract for football, did not apply the per se rule, instead choosing to use a "rule of reason" analysis. The rule of reason analysis has been utilized in all recent antitrust cases involving the NCAA as well.

The rule of reason analysis requires the court to determine if the harm from the restraint on competition outweighs the restraint's pro-competitive impact. The plaintiff bears the initial burden of showing the restraint causes significant anti-competitive effects in a relevant market. If this burden is met, the defendant must then produce evidence of the restraint's pro-competitive effects. If this is done, the plaintiff must finally show that any legitimate objectives of the restraint can be met through less restrictive means.

To date, the courts have also been consistent in upholding, against antitrust challenge, every regulatory action of the NCAA which has directly impacted athletes. The Supreme Court has, on the one occasion noted above, ruled against the NCAA in an antitrust action involving its proprietary action in entering into contracts for the televising of football games. There is, perhaps, reason to believe that even some of the NCAA's regulatory activities may now be suspect under the Sherman Act.

. . . . *[The author's analysis of* Law v. NCAA *is omitted.]*

The NCAA's limitations on scholarships, in so far as they prohibit stipends, are part of its regulatory program. The association would no doubt contend that these are noncommercial and, therefore, out of the purview of the Sherman Act. One jurist has labeled a similar assertion in regard to the NCAA's rules on eligibility and the professional football draft "incredulous."[57] It is quite clear that the rules act as a restraint on a relevant market, the labor market for collegiate athletes. They are obviously an attempt to perpetuate the amateur nature of collegiate athletics. But, this overlooks the key to the NCAA and collegiate athletics:

> Intercollegiate athletics programs shall be maintained as a vital component of the educational program, and student-athletes shall be an integral part of the student body. The admission, academic standing and academic progress of student-athletes shall be consistent with the policies and standards adopted by the institution for the student body in general.[58]

Amateurism has certainly been a significant part of the NCAA's programs, but there have been and continue to be exceptions to this requirement. As recently as the 1960s, the NCAA allowed schools to provide athletes on scholarship with "laundry money."[59] And, the NCAA has long allowed athletes who are clearly professionals, to continue to compete in collegiate athletics in other sports. The only restriction is that they may not receive financial aid from the school.[60] Collegiate athletics could survive if stipends were paid to the athletes. The strong allegiances to individual schools and traditions would survive if the athletes in certain sports received a stipend in addition to their tuition and room and board. The athletes would still be required to be full-time students. The stipend would not change the competition on the field, only the nature of the competition for players.

The present system is clearly a restraint. Many athletes do not have the funds to buy clothing, cannot fly home without going to the special assistance fund (except in an emergency), and often struggle to meet ordinary financial requirements of life.[61] The restrictions are not necessary to maintain collegiate athletics; as noted there is already precedent for chipping away at the amateur nature of the venture. And, a stipend, coupled with a "salary cap," is a less restrictive means of promoting collegiate athletics and maintaining competitive balance. It would not be possible under this proposal for a school to offer unlimited amounts of money and, in effect, act like a professional sports team during free agent signing periods.

B. Workers' Compensation Issues

If the proposal is adopted, even in some modified form, by the NCAA, it is likely that in most jurisdictions the athletes receiving stipends would then be covered by the workers' compensation laws of those states. Coverage brings with it legal and financial considerations for the athletic departments impacted.

Workers' compensation laws are state statutes enacted to compensate workers or their estates for job-related injuries or death, regardless of fault. The underlying premise of this legislation is that accidents in the workplace are inevitable, particularly in the industrial setting, and the burden of injuries caused by such accidents should be borne by the industries that benefit from the labor rather than the employees who are injured. This philosophy is implemented by providing an employee with a guaranteed remedy of benefits and medical care in the event of an injury occurring in the course of employment. Employers are generally required to self-insure, contract with a private insurance carrier, or pay into the state workers' compensation fund.[64] Under these statutes, each state has developed its own jurisprudence, and the determination of coverage under particular circumstances would necessitate analysis of the particular statute relevant to a particular circumstance. . . .

. . . . *[The author's analysis of various state provisions is omitted.]*

Under most state statutes, if the NCAA adopts a stipend provision the athletes on scholarship would probably fall within existing definitions of "employee." The stipend appears to be a wage paid for services rendered. Intent would, of course, be an issue in that a court would look to whether the stipend was any more tied to services rendered than the rest of the scholarship package. The analysis in *Rensing* focused on the amateur nature of collegiate athletics and the NCAA's prohibition on payment of players.[95] Such reasoning would no longer be available to a court. . . . As noted, collegiate athletics is big business. If additional money is paid to players, it is likely that the school will attempt to exercise more control over them. Control, of course, is a factor used in determining whether an employment relationship exists. Arguably, a college scholarship which includes a stipend begins to look more like a professional sports contract that happens to include tuition, fees, room, board, and books as well as a cash component. Under most definitions a recipient of this type of "scholarship" would be an employee.[96]

The best comparison would be to graduate assistants or teaching assistants on college campuses. The comparison is a valid one in that a graduate assistant in an English department or engineering college will often receive a tuition scholarship plus a stipend. The stipend and the scholarship are awarded in exchange for the student's serving as a teacher for a set number of classes or laboratory sessions. In the athletic setting, the scholarship and the proposed stipend would be awarded in exchange for the student's participation in the school's athletic program. This would include all practice sessions, team meetings, games, and off-season conditioning programs. Failure to participate would, of course, be cause for loss of the scholarship, as would failure to maintain a certain level of competence. At the University of Oklahoma, and perhaps many other universities, graduate assistants are treated as any other person on the payroll. In other words, the university includes them within its workers' compensation coverage. It is difficult to understand how collegiate athletes would be treated any differently.

C. Other Legal Issues Arising from the Proposal

1. Gender Equity.   Gender equity measures must be taken into account when adopting the proposal. Title IX requires not only equal opportunities for participation, but equal treatment and benefits for athletes with intercollegiate programs. Violations of the law will produce actions for injunctive relief and even for monetary damages. It is quite clear that schools providing stipends under the proposal would have to provide the stipends for a proportionate number of women athletes. Any disparities will wave red flags and likely subject the school to sanctions under the law.

2. Labor Law Issues.   Another question which arises in the context of consideration of stipends for collegiate athletes is whether the athletes would then be employees for purposes of the National Labor Relations Act. The act essentially gives employees of businesses engaging in interstate commerce the right to organize and engage in concerted activity for the purpose of collective bargaining or other mutual aid. The act further defines "employee" to mean any employee unless otherwise excluded by the act. The courts have construed the act to give the National Labor Relations Board great latitude in determining who is an employee under the act. In analyzing the question with regard to collegiate athletes receiving stipends along with their scholarships, one would have to look at the conditions of that scholarship.

Scholarships for collegiate athletes typically require enrollment as a full-time student, compliance with NCAA rules, compliance with athletic department rules, and requirements established by the coaches of the particular sport. The athlete does receive some benefits similar to those of a traditional employee. If the local definition of "employee" required additional benefits to be paid to an athlete, the stipend proposed would be added support for the determination that the athlete is an employee for federal labor law purposes. Certainly the "tools of the trade" are supplied by the athletic department and the university provides the place and time of work. No athlete could be viewed as an independent contractor. The only issue is whether this stipend is for services rendered or simply a part of the scholarship. Consistent with the position taken above, the stipend must be viewed as being paid for services rendered, just as would be the case for a traditional employee. The athlete in a Division I revenue-producing sport is at her institution to participate in sports, and, oh, by the way, get an education. Again, the comparison to a graduate assistant in an academic department is instructive. The stipend paid to the graduate assistant appears to trigger tax consequences and workers' compensation consequences similar to a traditional employee. It should also trigger labor law consequences, should the athletes desire to take advantage of them.

It is not hard to imagine the reaction throughout the world of collegiate sports should a court determine that college athletes have the right to form unions. What would be the bargaining unit? Would the linebackers be a separate unit or would they have to organize with the rest of the defensive squad? Again, one would expect significant efforts to influence Congress with regard to specific exclusions for intercollegiate athletics.

3. Taxation Issues.   Currently, athletic scholarships are not taxable to the athlete. Based upon experience with graduate assistants, it is clear that if the stipend is added, at least that portion of the scholarship would constitute taxable income to the athlete. This would also add the burden of withholding for income tax as well as for social security and Medicare. It might further provide fuel for those who advocate the general removal of the tax-exempt status of collegiate athletics. Providing the stipend could have an impact on evaluations of unrelated business income for NCAA member institutions.

IV. PRACTICAL FINANCIAL CONCERNS AND WHY IT WON'T HAPPEN OVERNIGHT

Assume for the moment that the legal issues raised above do not deter the membership's consideration of the proposal. There are nonetheless several serious political and practical concerns. The history and culture of the NCAA have for decades revolved around the concept of amateurism and the notion of the "student-athlete." Athletics are an integral part of the educational experience. Further professionalizing the programs, the argument goes, destroys this concept. The purists argue that any denigration of the amateurism concept is a giant step towards the destruction of intercollegiate athletics. The former president of the association, Joseph Crowley, said, "the day our members decide it's time to pay players will be the day my institution stops playing."[107] Even some people who favor increased attention to athletes' welfare believe that paying athletes is not a good idea.

There are, however, some very respected coaches who believe it is time to support the concept of paying stipends to athletes. Tom Osborne of the University of Nebraska has argued for many years that players should be able to receive money for living expenses. . . . However, even many who conceptually support the proposal acknowledge the enormous practical and financial difficulties presented. . . .

There are sources of revenue or ideas for revenue redistribution which could support the proposal. As noted, the NCAA budget is $239 million for 1996–97. That figure will go up in the coming years. *[The NCAA budget for 2002–2003 was $422 million.]* The bowl games following the 1996 college season paid out over $100 million to participating schools and their conferences. Estimates are that licensed products generate over $2 billion annually in sales, providing generous royalties for colleges and universities. Corporate sponsorship agreements with individual schools provide additional funds. The NCAA Basketball Championship generates in excess of $50 million annually for the member schools; and, if the NCAA ever approves a national football championship playoff system, an additional $100 million or more will be available for distribution to the schools. Finally, there are television contracts and gate receipts that add to the revenues of most of the Division I schools.

The other side of the equation begins with the reality that many of the Division I schools lose money on their athletic programs. Even those making money argue they have very little flexibility in their budgets, particularly those with gender equity pressures.[114] The proposal as structured above would cost approximately $29 million annually, with the impact as high as $400,000 for Division I-A football schools.

While there is no doubt that absorbing these costs would be difficult for most schools, there are sources of revenue which could support the proposal. It will require athletic administrators to be creative and to look for ways to cut costs in existing programs without cutting quality and equality. It is arguable that many, if not most, Division I athletic programs have unnecessary extravagance and duplication. It may also be time to suggest to the professional sports leagues that direct subsidies are due their "minor leagues," the college athletic programs. Corporate sponsors such as McDonald's or Nike should be considered as potential benefactors of this program. For the present, however, these outside sources are not available in any meaningful way. Therefore, existing funding would have to be utilized to implement the proposal for stipends for athletes.

The cost of the stipend is not the only cost presented. If the athlete is viewed as an employee in a given state for workers' compensation purposes, the schools may have to purchase insurance coverage. There may also be additional insurance or fringe benefit costs associated with a determination of employee status. If the program begins to look more professional than amateur, there may be tax consequences to the schools with very significant price tags. If athletes had success with either the potential claims under the Sherman Act or those under Title IX, costs would escalate. Then there is the possibility of added leverage through unionization and collective bargaining. This too would have additional costs.

It is difficult to be sympathetic to concerns for the loss of amateurism in collegiate sports as a result of consideration for stipends. When a school makes an estimated $4 million in revenues directly traceable to the participation of one basketball player, concerns over the loss of amateurism are difficult to swallow. Intercollegiate athletics revolves around big money. Winning brings more money to programs and, thus, coaches are under pressure to produce. Those who do produce at the Division I level can expect six and seven figure annual incomes. Athletes spend twelve months a year playing, practicing, and training for their particular sport. For approximately eight months per year they are also students. The athletes are primarily responsible for the generation of the revenues used to pay the aforementioned coaches and programs. In return, they receive, relatively speaking, incredibly poor compensation. The days of sports at the collegiate level, at least in Division I programs, being "just a game" are long gone. Sports have a way of putting educational institutions on the map. How many people would know of the College of Charleston without basketball?

Finally, it is suggested that amateurism in and of itself is not the reason most fans watch collegiate sports. Loyalties to educational institutions and to tradition are very important. Ticket prices for collegiate events are more affordable than for professional events, and a modest stipend for athletes will not alter that situation. Rivalries and the national championships sanctioned by the NCAA are a natural attraction. A retreat from pure amateurism will not detract from this attraction.

More attention must be paid to athletes' welfare. The relaxation of the work restrictions is well-intentioned, but is misdirected. It is counter to the association's own concerns over the amount of time the athletes have in a day for sports, school, and life. It throws one more factor into the mix, which is a mistake. There are, of course, natural concerns over athletes having jobs under this rule which pay good wages for little or no work. Policing will be a nightmare.

It is time for collegiate athletes to receive monthly stipends as part of their scholarship package. Even Walter Byers, former longtime Executive Director of the NCAA, now calls for fair treatment of athletes, including relaxation of restrictions on compensation and outside income. We are no longer in an age of innocence where there is no commercialism in college athletics. It is big business and those most responsible for the product put on the field, the players, should be compensated.

REFERENCES

31. Sherman Act, 15 U.S.C. 1 (1990).

35. NCAA v. Board of Regents of the Univ. of Okla., 468 U.S. 85, 101 (1984).

57. Banks v. NCAA, 977 F.2d 1081, 1098 (7th Cir. 1992). (Flaum, J., concurring in part and dissenting in part).

58. 1996–1997 NCAA Manual (1996), at 2.5.

59. Steve Wulf, Tote That Ball, Lift That Revenue; Why Not Pay College Athletes Who Put in Long Hours to Fill Stadiums and Coffers? Time, Oct. 21, 1996, at 94.

60. See NCAA Manual, supra note 58, at 12.1.2.

61. See, e.g., Brian Carnell, Another View: Free the Athletes and Scrap the NCAA, Detroit News, Jan. 23, 1997, at A15 (arguing that the players do most of the work and assume all of the risk, yet are prevented from sharing in the results of their labor); Ron Maly, Hawkeyes' Verba: Players Feeling Cheated, Des Moines Reg., Jul. 28, 1996, at Big Peach 4 (describing the financial struggles of scholarship athletes); Michael Costello, Some Cheating: Sharing the Booty with Athletes, Lewiston Morning Trib., Mar. 16, 1996, at A12 (stating that students "grind their bones into dust for next to nothing").

64. See Arthur Larson, Workers' Compensation Law: Cases, Materials, and Text 795 (1992).

95. Rensing v. Indiana State Univ. Bd. of Trustees, 444 N.E.2d 1170 (Ind. 1983) at 1172–73.

96. See generally Alan Roberts, Comment, College Athletes, Universities, and Workers' Compensation: Placing the Relationship in the Proper Context by Recognizing Scholarship Athletes as Employees, 35 S. Tex. L. Rev. 1315 (1996), at 1341 (noting Texas' liberal definition of employee on a quid pro quo basis); Ray Yasser, Essay: A Comprehensive Blueprint for the Reform of Intercollegiate Athletics, 3 Marq. Sports L.J. 123 (1993), at 137 (calling an athletic scholarship an oxymoron and comparing it more to a one-year renewable contract).

107. Curry Kirkpatrick, The Hoops Are Made of Gold, Newsweek, Apr. 3, 1995, at 62.

114. David Nakamura, Equity Leaves Its Mark on Male Athletes; Some Schools Make Cuts to Add Women's Sports, Wash. Post, Jul. 7, 1997, at A1.

THE GAME OF LIFE

James L. Shulman and William G. Bowen

KEY EMPIRICAL FINDINGS

. . . We have used the extensive institutional records of the 30 academically selective institutions in the study to learn about the pre-collegiate preparation of athletes and other students in the 1951, 1976, and 1989 entering cohorts and their subsequent performance in college. We have also followed the approach suggested more than a century ago by the Walter Camp Commission on College Football and analyzed the experiences and views of both former athletes and other students who attended these schools. In seeking to move the debate over intercollegiate athletics beyond highly charged assertions and strongly held opinions, we use this chapter to summarize the principal empirical findings that we believe deserve the attention of all those who share an interest in understanding what has been happening over the course of the past half century.

. . . .

Scale: Numbers of Athletes and Athletic Recruitment

1. *Athletes competing on intercollegiate teams constitute a sizable share of the undergraduate student population at many selective colleges and universities, and especially at coed liberal arts colleges and Ivy League universities.* In 1989, intercollegiate athletes accounted for nearly one-third of the men and approximately one-fifth of the women who entered the coed liberal arts colleges participating in this study; male and female athletes accounted for much smaller percentages of the entering classes in the Division I-A scholarship schools, which of course have far larger enrollments; the Ivies are intermediate in the relative number of athletes enrolled, with approximately one-quarter of the men and 15 percent of the women playing on intercollegiate teams. Some of the much larger Division I-A schools, public and private, enrolled a smaller absolute number of athletes than either the more athletically oriented coed liberal arts colleges or the Ivies — primarily because a number of the Division I-A schools sponsor fewer teams.

2. ***The relative number of male athletes in a class has not changed dramatically over the past 40 years, but athletes in recent classes have been far more intensely recruited than used to be the case.*** This statement holds for the coed liberal arts colleges as well as the universities. In 1989, roughly 90 percent of the men who played the High Profile sports of football, basketball, and hockey said that they had been recruited (the range was from 97 percent in the Division I-A public universities to 83 percent in the Division III coed liberal arts colleges), and roughly two-thirds of the men who competed in other sports such as tennis, soccer, and swimming said that they too had been recruited. In the '76 cohort, these percentages were much lower; there were many more "walk-ons" in 1976 than in 1989, and there were surely fewer still in the most recent entering classes.

3. ***Only tiny numbers of women athletes in the '76 entering cohort reported having been recruited, but that situation had changed markedly by the time of the '89 entering cohort; recruitment of women athletes at these schools has moved rapidly in the direction of the men's model.*** Roughly half of the women in the '89 cohort who played intercollegiate sports in the Ivies and the Division I-A universities reported that having been recruited by the athletic department played a significant role in their having chosen the schools they attended. The comparable percentages in the coed colleges and the women's colleges were much lower in '89, but women athletes at those schools are now also being actively recruited.

Admissions Advantages, Academic Qualifications, and Other "Selection" Effects

1. ***Athletes who are recruited, and who end up on the carefully winnowed lists of desired candidates submitted by coaches to the admissions office, now enjoy a very substantial statistical "advantage" in the admissions process — a much greater advantage than that enjoyed by other targeted groups such as underrepresented minority students, alumni children, and other legacies; this statement is true for both male and female athletes.*** At a representative non-scholarship school for which we have complete data on all applicants, recruited male athletes applying for admission to the '99 entering cohort had a 48 percent greater chance of being admitted than did male students at large, after taking differences in SAT scores into account; the corresponding admissions advantage enjoyed by recruited women athletes in '99 was 53 percent. The admissions advantages enjoyed by minority students and legacies were in the range of 18 to 24 percent.

2. ***The admissions advantage enjoyed by men and women athletes at this school, which there is reason to believe is reasonably typical of schools of its type, was much greater in '99 than in '89, and it was greater in '89 than in '76.*** The trend — the directional signal — is unmistakably clear.

3. ***One obvious consequence of assigning such a high priority to admitting recruited athletes is that they enter these colleges and universities with considerably lower SAT scores than their classmates.*** This pattern holds for both men and women athletes and is highly consistent by type of school. The SAT "deficit" is most pronounced for men and women who play sports at the Division I-A schools, least pronounced for women at the liberal arts colleges (especially the women's colleges), and middling at the Ivies. Among the men at every type of school, the SAT deficits are largest for those who play the High Profile sports of football, basketball, and hockey.

4. *Admitted athletes differ from their classmates in other ways too, and there is evidence of an "athlete culture."* In addition to having weaker academic qualifications, athletes who went on to play on intercollegiate teams were clearly different in other ways at the time they entered college. They were decidedly more competitive than students at large. The male athletes were also more interested than students at large in pursuing business careers and in achieving financial success (this was not true, however, of the women athletes); athletes placed considerably less emphasis on the goals of making original contributions to science or the arts. The differences between athletes and their classmates along many of these dimensions have widened with the passage of time. In addition, athletes who compete in the Lower Profile sports (such as track, swimming, lacrosse, and tennis) had begun, by the time of the '89 cohort, to share more of the attributes of the athlete culture that earlier were found mostly among the High Profile athletes. Similarly, whereas women athletes in the '76 cohort were largely indistinguishable from their classmates in most respects, by the time of the '89 cohort women who played sports had more and more in common with the male athletes (for example, entering college with both lower standardized test scores and more politically conservative views than other women students).

5. *Contrary to much popular mythology, recruitment of athletes has no marked effect on either the socioeconomic composition of these schools or on their racial diversity.* Male athletes (especially those who play High Profile sports at the Division I-A schools) are more likely than students at large to come from modest socioeconomic backgrounds and to be African Americans. Nonetheless, elimination of the athletic contribution to racial diversity in the '89 cohort would have caused the percentage of African American men enrolled at these schools to decline by just 1 percentage point — an estimate obtained by recalculating the percentage of African American students who would have been enrolled had the racial mix of athletes been the same as the racial mix of students at large. There would even be an opposite effect among the women, since the share of African American women playing college sports is much lower — often half the corresponding percentage — of African American women students at large. Moreover, until very recently, women athletes were more likely than other women students to come from privileged backgrounds. Those men who play Lower Profile sports continue to come from more advantaged backgrounds than either the other athletes or the rest of their male classmates.

Graduation Rates, Underperformance in the Classroom, and Choice of Major

1. *Despite their lower SATs, athletes who attended the selective schools included in this study, along with their classmates who participated in other time-intensive extracurricular activities, graduated at very high rates.* The national problem of low graduation rates — which has attracted the attention of both the NCAA and the public — does not afflict most athletes or other students who attend these schools.

2. *When we examine grades (rank-in-class), an entirely different picture emerges: the academic standing of athletes, relative to that of their classmates, has deteriorated markedly in recent years.* Whereas male athletes in the '51 cohort were slightly more likely than other students to be in the top third of their class, only 16 percent of those in the '89 cohort finished in the top third, and 58 percent finished in the bottom third. Women athletes in the '76 cohort

did as well academically as other women, but women athletes in the '89 cohort were more likely than other women to be in the bottom third of the class. This pattern is especially pronounced in those sets of schools where women athletes were highly recruited; the women's colleges are alone in showing no gap at all in academic performance between women athletes and other women students in the '89 cohort.

3. *Only part of this decline in the academic performance of athletes can be attributed to their lower levels of aptitude or preparation at the time they began college; they consistently underperform academically even after we control for differences in standardized test scores and other variables.* Academic underperformance among athletes is a pervasive phenomenon. In the '89 cohort, it is found among both male and female athletes and among those who played all types of sports (not just among the men who played football, basketball, and hockey); it is more pronounced within the Ivy League and the coed liberal arts colleges than it is within the Division I-A schools.

4. *Academic underperformance in college has roots in high school academic performance, in the priority assigned by athletes to academics, and in the "culture of sport."* The degree of underperformance varies not only with precollege academic indicators, but also with how many other athletes who played on the same teams underperformed (possible peer effects) and whether athletes cited a coach as a principal mentor. The "culture of sport" interpretation of this pattern is supported by evidence showing that students who were active in other time-intensive extracurricular activities *overperformed* academically, relative to their SAT scores and other predictors.

5. *Male athletes have become highly concentrated in certain fields of study, especially the social sciences, and female athletes have started to show different patterns of majors as well.* At one Ivy League university, 54 percent of all High Profile athletes majored in economics or political science as compared with 18 percent of male students at large. When considered in the light of differences in career and financial goals, many of the choices of field of study by male athletes seem to be driven by a desire for something akin to a business major. More generally, this evidence on academic concentrations is consistent with other data on rooming patterns in suggesting a greatly increased tendency for athletes to band together. In the 1950s, male athletes were much more broadly distributed across fields of study and, in general, were more like their classmates in all respects.

Advanced Degrees, Careers, and Earnings

1. *Women athletes in the '76 cohort (but not in the '89 cohort) were more likely than their peers to earn advanced degrees of every kind; this was not true of the men, however.* Male athletes were more likely than other male students to earn no advanced degree and also more likely to earn MBAs; they were less likely to earn Ph.D.s. Differences between athletes and other students in advanced degree attainment must be seen in context: all students who attended these selective schools, athletes and others, were far more likely to earn advanced degrees than were most graduates of four-year colleges.

2. *Consistent with patterns of advanced degree attainment, male athletes are more likely than other men in their classes to have chosen jobs in business and finance and less likely to have become scientists, engineers, academics, or doctors or lawyers.* These differences were smaller in the '51 cohort than in the '76 cohort (to the extent they existed at all in the

1950s), and they are magnified when we look at the early vocational choices made by the members of the '89 cohort. High Profile athletes have always been somewhat more interested in careers in marketing than either other athletes or students at large, and this vocational preference appears to have intensified in the most recent cohort. Athletes in the '89 cohort were appreciably *less* likely than their classmates to work in computer science and other technologically driven fields.

3. ***Male athletes consistently earned more money than their classmates.*** The average earnings of former athletes exceed the average earnings of students at large in the '51, '76, and '89 cohorts. This pattern is also found in every type of school, ranging from the coed liberal arts colleges to the Division I-A public universities. These consistent differences are on the order of 10 percent.

4. ***The earnings advantage of male athletes is attributable to both pre-college differences and post-college choices.*** Athletes are more likely than students at large to work in the for-profit and self-employment sectors; moreover, within the for-profit sector, the earnings advantage of athletes is highly concentrated in financial services occupations. There is no significant difference in the average earnings of athletes and of students at large in law and medicine, among those who are CEOs of for-profit enterprises, or in any of the fields within the not-for-profit and governmental sectors. Thus the earnings advantage of male athletes is not an across-the-board phenomenon, and its location in financial services suggests that it is mainly a function of some combination of (a) the vocational interests of male athletes; (b) the special advantages of athlete-alumni networks in fields such as financial services; and (c) the special contribution to marketplace success in these fields of personal traits often associated with being an athlete (such as a high level of competitiveness, discipline, focus on achieving well-defined goals, and ability to take direction and work in teams).

5. ***In general, the earnings of male athletes are not associated with how many years they played sports in college.*** This lack of any association leads us to believe that the earnings advantages enjoyed by athletes are related more to who they were, what they had already learned, and what they wanted when they entered college than to the amount of further "training" ("treatment") that they received by playing college sports. One clear exception to this pattern is that the small number of High Profile athletes who played for four years earned appreciably more than their teammates — a finding that we suspect indicates the presence of a kind of "credentialing" or "celebrity" effect. Those male athletes who earned letters for four years in the High Profile sports are likely to be the visible stars, who are most likely to have been known by alumni and who may then have had especially good opportunities to enter high-paying occupations in fields where connections are often especially useful.

6. ***Intensity of the level of play does not translate into superior later life outcomes for male athletes, as measured by earnings.*** On the contrary, the earnings advantage enjoyed by athletes is smallest among those who played at the Division I-A public universities and, if anything, larger for the men who played at the Division III level in coed liberal arts colleges than for those who participated in more elaborate programs in the Ivies or in the Division I-A private universities. Also, there is no relation between the won–lost record of the team on which a student played and how much that student earned later in life.

7. ***Women athletes in the '76 cohort were more likely than their female peers to be working full-time, to be either doctors or academics (unlike the male athletes, who were disproportionately found in business fields), and, like the men who played sports, to enjoy a sizable***

earnings advantage over their women classmates; moreover, within the for-profit sector, the relative earnings advantage of the '76 women athletes is even larger than the earnings advantage of their male counterparts. These patterns reflect both the high overall academic achievements of these '76 women athletes (who were only rarely recruited as athletes and met the same admissions requirements as all other women students) and the atypically high levels of drive and ambition often associated with playing college sports. In many respects, these '76 women athletes resemble the men who played sports in the 1950s.

8. *In contrast, women athletes in the '89 cohort are no more likely than other women to have earned, or to be earning, advanced degrees, and they do not enjoy any earnings advantages over their peers.* These women are of course at very early stages in their post-college lives, and much may change over time. But the '89 women athletes differ from their predecessors in having been more actively recruited as athletes, in having entered with weaker academic profiles, and in having subsequently underperformed academically. The experiences to date of the '76 women athletes may be poor predictors of what latter-day women athletes will go on to do.

9. *There is no evidence that earnings for women athletes are enhanced by larger "doses" of athletic framing in college.* There is no consistent association of any kind between years of play and earnings; nor is there any association between the earnings advantages enjoyed by women athletes and the intensity of the level of play. In fact, the Division I-A private universities are the only group of schools at which women athletes enjoyed *rio* earnings advantage; conversely, the highest earnings advantage accorded college athletes in the '76 cohort is found in the women's colleges.

Leadership

1. *Athletes were more likely than other students to rate themselves highly as leaders before college began and were also more likely to say, after college, that leadership had played an important role in their lives; yet, surprisingly, neither this greater inclination to provide leadership, nor this stronger expression of its importance, is associated with evidence of having actually provided more leadership.* Athletes and their classmates seem about on a par in this regard. Athletes were no more likely than other students to become CEOs, to earn top salaries in professional fields like law and medicine (where earnings may serve as a proxy for leadership), or to be leaders in most civic activities.

2. *Athletes are leaders in exceptionally large numbers in two specific arenas — alumni/ae activities and youth groups (men only) — and having been a college athlete appears to have measurable effects on the priorities that these leaders emphasize.* This is clearest in the case of alumni/ae leadership. Former athletes who now serve as trustees and in other leadership capacities are more likely to favor increasing the emphasis their school places on intercollegiate athletics than are other alumni leaders, alumni at large, or even other alumni who played sports in college.

3. *In the aggregate, alumni/ae from all three eras and from all types of institutions want their schools to place less, not more, emphasis on intercollegiate athletics than the schools do at present.* When asked about their schools' institutional priorities, the alumni/ae consistently wanted more emphasis placed on undergraduate teaching, residential life, and extracurricular activities — but not on intercollegiate athletics. Former athletes, on the other hand, favor placing more emphasis on intercollegiate athletics.

Giving Back to the College or University

1. *In common with high academic achievers and students who were heavily involved in extracurricular activities, former athletes have generally had above-average general giving rates.* All three of these groups have "bonded" more closely with their schools than have most students, in part because they may feel that they had unusually successful and enjoyable experiences as undergraduates. Such feelings of attachment may be the primary reason why these groups have been so supportive of the broad educational purposes of their institutions.

2. *The High Profile athletes at the Division I-A schools are a revealing exception to this pattern: they are much less likely than others to be contributors.* The main reason, we suspect, is that these High Profile athletes are more likely to be focused on their athletic pursuits and may see themselves as a group apart from the larger academic community (and may even disidentify with it). General giving rates among High Profile athletes have declined over time, relative to the giving rates of others, at both the Division I-A private universities and the coed liberal arts colleges (although not in the Ivies) — a finding that may reflect what appears to be a growing separation of athletes on many campuses from the rest of the campus community. Striking evidence in support of this interpretation is provided by the *lack* of any decline in general giving rates on the part of either the academic high achievers or the students active in extracurricular activities.

3. *The data flatly contradict one of the strongest myths about college athletics — namely, that winning teams, and especially winning football teams, have a large, positive impact on giving rates.* Winning football teams do not inspire increased giving on the part of alumni/ae at Division I-A private universities or Ivy League schools. Surprisingly, it is only at the coed liberal arts colleges, where teams generally receive less recognition, that winning is associated with increased alumni/ae giving, a finding that can be attributed mainly to the exceptionally large number of former athletes found among the alumni/ae of these schools.

The Financial Equation: Costs and Revenues Associated with Intercollegiate Sports

1. *Expenditures on intercollegiate athletics, excluding capital costs, vary tremendously depending on the level of play at which the institution competes.* Total expenditures, excluding capital costs, reach the $50 million level at a university such as the University of Michigan, which offers a wide range of highly competitive big-time programs; $20 to $25 million at a more "standard" Division I-A university; $10 million at an Ivy League university; and $1.5 million at a coed liberal arts college.

2. *Level of play has a surprisingly large effect on expenditures on sports such as tennis, swimming, and field hockey, as well as on football and basketball.* Direct annual expenditures on one of these Lower Profile sports may range from $350,000 at a Division I-A university, to $125,000 in the Ivy League, to $40,000 at a coed liberal arts college. Thus the budgetary consequences of choosing one level of competition over another are considerable.

3. *Revenues from athletics, including gate receipts and television and bowl revenues, can offset most, and sometimes all, of the costs of big-time programs if (and only if) teams are consistently successful; even in these settings, most schools lose money, and it is unlikely that any school comes close to covering its full costs if proper allowances are made for the*

capital-intensive nature of athletics. We estimate that the overall *net costs* of an intercollegiate sports program, exclusive of capital costs, may range from zero for the most competitively successful big-time programs, to $7 to $8 million at both the "standard" Division I-A private universities and the Ivies, to $1.5 million at a coed liberal arts college. Net spending ranges from $2,500 per intercollegiate athlete per year at a coed liberal arts college, to $9,000 per year at an Ivy League school, to $18,000 per year at a "standard" Division I-A private university.

4. ***Athletic budgets, seen on a "net" basis, should be regarded as expenditures by the institution that must be justified in terms of the contribution they do or do not make to the core educational mission of the school.*** In only the rarest case can athletic expenditures be justified as an "investment" that will somehow benefit the institution's bottom line. Moreover, the increasing volatility of athletic revenues (at those schools where revenues from sponsorships and licensing are consequential) means that the financial risk factor associated with big-time programs cannot be ignored.

A CALL TO ACTION: RECONNECTING COLLEGE SPORTS AND HIGHER EDUCATION

*Report of the Knight Foundation Commission
on Intercollegiate Athletics*

FOREWORD

In 1989, as a decade of highly visible scandals in college sports drew to a close, the trustees of the John S. and James L. Knight Foundation were concerned that athletics abuses threatened the very integrity of higher education. In October of that year, they created a Commission on Intercollegiate Athletics and directed it to propose a reform agenda for college sports.

In announcing this action, James L. Knight, then chairman of the Foundation, emphasized that it did not reflect any hostility toward college athletics. . . . "Our interest is not to abolish that role but to preserve it by putting it back in perspective. . . ."

. . . To understand their concern and the subsequent work of the Commission, it is necessary to look back on the extent to which corruption had engulfed big-time college sports in the 1980s.

In a cover story shortly before the Commission was created, *Time* magazine described the problem as ". . . an obsession with winning and moneymaking that is pervading the noblest ideals of both sports and education in America." Its victims, *Time* went on to say, were not just athletes who found the promise of an education a sham but "the colleges and universities that participate in an educational travesty — a farce that devalues every degree and denigrates the mission of higher education."

Here are some broad outlines of the problems the Commission saw then:

- In the 1980s, 109 colleges and universities were censured, sanctioned, or put on probation by the National Collegiate Athletic Association (NCAA). That number included more than half the universities playing at the NCAA's top competitive level — 57 institutions out of 106.
- Nearly a third of present and former professional football players responding to a survey near the end of the decade said they had accepted illicit payments while in college, and more than half said they saw nothing wrong with the practice.

- Another survey showed that among the 106 institutions then in the NCAA's Division I-A, 48 had graduation rates under 30 percent for their men's basketball players and 19 had the same low rate for football players.

At times it seemed that hardly a day passed without another story about recruiting violations . . . , under-the-table payoffs . . . [or] players who didn't go to classes or who took courses that would never lead to a meaningful degree. Even crime sprees at some athletic powerhouses were added to the list.

It was small wonder that eight out of 10 Americans questioned in a Louis Harris poll in 1989 agreed that intercollegiate sports had spun out of control. They agreed that athletics programs were being corrupted by big money, and felt that the many cases of serious rules violations had undermined the traditional role of universities as places where young people learn ethics and integrity.

A 1989 series in the *New York Times* raised another warning flag:

"High school athletics have become the latest entree on the American sports menu, served up to help satisfy the voracious appetite of the fan. As a result, scholastic athletes are on the verge of becoming as important to the billion-dollar sports industry as their college brothers and sisters — and just as vulnerable to big-time exploitation."

Somehow, the Knight Foundation concluded, sanity had to be restored to this bleak scene and the values of higher education put above all else in the world of intercollegiate athletics.

. . . .

The Commission laid out an analysis of the problems facing college sports and proposed a "new model for intercollegiate athletics." This analysis was straightforward: Following decades of presidential neglect and institutional indifference, big-time college sports were "out of control." The reform agenda Commission members proposed was equally straightforward, the "one-plus-three" model — presidential control directed toward academic integrity, financial integrity, and independent certification.

No claim was made that their recommendations would solve all the problems tarnishing college sports, or even that all problems would ever be solved to everyone's satisfaction. "Reform is not a destination but a never-ending process," said the Commission's last report.

. . . .

The report that follows presents the Commission's findings from a series of meetings in 2000 and 2001 with NCAA representatives, university presidents, a trustee board chair, faculty, conference commissioners, athletics directors, coaches, athletes, authors, professional sports executives, television officials, a sports apparel representative, a gambling lobbyist, leaders of national higher education associations, and a U.S. senator.

After assessing those hearings, the Commission concludes with some satisfaction that the NCAA has moved a long way toward achieving the goals laid out in the Commission's earlier reports . . . Many reform efforts have been undertaken over the last decade with sincerity and energy. We reiterate our strong conviction that college sports, when properly conducted, are worth saving. Sports at all levels have been a source of immense satisfaction, self-discipline, and achievement for tens of thousands of young men and women.

. . . .

TEN YEARS LATER

It is tempting to turn away from bad news. To the cynic, corruption has been endemic in big-time sports as long as they have existed. To the rationalizer, reform is already under way and things are not nearly as bad as the critics make them out to be. More time is all that is needed. But to the realist, the bad news is hard to miss. The truth is manifested regularly in a cascade of scandalous acts that, against a backdrop of institutional complicity and capitulation, threaten the health of American higher education. The good name of the nation's academic enterprise is even more threatened today than it was when the Knight Commission published its first report a decade ago. Despite progress in some areas, new problems have arisen, and the condition of big-time college sports has deteriorated.

Consider as an example some simple statistics: As noted in the foreword, 57 out of 106 Division I-A institutions (54 percent) had to be censured, sanctioned, or put on probation for major violations of NCAA rules in the 1980s. In the 1990s, 58 out of 114 Division I-A colleges and universities (52 percent) were similarly penalized. In other words, more than half the institutions competing at the top levels continue to break the rules. Wrongdoing as a way of life seems to represent the status quo.

The fact that such behavior has worked its way into the fiber of intercollegiate sports without provoking powerful and sustained countermeasures from the many institutions so besmirched speaks for itself. It appears that more energy goes into looking the other way than to finding a way to integrate big-time sports into the fabric of higher education.

At the heart of these problems is a profound change in the American culture of sports itself. At one time, that culture was defined by colleges, high schools, summer leagues, and countless community recreational programs. Amateurism was a cherished ideal. In such a context, it made sense to regard athletics as an educational undertaking. Young people were taught values ranging from fitness, cooperation, teamwork, and perseverance to sportsmanship as moral endeavor.

All of that seems somehow archaic and quaint today. Under the influence of television and the mass media, the ethos of athletics is now professional. The apex of sporting endeavor is defined by professional sports. This fundamental shift now permeates many campuses. Big-time college basketball and football have a professional look and feel — in their arenas and stadiums, their luxury boxes and financing, their uniforms and coaching staffs, and their marketing and administrative structures. In fact, big-time programs have become minor leagues in their own right, increasingly taken into account as part of the professional athletics system.

In this new circumstance, what is the relationship between sport and the university as a place of learning?

At the time the Knight Commission was formed in 1989, the answers to that question were already sounding alarm bells. For example, the late A. Bartlett Giamatti, a former president of Yale who went on to become commissioner of major league baseball, said that "failures of nerve, principle and purpose" were threatening to "engulf higher education in ways unfair and dangerous." He argued that what had been "allowed to become a circus — college sports — threatens to become the means whereby the public believes the whole enterprise is a sideshow."

Now, in this new millennium, informed critics are equally scathing in their evaluations. James Duderstadt, president emeritus of the University of Michigan, put it this way before the Knight Commission in late 2000: Major college sports "do far more damage to the university, to its students and faculty, its leadership, its reputation and credibility than most realize — or at least are willing to admit." The ugly disciplinary incidents, outrageous academic fraud, dismal graduation rates, and uncontrolled expenditures surrounding college sports reflect what Duderstadt and others have rightly characterized as "an entertainment industry" that is not only the antithesis of academic values but is "corrosive and corruptive to the academic enterprise."

. . . .

The most glaring ele ments of the problems outlined in this report — academic transgressions, a financial arms race, and commercialization — are all evidence of the widening chasm between higher education's ideals and big-time college sports.

Academics

When the accretions of centuries of tradition and the bells and whistles of the modern university have been stripped away, what remains is the university's essential mission as an institution for teaching, learning, and the generation of new knowledge. This is the mission that big-time college sports often mock and, in some cases, deliberately undermine.

Big-time athletics departments seem to operate with little interest in scholastic matters beyond the narrow issue of individual eligibility. They act as though the athletes' academic performance is of little moment. The historic and vital link between playing field and classroom is all but severed in many institutions. Graduation rates for athletes in football and basketball at the top level remain dismally low — and in some notable cases are falling. While the Commission recognizes that graduation rates for athletes subject to the NCAA's more stringent eligibility standards effective in the mid-1990s are not yet available, we cannot ignore these facts: The graduation rate for football players in Division I-A fell 3 percent last year and 8 percent in the last five years. The rate for men's basketball players at Division I-A institutions remained stable over the last year, but fell 5 percent over the last five years.

Graduation rates for both were already abysmal. The most recent NCAA graduation rate report reveals that 48 percent of Division I-A football players and 34 percent of men's basketball players at Division I-A institutions earned degrees. The graduation rate for white football players was 55 percent, the lowest since the Student Right to Know Act mandated that such records be made public. Only 42 percent of black football players in Division I-A graduate, according to the most recent figures.

Derrick Z. Jackson, a columnist for the *Boston Globe,* analyzed the graduation rates of African-American players on the 64 teams in the 2001 NCAA men's basketball tournament. He reports these shameful figures from the latest NCAA graduation rate report: Twenty-six of the 64 teams graduated fewer than 35 percent of their African-American players. Seven teams had African-American graduation rates of zero. Furthermore, he writes, "Of the 64 teams, a school was nearly twice as likely to have suffered a decline in its African-American player graduation rate since the mid-1990s than enjoy an increase. The rate in the 2000 NCAA graduation rate report was lower for 35 schools than the rate in the 1996 report. It was higher for only 19 schools."

An academic official at a Division I-A institution told Jackson in regard to the 10 percent graduation rate of its men's basketball team, "We have not in the past had the same high expectations of athletes in academics and not held them to as high a standard in the classroom."

In the face of these facts, many defend the overall graduation rates of Division I-A football and basketball players because in some instances they compare favorably to those of the student body as a whole. The Commission is unimpressed with this comparison of apples and oranges. The fact is that the rest of the student body does not have the advantage of full scholarships and the often extensive academic support services extended to athletes. Data from the U.S. Department of Education indicate that approximately 75 percent of high school graduates who enroll full-time in college immediately after graduation (and continue full-time in the same institution) will receive a bachelor's degree within five and a half years. This group of young full-time students is the appropriate comparison for Division I-A athletes.

Athletes are often admitted to institutions where they do not have a reasonable chance to graduate. They are athlete-students, brought into the collegiate mix more as performers than aspiring undergraduates. Their ambiguous academic credentials lead to chronic classroom failures or chronic cover-ups of their academic deficiencies. As soon as they arrive on campus, they are immersed in the demands of their sports. Flagrant violation of the NCAA's rule restricting the time athletes must spend on their sport to 20 hours a week is openly acknowledged. The loophole most used is that of so-called "voluntary" workouts that don't count toward the time limit. In light of these circumstances, academic failure, far from being a surprise, is almost inevitable.

Sadly though, it comes as a rude surprise to many athletes yearning for a professional sports career to learn that the odds against success are astronomically high. Approximately 1 percent of NCAA men's basketball players and 2 percent of NCAA football players are drafted by NBA or NFL teams — and just being drafted is no assurance of a successful professional career. "Student-athletes" whose sole and now failed objective was to make the pros suddenly find themselves in a world that demands skills their universities did not require them to learn.

The academic support and tutoring athletes receive is too often designed solely to keep them eligible, rather than guide them toward a degree. The instances of tutors or other counselors bending and breaking rules on athletes' behalf is a well-publicized scandal. NCAA case books clearly reveal multiple infractions stemming from "tutoring" involving completing athletes' assignments, writing their papers, and pressuring professors for higher grades. Beyond the breaking of the rules is the breaking of the universities' implicit covenant with all students, athletes included, to educate them. Despite new NCAA satisfactory progress requirements effective in the mid-1990s, press and NCAA reports repeatedly document instances of athletes being diverted into courses that provide no basis for meaningful degrees. A faculty member at a Division I-A institution who has recently spoken out against the transgressions she has witnessed on her campus said, "There are students on our football team this year [2000] who will graduate when both faculty and students know they cannot read or write."

The Arms Race

NCAA President Cedric Dempsey, along with many others, has been outspoken about what he calls an ever growing "arms race" of spending and building to reach impractical financial goals. There is evidence to support these concerns. The NCAA's latest study of revenues and expenses at Divisions I and II institutions shows that just about 15 percent operate their athletics programs in the black. And deficits are growing every year.

"Clearly, the rising revenues on most campuses have been overwhelmed by even higher costs," Dempsey told the NCAA convention this year. "At the more than 970 NCAA member schools, we are bringing in just over $3 billion a year, but we're spending $4.1 billion in that same period."

A frantic, money-oriented modus operandi that defies responsibility dominates the structure of big-time football and basketball. The vast majority of these schools don't profit from their athletics programs: At over half the schools competing at the NCAA's Division I-A level in 1999, expenses exceeded revenues by an average of $3.3 million, an increase of 18 percent over the previous two years. On the other hand, for the 48 Division I-A institutions where revenues exceeded expenses, the average "profit" more than doubled, increasing 124 percent from $1.7 million to $3.8 million from

1997 to 1999. In considering all these data, moreover, it must be understood that they do not take into consideration the full costs of athletics programs, in that the reported expenses do not include capital expenditures, debt service, and many indirect program costs. Nevertheless, competitive balance is crumbling as the gap between the haves and the have-nots widens. While a relative few programs flourish, many others have chosen to discontinue sports other than football or basketball to make ends meet. Even some of the "haves" react to intense financial pressure to control costs by dropping so-called minor sports.

Too much in major college sports is geared to accommodating excess. Too many athletic directors and conference commissioners serve principally as money managers, ever alert to maximizing revenues. And too many have looked to their stadiums and arenas to generate more money. In the last seven years, capital expenditures at Division I-A institutions (e.g., construction or remodeling of athletics facilities, capital equipment, etc.) increased 250 percent. From east to west, north to south, the test becomes who can build the biggest stadiums, the most luxurious skyboxes. Every one of the 12 schools in one major conference has built a new football stadium or refurbished its old one in recent years. All seem to have assumed they could not afford to do otherwise. The building boom in college sports facilities now under way across the nation will cost well over $4 billion, with the resulting debt stretching far into the future.

The arms race isn't entered into by NCAA fiat. Institutions, not the NCAA, decide what's best for themselves, and for many that means joining the arms race. Presidents and trustees accept their athletics department's argument that they have to keep up with the competition. When one school has a $50 million athletic budget and another gets along on $9 million, how can there be any pretense of competitive parity? And what about on-campus parity? A five-part series, "The Price of Winning," published by the *Philadelphia Inquirer* in fall 2000 revealed average annual costs as high as nearly $90,000 per athlete at one Division I-A institution. At some Division I-A schools, annual costs per football player are well over $100,000. How can such expenses be justified when the average salary of fully tenured professors at U.S. public research universities barely exceeds $84,000?

And what does higher education sacrifice when a school names its football stadium after a pizza chain or its new stadium club after any other commercial product or corporation? To what purpose, indeed, are luxury skyboxes built? Not to satisfy any legitimate institutional need; certainly not to accommodate more students, in whose name and for whose benefit collegiate sports were originally introduced. The central goal is to garner greater fiscal windfalls from wealthy boosters and alumni willing to spend thousands of dollars to acquire not only luxury boxes but choice seating throughout the stadium, while students are often relegated to the end zone if they can get tickets at all. Interestingly, repeated studies indicate that most contributions to colleges and universities come from those to whom athletic records have little import. Big athletic boosters, conversely, are far less likely to support other aspects of the universities' life and mission, again according to these studies.

There is a tangible downside to this arms race for most schools, that is, for the majority whose big-time programs are less successful and cannot pay for themselves. They must siphon funds from general revenue to try to keep up with the Joneses. Pursuit of success in this context jeopardizes not only the universities' moral heritage but also their financial security.

A glaring symptom of the arms race run amok is the salaries of so-called "star" coaches. At last count, some 30 college football and men's basketball coaches are paid a million dollars or more a year. A few are nearing twice that, or are already there. The irony is not lost on the critics. A college provost points out that his school spent more money hiring the head football coach than it did hiring five department heads — combined. A trustee laments that his university signed the basketball coach to a salary three times greater than its president's. Many players join the complaining chorus when they compare their scholarships to their coaches' salaries, and when their coaches break contracts and jump from team to team — just as their professional counterparts do. Some dissatisfied players have begun to organize in an attempt to increase their clout and have aligned with the United Steelworkers of America for help in doing so.

But coaches have quite a different perspective. They consider the pressures put on their teams' performance when football and basketball revenues are expected to produce the lion's share of the athletic department's budget. They weigh the dismissal rate of those in their ranks who do not win — or do not win soon enough, or big enough — in a win-at-any-cost environment. And they conclude that their salaries are justified.

The logical question for academia emerges: Is there any other department at a university where so much money is spent and justified primarily by reference to the nonacademic performance of its students, staff, or instructors? That is the crux of the matter. Coaches' salaries, like numerous athletics department expenditures, are considered as though they have nothing to do with the traditions and principles of the universities in which they are housed. This lack of academic connection is the fundamental corruption of the original rationale for both sports and coaches on campus: that they are integral components of a well-rounded student life and a useful complement to the universities' other central pursuits. What we have now is a separate culture of performers and trainers, there to provide bread and circuses but otherwise unconnected to the institution that supports them.

Commercialization

Over the last decade, the commercialization of college sports has burgeoned. Vastly larger television deals and shoe contracts have been signed, and more and more space in stadiums and arenas has been sold to advertisers. In too many respects, big-time college sports today more closely resemble the commercialized model appropriate to professional sports than they do the academic model. The NCAA's Dempsey warned the NCAA membership recently that "the level of cynicism over the commercialization of our most visible athletics programs has reached epidemic proportions."

Beginning in 2002, CBS will pay the NCAA $6.2 billion over an 11-year period for broadcast rights primarily for its Division I men's basketball tournament. Television accounts for nearly 80 percent of the NCAA's revenue. When all sources of revenues are accounted for, the Division I men's basketball tournament alone generates well over 90 percent of the NCAA's operating budget. And much of the television money is distributed based on winning basketball games. The NCAA's revenue distribution formula for its new CBS contract values each win in the Division I men's basketball tournament at $780,000. Thus, the stakes for a foul shot to win a game in the tournament will exceed three-quarters of a million dollars. The players are fully aware of these economics, and they feel the pressure.

With the money comes manipulation. Schools and conferences prostrate themselves to win and get on television. There is a rush now to approve cable and television requests for football and basketball games on weekday evenings, on Sundays, in the morning, and late at night. So much for classroom commitments. On the field, the essential rhythms of the games are sacrificed as play is routinely interrupted for television commercials, including those pushing the alcoholic beverages that contribute to the binge drinking that mars campus life.

Arguments that higher education should be above this commercial fray largely go unheeded, but concern is growing over the economic realities. The television money, when parceled around, never seems to be enough, and the benefits are never evenly distributed. The rich — that is, the schools more in demand by network schedule-makers — get richer, the poor go deeper into debt. Disparities have widened to the point where many underfunded programs trying to compete at the top level are perpetual losers, both on and off the field.

The winners are primarily those institutions that belong to the founding conferences in the Bowl Championship Series (BCS), namely, the Atlantic Coast Conference (ACC), the Big East, the Big Ten, the Big 12, the Pacific-10, and the Southeastern Conference (SEC). The BCS is a consortium originally designed and instituted in the early 1990s by conference commissioners to control Division I-A post-season football. The NCAA has no role in the BCS, and even presidents of BCS member institutions are marginalized: for negotiation of BCS television contracts, for example, only conference commissioners and representatives of the television network are at the table, with bowl representatives brought in for the revenue distribution discussions that follow. A small group of conference commissioners controls distribution of all Division I-A postseason football revenues. Conference commissioners are rewarded for successfully generating postseason revenues and so have little incentive to consider other priorities. In allowing commercial interests to prevail over academic concerns and traditions, presidents have abdicated their responsibilities.

Meanwhile, equipment manufacturers inundate prominent coaches and universities with goods and money in exchange for exposure — advertisements of all kinds on campuses, stadiums, and field houses, and logos on uniforms, shoes, and every other conceivable piece of equipment.

There is a clear and sharp message in such deals: This is business; show us the money. Over the last decade, the amounts of money involved have grown tremendously. The University of Michigan's latest contract with Nike, for example, doubled its cash payments from the shoe and apparel company to $1.2 million a year. With royalties, uniforms, and equipment added to that, the seven-year deal is expected to be worth $25 million to $28 million.

The sellout has made at least one longtime manufacturer's representative openly disdainful. He told the presidents on the Commission that they and their counterparts had "sold their souls" to him in the 1970s when he came bearing gifts, and it was their lack of courage to make changes in the interim that put them so deeply into the morass.

The influence of sneaker companies is now pervasive in high school sports as well, both in schools and in summer basketball leagues. These companies have become part of the college recruiting process in many instances, and contribute to the special treatment of athletes from a young age. This special treatment raises players' expectations, shields them from the consequences of their own actions, and teaches them that the rules applied to everyone else don't necessarily apply to them. It exploits athletes as they are eased through high school and college, finishing their years in school with no semblance of the education needed to negotiate life when their playing days are over.

High school sports today can reflect the worst of their collegiate counterparts. In addition to commercial influences, recruitment and transfer of high school players is far too common, leading to disjointed academic experiences and absurdly dominant teams in some communities. Academic compromises are made for high school athletes as well, leaving them with a diploma but ill-prepared for college-level work. And throughout high school sports, as throughout colleges and universities, the young athletes' ultimate goal has increasingly become a successful career at the professional level, with all the single-minded focus that requires.

College sports as an enterprise with vested commercial interests contradicts the NCAA's stated purpose: to maintain intercollegiate athletics "as an integral part of the educational program, and the athlete as an integral part of the student body, [and to] retain a clear line of demarcation between intercollegiate athletics and professional sports." The more that line is crossed, the more likely government intervention in the form of IRS challenges to the institutions' tax-exempt status becomes. Current proposed IRS regulations would tax as "business related income" revenues derived from such arrangements as "naming rights" for games or from contracts with such vendors as soft drink companies for exclusive rights in stadiums or arenas.

The NCAA Manual also says that postseason play is meant to be controlled to "prevent unjustified intrusions on the time student-athletes devote to their academic programs, and to protect [them] from exploitation by professional and commercial enterprises." Yet the number of postseason bowl games has grown from 18 to 25 over the past 10 years, and the men's Division I basketball tournament is three weeks long. Seasons now extend from August until January for football, and from October to April — nearly six months — for basketball.

Sports as big business is suitable for the marketplace and has proved to be a profitable way to tap into the national psyche. Sports as big business for colleges and universities, however, is in direct conflict with nearly every value that should matter for higher education. In the year 2001, the big business of big-time sports all but swamps those values, making a mockery of those professing to uphold them.

A CALL TO ACTION

. . . .

The Commission has pursued this work over the years because it believes the nation's best purposes are served when colleges and universities are strong centers of creative, constant renewal, true to their basic academic purposes. In the opening years of the new century, however, those basic purposes are threatened by the imbalance between athletic imperatives and the academy's values. To say it again, the cultural sea change is now complete. Big-time college football and basketball have been thoroughly professionalized and commercialized.

Nevertheless, the Commission believes that the academic enterprise can still redeem itself and its athletic adjunct. It is still possible that all college sports can be reintegrated into the moral and institutional culture of the university. Indeed, in sports other than football and basketball, for the most part that culture still prevails. Athletes can be (and are) honestly recruited. They can be (and are) true "student-athletes," provided with the educational opportunities for which the university exists. The joys of sport can still be honorably celebrated.

But the pressures that have corrupted too many major athletic programs are moving with inexorable force. If current trends continue, more and more campus programs will increasingly mirror the world of professional, market-driven athletics. What that could look like across the board is now present in high-profile form: weakened academic and amateurism standards, millionaire coaches and rampant commercialism, all combined increasingly with deplorable sportsmanship and misconduct.

Even if the larger picture is not yet fully that bleak, the trend is going in entirely the wrong direction. As it accelerates, so too does the danger that the NCAA might divide — with the major programs forming a new association to do business in very much the same way as the professional sports entertainment industry.

Perhaps 40 to 60 universities (mostly those with large public subsidies) could and might indefinitely operate such frankly commercial athletic programs. Critics might say good riddance. But the academic and moral consequences implicit in such an enterprise are unacceptable to anyone who cares about higher education in this nation.

Such a division must not be allowed to happen. It is time to make a larger truth evident to those who want bigger programs, more games, more exposure, and more dollars. It is this: Most Americans believe the nation's colleges and universities are about teaching, learning, and research, not about winning and losing. Most pay only passing attention to athletic success or failure. And many big donors pay no attention at all to sports, recognizing in Bart Giamatti's words that it is a "sideshow."

Part of this larger truth requires understanding something that sports-crazed fans are inclined to ignore or denigrate: Loss of academic integrity in the arenas and stadiums of the nation's colleges and universities is far more destructive to their reputations than a dozen losing seasons could ever be.

Time has demonstrated that the NCAA, even under presidential control, cannot independently do what needs to be done. Its dual mission of keeping sports clean while generating millions of dollars in broadcasting revenue for member institutions creates a near-irreconcilable conflict. Beyond that, as President Cedric Dempsey has said, the NCAA has "regulated itself into paralysis."

The Need to Act Together

The plain truth is that one clear and convincing message needs to be sent to every member of the academic community: What is needed today is not more rules from above, but instead a concerted grassroots effort by the broader academic community — in concert with trustees, administrators, and faculty — to restore the balance of athletics and academics on campus.

But a grassroots effort cannot be expected to flourish campus by campus. As long as there is an athletics arms race, unilateral disarmament on the part of one institution would most assuredly be punished swiftly by loss of position and increased vulnerability. Change will come, sanity will be restored, only when the higher education community comes together to meet collectively the challenges its members face.

Presidents and trustees must work in harness — not wage the battles so commonplace today over control of the athletic enterprise. Presidents cannot act on an issue as emotional and highly visible as athletics without the unwavering public support of their boards. As John Walda, president of the Indiana University board of trustees, told the Commission in early 2001:

> "Trustees must insist that their presidents not only be dedicated to recapturing control of college sports, but that they stand up to the media, the entertainment industry, coaches, and athletics directors when the institution's values are threatened. And when a president takes bold action . . . trustees must support and defend their president and his or her decision."

National higher education associations such as the American Council on Education (ACE) and the Association of Governing Boards of Universities and Colleges (AGB), in particular, can and should do more to help resolve the persistent problems addressed in this report. Intercollegiate athletics should loom larger in their programming priorities. New and creative programs and services should be offered directly to institutions and their governing boards through joint collaboration among these associations.

Conferences and the NCAA must work together as well. Tensions between conference commissioners and the NCAA must be resolved so that the best interests of intercollegiate athletics and higher education prevail. Power struggles for control of big-time football, revenue distribution, and other matters reflect a culture dominated by competitive rather than academic concerns, and one that often ignores the welfare of the athletes representing their institutions.

Faculty, too, have a critical role to play. Above all, they must defend the academic values of their institutions. Too few faculty speak out on their campus or fight aggressively against meaningless courses or degrees specifically designed to keep athletes eligible, suggesting they have surrendered their role as defenders of academic integrity in the classroom. Further, the academy has capitulated on its responsibility and allowed commercial interests — television, shoe companies, corporate sponsors of all sorts — to dictate the terms under which college sports operate. No academic institution would allow television to arrange its class schedule; neither should television control college athletic schedules. There are scattered signs of faculty awakening, but on many campuses, faculty indifference prevails even when informed critics make their case.

Athletics directors and coaches bear a huge responsibility. Directors of athletics steer the enterprise for their institutions and, in that regard, are in the best position to monitor its direction and raise flags and questions when it heads off course. Coaches are closest to the athletes and have the most influence on the quality of their collegiate experiences. Clearly, pressures on athletics directors and coaches to generate revenues and win at all costs must be mitigated. In turn, athletics directors must see to it that athletics programs are conducted as legitimate and respected components of their institutions. And coaches, quite simply, need to be held more accountable for what goes on around them. They set the tone. "When the cheating starts," the legendary Bear Bryant used to say, "look to the head coach. He's the chairman of the board."

Alumni pressure to escalate athletics programs and produce winning teams distorts and ultimately compromises the values of the institutions they claim to cherish. Alumni must offer strong and visible support to the president and trustees of their alma mater as they work to balance athletics and academics on their campuses. Alumni, better than anyone, should realize that the reputation of their institution depends not on its won–lost record but on its reputation for integrity in all that it undertakes.

A Coalition of Presidents

The Commission understands that collective action is key to overcoming the dynamic of the athletics arms race. No single college or university can afford to act unilaterally, nor can one conference act alone. But a determined and focused group of presidents acting together can transform the world of intercollegiate athletics. Just as Archimedes was convinced he could move the world with the right fulcrum for his lever, presidents from a group of powerful conferences could, in collaboration with the NCAA, create the critical mass needed to bring about the fundamental changes this Commission deems essential.

In its earlier reports, the Commission defined a "one-plus-three" model, with the "one" — presidential control — directed toward the "three" — academic integrity, financial integrity, and certification. The Commission here proposes a new "one-plus-three" model for these new times — with the "one," a Coalition of Presidents, directed toward an agenda of academic reform, de-escalation of the athletics arms race, and de-emphasis of the commercialization of intercollegiate athletics. The Coalition of Presidents' goal must be nothing less than the restoration of athletics as a healthy and integral part of the academic enterprise.

The creation of the Coalition is the first order of business, but its creation will be no panacea in and of itself. Given the enormous scope of this reform effort, the Commission recognizes that change will have to be accomplished in a series of steps over time. As in its earlier reports, the Commission feels no obligation to rewrite the NCAA Manual or propose solutions to every problem on campus.

Starting from the broad principle that athletic departments and athletes should be held to the same standards, rules, policies, and practices that apply elsewhere in their institutions, the Commission makes the following recommendations for the Coalition's agenda:

Academics.   Our key point is that students who participate in athletics deserve the same rights and responsibilities as all other students. Within that broad framework, the Coalition should focus on the following recommendations:

- Athletes should be mainstreamed through the same academic processes as other students. These specifically include criteria for admission, academic support services, choice of major, and requirements governing satisfactory progress toward a degree.
- Graduation rates must improve. By 2007, teams that do not graduate at least 50 percent of their players should not be eligible for conference championships or for postseason play.
- Scholarships should be tied to specific athletes until they (or their entering class) graduate.
- The length of playing, practice, and postseasons must be reduced both to afford athletes a realistic opportunity to complete their degrees and to enhance the quality of their collegiate experiences.
- The NBA and the NFL should be encouraged to develop minor leagues so that athletes not interested in undergraduate study are provided an alternative route to professional careers.

These recommendations are not new. What is novel is the Commission's insistence that a new and independent structure is needed to pursue these proposals aggressively.

The Arms Race.   The central point with regard to expenditures is the need to insist that athletic departments' budgets be subject to the same institutional oversight and direct control as other university departments. The Coalition should work to:

- Reduce expenditures in big-time sports such as football and basketball. This includes a reduction in the total number of scholarships that may be awarded in Division I-A football.
- Ensure that the legitimate and long-overdue need to support women's athletic programs and comply with Title IX is not used as an excuse for soaring costs while expenses in big-time sports are unchecked.
- Consider coaches' compensation in the context of the academic institutions that employ them. Coaches' jobs should be primarily to educate young people. Their compensation should be brought into line with prevailing norms across the institution.
- Require that agreements for coaches' outside income be negotiated with institutions, not individual coaches. Outside income should be apportioned in the context of an overriding reality: Advertisers are buying the institution's reputation no less than the coaches'.
- Revise the plan for distribution of revenue from the NCAA contract with CBS for broadcasting rights to the Division I men's basketball championship. No such revenue should be distributed based on commercial values such as winning and losing. Instead, the revenue distribution plan should reflect values centered on improving academic performance, enhancing athletes' collegiate experiences, and achieving gender equity.

Again, the recommendations put forth here have been heard before. The Coalition offers a chance to make progress on them at long last.

Commercialization. The fundamental issue is easy to state: Colleges and universities must take control of athletics programs back from television and other corporate interests. In this regard, the Coalition should:

- Insist that institutions alone should determine when games are played, how they are broadcast, and which companies are permitted to use their athletics contests as advertising vehicles.
- Encourage institutions to reconsider all sports-related commercial contracts against the backdrop of traditional academic values.
- Work to minimize commercial intrusions in arenas and stadiums so as to maintain institutional control of campus identity.
- Prohibit athletes from being exploited as advertising vehicles. Uniforms and other apparel should not bear corporate trademarks or the logos of manufacturers or game sponsors. Other athletic equipment should bear only the manufacturer's normal label or trademark.
- Support federal legislation to ban legal gambling on college sports in the state of Nevada and encourage college presidents to address illegal gambling on their campuses.

The Commission is not naïve. It understands that its recommendations governing expenditures and commercialization may well be difficult to accept, even among academics and members of the public deeply disturbed by reports of academic misconduct in athletics programs. The reality is that many severe critics of intercollegiate athletics accept at face value the arguments about the financial exigencies of college sports. In the face of these arguments, they conclude that little can be done to rein in the arms race or to curb the rampant excesses of the market.

Nothing could be further from the truth. The athletics arms race continues only on the strength of the widespread belief that nothing can be done about it. Expenditures roar out of control only because administrators have become more concerned with financing what is in place than rethinking what they are doing. And the market is able to invade the academy both because it is eager to do so and because overloaded administrators rarely take the time to think about the consequences. The Coalition of Presidents can rethink the operational dynamics of intercollegiate athletics, prescribe what needs to be done, and help define the consequences of continuing business as usual.

Membership and Financing

The Commission recommends that the president of the American Council on Education (ACE), working with the NCAA and the Association of Governing Boards of Universities and Colleges (AGB), bring together presidential and trustee leadership drawn from ACE, the NCAA, AGB, and Division I-A conferences to establish the Coalition of Presidents. We emphasize the importance of the commitment and active involvement of presidents; Coalition members must be drawn from their group. This is an extraordinary undertaking that cannot be delegated to conference commissioners or the executive staffs of the organizations represented. As we said in our initial report 10 years ago, "The Commission's bedrock conviction is that university presidents are the key to successful reform."

The presidents who must step forward should represent the conferences conducting the most visible and successful athletics programs — in terms of national championships and revenues produced. These are the conferences representing the lion's share of big-time programs. They include: the Atlantic Coast Conference (ACC), the Big East, the Big Ten, the Big 12, the Pacific-10, and the Southeastern Conference (SEC). But membership must not be restricted to presidents from those conferences alone. Institutional compromises in favor of athletics are not limited to the biggest sports schools. Coalition membership, therefore, should be strengthened by presidents from conferences that are not founding members of the BCS but that also compete at the Division I-A level.

The Coalition of Presidents should work collaboratively with the NCAA Division I Board of Directors, meeting jointly from time to time to identify priorities for review and discussion, focus on reform solutions, and develop a comprehensive timeline for appropriate action by the Division I board and by the officers of other higher education associations.

To protect the Coalition's objectivity and the credibility of its recommendations, it is absolutely critical in the Commission's view that it be financially independent of the athletics enterprises it is designed to influence, namely, the NCAA and the conference offices. The Commission believes the Coalition should be financed independently with assessments and dues from its member institutions, support from the higher education associations, and perhaps grants from the philanthropic community.

To complement and support the critical work that must be done, we recommend that the Knight Foundation consider helping fund the Coalition of Presidents with matching grants based on performance to the American Council on Education, and establishing, perhaps with other foundations and the Association of Governing Boards, a separate and independent body — an Institute for Intercollegiate Athletics. The Commission envisions the Institute not as an action agency but as a watchdog to maintain pressure for change. It should keep the problems of college sports visible, provide moral leadership in defense of educational integrity, monitor progress toward reform goals, and issue periodic report cards.

A Final Word

This Commission concludes its work with an admission and an exhortation. The admission first: Most of us who serve on the Knight Commission have held leadership positions while the excesses we deplore here have distorted American higher education. We offer our indictment of the existing situation painfully aware that it calls us, no less than others, to account.

The exhortation involves a strong reaffirmation of the role and purpose of higher education in enhancing the well-being of our nation. That role is best filled and these purposes best achieved when integrity, character, and honor are the hallmarks of academic activities across the board — on the playing field as much as in the classroom and laboratory.

There are no downsides to thoroughgoing reform. When and if accomplished, athletic contests would still be attended by their fans and covered by the media even if the players were students first and athletes second. None of the measures proposed here will diminish competitiveness. The games will continue and be just as exciting — perhaps more so if played without television timeouts interrupting and changing the very nature of the game. Although there might be some grumbling in the short term, the enthusiasm of students and alumni will not be abated over the long haul, largely because most will not notice the difference.

But if there is no downside to deep and sustained reform, continued inattention to the problems described here is fraught with potential dangers. Failure to engage in self-corrective action may leave higher education vulnerable to external interventions, especially legislative. In some areas that would be welcome, as in steps to control the influence of gambling. In others, it would be unwelcome, as in a possible attack on college sports' tax-exempt status.

Worse, some predict that failure to reform from within will lead to the collapse of the current intercollegiate athletics system. Early warning signs of just that are abundant and should not be ignored. If it proves impossible to create a system of intercollegiate athletics that can live honorably within the American college and university, then responsible citizens must join with academic and public leaders to insist that the nation's colleges and universities get out of the business of big-time sports.

The Knight Foundation Commission on Intercollegiate Athletics trusts that day will never arrive. The search now is for the will to act. Surely the colleges and universities of the land have within their community the concerned and courageous leaders it will take to return intercollegiate athletics to the mainstream of American higher education. If not, it is not the integrity of intercollegiate sports that will be held up to question, but the integrity of higher education itself.

 . . . . *[The Commission's discussion in Appendix A of additional issues that were raised for its consideration for which no specific recommendations were made is omitted. These issues included freshman ineligibility, recruiting restrictions, need-based financial aid, early departures to the NBA, certification and accreditation, and antitrust exemptions.]*

APPENDIX B: ACTION ON KNIGHT COMMISSION RECOMMENDATIONS OF MARCH 1991

Presidential Control

Trustees should explicitly endorse and reaffirm presidential authority in all matters of athletics governance, including control of financial and personnel matters. Trustees should annually review the athletics program and work with the president to define the faculty's role in athletics.

Implementation of this recommendation requires action on individual campuses. Following the release of the Commission's first report, more than 100 institutions and organizations reported adoption of these principles. Additionally, the Association of Governing Boards of Universities and Colleges (AGB) has worked to educate trustees about their appropriate role in intercollegiate athletics through articles and white papers in its periodicals and publications, and via speakers and meetings focused on this topic.

Presidents should act on their obligation to control conferences.

Based on testimony before the Commission during 2000–2001, presidents do not in practice control at least a handful of Division I-A conferences. At the national level, the 1992 NCAA convention amended the NCAA Constitution to require presidential approval of conference-sponsored legislative initiatives.

Presidents should control the NCAA.

In 1997 the NCAA restructured, giving presidents full authority for the governance of intercollegiate athletics at the national level. The Association's top body, the Executive Committee, is comprised entirely of CEOs, and the NCAA's three divisions are led by presidential groups.

Presidents should commit their institutions to equity in all aspects of intercollegiate athletics.

Opportunities for women to compete for NCAA member institutions in NCAA championship sports increased 57 percent between 1991 and 2000. Despite this tremendous progress, during the 1998–1999 academic year (the most recent year for which data are available), 41 percent of these varsity athletes were women even though women comprise 52 percent of the undergraduates at NCAA member institutions. Women at the Division I level in 1999–2000 — where they represent 53 percent of the student body — received 43 percent of athletic scholarship dollars and 32 percent of overall athletics budgets. Overall, 48 percent of all participants in NCAA-sponsored championships in 2000–2001 were women and 52 percent were men.

Presidents should control their institutions' involvement with commercial television.

Presidents have been actively involved with contract negotiations with CBS, which broadcasts the Division I men's basketball tournament, and with ESPN. Their involvement, however, has not led to institutional control over the commercial aspects of televised sports. Further, testimony before the Commission during 2000–2001 indicated that presidents are not actively involved in negotiations for televising the Bowl Championship Series (BCS) postseason football bowl games.

Academic Integrity

The NCAA should strengthen initial eligibility requirements:

The number of required units of high school academic work for initial eligibility should be raised from 11 to 15.

The 1992 NCAA convention raised the Divisions I and II core curriculum requirements from 11 to 13 units, effective in 1995.

High school students should be ineligible for reimbursed campus visits (or signing a letter of intent) until they show reasonable promise of being able to meet degree requirements.

Between 1991 and 1997 the NCAA adopted seven proposals related to proof of a prospect's academic credentials required before an official (expense paid) visit. Criteria included minimum required test scores and core academic courses completed. In 1997, however, in response to concerns expressed by the U.S. Department of Justice, the NCAA eliminated specific academic criteria and instead requires only that the prospect submit a test score and academic transcript prior to an official visit.

Junior college transfers who did not meet NCAA initial eligibility requirements upon graduation from high school should sit out a year of competition after transfer.

This recommendation has not been adopted by the NCAA. In 1996, however, the NCAA adopted higher minimum percentage of degree requirements for all junior college transfers in Division I football and men's basketball. These athletes must have completed 35 percent — versus 25 percent — of their degree requirements to be immediately eligible in their third year of collegiate enrollment (see below).

The NCAA should study the feasibility of requiring that the range of academic abilities of incoming athletes approximates the range of abilities of the entire freshmen class.

In its first five-year cycle, the NCAA certification program gathered data related to this recommendation by requiring that institutions compare the academic profiles of all incoming athletes with the rest of the incoming class as a whole. The next certification cycle improves upon this assessment by requiring that comparisons be made on a sport-by-sport basis, as well as by gender and racial subgroups. Significant differences in academic profiles must be noted and explained.

The letter of intent should serve the student as well as the athletics department.

Since 1991, no changes have been made in the national letter of intent program. However, athletes are permitted to appeal the terms and conditions of the letter of intent. Approximately 20,000 such documents are signed each year by prospects planning to attend NCAA Division I and II institutions. During the 1999–2000 academic year — a typical year — 170 letters of intent were appealed: 86 percent of the appeals were approved, 12 percent of the athletes were granted a partial release, and 2 percent of the appeals were denied. These data indicate flexibility in the administration of the national letter of intent program.

Athletics scholarships should be offered for a five-year period.

No action to date.

Athletics eligibility should depend upon progress toward a degree.

The 1992 NCAA convention adopted new Division I requirements stipulating minimum percentages of credits earned toward a specific degree, as well as a minimum grade point average toward that degree, for athletes' third and fourth years of eligibility, effective in 1996. Further, the permissible number of credits earned during the summer to maintain eligibility was capped, and the new satisfactory progress toward degree requirements was made applicable to midyear transfer students after a semester rather than a year on campus.

Graduation rates of athletes should be a criterion for NCAA certification.

NCAA certification incorporates graduation rates as a criterion. In the program's first five-year cycle, however, graduation rates of all athletes were compared with the student body as a whole. The next certification cycle improves upon this assessment by requiring that comparisons be made on a sport-by-sport basis, as well as by gender and racial subgroups. Significant differences in graduation rates must be noted and explained.

Financial Integrity

All funds raised and spent in connection with intercollegiate athletics programs will be channeled through the institution's general treasury. The athletics department budget will be developed and monitored in accordance with general budgeting procedures on campus.

Implementation of this recommendation requires action on individual campuses. Data concerning its adoption are unavailable. The NCAA certification program, however, addresses these issues specifically in the first operating principle under the Financial Integrity section of the program's self-study document, which each Division I institution must address in detail.

Athletics costs must be reduced.

Some efforts to reduce costs have been made, such as reducing the number of allowable scholarships in certain sports and limiting assistant coaches' salaries in men's basketball. In the latter instance, however, the salary caps were successfully challenged as a violation of antitrust law; the NCAA settlement with the coaches cost over $50 million. At the institutional level, athletics costs rose steadily during the 1990s, such that the NCAA's latest financial study reports that roughly just 15 percent of Divisions I and II institutions operate in the black. From 1997 to 1999, deficits at Division I-A institutions where expenses exceeded revenues increased 18 percent.

Athletics grants-in-aid should cover the full cost of attendance for the very needy.

No action to date, although the NCAA's Special Assistance Fund available to needy athletes has increased from $3 million in 1991 to $10 million in 1998, and is scheduled to increase to $10.4 million in 2002. Additionally, in 2002 the NCAA will institute a new $17 million Student Opportunity Fund, which can be broadly used for anything that benefits athletes but not, specifically, on salaries or facilities. Each fund is scheduled to increase annually throughout the duration of the NCAA's 11-year CBS contract.

The independence of athletics foundations and booster clubs must be curbed.

Implementation of this recommendation requires action on individual campuses. Data concerning changes in the numbers of independent athletics foundations and booster clubs are unavailable.

The NCAA formula for sharing television revenues from the Division I men's basketball tournament must be reviewed by university presidents.

The NCAA Executive Committee and the Division I Board of Directors, both composed entirely of presidents, have been actively involved in review of the formula for distribution of revenues from the new $6.2 billion CBS contract. The formula was approved in early 2001 by the NCAA Executive Committee.

All athletics-related coaches' income should be reviewed and approved by the university.

The 1992 NCAA convention adopted legislation requiring annual, prior written approval from the president for all athletically related income from sources outside the institution. That legislation, however, was eliminated in 2000 as part of an NCAA deregulation effort.

Coaches should be offered long-term contracts.

Implementation of this recommendation requires action on individual campuses. While it appears that more long-term contracts are being offered to big-time football and men's basketball coaches, the pressure to win has not diminished.

Institutional support should be available for intercollegiate athletics.

Progress in this regard has been minimal. The NCAA Division I Philosophy Statement, for example, still contains language recommending that its members strive "to finance [their] athletics programs insofar as possible from revenues generated by the program itself." Moreover, several states have laws prohibiting the use of state funds on intercollegiate athletics programs. In Division I-A, institutional support, direct government funding, and student activity fees have increased as a percentage of total revenues from 14 percent in 1993 to 16 percent in 1997.

Certification

The NCAA should adopt a certification program for all institutions granting athletics aid that would independently authenticate the integrity of each institution's athletics program.

Division I institutions must undergo NCAA certification of their athletics departments. When the program was first adopted, institutions were meant to be certified once every five years; since then, the cycle has been extended to once every 10 years. Division II institutions, which also award athletics aid, have not adopted the certification program.

Universities should undertake comprehensive, annual policy audits of their athletics programs.

The Division I certification program requires an annual compilation of athletics policy audits and other data.

The certification program should include the major themes advanced by the Knight Commission, i.e., the "one-plus-three" model.

The NCAA certification program substantially incorporates the fundamental principles of the "one-plus-three" model. The four major components of athletics certification are: governance and commitment to rules compliance; academic integrity; fiscal integrity; and equity, welfare, and sportsmanship.

DISCUSSION QUESTIONS

1. Which constituency is the most likely to be able to effectuate a change in intercollegiate athletics? Which is the least likely to effectuate change?

2. What is the likelihood that the reform measures suggested by the Knight Commission will be adopted by the NCAA?

3. Why do people cling to antiquated (and mythological) notions of amateurism when discussing intercollegiate athletics?

4. What, if any, reforms would you make to intercollegiate athletics? How could you make these reforms economically feasible?

5. What would be the impact if athletes in revenue-generating sports were paid a stipend?

6. What problems would arise if only athletes in men's basketball and football were paid?

7. Are there any potential racial repercussions to not fully contemplating pay for student-athletes?

8. Should the revenues of profitable sports be used to support those that are not profitable?

9. What justifications exist for the continuation of the existing amateurism model in collegiate sports?

10. Discuss the "athletic arms race" that universities are facing, including the aggravating factors and any suggestions that you feel would properly address the situation.

11. What factors have led to the commercialization of college sports? What are the implications of this commercialization?

PART IV

SOCIOLOGICAL CONSIDERATIONS

CHAPTER 19

DIVERSITY

INTRODUCTION

Sports business leaders, with greater public exposure and scrutiny than executives in other industries, have long been confronted with pressure to insure that their industry is diverse. The diversity emphasis has been focused primarily on race and gender. In recent years a global diversity element has come into play as well. In general, sports has attained a leadership position for its on-field diversity, but has long lagged in diversity in the front office.

Well before Jackie Robinson integrated Major League Baseball in 1947, municipalities led by New York City, often raised racial discrimination issues. The National Association for the Advancement of Colored People made a number of pronouncements as well. Questions of policy were raised such as, why should publicly financed facilities be used by enterprises that discriminate?

Even as far back as the search to find a "Great White Hope" to battle the first black heavyweight champion, Jack Johnson, race has been an important part of the business of sports. There, the race of the boxers was used to sell tickets and inspire interest. The race-baiting formula has been used over and over again including, notably, the Larry Holmes–Gerry Cooney heavyweight championship bout. Race sells in the marketing of a sporting contest.

The slow elimination of racial discrimination in sports has largely occurred for practical reasons. In post–World War II baseball, part of the motivation to recruit Negro Leaguers was simply to fill the need for more talent. Eventually it became the desire to expand the talent pool, realizing that much of the best talent was black. Ironically, this led to the demise of the Negro Leagues. That realization of the value of black talent ultimately occurred in other leagues as well. *[See Table 1, which shows the racial composition of players among leagues.]*

The issue of racial diversity has evolved from players to management and now to ownership. The following readings provide the sports business leader with a broad swipe at the issues as well as some of the approaches used to address them.

Other issues related to diversity beyond race have evolved over time as well. The 1973 Billie Jean King–Bobby Riggs "Battle of the Sexes" tennis match held in the then-novel Houston Astrodome is symbolic of some of the barriers that have been overcome in these other areas. That cross-gendered spectacle revealed to many that the potential of women's sports could extend beyond

TABLE 1.

Racial Composition of Players in Major Sports Leagues					
	NBA	*NFL*	*MLB*	*NHL*	*MLS*
2001–2002					
White	20%	33%	60%	98%	60%
African-American	78%	65%	10%	1%	16%
Latino	<2%	<1%	28%	0%	22%
Asian-American	<1%	1%	2%	<1%	1%
Other	0%	<1%	0%	<1%	1%
2000–2001					
White	21%	—	59%	98%	59%
African-American	78%	—	13%	2%	19%
Latino	1%	—	26%	<1%	20%
Other	0%	—	1%	<1%	2%
1999–2000					
White	22%	32%	60%	98%	63%
African-American	78%	67%	13%	2%	15%
Latino	<1%	<1%	26%	0%	21%
Other	0%	<1%	<1%	<1%	1%
1998–1999					
White	21%	32%	60%	98%	65%
African-American	78%	66%	13%	1%	16%
Latino	1%	<1%	26%	0%	18%
Other	0%	1%	<1%	1%	1%
1997–1998					
White	23%	33%	59%	98%	62%
African-American	77%	65%	15%	1%	16%
Latino	<1%	<1%	25%	0%	21%
Other	0%	1%	1%	1%	1%
1996–1997					
White	20%	31%	58%	—	—
African-American	79%	66%	17%	—	—
Latino	<1%	<1%	24%	—	—
Other	<1%	2%	1%	—	—

(Continued)

TABLE 1. (Continued)

RACIAL COMPOSITION OF PLAYERS IN MAJOR SPORTS LEAGUES					
	NBA	*NFL*	*MLB*	*NHL*	*MLS*
1995–1996					
White	20%	31%	62%	—	—
African-American	80%	67%	17%	—	—
Latino	0%	0%	20%	—	—
Other	<1%	<2%	1%	—	—
1994–1995					
White	18%	31%	62%	—	—
African-American	82%	68%	19%	—	—
Latino	0%	0%	19%	—	—
Other	0%	1%	0%	—	—
1993–1994					
White	21%	35%	64%	—	—
African-American	79%	65%	18%	—	—
Latino	0%	0%	18%	—	—
1992–1993					
White	23%	30%	67%	—	—
African-American	77%	68%	16%	—	—
Latino	0%	<1%	16%	—	—
Other	0%	1%	<1%	—	—
1991–1992					
White	25%	36%	68%	—	—
African-American	75%	62%	17%	—	—
Latino	0%	2%	14%	—	—
1990–1991					
White	28%	39%	68%	—	—
African-American	72%	61%	18%	—	—
Latino	0%	0%	14%	—	—
1989–1990					
White	25%	40%	70%	—	—
African-American	75%	60%	17%	—	—
Latino	0%	0%	13%	—	—

(Continued)

TABLE 1.   (Continued)

Racial Composition of Players in Major Sports Leagues

WNBA

2002

White	35%
African-American	61%
Latina	<3%
Asian-American	<1%
Other	<1%

2000

White	34%
African-American	63%
Latina	3%
Other	0%

1999

White	33%
African-American	65%
Latina	2%
Other	0%

1998

White	32%
African-American	64%
Latina	3%
Other	1%

College student-athletes (male): Division I

2000–2001	*Basketball*	*Football*	*Baseball*
White	32.5%	49.4%	81.3%
African-American	57.1%	42.1%	6.7%
Latino	1.4%	2.1%	5.6%
American Indian/Alaskan Native	0.4%	0.4%	0.4%
Asian-American/Pacific Islander	0.2%	1.3%	0.9%
Non-Resident Aliens	5.1%	1.7%	2.1%
Other	3.3%	2.9%	3.0%
			(Continued)

Note: Data provided by the NCAA. Historically Black institutions excluded. Only student-athletes receiving financial aid are included in this report.

TABLE 1. (Continued)

Racial Composition of Players in Major Sports Leagues			
College student-athletes (male): Division I (continued)			
1998–1999	*Basketball*	*Football*	*Baseball*
White	34.0%	46.9%	88.1%
African-American	55.9%	46.4%	2.8%
Latino	1.4%	1.9%	4.7%
American Indian/Alaskan Native	0.3%	0.4%	0.5%
Asian-American/Pacific Islander	0.3%	2.0%	0.8%
Non-Resident Aliens	5.5%	1.0%	1.4%
Other	2.6%	1.9%	1.7%
1996–1997			
White	33.8%	46.9%	89.5%
African-American	57.3%	47.6%	3.0%
Latino	1.5%	1.9%	4.3%
American Indian/Alaskan Native	0.2%	0.3%	0.5%
Asian-American/Pacific Islander	0.3%	1.2%	0.6%
Non-Resident Aliens	4.4%	0.6%	0.9%
Other	2.5%	1.5%	1.2%
1991–1992			
White	34.5%	53.2%	90.0%
African-American	61.8%	42.7%	4.3%
Latino	0.8%	1.4%	3.9%
American Indian/Alaskan Native	0.2%	0.3%	0.3%
Asian-American/Pacific Islander	0.2%	1.0%	0.7%
Non-Resident Aliens	**	**	**
Other	2.5%	1.4%	0.8%

**Not recorded at this date.
Note: Data provided by the NCAA. Historically Black institutions excluded. Only student-athletes receiving financial aid are included in this report.
Source: Institute for Diversity and Ethics in Sport, Racial and Gender Report Card.

the moral obligation to promote gender equality to the realization of profit. This certainly led to a number of women's sports leagues. Many of these are discussed in Chapter 11 on "Start-Up Leagues and Niche Sports." Other important issues related to women and diversity are discussed in Chapter 17, "Gender Equity."

Rimer's "Discrimination in Major League Baseball: Hiring Standards for Major League Managers, 1975–1994" illustrates some of the history of disparate standards used in managerial hiring decisions. It provides a clear message to managers to beware of applying disparate standards in hiring. A more recent study by Janice Madden examines the issue in the NFL. The Madden study may be viewed at http://www.findjustice.com/ms/nfl/frameIndex.htm.

The excerpt from Shropshire's "Diversity, Racism, and Professional Sports Franchise Ownership: Change Must Come from Within" focuses on ownership. The discussion in this selection highlights the limitations of the law in bringing about change. Sports owners are often confronted with demands to diversify their ranks. Currently, for example, Robert Johnson, the owner of the revived NBA franchise in Charlotte, North Carolina, is the lone African-American owner of a major league sports franchise. Arturo Moreno is the lone Latino owner with his 2003 purchase of the Anaheim Angels.

The excerpt from Kahn's "The Sports Business as a Labor Market Laboratory" focuses on salary discrimination and contract termination issues. The selection provides an overview of the research available on the issue of differences in pay to players based on race.

Vargas's article "The Globalization of Baseball: A Latin American Perspective" focuses on the diversity issues associated with the global recruitment of athletes into U.S. based pro leagues. This is a fairly harsh analysis. It is valuable for the sports business leader, as it provides a litany of red flags for those contemplating the recruitment of international athletes. Although the focus is on baseball and Latinos, the lessons may be valuable in any sport where global expansion and the recruitment of talent is an issue.

The lessons from all of the excerpts included here are applicable to broader diversity issues as well.

Managers and Coaches

Discrimination in Major League Baseball: Hiring Standards for Major League Managers, 1975–1994

Edward Rimer

In 1975, the Cleveland Indians hired Frank Robinson to be their manager, the first Black to hold such a position in Major League Baseball. This occurred 28 years after Jackie Robinson had successfully integrated professional baseball. As befalls most managers, Frank Robinson was fired and, subsequently, was rehired by two other teams *[now three]*. Although other Blacks have become managers and there have been several Hispanic managers, there remains a belief that minorities are not given an equal opportunity to assume administrative and managerial positions in the major leagues. *[See Figure 1 for racial comparisons of coaches in the NFL.]*

The purpose of this article is twofold. First, I analyze the backgrounds of those individuals who were managers during the past 20 years (1975–1994) to ascertain what were the implicit standards, if any, that the owners used in making their hiring decisions. Second, having identified such standards, I compare the backgrounds of Black, White, and Hispanic managers to determine whether the standards were applied equally to all managers.

This study differs from previous work in that it seeks to determine what were the standards used to hire managers and whether such standards were applied equally to Blacks, Hispanics, and Whites. The focus is on the hiring actions of the teams, and on whether the qualifications were applied uniformly to all who became managers, rather than on the behaviors of individuals seeking managerial positions.

Historically, employers have used two methods to screen out and discriminate against applicants for certain positions. Applicants [first] may be asked to possess some non-job-related attributes. Courts have continually ruled that employers must demonstrate that the requirements for a job must be essential for its successful completion.

Second, these job-related requirements must be applied equally to all applicants. Personnel management law is replete with edicts that standards must be applied equally in diverse areas such as hiring, firing, compensation, and benefits. In fact, current human resource management theory posits

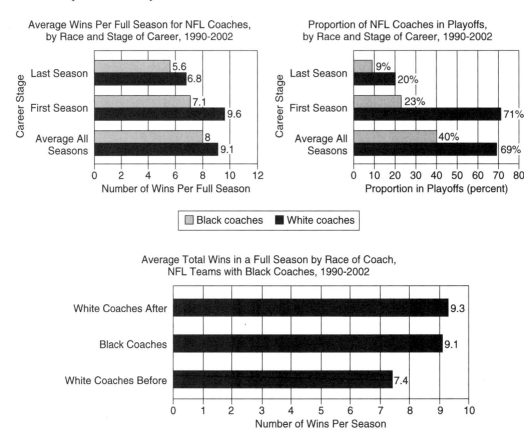

Source: Madden, "Differences in the Success of NFL Coaches by Race 1990-2002: Evidence of Last Hire, First Fire," (March 28, 2003)

Figure 1.   Black vs. White Coaching Success in NFL.

that other functions, such as performance appraisal, also suffer when dissimilar standards are used to evaluate employees. Employers have been able to defend their personnel actions when they have been able to demonstrate that the qualifications are job related and applied equally to all applicants.

. . . This study attempts to determine whether the job-related requirements were applied equally to all who became managers between 1975 and 1994. In this manner, we would have some indication as to how the courts might rule should an individual seek legal remedies against a team alleging discriminatory hiring/promotion practices.

This is accomplished by comparing the prior job-related work experiences of Whites, Blacks, and Hispanics who were managers during the past 20 years, 1975–1994. The purpose of this study is to ascertain whether White, Black, and Hispanic professional baseball players had to possess different attributes to be hired as major league managers. Further, I discuss the extent to which these different hiring standards may preclude or facilitate future success as a manager.

Managerial Skills, Knowledge, and Abilities

Managers need to possess a knowledge of baseball so that they can make strategic decisions as the game progresses. This normally involves setting the starting lineup, determining the starting pitching rotation, and determining when to pinch hit, remove the pitcher, and numerous other options (steal, hit-and-run, etc.) that may occur during a game. Whereas the average fan may have some rudimentary understanding of these aspects of the game, the manager is expected to make these decisions while being cognizant of his team's abilities as well as what the opposition will do to counter his actions. This knowledge of the game can be gained by anybody playing the game. It is not limited to those who play for specific teams or at certain positions.

Managers also serve as teachers, assisting their players in some of the finer points of the game. Aspects of hitting, fielding, and pitching are all within the purview of the manager. It is common to hear players give credit to their managers and to see photographs in the newspapers (particularly during spring training) of a manager holding a bat and demonstrating a swing or gripping a bat while a circle of players is gathered around him. Managers must also possess leadership abilities. Although their specific styles may differ, managers must be able to instill in their players the confidence and loyalty to perform at their peak performance levels. The ability to teach and be an effective leader is not limited to certain types of players. The literature on both teaching and leadership indicates that there is more than one effective style, and a cursory review of baseball history indicates that infielders, outfielders, pitchers, and catchers have been effective managers.

Whereas knowledge of the job, knowledge of the jobs of those they supervise (the players), and the ability to lead are quite similar to the case of generic management, baseball is unique in that the prior job-related experiences of managers (as players and/or coaches) are readily available and easily quantifiable. The ability to quantify performance has been an essential part of the studies on salary discrimination. Here, however, prior records are evaluated in terms of qualifications for the job as manager. Three distinct prior job-related experiences are analyzed. Specifically, I compare the records of the managers as players, focusing on longevity and several career performance statistics to measure their knowledge of Major League Baseball and potential ability to be major league managers.

Longevity provides the individual with a greater opportunity to learn about the game, leadership techniques, and the like. Managerial experience at the minor league level is used to assess previous opportunities to exercise leadership, and major league coaching background is used as a measure of their teaching and instructional expertise.

The Managerial Pool, 1975–1994

Between 1975 and 1994, 140 different individuals held the position of manager of a Major League Baseball team. Of these 140, 39 had managed prior to 1975; Frank Robinson was the only new manager to begin the 1975 season. In 1975, there were 24 teams. Two teams were added to the American League in 1977, and two teams were added to the National League in 1993. During this 20-year time period, major league teams changed managers 210 times, creating an average of more than 10 opportunities per year for major league teams to hire new managers. Of the 24 managers who started the 1975 season, none was managing the same team at the conclusion of the 1994 season. Of the original 24 managers in 1975, 20 were subsequently rehired by other teams after being terminated. There was a constant turnover of managers, thus providing ample opportunity for the hiring of Black and Hispanic managers.

Of the 140 managers, there were 7 Black managers (Don Baylor, Dusty Baker, Larry Doby, Cito Gaston, Hal McRae, Frank Robinson, and Maury Wills) and 5 foreign-born Hispanic managers (Felipe Alou, Preston Gomez, Marty Martinez, Tony Perez, and Cookie Rojas). *[See Table 2.]* In addition, 12 individuals managed fewer than 42 games or 25% of a full season. Marty Martinez, who managed 1 game with Seattle in 1986, is the only Black or Hispanic who managed fewer than 42 games. Many of these individuals who managed a limited number of games were hired on an interim basis. This is taken into account when I compare their managerial experiences.

TABLE 2.

RACIAL DIFFERENCES IN MANAGERIAL SELECTION		
Major League Baseball managers: 1975–1994		
	Number	*Percentage*
White	128	91.4
Black	7	5.0
Hispanic	5	3.6
Total	140	100.0
Major League Baseball managers and Major League playing experience: 1975–1994		
	Number	*Years*
White	89	9.0
Black	7	16.6
Hispanic	5	12.8
All managers	101	9.8
Managers with major league playing experience		
	Total	*Major League Experience*	*Percentage*
White	128	103	80.4
Black	7	7	100.0
Hispanic	5	5	100.0
Total	140	115	82.1

Source: Edward Rimer, "Discrimination in Major League Baseball: Hiring Standards for Major League Managers, 1975–1994." *Journal of Sport and Social Issues,* May 1996: 20(2), p. 123.

RESULTS

Managers as Major League Players

The most notable prerequisite to being a major league manager is to have played in the major leagues. By performing at the major league level, players demonstrate their abilities under the most repetitive conditions and gain firsthand knowledge of how the game is played and the performance required to succeed at the highest level.

Of the 140 managers, 25 never played at the major league level. Of the remaining 115, 6 were pitchers. Consistent with earlier findings, most played second base or short stop (47), followed by catcher (25). . . . All 25 who did not have major league experience as players were White. All 6 managers who were pitchers in the major leagues were White.

A comparison of the experience of White, Black, and Hispanic managers as major league players reveals that the Black and Hispanic managers have had more extensive and productive careers than have their White counterparts. This is true even after eliminating from the comparison all of the White managers who never played at the major league level. . . .

Even after excluding White managers who never played at the major league level and therefore raising the mean experience for Whites, Black managers have approximately twice as much major league experience as do White managers (i.e., 84% longer, 136% more games, and 159% more at bats). The major league careers of Hispanic managers are 42% longer, having played in 72% more games and with 82% more plate appearances.

Because there is a limited number of Black and Hispanic managers compared to White managers, and because the analysis includes the entire population, no test for statistical significance was performed. I did calculate the standard deviation of each mean to reveal the extent to which there is variation within the White, Black, and Hispanic managers. The greatest variance is among the Hispanic managers, whereas the least is among the Black managers.

As with career longevity, Black and Hispanic managers outperformed the White managers in all offensive categories [as major league players]. Blacks, on average, scored more than twice as many runs and had 176% more hits, 406% more home runs, 249% more runs batted in, and a batting average 7% higher than did White managers. Hispanics also outperformed White managers, but not to the same extent as did the Black managers: 88% more runs, 91% more hits, 163% more home runs, 120% more runs batted in, and a batting average 5% higher than those of White managers. Interestingly, there is less variance among White managers regarding the performance criteria, with Hispanics showing the greatest variance.

Minor League Managerial Experience

In addition to being a player, managing at the minor league level is often considered a prerequuisite for obtaining a major league managerial job. It is as a manager that the individual gains experience in game strategy, leadership, and interactions with team administration. Of the 140 managers, almost 70% had managed at the minor league level. . . .

Felipe Alou, Frank Robinson, and Preston Gomez are the only minority major league managers with prior experience as minor league managers. . . .

Whereas the length of experience and performance appears similar, the percentage of Blacks and Hispanics with minor league managerial experience is less than the percentage of Whites with minor league managerial experience. The variance between those who have managed at the minor league level is also similar.

. . . .

DISCUSSION

Standard employment practices compel employers to demonstrate that requirements for a position are job related and that such job requirements are applied equally to all candidates for the position. Baseball managers need to have a knowledge of the game, the ability to teach, and the ability to lead. I identified three prior job-related experiences that are likely to provide the individual with these necessary skills, knowledge, and abilities: major league playing experience, minor league managerial experience, and major league coaching experience.

All but one of the men who managed between 1975 and 1994 had some experience as either a major league player, a minor league manager, or a coach of a major league team. The lone exception, Atlanta Braves owner Ted Turner, managed for one game in 1977. It thus appears that these three conditions are used by teams as part of the hiring process and are considered to be job-related prerequisites for employment as a manager. It is also evident from the analysis that these three qualifications are not considered to be an absolute requirement. Only 55 of the 140 managers (39%) had experience in all three areas studied. Some combination of playing experience, minor league managerial experience, and major league coaching experience is deemed appropriate to be hired as a manager.

The requirement that a manager have major league playing experience was not applied equally to all who were managers between 1975 and 1994. All Black and Hispanic managers had to have played at the major league level and had to have had longer and more productive careers as players than was the case with White managers. This is true even after eliminating from consideration the 25 White managers who never played major league baseball. Only 80% of the White managers had major league playing experience, whereas 100% of the minority managers had performed at the major league level. The data reveal that heightened expectations regarding length of time in the major leagues were applied consistently to all Black managers.

Previous studies would lead one to conclude that this difference in the performance standards is attributable to position segregation. Seven of the minority managers were primarily outfielders (58% of all minority managers as compared to only 9% of White managers were outfielders), and outfielders have consistently had to be more productive in terms of offensive performance. The data reveal, however, that minority outfielders who became managers had longer and more productive careers than did White outfielders who became managers.

. . . .

Between 1975 and 1994, only 18 outfielders became managers. This is consistent with previous research regarding position centrality. However, the total playing, coaching, and minor league managerial experience of minority and White outfielders is different. The minority outfielder/managers spent an average of 23 years as player, coach, and minor league manager; whereas the average was 17 years for the White outfielders with major league playing experience who became managers. There were several White managers who were outfielders but had not played at the major league level.

Minority outfielders who became managers were coaches for an average of 4 years, whereas the White outfielder/managers were coaches for an average of 2 years. Only 28% of the minority outfielder/managers had minor league managerial experience, whereas 55% of the White outfielder/

managers managed at the minor league level. The average number of years of managing in the minor leagues was almost equal: 1.8 for the minority outfielders and 2.7 for the White outfielders. The limited number of Black or Hispanic managers who played positions other than outfielder precludes any meaningful comparison to the White managers.

The data show that no marginal Black players, either those who did not make it to the major leagues or those who had limited major league careers, were ever selected to be major league managers during the past 20 years. Although it is not known with any certainty who may have applied for these positions, there are several Blacks with limited playing careers who became coaches but never became managers (e.g., Tommie Aaron, Gene Baker, Curt Motton, and, most recently, Tom Reynolds).

A cursory look at the White managers who did not play at the major league level indicates that a lengthy playing career cannot be considered an essential prerequisite for superior performance as a manager. Two of the more successful managers in the past and present, Earl Weaver and Jim Leyland, are among the 25 who never played Major League Baseball. This leads one to consider the impact on the effectiveness of minority managers who, it appears, are required to possess certain characteristics that are not necessarily correlated with success as a manager. Further analysis of the relationship between a manager's playing career and managerial record is necessary.

The situation is somewhat reversed when we examine managerial experience in the minor leagues. Although it is the weakest of the three elements (only 69% of all managers had minor league managerial experience), the majority of Black and Hispanic managers did not have an opportunity to manage in the minor leagues. The length and performance of those who did are similar for Blacks, Whites, and Hispanics.

Star players may be hesitant to spend time in the minor leagues, even if it is as the manager of the team. Data on player performance at the major league level indicate that most of the minority managers could be considered star players. Offers to coach at the major league level may appeal to both the player and team, as the player is more visible to the fans. It should be noted that there are numerous star White players who became managers without first obtaining managerial experience in the minor leagues. Yogi Berra, Alvin Dark, Toby Harrah, and Pete Rose are some of the more prominent to follow this career path. Further study is needed to determine the extent to which being a minor league manager provides invaluable experience that is not obtained by either playing or coaching.

. . . .

The large variance in the means for player longevity, performance categories, and years and games managed in the minor leagues indicates the absence of precise prerequisite criteria. A total of 65 managers (46%) had experience in two of the three categories. In addition, 20 were players and minor league managers, 30 were players and had prior coaching experience, and 15 had managed minor league teams and coached. Previous studies of managerial performance have taken into account the abilities of the players managed and the teams' won–lost records (Horowitz, 1994; Jacobs & Singell, 1993; Kahn, 1993; Porter & Scully, 1982), and neglected to include the backgrounds of the individual managers. Porter and Scully's evaluation of managers with 5 or more years of experience between 1961 and 1980 determined that Earl Weaver, Sparky Anderson, and Walter Alston were the most efficient. Horowitz's methodology also concluded that Weaver and Alston were among the best major league managers. Given that these three had limited, if any, major league experience as players (Alston, 1 at bat; Anderson, 1 year with 477 at bats; Weaver, no major league playing experience), we should be cautious before assuming that playing can substitute for minor league [managing] or coaching experience. To the extent that Blacks and Hispanics have longer playing careers and limited coaching and previous managerial experience, they may be at a disadvantage in terms of the training and background necessary to succeed as a manager. Further study is needed to determine what combination of the three job-related activities is most closely related to superior performance as a manager. Additionally, further study is needed to determine whether and to what extent the position played at the major league or minor league level affects the number of years considered appropriate experience and, therefore, the need to be a minor league manager or major league coach before becoming a major league manager.

This study examined the background of all major league managers from 1975 through 1994. Specifically, it compared the playing records, minor league managerial experience, and coaching experience of all those who managed during the past 20 years. All but one (Ted Turner, a team owner) had some combination of the specified job-related experiences. We can thus conclude that these criteria are considered by owners when they hire managers. The amount of experience required as a player, minor league manager, or coach was different for Black, White, and Hispanic managers. Blacks and Hispanics had longer and more productive careers as players than did their White counterparts. Further, there were differences between the minority and White outfielders who became managers. A comparison of the playing careers of the minority and White outfielders who became managers revealed that the minority outfielder/managers outperformed the Whites in all offensive categories and had nearly an identical batting average. Minority managers tended to be outfielders, a position in which they are overrepresented but a position that has produced a limited number of managers. Black and Hispanic managers had less minor league managerial experience than did White managers and had similar experience as major league coaches. It would appear that major league baseball teams, although using appropriate job-related criteria in the hiring of managers, did not apply these criteria in an equitable manner.

REFERENCES

1. Horowitz, I. (1994). Pythagoras, Tommy Lasorda, and me: On evaluating baseall managers. *Social Science Quarterly, 75,* 187–194.
2. Jacobs, D., & Singell, L. (1993). Leadership and organizational performance: Isolating links between managers and collective success. *Social Science Research, 22,* 165–189.
3. Kahn, L. (1993). Managerial quality, team success, and individual player performance in major league baseball. *Industrial and Labor Relations Review, 46,* 531–547.
4. Porter, P., & Scully, G. (1982). Measuring managerial efficiency: The case of baseball. *Southern Economic Journal, 49,* 642–650.

DIVERSITY, RACISM, AND PROFESSIONAL SPORTS FRANCHISE OWNERSHIP: CHANGE MUST COME FROM WITHIN

Kenneth L. Shropshire

One possible path for decreasing actual or perceived racism against African Americans in any business setting is to increase African American ownership. The broad assumption underlying the advocacy of this remedy is that increased diversity in the ownership of an industry will decrease occurrences of discrimination.

. . . .

II. IDEAL STATE: VALUE OF DIVERSITY IN OWNERSHIP

A. General Benefit

What would be the primary benefits of greater African American ownership in professional sports? Two of the major benefits would be (1) the social value of diversity and (2) the financial value of diversity. The social value of diversity consists of both the actual value that diversity can bring to an enterprise through the presentation of different points of view and the perceived value that diversity may have in improving the image of an almost all white ownership. The financial value of diversity includes allowing minorities access to a piece of the lucrative sports ownership pie and front office employment, expanding the individual franchise revenues by attracting more fan support and attendance from minorities, and bringing about equity in player salaries without regard to race.

. . . . *[The author's discussion of the actual and perceived values of diversity is omitted.]*

C. Ownership Glass Ceilings and Differential Racism

Glass ceilings are present in much of American society. Part of the reason for the existence of such ceilings is the discomfort that many white Americans feel with African Americans in positions of power. African Americans may not be treated dramatically differently by whites in the business setting until they seek a position of power — until they seek to break through the glass ceiling. This has been referred to as a form of "differential racism." The best recent example of America's glass ceilings may have been Colin Powell's contemplation of running for the presidency of the United States. Although Powell undoubtedly held many of the traditional qualifications for the office, he hesitated and eventually decided not to run. Given the tremendous media attention paid to Powell's African American heritage, part of his thought process in deciding whether to run presumably included the role that his race plays in how people view him. The question Powell apparently heard many asking was whether a black man could really hold the top job in the world.

. . . .

Just as this glass ceiling, or differential racism, may be the reason for an absence of African Americans in top-level positions on the field in sports, in politics, in corporate America, and in the entertainment industry, glass ceilings that keep African Americans from acquiring ownership interests in sports franchises probably exist as well.

III. LEGAL RECOURSE: CAN THE LAW COMPEL DIVERSITY?

. . . . One may question whether existing law provides any possible causes of action or remedies by which to increase diversity and African American ownership of professional sports franchises. The conclusion is that present law can only play a limited role in bringing about increased African American ownership in professional sports.

. . . . *[The author's discussion of affirmative action and other applicable laws is omitted.]*

It cannot be disputed that trust and confidence among fellow owners of a sports league is desirable for the efficiency and success of the league. A bad choice can doom the partnership. There are thirty *[now 32]* or fewer franchises in each of the professional leagues. Consequently, individuals who enter into a partnership or who expand their partnerships are very selective of whom they permit to join, and the courts are aware of this selectivity. The necessary trust and confidence will not exist if the partnership is compelled by force of law to admit an individual whom the partnership does not want. There will just be too much bad blood and distrust. Once a legal action is brought, the possibility that the petitioner and the partners could work together harmoniously is minimal. Moreover, such legal action could jeopardize the partnership. This is why reinstatement is a disfavored remedy for high-level employees, both in the employment and partnership contexts, and why a judicial mandate of minority sports franchise ownership is even more unlikely.

Thus, antidiscrimination law provides only limited protections to minorities seeking to own professional sports franchises. Title VII does not apply directly, because there will normally not be an existing employer–employee relationship at stake, and Section 1981 only prevents owners from flagrantly discriminating on the basis of race in choosing their co-owners.

. . . .

As it currently stands, the law is clear that the owners in a given league may sell or grant franchises to whomever they choose, and, provided nothing in their decision-making process violates any . . . laws . . . , no legal action can force the existing owners to sell to a particular group. The plaintiffs in . . . two cases based their actions on antitrust laws, arguing against the anti-competitive nature of a league not accepting them as franchise owners. Neither bidder was African American, and neither was successful.

In both the existing franchise purchase and expansion areas, the choice as to which potential owners to bring on board is that of the respective league owners. Just as in any other business, courts are reluctant to compel business owners to take on new partners. So long as the reason for rejection is not illegal, courts are not likely to intervene.

   . . . . *[The author's discussion of the impact of litigation and litigation threats is omitted.]*

IV. WILL IT HAPPEN?: NEED FOR VOLUNTARY EFFORTS

As the previous section indicates, courts are not likely to interpret existing law as a mandate to compel existing professional club owners to admit minority ownership into their league memberships without flagrant racism. . . . What is likely to be much more effective — at least in the short term — is increased commitment from existing owners and players to recognize the important benefits that diverse ownership in sports can bring about.

V. CONCLUSION

There are many difficulties in breaking African Americans into the ownership ranks of professional sports. The greatest obstacles are not financial but structural. The owners themselves must somehow be compelled to desire change; however, they likely suffer from the same levels of conscious and unconscious racism as the rest of society. Indeed, the issues discussed in this article are applicable to businesses beyond sports.

The key barrier to change is the legally protected clubbiness of the owners. They have the nearly exclusive right to select their co-owners. There is no requirement, unless self-imposed, that the owners accept the best financial offer. As a group, the owners of any league certainly could mandate that any multiowner group seeking a franchise must include African American investors. The NFL took a step in this regard with the new Jacksonville franchise, in which African American and former NFL player Deron Cherry has an ownership interest. Similarly, Charlotte African American businessman Bill Simms is part of the ownership group for the Charlotte franchise.

It will be difficult to use legal pressure to compel greater African American ownership. No current legislation on either the state or federal level regulates sports franchise ownership. Given the constitutional problems that would arise if such legislation were implemented and the recent public backlash against affirmative action in general, it does not appear that the lack of diversity in franchise ownership will be addressed by statute. In addition, although Section 1981 offers protection from flagrant discrimination, it is ineffective to put any real pressure on the owners to diversify their group.

The burden is thus on league leaders and the athletes to bring about such change.

SALARIES

THE SPORTS BUSINESS AS A
LABOR MARKET LABORATORY

Lawrence M. Kahn

Among the forms of discrimination in sports, salary discrimination is the most studied issue. The typical research design — similar to much work in this area in labor economics — is a regression in which log salary is the dependent variable, and the independent variables include performance indicators, team characteristics, and market characteristics, with a dummy variable for white race. If the coefficient on the white indicator is positive and significant, then this potentially offers evidence of discrimination. Alternatively, some researchers have used separate regressions for white and nonwhite players, testing the possibility that performance is rewarded differently by race.

A major difficulty for all labor market research on discrimination is the problem of unobserved or mismeasured variables, such as the quality of schooling among workers in general. However, such problems must surely be less severe in sports than elsewhere. For example, the *Baseball Encyclopedia* and other baseball data sources allow one to control for very detailed performance indicators like batting average, stolen bases, home runs, career length, team success, and many more. "Occupation" in baseball is one's position, a far more detailed indicator than, say, "machine operative." The accuracy of the compensation data in sports, in many cases supplied by the relevant players' union that keeps copies of the actual player contracts, is very high.

The sport where regression analyses have produced the most evidence of salary discrimination is professional basketball. In the mid-1980s, several studies found statistically significant black salary shortfalls of 11–25 percent after controlling for a variety of performance and market-related statistics (for example, Kahn and Sherer, 1988; Koch and Vander Hill, 1988; Wallace, 1988; Brown, Spiro, and Keenan, 1991).* However, by the mid-1990s, there were no longer any overall significant racial salary

---

* While there may still be omitted variables that could have explained the *ceteris paribus* white salary advantage, reverse regression tests, which can under some restricted circumstances take account of such problems (Goldberger, 1984), showed even larger apparent discrimination coefficients against black players (Kahn and Sherer, 1988). In fact, these larger effects suggest that black players had better unmeasured productivity characteristics than whites, at least under the statistical assumptions outlined by Goldberger (1984).

differentials in the NBA, holding performance constant (Hamilton, 1997; Dey, 1997; Bodvarsson and Brastow, 1998). One caveat to this finding is seen in Hamilton's (1997) results from quantile regressions, which estimate the extent of discrimination at different points of the salary distribution, conditional on productivity. He did not find evidence of discrimination at the 10th, 25th, and 50th salary percentiles, but there was a significant white salary premium of about 20 percent, other things equal, at the 75th percentile of the salary distribution and above.*

Customer preferences may have something to do with the racial pay gap observed in basketball in the 1980s. For example, Kahn and Sherer (1988) found that, all else equal, during the 1980–86 period each white player generated 5,700 to 13,000 additional fans per year. The dollar value of this extra attendance more than made up for the white salary premium, a finding consistent with the existence of monopsony. Other researchers found a close match between the racial makeup of NBA teams in the 1980s and of the areas where they were located, again suggesting the importance of customer preferences (Brown, Spiro, and Keenan, 1991; Burdekin and Idson, 1991; Hoang and Rascher, 1999). However, by the 1990s, customer preferences for white players were less evident. Dey (1997), for example, found that all else equal, white players added a statistically insignificant 60 fans apiece per season during the 1987–93 period. This evidence is consistent with the decline in the NBA's overall unexplained white salary premium from the 1980s to the 1990s, although Hamilton's (1997) results suggest that it is possible that white stars add fans even if the average white player does not.

If NBA fans do have preferences for white players, having white benchwarmers may be a cheap way for teams to satisfy such demands. While early research found that white benchwarmers had longer careers than black benchwarmers (Johnson and Marple, 1973), more recent work does not find that benchwarmers are disproportionately white (Scott, Long, and Somppi, 1985).

In contrast to these findings in basketball, similar regression analyses of salaries in baseball and football have not found much evidence of racial salary discrimination against minorities. For example, in baseball, these kinds of analyses never seem to find a significantly positive salary premium for white players. Among nonpitchers, some studies actually have found significantly negative effects of being white in the late 1970s and 1980s (Christiano, 1986, 1988; Irani, 1996); however, my own reanalysis of the same data used in one of these studies found that these differentials disappeared when a longer list of productivity variables was added (Kahn, 1993). In football in 1989, Kahn (1992) found only very small salary premia (discrimination coefficients) in favor of whites of only 1–4 percent, and these differences were usually not statistically significant. However, nonwhite NFL players earned more in areas with a larger relative nonwhite population than nonwhites elsewhere, and whites earned more in more white metropolitan areas than whites elsewhere. These findings suggest the influence of customers, but they did not add up to large overall racial salary differences in the NFL.†

---

* Logically, if there is no *ceteris paribus* pay gap on average, and white stars receive a premium, then blacks at the bottom should earn more than whites. Hamilton (1997) finds point estimates in this direction, but they are not statistically significant.

† A lively literature has developed on the issue of discrimination against French Canadians in the National Hockey League. Some authors have found apparent salary discrimination against this group in Canadian cities outside Quebec province, a pattern consistent with the notion of customer discrimination (Jones and Walsh, 1988; Longley, 1995). Yet others have disputed this interpretation and the findings as well (Krashinsky and Krashinsky, 1997). There is also a debate over whether French Canadians face entry barriers into the NHL (Walsh, 1992; Lavoie, Grenier, and Coulombe, 1992).

Although little evidence exists of a discriminatory salary premium in baseball or football, there is evidence of other forms of discrimination in sports, some of it among customers, and also in hiring, retention, and assignment of players. For example, a larger number of white players seem to lead to added baseball fans, over the time period from the mid-1950s through the 1980s (Hanssen, 1998; Irani, 1996). Moreover, baseball cards for white players sold at a significantly higher price than those of comparable black players in 1989 (Nardinelli and Simon, 1990).

On hiring, there is indirect evidence that black players went later in the NFL draft than whites of equal playing ability during the 1986–91 period (Conlin and Emerson, 1998). However, in basketball, a study found only small, insignificant racial differences in draft order among NBA players on rosters in 1985, conditional on college performance — and these differences favored black players (Kahn and Sherer, 1988). All studies of drafts suffer somewhat from the fact that there is no systematic information available on those not drafted and not on rosters.

On player retention, Jiobu (1988) found that from 1971 to 1985, black players in Major League Baseball had a significantly higher exit rate than whites, other things equal, and Hoang and Rascher (1999) obtained a similar result for the NBA for 1980–91. A reasonable interpretation of these differences in exit rates is that they reflect team decisions not to offer players a new contract. Whether this disparity held up in the 1990s or whether the effects are similar for benchwarmers and more regular players are interesting questions for future researchers.

REFERENCES

1. Bodvarsson, Orn and Raymond T. Brastow. 1998. "Do Employers Pay for Consistent Performance?: Evidence from the NBA." *Economic Inquiry.* 36:1, pp. 145–60.

2. Brown, Eleanor, Richard Spiro, and Diane Keenan. 1991. "Wage and Nonwage Discrimination in Professional Basketball: Do Fans Affect It?" *American Journal of Economics and Sociology.* 50:3, pp. 333–45.

3. Burdekin, Richard C. K. and Todd L. Idson. 1991. "Customer Preferences, Attendance and the Racial Structure of Professional Basketball Teams." *Applied Economics.* 23:1, Part B, pp. 179–86.

4. Christiano, Kevin J. 1986. "Salary Discrimination in Major League Baseball: The Effect of Race." *Sociology of Sport Journal.* 3:2, pp. 144–53.

5. Christiano, Kevin J. 1988. "Salaries and Race in Professional Baseball: Discrimination 10 Years Later." *Sociology of Sport Journal.* 5:2, pp. 136–49.

6. Conlin, Mike and Patrick M. Emerson. 1998. "Racial Discrimination and Organizational Form: A Study of the National Football League." Working Paper, Cornell University.

7. Dey, Matthew S. 1997. "Racial Differences in National Basketball Association Players' Salaries: Another Look." *The American Economist.* 41:2, pp. 84–90.

8. Goldberger, Arthur S. 1984. "Reverse Regression and Salary Discrimination." *Journal of Human Resources.* 19:3, pp. 293–318.

9. Hamilton, Barton Hughes. 1997. "Racial Discrimination and Professional Basketball Salaries in the 1990s." *Applied Economics.* 29:3, pp. 287–96.

10. Hanssen, Andrew. 1998. "The Cost of Discrimination: A Study of Major League Baseball." *Southern Economic Journal.* 64:3, pp. 603–27.

11. Hoang, Ha and Dan Rascher. 1999. "The NBA, Exit Discrimination, and Career Earnings." *Industrial Relations.* 38:1, pp. 69–91.

12. Irani, Daraius. 1996. "Estimating Customer Discrimination in Baseball Using Panel Data," in *Baseball Economics: Current Research*. John Fizel, Elizabeth Gustafson, and Lawrence Hadley, eds. Westport, CT.: Praeger, pp. 47–61.

13. Jiobu, Robert M. 1988. "Racial Inequality in a Public Arena: The Case of Professional Baseball." *Social Forces*. 67:2, pp. 524–34.

14. Johnson, Norris R. and David P. Marple. 1973. "Racial Discrimination in Professional Basketball: An Empirical Test." *Sociological Focus*. 6:4, pp. 6–18.

15. Jones, J. C. H. and William D. Walsh. 1988. "Salary Determination in the National Hockey League: The Effects of Skills, Franchise Characteristics, and Discrimination." *Industrial & Labor Relations Review*. 41:4, pp. 592–604.

16. Kahn, Lawrence M. 1992. "The Effects of Race on Professional Football Players' Compensation." *Industrial & Labor Relations Review*. 45:2, pp. 295–310.

17. Kahn, Lawrence M. 1993. "Free Agency, Long-term Contracts and Compensation in Major League Baseball; Estimates from Panel Data." *The Review of Economics and Statistics*. 75:1, pp. 157–64.

18. Kahn, Lawrence M. and Peter D. Sherer. 1988. "Racial Differences in Professional Basketball Players' Compensation." *Journal of Labor Economics*. 6:1, pp. 40–61.

19. Koch, James V. and C. Warren Vander Hill. 1988. "Is There Discrimination in the 'Black Man's Game'?" *Social Science Quarterly*. 69:1, pp. 83–94.

20. Krashinsky, Michael and Harry A. Krashinsky. 1997. "Do English Canadian Hockey Teams Discriminate Against French Canadian Players?" *Canadian Public Policy-Analyse de Politiques*. 23:2, pp. 212–6.

21. Lavoie, Marc, Gilles Grenier, and Serge Coulombe. 1992. "Performance Differentials in the National Hockey League: Discrimination Versus Style-of-Play Thesis." *Canadian Public Policy-Analyse de Politiques*. 18:4, pp. 461–69.

22. Longley, Neil. 1995. "Salary Discrimination in the National Hockey League: The Effects of Team Location." *Canadian Public Policy-Analyse de Politiques*. 21:4, pp. 413–22.

23. Nardinelli, Clark and Curtis Simon. 1990. "Customer Racial Discrimination in the Market for Memorabilia: The Case of Baseball." *Quarterly Journal of Economics*. 105:3, pp. 575–95.

24. Scott, Jr., Frank A., James E. Long, and Ken Somppi. 1985. "Salary vs. Marginal Revenue Product Under Monopoly and Competition: The Case of Professional Basketball." *Atlantic Economic Journal*. September 13:3, pp. 50–59.

25. Wallace, Michael. 1988. "Labor Market Structure and Salary Determination Among Professional Basketball Players." *Work and Occupations*. 15:3, pp. 294–312.

26. Walsh, William D. 1992. "The Entry Problem of Francophones in the National Hockey League: A Systemic Interpretation." *Canadian Public Policy-Analyse de Politiques*. 18:4, pp. 443–60.

THE GLOBALIZATION OF BASEBALL: A LATIN AMERICAN PERSPECTIVE

Angel Vargas

INTRODUCTION

The global reach of Major League Baseball (MLB) has never been more evident. MLB has been engaging in high-profile efforts to globalize America's pastime by staging exhibition and regular season games in foreign nations, such as the Dominican Republic, Mexico, Venezuela, Cuba, and Japan. The presence of foreign players, especially those from Latin American countries, is at an all-time high. . . . In the globalization of baseball, Latin American countries, particularly the Dominican Republic and Venezuela, are at the forefront of MLB teams' attention and activities as they deepen their search for the next generation of Latino superstars.

Virtually everything about the globalization of baseball that comes out of the MLB Commissioner's Office in New York is, however, one-sided propaganda. A critical Latin American perspective has been missing from the discourse about the globalization of baseball. The most serious problem today is the lack of MLB interest in, and respect for, what people in Latin America perceive as the problem with the way MLB teams behave in Latin America. In this Article, I provide my perspective as a Venezuelan active in the world of professional baseball on MLB mistreatment of Latin Americans.

My arguments do not depend on academic theories about globalization, or flow from nostalgic myths about baseball as a national pastime, but arise out of MLB mistreatment of Latino children and their parents that unfortunately I and my Latin American colleagues see almost every day. I am the President of the Venezuelan Baseball Players Association (Association). Since 1988, I have been working with the Association on behalf of Venezuelan baseball players. I also serve as the General Secretary of the Caribbean Baseball Players Confederation, which represents professional baseball players from the Dominican Republic, Puerto Rico, Mexico, and Venezuela. My professional baseball experiences also include three years in the U.S. minor leagues, where I played in the Philadelphia Phillies and Boston Red Sox organizations. . . .

In this Article, I lead the reader through the steps by which a typical Venezuelan or Dominican boy with baseball talent becomes involved in professional baseball and with MLB. I analyze four steps in this process: (1) how MLB teams initially contact the boy and his parents (Part I); (2) signing the boy to a MLB professional baseball contract (Part II); (3) the experience of the boy in the "baseball academies" that each year serve as training grounds for hundreds of Latino children (Part III); and (4) the experience of the Latino player if he is lucky enough to play in the U.S. minor or major leagues (Part IV). . . . Most of my arguments focus on the first three steps in this process because that is where the greatest MLB abuses occur. As the process of bringing a Latino boy into professional baseball progresses, the number of recruits affected declines. The initial contacts, signing, and training in baseball academies take place in Latin America. I and those who are involved in professional baseball in Latin America are well-placed to comment on the problems we see daily.

In Part V, I outline responses from key actors in the globalization of baseball that are necessary to solve the problems I discuss. I conclude with a plea to the baseball world to end the discrimination against Latino children and their parents and make equal treatment the norm for MLB in the twenty-first century.

I. INITIAL CONTACT

Historically, initial contacts with Latino children were made by MLB team scouts. Scouts often rely on people known as buscones to help them comb the country for baseball talent. Often the initial contacts are innocent, involving a scout or buscon making favorable comments to parents about a child's performance in a youth league game and giving them his card. The idea is to foster the parents' and the child's loyalty to the team that the scout or buscon represents. With very talented children, the initial contacts can be more serious and intense, involving gifts of uniforms, bats, gloves, and money, or an invitation to attend a baseball academy where the child can train at a big-league facility. Many times the academy is used to hide talented children who are too young to sign from other team scouts and buscones.

MLB scouts and buscones have, for many years, competed fiercely with each other for Latino talent. Today, they face new competitive pressures from agents, who have sensed a market opportunity in the frenzy that MLB teams display trying to find young Latino talent. The rise of agents in the process of initial contacts has good and bad aspects. On the positive side, a qualified, professional agent can act in the best interests of a child and balance the power and influence possessed by MLB teams. Young prospects who are represented by agents usually receive, for example, much higher signing bonuses than players who are not represented. On the negative side, some agents are just as eager as MLB teams to exploit naive, poor children and their families to get a piece of any signing bonus that may come along. The greatest legal concern about how Latino children are contacted is that the actions of scouts, buscones, and agents are unregulated in the two biggest markets: Venezuela and the Dominican Republic. In Venezuela, for example, we do not have laws that adequately regulate the qualifications or activities of scouts and agents. We, as a country, have to change our attitudes about this as the situation is out of control, and we have to take our share of the blame for letting this happen. But we are also deeply disappointed that MLB has not taken any serious action to mitigate the problems that its hunger for cheap Latino talent has created. Let me make clear that MLB knows, and has known for a long time, that these problems exist; but, to date, it prefers the current system because it produces cheaper talent.

II. SIGNING

The next step is signing a Latino child to a professional contract with a MLB team. There are enormous problems with how MLB teams sign Latino children to contracts. The first problem concerns underage signing. MLB teams routinely sign Latino children younger than is permitted by MLB rules. . . . The rule provides that a player who is not subject to the draft and who is not under contract with a MLB team can be signed by any team if (1) he is seventeen years old at the time of signing, or (2) he is sixteen years old at the time of signing and he will turn seventeen prior to the later of (i) the conclusion of the baseball season in which he signed and (ii) September 1 of the year he signs. The seventeen-year-old rule does not apply to players in the United States, Canada, and Puerto Rico, because they are subject to the MLB draft. The rule, thus, applies to children who live in Latin America. MLB teams act, however, as if this rule allows them to sign players immediately when they turn sixteen, but this is not what the rule provides. Thus, many signings that MLB teams trumpet to the world as legal are in fact violations of the MLB rule.

. . . .

Another problem in Venezuela is that MLB signs too many players, most of whom they release within two years. Over-signing players is part of MLB team strategy to get Latino talent as cheaply as possible. Dick Balderson, formerly of the Colorado Rockies, referred to this strategy as the "boat-load mentality": "The boatload mentality means that instead of signing 4 American guys at $25,000 each, you sign 20 Dominicans for $5,000 each." . . .

Another significant problem is that MLB scouts and teams never, to my knowledge, give the children and their parents a Spanish-language version of the contract or give them any Spanish-language document that explains the contract that they are signing. Most of these children and their parents do not speak or read English; yet, they are presented with a lengthy, complex English-language contract and asked to sign.

We also experience problems with signing bonuses. The Association routinely receives calls from players who never received a promised signing bonus or received only part of a promised signing bonus. Scouts sometimes also take a significant chunk of a signing bonus for unspecified reasons not written down in any contract, and unscrupulous agents also ask for fifteen to twenty percent of a signing bonus (agents in the United States can only take five percent). These problems occur routinely despite the fact that signing bonuses for Latino players are significantly less than bonuses received by American players drafted by MLB teams.

III. THE BASEBALL ACADEMIES

Many Latino players who are signed by MLB teams attend so-called "baseball academies" in the Dominican Republic and Venezuela. Most MLB teams have these facilities in these two countries. In Venezuela, twenty-eight of the thirty MLB teams operate academies. The numbers are similar in the Dominican Republic. The scale of MLB involvement in baseball academies means that for years, hundreds of Latino children and young men have passed through these training facilities.

One reason behind the development of baseball academies in Latin American countries is the restricted number of visas available to MLB teams from the U.S. government for foreign baseball players. MLB teams do not have enough visas to send all Latino players to the United States, so academies hoard the promising players by keeping them from other teams that might like to sign them. The visa bottleneck created by the U.S. government has driven the development of the baseball academies.

Many problems exist in connection with these baseball academies, including significant violations of Venezuelan and perhaps Dominican law. The first problem has to do with the ages of players who attend academies. Although MLB rules prohibit MLB teams from signing players younger than seventeen, these rules do not prohibit MLB teams from sending players between the ages of twelve and sixteen to the academies. Such children are not technically employees, because they have not signed a contract, but they nevertheless participate in the full regimen of the academy. It is my experience that in many Dominican and Venezuelan academies, the persons responsible do not treat the players according to their ages. This means that thirteen- and fourteen-year-olds are expected to complete workouts designed for players seventeen years and older. In my opinion, treating boys this way is neither right nor necessary, unless Latino boys are regarded as cheap commodities. But again, this practice is unregulated by MLB and the Dominican Republic and Venezuela.

A second problem is the deplorable conditions in which players live and train in many of these academies. Common complaints that I hear about academies in Venezuela include a lack of:

- security against personal and property crimes;
- consistent and adequate supplies of clean water;
- consistent and adequate sanitary services (e.g., toilets);
- well-maintained buildings;
- sufficient food and nutrition;
- trained medical staff;
- serious educational activities; and
- high-quality playing facilities.

I hear these complaints not only about MLB-run baseball academies but also about the Summer League programs organized by MLB teams in Venezuela and the Dominican Republic, and the so-called "parallel" league organized and operated by Venezuelan professional baseball teams.

To be fair, a small number of baseball academies do not have these problems. I believe that the facilities used by the Houston Astros in Venezuela and by the Los Angeles Dodgers and Oakland A's in the Dominican Republic exhibit none of these problems, because the teams have invested money in the physical facilities and in trained professional staff to manage the enterprise. But I have to stress that these academies are the exception and not the rule in the Dominican Republic and Venezuela. I believe that most MLB teams, in the pursuit of cheap Latino talent, have not bothered to invest in physical facilities or proper management at the academies. The "boatload mentality" is at work in the academies. MLB teams sign many Latino players cheaply and then as cheaply as possible weed out the promising players from the rest.

Particularly disturbing to me is the lack of adequate food and medical attention, because the players work in the academies very hard and expend significant [amounts of] energy. Their bodies need proper nutrition. Yet, I repeatedly hear complaints and stories in Venezuela and the Dominican Republic about academies that provide inadequate food and water to players. I also receive complaints about players who do not receive adequate medical attention after they are injured while playing in academies or on Summer League teams. Often, injured players are immediately released, and MLB teams try to avoid paying for medical costs that the player incurs treating the injury. In addition, firing an employee who is injured on the job is illegal under Venezuelan labor law, as is the refusal to pay for the medical expenses that the employee incurs treating the injury.

MLB rules require that major league clubs provide qualified medical trainers or personnel to their minor league teams. Most academies and Summer League teams have a "trainer," usually someone who has little or no qualifications to treat sports injuries. MLB teams apparently do not require that academy or Summer League team "trainers" be trained to handle baseball injuries. Under Venezuelan law, someone who claims to be a medical trainer must be certified by the government. Here is another example where MLB teams routinely ignore MLB rules and Venezuelan law.

The reader might be wondering why the Association has not taken action to address these problems. The first problem is that the players in the academies and Summer League facilities are not members of the Association. Technically, the Association does not represent their interests; it only represents players in the Venezuelan professional league. The second problem is that, even if the Association did represent these players, it does not have the resources to cope with problems in the academies and Summer League in addition to all the other problems that it faces. The Association staff consists of myself and four other people. That is all. We are under-staffed and under-funded. Despite the representation and resource problems, I have confronted the persons in Venezuela who are responsible for the MLB academies and Summer Leagues only to be told not to interfere, because MLB would "get mad" at me and the Association. Behind this threat was a desire to prevent exposing the entire system to much-needed critical scrutiny.

MLB teams are also violating a host of other Venezuelan laws. To my knowledge, MLB teams do not comply with the following requirements of Venezuelan law:

- If an employee is fired before the employment contract terminates, the employer must pay the rest of the salary due under the contract. MLB teams routinely release players under contract without providing the rest of the salary due under the contract.
- Employers must pay ten days of salary for every three months an employee works. MLB teams do not make such payments to players under contract.
- Companies must make social security payments to the Venezuelan federal government for all Venezuelan employees. MLB teams make no such payments.
- To employ foreign workers in Venezuela, companies must obtain working visas for the workers. MLB teams routinely ignore the working visa requirements for foreign players, such as Dominicans, who play in the academies and in the Summer League.

We also have concerns about how the academies interfere with the education of children in Venezuela. When attendance at the academies occurs during the school year, as it often does, the players have no chance to attend school and a baseball academy. In the academies, MLB teams provide little more than simple English lessons narrowly related to playing baseball. Often the English courses are not mandatory. This situation shows that MLB teams have little interest in educating the Latino children that are brought into the system. Under Venezuelan law, it is arguable that MLB academies are unlawfully interfering with the attendance of children at school. I do not believe that Venezuelan companies can formally or informally employ children and prejudice their attendance at school under law. Why should MLB academies be allowed to do so?

IV. LATINO PLAYERS IN THE MINOR AND MAJOR LEAGUES IN THE UNITED STATES

The overwhelming majority of Latino children brought into the MLB system through initial contacts, signing, and the academies never make it to the United States to play in the minor or major leagues. The attrition rate for Latinos who make the minor leagues in the United States is also very high. One problem created by this high attrition rate is the large number of illegal immigrants in the United States who were once part of the minor leagues but who were cut from the teams. . . .

But even for the Latino player who survives to secure a place in the minor or major leagues, the problems continue. I do not discuss these problems in detail, because other authors. . . . have analyzed these problems with more authority than I could. But I mention briefly some important problems that Latino players face in the minor and major leagues in the United States:

- There is deeply ingrained prejudice against Latino players in MLB. Latino major leaguers routinely say that they are treated under a different, tougher standard than American players.
- Latino players face cultural obstacles that do not confront American players. Making the cultural transition from the Dominican Republic or Venezuela to life in the United States is very difficult for Latino players, because they often do not have the language and other skills to make a successful transition.
- Increasingly, Latino players in both the minor and major leagues are having difficulty obtaining visas for their families to come to the United States during the North American baseball season. Isolation from family members exacerbates the difficulties Latinos face in succeeding in las Grandes Ligas and the minor leagues.

Latino major league players often find that there are no career opportunities for them in MLB when their active playing careers are over. MLB teams have systematically denied Latino players opportunities to coach, manage, and be a part of baseball management, despite the importance of Latino players to the success of MLB teams. This is a different type of "boatload mentality": after the teams are finished with the players, put the players back on the boat and send them home.

V. NEEDED RESPONSES

I offer some solutions:

The MLB Commissioner's Office must credibly sanction MLB teams for misbehavior in Latin American countries. What I criticize in this Article has been widely known in MLB circles for many years, but the Commissioner's Office has done little to curb the abuses. In February 2000, I met with a very senior official from the Commissioner's Office. I expressed my opinions about the problems created by MLB teams in Venezuela and the Dominican Republic. His response was the response I have heard a hundred times: "We are aware of the problems, and we are working on them." The first half of his statement is correct, but I have seen no serious evidence of the Commissioner's Office working to resolve these problems in a systematic way.

Scouts, MLB teams, MLB academies, and agents must be better regulated by governments. Right now, the system is out of control and exploitative. The system is not characterized by respect for the rule of law or by respect for Latino children and their families. In Venezuela, support is growing for a baseball law to halt many of the current abuses. Our President, Hugo Chavez, has expressed interest in this proposed legal reform, and newly-elected national legislators have also expressed a desire to adopt such a baseball law. It is my hope that this baseball law can become a model for other Latin American countries and form the template for a global baseball law.

The MLBPA could assist the efforts of the Association and the Caribbean Confederation by voicing clearer and stronger opposition to MLB team actions in Latin America. Cross-border labor union solidarity is often necessary in the era of globalization to cope with the mistreatment of laborers in many fields of economic activity. We need such solidarity in the face of the globalization of baseball.

Major league Latin American baseball players, especially the very big stars, should speak out. These superstars have status and influence in their home countries that can be used to improve MLB treatment of Latino children and their parents. I realize that these players are not trained social activists, but I believe that Latin Americans must take responsibility for what we have allowed to happen to us.

CONCLUSION

. . . . I ask the baseball world to support my plea for equal treatment for internationally recognized standards that should be applied to all baseball prospects regardless of their race or national origin. . . .

DISCUSSION QUESTIONS

1. Is there any analogy with the alleged treatment of young athletes in Latin America and the treatment of inner city youth by those in search of basketball talent?

2. What is a counterargument to the negative portrayal of the baseball academies in Latin America?

3. Is there any applicability of the solutions presented regarding the treatment of Latin American athletes to inner city basketball youth? Is there applicability to Eastern European basketball players? What about Japanese and Korean baseball players?

4. What use can sports business leaders make of the statistics presented in the Rimer article?

5. Is there business value to increased minority sports franchise ownership?

6. Not too long ago, a key diversity issue was the absence of African-American NFL quarterbacks. Why has that issue, and many related player diversity issues, largely disappeared?

7. Why doesn't the law compel greater diversity at the ownership level?

8. What impact does the addition of two owners of color — Arturo Moreno and Robert Johnson — have on the overall sports diversity picture?

9. Why are there fewer minorities in the niche and individual sports than in team sports?

10. If you were to begin a league from scratch today, how might you avoid many of the diversity issues confronting leaders in existing sports enterprises?

ETHICS

INTRODUCTION

No modern-day business plan or existing enterprise is complete or current without the incorporation of ethical guidelines. In sports, arguably, the most public ethical issues have been raised in relation to the Olympic Games and a variety of taints associated with collegiate athletics.

It is now the case that the teaching of ethics at America's colleges and universities has moved from being the exclusive domain of Philosophy departments to being a required part of the undergraduate and graduate business programs. The names Enron, WorldCom, and Arthur Andersen play no small role in this development.

The Enron, WorldCom, Arthur Andersen, Olympic, college stew makes this an important area of study for sports business leaders. Most of the issues are generic as they refer to questions of honesty, deception, and corruption. There are, however, issues that only impact sports. It is these unique issues that the readings in this chapter focus upon.

The role of sports in this ethical realm is made even more complex because of the lessons many of us expect these games to teach our children. Right or wrong, virtually every aspect of sport is held on an ethical pedestal.

The first excerpt, "The Ethical Issues Confronting Managers in the Sport Industry," provides the broad overview of the ethical issues confronting sports business leaders. The article is useful in giving readers a list of topics to pause and reflect upon in their ethical overview of sports-related business decisions.

The second selection, "The Olympics and the Search for Global Values," provides a micro view of ethics in a specific sector of the sports business. The piece is, noticeably, highly opinionated. It relates two bits of business well. First, it appropriately positions the sports ethics issue in the global setting. As leagues globalize, an understanding of these issues becomes increasingly important. Second, and probably most importantly, the article points to the need for the improvement of ethics issues to begin at the top of an organization. It is now broadly understood, outside of the sports context, that ethical standards in business entities are most successful when clearly mandated from the top down.

OVERVIEW

THE ETHICAL ISSUES CONFRONTING MANAGERS IN THE SPORT INDUSTRY

Mary A. Hums, Carol A. Barr, and Laurie Gullion

PROFESSIONAL SPORT

. . . . Professional sport has very different ethical issues than amateur or school sport, since the purposes of professional sport are entertainment and profits. Sport managers working in professional sport face ethical issues in relation to a number of different constituencies, specifically 1) local communities which support teams, 2) the players, and 3) the front office personnel.

Local Communities

What obligations do professional sport organizations have to their fans and the communities in which the organizations reside? One ethical decision sport managers face is determining ticket prices for fans. Every year teams raise ticket prices. Factors influencing ticket prices come from both outside and inside sport, and range from economic recessions and world wars to team success, strikes, and moving into new facilities. It is in this last category where many questions arise. When new stadiums and arenas are built, they have a positive impact on attendance. Given the predictable increase in ticket prices however, a not so obvious change occurs in the fan base. Fans who were able to have season tickets in the past, but who cannot afford to renew them when the new arena is constructed, are effectively shut out of the new arena, and replaced by fans with higher disposable incomes. In effect, the consumption of spectator sport in person is beginning to become an activity for the elite, while others are denied access. . . . The underlying question here is who really are the team's "most valuable customers" — the casual attendees who come to the game only when their disposable income allows a ticket purchase, the traditional season ticketholders, the new higher income season ticketholders, or the corporate luxury box holders? The answer to that question speaks to the stance teams take in the industry. Is it only about increasing corporate revenues or is there still some consideration for the average fan on whom the success of these teams was originally built?

What commitments do professional franchises have to the communities in which they do business? The recent rash of "free agent franchises" has brought this question to the forefront. Cities such as Baltimore, Cleveland, and Los Angeles, which lost NFL teams, as well as Canadian cities like Quebec City and Winnipeg, which have lost NHL franchises, have been left with empty stadiums and arenas while teams and their owners move on to more lucrative locations. . . . Why are owners lured to new locations? In a nutshell, owners look to determine if they can acquire 1) better lease arrangements including greater cuts of parking and concessions, 2) public financing of the project which relieves them of any debt incurred in stadium or arena construction, and 3) an increased number of luxury boxes. And how do owners convince cities that a sport franchise is a "good" use of public dollars? Usually three arguments are made — 1) the city will benefit from direct spending on events, 2) the city will benefit from money spent by fans as that money recycles through the economy via the multiplier effect, and 3) the city needs the franchise to have a "major league" image. Research by a number of authors . . . has indicated that these arguments may not always hold up. The bottom line question remains — who really profits from franchise relocation? The answer is the owners. So the question becomes for sport managers — is this an ethical stance to take? Is it ethical to "hold cities hostage" with the threat to leave for a better offer, oftentimes leaving the cities with massive amounts of long-term debt and an empty facility to maintain?

Players

Volumes have been written relating to the recent labor unrest and work stoppages in Major League Baseball and the National Hockey League. Whether one sides with management or labor in these discussions, there are still the same questions of fundamental fairness involved in any labor dispute. What made these disputes different to the general public was the fact [that] the "laborers" in these cases happened to be highly paid professional athletes instead of coal miners or factory workers. What constitutes fair working conditions for these athletes? Just how much control is management allowed to have over them? And where does the phrase "in the best interest of the game" enter into the discussion? Although the salaries are high, sport managers must still keep in mind the basic principles of fairness when dealing with these athlete-employees.

. . . . *[The authors' discussion of the HIV issue is deleted.]*

Front Office Personnel

Finally, there are ethical issues related to front office staffs of professional franchises. The most important has to do with diversification of front office staffs. Traditionally, professional sport management has been the exclusive realm of white males. Sport is often regarded as one of society's most traditionally male institutions. Given the changing face of the international workforce, sport managers now must make ethical decisions in hiring in order to make the management of sport more inclusive for women, minorities, and people with disabilities.

. . . .

In addition to diversifying the workforce in terms of women and minorities, special attention needs to be turned to increasing opportunities for people with disabilities. While athletes with disabilities continue to make slow progress with recognition and acceptance on the playing field, relatively little data is available on the numbers of people with disabilities in sport management positions. The following suggestions have been offered . . . for increasing opportunities for people with disabilities in sport management positions:

1. Value diversity within the organization.
2. Redefine who is a "Qualified Individual" by:
   a) Being knowledgeable of existing labor laws related to discriminatory work practices.
   b) Increasing knowledge and awareness of multiculturalism in general.
   c) Being knowledgeable and supportive of issues of importance to all groups in the workplace.
   d) Writing statements about valuing diversity into the organization's code of ethics.
   e) Expanding personal and professional networks.
   f) Acting as a "mentor" or "womentor" to people with disabilities in one's sport organization.
3. Create organizational visions inclusive of people with disabilities.
4. Create organizational mission statements inclusive of people with disabilities.
5. Actively recruit and retain people with disabilities as employees.

INTERCOLLEGIATE ATHLETICS

The world of intercollegiate athletics is certainly not without its share of ethical issues. Examples of ethical issues within intercollegiate athletics include, but are not limited to, 1) whether student-athletes are being exploited by not being paid for their athletic endeavors, 2) the courting of amateur student-athletes by professional player agents, 3) gender equity, 4) diversity issues, and 5) improprieties by intercollegiate coaches and administrators.

Paying Student-Athletes

The National Collegiate Athletic Association's (NCAA) 1995–96 budget projected revenues of $234.2 million. Of this total, $180.9 million or 77% came from television rights fees, with $178.3 million directly attributed to the NCAA's broadcast contract with CBS covering the men's basketball tournament. Thus, 64 college basketball teams and their roughly 12–15 student-athletes per team generate nearly 77% of the NCAA's total revenue. This figure does not include revenue the NCAA collects from ticket sales, merchandise sales, or sponsorship deals connected with the men's basketball tournament. In addition, base salaries of Division I men's basketball coaches routinely approach or exceed the six-digit mark. Including additional shoe and apparel contracts, TV and radio contracts, and endorsement deals, this base salary is likely to more than double or even triple. Some of these contracts, such as shoe and apparel deals, involve the student-athlete to a greater extent than the coach, and yet the coach receives the paycheck while the athlete is required to wear the shoes and apparel.

Bylaws 15.02.5 and 15.2.4.1 of the NCAA rules prohibit a college student-athlete on an athletic scholarship from receiving anything more than the monetary equivalent of tuition, room, board, books, and fees plus Pell Grant money up to the student-athlete's full cost of attendance. . . . In 1989,

University of New Haven sociology professor Allen Sack surveyed approximately 3,500 current and former professional athletes. Of the 1,182 athletes who responded, nearly one-third admitted receiving illegal payments while they were in college.

. . . . The more controversial and difficult issue may not be determining whether student-athletes should be paid, but rather determining *which* student-athletes should get paid and how much. Should differences be put in place for male versus female student-athletes, football players versus field hockey players, starters or star players versus second or third string athletes? The actual implementation of a system may be the more difficult of the ethical concerns surrounding the paying of student-athletes.

Player Agents

A growing problem within intercollegiate athletics is the courting of highly talented student-athletes by professional player agents. Player agents, depending upon the athlete's sport, receive between 3% and 15% of a professional athlete's salary. This income potential is extremely enticing to the professional player agent. Many player agents, therefore, disregard the NCAA rules restricting a collegiate student-athlete from signing or accepting anything from a player agent and instead use various methods to lure the student-athlete into signing with them. NCAA Bylaw 12.3.1 states that an individual shall be ineligible for participation in an intercollegiate sport if he or she ever has agreed (orally or in writing) to be represented by an agent for the purpose of marketing his or her athletics ability or reputation in a sport. Player agents have been known to offer cash, cars, airline tickets, and other amenities to the student-athlete in exchange for the student-athlete signing with them. Player agents have also used "runners" who act on behalf of the player agent trying to persuade the student-athlete to sign with that particular player agent. These "runners" exert pressure on the student-athlete by getting close to the student-athlete and his/her family or friends, and attempting to persuade the student-athlete to sign with the player agent.

This problem is compounded because of lack of regulation of player agents. The NCAA lacks any authority or enforcement power over the player agents. The NCAA can punish the school and student-athlete, but possesses no enforcement power over the player agent. Individual states have become more involved in this area by passing their own legislation and/or agent registration systems. The state of Florida has already handed down fines and jail sentences to agents who contacted Florida's student-athletes without first registering with the state. Individual colleges and universities are also getting more involved by instituting their own agent registration systems and trying to educate student-athletes as to illicit player agent behavior.

Gender Equity

Perhaps the most important phrase of the 1990s in intercollegiate athletics is "gender equity," that is, offering equal opportunities for both men and women to participate in sport. A piece of legislation referred to as Title IX provides guidelines for gender equity. Title IX prohibits sex discrimination in any educational program or activity receiving federal financial assistance. A 1990–91 NCAA Gender Equity study found that although college campuses were comprised of approximately 50% male students and 50% female students, college athletic departments were comprised of 70% male athletes and 30% female athletes. In addition, the male student-athletes were receiving 70% of the athletic scholarship money, 75% of the operational budget, and 80% of the recruiting moneys available.

Institutions have been slow to comply with Title IX, though, given the potential financial impact of instituting a new women's sport program, increasing scholarship, operational, and recruiting funding for women, or instituting other changes dictated by Title IX legislation involving areas such as facilities, equipment, travel and per diem, or coaches' compensation. A 1994–95 NCAA participation study found the percentage of female athletes has increased to 36.9% of all athletic participants, but this number still lacks in comparison to the 63.1% of student-athletes who are male.

Gender equity also involves coaches and administrators. In 1972, the year Title IX was passed, more than 90% of women's teams were coached by women. In 1994, 49.4% of women's teams were coached by women and only about 2% of the head coaches of men's teams within the NCAA were women with almost all of these sport programs involving combined gender teams. In 1972, more than 90% of women's programs were directed by a female head administrator. In 1994, 20.98% of women's programs were directed by a woman, and the average number of women included in the athletic administrative structure at each school was less than one.

Historically, although Title IX is the law, its enforcement policy was weak, therefore it was often simply ignored by college athletic directors. It became an ethical choice for athletic directors to attempt to comply with the law, and many athletic directors, for reasons including money or tradition or sexism, simply chose not to comply. Others, however, made the ethical choice to increase opportunities for female athletes, simply because it was the right thing to do.

Diversity

The NCAA's Minority Opportunity and Interests Committee studied the minority composition of intercollegiate student-athletes, coaches, and administrators and found in 1993–94 that Black student-athletes comprised 25.3% of Division I college scholarship student-athletes, but accounted for only 4.1% of athletic directors and 4.4% of head coaches when predominantly Black institutions were excluded. These percentages were an increase from a 1990–91 study which found 2.2% of athletic directors and 3.3% of head coaches were Black, but still fall short of the percentage of Black student-athletes which has remained unchanged since 1990–91.

Improprieties

On June 28, 1996, *The Chronicle of Higher Education* reported 23 institutions on NCAA probation. Violations included improper academic certification of student-athletes, playing ineligible student-athletes, recruiting violations, providing extra benefits to student-athletes, lack of institutional control, and unethical conduct by head and assistant coaches. A "win at all costs" attitude still dominates intercollegiate athletics, pressuring coaches and even administrators to violate NCAA rules in an attempt to sign highly talented student-athletes or win big games. The financial payoff associated with athletic success still dominates in "big-time" football and basketball. Coaches and athletic administrators feel pressure from alumni, boosters, and even university administrators to win. The enforcement and investigative staff of the NCAA is small and cannot keep up with the many activities of the 991 member institutions. Coaches may feel the odds of not being caught are in their favor, and administrators may look the other way in order to keep the revenue streams flowing.

　. . . . [The authors' discussion of facility management ethical issues is omitted.]

SPORT MANAGERS AND ETHICAL DECISION MAKING

. . . .

An adaptation of Zinn's[1] ethical decision-making model has also been suggested, which could be applied across the different industry segments:

1. Identify the correct problem to be solved.
2. Gather all the pertinent information.
3. Explore codes of conduct relevant to one's profession or to this particular dilemma.
4. Examine one's own personal values and beliefs.
5. Consult with peers or other individuals in the industry who may have experience in similar situations.
6. List decision options.
7. Look for a "win-win" situation if at all possible.
8. Ask the question, "How would my family feel if my decision and how I arrived at my decision were printed in the newspaper tomorrow?"
9. Sleep on it. Do not rush to a decision.
10. Make the best decision possible, knowing it may not be perfect.
11. Evaluate the decision over time.

The development of an ethical decision-making model for sport managers is obviously an area ripe for additional research and thought.

CONCLUSION

As illustrated above, the sport industry is a broadly defined industry encompassing a number of diverse segments. Managers in each of these segments, professional sport, intercollegiate sport, the health and fitness industry, recreational sport and facility management, are challenged daily by the changes occurring in the industry as it grows and matures. Along with growth comes an increasing number of complicated ethical questions, many of which are unique to given segments of the industry. Sport managers need to stay current with the ethical issues they may confront, so they will be proactive in their approaches rather than reactive.

REFERENCES

1. Zinn, Z. M. "Do the Right Thing: Ethical Decision Making in Professional and Business Practice," *Adult Learning* 5, 7–8, 27.

THE OLYMPICS AND THE SEARCH FOR GLOBAL VALUES

John Milton Smith

Disillusionment with the Olympics mirrors the mounting disenchantment with the values of globalization. Indeed, the recent history of the Games has been characterized by the growth of a culture which reifies the worst features of global competition, including: winning at any price, commercial exploitation by MNCs, corruption, intense national rivalry, [and] the competitive advantage of advanced nations.

There can be little argument that the global institutions have been a miserable failure in dealing with the social and ethical consequences of globalization. Their performance has been particularly dismal in addressing issues involving poverty, terrorism, environmental protection, natural disasters and humanitarian crises involving the weak and defenseless.

. . . . *[The author's background discussion on Olympic corruption is deleted.]*

THE IOC'S LEADERSHIP CHALLENGE

Ironically, the last vestige of amateurism associated with the Games is its management. Despite the scandals and controversies of recent years, the IOC [International Olympic Committee] displays few signs of the professional management techniques and processes which characterize the successful international business organizations of today. The IOC has not been proactive in addressing the key corporate governance issues such as accountability, social responsibility, risk management, transparency, and the implementation of codes of conduct. Furthermore, the Olympic leadership has failed to define and communicate a clear unifying purpose. The Olympic ideals remain at the level of platitude; they do not constitute a unifying sense of purpose. There has been no rigorous public discussion of the multiple and sometimes conflicting objectives of the Games. Not only is there a lack of vision and coherent mission, there are also no major mechanisms in place to provide for public input into planning processes.

Despite heavy emphasis on the so-called Olympic ideals, the leaders of the movement have singularly failed to articulate its core values and relate them to contemporary mores and behavior. Again, by comparison with management best practiced in major MNCs, the IOC has lagged badly. This is further reflected in the lack of a comprehensive Code of Conduct and ethics training regime. Only recently, after an extremely damaging period of adverse publicity, has an Ethics Commission been established, and there is still no regular ethics auditing system. Instead, President Samaranch continues to talk paternalistically about "the Olympic Family" and of the need for more loyalty and better housekeeping. The "family" analogy is doubly unfortunate because, on the one hand, it implies a degree of unity which clearly does not exist and, on the other, a closed community with the potential to become a corrupt, self-serving community more akin to the Mafia than to a modern, professional organization.

Juan Antonio Samaranch, the long-standing President of the IOC, has been the architect of the Olympic Games as a scandal-ridden media spectacle and business enterprise. It is claimed that he has transformed the Games "from a global sporting get-together to a corporate spectacle sadly replete with corruption and kickbacks." Aloof, arrogant, and imperious, Samaranch operates not as an inspiring leader but as a banana-republic dictator, cultivating a shameless culture of extravagance and excess around him. Once a senior member of General Franco's fascist regime, he presides over the IOC as if it were a personal fiefdom. Until the Salt Lake City kickback scandal, Samaranch expected to be called "Excellency," demanded a royal standard of hospitality wherever he traveled, and turned a blind eye to the blatant corruption of his colleagues.

As President of the IOC, Samaranch has clearly failed to provide inspiring values leadership. Instead, the Olympic Games are enveloped in a culture of shame, disappointment, and uncertainty. While Samaranch has certainly succeeded in addressing the commercial challenges facing the Games as a global sporting event, he has been much less successful in articulating what they stand for or in realizing their potential influence as a moral force. Apart from vague rhetoric about Olympic ideals, he has never been convincing as the champion for Olympic values. Despite his long tenure, Samaranch has not created a transcending Olympic ethos based on human excellence, and he himself falls far short of what such a challenge demands of a leader.

Despite intense world-wide interest in the Games and attraction to the values they are perceived to represent, they have failed dismally in recent years to celebrate and reinforce the values which are embedded in their history. The opportunity is still there for a future leader to tap into this history and to liberate the massive moral authority and potential ethical influence which it contains. Above all, and certainly more than any other regular global event, the Olympic Games are a potential forum for rekindling the human spirit, lifting morale, and bringing people together in pursuit of common goals. They are also a reaffirmation of the importance of setting ambitious objectives, having a sense of purpose, making painful sacrifices, persevering when the going gets tough, giving loyalty to one's teammates, and being proud of doing one's best.

Unfortunately, the administration of the Games has become remote from the world of the athletes and a source of embarrassment to virtually every group of stakeholders. Based on their track record, most senior officials are perceived to be self-seeking power brokers rather than inspiring leaders. How could this sad situation be transformed, and what changes would be required to convert the Olympic ideology and rhetoric into practical reality?

The most important change would be in the area of leadership. Rekindling and revitalizing the Olympic spirit will involve much more than the sort of leadership which produces plans and profits. Character and credibility will be critical success factors, as will the communication skills needed to articulate the Olympic values and create an uplifting ethos. . . . This should not be a purely top-down exercise.

Instead, all stakeholders should be given the opportunity to provide input and discuss options openly and without intimidation. In reviewing the Mission and charting the future direction of the Olympic Games, participants from all over the world would come together in developing a set of global human values which could become the touchstone for future international relations and problem-solving. At every level — local, national, regional, global — the key to transforming society is to reform the critical organizations first. And that is why there is such an urgent need for an outstanding leader at the helm of the IOC.

In defining the task and revising the position description for the next President of the IOC, there is an exciting opportunity to conceptualize the Games as a major vehicle and catalyst for developing and propagating a set of widely shared global ethical standards.

The transformation of the Games will require nothing short of a leadership revolution. Apart from changes to the decision-making process and a radical restructuring, the new leadership must have the ability to create an inspiring global festival of human attainment.

. . . .

The reinvention of the Games will require not only transformational leadership but also a solid framework of strategic management as well. This will entail a more focused and well-defined mission, more democratic and representative structures, more transparent and accountable processes, and more emphasis upon the creation of brand equity. Because the strength and credibility of the Olympic brand hinges so heavily upon core values, high priority should be given to the development of a code of practice, to the role of the new Ethics Commission and to the use of audit mechanisms.

There is still an opportunity for a visionary IOC leader to seize the initiative in making the Games a platform for promoting positive global values. Such a leader will need to be a strategic thinker and an outstanding communicator. Just as the most recent leaders of the UN, IMF, and the World Bank have begun to reshape the agendas of their organizations to place greater emphasis upon human rights and the welfare of people, so the IOC needs a leader who is able to create a shared vision for the Games which is a beacon for inspiring people all over the world to strive for excellence and to work together in harmony. As Sir Roger Bannister, the first person to run a four-minute mile, has put it: "The Olympic Games should remain one of the great hopes of the world."

DISCUSSION QUESTIONS

1. What obligations do professional teams have to the communities in which they play? What about college teams?

2. What ethical dilemmas are raised by not paying college athletes? What dilemmas would be raised by paying them?

3. What are the ethical issues associated with Title IX? What are the ethical issues associated with diversity generally?

4. What are the elements of the suggested model to confront ethical issues as a sports business leader?

5. What are the unique ethical problems of the leaders in the Olympic movement?

6. How might the Olympic-related ethical guidelines presented in the readings apply to the NFL, the NCAA, and the WTA?

7. Why is it "good" to have a major league franchise move into your home city? Who actually benefits?

8. As a local middle-class citizen would it *really* be good for a team to move to your city? Why or why not?

9. Why is it more common to see fans side against "athletes" when it is quite common for the masses to side with "laborers" when dealing with work stoppages? Who do you tend to side with during a work stoppage in sports?

10. What are the risks associated with franchise relocation that are faced by owners?

11. Why is there not more internal self-regulation by NCAA member institutions?

PART V

THE FUTURE

FUTURE CHALLENGES

INTRODUCTION

The successful sports business leader must give the requisite amount of attention to both current and future operations. Long-term strategic planning is a necessity for survival, but is often difficult given the dynamic nature of the sports industry. While peering into the crystal ball and making specific predictions about the future is typically a fruitless and ultimately humbling endeavor, it is possible to make informed generalizations about the future of the business of sports. At the outset, it is likely that the leaders of professional, Olympic, intercollegiate, and even interscholastic sports will further adopt a more global, business-like approach in the management of their organizations. Despite the differences between the sports and nonsports-related organizations discussed throughout this book, there is a need for increased homogeneity in the operation of these businesses. To that end, the education of the future sports industry leaders must become more business-oriented. Those aspiring to be the best sport managers will need the business training of an MBA along with knowledge of the sports industry. Educational programs must adapt to this need.

Professional sports are unlikely to undergo any radical changes in the near future. The ownership ranks will continue to be dominated by wealthy individuals and corporations, and franchise values will continue to appreciate. However, there is likely to be some reduction in the publicly traded corporations that are involved in ownership. Instead of considering franchise ownership as merely an ancillary activity, it is likely that those corporations that remain involved will be more closely aligned with sports, such that their core missions will be furthered by the ownership of a professional sports franchise. Unlike other publicly traded corporations that have been forced to sell their teams in troubled times, these publicly traded corporations will be able to avoid investor and analyst pressure to divest themselves of their sports holdings in the event of a company downturn. Similarly, there will not be any new publicly traded teams until these franchises can figure out a way to provide value to investors and shareholders.

The structure of the major professional leagues is unlikely to change in the next decade. Though there may be some very limited global expansion and perhaps even domestic contraction, the status quo will likely persist, with owners continuing to argue about the appropriate amount of revenue sharing within their respective leagues. The struggles between the owners and the player unions will also endure, with the collective bargaining process remaining fraught with problems. Though athlete compensation is likely to keep increasing along with owner revenues, the parties will continue to argue about whether salaries should be unrestrained in accordance with free market principles or artificially limited via salary caps, luxury taxes, and the like.

A slowdown in the building boom in the major professional sports leagues is inevitable, as most of the playing facilities have already been renovated or replaced. Facilities in New York City and classic ballparks such as Fenway Park and Wrigley Field are among the last bastions. Expect this to change in the next decade, with the construction of new stadia and an arena in New York City and substantial changes made to the classics. The next wave of construction in professional sports will not occur until approximately 2020.

Media rights, the other major source of revenue for the major sports leagues, will continue to increase, albeit at a slower rate than in the 1990s. Expect broadcasters to try to reduce their risk in these expensive ventures through profit sharing arrangements with the leagues similar to the current NBA deal. Though the biggest events will continue to thrive on network television, the future of sports broadcasting is likely to be largely based on a cable television model, so as to allow broadcasters to generate revenues from both advertisers and subscribers.

Finally, professional sports outside of the major sports leagues will continue to meet varying degrees of success. Some start-up leagues and niche sports that demonstrate both appropriately modest goals and attractive products will be moderately successful, but most will fail. Though they will always have a core of loyal followers, the popularity of individual sports such as tennis, golf, and auto racing will ebb and flow depending primarily on the presence of transcendent athletes who are able to bring the sports into the mainstream of the nation's sporting conscience.

There are also likely to be changes in the realm of big-time intercollegiate athletics. This segment of the sports industry is fundamentally flawed at its core, in that there is no logical connection between education and athletics. Indeed, this nexus is largely an American phenomenon, with most of the world adhering to the club system of athletics. Nonetheless, college sports are so deeply ingrained in American culture that it is likely to endure, albeit in a slightly altered form. Radical reform efforts led by university presidents and governing bodies to scale back the emphasis of athletics are likely to be unsuccessful. To the contrary, it is far more likely that intercollegiate athletics will continue to be increasingly professionalized. Institutions will seek to limit the ever-increasing financial burden created by big-time sports programs by engaging in the same revenue-generating tactics seen in professional sports. Luxury seating, corporate naming rights, and signage will become the rule rather than the exception in college athletic facilities, and increasingly sophisticated sales and marketing efforts will result in enhanced sponsorships.

A playoff in Division I-A football is inevitable for two reasons. First, the revenue potential is too great to continue to ignore. Second, it is very likely that the Bowl Championship Series in its current form violates the antitrust laws and will not withstand a legal challenge. Meanwhile, the increasing professionalization will continue to result in increased pressure to compensate athletes beyond the value of tuition, room, and board, a movement that institutions will doubtlessly continue to resist. Ultimately, the best chance for decreasing the commercialism in college basketball and football may, ironically, come from the professional leagues in these sports. A decision by the NBA or NFL to vertically integrate their player development systems in the manner of MLB and the NHL — rather than rely on colleges to train their future labor pool — would dramatically alter the landscape of intercollegiate athletics. However, the cost associated with doing so makes this unlikely in the NFL, although it remains a distinct possibility for the NBA.

In this chapter, we present the commentary of several well-respected "visionaries" offering their thoughts on the future of the business of sports. In the first excerpt, Sheehan considers the future of each major North American professional sports league and big-time college football and basketball. In the next article, Mahony and Howard discuss the trends of the 1990s and examine various strategies that sports organizations are likely to adopt in the future. In the final selection, Gladden, Irwin, and Sutton predict that professional sports teams will exert considerable effort to build the equity of their brands through both the acquisition of assets and the enhancement of their customer relationships.

BIG-TIME SPORTS

KEEPING SCORE: THE ECONOMICS
OF BIG-TIME SPORTS

Richard G. Sheehan

WHAT DO THE FINANCIAL NUMBERS
IMPLY FOR THE FUTURE OF SPORTS?

Turning to the future, let me briefly consider where each league appears headed based upon its current financial situation.

Baseball. The easiest prediction is for increasing reliance on cable and pay-per-view and additional efforts to obtain municipally subsidized new stadiums. Owners keep searching for additional revenues in an entirely futile attempt to stay one step ahead of the players. Pay-per-view represents the only obvious new revenue source on the horizon. Some clubs will push for additional revenue from a new stadium. Following Chicago, Baltimore, Cleveland, and Texas, it is likely that the push for new stadiums will continue with owners . . . aggressively lobbying for municipal support. The spectacle of George Steinbrenner, netting $20 million plus per year from the Yankees, trying to shake down a financially threadbare New York City (or state) may make sense to Steinbrenner and other MLB owners. . . .

It would appear that greater revenue sharing is in the cards for baseball. I say this not because I have recommended it or even because it is economically justified. It will come because the number of clubs that believe they would gain from such a plan is growing close to a majority.

I would like to say that further expansion is in the cards for baseball because a number of cities could support a well-run franchise. Expansion is economically justified. The cities at the top of the expansion list should include New York City, Washington, D.C., and Mexico City. . . . However, the owners have shown no enthusiasm for the prospect of expansion.

Ultimately, one would hope that baseball's owners and union would recognize that they are partners and may gain more by collaborating than by fighting. I am not optimistic. There has been too much bad blood. The owners have exploited the players for too long for the players to trust the owners, and the players have won for too long at the negotiating table for the owners not to seek victory regardless of the cost. At some point the owners' and players' economic self-interests will bring about a long-term settlement. Baseball politics, however, may postpone that settlement for a long time.

Basketball.   Basketball will see the demise of the owners' cherished salary cap. It is simply a matter of time, if not this contract, then the next. It served a purpose ten years ago; it serves none today. The NBA has been in the forefront of most economic trends in sports. Unfortunately, the union split also is a likely future trend. All owners do not have the same goals and incentives and constraints, and it would be unreasonable to think that all players do. In the past, splits among players have been masked by [the players'] desire to raise the total income of all players. At some point players will recognize that more for the stars means less for the journeymen. This will greatly complicate labor negotiations. Future labor negotiations in sports could be dramatically uglier and messier unless all parties have a dramatic change of heart. Again, the question is will there be cooperation or confrontation?

Basketball has taken the lead in terms of aggressively seeking expansion franchises and then imposing stringent restrictions on those franchises. I expect this trend to continue, ultimately with two twists. First, the expansion to Europe is inevitable. The only question is how soon. The NBA wants to continue to increase revenues, and Europe is the likely source for the next big increase. The other expansion twist will involve owners like Disney. The only surprise about Disney's entry into sports was that it did not happen in the NBA first. The cross-marketing opportunities for companies like Disney or SONY or Busch or a Baby Bell or a network, perhaps Fox, are too rich to ignore. The economic pressures will lead to these linkages. The only question is how soon. The building boom also will continue. New facilities draw more fans, even with the same old team. More importantly, however, a new arena gives a franchise the opportunity to maximize the number of luxury boxes and substantially increase revenues. . . . A corollary is that players will get a slice of that revenue.

The last prediction for basketball: those long-term contracts are not the wave of the future. The most recent union contract begins to address this issue. Teams and players will both get burned. Teams will sign mediocre talent and be stuck with big-money payouts that will lower profits and — if the salary cap is still in place — reduce their ability to field a competitive team. Players will sign for what looks like a fortune but in a few years find that they are at the top of the talent pool but only in the middle of the salary ranking. (No one should be surprised when a Glenn Robinson or a Chris Webber is a holdout in five years!)

Football.   Football has followed a very different path from the other three leagues, largely due to a more restricted schedule. One thing to change: the schedule. The NFL already has cut back the exhibition schedule and increased the length of the regular season. Ultimately it will do it again. The economics make it inevitable. The payoff from changing the last two preseason games to regular season games is just too great to ignore. Increase the season by two games or 12 percent and each team could pick up another $1 million in television money and perhaps another $1 million in gate revenues.

Non-gate stadium revenues will be the main growth area in the immediate future for the NFL. Franchises are going to increasingly search for income like additional luxury boxes, personal seat licenses, and individual deals with major sponsors. All give the team additional revenue. Perhaps more importantly, however, all give the team additional revenue that does not have to be shared with the league. Ultimately, NFL revenue sharing will have to be expanded to include these revenue sources or current revenue-sharing agreements are going to break down. No middle ground is possible.

More teams will attempt to shake down more cities for publicly subsidized stadiums and deals like St. Louis gave the Rams. Every deal that is signed puts further pressure on financially weaker franchises to cut their own deal, because each deal increases next year's salary cap. Expansion into Los Angeles is a no-brainer. Overseas expansion appears premature. Football has yet to set the stage for successful international expansion. One revenue concern: if the next round of negotiations for national television broadcast rights does not match the last round, many NFL franchises [will] be in deep financial trouble.

The salary cap in football is an interesting experiment that will soon be history — by the owners' request. It makes no more sense in the NFL than it makes in the NBA. The San Francisco 49ers first demonstrated in 1994 how meaningless it was with creatively written — and rewritten — contracts. Teams like the Cincinnati Bengals thought they would be able to increase their payroll, sign talent that other teams had to waive, and then be a contender on the field. They got one of three. They spent more but had nothing to show other than a bigger payroll and lower profits. The owners may be greedy, but they are not that stupid. When they see the salary cap does not deliver as promised, it's history.

Also coming in football, more reliance on guaranteed contracts. Players are going to look at still-performing veterans . . . being cut and realize that the big contracts are meaningless unless you collect. Given a choice between a 3-year $2 million contract with no guarantee and a 3 year $1.4 million contract with a guarantee, players are going to start taking guarantees and the clubs will go along because it saves them money and makes it easier to fit under the cap. (Bonuses are a form of guarantees, generally paid in advance and used to circumvent the salary cap. Teams will attempt to move from bonuses to guarantees when the salary cap is removed, because bonuses are paid up front while guarantees are paid in the future.)

Hockey.   The primary question facing the NHL is the future of the small Canadian markets, and there is no easy call on that. If NHL owners are willing to agree on a generous revenue-sharing plan, then cities . . . will retain their franchises. Without substantial revenue sharing, goodbye . . . Edmonton, and possibly Calgary, and even Ottawa in the long term. NHL owners have not been generous to anyone but themselves; thus I am not optimistic about more revenue sharing. Nevertheless, the choice is clear from an economic standpoint.

The wisdom of additional expansion is in doubt. Adding franchises in large southern cities would dilute the talent pool. It would not be profitable to the league unless the southern franchises had exceptional strength such as that brought by owners like Disney. Remember that Calgary has a franchise because the Flames could not make it in Atlanta. Nevertheless, adding franchises would make a national television contract more likely. In terms of expansion, the NHL is in a unique position with a receptive international audience in Europe. However, while a franchise in Moscow could be extremely popular it may not be profitable and would not help to secure a national television contract in the United States.

The main economic step that the NHL must take to maintain its status as a major league sport is to package the game to make it attractive to U.S. television networks. Bringing in Disney and taking out fighting were two major steps forward. Unfortunately, the 1994 strike was a major step backward. Ultimately, though the purists will wail, the timing of the game will change to accommodate TV. From an economic perspective, hockey needs a network television contract and that contract will not come without breaks in the action for commercials and probably a shorter game.

College Football. The top college programs make tons of money while most of the rest lose money. Does this mean that colleges will drop or scale back their football programs? Probably not. There is too much pride at stake for many college administrators to look just at the economics of their football programs. (What state legislators might do is a different question.) In the late 1960s Holy Cross commissioned a study to see whether its football program was economically justified. The answer was no, and the recommendation was made to drop football. Holy Cross still has a football program — based largely and explicitly on considerations of school pride.*

As in the pros, the search goes on for ways to increase revenues and decrease costs. One thing that will come: a college football playoff. Would it do away with the bowls? Perhaps, but in general who would care? With the exception of Notre Dame, the teams that gain the most from the bowls are the Vanderbilts and Northwesterns. They generally do not go, yet split the conference revenues of the teams that do. Would it further detract from the academic performance of student-athletes? The argument rings hollow. If football players need more time to study, do away with spring practice; don't leave for a Saturday away game on Thursday morning making the players miss Thursday and Friday classes; and further restrict the amount of hours that players must put in both during the season and off-season. Division I-AA has a tourney and there has been no obvious impact on academic performance. Division I-A could do things one better. Take the top eight teams for a three game tourney; begin with the traditional January 1 bowls and end two weeks later about January 15th. For most schools that is an academic break period anyway. The tourney will come. The potential revenues are too great to ignore.

Also on revenues, colleges will place much greater emphasis on marketing. The pros have moved far beyond colleges in terms of marketing their games (one might also argue that they have moved far beyond good taste). Nevertheless, a horde of marketing ideas and tie-ins — many extraordinarily tacky — will creep into collegiate sports over the next ten years simply because athletic directors will not be able to turn down the money. . . . Revenue sources also include items like shoe contracts. . . .

On costs, college presidents may continue reducing the maximum number of allowed grants-in-aid as a means of holding down costs. Frankly, I think those actions are largely window-dressing. Grants-in-aid are not the major factor driving the cost of college football. Coaches salaries, administrative overhead, maintenance of frequently palatial facilities, and even travel and recruiting all may exceed the cost of grants-in-aid. If college presidents are sincere about cutting expenses there are other items that need their attention including athletic administrative costs, facilities costs, and recruiting costs.

On compensating student-athletes . . . if changes are not made to increase the implicit compensation, then athletes will take it in their own hands, perhaps hiring agents to negotiate with colleges. The NCAA's only choice is to do something substantial quickly or wait for the athletes to take the initiative.

On gender equity and Title IX . . . requiring colleges to go to a 50–50 ratio could dramatically change the face of collegiate athletics, either by substantially increasing the costs of athletic programs or by dramatically cutting men's programs in sports like wrestling, gymnastics, volleyball, and soccer. The rationale for only forty percent female athletes was ad hoc at best, and dollar subsidies to male sports dwarf those to female sports at many universities that do not make money on football.

---

* Holy Cross's football program now is Division I-AA and offers no athletic grants-in-aid. However, scholarship costs are but a small part of the total cost of a football program. Thus, it is likely that Holy Cross's football program still is not justified simply from an economic perspective. It would appear that school pride is the primary factor maintaining Crusader football.

College Basketball.   Basketball presents a very different picture from college football. The successful schools . . . make substantial money from their programs but not nearly as much as the top football programs. While the maximums are much smaller, the losses also are much smaller. The primary difference between basketball and football is that the lower costs have prompted many more schools to go Division I in basketball. . . . For schools like Robert Morris, Coppin State, Murray State, or Santa Clara, an NCAA tourney bid is like winning the lottery in terms of publicity and revenue. In addition, this lottery ticket is relatively cheap. Thus we see a proliferation of Division I basketball schools although most make at best only a small profit.

Reorganization is coming to major college basketball. Nothing too dramatic and nothing that would pose a danger to the golden goose of the NCAA tourney. But the number of teams joining Division I just for a piece of the tourney pie keeps growing and the pieces are getting smaller. It is only a matter of time before basketball divides Division I into the real basketball schools and the ersatz schools. The split will come for the same reason it came in football. The North Carolinas, Kentuckys, and UCLAs simply do not need to split the tourney revenue with Brooklyn College, Florida Atlantic, or Prairie View. As economic pressures grow on the former schools they will surely cut the latter out of the pie.

THE FINAL SCORE

The bottom line is that professional franchises have been very profitable endeavors, despite cries of poverty far and wide. Economic pressures have shaped the way sports has evolved and will continue to shape the way it evolves. The games themselves, however, all appear quite healthy. As a number of people have stated, "Baseball must be a great game to survive the people that run it." The same can be said for basketball, football, and hockey. Each sport seems to have a way of muddling along, perhaps not finding the best solution to its problems, but always finding the next batter in the lineup. I expect that situation to continue.

We have all heard owners cry poverty, fans decry that the games are not what they used to be, and sports analysts speculate whether a sport can survive recent economic turmoil. . . . Each sport has real economic problems. Tell me an area of life that does not! But each sport also has some major strengths and appears financially sound overall. In addition, each sport has been around a long time despite management that has sometimes been just a cut above indictable. It is reasonable to assume that all will continue to muddle along.

Strategic Planning

Sport Business in the Next Decade: A General Overview of Expected Trends

Daniel F. Mahony and Dennis R. Howard

CHALLENGES AHEAD: WILL THE '90s BOOM TURN TO A BUST?

The facility boom of the 1990s has profoundly altered the economic landscape of sports in North America in ways . . . analysts could not have imagined in 1989. Unfortunately, the building trend that held so much promise at the beginning of the 1990s has left the industry at the end of the decade in a precarious position.

Growing Disparity

At the start of the past decade, analysts were optimistically predicting that the gap between large and small market teams would be effectively closed because teams in new facilities would generate substantially more income, enough to remain competitive with teams in larger cities.[1] But, unfortunately, the reality emerging at the end of the decade is that new stadiums and arenas have provided only temporary and partial relief to smaller market teams. Once big-market teams in New York, Boston, and Los Angeles build new or revenue-enhanced facilities, the gap between the high-end markets and those in the middle, like San Francisco, or the lower-end, like Pittsburgh, will be even more dramatic. . . .

While the revenue gap among teams in baseball is becoming more and more a yawning chasm, the income-producing disparity of new venues is substantial across the other leagues as well. Consider that the Dallas Cowboys gross around $29 million a year from their 389 luxury suites alone, compared to the Minnesota Vikings, who receive about $6 to $7 million annually from their suite rentals.[2] Suite revenues are one of the few income streams produced by NFL teams that do not have to be shared.

Jerry Jones, owner of the Dallas Cowboys, gets to keep all of that $29 million, providing him with a decided competitive advantage.

While the abundant number of new venues has created more revenue for sport teams than ever before, it appears that rather than leading to greater economic parity and prosperity among teams, the building boom has exacerbated the gap between the haves and the have-nots. The imbalance in the economic fortunes of professional teams is further aggravated by the enormous debt incurred by those franchises that got a late start in the recent building boom. In the early 1990s, a number of teams . . . were able to leverage their way into new publicly-financed venues by threatening to move their teams to other cities. During that same period, a number of cities built new arenas and stadiums at *public expense* on the promise that these new sport edifices would produce thousands of new jobs, substantial tax revenues, and in effect, serve as engines of economic redevelopment.[3]

Teams able to cash in on this arrangement, like the Baltimore Orioles and Phoenix Suns, were able to occupy fully-subsidized state-of-the-art venues and through the conveyance of "sweet-heart" lease agreements, receive the lion's share, if not all, of the income from the sale of premium seating, naming rights, venue signage, etc. In contrast to the many teams benefiting from the public's largesse early in the decade, those clubs occupying new facilities, especially after 1996, found themselves in a completely different situation. The public's generosity began to wane in the mid-1990s. Voter resistance grew as economists like Noll and Zimbalist[4] and Rosentraub[5] provided compelling evidence that sports facilities did not produce the extensive economic benefits the proponents claimed.

At the close of the 1990s, the prospects for teams to receive large-scale public support had diminished greatly. In 1998 and 1999, in cities across the United States, local voters rejected 9 of 13 proposals to devote pubic tax monies toward the construction of new sports venues. In the four cities . . . where projects were approved, a sufficient number of voters were willing to support "soft" tax mechanisms like increased "bed" or car rental taxes, in which the biggest burden would be borne by visitors to the area. As a result, owners/teams have been forced to pay an increasingly greater share of the facility construction costs over the last half of the 1990s. Of the 24 major projects completed over the last two years of the 1990s, the owners contributed on average $120 million.[6]

Leveraged to the Hilt

This dramatic shift over the last half of the 1990s toward increased team or private financing has profoundly affected the economics of professional sport. As teams have had to pay more, a number of interrelated and unanticipated impacts have resulted. First, almost every team with a new facility or committed to building a new facility through 2003 is "hocked to the gills" according to CNBC's Dom Daliller.[7] The average of $120 million teams have borrowed to finance their share of facility construction actually grows to over $200 million when the interest costs are added to the full debt service obligation. In most every instance, the teams' annual debt service, often ranging from $15 to $30 million per year, has been secured largely from pledging a significant share of the teams' anticipated revenues from luxury suite rentals, club seat sales, parking, concessions, etc. The net result is that the team often realizes only modest amounts of "incremental" revenue. Rather than being awash in new money, ironically, teams find themselves increasingly awash in more debt.

Squeeze Play on Corporations and Fans

The highly-leveraged position of many teams — we estimate that entering the new millennium one-third of all major league teams will be in debt over 50% of their actual franchise value — has led to a second major consequence. The pressure to service debt and still realize enough excess revenue from the facility to pay escalating player salaries has meant that teams have to squeeze more from both corporations and fans. Clearly, teams have asked their fans to bear an increasing share of their growing debt and payroll burdens. During the 1990s, while salaries across the major leagues rose an average of 175%, the average cost of attending a league game increased almost 90%. . . .[8]

. . . .

While individual fans have borne a considerable share of teams' needs to raise more and more revenue, many teams, particularly those in heavily leveraged venues, find themselves in a financially dependent relationship with the corporate community. This dependency relationship is at its most vulnerable in those situations where the revenue derived from the sale of luxury suites serves as the primary source of income for repaying the team's large debt obligation. The substantial dependency on corporations is based on the fact that companies lease over 90% of the luxury suites occupied in sports venues.[9] In most instances, these corporations lease suites for three, five, and/or seven year periods. The vulnerability aspect becomes apparent when one considers that the team must generate sufficient suite revenues to pay off debt obligations that typically extend 20 to 25 years. Teams are liable for making debt service payments of as much as $10 to $20 million a year. For example, Daniel Snyder, who paid $800 million to purchase the Washington Redskins, is allegedly making debt service payments of $55 million. This means that in order to ensure a steady income flow from suite rentals over the entire length of the borrowing period, teams must resell or renew suite lease agreements from three to seven times.

With more and more leases due to expire in the early 2000s, teams in heavily leveraged situations face a critical challenge. Will current corporate suite holders renew existing leases for another three to seven years and, if not, can teams find enough companies willing to step in and replace them? . . . There is mounting concern that suite renewals are anything but automatic. In fact, most evidence suggests renewals have been very "soft" in many venues facing their first wave of widespread suite lease expirations.[10] Industry analysts concede that it will be particularly difficult to get corporations to renew suite leases in those market areas that are heavily saturated with premium facilities. At least nine markets, including Dallas, Tampa–St. Petersburg, Seattle, and Washington, D.C., have already become oversaturated with more suites available than large companies able or willing to fill them. . . .[11]

. . . . *[The authors' discussion of the emergence of new major competitors is omitted.]*

What If the Economy Falters?

The most serious "what if" question looming for sports teams in the decade ahead is "What if the economy should falter?" Will companies still be willing to invest their currently estimated $8 billion a year in sport properties to entitle new venues, occupy luxury suites, and to sponsor teams and/or special events? We feel pretty confident in predicting that the economy will slow down dramatically during the next decade. When and how severely is difficult to gauge, but many prominent economists believe a downturn is inevitable, and in a recessionary economy, the sports industry would be particularly vulnerable. . . .[12] Even the most remote prospect for an economic downturn should send a shiver through an industry so dependent on consumer spending. As Samuelson pointed out, "People spend when they believe in endless economic growth; businesses invest because people spend."[13] . . .

The repercussions for many corporate-dependent segments of the sport industry reliant on sponsorships, suites, and large-scale media deals could be devastating. According to Randy Vataha, a principal in an investment banking firm specializing in sports properties, "the number of teams and amount of money tied up in luxury suites and club seats clearly creates a greater risk today than it did 10 years ago."[14] The teams at greatest risk are those that built privately financed venues in the last few years. . . .

As the sports industry rides the crest of extended economic prosperity into the new millennium, it must recognize its vulnerabilities. While most acute at the major property levels (e.g., major leagues, big-time collegiate sports, men's and women's golf and tennis tours), a major recession would have an adverse impact on all segments of the sport industry. While serious challenges already face this industry, like sliding attendance in many segments, widespread declining television ratings, and a growing "corporate welfare" dependence, we are not ready to pronounce that the apocalypse is now upon us. These realities do suggest, however, the need for sport managers to prudently plan for the uncertainties of the new decade. Worst case or "what if" scenarios must be considered, and contingency plans drawn. The keys to maintaining economic vitality at the organizational level depend on tried and true survival mechanisms: cutting (or at least controlling) costs, and growing revenues. The managers who are most adept at achieving both these operational goals will be in the best position to flourish under any kind of economic circumstance in the decade ahead. For those hoping to ride out the inevitable economic downturn, finding a way to achieve at least one of those goals will be the key to survival.

WHAT IT WILL TAKE TO REMAIN VIABLE IN THE NEXT DECADE

Because we believe the general growth in the economy will not continue during the next decade, sport organizations will have to use a variety of strategies to remain viable. Although each of these strategies is ultimately designed to maximize profits, they present a variety of ways to accomplish this goal. The focus of some strategies will be to help improve revenue generation. This will be difficult for many sport products and services when the economy declines because they are often viewed as luxuries, not necessities. Therefore, many of the strategies will involve seeking new revenue streams previously unavailable or not thoroughly explored. Creative sport organizations that capture the consumers' imagination will be rewarded. Meanwhile, other strategies will focus more on cost containment. While the tendency of some organizations is to simply try to generate more revenue when times are tough, the next decade will be particularly challenging and sport organizations will have to find ways to increase efficiency and cut costs. Although it would be impossible to discuss all of the revenue-generating and cost containment strategies that sport organizations may use in the next decade, we will make a brief attempt to summarize some of the most common and the most creative strategies.

Taking Advantage of New Technology

Striving to take full advantage of the great potential of the Internet will be a focal point for many, if not most, sport organizations over the next decade. As Kahle and Meeske[15] pointed out, the sports industry has barely begun to take advantage of the promise the new technology offers with respect to revenue generation and fan development. The early rush by sports properties to adopt the technology was primarily concerned with simply getting on-line. Establishing a net presence usually involved creating a communication vehicle full of fan-friendly information (i.e., scores, player bios, schedules), "eye-popping graphics," and some interactivity.[16] It wasn't until the very end of the 1990s that major sport entities began to develop coherent, long-term web strategies. By 2000, most leagues and many teams have established Internet marketing divisions, dedicated to fully capitalizing on the enormous potential of the Web to sell licensed merchandise, engender fan loyalty, increase ticket sales, and for reaching disaffected fans.

. . . .

Other sports organizations are also taking advantage of the Internet's unique ability to access their fans in highly personalized ways. The New York Yankees have induced more than 150,000 website visitors to register for their listserve. The San Francisco Giants recently unveiled an innovative electronic ticket exchange program which should become a model for other sports organizations.[17] Season ticketholders will be able to use the Giants' website to sell tickets they can't use at face value or higher. The exchange program is designed to reduce no-shows by at least 50% and to increase ticket renewal rates by ensuring season ticketholders that they won't be holding a drawer full of unused tickets at season's end.

. . . .

. . . . It is imperative that sport managers closely monitor this quickly evolving technology. No matter what form or to what extent convergence may occur, it is clear that the integration of television and the computer will require managers to carefully consider a whole range of critical issues, from how to both protect and enhance broadcast rights to fully leveraging the considerable revenue opportunities related to virtual advertising, sponsorship, and merchandising.

It is conceivable that advances in technology will make paper tickets and ticket sellers all but disappear by the end of the decade, to be replaced by electronic tickets and electronic turnstiles. Fan card technology is advancing at such a rapid rate that soon fans will not have to bring money to the ballpark. The card-swipe technology will allow fans to purchase concessions and team merchandise at the same time they will be collecting points for prizes provided by the team. Fan cards allow teams to reward their most loyal fans, and at the same time, provide teams with the ability to develop sophisticated databases on fan purchase behaviors (who buys what, how often, at what point in a game, etc.). In addition, there are a number of other exciting technological advancements that will become increasingly prominent in the next few years, such as "smart" seats, video-based data systems, and virtual signage.

However, not all technological changes will be good for sport organizations. First, some of the improvements in technology will make some currently strong areas less profitable. For example, with the advent of cable, viewers have far more viewing options, which has led to very few sporting events drawing a large viewership. Even those with great ratings are seeing some general declines, and with the number of stations expected to increase at an even faster rate in the next decade, this decline should be expected to continue. Therefore, when some organizations find ways to generate revenue from new technology they may simply be replacing revenue lost due to new technology.

Second, there will be considerable pressure on sport organizations to keep up with their competitors by investing in new "state of the art" technology. Due to this pressure, many sport organizations will make poor technological investments. They will invest in technology that quickly becomes obsolete or was never worth the money invested. Overall, the potential for both positive and negative outcomes will lead many sport organizations to seek technology experts as consultants or full-time employees if they do not already have them. These individuals will be critical in making investment and usage decisions regarding this new technology. Organizations that do not seek these individuals will make many mistakes in the constantly changing world of technology that will frequently cost far more than the services of the experts.

Exploit the Big Events, Rivalries, and Stars

Whether it's the Super Bowl or the World Cup . . . sport organizations will seek to exploit anything or anyone that is popular to the maximum extent possible. In a highly competitive marketplace, organizations frequently exploit their most popular assets.[18] Although some fans may complain about the excessive coverage of some events and stars, the fact remains these big events and big stars draw considerable interest and organizations can only assure they will get the most out of them if they take full advantage of them when they are popular. The NBA, Chicago Bulls, Nike, and other corporate sponsors never stopped exploiting Michael Jordan's popularity because even if some fans may have had enough of Mike, he still drew larger audiences and greater sales than other American athletes.

In addition to exploiting popular assets, the desire for big events and stars will have two related impacts. First, sport organizations will no longer pay big money for events and stars not popular enough to be exploited this way. The recent move by many sporting good manufacturers to dump most of their high priced endorsers is the beginning of a trend, not a unique situation that will soon pass. Essentially, there will be only a few truly exploitable events, rivalries, and stars in the next decade and those associated with them will reap the rewards. However, there will be a much larger group of also-rans, which will never be able to attract a large enough interest.

Second, sport organizations will continue to seek the next mega-event, mega-rivalry, and mega-star to exploit and will often try to create them when they do not emerge on their own. For example, it appears likely to us that the NCAA will either start or have in the works a true National Championship in Division I-A football by the end of the next decade. The current Bowl Championship Series (BCS) format has led to one exploitable game and a number of also-ran bowls with decreasing fan interest and ratings. In contrast, a 16 team playoff could be exploited for at least a month and generate far more fan and advertising interest and more revenue.[19] The recent purchase of the broadcasting rights for the NCAA Men's Basketball Tournament by CBS for $6.2 billion over 11 years, a 252% increase from the previous contract, is a clear indication of the tremendous value of the big events. Essentially, CBS will be paying an average $545 million each year for a tournament that lasts only three weeks.

Overall, the search for the next Michael Jordan, the next World Cup, and the next Arnold Palmer–Jack Nickalus rivalry will not end. In the last year professional golf twice tried to find a rival for Tiger Woods, first with David Duval and later with Sergio Garcia, with the hope of exploiting such a rivalry to increase fan interest. Meanwhile, the NBA focused on promoting Toronto Raptor star Vince Carter as the next "Michael Jordan." However, sport organizations will be quicker to abandon these efforts if the star or event does not emerge as being truly capable of being exploited.

Improved Targeting Efforts by Small Organizations

While the previous section highlighted the increasing importance of the big events, rivalries, and stars, this does not mean the sport industry will decrease in size and eliminate all of the smaller events and organizations. Although not all of the organizations that have emerged in the last decade or will emerge in the next decade will survive, many will do very well, albeit on a smaller scale. What will distinguish the survivors from the rest will be their ability to reach a distinct target market. If they can obtain consistently strong loyalty from a relatively small, but distinct, group of fans and/or consumers, they will be able to match their target market with the target markets of advertisers and sponsors. Although they will never be able to be competitive with the larger events and organizations, this strategy will provide a steady flow of income that, combined with good cost controls, will allow these organizations to be financially successful over the long term. In the United States, both women's professional softball and bass fishing have achieved some success using this approach. However, new organizations that try to reach a mass audience and do not find their own distinct niche in the marketplace will be the organizations that fail. In this highly competitive sport marketplace, they will certainly have plenty of company.

Tapping New Markets

As suggested above, the small organizations that achieve success will be those that find their own unique target market. In fact, the most successful will probably be those that are able to find a market which has largely been ignored in the past. However, the small organizations will not be alone in their efforts to seek demographically and/or geographically distinct groups. Large organizations will also be looking to expand into new markets. Within the United States, we expect to see more organizations targeting those groups who are generally marginalized by society including minority groups, people with disabilities, gays and lesbians, and women. The recent success of the Women's World Cup and the WNBA has been related in part to their ability to appeal to female fans, particularly young girls. In another example, a number of baseball teams have begun to try and improve their efforts at marketing to Hispanic fans.

Finally, the global expansion predicted by Rosner[20] is far from over. Sporting goods manufacturers and professional sport leagues and teams will continue their efforts to generate additional revenue from the world marketplace. While the possibility for World Leagues still appears to be a distant dream, the potential to generate increased merchandise sales and broadcast fees makes Europe and Asia particularly appealing to the North American based organizations. Likewise, it appears quite possible European and Asian sport organizations will increase their efforts to capture revenue in North America. For example, the potential to earn revenue from broadcasting Premier League soccer games on one or more of the ever expanding North American television stations would appear to be fairly strong. Essentially, while the predictions by Rosner and his experts related to the changes in the world sport marketplace may have been slightly premature, they will prove to be quite accurate over the long term.

Reconnect with Traditional Fans/Consumers

While seeking new markets appears to have been a relatively common goal among sport organizations for some time (the expansion of Major League Baseball into Canada began about 30 years ago), the bigger change in strategy in the next decade will be an effort to reconnect with traditional fans/consumers. Despite the tremendous growth in the field of sport marketing, it is still amazing that many sport organizations will readily admit they know virtually nothing about their current fan base. However, the difference is now many of them recognize this as a problem and are trying to do something about it. More sport organizations are talking about the need to establish strong relationships with their fans, particularly those who have left or are on the verge of leaving.

For example, college football administrators recognized a couple of years ago that they were losing the student fans. Not only were they concerned about losing a traditional fan base, they were particularly concerned because this is a group they expect long-term support from as alumni. After realizing they had a problem, the NCAA put together a marketing campaign aimed at bringing students back to college football games. Although their problem may not yet be solved, they certainly made an effort to reconnect. In another example, Nike made considerable efforts to appeal to African-American consumers after receiving criticism for exploiting this demographic group.[21] Although Nike's sales were still strong at that time, they did not want to risk losing a large number of African-American consumers. This need to maintain strong support from the traditional consumers will only become stronger as the market declines and becomes more competitive in the next decade. Those sport organizations seeking only to exploit their relationship with their consumers to maximize profits will certainly suffer in the upcoming decade.

Creative Financing

While North American fans will likely receive increased exposure to overseas sports leagues, such as the English Premier League and Australian Rules Football, it is also quite likely that managers of sports organizations in Canada and the United States will import more marketing and financing innovations that have been successfully implemented in Europe and other places around the world. In fact, as surprising as it may be to many managers of sports properties in North America, some of the most recent innovations in sport financing originated in Europe. For example, asset-backed securitizations (ABS bonds) and public stock sales (IPOs) were pioneered by soccer clubs in England, Spain, and Italy. . . .

. . . . As sports become increasingly global, over the next decade we should expect to see a great deal more importation of the latest marketing and financing applications from Europe and other places around the world.

. . . .

. . . . It is clear that as more creative forms of financing become necessary, those sport managers that will be the most successful in adopting these innovations will have developed at least a basic understanding of the nuances of both debt and equity financing. In addition, it will be necessary for those organizations attempting to put together complex projects to hire consultants or full-time employees with strong financial expertise. Similar to our discussion related to technology, financing decisions involve considerable sums of money, so mistakes can be costly. Therefore, the expertise needed to make such decisions will need to be far greater than many sport organizations have had in the past.

Budget Cuts

Although many sport organizations have been seen as free spenders without concern for cost,[22] the highly competitive environment in the next decade will force many organizations to focus on cutting the budget and controlling expenses in addition to increasing revenue. Colleges and universities in the United States have been regularly cutting sports since the late 1980s and there is no reason to believe this trend will not continue.[23] All of the major professional sport leagues have attempted to bring labor costs under control with varying degrees of success. The labor wars of the last 20 years will continue in the next decade as owners continue their efforts to control costs.

This does not mean, however, that sport organizations will cut all costs equally. It is our prediction that sport organizations will continue to spend heavily on players, teams, endorsers, and other employees when they believe there will be a payoff for this investment, while significantly cutting areas not expected to have a great payoff.[24] The decision by many colleges to eliminate men's non-revenue sports rather than decrease the budget for football or men's basketball is reflective of such a strategy. We are also seeing an increasing gap between the salaries of the star players and the bench players on many professional teams. This compensation gap between the haves and the have-nots will become even stronger in the next decade.

Synergy

Another recent trend is the attempt by sport organizations to control costs and increase efficiency through mergers and acquisitions. Stotlar's[25] article thoroughly detailed the increasing number of mergers and acquisitions involving sport organizations. He ended his article by asking the question on the mind of most observers — "where does . . . this madness end?"[26] It is our prediction that the "madness" is far from over and the increased activity in 1999 would appear to indicate the efforts toward synergy may actually increase in the next decade. Mergers between teams (e.g., the New York Yankees and the New Jersey Nets), leagues (e.g., the National Football League and the Arena Football League), and organizations in the same industry (e.g., sport agent firms) will continue to increase in number.

Although horizontal integration such as the examples discussed above will remain popular, vertical integration, particularly when it involves sport organizations and media corporations, may become the most popular.[27] These combinations allow the sport organization access to large amounts of "free" promotion and the media corporation access to "free" programming for their outlets (e.g., television stations, radio stations). In fact, some observers have noted that it can be less expensive for the media outlet to buy the sport organization as opposed to paying the rapidly increasing television rights fees.[28] Stotlar also notes that there are clear benefits from successful vertical integration including the "cost savings through a reduction of redundant services and personnel."[29] While the growing number of combinations in the sport industry may appear to be "insane" to many observers, the increased efficiency and cost savings resulting from successful mergers and acquisitions would indicate [that] those who were involved in bringing these organizations together are quite sane and are helping their organizations to achieve long-term security and success. In fact, we believe this trend toward integration will stop only if the government becomes concerned that these mergers and acquisitions are having a detrimental effect on competition, which does not appear to be the case at this point.[30]

CONCLUSION

Overall, it appears the next decade will be particularly challenging for many sport organizations. The sport industry boom of the 1990s will end, and declines in the economy and increasing competition will make success harder for many organizations to attain. In this new sport marketplace, more sophisticated and innovative organizations will be the most successful, while those holding to the "build it and they will come" philosophy of sport management will surely suffer. While the strategies discussed in this article do not address every innovative strategy that will be used by successful sport organizations in the next decade, we do provide a thorough list of some of the strategies that will be more commonly used. The strategies discussed in this article included: the aggressive adoption of Internet marketing and other emerging technological developments; a focus on the big events, rivalries, and stars; the tapping of new markets; improved targeting efforts; attempts to reconnect with traditional fans/consumers; the creative use of more complex equity and debt financing techniques; increased budget cuts; and promoting cost and service efficiencies through organizational consolidation and vertical integration. A number of these strategies will require a level of sophistication not generally associated with the sport marketplace. However, such high levels of sophistication will be common by the end of the next decade among those sport organizations that will continue to be successful in the challenging times that lie ahead.

REFERENCES

1. Ozanian, M., & Taub, S. (1992, July 7). Big leagues, bad business. *Financial World,* 34–42.

2. Fisher, D., & Ozanian, M. (1999, September 20). Cowboy capitalism. *Forbes,* 171–177.

3. Rosentraub, M. (1997). *Major league losers: The real cost of sports and who's paying for it.* New York: Basic Books.

4. Noll, R., & Zimbalist, A., (1997). *Sports, Jobs, and Taxes: The Economic Impact of Sports Teams and Stadiums.* Washington, DC: The Brookings Institution Press.

5. Rosentraub, M. (1997). *Major league losers: The real cost of sports and who's paying for it.* New York: Basic Books.

6. Howard, D. R. (1999). *The future of stadium financing.* Paper presented at the International Sport Summit '99, New York, NY, January 18.

7. Howard, D. R. (1999). The changing fanscape of big-league sports: Implications for sport managers. *Journal of Sport Management, 13,* 78–91.

8. Cohen, W. (1999, November 15). Oysters, scotch, and hoops. *U.S. News & World Report,* 92–93; Howard, D. R. (1999). The changing fanscape of big-league sports: Implications for sport managers. *Journal of Sport Management, 13,* 78–91.

9. Howard, D. R. (1999). *The future of stadium financing.* Paper presented at the International Sport Summit '99, New York, NY, January 18.

10. Maloney, R. (1999, August 3). Sabres hunt suite re-signees. *Street & Smith's Sports Business Journal,* 1, 6; Van Alphen, T. (1999, November 11). Skydome slashes suite lease prices. *Toronto Star,* Web site.

11. Howard, D. R. (1999). The changing fanscape of big-league sports: Implications for sport managers. *Journal of Sport Management, 13,* 78–91.

12. Kaplan, D. (1998, October 19). Is sports business recession-proof? Talk of a downturn prompts debate. *Street & Smith's Sports Business Journal,* 1, 1, 37.

13. Samuelson, R. (1998, July 27). Is this too good to last? *Newsweek,* 39.

14. Kaplan, D. (1998, October 19). Is sports business recession-proof? Talk of a downturn prompts debate. *Street & Smith's Sports Business Journal,* 1, 1, 37.

15. Kahle, L. & Meeske, C. (1999). Sports marketing and the internet: It's a whole new ballgame. *Sports Marketing Quarterly, 8* (2), 9–12.

16. Duncan, M. & Campbell, R. (1999). Internet users: How to reach them and how to integrate the internet into the marketing strategy of sports businesses. *Sport Marketing Quarterly, 8* (2), 35–42.

17. Dickey, G. (2000, June 14). Giants' new ticket plan a winner. *San Francisco Chronicle,* Web site; Migala, D. (2000, June 5). Make online ticketing a winner with these 4 tips. *Street & Smith's Sports Business Journal, 3,* 22.

18. Stevens, E. L. & Grover, M. (1998, February 16). The entertainment glut. *Business Week,* 88–95.

19. Dunnavant, K. (1998, December 28). Redoing the game. *Street & Smith's Sports Business Journal, 1,* at 19, 28–29.

20. Rosner, D. (1989, January 2). The world plays catch-up. *Sports, Inc.,* 6–13.

21. Armstrong, K. L. (1999). Nike's communication with black audiences: A sociological analysis of advertising effectiveness via symbolic interactionism. *Journal of Sport and Social Issues, 23,* 266–286.

22. Basralian, J. (1995, February 14). Financial controls? What financial controls? *Financial World,* 121.

23. Mahony, D. F., & Pastore, D. (1998). Distributive justice: An examination of participation opportunities, revenues, and expenses at NCAA institutions — 1973–1993. *Journal of Sport and Social Issues, 22,* 127–148.

24. Mahony, D. F., & Pastore, D. (1998). Distributive justice: An examination of participation opportunities, revenues, and expenses at NCAA institutions — 1973–1993. *Journal of Sport and Social Issues, 22,* 127–148.

25. Stotlar, D. (2000). Vertical integration in sport. *Journal of Sport Management, 14,* 1–7.

26. Stotlar, D. (2000). Vertical integration in sport. *Journal of Sport Management, 14,* 1–7, at 6.

27. Miller, S. (1999, August 23). Taking sports to the next level. *Street & Smith's Sports Business Journal, 2,* 23, 32; Stotlar, D. (2000). Vertical integration in sport. *Journal of Sport Management, 14,* 1–7.

28. Stotlar, D. (2000). Vertical integration in sport. *Journal of Sport Management, 14,* 1–7.

29. Stotlar, D. (2000). Vertical integration in sport. *Journal of Sport Management, 14,* 1–7, at 1.

30. Stotlar, D. (2000). Vertical integration in sport. *Journal of Sport Management, 14,* 1–7.

BRANDING

MANAGING NORTH AMERICAN MAJOR PROFESSIONAL SPORT TEAMS IN THE NEW MILLENNIUM: A FOCUS ON BUILDING BRAND EQUITY

James M. Gladden, Richard L. Irwin, and William A. Sutton

Following a decade that produced astonishing player salaries, continued player mobility, widespread corporate involvement, and skyrocketing ticket prices and broadcast rights fees, North American major league professional sport teams enter the 21st century encountering a number of significant challenges. An analysis of the aforementioned trends yields valuable insight into the future of professional team sport management in North America and leads to the identification of a primary concern of team owners and operators, that of managing the franchise's brand equity. With team owners increasingly reaping profits from the long-term appreciation of the team's value while continuing to lose money on a yearly basis, there will be an increased focus on strengthening team brands. This new focus will lead management to build and maintain brand equity through two primary means: the acquisition of assets and the enhancement of customer relationships. Each of these predictions is explained in depth in this paper and examples are provided.

. . . .

Hereafter, we contend that 2000 to 2010 will be the decade in which team management activities evolve from a focus on winning as a means of realizing short-term profits to a focus on strategic management of the team brand as a means of realizing long-term appreciation in franchise value. Beyond the fact that each league produces only one champion per year, there are a variety of reasons that such a paradigm shift will occur. As the merger between the Yankees and Nets demonstrates, team owners are now beginning to focus on the accumulation of assets to increase the value of the team. In addition, brand management will be needed if major league professional teams hope to curb the trend of alienating the individual fan in the interest of courting corporate dollars.

. . . . *[The authors' review of the 1990s is omitted.]*

THE FOCUS ON BUILDING BRAND EQUITY

. . . North American professional sport franchises will continue to be challenged by issues of profitability. As a result, the corporate involvement in sport and the focus of selling the sport product to corporations will not decrease. Further, the manner in which owners view their teams will continue to evolve. Given the rapid escalation in franchise values, a long-term focus on the appreciation of the franchise's value, or equity, will increasingly dictate the actions of North American team sport managers. This will cause a shift in the way teams are viewed and managed.

Specifically, we contend that teams in this decade will increasingly be viewed as brands and managed accordingly. The goal of such efforts will be to build brand equity. . . . The key for professional teams will be to differentiate their brand by developing and/or strengthening positive associations with team brands in the minds of their consumers. . . . Adaptation and responsiveness will become the focus of professional teams because it will help owners satisfy the desire to increase franchise value.

. . . In sport, though, managers have largely demonstrated a consistently myopic view that winning is the only means to generate equity.[1] While it is not disputed that winning greatly enhances brand equity, and consistent losing detracts from equity, Gladden and Milne[2] documented the fact that success and brand equity are distinct constructs that result in the realization of positive marketplace outcomes (e.g., merchandise sales). Thus, in this decade, sport teams will look to other ways to create brand equity for their respective sport teams. While success in competition is vitally important and can drive a brand, a broader, more long-term approach is needed in the present context. We have argued that the owner's financial return is not in the short-term profits, but rather in the long-term appreciation of assets. Central to appreciation then is the enhancement of such assets. . . . Further, mainstream marketing research has already demonstrated that brand-building efforts play a significant role in increasing the value of companies in a variety of industries.[3]

. . . . We envision that during the early stages of the 21st century, team owners and managers will be charged with building and maintaining brand equity with the individual fans, corporations, and media outlets that are crucial to the success of sport teams. At the crux of these efforts will be strategic efforts to build relationships with these groups that result in brand loyalty. . . . "The advent of the term 'relationship management' captures this new awareness."[4] This view will be increasingly applied to strengthen team brands in this decade.

These relationship-building efforts will focus on two aspects that are consistent with the definitions of brand equity management set forth above. First, professional teams will focus on acquiring assets (thus creating additional channel relationships) that will enhance the equity of the brand by allowing it to better serve its varied customers in a cost effective and profit maximizing manner. To do this, we contend that strategies such as integration, strategic alliances, and mergers will be more common in the next decade. The second focus of this paper is on the individual fans of professional team sport. While a team needs corporations to purchase its luxury suites, the luxury suites are meaningless as hospitality tools if people are not interested in attending the games. Similarly, the corporations interested in sponsoring teams and media entities are interested in broadcasting games because of the audiences that team sport deliver. For these two reasons, the second prong of the team sport manager's brand management efforts will be to increase their efforts to develop long-term relationships with fans.

BUILDING BRAND EQUITY THROUGH
THE ACQUISITION OF ASSETS

Acquiring assets will be a primary brand management strategy employed by professional teams in the future. As it relates to major league professional sport, it will increasingly appear that there is a great deal of truth in the axiom "there is strength in numbers." Through the acquisition of assets, namely product offerings, sport managers will be able to more effectively integrate and bundle packages of inventory for corporate consumers (sponsors and advertisers). In addition, this will allow for the seasonal focus on different sport holdings by one single staff, as opposed to the past where one staff focused on one property. Taken together, the bundling and increased operational efficiency will lead to profit maximization and brand equity through the achievement of economies of scale, particularly as it relates to corporate sales.

Thus, consistent with the view of Pitts and Stotlar,[5] we contend that North American professional teams will choose to pursue practices common among their chief competitors (in entertainment) and amass synergistic assets that not only enhance production, delivery, and consumption, but also the financial value of the franchise. These efforts will focus on asset acquisition through the following means: (a) integration strategies, (b) strategic alliances, and (c) mergers. . . .

Integration Strategies

Integration strategies, or the acquisition of distributors, suppliers, and/or competitors[6] will continue to impact the major league professional sport industry. . . . Mass media owners were focused on sport teams because it allowed them to acquire content for distribution. In turn, this gave the corporate owner more control over the production and distribution of the sport product. This allowed for operational efficiencies, such as the bundling of advertising inventory, which resulted in more attractive offerings for corporations, thus leading to profit maximization. . . .

Integration strategies have also been increasingly popular among Major League Baseball teams. Purchasing ownership of minor league teams and then relocating these teams within reasonable proximity to the major league team creates a feeder system designed to nurture fan affiliation from the time a player is 18 through their major league career. This integration ensures that fans have a longer relationship with the organization to not only attend games, but also to view them on television, access their Web sites, and purchase merchandise and sponsors' products. From a business perspective, integration provides packaging for regional sports channels and the reduction of travel costs because they can be shared throughout the system. . . .

Integration strategies will become even more prevalent for two reasons. The first is that the increased prevalence of Regional Sports Networks and their ownership of professional sports teams (i.e., Comcast Spectacor and the Philadelphia Flyers and minor league hockey Philadelphia Phantoms) can greatly enhance the equity of team brands by broadening product offerings such that more diverse audiences are delivered. This will allow teams to bundle the consolidated property's rights, ultimately increasing sponsorship fees, and in some cases media rights. In the case of the Philadelphia Phantoms, Comcast Spectacor is able to broaden the audience it delivers by expanding beyond the typical corporate client that pays an average of $40 for a ticket to attend a Flyers game to a more middle-class or family-oriented fan that can afford to attend a smattering of Phantoms games less expensively. This strategy must be working for Comcast because it recently purchased three minor league baseball teams. Second, as is evidenced by the WNBA, with more team owners also owning their facilities, these owners will seek complimentary programming for their facilities, which not only makes the facility profitable, but also delivers a broader and more diverse audience to sponsors. Integration will continue to occur this decade due to expansion of the WNBA, Arena Football League, and Minor League Hockey.

While integration appears to make conceptual sense, the actual implementation of such acquisitions will provide a challenge to sport managers of the future. Sport entities will not be immune to some of the typical problems that arise when corporations integrate. For example, integration often creates problems meeting capacity at each stage in the value chain.[7] In the case of Comcast Spectacor, the challenges of coordinating the sales of packaged inventory across two hockey teams and three baseball teams using one combined sales staff are immense. Thompson and Strickland[8] also note [that] integration requires different business skills. As part of their burgeoning entertainment conglomerate, Comcast Spectacor has also created public skating rinks called Flyers Skate Zones. In this case the business challenges of managing a skating rink are much different than those of managing a baseball or hockey team. Such problems have often led companies to consider strategic alliances and joint ventures rather than integration. This will be true in sport as well.

Strategic Alliances

. . . . As we move to the next millennium, strategic alliances and joint ventures will play an important role in assisting teams to develop brand equity. . . . Varadarajan and Cunningham[9] contend one of the motives of strategic alliances is to shape the structure of the industry. Already, there are . . . visible examples of this. First, the NBA has entered into a strategic alliance with sports and entertainment giant SFX to promote the NBA's new minor league.[10] In doing so, the NBA is taking an innovative step to create formal synergies between sport and musical entertainment offerings. . . .

. . . .

In the future, we agree with Lachowetz[11] that strategic alliances will be broadened to include the sales of tickets. Lachowetz contends that "regional sports alliances"[12] will begin to emerge in metropolitan markets. These alliances will serve to package inventory targeted to both corporations and individuals (i.e., tickets). In doing so, traditional non-users might be introduced to another team's product via a "sample" of the sport options in a market. Such alliances have been completed between two teams already (the NBA's Toronto Raptors and the NHL's Toronto Maple Leafs) but have yet to include more than two entities. Rest assured, such variations of the regional sports alliance will emerge in the future, for they allow for a broader population to be served, thus increasing and improving customer relationships between the fan and the team brand.

While strategic alliances will definitely become more prominent as a means of enhancing brand equity, some of the typical problems associated with strategic alliances will also occur. Day[13] suggests the greatest costs associated with a strategic alliance are when the alliance fails to meet expectations and/or is dissolved for poor performance. While these alliances to sell broadcast time, sponsorships, and tickets may work for some markets, in others they will not be successful. This will be particularly true in situations where an entity in the alliance possesses more brand equity than its partners. . . . In fact, according to Aaker and Joachimsthaler,[14] a corporation would be wise to stay away from sponsoring a brand that did not provide associative brand image benefits. Another problem with strategic alliances is that organizational cultures may clash. . . .[15] Thus, the sponsor benefits realized by the teams, particularly from a promotional perspective, might vary, thus creating resentment between the partners in the alliance.

Mergers

The recent formation of YankeeNets through the merger of MLB's New York Yankees with the NBA's New Jersey Nets, marked a departure from accepted practice into a realm of virtually uncharted reality and unlimited possibility. It represents a model whereby individual teams can merge to enhance each other's operational revenue, while at the same time building brand equity. . . .

At the root of the merger was Yankees owner George Steinbrenner's desire to create a Regional Sports Network and control the broadcasts of Yankees games.[16] While the Yankees, fresh off three championships in 4 years would provide programming for the spring, summer, and early fall, Steinbrenner needed programming for the late fall and winter. The NBA's New Jersey Nets provided just such programming. A merger resulted, which provides synergies that can enhance the brands of both teams. First, it creates operational efficiencies. While each team's on-field and on-court activities (including player personnel decisions) will be handled separately, the business and marketing operations will be handled by one unit. This allows for the two-team entity to package the sale of local television rights, sponsorships, advertising, and luxury suites. . . . In effect, by merging, the Yankees and Nets created an entity with enhanced equity due to the increased breadth of packages that can be offered to advertisers. In an effort to enhance equity further, YankeeNets purchased a stake in the New Jersey Devils professional hockey team and formed a strategic alliance with the Manchester United of the English Premier League to promote each other's brands.

. . . .

While YankeeNets provides numerous opportunities to enhance brand equity, the Yankees may not have selected the optimal partner. As a perennial champion, the Yankees have a high perception of quality and are certainly one of the top brand names in Major League Baseball. By contrast, the Nets have a history of poor performance, and it could be argued that they are one of the weaker brand names in the NBA. In the context of brand management then, does the acquisition of an inferior property decrease the prestige and image of the Yankees organization? . . . . A more appropriate fit, that is a merger where the brand strength of the two entities would be more comparable, would have been between the Yankees and Knicks. However, given the fact that the Knicks (and Rangers) are owned by Cablevision, which operates the MSG Network (that televises Yankee games until the 2001 season), such a merger was not possible. The direct impact of taking on an entity whose image is different is yet to be seen. *[YankeeNets formally dissolved in March 2004, though the teams remain partners in the YES Network.]*

Summary

Based on the recent efforts by major league professional teams (and/or their owners), we contend that the acquisition of assets, via integration, strategic alliances, and mergers, will be a primary tool utilized by sport managers to enhance the equity associated with their teams. While these efforts are not commonplace yet, they will be necessary if team owners hope to continue realizing appreciation in the values of their franchises. However, we also caution that such efforts will not be achieved without problems. Specifically, in acquiring additional assets, sport managers will need to overcome problems associated with the integration of inventories, personnel, and brand imagery.

BUILDING BRAND EQUITY THROUGH CUSTOMER RELATIONSHIPS

Much has been written regarding the need for professional sports to win back the consuming public. Escalating ticket prices, franchise relocation, and free agency all pose serious threats to the maintenance of a core base of consumers into the future. While corporations, rather than individuals, purchase the majority of in-stadium/arena tickets, the individual sport fan is still vitally important to the team's brand equity. The individual sport consumer influences both the corporate and media entities that are helping to underwrite sport. Without the large base of individual fans, there is no television audience for broadcasting entities. Similarly, without the large base of individual fans, teams would be much less attractive to sponsors as vehicles to target fans. We are already seeing hints of this. . . . Another reason teams may refocus on individuals is that they will be more recession/depression-proof than the corporation. Howard[17] suggested the corporate consumer is not nearly as emotionally connected and involved with professional teams as the individual fan. Thus, in the advent of a recession, the hospitality budgets that finance corporate season tickets and luxury suites will be one of the first line items eliminated.

So, the question becomes, how can pro sport managers enhance relationships with individual fans? This question is even more perplexing given the fact that the glut of technology-based entertainment offerings (e.g., Internet, virtual reality games) will further compete for the sport consumer's time and money. In response, professional teams of this decade will focus on developing positive mental associations with their team brands as a means of fostering long-term loyalty. Such associations provide the basis for brand differentiation, ultimately leading to loyalty and brand equity.[18] Keller[19] suggests that there are three keys to forming brand associations in the consumer's mind: strength, favorability, and uniqueness. Given its unpredictable and subjective nature, sport offers a very unique offering in the entertainment marketplace.[20] However, sport teams have recently fostered unfavorable brand associations for a variety of reasons, including franchise relocation (or the threat of) and the trading of key players in order to reduce team expenditures. Out of necessity then, sport managers in this decade will both recognize and centralize their focus on building relationships with their fans as a means of fostering positive brand associations. . . .

Specifically, we contend that teams will seek to enhance their relationships with individual fans by increasingly utilizing four broad-based strategies:

1. Developing an enhanced understanding of the consumer
2. Increasing the interactions between the consumer and the brand
3. Reinforcing and rewarding loyalty to the team brand
4. Consistent integrated marketing communication to reinforce key brand associations

Toward a Better Understanding of the Team Sport Consumer

Before teams can create or take advantage of the brand associations consumers have with their teams, they must first understand consumers' existing perceptions of their brands. As such, an important component of teams' efforts to build better relationships with their customers will be an increased focus on soliciting, listening, and responding to consumer needs. . . . It is amazing that the market research conducted by sport teams is not more sophisticated. . . . For the major professional sport team of this next decade, the challenge is to learn as much as possible about their consumers. . . .

Dialogue with customers is bound to increase after years [of] decline. . . . It is not outside the realm of possibility that brand focused teams will poll fans prior to trading a popular player.

In the next decade, team managers will make better use of technology to garner a more intricate understanding of their consumers. The focus of these efforts will be to build detailed databases so that more personal interactions and appeals can be made. For example, the fan loyalty programs where consumers "swipe" their identification card at a kiosk every time they attend provide resources to build a database of people attending games. While such technology is only starting to become prevalent, its use will be expanded such that the team will be able to track not only when someone attends, but where they park, how much food, beverage, and merchandise they purchase, and when they leave. While numerous retail organizations have been employing this technology for over a decade (e.g., grocery stores), teams are just now awakening to its utility. Similarly, teams will become adept at using their Web page to gather information about their consumers. . . . Thus, both surveys and on-line focus groups (through the team chat rooms) will become an increasingly common practice among teams.

Increasing Consumer Interactions with the Team Brand

In addition to learning more about their customers in an effort to better satisfy needs, professional sport managers will also realize the importance of fostering regular interactions between the consumer and their brands. The end goal of such interactions would be what Rozanski, Baum, and Wolfsen[21] call "emotional loyalty." Such loyalty is formed in two ways: from a consumer's personal relationship with a brand and through the formation of strong user communities around the brand. Sport is unique in that it allows for direct experience with the team brand. In this sense, sport has advantages over consumer products because it fosters more direct experiences, which are vital to brand building.[22] . . . . As such, we suggest that teams will focus on the ease with which positive brand associations with a particular team can be created given a consumer's willingness and desire to belong to a particular group. . . .

Central to the enhanced interactions found in user groups will be the ability of team marketers to involve players and coaches in these efforts. Today, given the ever-heightening media scrutiny associated with these figures' celebrity, there is very little interaction between fans and players and coaches.[23] Out of the necessity to build relationships in an effort to build brand equity, team managers will seek to alter this trend. One way this may happen is through providing players and coaches with an ownership stake in the team. Productivity and motivation among employees, whether it be players, coaches, or account executives, can be affected by watching stock values rise and fall.[24] Therefore, we speculate that player and coach contracts will offer a stake in ownership as an incentive. One outcome of this strategy is that players will pay more attention to fan interaction and personal appearances.

Product extensions using the team's brand name will also be used to enhance consumer interactions with the brand. Consistent with owners' efforts to integrate as a means of creating an entity with many complementary product offerings, we predict that teams will own and operate off-site viewing venues such as sports grills and theaters as well as merchandise outlets. In response to escalating ticket prices, Howard[25] contends that those unable to afford a ticket will turn to sports bars for professional team sport consumption. Therefore, it makes sense that teams seize this opportunity to control the consumption environment and add to its asset portfolio in much the same fashion as several English Premier Soccer clubs.[26] By controlling the consumption environment, the team will also be controlling and enhancing consumer interactions with the brand.

Integrated Brand Communications to Reinforce Positive Associations

Consistent with a focus on fostering positive associations as a means of building a strong relationship with consumers, professional team managers will also recognize the importance of taking a consistent, long-term approach to marketing their brands. . . . This speaks to the need for a long-term vision to guide the planning of marketing activities. Consistent communication about the brand is also important to maintaining positive associations over time.[27] However, a main challenge to maintaining consistency for the sport team is the disasters that occur in the form of unexpected losing seasons, player misconduct and injuries, and coaching changes. The pro team will often react to such problems by amending their marketing communications in an effort to reduce the fallout from the problem. Instead of being reactive, pro teams will become more proactive.

. . . . The challenge for sport teams will be to identify the core values that the organization wants to promote and to communicate them throughout the organization and to current and prospective consumers. This need is already being recognized. . . . Several values that will emerge have already been discussed: a focus on creating a connection between the team and the consumers and an emphasis on rewarding consumer loyalty. Pro teams of the future will concentrate on communicating these core values and others across all marketing platforms including promotional events, advertising campaigns, community relations efforts, public relations efforts, and Web marketing.

As teams pay more attention to their brand's core values, the personnel side of the business will be impacted. For example, if a team brand is focusing on families, then the team will avoid signing or trading for players that have poor personal reputations. While winning is important, doing so at the expense of contradicting a key brand association is poor brand management practice. Thus, look for brand management efforts to impact the personnel side of professional teams of the future. Such efforts have already been implemented in several instances. . . .

This emphasis on brand management practices will also lead teams to focus less on success when marketing their teams. While success may be fleeting, a focus on commitment to customers is not. . . .

Reinforcing and Rewarding Loyalty

Much like any interpersonal relationship, people form relationships with brands. In order for these relationships to be long-term and positive, the brand must represent values that are meaningful to the consumer and must behave in a manner consistent with these values.[28] Such thinking clearly transfers to the professional sport setting. However, such a philosophy has truly only been adopted by minor league sport franchises.[29] Further, one such value that is very important to all business, but in particular to sport entities, is loyalty. Yet, professional team sport is one of the only business environments in which customers are forced to pay for the right to be loyal. While personal seat licenses have been invaluable as funding mechanisms for new stadium-arena construction, their impact on brand equity can be questioned. Brand loyalty provides an organization with protection against the competition and allows for reduced marketing costs.[30] By placing a premium on the right to be loyal, pro teams are instantly giving some of their most loyal consumers a reason to reconsider their commitment. According to this logic, what is a pro sport team brand saying to its most loyal customers when it asks them to pay thousands of dollars for the *right* to purchase season tickets? Does this serve to foster a lasting relationship? We argue that such a practice fosters both negative associations and increased expectation of value and therefore will decrease in the next decade. Sport teams are beginning to realize this. . . .

In the next decade, efforts to reward and recognize fan loyalty will become more prevalent. Already, through the fan loyalty card programs, teams are making more of an effort to recognize their patrons.[31] Such programs that attempt to reinforce and recognize loyalty will continue well into the future. In a further effort to inextricably connect fans with their favorite team, owners will increasingly offer ownership stock in their teams. Rather than forcing fans to pay for a personal seat license, teams will appeal to a broader spectrum of fans with stock offerings, where purchases are voluntary and symbolic. . . . Ownership of team stock will ultimately create a new and elite user group of highly committed and vested fans. However, teams will have to respond with recognition programs for the new owners if the stock offering is to successfully reinforce loyalty. Special access to players and coaches as well as extremely regular communication with the team will be integral to rewarding the loyalty demonstrated by these groups.

Summary

The second major focus of team brand management efforts this decade will be focused on developing deeper relationships with customers. Ultimately, this will be accomplished by creating positive brand associations with professional sport team brands. Central to this will be understanding what consumers want from the team and then focusing on enhancing interactions between the consumer and the team brand as a means to satisfy consumer needs. Such a focus will allow teams to more effectively build and remind consumers of their positive associations with team brands. Additionally, the team's marketing communications will become more integrated as a means of further reinforcing such positive associations. Finally, such a focus will lead teams to actively seek ways to recognize and reinforce the loyalty that results from a strong relationship between the consumer and the brand.

CONCLUSION

. . . . This paper has one overarching premise — that the business management of major league professional teams will become more strategic. Specifically, we contend that brand management will be the prevailing focus of sport managers. This is necessary because the focus of team owners is increasingly toward the appreciation of their asset, the franchise, over the long term. Central to this is optimally serving all of the team's customers in a cost efficient manner.

Therefore, we suggest sport managers will employ brand management practices through two broad strategies: the acquisition of assets to enhance competitive position and the building of customer relationships to ensure long-term loyalty. . . .

We offer these predictions for two reasons. First, brand management is increasingly discussed by sport managers.[32] Second, such practices are essential if teams are to thrive in the increasingly competitive entertainment marketplace. In fact, we suggest some teams may not succeed. . . . Further, such strategies have global implications as well. The YankeeNets organization's strategic alliance with the Manchester United suggests that there may be few boundaries for these brand-based efforts in the future.

REFERENCES

1. Mullin, B., Hardy, S., & Sutton, W.A. (2000). *Sport marketing* (2nd ed.). Champaign, IL: Human Kinetics.

2. Gladden, J.M., & Milne, G.R. (1999). Examining the importance of brand equity in professional sport: Examining the link between brand associations and brand loyalty. *International Journal of Sports Marketing and Sponsorship,* 3(1), 45–69.

3. Aaker, D.A., & Joachimsthaler, E. (2000). *Brand leadership.* New York: The Free Press.

4. Shocker, A.D., Srivastava, R.K., & Ruekert, R.W. (1994). Challenges and opportunities facing brand management: An introduction to the special issue. *Journal of Marketing Research,* 31, 152.

5. Pitts, B.G., & Stotlar, D.K. (1996). *Fundamentals of sport marketing.* Morgantown, WV: Fitness Information Technologies.

6. David, F.R. (1999). *Strategic management: Concepts and cases.* Upper Saddle River, NJ: Prentice Hall.

7. Thompson, A.A., & Strickland, A.J. (1998). *Creating and implementing strategy* (10th ed.). Boston: McGraw Hill.

8. Thompson, A.A., & Strickland, A.J. (1998). *Creating and implementing strategy* (10th ed.). Boston: McGraw Hill.

9. Varadarajan, P.R., & Cunningham, M. (1995). Strategic alliances: A synthesis of conceptual foundations. *Journal of the Academy of Marketing Science,* 23(4), 282–296.

10. Humbles, A. (2000, July 21). Nashville not likely to get NBA developmental team. *The Tennesseean.* Available: http://www.tennessean.com/sii/00/07/21/nbd121.html.

11. Lachowetz, T. (2000, June 26–July 2). Turn your competitor into a sales partner. *Street & Smith's SportsBusiness Journal,* 57.

12. Lachowetz, T. (2000, June 26–July 2). Turn your competitor into a sales partner. *Street & Smith's SportsBusiness Journal,* 57.

13. Day, G.S. Advantageous Alliances. *Journal of the Academy of Marketing Science,* 23(4), 297–300.

14. Aaker, D.A., & Joachimsthaler, E. (2000). *Brand leadership.* New York: The Free Press.

15. Day, G.S. Advantageous Alliances. *Journal of the Academy of Marketing Science,* 23(4), 297–300.

16. Akasie, J. (1999). Out of his league. *Forbes,* September 20, 1999, 54.

17. Howard, D.R. (1999). The changing fanscape for big-league sports: Implications for sport managers. *Journal of Sport Management,* 13, 78–91.

18. Aaker, D.A. (1991). *Managing brand equity.* New York: The Free Press; Gladden, J.M., & Funk, D.C. (2001). Understanding brand loyalty in professional sports: Examining the link between brand association and brand loyalty. *International Journal of Sport Marketing and Sponsorship,* 3(1), 45–69.

19. Keller, K.L. (1998). *Strategic brand management: Building, measuring, and managing brand equity.* Upper Saddle River, NJ: Prentice Hall.

20. Mullin, B., Hardy, S., & Sutton, W.A. (2000). *Sport marketing* (2nd ed.). Champaign, IL: Human Kinetics.

21. Rozanski, H.D., Baum, A.G., & Wolfsen, B.T. (1999). Brand zealots: Realizing the full value of emotional loyalty. *Strategy & Business,* 17, 51–62.

22. Joachimsthaler, E., & Aaker, D.A. (1999). Building brands without mass media. In: *Harvard business review on brand management* (1–22). Boston: Harvard Business School Publishing.

23. Burton, R. (1998, November 2). Apocalypse soon: Pro sports teetering on the edge of an abyss. *Street & Smith's SportsBusiness Journal,* 30–31.

24. Henry, D. (1999, December 23). Fiber-optics firm CEO faces a sweet dilemma. *USA Today,* 3B.

25. Howard, D.R. (1999). The changing fanscape for big-league sports: Implications for sport managers. *Journal of Sport Management,* 13, 78–91.

26. Cowell, A. (1999). How Manchester United scores on its balance sheets. *Strategy & Business,* 17, 79–87.

27. Aaker, D.A. (1991). *Managing brand equity.* New York: The Free Press; Schultz, D.E., & Barnes, B.E. (1999). *Strategic brand communication campaigns.* Lincolnwood, IL: NTC Business Books.

28. Fournier, S. (1998). Consumers and their brands: Developing relationship theory in consumer research. Journal of Consumer Research, 24(4), 343–363; Kapferer, J.N. (1992). *Strategic brand management.* New York: The Free Press.

29. Arnott, D. (1998, September 21–27). Minor leagues teach major business lessons. *Street & Smith's SportsBusiness Journal,* 39.

30. Aaker, D.A. (1991). *Managing brand equity.* New York: The Free Press.

31. Mullin, B., Hardy, S., & Sutton, W.A. (2000). *Sport marketing* (2nd ed.). Champaign, IL: Human Kinetics.

32. Alm, R. (1997, August 4). Mavericks would like to get into brand name game. *The Dallas Morning News,* 2B.

DISCUSSION QUESTIONS

1. What do you think of Sheehan's predictions about the future of MLB, the NBA, the NFL, the NHL, and college basketball and football?

2. Do you think Sheehan's prediction that salary caps will disappear in the four major sports is accurate?

3. Can you think of any untapped sources of revenue that owners could turn to in the case of an economic downturn?

4. Do you think technological advances will lead to increased or decreased revenues for owners? Can you think of any additional ways technology can be used to generate revenues? Can you think of other ways technology may reduce revenues?

5. Which of the proposed sources of increased revenue do you think is best or most likely to be successful? Why?

6. Which of the proposed sources of increased revenue do you think is worst or least likely to be successful? Why?

7. Do you think that strategic management of a team brand will be more important to the financial success of an organization than having a winning team?

8. What are some of the brand management strategies discussed by the authors?

9. What will fans think of the strategies that sport organizations will seek to utilize in order to enhance their relationships with individual fans? Are they likely to influence fan loyalty or consumption levels? What types of things would make fans more loyal?

10. What possible negative outcomes can result from integration?

INDEX